CW01468303

philosophy – values
strategy
→ theory.

policy.

plan.

tactics.
– practice.

process

doing

Cambridge Handbook of Strategy as Practice

Now in its second edition, this extended and thoroughly updated handbook introduces researchers and students to the growing range of theoretical and methodological perspectives being developed in the vibrant field of strategy as practice. With new authors and additional chapters, it shows how the strategy-as-practice approach in strategic management moves away from disembodied and asocial studies of firm assets, technologies and practices to explore and explain the contribution that strategizing makes to people working at all levels of an organization. It breaks down many of the traditional paradigmatic barriers in strategy to investigate who the strategists are, what they do, how they do it and what the consequences or outcomes of their actions are. This essential work summarizes recent developments in the field while presenting a clear agenda for future research.

DAMON GOLSORKHI is Associate Professor of Strategic Management at Grenoble Ecole de Management, France.

LINDA ROULEAU is Professor in the Department of Management at HEC Montréal.

DAVID SEIDL is Professor of Organization and Management at the University of Zurich, Switzerland.

EERO VAARA is Professor of Organization and Management at Aalto University School of Business in Helsinki, Finland, Permanent Visiting Professor at EMLYON Business School, France and Distinguished Visiting Scholar at Lancaster University, UK.

Cambridge Handbook of Strategy as Practice

Second Edition

Edited by

DAMON GOLSORKHI

LINDA ROULEAU

DAVID SEIDL

EERO VAARA

CAMBRIDGE
UNIVERSITY PRESS

CAMBRIDGE
UNIVERSITY PRESS

University Printing House, Cambridge CB2 8BS, United Kingdom

Cambridge University Press is part of the University of Cambridge.

It furthers the University's mission by disseminating knowledge in the pursuit of education, learning and research at the highest international levels of excellence.

www.cambridge.org
Information on this title: www.cambridge.org/9781107421493

© Cambridge University Press 2015

First published 2010
Second edition 2015
First paperback edition 2016

A catalogue record for this publication is available from the British Library

Library of Congress Cataloguing in Publication data
Cambridge handbook of strategy as practice / edited by Damon Golsorkhi, Linda Rouleau, David Seidl, Eero Vaara. – Second edition.
        pages   cm
Includes index.
ISBN 978-1-107-07312-8 (Hardback)
1. Strategic planning–Handbooks, manuals, etc.   I. Golsorkhi, Damon.
HD30.28.C348 2015
658.4′012–dc23   2014050243

ISBN 978-1-107-07312-8 Hardback
ISBN 978-1-107-42149-3 Paperback

Additional resources for this publication at www.cambridge.org/golsorkhi.

Contents

Figures

Tables

Boxes

Contributors

Florence Allard-Poesi is Professor of Strategic Management and Organizational Theory and director of the Institut de Recherche en Gestion at the University Paris–East. Her research focuses principally on sensemaking in organizations and the role that discursive practices play in this context. She also works on the methodological and epistemological problems that these issues present. Her work has been published notably in *Organization*, *@grh*, *Management International*, *M@n@gement* and *Economies et Sociétés*.

Mats Alvesson is Professor of Business Administration at the University of Lund, Sweden, Cass Business School, City University, London, and at University of Queensland Business School, Australia. His research interests include critical theory, gender, power, the management of professional service (knowledge-intensive) organizations, leadership, identity, organizational image, organizational culture and symbolism, qualitative methods and the philosophy of science. Recent books include *The Triumph of Emptiness* (2013), *Qualitative Research and Theory Development* (2011, with Dan Kärreman), *Constructing Research Questions* (2013, with Jörgen Sandberg), *Interpreting Interviews* (2011), *Metaphors We Lead By. Understanding Leadership in the Real World* (2011, edited with André Spicer), *Oxford Handbook of Critical Management Studies* (2011, edited with Todd Bridgman and Hugh Willmott), *Understanding Gender and Organizations* (2009, second edition, with Yvonne Billing) and *Reflexive Methodology* (2009, second edition, with Kaj Skoldberg).

Widar von Arx is Professor of Business Administration at the Lucerne University of Applied Sciences and Arts, where he leads a research team on mobility and transportation. His research interests include organizational change, leadership and innovation in complex organizations. He works with theoretical perspectives such as convention theory, social constructivism and other practice theories to explore his ethnographic data on managerial actions and interactions in organizations. In addition, he is engaged in many applied research projects specifically with public transport companies, on issues such as new service development, process management and strategy.

Julia Balogun is Associate Dean (Research) and Professor of Strategic Management at the University of Bath School of Management. Her research focuses on strategy as practice with a particular concern for strategic change and renewal, predominantly within large mature corporations. She is particularly interested in how strategists accomplish their work through political, cultural, cognitive and discursive processes and practices. She has published widely in the area of strategy and strategic change in journals such as the *Academy of Management Journal*, *Organization Studies*, the *Journal of International Business Studies* and the *Journal of Management Studies*. Her book *Exploring Strategic Change* (2013, with Veronica Hope-Hailey) is in its fourth edition.

Nic Beech is Vice-Principal for Governance, Planning and Policy at the University of St Andrews and Chair of the British Academy of Management. His research interests are in management practice, change and the construction of identity, particularly in music and the creative industries and in health services. He is a fellow of the Royal Society of Arts, the British Academy of

Management, the Chartered Institute of Personnel and Development and the Academy of Social Sciences. His publications include the following with Cambridge University Press: *Managing Creativity: Exploring the Paradox* (2010, with Barbara Townley), *Managing Change: Enquiry and Action* (2012, with Robert MacIntosh) and *Organising Music: Theory, Practice, Performance* (2015, with Charlotte Gilmore).

Nicolas Bencherki is an Assistant Professor of Communication at the University at Albany, State University of New York. His current research focuses on the contribution of the philosophy of individuation and of possession to organizational communication's understanding of the constitution and action of organizations, and to its conception of themes such as membership, strategy or ethics. His theoretical investigations are informed by ethnographic fieldworks among community and nonprofit organizations.

Martin Blom is a Senior Lecturer in Strategic Management at Lund University School of Economics and Management, Department of Business Administration. His research interests cover topics such as strategy, corporate governance and leadership/followership. His more recent publications include 'Leadership on demand: followers as initiators and inhibitors of managerial leadership' (*Scandinavian Journal of Management*, 2014, with Mats Alvesson); 'Strategy consultants doing strategy: how status and visibility affect strategizing' (*African Journal of Business Management*, 2013, with Mikael Lundgren); and 'Corporate governance' (with Jaan Grünberg, in *Management: An Advanced Introduction*, 2013, edited by Lars Strannegård and Alexander Styhre).

Ethel Brundin is Professor in Entrepreneurship and Business Development at Jönköping International Business School, Sweden. She is affiliated with the Centre for Family Enterprise and Ownership, which is ranked number one in Europe for family business research and number four in the world. She is an active research member of the European chapter of STEP (Successful Transgenerational Entrepreneurship Practices – a worldwide research project. She is a Permanent Visiting Professor at the Witten Herdecke University in Germany and Extra Ordinary Professor at the University of the Western Cape, South Africa. The focus of her research interest is micro-processes, including emotions, entrepreneurship and strategic leadership – often in combination. She has published in leading international journals and edited books about emotions and strategizing among strategic leaders and entrepreneurs as well as about entrepreneurship in the emergent market of South Africa.

Chris S. Chapman is Professor of Management Accounting at Copenhagen Business School. He is editor-in-chief of *Accounting, Organizations and Society*. His research has focused on the ways in which people work to make accounting relevant to operational decision-making in a variety of contexts, including restaurants and professional service firms, and more recently on the design of cost systems for health care providers.

Mathieu Chaput teaches at the Department of Communication of the Université de Montréal, where he earned his PhD in 2012. His research covers the communicative constitution of organizations, the analysis of rhetoric and the study of interactions.

Robert Chia is Research Professor of Management at the Adam Smith Business School, University of Glasgow. He received his PhD in organizational analysis from Lancaster University. He has published extensively in the top international management journals and is the author/editor of five books. His latest books include *Strategy without Design: The Silent Efficacy of Indirect Action* (2009, with Robin Holt, Cambridge University Press) and *Philosophy and Organization Theory* (2011, edited with Haridimos Tsoukas). His research interests include process thinking in organization theory; strategy practices; east–west philosophies; and managerial wisdom. Prior to entering academia Robert worked for seventeen years in shipbuilding, aircraft engineering, human resource management and manufacturing management.

Wai Fong Chua is Pro-Vice-Chancellor (Students) at the University of New South Wales, Sydney. She is an editor of *Accounting, Organizations and Society* and sits on the editorial boards of a range of international journals. Her research interests include the operation of accounting inscriptions in organizational arenas, the interactions between accounting and affect and the historical professionalization of accounting work.

Stewart Clegg's career has been spent mostly in Australia, from where he now travels frequently to Europe, where he is a Visiting Professor at EM-Lyon Business School and the Nova School of Business and Economics in Lisbon, and Strategic Research Advisor at Newcastle University Business School, in the United Kingdom. Widely acknowledged as one of the most significant contemporary theorists of power relations in social science generally, he is also a well-known contributor to organization studies, in which his theoretical interests in power connect with many substantive issues. The author and editor of a large number of books and hundreds of journal articles, as well as being active in many other fields, he is Professor and Director of the Centre for Management and Organisation Studies at the University of Technology, Sydney, which recently awarded him a D.Litt. for a thesis entitled 'Works/ words of power'.

Charlotte Cloutier is currently Assistant Professor of Strategy at HEC Montréal, the business school of the Université de Montréal. Her research focuses on understanding strategy processes as they unfold in pluralistic organizations (nonprofit organizations, trade associations, hospitals, universities, government ministries or agencies, etc.), notably from a strategy-as-practice perspective.

François Cooren is a Professor at the Université de Montréal, where he is the Chair of the Department of Communication. His research focuses on organizational communication, language and social interaction, as well as communication theory. He is the author of three books – *The Organizing Property of*

Communication (2000), *Action and Agency in Dialogue: Passion, Incarnation, and Ventriloquism* (2010) and *Organizational Discourse: Communication and Constitution* (2015) – and has also edited five volumes. He is also the author of close to fifty articles, published, for the most part, in international peer-reviewed journals, as well as more than twenty book chapters. In 2010–2011 he was the President of the International Communication Association, and was elected a fellow of this association in 2013. He is also the current President of the International Association for Dialogue Analysis (2012–2015).

Joep Cornelissen is Professor of Corporate Communication and Organization Theory and Associate Dean for Research at the Faculty of Economics and Business Administration, VU University Amsterdam. The main focus of his research is the role of communication and sensemaking in processes of innovation, entrepreneurship and change, but he also has an interest in questions of reasoning and theory development in organization theory. His papers have been published in the *Academy of Management Review*, *Journal of Management Studies*, *Organization Science* and *Organization Studies*, and he has written a general text on corporate communication – *Corporate Communication: A Guide to Theory and Practice* (2014) – that is now in its fourth edition. He is a Council member of the Society for the Advancement of Management Studies and a former general editor of the *Journal of Management Studies* (2006–2012), and he serves on the editorial boards of the *Academy of Management Journal*, *Journal of Management*, *Journal of Management Studies* and *Organization Studies*.

Ann L. Cunliffe is Professor of Organisation Studies at the School of Management of the University of Bradford, United Kingdom, where she has recently been awarded a Fiftieth Anniversary Professorial Chair. Her current research lies at the intersection of organizational studies, philosophy and communications, and focuses on examining the relationship between language, conversation and responsive and ethical ways of managing organizations. Other interests include leadership, selfhood, embodied sensemaking, reflexivity and expanding the reach and rigour of qualitative research.

Katharina Dittrich is a postdoctoral fellow at the Institute of Business Administration at the University of Zurich. In her PhD studies she focused on the accomplishment and change of organizational routines and practices from a practice-theoretical perspective. She carried out a one-year ethnographic study at a start-up company in the pharmaceutical industry, observing interactions at the board, management and employee levels. Her working paper on the role of meetings in the strategy process has received the 'Best Student Paper' award of the SAP Interest Group at the 2011 Academy of Management meeting. In her postdoctoral studies, she investigates how organizational routines interact and how they work together as an ecology of interdependent patterns of action.

Mona Ericson is Professor of Strategy and Organization at Jönköping International Business School. She received her doctoral degree from the Stockholm School of Economics, where she also earned an associated professorship. Her principal research interests are in strategy practice and change, with a focus on human activity and a polyphony of voices. Mona is the author of seven monographs. She has also published in academic journals such as the *Human Resource Development Quarterly, International Journal of Qualitative Methods, Management Decision* and *Scandinavian Journal of Management*. Her most recent publication is 'On the dynamics of fluidity and open-endedness of strategy process toward a strategy-as-practic*ing* conceptualization' (*Scandinavian Journal of Management*, 2014).

Elana Feldman is a PhD candidate in organizational behaviour at the Boston University School of Management. Her primary research interests include temporality and relationships at work. She has also published co-authored articles and book chapters in the areas of careers and social change in organizations. She helped found and serves on the Steering Committee for the Positive Relationships at Work Microcommunity.

She holds a Bachelor of Arts from Brown University, Providence, Rhode Island.

Martha S. Feldman (Stanford University PhD, 1983) is the Johnson Chair for Civic Governance and Public Management and Professor of Social Ecology, Business, Political Science and Sociology at the University of California, Irvine. Her current research on organizational routines explores the role of performance and agency in creating, maintaining and altering these fundamental organizational phenomena. She is a senior editor for *Organization Science* and serves on the editorial boards of several management journals. She received the *Administrative Science Quarterly*'s 2009 award for 'Scholarly Contribution' and the 2011 Academy of Management 'Practice Scholarship' award. In 2014 she received an honorary doctorate in economics from St. Gallen University Business School, Switzerland, and was listed by Thomson Reuters as a highly cited author.

Steven W. Floyd is the Isenberg Professor of Innovation and Entrepreneurship at the Isenberg School of Management at the University of Massachusetts, Amherst. His research focuses on the strategy development process, and much of it takes a middle management perspective on how strategy forms. Recent papers focus on group influence activities and networks in strategic initiatives and the ritualized practices associated with deliberate strategy-making. His co-authored research has won the Academy of Management's 'Sumantra Ghoshal Research and Practice' award and the 'Best Conference Paper' prize of the Strategic Management Society. He is a former general editor of the *Journal of Management Studies*. Currently he serves on the editorial board of the *Academy of Management Journal* and as an associate editor of the *Strategic Management Journal*.

Karen Golden-Biddle is the Questrom Professor in Management at Boston University's School of Management. Working in the interdependent arenas of large-scale organizational change and theorizing in research, she has a keen interest in the cultural and relational micro-processes constituting and motivating active, engaged change efforts that enrich human lives at work and in society. She has received the Douglas McGregor Award and the Academy of Management's Robert McDonald Award for the Advancement of Organizational Research Methodology. Her book *Composing Qualitative Research* (2007, with Karen Locke) is in its second edition and has been widely used in doctoral programmes across the world.

Damon Golsorkhi is Associate Professor of Strategy and Innovation at Grenoble Ecole de Management, France. His research is at the crossroad of sociology and management, and he focuses on strategy as practice, power and resistance, and social change. He has published in academic journals such as *Organization*, *M@n@gement* and *Revue Française de Gestion*. He has also edited several books, including the first French book on strategy as practice (*La fabrique de la stratégie*, 2006) and *Rethinking Power in Organizations, Institutions, and Markets* (2012, with David Courpasson and Jeff Sallaz).

Marie-Léandre Gomez is Associate Professor of Management Control at ESSEC Business School, Cergy-Pontoise, France. Her current research topics include strategizing, creativity, learning and power in organizations, with a practice-based approach and a process perspective. She is particularly interested in the role of performance evaluation tools for professional organizations. She has recently conducted empirical fieldwork in grand restaurants and hospitals.

Jean-Pascal Gond is Professor of Corporate Social Responsibility at Cass Business School, City University, London. His research mobilizes organization theory and economic sociology to investigate corporate social responsibility. His research in economic sociology is concerned with the influence of theory on managerial practice (performativity), organizational approaches to justification and valuation, and the governance of self-regulation. He has published in leading academic journals, such as *Business and Society*, *Economy and Society*, *Journal of Management Studies*, *Organization Science* and *Organization*

Studies, and French journals such as *Finance Contrôle Stratégie*.

Simon Grand is a management researcher, knowledge entrepreneur and strategy designer. He is Professor of Strategic Management and founder and academic director of the RISE Management Innovation Lab at the University of St. Gallen, Switzerland (www.rise.ch), research fellow at the Zurich University of the Arts and a member of the supervisory board of several companies. In his research, he examines the interplay between routine dynamics and strategy processes, and in particular their managerial enactment, with an empirical focus on entrepreneurial companies and technology corporations in various industry contexts. He also works and publishes on the practice of executive management and corporate governance, as well as on their foundation in management and organization theory.

Royston Greenwood is the Telus Professor of Strategic Management in the School of Business, University of Alberta, and a Visiting Professor at the University of Edinburgh. He is a fellow of the Academy of Management and a former Chair of the Academy's Organization and Management Theory Division. His research interests focus on institutional and organizational change, though recently he has begun to explore the institutional foundations of corporate fraud. He has twice won the 'Best Paper' award from the *Academy of Management Journal*, and has also received the 'Scholarly Contribution' award from the *Administrative Science Quarterly*. He also received the 'Greif Research Impact' award from the Entrepreneurship Division and the 'Distinguished Scholar Award' from the Organization and Management Theory Division of the Academy.

Stéphane Guérard is Assistant Professor (Oberassistent) at the University of Zurich. With an emphasis on processual and qualitative research approaches, his research focuses on understanding how practices and framing activities shape institutions, technology adoption, meetings and strategy. He has published, among others, in *Organization Studies*, the *International Journal of Management Reviews* and *M@n@gement*.

For several years he has been teaching courses entitled 'The practice of strategy' and 'Designing effective organizations'.

Paula Jarzabkowski is a Professor of Strategic Management at Cass Business School, City University, London. Her research takes a practice theory approach to studying strategizing in pluralistic contexts, such as regulated firms, third-sector organizations and financial services, particularly insurance and reinsurance. She is experienced in using and extending ethnographic research methods in her work. Her research on these topics and using these methods has been published widely in the leading journals, and she also published the first research monograph on strategy as practice, entitled *Strategy-as-Practice: An Activity-Based Approach*, in 2005.

Phyl Johnson is a psychologist and a Visiting Professor of Executive Education at Strathclyde Business School in Scotland. She is also the Senior Partner in the Strategy Explorers consulting firm. She works as an executive coach and specializes in supporting senior executives through strategic change. In her consulting role, she has worked in a wide range corporations in Europe. She has held faculty positions at Cranfield School of Management, England, and Strathclyde Business School, where her research interests focused on the psychology of the strategist.

Martin Kornberger received his PhD in philosophy from the University of Vienna in 2002, followed by a decade at the University of Technology, Sydney, where he worked last as Associate Professor for Design and Management and Research Director of the Australian government's Creative Industry Innovation Centre. Currently he works as Professor for Strategy and Organization at Copenhagen Business School. He is also a Professorial Fellow at the University of Edinburgh Business School and a Visiting Researcher at the WU Vienna University of Economics and Business.

Tomi Laamanen is Chaired Professor of Strategic Management, Director of the Institute of Management, and Director of the PhD Program of Strategy and Management of the University of St. Gallen, Switzerland. He holds two D.Sc. degrees (in strategy and finance). His research focuses on strategic management, with a special emphasis on strategy process, mergers and acquisitions, capability dynamics and management's cognition. His work has appeared in European and North American journals, including the *Strategic Management Journal*, *Journal of Management*, *Journal of Management Studies*, *Research Policy*, *Long Range Planning* and *Harvard Business Review*. He is associate editor of the *Strategic Management Journal* and a member of the editorial review boards of the *Academy of Management Journal*, *Academy of Management Discovery* and *Journal of Management*. In addition to teaching and research, he has actively worked with a number of firms as chairman, member of the board or strategy consultant.

Pikka-Maaria Laine works as an Associate Professor of Management at the University of Lapland, Finland. She also holds the position of Adjunct Professor of Strategic Management at the University of Eastern Finland. She is interested in strategy work, especially its participative and dialogical aspects. In addition to her university position she also works as a facilitator in dialogical strategy work. Her research interests revolve around strategy-making, subjectivities, power and resistance, and she has published in academic journals. She has acted as a leading member of the strategy-as-practice standing working group at the European Group for Organizational Studies, and as a board member of the Finnish Strategic Management Society.

Ann Langley is Professor of Management and Research Chair in Strategic Management in Pluralistic Settings at HEC Montréal. Her research focuses on strategic change, leadership, identity and the use of management tools in complex organizations, with an emphasis on processual and qualitative research approaches. She has published over seventy articles and six books She is co-editor of *Strategic Organization* and series editor, with Haridimos Tsoukas, of 'Perspectives on Process

Organization Studies', published by Oxford University Press.

Jane Lê is a Senior Lecturer in Work and Organisational Studies at the University of Sydney. Her research centres on organizational practices and processes in complex, dynamic and pluralistic organizations. She is particularly interested in social processes such as conflict, coordination and information-sharing, and has a passion for qualitative research and qualitative research methods. She received her PhD from Aston Business School, Birmingham. She has published in journals such as *Organization Science, Strategic Organization* and the *International Journal of Human Resource Management*.

Bernard Leca is Professor of Management Control at ESSEC Business School, Cergy-Pontoise. His main research focuses on the way organizations or individuals can initiate and implement institutional change, in particular through institutional work. He has published in academic journals such as *Annals of the Academy of Management, Organization Studies, Organization* and *M@n@gement*.

Feng Liu is Assistant Professor of Strategy at Warwick Business School, University of Warwick, United Kingdom. Her research interests focus on top management team and board team strategizing activities and emotion in organizations. Her recent publications include 'Emotional dynamics and strategizing processes: a study of strategic conversations in top team meetings' (with Sally Maitlis, *Journal of Management Studies*, 2014).

Karen Locke is W. Brooks George Professor in the School of Business Administration at the College of William and Mary, Williamsburg, Virginia. She joined the faculty there in 1989 after earning her PhD in organizational behaviour from Case Western Reserve University, Cleveland. She focuses on developing a sociology of knowledge in organizational studies and on the use of qualitative research for the investigation of organizational phenomena. Her work appears in journals such as the *Academy of Management Journal, Organization Science, Journal of Organizational Behavior,*

Journal of Management Inquiry, Organizational Research Methods and Studies in Organization, Culture and Society. In addition, she has authored *Grounded Theory in Management Research* (2001) and co-authored *Composing Qualitative Research* (with Karen Golden-Biddle, second edition, 2007). Her current work continues her interest in the processes of qualitative researching and focuses on exploring and explicating their creative and imaginative dimensions.

Michael Lounsbury is a Professor, Thornton A. Graham Chair, and Associate Dean of Research at the Alberta School of Business. He is interested in the relationship of institutions, entrepreneurship and innovation. He has published extensively in top journals, such as the *Academy of Management Annals, Academy of Management Journal, Academy of Management Review, Administrative Science Quarterly, Journal of Management Studies, Organization Studies and Strategic Management Journal. His book The Institutional Logics Perspective: A New Approach to Culture, Structure, and Process* (with Patricia H. Thornton and William Ocasio, 2012) received the George R. Terry book award from the Academy of Management in 2013. Formerly he was a co-editor of the *Journal of Management Inquiry and Organization Studies*, and associate editor of the *Academy of Management Annals*. His PhD is from Northwestern University, Evanston, Illinois, in sociology and organization behaviour.

Maria Lusiani is Assistant Professor of Management at the University of Venice. She previously held a postdoctoral position at HEC Montréal within the Canada Research Chair of Strategic Management in Pluralistic Settings. She teaches strategic management, public management and qualitative research methods. Her research interests include management practices in pluralistic settings, management–profession tensions in professional work and new public management studies. She mainly conducts qualitative research, and has some expertise in ethnography, process research and discourse analysis. Her empirical research focuses on public, professional services in the fields of culture and health care.

Habib Mahama is an Associate Professor of Accounting at the United Arab Emirates University. He serves on the editorial boards of a number of international journals. His research interest is in the area of management accounting, with a specific focus on management accounting controls in inter-firm relationships, management control of operational risk and behavioural management accounting.

Saku Mantere is Associate Professor of Strategy and Organization at the Desautels Faculty of Management, McGill University, Montreal. His research is focused on what makes organizations strategic and how strategic management influences organizations. He is particularly interested in strategic change, middle management and strategy discourse, as well as reasoning as a methodological issues in management studies.

Leif Melin is Professor of Strategy and Organization and the Hamrin Professor of Family Business Strategy at Jönköping International Business School. His research interest includes several topics related to strategizing and strategic change applying the strategy-as-practice perspective, such as strategic dialogues as an important practice. His publications include *Strategy as Practice: Research Directions and Resources* (with Gerry Johnson, Ann Langley, and Richard Whittington, 2007, Cambridge University Press) and *Sage Handbook of Family Business* (with Mattias Nordqvist and Pramodita Sharma, 2014), and he has published articles on strategy in the *Strategic Management Journal*, *Strategic Organization*, *Journal of Management Studies*, *Family Business Review*, *Entrepreneurship Theory and Practice*, *Long Range Planning* and *Journal of Family Business Strategy*.

Eléonore Mounoud is Associate Professor in Business Strategy and Organization Studies at École Centrale Paris. After graduating in agricultural engineering from INA-PG, in France, she worked as a consultant on environmental issues and technological change. She holds a PhD in business strategy from HEC Paris. She studies texts (discourses), talks (narratives) and tools

(management systems) in daily business practice. She is currently co-chairing the 'Operational efficiency and management systems' research programme, sponsored by BNP Paribas, at Ecole Centrale Paris.

David Oliver is Senior Lecturer in Work and Organisational Studies at the University of Sydney Business School. His research interests include organizational identity, contemporary strategy practices and tools, and stakeholder engagement. He has worked at HEC Montréal and the IMD Business School and Imagination Lab, Lausanne, Switzerland. His publications have appeared in management journals such as *Organization Studies*, the *British Journal of Management*, *Human Relations*, *Journal of Applied Behavioral Science* and *Journal of Business Ethics*. He is a member of the Strategy as Practice Research Group at HEC Montréal and the Organisational Discourse, Strategy and Change Group at the University of Sydney.

Wanda J. Orlikowski is the Alfred P. Sloan Professor of Information Technologies and Organization Studies at the Massachusetts Institute of Technology's Sloan School of Management. She received her PhD from New York University. Her research examines technologies in the workplace, with a particular focus on the ongoing relations between technologies, organizing structures, cultural norms, control mechanisms, communication and work practices. She is currently exploring sociomaterial practices in social media.

Andrew Popp is Professor of Business History at the University of Liverpool Management School. He has published two monographs, one edited collection and more than thirty articles. He is Co-Director of the Centre for Port and Maritime History, based in Liverpool, and co-edits the book series 'Studies in Port and Maritime History' for Liverpool University Press. He is editor-in-chief at *Enterprise and Society: The International Journal of Business History* . His research interests focus primarily on the history of business in Britain in the nineteenth century, including industrial districts, regional business networks, trust and other forms of social capital, cultural representations of business, commercial salesmen and occupational cultures. Most recently he has focused on entrepreneurship and family business, and he is currently beginning a project on oral histories of entrepreneurship in the 1980s. In addition, he has recently developed a focus on sources and methods in business history. His work is characterized by methodological innovation and a desire to examine the relationship between business, society and history in the widest possible terms.

Andreas Rasche is Professor of Business in Society at the Centre for Corporate Social Responsibility at Copenhagen Business School (CBS) and Research Director of the CBS World-Class Research Environment on 'Governing responsible business'. His research focuses on corporate responsibility standards (particularly the UN Global Compact), the political role of corporations in transnational governance and the governance of global supply networks. He regularly contributes to international journals in his field of study and has lectured on corporate social and environmental responsibility at different institutions. He has co-edited *The United Nations Global Compact: Achievements, Trends and Challenges* (with Georg Kell, 2010, Cambridge University Press) and published *Building the Responsible Enterprise: Where Vision and Values Add Value* (with Sandra Waddock, 2012). He is associate editor of *Business Ethics Quarterly*. He joined Copenhagen Business School from Warwick Business School in August 2012 (more information is available at www.arasche.com).

Patrick Regnér is a Professor of Strategic Management at the Stockholm School of Economics and has been a Director of its Institute of International Business. His research interests focus on strategy creation and change and how practices, actors, activities and social interactions shape strategies. His current research examines normative institutional embeddedness and social complexities in imperfect imitation and firm's responses to institutions. His research is published in leading journals, such as the *Strategic Management Journal, Journal of International*

Business, Journal of Management Studies, Management International Review, British Journal of Management and *Human Relations*. He co-authors the leading European strategy textbook, *Exploring Strategy: Text and Cases* (with Gerry Johnson, Richard Whittington, Kevan Scholes and Duncan Angwin, tenth edition, 2013), and is a member of the editorial boards of the *Journal of Management Studies, Organization Studies* and *Strategic Organization*.

Emmanuelle Reuter Emmanuelle Reuter is a postdoctoral research fellow and lecturer at the University of St Gallen, Switzerland. Her main research interests surround the cognitive underpinnings of strategy practices and processes, particularly in changing industry environments, with a particular emphasis on regulatory transformations and sustainability issues. Her ongoing projects focus on how executives attend to and interpret such environments, and make strategic decisions when faced with changes in it. In her dissertation, a primary focus has been on the private banking industry as a research site. She won the outstanding reviewer awards by the Managerial and Organizational Cognition division at the Academy of Management. Her working paper on processes of strategy making in unfamiliar environments has received the '2012 Best Conference Proposal' award of the Strategy Process IG at the Strategic Management Society.

Linda Rouleau is a Professor in the Department of Management of HEC Montréal, where she holds a professorship in strategy, organization and social practices. She teaches strategic management and organization theories. Her research work focuses on micro-strategy and strategizing in pluralistic contexts, and she also researches into the strategic sensemaking role of middle managers and leaders. In the last few years she has published in peer-reviewed journals such as the *Academy of Management Review, Organization Science, Accounting, Organization and Society, Journal of Management Studies* and *Human Relations.* She is jointly responsible for the GéPS (Study Group of Strategy as Practice, HEC Montréal) and research member of the CRIMT (a Canadian research centre focusing on globalization and work).

Johannes Rüegg-Stürm is Professor for Organizational Studies and Director of the Institute for Systemic Management and Public Governance at the University St. Gallen, Switzerland. He is the founder and Academic Director of the interdisciplinary master programme MA in management, organization studies and cultural theory. His research interests include systemic perspectives on management and organization studies; the management of pluralistic organizations, with a focus on health care organizations; and management innovation and strategic change. His work has earned several academic awards. He (together with Simon Grand) is author of the forthcoming book *The St. Gallen Management Model*, which will be published in English in the next few months.

Dalvir Samra-Fredericks is Professor of Organization Studies at Nottingham Business School, United Kingdom, and a Visiting Professor at Hanken School of Economics, Helsinki. Her research focuses on blending the ethnographic and ethnomethodological stances, and in particular involves audio-video recording strategists talking in interactions over time and space. By accessing such real-time interactions, fine-grained analyses of how they combine an array of elusive linguistic skills and forms of knowledge to do their work effectively can be achieved. This work has been singled out as 'exemplary', most recently, in a major review ('Qualitative research in management: a decade of progress', by Dustin J. Bluhm, Wendy Harman, Thomas W. Lee and Terence R. Mitchell, 2011, *Journal of Management Studies*). She has also guest-edited with colleagues two special issues of *Organization Studies*; one was a symposium issue (2008), on the 'The foundations of organizing', and the second captured a central thrust of her work in its title: 'Re-turn to practice: understanding organization as it happens' (2009).

Henri Schildt is an Associate Professor in Strategy at Aalto University, Helsinki, with joint appointments in the Department of Management Studies and the Department of Industrial Engineering and Management. He received his PhD from Helsinki University of Technology, and

he has previously worked at Imperial College London and Hanken School of Economics, Helsinki. His research on topics such as technology strategy, organizational change and entrepreneurial narratives has been published in the *Academy of Management Journal, Organization Science, Strategic Management Journal* and other outlets. He is currently the principal investigator in a four-year project funded by the Academy of Finland that studies the strategy practices and strategy work related to advanced business analytics and 'big' data.

Markus Schimmer is a postdoc at the Institute of Management of the University of St. Gallen, Switzerland, where he received his PhD in strategy. During his PhD studies he was a visiting research scholar at the University of Virginia's Darden School of Business. His research interests are directed towards firm and industry dynamics, with a focus on the impacts of the digital revolution. His research deploys competitive dynamics and industrial organization as theoretical perspectives. His work has appeared in various journals, such as *Strategic Organization*, the *Journal of Strategy and Management* and *Harvard Kennedy School Review*. Prior to his studies he worked in the headquarters of a multinational insurance group.

David Seidl is a chaired Professor of Organization and Management at the University of Zurich and Research Associate at the Centre for Business Research (CBR) at the University of Cambridge. He received his PhD from the Judge Business School, University of Cambridge, and has previously worked at the University of Munich. He is also a senior editor of *Organization Studies* and serves on the editorial boards of several journals, including the *Journal of Management Studies, Organization, Scandinavian Journal of Management* and *Strategic Organization*. In his research he has been interested in strategy as practice, strategic change, standardization and the philosophy of science, on which he has published widely in leading international journals.

Michael Smets is an Associate Professor of Management and Organisation Studies at the Saïd

Business School, University of Oxford, where he also received his D.Phil. and a member of the Centre for Professional Service Firms, part of the Saïd Business School. His research focuses on the interplay of work and institutions, especially on how professionals at work generate, respond to and resolve institutional complexity in areas such as law, consulting and reinsurance. In doing so, he draws heavily on institutional theory and strategy as practice in order to theorize from rich qualitative – often ethnographic – data. Recent publications in this vein include 'From practice to field: a multilevel model of practice-driven institutional change' (with Tim Morris and Royston Greenwood, 2014, *Academy of Management Journal*) and 'Reinsurance trading in Lloyd's of London: balancing conflicting-yet-complementary logics in practice' (with Paula Jarzabkowski, Gary Burke and Paul Spee, 2015, *Academy of Management Journal*).

Paul Spee is a Senior Lecturer in Strategy at the University of Queensland Business School. His research interests are underpinned by social practice theory and revolve around exploring the use of artefacts enabling and constraining situated activities. Paul received his PhD from Aston Business School, Birmingham. His work has appeared in the *Academy of Management Journal*, *Organization Studies*, *Strategic Organization* and Oxford University Press, among others.

Violetta Splitter is a Research Associate at the Chair of Organization and Management at the University of Zurich. Her research interests include strategy as practice, the transferability of management ideas and concepts, the practical relevance of management education and research and a Bourdieusian perspective on organizational phenomena. She has published her work in the *Journal of Applied Behavioural Science* and *Organization*.

Haridimos Tsoukas (www.htsoukas.com) holds the Columbia Ship Management Chair in Strategic Management at the Department of Public and Business Administration, University of Cyprus, and is a Distinguished Research Environment

Professor of Organization Studies at Warwick Business School, University of Warwick, United Kingdom. He obtained his PhD at the Manchester Business School (MBS), University of Manchester, and has worked at MBS, the University of Essex, the University of Strathclyde, and at the ALBA Graduate Business School, Greece. He was editor-in-chief of Organization Studies (2003–2008). He is the co-founder and co-organizer of the International Symposium on Process Organization Studies and co-editor of the book series 'Perspectives on process organization studies', published by Oxford University Press (both with Ann Langley). His research interests include knowledge-based perspectives on organizations, organizational becoming, practical reason in management and policy studies, and meta-theoretical issues in organizational and management research.

Florian Ueberbacher is a lecturer and Senior Research Fellow at the University of St. Gallen, Switzerland. He received his PhD from the same institution. His research encompasses organization theory, strategic management and entrepreneurship. He is specifically interested in how organizations gain and maintain legitimacy and power in contested environments. His research has been published in the *Academy of Management Proceedings*, *Journal of Management Studies* and *Technology Analysis and Strategic Management*.

Eero Vaara is a Professor of Organization and Management at Aalto University School of Business, Helsinki, a Permanent Visiting Professor at EM-Lyon Business School and a Distinguished Visiting Scholar at Lancaster University, United Kingdom. His research interests focus on organizational, strategic and institutional change, strategic practices and processes, multinational corporations and globalization, management education, and methodological issues in organization and management research. He has worked especially on discursive and narrative approaches. His work has been published in leading journals and several books, and he has received several awards for his contributions.

Valérie-Inés de La Ville graduated from EM-Lyon Business School in 1985 and has held a PhD in entrepreneurial strategies from the University Lyon 3 since 1996. She is currently Full Professor in Strategic Marketing and Business Policy at the University of Poitiers, France. In 2003 she created the European Centre for Children's Products, a training and research unit focused on youth-oriented markets. Her fields of interest lie in entrepreneurship and strategic innovations in children-oriented markets, as well as in the ethical issues raised by addressing children as consumers or economic actors (http://cepe.univ-poitiers.fr).

Consuelo Vásquez is an Associate Professor in the Département de Communication Sociale et Publique at the Université du Québec à Montréal. She has been a Visiting Scholar at the University of Costa Rica since 2012 and at the Université catholique de Louvain, Belgium, since 2013. In 2012 she co-edited a special issue on organizational communication studies in *Diálogos de la Comunicación*, the Latin American Federation of Communication School's journal, which brings together the work of scholars from Europe and North and South America. Her work has been published in *Communication Theory*, *Communication Measures and Methods*, *Discourse and Communication, Qualitative Research in Organization and Management*, the *Scandinavian Journal of Management* and other international peer-reviewed journals. She has also served as an editorial board member of the *Revue Internationale de Communication Sociale et Publique* and *Studies in Communication Sciences*. Her current research looks at the constitutive role of spacing and timing in 'fragile' organizations.

Xena Welch Guerra is a Research Associate and PhD student in strategy and management at the Institute of Management, University of St. Gallen, Switzerland. Her main research interests centre on mergers and acquisitions, cognitive and behavioural theories, and research methods. Her dissertation research focuses on serial acquirers and applies a variety of both qualitative and quantitative approaches to examine the formation and implementation of acquisition sequences.

Richard Whittington is Professor of Strategic Management at the Saïd Business School, and Millman Fellow at New College, University of Oxford. He is a board member of the Strategic Management Society and associate editor of the *Strategic Management Journal*. He is also a former Chair of the 'Strategizing activity and practices' interest group at the Academy of Management. He is co-author of *Strategy as Practice: Research Directions and Resources* (with Gerry Johnson, Ann Langley and Leif Melin, 2007) and a review of strategy-as-practice research in the *Academy of Management Annals* (with Eero Vaara, 2012). He is co-author of a leading strategy textbook, *Exploring Strategy: Text and Cases* (with Gerry Johnson, Kevan Scholes, Duncan Angwin and Patrick Regnér, tenth edition, 2013). He is currently working on a book on the long-term trajectory of strategy as a professional field of practice.

Carola Wolf is Lecturer in Strategy at Aston Business School, Birmingham. Her research applies a sociological perspective on strategy processes and practices, with a particular focus on middle managers. Her most recent publications include 'Strategic planning research: toward a theory-driven agenda' (with Steven Floyd, forthcoming, *Journal of Management*), which is based on her research on the role of strategic planning processes on middle management engagement in strategy-making. Her further research interests include topics such as strategic change and the emergence of strategy.

Preface to the Second Edition

We did not anticipate the first edition of the *Cambridge Handbook of Strategy as Practice* to be followed by a new version this soon. In the five years since the first edition was published, however, the field of practice-based strategy research has moved on considerably. New theoretical perspectives have been advanced, alternative methodologies have been suggested and new topics have been explored. In reaction to these developments, we have put this second edition together. We have included twenty new chapters and have substantially revised and updated all the original ones. In addition, the overall structure of the handbook has been changed: We have added Part III, covering organization and management theory perspectives on strategy as practice (SAP), such as the institutional perspective, alternative strategy perspectives, the routine dynamics perspective, the identity theory perspective, the communicative constitution of organizations perspective, the power perspective and the critical perspective. We have also added Part V, on substantive topic areas in strategy as practice research, which includes chapters on strategic planning, strategy meetings, the role of materiality in strategy, the strategic role of middle managers, participation in strategy and the role of emotions in strategy. Moreover, we decided to drop the original Part IV, on exemplary empirical research, as we felt that it was no longer possible to provide a representative overview of the wide variety of empirical studies conducted in the area of strategy as practice. Since the respective empirical chapters are still of great value to practice-based researchers, however, we have made them freely available on the website of Cambridge University Press: to access the papers, please visit www.cambridge.org/golsorkhi.

Working on this second edition has been a wonderful journey, as we have had the opportunity to learn new things and get to know new people. This book project has been an important way for us to participate in the development of the SAP agenda, and we are especially happy about the dialogue that has been established with those who have not usually been considered to be part of the SAP community. All this has required a great deal of effort from the authors. We are grateful to the authors of the previous edition, who without hesitation agreed to revise and update their chapters, and to the new ones, for so generously accepting the challenge to join us in this great adventure. This second edition literally would not have happened had not Paula Parish from Cambridge University Press approached us, and she has been a fantastic key person to work with. We also want to thank all the others in the great CUP team facilitating this editing process.

Damon, Linda, David and Eero

Introduction: what is strategy as practice?

DAMON GOLSORKHI, LINDA ROULEAU,
DAVID SEIDL and EERO VAARA

Strategy as practice as a research approach

Since early 2000 strategy as practice (SAP) has emerged as a distinctive approach for studying strategic management, strategic decision-making, strategizing, strategy-making and strategy work (Whittington 1996; Johnson, Melin and Whittington 2003; Jarzabkowski, Balogun and Seidl 2007). In recent years SAP research has confirmed its vitality and fulfilled its promise by being more lively than ever (Golsorkhi *et al.* 2010; Vaara and Whittington 2012; Balogun *et al.* 2014; Seidl and Whittington 2014). This second edition of the handbook confirms the strong enthusiasm for the generation of new ideas about the way practitioners are doing their strategy work. Strategy-as-practice research focuses on the micro-level social activities, processes and practices that characterize organizational strategy and strategizing. This provides not only an organizational perspective into strategic decision-making but also a strategic angle for examining the process of organizing, and thereby serves as a useful research programme and social movement for connecting contemporary strategic management research with practice-oriented organizational studies.

Strategy as practice can be regarded as an alternative to the mainstream strategy research via its attempt to shift attention away from a 'mere' focus on the effects of strategies on performance alone to a more comprehensive, in-depth analysis of what actually takes place in strategy formulation, planning and implementation and other activities that deal with the thinking and doing of strategy. In other words, SAP research is interested in the 'black box' of strategy work that once led the research agenda in strategic management research

(Mintzberg 1973; Mintzberg and Waters 1985; Pettigrew 1973), but has thereafter been replaced by other issues, not least because of the increasing dominance of the micro-economic approach and a methodological preoccupation with statistical analysis. Because of its micro-level focus, studies following the strategy-as-practice agenda tend to draw on theories and apply methods that differ from the common practices of strategy scholars. In this way, SAP research can contribute to the evolution of strategic management as a discipline and body of knowledge with new theories and methodological choices.

It would be a mistake, however, not to link strategy-as-practice research to the broader 'practice turn' in contemporary social sciences. In fact, 'practice' has emerged as a key concept for understanding central questions about how agency and structure, and individual action and institutions, are linked in social systems, cultures and organizations (Bourdieu 1990; Foucault 1977; Giddens 1984; de Certeau 1984; Sztompka 1991; Schatzki 2002). This practice turn is visible in many areas of the social sciences today, including organizational research (Brown and Duguid 1991; Orlikowski 2000; Nicolini, Gherardi and Yanow 2003; Feldman and Orlikowski 2011; Nicolini 2012). It is about time that we utilized this paradigm to enrich our understanding of organizational strategy.

'Practice' is a very special concept, in that it allows researchers to engage in a direct dialogue with practitioners. Studying practices enables one to examine issues that are directly relevant to those who are dealing with strategy, either as strategists engaged in strategic planning or other activities linked with strategy, or as those who have to cope with the strategies and their implications. By so doing, studies under this broad umbrella promise

1

to accomplish something that is rare in contemporary management and organization research: to advance our theoretical understanding in a way that has practical relevance for managers and other organizational members.

Like any emergent research approach, strategy as practice can either develop into a clearly defined but narrow theoretico-methodological perspective, or grow into an open and versatile research programme that is constantly stretching its boundaries. A key motivation behind this handbook, reinforced in this second edition, is to actively pursue the latter alternative. By spelling out and elaborating various alternative perspectives on strategy as practice, we wish to contribute to the expansion and further development of this research approach. Although there exists a risk of eclecticism and ambiguity, we believe that the benefits of theoretical and methodological innovation and continued discussion outweigh such concerns. Our view of strategy as practice emphasizes the usefulness of studying 'practical reason' – the starting point in Dewey's (1938) and Bourdieu's (1990) analyses of social practice. According to this view, we must focus on the actual practices that constitute strategy and strategizing while at the same time reflecting on our own positions, perspectives and practices as researchers. This includes a need to draw from, apply and develop various theoretical ideas and empirical methods.

This handbook represents a unique collection of ontological, epistemological, theoretical and methodological perspectives as well as work on substantive topic areas on strategy as practice, as written by leading scholars in the field. When compiling the handbook, we as editors had three specific goals in mind. First, as explained above, we wished to open up more extensively than in the first edition the multiple ways in which academics from other perspectives think about and conduct SAP research. This is shown in the multiplicity of approaches presented in our five parts, which are complementary to each other in various ways. In this endeavour, we emphasize the need to study both concrete instances of organizational strategizing and broader issues, such as the institutionalization of strategy as a body of knowledge and praxis (Seidl and Whittington 2014). Second, we were

determined to promote critical thinking. This is important to make sure that strategy-as-practice research does not dissolve into a restricted study of top management but includes analysis of how others contribute to strategizing and how they at times may resist strategies and their implications. Moreover, reflection on strategy as a body of knowledge (Knights and Morgan 1991) and praxis (Whittington 2006) that has all kinds of power implications must continue. Third, unlike many handbooks, we emphasize the future. Thus, the chapters included in this book not only provide overviews of what has already been done in this field but also spell out theoretical or methodological ideas for the future.

The rest of this introduction is organized as follows. First, there is a brief overview of the practice turn in social science, followed by a review of strategy-as-practice research. We then introduce the contributions of this handbook, starting with ontological and epistemological questions and proceeding to the various alternative theories. Then several methodological choices are laid out, before introducing some substantive topic areas of strategy as practice that have been developed to date.

The practice turn in social sciences

The purpose of this section is to highlight central ideas in the so-called practice turn in social sciences. A comprehensive review of the various perspectives is beyond the scope of this introduction, however (see, for example, Turner 1994; Schatzki, Knorr Cetina and von Savigny 2001; Reckwitz 2002). To begin with, it is important to note that representatives of several schools of thought have contributed to our understanding of the central role of practices in social reality. These include philosophers (Wittgenstein 1953 [1951]; Foucault 1977; Dreyfus 1991; Tuomela 2005), sociologists (Giddens 1984; de Certeau 1984; Bourdieu 1990), anthropologists (Ortner 2006), activity theorists (Vygotsky 1978; Engeström, Miettinen and Punamäki 1999), discourse analysts (Fairclough 2003), feminist scholars (Martin 2003) and many others.

Although there is no single motive behind this collective interest, three things should be emphasized. First, a focus on practice provides an opportunity to examine the micro-level of social activity and its construction in a real social context or field. Thus, a practice approach allows one to move from general and abstract reflection on social activity to an increasingly targeted analysis of social reality. This is not to say that all practice-oriented research would have to engage in ethnographic, discourse or conversation analysis, or activity theory or any other type of micro-level empirical study. On the contrary, a key part of the practice literature has been very theoretical in nature. Nevertheless, the advantage that a practice approach brings to areas such as strategy lies predominantly in its ability to elucidate the micro-level foundations of social activity in a particular setting – in either theoretical or empirical studies. Furthermore, the flexibility and multiplicity of variations in the notion of practice make it possible to analyse activities from multiple angles. Activity can be studied as more or less intentional action, cognition, embodied material practice, discourse or text – and the list does not stop here.

Second, the practice approach breaks with methodological individualism by emphasizing that activities need to be understood as enabled or constrained by the prevailing practices in the field in question. Thus, a practice approach to strategy should not merely focus on the behaviours or actions of managers but seek to examine how these behaviours or actions are linked with prevailing practices. A fundamental insight in practice theories is that individual behaviours or actions – however they are defined – are always related to the ways in which social actors are supposed to think or feel or communicate in and through language in a given situation. Moreover, most practice theories emphasize the latent connection to material aspects of social reality. In other words, specific behaviours or actions are closely linked with or mediated by material resources.

Third, the notion of practice allows one to deal with one of the most fundamental issues in contemporary social analysis: how social action is linked with structure and agency. Although views on the linkage of practice and activity differ, most

scholars emphasize the potential of the concept of practice to explain why and how social action sometimes follows and reproduces routines, rules and norms and sometimes doesn't. For example, Giddens' (1984), Foucault's (1980) and Bourdieu's (1990) seminal works all focus on 'practice' as a key theoretical concept when dealing with social activity. For Giddens (1984), structuration is the key issue; practices are reproduced and at times transformed in social action, thus reifying social structures. For Foucault (1977; 1980), the point is that we are all constrained and enabled by discursive practices that include all kinds of social practices in addition to pure discourse. And, for Bourdieu (1990; 1994), practices constitute an essential part of all human activity; they are part of a grammar of dispositions (inculcated in 'habitus') that defines what can and will be done in social fields.

This may all give the impression that a meta-theory of social practice exists that could be applied to areas such as strategy research. The fact remains, however, that a closer look at the various perspectives referred to above reveals fundamental epistemological, theoretical and methodological differences. This multiplicity of perspectives does not have to be seen as an impediment to the development of practice-based approaches, but a richness that can help us to better understand various aspects of social activities and practices in contexts such as strategy as practice.

Overview of strategy-as-practice research

Strategy-as-practice research developed from several sources. Classics of strategy process research (Pettigrew 1973; Mintzberg, Raisinghani and Théoret 1976; Mintzberg and Waters 1985; Burgelman 1983) and various attempts to broaden and renew strategic management (Eisenhardt 1989; Gioia and Chittipeddi 1991; Knights and Morgan 1991; Johnson and Huff 1998; Langley 1989; Oakes, Townley and Cooper 1998) can be seen as its intellectual roots. Despite its many important predecessors, however, it has only been from the mid-2000s that strategy as practice has established itself as a clearly defined sub-field in strategy research, bringing together like-minded colleagues whose ideas might otherwise have 'remained marginal and isolated voices in the wilderness' (Johnson et al. 2007: 212). Since the publication of the seminal *Journal of Management Studies* special issue on 'micro strategy and strategizing' (Johnson, Melin and Whittington 2003), which defined the SAP research agenda for the first time, we have seen more than 100 journal articles in leading journals, eight special issues, several foundational books, at least two comprehensive review papers and numerous book chapters, not to speak of the wealth of conference papers presented every year since then. In the following we provide a short overview of this research stream (see Appendix). We focus first on the contributions that have aimed at developing the strategy-as-practice research agenda, and then turn to important themes within this area.

Development of the research agenda

Important efforts have been made to define and develop the strategy-as-practice approach per se. These include analyses that have focused on *the role and characteristics of strategy-as-practice research in relation to other sub-fields of strategy.* The first paper to do so was that of Whittington (1996), who positions strategy as practice with reference to the policy, planning and process approaches as the major perspectives on strategy. Given the affinities of the SAP approach with the process approach, it is not surprising that others have elaborated on the similarities and differences between the two (Johnson et al. 2007; Whittington 2007; Chia and MacKay 2007; Floyd et al. 2011). In addition, there are several works that show how strategy as practice can be understood as a complementary approach to the resource-based view in general (Johnson, Melin and Whittington 2003; Johnson et al. 2007) and dynamic capabilities in particular (Regnér 2008).

Strategy-as-practice research has included publications that have *developed the research agenda and offered explicit frameworks.* This includes the seminal paper by Johnson, Melin and Whittington (2003), in which the SAP approach – at that time labelled the 'activity-based view of strategy' – was introduced for the first time. The approach is

characterized as concern 'for the close understanding of the myriad, micro activities that make up strategy and strategizing in practice' (Johnson, Melin and Whittington 2003: 3). This characterization was refined by Whittington (2006), who emphasizes that the strategizing activities needed to be understood in their wider social context: actors are not working in isolation but are drawing upon the regular, socially defined *modus operandi* that arise from the plural social institutions to which they belong. Based on this, Whittington proposes an overarching framework of 'practitioners' (that is, those who do the actual work of making, shaping and executing strategy), 'praxis' (the concrete, situated doing of strategy) and 'practices' (the routinized types of behaviour drawn upon in the concrete doing of strategy) as the three building blocks that make up strategizing.

This framework was further developed by Jarzabkowski, Balogun and Seidl (2007), who argue that, because of pragmatic reasons, empirical works would do well to focus on the relation between any two of the building blocks while (temporarily) bracketing out the third. In their review of the strategy-as-practice literature of the time, they show how all papers can be placed within this framework, identifying particular gaps from which they develop a research agenda for future work. Johnson et al. (2007) propose another overarching framework, which positions different research projects according to the level of analysis (the level of actions, the organizational level and the field level) and according to whether they are concerned with content or process issues. The authors use this framework to examine the strength and distinctiveness of the existing research and propose their own agenda for future work. A literature review and research agenda on the basis of this framework is provided by Jarzabkowski and Spee (2009). More recently, Vaara and Whittington (2012) offer an extensive literature review on SAP research, attesting its vitality and contributions regarding the tools and methods of strategy-making (practices), how strategy work takes place (praxis) and the role and identity of the actors involved (practitioners).

There are several useful discussions of various *theoretical perspectives* on strategy-as-practice research. Jarzabkowski, for example, explores activity theory (Jarzabkowski 2003; 2005), different theories of social practice (Jarzabkowski 2004) and structuration theory in particular (Jarzabkowski 2008). Denis, Langley and Rouleau (2007) compare potential contributions from theories of social practice, convention theory and actor–network theory. Johnson *et al.* (2007) provide an exploration of situated learning theory, actor–network theory, the Carnegie tradition of the sensemaking and routines perspective, and institutional theory. In addition, Chia and Holt (2006) have explored the potential of the Heideggerian perspective, Campbell-Hunt (2007) complexity theory, Seidl (2007) systemic-discursive theories (such as those by Wittgenstein, Lyotard and Luhmann), Fenton and Langley (2011) and Brown and Thompson (2013) the narrative perspective, Ezzamel and Willmott (2010) poststructuralist analysis and Vaara (2010) critical discourse analysis as fruitful bases for SAP research. Following Hendry and Seidl (2003), Katzberg (2013) has drawn on Luhmann's system theory for theorizing the interconnectedness between different organizational arenas. Balogun *et al.* (2014) have, in turn, elaborated on the role of discourse as the central foci of SAP research, and Guérard, Langley and Seidl (2013) have explored the potential of different performativity perspectives, such as those of Austin, Butler, Lyotard and Callon. In a recent article, Seidl and Whittington (2014) provide an overview of different theoretical perspectives in terms of the ways in which they allow the linking of local strategizing activity to larger social phenomena.

Closely related, there also are a few *methodological reflections on strategy as practice*, though explicit contributions have been rare. The paper of Balogun, Huff and Johnson (2003) was the first to address this issue and to suggest particular methodological approaches. The paper summarizes the particular methodological challenges of SAP research as follows: 'The growing need of researchers to be close to the phenomena of study, to concentrate on context and detail, and simultaneously to be broad in their scope of study, attending to many parts of the organization, clearly creates conflicts' (Balogun, Huff and Johnson 2003: 198). This issue is also taken up by Johnson *et al.* (2007), providing illustrations of various methodological choices and their respective advantages and disadvantages. Rasche and Chia (2009) also deal with methodological challenges in a section of their paper that propagates ethnographic approaches as most suitable for strategy-as-practice research. Venkateswaran and Prabhu (2010) argue for process and clinical studies for advancing our knowledge of the practice of strategy-making. For a broad range of novel ways of interacting with informants, collecting data, involving collaborators and so on, the chapter written by Huff, Neyer and Moslein (2010) in the *Handbook*'s first edition remains an important methodological piece to consult.

Others have *criticized the predominant definitions and approaches to SAP research*, however. In particular, Chia and his colleagues have provided alternative perspectives on the analysis of strategy (Chia and MacKay 2007; Rasche and Chia 2009; Chia and Holt 2009). Rather than building on the proposed frameworks, they criticize current research for its lack of distinctiveness, and call for a more focused approach that breaks away from the methodological individualism that still dominates strategy-as-practice work. In addition, Clegg, Carter and Kornberger (Clegg, Carter and Kornberger 2004; Carter, Clegg and Kornberger 2008; 2010; Carter 2013) have critiqued the conceptual and methodological bases of much of the research in this area. In a nutshell, they argue for more theoretically advanced and critically oriented studies to explore fundamental issues of identity and power. This critique served as a key motivator for the expansion and development of the strategy-as-practice research agenda in this second edition, with several implicit and explicit chapters around these issues (including a chapter by Clegg and Kornberger on strategy as practice and power, and another by Blom and Alvesson on strategy as practice and critical approaches). In a more optimistic tone, Rouleau (2013) provides a reflexive view of the knowledge production project underlying the development of this research perspective. She considers that this perspective is now at the crossroads, and invites researchers to discuss how in a more advanced stage of institutionalization and development this new knowledge project will be able to cultivate its inherent diversity while consolidating its agenda.

Central themes in strategy-as-practice research

Strategy-as-practice research has examined various important themes, including strategy work in different settings, formal strategic practices, sensemaking in strategizing, materiality and tools in strategy work, discursive practices of strategy, roles and identities in strategizing and power in strategy.

The thrust of existing research has focused on *ways in which strategy work is conducted in specific organizational settings*. In fact, most studies in this area have concentrated on organizational processes, activities and practices in particular contexts. In addition to studying business organizations, such as venture capital firms (King 2008), financial services organizations (Ambrosini, Bowman and Burton-Taylor 2007), airlines (Vaara, Kleymann and Seristö 2004), clothing companies (Rouleau 2005) or multi-business firms (Paroutis and Pettigrew 2007; Jarzabkowski and Balogun 2009), scholars have examined strategizing in orchestras (Maitlis and Lawrence 2003), artistic organizations (Daigle and Rouleau 2010), hospitals (Denis *et al.* 2011), cities (Kornberger and Clegg 2011; Pälli, Vaara and Sorsa 2009) and universities (Jarzabkowski 2003; 2004; 2005; Jarzabkowski and Seidl 2008). These analyses have also revealed general patterns of strategizing; for example, Regnér (2003) shows that there are significant differences in the way that people in the centre of a firm strategize compared to those who work on the periphery. Hydle (forthcoming) draws attention to the way that strategy work is organized both temporally and spatially.

Researchers have also focused special attention on *formal strategic practices*. Studies have examined strategy workshops (Hendry and Seidl 2003; Hodgkinson *et al.* 2006; Bourque and Johnson 2008; Whittington *et al.* 2006; MacIntosh, Maclean and Seidl 2010; Healey *et al.* forthcoming), strategy meetings (Jarzabkowski and Seidl 2008; Spee and Jarzabkowski 2011; Wodak, Kwon

and Clarke 2011; Asmuß and Oshima 2012; Liu and Maitlis 2014; Kwon, Clarke and Wodak 2014), committees (Hoon 2007), formal teams (Paroutis and Pettigrew 2007; Hendry, Kiel and Nicholson 2010) and various formal administrative routines (Jarzabkowski 2003; 2005; Jarzabkowski and Wilson 2002). These formal practices play a key role in strategy formation, and, for this reason, Whittington and Cailluet (2008) have dedicated an entire special issue of *Long Range Planning* to the exploration of new avenues for research into strategic planning.

A significant part of strategy-as-practice research to date has been devoted to the study of *sensemaking in strategizing*. In contrast to earlier works on cognitive aspects, SAP scholars have been interested in the social dimensions of sensemaking. Accordingly, researchers have focused on the socially negotiated nature of sensemaking (Balogun and Johnson 2004; 2005; Rouleau and Balogun 2011), the political contests around the framing of strategic issues (Kaplan 2008), the temporal dimension of sensemaking (Kaplan and Orlikowski 2013), the interaction between individual-level and organizational-level sensemaking (Stensaker and Falkenberg 2007), the influence of the wider societal context on sensemaking activities at the organizational interface (Rouleau 2005; Teulier and Rouleau 2013), the political aspects (Mueller *et al.* 2013) and the role of emotions in sensemaking (Liu and Maitlis 2014). The role of emotions in particular is a topic that deserves more attention in future research.

Studies on the *discursive aspects of strategy* have become increasingly popular in recent years. A seminal paper by Knights and Morgan (1991) examines the historical emergence of strategic management discourse, and its assumptions and implications for management. Hendry (2000) provides another influential account of strategy as an essentially discursive practice. Based on ethnomethodology and conversation analysis, Samra-Fredericks (2003; 2004; 2005) has focused on the rhetorical micro-processes of strategizing and the ways in which conversations impact strategy, and thereafter strategy conversations have been examined from other perspectives too (Whittle *et al.* 2014; Wodak, Kwon and Clarke

2011). Coming from a somewhat different perspective, Seidl (2007) points to the differences between different types of strategy discourses and the problematic relations between them. Drawing on critical discourse analysis, Vaara and his colleagues have examined how discursive practices make up strategy (Vaara, Kleymann and Seristö 2004), how strategy discourse is appropriated and resisted (Laine and Vaara 2007) and how discourses may impede or promote participation in strategic decision-making (Mantere and Vaara 2008). Phillips, Sewell and Jaynes (2008) have followed suit to provide an integrative model of the role of discourse in strategic decision-making, and Hardy and Thomas (2014) provide an illuminative analysis of how strategy discourses construct objects and subjects. Drawing on seminal work on strategy and narratives (Barry and Elmes 1997), strategy-as-practice researchers have focused on the role of narratives and storytelling in strategy work (Fenton and Langley 2011; Brown and Thompson 2013: Vaara and Reff Pedersen 2013). Strategic plans have also received special attention in recent years (Cornut, Giroux and Langley 2012; Spee and Jarzabkowski 2011; Vaara, Sorsa and Pälli 2010). The discursive perspective of strategy as practice has been one of the most fast-growing perspectives since 2010, including a special issue in the *Journal of Management Studies* (Balogun *et al.* 2014).

Research around the role of *materiality and tools* in strategizing is a growing area of contribution. In the wake of this research stream, Heracleous and Jacobs (2008), show how material artefacts are purposefully employed in change interventions in order to stimulate particular sensemaking processes. Whittington *et al.* (2006) discuss physical objects as particular means of communication. Some authors have studied the ways in which tools and techniques change according to context (Seidl 2007; Jarzabkowski and Wilson 2006). Others have examined strategy tools as potential boundary objects that can span across different organizational contexts (Spee and Jarzabkowski 2009). Kaplan's (2011) analysis of PowerPoint has elucidated the specific ways in which material objects influence strategy processes. Wright, Paroutis and Blettner (2013) study how, when and to what effect strategy tools are used in strategy work. Jarzabkowski, Spee and Smets (2013), as well as Werle and Seidl (forthcoming), focus on how knowledge is inscribed in visual artefacts and the way these shape unfolding strategy processes. Jarzabkowski and Kaplan (2015) provide a framework for understanding the reciprocal relationship between the agency of actors and the selection, application and outcomes of tools. Moreover, there have been calls to analyse the ways in which strategizing work has changed through the use of technologies such as mobile phones and the like (see, for example, Molloy and Whittington 2005).

Researchers have also examined the *roles and identities of managers and other organizational members engaged in strategy work*. Accordingly, a great deal of research has been devoted to the strategic role of middle managers (Fauré and Rouleau 2011; Mantere 2005; 2008; Sillince and Mueller 2007; Balogun and Johnson 2004; 2005; Rouleau 2005; Rouleau and Balogun 2011; Thomas, Sargent and Hardy 2011). Other actors who have received specific attention are consultants (Nordqvist and Melin 2008; Schwarz 2004) and regulators (Jarzabkowski, Matthiesen and Van de Ven 2009). In addition, scholars have pointed out the need for research into the strategic roles of strategy teachers and strategy gurus (Hendry 2000; Whittington *et al.* 2003). Furthermore, Rouleau (2003) has examined the impact of gender on strategizing practice. Beech and Johnson (2005) in turn show the recursive relation between a strategist's identity and strategizing activities during a larger change project. In another study, Lounsbury and Crumley (2007) provide a conceptualization of agency that accounts for the way in which practitioners are constrained by wider societal belief systems, providing meaning to their activities and prescribing them specific roles that delimit the scope for performativity. Following Knights and Morgan (1991), others have focused on the social construction of the identity and subjectivity of strategists (Dameron and Torset 2014; Dick and Collings 2014; Laine and Vaara 2007). These analyses have been closely connected with discourse and power, as explained below.

Ever since the beginning of strategy-as-practice research, scholars have also been interested in *issues of power*. Knights and Morgan (1991) set out on an analysis of the 'disciplinary force' of strategy as a particular institutional practice. Studies drawing on critical discourse analyses have also focused on the ways in which strategy discourse can be used to legitimize or resist specific ideas and to promote or protect one's own power position (Laine and Vaara 2007; Mantere and Vaara 2008). This has been followed by studies by Ezzamel and Willmott (2008) and McCabe (2010), who examine the power differentials and inequalities in the strategizing processes occurring in a global retailer and manufacturing company and a UK building society, respectively, focusing attention on various modes of resistance. Other studies focus on power as the central issue of strategic processes and practices. Samra-Fredericks (2005), for example, provides a fine-grained study of the everyday interactional constitution of power based on an analysis of the talk within a strategy meeting. Kornberger and Clegg (2011) in their study of the strategy-making process undertaken by the city of Sydney highlight the power effects resulting from the simultaneous representation of facts and values. They argue that strategy is a sociopolitical practice aimed at mobilizing people, marshalling political will and legitimizing decisions. Mueller *et al.* (2013) studied a multinational apparel company, and they highlight how politics constitutes a central interpretive method through which organizational reality is constructed and strategic decisions are made. Based on a case study of global telecommunication company, Hardy and Thomas (2014) in turn show how the power effects of discourses are intensified through particular discursive and material practices, leading to the production of objects and subjects that are clearly aligned with the strategy.

Ontological and epistemological questions

The strategy-as-practice approach was born from a break with the traditional notion of strategy as a property of organizations. Instead, strategy was to be understood as an activity or practice: strategy is not something that firms *have*, but something that

people *do* (Johnson, Melin and Whittington 2003; Jarzabkowski *et al.* 2007). If taken seriously, this reconceptualization implies a fundamental ontological shift in several respects. First, the world of strategy is no longer taken to be something stable that can be observed but, rather, constitutes a reality in flux (a dynamic and processual perspective). Second, strategy is no longer regarded as 'located' on the organizational level; instead, it is spread out across many levels, from the level of individual actions to the institutional level (multilevel perspective). Third, the world of strategy constitutes a genuinely social reality created and recreated in the interactions between various actors inside and outside the organization (open perspective). Accordingly, there are several fundamental epistemological consequences for both researchers and practitioners. So far, however, strategy-as-practice scholars have focused relatively little attention on epistemological questions. In this sense, the chapters in Part I of this second edition of the handbook pave the way for a better understanding of these fundamental issues.

Wanda Orlikowski in her chapter distinguishes three different types of practice research in organization studies in general and strategy-as-practice research in particular. These three types of research result from fundamentally different understandings of 'practice' among the respective researchers. The first type treats practice merely as *phenomenon*: researchers study what happens 'in actual practice', as opposed to what is merely derived theoretically. The second type emphasizes practice as a theoretical *perspective*: apart from attending to actual practice, researchers draw on practice-centred theory in their studies. Incorporating the assumptions of the other two types, the third mode highlights the notion of practice as a particular *philosophy* (ontology): researchers conceive of practice as constitutive of all social reality – i.e. actors and agency are treated as a product of their practices. This mode of engagement with practice is the most extreme form, rarely found in existing publications. Orlikowski discusses the general challenges of the three different practice views and the implications for research practice.

The next two chapters elaborate on Orlikowski's third mode of practice engagement. Drawing on

Heidegger, Robert Chia and Andreas Rasche characterize this mode as a 'dwelling worldview', in contrast to what they refer to as a 'building worldview'. The latter is the dominant view inherent in traditional strategy research, accounting for a large percentage of existing strategy-as-practice work. This view is characterized by two basic assumptions: (1) individuals are treated as discretely bounded entities, and (2) there is a clear split between the mental and physical realms; cognition and mental representation of the world necessarily precede any meaningful action. Accordingly, strategic action is explained through recourse to the intention of actors. In contrast, the dwelling worldview does not assume that the identities and characteristics of persons pre-date social interactions and social practices. Social practices are given primacy over individual agency and intention. Thus, strategic actions are explained not on the basis of individual intentions but as the product of particular, historically situated practices. Chia and Rasche discuss the epistemological consequences of these two worldviews. They argue that the research findings depend greatly on the chosen worldview.

In the following chapter, Haridimos Tsoukas develops the argument of Chia and Rasche further. In line with earlier works by Chia (Chia and Holt 2006; Chia and MacKay 2007), he argues that strategy-as-practice researchers need to follow Orlikowski's third mode of practice engagement. Only this would allow them to go beyond the process approach in strategy. He supports the call for a clear break with methodological individualism in favour of a view that gives primacy to practice. He warns about pushing research too much in the opposite direction, however, where strategy is treated as emergent by definition. Instead, we need to reconcile – from a practice-based approach – the possibility of both non-deliberate and deliberate types of action in strategy. Drawing on Heidegger's philosophy, he develops a framework that distinguishes between four different types of actions according to the involved form and degree of intentionality: (1) 'practical coping' (based on tacit understandings); (2) 'deliberate coping' (based on explicit awareness); (3) 'detached coping' (based on thematic awareness); and (4) 'theoretical coping' (based on theoretical understanding). These four forms of action are then linked to four forms of strategy-making.

Simon Grand, Widar von Arx and Johannes Rüegg-Stürm argue in their chapter that serious practice research needs to be accompanied by constructivist epistemologies. They show that, while there are many variants of constructivism, they all share four central concerns: (1) they question a concept of 'reality' as something that is 'objectively given'; (2) they study the status of knowledge and the processes through which it is constructed; (3) they treat agency in the construction of reality as distributed among heterogeneous actants; and (4) they challenge the predominance of unquestioned dichotomies in the social sciences, such as micro versus macro or situated activities versus collective practices. After introducing and comparing the three most central constructivist perspectives, Grand, von Arx and Rüegg-Stürm discuss the implications of the four central assumptions of strategy-as-practice research, useful for the study of strategizing practices, the understanding of strategy and the conduct of strategy research. Above all, they emphasize that the very notion of strategy and strategizing practice contains nothing that can be taken as given, but is instead the result of continuous (re)construction by the activities of the practitioners and researchers involved.

The chapter by Katharina Dittrich, Karen Golden-Biddle, Elana Feldman and Karen Locke continues the same theme by examining how SAP articles construct their contribution to the field of organizational studies. Based on earlier work (Locke and Golden-Biddle 1997), they argue that the construction of academic contributions can be examined along two dimensions: (1) the article needs to make connections among extant work, and between extant work and the respective article; this can be accomplished in several different ways, for example by presenting progressive coherence in the literature; and (2), in order to make a contribution, the article has to problematize the current state of research. Again, there are different methods for doing this, such as by presenting it as incomplete or contradictory. Combining the two dimensions, the authors create a framework of nine generic choices for constructing contributions. By placing the existing strategy-as-practice papers within the framework, Dittrich, Golden-Biddle, Feldman and Locke identify opportunities for the construction of contributions yet to be examined by strategy-as-practice researchers.

Ann Langley addresses a central question in strategy-as-practice research: how can we build a cumulative body of knowledge when SAP interests tend to favour small, intensive samples and fine-grained analysis, leading to corresponding limitations in terms of generalizability? Langley addresses this question from three different perspectives on the nature and purpose of science: (1) the 'normal-science view' is based on the ongoing search for more accurate, general and useful causal statements about the relationships between important phenomena; (2) rather than striving for a single truth, the 'practice view' calls for increasingly insightful interpretations or representations of the social world; and (3) the 'pragmatic view' puts the emphasis on the instrumentality of knowledge. Accordingly, the researcher ought to uncover the knowledge of the practitioners, render it explicit and make it available to others. Langley shows how the different publications in the field of strategy as practice invariably fall into one of the three views of science. She concludes by discussing the advantages and disadvantages were strategy as practice to adhere to any one of these models of science.

In the final chapter of Part I, Violetta Splitter and David Seidl address the practical relevance of practice-based research on strategy. They review practice-based studies that have examined the ontological and epistemological conditions for producing strategy research that proves relevant to management practice. Drawing on these works, they argue that researchers inevitably adopt a scholastic point of view, which makes it impossible to capture directly the logic of strategy practice. Strategy-as-practice scholars can increase the practical relevance of their research, however, by developing theories based on practical logic. They outline three approaches to capture the logic of management practice: (1) theorizing through practical rationality, (2) the application of 'participant objectivation' and (3) the consideration of the dissociation process. They argue that, if strategy-as-

practice research builds on these insights, it can prove a particularly fruitful approach for generating knowledge that is of conceptual relevance to strategy practice.

Theoretical resources: social theory

With Lewin's adage that 'nothing is so practical as a good theory' in mind, it is important to focus attention on the theoretical basis of strategy as practice. A 'good' theory allows us to advance knowledge without having to reinvent the wheel. By offering a means to make sense of the very processes, activities and practices that constitute strategy and strategizing, it can also serve practitioners. There is no one theory of practice, however, that can provide a basis for all relevant research questions at various levels of analysis, which range from reflections on strategy as a body of knowledge and praxis to studies of the idiosyncrasies of specific strategic and organizational processes in different institutional and cultural contexts. Nor should a unified theory be the objective if we wish to advance the theoretical discussion of practices and their implications. Consequently, strategy-as-practice research can and must be informed by alternative conceptions of practice and strategy. Various approaches have been offered and applied, the most important of which are presented and discussed in Parts II and III of this handbook; while Part II focuses on general social theories, Part III contains organization and management theories. The chapters in these two parts serve to explain how specific approaches are able to elucidate our understanding not only of concrete strategic decision-making but also of strategy as a body of knowledge and praxis.

In the first chapter of Part II, Richard Whittington explains how Giddens' (1984) structuration theory can be applied to strategy-as-practice research. Giddens has been a key source of inspiration in seminal pieces of strategy as practice, including Whittington's own influential work (Whittington 1992; 2006). In his chapter, Whittington demonstrates how management researchers have already applied structuration theory in strategy-as-practice research. He explains how

structuration theory differs from two close alternatives: the practice-theoretic approach of Bourdieu
and the critical realist approach of Bhaskar and
Archer. Whittington focuses on the advantages of
structuration theory and highlights its usefulness
for analysis that deals with the ever-present issues
of agency and structure. He also points out, however, that there is more to structuration theory than
has been realized in previous research. In particular, he argues that the institution of strategy has
received far too little attention, and he concludes
by calling for further studies in this area.

Paula Jarzabkowski and Carola Wolf focus on
activity theory as an approach for studying strategy
as practice. They introduce the origins of activity
theory in Russian social psychology before showing how scholars in areas as diverse as technology
studies, education and organization theory have
drawn upon it to explain how human activity
develops within its cultural and historical context.
A conceptual framework is then developed, to
show how activity theory can contribute to understanding organizational practices generally and
strategy-as-practice topics specifically, building
on the concepts of strategy practitioners, practices
and praxis. In particular, their framework focuses
on the way that strategy practices mediate human
activity. Throughout the chapter they outline a
series of pertinent research areas in which strategy-as-practice scholars may benefit from an activity theory approach.

Marie-Léandre Gomez provides a Bourdieusian
perspective on strategy as practice. This is a contribution that is very much needed, given the
impact of Bourdieu's work on practice theory in
general. Gomez explains how Bourdieu offers a
systemic view of practice that highlights the
importance of relations between agents and with
the field, the capital possessed by these actors, and
their habitus. She argues that research on strategy
can benefit greatly from Bourdieu's praxeology. In
particular, a Bourdieusian perspective allows one
to overcome false dichotomies in strategy and strategizing: the micro/macro alternative, the opposition between structure and agency, and the
dilemma between rationality and emerging strategy. In addition, the perspective can help us
achieve a better understanding of the various

struggles that characterize strategy and the role of
academics in these struggles.

Jean-Pascal Gond, Bernard Leca and Charlotte
Cloutier introduce the economies-of-worth (EW)
perspective to strategy-as-practice scholars, emphasizing its critical distance from earlier forms of
critical sociology and its distinctiveness from the
concept of institutional logic. They clarify the EW
assumptions, introduce its key concepts and explain
its usefulness for understanding the formation of
social agreement in the context of disputes. Based
on a review of existing economies-of-worth studies,
the chapter shows how the EW framework might
inform new lines of inquiry and conceptual developments for future SAP research, focusing on the
core topics of justification, valuation and critiques.

Saku Mantere turns his attention to Wittgenstein
and the potential of the philosopher's ideas for
elucidating our understanding of strategy as practice. This is an important contribution in view of
the fact that, apart from Wittgenstein being one of
the most influential philosophers, his ideas have
paved the way for the 'practice turn' in social
science. Both Giddens and Bourdieu, for example,
have been greatly influenced by Wittgenstein.
Mantere focuses on the idea of the 'language game'
as a powerful concept to make sense of strategy as
practice. He argues that language games shed more
light on the discursive struggles endemic to the
practice of strategy. He also maintains that the
notion of 'forms of life', used to characterize
the non-linguistic background of social practice,
can direct our attention onto a number of important
yet often neglected aspects of strategy. Examples
from real-life strategy conversations provide concrete illustrations of these ideas.

Florence Allard-Poesi adopts a Foucauldian view
on strategy as practice. This reflection explains the
seminal role of Foucault's work in more critical
studies of strategy as practice, as well as pointing
to new ways in which we can look at strategy as a
body of knowledge. From this perspective, strategic
management may be seen as a heterogeneous set of
discursive and material practices. These discursive
and material practices are governed by specific rules
that structure what can be read, said and done in and
around strategy. They are techniques utilized for
controlling from a distance in the modern

enterprise, with both enabling and constraining implications for organizations and their members. Allard-Poesi argues that strategic management is similar to a monitoring technique in which the strategist is led to reveal one's intentions, say aloud what is hidden and 'objectify' one's subjectivity. This has all kinds of effects on the individuals in question and the way in which people can and will make sense of strategy.

Valérie-Inès de La Ville and Eléonore Mounoud outline a narrative approach to strategy as practice. They draw on the work of Riceour and de Certeau in order to elucidate the various narrative practices that constitute an inherent part of strategy and strategizing. This involves the production of texts in strategy formulation, but also the consumption of texts in the 'implementation' of strategies. De La Ville and Mounoud offer a model that focuses on the writing and reading of texts and narratives as ongoing activities in organizations. This view allows one to understand the crucial role of strategy texts and ongoing interpretations in strategizing – and thus challenges the conventional view, which focuses solely on formal strategies without considering the ways in which they are 'talked into being'.

Christopher Chapman, Wai Fong Chua and Habib Mahama discuss the varieties of points of contact between actor–network theory and strategy-as-practice research. They review the origins of actor–network theory and discuss three of its foundational principles, namely generalized symmetry, recursivity and radical indeterminacy. The authors describe how various streams of preoccupations related to strategic decision-making, planning, accounting and control have dealt with these principles over time. By showing how these principles have been drawn on in empirical studies, Chapman, Chua and Mahama elaborate on how strategy-as-practice researchers can draw on actor–network theorizing to fruitfully advance our understanding of the dispersed, complex and non-linear trajectory of strategy-making.

Theoretical resources: management and organization theory

In Part III we continue our theoretical exploration and exploitation of useful perspectives to understand strategy as practice. in contrast to the chapters in Part II, however, the focus here is not on general social theories but on management and organization theories. Strategy-as-practice research is characterized by a high degree of theoretical pluralism. Its rapid expansion in the last decade is partly a consequence of the interests for this perspective demonstrated by other areas in management and organization theories. For example, Suddaby, Seidl and Lê (2013) examine the foundational assumptions and methods in strategy as practice and neo-institutionalism to investigate their complementaries and differences. Whittington (2011; 2014) takes the view that promising features will necessarily come out from bridging initiatives between strategy as practice and accounting or information systems. This section goes over these calls for joint work and proposes new ways to advance strategy-as-practice research by drawing on theoretical anchorings that are closer to the strategy field.

Michael Smets, Royston Greenwood and Mike Lounsbury show the applicability of institutional theory for strategy as practice. As one of the most vital research areas of organization theory, institutional perspectives have the potential to bring new insights for the understanding of strategic practices and activity. More precisely, they could help to understand the linkage between not just the different levels of strategic activities but also the internal life of institutions. As a result, scholars in the fields of institutional theory and strategy as practice have recently begun to reach out to each other to broaden and nuance their theorizing of current puzzles. This chapter identifies natural points of connection between the two literatures and outlines a research agenda for future studies at the intersection of institutional theory and strategy as practice.

Patrick Regnér examines commonalities and differences between strategy as practice and other contemporary approaches in strategy research, in particular the resource-based view (RBV), the capabilities perspectives and the micro-foundations approach. He highlights four types of insights that can be gained from research at their intersection. (1) The research provides insights into how practices, praxis and practitioners underlie resources and capabilities that maintain competitive advantage. (2) It highlights how praxis, practices and practitioners are influenced by the resources and capabilities in which they are embedded. (3) Linking the 'micro' descriptions and explications of strategizing that the practice view provides with more 'macro' organizational resources and capabilities may help develop a more integrated view of strategic management. (4) Finally, relating strategy practices to strategy content and outcomes may also be of benefit to managerial practice.

Martha Feldman discusses similarities and synergies between the study of routines as dynamic processes and the study of strategy as practice. She argues that strategy as practice and the theory of routine dynamics are distinct but related theories of organizing. Recent research in the fields of both routines and strategy has used practice theory to focus attention on the dynamic and generative processes that result in strategy and routines and that have previously been studied as relatively static entities. Feldman seeks to identify some of the ways in which routine dynamics can contribute to strategy as practice research, showing that the theory of routine dynamics is not just a compatible theory but also a useful tool for studying the practice of strategy.

David Oliver interestingly advances the perspective of 'identity work' as a form of strategic practice. He begins by reviewing the literature on identity and identification at the individual, collective, and organizational levels in the organization studies literature. The author then examines existing research linking identity with strategy, and organizes this work into three broad perspectives: identity as resource, identity as lens, and identity as work. Each of the three perspectives is linked to one of the three foci of strategy research, i.e. strategy content, strategy process, and strategy as practice. Oliver finally draws on the growing number of processual studies of identity to elaborate the notion of identity work as a strategic practice – one that operates across different levels of analysis and integrates past, present and future temporal orientations. A concluding discussion proposes five avenues of future research that might potentially be of interest to strategy-as-practice scholars, namely identity emergence, identity across levels of analysis, identity and time, identity talk, and identity and materiality.

Joep Cornelissen and Henri Schildt concentrate on sensemaking and its potential for strategy as practice. Their review of past SAP research suggests that sensemaking is used in a largely perfunctory manner in strategy-as-practice research. They argue that sensemaking provides in effect a rich smorgasbord of theoretical constructs and models that is useful for SAP research. Cornelissen and Schildt also maintain, however, that moving beyond the application of sensemaking as an umbrella construct will provide important opportunities for more specific contributions. In particular, they discuss specific opportunities related to temporality, materiality, and sensegiving in strategy-as-practice research and the role that a sensemaking lens might play in exploring these topics.

François Cooren, Nicolas Bencherki, Mathieu Chaput and Consuelo Vásquez develop a communicational approach to strategy and strategy-making as an attempt to dialogue with the strategy-as-practice literature and its latest developments regarding talk and text. Based on a communicative constitution of organization (CCO) approach, it provides a conceptual framework to define strategy-making as a series of communication episodes in which specific matters of concerns are invoked, evoked and negotiated, defining and appropriating value to the organization. More specifically, Cooren, Bencherki, Chaput and Vásquez propose focusing on fleeting moments of strategy to highlight how collective endeavours are progressively born as effects, and therefore do not exist prior to the practices that generate them. Applying this framework to the analysis of a board meeting in a community organization, the authors show that favouring a constitutive view of communication allows the researcher to de-centre his/her analysis from human practices, broadening it to a 'web of practices' (Vaara and Whittington, 2012: 310) that are created through talk and text.

Then Stewart Clegg and Martin Kornberger focus on one of the most important but still under-studied dimensions in strategy as practice: power. Their chapter investigates how power theories can inform the study of strategy as practice, and vice versa. Understanding strategy as the 'art of creating power', the study of the ways in which power and strategy interact, and how one leads to the other, should be a central concern for scholars of strategy. While providing an overview of the key writings that have emerged at the interface between power and strategy, Clegg and Kornberger also attempt to point towards several possible future lines of inquiry. Their chapter is organized following a rather simple heuristic device ('strategy' as noun, 'strategizing' as verb, 'strategic' as adjective), which emphasizes the different agents, mechanisms and effects that can guide the analysis of power and strategy.

In the last chapter of Part III, Martin Blom and Mats Alvesson talk about the need for strategy-as-practice scholars to have a 'critical eye' on their research. Indeed, the purpose of their chapter is to review and comment on strategy as practice from a critical perspective, and to suggest how a critical perspective can be leveraged in a future research agenda. For this purpose, Blom and Alvesson outline five themes oriented towards critical management studies (CMS) for future SAP research, partly based on previous studies with a 'critical touch', but with the addition of some new – and perhaps more radical – questions and contributions in relation to previous strategy-as-practice literature.

Methodological resources in strategy-as-practice research

At the inception of the strategy-as-practice movement, scholars pointed to its methodological challenges (Balogun, Huff and Johnson 2003), which require the researcher simultaneously to be close to actual practice while employing a broad range of theoretical and methodological tools. There have been calls for an exploration of methods that allow us to observe and understand the longitudinal and processual dynamics of the practices, routines and actions of the situated actors, to uncover their interdependences and interactions and also to focus on discourses and their performativity – the disclosure of the 'non-says', of what is implicit or couched in rhetoric. While longitudinal case studies remain the most frequently used research design in strategy as practice, there is a notable trend towards applying and developing other methodologies. Some of the most promising approaches are presented and discussed in Part IV of this

handbook. As will become clear, the call for 'methodologically innovative' approaches does not necessarily mean that one has to develop entirely new methodologies; it suggests, rather, that we look at them through a 'practice lens' and use innovative ways to approach managers and reconstruct their strategizing activities and roles.

Ann Cunliffe proposes in the first chapter of Part IV some key considerations and a stimulating reflection on the connection between ethnography and practice. In her chapter, she argues that ethnography is particularly suited to strategy-as-practice research because of its focus on the rich description of the micro-practices of organizational life. By examining taken-for-granted activities and interactions, it is possible to better understand new or unanticipated processes and practices that are at the core of strategy-making. Cunliffe urges SAP researchers to embrace more deeply a subjectivist or intersubjective view when using an ethnographic methodology, however, in order to offer new insights into the relational and reflexive nature of strategizing as an emergent and lived experience. In order to do so, she considers there to be a number of questions that need to be better considered. What philosophical assumptions underpin the ethnographer's work? How do these influence the method(s) used, the form of analysis and theorizing? How does the researcher position him-/herself in the research? How does an ethnographer write a convincing research account?

Phyl Johnson, Julia Balogun and Nic Beech propose that strategy practitioners and their strategy-making practices should be examined through an 'identity lens', and urge strategy-as-practice researchers to move to a 'close-with' relationship with research subjects. Drawing on an empirical example, they propose a generic methodological approach to access identity through narratives captured from longitudinal engagement, multiple performances and back-stage access to the strategic practitioner. Their chapter encourages researchers to produce collaborative research and engage themselves in long-term relationships with practitioners. Even though Johnson, Balogun and Beech provide some ground rules for establishing close relationships with strategists, they nevertheless maintain a critical and reflexive stance towards the position of researchers engaged in a collaborative agenda.

Linda Rouleau suggests that biographical methods, such as narratives of practices and the life trajectories of practitioners, constitute a set of relevant qualitative methods of inquiry that offer many opportunities for developing typologies of practices and propositions regarding the skills needed in strategizing. Focusing on work experience and professional trajectories, narratives of practices provide privileged access to the subjective accounts of what managers and others 'do'. Rouleau draws on results and illustrative data extracted from a previous study, which examined how middle managers deal with the restructuring of their organization. She explains with clarity how biographical methods, in general, and narratives of practices, in particular, can be used to gain access to explicit and tacit knowledge, and how the depth of the relationship between narrator and researcher is central to the thorough understanding of strategizing practices.

In the following chapter, Dalvir Samra-Fredericks explores select aspects of the ethnomethodological and conversation-analytical (EM/CA) traditions in order to explain their relevance to the study of various strategizing practices. Drawing on two extracts from transcribed interaction reproduced from previous studies, she discusses some of the practical challenges one faces when accessing, selecting and interpreting accounts, and raises many theoretical issues related to the understanding of the elusive nature of practice. Samra-Fredericks delves into the reasoning processes that underlie EM/CA, and offers strategy-as-practice researchers an insightful discussion on the skills and forms of knowledge that effective leaders use in 'talk-in-interaction'. The author simply and clearly demonstrates through her own EM/CA perspective how the tiniest moment of interaction contains the essence of strategic and social order.

Eero Vaara looks at the discursive aspects of strategy and strategizing from a critical angle. He emphasizes that critical discourse analysis (CDA) differs from relativist forms of discourse analysis, which reduce everything to discourse. After an overview of the characteristic features of CDA, he presents various ways in which this methodology can be applied to advancing our understanding of different forms of strategic discourse: (1) the central role of formal strategy texts; (2) the use of discursive practices in strategy conversations; (3) the discursive construction of conceptions of strategy and subjectivity in organizational strategizing; (4) the processes of legitimization in and through strategy discourse; and (5) the ideological underpinnings of strategy discourse as a body of knowledge and praxis. Vaara also provides an example of CDA as applied to the analysis of a media text. By focusing on 'strategic text', his chapter addresses the fundamental questions of how texts are selected and to what extent findings are generalizable in the SAP perspective.

Mona Ericson, Leif Melin and Andrew Popp talk about the usefulness of historical methods for strategy-as-practice research. First they direct our attention to the specific characteristics of business historians' writing on strategy, as their work has generally been inductive and built on corporate archives, thus generally silencing what goes on inside a firm. Drawing on their rich and wide-ranging background in historical research, they then introduce four different categories of methods suitable for giving a voice to practitioners in strategy-making over time. These categories refer to written sources and narratives, micro-history, ego documents and lived experience. By drawing on their own expertise, Ericson, Melin and Popp introduce each of these categories of historical methods and provide insightful reflections on their challenges and limits. According to these authors, it is important to stress that practice is an inherently temporal experience, and that methods allowing for a historical perspective open a window for critical reflection on time, providing us with alternatives for evaluating present occurrences.

In the final chapter of Part IV, Tomi Laamanen, Emmanuelle Reuter, Markus Schimmer, Florian Ueberbacher and Xena Welch Guerra look at one of the most ignored methodological procedures in strategy-as-practice research, namely the quantitative one. Strategy-as-practice research has historically had a strong reliance on qualitative research methods, in order to enable the researcher to develop a deeper understanding of the micro-level strategy practices and activities that quantitative research designs have not been able to capture. SAP research does not necessarily always have to be qualitative, however. Laamanen, Reuter, Schimmer, Ueberbacher and Welch Guerra see major potential in enriching SAP research with quantitative research design. In their chapter, they discuss some of the quantitative work published in related research streams, draw lessons from them that are applicable to strategy-as-practice research, identify innovative ways to examine strategy practices through innovative research designs and outline possible novel sources of data that a quantitative researcher interested in strategy practices could utilize.

Substantive topic areas in strategy as practice

In this new part of the handbook we focus on central substantive topic areas in strategy-as-practice research, by which we mean areas that can be viewed as important sub-streams of strategy-as-practice research. They have effectively succeeded in becoming attractive to a group of researchers concerned to advance our knowledge around them. Therefore, their interests reside in the fact that they provide potential and possibilities for building some cumulative knowledge in SAP research.

Ann Langley and Maria Lusiani focus on the process of strategic planning. After a review of prior research, they elaborate on what it means to view strategic planning as a social practice. They argue that 'strategic planning' is essentially a label that is applied to a shifting set of practices that relate to the articulation of organizational strategic intent in the form of strategic plans. In their analysis, Langley and Lusiani focus on the textual practices that can be seen as the core of the production and consumption of strategic plans. The rest of their chapter then elaborates on their shape, content and dynamics, as well as suggesting avenues for future research.

David Seidl and Stéphane Guérard review and synthesize the extant literature on the role of meetings in the context of strategy. They show that meetings involve various meeting practices, that they serve many different (both manifest and latent) functions and that their concrete effects on the respective organizations depend on the ways in which they are integrated into larger series of meetings. In addition to this, Seidl and Guérard examine the literature on strategy workshops, as particular types of meetings. They explain that workshops allow the existing organizational structures to be suspended, and in this way provide a platform for strategic reflection. They also report on various empirical studies that have examined the effectiveness of different workshop designs. Based on the review of the existing literature, the authors outline an agenda for future research on meetings and workshops.

Jane Lê and Paul Spee set an agenda for the nascent body of research exploring the role of materials in strategy research. They provide an overview of different approaches to materiality: the communication approach; the technology approach; the sensemaking approach; and the positivist approach. Lê and Spee explain the assumptions inherent in each approach and how these assumptions alter the way we understand and study strategizing. Their chapter concludes with suggested avenues for future research into exploring the way that embracing materiality may alter our understanding of strategy and organization.

Co-authored by Linda Rouleau, Julia Balogun and Steve Floyd, the next chapter reviews the existing research on middle managers, strategy and strategic change from a strategy-as-practice perspective. According to these authors, SAP research into middle managers has been burgeoning in the last decade, and now constitutes a lively research sub-stream on which strategy-as-practice researchers can build cumulatively. They suggest that strategy-as-practice researchers have until now drawn on four theoretical lenses to acquire a better understanding of what middle managers do in their strategy work and how they do it. Besides the sensemaking and discursive lenses, SAP research on middle managers has seen the emergence of studies examining their strategic work under the political and institutional lenses. Nevertheless, Rouleau, Balogun and Floyd maintain that five main challenges should be addressed in order to develop the full potential of strategy-as-practice research on middle managers. These challenges are related to the theoretical, methodological, epistemological, ontological and practical relevance of these studies. The chapter ends by suggesting ways by which future SAP research could begin to meet these challenges.

Pikka-Maaria Laine and Eero Vaara examine participation in strategy research in general and in strategy-as-practice research in particular. Participation is, arguably, a key issue in strategy process, but it has received relatively little explicit attention in strategy research. Thus, this chapter provides an overview of research into participation. Laine and Vaara spell out four perspectives on participation: participation as a non-issue, participation as a part of strategy process dynamics, participation as produced in and through organizational practices, and participation as an issue of subjectivity. They also offer ideas for future research on participation. These include extending strategic agency to non-managerial actors, focusing on co-orientation in the interaction of actors in multifaceted strategy processes, analysing institutional and cultural differences in participation, studying sociomateriality and its role in enabling or promoting participation, analysing polyphony and dialogicality, and developing the critical perspectives needed to deal with issues such as resistance and empowerment in a more comprehensive manner.

In the final chapter of this handbook, Ethel Brundin and Feng Liu examine an emerging topic in strategy-as-practice research: the role of emotions in strategizing. They suggest that the study of emotions has enriched our knowledge of strategy as discursive practices, as part of board team and top management dynamics and in decision-making. They explain how and why emotions can be used as a tool to obtain intended outcomes but also be a part of practices that lead to unintended outcomes during strategic change. Brundin and Liu conclude that the topic of emotion leaves us with a set of openings for future research. These include a critical approach to emotions, a widening up to include more strategists and a diversity of organizational and cultural contexts. In addition, opening up for the psychodynamic of emotions

can further our understanding of emotions and strategizing. Finally, they conclude that there is little evidence in current studies of developed emotion constructs making contributions 'to theory' in order to further our knowledge about emotion per se in strategizing.

Challenges for future research: a research agenda

As previously mentioned, this handbook strives to be future-oriented. Each of the chapters provides innovative ideas to further advance our understanding of strategy as practice. With this in mind, the editors wish to take this opportunity to spell out a renewed agenda for strategy-as-practice research. First and foremost, it is vital to make sure that these new insights connect with other streams of strategic management. Otherwise, strategy as practice stands the risk of becoming an isolated research approach or a social movement that does not interact with other communities. Hence, one of the key challenges for the future is to strengthen, both on theoretical and on empirical fronts, its linkages to other important sub-fields in strategy, such as the strategy process school, institutional approaches to strategy, the resource-based view and its new applications, cognition and sensemaking in and around strategy, evolutionary perspectives, materiality, learning, and communication in strategic management.

Future research on strategy as practice holds great promise if it can continue to draw from and apply the theories and methodologies of the social sciences in novel ways. It is paramount that this research approach does not reinvent the wheel or develop in a vacuum, but is linked with other areas of social science. The goal should be not only to be informed but to be able to contribute to other fields. As the chapters of this handbook demonstrate, research on strategy as practice has a great deal to offer to contemporary social research on practice, activity, institutions and discourse. For example, focused analyses of strategy and strategizing can add to the ways in which Giddensian, Foucauldian or Bourdieusian traditions can be applied in addressing crucial issues in contemporary organizations or society at large.

It is crucial that SAP research continue on the trajectory of theoretical and empirical analysis, however, aiming at an increasingly better understanding of the activities, processes and practices that characterize organizational strategy and strategizing. The contributions of this handbook illustrate how much we have learned since this research approach came into being. Many issues still warrant targeted research efforts, though. They include the following.

Linkage of the macro and micro in strategy. One of the great advantages of the practice approach is that it provides an opportunity to analyse how concrete micro-level activities are linked with broader institutionalized practices. This link is visible, for example, in discursive analyses of strategy, but many other aspects of the social and organizational practices that constitute strategy and strategizing remain unexplored. Whether we call it 'institutionalization', 'legitimization', 'naturalization' or 'normalization', there is a great deal of work still to be done to explain how widely held assumptions about appropriate strategizing methods influence what is actually done in organizations, and how these activities, then, reproduce or at times transform prevailing understandings and practices. Even though, since the first edition in 2010, we have new avenues in the connections of institutional perspectives and strategy as practice, the macro–micro linkage remains one of the central challenges facing future research.

Agency in strategy and strategizing. A key reason for the emergence of practice theories was the need to develop concepts that explain how structure and agency are linked. Strategy-as-practice studies have added to our understanding of the role, identity and subjectivity of the strategists in many ways, and yet we still know little about those who are unable to participate in strategic decision-making. Furthermore, there are still few analyses that specify the ways in which organizational actors are at one and the same time constrained and enabled by prevailing practices. We must go beyond the conventional view in strategic management, which assumes that all strategists are omnipotent actors, but we must also not succumb to the gloomy perspective that everything is predetermined. This is a major theoretical question, but there is no doubt that empirical analyses of agency have a great deal to offer to practitioners.

Spread of strategy as discourse and praxis to new areas. SAP research is by definition contextual; the focus of the analysis lies in the activities and practices that constitute strategy and strategizing in a given setting. Apart from studies of strategizing in business organizations, it is important and interesting to analyse the spread of strategy as a body of knowledge and praxis to other types of context, in particular public organizations such as government, municipalities, universities, hospitals and kindergartens. As the few existing studies show, such settings are often characterized by all kinds of struggles and clashes. At the same time, however, they provide examples of the recontextualization and hybridization of practices, as well as innovations for dealing with problems and challenges.

Cross-national comparisons. Decision-making and strategizing practices have evolved in distinctive ways in different national contexts. Future research on strategy as practice could zoom in on these differences and examine trends of practice convergence or divergence.

Longitudinal analyses and the role of history. Not all research has to be longitudinal, but a more fine-grained understanding of the processes of strategic decision-making and change would benefit from longer-term analyses that elucidate changes in strategy and strategizing. Furthermore, historical studies can help us to better understand how practices have evolved and developed and the role of innovation in strategy and strategizing.

Coping and resistance. Conventional research tends to virtually ignore resistance; it is often framed as an obstacle to be dealt with and/or as illegitimate behaviour. If we want to gain a better understanding of the social processes in strategizing, we need to take the issue of resistance seriously. As demonstrated in the contributions to this handbook, such analysis involves a reconceptualization of the ways in which organizational actors interpret, make sense of, consume or react to strategies that are imposed upon them. The reactions range from various modes of coping to outright resistance. Future research on strategy as practice would do well to draw from existing critical analyses of power and resistance in this endeavour.

Temporal and spatial dimension of strategizing. As various practice theorists have highlighted, we cannot properly understand human activity without paying attention to its temporal and spatial dimensions. Surprisingly, however, there is only very little research so far that has examined how strategy work is organized in time and space (see, however, Kaplan and Orlikowski 2013; and Hydle forthcoming). In terms of 'objective' time and space, we need to analyse where and when strategy work is being carried out. Strategy work is both dispersed across different physical and discursive spaces and taking place at various different points in time. In terms of 'subjective' time and space – or, better, temporality and spatiality – we need to study how the temporal and spatial dimensions are constructed in and though our strategizing practices.

Emotions in strategy work. Closely related to sensemaking, several calls have been made for taking emotions seriously in strategy-making. Recently, it seems that this topic has been emerging as an insightful and stimulating dimension that is transversal to any strategic practices and situations (Brundin and Melin 2006; Brundin and Nordqvist 2008; Sloan and Oliver 2013; Liu and Maitlis 2014). As 'emotion' is literally related to sentiments and feelings that are part of 'movement', there is a need for us to develop a better understanding of their role in strategic planning and change. Related to cognition and sensemaking, emotions can either support or weaken strategic intents. Moreover, they are gendered and culturally and institutionally embedded, as they are sites of power relations in action. In this sense, emotions appear to be an interesting topic to advance our view of strategy-making as a social practice.

Mediation and technologization of discourse and practice. In many ways the prevailing theories and methods of strategic management and organization studies tend to follow the social science tradition of forgoing tools, technologies, artefacts and other objects. Although there are interesting possibilities in such strategy-as-practice research as activity theory, most theory and methods trail behind practice when it comes to analysing the ways in which the various information technology (IT) and other tools of communication affect contemporary organizations. Moreover, if comprehensively understood, mediation (the use of media to communicate and interact) and technologization (the use of conceptual tools, IT and other means in decision-making and organizational actions) are fundamental features of contemporary organizations and society that warrant attention in their own right.

Practitioners and their knowledge. Finally, practice research should be accessible to practitioners. Increasingly sophisticated theoretical analysis runs the risk of becoming alienated from the problems and challenges of the practitioners. Researchers should be mindful of this and strive to better understand the world of the practitioner with new epistemological, theoretical and methodological perspectives. For example, future research could challenge the prevailing view that academic knowledge is superior to practical knowledge. Theoretical work could develop concepts and ideas that draw from what is relevant – either useful or problematic – in the practitioners' world. In addition, new research could aim at a reappropriation of methods such as action research.

Appendix

Example papers	Contribution
Development of the research agenda	
Relation to other sub-fields of strategy	
Chia and MacKay 2007	Relation to process approach
Fauré and Rouleau 2011	Relation to accounting
Johnson, Melin and Whittington 2003; Johnson *et al.* 2007	Relation to process approach and resource-based theory
Regnér 2008	Relation to dynamic capabilities/resource-based theory
Suddaby, Seidl and Lê 2013	Relation to institutional theory
Teulier and Rouleau 2011	Relation to information technology
Whittington 1996	Relation to policy, planning and process approach
Whittington 2007	Relation to process approach
Whittington 2011	Relation to transdisciplinarity
Whittington 2014	Relation to strategic information systems
Definition of the strategy-as-practice agenda and/or frameworks	
Balogun *et al.* 2014	Characterization of strategy as practice with a particular emphasis on discursive perspectives, literature review and research agenda
Jarzabkowski 2005	Characterization of strategy as practice with an emphasis on the activity theory perspective
Jarzabkowski, Balogun and Seidl 2007	Characterization of strategy as practice together with a research framework, literature review and research agenda
Jarzabkowski and Spee 2009	Review of the strategy-as-practice literature and future directions
Johnson, Melin and Whittington 2003	Characterization of strategy as practice as 'activity-based view'
Johnson *et al.* 2007; Whittington 2006	Characterization of strategy as practice together with a research framework and research agenda
Seidl and Whittington 2014	Review of strategy-as-practice literature in terms of connecting 'micro' and 'macro' and directions for future research
Vaara and Whittington 2012	Review of strategy as practice literature and future directions
Exploration of different theoretical perspectives	
Brown and Thompson 2013	Narrative perspective
Campbell-Hunt 2007	Complexity theory
Chia and Holt 2006	Heideggerian perspective
Denis, Langley and Rouleau 2007	Actor–network theory, theories of social practice, convention theory
Denis *et al.* 2011	Actor–network theory (Latour)
Herepath 2014	Archerian critical realism
Jarzabkowski 2003; 2005	Activity theory
Jarzabkowski 2004	Theories of social practice (Bourdieu, Giddens, de Certeau)
Johnson *et al.* 2007	Situated learning, actor–network theory, Carnegie tradition (sensemaking, routines), institutionalist theories
Jørgensen and Messner 2010	Practice theory (Schatzki)
Seidl 2007	Systemic-discursive approaches
Vaara, Kleymann and Seristö 2004; Vaara, Sorsa and Pälli 2010	Critical discourse analysis

Example papers	Contribution
Whittington, Cailluet and Yakis-Douglas 2011	Sociology of professions
Methodological reflections	
Balogun, Huff and Johnson 2003; Johnson *et al.* 2007	Reflection on methodological challenges and exploration of novel methodologies
Huff, Neyer and Möslein 2010	Broader methods to support new insights
Rasche and Chia 2009	Propagation of ethnographic approaches
Venkateswaran and Prabhu 2010	Propagation of processual and clinical methodologies
Critical reflections on strategy as practice	
Carter, Clegg and Kornberger 2008; Clegg, Carter and Kornberger 2004	Need for more theoretically advanced and critically oriented studies
Chia and MacKay 2007	Criticism for lack of differentiation from process research
Rasche and Chia 2009	Criticism for lack of reflection of different strands of practice thinking
Rouleau 2013	Critical reflection about the development of strategy as practice

Central themes within strategy-as-practice research

Strategy work in different contexts	
Hydle forthcoming	Spatio-temporal organization of strategy work
Jarzabkowski 2003; 2004; 2005; 2008; Jarzabkowski and Seidl 2008	Strategizing in universities
Jarzabkowski and Balogun 2009	Strategizing in multinationals
King 2008	Strategizing of venture capital firms
Maitlis and Lawrence 2003	Strategizing in an orchestra
Paroutis and Pettigrew 2007	Strategizing in multi-business firms
Regnér 2003	Strategizing in the centre vs. periphery
Formal practices	
Bourque and Johnson 2008	Strategy workshops
Clarke, Kwon and Wodak 2012	Strategy meetings
Healey *et al.* forthcoming	Strategy workshops
Hendry and Seidl 2003	Strategic episodes, workshops, meetings
Hodgkinson *et al.* 2006	Strategy workshops
Hoon 2007	Committees
Jarzabkowski 2003; 2005; Jarzabkowski and Wilson 2002	Administrative practices
Jarzabkowski and Seidl 2008	Strategy meetings
Kwon, Clarke and Wodak 2014	Strategy meetings
Johnson *et al.* 2010	Strategy workshops
Liu and Maitlis 2014	Strategy meetings
MacIntosh, MacLean and Seidl 2010	Strategy workshops
Paroutis and Pettigrew 2007	Formal teams
Spee and Jarzabkowski 2011	Strategy meetings
Van Aaken *et al.* 2013	Strategy workshops
Whittington *et al.* 2006	Strategy workshops
Whittington and Cailluet 2008	Strategic planning practices
Wodak, Kwon and Clarke 2011	Strategy meetings

Example papers	Contribution
Sensemaking	
Balogun and Johnson 2004; 2005	Socially negotiated nature of sensemaking
Heracleous and Jacobs 2008	The role of embodied metaphors in sensemaking
Hodgkinson and Clarke 2007	Cognition in action
Kaplan 2008	Framing contests
Kaplan and Orlikowski 2013	Temporal dimension of sensemaking
Liu and Maitlis 2014	Emotional dynamic in top management teams (TMTs) and their impact on strategic sensemaking
Mueller *et al.* 2013	The role of politics in sensemaking
Rouleau and Balogun 2011	Discursive competence in strategic sensemaking
Rouleau 2005	Contextual factors of sensemaking/sensegiving and context
Stensaker and Falkenberg 2007	Interaction between individual-level and organizational-level sensemaking
Thomas, Sargent and Hardy 2011	Sensemaking in meetings
Materiality, tools and techniques	
Giraudeau 2008	Strategic plans as visual and textual representation of contexts and strategies
Heracleous and Jacobs 2008	Embodied metaphors
Jarzabkowski, Spee and Smets 2013	Knowledge inscription in strategy tools
Jarzabkowski and Kaplan 2015	Interrelation between affordances of strategy tools and the agency of strategy-makers
Kaplan 2011	PowerPoint as facilitating collaboration and cartography
Jarzabkowski and Wilson 2006; Seidl 2007	Change of tools and techniques according to context
Molloy and Whittington 2005	Impact of everyday technologies on strategizing
Spee and Jarzabkowski 2009	Tools as boundary objects
Werle and Seidl forthcoming	Epistemic and partial objects in the strategy process
Whittington *et al.* 2006	Physical objects as means of communication
Wright, Paroutis and Blettner 2013	The usefulness of strategy tools
Discursive aspects	
Barry and Elmes 1997	Strategy narratives
Brown and Thompson 2013	Strategy narratives
Cornut, Giroux and Langley 2012	Strategic plans
Fenton and Langley 2011	Strategy narratives
Hardy and Thomas 2014	Discursive production of strategic objects and subjects
Hendry 2000	Strategy as technological and appropriative discourse
Knights and Morgan 1991	Historical emergence of the strategy discourse
Kwon, Clarke and Wodak 2014	Discursive strategies to create consensus or shared views
Laine and Vaara 2007	Discursive struggles in strategy work
Mantere 2013	A language-based view on strategy
Mantere and Vaara 2008	Discourses impeding or promoting participation
Mirabeau and Maguire 2014	Practices of strategy articulation
Pälli, Vaara and Sorsa 2009	Discursive practices in the production of strategic plans
Paroutis and Heracleous 2013	First-order strategy discourse in institutional adoption
Samra-Fredericks 2003; 2004; 2005	Rhetorical micro-processes of strategizing and their impact on strategy

Example papers	Contribution
Seidl 2007	Differentiation between different strategy discourses
Sillince, Jarzabkowski and Shaw 2012	Rhetorical dimension of strategy
Sminia 2005	Layering of the strategy discussions
Spee and Jarzabkowski 2011	Interplay between the talk and text during planning conversation
Vaara, Kleymann and Seristö 2004	Discursive practices in the construction of strategies
Vaara, Sorsa and Pälli 2010	Strategy discourse as a multifaceted interdiscursive phenomenon
Vaara and Reff Pedersen 2013	Strategy narratives
Whittle *et al.* 2014	Power and politics in a strategy conversation
Wodak, Kwon and Clarke 2011	Discursive strategies to create consensus or shared views
Roles and identities	
Balogun and Johnson 2004; 2005	Middle managers
Beech and Johnson 2005	Recursive relation between strategist's identity and his/her strategizing activities
Dameron and Torset 2014	Subjectivity of senior managers
Jarzabkowski, Matthiesen and Van de Ven 2009	Regulators
Knights and Morgan 1991	Impact of the emergence of strategic management on managers' identity
Lounsbury and Crumley 2007	Constraining and enabling of agency through wider/societal theories and belief systems
Mantere 2005, 2008	Middle managers
Nordqvist and Melin 2008	Consultants
Rouleau 2003	Impact of gender on strategizing
Rouleau 2005; Rouleau and Balogun 2011	Middle managers
Schwarz 2004	Consultants
Sillince and Mueller 2007	Middle managers
	Power
Dick and Collings 2014	Strategy discourse, senior management subjectivity and power effects
Ezzamel and Willmott 2008	Power diffentials and modes of resistance in strategizing processes
Knights and Morgan 1991	'Disciplinary force' of strategy as institutional practice
Kornberger and Clegg 2011	The power effects of strategic plans
Laine and Vaara 2007; Mantere and Vaara 2008; McCabe 2010	Power diffentials and modes of resistance in strategy processes
Mueller *et al.* 2013	Role of power and politics in sensemaking
Whittle *et al.* 2014	Power and politics in a strategy conversation

References

Ambrosini, V., Bowman, C., and Burton-Taylor, S. (2007), 'Inter-team coordination activities as a source of customer satisfaction', *Human Relations*, 60/1: 59–98.

Asmuß, B., and Oshima, S. (2012), 'Negotiation of entitlement in proposal sequences', *Discourse Studies*, 14/1: 67–86.

Balogun, J., Huff, A. S., and Johnson, P. (2003), 'Three responses to the methodological challenges of studying strategizing', *Journal of Management Studies*, 40/1: 197–224.

Balogun, J., Jacobs, C. D., Jarzabkowski, P., Mantere, S., and Vaara, E. (2014), 'Placing strategy discourse in context: sociomateriality, sensemaking, and power', *Journal of Management Studies*, 51/2: 175–201.

Balogun, J., and Johnson, G. (2004), 'Organizational restructuring and middle manager sensemaking', *Academy of Management Journal*, 47/4: 523–49.

Balogun, J. (2005), 'From intended strategies to unintended outcomes: the impact of change recipient sensemaking', *Organization Studies*, 26/11: 1573–601.

Barry, D., and Elmes, M. (1997), 'Strategy retold: toward a narrative view of strategic discourse', *Academy of Management Review*, 22/2: 429–52.

Beech, N., and Johnson, P. (2005), 'Discourses of disrupted identities in the practice of strategic change', *Journal of Organizational Change Management*, 18/1: 31–47.

Bourdieu, P. (1990), *The Logic of Practice*. Cambridge: Polity.

(1994), *Raisons pratiques: Sur la théorie de l'action*. Paris: Éditions du Seuil.

Bourque, N., and Johnson, G. (2008), 'Strategy workshops and "away-days" as ritual', in Hodgkinson, G. P., and Starbuck, W. (eds.), *Oxford Handbook of Organizational Decision Making*: 552–64. Oxford University Press.

Brown, J. S., and Duguid, P. (1991), 'Organizational learning and communities of practice: toward a unified view of working, learning and innovation', *Organization Science*, 2/1: 40–57.

Brown, A. D., and Thompson, E. R. (2013), 'A narrative approach to strategy-as-practice', *Business History*, 55/7: 1143–67.

Brundin, E., and Melin, L. (2006), 'Unfolding the dynamics of emotions: how emotion drives or counteracts strategizing', *International Journal of Work Organization and Emotion*, 1/3: 277–302.

Brundin, E., and Nordqvist, M. (2008), 'Beyond facts and figures: the role of emotions in boardroom dynamics', *Corporate Governance*, 16/4: 326–41.

Burgelman, R. A. (1983), 'A process model of internal corporate venturing in the diversified major firm', *Administrative Science Quarterly*, 28/2: 223–44.

Campbell-Hunt, C. (2007), 'Complexity in practice', *Human Relations*, 60/1: 793–823.

Carter, C. (2013), 'The age of strategy: strategy, organizations and society', *Business History*, 55/7: 1047–57.

Carter, C., Clegg, S., and Kornberger, M. (2008), 'Strategy as practice?', *Strategic Organization*, 6/1: 83–99.

(2010), 'Re-framing strategy: power, politics and accounting', *Accounting, Auditing and Accountability Journal*, 23/5: 573–94.

Chia, R., and Holt, R. (2006), 'Strategy as practical coping: a Heideggerian perspective', *Organization Studies*, 27/5: 635–55.

Chia, R. (2009), *Strategy without Design: The Silent Efficacy of Indirect Action*. Cambridge University Press.

Chia, R., and MacKay, B. (2007), 'Post-processual challenges for the emerging strategy-as-practice perspective: discovering strategy in the logic of practice', *Human Relations*, 60/1: 217–42.

Clarke, I., Kwon, W., and Wodak, R. (2012), 'A context-sensitive approach to analysing talk in strategy meetings', *British Journal of Management*, 23/4: 455–73.

Clegg, S., Carter, C., and Kornberger, M. (2004), 'Get up, I feel like being a strategy machine', *European Management Review*, 1/1: 21–8.

De Certeau, M. (1984), *The Practice of Everyday Life*. Berkeley: University of California Press.

Cornut, F., Giroux, H., and Langley, A. (2012), 'The strategic plan as a genre', *Discourse and Communication*, 6/1: 21–54.

Daigle, P., and Rouleau, L. (2010), 'Strategic plans in arts organizations: a compromising tool between artistic and managerial values', *International Journal of Arts Management*, 12/3: 13–30.

Dameron, S., and Torset, C. (2014), 'The discursive construction of strategists' subjectivities: towards a paradox lens on strategy', *Journal of Management Studies*, 51/2: 291–319.

Denis, J.-L., Dompierre, G., Langley, A., and Rouleau, L. (2011), 'Escalating indecision: between reification and strategic ambiguity', *Organization Science*, 22/1: 225–44.

Denis, J.-L., Langley, A., and Rouleau, L. (2007), 'Strategizing in pluralistic contexts: rethinking theoretical frames', *Human Relations*, 60/1: 179–215.

Dick, P., and Collings, D. G. (2014), 'Discipline and punish? Strategy discourse, senior manager subjectivity and contradictory power effects', *Human Relations*, 67/12: 1513–36.

Dewey, J. (1938), *Experience and Education*. New York: Touchstone.

Dreyfus, H. (1991), *Being-in-the-World: A Commentary on Heidegger's Being and Time, Division 1.* Cambridge, MA: MIT Press.

Eisenhardt, K. (1989), 'Making fast strategic decisions in high-velocity environments', *Academy of Management Journal*, 32/3: 543–76.

Engeström, Y., Miettinen, R., and Punamäki, R.-L. (eds.) (1999), *Perspectives on Activity Theory*. Cambridge University Press.

Ezzamel, M., and Willmott, H. (2008), 'Strategy as discourse in a global retailer: a supplement to rationalist and interpretive accounts', *Organization Studies*, 29/2: 191–217.

Ezzamel, M. (2010), 'Strategy and strategizing: a poststructuralist perspective', in Baum, J. A. C., and Lampel, J. (eds.), Advances in Strategic Management, vol. XXVII, The Globalization of Strategy Research: 75–109. Bingley, UK: Emerald.

Fairclough, N. (2003), *Analyzing Discourse: Textual Analysis for Social Research*. London: Routledge.

Fauré, B., and Rouleau, L. (2011), 'The strategic competence of accountants and middle managers in budget making', *Accounting, Organizations and Society*, 36/3: 167–82.

Feldman, M. S., and Orlikowski, W. J. (2011), 'Theorizing practice and practicing theory', *Organization Science*, 22/5: 1240–53.

Fenton, C., and Langley, A. (2011), 'Strategy as practice and the narrative turn', *Organization Studies*, 32/9: 1171–96.

Floyd, S., Cornelissen, J., Wright, M., and Delios, A. (2011), 'Processes and practices of strategizing and organizing: review, development, and the role of bridging and umbrella constructs', *Journal of Management Studies*, 48/5: 933–52.

Foucault, M. (1977), *Discipline and Punish: The Birth of the Prison*. New York: Pantheon Books.

Foucault, M. (1980), *Power/Knowledge: Selected Interviews and Other Writings 1972–1977*, ed. Gordon, C. New York: Pantheon Books.

Giddens, A. (1984), *The Constitution of Society*. Cambridge: Polity.

Gioia, D. A., and Chittipeddi, K. (1991), 'Sensemaking and sensegiving in strategic change initiation', *Strategic Management Journal*, 12/6: 433–48.

Giraudeau, M. (2008), 'The drafts of strategy: opening up plans and their uses', *Long Range Planning*, 41/3: 291–308.

Golsorkhi, D., Rouleau, L., Seidl, D., and Vaara, E. (eds.) (2010), *Cambridge Handbook of Strategy as Practice*. Cambridge University Press.

Guérard, S., Langley, A., and Seidl, D. (2013), 'Rethinking the concept of performance in strategy research: towards a performativity perspective', *M@n@gement*, 16/5: 566–78.

Hardy, C., and Thomas, R. (2014), 'Strategy, discourse and practice: the intensification of power', *Journal of Management Studies*, 51/2: 320–48.

Healey, M. P., Hodgkinson, G. P., Whittington, R., and Johnson, G. (forthcoming), 'Off to plan or out to lunch? Relationships between design characteristics and outcomes of strategy workshops', *British Journal of Management*.

Hendry, J. (2000), 'Strategic decision making, discourse and strategy as social practice', *Journal of Management Studies*, 37/7: 955–77.

Hendry, J., and Seidl, D. (2003), 'The structure and significance of strategic episodes: social systems theory and the routine practices of strategic change', *Journal of Management Studies*, 40/1: 175–96.

Hendry, K. P., Kiel, G. C., and Nicholson, G. (2010), 'How boards strategise: a strategy as practice view', *Long Range Planning*, 43/1: 33–56.

Heracleous, L., and Jacobs, C. D. (2008), 'Understanding organizations through embodied metaphors', *Organizations Studies*, 29/1: 45–78.

Herepath, A. (2014), 'In the loop: a realist approach to structure and agency in the practice of strategy', *Organization Studies*, 35/6: 857–79.

Hodgkinson, G. P., and Clarke, I. (2007), 'Conceptual note: exploring the cognitive significance of organizational strategizing: a dual-process framework and research agenda', *Human Relations*, 60/1: 243–55.

Hodgkinson, G. P., Whittington, R., Johnson, G., and Schwarz, M. (2006), 'The role of strategy workshops in strategy development processes:

formality, communication, co-ordination and inclusion', *Long Range Planning*, 39/5: 479–96.

Hoon, C. (2007), 'Committees as strategic practice: the role of strategic conversation in a public administration', *Human Relations*, 60/6: 921–52.

Huff, A. S., Neyer, A.-K., and Möslein, K. (2010), 'Broader methods to support new insights into strategizing', in Golsorkhi, D., Rouleau, L., Seidl, D., and Vaara, E. (eds.), *Cambridge Handbook of Strategy as Practice*: 201–16. Cambridge University Press.

Hydle, K. (forthcoming), 'Temporal and spatial dimensions of strategizing', *Organization Studies*.

Jarzabkowski, P. (2003), 'Strategic practices: an activity theory perspective on continuity and change', *Journal of Management Studies*, 40/1: 23–55.

(2004), 'Strategy as practice: recursive, adaptive and practices-in-use', *Organization Studies*, 25/4: 529–60.

(2005), *Strategy as Practice: An Activity-Based Approach*. London: Sage.

(2008), 'Shaping strategy as a structuration process', *Academy of Management Journal*, 51/4: 621–50.

Jarzabkowski, P., and Balogun, J. (2009), 'The practice and process of delivering integration through strategic planning', *Journal of Management Studies*, 46/8: 1255–88.

Jarzabkowski, P., Balogun, J., and Seidl, D. (2007), 'Strategizing: the challenges of a practice perspective', *Human Relations*, 60/1: 5–27.

Jarzabkowski, P., and Kaplan, S. (2015), 'Strategy tools-in-use: a framework for understanding "technologies of rationality" in practice', *Strategic Management Journal*, 36/4: 537–58.

Jarzabkowski, P., Matthiesen, J., and Van de Ven, A. H. (2009), 'Doing which work? A practice approach to institutional pluralism', in Lawrence, T., Leca, B., and Suddaby, R. (eds.), *Institutional Work: Actors and Agency in Institutional Studies of Organizations*: 284–316. Cambridge University Press.

Jarzabkowski, P., and Seidl, D. (2008), 'The role of meetings in the social practice of strategy', *Organization Studies*, 29/11: 1391–426.

Jarzabkowski, P., and Spee, P. (2009), 'Strategy-as-practice: a review and future directions for the field', *International Journal of Management Reviews*, 11/1: 69–95.

Jarzabkowski, P., Spee, P., and Smets, M. (2013), 'Material artifacts: practices for doing strategy with "stuff"', *European Management Journal*, 31/1: 41–54.

Jarzabkowski, P., and Wilson, D. C. (2002), 'Top teams and strategy in a UK university', *Journal of Management Studies*, 39/3: 355–81.

(2006), 'Actionable strategy knowledge: a practice perspective', *European Management Journal*, 24/3: 348–67.

Johnson, G., and Huff, A. S. (1998), 'Everyday innovation and everyday strategy', in Hamel, G., Prahalad, C. K., Thomas, H., and O'Neal, D. (eds.), *Strategic Flexibility: Managing in a Turbulent Environment*: 3–27. Chichester, UK: John Wiley.

Johnson, G., Langley, A., Melin, L., and Whittington, R. (2007), *Strategy as Practice: Research Directions and Resources*. Cambridge University Press.

Johnson, G., Melin, L., and Whittington, R. (2003), 'Guest editors' introduction: micro strategy and strategizing: towards an activity-based view', *Journal of Management Studies*, 40/1: 3–22.

Johnson, G., Prashantham, S., Floyd, S., and Bourque, N. (2010), 'The ritualization of strategy workshops', *Organization Studies*, 31/12: 1589–618.

Jørgensen, B., and Messner, M. (2010), 'Accounting and strategising: a case study from new product development', *Accounting, Organizations and Society*, 35/2: 184–204.

Kaplan, S. (2008), 'Framing contests: strategy making under uncertainty', *Organization Science*, 19/5: 729–52.

(2011), 'Strategy and PowerPoint: an inquiry into the epistemic culture and machinery of strategy making', *Organization Science*, 22/2: 320–46.

Kaplan, S., and Orlikowski, W. J. (2013), 'Temporal work in strategy making', *Organization Science*, 24/4: 965–95.

Katzberg, G. (2013), 'Separation and reconnection: episodic organizational arenas in the strategic process', *Journal of Strategy and Management*, 6/3: 212–28.

King, B. (2008), 'Strategizing at leading venture capital firms: of planning, opportunism and deliberate emergence', *Long Range Planning*, 41/3: 345–66.

Knights, D., and Morgan, G. (1991), 'Corporate strategy, organizations, and subjectivity: a critique', *Organization Studies*, 12/2: 251–73.

Kornberger, M., and Clegg, S. (2011), 'Strategy as performative practice: the case of Sydney 2030', *Strategic Organization*, 9/2: 136–62.

Kwon, W., Clarke, I., and Wodak, R. (2014), 'Micro-level discursive strategies for constructing shared views around strategic issues in team meetings', *Journal of Management Studies*, 51/2: 265–90.

Laine, P.-M., and Vaara, E. (2007), 'Struggling over subjectivity: a discursive analysis of strategic development in an engineering group', *Human Relations*, 60/1: 29–58.

Langley, A. (1989), 'In search of rationality: the purposes behind the use of formal analysis in organizations', *Administrative Science Quarterly*, 34/4: 598–631.

Liu, F., and Maitlis, S. (2014), 'Emotional dynamics and strategizing processes: a study of strategic conversations in top team meetings', *Journal of Management Studies*, 51/2: 202–34.

Locke, K., and Golden-Biddle, K. (1997), 'Constructing opportunities for contribution: structuring intertextual coherence and "problematizing" in organizational studies', *Academy of Management Journal*, 40/5: 1023–62.

Lounsbury, M., and Crumley, E. (2007), 'New practice creation: an institutional perspective on innovation', *Organization Studies*, 28/7: 993–1012.

MacIntosh, R., MacLean, D., and Seidl, D. (2010), 'Unpacking the effectivity paradox of strategy workshops: do strategy workshops produce strategic change?', in Golsorkhi, D., Rouleau, L., Seidl, D., and Vaara, E. (eds.), *Cambridge Handbook of Strategy as Practice*: 291–309. Cambridge University Press.

Maitlis, S., and Lawrence, T. B. (2003), 'Orchestral manoeuvres in the dark: understanding failure in organizational strategizing', *Journal of Management Studies*, 40/1: 109–39.

Mantere, S. (2005), 'Strategic practices as enablers and disablers of championing activity', *Strategic Organization*, 3/2: 157–84.

(2008), 'Role expectations and middle manager strategic agency', *Journal of Management Studies*, 45/2: 294–316.

(2013), 'What is organizational strategy? A language-based view', *Journal of Management Studies*, 50/8: 1408–26.

Mantere, S., and Vaara, E. (2008), 'On the problem of participation in strategy: a critical discursive perspective', *Organization Science*, 19/2: 341–58.

McCabe, D. (2010), 'Strategy-as-power: ambiguity, contradiction and the exercise of power in a UK building society', *Organization*, 17/2: 151–75.

Martin, P. Y. (2003), '"Said and done" versus "saying and doing": gendering practices, practicing gender at work', *Gender and Society*, 17/3: 342–66.

Mintzberg, H. (1973), *The Nature of Managerial Work*. New York: Harper & Row.

Mintzberg, H., Raisinghani, D., and Théoret, A. (1976), 'The structure of "unstructured" decision processes', *Administrative Science Quarterly*, 21/2: 246–75.

Mintzberg, H., and Waters, J. A. (1985), 'Of strategies, deliberate and emergent', *Strategic Management Journal*, 6/3: 257–72.

Mirabeau, L., and Maguire, S. (2014), 'From autonomous strategic behavior to emergent strategy', *Strategic Management Journal*, 35/8: 1202–29.

Molloy, E., and Whittington, R. (2005), 'Practices of organizing: inside and outside the processes of change', in Szulanski, G., Porac, J., and Doz, Y. (eds.), Advances in Strategic Management, vol. XXII, Strategy Process: 491–515. Bingley, UK: Emerald.

Mueller, F., Whittle, A., Gilchrist, A., and Lenney, P. (2013), 'Politics and strategy practice: an ethnomethodologically-informed discourse analysis perspective', *Business History*, 55/7: 1168–99.

Nicolini, D. (2012), *Practice Theory, Work, and Organization: An Introduction*. Oxford University Press.

Nicolini, D., Gherardi, S., and Yanow, D. (2003), *Knowing in Organizations: A Practice-Based Approach*. Armonk, NY: M E Sharpe.

Nordqvist, M., and Melin, L. (2008), 'Strategic planning champions: social craftspersons, artful interpreters and known strangers', *Long Range Planning*, 41/3: 326–44.

Oakes, L. S., Townley, B., and Cooper, D. J. (1998), 'Business planning as pedagogy: language and control in a changing institutional field', *Administrative Science Quarterly*, 43/2: 257–92.

Orlikowski, W. J. (2000), 'Using technology and constituting structures', *Organization Science*, 11/4: 404–28.

Ortner, S. B. (2006), *Anthropology and Social Theory: Culture, Power and the Acting Subject*. Durham, NC: Duke University Press.

Pälli, P., Vaara, E., and Sorsa, V. (2009), 'Strategy as text and discursive practice: a genre-based approach to strategizing in city administration', *Discourse and Communication*, 3/3: 303–18.

Paroutis, S., and Heracleous, L. (2013), 'Discourse revisited: dimensions and employment of first-order strategy discourse during institutional adoption', *Strategic Management Journal*, 34/8: 935–56.

Paroutis, S., and Pettigrew, A. M. (2007), 'Strategizing in the multi-business firm: strategy teams at multiple levels and over time', *Human Relations*, 60/1: 99–135.

Pettigrew, A. M. (1973), *The Politics of Organizational Decision-Making*. London: Tavistock.

Phillips, N., Sewell, G., and Jaynes, S. (2008), 'Applying critical discourse analysis in strategic management research', *Organizational Research Methods*, 11/4: 770–89.

Rasche, A., and Chia, R. (2009), 'Researching strategy practices: a genealogical social theory perspective', *Organization Studies*, 30/7: 713–34.

Reckwitz, A. (2002), 'Toward a theory of social practices: a development in culturalist theorizing', *European Journal of Social Theory*, 5/2: 243–63.

Regnér, P. (2003), 'Strategy creation in the periphery: inductive versus deductive strategy making', *Journal of Management Studies*, 40/1: 57–82.

— (2008), 'Strategy-as-practice and dynamic capabilities: steps towards a dynamic view of strategy', *Human Relations*, 61/4: 565–88.

Rouleau, L. (2003), 'Micro-strategy as gendered practice: resisting strategic change through the family metaphor', paper presented at the nineteenth European Group for Organizational Studies colloquium, Copenhagen, 5 July.

— (2005), 'Micro-practices of strategic sensemaking and sensegiving: how middle managers interpret and sell change every day', *Journal of Management Studies*, 42/7: 1414–41.

— (2013), 'Strategy-as-practice research at a crossroads', *M@n@gement*, 16/5: 547–65.

Rouleau, L., and Balogun, J. (2011). 'Middle managers, strategic sensemaking, and discursive competence', *Journal of Management Studies*, 48/5: 953–83.

Samra-Fredericks, D. (2003), 'Strategizing as lived experience and strategists' everyday efforts to shape strategic direction', *Journal of Management Studies*, 40/1: 141–74.

— (2004), 'Understanding the production of "strategy" and "organization" through talk amongst managerial elites', *Culture and Organization*, 10/2: 125–41.

— (2005), 'Strategic practice, "discourse" and the everyday interactional constitution of "power effects"', *Organization*, 12/6: 803–41.

Schatzki, T. R. (2002), *The Site of the Social: A Philosophical Account of the Constitution of Social Life and Change*. University Park: Pennsylvania State University Press.

Schatzki, T. R., Knorr Cetina, K., and von Savigny, E. (eds.) (2001), *The Practice Turn in Contemporary Theory*. London: Routledge.

Schwarz, M. (2004), 'Knowing in practice: how consultants work with clients to create, share and apply knowledge?', *Academy of Management Proceedings*, Supplement: D1–D6.

Seidl, D. (2007), 'General strategy concepts and the ecology of strategy discourses: a systemic-discursive perspective', *Organization Studies*, 28/2: 197–218.

Seidl, D., and Whittington, R. (2014), 'Enlarging the strategy-as-practice research agenda: towards taller and flatter ontologies', *Organization Studies*, 35/10: 1407–21.

Sillince, J., and Mueller, F. (2007), 'Switching strategic perspective: the reframing of accounts of responsibility', *Organization Studies*, 28/2: 155–76.

Sillince, J., Jarzabkowski, P., and Shaw, D. (2012), 'Shaping strategic action through the rhetorical construction and exploitation of ambiguity', *Organization Science*, 23/3: 630–50.

Sloan, P., and Oliver, D. (2013), 'Building trust in multi-stakeholder partnerships: critical emotional incidents and practices of engagement', *Organization Studies*, 34/12: 1835–68.

Sminia, H. (2005), 'Strategy formation as layered discussion', *Scandinavian Journal of Management*, 21/3: 267–91.

Spee, P., and Jarzabkowski, P. (2009), 'Strategy tools as boundary objects', *Strategic Organization*, 7/2: 223–32.

Spee, P. (2011), 'Strategic planning as communicative process', *Organizational Studies*, 32/9: 1217–45.

Stensaker, I., and Falkenberg, J. (2007), 'Making sense of different responses to corporate change', *Human Relations*, 60/1: 137–78.

Suddaby, R., Seidl, D., and Lê, J. (2013), 'Strategy-as-practice meets neo-institutional theory', *Strategic Organization*, 11/3: 329–44.

Sztompka, P. (1991), *Society in Action: The Theory of Social Becoming*. Cambridge: Polity.

Teulier, R., and Rouleau, L. (2013), 'Middle managers' sensemaking and interorganizational change initiation: translation spaces and editing practices', *Journal of Change Management*, 13/3: 308–37.

Thomas, R., Sargent, L. D., and Hardy, C. (2011), 'Managing organizational change: negotiating meaning and power–resistance relations', *Organization Science*, 22/1: 22–41.

Tuomela, R. (2005), *The Philosophy of Social Practices: A Collective Acceptance View*. Cambridge University Press.

Turner, S. (1994), *The Social Theory of Practices: Tradition, Tacit Knowledge, and Presuppositions*. University of Chicago Press.

Vaara, E. (2010), 'Taking the linguistic turn seriously: strategy as multifaceted and interdiscursive phenomenon', in Baum, J. A. C., and Lampel, J. (eds.), *Advances in Strategic Management*, vol. XXVII, *The Globalization of Strategy Research*: 29–50. Bingley, UK: Emerald.

Vaara, E., Kleymann, B., and Seristö, H. (2004), 'Strategies as discursive constructions: the case of airline alliances', *Journal of Management Studies*, 41/1: 1–35.

Vaara, E., and Reff Pedersen, A. (2013), 'Strategy and chronotopes: a Bakhtinian perspective on the construction of strategy narratives', *M@n@gement*, 16/5: 593–604.

Vaara, E., Sorsa, V., and Pälli, P. (2010), 'On the force potential of strategy texts: a critical discourse analysis of a strategic plans and its power effects in a city organization', *Organization*, 17/6: 685–702.

Vaara, E., and Whittington, R. (2012), 'Strategy-as-practice: taking social practices seriously', *Academy of Management Annals*, 6/1: 285–336.

Van Aaken, D., Koob, C., Rost, K., and Seidl, D. (2013), 'Ausgestaltung und Erfolg von Strategieworkshops: eine empirische Analyse', *Zeitschrift für betriebswirtschaftliche Forschung*, 65/7: 588–616.

Venkateswaran, R., and Prabhu, G. N. (2010), 'Taking stock of research methods in strategy as practice', *Electronic Journal of Business Research Methods*, 8/2: 156–62.

Vygotsky, L. (1978), *Mind in Society: The Development of Higher Psychological Processes*. Cambridge, MA: Harvard University Press.

Werle, F., and Seidl, D. (forthcoming), 'The layered materiality of strategizing: epistemic objects and the interplay between material artefacts in the exploration of strategic topics', *British Journal of Management*.

Whittington, R. (1992), 'Putting Giddens into action: social systems and managerial agency', *Journal of Management Studies*, 29/6: 693–712.

(1996), 'Strategy as practice', *Long Range Planning*, 29/5: 731–5.

(2006), 'Completing the practice turn in strategy research', *Organization Studies*, 27/5: 613–34.

(2007), 'Strategy practice and strategy process: family differences and the sociological eye', *Organization Studies*, 28/10: 1575–86.

(2011), 'The practice turn in organization research: a disciplined transdisciplinarity', *Accounting, Organization and Society*, 36/3: 183–6.

(2014), 'Information systems strategy and strategy-as-practice: a joint agenda', *Journal of Strategic Information Systems*, 23/1: 87–91.

Whittington, R., and Cailluet, L. (2008), 'The crafts of strategy: special issue introduction by the guest editors', *Long Range Planning*, 41/3: 241–7.

Whittington, R., Cailluet, L., and Yakis-Douglas, B. (2011), 'Opening strategy: evolution of a precarious profession', *British Journal of Management*, 22/3: 531–44.

Whittington, R., Jarzabkowski, P., Mayer, M., Mounoud, E., Nahapiet, J., and Rouleau, L. (2003), 'Taking strategy seriously: responsibility and reform for an important social practice', *Journal of Management Inquiry*, 12/4: 396–409.

Whittington, R., Molloy, E., Mayer, M., and Smith, A. (2006), 'Practices of strategising/organising: broadening strategy work and skills', *Long Range Planning*, 39/6: 615–29.

Whittle, A., Housley, W., Gilchrist, A., Mueller, F., and Lenney, P. (2014), 'Power, politics and organizational communication: an ethnomethodological perspective', in Cooren, F., Vaara, E., Langley, A., and Tsoukas, H. (eds.), *Language and Communication at Work: Discourse, Narrativity, and Organizing*: 71–94. Oxford University Press.

Wittgenstein, L. (1953 [1951]), *Philosophical Investigations*. Oxford: Blackwell.

Wodak, R., Kwon, W., and Clarke, I. (2011), '"Getting people on board": discursive leadership for consensus building in team meetings', *Discourse and Society*, 22/5: 592–644.

Wright, R. P., Paroutis, S., and Blettner, D. P. (2013), 'How useful are the strategic tools we teach in business schools?', *Journal of Management Studies*, 50/1: 92–125.

PART I

Ontological and Epistemological Questions

Practice in research: phenomenon, perspective and philosophy

WANDA J. ORLIKOWSKI

The focus on practice in management studies – and the strategy field more specifically – is a recent and important development in what organizational scholars pay attention to and how. Reflecting the more general social-theoretic 'practice turn' (Ortner 1984; Schatzki, Knorr Cetina and von Savigny 2001; Reckwitz 2002), this development is diverse and dynamic, expressing both a range of approaches and a set of emerging possibilities (Gherardi 2006; Feldman and Orlikowski 2011; Molloy 2007; Postill 2010; Whittington 2006). Schatzki (2001a: 4) argues that, given the broad array of interpretations and interests, the most effective notion of practice may be in its framing and orienting of research. It is in this spirit of exploring various ways of structuring practice research that I offer the discussion below, and not to propose or defend any particular conception or appropriation of practice ideas.

In what follows, I want to distinguish three modes of engaging with practice in research, and highlight some of their attending entailments. I then discuss some of the challenges and implications associated with taking practice seriously in studies of organizations. Throughout this commentary, I will draw on illustrations from the arena of organizational research that I am most familiar with: technology studies. These examples should offer some useful analogies and applications for strategy-as-practice research, in which parallel considerations and formations are evident.

Modes of engaging practice in research

I find it useful to differentiate between the different ways that the notion of practice has been attended to in the management literature (including the strategy-as-practice literature). These variations arise as

a result of differences in the locus of researchers' attention and the logic of their inquiry. Three modes of engaging practice in research are evident. The first mode emphasizes practice as a *phenomenon* – the notion that what is most important in organization research is understanding what happens 'in practice', as opposed to what is derived or expected from 'theory'; the second mode advocates practice as a *perspective* – the articulation of a practice-centred theory about some aspect of organizations; and the third mode highlights the notion of practice as a *philosophy* – the commitment to an ontology that posits practice as constitutive of all social reality, including organizational reality.

These three modes of engaging practice in research are not mutually exclusive, but they can be understood as entailing differing assumptions about the power of practice to produce the world. As a result, they have different implications for how practice studies are understood and performed. Researchers engaging in studies of practice as a phenomenon may choose to do so without employing either a practice theory or a practice ontology. Researchers drawing on a practice perspective will certainly focus on some form of practice phenomenon and do so through a practice-theoretic lens, but they need not also take on board a practice ontology. Researchers drawing on a practice philosophy believe in the primacy of practices in constituting social life, and will thus necessarily engage with practice through all three modes: philosophically, theoretically (practice as a perspective) and empirically (practice as a phenomenon).

Practice as a phenomenon

The first mode of engaging with practice involves a specific commitment to understanding what

33

practitioners do 'in practice', with 'practice' here signifying the commonsensical notion of practical activity and direct experience. In this view, practice is recognized as a central locus of organizing, and thus critical in producing consequential organizational outcomes. This is a claim that, notwithstanding elegant theories and sophisticated models, it is practice that matters in organizational life, and that researchers ignore this to the detriment of their understanding of organizations, specifically running the risk that their work will be irrelevant at best, or misleading at worst.

In this mode, there is an explicit distinction between 'practice' and 'theory' – or, put another way, a distinction between what 'actually happens' and what researchers claim is happening through their representations, frameworks, narratives, models, propositions and theories. This distinction recognizes that there is typically a large gap between scientific knowledge and lived reality, and thus what is sought are means of bridging this gap by engaging more deeply in the empirical details of organizational life on the ground. The techniques used to do this vary, but all endeavour to get closer to practitioners and to their situated, practical activities. Examples of such gap-closing research range from immersive participant observation studies to various kinds of action research projects.

With respect to participant observation, researchers tend to perform in-depth field investigations and ethnographies of practitioners at work (Barley and Kunda 2006; Bucciarelli 1994; Burawoy 1979; Hutchins 1995; Orr 1996; Lave and Wenger 1991), focusing on specific social groups, professions, occupations or communities such as engineers, managers, midwives and technicians in order to understand how it is that they do what they do. Studies of such practitioners 'in the wild' recount the myriad and detailed ways in which work is an ongoing and contingent accomplishment, typically relying less on explicit knowledge, specific prescriptions and canonical procedures, and more on tacit knowing, situated experiences and reflective improvisations. In other words, focusing on what practitioners do in practice reveals an adaptive and pragmatic intelligibility that is not easily captured in abstract models and formal theoretical propositions (Brown and Duguid 1991; Schön 1983).

With respect to action learning, researchers choose to engage practice more directly by partnering with practitioners on various projects (Rynes, Bartunek and Daft 2001; Van de Ven and Johnson 2006). Methodologies include action science (Lewin 1946; Argyris, Putnam and Smith 1985; Whyte 1991), clinical fieldwork (Schein 1987), process consultation (Schein 1999), insider/outsider team research (Bartunek and Louis 1996) and collaborative interactive action research (Rapoport et al. 2002). All these various techniques explicitly design research studies as joint interventions aimed at addressing some substantial problem or challenge within an organization. In the process of collectively intervening in practice, researchers and practitioners generate data that are then analysed to help create and implement specific and more substantive practical changes in the workplace. One of the premises guiding this work is the notion that the best way to understand a system is to try to change it (Schein 1985).

This mode of engaging practice as a phenomenon has been particularly useful in technology studies. Here, there is a similar range of methodological approaches aimed at getting closer to what happens on the ground, from detailed field studies (Gasser 1986; Kling 1991; Thomas 1994; Zuboff 1988) to participative systems design (Checkland 1999; Dourish and Button 1998; Mumford and Hensall 1979; Sachs 1995) and action research (Baskerville and Myers 2004). Recognizing the importance of what happens in practice has led researchers to focus on specific instances of technology use, as opposed to examining technologies abstractly 'in theory', or in isolation from specific situated conditions. An important insight of this work is that technology matters only to the extent that it is incorporated into users' practices. Studying the designed functionality or inscribed features of a technology is insufficient to understand the effects of that technology, because practice departs (sometimes substantially) from theory, design, plan or mandate (Button 1993; Ciborra 2002).

An important genre of this kind of work is represented by ethnomethodological accounts of technological use in the workplace (Luff,

Hindmarsh and Heath 2000). For example, Suchman (1987) describes a study she conducted into people's use of a photocopier that had been designed with an intelligent user interface, but that had been found to be particularly difficult to operate in practice. Suchman investigated users' actual interactions with the photocopier in practice (via detailed transcripts and videotaped recordings of users attempting to photocopy documents), and identified a range of breakdowns, misconceptions and communicative troubles that emerged in the gap between the assumptions embedded within the design of the machine's expert system interface and the actual expectations, intentions and actions of the users interacting with the machine. By showing in detail what happened in practice, Suchman argues persuasively that situated forms of social action can never be fully specified a priori, and thus that human–computer interaction should be understood as an ongoing contingent co-production that emerges in practice.

A key contribution of studies focusing on practice as a phenomenon is both the claim and the emerging grounded evidence that *practices matter*, and thus have to be empirically engaged with in order to understand/improve organizational reality.

Practice as a perspective

A second mode of engaging practice in research identifies it as a powerful lens for studying particular social phenomena. The ascendancy of this analytical perspective represents an important departure from traditional perspectives on organizations that have tended to privilege either macro-level structural relations or micro-level psychological attributes. As Lave (1988: 15) puts it, a practice perspective shifts attention to the routine, lived character of the everyday world, and it is this everyday activity that now serves as the object of analysis. But this everyday activity is not simply a focus on the mundane and micro-aspects of organizations. On the contrary, a practice perspective posits that it is through the situated and recurrent nature of everyday activity that structural consequences are produced and become reinforced or changed over time.

This view of practice entails a specific conceptual grounding in what have come to be known as 'practice theories'. Postill (2010) offers a useful distinction between two generations of practice theorists. The first generation, represented by such scholars as Bourdieu (1977), de Certeau (1984), Foucault (1977), Garfinkel (1967), Giddens (1984) and Taylor (1985), has provided the theoretical foundations on which the second generation, represented by scholars such as Ortner (1984), Pickering (1995), Reckwitz (2002), Rouse (1996) and Schatzki (2002), are producing analyses, building extensions and generating elaborations. A particularly useful compilation of second-generation developments is available in the co-edited collection *The Practice Turn in Contemporary Theory* (Schatzki, Knorr Cetina and von Savigny 2001), which includes chapters by such contributors as Barnes, Knorr Cetina, Lynch, Swidler and Turner.

The first generation of practice theorists emphasized agents' actions, interactions and improvisations and focused on how these produce/reproduce/ transform social structures, while also acknowledging the imprinting of structure and power on the human body and recurring forms of human activity (e.g. habitus, discipline). The second generation of practice scholars sought to advance the central tenets proposed by the first generation theorists while also developing new concepts and understandings. An important scholar in this regard is Schatzki, a philosopher, whose recent writings (2001a; 2001b; 2002; 2005) have been especially influential in stimulating the growing interest in a practice perspective among social scientists. *The Practice Turn* has done much to inform researchers of the generative possibilities entailed in adopting a practice lens on social phenomena. In particular, Schatzki's definition of practices as 'embodied, materially mediated arrays of human activity centrally organized around shared practical understandings' (Schatzki 2001a: 2) has been widely taken up by scholars interested in employing a practice perspective in their own research studies.

While many of the practice theorists also advocate a practice philosophy (more on which in the next section), their practice theories have also been appropriated to inform the study of quite specific social phenomena. Such application of practice theory has in some cases stimulated valuable and innovative reconceptualizations of established notions in social science. For example, Lave (1988) has done significant work in using a practice perspective to shift understanding of human cognition. Rather than assuming that cognition occurs 'in the head' (the conventional view adopted by psychologists and cognitive scientists), she draws on practice theory to offer a powerful argument for an understanding of cognition as enacted 'in practice'.

Lave's research involved studying mathematical problem-solving activities in adults in different settings, observing participants in routine activities such as grocery shopping in the supermarket (calculating best buys), and assessing them on their general arithmetic knowledge through standardized mathematical achievement tests. She found considerable variation in participants' arithmetic procedures and performances across these two contexts. Even though the mathematics test was designed to evaluate the same arithmetic knowledge that the participants had used in the supermarket, participants scored an average of 59 per cent on the test of arithmetic knowledge, as opposed to achieving an average of 98 per cent for arithmetic knowledge in the supermarket. Lave argues that competence in arithmetic is not abstract knowledge that individuals either do or do not have (and that they can easily apply in any context), but a 'knowledge-in-practice', embodied and enacted by a person acting in a particular setting and engaging aspects of the self, the body and the physical and social worlds (Lave 1988: 180–1). In Lave's practice-theoretic reformulation, cognition is not separate from doing. Rather, cognition is an activity grounded in practice.

In the case of technology studies, the adoption of a practice perspective has led researchers to focus on the structured practices through which people engage with particular technologies in their daily work. One such stream of research draws on Giddens' (1984) structuration theory, which posits structures as recursively produced, reproduced and changed in social practices. In some of my prior work, I have applied this understanding to the use of technology (Orlikowski 1992; 1996; 2000), and

argued that, through their regularized engagement with a particular technology (and some of its inscribed features), users recurrently enact technology structures – what I term 'technologies-in-practice' – which are the sets of rules and resources that are (re)constituted in people's ongoing interactions with the technologies at hand. I argue that such technologies-in-practice are consequential for shaping the kinds of institutional, interpretive and practical outcomes that emerge from engagement with technologies.

In particular, drawing on a series of studies into the use of a groupware technology, I distinguish a number of different technologies-in-practice that were enacted with the Lotus Notes groupware technology in both similar and disparate contexts (Orlikowski 2000). For example, in a large multinational consulting company, I found that the consultants were strongly inhibited from using the technology for knowledge-sharing (its intended use) by their firm's hierarchical career path, individual criteria for evaluation and promotion, a client-focused billing system and their lack of understanding of the technology. As a result, their work practices used none or very few of the collaborative features of Lotus Notes, and were oriented towards personal rather than collaborative benefit. Through such practices they enacted technologies-in-practice of limited use and individual productivity that had minimal impact on knowledge-sharing and project performance within the organization. In contrast, the technologists in this firm, influenced by an institutional context that supported and rewarded cooperation in technical support work and a deep understanding of technology, used the collaborative features of Lotus Notes in their work practices, and in doing so enacted a technology-in-practice of collective problem-solving that led to improved knowledge-sharing and technical performance. The use of a practice perspective thus allowed me to identify the various conditions (institutional, interpretive and technological) that shaped the enactment of different technologies-in-practice, and how those different enactments, in turn, reinforced or modified the institutional, interpretive and technological conditions.

A key contribution of a practice perspective is the claim that *practices shape reality*, and thus that analytical purchase is gained by treating practices as a focal lens through which to inquire into social reality. A practice perspective, because it entails a theoretically grounded understanding of the recursive interaction among people, activities, artefacts and contexts, is particularly well positioned to address organizational phenomena that are posited to be relational, dynamic and emergent.

Practice as a philosophy

A third mode of engaging practice in research represents a commitment to the ontological primacy of practice in social life. All social reality is understood to be constituted in and through practices, and as such is seen to be an ongoing dynamic and practical accomplishment. Compared to the modes of engaging practice in research discussed above, this mode entails the strongest ontological assertion about the constitution of social reality. The first mode's focus on practice as a phenomenon is an empirical claim that *practices matter*, and thus should be investigated when studying organizational reality. The second mode's focus on practice as a perspective is a theoretical claim that *practices shape reality* in particular ways, and these need to be explicated through practice-theoretic accounts of organizational phenomenon. The third mode's focus on practice as a philosophy is a meta-theoretical claim that *practices are reality*, and therefore studies of organizations must be grounded ontologically, theoretically and empirically in ongoing, lived practice.

Claiming that all social life – not just specific phenomena – is constituted in ongoing practices represents a distinct social ontology, which Schatzki (2002; 2005) sets apart from the dominant alternative ontologies: individualism and societism. Ontological individualism claims 'that social phenomena are either constructions out of or constructions of individual people and – on some versions – their relations' (Schatzki 2005: 466). The assumption is that 'all social matters ultimately consist in and are explained by facts about people – either individual people or groups thereof' (467). In contrast, societism rejects this view, denying that all there is to social phenomena are individuals and their relations. Different scholars emphasize different additional elements that are not decomposable to individuals, such as modes of production, structures, discourses, institutions, etc. Ontological societism thus claims that social phenomena are composed of something other than features of individuals or groups (Schatzki 2005: 467). Arguing that both these dominant ontologies are problematic, Schatzki proposes an alternative approach that steers a path between individualism and societism and identifies practice as 'the primary generic social thing' (2001a: 1). In this alternative ontology, practices are constitutive of social reality.

In the case of technology studies, the recognition that social life transpires as 'nexuses of practices and material arrangements' (Schatzki 2005: 471) has led scholars to draw attention to how relations and boundaries between humans and technologies are not fixed, but enacted in practice. This approach entails a shift from positing humans and technologies as discrete, preformed entities to viewing them as intertwined through dynamic, unfolding relations (Emirbayer 1997). Prior perspectives – including practice-theoretic perspectives on technologies such as my own (Orlikowski 1992; 2000) – have tended to view technology and humans as interacting through relations of mutual or reciprocal influence. While useful, such views still tend to assume that humans and technology are distinct entities with some a priori independence from each other. Speaking of humans and technology as mutually shaping each other necessarily maintains their ontological separation. It is this presupposition of ontological separatism between humans and technologies that is set aside here in favour of a position of ontological entanglement.

Ontological entanglement posits that there are no independently existing entities with inherent characteristics (Barad 2003: 816). Rather, these separate entities are reconceptualized as heterogeneous and shifting associations (Pickering 2001; Latour 2005) that are enacted in practice as an 'ongoing, contingent coproduction of a shared sociomaterial world' (Suchman 2007: 23). These sociomaterial reconfigurations are quite fluid, mutating over times and places, and entangling people, meanings, materialities and practices in the performance of work (Suchman 2007). The contingency of the sociomaterial reconfigurations enacted in practice challenges assumptions that are deeply taken for granted about the relative independence, singularity and stability of reality, and opens up the radical possibility of multiple sociomaterial realities being performed in practice.

One example of what this proposition might involve in research practice is offered by Mol's (2002) investigation of the diagnosis and treatment of a particular cardiovascular disease, atherosclerosis, which involves a thickening and hardening of large and medium-sized arteries. In examining the practices entailed in constituting this disease, she conducted, as she puts it, 'an ethnography of a disease'. What she found through detailed fieldwork in a hospital is that what atherosclerosis *is* varies significantly depending on where, when, how and with whom the disease is being discussed, evaluated and treated. As she powerfully argues, what the disease is then depends on how the disease is sociomaterially enacted in practice within different sites across the hospital.

For example, in the outpatient clinic, the disease is enacted through a conversation about pain and inability to walk distances or up stairs that takes place between the vascular surgeon and the patient. It also involves manipulation of the patient's legs by the surgeon, and a consideration of the leg's skin colour and texture, as well as measurements of blood pressure in the legs. In the pathology lab, in contrast, the disease is enacted through dissecting arteries taken from an amputated limb and then examining cross-sections of the arterial walls under the microscope. As Mol (2002: 35, emphasis in original) writes:

> The practices of enacting clinical atherosclerosis and pathological sclerosis *exclude* one another. The first requires a patient who complains about pain in his legs. And the second requires a cross section of an artery visible under the microscope... It is not a question of *looking from different perspectives.* [...] The incompatibility is a *practical* matter. It is a matter of patients who speak, as against body parts that are sectioned. Of talking about pain, as against estimating the size of cells. Of asking questions, as against preparing slides. In the outpatient clinic

and in the department of pathology, atherosclerosis is *done differently.*

Mol argues that the disease is not a self-standing and discrete entity. It does not stand by itself. It is not independent or fixed or singular. Rather, it is sociomaterially configured by the practices that involve particular bodies, skills, places, instruments, interactions, tests, measures, and so on. In other words, the disease – and, by extension, social life more generally – is thoroughly constituted by contingent practices.

Implications of researching practice

Each of the three modes of engaging practice in research makes different contributions to knowledge, and represents different challenges and implications for the conduct and outcomes of organizational research.

A focus on *practice as a phenomenon* establishes the centrality of practice in the ongoing conduct of organizational life. It argues compellingly that, to develop an understanding of how it is that organization – or, more specifically, organizing – happens, we must understand what organizational members do every day when they show up for work (wherever and whenever that may be). This focus on the details of everyday doings – both the mundane and the novel – recognizes that organizational life tends not to be the rational, orderly, homogeneous and invariant phenomenon that is often portrayed in formal theories and abstracted models. On the contrary, as studies of practice highlight, organizational realities are rich with contingency, complexity, interdependence and emergence. And, while such 'messiness' is difficult to parse and represent, assuming it away does a disservice to the practitioners and to knowledge. A focus on the phenomenon of practice in organizational research thus insists on taking seriously the everyday realities of organizing as they show up in practice, however inconvenient or complicating these render the processes and products of research.

A commitment to the phenomenon of practice requires deep engagement in the field, observing or working with practitioners in action. Such intensive and extensive fieldwork is time-consuming and generates large amounts of qualitative data that are demanding to analyse. It also requires committed and open access from participating organizations and their members, who will need to engage in, or at least be tolerant of, the ongoing research effort. Whether researchers are conducting a participant observation study or an action research project, they will need to carefully navigate and negotiate the terms of their engagement in and their intellectual and ethical obligations to the participating organization. Expectations of researchers by organization members will vary from sharing insights, offering practical suggestions and making normative recommendations to facilitating specific changes in practitioners' capabilities and shifts in their practice.

Knowledge outcomes from immersive practice studies tend to take on a different form from traditional academic research. They are much more likely to be directly relevant to the practitioners and contexts studied. Whether through detailed field study or through active intervention, the deep engagement in particular sites allows for the findings generated to be very applicable to the situations at hand. Extending these specific findings to other contexts is more challenging. In particular, such insights are bounded, historically and contextually, and any theory that is built from participant observation studies is necessarily grounded in specific conditions. Action research projects do not seek to test or build theory but to understand living systems in action and how to change them. They design and implement distinct interventions the effects of which are necessarily local and situated. Nevertheless, the experiential learning to be had from attempting to shift organizational practice (and then studying what happens) typically generates valuable process lessons that can be usefully applied in other contexts.

A focus on *practice as a perspective* involves employing, to a greater or lesser extent, the conceptual scaffolding afforded by one or other existing practice theory. It entails treating practices as a central lens through which to understand organizations, examining the recurrent doings and saying of actors and how these both shape and are shaped by structural conditions and consequences. The appropriation of a practice-theoretic lens requires researchers to attend to certain aspects of social phenomena, the specifics varying by the particular practice theory taken up – for example, the emergent and contingent nature of everyday activity, its human embodiment, material mediation, embeddedness in sociopolitical contexts and the enactment of social structures. This raises the question of how to effectively account for such emergent, contingent, embodied, mediated, embedded and enacted aspects of everyday life. Furthermore, given that a practice perspective theorizes situated activities and institutional consequences, as well as their recursive interaction, a key empirical issue is where and how to pay attention to all these aspects. As some bracketing is practically necessary, how is this to be done? Where should researchers draw boundaries around actors, objects, activities and political/institutional/cultural structures? And what are the implications for knowledge of what is left in and what is left out? Making these methodological choices has important theoretical and practical consequences, highlighting what we choose to keep in view and obscuring what we choose to cut out – 'the brighter the light, the darker the shadow'.

While the theoretical insights developed through a practice perspective may, at first blush, appear less directly influential in practice, theories too have powerful pragmatic implications. Indeed, Giddens makes a strong argument for what he calls the 'double hermeneutic' in the social sciences – that is, the discourse of social studies circulates in and out of its subject matter, reflexively restructuring it (Giddens (1993: 15):

One consequence of the double hermeneutic is that original ideas and findings in social science tend to 'disappear' to the degree to which they are incorporated within the familiar components of practical activities. This is one of the main reasons why social science...typically sustains less prestige in the public eye... In reality, the impact of social science – understood in the widest possible way, as systematic and informed reflection upon the conditions of social activity – is of core significance to modern institutions, which are unthinkable without it.

The people we study appropriate the concepts we develop and, in so doing, change the reality that we have studied. As Geertz (1973) puts it, our models *of* reality become models *for* reality.

A focus on *practice as a philosophy* entails the claim that all social life is constituted in practices, and thus pushes this notion of the double hermeneutic even further. If social life is constituted in practices then so too do practices of social science participate directly in the constitution of social reality. A practice philosophy thus has strong epistemological implications for the nature and politics of social science research, suggesting in particular that the long-standing commitment to a representational meta-theory needs to be displaced. Barad (2007: 46) writes, 'Representationalism is the belief in the ontological distinction between representations and that which they purport to represent... That is, there are assumed to be two distinct and independent kinds of entities – representations and entities to be represented.' In this form of social science research there is 'a bracketing out of the significance of practices; that is, representationalism marks a failure to take account of the practices through which representations are produced' (53). In contrast, a performative meta-theory 'takes account of the fact that knowing does not come from standing at a distance and representing, but rather from a direct material engagement with the world' (49). As Tsoukas (1998: 792, emphasis in original) notes, '[T]he models through which we view the world are not mere mirrors upon which the world is passively reflected but, in an important sense, our models also help *constitute* the world we experience.'

A similar argument is made by Law and Urry (2004: 391), who observe that social inquiry and its methods are profoundly productive: '[T]hey do not simply describe the world as it is, but also enact it.' This, they argue, is a recognition that the methods of social science 'have effects; they make differences; ...and they can help to bring into being what they also discover' (393). As a result, 'social science is performative. It *produces* realities' (395, emphasis in original). The shift away from a representational meta-theory towards a performative one raises important political and ethical questions (Rouse 2001). In particular, it begs the question of

what kinds of realities are being produced through our social science. Law and Urry (2004: 397) argue that the kind of reality that social science has tended to produce is a singular one, 'composed of discrete entities standing in hierarchical or inclusive relations with one another'. And, as they argue, such a reality is not productive in a twenty-first century in which social relations are increasingly entangled, ephemeral, non-linear, unpredictable, global and mobile. Shifting towards a practice ontology, and thus a performative meta-theory, may help to provide more productive metaphors and approaches for studying contemporary organizational life. But it will challenge established institutional norms, practices and criteria of organizational research that are premised on representationalism.

Conclusion

The turn to practice in management studies – and particularly in the strategy-as-practice school of thought – has been a welcome addition to the repertoire of ideas and approaches that scholars use to study organizational phenomena. In focusing on *practice as a phenomenon,* the value of engaging with the everyday doings of organizing has been foregrounded. In focusing on *practice as a perspective,* the value of practice theories in examining and explicating specific organizational phenomena has been articulated. In focusing on *practice as a philosophy,* the value of understanding practice as constitutive of reality has been highlighted. Furthermore, the entailments of a practice philosophy within management studies help us to see that engaging with practice in research – whether through descriptions, interventions, appropriations or enactments – is itself performative and thus implicated in constituting particular kinds of practices and organizations.

Law and Singleton (2000: 767) note that 'every description of the world also participates in social and material agenda-setting'. Thus, key questions the community of strategy-as-practice scholars might want to ask going forward are these. What and whose agenda is being set in our research, and by whom? What are the performative consequences of our various modes of engaging with practice? And, more pointedly, if our research helps to produce certain organizational outcomes, then what kinds of organizational outcomes do we want to help produce?

References

Argyris, C., Putnam, R., and Smith, D. (1985), *Action Science: Concepts, Methods and Skills for Research and Intervention*. San Francisco: Jossey-Bass.

Barad, K. (2003), 'Posthumanist performativity: toward an understanding of how matter comes to matter', *Signs*, 28/3: 801–31.

—— (2007), *Meeting the Universe Halfway: Quantum Physics and the Entanglement of Matter and Meaning*. Durham, NC: Duke University Press.

Barley, S. R., and Kunda, G. (2006), *Gurus, Hired Guns, and Warm Bodies: Itinerant Experts in a Knowledge Economy*. Princeton University Press.

Barnes, B. (2001), 'Practice as collective action', in Schatzki, T. R., Knorr Cetina, K., and von Savigny, E. (eds.), *The Practice Turn in Contemporary Theory*: 17–28. London: Routledge.

Bartunek, J. M., and Louis, M. R. (1996), *Insider/Outsider Team Research*. Thousand Oaks, CA: Sage.

Baskerville, R., and Myers, M. D. (2004), 'Foreword to special issue on action research in information systems: making IS research relevant to practice', *MIS Quarterly*, 28/3: 329–33.

Bourdieu, P. (1977), *Outline of a Theory of Practice*. Cambridge University Press.

Brown, J. S., and Duguid, P. (1991), 'Organizational learning and communities of practice: toward a unified view of working, learning and innovation', *Organization Science*, 2/1: 40–57.

Bucciarelli, L. L. (1994), *Designing Engineers*. Cambridge, MA: MIT Press.

Burawoy, M. (1979), *Manufacturing Consent: Changes in Labor Process under Monopoly Capitalism*. University of Chicago Press.

Button, G. (ed.) (1993), *Technology in Working Order: Studies in Work, Interaction and Technology*. London: Routledge.

Checkland, P. (1999), *Systems Thinking, Systems Practice*, 2nd edn. Chichester, UK: John Wiley.

Ciborra, C. (2002), *The Labyrinths of Information: Challenging the Wisdom of Systems*. Oxford University Press.

De Certeau, M. (1984), *The Practice of Everyday Life*. Berkeley: University of California Press.

Dourish, P., and Button, G. (1998), 'On "technomethodology": foundational relationships between ethnomethodology and system design', *Human–Computer Interaction*, 13/4: 395–432.

Emirbayer, M. (1997), 'Manifesto for a relational sociology', *American Journal of Sociology*, 103/2: 281–317.

Feldman, M. S., and Orlikowski, W. J. (2011), 'Theorizing practice and practicing theory', *Organization Science*, 22/5: 1240–53.

Foucault, M. (1977), *Discipline and Punish: The Birth of the Prison*. New York: Pantheon Books.

Garfinkel, H. (1967), *Studies in Ethnomethodology*. Englewood Cliffs, NJ: Prentice Hall.

Gasser, L. (1986), 'The integration of computing and routine work', *ACM Transactions on Office Information Systems*, 4/3: 205–25.

Geertz, C. (1973), *The Interpretation of Cultures*. New York: Basic Books.

Gherardi, S. (2006), *Organizational Knowledge: The Texture of Workplace Learning*. Oxford: Blackwell.

Giddens, A. (1984), *The Constitution of Society*. Cambridge: Polity.

—— (1993), *New Rules of Sociological Method*, 2nd edn. Redwood City, CA: Stanford University Press.

Hutchins, E. (1995), *Cognition in the Wild*. Cambridge, MA: MIT Press.

Kling, R. (1991), 'Computerization and social transformations', *Science, Technology, and Human Values*, 16/3: 342–67.

Knorr Cetina, K. (2001), 'Objectual practice', in Schatzki, T. R., Knorr Cetina, K., and von Savigny, E. (eds.), *The Practice Turn in Contemporary Theory*: 175–88. London: Routledge.

Latour, B. (2005), *Reassembling the Social: An Introduction to Actor–Network Theory*. Oxford University Press.

Lave, J. (1988), *Cognition in Practice: Mind, Mathematics and Culture in Everyday Life*. Cambridge University Press.

Lave, J., and Wenger, E. (1991), *Situated Learning: Legitimate Peripheral Participation*. Cambridge University Press.

Law, J., and Singelton, V. (2000), 'Performing technology's stories: on social constructivism, performance and performativity', *Technology and Culture*, 41/4: 765–75.

Law, J., and Urry, J. (2004), 'Enacting the social', *Economy and Society*, 33/3: 390–410.

Lewin, K. (1946), 'Action research and minority problems', *Journal of Social Issues*, 2/4: 34–46.

Luff, P., Hindmarsh, J., and Heath, C. (eds.) (2000), *Workplace Studies: Recovering Work Practice and Informing System Design*. Cambridge University Press.

Lynch, M. (2001), 'Ethnomethodology and the logic of practice', in Schatzki, T. R., Knorr Cetina, K., and von Savigny, E. (eds.), *The Practice Turn in Contemporary Theory*: 131–48. London: Routledge.

Mol, A. (2002), *The Body Multiple: Ontology in Medical Practice*. Durham, NC: Duke University Press.

Molloy, E. (2007), 'Practice theory and management research', in Thorpe, R., and Holt, R. (eds.), *The Sage Dictionary of Qualitative Management Research*: 163–5. London: Sage.

Mumford, E., and Hensall, D. (1979), *Participative Approaches to Computer Systems Design*. London: Associated Design Press.

Orlikowski, W. J. (1992), 'The duality of technology: rethinking the concept of technology in organizations', *Organization Science*, 3/3: 398–427.

——(1996), 'Improvising organizational transformation over time: a situated change perspective', *Information Systems Research*, 7/1: 63–92.

——(2000), 'Using technology and constituting structures'. *Organization Science*, 11/4: 404–28.

Orr, J. E. (1996), *Talking about Machines: An Ethnography of a Modern Job*. Ithaca, NY: ILR Press.

Ortner, S. B. (1984), 'Theory in anthropology since the sixties', *Comparative Studies in Society and History*, 26/1: 126–66.

Pickering, A. (1995), *The Mangle of Practice: Time, Agency, and Science*. University of Chicago Press.

Pickering, A. (2001), 'Practice and posthumanism: social theory and a history of agency', in Schatzki, T. R., Knorr Cetina, K., and von Savigny, E. (eds.), *The Practice Turn in Contemporary Theory*: 163–74. London: Routledge.

Postill, J. (2010), 'Introduction: theorising media and practice', in Bräuchler, B., and Postill, J. (eds.), *Theorising Media and Practice*: 1–32. New York: Berghahn.

Rapoport, R., Bailyn, L., Fletcher, J. K., and Pruitt, B. H. (2002), *Beyond Work–Family Balance: Advancing Gender Equity and Workplace Performance*. San Francisco: Jossey-Bass.

Reckwitz, A. (2002), 'Toward a theory of social practices: a development in culturalist theorizing', *European Journal of Social Theory*, 5/2: 243–63.

Rouse, J. (1996), *Engaging Science: How to Understand Its Practices Philosophically*. Ithaca, NY: Cornell University Press.

——(2001), 'Two concepts of practices', in Schatzki, T. R., Knorr Cetina, K., and von Savigny, E. (eds.), *The Practice Turn in Contemporary Theory*: 189–98. London: Routledge.

Rynes, S. L., Bartunek, J. M., and Daft, R. L. (2001), 'Across the great divide: knowledge creation and transfer between practitioners and academics', *Academy of Management Journal*, 44/2: 340–55.

Sachs, P. (1995), 'Transforming work: collaboration, learning, and design', *Communications of the ACM*, 38/9: 36–44.

Schatzki, T. R. (2001a), 'Introduction: practice theory', in Schatzki, T. R., Knorr Cetina, K., and von Savigny, E. (eds.), *The Practice Turn in Contemporary Theory*: 1–14. London: Routledge.

Schatzki, T. R. (2001b), 'Practice mind-ed orders', in Schatzki, T. R., Knorr Cetina, K., and von Savigny, E. (eds.), *The Practice Turn in Contemporary Theory*: 42–55. London: Routledge.

——(2002), *The Site of the Social: A Philosophical Account of the Constitution of Social Life and Change*. University Park: Pennsylvania State University Press.

——(2005), 'The sites of organizations', *Organization Studies*, 26/3: 465–84.

Schatzki, T. R., Knorr Cetina, K., and von Savigny, E. (eds.) (2001), *The Practice Turn in Contemporary Theory*. London: Routledge.

Schein, E. H. (1985). *Organizational Culture and Leadership: A Dynamic View*. San Francisco: Jossey-Bass.

——(1987), *The Clinical Perspective in Fieldwork*. Newbury Park, CA: Sage.

——(1999), *Process Consultation Revisited*. Reading, MA: Addison-Wesley.

Schön, D. A. (1983), *The Reflective Practitioner*. New York: Basic Books.

Suchman, L. A. (1987), *Plans and Situated Actions: The Problem of Human–Machine Communication*. Cambridge University Press.

——(2007), *Human–Machine Reconfigurations: Plans and Situated Actions*. Cambridge University Press.

Swidler, A. (2001), 'What anchors cultural practices', in Schatzki, T. R., Knorr Cetina, K., and von Savigny, E. (eds.), *The Practice Turn in Contemporary Theory*: 74–92. London: Routledge.

Taylor, C. (1985), *Philosophy and the Human Sciences*. Cambridge University Press.

Thomas, R. J. (1994), *What Machines Can't Do: Politics and Technology in the Industrial Enterprise*. Berkeley: University of California Press.

Tsoukas, H. (1998), 'The word and the world: a critique of representationalism in management research', *International Journal of Public Administration*, 21/5: 781–817.

Turner, S. (2001), 'Throwing out the tacit rule book: learning and practices', in Schatzki, T. R., Knorr Cetina, K., and von Savigny, E. (eds.), *The Practice Turn in Contemporary Theory*: 120–30. London: Routledge.

Van de Ven, A. H., and Johnson, P. E. (2006), 'Knowledge for theory and practice', *Academy of Management Review*, 31/4: 802–21.

Whittington, R. (2006), 'Completing the practice turn in strategy research', *Organization Studies*, 27/5: 613–34.

Whyte, W. F. (ed.) (1991), *Participatory Action Research*. Newbury Park, CA: Sage.

Zuboff, S. (1988), *In the Age of the Smart Machine*. New York: Basic Books.

Epistemological alternatives for researching strategy as practice: building and dwelling worldviews

CHAPTER 2

ROBERT CHIA and ANDREAS RASCHE

The ordinary practitioners...live 'down below', below the threshold at which visibility begins... [T]heir knowledge...is as blind as that of lovers in each other's arms... It is as though the practices were characterized by their blindness.

De Certeau (1984: 93)

Introduction

Most traditional approaches to strategy research have tended to consist of a complex amalgam of activities comprising the analyses of dependent and independent variables, theoretical conjecturing and the testing of theories and models developed to capture the essence of strategic realities (Rasche 2008). In this regard, the strategy-as-practice approach to research is a welcome departure in its single-minded insistence on focusing primarily on what strategy practitioners actually do. Although the strategy-as-practice field has attracted a mass of empirical work (Balogun and Johnson 2005; Jarzabkowski 2005; Jarzabkowski and Wilson 2002; Paroutis and Heracleous 2013; Regnér 2003; Samra-Fredericks 2003) and theoretical clarification (Denis, Langley and Rouleau 2007; Jarzabkowski, Balogun and Seidl 2007; Johnson, Melin and Whittington 2003; Whittington 1996; 2003; 2006; for a recent review, see Vaara and Whittington 2012), the alternative epistemological groundings available and how they may affect further efforts at conceptualizing strategy as practice remain relatively unarticulated. This is despite the fact that there have been some notable attempts to clarify research and methodological priorities for the SAP movement (Balogun, Huff and Johnson 2003; Ezzamel and Willmott 2010; Jarzabkowski 2003; 2004; 2005; Johnson, Melin and Whittington 2003; McCabe 2010; Tsoukas 2010; Whittington 2006).

For researchers it is vital to give substantial consideration to the manner in which accounts and explanations proffered on strategy practice are reflexively moderated by an acute awareness of the inherent problems relating to the 'situatedness' of strategic action, and hence the epistemological issues associated with such attempted representations. The manner in which academically articulated accounts of strategy practice tend to create a schism between such accounts and the very practices they purport to explain is one of the most intractable problems of the research process. Such a schism can be addressed and rectified only through a careful examination of the dominant research dispositions and the nature and limitations of the resultant explanatory outcomes involved.

In this chapter, we explore how the explanatory rupture between research accounts of strategy practice and the practice itself is intimately linked to the adoption of a widely held set of epistemological premises that we term here the *building* worldview. This dominant view relies on two core assumptions. The first is that each individual is a discrete bounded entity relating externally to its social environment and to other individuals in such a way as to leave its basic internally specified identity and agentic qualities relatively unchanged. A 'social atomism' (de Certeau 1984: xi) or methodological individualism (Weber 1968 [1922]: 15) is presupposed. Individuals are conceived of as being separated by a structure of invisible 'walls', and this tends to 'obscure and distort our understanding of our own life in society' (Elias 1978: 15).

Second, the building worldview presupposes a Cartesian split between the mental and the physical realms, so that proper knowledge is construed as the ability to represent the world around us in the mind in the form of mental images. Cognition and mental representation necessarily precede any meaningful action. What distinguishes 'action' as opposed to 'mere' behaviour, as such, is that actors are deemed to be motivated by prior thought-out intentions and to act *purposefully* to attain pre-specified goals. By 'purposeful', we mean a *deliberately designed and planned form of intervention*. Strategic action is thus explained through recourse to the meaning and intention of actors, and a means–ends logic of action is presumed.

We contrast this building worldview with a *dwelling* one, in which the identities and characteristics of persons are not deemed to pre-exist social interactions and social practices. Rather, the individual person is viewed as a product of the 'condensations of histories of growth and maturation within fields of social relations... [E]very person emerges as a locus of development within such a field' (Ingold 2000: 3). Hence, neither the individual nor society is to be construed as self-contained entities interacting externally with each other (Elias 1991: 456). Instead, both the individual and society are viewed as mutually constitutive and co-defining impulses relying on 'complex responsive processes' (Stacey 2007: 247) to become who and what they are. Social practices themselves are given primacy over individual agency and intention (Chia and Holt 2006; Ezzamel and Willmott 2008) – so much so that the individual is understood as a locus 'in which an incoherent (and often contradictory) plurality of such relational determinations interact' (de Certeau 1984: xi). Neither individuals nor some overarching deterministic super-structures are the real 'co-authors' of action. In this regard, a *relational* ontology of individuation is presupposed (Chia and MacKay 2007; Chia and Holt 2006: 635; Ezzamel and Willmott 2008: 197).

What this implies is that individual agents are so constituted by everyday social practices that they act and interact, for the most part, spontaneously and *purposively* (in contrast to purposefully) in a self-referential manner to overcome immediate problems and obstacles without any need for theoretical distancing, conscious deliberation or an overall pre-designed plan of action. There is, on this view, no presupposed prior distinction between individual and society, no dualism between mind and matter and no prior distance between thought and action; these are deemed to be secondary distinctions generated through social practices themselves.

The delineation of such a dwelling worldview enables us to establish an alternative set of epistemological premises whereby knowledge is not some representational commodity that is digested, processed and then acted upon but, rather, is 'grown' and regrown through social practice within specific sociocultural and historical contexts; unconsciously internalized and incorporated into the *modus operandi* of the individual in the form of skills, sensitivities and overriding predispositions (Bourdieu 1990). Both the building and the dwelling modes of explanation may be employed to explain the actual practice of strategizing. Each produces significantly different explanatory outcomes, however. Thus, while it is possible to straightforwardly identify and catalogue the explicit and purposeful 'doings' of assigned strategists – the tools, artefacts, talk, awayday meetings and strategy presentations, etc. – it is also true to say that much of what goes on in the actual process of evolving a coherent strategy consists of small, unspectacular everyday coping actions throughout an organization. These are carried out in a self-absorbed manner by individuals with no presumption of deliberate forethought or conscious planning on their part. We believe that strategy-as-practice scholars have not given adequate attention to this latter aspect of strategy-making and the tacit form of practical knowledge associated with it, even though there are now signs that some strategy researchers are beginning to address these issues (Baumard 1999; Ezzamel and Willmott 2010; McCabe 2010; Nonaka and Toyama 2007; Regnér 2003). Hence, our aim here is to draw on these insights to enrich accounts of strategy practice by expanding the epistemological possibilities available to the strategy-as-practice research movement.

Our analysis proceeds as follows. In the next section, we lay the ground for our argumentation *apollo s deo.   >.   buich s duch.*

by discussing (1) how epistemological considerations interact with the strategy research process and (2) how traditional epistemological assumptions have informed strategy scholars' thinking. In the third section, we draw on these insights to distinguish between a building and a dwelling worldview and the specific epistemologies associated with each of these. We show that two types of knowledge, *episteme* and *techné*, are intimately linked to the dominant building worldview while another two, *phronesis* and *mētis*, constitute the form of practical knowing characterized by a dwelling mode. In the final section, we first argue that a lot of strategy-as-practice research is still rooted in the building epistemology, and then explore the implications of adopting a dwelling worldview for the future direction of the SAP movement. We show that adopting a dwelling set of epistemological premises opens up new avenues for explaining the acquired disposition towards strategy practice as a form of mundane or opportunistic everyday strategizing that is inherently unspectacular but that is yet unquestionably efficacious and transformational in its overall conduct.

"drifty into excellera"

Epistemology and the research process

Problems and tensions of researching strategy practice

The term 'epistemology' is based on the Greek words *episteme* (knowledge) and *logos* (account/ explanation), and is often misperceived to be solely about propositional forms of knowledge claims underpinned by a rationally inspired mode of thought. In 'proper' epistemological inquiry, therefore, the facts, the theory, the alternatives and the ideals are brought together and weighed against each other in the creation of knowledge. The prevailing emphasis on this specific form of knowledge has meant that only that which can be subjected to linguistic explication, propositional articulation and universal generalization or precise measurement is deemed to be proper knowledge.

The problem with relying solely on this type of knowledge in academic research is that it misses out on a wealth of tacit, inarticulate and often inarticulatable understandings of strategy practitioners as they go about their practical affairs. Indeed, for most of the time, practitioners themselves may be unaware of this tacit knowledge that they possess. This means that, when they are questioned in the research process, respondents may unsuspectingly feel pressurized to justify, account for or clarify their actions in an explicitly logical and coherent manner that is readily understandable to the researcher, thereby distorting what they actually know and do. They are required to respond to the questions, concerns and preoccupations of researchers in a social context that is distant from the immediate demands of practical engagements, and do so using a logic and vocabulary foreign to that of everyday application – so much so that they may unwittingly conceal from themselves and their interrogators the true nature of their practical mastery (Bourdieu 1977: 19). This means that the practice-naïve academic researcher and the research-naïve practitioner may actually unintentionally collude in producing an overly deliberate and rationalistic account of what has actually happened through their *retrospective* sensemaking (Weick 2001). The situation is far less problematic when successful strategists express their own views in autobiographical accounts, for instance, because there they are less constrained by academic protocols.

In the case of formalized research, however, the conversion from the prospective orientation of inventive, opportunistic and timely action on the part of practitioners to the retrospective theoretical schema of logical explanation connives to transform the reality of practice in process to an efficiency 'model' of action and the framing of experience in strictly instrumental causal terms, thereby 'flattening out' the more enfolded and circuitous reality of everyday strategic coping practices. This is partly because, for research to be acceptable and publishable in respected journals, scholars are required to adopt 'discursive practices' that conform to the tight demands of an academic community that recognizes only propositional forms of knowledge and explicit causal explanations as the legitimate form of knowledge. Producing knowledge acceptable to the exacting demands of academic scholarship, therefore, risks killing off that very thing that makes research itself a worthwhile activity (Mintzberg 2004: 399). It tends to leave out the tacit 'feel' for a strategy situation that is intuitively understood by the strategy practitioner but that is hardly ever acknowledged in research accounts.

The epistemological legacy of Western thought

To understand the grounds on which the described schism between theory and practice has been generated, we explore deeper into the epistemological legacy of Western thought in this section. In the *Nichomachean Ethics*, Plato's successor, Aristotle distinguished between three types of knowledge, which he called *episteme, techné* and *phronesis*. *Episteme* is universal truth that is context-independent, rationally based and objective. Baumard (1999: 53) maintains that *episteme* is propositional knowledge and expertise 'about' things. It is abstract, universal and hierarchical knowledge that can be 'written, recorded, and validated'. It is explicitly articulated in causal terms and can be systematically verified empirically. Similarly, *techné* is about craftsmanship and involves precise codifiable techniques or practical instructions that are amenable to linguistic explication. *Episteme* and *techné* were both often used interchangeably among the ancient Greeks, as Nussbaum (1986: 94) has noted, and both reflect aspirations towards explicitness, universality, precision, clarity and teachability – all values that were associated with what was deemed desirable in ancient Greece, and that are still held in the highest esteem, particularly in academic circles (Raphals 1992: 227). Knowledge is thus considered such only if it is capable of being expressed linguistically in terms of principles, causes or actor meanings and intentions.

In addition to *episteme* and *techné*, however, Aristotle also posited (though less emphatically) the existence of *phronesis* (practical wisdom) as a less accessible form of personal knowing that differs qualitatively from *episteme* and *techné* in that it 'expresses the kind of person that one is' (Dunne 1993: 244). While *episteme* and *techné* imply the explicitness and transmissibility of

knowledge, *phronesis* alludes to a form of *tacit* knowing that emerges through a person's striving and that is inseparable from an individual's entire cultural attitude and predisposition. Although both *episteme* and *techné* can be consciously learned and hence can be forgotten, '*phronesis* cannot' (Aristotle, *Nichomachean Ethics*, 6.5.1140b, 28–30, cited by Dunne 1993: 265), since it is always already integral to an individual's make-up. Unlike *episteme* or *techné*, in which it is possible to make a distinction between intention and behaviour, and hence between what one *is* and what one *does*, in *phronesis* what one *does* is inextricable from what one *is*. Unlike *episteme* and *techné*, which produce outcomes that are clearly separable from the producer, *phronesis* gives rise to *praxis,* which cannot be instrumentalized: it is action that seeks no outcomes other than its own self-realization (Dunne 1993: 262). In *phronetic* action (that is, *praxis*),

> the agent...is constituted through the actions... [H]e becomes and discovers 'who' he is through these actions. And the medium for this becoming through action is not one over which he is ever sovereign master; it is, rather, a network of other people who are also agents and with whom he is bound in relationships of interdependence (262–3).

This intimate relationship between being and doing, between intention and action and between identity and strategy makes *phronesis* extremely difficult to apprehend, and hence it remains very much an unexplored feature in strategy research (Baumard 1999; Nonaka and Toyama 2007).

Moreover, recent studies of pre-Socratic Greek culture and society, including especially the insights expressed in Homer's *Iliad* and Hesiod's *Theogony* (Detienne and Vernant 1978), suggest the existence of yet another form of practical knowing on which even Plato and Aristotle remained surprisingly silent. Detienne and Vernant call this form of 'cunning intelligence' *mētis. Mētis* is 'a type of intelligence and of thought, a way of knowing; it...combines flair, wisdom, forethought, subtlety of mind, deception, resourcefulness, vigilance, opportunism, various skills and experience acquired over years' (Detienne and

Vernant 1978: 4). The field of application for *mētis* is a world that is shifting, multiple, disconcerting and ambivalent. While *phronesis* was still considered in Aristotelian thought, and is increasingly recognized and acknowledged as, a form of 'tacit knowledge' or 'practical wisdom' (Baumard 1999; Nonaka and Toyama 2007), the quality of *mētis* was ignored by the Greek philosophers – and this has also been the case in strategy research. *Mētis* corresponds to what we mean when we say that someone is 'street-smart', or seems able to 'get away with things' or 'get out of difficult situations' with cunning and ease. Both *phronesis* and *mētis* remain relatively unexplored in the strategy-as-practice research agenda, yet they are vital tacit qualities of an effective strategy practitioner. In what follows, we show that *phronesis* and *mētis* are alternative epistemologies intimately linked to a dwelling mode of thinking.

Building and dwelling: two worldviews for strategy-as-practice research

Comparing the building and dwelling worldviews

In *The Practice of Everyday Life*, de Certeau (1984: 91–3) finds himself at the top of the ill-fated World Trade Center in New York musing on the distinction between the view looking down on the city, and enjoying the voyeuristic pleasures of seeing it all neatly laid out below as one would view a map of a city, and the view of the city as most ordinary people would see it: pedestrians engrossed in their specific circumstances and unthinkingly finding their way around at the street level itself. Unlike the detached transcendent observer looking from atop the building, the pedestrians on the streets down below do not have a map-like view or comprehensive picture of the city but experience a series of continuously changing migrational outlooks as they actually walk the streets at 'ground zero' – unthinkingly but deftly avoiding traffic, sidestepping and negotiating their way around obstacles, ignoring the honking, but noticing the displays on the sidewalk, passing by, reaching towards and generally 'muddling

through' (Lindblom 1959) on their way to work. This is the creative experience of weaving spaces, events and situations together in a subjective self-referential manner. The richness of experiences involved in such pedestrian journeys cannot be captured by static maps, tracing routes or locating positions. Nor can they be even descriptively exhausted through seeking out and clarifying the meanings and intentions of actors, since such everyday activities are often conducted unthinkingly *in situ*. The pedestrians 'down below' have no privileged 'bird's-eye' view and must act by 'reaching out' from wherever they find themselves, feeling their way towards a satisfactory resolution of their immediate circumstances. In this astute observation, de Certeau is making a vital distinction between two different outlooks and their associated modes of engagement and knowing that we label here the 'building' and 'dwelling' worldviews.

In the *building* mode, researchers suppose that there is an initial pre-cognitive separation between the actor and the world – so much so that the strategy actor has first a need to 'construct mental representations and models of the world prior to any practical engagement with it' (Ingold 2000: 178). As such, the strategy actor is assumed to be distinct and detached from the situation he/she finds him-/herself in, much like de Certeau's viewer looking from atop the World Trade Center building. Strategizing is thus construed as the act of planning purposeful 'interventions' into the flow of reality to effect a desired outcome. Such action is necessarily 'heroic', in that it presupposes the attempt on the part of the actor to *impose* his/her will and ideal onto an otherwise recalcitrant reality. It directs attention to the meaning, intention and purposefulness of the individual actor and portrays the strategy actor as a self-contained entity engaging externally with reality.

In the *dwelling* mode of theorizing, on the other hand, people are assumed to be intimately immersed and inextricably intertwined with what surrounds them, in all its complex interrelatedness. They have no privileged 'bird's-eye' view of their situation, and hence have to act from wherever they find themselves in order to achieve a satisfactory resolution of their immediate predicament. In

Table 2.1 Contrasting a building and a dwelling epistemology

Building worldview	Dwelling worldview
Actors are self-conscious, intentional and self-motivated.	Actors as non-deliberate, relationally constituted nexus of social activities.
Actions are guided by predefined goals directing efforts towards outcomes – purposeful action.	Actions are directed towards overcoming immediate impediment – purposive practical coping.
Consistency of action assumed to be ordered by deliberate intent.	Consistency of action assumed to be ordered by a *modus operandi* – an internalized disposition.

Source: Adopted and modified from Chia and Holt (2006: 644).

their everyday activities, people engage in 'way-finding' (Hutchins 1995), creating action pathways that radiate outwards from their concrete existential situations. Like the pedestrians in de Certeau's (1984) observation, people experience the city streets by reaching out and feeling 'their way *through* a world that is itself. . .continually coming into being' (Ingold 2000: 155, emphasis added). Self and world (e)merge in the concrete activities of dwelling, in which skills are acquired and developed 'without necessarily passing through consciousness' (Dreyfus 1991: 27). In such a dwelling mode, decisions and actions emanate from being *in situ* and occur *sponte sua*. Here, the efficacy of action does not depend upon some pre-thought plan of action but results from internalized predispositions that facilitate continuous timely and ongoing adjustment and adaptation to local circumstances.

What is crucial to the dwelling mode of explanation is that it acknowledges the primacy of tacit knowledge over explicit knowledge. It recognizes that such forms of tacit knowing are acquired through living within and becoming intimately acquainted with local conditions 'on the ground', and not from some detached observer's point of view. In other words, the *dwelling* mode of engagement presupposes the possession of *phronesis* and/or *mētis*. Actions are taken in *relation* to changes observed in a specific local context and not as a universal rule or principle. Moreover, such small local adaptations and the timeliness involved in doings are incremental and 'unheroic', so that they often go unnoticed. The practical intelligence involved is subtle, tacit and oblique, unlike the kind of direct means–ends logic of explanation used to account for purposeful human action.

Table 2.1 summarizes the relationship between a building and a dwelling worldview.

Towards a dwelling worldview: phronesis and mētis

To better understand what we mean by a dwelling epistemology and its implications, we now link the concepts of *phronesis* and *mētis* to our discussion. As we have maintained, unlike *episteme* or *techné*, *phronesis* and *mētis*, though different forms of tacit knowing, are acquired through the immersion and internalizing of embedded social practices. These are learned unconsciously and unintentionally through exemplification, and unthinkingly emulated. Such practical knowing is generated in the immediate intimacy of lived experience, tacitly acquired through trial and error and the process of the gradual modification of behaviour, and hence does not easily lend itself to research scrutiny. *Phronesis*, in particular, is the tacit form of prudent practical intelligence and wisdom, acquired through experience, that accounts for the ability to perform expediently and appropriately in defined social circumstances.

Nonaka and Toyama (2007: 6), in a relatively recent paper on strategic management, suggest that strategy-in-practice may be better understood as 'distributed phronesis'. In largely agreeing with the emphasis on strategy as practice, Nonaka and Toyama make the point that strategy as practical wisdom arises from the desire to pursue a 'common goodness' and hence necessarily involves subjective value judgements. This is where *phronesis* differs qualitatively from *episteme* and *techné*. Thus, 'if *techné* is the knowledge of how to make the car well, *phronesis* is the knowledge of what a good car is...and how to endeavour to build such a car' (Nonaka and Toyama 2007: 8). Neither *episteme* nor *techné* can answer the question of what a 'good' car is, since this is a subjective valuation. Only through *phronesis* can one answer that question.

By couching the problematic in this manner, however, Nonaka and Toyama are in danger of 'instrumentalizing' *phronetic* action (*praxis*), which, as we have shown, is inseparable from a person's being and internalized predisposition. Someone with *phronesis* cannot help acting in the way he/she does. He/she is internally predisposed to building a 'good' car in this instance; it is part of being, as we have argued above. Our view is that Nonaka and Toyama overlook the most important aspect of *phronesis*; that it is a culturally shaped and socially internalized *modus operandi* or *habitus* (Bourdieu 1990), integral and inextricable from one's own self-identity. *Phronesis* denotes a shared propensity to act in a manner congruent with our own sense of who we are. For this reason, we can agree with Nonaka and Toyama that *phronesis* may indeed be an immanent, and socially distributed, strategic orientation that is enacted and re-enacted through the everyday coping actions of a collectivity.

Mētis, on the other hand, is the kind of practical intelligence required to escape puzzling and ambiguous situations, and is particularly applicable to those research settings that do not lend themselves to precise measurement, exact calculation or rigorous logic (Baumard 1999: 65). Raphals (1992: 5) points out that, while *phronesis* is 'practical but not inherently oblique, devious or indirect', *métic* intelligence operates with a 'peculiar twist'; it reflects the internalized ability to attain a surprising reversal of situations. So, while *phronesis* is tacit shared practical wisdom associated with goodness and virtue, *métis* has no such moral compunctions. It is more associated with clandestine and seemingly 'unsavoury' ruses, cunning and opportunism; with the ability to 'get away' with things as and when needed.

Mētis operates through duplicity and disguise, concealing its true lethal nature beneath a reassuring exterior. It is characterized by agility, suppleness, swiftness of action and the art of dissimulation (seeing without being seen or acting without being seen to act). It is a form of primordially acquired 'strategy', in which the emphasis is on constantly seeking out practical ways to survive dangerous situations or to 'outwit' the competition. The eminent Yale anthropologist James Scott maintains that '[k]nowing how and when to apply the rules of thumb *in a concrete situation* is the essence of *mētis*' (Scott 1998: 316, emphasis in original). *Mētis* reflects the ability to attain a surprising reversal of unfavourable situations to achieve favourable outcomes through diversionary practices such as poachings, surprises, trickery and deceit. *Mētis* is quintessentially the strategy of the 'weak', the disempowered or the disadvantaged (de Certeau 1984: 37–40).

Both *phronesis* and *mētis* point to the myriad ways by which strategy actors, finding themselves in a given situation, are still able to spontaneously and without much forethought transform unfavourable circumstances into favourable outcomes through their practical wisdom, alertness, resourcefulness and guile. When referring to *phronesis* and *mētis*, researchers can distinguish the everyday *purposiveness* of absorbed practical coping action from the *purposefulness* of planned action (Chia and Holt 2006: 648). *Phronetic* and *mētic* intelligence are both internalized predispositions inscribed onto material bodies that generate the propensity to act in a manner congruent with the demands of shifting material situations. They constitute the authentic art of strategizing that is peculiarly sensitive to time – duration as well as simultaneity – and hence they are particularly well suited for dealing with transient, shifting, disconcerting and ambiguous situations. It is quintessentially that which often continues to remain 'outside' the remit of strategy-as-practice theorizing, yet is everywhere to be seen in practice.

Building and dwelling worldviews: consequences for strategy-as-practice research

Both the building and the dwelling modes of comprehension may be employed to understand the actual practice of strategizing, each with its own merit. To date, however, it has been the former that has primarily occupied the attention of the SAP research community.

Strategy-as-practice research and the building epistemology

Although strategy-as-practice scholars have taken much care to conceptualize strategy practices as flexible and being based on practitioners' improvizations in praxis (Whittington 2006: 620), and although they have encouraged methodological pluralism in research (Balogun, Huff and Johnson 2003; Whittington 2003), we contend here that their underlying epistemological assumptions remain largely within the realms of traditional scholarship and that their attention is restricted to considering practitioners' actions in terms circumscribed by *episteme* and *techné*. Neither *phronesis* nor *mētis*, as equally legitimate tacit forms of knowledge possessed by practitioners, features much in their studies. The central assumption of the autonomous strategic actor relying on explicit knowledge to deliberately analyse, plan and then purposefully act to attain predefined ends remains a core feature of the research agenda. To be sure, the focus is directed to more micro-level everyday strategic sensemaking activities, but the focus remains on what formally assigned organizational strategists actually do and the rational choices they make.

Ezzamel and Willmott (2008) maintain that strategy-as-practice advocates such as Jarzabkowski (2005) and Whittington (2006) continue to rely on an interpretive approach to peer into the black box of everyday strategizing and to examine 'how, for example, decision-makers' cognitive frameworks yield their sense of the context; and how these frameworks inform their actions' (Ezzamel and Willmott 2008: 196), without acknowledging that such research accounts are 'inescapably constitutive of what [they] claim to capture or reflect' (196). Ezzamel and Willmott insist – rightly, in our view – that, even though strategy-as-practice theorists continue to employ and emphasize the primacy of practice, citing seminal thinkers such as Bourdieu (1990) and Foucault (1972: 1984) as key advocates, they have not

actually embraced the latter's relational ontology. 'SAP analysis incorporates little consideration of how, for example, engaging in practices is constitutive of practitioners as subjects' (Ezzamel and Willmott 2008: 197). Instead, practices are mainly construed in terms of how assigned strategists 'think, talk, reflect, act, interact, emote, embellish, politicise' (Jarzabkowski 2005: 3). It is these explicit doings of strategists that feed into strategy-as-practice theorizing. Practices themselves remain secondary outputs of individuals. In maintaining this epistemological stance, strategy-as-practice researchers continue to subscribe to what we have called here a building worldview.

Such a research orientation overlooks the formative character of social practices on the individual's or organization's identity. In other words, it fails to consider the fact that so-called strategic 'choices' are shaped by deeply embedded internalized tendencies distributed throughout the organization and acquired through socialization/acculturation, and that this predisposition, or habitus, itself constitutes an *immanent* strategy of sorts. Instead, the impression conveyed of organizational strategy-making is one in which important individuals gather themselves in corporate boardrooms, away-days and summer retreats, enjoying fresh air and/or distance from the cacophony of business operations, to make glitzy presentations and produce glossy reports with a view to charting out the future direction of the organization. This view of strategy-making as a deliberate, intentional and goal-driven activity is itself dispositionally embedded into much of strategy-as-practice research because of the continuing commitment to proper explicit knowledge (i.e. *episteme* and *techné*).

Hendry and Seidl (2003: 176), for instance, characterize strategic episodes as 'a sequence of communications structured in terms of a beginning and ending'. Although we agree that such episodes exist (e.g. meetings and occasions in which senior managers separate themselves deliberately from their day-to-day routines), and that they might constitute a useful unit of strategy research and analysis, over-focusing on these formalized aspects of strategizing leads to an overlooking of the less conscious and more *tacit* elements involved in the build-up to those episodes in the first place.

Similarly, strategy practices are often viewed in a manner that allows a researcher to document and classify precise outcomes and to establish causal relations. Mantere (2005), for instance, uses Jarzabkowski's (2004) distinction between recursive and adaptive practices to assign clear outcomes (e.g. task definition) to the identified practices (e.g. organizing) and to then characterize key strategy practices in terms of their causes and effects. Similarly, Paroutis and Heracleous (2013) show how top management and the central strategy team (i.e. 'strategists') of a firm made sense of the concept of strategy. Their analysis neatly packs the strategy discourse of an organization into four distinct dimensions, ranging from an understanding of strategy as being goal-oriented to a perspective highlighting its aspirational character. This kind of explanation rests squarely on the notion of knowledge as *episteme* and/or *techné*: both forms of knowledge are characterized by explicitness, classifiability and clarity and are linguistically expressible in propositional terms or in terms of actor meanings and intentions.

We are *not* arguing that all research into strategy practice must eschew such manifest elements of the strategic activity. Rather, strategy-as-practice research should not be *limited* to these visible 'doings'. Strategy as practice consists of both visible and manifest purposeful activities *and* more mundane everyday practical coping actions. This idea that strategy researchers, like astute business investors, must eschew the visible and manifest and look towards the inarticulate and implicit is well understood by successful strategists themselves. Observing that it is often the hidden practical activities and not the surface glitter that are most important in accessing what is really going on in organizational reality, the chairman of Channel 4 and the private equity firm Risk Capital Partners, Luke Johnson, writes in an article in the *Financial Times*:

> 'Beware form over substance'... [L]ook at the underlying reality rather than the surface appearance of things... Terry Smith, who runs the UK inter-dealer broker Tullett Prebon, once told me his *footwear test of investment analysis*: *back the captain of industry who wears practical shoes with plastic soles rather than the ones who*

wear ultra-posh brogues from Church's. The former visits factories to find out what's going on, the latter is unlikely to be found outside London's West End ('Seek hidden value, not surface glitter', *Financial Times*, 5 March 2008: 14, emphasis added).

Johnson is reminding us, whether as investors or researchers, to resist the seductions of the apparent and to look beneath the surface of things, to the 'rough ground' (Dunne 1993), to discover the true reality of the practitioner world. Similarly, while the SAP movement has rightly directed attention towards the less 'glittery' aspects of strategy-making and the more ordinary activities, it is now timely to take the next logical step and focus attention on what escapes the building worldview on strategy-making; the *tacit dimension* of strategy as practice.

Strategy-as-practice research and the dwelling worldview

This turn towards the *tacit dimension* in strategy as practice reflects a commitment to a dwelling mode of explanation and a deliberate focus on the role that *phronesis* and *mētis* play in the non-deliberate shaping of strategic outcomes. This is what is required to further expand the field of strategy-as-practice research; to try to track the spontaneous emergence of strategy through direct local action *before* deliberate planning and purposeful intention kick in. What is really needed to truly appreciate how 'the myriad, micro activities that make up strategy and strategising in practice' (Johnson, Melin and Whittington 2003: 3) cumulatively add up to a consistent pattern of actions is a redirection of attention to the inarticulate and unexpressed but implied elements of the strategy process. This requires a more sympathetic grasping of the internal logic of local coping actions that take place largely unplanned and *in situ* in dealing with the exigencies of an evolving situation. In other words, attending to and dealing with the problems, obstacles and concerns confronted in the here and now may actually generate a surprising consistency of action that, through hindsight, may appear as a relatively stable pattern to which we might ascribe the label 'strategy'. In this sense, strategy may be latent or *immanent* in such everyday coping actions. To grasp this immanent aspect of strategy practice we need to embrace the reality of tacit forms of understanding and the dispositional tendencies associated with these local forms of knowing.

The difference between a building and dwelling worldview is well reflected in Regnér's (2003) distinction between strategy-making at the centre and at the periphery. According to Regnér, strategy-making at the centre is much about using deductive methods based on well-defined representations. This, from our perspective, would be much in line with a building worldview. By contrast, at the periphery, decision-makers develop a *phronetic* awareness of the local context, and strategy-making is largely improvisational; strategy slowly emerges through the internalized predispositions that actors refer to. A dwelling epistemology, thus, would be a necessary supplement while studying strategy-making in the periphery. This shows that we do not think of building and dwelling epistemologies as mutually exclusive alternatives but, rather, like to encourage scholars to use both while making sense of research settings.

Laine and Vaara (2007) also shed light on the *phronetic* awareness developed by employees who would normally not be described as strategists. Their analysis focuses on the discursive construction of subjectivity within strategy-making. The study shows how project engineers distanced themselves from the strategy discourse, which was initiated by management (mostly questioning the rationality underlying this dominating discourse). Having developed their own (competing) discourse, the engineers protected their own professional identity and autonomy and portrayed themselves as legitimate actors in the overall process of strategy development (e.g. because of their extensive customer contacts and 'on-the-ground' knowledge). Laine and Vaara (2007) emphasize that strategy-making happens in different parts of the organization, and that struggles over what counts as strategy and strategizing influence the kind of subjectivities that are developed by different organizational actors. Adopting such a view on strategizing plays down the role of pre-thought plans, highlighting how practical coping on the ground can produce alternatives to centrally developed strategic plans (see also McCabe 2010 for a perspective on strategizing that reaches beyond that of management).

Another more practical example of how practical coping actions, shaped by an internalized *modus operandi* (Bourdieu 1990) and characterized by *phronesis* and *mētis*, provide the seeds for the non-deliberate development of a strategy is reflected by the case of Virgin Airways. Sir Richard Branson's airline was born serendipitously as a consequence of him and his then girlfriend being stranded on one of the Virgin Islands during a holiday in the Caribbean in the late 1970s. When they got to the local airport on the island to return home, they found, together with other waiting passengers, that their flight to Puerto Rico had been cancelled.

> No one was doing anything. So I did – someone had to. *Even though I hadn't a clue what I was really doing*, with a great deal of aplomb I chartered a plane for $2,000 and divided that by the number of passengers. It came to $39 a head. I borrowed a blackboard and wrote on it: VIRGIN AIRWAYS. $39 SINGLE FLIGHT TO PUERTO RICO. All the tickets were snapped up by grateful passengers. I managed to get two free tickets out of it and even made a small profit! The idea for Virgin Airways was born, right there in the middle of a holiday (Branson 2007: 39–40, emphasis added).

This spontaneous coping action, borne of necessity given the circumstances he found himself in, provided the embryonic start to the idea of running a trans-Atlantic airline. Today Virgin Airways is flying to over 300 destinations all over the world.

The success of Virgin Airways, among many others, shows that the idea of strategy-making as a formal affair conducted primarily by assigned top managers and highly paid strategists is only partially correct. Often, strategy emergence in actual practice happens quite serendipitously and relies more on an initial opportunistic intervention or on deeply embedded and unconscious dispositional tendencies than on expressed meanings, intentions and choices. To be sure, there may be some vague directional aspirations and internalized tendencies that may serve as the driving force behind such initially insignificant initiatives. To understand these hidden motives, however, we need to resort more to *phronesis* and *mētis* as fertile modes of explanation.

Only through an appreciation of how *phronesis* and *mētis* actively shape strategic behaviour can we begin to follow more closely the twists and turns of everyday absorbed practical coping; the opportunism, reversals, ruses, duplicities, disguises and inventiveness that is entailed in strategic doing. This, after all, is really what constitutes strategy-in-practice, as opposed to strategy-in-theory, which we all know and read about in prestigious journals. This 'underbelly' of strategy practice has been considered either too obscure or morally repugnant to warrant serious study. Curiously, however, the more popular 'airport-type' books on the practice of strategy are far more likely to acknowledge the existence of these elusive and/or 'unsavoury' strategic ruses. These books often relate to the thinking of ancient Greeks, von Clausewitz, Machiavelli and Sun Tzu, who were centrally concerned with the oblique and circuitous elements of strategizing, as described in the dwelling worldview.

The importance of timing and surprise, as well as deception and clever manoeuvres, in gaining strategic advantage is well documented in the classic text of Carl von Clausewitz, which has been taken up by practitioner-friendly books and which is studiously internalized and put into practice by successful strategists. The entrepreneur Reinhold Würth, founder of the German Würth Group, confesses to be an ardent devotee of Carl von Clausewitz. He writes: 'Von Clausewitz writes that if you have to defend a fortress and you are surrounded by enemies you should send out a minor part of your troops to engage the enemy as far away as possible to enable the rest of your troops time to prepare' (*Financial Times*, 5 March 2008: 14). In relating this lesson to his own business, Würth is endorsing the use of deception and dissimulation in business affairs as a legitimate strategy. He is acknowledging the reality of *mētis* in practically coping with the strategic challenges of a globalized economy. This is something the more ponderous academic literature on business strategy taught in business schools with its economics-based concern seems to leave out.

From a dwelling worldview, practices intimated by *phronesis* and *mētis*, as the ones described in the above-mentioned examples, constitute legitimate 'objects' of strategy-as-practice research. Such practices are resistant to traditional conceptual analysis, and it is only *obliquely* that they can be approached. Clearly, the shift in focus, initiated by the SAP movement, to micro-strategizing and flexible adaptation is to be complimented. Yet an emphasis on flexibility by itself is not sufficient to move research from a *building* to a *dwelling* worldview, with all its attendant consequences. What is needed in strategy-as-practice research is a redirection of attention from the declared overt activities traditionally associated with strategizing to the subtle manoeuvres adopted by individuals, organizations and businesses over the course of dealing with pressing immediate concerns that threaten their survival, growth and development.

To truly appreciate the hidden workings that make up strategy and strategizing, the importance of *phronetic* and *mētic* intelligence and how it is multifariously deployed to gain momentary strategic advantage in any given situation must be fully recognized. This requires a sympathetic grasping of the internal logic of practice through following closely the everyday practical coping behaviour of strategists, and not through the retrospective reasons and meanings offered by actors themselves in restricted academic research contexts. Strategy-as-practice scholars need to get 'inside' the experiences of strategy practitioners and to use an alternative vocabulary for describing how practitioners cope on an everyday basis where they find themselves and not where they think they ought to be. Adopting this dwelling research stance will give us a different and more enriched account of strategy as practice.

Conclusion

This chapter contrasts two major epistemological alternatives for strategy-as-practice research. On the one hand, the *building* worldview leads to a detached, spectator's apprehension of social situations that privileges a 'knowledge about' typically characterized by *episteme* (abstract, universal generalizations using propositional forms) and/or *techné* (precise, measurable, codifiable instruction) (Raphals 1992; Baumard 1999; Nonaka and Toyama 2007). Research in line with the building worldview is directed towards the visible, the manifest and often the 'spectacular' interventions carried out by relatively autonomous strategy actors. On the other hand, a *dwelling* worldview leads to an intimate, engaged and involved comprehension of the local mindsets and proficiencies required to skilfully perform the everyday practices of strategizing. It directs attention to the minutiae of tacit and almost imperceptible interventions that, cumulatively, produce the gradual transformation of strategic situations. An 'unheroic' stance is adopted so that research attention is redirected to the mundane, everyday practical forms of intelligence and knowledge that are more associated with *phronesis* and *mētis*. Both *phronesis* and *mētis* are forms of knowing-in-practice that are recognizable as such only in their articulation: ingrained propensities, dispositions and capabilities associated with a dwelling worldview.

A dwelling epistemology also points to a different understanding of strategy in general. Often, strategy is construed in terms of clarity of vision, of transparent purposefulness, of goal-directed action and systematic resource mobilization (Chia and Holt 2009). This approach is practically 'naïve', however, in that it does not take into account the fleeting, transient and shifting nature of competitive realities, whereby competitive advantage may last for only a short while. It is surprise and the capitalizing on momentary advantage that constitute the real strategizing-in-practice. Researching ephemeral and *immanent* strategies involves the adoption of a dwelling epistemology – one that pays attention to the unconscious parts of strategizing and the internalized and culturally mediated *modus operandi* that underlies strategy practices.

Although the SAP research movement rightly aspires to document the micro-moments of strategizing, we conclude that it can be enriched by incorporating the tacit dimension of strategizing to leverage the full potential of an alternative dwelling

epistemology. Although the building worldview remains dominant in existing theoretical and empirical studies on the practice of strategy, we see much potential for the dwelling worldview to supplement and extend this more traditional position. It can teach us, above all, that those who are researched do not necessarily have a 'bird's-eye' view of their situation and that, consequently, the resulting knowledge they operate with is of a different genre from that of *episteme* and *techné*. To better understand and appreciate the world of practitioners, strategy-as-practice researchers must attune themselves to the more subtle nuances of strategizing: to the possibility of *phronesis* as a distributed practical wisdom and tacit understanding that underpins strategic actions; and to the importance of *mētis* in strategic manoeuvrings that appear to be more recognized and accepted by astute business practitioners themselves.

References

Baumard, P. (1999), *Tacit Knowledge in Organizations*. London: Sage.

Balogun, J., Huff, A. S., and Johnson, P. (2003), 'Three responses to methodological challenges of studying strategizing', *Journal of Management Studies*, 40/1: 197–224.

Balogun, J., and Johnson, G. (2005), 'From intended strategy to unintended outcomes: the impact of change recipient sensemaking', *Organization Studies*, 26/11: 1573–601.

Bourdieu, P. (1977), *Outline of a Theory of Practice*. Cambridge University Press.

(1990), *The Logic of Practice*. Cambridge: Polity.

Branson, R. (2007), *Screw It, Let's Do It: Lessons in Life*. London: Virgin Books.

Chia, R., and Holt, R. (2006), 'Strategy as practical coping: a Heideggerian perspective', *Organization Studies*, 27/5: 635–55.

Chia, R. (2009), *Strategy without Design: The Silent Efficacy of Indirect Action*. Cambridge University Press.

Chia, R., and MacKay, B. (2007), 'Post-processual challenges for the emerging strategy-as-practice perspective: discovering strategy in the logic of practice', *Human Relations*, 60/1: 217–42.

De Certeau, M. (1984), *The Practice of Everyday Life*. Berkeley: University of California Press.

Denis, J.-L., Langley, A., and Rouleau, L. (2007), 'Strategizing in pluralistic contexts: rethinking theoretical frames', *Human Relations*, 60/1: 179–215.

Detienne, M., and Vernant, J. P. (1978), *Cunning Intelligence in Greek Culture and Society*. Brighton: Harvester Press.

Dreyfus, H. (1991), *Being-in-the-World: A Commentary on Heidegger's Being and Time, Division 1*. Cambridge, MA: MIT Press.

Dunne, J. (1993), *Back to the Rough Ground: 'Phronesis' and 'Techné' in Modern Philosophy and in Aristotle*. University of Notre Dame Press.

Elias, N. (1978), *What Is Sociology?* Oxford: Blackwell.

—— (1991), *The Society of Individuals*. Oxford: Blackwell.

Ezzamel, M., and Willmott, H. (2008), 'Strategy as discourse in a global retailer: a supplement to rationalist and interpretive accounts', *Organization Studies*, 29/2: 191–217.

—— (2010), 'Strategy and strategizing: a poststructuralist perspective', in Baum, J. A. C., and Lampel, J. (eds.), *Advances in Strategic Management*, vol. XXVII, *The Globalization of Strategy Research*: 75–109. Bingley, UK: Emerald.

Foucault, M. (1972), *The Archaeology of Knowledge*. New York: Harper Colophon.

—— (1984), 'Truth and power', in Rabinow, P. (ed.), *The Foucault Reader*: 51–75. Harmondsworth, UK: Penguin Books.

Hendry, J., and Seidl, D. (2003), 'The structure and significance of strategic episodes: social systems theory and the routine practices of strategic change', *Journal of Management Studies*, 40/1: 175–96.

Hutchins, E. (1995), *Cognition in the Wild*. Cambridge, MA: MIT Press.

Ingold, T. (2000), *The Perception of the Environment*. London: Routledge.

Jarzabkowski, P. (2003), 'Strategic practices: an activity theory perspective on continuity and change', *Journal of Management Studies*, 40/1: 23–55.

—— (2004), 'Strategy as practice: recursiveness, adaptation, and practices-in-use', *Organization Studies*, 25/4: 529–60.

—— (2005), *Strategy as Practice: An Activity-Based Approach*. London: Sage.

Jarzabkowski, P., Balogun, J., and Seidl, D. (2007), 'Strategizing: the challenges of a practice perspective', *Human Relations*, 60/1: 5–27.

Jarzabkowski, P., and Wilson, D. C. (2002), 'Top teams and strategy in a UK university', *Journal of Management Studies*, 39/3: 355–81.

Johnson, G., Melin, L., and Whittington, R. (2003), 'Guest editors' introduction: micro strategy and strategizing: towards an activity-based view', *Journal of Management Studies*, 40/1: 3–22.

Laine, P.-M., and Vaara, E. (2007), 'Struggling over subjectivity: a discursive analysis of strategic development in an engineering group'. *Human Relations*, 60/1: 29–58.

Lindblom, C. (1959), 'The science of muddling through', *Public Administration Review*, 19/2: 79–88.

Mantere, S. (2005), 'Strategic practices as enablers and disablers of championing activity', *Strategic Organization*, 3/2: 157–84.

McCabe, D. (2010), 'Strategy-as-power: ambiguity, contradiction and the exercise of power in a UK building society', *Organization*, 17/2: 151–75.

Mintzberg, H. (2004), *Managers Not MBAs: A Hard Look at the Soft Practice of Managing and Management Development*. San Francisco: Berrett-Koehler.

Nonaka, I., and Toyama, R. (2007), 'Strategic management as distributed practical wisdom (phronesis)', *Industrial and Corporate Change*, 16/3: 1–24.

Nussbaum, M. C. (1986), *The Fragility of Goodness: Luck and Ethics in Greek Tragedy and Philosophy*. Cambridge University Press.

Paroutis, S., and Heracleous, L. (2013), 'Discourse revisited: dimensions and employment of first-order strategy discourse during institutional adoption', *Strategic Management Journal*, 34/8: 935–56.

Raphals, L. (1992), *Knowing Words: Wisdom and Cunning in the Classical Traditions of China and Greece*. Ithaca, NY: Cornell University Press.

Rasche, A. (2008), *The Paradoxical Foundation of Strategic Management*. Heidelberg: Physica-Verlag.

Regnér, P. (2003), 'Strategy creation in the periphery: inductive versus deductive strategy making', *Journal of Management Studies*, 40/1: 57–82.

Samra-Fredericks, D. (2003), 'Strategizing as lived experience and strategists' everyday efforts to shape strategic directions', *Journal of Management Studies*, 40/1: 141–74.

Scott, J. (1998), *Seeing Like a State: How Certain Schemes to Improve the Human Condition Have Failed*. New Haven, CT: Yale University Press.

Stacey, R. (2007), *Strategic Management and Organizational Dynamics*. London: Prentice Hall.

Tsoukas, H. (2010), 'Practice, strategy making and intentionality: a Heideggerian onto-epistemology for strategy as practice', in Golsorkhi, D., Rouleau, L., Seidl, D., and Vaara, E. (eds.), *Cambridge Handbook of Strategy as Practice*: 47–62. Cambridge University Press.

Vaara, E., and Whittington, R. (2012), 'Strategy-as-practice: taking social practices seriously', *Academy of Management Annals*, 6/1: 285–336.

Weber, M. (1968 [1922]), *Economy and Society*. New York: Bedminster Press.

Weick, K. E. (2001), *Making Sense of the Organization*. Oxford: Blackwell.

Whittington, R. (1996), 'Strategy as practice', *Long Range Planning*, 29/5: 731–5.

(2003), 'The work of strategizing and organizing: for a practice perspective', *Strategic Organization*, 1/1: 117–25.

(2006), 'Completing the practice turn in strategy research', *Organization Studies*, 27/5: 613–34.

Making strategy: meta-theoretical insights from Heideggerian phenomenology

CHAPTER 3

HARIDIMOS TSOUKAS

My purpose in this chapter is to lay out an onto-epistemological framework for strategy as practice by drawing on Heideggerian phenomenology. The need for such a framework comes from the recent proliferation of strategy-as-practice studies and the concomitant advancement of relevant knowledge claims, which do not necessarily share the same understanding of 'strategy' or 'practice'. Bringing clarity to what strategy as practice can achieve, how it relates to similar perspectives and how it can be further advanced will help dissolve ambiguities, spot contradictions and integrate various theoretical lenses. Heideggerian phenomenology is highly relevant for such a task, as it foregrounds the notion of practice and the modes of human involvement in practice. Since strategy relates to intentionality and the use of tools and artefacts, especially language, how intentions and language are implicated in the making of strategy is of critical importance. By way of example, consider the following three vignettes.

(1) The contrasting accounts of Honda's spectacular success in capturing two-thirds of the motorcycle industry in the United States, in the early 1960s, are well known. Pascale's (1984) account, drawn from interviews with the Honda executives who were in charge of the US project at the time, shows the largely improvisational nature of Honda's responses to unexpected problems and unfolding events on the ground, as the company made the effort to enter the US market. One of the Honda executives remarked: 'In truth, we had no strategy other than the idea of seeing if we could sell something in the United States. It was a new frontier, a new challenge, and it fit

the "success against all odds" culture that Mr Honda had cultivated' (Pascale 1984: 54). By contrast, the Boston Consulting Group (BCG) study of the same phenomenon accounted for Honda's success in terms of microeconomic concepts, such as 'low cost producer' and 'economies of scale' (BCG 1975). While, for Pascale, Honda's success was accountable in terms of the unique processes through which the particular Honda executives experimented, adapted and learned, for the authors of the BCG report, Honda's success was an illustration of the microeconomic strategy model. Whereas both accounts point at patterns of action over time, they explain those patterns differently. Adaptationists highlight the absence of well-defined, elaborately articulated plans and intentions, whereas microeconomists allude to the advantages firms enjoy by pursuing the precepts of the strategy model.

Although not theory-driven, Pascale's account attributes the consistency evident in Honda's pattern of actions to organizational and extra-organizational sources: shared corporate values and Japanese culture, respectively. Goold (1996), by contrast, attributes the sources of consistency to microeconomic factors that enabled the experimentation of Honda executives. Those microeconomic factors were critical in the formulation of the generic corporate intentions to enter the new, unfamiliar and vast US market. Thus, while one school of thought does not anticipate and, therefore, does not look for explicit corporate intentions, highlighting the importance of strategy emerging out of the interplay of unique circumstances with local agent's choices, the other school of thought looks for how corporate intentions (variously elaborate) guide corporate policy. In view of the above, the question is: how can we account for strategy, understood as a pattern of actions over time, in terms that do justice to both 'local' responses to unfolding situations and 'global' intentions to realize a general idea or plan?

(2) In his study of telecommunications firms, Regnér (2003) identifies two distinct types of strategy creation in organizational centres and peripheries. Strategy-making in the corporate periphery was 'inductive', including trial and error, experiments and local initiatives in response to local problems, while strategy-making at the corporate centre was 'deductive', involving planning and analysis. This parallels Mintzberg's (2007) claim that, in entrepreneurial organizations, strategy creation tends to be 'intuitive', in contrast with strategy in machine organizations, where strategy-making is overtly 'analytical'. The question that arises is this: how can we account for strategy-making in a way that does justice to both its intuitive and analytical elements?

(3) In their study of participation in strategy making in twelve professional organizations in Nordic countries, Mantere and Vaara (2008) report and analyse the discourses that impede or facilitate participation in strategy work. The authors do not so much report how strategy is created in these organizations as how organizational members talk about the making of strategy in their organizations. Thus, in discourses impeding participation, interviewees explicitly refer to their conceptions of what strategy is about. A top management team individual, for example, explained his involvement as follows: 'This is the order of things in my mind: First top management defines a vision, a desired end state, which is then pursued. . .' A lower-rank organizational member held a different view, however: 'I used to work in a smaller firm where people could participate in strategic planning. In my new role in this large firm, I have had to teach myself that planning is none of my business' (Mantere and Vaara, 2008: 348). In view of such evidence, the

question is: what understanding of strategy will do justice to studies that do not deal with strategy-making per se but with talking about strategy-making?

In this chapter I argue that Heideggerian phenomenology will help us address the preceding questions. By distinguishing between different types of action and mapping onto them different types of intentionality-cum-language use, we obtain a broad picture that enables us to see the contributions of different kinds of SAP research. The chapter is organized as follows. In the next section, I undertake a brief literature review. It aims to give the reader a sense of the issues at hand rather than to exhaustively map the terrain. This is followed by outlining a Heideggerian vocabulary, which centres on the notions of practice and the various modes of intentionality involved in applying practice. The relevance of such a vocabulary is demonstrated subsequently, in the section dealing with strategy as practice from a Heideggerian perspective. Finally, in the discussion and conclusion sections the argument is summarized, a discussion of relevant pieces of the literature is offered and the benefits of the Heideggerian meta-theoretical framework are outlined.

What are the challenges for strategy-as-practice research?

Strategy as practice calls for nothing less than a reorientation of the field of strategy research. By reconceiving strategy as not something organizations have but as something organizations *do*, strategy as practice shifts the focus of analytical attention towards the *making* of strategy (Whittington 2006; Mantere 2010; 2013; Kaplan 2011; Kaplan and Orlikowski 2013), thus departing from traditional variance model approaches (Tsoukas and Knudsen 2002).

Insofar as this is the case, strategy as practice shares important assumptions with an earlier perspective in strategy research, namely the strategy process (SP) approach. The SAP and SP approaches both avoid treating strategy as a dependent variable, the variance of which is to be explained through the construction of a model consisting of a set of contributory variables, each one of which has its own variance (Langley 2007; Pettigrew 1992; Van de Ven and Poole 2005). Rather, the main research question these two perspectives seek to address is: *how do organizations make strategies*? Focusing on and accounting for process is of great importance if we are to understand *how* strategy is created (Langley 2007).

Given their strong affinities and overlaps, what more does strategy as practice add to what we know from the SP approach? For several researchers, strategy-as-practice advances process theorizing by overcoming the limitations of the process perspective. What are these limitations? Johnson, Melin and Whittington (2003: 10–13) have suggested that SP research suffers from six shortcomings: (1) SP researchers have largely relied on second-hand retrospective accounts rather than on ethnographic research methods that stay close to the actual work that makes up organizational life; (2) SP research has focused too strongly on managerial agency at the expense of other actors; (3) SP research has tended to be mainly descriptive, offering little practical advice to managers; (4) SP has forced a dichotomy between process and content; (5) SP research often lacks explicit links to strategy outcomes; and (6), by focusing heavily on the particular, SP research has eschewed offering generalizable frameworks, thus impeding knowledge accumulation.

It is worth noting, however, that even if some, or all, of these criticisms are accepted, there is nothing inherent in SP that would stop it from taking them on board. Such a critique does not impinge on the 'hard core' (Lakatos 1978 [1968]) of SP research. To use Lakatos's terms, all the preceding critical points can be accommodated within the 'protective belt' of SP research. What is there, for example, in SP that would stop researchers from employing ethnographic methods, extending the reach of their empirical research to actors other than managers, being more prescriptive as well as generic in their theories or bringing together process and content issues (Langley 2007)? Hardly anything.

For other researchers, the distinctive feature of strategy as practice is 'the sociological eye'

(Whittington 2007) it brings to the study of strategy. The chief characteristics of the sociological eye are (1) the treatment of social processes not as unique processes but as consisting of the enactment, over time, of social roles, embedded in broader contexts and (2) sensitivity for the neglected, the unintended and the unexpected. No one can fairly criticize SP for insensitivity to the unintended or the unexpected, however. Indeed, Mintzberg and his associates (Mintzberg and McHugh 1985; Mintzberg and Waters 1982; 1985; Mintzberg 2007), to take the most prominent advocates of a process perspective on strategy, have done a lot to sensitize us to the importance of the *emergent* features of strategy. What Whittington usefully adds, however, is the concern with the *social embeddedness* of strategy-making, which has, admittedly, been missing from much of SP research, although the role of professional associations has been mentioned (Mintzberg 2007: 357).

By 'social embeddedness' Whittington means seeking connections between organizational and institutional changes, such as, for example, the rise of neoliberal ideology in the political sphere and the introduction of new public management in the public sector; the rise of strategic management as a discipline and the entry of 'strategy' vocabulary into organizational practice (Knights and Morgan 1991; Allard-Poesi 2010; Ezzamel and Willmott 2008; Mantere 2013); or the professionalization of management in the United Kingdom, in the 1980s, and particular changes at firm level. Looking for the sources of strategy outside the organization is useful and interesting. At the same time, it has been the least studied feature of strategy-making. The tendency among SAP researchers has been to focus on strategy practitioners *within* the organization, refraining from systematically connecting organizational changes with extra-organizational contexts. Insofar as this has been the case, it is not particularly clear how SAP research – as it has been pursued so far, at least – differs from that of its process cousin.

Moreover, much as looking into social roles and the institutional embeddedness of strategies is important, this should not be at the expense of looking into the *creative* process of strategy-making, which is inextricably tied to *local* contexts of action and to experiential trials and errors in perceived unique conditions (Mintzberg 1987; 1990; Weick 2001). Searching for the novelty of strategic behaviour has been a distinguishing feature of the SP approach, especially in the studies conducted by Mintzberg and his associates (see especially Mintzberg 2007). As the aforementioned case of Honda shows, the challenge is to retain sensitivity both to local conditions and actors' responses to them *and* to the institutional embeddedness and the interconnections across levels of analysis. How can this be achieved? What kind of onto-epistemology is needed to frame inquiry accordingly?

For a third stream of researchers, strategy as practice is beset by the same weaknesses as SP research, chief among which is adherence to methodological individualism – namely the explanation of strategic behaviour in terms of atomistic agents, deliberately acting on their environment. The patterns that strategy researchers note are thought to be generated by agents conceived in individualistic terms, hence the emphasis on what individual agents say or do to one another. Analytical primacy is given to agents' visible doings rather than to 'culturally and historically shaped tendencies and dispositions acquired through social practices internalized by the actors' (Chia and MacKay 2007: 226). Moreover, as will be argued later in this chapter, the individualist bias of influential versions of SAP research is shown when 'strategy-making' is identified with 'strategizing' (Jarzabkowski, Balogun and Seidl 2007). It is not often appreciated that, while the making of strategy may occur in both non-deliberate and deliberate ways, strategizing is a conscious activity, typically involving deliberate actions. By conflating the two, an important distinction is abolished.

Methodological individualism should be avoided and the focus should shift to 'trans-individual social practices', argue Chia and MacKay (2007: 226), drawing inspiration from Heideggerian phenomenology (see also Chia and Holt 2006; 2009). Change should be seen as *immanent* in things and human situations, not as externally brought about. Again, as Pascale's account of Honda suggests, individuals are primarily defined by their membership of practices, which are carriers of cultural dispositions and tacit understandings (Sandberg

and Tsoukas 2011). Consequently, for the proponents of this view ('post-processual', as Chia and MacKay 2007 call it), individual actions are less the outcomes of individual choices and more the unself-conscious responses to surrounding circumstances. Strategies are secondary (stabilized) effects of culturally transmitted practices. To put it simply, actors are culturally predisposed to act in particular ways due to their membership of practices. Once observers retrospectively recognize consistency in actors' actions, they label the resulting pattern *strategic*. This is a second-order characterization, however, imposed retrospectively by observers, while, as in the Honda case, actors tend to act non-deliberately. What observers, such as the BCG consultants, secondarily recognize as strategy is the outcome of the primary propensity to act non-deliberately in particular situations; strategy is immanent in practical action (Chia and Holt 2006; 2009).

The 'post-processual' approach is undoubtedly promising, in that it allows for *trans*-individualist explorations of strategy and for non-deliberate modes of action to be taken into account. Unless it is further developed, however, it risks pushing us too much in the opposite direction. When Chia and MacKay (2007: 235, emphasis in original) argue that 'strategy *subsists* on each and every mundane and seemingly isolated act we perform', they are right, but tell only part of the story. Another part is about *deliberate action*, which, although recognized in passing in their paper, is not analytically related to non-deliberate action. While it is true that the infusion of practitioners with an internalized style of engagement, grounded in culturally transmitted social practices, affords action consistency over time and, thus, apparent purposefulness, it is also true that goal-directed actions and reflexive monitoring are not only possible but systemically built into formal organizations (Giddens 1991: 16). Strategy awaydays, for example, or scenario-planning exercises, aim at creating the sort of reflective distance between the non-deliberate mode of ordinary, improvisational practical coping and the more explicitly articulated, deliberate mode of acting that is characteristic of strategic episodes (Hendry and Seidl 2003). Clearly, we have evidence of both: patterns of non-deliberate actions that may *retrospectively* be seen as forming a strategy *and* deliberate actions that commit an organization to a new course of action. How can we be attentive to both? How can we make room for both types of engagement?

To be sure, for all their differences of vocabulary, Whittington and Chia and MacKay agree that strategy as practice will live up to its name, and thus differentiate itself from SP research, insofar as it widens its attention to embrace the broader contexts that make organizational patterns of actions possible. Both sets of researchers argue for the need to 'de-centre' (Whittington 2007: 1578; Chia and MacKay 2007) the organization as the locus of strategy-making. Whittington points to the analytical levels of the industry (or field) and society over and above the organization, while Chia and MacKay point to 'practice complexes' (2007: 233) – namely to extra-organizational discourses, artefacts, techniques and canonical examples – through which propensities to act in particular ways are transmitted.

Finally, following the linguistic turn, a fourth stream of research has focused on language use in strategy. This has taken two forms. First, the focus has been on exploring the discourses that shape the identities and the practices of those involved in strategy work, and the implications of those discourses for how power is enacted in particular contexts (Ezzamel and Willmott 2008). Such an approach focuses on the constitution of strategic management as a discipline and its key conceptual categories, the relevant knowledge/power claims advanced, the truth regimes that strategic management discourse helps institute (Knights and Morgan 1991; Rasche and Chia 2009) and the discursive practices pursued for the legitimization of new policies. Second, the focus on language has taken a more pragmatic turn, exploring how strategy is formed through narration, rhetoric and storytelling (Barry and Elmes 1997; Küpers, Mantere and Statler 2013; Vaara, Kleymann and Seristö 2004; Sillince, Jarzabkowski and Shaw 2012).

A focus on language is particularly insightful since it extends research upwards towards extra-organizational discourses, whose achievement of hegemony as well as effects may be researched, and downwards to the particular words, frames and

narratives that organizational members use to account for their, and to influence others', experiences. SAP research ought to be able to show how language is used, aided by particular artefacts and objects, at several levels of analysis, with what effects. As I show later, Heideggerian phenomenology helps clarify the uses of language.

In the rest of the chapter I argue that an onto-epistemological framework inspired by Heideggerian phenomenology (see Dreyfus 1991a; 1991b; 2000; Heidegger 1962; Spinosa, Flores and Dreyfus 1997; Schatzki 2000; 2005) enables us to see how the organization may be 'de-centred' and how strategy-making may be studied in its various manifestations. The contribution of such a framework will be to (1) enable SAP researchers to overcome the individualist bias Chia and MacKay have rightly identified in dominant conceptions of strategy as practice, while allowing space for creative action; (2) analytically relate non-deliberate and deliberate types of action; and (3) suggest how strategy as practice, conceived along Heideggerian lines, differs substantially from the SP approach, at least as the latter has been traditionally practised. Below I outline a Heideggerian vocabulary, in terms of which SAP research will be discussed in the subsequent section.

Practice, coping and awareness: a Heideggerian vocabulary

Human agency is necessarily exercised in the context of sociomaterial practices. Whether one makes flutes (Cook and Yanow 1996), repairs photocopiers (Orr 1996) or treats patients (Benner 1994), one is enabled to do so insofar as one is entwined with others and artefacts in specific sociomaterial practices, which endow one's activities with significance and meaning (Sandberg and Tsoukas 2011). *Sociomaterial practices* are organized, open-ended human activities transpiring within material arrangements, unfolding in time and carried out by skilful agents whose actions are based on: tacit understandings, explicit rules and teleo-affective structures; the bodily coordination and orientation of an agent to the task at hand; and the incorporation of tools within the field of an agent's bodily comportment (Dreyfus 1991b: 27; Orlikowski 2007; Reckwitz 2002: 249; Rouse 2000: 9; Schatzki 2005: 471; Rasche and Chia 2009).

Particular human *activities* and sociomaterial *practices* are mutually constituted. For example, the practice of grading students' scripts in a university consists of activities such as pondering grades and recording them. The activities are moments of the practice; one cannot exist without the other. Broadly speaking, grading is a sociomaterial practice that incorporates certain tacit understandings of how to grade; it is based on certain explicit rules about grading; and it incorporates a teleo-affective structure consisting of the appropriate ends to be pursued and the relevant emotions to be experienced (assessing and developing students through grading their written work, for example), the activities to be pursued for these ends (e.g. pondering and recording grades) and acceptable uses of relevant equipment. Thus, a particular episode of grading consists of the activities of 'pondering' and 'recording grades', which are inextricably tied to a particular 'grading' sociomaterial practice. Similarly, what a particular grading practice is depends on the exercise of the particular grading activities. In scrutinizing a grading episode, one scrutinizes the practice, and vice versa (Schatzki 2005: 468).

To enter a sociomaterial practice – to become, say, a repair technician, an academic, a manager or a surgeon – is to enter a practice the identity of which is constituted through the normative use of language, body and equipment (Hardy, Lawrence and Grant 2005: 61; Harré and Gillett 1994: 28–9). To be a human agent is to experience one's situation in terms of *already* constituted meanings and acceptable emotions, articulated through the discourse that defines the practice (Dreyfus 1991a: ch. 5; Taylor 1985b: 27; 1985a: 54–5). This is so because a human being is, in Taylor's (1985a: 45) well-known phrase, a 'self-interpreting animal'. It is a being for whom things matter; whose identity is constituted by qualitative distinctions made in language, worked out within a form of life (Dreyfus 1991a: 23). The already constituted distinctions of a sociomaterial practice make up what Wittgenstein (1979: para. 94) calls the 'inherited

background', against which practitioners make sense of their particular tasks (Tsoukas 2009: 943). The distinctions constituting the 'inherited background' situate humans relative to some standards of excellence, obligations (MacIntyre 1985: 187–94; Taylor 1991: 305) or 'normative boundaries' (Kogut and Zander 1996: 515).

For example, Gawande (2002: 13–15), a surgical resident at a hospital in Boston, describes the sense of 'ineptitude' he felt when, in his fourth week in surgical training, he tried for the first time to install a central line into a patient's chest so that the patient could be fed intravenously (see also Benner 1994: 137–40). The trainee surgeon's felt inadequacy came from the realization, following an exchange with the chief resident who was supervising the procedure, of not having done certain things as well as he should – not having attained a level of professional competence.

This example is instructive in reminding us that to have an experience, such as 'ineptitude' in this case, involves the application of a particular meaning concerning work standards – namely seeing that certain descriptions apply, along with the associated emotions they typically come with – and an appropriate use of bodily skills and equipment. No wonder why, later, Gawande (2002: 14) chastised himself: 'I failed to check his platelet count. [. . .] I forgot to bring the extra syringe for flushing the line when it's on.' Admissions of perceived inadequacy or failure are possible insofar as certain standards of excellence are not achieved or normative boundaries are transgressed.

Practitioners are initiated into a sociomaterial practice by learning to make relevant distinctions in practice (Benner, Hooper-Kyriakidis and Stannard 1999: 30–47; Polanyi 1962: 101; Yanow 2015). Gawande gives a vivid account of his initiation in medical practice. Through dealing with particular incidents involving patients, initially under the supervision of, and later in collaboration with, more experienced members of his practice, the trainee surgeon was learning to use the key categories implicated in a surgeon's job; to make proper use of the relevant equipment; and to bring his body into a certain level of coordination with the task at hand. Through his participation in this practice he was gradually learning to relate to his circumstances 'spontaneously' (Wittgenstein 1980a: para. 699): to use medical equipment, to recognize certain symptoms, to relate to colleagues and patients. The needles and how to use them in patients´ chests, the X-rays and how to read them, and his relationships to others were not objects of thought for him but 'subsidiary particulars' (Polanyi and Prosch 1975: 37–8) – taken-for-granted aspects of the normal setting in all its recognizable stability and regularity. As Wittgenstein (1979: paras. 473–9) aptly notes, the basis of a sociomaterial practice is *activity*, not knowledge; *practice*, not thinking; *certainty*, not uncertainty. With the help of more experienced others we first learn to act – that is to accept the *certainties* of our particular sociomaterial practice (e.g. to use needles, to recognize the symptoms of pulmonary disease, to relate to patients) – and, thus, to relate spontaneously to our surroundings, and *later* we reflect on them. Experience comes first, knowledge later. 'Language…,' as Wittgenstein (1980b: 31) has famously remarked, 'is a refinement and in the beginning was the deed.'

The 'spontaneous' aspects of the activities that practitioners undertake are primary and constitute Wittgenstein's 'inherited background', against which practitioners make sense of their particular tasks (Shotter and Katz 1996: 225; Taylor 1993: 325; 1995: 69). Practitioners are aware of the background but their awareness is largely 'inarticulate' (Taylor 1991: 308) and implicit in their activity (Ryle 1963: 40–1; Tsoukas 2009; 2011). The 'inherited background' provides the teleo-affective structure that renders their explicit representations comprehensible and makes certain emotions acceptable (Dreyfus 1991a: 102–4; Taylor 1993: 327–8; 1995: 69–70). As Dreyfus (1985: 232; emphasis added) notes, 'What makes up the background is not beliefs, either explicit or implicit, but habits and customs, embodied in the sort of subtle skills which we exhibit in our everyday interaction with things and people. [. . .] *We just do what we have been trained to do. . .*' In other words, the exercise of particular skills within sociomaterial practices is *non-deliberate* – an array of spontaneous responses to the developing situation at hand. At the same time, this non-deliberate activity is oriented towards attaining certain ends that determine it as the activity it is.

For example, while explaining strategy as practice to students in class, prompted by a question, a lecturer may use the whiteboard in order to draw a chart. This is non-deliberate (spontaneous) acting oriented towards a particular end. Not unlike driving a car, the lecturer, immersed in his/her activity, does what the situation calls for without paying attention to his/her actions. The teleological structure of the sociomaterial teaching practice makes the particular act of drawing a chart on the board sensible. As Schatzki (2000: 33, emphasis added) notes:

> These 'in order tos,' 'toward whichs,' and 'for the sake ofs' – in more conventional terms, purposes, tasks, and ends – orient [the teacher's] activity in the sense of structuring what he is up to: in conjunction with the current situation, they specify that writing on the board *makes sense* – that is, is the appropriate and needed thing (given the situation and the purposes and ends involved). They determine, in other words, what might be called the *practical intelligibility* that informs nondeliberate activity.

To sum up, when agents act non-deliberately, they respond spontaneously to circumstances in order to get on with the tasks at hand. They do not pay explicit attention to what they do; they do what makes sense to them. What makes sense to them, however, is teleologically structured: their sense-making is oriented towards certain ends. This is why it can be said that agents act purposively without necessarily having a purpose in mind (Chia and MacKay 2007: 235; Schatzki 2000: 33).

When responding spontaneously to the solicitations of the task at hand, not only do agents not pay attention to what they do, they do not, moreover, have a representation of the goal they pursue (Wakefield and Dreyfus 1991). Non-deliberate acting is *practical coping* with the situation at hand; it is not mediated by mental representations; it results from an ongoing integration of one's activity *as* a teacher, a manager, a physician, etc., within a sociomaterial practice (Rouse 2000: 12). When language is used in practical coping, as is often the case, it is used as equipment assimilated in the activity and, thus, it functions in a non-propositional way. When, for example, in the middle of an operation, a surgeon says 'Scalpel!'

and a nurse hands him one, he is using language non-propositionally, namely in a way to enable him get on with the task at hand rather than make assertions about the task or the world at large (Dreyfus 2000: 317).

When practical coping is interrupted by a 'breakdown', intentional directedness takes over, and it can take two forms: explicit awareness and thematic awareness (Yanow and Tsoukas 2009). With *explicit awareness*, agents pay attention to what they do when their activities run into trouble. The computer does not respond as expected and the operator cannot do what he/she wants; the violinist finds he/she is unable to play smoothly because a string has broken; or a teacher is facing a rather unresponsive class. In such instances of breakdown the agent becomes aware of his/her activity, of what he/she was trying to accomplish, the equipment he/she was using: he/she starts acting *deliberately.* When the situation requires attention, mental content arises, consisting of beliefs, desires and propositional attitudes. Subject–object polarity emerges, and now the deliberate agent is oriented towards his/her activity through mental states causing deliberate actions. Drawing on an illustration by Dreyfus (1991a: 69–70), Schatzki (2000: 35, emphasis added) aptly notes:

> When the door knob sticks, one's focused efforts to move it are caused by the *desire* to open it in conjunction with the *belief* that greater force will accomplish this, and repeated attempts are guided by the intention in action to budge it. [...] The content of each of these *mental states* – what one is up to, how things work, what needs to be done – is explicit to the actor. Hence not only does deliberate action differ from its nondeliberate cousin by virtue of actors paying attention to their activity; whereas nondeliberate action rests on the exercise of skills, deliberate action is caused by mental states (where mental states are causally efficacious states of being explicitly aware of something). As a result, when someone deliberately acts purposively, she has a purpose in mind, that is, she is explicitly aware of what she is out to accomplish (this purpose can be said to constitute the content of one's desires).

Moreover, when someone is explicitly aware of something, that act of awareness is brought to one's awareness too; the agent is aware that he/she is aware. By contrast, when the agent is absorbed in the task, as is the case with practical coping (namely when the agent is non-explicitly aware of something), the agent is not aware that he/she is aware of it. Self-consciousness and the accompanying subject–object split have not yet arisen (Schatzki 2000: 36).

Notice that, when practical coping is interrupted, the agent stays involved in the activity, although he/she now pays attention to what he/she does. Explicit awareness is still oriented towards practical ends. When the agent detaches him-/herself from a specific practical situation, however, and stares at it from a reflective distance, aiming to know its *properties*, then the practical situation becomes *occurrent* and the agent develops *thematic awareness*. The latter brackets particular, immediate practical concerns and aims at finding out about, or reflecting on, abstract properties of the situation at hand. Thus, whereas in explicit awareness the physician might say 'This scalpel is not sharp enough', thus becoming explicitly aware of its limited sharpness, in thematic awareness the physician comes to know that the object he/she has been using as a scalpel is an object with the property 'sharpness'. Whereas in the former case the proposition refers to a situated *aspect* of the scalpel ('It is not sharp enough for me to do this job'), in the latter case it refers to a desituated *property* of the scalpel (i.e. it has 'bluntness' in any situation) and, thus, to 'scalpel' in general (Dreyfus 2000: 317–18). With thematic awareness the agent moves from aspects to properties and from practical to quasi-theoretical understanding.

Finally, when one is completely detached from a practical situation, approaching it through the lens of another 'world' (namely through what may be called theoretical coping), one engages in *theoretical understanding.* The latter, typically, is the concern of theorists. Recall that, in practical coping, language is used as a situational coping skill; in deliberate coping (explicit awareness), it is used propositionally to refer to a particular aspect of a situation, with a particular practical purpose in mind; and, in detached coping (thematic awareness), it is used propositionally to make assertions about properties that bear no relevance to a particular practical situation but that enable one to refer to things and events in the rest of the world. Now, when not only a practical situation is bracketed but a shared meaningful world of a particular sociomaterial practice is bracketed too (e.g. the world of clinical medicine), we can talk of *theoretical understanding*. In such a case, an object is 'de-worlded' (Dreyfus 2000: 317) and, insofar as this is the case, reinserted into a different world ('re-worlded') – the world of theory. Thus, the scalpel is not just an occurrent object with the property 'sharpness' but an entity whose material composition, design and making may be studied independently, and a system of causal relationships ascertained.

Theoretical understanding goes beyond thematic awareness in that it goes beyond merely detaching an object from a practical situation and recontextualizes it into a corpus of theory. For example, organizational properties such as 'strategy', 'cost leadership', 'dynamic capabilities', etc., when studied by organization theorists, are concepts that are parts of *theories* (and, thus, parts of the *world* of academic theories), not of the (business) world. Theoretical understanding focuses either on the uses of concepts by practitioners and what such uses achieve or on the processes of conceptual construction in a discursive field over time.

This Heideggerian phenomenological line of thinking has important implications for how we view strategy-making, and, crucially, it helps furnish strategy as practice with an onto-epistemology that makes room for different types of action and intentionality. In the next section I show its relevance for strategy as practice.

Strategy as practice from a Heideggerian perspective

As Mintzberg and his associates have shown, when streams of actions may be identified over time, one can speak of an emergent strategy. Whether we talk about Steinberg's entrepreneurship, McLaren's films in the National Film Board of Canada (Mintzberg and Waters 1982; 1985), Honda's incursion into the US motorcycle industry or the inductive-cum-exploratory strategies developed in

the organizational periphery in Regnér's (2003) firms, we are talking about 'strategy' *ex post facto*. Notice, however, that practitioners do not necessarily have the sense that they strategize; this is, usually, researchers' attribution. Often, practitioners respond spontaneously – that is to say, non-deliberately – to the developing practical situation they find themselves in. The label for a particular 'strategy' they pursue is given to a patterned stream of actions either by practitioners themselves when they *retrospectively* make sense of what they do (Weick 1995: 76–80; 2001: 354) – namely when they become explicitly aware of what they do because of some difficulty or interruption they have encountered – or by theorists who 'de-world' the stream of action they study and re-insert it in their world of theory.

The ex post facto ascription of 'strategy' is clearly shown in the analysis of Porac, Thomas and Baden-Fuller (1989) of seventeen high-quality manufacturers of knitted outwear, predominantly from the Hawick area in Scotland. As the authors note, the Scottish firms are embedded in a part of the United Kingdom that has had a long history in the production of wool, with formal wool trade associations dating as far back as the mid-1600s. Scottish expertise in the preparation of cashmere and its use in the production of knitted and woven garments has been historically strong. The Industrial Revolution facilitated the establishment of several Scottish knitwear manufacturers. The seventeen firms studied have been following a long tradition of wool production; they buy the dyed yarn from local spinners and employ mostly local people, trained in several local, well-respected colleges.

Against such a background, Porac, Thomas and Baden-Fuller (1989: 404) describe the 'strategy' their firms have followed as follows:

In Porter's (1980) terms, the Scottish knitwear manufacturers seem to be following a 'focus' strategy by concentrating their efforts upon a narrow segment of the retail market. The aim is to sell premium quality, expensive garments through specialist distribution channels to a limited number of high income consumers. Two aspects of this strategy are noteworthy. First, the strategy seems more evolutionary than planned, having developed over several decades in response to problems encountered in the market place. Ten years ago, the Scottish firms sold in fewer international markets and with a more limited product range than is currently the case. They have gradually been forced by competing knitwear firms to expand both their range and their international customer base.

Although the Scottish firms manufacture with up-to-date electronic knitting equipment, they have historically used traditional, labour intensive methods of hand finishing. Such methods permit the manufacture of very high quality sweaters, and the pool of skilled workers available to these companies has allowed them to exploit fully the traditional methods. On the other hand, traditional methods are not as efficient as more modern manufacturing techniques. As other domestic and foreign firms began to produce lower cost, higher volume, and lesser quality garments, the Scottish manufacturers, intendedly or unintendedly used the 'high quality' strategy to defend their position in the market. This strategy seems to be based upon certain beliefs about the nature of demand for Scottish products and the skills necessary to satisfy such demand".

A number of points are worth stressing in this account. First, the 'focus strategy' – namely 'sell [ing] premium quality, expensive garments through specialist distribution channels to a limited number of high income consumers' – is Porac, Thomas and Baden-Fuller's ascription, in an effort to make sense of the patterned stream of actions they found in the behaviour of the Scottish firms. Second, the researchers perceptively note that this 'strategy' developed over a long stretch of time, in a piecemeal, pragmatic way, 'in response to problems encountered in the marketplace'. We are not given historical evidence as to what these responses were responses *to*, but we are usefully told that the sociomaterial practice of knitwear manufacturing has, among other things, historically used traditional, labour-intensive methods of hand-finishing. In other words, the Scottish firms have been drawing on their 'inherited background' – the resources of the environment they have found themselves embedded into – in order to produce their knitwear. They had to make do with whatever was available to them, and, in that sense,

their actions were non-deliberate, having been shaped instead by historically and culturally transmitted propensities. The practical coping with the surrounding situation (i.e. to produce knitwear in that particular environment) was shaped by what Chia and MacKay (2007: 232) aptly call, drawing on Bourdieu (1990), a 'sociality of inertia' – namely the social, cultural and technological tradition these firms found themselves in, which infused their practical coping and enabled agents to act appropriately (that is, according to the norms and with the materials at hand), though not necessarily deliberately. Approached this way, Chia and MacKay (2007: 236) are certainly right in construing strategy-making as 'a collective, culturally shaped accomplishment attained through historically and culturally transmitted social practices and involving dispositions, propensities and tendencies'. This type of analysis meets Whittington's criterion of 'de-centring' upwards the organization, since it shifts the focus from the activities *within* particular organizations to the historically and culturally transmitted fields of sociomaterial practice that are constitutive of those activities (Mantere 2013; Seidl 2007; Gomez 2010).

In view of this, empirical research on the making of strategy, informed by Heideggerian phenomenology, would seek to describe the practical-coping activities of organizational actors embedded within a broader field of sociomaterial practice: how actors spontaneously (non-deliberately) draw on particular sociocultural norms and material resources available to respond to developing practical situations. Such studies could range from micro-sociological studies of the practical-coping activities of particular individuals in particular circumstances of situated interaction (as, for example, in the case of Honda's senior managers efforts to sell the 50cc Supercubs in the United States in the late 1950s, see Pascale 1984) to more historically or anthropologically oriented studies, aimed at describing the mutual constitution of a sociomaterial practice and its component activities (Langley 2007: 273–4). In both cases, 'strategy' is a second-order label aiming to capture, *in retrospect*, a pattern of actions coping with a developing practical situation over time – as, for example, in the phrase '[traditional, labour-intensive methods of hand-finishing] permit the manufacture of very high quality sweaters, and the pool of skilled workers available to these companies has allowed them to exploit fully the traditional methods' (Porac, Thomas and Baden-Fuller 1989: 404). The rationalizing language of retrospectively accounting for strategy should be minimal, however, so that it does not obscure the practical coping involved when actors act in the context of broader, open-ended sociomaterial practices.

The non-deliberate acting that is associated with practical coping may be interrupted by breakdowns, crises or unexpected events and developments, several of which are caused by competitors, technological change and/or governmental interventions. In such cases, *deliberate* coping takes over, whereby agents pay explicit attention to what they do; it marks the beginning of strategic *thinking*. For example, when costs became an issue (namely when a 'breakdown' occurred), Scottish knitwear manufacturers were forced to think explicitly about what it was that had enabled them to develop with success so far and what might give them the edge from now on. Thus, they consciously articulated what they had been doing all along as a strategy of 'high quality' (Weick 1995: 78). Porac, Thomas and Baden-Fuller (1989: 404) note: 'On the other hand, traditional methods are not as efficient as more modern manufacturing techniques. As other domestic and foreign firms began to produce lower cost, higher volume, and lesser quality garments, the Scottish manufacturers, intendedly or unintendedly used the "high quality" strategy to defend their position in the market. This strategy seems to be based upon certain beliefs about the nature of demand for Scottish products and the skills necessary to satisfy such demand.' As Weick (1995: 78) playfully notes, 'How can I know what I've made until I see how it's sewn?'

On this view, strategy-making is articulating or reinterpreting what an agent has *already* been doing as a matter of course (i.e. non-deliberately). Capitalizing on retrospective reframing is what effective strategists do all the time, notes Weick (1995: 78; see also Kaplan and Orlikowski 2013). *Articulating* occurs when a hitherto non-deliberate activity is brought into sharper focus – when an *aspect* of an activity is revealed (Spinoza, Flores and Dreyfus 1997: 24–5). *Reinterpreting* occurs when an *aspect* of an activity is embedded within a new conversation and acquires new meaning. The case of Scottish knitwear manufacturers is a case of articulating. The now legendary story of how 3M developed its famous Post-it notepads is a case of reinterpreting (Garud, Gehman and Kumar swamy 2011). Here is how the story goes according to Sawyer (2007: 45).

Spence Silver, a research scientist at 3M, tries to improve the adhesive used in tape. *As* a research scientist he acts non-deliberately, pretty much like the lecturer explaining strategy as practice to his/her students, discussed earlier. The kind of new adhesive he develops bonds rather weakly, however, and thus is not quite the improvement he has been hoping for. Silver describes the new adhesive to several colleagues for five years, but no one can think of ways of using it into a product. No one except Art Fry, working in new product development, who, frustrated by paper bookmarks falling out of his hymnal when singing in church, realizes that Silver's adhesive can be used to make the sort of bookmark he has always wanted. The now legendary Post-it note was invented!

Notice that the new adhesive Silver had created assumed importance in *retrospect* – after it had been taken up by someone else. The organizational significance of a new initiative cannot be assessed except in retrospect, namely after the initiative has been discursively woven into other ideas and initiatives created by others. A mundane change today may turn out to be important tomorrow, or may give rise to further, more consequential, changes later. Serendipity is the term normally given to the process of favourable consequences arising when we are aiming at something else. As the case of Honda also shows, consequences are recognized as being favourable *in retrospect*, after they have been embedded in subsequent conversations and projects. Spencer's new adhesive had not been recognized as usefully new until another organizational member could see it as *relevant* to his practical concerns. Strong adhesives were what 3M had been making all along, until it saw potential in weak adhesives – that is, until it distanced itself from (i.e. reinterpreted) the habitual (i.e. non-deliberate) way of approaching adhesives.

Thus, retrospective reframing – articulating or reinterpreting the premises of non-deliberate actions – discloses an *aspect* of the practice and enables an agent to be explicitly aware of it. The agent now forms beliefs, desires and propositional attitudes concerning the task at hand. The agent's actions are no longer solicited by the practical task at hand but deliberately caused by mental content – certain desires and beliefs.

Moreover, as discussed in the previous section, when a practical situation is looked at from a reflective distance, detached from a specific practical concern, the latter becomes occurrent, and the agent develops thematic awareness. This is typically the case with strategizing (strategic planning sessions, scenario-planning interventions, narrative workshops and strategic episodes in general). Planners and strategy practitioners at large, especially consultants and academics, look at the organization as a detached object the properties of which may be discerned and/or redescribed. Unlike the case of explicit awareness, in which practitioners try to coherently find their way around by articulating or reinterpreting what they do, planners bracket any immediate, particular practical concerns, aiming to highlight relatively abstract organizational *properties*, such as organizational strengths and weaknesses, capabilities, past strategies, competitors' strategies, scenario-based threats and opportunities or discourses and narratives used, in order to articulate their intent for the organization. This bracketing is often symbolically manifested in awayday strategy meetings, in which the hurly-burly of organizational life is pushed back to create space for detached, analytical thinking (Wright, Paroutis and Blettner 2013), whereby those involved try to experience the organization as occurrent and, thus, bring it to their thematic awareness as an object of reflection (Küpers, Mantere and Statler 2013)

For example, in the case of the Scottish firms, a strategy for 'premium quality' was at some stage deliberately articulated. Furthermore, certain organizational-cum-environmental properties, such as 'expensive garments', 'specialist distribution channels' and 'high-income consumers' (see Porac, Thomas and Baden-Fuller 1989: 404) were highlighted and sought to be related to one another

in a coherent and mutually reinforcing manner. Similarly, as Jarzabkowski and Wilson (2002: 363–4) found in their study of the strategy-making of the top management team at Warwick University, the strategic intent of consolidating and maintaining the institution's position as a leading research university in an increasingly competitive environment was clearly articulated in the Warwick Strategic Plan, which included four main areas of strategic action. The language of such a plan was relatively abstract and included setting targets, highlighting properties (e.g. strengthen the capacity for income generation, achieve research excellence, etc.) and describing an array of actions to operationalize the plan. Coherence between strategic intent and actions was noted by the researchers.

In strategizing episodes, formal representations that depict the organization and its environment in abstract terms are typically used, and reasoning often acquires a quasi-syllogistic form (Regnér 2003: 71–4). Thematic awareness, abstract language and desituated organizational properties and their relationships are developed. Looked at as an outcome, strategy forms a quasi-theoretical framework – namely a relatively abstract description of the organization causally related to some desired outcomes, the components of which, ideally, are consistent with one another. The aim is for action to be guided by explicit intentionality (formulated through a variable composition of stakeholders in different settings), which sets priorities and deadlines, commits resources, and outlines actions for the organization to implement, in order for particular outcomes to be attained. Setting strategy amounts to achieving thematic awareness in a way that reaches analytical clarity and enables intent to be realized coherently through prioritized actions.

If the outcome of a strategizing episode is a strategic plan, or at least the elements of a strategic awareness or orientation, an SAP perspective can shed light on how such a plan (i.e. a discursive object) is generated, and how it is further related to the rest of the organization. How do actors interact and what broader practices do they draw upon (Jarzabkowski, Balogun and Seidl 2007: 8)? Which particular issues are brought to the attention of which organizational members (especially senior and middle managers), in what ways? How are issues discursively framed, by whom, and why (Laine and Vaara 2007; Rouleau 2005)? What technologies (symbolic and material) are used in the making of strategy (Kaplan 2011; Wright, Paroutis and Blettner 2013)? What 'strategy labels' are used and how is their use reinforced through a division of linguistic labour (Mantere 2013)? Different theories, such as actor–network theory, conventionalist theory, communication theory, etc., may be used to address these questions (Denis, Langley and Rouleau 2007).

In other words, the very process of developing thematic awareness merits attention in its own terms, and it is here where, predominantly, strategy as practice has usefully contributed so far. Maitlis and Lawrence (2003: 125), in their case study of the (failed) attempt to develop an artistic strategy in a British symphony orchestra, allude to this when they note: 'As actors begin to discuss [an] issue, both formally and informally, it becomes a strategic organizational issue – an event, development or trend that is seen as having organizational implications.' Notice the pattern: an issue becomes *strategic* when actors begin developing thematic awareness about it – namely when actors bracket any immediate, particular practical concern and focus on relatively abstract organizational properties, the appropriate manipulation of which is aimed to benefit the organization by sustainably differentiating it from the rest. This is far from being a straightforward process, as is shown by Maitlis and Lawrence (2003).

For some, for example, the orchestra was lacking a 'commercially viable strategy', for others the problems lay with an 'incoherent artistic product', while for the musicians 'the artistic strategy had neither coherence nor commercial viability' (Maitlis and Lawrence 2003: 125). Each one of these statements points to an 'issue' that was brought, in rather abstract terms, to the thematic awareness of the people involved in strategizing. Clearly, how language is used to frame issues (Mantere 2013), how certain organizational events are rhetorically mobilized and how outside influences and developments are rhetorically brought 'into' the organization (Sillince, Jarzabkowski and Shaw 2012), how relevant meetings are conducted (Hodgkinson and Wright 2002), how objects and artefacts (such as PowerPoint presentations, flip charts, etc.) are used (Kaplan 2011), how emotions are handled (Huy 2012) and what forms of knowledge are mobilized are all highly relevant facets of strategizing episodes that merit empirical investigation, especially with the help of ethnographic and ethnomethodological methods (Samra-Fredericks 2003; Rasche and Chia 2009).

Discussion

To appreciate what strategy as practice has to offer to strategy researchers, and to fully realize its potential, it needs to be grounded on an onto-epistemology that acknowledges the various ways through which strategies *qua* practices may develop as well as the various modes of intentionality and language use that underlie strategy-making. Strategy as practice will add to the valuable insights offered by the strategy process approach to the extent that it de-centres the organization, in order to focus on the macro-practices agents draw upon, as well as the micro-practices they engage in. SAP researchers should be particularly alert to exploring the tacit understandings and internalized styles of practical coping; the body and its constitutive involvement in skilled action; and the use of tools (including techniques, models and language at large) by agents. At the same time, strategy as practice should make space for deliberate modes of acting, which have been traditionally downplayed by process researchers and, more recently, by scholars who privilege trans-individualistic analyses. I have tried to show in this chapter that a fully developed Heideggerian onto-epistemological framework provides a coherent way for different types of strategy-making to be researched from a practice perspective.

More specifically, my argument has been as follows (see Table 3.1). As members of sociomaterial practices, agents act on the basis of distinctions they have internalized through their involvement in practice(s). Such distinctions constitute an inherited background that enables agents to relate spontaneously to the solicitations of the

Table 3.1 Action, intentionality and strategy-making: a Heideggerian framework

Type of action	Practical coping	Deliberate coping	Detached coping	Theoretical coping
Type of intentionality	Tacit understanding (non-deliberate)	Explicit awareness • Articulation • Reinterpretation	Thematic awareness	Theoretical understanding
Type of language use	Situational coping skill	Propositional (aspects)	Propositional (properties)	Abstraction
Type of strategy-making/research	Emergent pattern of actions	Retrospective reframing	Strategizing	Theorizing strategy-making

tasks at hand and, therefore, to act non-deliberately. Non-deliberate acting is *practical coping* with a developing situation; it is not mediated by mental representations, and comes about from an ongoing integration of one's activity *as a* practitioner within a particular sociomaterial practice. The latter has a teleo-affective structure, making action within it purposive and sensible. The patterned action that is often discernible in practical coping is mainly a result of agents' acting from the same inherited background that shapes their actions. Strategy here emerges over time from the coherent coping of actors with developing practical situations. Although one may speak of strategy as a pattern in a stream of actions, one may not speak of strategic thinking or strategizing. In practical coping, language is not used propositionally but as a situational coping skill.

When actors encounter breakdowns in the spontaneous flow of their activities, they develop explicit awareness and move to *deliberate coping*: they pay explicit attention to what they do and retrospectively try to make sense of it through articulation or reinterpretation. Strategy here is retrospective reframing. Capturing those reframings in action – describing 'the ways in which new interpretations of old actions bubble up in ongoing events' (Weick 1995: 78) shows an additional way through which patterned action may emerge over time. Now it is not merely the acting out of taken-for-granted assumptions and propensities but also the deliberate thinking about past patterns of actions in order for them to be further advanced or reconstituted. Strategic thinking emerges as a process of deliberately 'looking-back-in-order-to-look-forward', and it arises from

a practical concern with the task at hand. Language is now propositionally used to refer to a particular aspect of a situation, with a particular practical purpose in mind. Creativity here is potentially at its highest, insofar as meaning is attributed to past actions in order to provide the basis for future actions.

Finally, when agents develop thematic awareness about the organization, the latter becomes a detached object of reflection to be described in terms of abstract properties. This is when strategic thinking proper – or, to be more precise, *strategizing* – takes place, typically in strategic planning sessions, strategy awaydays, narrative workshops, scenario-planning sessions and strategic episodes in general. In strategizing, agents move from deliberately coping with situational aspects of practical situations to being thematically aware of desituated properties of occurrent objects of attention. Strategy-making practitioners (typically senior managers, as well as internal and external consultants and, perhaps, other stakeholders) bracket immediate, task-related practical concerns, in order to discern relatively abstract organizational *properties* that, when systematically and coherently interrelated, will probably make up strategic intent. Thinking tends to be analytical, either deductive or narrative, or a combination of both. Past and future are usually brought together, although the emphasis on each may vary. The organization is represented through abstract formulations or narrative genres, and explicit beliefs and desires are articulated. Note that, although strategizing involves abstraction and the formulation of intentionality, this is still a sociomaterial and thoroughly political process involving the use of artefacts and tools, especially language (Heracleous and Jacobs 2012). In thematic awareness, language is used propositionally or narratively to make assertions about organizational properties that bear no relevance to a particular practical situation. Strategic learning is an outcome of such a use of language.

The Heideggerian onto-epistemology advanced here overcomes some of the problems in SP and SAP research correctly identified by Whittington, and Chia and MacKay. Whittington has rightly criticized SP research for reifying organizations and for not paying sufficient attention to strategic intent. In his words (Whittington 2007: 1581, emphasis added): '[F]irst, by defining strategy as what the organizations does, [Mintzberg] denies the sense of strategy as a kind of *work* that people do; second, by stressing how organizational outcomes are so frequently detached from strategic intent, he reduces that strategy work to a vain, even absurd endeavor to control the uncontrollable. [. . .] For Mintzberg, why bother to explore the actual roles, adaptations and impacts of planning in practice, if strategic plans are typically not realized in organizational outcomes?'

The above are sensible points, which can be accommodated within the framework offered here. More specifically, strategy has been shown to emanate from the practical coping, deliberate coping or strategizing of individuals situated in sociomaterial practices. In *practical coping*, the inherited background of sociomaterial practices is the launching pad for non-deliberate actions, in response to a practical situation at hand (recall the Scottish knitwear firms in their early days or the Honda responses to unexpected problems when attempting to enter the US motorcycle market). In *deliberate coping*, both the inherited background and the explicit awareness of individuals are intertwined in the face of breakdowns. Strategy is making retrospective sense of what has been going on in order to consolidate, further refine or change a pattern of actions (think of the Post-it notepad story discussed earlier). In *strategizing*, the organization is an occurrent object, which enters the thematic awareness of the participants, and its properties are identified (think of strategic planning meetings conducted at the British symphony

orchestra mentioned earlier). Notice that each one of these three modes of strategy-making involves *work* that is carried out within sociomaterial practices consisting of tacit understandings, bodily involvement and the use of tools. Finding out how such work is organized and carried out over time, and with what effects, are important themes that SAP researchers typically aim at exploring.

Chia and MacKay (2007) have rightly criticized both the SP approach and the dominant understanding of strategy as practice for an individualistic bias, which tends to portray strategy-making as the doing of purposeful agents. Subscribers to a Heideggerian phenomenology are alert to the tacit understandings, embodied capacities and historically shaped tendencies that reside in extra-organizational sociomaterial practices (Tsoukas 2009; 2011). That much is eloquently said by Chia and MacKay, who also share a Heideggerian onto-epistemology. What they seem to underestimate, however (although they mention its possibility without developing it: see Chia and Mackay 2007: 238), is deliberate action and the associated practice of strategizing. From a Heideggerian perspective, strategizing – the process of forming thematic awareness – is a distinctive moment of 'being-in-the-world' that comes about when people step back from immediate practical tasks and reflect on an entity in a detached manner, seeking to identify its properties *in abstracto*. How thematic awareness develops, and with what results, are fascinating topics to study from a practice perspective.

It should be noted, however, that thematic awareness, although it aims at decontextualization, detached thinking and abstraction, itself constitutes a *practical* task. Detached reflection does not come ready-made but involves *work* too, and therefore draws on relevant sociomaterial practices and skills; like any practice, it relies on tacit understandings, the body and particular tools (especially language). Thematic awareness is a social accomplishment and is explored through theoretical understanding. How agents abstract, what concepts they use, how they argue and draw each other's attention to certain things and how they relate to others are activities shaped by broader sociomaterial practices on which people draw (Latour 2005).

Post-structuralist approaches, with their macro-focus on *epistemes*, truth regimes and disciplinary practices (Allard-Poesi 2010; Knights and Morgan 1991; Ezzamel and Willmott 2008; Rasche and Chia 2009), as well as more micro-oriented ethno-methodological and discursive-narrative studies, focusing on discursive practices, narrative-rhetorical frames and conversation analyses (Samra-Fredericks 2003; Mantere and Vaara 2008; Vaara, Kleymann and Seristö 2004), are most relevant here. Chia and MacKay (2007: 229) are right in pointing out that a particular strategist's relational-rhetorical skills, as studied by Samra-Fredericks (2003), are no mere individual traits but social accomplishments – namely *ways* of arguing and relating that are grounded on established practices with which participants can identify. The micro-practices agents engage in (i.e. the patterns of interactions locally instantiated) and the macro-practices agents draw upon (i.e. the discourses, the tacit understandings, the bodily comportment and the tools used) are important topics to study, though it may not be always possible to do both things at once.

Heideggerian phenomenology enables us to better appreciate the different uses of language in the strategy-making process. Some researchers, espousing a language-based view of strategy, have argued that 'for a strategy to be organizational, there needs to be a shared language game attached to "strategy" and associated labels' (Mantere 2013: 1414). In other words, organizational strategy is a language game 'that governs the proper use of strategy labels at the level of the organization' (1420). Such a view of strategy leaves unaccounted the making of strategy when 'strategy labels' are *not* explicitly used, however. Such was the case with Scottish knitwear firms, 3M's Post-it notepads and Honda's entry in the US motorcycle market. As far as we know, in all these cases, 'strategy labels' were not explicitly used by the actors involved and a strategy vocabulary was not in evidence. 'Strategy labels' were, instead, researchers' *ex post facto* attributions – second-order concepts to analytically understand firm behaviour.

Thus, when Mantere argues, addressing the question 'Who are the strategists?' (Mantere

2013: 1410), that 'significant strategic actors are those who have linguistic expert roles in the strategy language game' (1420), he leaves out actors who retrospectively turned out to be of 'strategic' importance but who did not have 'linguistic expert roles in the strategy language game' in their organizations. Were Silver Spence (research scientist, 3M), Kihachiro Kawashima (American Honda executive), or Norman McLaren (film-maker, National Film Board, Canada) 'strategic actors' in Mantere's sense? Clearly not, at least by his criterion of whether they had been active in authoritatively influencing the rules of the use of 'strategy labels'. These people were too busy doing their particular jobs in their respective organizations. Like Mintzberg's (2007) professionals and experts, these individuals were not part of 'strategy units', nor, as far as we know, were they taking part in strategizing sessions. They were, however, making strategy.

From the perspective advanced here, the making of organizational strategy is a more multi-faceted process than Mantere's conceptualization allows. Organizational members may be involved non-deliberately in the making of strategy (in the practical coping mode) or they may be deliberately using 'strategy vocabulary' (in the thematic awareness mode), when approaching their organization as an occurrent object, the properties of which they need to figure out. To identify strategy-making with the use of 'strategy labels' is to miss the non-deliberate modes of strategy-making.

Similarly, a Heideggerian framework enables us to avoid the circular definitions of strategy that so often beset the field. Jarzabkowski, Balogun and Seidl (2007: 8, emphasis added) argue that 'an activity is considered *strategic* to the extent that is consequential for the *strategic* outcomes, directions, survival and competitive advantage of the firm'. As in Mantere's case, the problem with such a definition is that it conflates 'strategy-making' with 'intentionality' – two distinct and contingently linked phenomena. Some types of activity are considered 'strategic' because participants define them as such, and a division of linguistic labour has developed to control the use of 'strategy labels' (Mantere 2013), not because they are necessarily consequential for the organization. This is what has been described in this chapter as *strategizing*, and it is linked with intentionality and thematic awareness. Mintzberg (1994) was right to point out, however, that it is not uncommon for strategic planning exercises to be just that: ritual exercises, bearing no clear relationship to organizational outcomes. What is intended is not necessarily consequential.

Reversely, what may turn out to be of major consequence for the competitive advantage of an organization may not be an outcome of a 'strategic' activity as such (namely an outcome of strategizing) but may emerge from a pattern of actions practically coping with a developing situation, as, for example, was the case of the Scottish knitwear firms relying on traditional methods of hand-finishing their sweaters. Alternatively, a competitive advantage may emerge from a stream of practical-coping activities after they have been retrospectively made sense of by practitioners. Non-deliberate practical coping, although purposive, is not directed at generating particular (consequential) outcomes, and thus it is not purposeful; it merely enacts a particular inherited background over time. Deliberate coping interweaves spontaneous responses to a developing practical situation with articulating or reinterpreting the emerged pattern of actions. What is consequential is a retrospective attribution.

Conclusion

I have argued in this chapter that keeping 'strategy-making' separate from 'intentionality' is beneficial, since it allows us to better see their connections. 'Strategy' was traditionally considered to be identical with senior managerial intentionality and its manifestations – that is, strategic plans. The strategy process approach widened our appreciation of 'strategy' by enabling us to see how patterns in streams of non-deliberate actions can be seen as de facto forming a strategy. Whereas traditional approaches attributed a coherent pattern of organizational actions to the strategic intent of relevant practitioners, SP researchers bracketed that assumption in search for patterns of action independently of their origin.

A Heideggerian lens on strategy as practice makes the following contribution: first, it brings intentionality under scrutiny and shows *how* it is constructed in strategizing episodes through practitioners drawing upon particular sociomaterial practices (something that the SP approach refrained from doing); and, second, it shows the 'inherited background' from which practitioners engage in coherent practical coping and explores how aspects of this 'inherited background' are brought to explicit awareness in the face of breakdowns, and with what effects (something that has been immanent in the SP approach but not fully realized, nor explicitly theorized, because of its individualist bias).

Heideggerian phenomenology provides a meta-theoretical vocabulary to account for the various streams of strategy research. The framework suggested here helps us to coherently acknowledge the various streams of SAP research, and to address associated ambiguities and misconceptions. Moreover, it suggests research questions to be asked and offers ways for insights from different SAP studies to be integrated.

References

Allard-Poesi, F. (2010), 'A Foucauldian perspective on strategic practice: strategy as the art of (un)folding', in Golsorkhi, D., Rouleau, L., Seidl, D., and Vaara, E. (eds.), *Cambridge Handbook of Strategy as Practice*: 168–82. Cambridge University Press.

Barry, D., and Elmes, M. (1997), 'Strategy retold: toward a narrative view of strategic discourse', *Academy of Management Review*, 22/2: 429–52.

Benner, P. (1994), 'The role of articulation in understanding practice and experience as sources of knowledge in clinical nursing', in Tully, J. (ed.), *Philosophy in an Age of Pluralism*: 136–55. Cambridge University Press.

Benner, P., Hooper-Kyriakidis, P., and Stannard, D. (1999), *Clinical Wisdom and Interventions in Critical Care*. Philadelphia: Saunders.

Boston Consulting Group (1975), *Strategy Alternatives for the British Motorcycle Industry*. London: Her Majesty's Stationery Office.

Bourdieu, P. (1990), *The Logic of Practice*. Cambridge: Polity.

Chia, R., and Holt, R. (2006), 'Strategy as practical coping: a Heideggerian perspective', *Organization Studies*, 27/5: 635–55.

(2009), *Strategy without Design: The Silent Efficacy of Indirect Action*. Cambridge University Press.

Chia, R., and MacKay, B. (2007), 'Post-processual challenges for the emerging strategy-as-practice perspective: discovering strategy in the logic of practice', *Human Relations*, 60/1: 217–42.

Cook, S., and Yanow, D. (1996), 'Culture and organizational learning', in Cohen, M., and Sproull, L. (eds.), *Organizational Learning*: 430–59. Thousand Oaks, CA: Sage.

Denis, J.-L., Langley, A., and Rouleau, L. (2007), 'Strategizing in pluralistic contexts: rethinking theoretical frames', *Human Relations*, 60/1: 179–215.

Dreyfus, H. (1985), 'Holism and hermeneutics', in Hollinger, R. (ed.), *Hermeneutics and Praxis*: 227–47. University of Notre Dame Press.

(1991a), *Being-in-the-World: A Commentary on Heidegger's Being and Time, Division 1*. Cambridge, MA: MIT Press.

(1991b), 'Reflection on the workshop on "the self"', *Anthropology and Humanism Quarterly*, 16/1: 27–31.

(2000), 'Responses', in Wrathall, M., and Malpas, J. (eds.), *Heidegger, Coping, and Cognitive Science: Essays in Honor of Hubert L. Dreyfus*: 313–49. Cambridge, MA: MIT Press.

Ezzamel, M., and Willmott, H. (2008), 'Strategy as discourse in a global retailer: a supplement to rationalist and interpretive accounts', *Organization Studies*, 29/2: 191–217.

Garud, R., Gehman, J., and Kumaraswamy, A. (2011), 'Complexity arrangements for sustained innovation: lessons from 3M Corporation', *Organization Studies*, 32/6: 737–67.

Gawande, A. (2002), *Complications: A Surgeon's Notes on an Imperfect Science*. New York: Metropolitan Books.

Giddens, A. (1991), *Modernity and Self-Identity: Self and Society in the Late Modern Age*. Cambridge: Polity.

Gomez, M.-L. (2010), 'A Bourdieusian perspective on strategizing', in Golsorkhi, D., Rouleau, L., Seidl, D., and Vaara, E. (eds.), *Cambridge Handbook of Strategy as Practice*: 141–54. Cambridge University Press.

Goold, M. (1992), 'Design, learning and planning: a further observation on the design school debate', *Strategic Management Journal*, 13/2: 169–70.

Hardy, C., Lawrence, T. B., and Grant, D. (2005), 'Discourse and collaboration: the role of conversations and collective identity', *Academy of Management Review*, 30/1: 58–77.

Harré, R., and Gillett, G. (1994), *The Discursive Mind*. Thousand Oaks, CA: Sage.

Heidegger, M. (1962), *Being and Time*. New York: Harper & Row.

Hendry, J., and Seidl, D. (2003), 'The structure and significance of strategic episodes: social systems theory and the routine practices of strategic change', *Journal of Management Studies*, 40/1: 175–96.

Heracleous, L., and Jacobs, C. D. (2012), *Crafting Strategy: Embodied Metaphors in Practice*. Cambridge University Press.

Hodgkinson, G. P., and Wright, G. (2002), 'Confronting strategic inertia in a top management team: learning from failure', *Organization Studies*, 23/6: 949–77.

Huy, Q. N. (2012), 'Emotions in strategic organization: opportunities for impactful research', *Strategic Organization*, 10/3: 240–7.

Jarzabkowski, P., Balogun, J., and Seidl, D. (2007), 'Strategizing: the challenges of a practice perspective', *Human Relations*, 60/1: 5–28.

Jarzabkowski, P., and Wilson, D. C. (2002), 'Top teams and strategy in a UK university', *Journal of Management Studies*, 39/3: 355–81.

Johnson, G., Melin, L., and Whittington, R. (2003), 'Guest editors' introduction: micro strategy and strategizing: towards an activity-based view', *Journal of Management Studies*, 40/1: 3–22.

Kaplan, S. (2011), 'Strategy and PowerPoint: an inquiry into the epistemic culture and machinery of strategy making', *Organization Science*, 22/2: 320–46.

Kaplan, S., and Orlikowski, W. J. (2013), 'Temporal work in strategy making', *Organization Science*, 24/4: 965–95.

Knights, D., and Morgan, G. (1991), 'Corporate strategy, organizations, and subjectivity: a critique', *Organization Studies*, 12/2: 251–73.

Kogut, B., and Zander, U. (1996), 'What firms do? Coordination, identity, and learning', *Organization Science*, 7/5: 502–18.

Küpers, W., Mantere, S., and Statler, M. (2013), 'Strategy as storytelling: a phenomenological collaboration', *Journal of Management Inquiry*, 22/1: 83–100.

Laine, P.-M., and Vaara, E. (2007), 'Struggling over subjectivity: a discursive analysis of strategic development in an engineering group', *Human Relations*, 60/1: 29–58.

Lakatos, I. (1978 [1968]), *The Methodology of Scientific Research Programmes*. Cambridge University Press.

Langley, A. (2007), 'Process thinking in strategic organization', *Strategic Organization*, 5/3: 271–82.

Latour, B. (2005), *Reassembling the Social: An Introduction to Actor–Network-Theory*. Oxford University Press.

MacIntyre, A. (1985), *After Virtue*, 2nd edn. London: Duckworth.

Maitlis, S., and Lawrence, T. B. (2003), 'Orchestral manoeuvres in the dark: understanding failure in organizational strategizing', *Journal of Management Studies*, 40/1: 109–39.

Mantere, S. (2010), 'A Wittgensteinian perspective on strategizing', in Golsorkhi, D., Rouleau, L., Seidl, D., and Vaara, E. (eds.), *Cambridge Handbook of Strategy as Practice*: 155–67. Cambridge University Press.

——— (2013), 'What is organizational strategy? A language-based view', *Journal of Management Studies*, 50/8: 1408–26.

Mantere, S., and Vaara, E. (2008), 'On the problem of participation in strategy: a critical discursive perspective', *Organization Science*, 19/2: 341–58.

Mintzberg, H. (1987), 'Crafting strategy', *Harvard Business Review*, 65/4: 66–75.

——— (1990), 'The design school: reconsidering the basic premises of strategic management', *Strategic Management Journal*, 11/3: 171–95.

——— (1994), *The Rise and Fall of Strategic Planning*. New York: Free Press.

——— (2007), *Tracking Strategies: Toward a General Theory*. Oxford University Press.

Mintzberg, H., and McHugh, A. (1985), 'Strategy formation in an adhocracy', *Administrative Science Quarterly*, 30/2: 160–97.

Mintzberg, H., and Waters, J. A. (1982), 'Tracking strategy in an entrepreneurial firm', *Academy of Management Journal*, 25/3: 465–99.

——— (1985), 'Of strategies, deliberate and emergent', *Strategic Management Journal*, 6/3: 257–72.

Orlikowski, W. J. (2007), 'Sociomaterial practices: exploring technology at work', *Organization Studies*, 28/9: 1435–48.

Orr, J. E. (1996), *Talking about Machines: An Ethnography of a Modern Job*. Ithaca, NY: ILR Press.

Pascale, R. T. (1984), 'Perspectives on strategy: the real story behind Honda's success', *California Management Review*, 26/3: 47–72.

Pettigrew, A. M. (1992), 'The character and significance of process strategy research', *Strategic Management Journal*, 13/S2: 5–16.

Polanyi, M. (1962), *Personal Knowledge: Towards a Post-Critical Philosophy*. University of Chicago Press.

Polanyi, M., and Prosch, H. (1975), *Meaning*. University of Chicago Press.

Porac, J. F., Thomas, H., and Baden-Fuller, C. (1989), 'Competitive groups as cognitive communities: the case of Scottish knitwear manufacturers', *Journal of Management Studies*, 26/4: 397–416.

Rasche, A., and Chia, R. (2009), 'Researching strategy practices: a genealogical social theory perspective', *Organization Studies*, 30/7: 713–34.

Reckwitz, A. (2002), 'Toward a theory of social practices: a development in culturalist theorizing', *European Journal of Social Theory*, 5/2: 243–63.

Regnér, P. (2003), 'Strategy creation in the periphery: inductive versus deductive strategy making', *Journal of Management Studies*, 40/1: 57–82.

Rouleau, L. (2005), 'Micro-practices of strategic sensemaking and sensegiving: how middle managers interpret and sell change every day', *Journal of Management Studies*, 42/7: 1413–41.

Rouse, M. (2000), 'Coping and its contrasts', in Wrathall, M., and Malpas, J. (eds.), *Heidegger, Coping, and Cognitive Science: Essays in Honor of Hubert L. Dreyfus*: 7–28. Cambridge, MA: MIT Press.

Ryle, G. (1963), *The Concept of Mind*. London: Penguin Books.

Samra-Fredericks, D. (2003), 'Strategizing as lived experience and strategists' everyday efforts to shape strategic direction', *Journal of Management Studies*, 40/1: 141–74.

Sandberg, J., and Tsoukas, H. (2011), 'Grasping the logic of practice: theorizing through practical rationality', *Academy of Management Review*, 36/2: 338–60.

Sawyer, K. (2007), *Group Genius: The Creative Power of Collaboration*. New York: Basic Books.

Schatzki, T. R. (2000), 'Coping with others with folk psychology', in Wrathall, M., and Malpas, J. (eds.), *Heidegger, Coping, and Cognitive Science: Essays in Honor of Hubert L. Dreyfus*: 29–52. Cambridge, MA: MIT Press.

(2005), 'The sites of organizations', *Organization Studies*, 26/3: 465–84.

Seidl, D. (2007), 'General strategy concepts and the ecology of strategy discourses: a systemic-discursive perspective', *Organization Studies*, 28/2: 197–218.

Shotter, J., and Katz, A. M. (1996), 'Articulating a practice from within the practice itself: establishing formative dialogues by the use of a "social poetics"', *Concepts and Transformation*, 1/2–3: 213–37.

Sillince, J., Jarzabkowski, P., and Shaw, D. (2012), 'Shaping strategic action through the rhetorical construction and exploitation of ambiguity', *Organization Science*, 23/3: 630–50.

Spinosa, C., Flores, F., and Dreyfus, H. (1997), *Disclosing New Worlds: Entrepreneurship, Democratic Action, and the Cultivation of Solidarity*. Cambridge, MA: MIT Press.

Taylor, C. (1985a), Philosophical Papers, vol. I, Human Agency and Language. Cambridge University Press.

(1985b), Philosophical Papers, vol. II, Philosophy and the Human Sciences. Cambridge University Press.

(1991), 'The dialogical self', in Hiley, D., Bohman, J., and Shusterman, R. (eds.), *The Interpretive Turn: Philosophy, Science, Culture*: 304–14, Ithaca, NY: Cornell University Press.

(1993), 'Engaged agency and background in Heidegger', in Guignon, C. (ed.), *The Cambridge Companion to Heidegger*: 317–36. Cambridge University Press.

(1995), *Philosophical Arguments*. Cambridge, MA: Harvard University Press.

Tsoukas, H. (2009), 'A dialogical approach to the creation of new knowledge in organizations', *Organization Science*, 20/6: 941–57.

(2011), 'How should we understand tacit knowledge? A phenomenological view', in Easterby-Smith, M., and Lyles, M. A. (eds.), *Handbook of Organizational Learning and Knowledge Management*, 2nd edn: 453–76. Oxford: Blackwell.

Tsoukas, H., and Knudsen, C. (2002), 'The conduct of strategy research', in Pettigrew, A. M., Thomas,

H., and Whittington, R. (eds.), *Handbook of Strategy and Management*: 411–35. London: Sage.

Vaara, E., Kleymann, B., and Seristö, H. (2004), 'Strategies as discursive constructions: the case of airline alliances', *Journal of Management Studies*, 41/1: 1–35.

Van de Ven, A. H., and Poole, M. S. (2005), 'Alternative approaches for studying organizational change', *Organization Studies*, 26/9: 1377–404.

Wakefield, J., and Dreyfus, H. (1991), 'Intentionality and the phenomenology of action', in Lepore, E., and van Gulick, R. (eds.), *John Searle and His Critics*: 259–70. Oxford: Blackwell.

Weick, K. E. (1995), *Sensemaking in Organizations*. Thousand Oaks, CA: Sage.

(2001), 'Substitutes for strategy', in *Making Sense of the Organization*: 345–60. Oxford: Blackwell.

Whittington, R. (2006), 'Completing the practice turn in strategy research', *Organization Studies*, 27/5: 613–34.

(2007), 'Strategy practice and strategy process: family differences and the sociological eye', *Organization Studies*, 28/10: 1575–86.

Wittgenstein, L. (1979), *On Certainty*, ed. Anscombe, G. E. M., and von Wright, G. H. Oxford: Blackwell.

Wittgenstein, L. (1980a), *Remarks on the Philosophy of Psychology*, vol. II, ed. von Wright, G. H., and Nyman, H. University of Chicago Press.

Wittgenstein, L. (1980b), *Culture and Value*, ed. von Wright, G. H., and Nyman, H. University of Chicago Press.

Wright, R. P., Paroutis, S., and Blettner, D. P. (2013), 'How useful are the strategic tools we teach in business schools?', *Journal of Management Studies*, 50/1: 92–125.

Yanow, D. (2015), 'After mastery: insights from practice theorizing', in Garud, R., Simpson, B., Langley, A., and Tsoukas, H. (eds.), *The Emergence of Novelty in Organizations*: ch. 11. Oxford University Press.

Yanow, D., and Tsoukas, H. (2009), 'What is reflection-in-action? A phenomenological account', *Journal of Management Studies*, 46/8: 1339–64.

Constructivist paradigms: implications for strategy-as-practice research

SIMON GRAND, WIDAR VON ARX and JOHANNES
RÜEGG-STÜRM

Introduction

The practice turn in strategy research (Johnson, Melin and Whittington 2003; Johnson *et al.* 2007; Golsorkhi *et al.* 2010; Vaara and Whittington 2012) implies an explicit reconsideration of paradigmatic premises (Tsoukas and Knudsen 2002; Feldman and Orlikowski 2011; Vaara and Whittington 2012). The strategy-as-practice research programme challenges concepts of strategy that have long been taken for granted, uncovering the complexities of the 'social fabric' of strategy-making (Latour 1996). Furthermore, it undermines the apparently self-evident premises of strategy research and its relation to strategy-making by referring to various constructivist perspectives, theories and methodologies.

Looking at the main contributions to strategy-as-practice research of the last few years, a handful of patterns seem dominant. One can distinguish between three dimensions (Johnson *et al.* 2007; Orlikowski in this volume). On an empirical level ('*phenomenon*'), strategy-making is seen as involving multiple construction processes and activities and multiple actors inside and outside the organization, distributed across multiple organizational layers (Johnson, Melin and Whittington 2003; Jarzabkowski and Spee 2009). While strategies and strategy processes are traditionally treated as defined entities, the strategy-as-practice research programme emphasizes their constructedness, and thus their heterogeneity, processuality and fragility. On a theoretical level ('*perspectives*'), the study of strategy-making requires approaches that provide conceptual cover for this heterogeneous mesh of

processes, activities and actors, as well as the fact of their situatedness and embeddedness. It is argued that a focus on the practice of strategy-making therefore implies a discussion of the underlying action theories (Grand and MacLean 2007; Jarzabkowski 2004; Tsoukas and Knudsen 2002) and, specifically, theories of practice (Schatzki, Knorr Cetina and von Savigny 2001). On a philosophical level ('*philosophies*'), this emphasis on strategy-making as social practice requires a consideration of scientific research itself from the vantage point of practice (Knorr Cetina 2002; Tsoukas 2005). How do scientific research itself and particular research practices contribute to the construction of the field of strategy, both scientifically and organizationally (Knights and Morgan 1991)?

In this chapter, we explore specifically why an interest in strategy practice(s) promotes constructivist perspectives. For this purpose, constructivism is understood as a paradigm (Kuhn 1996; Guba and Lincoln 1994), a set of fundamental assumptions and worldviews underlying most of the theories used by strategy-as-practice researchers. It is our aim to uncover some of the basic premises underlying constructivist epistemologies as well as their potential for advancing the SAP research programme, and strategy research more generally. To focus our discussion, we ask two main questions.

> How do constructivist paradigms shape strategy-as-practice research? How could constructivist paradigms contribute to the future advancement of the field?

We explore these questions in two steps. First, we introduce three influential, archetypal constructivist approaches – the programme of social construction, systemic constructivism, and the empirical programme of constructivism – by exploring their idiosyncrasies and the differences and/or common ground between them. Second, we discuss the impact of constructivist paradigms on research in the strategy-as-practice field. The analysis is structured along four dimensions: (1) the identification of practices, activities and actors as the main constituents of scientific descriptions and explanations in strategy research (addressing *ontological issues*); (2) the understanding and conceptualization of 'strategy' and 'strategic' (addressing *epistemological issues*); (3) the conduct of strategy research understood as a construction process (identifying the *methodological issues* of the programme); and (4) the practical relevance and political aspect of a strategy-as-practice perspective (and, by implication, *normative issues*).

By doing so, we combine a discussion of the field as it has emerged over recent years with the discussion of prospects for its future development. We conclude this chapter by identifying critical issues that are essential for extending SAP research on the side of constructivist research paradigms.

Constructivist paradigms

With a wide choice of constructivist perspectives and approaches available (Hacking 1999), we focus on three central, but distinct approaches that represent both the commonalities and the differences in the constructivist research programme. To this end, we discuss the research programme of social construction (Berger and Luckmann 1967; Luckmann 1992), systemic constructivism (Maturana and Varela 1987; Luhmann 1996) and the empirical programme of constructivism (Latour and Woolgar 1986; Knorr Cetina 1981; Latour 2005). These programmes share four major concerns, which are also explicitly addressed in contributions to the strategy-as-practice research programme. By 'concerns', we mean controversial issues that are raised, discussed and addressed explicitly in these approaches, instead of being covered as theoretical and philosophical pre-conceptualizations and thus black-boxed as self-evident and taken for

granted (Latour 2005). This implies that we see constructivist paradigms as opportunities for questioning established research paradigms, while introducing alternative paradigmatic orientations.

Concern 1. The constructivist programmes question a concept of 'reality' as something that is 'objectively given', instead focusing on the construction processes implied in the creation, establishment and stabilization of 'reality'. This explains why constructivist perspectives imply ontological considerations, as embedded in (social) practice itself.

Concern 2. Constructivist research programmes specifically study the status of 'knowledge' (Tsoukas 2005), the relation to the 'world' (Goodman 1987) and the process of the scientific generation of knowledge (Knorr Cetina 2002), thus reflecting research as a construction process, which inherently implies epistemological considerations.

Concern 3. Agency in the creation process cannot automatically be associated with particular entities ('individual', 'organization', 'institutional'), but must be studied as distributed among heterogeneous actants (Latour 2005). This makes the methodological consideration of the creative qualities of research essential (Lury and Wakeford 2012).

Concern 4. They challenge the predominance of unquestioned dichotomies in the social sciences, between micro and macro, between subjective and objective or between situated activities and collective practices (Bourdieu and Wacquant 1992), including the recognition of the normative qualities of any such distinction (Thévenot 2006).

Although the three constructivist paradigms discussed in the next section of the chapter share these four concerns, they differ with respect to their basic premises as well as the ways in which they address these concerns (Knorr Cetina 1989; Hacking 1999).

Research programme of social construction

The research programme of social construction is embedded in a phenomenological reinterpretation of the social sciences (Husserl 1931; Schütz 1932), studying 'reality' and 'knowledge' as resulting from social construction processes; reality is always a reality for and by humans. The social construction of reality is seen as ingrained in mundane activities and multiple practices, continuously enacted by the social actors themselves. Thereby, it is important to understand how it is possible for particular 'realities' to be accepted as 'objective', 'given', 'external' or 'natural'. From the vantage point of this research programme, knowledge is understood as resulting from social construction processes, in particular institutionalization, objectivation and legitimization (Berger and Luckmann 1967). These processes are described as leading to the experience of a legitimate backdrop of established knowledge and social order.

Scientific knowledge results from the generation of second-order knowledge, the construction of scientific 'knowledge' on the social construction of 'knowledge' (Schütz 1967 [1932]). Every social phenomenon can be studied as the result of a construction process (Hacking 1999). The starting point for any inquiry in social constructivism is subjective, individual meaning ('Lebenswelt'). The purpose of empirical reconstruction is to shed light on the process of 'objectivation' from subjective meaning to shared understanding and common knowledge. More recently the research programme has turned towards a theory of social action (Luckmann 1992), identifying social action as the primary locus of social meaning in the making. This is a coherent extension of the initial programme, which emphasizes that common-sense knowledge is a meaningful focus of any sociology of knowledge (Knoblauch 2005).

Social action is predominantly shaped by implicit everyday knowledge, which is legitimate and objective in a particular situation or context, but which gains its legitimacy and objectivity through the social construction processes that transcend these situations and contexts (concern 1). Social constructivism thereby refers to anthropological premises concerning the 'creation of knowledge; and 'making of meaning' (discussed as implied 'proto-sociology': Eberle 1992) (concern 2). Thereby, the research programme is understood as 'sociology of knowledge' (Knoblauch 2005), with a particular interest in the situated and social construction of knowledge in everyday activities and scientific research (concern 3). Social 'reality' is considered 'objective' and 'subjective' at the same time. Objective reality, although the outcome of social construction, appears to individuals as a given, while subjective reality refers to the continuous making of meaning in everyday social interactions (concern 1).

While this perspective is influential in discussions of constructivist paradigms, it is often cited without a careful consideration for these underlying premises. Furthermore, various difficulties with this perspective have been discussed over time. It has been argued that the application of this perspective can become tautological when 'social' phenomena are seen as resulting from 'social' construction (Latour 2005). It remains difficult to demonstrate in an empirical study that 'something' is socially constructed (Hacking 1999). The approach assumes a collectively shared common understanding of 'reality' and 'knowledge', while its fragility and heterogeneity remain underexplored. Overall, the intuition behind the research programme is a central reference for constructivist epistemologies, but, without a careful consideration for the underlying premises, the simple assertion of 'reality' and 'knowledge' as being constructed becomes trivial.

Systemic constructivism

In line with this critique, and in order to identify more explicit conceptual foundations, constructivism can be understood as the epistemology of systems theory. Human cognition in everyday activities and scientific practice does not represent an objective, given world but, instead, resembles an active process of inventing reality (Watzlawick 1984) by drawing analytical distinctions. There is no correspondence between an outer world and its 'representation' or construction in our brains (Maturana and Varela 1987). The brain operates according to structures and criteria the purpose of which is not to represent the world correctly. The only relevant criterion is viability, understood as the capacity to cope successfully with the world. As a consequence, the cognition process itself undergoes historical development and differentiation processes in response to previous cognition and experience. Whatever is recognized as real, relevant and true has an impact back on the cognition process itself, and vice versa. Cognitive structures and content are mutually dependent; this phenomenon is called 'self-referentiality'. On the basis of such an understanding, information and knowledge are not regarded as given entities but as the processes of informing and knowing.

What we identify as 'reality' or 'knowledge' is an ongoing contingent process of enactment (Weick 1979). Constructivism is thus understood as 'operative epistemology' (von Foerster 1981): any information is 'a difference which makes a difference' (Bateson 1972: 315). This anti-realist ontological conceptualization challenges traditional ideas of reality and knowledge. Whereas so-called radical constructivism (Glasersfeld 1995; Watzlawick 1984) focuses on processes of cognitive constructions, in systemic constructivism these processes of reality construction occur in communicative systems (Luhmann 1986; 1996). In this perspective, instances of communication are the basic elements of social systems. What is considered real, relevant and true is continuously co-created in communication. From a systems theory perspective, cognitive (individual) systems and communicative systems work independently (operationally closed). Any data are processed according to the (cognitive or communicative) structures that have evolved. Organizational phenomena cannot be ascribed directly to individual activities. Cognitive and communicative systems operate in structural coupling, however: they both process meaning and enact structures. Thoughts and communications need to be mutually connective, so that ongoing sensemaking is possible. Systemic constructivism thus strives to explain the social not from individuals' mental structures but by conceptualizing the social as an autonomous, communicative domain (Luhmann 1996; Seidl 2007).

Systemic constructivism addresses some of the open issues in the research programme of social construction (see above). In particular, systemic constructivism makes a distinction between cognitive and social systems, not taking individual agency or social 'entities' as the basis for studying social phenomena but the ongoing processes of communication (concern 1). This leads to a decentralization of agency, which implies that research relies on communication itself that has always already taken place and that creates 'reality', irrespective of individual consciousness (concern 3). Accordingly, one focus lies on the processes of drawing distinctions as the fundamental premise for shaping social 'reality' and the organization of 'knowledge' (concern 2). This allows for internalizing the difficulties associated with many unquestioned dichotomies in the social sciences. As a consequence, systemic constructivism is inherently reflexive. It emphasizes the necessity of observing the process of observation as the essence of research (concern 4). Therefore, systemic constructivism is an operative epistemology insofar as there is never a final description of a phenomenon, since knowledge creation is inherently processual and open for future development.

The fundamental shift in systemic epistemology lies in its focus on communication. One main difference from other constructivist epistemologies lies in the conceptualization of situated activities, which are reduced to manifestations and actualizations of communication. Thereby, some issues and problems of this perspective have been raised over time: while most social theories explicitly take the everyday theorizing of the social actors as an important informant about social meaning, systemic constructivism neglects individual consciousness as not being important for the study of communication or social reality; furthermore, the process of making distinctions assumes the possibility of rather clear-cut distinctions, while it can be argued that most empirical phenomena and social references are characterized by inherent ambiguity and fuzziness (Latour 1999).

The empirical programme of constructivism

By contrast to the first two constructivist versions explored here, the empirical programme of constructivism argues that it is problematic to preassume any theory of construction. The study of construction processes should not be subject to pre-conceptualized assumption but, rather, analysed empirically (Latour 2005). The creation of 'reality', the 'world' and 'knowledge' is studied as the product of heterogeneous, situated and fragile activities (Knorr Cetina 1989). The research process is not primarily guided by theoretical premises, which tend to 'black-box' what would actually require explicit description and explanation. The empirical programme develops a specific repertoire of research devices and methodological practices guiding the empirical research process in all its openness, messiness and fragility (Law 2004). By doing so, the empirical programme is looking for the self-evident that is taken for granted and must be deconstructed by the research process, opening the black boxes of so-called social 'reality' (Latour 1999; 2005). As a consequence, this research programme is interested in studying the inherently controversial, heterogeneous, fragile nature of social phenomena.

This explains the prominent status of the sciences in this research programme. Scientific research as the locus of knowledge creation is a prototypical context for understanding the construction of 'true', 'objective', 'valid', 'natural' worldviews in modern societies (Knorr Cetina 2002; Latour and Woolgar 1986). Furthermore, this line of research is closely related to the so-called 'practice turn' in the social sciences (Bourdieu 1977; Foucault 1971; Schatzki, Knorr Cetina and von Savigny 2001). Both are interested in understanding how the 'stability' and 'objectivity' of 'reality' is created in mundane activities, situated actions and local practices. Finally, this explains the relation of this research programme to anthropological perspectives (Geertz 1973), which cultivate the creation of an alienated view on the self-evident. Neither pre-specified theories, as in systemic constructivism, nor everyday theories of the actors involved, as in the research programme of social construction, can guide the research process, but they must be empirically reconstructed and described in their creation (Latour 2005). The main preoccupation of research is thus to develop methodologies as research practices that allow us to study 'world creation' (Knorr Cetina 1989) as the continuous 'manufacturing' of knowledge under conditions of uncertainty (Knorr Cetina 2002).

This reconceptualization of research provides several insights: the empirical programme of constructivism not only challenges unquestioned dichotomies in the social sciences, but any foundations that are taken for granted (concern 4). This is relevant for the study of 'reality', 'knowledge' and 'fact', which cannot be taken for granted, but must be described in their creation (concern 1). In parallel, it is relevant for the study of 'agency', which cannot be seen as inherent to any 'individual' or 'organization', but must be seen as resulting from inscriptions and enacted networks (concern 3). As a consequence, this research programme always reflects epistemological issues, including the status of (scientific) 'knowledge' and the idiosyncratic procedures of (scientific) knowledge creation (concern 2). The research programme propagates an understanding of research practice that is concerned with the world 'as it could be' (Law 2004; Lury and Wakeford 2012), instead of focusing on the world 'as it is'. The criterion for 'good' research is the creation of unconventional, new worldviews and perspectives (Knorr Cetina 1989), which requires 'discovery technologies', not theories.

This perspective is related to multiple approaches that came about as part of the practice turn (Schatzki, Knorr Cetina and von Savigny 2001). Among others, it resonates with grounded theory-building (Strauss and Corbin 1990) and related pragmatist epistemologies (Joas 1992), emphasizing the creative nature of action and research (Joas 1992; Tsoukas and Knudsen 2002). Moreover, it is in line with the approaches of social practice (Foucault 1971; Bourdieu and Wacquant 1992), emphasizing the importance of reflecting the practice of doing research, shifting the focus from social theories to methodological issues (Latour 2005). For example, the empirical programme insists on 'symmetry' regarding the importance of objects, actors and actions as central for 'good' research (Knorr Cetina 1989), as well as on the 'relational' aspect of knowledge creation (Law 2004). It implies that what it explores in terms of the creation of 'reality' and the 'world' also holds for scientific research itself. It also implies that – while the other constructivist epistemologies argue for particular theoretical perspectives – the empirical programme of constructivism focuses on the heterogeneity and variety of situated mechanisms and idiosyncratic activities, relevant for the construction and stabilization of 'reality' in particular contexts (Knorr Cetina 1989; Law 2004).

Implications for strategy-as-practice research

We now turn to recent contributions and discussions of the strategy-as-practice research programme, as seen in the light of a constructivist paradigm. The discussion follows the 'disciplinary matrix' of the constructivist paradigm (Kuhn 1974). The matrix includes issue such as the perspective from which something is explained, the kind of questions that are asked and the modes of explanations identified as particularly promising and attractive by the research programme. As in the case of a laboratory experiment, the disciplinary matrix contours the possibilities and limitations of the knowledge that can be generated within the action spaces it delineates. In our understanding, the instantiation of the constructivist paradigm takes place in four dimensions.

Dimension 1. One important starting point for strategy-as-practice research is set out by saying that the social scene consists of 'practices, practitioners, and praxis', on the basis of which strategy-making, strategy processes and strategic outcomes can be described, interpreted and explained in new ways (Jarzabkowski, Balogun and Seidl 2007). This introduces an ontological convention. It defines the 'building blocks' and taken-for-granted 'constituents' that researchers accept as given for explaining particular phenomena, activities and processes (Rheinberger and Hagner 1997; Knorr Cetina 1989).

Dimension 2. Furthermore (and this is particularly central to a constructivist paradigm), there are epistemological questions implied by studying strategy, understood as types of knowledge (Elkana 1986) and modes of knowing (Tsoukas 2005; Grand and Ackeret 2012) implied in strategy-making. This implies the question of whether strategy can be seen as a predefined academic concept (Chandler 1990), a multifaceted construction process (Mantere and Vaara 2008) or an ex-post ascription of a certain pattern of actions that lead to a certain outcome (Mintzberg 1978).

Dimension 3. Moreover, addressing ontological and epistemological issues in this perspective also has consequences for the methodological dimension: it enables research to gain insights into strategy-making, strategy processes and the dynamic mechanisms of strategic outcomes affecting those who practise strategy every day as their profession (Schütz 1932), not least beyond the insights generated by established research areas within strategy research (Johnson, Melin and Whittington 2003). In the perspective of a constructivist paradigm, this addresses the issue of research methods as 'discovery technologies' (Knorr Cetina 1989).

Dimension 4. Finally, any research programme, particularly if viewed from a constructivist perspective, asks the 'normative question': why is it important and relevant to research strategy-making in organizations by focusing on strategy as practice? In which way does such research generate novel or relevant knowledge for practice, impact on practice or even contribute to a better world? The normative question is more important than sometimes assumed, because it shapes the kind of research interests, discourses and types of presentations that will be accepted in a particular research programme.

Focusing on practice: ontological issues

Practice as constructed, yet taken-for-granted reality

Strategy as practice studies how strategy is produced, stabilized and changed in organizations through 'practices, practitioners, and praxis' (Jarzabkowski, Balogun and Seidl 2007). This focus implies a particular ontology as well as 'ontological politics' (Mol 1999), defining what is seen as existing and thus constituting the taken-for-granted, unquestioned reality, while at the same time questioning the taken-for-grantedness of other 'things' (Latour 2005) such as 'strategy', 'process' or 'performance' that is characteristic for alternative ontologies in strategy research. Constructivist paradigms are characterized by explicitly addressing such ontological issues, refocusing scientific research from 'describing reality' to an exploration of 'reality construction' through scientific research and social practice (Knorr Cetina 1989; Schatzki, Knorr Cetina and von Savigny 2001): there is no unbiased correspondence between the 'reality out there' and our systems of representation. At the same time, it is essential to understand the importance of 'elements' that are taken for granted in any construction process. Social constructivism suggests a pragmatic approach: 'It will be enough, for our purposes, to define "reality" as a quality appertaining to phenomena that we recognize as having a being independent of our volition (we cannot "wish them away"), and to define "knowledge" as the certainty that phenomena are real and that they possess specific characteristics' (Berger and Luckmann 1967: 13, cited by Eberle 1992). Practices, practitioners and praxis can be understood as such realities within the strategy-as-practice research programme.

From activities to practices in context

A fundamental shift that comes with the SAP programme is the focus on social practices: how they are created, mobilized, actualized and changed in the everyday micro-activities of managers engaged in strategy-making (Johnson, Melin and Whittington 2003; Whittington 1996), and how activities become socially accepted patterns of action (Feldman and Orlikowski 2011; Vaara and Whittington 2012). The main inroad consists in opening the 'black box' of strategy as created in heterogeneous strategizing activities, instead of relying on taken-for-granted pre-conceptualizations of what strategy is and how strategy is made (Mintzberg 1971; 2009). The focus is on understanding the production of particular strategies through distributed activities and the mobilization of related practices (Johnson, Melin and Whittington 2003), which is not covered by existing strategy research (Johnson, Melin and Whittington 2003; Samra-Fredericks 2003; Whittington 1996). Furthermore, it is important to understand that practices are understood as socially accepted, functional heuristics on

how to decide and act. Practices are only necessary regarding recurrent, important issues. This is what constitutes the distinction from an ordinary activity (Knoblauch 2005; Orlikowski and Yates 1994). Eventually, these practices are so obvious that they are unquestioned and start to represent the objectified context for members of a community: '[S]ocial reality is practices' (Taylor 1985, cited by Schatzki 2005: 470). The routinized and collectively held repertoires of practices of an organization thus represent the most relevant context for strategy-making (Endrissat and von Arx 2013). This is an object of interest very close to the empirical programme of constructivism, arguing *ex ante* that every managerial activity and social interaction of people within and outside an organization can potentially lead to an idea, opportunity or initiative that can gain strategic importance.

From a single actor to dispersed agency and power

Understanding strategy creation from a constructivist perspective also implies that the empirical focus must be extended beyond the interaction of top management teams in formal settings dedicated to strategy. Middle managers (Balogun and Johnson 2004; Floyd and Lane 2000; Westley 1990) and specialized strategists (Grant 2003; Pettigrew 1985, Rouleau 2005), line managers and specialized units (Ahrens and Chapman 2007; Brown and Eisenhardt 1997; Orlikowski 2002), external stakeholders, including customers (Christensen and Bower 1996), investors (Bower and Gilbert 2005), strategic partners (Dyer and Singh 1998), technology partners (von Hippel and von Krogh 2003) and consultants are involved in strategy-making. A constructivist research approach abstains from any 'great man' concept of strategy-making. Instead, constructivism in particular treats everything as a continuously generated effect of a web of relations. Nothing has reality outside the enactment of these relations. There is no stable prime mover, but there is enactment and there is performance through a multitude of actors, practices and other actants, who enact together a more or less precarious reality (Law 2008). This implies that agency does not come automatically   from   practices   and   routines

(Feldman and Pentland 2003), heterogeneous actors or artefacts but, instead, lies in their 'embeddedness' in the network. It is these 'collective' qualities that make them 'strategic', on account of their relation to 'how an organization moves forward' (Rumelt 2011). In strategy-as-practice research, such concepts as recursiveness (Jarzabkowski 2004), styles of engagement (Chia and MacKay 2007) and leadership practices (Denis, Lamothe and Langley 2001) attempt to incorporate this relational aspect into the conceptualization of agency in strategy-making.

Practices as related to tools and artefacts

The multiple strategy tools, with artefacts involved, as well as the strategizing methods mobilized in an organization, are, on the one hand, an expression of multiple ways of systematizing strategizing activities, in addition to expressing strategic practices. The same holds for the multiple conceptual frameworks, models and tools in strategy research, which are an expression of different ways of conceptualizing such activities and practices. On the other hand, they can differ in their degree of 'generality', 'objectivity' and 'self-evidence', thus influencing the extent to which they gain their own agency (Latour and Woolgar 1986; Orlikowski 2000) and become relevant actants in the strategy-making process (Latour 2005). Routinization processes transform the usage of concepts and the enactment of particular patterns of action into stable structures and tangible references, which are used by the managers and researchers involved. From the perspective of a constructivist research programme, studying strategy-making suggests explicitly describing and reflecting the various construction technologies implied (Knorr Cetina 1989) that managers and researchers use to establish and maintain, but also to advance and change, particular strategy concepts and strategizing practices.

The strategy-as-practice research programme successfully complements strategy research by opening the black box of strategy-making. Constructivist research paradigms challenge the self-evidence of such processes, emphasizing the ontological issues implied by the identification of primary starting points for such descriptions, as well

as exploring how they shape our understanding of strategy-making. Thereby, constructivist paradigms have emphasized the importance of considering a multitude of heterogeneous activities, actors, tools and artefacts involved in strategy-making. Furthermore, they insist on the importance of understanding the creation, actualization and transformation processes involved in the generation of stabilized action patterns as repertoires of practices.

Framing strategy in relation to practice: epistemological issues

Double hermeneutic in conceptualizing strategy

SAP research emphasizes the importance of explicitly considering the multitude of strategy concepts that are enacted in practice. This raises epistemological issues concerning the status of different concepts of strategy, as well as the knowledge base involved in their description, interpretation and conceptualization. A 'double hermeneutic' is implied in the conceptualization of any social phenomenon (Giddens 1987), including 'strategy'. Scientific research is seen as studying a world that is already interpreted by the social actors involved in the constitution of this reality. Out of this 'first-order' knowledge, research produces 'second-order' descriptions, concepts and models. Scientific and practical knowledge creation on strategy and strategy-related issues can thus benefit from this interplay between first-order and second-order concepts. It leads to an ongoing actualization, revision and transformation of such concepts within and in between academic and practical approaches to strategy. Constructivist paradigms emphasize this mechanism as an important source of understanding, viewing practitioners themselves as researchers on the social fabric of strategy, mobilizing similar methods as social scientists (Schütz 1967 [1932]).

The implications for the strategy-as-practice research stream are twofold. First, as we build on first-order knowledge, it is useful to foster new forms of collaborative and dialogical research methodologies to learn from the practitioner's knowledge (Grand 2003). Second, strategy concepts are always historically bound and context-dependent phenomena that are in a constant state of becoming, depending on the productiveness of the exchange between praxis and academia (Tsoukas and Chia 2002).

Strategy concepts as constituted in interactions

SAP research thus emphasizes the situatedness of strategizing activities (Johnson, Melin and Whittington 2003) and strategy creation (Tsoukas and Chia 2002). Strategy-making takes place in concrete communicative interactions; it emerges from and gains relevance and significance in specific contexts, and it must be interpreted in the perspective of these contexts. Hence, words and ideas, concepts and terms, including concepts of 'strategy', cannot be understood independently of the language games, communicative interactions and sensemaking processes in which they are produced and actualized (Seidl 2007). This implies that similar activities have different meanings according to the contexts in which they occur, as well as depending on the particular perspectives of the actors involved (Engström and Blackler 2005; Samra-Fredericks 2003; Suchman 1987). The definition of what 'strategy' means must be seen to be processual (Van de Ven 1993). Often, parallel worlds of a strategy discourse exist. One world is more aligned with the expectations implied in strategy textbooks and known strategy concepts (Porter 1985). And there is a living world of strategy-making, which is messy, implicit and embodied. Hence, the standardized concepts of strategy and the locally embedded and embodied concepts of strategy are intertwined within a singular practice or practitioner. This raises the epistemological issue of how academic research is able to reconstruct an 'objective picture' of strategy-making in practice when it is exactly the academic output that holds as a best-practice benchmark in organizations.

Strategy in the face of multiple uncertainties

'Strategy' is often conceptualized as crucial for organizational agency in future-oriented, fundamentally uncertain, contested or open situations (Schendel and Hitt 2007). It is in these situations that it is challenging, but important, to build and stabilize strategy concepts and strategizing

practices as taken for granted and self-evident (Gomez and Jones 2000). Binding concepts of performance, established repertoires of methods and unquestioned issues are central for productive, coordinated strategy-making under conditions of uncertainty and ambiguity, but also for strategy research itself. In this perspective, strategy-making itself can be understood as an epistemological practice (Spender 1996; Tsoukas 1996; 2005). Such justified concepts are necessary to conclude otherwise endless scientific and managerial discussions about the appropriate conceptualization of 'strategy' and infinite regresses of defining such references as 'performance'. Accordingly, it is essential to distinguish between three sources of uncertainty (Gomez and Jones 2000; Karpik 2010; Grand 2015): uncertainty due to the impossibility of knowing the future ('Knightian uncertainty': Gomez and Jones 2000), due to the impossibility of overseeing distributed activities and processes ('Keynesian uncertainty': Gomez and Jones 2000) or due to the contingency of valuation ('Karpikian uncertainty': Karpik 2010). Strategy-making and strategy research in the face of these uncertainties are thus at one and the same time difficult (systemic constructivism would argue: it is impossible) and particularly important (systemic constructivism would argue: it is necessary).

Stabilizing strategy concepts in practice

The enactment of formalized strategy concepts is changing across situations and over time, and it must therefore be (re)created, actualized and confirmed in each situation. Strategy-as-practice research studies the heterogeneity of concepts and practices, and the reduction and extension of this heterogeneity, as central approaches to reduce uncertainty (Grand and Ackeret 2012). Talking about strategy-making and strategizing practices cannot automatically imply that they are 'stable'. From a constructivist perspective, they must, rather, be seen as 'stabilized', emerging through multiple, dispersed processes of institutionalization, socialization and routinization (Vaara and Whittington 2012; Berger and Luckmann 1967). To transcend the contingency of decisions and actions, managers use strategy concepts that are stabilized and anchored as self-evident and unquestionable. In this context, the practice turn provides important insights, conceptualizing construction and stabilization as discourse formation (Foucault 1978), language games (Wittgenstein 1967 [1951]), circulating references (Latour 1999), translation (Callon 1986), black-boxing (Latour 2005), materialization (Orlikowski 2000; 2002) or routinization (Gomez and Jones 2000). Dispersed strategy-related activities are coordinated in the organization because of the formation of shared expectations and 'objectivized' interpretations. Tools and methods become recognized as self-evidently relevant for strategy-making (Bower and Gilbert 2007). Practice communities not only actualize routines of strategy-making but also construct their identity as those who make strategy (Brown and Duguid 2001). The notion of 'porte parole' stresses that the ability to construct reality depends on such positions of power (Bourdieu 1982). They condense repertoires of strategy-making in the form of taken-for-granted templates, 'normal' ways of representation, visualizations and documentations (Orlikowski 2000; 2002).

A constructivist research programme brings the contingency of 'strategy', as well as the uncertainty and ambiguity of related concepts of performance, to the centre of research (Gomez and Jones 2000; Karpik 2010). As a result, strategic management as an academic discipline, scholarly field and managerial practice has an impact on the stabilization and destabilization of particular definitions within particular organizations and scientific and managerial communities alike. The impact of heterogeneous actors, activities and artefacts on such stabilization or destabilization, and thus on the confirmation or deconstruction of established power structures, is identified by the empirical programme of constructivism as essential for any in-depth understanding of these processes (Callon 1986; Latour 2005). The dynamic interaction and reflexive relationship between the construction of strategy *in managerial practice* and the construction of strategy *in strategy research* – between situated, subjective concepts of strategy and generalized, objectivizing conceptualizations – is a central precondition for conducting strategy research (Tsoukas 2005; Rüegg-Stürm and Grand 2014).

Research as practice: methodological issues

Empirical research as questioning and pre-assuming stabilized concepts

The decisive activities in shaping the strategy of an organization can only be identified ex post (Bower 1970; Burgelman 1994; Johnson 1987; Mintzberg and McHugh 1985; Pettigrew 1987). While research in the area of strategic management in most cases pre-assumes that it is clear what 'strategic' means, however, the SAP research programme emphasizes the need to empirically follow, describe, understand and reflect the ongoing construction of what 'strategic' means (Latour 1999; Callon 1986: Langley 1989). This implies that the concept of 'strategy' is so central, but at the same time not self-evident, that it must be explicitly reflected, conceptualized and defined in any strategy research project. Paradoxically, strategy-making under uncertainty requires that taken-for-granted strategy concepts and strategizing practices have to be stabilized as given, knowing that they are contingent and potentially questionable. This is in line with a constructivist research programme, which focuses on the dynamic interplay of confirming and transforming such concepts and practices. The 'practice turn' in the social sciences emphasizes promising perspectives here, including the concepts of routines as routinization (Feldman 2003), habitus as the embodied repertoire of practices that define whether someone is part of a particular community (Bourdieu 1977), structuration as the continuous confirmation and adaptation of action patterns (Giddens 1984), black-boxing as the activities and artefacts that translate and transform situated ideas into stable references (Latour 1999), conventions as a way of understanding the constructive but unquestioned nature of the references (Boltanski and Thévenot 1991; Gomez and Jones 2000) and common knowledge that results from the collective objectivation and typification of embedded experiences and situated interactions (Berger and Luckmann 1967; Wenger 1998). Exploring the creation of 'strategy concepts' and their situated enactment becomes a focus in itself (Tsoukas and Knudsen 2002; Vaara and Whittington 2012).

Empirical research as generating novel descriptions, interpretations, and explanations

Constructivist paradigms have a particular view on the generative qualities of scientific research: Research not only discusses the world 'as it is' but reflects the contingency of 'reality' and 'knowledge' as it is, which leads to an interest in identifying, exploring and describing possible worlds 'as they could be' (Latour 2005; Chia and Holt 2009), or even in changing the world 'as it is' (Hacking 1999). This implies that it is essential for research to explicitly consider the inherent uncertainty and openness of any social interaction and future development as crucial (Gomez and Jones 2000). As a consequence, research itself must be seen as constructing 'reality' and 'knowledge', emphasizing the creativity and self-reflexivity of research. In particular, this includes a conceptualization of strategy-making and strategy research from the perspective of the creativity of action (Joas 1992), situated action (Suchman 1987) or interpretative flexibility (Callon 1986). Strategy-as-practice research considers this creativity in strategy-making and the distinctive forms of how this happens in practice fields (Tsoukas and Knudsen 2002). Such creative reinvention of strategy practices explains why taken-for-granted references and practices transform themselves across situations and over time (Joas 1992). Stories and repertoires, tools and artefacts referring to strategy are never unambiguous. They have to be reinterpreted and recreated in any given new situation. The same holds for the mobilization of research methods as inventive methods (Lury and Wakeford 2012).

From the perspective of constructivist paradigms, research methods have the role of enabling the study of the creation and construction, as well as the deconstruction and transformation, of important black boxes such as 'strategies' or 'strategizing' activities. Furthermore, strategy research must be seen as creative and generative itself, not focusing primarily on descriptions, interpretations or explanations of the world 'as it is' but on opening up for new perspectives, alternative interpretations and novel explanations, in the sense of construction technologies (Knorr Cetina 1989) as well as inventive methods (Lury and Wakeford 2012). In this way, the constructivist paradigms introduced above differ in their approaches to the generative quality of research. The research programme of social construction builds on the inherent creativity of social action itself, exploring 'strategy-making' as a generative practice, and thus as a source for novel insights into alternative approaches to strategy. Systemic constructivism sees its conceptual contributions as triggers for establishing novel perspectives on strategy. Finally, the empirical programme of constructivism challenges the taken-for-granted nature of many concepts in strategizing activities and in strategy research, at the same time exploring their necessity and contingency.

Reflecting practical relevance: normative issues

An underlying ambition of the strategy-as-practice research programme has always been to develop results that are of 'practical relevance' (Splitter and Seidl 2011). By doing so, the programme implicitly assumes that such relevance results directly or indirectly from explicitly considering the praxis involved in strategy-making (Johnson *et al.* 2007). At the same time, it is exactly this ambition that is still seen as unfulfilled by most researchers who have been working from the perspective of the SAP research programme so far (Vaara and Whittington 2012). Constructivist epistemologies allow the identification of some specific issues and challenges implied in the attempt to claim 'practical relevance'. If the world is seen as 'constructed', as it is argued in constructivist epistemologies, this implies that 'it could be otherwise'. Obviously, this awareness of contingency is a methodological issue, but it can also be seen as the starting point for changing the world as it is, and thus as a pragmatic and normative stance, in various degrees of engagement (Hacking 1999).

This is of importance for the issue of the 'practical relevance', as it identifies different types of relevance (Grand 2003). Four types of engagement are particularly interesting (as discussed by Hacking 1999).

First, a constructivist perspective can be conceptualized as a methodology emphasizing the construction mechanisms underlying particular phenomena. The value of an *'analytical' engagement* (Foucault 1971) lies in reconstructing phenomena as they are and identifying alternatives of how they could be. Emphasizing such alternatives is a very implicit and indirect way of identifying potentially critical aspects of a current strategic practice or an established theoretical conceptualization. It can be a reference for more explicitly exploring how and why these alternatives have not emerged so far, however, for example because they have not been supported by established power structures (Guba and Lincoln 1994), have been purposefully neglected (Elkana 1986) or are discursively marginalized (Foucault 1971).

Second, this can lead to an *'ironic' engagement*, which means that the contingency of a phenomenon is taken as a starting point for ironically discussing positions that accept phenomena as 'real' or 'objective' (Rorty 1989). To address such topics ironically implies a distant mode of commenting, framing and criticizing, however, without necessarily proposing alternative perspectives or practices. It remains for others in strategy research and strategic management to take up such criticism and turn it into actual changes in the strategy concepts and strategizing practices used in research projects or mobilized in organizations, and thus to develop alternative views, possibilities and opportunities.

Third, based on a normative valuation of a phenomenon, this can lead to a *'reformist' engagement*, in which the fact that something could be otherwise is used to criticize the phenomenon as it is (Hacking 1999: 40); it is here that we can see the transition towards a practical engagement (Dahrendorf 2005; Elkana 1986). Here, critique turns into correction, the initial understanding of what critique is for: to correct what is currently present into something better (Walzer 1988).We can think of many different ways in which strategy research and strategic management can jointly engage in such reformist engagements: through joint research projects generating new descriptions, interpretations and explanations; through many different modes of executive education (Mintzberg 2009); and through innovation and development partnerships between academia and practice (Rüegg-Stürm and Grand 2014).

Fourth, this can lead to a *'transformative' engagement*, which opts for fundamental change in the conceptualization and practice of strategy-making as the only possibility of changing and transforming the phenomenon and praxis as it is. Especially in recent attempts to rethink strategy-making from a philosophical perspective, for example on the basis of process ontology (Chia and Holt 2009), reflexive epistemology (Spender 1996; Tsoukas 2005) or inventive methods (Law 2004; Lury and Wakeford 2012), we see various suggestions for rethinking how strategy research is understood and realized, as well as how it re-shapes strategic management (Vaara and Whittington 2012). Such perspectives explicitly or implicitly mobilize the normative, political and ideological critique implied in many practice theories and epistemologies (Foucault 1971; Bourdieu and Wacquant 1992; Schatzki, Knorr Cetina and von Savigny 2001; Thévenot 2006; Latour 2005).

These degrees of constructivist engagement are an inherent aspect of a constructivist paradigm and its realization in the strategy-as-practice research programme. Throughout its development as a research programme, it has not only focused on describing the practice of strategy making, as well as reflecting research practice in relation to strategy making, but explored alternative ways and future possibilities of making strategy (Mantere and Vaara 2008; Whittington 2007).

Conclusion

A constructivist research programme in strategy research implies the development of alienating perspectives as they are established and changed in strategy research and strategizing practice. Although constructivist epistemologies differ in their premises, they thus share a scepticism about anything that is simply taken for granted, self-evident or unquestioned (Hacking 1999). At the same time, more recent perspectives in these epistemologies share an emphasis on understanding better how taken-for-granted, self-evident, unquestioned references, concepts and practices for robust managerial action and scientific research are emerging, are enacted and are established, given the fundamental uncertainty and ambiguity implied (Gomez and Jones 2000). From the perspective of constructivist epistemologies, it would be of particular importance to transcend some fundamental opposition that underlies the distinction between strategy as practice as a new research programme and strategy research as it is understood in dominant academic and managerial discourses (Johnson *et al.* 2007). In particular, five points are important.

Strategy research should emphasize the importance of constantly unpacking and *deconstructing fundamental, taken-for-granted concepts* in strategy research and strategic management. Opening the black boxes and disassembling and reassembling strategy (Latour 2005) can be identified as a primary focus. Obviously, this focus is ambiguous, as the pre-assumption of unquestioned black boxes is a precondition for establishing a research programme. It is this ambiguity of relying on and at the same time deconstructing strategy-related black boxes that ensures the dynamism and creativity of this research programme, however.

In order to be able to disassemble the black box 'strategy' and strategy-related black boxes, it is important to *cultivate alienating perspectives* (Latour 2005). One common pattern of constructivist epistemologies is exactly this alienating effect, which is often criticized for its usage of abstract terminology (Luhmann 2002; Latour 2005). This is central to these research programmes, however, because they explicitly do not build on common sense or everyday theorizing concerning central concepts and terms. They introduce concepts and terms that have to gain meaning through their translation in particular contexts and specific situations (Latour 1999). This leads to an ongoing reflection and reconstruction of concepts and terms in research practice.

It is exactly the insistence on alienating perspectives that, at the same time, creates a precondition for being able to *consider particularities, contexts and idiosyncrasies* in empirical research. A related approach in empirical research is the attempt to exclude any theoretical perspective and concept from the initial entry into the field (Glaser and Strauss 1967). Obviously, both extremes – alienation through abstraction and alienation through the absence of abstract notions – are impossible

to realize in research practice (Latour 1999). To take them as references leads to a continuous reflection of the premises and black boxes, however, which is important for any research programme in the perspective of constructivist epistemologies (Law 2004).

This reflection of research indicates that *research is creation and construction*. Whereas traditional epistemologies discuss the inherent creativity of research as a problem, which must therefore be disciplined through particular methodological tools, constructivist epistemologies would, on the contrary, insist on the central importance of creativity for (good) research (Joas 1992). In this line of thought, the empirical programme of constructivism explicitly emphasizes the importance of understanding methodology as 'discovery technologies' (Knorr Cetina 1989). Research methodologies are understood as enabling, ensuring and fostering creativity in research practice (as it is discussed in the science studies; see Knorr Cetina 2002).

If research is interpreted as creation and construction, it needs to be enabled by particular *methodologies, technologies and practices of creation or construction* (Knorr Cetina 1989). This implies that any closure of a research programme, any predefinition of central concepts and terms or any unquestioned foundation of research on one particular theory must be understood as relying on black boxes (Latour 1999). As discussed above, such black boxes are necessary for research practice, but they are also always inherently problematic at the same time (Elkana 1986); they are an expression of a particular thought style and thought community (Fleck 1980) that result from particular creation and construction processes.

From the perspective of constructivist paradigms, strategy research would focus especially on the *creation and construction, routinization and stabilization, translation and transformation of strategy concepts and strategizing practices*. In this respect, it is important to study the self-evident, unquestioned qualities of such concepts and practices at the same time, as well as their situatedness, idiosyncrasy and contingency. Strategies and strategizing practices are objects that strategy research and strategic management cannot assume as given, and neither are they only contingent. Strategies and strategizing practices are the result of continuous scientific and practical (re)construction processes, through the creative activities of the organizational actors and strategy researchers involved, and through interactions between organizational actors and strategy researchers. Specifically, constructivist paradigms suggest that SAP research should focus on advancing strategy research and the practice of strategic management, by exploring the situated construction of strategy concepts and strategizing practices, the importance of explicitly considering the uncertainty implied in strategizing, the importance of routinization processes for the establishment of strategy concepts and strategizing practices in specific organizational contexts, and the deconstruction of such concepts and practices, as it takes place in any process of translation and transformation.

References

Ahrens, T., and Chapman, C. S. (2007), 'Management accounting as practice', *Accounting, Organizations and Society*, 32/1: 1–27.

Balogun, J., and Johnson, G. (2004), 'Organizational restructuring and middle manager sensemaking', *Academy of Management Journal*, 47/4: 523–49.

Bateson, G. (1972), *Steps to an Ecology of Mind: Collected Essays in Anthropology, Psychiatry, Evolution, and Epistemology*. University of Chicago Press.

Berger, P. L., and Luckmann, T. (1967), *The Social Construction of Reality: A Treatise in the Sociology of Knowledge*. London: Penguin Books.

Boltanski, L., and Thévenot, L. (1991), *De la justification: Les économies de la grandeur*. Paris: Éditions Gallimard.

Bourdieu, P. (1977), *Outline of a Theory of Practice*. Cambridge University Press.

—— (1982), *Ce que parler veut dire*. Paris: Fayard.

Bourdieu, P., and Wacquant, L. (1992), *An Invitation to Reflexive Sociology*. University of Chicago Press.

Bower, J. L. (1970), *Managing the Resource Allocation Process: A Study of Corporate Planning and Investment*. Cambridge, MA: Harvard Business School Press.

Bower, J. L., and Gilbert, C. G. (2005), *From Resource Allocation to Strategy*. Oxford University Press.

Bower, J. L., and Gilbert, C. G. (2007), 'How managers' everyday decisions create or destroy your company's strategy', *Harvard Business Review*, 85/2: 72–9.

Brown, J. S., and Duguid, P. (2001), 'Knowledge and organization: a social-practice perspective', *Organization Science*, 12/2: 198–213.

Brown, S. L., and Eisenhardt, K. M. (1997), 'The art of continuous change: linking complexity theory and time-paced evolution in relentlessly shifting organizations', *Administrative Science Quarterly*, 42/1: 1–34.

Burgelman, R. A. (1994), 'Fading memories: a process theory of strategic business exit in dynamic environments', *Administrative Science Quarterly*, 39/1: 24–56.

Callon, M. (1986), 'Some elements of a sociology of translation: domestication of the scallops and the fishermen of St Brieuc Bay', in Law, J. (ed.), *Power, Action and Belief: A New Sociology of Knowledge?*: 196–223. London: Routledge & Kegan Paul.

Chandler, A. D. (1990), *Strategy and Structure: Chapters in the History of the American Industrial Enterprise*. Cambridge, MA: MIT Press.

Chia, R., and Holt, R. (2009), *Strategy without Design: The Silent Efficacy of Indirect Action*. Cambridge University Press.

Chia, R., and MacKay, B. (2007), 'Post-processual challenges for the emerging strategy-as-practice perspective: discovering strategy in the logic of practice', *Human Relations*, 60/1: 217–42.

Christensen, C. M., and Bower, J. L. (1996), 'Customer power, strategic investment, and the failure of leading firms', *Strategic Management Journal*, 17/3: 197–218.

Dahrendorf, R. (2005), *Engagierte Beobachter: Die Intellektuellen und die Versuchungen der Zeit*. Vienna: Passagen Verlag.

Denis, J.-L., Lamothe, L., and Langley, A. (2001), 'The dynamics of collective leadership and strategic change in pluralistic organizations', *Academy of Management Journal*, 44/4: 809–37.

Dyer, J. H., and Singh, H. (1998), 'The relational view: cooperative strategy and sources of interorganizational competitive advantage', *Academy of Management Review*, 23/4: 660–79.

Eberle, T. (1992), 'A new paradigm for the sociology of knowledge: "the social construction of reality" after 25 years', *Schweizerische Zeitschrift für Soziologie*, 18/2: 493–502.

Elkana, Y. (1986), *Anthropologie der Erkenntnis*. Frankfurt: Suhrkamp Verlag.

Endrissat, N., and von Arx, W. (2013), 'Leadership practices and context: two sides of the same coin', *Leadership*, 9/2: 278–304.

Engström, V., and Blackler, F. (2005), 'On the life of the object', *Organization*, 12/3: 307–30.

Feldman, M. S. (2003), 'A performative perspective on stability and change in organizational routines', *Industrial and Corporate Change*, 12/4:727–52.

Feldman, M. S., and Orlikowski, W. J. (2011), 'Theorizing practice and practicing theory', *Organization Science*, 22/5: 1240–53.

Feldman, M. S., and Pentland, B. T. (2003), 'Reconceptualizing organizational routines as a source of flexibility and change', *Administrative Science Quarterly*, 48/1: 94–118.

Fleck, L. (1980), *Entstehung und Entwicklung einer wissenschaftlichen Tatsache: Einführung in die Lehre vom Denkstil und Denkkollektiv*. Frankfurt: Suhrkamp Verlag.

Floyd, S. W., and Lane, P. J. (2000), 'Strategizing throughout the organization: managing role conflict in strategic renewal', *Academy of Management Review*, 25/1: 145–75.

Foucault, M. (1971), *Die Ordnung der Dinge: Eine Archäologie der Humanwissenschaften*. Frankfurt: Suhrkamp Verlag.

(1978), *The History of Sexuality*, vol. I, *An Introduction*. New York: Random House.

Geertz, C. (1973), *The Interpretation of Cultures: Selected Essays*. New York: Basic Books.

Giddens, A. (1984), *The Constitution of Society*. Cambridge: Polity.

(1987), *Social Theory and Modern Sociology*. Cambridge: Polity.

Glaser, B. G., and Strauss, A. (1967), *The Discovery of Grounded Theory: Strategies for Qualitative Research*. Chicago: Aldine.

Glasersfeld, V. (1995), *Radical Constructivism: A Way of Knowing and Learning*. London: Falmer Press.

Golsorkhi, D., Rouleau, L., Seidl, D., and Vaara, E. (eds.) (2010), *Cambridge Handbook of Strategy as Practice*. Cambridge University Press.

Gomez, P.-Y., and Jones, B. C. (2000), 'Conventions: an interpretation of deep structure in organizations', *Organization Science*, 11/6: 696–708.

Goodman, N. (1987), *Ways of Worldmaking*. Indianapolis: Hackett.

Grand, S. (2003), 'Praxisrelevanz versus Praxisbezug der Forschung in der Managementforschung', *Die Betriebswirtschaft*, 63/5: 599–604.

(2012), 'Routines, strategies and management: engaging for recurrent creation "at the edge"', *Habilitation* manuscript. University of St Gallen, Switzerland.

Grand, S., and Ackeret, A. (2012), 'Managing knowledge: a process view', in Schultz, M., Maguire, S., Langley, A., and Tsoukas, H. (eds.), *Constructing Identity in and around Organizations*: 261–305. Oxford University Press.

Grand, S., and MacLean, D. (2007), 'Researching the practice of strategy as creative action: toward an action theoretics foundation of the research program', paper presented at the twenty-third European Group for Organizational Studies colloquium, Vienna, 7 July.

Grant, R. M. (2003), 'Strategic planning in a turbulent environment: evidence from the oil majors', *Strategic Management Journal*, 24/6: 491–517.

Guba, E., and Lincoln, Y. (1994), 'Competing paradigms in qualitative research', in Denzin, N., and Lincoln, Y. (eds.), *Handbook of Qualitative Research*: 105–17. Thousand Oaks, CA: Sage.

Hacking, I. (1999), *The Social Construction of What?* Cambridge, MA: Harvard University Press.

Husserl, E. (1931), *Cartesianische Meditationen: Eine Einleitung in die Phänomenologie*. Hamburg: Meiner.

Jarzabkowski, P. (2004), 'Strategy as practice: recursiveness, adaptation, and practices-in-use', *Organization Studies*, 25/1: 529–60.

Jarzabkowski, P., Balogun, J., and Seidl, D. (2007), 'Strategizing: the challenges of a practice perspective', *Human Relations*, 60/1: 5–27.

Jarzabkowski, P., and Spee, P. (2009), 'Strategy-as-practice: a review and future directions for the field', *International Journal of Management Reviews*, 11/1: 69–95.

Joas, H. (1992), *Die Kreativität des Handelns*. Frankfurt: Suhrkamp Verlag.

Johnson, G. (1987), *Strategic Change and the Management Process*. Oxford: Blackwell.

Johnson, G., Langley, A., Melin, L., and Whittington, R. (2007), *The Practice of Strategy: Research Directions and Resources*. Cambridge University Press.

Johnson, G., Melin, L., and Whittington, R. (2003), 'Guest editors' introduction: micro strategy and strategizing: towards an activity-based view', *Journal of Management Studies*, 40/1: 3–22.

Karpik, L. (2010), '*Valuing the Unique: The Economics of Singularities*. Princeton University Press.

Knights, D., and Morgan, G. (1991), 'Corporate strategy, organizations, and subjectivity: a critique', *Organization Studies*, 12/2: 251–73.

Knoblauch, H. (2005), *Wissenssoziologie*. Konstanz: UVK Verlag.

Knorr Cetina, K. (1981), *The Manufacture of Knowledge: An Essay on the Constructivist and Contextual Nature of Science*. Oxford: Pergamon Press.

Knorr Cetina, K. (1989), 'Spielarten des Konstruktivismus: einige Notizen und Anmerkungen', *Soziale Welt*, 40/1–2: 86–96.

(2002), *Die Fabrikation von Erkenntnis: Zur Anthropologie der Naturwissenschaft: Erweiterte Neuaissenschaft*. Frankfurt: Suhrkamp Verlag.

Kuhn, T. S. (1974), 'Second thoughts on paradigms', in Suppe, F. (ed.), *The Structure of Scientific Theories*: 459–82. Urbana: University of Illinois Press.

(1996), *The Structure of Scientific Revolutions*, 3rd edn. University of Chicago Press.

Langley, A. (1989), 'In search of rationality: the purposes behind the use of formal analysis in organizations', *Administrative Science Quarterly*, 34/4: 598–631.

Latour, B. (1996), 'On actor–network theory: a few clarifications plus more than a few complications', *Soziale Welt*, 47/4: 369–81.

(1999), *Pandora's Hope: Essays on the Reality of Science Studies*. Cambridge, MA: Harvard University Press.

(2005), *Reassembling the Social: An Introduction to Actor–Network-Theory*. Oxford University Press.

Latour, B., and Woolgar, S. (1986), *Laboratory Life: The Construction of Scientific Facts*, 2nd edn. Princeton University Press.

Law, J. (2004), *After Method: Mess in Social Science Research*. Abingdon: Routledge.

(2008), 'Actor network theory and material semiotics', in Turner, B. S. (ed.), *The New Blackwell Companion to Social Theory*: 141–58. Oxford: Wiley-Blackwell.

Luckmann, T. (1992), 'Social construction and after', *Perspectives,* 15/2: 4–5.

Luhmann, N. (1986), 'The autopoiesis of social systems', in Geyer, F., and van der Zouwen, J. (eds.), *Sociocybernetic Paradoxes: Observation, Control and Evolution of Self-Steering Systems*: 176–92. London: Sage.

(1996), *Social Systems*. Redwood City, CA: Stanford University Press.

(2002), *Einführung in die Systemtheorie*. Heidelberg: Carl-Auer-Systeme Verlag.

Lury, C., and Wakeford, N. (eds.) (2012), *Inventive Methods: The Happening of the Social*. London: Routledge.

Mantere, S., and Vaara, E. (2008), 'On the problem of participation in strategy: a critical discursive perspective', *Organization Science*, 19/2: 341–58.

Maturana, H., and Varela, F. (1987), *The Tree of Knowledge: The Biological Roots of Human Understanding*. Boston: Shambhala.

Mintzberg, H. (1971), 'Managerial work: analysis from observation', *Management Science*, 18/2: 97 –110.

(1978), 'Patterns in strategy formation', *Management Science*, 24/9: 934–48.

(2009), *Managing*. San Francisco: Berrett-Koehler.

Mintzberg, H., and McHugh, A. (1985), 'Strategy formation in an adhocracy', *Administrative Science Quarterly*, 30/2: 160–97.

Mol, A. (1999), 'Ontological politics: a word and some questions', in Law, J., and Hassard, J. (eds.), *Actor Network Theory and After*: 74–89. Oxford: Blackwell.

Orlikowski, W. J. (2000), 'Using technology and constituting structures: a practice lens for studying technology in organizations', *Organization Science*, 11/4: 404–28.

Orlikowski, W. J. (2002), 'Knowing in practice: enacting a collective capability in distributive organizing', *Organization Science*, 13/3: 249–73.

Orlikowski, W. J., and Yates, J. (1994), 'Genre repertoire: the structuring of communicative practices in organizations', *Administrative Science Quarterly*, 39/4: 541–74.

Pettigrew, A. M. (1985), *The Awakening Giant: Continuity and Change in Imperial Chemical Industries*. Oxford: Blackwell.

(1987), 'Context and action in the transformation of the firm', *Journal of Management Studies* 24/6: 649–70.

Porter, M. E. (1985), *Competitive Advantage: Creating and Sustaining Superior Performance*. New York: Free Press.

Rheinberger, H. J., and Hagner, M. (1997), 'Plädoyer für eine Wissenschaftsgeschichte des Experiments', *Theory in Biosciences*, 116/1: 11–32.

Rorty, R. (1989), *Contingency, Irony, and Solidarity*. Cambridge University Press.

Rouleau, L. (2005), 'Micro-practices of strategic sensemaking and sensegiving: how middle managers interpret and sell change every day', *Journal of Management Studies*, 42/7: 1413–41.

Rüegg-Stürm, J., and Grand, S. (2014), *Das St Galler Management-Modell: 4. Generation: Einführung*. Bern: Haupt.

Rumelt, R. (2011), *Good Strategy Bad Strategy: The Difference and Why It Matters*. New York: Crown Business.

Samra-Fredericks, D. (2003), 'Strategizing as lived experience and strategists' everyday efforts to shape strategic direction', *Journal of Management Studies*, 40/1: 141–74.

Schatzki, T. R. (2005), 'Peripheral vision: the sites of organizations', *Organization Studies*, 26/3: 465–84.

Schatzki, T. R., Knorr Cetina, K., and von Savigny, E. (eds.) (2001), *The Practice Turn in Contemporary Theory*. London: Routledge.

Schendel, D., and Hitt, M. A. (2007), 'Comments from the editors: introduction to volume 1', *Strategic Entrepreneurship Journal*, 1/1: 1–60.

Schütz, A. (1932), *Der sinnhafte Aufbau der sozialen Welt*. Frankfurt: Suhrkamp Verlag.

(1967 [1932]), *The Phenomenology of the Social World*. Evanston, IL: Northwestern University Press.

Seidl, D. (2007), 'General strategy concepts and the ecology of strategy discourses: a systemic-discursive perspective', *Organization Studies*, 28/2: 197–218.

Spender, J. C. (1996), 'Making knowledge the basis of a dynamic theory of the firm', *Strategic Management Journal*, 17/S2: 45–62.

Splitter, V., and Seidl, D. (2011), 'Does practice-based research on strategy lead to practically relevant knowledge? Implications of a Bourdieusian perspective', *Journal of Applied Behavioral Science*, 47/1: 98–120.

Strauss, A., and Corbin, J. (1990), *Basics of Qualitative Research: Techniques and Procedures for Developing Grounded Theory*. Newbury Park, CA: Sage.

Suchman, L. (1987), *Plans and Situated Actions: The Problem of Human–Machine Communication*. Cambridge University Press.

Taylor, C. (1985), *Philosophical Papers*, vol. I, *Human Agency and Language*. Cambridge University Press.

Thévenot, L. (2006), *L'action au pluriel: Sociologie des régimes d'engagement*. Paris: Éditions La Découverte.

Tsoukas, H. (1996), 'The firm as a distributed knowledge system: a constructionist approach', *Strategic Management Journal*, 17/S2: 11–25.

(2005), *Complex Knowledge: Studies in Organizational Epistemology*. Oxford University Press.

Tsoukas, H., and Chia, R. (2002), 'On organizational becoming: rethinking organizational change', *Organization Science*, 13/5: 567–82.

Tsoukas, H., and Knudsen, C. (2002), 'The conduct of strategy research', in Pettigrew, A. M., Thomas, H., and Whittington, R. (eds.), *Handbook of Strategy and Management*: 411–35. London: Sage.

Vaara, E., and Whittington, R. (2012), 'Strategy-as-practice: taking social practices seriously', *Academy of Management Annals*, 6/1: 285–336.

Van de Ven, A. H. (1993), 'Managing the process of organizational innovation', in Huber, G. P., and Glick, W. (eds.), *Organizational Change and Redesign: Ideas and Insights for Improving Performance*: 269–94. New York: Oxford University Press.

Von Foerster, H. (1981), *Observing Systems*. Seaside, CA: Intersystems Publications.

Von Hippel, E., and von Krogh, G. (2003), 'Open source software and the "private-collective" innovation model: issues for organization science', *Organization Science*, 14/2: 209–23.

Walzer, M. (1988), *The Company of Critics: Social Criticism and Political Commitment in the Twentieth Century*. New York: Basic Books.

Watzlawick, P. (ed.) (1984), *The Invented Reality: How Do We Know What We Believe We Know?* New York: W. W. Norton.

Weick, K. E. (1979), *The Social Psychology of Organizing*, 2nd edn. New York: McGraw-Hill.

Wenger, E. (1998), *Communities of Practice: Learning, Meaning and Identity*. Cambridge University Press.

Westley, F. (1990), 'Middle managers and strategy: microdynamics of inclusion', *Strategic Management Journal*, 11/5: 337–51.

Whittington, R. (1996), 'Strategy as practice', *Long Range Planning*, 29/5: 731–35.

(2007), 'Strategy practice and strategy process: family differences and the sociological eye', *Organization Studies*, 28/10: 1575–86.

Wittgenstein, L. (1967 [1951]), *Philosophical Investigations*, repr. edn. Oxford: Blackwell.

Constructing contribution in strategy-as-practice research

KATHARINA DITTRICH, KAREN GOLDEN-BIDDLE, ELANA FELDMAN and KAREN LOCKE

As with all knowledge-creating communities, strategy-as-practice scholarship constitutes itself through the production of networks of texts that frame and focus topics of interest. SAP scholarship seeks to advance knowledge in 'the doing of strategy: who does it, what they do, how they do it, what they use, and what implications this has for shaping strategy' (Jarzabkowski and Spee 2009: 69). In mapping the growing work in this area (Jarzabkowski and Spee 2009; Vaara and Whittington 2012), reviews have shown that recent SAP texts advance a research agenda developed in foundational publications (such as those of Jarzabkowski, Balogun and Seidl 2007; Johnson *et al.* 2007; and Whittington 2006) and contribute to strategic management by moving 'beyond the strategy discipline's usual focus on economic performance *per se*' (Vaara and Whittington 2012: 3) to actively integrate social theories of practice and broaden the scope of outcomes regarded as important to study.

Although these reviews discern specific findings and a general understanding of what knowledge is being produced, they yield little insight into *how* SAP authors position their work and make claims of knowledge regarded as *contributions* by the academic community. Understanding how authors craft arguments to persuade an intended audience is important, because written texts 'do not simply array "facts" and evidence logically' (Locke and Golden-Biddle 1997: 1060) but, rather, use certain rhetorical strategies to convey novelty and even surprise vis-à-vis existing knowledge (Davis 1971).

In order to consider how strategy-as-practice research constructs opportunities for contribution, its written texts must be regarded as 'first-order data' and examined directly for rhetorical strategies. For this purpose, we turn our analytic attention to the genre of journal articles that are the location of crucial public discourse among researchers (Winsor 1993; Yearley 1981; Zuckermann 1988). Our sample consisted of seventy empirical SAP studies published in peer-reviewed journals from 2002 to early 2014. We divided our sample into two subsets in order to analyse the development of contribution constructions over time: (1) the first wave contained articles published from 2002 to 2008; and (2) the second wave contained articles published from 2009 to 2014. To guide our analysis, we drew on an extant framework of constructing opportunities for contribution in management and organization studies (Locke and Golden-Biddle 1997).

Our analysis revealed three insights about how SAP scholars construct opportunities for contribution in their written texts. First, we found that a majority of articles utilize strategies for constructing contributions aimed at building on or elaborating extant work in strategy as practice and strategic management. Second, we observed that some articles use SAP research and its approach to challenge the extant work of other streams of research in strategic management, as well as to provoke research in other fields such as accounting or marketing. Third, we found that, to date, only 10 per cent of SAP empirical research uses a strategy of explicit disagreement with extant literature. In the original study by Locke and Golden-Biddle (1997), these contribution strategies accounted for 31 per cent of articles across all management and organization studies' domains; we therefore suggest that there is further room for SAP scholars to provoke and challenge how the field of strategic management theorizes strategy. Hence, we reinforce the call in the 2010 version of this volume's chapter (Golden-Biddle and Azuma

2010) to make disagreement with the existing literature more explicit and thus follow SAP's original vocation to challenge mainstream strategy research.

How SAP research constructs opportunities for contribution

To analyse how strategy-as-practice research develops theoretically relevant insights regarded as contributions by academic readers, we identified seventy empirical articles that explicitly drew upon or sought to contribute to SAP research. We assembled these papers in two steps. First, we searched the SAP-IN website database (www.sap-in.org) and then checked the two recent review articles (Jarzabkowski and Spee 2009; Vaara and Whittington 2012) for additional papers. Second, following the approach taken by Jarzabkowski and Spee (2009), we applied two qualifying criteria: (1) that the paper explicitly identified itself with the SAP perspective (i.e. by mentioning 'strategy as practice,' 'practice turn in strategy' or 'strategizing practices'); and (2) that the paper cited at least one of the foundational works of strategy as practice (Hendry 2000; Jarzabkowski 2004; Jarzabkowski, Balogun and Seidl 2007; Johnson *et al.* 2007; Johnson, Melin and Whittington 2003; Whittington 1996; 2003; 2006; 2007) or one of the two SAP review articles (Jarzabkowski and Spee 2009; Vaara and Whittington 2012).

As noted earlier, we divided our sample into two subsets. The first wave of articles (2002–2008) reflects the period in which strategy as practice constituted itself as a *field of research*; the end of this period is marked by the publication of the first review article on SAP research, namely that by Jarzabkowski and Spee (2009). The second wave of articles (2009–2014) reflects the period when SAP research was further established and expanded its reach; this is marked by the publication of the second review article, that by Vaara and Whittington in 2012. Each subset of our sample comprised thirty-five articles, making seventy in total.

Our analysis focused on the articles' introductions, because, as prior work has shown, authors typically offer readers plausible proposals of knowledge in the introduction (Bazerman 1993; Golden-Biddle and Locke 2007; Knorr Cetina 1981; Locke and Golden-Biddle 1997; Swales and Najar 1987). Following Locke and Golden-Biddle (1997), we defined the introduction as beginning with the first line after the abstract of each paper up to the methods section. In cases when we did not identify a contribution related to strategy as practice in the introduction, we carefully screened the remaining sections of the paper to evaluate whether the authors position their work as strategy as practice at a later point in the text (for example, Eppler and Platts 2009).

To assess how SAP authors construct opportunities for contribution, we drew on the framework developed by Locke and Golden-Biddle (1997), which describes two primary processes: (1) constructing *intertextual coherence*, and (2) *problematizing the situation*. These two processes reflect 'the tension between, on the one hand, authors' needing to relate present works to existing research programmes so that the works' importance and relevance to the scholarly community are established and, on the other hand, needing to demonstrate that the works identify occasions for original contribution' (Locke and Golden-Biddle 1997: 1029). Thus, in developing texts for peer-reviewed journals, authors must position their work and claim a contribution by constructing and connecting to the literature to which they intend to contribute while also problematizing that very literature in order to carve out space for their contribution. Below, we describe these two processes separately, along with the strategies used for their construction, and then apply them to our sample in order to identify the different ways in which SAP authors construct opportunities for contribution.

Process 1: constructing the intertextual field

To situate manuscripts within the literature, SAP authors do not simply report 'what is out there' but, rather, use the ambiguity and multiplicity of extant work to shape the construction of the 'literature' – or the relationship among identified texts – to make space for their research to make a contribution. How authors construct their scholarly work is an important resource (Golden-Biddle and Locke 2007) in developing opportunities for contribution, as well as for shaping a growing research stream such as strategy as practice. These networks of existing studies within a manuscript are conceptualized as *intertextual fields* (Bazerman 1993; Gephart 1988; Golden-Biddle and Locke 2007; Locke and Golden-Biddle 1997) and represent how existing works relate to each other as well as to the proposed study. Analysing our sample, we found that SAP scholars use all three strategies identified by Locke and Golden-Biddle (1997) to construct the intertextual field: *progressive coherence*, *synthesized coherence* and *non-coherence*. Next we describe each strategy and its prevalence in our sample, and provide examples of how SAP scholars have applied it.

Progressive coherence

The first strategy of constructing an intertextual field depicts the literature as an existing and well-established stream of research that has produced cumulative knowledge about a specific topic. Authors constructing *progressive coherence* emphasize shared theoretical perspectives or empirical methods, as well as consensus among scholars working on this topic. *Progressive coherence* is indicated in the text through the use of multiple and often intensive references. For example, the article by Rouleau and Balogun (2011) uses this strategy to depict a 'growing body of research' on the role of middle managers in strategic change, particularly in terms of their sensemaking capacity:

> There is a growing body of research which shows the important strategic role middle managers play in both the formulation and implementation of strategic change (see for example, *Balogun, 2003; Balogun & Johnson, 2004, 2005; Currie & Proctor, 2005; Dutton, et al., 2001; Floyd & Wooldridge, 1994, 1997; Hoon, 2007; Ling, et al., 2005; Mantere, 2008; Rouleau, 2005; Westley, 1990).* This research also highlights middle manager sensemaking capabilities as critical to the roles they perform... There is increasing evidence from existing research on both senior and middle managers of the need for them to

exercise their strategic influence *(Alexiev, et al., forthcoming; Balogun, et al., 2005, 2008; Buchanan, 2008; Fairhurst, 2007; Mangham & Pye, 191; Pye & Pettigrew, 2005)* (Rouleau and Balogun 2011: 953, emphasis added).

More than three-quarters of the articles in our overall sample (fifty-four out of seventy) use a *progressive coherence* strategy to construct the intertextual field. Comparing analyses over time, we observed a slight decline in the use of this strategy, from 83 per cent (twenty-nine out of thirty-five) in the first wave to 74 per cent (twenty-six out of thirty-five) in the second wave of SAP articles.

Synthesized coherence

The second strategy of constructing an intertextual field draws together previously unrelated work by pointing out connections and common ideas not yet explored. The use of this *synthesized coherence* strategy brings attention to or invents topics for inquiry that have been implicit in previous works. Some articles point out the commonalities and underlying consensus between two previously unrelated and distinct research programmes. Other articles assemble disparate research areas around an overarching idea. For example, Denis and his colleagues (2011) bring together four different empirical studies in order to develop the idea of 'escalating indecision'. They highlight the common characteristics of the phenomenon observed across the studies, suggesting that they represent a distinct kind of decision pathology:

> We have all come across situations where it seemed that people were gridlocked in cycles of perpetual decision making – bound to continue investing time and energy in a project or issue, but apparently unable to move it forward to implementation. *A classic case*, immortalized in an Emmy-Award-winning satirical documentary (Brown 2005), is the project to construct the new eastern span of the San Francisco–Oakland Bay Bridge... *Another example* concerns the failed project to implement a new form of personal public transportation, called Aramis, in Paris (Latour 1996). [. . .] *Another example* documented

by Silva (2002) is the decision surrounding the location of the new international airport in Lisbon... *We use the term 'escalating indecision' to refer to these situations* in which people and organizations continually make, unmake, and remake strategic decisions, resulting over the long term in a large expenditure of energy with little concrete strategic action, the constant possibility of reversal or reorientation, and potential widening scope of decision activity (Denis *et al.* 2011: 225, emphasis added).

In our total sample, 16 per cent of the articles (eleven out of seventy) construct a synthesized coherence intertextual field. Comparing analyses over time, we observed a noticeable increase in the use of a synthesized coherence strategy, from 11 per cent (four out of thirty-five) in the first wave to 20 per cent (seven out of thirty-five) in the second wave of SAP articles. The authors in our sample use the synthesized coherence strategy for three particular reasons: (1) to identify new topics for research (for example, Denis *et al.* 2011 identify the decision pathology of escalating indecision); (2) to expose commonalities between strategy as practice and other streams of research, thereby broadening the scope of topical areas for which strategy as practice is relevant; and (3) to illuminate implicit assumptions in different areas of research. Gomez and Bouty's (2011) article is an example of the second category; the authors bring together two previously unrelated streams of research, SAP and neo-institutional theory, to investigate the emergence of influential practices. In contrast, the paper by Mantere, Schildt and Sillince (2012) is an example of the third category. The authors assemble and relate discrepant references from different areas in order to argue that the existing literature implicitly views change reversal as unproblematic; they then challenge the literature by showing how change reversal is anything but unproblematic.

Non-coherence

In contrast to the two previous forms of constructing the intertextual field, the third strategy presents referenced work as belonging to a common research programme, but links it together in *disagreement*. While scholars may agree on the

importance of a particular research topic, they are depicted as *non-coherent* on one or more important dimensions. Often the discord among scholars is portrayed as two opposing camps, and highlights the major controversy that characterizes this field of research. For example, the article by Jarzabkowski and Balogun (2009) constructs disagreement within the strategic planning literature about the benefits of planning and how they might be realized. Two opposing camps are described; the first camp argues that strategic planning is useless, while the second camp claims strategic planning is of value:

> *While some authors* have described strategic planning as an annual ritual that delivers little in the way of strategic thinking or genuine change (Mintzberg, 1994), *others find* that strategic planning remains a widely used organizational practice (Rigby, 2003; Whittington & Cailluet, 2008). *Furthermore, organizations are placing increased emphasis* on planning as a means of enabling communication, participation, and integration around common goals (Andersen, 2004; Grant, 2003; Ketokivi & Castañer, 2004). *Yet* empirical evidence for these espoused integration benefits remains mixed (Wooldridge, et al., 2008) ... *Various claims have been made about the efficacy of strategic planning.* While planning was a staple in earlier strategy studies (e.g., Ackoff, 1970; Lorange, 1975), it has been subjected to considerable *critique*. For example, Mintzberg (1994) claimed that *strategic planning had failed* wherever it had been implemented, whereas Miller and Cardinal [1994] found that *strategic planning did add value* by focusing on the link between strategic planning and firm performance (Jarzabkowski and Balogun 2009: 1255–7, emphasis added).

The non-coherence form of constructing the intertextual field remains seldom used in SAP research, being represented in only 6 per cent of the overall sample of articles (four out of seventy), with no increase in proportionate use across the two subsamples.

Process 2: problematizing the situation

After constructing the intertextual field in which a manuscript is located, SAP authors need to call into question that same literature in order to carve out a space for their own contributions. Authors thus intentionally subvert the very literature just constructed by disclosing a puzzle or 'complication' that signals this new contribution. Locke and Golden-Biddle (1997) find three distinct strategies of problematizing the situation: *incompleteness*, *inadequacy* and *incommensurateness*. They use the prefix 'in' deliberately in order to convey the negation, or even subversion, of the intertextual field that has just been constructed. The three strategies of problematizing the situation represent a continuum with increasing negation and upheaval of the extant literature. In our sample, all three strategies for problematizing the situation were present, albeit with different weights.

Incompleteness

The first strategy of problematizing the situation, *incompleteness*, claims that the existing literature is not fully specified, and so it proposes a contribution through further development. In this form of problematization, authors approach the existing literature politely and present their contribution tentatively and with humility (Locke and Golden-Biddle 1997). For example, Liu and Maitlis (2014) aver that emotions in strategizing need further specification because of a lack of understanding of emotional display patterns among management team members in their continuing conversations about strategic issues:

> *Although existing research has demonstrated the importance of emotion in strategy, it has neglected some important dynamics.* Much of the extant research focuses on the emotions displayed by just one team member (typically the leader), *and pays less attention* to the emotional reactions of others (e.g., Brundin & Melin, 2006; Kisfalvi & Pitcher, 2003; Samra-Fredericks, 2004) [...] Where strategy research has examined the emotions of multiple team members, the focus has typically been on small segments of conversation about a single issue (e.g., Mangham, 1998; Tracy, 2007). This is inconsistent with the realities of strategy discourse in organizations, where management teams engage in long running conversations that span multiple issues within a

single meeting (Jarzabkowski & Seidl, 2008). *An important area for research, therefore, concerns the emotional dynamics* generated by multiple team members in longer episodes of strategizing about a variety of issues   (Liu and Maitlis 2014: 2, emphasis added).

In our total sample, 53 per cent of the articles (thirty-seven out of seventy) constructed the complication in the literature as *incomplete*. This approach has remained the dominant strategy for problematizing the situation, with a slight increase between the first wave (49 per cent, or seventeen out of thirty-five) and the second (57 per cent, or twenty out of thirty-five) of SAP articles.

Inadequacy

The second strategy for problematizing clears a space for contribution by arguing that the literature requires an alternative perspective in order to understand a specific phenomenon. Hence, authors reason that it is not sufficient to simply further specify the existing literature; rather, a different perspective needs to be offered in order to correct an important oversight. Manuscripts that construct the literature as *inadequate* often reference other studies in order to support their alternative perspective and to convey their partisanship for that position. Illuminating oversights or absent perspectives constitute the hallmark of those texts that problematize the field as *inadequate*. For example, Paroutis and Heracleous (2013) argue that, in order to understand strategic change, it is not sufficient to simply study change processes; it is equally important to understand how strategists 'conceive of and employ the concept of strategy'. The authors argue for the use of a discursive lens in order to investigate how strategists understand *strategy*:

> *Despite advancements in strategy-as-practice, our understanding* of the meanings of strategy as perceived by organizational actors 'in practice' is *still fairly limited. Our study extends this* approach by employing a discursive lens to understand strategy practices back to a point *more primary and foundational* than the strategy process, *back to the very concept* of strategy as understood by practitioners. Such an investigation is important

since language is a constituting element of daily practice and strategy making (Tsoukas, 2010) [...] While most prior studies have highlighted the substantive importance of strategic change for organizational survival, the processes by which strategists conceive of and employ the concept of strategy in the context of institutional adoption have rarely been studied. *However, discourse is fundamental and constitutive of strategic change*, and therefore understanding this dimension can be enlightening to our understanding of change itself (Oswick, et al., 2010). Overall, *we propose that a more comprehensive approach* to the micro level activities of actors during strategic change *needs to start with an understanding of the dimensions of the first-order discourse these actors employ* (Paroutis and Heracleous 2013: 936, emphasis added).

Our analysis has revealed that 41 per cent of the articles (twenty-nine out of seventy) in the overall sample problematized the puzzle or complication in the literature as *inadequate*. Comparing the findings over time, we observed a decline in the use of this approach, from 46 per cent (sixteen out of thirty-five) in the first wave to 37 per cent (thirteen out of thirty-five) in the second wave.

Incommensurateness

In contrast to the other two strategies, authors who adopt the *incommensurateness* approach for problematizing the situation argue that the literature is wrong or misguided, and so propose an alternate thesis to address this fault. A defining characteristic of this construction is that the existing body of knowledge is challenged head-on; thus, the paper introduces an often very different perspective. An illustrative example is provided by Ezzamel and Wilmott (2008: 191), who criticize 'mainstream' strategy literature for assuming that 'strategy exists "out there"' and ignoring the effects of strategy discourse. The authors draw on a Foucauldian perspective, investigating the disciplinary effects of a specific strategic discourse:

> In general, what we will term 'mainstream' literatures on strategy are underpinned by an assumption that such philosophical or metatheoretical issues are effectively settled or

can be safely ignored for all practical purposes. *It is assumed that strategy exists 'out there'*, either in the variables that comprise or govern it (Barney 1991; Porter 1980), or in the meanings of organizational members and others (e.g., consultants) who formulate and implement it (Mintzberg et al. 1995; Pettigrew 1987). *Debate is confined* to the question of which approach and methodology best captures key — 'objective' and 'subjective' — features of strategic management. *Excluded from analysis* is consideration of the constitutive effects of the use of strategy as a discourse *even though, arguably, it is through* discourse(s) that the plurality of conceptions and accounts of 'strategy' and 'strategic management' are articulated. *It is not (just) that* 'authors of traditional strategy frameworks *virtually ignore the role of language* in strategic decision making' (Barry & Elmes 1997: 432; see also Vaara et al. 2005) *but (also) that the conceptions* of strategy developed by mainstream frameworks *exclude recognition and exploration of how* discourse 'works to create some sense of stability, order and predictability and thereby produce a sustainable, functioning and liveable world' (Chia 2000: 514, emphasis added). Discourse is here understood to give social existence to the objects (e.g., 'opportunities', 'markets', 'competencies') that researchers are urged to study; that students are expected to know about; and which managers are urged to act upon. Understood in this way, *the neglect of strategy as a discourse* is a *glaring omission from* the study of strategy. *By advancing an approach* guided by Foucauldian analysis (see Knights 1992; Knights & Morgan 1991), the paper explicates the theoretical basis for generating an alternative corpus of knowledge of the world of management and organization in which recognition of its discursive constitution is placed at the centre of analysis. *It advances and illustrates an alternative to* (empirical) realist analyses of strategy in which the objects of analysis — variables and meanings — are assumed to be self-evident and accessible by applying an appropriate method (Ezzamel and Willmott 2008: 191–2, emphasis added).

Only four papers, 6 per cent of our total sample, utilized an incommensurate problematization. The use of this strategy has remained constant over time, with two articles in each of the two waves.

Considering contribution opportunities in SAP research

When considered in combination, the two processes of *constructing the intertextual field* and *problematizing the situation*, along with their associated strategies, yield nine different opportunities for contribution (Locke and Golden-Biddle 1997). We mapped the seventy articles that comprised our sample onto this framework, represented in Table 5.1, which enabled us to examine the distribution of opportunities for contribution created through SAP research as published in journal articles to date.

Although our sample includes all opportunities for contribution, five of the nine opportunities are represented by only one or two articles. Here, we share observations from our analyses of the sample and offer a comparison between the two subsets (i.e. the first and second waves) of this sample.

Observation 1

SAP empirical research relies heavily on two primary opportunities for contribution: progressive-incomplete and progressive-inadequate. The construction of these two opportunities for contributions is directed towards building strategy as practice's legitimacy as a research domain.

A majority of the articles (76 per cent, or fifty-three out of seventy) use two approaches for contributing scholarly knowledge to the literature: (1) *progressive incompleteness* and (2) *progressive inadequacy*. Both these approaches connect SAP research with an intertextual field that is represented as 'well established' per the production of cumulative knowledge. They differ in their problematization, or *negation*, of that literature, however: not fully specified (*incompleteness*) versus missing an important perspective or idea (*inadequacy*).

An example of *progressive incompleteness* can be found in the 2013 study by Jarzabkowski and her colleagues. Here the authors depict SAP as an established stream of research that has recognized the importance of material objects in the 'doing' of strategy. They argue that the literature needs further specification, however, about how these material objects interact with human activity in strategy-making:

> From a strategy-as-practice perspective, strategy is not a static property of a firm but is continuously created in the doing of strategy work. *Embedded in such doing are all kinds of 'stuff' to make strategy happen* including routines and procedures, discursive resources and material artifacts (Whittington, 2007). There are increasing calls within the strategy-as-practice literature to focus on those material objects, such as whiteboards, spreadsheets, and PowerPoints, through which people do strategy work (Jarzabkowski, Balogun & Seidl, 2007; Jarzabkowski & Whittington, 2008; Kaplan, 2011; Whittington, 2003). However, the study of such objects and, in particular, *the implications of the way that they interact with human activity in strategy making remains relatively underexplored* (Jarzabkowski & Spee, 2009), with some exceptions (e.g., Kaplan, 2011; Molloy & Whittington, 2005) (Jarzabkowski, Spee and Smets 2013: 41, emphasis added).

In comparison, an example of *progressive inadequacy* is evident in the work of Wright and his colleagues (2013), who demonstrate the literature's accumulation of knowledge on strategic tools and techniques. These authors go further than Jarzabkowski, Spee and Smets (2013) in problematizing the literature by arguing that understanding the use of strategy tools in practice requires going beyond what is visible and observable in order to investigate the internal logic of practitioners:

> We focus on strategic tools and techniques because they form a critical and cognitively demanding element in the practice of effective strategy workers (*Jarzabkowski, 2004; Jarzabkowski & Spee, 2009; Liedtka, 1998; Whittington, 1996, 2007*). The literature on strategic tools has shown how these knowledge artefacts are used (and abused) in organizational settings... *A number of studies* provide interesting insights into how many, which, and when certain tools are used in the strategy-making process, along with who uses these tools (see, for example, *Clark, 1997; Jarzabkowski, et al., 2010b; Rigby & Bilodeau, 2011; Stenfors, 2007*) ... *However, many of these noteworthy studies are based on snapshot survey data,*

Table 5.1 Opportunities for contribution in strategy-as-practice research

Process 1: structuring the intertextual field	Process 2: problematizing the situation		
	Incompleteness	*Inadequacy*	*Incommensurability*
Progressive coherence	*First wave (2002–2008)* Balogun and Johnson 2004 Balogun and Johnson 2005 Beech and Johnson 2005 Heracleous and Jacobs 2008 Hodgkinson *et al.* 2006 Hoon 2007 Jarzabkowski 2003 Jarzabkowski and Seidl 2008 Jarzabkowski and Wilson 2002 King 2008 Mantere 2008 Nordqvist and Melin 2008 Salvato 2003 Sillince and Mueller 2007 Sminia 2005	*First wave (2002–2008)* Ambrosini, Bowman and Burton- Taylor 2007 Jarzabkowski 2008 Laine and Vaara 2007 Maitlis and Lawrence 2003 Mantere and Vaara 2008 Nayak 2008 Paroutis and Pettigrew 2007 Regnér 2003 Rouleau 2005 Samra-Fredericks 2003 Vaara, Kleymann and Seristö 2004 Voronov 2008 Whittington et al. 2006	*First wave (2002–2008)* Ezzamel and Willmott 2008
	Second wave (2009–2014) Aggerholm, Asmuß and Thomsen 2012 Angwin, Paroutis and Mitson 2009 Balogun, Jarzabkowski and Vaara 2011 Corbett-Etchevers and Mounoud 2011 Daigle and Rouleau 2010 Eppler and Platts 2009 Fauré and Rouleau 2011 Jarzabkowski, Spee and Smets 2013 Johnson *et al.* 2010 Kaplan 2011 Kornberger and Clegg 2011 Küpers, Mantere and Statler 2012 O'Brien 2011 Rouleau and Balogun 2011 Vaara, Sorsa and Pälli 2010 Whittle and Mueller 2010	*Second wave (2009–2014)* Abdallah and Langley 2014 Clarke, Kwon and Wodak 2012 Hendry, Kiel and Nicholson 2010 Järventie-Thesleff, Moisander and Laine 2011 Jørgensen and Messner 2010 Nordqvist 2012 Spee and Jarzabkowski 2011 Van Wessel, van Buuren and van Woerkum 2011 Voronov 2008 Wright, Paroutis and Blettner 2013	*Second wave (2009–2014)* Mueller *et al.* 2013
Synthesized coherence	*First wave (2002–2008)* Mantere 2005	*First wave (2002–2008)* Samra-Fredericks 2005 Lounsbury and Crumley 2007 Kaplan 2008	*First wave (2002–2008)*
	Second wave (2009–2014) Denis *et al.* 2011 Gomez and Bouty 2011 Liu and Maitlis 2014 McCabe 2010	*Second wave (2009–2014)* Moisander and Stenfors 2009 Paroutis and Heracleous 2013	*Second wave (2009–2014)* Mantere, Schildt and Sillince 2012
Non-coherence	*First wave (2002–2008)* Stensaker and Falkenberg 2007	*First wave (2002–2008)*	*First wave (2002–2008)* Giraudeau 2008
	Second wave (2009–2014)	*Second wave (2009–2014)* Jarratt and Stiles 2010 Jarzabkowski and Balogun 2009	*Second wave (2009–2014)*

which are *merely* descriptive and explore *only* the behavioural level. We contend that *it is this very lack of understanding beyond the visible and observable layer of practice* that results in a situation where the knowledge we produce ill-prepares practitioners who are striving for new ways of thinking and doing that addresses their everyday challenges (Mintzberg, 2004). *Very little research has investigated the internal logic of practitioners* to gain a deeper insight into how tools shape (and are shaped by) strategy workers (see Hodgkinson & Clarke, 2007; Jarzabkowski & Wilson, 2006; Whittington, 2006). . . We therefore contend in the present paper that, *to understand the usefulness of strategic tools, we first need to understand a different type of logic at play* (Bourdieu, 1990). . . *Only by understanding this internal logic* can we come to comprehend fully whether the logics applied through our tools meet the needs of practicing managers (Wright, Paroutis and Blettner 2013: 92–3, emphasis added).

The above examples also illuminate how these two opportunities for contribution act in the service of *building* or *elaborating* extant work in strategy as practice or strategic management. For instance, the Jarzabkowski, Spee and Smets (2013) example of a progressive-incomplete construction includes the authors' claim that they will elaborate an 'underexplored' part of the SAP literature by investigating the way that objects interact with human activity in strategy-making. In the Wright, Paroutis and Blettner (2013) example of a progressive-inadequate construction, the authors claim that they will build upon the SAP literature by illuminating a different logic at play in the use of strategic tools.

In comparing the two subsets of our sample, we noticed that the use of these two opportunities declined from 80 per cent (twenty-eight out of thirty-five) of articles in the first wave to 71 per cent (twenty-five out of thirty-five) in the second wave. This suggests a slight broadening in how SAP scholars construct the literature as they seek opportunities for contribution. Room for further broadening through the use of other strategies for constructing a contribution seems to exist, however, because, in the framework's originating study, these contribution opportunities represent only slightly more than one-third

of the sample (35 per cent) (Locke and Golden-Biddle 1997).

Observation 2

SAP empirical research uses an 'inadequate' problematization that, when paired with a 'progressive' or 'synthesized' intertextual field, positions the text to challenge extant work in strategic management and other fields of research.

In line with strategy as practice's initial aim of challenging traditional research in strategic management, we observed that articles in this area tend to use an 'inadequate' problematization of the literature, paired with a 'progressive' or 'synthesized' literature construction, in order to challenge other streams of research in strategic management, such as research on corporate boards (Hendry, Kiel and Nicholson 2010) or upper echelon research (Angwin, Paroutis and Mitson 2009). For example, the excerpt below establishes the existence of an extensive literature on the strategy role of corporate boards, but then problematizes this literature by suggesting that the field's understanding of how boards address this role is still missing:

> *Global research in recent years has clearly established that* directors are devoting more time to strategy and that many see this as an increasingly important role for boards. [. . .] *While there is extensive literature on the strategy role of boards, our understanding of how boards address this role is limited*, particularly the behavioural aspects of boards working with management on strategy. [. . .] *With this gap in the literature in mind*, two key questions underpin this paper. First, what does strategic involvement on the part of boards mean in terms of board behaviour? Alternatively, how do boards strategise? Second, how is this strategising behaviour affected by contextual factors within the organisation, especially within the board–management interface? *In addressing these questions, we take a micro-perspective on board strategising*, drawing on an in-depth qualitative analysis of directors' and senior managers' behaviour in a small number of selected cases. *In particular, we use the Strategy as Practice perspective to identify and explore this strategising behaviour. This perspective is of*

particular value to our research questions in that it views strategy as a context-dependent, socially-accomplished activity constructed through the actions and interactions of multiple actors or groups within organisations (Hendry, Kiel and Nicholson 2010: 33–4, emphasis added).

During our analysis, we observed that authors in the second wave increasingly use strategy as practice to challenge research in fields other than strategic management, such as accounting (Jørgensen and Messner 2010) and marketing (Järventie-Thesleff, Moisander and Laine 2011). This broadening of SAP research is also reflected in the outlets used for publication: SAP articles are now also published in journals considered networks of texts in other disciplines, such as *Accounting, Organizations and Society*; *International Public Management Journal* and *Business History*. For example, Järventie-Thesleff and her colleagues (2011) import strategy as practice into the domain of brand management – a purpose indicated in their article's title: 'Organizational dynamics and complexities of corporate brand building: a practice perspective'. The authors develop a progressive literature construction treated as inadequate:

> *Much of the current research* on corporate branding is conceptual and *typically takes the 'content perspective'* (Whittington, 2007: 1576) on brand strategy, discussing the nature and dimensions of different types of brand strategy (e.g., Aaker, 2004; Balmer & Gray, 2003; Knox & Bickerton, 2003). *Relatively little empirical research* has been focused on the specific activities, processes and routinized practices through which corporate brand strategies are developed and implemented in the organization. Consequently, *there appears to be a need* for empirically well grounded research on the praxis and practices of corporate brand building as well as on the managerial challenges that it involves. In this paper, our aim is to respond to these research needs. *Drawing on the practice turn in contemporary social theory* (Schatzki, Cetina & Savigny, 2001) *and the emerging strategy-as-practice tradition* (Jarzabkowski, Balogun & Seidl, 2007; Johnson, Langley, Melin & Whittington, 2007; Laine & Vaara, 2007; Whittington, 2006, 2007), *we build a practice-based approach to corporate brand management* to shed light onto the day-to-day

activities and organizational practices through which corporate brand strategies get managed in business organizations. More specifically, *we extend the post-processual approach to theorizing strategy as practice* (Carter, Clegg & Kornberger, 2008; Chia & MacKay, 2007) *to the domain of brand management.* (Järventie-Thesleff, Moisander and Laine 2011: 196–7, emphasis added).

Despite this expansion of SAP research to other domains, we observed a slight decrease in the use of *progressive-inadequate* and *synthesized-inadequate* contribution constructions, from 46 per cent of articles (sixteen out of thirty-five) in the first wave to 31 per cent (eleven out of thirty-five) in the second wave of SAP research.

Observation 3

SAP empirical research continues to use only rarely five of the nine contribution opportunities – all of which make disagreement more explicit.

In contrast to the other opportunities for contribution, the five opportunities of the outer cells of our framework employ rhetorical strategies of disagreement with extant literature via *non-coherence structuring* of the intertextual field and/or *incommensurate problematization*, thus challenging prior literature. Instead of suggesting refinements or oversights in problematizing extant literature, articles using these five approaches directly challenge extant work as 'misguided' or 'wrong', or they construct an intertextual field with contentious characterizations and depictions of internal challenges (Locke and Golden-Biddle 1997). In our overall sample, only 10 per cent of articles (seven out of seventy) take this approach, and the use of these five opportunities for contribution has remained stable over time (three articles in the first wave and four in the second).

Mueller and his colleagues (2013) represent one example of this approach in their use of a *progressive-incommensurate* opportunity for contribution: they explicitly disagree with extant SAP research by challenging a 'taken-for-granted assumption' about how strategy relates to power and politics, and thus propose a different perspective to redress this misunderstanding.

The rapidly growing and influential field of 'strategy-as-practice' (SAP) research focuses on the 'micro-level social activities, processes and practices that characterize organizational strategy and strategizing'. [. . .] *Existing SAP research has focused on* the role of managerial sensemaking and leadership, discourse, metaphors, rhetoric, emotion, norms and values, habitus. . . Within existing literature, strategy has been studied as a process of sensemaking and as a process imbued with power and politics. However, *there remains a taken-for-granted assumption about* how the former relates to the latter. *Existing work has been restricted to* studying the role of power and politics in shaping sensemaking processes, a kind of 'one way street' of influence. *This work views* power and politics as something that actors have (as a possession or property) and that affects their strategic behaviour, including their sensemaking. *We challenge this taken-for-granted assumption and propose a different perspective* that views politics as an interpretive procedure that enables actors to author accounts that make sense of the organizational landscape (what political motives and allegiances could be at play?) and envision a strategic direction for the future (where should we go next?). Thus, *our aim is to do more than 'fill a gap' in existing research* on power and politics by simply adding another dimension to the influence that politics is understood to wield over strategic behaviour. *Rather, our aim is to challenge the dominant assumption that* organizational politics is simply an input into – and force acting over – processes of strategic sensemaking. [. . .] Politics, *we propose, is not simply an objective force* that acts over strategists, *but rather is rendered into* a 'social fact' through ongoing processes of discursive sensemaking. ([Mueller *et al.* 2013: 1169–70, emphasis added).

Giraudeau (2008) exhibits the strongest form of disagreement: he uses both a contentious characterization of the literature and a head-on challenge to existing work by explicitly rejecting the two opposing models of strategic planning. The article is thus a vivid example of a *non-coherence-incommensurability* strategy:

These criticisms of corporate strategic planning *oppose two models of action.* Mintzberg suggests this when he appeals to *the distinction between 'deliberate' and 'emergent' strategies* so as to justify his critical insights into planning. This distinction, which later *crystallised into the 'planning' vs. 'learning' controversy,* can be summarised as opposing a type of action that would exclusively follow a predefined plan with an action that would build progressively according to the situations actors are confronted with. [. . .] Indeed, although studies dealing with strategic planning are innumerable, *most don't actually analyse strategic plans themselves.* Their focus is on the planning process, which is responsible for the 'detachment' of strategic planning from the other activities of the firm. The planning sequence appears to be too rigid, too bureaucratic for contemporary firms in their rapidly changing environments. *But this tells us more about the rigidity of predefined processes than about the specificities of planning itself.* On the other hand, the supposedly fallacious 'predetermination' and 'formalisation' of plans are made stable and exclusively negative properties of plans, without their actual uses being questioned. *But the predetermination of strategies could just as well be considered as an imaginative practice, which could lead to the invention of new strategies.* And formalisation may be used as a means to synthesise possible strategies in order to make their collective discussion easier. *Hence the necessity for a closer empirical scrutiny of plans and their uses.* This focus leads us not only, as some authors have tried, to articulate the two (planned and situated) models of action, *but to reject them both at the same time. Their existence appears as a strong cognitive bias.* [. . .] *Our aim here is therefore to do things the other way around: rather than presupposing any 'essence' of planning, we start our analysis from the close study of plans and their uses.* We won't consider the strategising process before examining the specific arts, facts and artifacts that compose it. In so doing, we draw widely on the strategy-as-practice (SAP) perspective, which insists on the necessity to take 'the practice inside the [strategy formation] process' into account. (Giraudeau 2008: 293, emphasis added).

While these examples of articles occupying the outer cells of our framework show that SAP research can be provocative and creative in constructing its contributions, it is clear that there is still room for further diversification of contribution opportunities: only 10 per cent of the SAP articles in our total sample (seven out of seventy) base their contributions on disagreement with the existing literature, as compared with 31 per cent in the framework's originating study (Locke and Golden-Biddle 1997). We recognize that the use of these five strategies to construct a contribution may be more risky because bold claims of disagreement with the current literature need to be well substantiated in the text in order to convince reviewers and readers. Nevertheless, as top journals are increasingly looking for strong theoretical contributions, and in line with strategy as practice's original goal of challenging traditional, mainstream strategy literature, we reinforce the call in the 2010 version of this chapter (Golden-Biddle and Azuma 2010) that disagreement with the existing literature should be made more explicitly. The excerpts presented in this chapter provide portraits that can catalyse ideas of how SAP research can achieve this goal.

Conclusion

Our updated analyses indicate that, in the intervening years since the first edition of the handbook in 2010, SAP authors have moved away from framing contributions within 'established' topics in order to develop their own research concerns and become more contentious. These authors have broadened the repertoire of their rhetorical strategies for constructing contributions and are increasingly drawing on other streams of research in order to construct opportunities for contribution. Directionally, this points to a stream of research increasingly comfortable with its place in the strategy conversation and beyond. Nevertheless, we note that there are still relatively few SAP empirical studies that directly challenge the existing literature by basing their contributions on disagreement.

By explicating the different strategies for contribution and providing examples for how they have been used, we hope that our results spark productive discussions about strategy as practice and energize readers to consider the contributions they can make to the now extant body of SAP knowledge. Being sensitive to and noticing how authors construct contributions – and thus convey the import

and relevance of their findings to academic readers – is imperative, because scientific knowledge is not 'an objective entity that exists independent of the knower' (Locke and Golden-Biddle 1997: 1025) but, rather, is socially constructed (see, for example, Knorr Cetina 1981; Latour and Woolgar 1979; Zuckermann 1988). Hence, authors need to relate to and convey to readers the novelty or uniqueness of their studies. Indeed, Mone and McKinley (1993) note that a 'uniqueness value' exists in organization science studies, and several studies (such as those by Beyer, Chanove and Fox 1995; Cole and Cole 1967; Crane 1965; 1967) have revealed that publication in organization studies journals is more likely when novelty is present in manuscripts. Given that the number one question that reviewers ask of submitted manuscripts is 'What's new?' (Whetten 1989), authors need to convey clearly to reviewers, and subsequent readers of their work, that which is novel and unique about their findings.

The achievement of uniqueness is far from simple, and, as Locke and Golden-Biddle's (1997) study already indicates, there are several different strategies that authors implement to make their articles 'interesting' (Davis 1971). Our analysis reveals that strategy-as-practice scholars do employ all of the nine strategies for constructing contributions, but are heavily biased towards two in particular, *progressive-incomplete* and *progressive-inadequate*. This shows limited creativity in constructing the intertextual field in which authors position their work, since they do not directly challenge existing works. Comparing the distribution of SAP articles across the contribution matrix (depicted in Table 5.1) to the distribution in Locke and Golden-Biddle's (1997) original study of organization studies' articles, we suggest that there is room to further broaden the use of different contribution strategies, particularly in terms of constructing contributions through explicit disagreement with the literature. Given that Locke and Golden-Biddle's (1997) sample consisted of empirical studies in two highly regarded, well-established journals in the field of organization studies (*Academy of Management Journal* and *Administrative Science Quarterly*), embracing the use of different contribution opportunities might also support the publication of SAP research in top management journals. At the same time, of course, bold claims, especially those that directly challenge the existing literature, need to be well substantiated in the subsequent text in order to convince reviewers and readers of the contribution's validity.

As scholars embark on the next wave of SAP research, we encourage them to continue to cultivate an alternative perspective on the strategy phenomenon. One way to do so, and therefore construct significant contributions to extant work, is to be more conscious about the rhetorical practices used to inscribe findings into a written text. In particular, attending to the five outer cells of the contribution matrix could help SAP authors strengthen their claims of knowledge vis-à-vis extant scholarship.

References

Abdallah, C., and Langley, A. (2014), 'The double edge of ambiguity in strategic planning', *Journal of Management Studies*, 51/2: 235–64.

Aggerholm, H. K., Asmuß, B., and Thomsen, C. (2012), 'The role of recontextualization in the multivocal, ambiguous process of strategizing', *Journal of Management Inquiry*, 21/4: 413–28.

Ambrosini, V., Bowman, C., and Burton-Taylor, S. (2007), 'Inter-team coordination activities as a source of customer satisfaction', *Human Relations*, 60/1: 59–98.

Angwin, D., Paroutis, S., and Mitson, S. (2009), 'Connecting up strategy: are senior strategy directors a missing link?', *California Management Review*, 51/3: 74–94.

Balogun, J., Jarzabkowski, P., and Vaara, E. (2011), 'Selling, resistance and reconciliation: a critical discursive approach to subsidiary role evolution in MNEs', *Journal of International Business Studies*, 42/6: 765–86.

Balogun, J., and Johnson, G. (2004), 'Organizational restructuring and middle manager sensemaking', *Academy of Management Journal*, 47/4: 523–49.

(2005), 'From intended strategies to unintended outcomes: the impact of change recipient sensemaking', *Organization Studies*, 26/11: 1573–601.

Bazerman, C. (1993), 'Intertextual self-fashioning: Gould and Lewontin's representations of the literature', in Selzer, J. (ed.), *Understanding Scientific Prose*: 20–41. Madison: University of Wisconsin Press.

Beech, N., and Johnson, P. (2005), 'Discourses of disrupted identities in the practice of strategic change: the mayor, the street-fighter and the insider-out', *Journal of Organizational Change Management*, 18/1: 31–47.

Beyer, J. M., Chanove, R. G., and Fox, W. B. (1995), 'The review process and the fates of manuscripts submitted to AMJ', *Academy of Management Journal*, 38/5: 1219–60.

Clarke, I., Kwon, W., and Wodak, R. (2012), 'A context-sensitive approach to analysing talk in strategy meetings', *British Journal of Management*, 23/4: 455–73.

Cole, J. R., and Cole, S. (1967), 'Scientific output and recognition: a study in the operation of the reward system in science', *American Sociological Review*, 32/3: 377–90.

Corbett-Etchevers, I., and Mounoud, E. (2011), 'A narrative framework for management ideas: disclosing the plots of knowledge management in a multinational company', *Management Learning*, 42/2: 165–81.

Crane, D. (1965), 'Scientists at major and minor universities: a study of productivity and recognition', *American Sociological Review*, 30/5: 699–714.

(1967), 'The gatekeepers of science: some factors affecting the selection of articles for scientific journals', *American Sociologist*, 2/4: 195–201.

Daigle, P., and Rouleau, L. (2010), 'Strategic plans in arts organizations: a tool of compromise between artistic and managerial values', *International Journal of Arts Management*, 12/3: 13–30.

Davis, M. S. (1971), 'That's interesting! Toward a phenomenology of sociology and a sociology of phenomenology', *Philosophy of the Social Sciences*, 1/2: 309–44.

Denis, J.-L., Dompierre, G., Langley, A., and Rouleau, L. (2011), 'Escalating indecision: between reification and strategic ambiguity', *Organization Science*, 22/1: 225–44.

Eppler, M. J., and Platts, K. W. (2009), 'Visual strategizing', *Long Range Planning*, 42/1: 42–74.

Ezzamel, M., and Willmott, H. (2008), 'Strategy as discourse in a global retailer: a supplement to rationalist and interpretive accounts', *Organization Studies*, 29/2: 191–217.

Fauré, B., and Rouleau, L. (2011), 'The strategic competence of accountants and middle managers in budget making', *Accounting, Organizations and Society*, 36/3: 167–82.

Gephart, R. P. (1988), *Ethnostatistics: Qualitative Foundations for Quantitative Research*. Newbury Park, CA: Sage.

Giraudeau, M. (2008), 'The drafts of strategy: opening up plans and their uses', *Long Range Planning*, 41/3: 291–308.

Golden-Biddle, K., and Azuma, J. (2010), 'Constructing contribution in "strategy as practice" research', in Golsorkhi, D., Rouleau, L., Seidl, D., and Vaara, E. (eds.), *Cambridge Handbook of Strategy as Practice*: 79–90. Cambridge University Press.

Golden-Biddle, K., and Locke, K. (2007), *Composing Qualitative Research*, 2nd edn. Thousand Oaks, CA: Sage.

Gomez, M.-L., and Bouty, I. (2011), 'The emergence of an influential practice: food for thought', *Organization Studies*, 32/7: 921–40.

Hendry, J. (2000), 'Strategic decision making, discourse and strategy as social practice', *Journal of Management Studies*, 37/7: 955–77.

Hendry, K. P., Kiel, G. C., and Nicholson, G. (2010), 'How boards strategise: a strategy as practice view', *Long Range Planning*, 43/1: 33–56.

Heracleous, L., and Jacobs, C. D. (2008), 'Crafting strategy: the role of embodied metaphors', *Long Range Planning*, 41/3: 309–25.

Hodgkinson, G. P., Whittington, R., Johnson, G., and Schwarz, M. (2006), 'The role of strategy workshops in strategy development processes: formality, communication, co-ordination and inclusion', *Long Range Planning*, 39/5: 479–96.

Hoon, C. (2007), 'Committees as strategic practice: the role of strategic conversation in a public administration', *Human Relations*, 6/6: 921–52.

Jarratt, D., and Stiles, D. (2010), 'How are methodologies and tools framing managers' strategizing practice in competitive strategy development?', *British Journal of Management*, 21/1: 28–43.

Järventie-Thesleff, R., Moisander, J., and Laine, P.-M. (2011), 'Organizational dynamics and complexities of corporate brand building: a practice perspective', *Scandinavian Journal of Management*, 27/2: 196–204.

Jarzabkowski, P. (2003), 'Strategic practices: an activity theory perspective on continuity and change', *Journal of Management Studies*, 40/1: 23–55.

(2004), 'Strategy as practice: recursiveness, adaptation, and practices-in-use', *Organization Studies*, 25/4: 529–60.

(2008), 'Shaping strategy as a structuration process', *Academy of Management Journal*, 51/4: 621–50.

Jarzabkowski, P., and Balogun, J. (2009), 'The practice and process of delivering integration through strategic planning', *Journal of Management Studies*, 46/8: 1255–88.

Jarzabkowski, P., Balogun, J., and Seidl, D. (2007), 'Strategizing: the challenges of a practice perspective', *Human Relations*, 60/1: 5–27.

Jarzabkowski, P., and Seidl, D. (2008), 'The role of meetings in the social practice of strategy', *Organization Studies*, 29/11: 1391–426.

Jarzabkowski, P., and Spee, P. (2009), 'Strategy-as-practice: a review and future directions for the field', *International Journal of Management Reviews*, 11/1: 69–95.

Jarzabkowski, P., Spee, P., and Smets, M. (2013), 'Material artifacts: practices for doing strategy with "stuff"', *European Management Journal*, 31/1: 41–54.

Jarzabkowski, P., and Wilson, D. C. (2002), 'Top teams and strategy in a UK university', *Journal of Management Studies*, 39/3: 355–81.

Johnson, G., Langley, A., Melin, L., and Whittington, R. (2007), *Strategy as Practice: Research Directions and Resources*. Cambridge University Press.

Johnson, G., Melin, L., and Whittington, R. (2003), 'Guest editors' introduction: micro strategy and strategizing: towards an activity-based view', *Journal of Management Studies*, 40/1: 3–22.

Johnson, G., Prashantham, S., Floyd, S., and Bourque, N. (2010), 'The ritualization of strategy workshops', *Organization Studies*, 31/12: 1589–618.

Jørgensen, B., and Messner, M. (2010), 'Accounting and strategising: a case study from new product development', *Accounting, Organizations and Society*, 35/2: 184–204.

Kaplan, S. (2008), 'Framing contests: strategy making under uncertainty', *Organization Science*, 19/5: 729–52.

(2011), 'Strategy and PowerPoint: an inquiry into the epistemic culture and machinery of strategy making', *Organization Science*, 22/2: 320–46.

King, B. L. (2008), 'Strategizing at leading venture capital firms: of planning, opportunism and deliberate emergence', *Long Range Planning*, 41/3: 345–66.

Knorr Cetina, K. (1981), *The Manufacture of Knowledge: An Essay on the Constructivist and Contextual Nature of Science.* Oxford: Pergamon Press.

Kornberger, M., and Clegg, S. (2011), 'Strategy as performative practice: the case of Sydney 2030', *Strategic Organization*, 9/2: 136–62.

Küpers, W., Mantere, S., and Statler, M. (2012), 'Strategy as storytelling: a phenomenological collaboration', *Journal of Management Inquiry*, 22/1: 83–100.

Laine, P.-M., and Vaara, E. (2007), 'Struggling over subjectivity: a discursive analysis of strategic development in an engineering group', *Human Relations*, 60/1: 29–58.

Latour, B., and Woolgar, S. (1979), *Laboratory Life: The Construction of Scientific Facts.* Beverly Hills, CA: Sage.

Liu, F., and Maitlis, S. (2014), 'Emotional dynamics and strategizing processes: a study of strategic conversations in top team meetings', *Journal of Management Studies*, 51/2: 202–34.

Locke, K., and Golden-Biddle, K. (1997), 'Constructing opportunities for contribution: structuring intertextual coherence and "problematizing" in organizational studies', *Academy of Management Journal*, 40/5: 1023–62.

Lounsbury, M., and Crumley, E. T. (2007), 'New practice creation: an institutional perspective on innovation', *Organization Studies*, 28/7: 993–1012.

Maitlis, S., and Lawrence, T. B. (2003), 'Orchestral manoeuvres in the dark: understanding failure in organizational strategizing', *Journal of Management Studies*, 40/1: 109–39.

Mantere, S. (2005), 'Strategic practices as enablers and disablers of championing activity', *Strategic Organization*, 3/2: 157–84.

—— (2008), 'Role expectations and middle manager strategic agency', *Journal of Management Studies*, 45/2: 294–316.

Mantere, S., Schildt, H. A., and Sillince, J. (2012), 'Reversal of strategic change', *Academy of Management Journal*, 55/1: 172–96.

Mantere, S., and Vaara, E. (2008), 'On the problem of participation in strategy: a critical discursive perspective', *Organization Science*, 19/2: 341–58.

McCabe, D. (2010), 'Strategy-as-power: ambiguity, contradiction and the exercise of power in a UK building society', *Organization*, 17/2: 151–75.

Moisander, J., and Stenfors, S. (2009), 'Exploring the edges of theory–practice gap: epistemic cultures in strategy-tool development and use', *Organization*, 16/2: 227–47.

Mone, M. A., and McKinley, W. (1993), 'The uniqueness value and its consequences for organization studies', *Journal of Management Inquiry*, 2/3: 284–96.

Mueller, F., Whittle, A., Gilchrist, A., and Lenney, P. (2013), 'Politics and strategy practice: an ethnomethodologically-informed discourse analysis perspective', *Business History*, 55/7: 1168–99.

Nayak, A. (2008), 'Experiencing creativity in organisations: a practice approach', *Long Range Planning*, 41/4: 420–39.

Nordqvist, M. (2012), 'Understanding strategy processes in family firms: exploring the roles of actors and arenas', *International Small Business Journal*, 30/1: 24–40.

Nordqvist, M., and Melin, L. (2008), 'Strategic planning champions: social craftspersons, artful interpreters and known strangers', *Long Range Planning*, 41/3: 326–44.

O'Brien, F. (2011), 'Supporting the strategy process: a survey of UK OR/MS practitioners', *Journal of the Operational Research Society*, 62/5: 900–20.

Paroutis, S., and Heracleous, L. (2013), 'Discourse revisited: dimensions and employment of first-order strategy discourse during institutional adoption', *Strategic Management Journal*, 34/8: 935–56.

Paroutis, S., and Pettigrew, A. M. (2007), 'Strategizing in the multi-business firm: strategy teams at multiple levels and over time', *Human Relations*, 60/1: 99–135.

Regnér, P. (2003), 'Strategy creation in the periphery: inductive versus deductive strategy making', *Journal of Management Studies*, 40/1: 57–82.

Rouleau, L. (2005), 'Micro-practices of strategic sensemaking and sensegiving: how middle managers interpret and sell change every day', *Journal of Management Studies*, 42/7: 1413–41.

Rouleau, L., and Balogun, J. (2011), 'Middle managers, strategic sensemaking, and discursive competence', *Journal of Management Studies*, 48/5: 953–83.

Salvato, C. (2003), 'The role of micro-strategies in the engineering of firm evolution', *Journal of Management Studies*, 40/1: 83–108.

Samra-Fredericks, D. (2003), 'Strategizing as lived experience and strategists' everyday efforts to shape strategic direction', *Journal of Management Studies*, 40/1: 141–74.

Samra-Fredericks, D. (2005), 'Strategic practice, "discourse" and the everyday interactional constitution of "power effects"', *Organization*, 12/6: 803–41.

Sillince, J., and Mueller, F. (2007), 'Switching strategic perspective: the reframing of accounts of responsibility', *Organization Studies*, 28/2: 155–76.

Sminia, H. (2005), 'Strategy formation as layered discussion', *Scandinavian Journal of Management*, 21/3: 267–91.

Spee, P., and Jarzabkowski, P. (2011), 'Strategic planning as communicative process', *Organization Studies*, 32/9: 1217–45.

Stensaker, I., and Falkenberg, J. (2007), 'Making sense of different responses to corporate change', *Human Relations*, 60/1: 137–77.

Swales, J., and Najar, H. (1987), 'The writing of research article introductions', *Written Communication*, 4/2: 175–91.

Vaara, E., Kleymann, B., and Seristö, H. (2004), 'Strategies as discursive constructions: the case of airline alliances', *Journal of Management Studies*, 41/1: 1–35.

Vaara, E., Sorsa, V., and Pälli, P. (2010), 'On the force potential of strategy texts: critical discourse analysis of a strategic plan and its power effects in a city organization', *Organization*, 17/6: 685–702.

Vaara, E., and Whittington, R. (2012), 'Strategy-as-practice: taking social practices seriously', *Academy of Management Annals*, 6/1: 285–336.

Van Wessel, M., van Buuren, R., and van Woerkum, C. (2011), 'Changing planning by changing practice: how water managers innovate through action', *International Public Management Journal*, 14/3: 262–83.

Voronov, M. (2008), 'Toward a practice perspective on strategic organizational learning', *The Learning Organization*, 15/2: 195–221.

Whetten, D. A. (1989), 'What constitutes a theoretical contribution?', *Academy of Management Journal*, 14/4: 490–5.

Whittington, R. (1996), 'Strategy as practice', *Long Range Planning*, 29/5: 731–5.

(2003), 'The work of strategizing and organizing for a practice perspective', *Strategic Organization*, 1/1: 117–25.

(2006), 'Completing the practice turn in strategy research', *Organization Studies*, 27/5: 613–34.

(2007), 'Strategy practice and strategy process: family differences and the sociological eye', *Organization Studies*, 28/10: 1575–86.

Whittington, R., Molloy, E., Mayer, M., and Smith, A. (2006), 'Practices of strategising/organising: broadening strategy work and skills', *Long Range Planning*, 39/6: 615–29.

Whittle, A., and Mueller, F. (2010), 'Strategy, enrolment and accounting: the politics of strategic ideas', *Accounting, Auditing and Accountability Journal*, 23/5: 626–46.

Winsor, D. A. (1993), 'Constructing scientific knowledge in Gould and Lewontin's "The spandrels of San Marco"', in Selzer, J. (ed.), *Understanding Scientific Prose*: 127–43. Madison: University of Wisconsin Press.

Wright, R. P., Paroutis, S., and Blettner, D. P. (2013), 'How useful are the strategic tools we teach in business schools?', *Journal of Management Studies*, 50/1: 92–125.

Yearley, S. (1981), 'Textual persuasion: the role of social accounting in the construction of scientific arguments', *Philosophy of the Social Sciences*, 11/3: 409–35.

Zuckermann, H. (1988), 'The sociology of science', in Smelser, N. J. (ed.), *Handbook of Sociology*: 511–74. Newbury Park, CA: Sage.

The ongoing challenge of developing cumulative knowledge about strategy as practice

ANN LANGLEY

The strategy-as-practice perspective has attracted a substantial following of scholars interested in developing a better understanding of strategy as 'something people do' rather than something that 'organizations have' (Jarzabkowski and Spee 2009; Johnson *et al.* 2007; Vaara and Whittington 2012). Under this banner, researchers have examined issues such as what happens in strategy meetings (Hodgkinson *et al.* 2006; Jarzabkowski and Seidl 2008; Johnson *et al.* 2010), how various strategic management tools are used (Abdallah and Langley 2014; Jarzabkowski and Kaplan 2015; Kaplan 2011; Stenfors *et al.* 2007) and how middle managers can and do contribute to strategy-making (Balogun and Johnson 2004; Mantere 2008; Rouleau 2005). There is also a more critical stream in strategy-as-practice writing that has focused on the discursive practices of strategists (Ezzamel and Willmott 2008; Kornberger and Clegg 2011; Laine and Vaara 2007; Mantere and Vaara 2008). Finally, there have been several attempts to position the SAP perspective with respect to broader currents in theories of practice (Chia and MacKay 2007; Hendry and Seidl 2003; Jarzabkowski 2004; Seidl 2007; Whittington 2006).

This chapter addresses a set of key but deceptively simple questions about this emerging body of work. Where is it heading? Is it, as many of its advocates hope, following a path likely to generate cumulative learning about the practice of strategy that will result in 'a societal shift towards better everyday strategizing praxis, empowered by more effective practices and a deeper pool of skilled practitioners' (Whittington 2006: 629)? Indeed, is this ambition even reasonable or desirable? If so, how might it be achieved? More generally, how can progress in the understanding of strategy as

practice be achieved in a sub-field whose empirical focus remains rather loosely defined, whose theoretical roots emphasize the situated and the particular and whose corresponding research methods tend to be qualitative and exploratory? Some scholars might consider this question as irrelevant, seeing situated knowledge of particular episodes of strategy practice as sufficient unto themselves for the local insight they offer over and above more traditional models of strategy. I believe that more is needed if the strategy-as-practice perspective is to develop fully and be taken seriously.

I was originally inspired to think about these issues following an exchange with Leif Melin, co-author on a book that we wrote jointly with Gerry Johnson and Richard Whittington (Johnson *et al.* 2007). Our book introduces the SAP perspective and presents some theoretical and methodological resources for developing it. The book also includes eight illustrative articles that, in our view at the time, began to offer some insights into strategy as a social practice. As co-authors, we were discussing how to formulate the conclusion of the book when Leif pointed out that, while we had devoted considerable space to the theoretical and methodological implications of the eight illustrative articles, we had not devoted much space to what they actually told us about the practice of strategy – that is, the substantive knowledge that emerged from them. We did not resolve this issue in the book; indeed, that was not its purpose. The illustrative articles were merely that: they examined different issues relevant to practice but came nowhere near to providing a basis to generalize. Leif's point was important, however, and the remark stimulated me to think about what it is that we actually know about the practice of strategy, and whether the work currently being undertaken in its name could one day be integrated into another kind of book – one that would be comprehensive, credible, insightful and substantively useful to strategists. If so, what might that book look like? And what should we be doing now to make it possible?

In this chapter, I present three alternative sets of answers to the questions raised in the last two paragraphs, each based on a different conception of the nature of knowledge accumulation and progress in organization studies and the social sciences that I label the normal science perspective, the practice-theory-based perspective and the pragmatic perspective. These should be viewed as extreme 'ideal types' that do not necessarily reflect realistic predictions or prescriptions but, rather, establish the palette of orientations to cumulative knowledge that might be considered. The normal science perspective is empiricist in focus, and emphasizes the accumulation of knowledge through the extension and elaboration of nomological networks of relationships among variables. The practice-theory-based perspective views progress in terms of increased idiographic understanding of the nature of practical activity. Its contribution to the improvement of practice appears largely conceptual rather than instrumental. Finally, the pragmatic perspective views knowledge *of* practice as deeply embedded *in* practice, and thus accumulating principally through direct experience. I illustrate each of the perspectives with an exemplar: a published book that represents the materialization of the perspective in an area of study adjacent to strategy as practice. Finally, I examine the extent to which the different perspectives are compatible with the nature of the SAP field of research as it is currently organized, and I conclude with some personal reflections on the potential for knowledge accumulation and improvement in the practice of strategy.

Note that, since the original version of this chapter was published in the first edition of the *Cambridge Handbook of Strategy as Practice*, research in the area has developed considerably. Indeed, the present volume of the handbook bears witness to this development, and several of its chapters attempt explicitly to integrate emerging findings,

hopefully providing an indication of the state of knowledge accumulation. Nonetheless, I believe that the questions of this chapter remain relevant. As an eclectic domain of study, strategy as practice means different things to different people. It is not clear that the body of knowledge – even as expressed in this handbook – yet hangs together with any degree of coherence (Rouleau 2013).

A normal science view of progress and knowledge accumulation

Focus and precepts: extension and elaboration of nomological networks

Beyond the specific question of developing knowledge about strategy as practice, the strategic management field overall has been characterized for some time by considerable soul-searching concerning progress and knowledge accumulation. Various authors have declared the field to be unduly fragmented (Hambrick 2004; Volberda 2004), several have called for researchers to invest more intensively in replication (Mezias and Regnier 2007; Singh, Ang and Leong 2003) and others have deplored the journals' overemphasis on theoretical novelty at the expense of rigour and the accumulation of empirical findings (Miller 2007; Oxley, Rivkin and Ryall 2010). Even those who have lauded the progress of 'strategic management' since its inception in the late 1970s have recognized the diversity of perspectives inhabiting the field and have drawn attention to its tendency to advance through pendulum swings between internal and external foci (Hoskisson *et al.* 1999). Soul-searching of a similar nature has characterized organization studies more generally (Davis 2010; Hambrick 2007; McKinley 2007; Pfeffer 1993; 1995; 2007; Tsang and Kwan 1999) as well as the related disciplinary field of sociology (Cole 2001; Davis 2001). The concern that overemphasis on theoretical novelty and disdain for replication have inhibited knowledge accumulation recently contributed to the foundation of a new journal: *Academy of Management Discoveries*.

With some exceptions, those initiating discussion on these issues tend to view scientific progress in terms of the development of ever more accurate, general and useful causal statements about the relationships between important phenomena observable in the empirical world. The orientation thus tends to be resolutely positivist in tone and based on a 'normal science' conception of knowledge, as expressed in the form of established relationships between variables, with dependent variables generally representing some notion of performance.

'Normal science' perspectives are not necessarily the espoused norm for strategy-as-practice scholars, who have tended to favour social constructivist assumptions and qualitative methodologies. Nevertheless, it is worth considering what, if anything, can be said about the potential for cumulative knowledge about the practice of strategy from an angle that considers the social world to be patterned by underlying relationships that can be expressed in nomothetic terms. In Johnson *et al.* (2007), Johnson insists that the SAP perspective will be irrelevant if it does not help explain or predict outcomes that are important to successful practice. Jarzabkowski, Balogun and Seidl (2007), Johnson *et al.* (2007) and Whittington (2006) have argued that, while it would be illusory to expect micro-level strategy research to explain *organizational* performance outcomes directly, it can and should focus on intermediate outcomes related for example to the effectiveness of strategists or to the effectiveness of the practices they engage in. Thus, it certainly makes sense to ask whether current research is heading towards building better explanations of the performance of strategic practices, and what exactly researchers should be doing to achieve this.

Writers from the mainstream literature on strategy and organization studies offer some specific suggestions for improving this kind of knowledge accumulation. For example, Carlson and Hatfield (2004) argue that, to enhance cumulative knowledge development in strategic management, scholars need to focus on the twin objectives of improving prediction (expressed as the amount of variance explained) and improving generality (by testing relationships established in earlier studies in a variety of new contexts). They therefore propose that researchers should take as their starting point

the phenomenon to be explained or predicted rather than the testing of any particular theory, and that a variety of theories should be mobilized as needed to help explain more of the variance. These authors argue emphatically for the need to build on prior research by including in each study all the variables that have been found important in the past. They further urge the use of valid and reliable measures and samples that are as large as possible to enhance generalizability. In the same vein, McKinley (2007) insists on the need for the standardization of measures across studies to ensure that they are comparable and to allow research results to accumulate. Finally, Mezias and Regnier (2007) cite the practices of certain prestigious political science and economics journals, which demand that authors' databases be archived and made available to other researchers, and that a fixed proportion of pages be allocated to replication. All these prescriptions are based on the idea that each individual study is a small piece in the collective construction of an increasingly robust edifice of 'truth' that will ultimately enable scholars to offer stronger and more valid recommendations to practitioners.

Example: Finkelstein, Hambrick and Cannella (2009) on strategic leadership

In 1984 Hambrick and Mason wrote a now famous paper in *Academy of Management Review* proposing an 'upper echelons' theory of strategy, which subsequently stimulated a very productive stream of research (Hambrick and Mason 1984). Finkelstein and Hambrick followed up in 1996 with a book that elaborated the theory and reviewed the state of accumulated knowledge about the 'impact of top executives on organizations' at that point in time (Finkelstein and Hambrick 1996). Research in this stream has continued since then. In 2007 the authors of the original article, Donald Hambrick and Phyllis Mason, received the *Academy of Management Review*'s award for the most 'innovative and frame-breaking' article during its first decade of existence (Kilduff 2007: 332). To commemorate the occasion, Hambrick was invited to present an update of 'upper echelons theory' in the journal (Hambrick 2007). In parallel with this, at least one systematic review and two meta-analyses of the upper echelons research programme have appeared – another sign that researchers have replicated previous work and that some kind of accumulation is occurring (Carpenter, Geletkanycz and Sanders 2004; Certo *et al.* 2006; Homberg and Bui 2013). Finally, a significantly updated version of the Finkelstein and Hambrick book (with the addition of a new author) was published in 2009 (Finkelstein, Hambrick and Cannella 2009). Finkelstein, Hambrick and Cannella (2009) and Carpenter, Geletkanycz and Sanders (2004) summarize the conceptual frameworks driving the research programme using a set of diagrams illustrating relationships between variables associated with top management team characteristics, team behaviour and performance.

Of course, Finkelstein, Hambrick and Cannella's book is not a volume about strategy as practice. It focuses not so much on what top executives or strategists do but on who they are, and on how this affects what organizations do and thence organizational performance, generally with little attention to what happens in between. Interestingly, however, Hambrick (2007) shows signs of moving closer to the interests of SAP scholars, by calling for more attention to what he calls the 'black box' of upper echelons research – specifically, the 'actual psychological and social processes that serve to transform executive characteristics into strategic action' (Hambrick 2007: 337). He argues that this is essential to improve relevance to practitioners. Hambrick is somewhat pessimistic about progress in this area, however, as it 'requires very intrusive access to large numbers of executives and TMTs who are notoriously unwilling to submit themselves to scholarly probing and poking' (337). Of course, this is exactly what many practice scholars have successfully embraced (such as Balogun and Johnson 2004; Jarzabkowski, Lê and Van de Ven 2013; Kaplan and Orlikowski 2013; Rouleau 2005). As an alternative, he proposes the development and use of a highly complex strategy simulation game that would provide a controlled context to observe and learn from pseudo-top management team dynamics in the laboratory. While moving closer to a practice perspective, the emphasis remains on developing the theory through elaboration of the patterns of relationships among decontextualized variables, and identifying the moderating factors that influence these relationships.

The overall point, however, is that, so far, the upper echelons approach as a sub-field of strategy has been fairly successful in gathering adherents and in developing a cumulative and relatively coherent body of knowledge. Will the strategy-as-practice community have as much to show for itself after a similar period of development?

Application and limitations: normal science and strategy as practice

To consider the implications and relevance of the above perspective for strategy as practice, I take the example of strategy workshops or meetings as a phenomenon for which there seems to be some attempt at cumulative understanding. Several researchers – most in the United Kingdom, but also elsewhere in Europe – have invested considerable effort on this (Blackler, Crump and McDonald 2000; Bowman 1995; Bürgi, Jacobs and Roos 2005; Healey *et al.* forthcoming; Hodgkinson *et al.* 2006; Hodgkinson and Wright 2002; Jarzabkowski and Seidl 2008; Johnson *et al.* 2010; Schwarz and Balogun 2007; Seidl, MacIntosh and MacLean 2006; Seidl, MacLean and MacIntosh 2011). Workshops to discuss the research were organized in 2003 and 2008, and, indeed, a chapter on this stream of research – chapter 32, by Seidl and Guérard – appears in this volume. It would seem that, if there is any focused strategy-as-practice topic that has engaged some kind of enthusiasm from a large number of researchers, this is it.

To develop cumulative knowledge about strategy workshops in a normal science vein, Carlson and Hatfield (2004) would require researchers to begin by defining a clear dependent variable that might be called, say, 'strategic workshop effectiveness', and then mobilize their energies towards explaining it, drawing on a variety of theoretical resources. One can see the beginnings of such attempts in MacIntosh, MacLean and Seidl's (2010) study of the determinants of effectiveness of workshops in achieving change in ten different organizations as well as in two recent quantitative studies (one in the United Kingdom and one in Germany) of factors affecting the effectiveness of strategy workshops using identical questionnaires (Healey *et al*. forthcoming; van Aaken *et al*. 2013).

After an initial period of exploration, McKinley (2007) would argue that everyone working in the focal research area should then converge on the same measure of the dependent variable and of its predictors to ensure that different studies are comparable. At some point, after some inductive studies that investigate the phenomenon in depth to identify key constructs (Carlile and Christensen 2005), there would be a need to isolate the variables that affect these outcomes, defining them in a general enough way that they will be widely applicable, and testing the research apparatus on a sufficiently large number of contexts to be able to argue for their generalizability. The community could then begin to construct – through successive studies that built upon each other – a valid and tested theory of strategy workshops that would enable managers to understand the practices and conditions that lead to their success. The studies by Healey *et al*. (forthcoming) and van Aaken *et al*. (2013), as reported by Seidl and Guérard in this volume, constitute an embryonic corpus that moves in this direction. The style of research on practice favoured by this normal science approach is reflected in Bromiley and Rau's (2014) formulation of what they call a 'practice-based view'.

This image has several problems, of course, not least of which is the relatively poor fit of the normal science perspective with the constructivist epistemological assumptions preferred by many practice scholars. Four concrete issues that may concern them will be mentioned here. First (and notwithstanding the measurement attempts mentioned above) is the question of what one might mean by the 'effectiveness' of strategy workshops and how one might isolate this notion independently of its context or of a moment in time at which it might be recognized. While participants may feel that an event was successful in the short term, its longer-term impact may be quite a different thing (Bowman 1995; Healey *et al*. forthcoming; Schwarz and Balogun 2007). As some of the work

on workshops has suggested, strategy development activities are often imbued with paradox; the more radically innovative they are in conceptual terms, the harder they may be to reconnect with daily action (Hendry and Seidl 2003; Johnson *et al*. 2010). Thus, agreeing on what effectiveness means may be problematic.

Second, while an individual workshop may accomplish or 'perform' things (such as producing a new strategic planning document, reinforcing a leader's credibility or patching up a conflict), those effects are highly context-dependent and, indeed, constituted by and imperfectly distinguishable from the micro-activities and specific practices that compose them, as well as the implicit or explicit strategies of their participants. What ultimately occurs depends partly on people's conceptions of what they are doing, partly on the cultural, material and practical resources that they draw on and partly on how they creatively and recursively mobilize these resources in interaction. Thus, the assumption of the separability and generality of dependent variables representing outcomes and independent variables representing practices is simplistic. The vast quantitative literature on strategic planning illustrates this problem. Although meta-analyses (Boyd 1991; Miller and Cardinal 1994) have suggested that the use of planning is somewhat related to organizational performance, the results of this research provide little guidance about precisely what a given company should do in any particular case.

Third, and related to the points above, the normal science perspective on knowledge accumulation in strategic management promoted by Carlson and Hatfield (2004) and others seems to focus exclusively on variance-based understandings, to the exclusion of process thinking that considers *how* phenomena evolve over time (Langley 2007; Van de Ven and Poole 2005). Indeed, Carlson and Hatfield's (2004) conception of knowledge as virtually time-independent is astonishing when one considers the inescapability of temporal influence. Thus, such a perspective will not be sensitive to important practical questions such as how workshops play themselves out over time, how they are linked to the chains of events that precede them and how they are connected to those that follow.

Finally, the 'strategy workshop', like any social or managerial practice, is a historically embedded phenomenon. Tools of strategizing wax and wane, shift and mutate, with fashion, experience, technology and institutional mores, as well as through their recursive reproduction and adaptation in the routines of particular firms (Jarzabkowski 2004). Using the example of gender relations, Cole (2001) suggests that one of the reasons for the lack of cumulative knowledge in sociology is that the phenomena of interest change more rapidly than the speed at which scholars are able to understand and describe them. Thus, any empirical regularities that might be detected concerning the determinants of the performance of strategy workshops can quickly become obsolete and anachronistic as the tools and techniques that generated the regularities are replaced by others and as the label 'strategy workshop' comes to mean something different.

In summary, although the normal science perspective is the dominant mode of thinking about scientific progress – and indeed, for some, still the *only* way of conceiving the possibility of progress – its usefulness as a model for the development of knowledge about strategy as practice is rather questionable. What alternative models might be helpful?

A practice-theory-based view of progress and knowledge accumulation

Focus and precepts: deeper theoretical understanding

My second attempt to define what knowledge accumulation might mean for strategy as practice is based not on the ideal of a single truth but on the search for increasingly insightful interpretations or representations of strategy viewed as a social practice. Rather than building increasingly elaborate nomological networks to explain or predict the performance of practical activity, this perspective involves placing stronger and deeper bets on the *theories of practice* that SAP scholars have often claimed as their intellectual inspiration (as described in Part II of this handbook) and developing these concertedly, determinedly and coherently to enrich the understanding of strategy.

This view thus rejects the rather backward-looking normal science conception of a single legitimate path to scientific progress based on enhanced prediction and generalization, and is more compatible with current ideas from the philosophy of science in which scholarly disciplines are seen to form a number of distinct epistemic communities that develop different sets of ontological and methodological commitments and pursue different research programmes (Laudan 1977; Zald 1995). Each of these communities has its own internal conceptions of progress, and its own modes of evaluation concerning what constitutes a valuable contribution (Zald 1995). From this angle, the question that then arises is: does the SAP community qualify as an 'epistemic community'? If so, what are its specific ontological and methodological commitments? How and to what extent are they different from those described previously?

The answer to this question remains rather ambiguous, and this is in many ways the central puzzle underlying this chapter. Strategy as practice currently has a rather loose identity organized around an interest in an empirical phenomenon (the doing of strategy), an appeal to the theoretical resources from practice theory and the use of qualitative research methods to capture and analyse the micro-activities associated with strategizing (Johnson *et al.* 2007). Beyond the general reference to theories of practice, Whittington (2006) and Jarzabkowski, Balogun and Seidl (2007) have drawn on Reckwitz (2002) in an attempt to offer a tripartite conceptual framework that might serve to integrate work in this sub-field around the notions of *practices* (routines, tools or discourses at organizational and extra-organizational levels), *praxis* (the concrete activities actually carried out in a specific situation) and *practitioners* (the sets of people who mobilize practices in their everyday strategy praxis). There are many different ways in which the elements of this framework could be used, however, and there is as yet no clear consensus concerning its completeness or relevance. Indeed, Chia and McKay (2007: 223) argue that, while there is some 'straining towards a revised vocabulary for theorizing strategy practice', much of the empirical work published so far under the banner of strategy as practice does not necessarily reveal a strongly practice-based ontology in which *practices* rather than the activities of individuals or organizational processes are taken to be the central focus of attention (Feldman and Orlikowski 2011). Indeed, Rouleau (2013) suggests that SAP scholars have been using the term 'practice' in five quite distinctive ways: as referring to managerial action, as a set of tools, as knowledge, as organizational resources and as global discourse.

To complicate matters further, even within the broader 'practice turn' in social theory, the definition of what constitutes a practice and how this concept should be used remains a topic of debate (Feldman and Orlikowski 2011; Schatzki, Knorr Cetina and von Savigny 2001). Furthermore, the language of this debate is highly complex, not to say opaque. It is widely recognized even by those who have used them in empirical studies that the writings of key theorists such as Giddens, Bourdieu, Vygotsky and Latour can be challenging to master and operationalize credibly in empirical research (see, for example, Pozzebon 2004), let alone to communicate to practitioners. There are many competing but somewhat overlapping theories of practice that vie for attention, each of which requires its adherents to invest considerable intellectual effort. The 'barriers to entry' into the world of sophisticated practice theorizing are as high as if not higher than the methodological and statistical barriers that have been mounting around the world of normal science-based strategic management research.

Nevertheless, as its proponents have argued, a practice-theory-based perspective offers a number of distinctive contributions (Chia and MacKay 2007; Feldman and Orlikowski 2011; Rouleau 2013; Whittington 2006) that are encouraging many strategy researchers to aspire to penetrate that world. The focus on practices brings strategy down to the level of the activities of human beings interacting in observable situations. It bridges notions of agency and structure by recognizing the individual skills and knowledge involved in the enactment, adaptation and regeneration of practices within strategizing activities while acknowledging the partly extra-individual, and even extra-organizational, source of those practices. Moreover,

practice theories recognize to different degrees the roles of material artefacts in enabling and constraining practical activity. What kinds of contributions might be generated, then, by running sufficiently hard with these ideas to build them into more substantial cumulative insights?

Example: Gherardi (2006) on organizational knowledge and knowing in practice

I have chosen Gherardi's (2006) book *Organizational Knowledge: The Texture of Workplace Learning* to illustrate the potential for the development of cumulative knowledge from a practice-theory-based perspective because it represents a strong example of a long-term research programme that has taken practice ideas seriously and developed them into a comprehensive contribution within the broader field of organization studies.

This book does not offer a perfect parallel to the Finkelstein, Hambrick and Cannella (2009) book described earlier, however, because it does not integrate other related research perfectly into its conceptualization and it emphasizes only one – albeit very extensive – programme of empirical study carried out specifically by Silvia Gherardi and her colleagues (particularly Nicolini and Strati) since 1994. Gherardi draws on other work dealing with communities of practice, learning and knowledge development as a backdrop to her own thinking rather than as an inherent part of it. A complementary article by Østerlund and Carlile (2005) goes some way towards integrating and connecting the diverse contributions of key theorists on communities of practice (Brown and Duguid 1991; 2001; Lave and Wenger 1991; Wenger 1998). A book that fully cumulates the stream of research on workplace learning has yet to be written, however.

Nevertheless, Gherardi's (2006) book is impressive in the way it has taken a single key workplace issue – safety – and explored its multiple ramifications in social practices across different levels. Inspired by Cooper and Fox (1990), Gherardi uses the notion of a 'texture' of knowing in practice to describe interconnectedness across a complex field of layered and interwoven practices that all have something to do with the way that safety is constructed in situated contexts. The work involved a series of interrelated research initiatives, giving rise to separate publications with a variety of co-authors constituting what Gherardi calls a 'spiral' case study. For example, one study looked at how novice building site managers become practitioners and learn about safety on the job. Another study looked at how understandings of safety are enacted within a community of practitioners. A third described how different communities of practice in the construction industry interact around questions of safety. A fourth examined repair practices following breakdown. A fifth looked at the distributed network of actors influencing the construction of safety in the wider context. Together, these studies generate a rich portrait of how safety and knowledge of safety are embedded in a field of interrelated practices.

Application and limitations: practice theories and strategy as practice

Again, Gherardi's book is not about strategy as practice. The book inspires reflection, however, as to whether it might be possible to do for strategy what Gherardi has done for safety. A similar texture of interwoven practices could be seen to constitute knowledge about strategy and strategizing. At the risk of overdrawing the parallels, novice strategists learn strategy practices on the job and strategy is enacted within communities of practitioners and between different communities in interaction. Strategic practices may take rather different forms when a firm needs to repair its position than under routine circumstances. Finally, as Whittington et al. (2003) indicate, a network of distributed actors contributes to the construction of what strategy means and to which forms of strategy are considered legitimate. Moreover, practices of strategy are at one and the same time locally situated, interconnected across communities and organizations and in perpetual flux. If the SAP research community could draw on practice theorizing to fill out the portrait of how this occurs, perhaps it might come closer to developing a cumulative and integrated body of knowledge.

So far, however, most research programmes in the strategy-as-practice area have had a narrower focus, and the use of practice theory has been both more opportunistic and more eclectic than the work described above. Only Jarzabkowski's (2005) monograph has so far attempted to offer an empirical analysis drawing on practice theories in book-length form. Jarzabkowski (2005) used an activity theory lens to examine strategy-making in universities. This lens is not necessarily pursued in her other very prolific streams of work, however, which draw also on theoretical resources such as structuration theory (Jarzabkowski 2008; Jarzabkowski and Wilson 2002), institutional theory (Jarzabkowski, Matthiesen and Van de Ven 2009; Smets et al. forthcoming) and theories of communication (Jarzabkowski and Sillince 2007; Spee and Jarzabkowski 2011) to address topics related to strategy-as-practice topics. Like many scholars whose work has been associated with strategy as practice (including me), Jarzabkowski has chosen to draw on multiple theories to multiply insights rather than deepening the insights derived from applying a single integrated theoretical frame to a range of topics. As I argue later, this approach has its advantages, and it is something that I have personally found enriching. I have even argued in favour of it in previous publications (Denis, Langley and Rouleau 2007). Nevertheless, it is true that such an approach does not necessarily enable individual studies to build strongly on one another, with the result that the SAP perspective does not yet have the clarity and unity of other perspectives on strategy (such as the resource-based view) or of other perspectives in organizational theory. Indeed, another book – that by Scott (2013) on institutional theory, now in its fourth edition – might suggest another valuable model for cumulative and integrative theorizing that practice theorists of organization would find inspiring. Another potential exemplar might be Thornton, Ocasio and Lounsbury's (2012) treatise on institutional logics.

The requirements for developing a more comprehensive and cumulative understanding of strategy as practice building on practice theory would seem to be quite difficult to meet, however. The convergence of teams of researchers around relatively similar practice-based theoretical frames is hampered by the complexity and interpretive flexibility of these frames, as well as by a research culture that tends to favour the distinctiveness of individual contributions (Hambrick 2004). Should pockets of convergence occur, narrow adherence to one or another theoretical approach (especially the more complex practice theories) may be accompanied by blinders and barriers to communication with adherents of other frames, leading, paradoxically, to a splintering of what is currently a fairly cohesive though eclectic and open community. Unfortunately, it is quite difficult to remain both open to different approaches to understanding and committed to a focused theoretical perspective. Since the practice of strategy is an empirical phenomenon, it would seem desirable that those working in this area remain able to transcend this paradox.

Another, rather different issue is raised by the emphasis on practice theory, however. This concerns the potential for developing knowledge that might be useful to practitioners. Clearly, academic research that draws on theories of practice may assist in describing the nature of such practices, and this in itself may be of interest. For example, practice theorists have revealed how storytelling among practitioners within the same community of practice contributes to learning to a greater extent than codified explicit knowledge of the type found in formal education programmes or procedures manuals (Gherardi 2006; Orr 1996). At the same time, and perhaps paradoxically, practice theorists have also revealed how boundary objects such as documents and other artefacts serve to connect different groups of practitioners embedded in different thought-worlds (Carlile 2002; 2004; Star and Griesemer 1989)

These are interesting insights, typical of practice-based theorizing and research. All the same, are insights such as these sufficient to meet Whittington's ambition, quoted earlier, of 'a societal shift towards better everyday strategizing praxis, empowered by more effective practices and a deeper pool of skilled practitioners' (Whittington 2006: 629)? Interestingly, Gherardi's (2006) book includes a three-and-a-half-page section at the end of the final chapter entitled 'Actionable knowledge'. This is the only part of a 265-page volume that addresses the implications of her research for practice. To be fair, this was not her primary objective. The thinness of this section might give us pause, however. Is that all there is? What does a practice-theory-based approach add over and above a normal science perspective that might be immediately useful?

Drawing on Pelz (1978), Astley and Zammuto (1992) identify three potential ways in which academic research may be practically useful: instrumental (the immediate and direct application of knowledge), conceptual (a more diffuse application of the theoretical ideas in reflexive practice) and symbolic (the mobilization of the results of research to support preconceived ideas). I believe that the contributions of the approach described in this section are likely to be largely at the conceptual rather than the instrumental or symbolic levels. At its best, practice-based research may help provide valuable conceptual tools for reflecting on concrete situations. It is unlikely to be directly usable in instrumental ways, however, or even to serve as a source of legitimization (symbolic use), given its relatively situated nature. In contrast, normal science-based research may be more widely mobilized in symbolic mode, because it bears the more traditional stamp of 'science' while providing insufficiently detailed prescriptions to enable instrumental use in particular cases. I would argue that another type of approach, described in the next section, offers more potential for 'instrumental' use than either of those described so far.

A pragmatic view of progress and knowledge accumulation

Focus and precepts: learning through practice and experience

The third perspective on what knowledge accumulation and progress might mean for strategy as practice is labelled here 'pragmatic' in reference to the pragmatist philosophy of Pierce, Dewey and James, revived by Rorty (1980), which has offered inspiration for practice theories in general and strategy as practice in particular (Johnson *et al*

2007). Pragmatism values the instrumental nature of knowledge and emphasizes the way in which knowing is embedded in and regenerated through practical activity (Cook and Brown 1999). Specifically, as I define it here, a pragmatic view of progress and knowledge accumulation considers practical knowledge to be constituted through direct participation in practice (Calori 2002; Gherardi 2006).

Taking this as a starting point, it is clear that competent and experienced practitioners of strategy can be viewed as possessing a rich store of cumulative tacit knowledge about strategy. From a pragmatic perspective, then, one of the most important aims of SAP researchers ought to be to uncover this knowledge, render it explicit and make it available to others – a process that Pearce labelled 'abduction' (Locke, Golden-Biddle and Feldman 2008). And the best way to capture such knowledge would actually be to become a practitioner.

Of course, many academics *are* indeed also strategy consultants. When this happens, however, their writings usually tend to emphasize formal techniques and not the everyday experience of doing strategy. The other problem is that, as soon as a strategy practitioner becomes an expert, the tacit knowledge involved in the practice may become quite unconscious (Polanyi 1966). The people who are perhaps the most able to render the tacit explicit are 'apprentice-novices', those who learn the practice through experience in close contact with experts and yet who are still able to articulate that learning. All this suggests that one potentially valuable approach to developing knowledge on practice is actually to find a 'master' (a recognized strategy practitioner expert or consultant), to become an 'apprentice' and then to commit one's cumulatively developing learning to writing. This does in some sense represent the logical conclusion of accepting a strong-form practice-based view of strategy.

It is also in this context that different forms of collaborative research may be relevant (Balogun, Huff and Johnson 2003; Calori 2002). For example, Balogun and Johnson (2004) used diaries and focus groups to collect data on practices at the same time as engaging the practitioners involved in

their study in reflection about what they were doing and how well it was working. In an initiative based on Argyris, Putnam and Smith's (1985) action science framework, Stronz (2005) videotaped naturally occurring strategy implementation team meetings over a period of several months. She then chose excerpts from these meetings to present to implementation team members individually, questioning them about their goals during meetings, their action strategies, what they felt they could have done differently and how they viewed the results of these meetings. The capacity to engage practitioners in productive reflection on their own practice developed by Balogun and Johnson and Stronz creatively combines data collection for academic research with constructive learning opportunities for those involved.

If this kind of work produces only local learning for participants and abstract formalized knowledge in the form of academic articles and monographs, however, its subsequent wider usefulness in developing better praxis, practices and practitioners will remain limited. Thus, a truly pragmatic (i.e. instrumentally useful) perspective on progress and knowledge accumulation should also mean finding ways to transfer the practical knowledge. Clearly, there is an embedded paradox here. If practice is needed to learn about practice, then the academic researcher may simply be a redundant intermediary. Some researcher-practitioners in the field of strategy have made an effort to render their own practical learning accessible in written form, however, and it is worth examining one of these contributions as an example of what can be achieved.

Example: Eden and Ackermann (1998) on making strategy

Taking a pragmatic view of progress and knowledge accumulation, Eden and Ackermann's (1998) book *Making Strategy: The Journey of Strategic Management* is a remarkable achievement. In one sense, it is a manual or a textbook. Unlike other textbooks, however, which generally provide an overview of different dimensions of the phenomenon, drawing on classic literature, Harvard-style case studies and a loose integrative frame, Eden and Ackermann's book represents the delineation, development and illustration of a very distinctive practical approach to making strategy that evolved through the consulting experience of the authors over a period of almost twenty years. The approach developed in the book is grounded in Colin Eden's early experimentation with cognitive mapping tools in the late 1970s, followed by the development of the SODA (Strategic Options Development and Analysis) software based on these tools in the 1980s and 1990s and many subsequent strategy-consulting applications.

The book itself is structured in a quite unusual way. The first part presents an overall normative model of strategy-making called 'the journey'. It is perhaps the most classic part of the book, introducing the authors' theory of strategy-making as a process and insisting on the objective of building political feasibility. The approach demonstrates a sensitivity to the practical activities of negotiating strategy that is unusual in strategy texts and could be acquired only through experience. The last part of the book is a presentation of some specific techniques and tools that the authors have developed over time, including an impressive degree of detail on how to analyse the information generated and how to organize strategy workshops, again based on the experience of the authors. Meanwhile, the middle part of the book bridges the other two sections and embeds the overall conceptual model and the specific tools in concrete situations. The ten so-called 'vignettes' offer blow-by-blow accounts of doing strategy using the tools and ideas presented. Although no doubt a little sanitized to protect individuals (including the authors), these accounts read as genuine and earthy. In addition to illustrating how the tools were used, they offer insight into the tensions that developed during workshop sessions, they reveal the micro-decisions made on the fly and they show the high commitment, minute attention to detail and improvisational skills needed by workshop facilitators. In other words, they come closer to describing the *doing* of strategy than many more academically oriented contributions in the strategy-as-practice field. To the extent that their approach is comprehensive and builds on a lifetime of experience, we have here an example of the development of a cumulative body of knowledge. Is this a perspective that might be mobilized more systematically to achieve the objectives of improving strategy as practice?

Application and limitations: pragmatism and strategy as practice

If knowledge *of* practice is to a large extent embedded *in* practice, then some would argue that it is only through practice that knowledge of it may be acquired and transferred. As noted above, this would seem to suggest an increased role for action research or collaborative research to develop and test better tools and techniques and to cumulatively refine skills in everyday strategizing. In addition to the book mentioned above, there have been a limited number of published studies that have taken such an action-oriented approach. For example, Macintosh and Maclean (1999) propose and test a complexity-theory-based approach to strategy intervention, Hodgkinson and Wright (2002) present an analysis of a failed scenario-planning intervention in which they were consultants, and a research group at the Imagination Lab in Lausanne in the 2000s produced a continuous stream of research results based on experimentation with construction kits (specifically LEGO) as strategy-making tools (Bürgi, Jacobs and Roos 2005; Heracleous and Jacobs 2008; Jacobs, Oliver and Heracleous 2013; Oliver and Roos 2007). These streams, and particularly the last, may perhaps have some cumulative potential.

Action research is not currently a central focus for most of those interested in strategy as practice, however. While willing and eager to learn about strategy as flies on the wall, many of us are not so inclined to place ourselves on the front lines as practitioners – or, if we are, to then reveal all in the first person in academic publications. An exchange in *Organization Studies* (Hodgkinson and Wright 2006; Whittington 2006) suggests one reason why. An important part of the learning involved in practice includes learning from negative experiences, such as that recounted by Hodgkinson and Wright (2002). Revealing one's role in such experiences can be a risky proposition, however, that can leave one open to unexpected critique. Many practitioners would no doubt prefer that the learning from their less successful experiences remain confidential. Learning from experience is, of course, the stock in trade of professional consultants. Nevertheless, they often have other, more commercial reasons for retaining information that might be critical in helping others replicate their approach, while exaggerating its successes. Overall, when researchers are also actors in the scenes they are reporting, issues of validity, completeness and trustworthiness may be more than usually challenging to address well.

In addition to this limitation, one may also ask whether work that *does* involve first-person involvement in practice is then truly able to communicate it formally in ways that may be effectively mobilized by others. My own feeling has always been in reading books such as that by Eden and Ackermann (1998) – excellent as it is in its genre – that, somehow, the 'magic' that makes their approach work is not really there on the written page. This is not because they have tried to hide it. On the contrary, particularly in the case of the Eden and Ackermann book, I sense a genuine desire to assist others in replicating their approach. Even so, I know that, if I spent the time needed to learn by heart the details of their techniques and practices by reading the book (including the many vignettes, and the extensive practical wisdom embedded in the 507-page tome), and if I got myself a contract with a firm to use it to help the company develop a strategy, the results might well be dismal. To learn to do what they do, I would have to – yes – maybe read the book, but also join them on a consulting assignment or two. There might then be some hope that I would pick up some of that magic that makes their approach work. I also suspect that, as I learned, I would begin to improvise with the tools and perhaps invent some of my own, which I might then pass on through a similar process to others. Thus, cumulative knowledge development from this perspective would merge research, professional development and teaching into one continuous process – something that would demand a radical and rather unlikely change in the way academia is currently organized.

Discussion and conclusion: prospects for developing cumulative knowledge

In the last three sections, I have presented three distinct models of progress and knowledge accumulation that might be relevant to strategy as practice. These should be seen as ideal types. None of them reflects a fully realistic perspective. I believe, however, that between them they delineate the range of possibility. I suspect that most SAP scholars would tend to explicitly espouse the second approach. The normal science perspective remains dominant in the major journals, however, and acts as a powerful attractor that tends to draw empirical work in that direction. Thus, many contributions relevant to the practice of strategy are formulated using propositional logic or conform in other ways to the normal science model in which prediction and generalization are emphasized (Maitlis and Lawrence 2003; Regnér 2003; Stensaker and Falkenberg 2007). At the same time, the pragmatic perspective I presented last has been somewhat underemphasized despite the seemingly obvious implications of a practice-based understanding of the nature of knowledge (but see the work of the Imagination Lab team cited earlier).

Having elaborated these various orientations, their foundations, their strengths and their limitations, I return to the questions that stimulated this reflection. Where is the strategy-as-practice subfield heading? Are its proponents' ambitions to improve and transform the practices of strategy desirable or realistic? What might be done to achieve them?

I believe that there is some doubt as to whether strategy as practice is currently heading strongly in the direction of developing knowledge that will improve practice through the concrete instrumental use of research findings. To achieve this, more researchers would have to invest in action research adopting what I have called the pragmatic perspective. Moreover, for those who do invest in this way, the rewards of consulting and the localized benefits that this brings may divert attention from any kind of formalization of the resulting practical knowledge. The result is that, while individual organizations may benefit from the learning, the wider community may not.

I do see more potential for strategy-as-practice scholarship to offer knowledge of conceptual value to practice. The frameworks that SAP scholars draw on combined with in-depth empirical studies in situated contexts provide modes of thinking that can illuminate strategizing and strategic issues. Since multiple theories have the potential to offer multiple insights, I believe that it is important to nurture pluralism and to maintain a strategy-as-practice area that is open to diversity.

Within this pluralism, however, I also see a need to deepen and strengthen the strands of work that are being accomplished. There are at least two possible ways of achieving this. The first way involves focusing on a specific empirical phenomenon. The current work on strategy workshops and meetings is an interesting case where this is happening, although it is unlikely that the diverse contributions will add up to a clear picture unless there is a concerted effort to bring the findings together. While the normal science model of standardized indicators and variance relationships I described earlier looks out of place, there may be scope for various forms of qualitative meta-analysis such as those revealed in several chapters in this volume. The second way of improving integration involves developing long-term research programmes within a distinct theoretical tradition, and expanding the focus gradually to different empirical dimensions of strategy. This idea generalizes from the model suggested by Gherardi's work (2006). The related field of organizational routines (Feldman and Pentland 2003), which seems to be building on a common theoretical foundation in practice theory that views routines as generative systems, may constitute a valuable model for this approach (see also Chapter 18 by Martha Feldman in this volume).

Of course, no one can construct the future of a field or epistemic community by simply saying how they think it should develop. The future of the community will be enacted in the activities of those who associate themselves with it. This chapter has simply drawn attention to some issues underlying that development. In my presentation of alternative knowledge accumulation perspectives, I have identified three books, each of which represents a different form of contribution

symbolizing the progress of a field. There is of course another kind of volume that contributes to enacting an epistemic community and to establishing its identity, its past success and its future potential: the handbook, a collection of writings that report on the work achieved so far, and the options for development. At the time of writing, this new edition of the *Cambridge Handbook of Strategy as Practice*, and more specifically, the additions over and above the previous 2010 volume, offer a valuable opportunity to assess the state of the field, and take stock of its 'progress'. Much indeed has been done. Whether or not this vibrant stream of research is developing into a coherent body of knowledge remains an open question, however.

References

Abdallah, C., and Langley, A. (2014), 'The double edge of ambiguity in strategic planning', *Journal of Management Studies*, 51/2: 235–64.

Argyris, C., Putnam, R., and Smith, D. M. (1985), *Action Science*. San Francisco: Jossey-Bass.

Astley, W. G., and Zammuto, R. F. (1992), 'Organization science, managers, and language games', *Organization Science*, 3/4: 443–60.

Balogun, J., Huff, A. S., and Johnson, P. (2003), 'Three responses to the methodological challenges of studying strategizing', *Journal of Management Studies*, 40/1: 197–224.

Balogun, J., and Johnson, G. (2004), 'Organizational restructuring and middle manager sensemaking', *Academy of Management Journal*, 47/4: 523–49.

Blackler, F., Crump, N., and McDonald, S. (2000), 'Organizing processes in complex activity networks', *Organization*, 7/2: 277–300.

Bowman, C. (1995), 'Strategy workshops and top-team commitment to strategic change', *Journal of Managerial Psychology*, 10/8: 4–12.

Boyd, B. K. (1991), 'Strategic planning and financial performance: a meta-analytic review', *Journal of Management Studies*, 28/4: 353–74.

Bromiley, P., and Rau, D. (2014), 'Towards a practice-based view of strategy', *Strategic Management Journal*, 35/8: 1249–56.

Brown, J. S., and Duguid, P. (1991), 'Organizational learning and communities-of-practice: toward a unified view of working, learning, and innovation', *Organization Science*, 2/1: 40–57.

(2001), 'Knowledge and organization: a social-practice perspective', *Organization Science*, 12/2: 198–213.

Bürgi, P. T., Jacobs, C. D., and Roos, J. (2005), 'From metaphor to practice in the crafting of strategy', *Journal of Management Inquiry*, 14/1: 78–94.

Calori, R. (2002), 'Real time/real space research: connecting action and reflection in organization studies', *Organization Studies*, 23/6: 877–83.

Carlile, P. R. (2002), 'A pragmatic view of knowledge and boundaries: boundary objects in new product development', *Organization Science*, 13/4: 442–55.

(2004), 'Transferring, translating, and transforming: an integrative framework for managing knowledge across boundaries', *Organization Science*, 15/5: 555–68.

Carlile, P. R., and Christensen, C. M. (2005), *The Cycles of Theory Building in Management Research*, Working Paper no. 05–057. Boston: Harvard Business School.

Carlson, K. D., and Hatfield, D. E. (2004), 'Strategic management research and the cumulative knowledge perspective', in Ketchen, D. J., and Bergh, D. D. (eds.), *Research Methodology in Strategy and Management*, vol. I: 273–301. Bingley, UK: Emerald.

Carpenter, M. A., Geletkanycz, M. A., and Sanders, W. G. (2004), 'Upper echelons research revisited: antecedents, elements, and consequences of top management team composition', *Journal of Management*, 30/6: 749–78.

Certo, S. T., Lester, R. H., Dalton, C. M., and Dalton, D. R. (2006), 'Top management teams, strategy and financial performance: a meta-analytic examination', *Journal of Management Studies*, 43/4: 813–39.

Chia, R., and MacKay, B. (2007), 'Post-processual challenges for the emerging strategy-as-practice perspective: discovering strategy in the logic of practice', *Human Relations*, 60/1: 217–42.

Cole, S. (2001), 'Why sociology doesn't make progress like the natural sciences', in *What's Wrong with Sociology?*: 37–60. Edison, NJ: Transaction Books.

Cook, S. D., and Brown, J. S. (1999), 'Bridging epistemologies: the generative dance between organizational knowledge and organizational knowing', *Organization Science*, 10/4: 381–400.

Cooper, R., and Fox, S. (1990), 'The "texture"of organizing', *Journal of Management Studies*, 27/6: 575–82.

Davis, G. F. (2010), 'Do theories of organizations progress?', *Organizational Research Methods*, 13/4: 690–709.

Davis, J. A. (2001), 'What's wrong with sociology?', in Cole, S. (ed.), *What's Wrong with Sociology?*: 99–120. Edison, NJ: Transaction Books.

Denis, J.-L., Langley, A., and Rouleau, L. (2007), 'Strategizing in pluralistic contexts: rethinking theoretical frames', *Human Relations*, 60/1: 179–215.

Eden, C., and Ackermann, F. (1998), *Making Strategy: The Journey of Strategic Management*. London: Sage.

Ezzamel, M., and Willmott, H. (2008), 'Strategy as discourse in a global retailer: a supplement to rationalist and interpretive accounts', *Organization Studies*, 29/2: 191–217.

Feldman, M. S., and Orlikowski, W. J. (2011), 'Theorizing practice and practicing theory', *Organization Science*, 22/5: 1240–53.

Feldman, M. S., and Pentland, B. T. (2003), 'Reconceptualizing organizational routines as a source of flexibility and change', *Administrative Science Quarterly*, 48/1: 94–118.

Finkelstein, S., and Hambrick, D. C. (1996), *Strategic Leadership: Top Executives and Their Effects on Organizations*. St Paul, MN: West Educational Publishing.

Finkelstein, S., Hambrick, D. C., and Cannella, A. A. (2009), *Strategic Leadership: Theory and Research on Executives, Top Management Teams, and Boards*. New York: Oxford University Press.

Gherardi, S. (2006), *Organizational Knowledge: The Texture of Workplace Learning*. Malden, MA: Blackwell.

Hambrick, D. C. (2004), 'The disintegration of strategic management: it's time to consolidate our gains', *Strategic Organization*, 2/1: 91–8.

(2007), 'The field of management's devotion to theory: too much of a good thing?', *Academy of Management Journal*, 50/6: 1346–52.

Hambrick, D. C., and Mason, P. A. (1984), 'Upper echelons: the organization as a reflection of its top managers', *Academy of Management Review*, 9/2: 193–206.

Healey, M. P., Hodgkinson, G. P., Whittington, R., and Johnson, G. (forthcoming), 'Off to plan or out to lunch? Relationships between design characteristics and outcomes of strategy workshops', *British Journal of Management*.

Hendry, J., and Seidl, D. (2003), 'The structure and significance of strategic episodes: social systems theory and the routine practices of strategic change', *Journal of Management Studies*, 40/1: 175–96.

Heracleous, L., and Jacobs, C. D. (2008), 'Understanding organizations through embodied metaphors', *Organization Studies*, 29/1: 45–78.

Hodgkinson, G. P., Whittington, R., Johnson, G., and Schwarz, M. (2006), 'The role of strategy workshops in strategy development processes: formality, communication, co-ordination and inclusion', *Long Range Planning*, 39/5: 479–96.

Hodgkinson, G. P., and Wright, G. (2002), 'Confronting strategic inertia in a top management team: learning from failure', *Organization Studies*, 23/6: 949–77.

—— (2006), 'Neither completing the practice turn, nor enriching the process tradition: secondary misinterpretations of a case analysis reconsidered', *Organization Studies*, 27/12: 1895–901.

Homberg, F., and Bui, H. T. (2013), 'Top management team diversity: a systematic review', *Group and Organization Management*, 38/4: 455–79.

Hoskisson, R. E., Hitt, M. A., Wan, W. P., and Yiu, D. (1999), 'Theory and research in strategic management: swings of a pendulum', *Journal of Management*, 25/3: 417–56.

Jacobs, C. D., Oliver, D., and Heracleous, L. (2013), 'Diagnosing organizational identity beliefs by eliciting complex, multimodal metaphors', *Journal of Applied Behavioral Science*, 49/4: 485–507.

Jarzabkowski, P. (2004), 'Strategy as practice: recursiveness, adaptation, and practices-in-use', *Organization Studies*, 25/4: 529–60.

—— (2005), *Strategy as Practice: An Activity-Based Approach*. London: Sage.

—— (2008), 'Shaping strategy as a structuration process', *Academy of Management Journal*, 51/4: 621–50.

Jarzabkowski, P., Balogun, J., and Seidl, D. (2007), 'Strategizing: the challenges of a practice perspective', *Human Relations*, 60/1: 5–27.

Jarzabkowski, P., and Kaplan, S. (2015), 'Strategy tools-in-use: a framework for understanding "technologies of rationality" in practice', *Strategic Management Journal*, 36/4: 537–58.

Jarzabkowski, P., Lê, J., and Van de Ven, A. H. (2013), 'Responding to competing strategic demands: how organizing, belonging, and performing paradoxes coevolve', *Strategic Organization*, 11/3: 245–80.

Jarzabkowski, P., Matthiesen, J., and Van de Ven, A. H. (2009), 'Doing which work? A practice approach to institutional pluralism', in Lawrence, T., Leca, B., and Suddaby, R. (eds.), *Institutional Work: Actors and Agency in Institutional Studies of Organizations*: 284–316. Cambridge University Press.

Jarzabkowski, P., and Seidl, D. (2008), 'The role of meetings in the social practice of strategy', *Organization Studies*, 29/11: 1391–426.

Jarzabkowski, P., and Sillince, J. (2007), 'A rhetoric-in-context approach to building commitment to multiple strategic goals', *Organization Studies*, 28/11: 1639–65.

Jarzabkowski, P., and Spee, P. (2009), 'Strategy-as-practice: a review and future directions for the field', *International Journal of Management Reviews*, 11/1: 69–95.

Jarzabkowski, P., and Wilson, D. C. (2002), 'Top teams and strategy in a UK university', *Journal of Management Studies*, 39/3: 355–81.

Johnson, G., Langley, A., Melin, L., and Whittington, R. (2007), *Strategy as Practice: Research Directions and Resources*. Cambridge University Press.

Johnson, G., Prashantham, S., Floyd, S., and Bourque, N. (2010), 'The ritualization of strategy workshops', *Organization Studies*, 31/12: 1589–618.

Kaplan, S. (2011), 'Strategy and PowerPoint: an inquiry into the epistemic culture and machinery of strategy making', *Organization Science*, 22/2: 320–46.

Kaplan, S., and Orlikowski, W. J. (2013), 'Temporal work in strategy making', *Organization Science*, 24/4: 965–95.

Kilduff, M. (2007), 'Celebrating thirty years of theory publishing in AMR: award-winning articles from the first two decades revisited', *Academy of Management Review*, 32/2: 332–3.

Kornberger, M., and Clegg, S. (2011), 'Strategy as performative practice: the case of Sydney 2030', *Strategic Organization*, 9/2: 136–62.

Laine, P.-M., and Vaara, E. (2007), 'Struggling over subjectivity: a discursive analysis of strategic development in an engineering group', *Human Relations*, 60/1: 29–58.

Langley, A. (2007), 'Process thinking in strategic organization', *Strategic Organization*, 5/3: 271–82.

Laudan, L. (1977), *Progress and Its Problems: Towards a Theory of Scientific Growth*. Berkeley: University of California Press.

Lave, J., and Wenger, E. (1991), *Situated Learning: Legitimate Peripheral Participation*. Cambridge University Press.

Locke, K., Golden-Biddle, K., and Feldman, M. S. (2008), 'Making doubt generative: rethinking the role of doubt in the research process', *Organization Science*, 19/6: 907–18.

MacIntosh, R., and MacLean, D. (1999), 'Conditioned emergence: a dissipative structures approach to transformation', *Strategic Management Journal*, 20/4: 297–316.

MacIntosh, R., MacLean, D., and Seidl, D. (2010), 'Unpacking the effectivity paradox of strategy workshops: do strategy workshops produce strategic change?', in Golsorkhi, D., Rouleau, L., Seidl, D., and Vaara, E. (eds.), *Cambridge Handbook of Strategy as Practice*: 291–309. Cambridge University Press.

Maitlis, S., and Lawrence, T. B. (2003), 'Orchestral manoeuvres in the dark: understanding failure in organizational strategizing', *Journal of Management Studies*, 40/1: 109–39.

Mantere, S. (2008), 'Role expectations and middle manager strategic agency', *Journal of Management Studies*, 45/2: 294–316.

Mantere, S., and Vaara, E. (2008), 'On the problem of participation in strategy: a critical discursive perspective', *Organization Science*, 19/2: 341–58.

McKinley, W. (2007), 'Managing knowledge in organization studies through instrumentation', *Organization*, 14/1: 123–46.

Mezias, S. J., and Regnier, M. O. (2007), 'Walking the walk as well as talking the talk: replication and the normal science paradigm in strategic management research', *Strategic Organization*, 5/3: 283–96.

Miller, C. C., and Cardinal, L. B. (1994), 'Strategic planning and firm performance: a synthesis of more than two decades of research', *Academy of Management Journal*, 37/6: 1649–65.

Miller, D. (2007), 'Paradigm prison, or in praise of atheoretic research', *Strategic Organization*, 5/2: 177–84.

Oliver, D., and Roos, J. (2007), 'Beyond text: constructing organizational identity multimodally', *British Journal of Management*, 18/4: 342–58.

Orr, J. E. (1996), *Talking about Machines: An Ethnography of a Modern Job*. Ithaca, NY: ILR Press.

Østerlund, C., and Carlile, P. (2005), 'Relations in practice: sorting through practice theories on knowledge sharing in complex organizations', *The Information Society*, 21/2: 91–107.

Oxley, J. E., Rivkin, J. W., and Ryall, M. D. (2010), 'The strategy research initiative: recognizing and encouraging high-quality research in strategy', *Strategic Organization*, 8/4: 377–86.

Pelz, D. C. (1978), 'Some expanded perspectives on use of social science in public policy', in Yinger, M. J., and Cutler, S. J. (eds.), *Major Social Issues: A Multidisciplinary View*: 346–57. New York: Free Press.

Pfeffer, J. (1993), 'Barriers to the advance of organizational science: paradigm development as a dependent variable', *Academy of Management Review*, 18/4: 599–620.

— (1995), 'Mortality, reproducibility, and the persistence of styles of theory', *Organization Science*, 6/6: 681–6.

— (2007), 'A modest proposal: how we might change the process and product of managerial research', *Academy of Management Journal*, 50/6: 1334–45.

Polanyi, M. (1966), *The Tacit Dimension*. Garden City, NY: Doubleday.

Pozzebon, M. (2004), 'The influence of a structurationist view on strategic management research', *Journal of Management Studies*, 41/2: 247–72.

Reckwitz, A. (2002), 'Toward a theory of social practices: a development in culturalist theorizing', *European Journal of Social Theory*, 5/2: 243–63.

Regnér, P. (2003), 'Strategy creation in the periphery: inductive versus deductive strategy making', *Journal of Management Studies*, 40/1: 57–82.

Rorty, R. (1980), *Philosophy and the Mirror of Nature*. Cambridge University Press.

Rouleau, L. (2005), 'Micro-practices of strategic sensemaking and sensegiving: how middle managers interpret and sell change every day', *Journal of Management Studies*, 42/7: 1413–41.

— (2013), 'Strategy-as-practice research at a crossroads', *M@n@gement*, 16/5: 574–92.

Schatzki, T. R., Knorr Cetina, K., and von Savigny, E. (eds.) (2001), *The Practice Turn in Contemporary Theory*. London: Routledge.

Schwarz, M., and Balogun, J. (2007), *Strategy Workshops for Strategic Reviews: A Case of Semi-Structured Emergent Dialogues*, Working Paper no. 054. London: AIM Research.

Scott, W. R. (2013), *Institutions and Organizations: Ideas, Interests, and Identities*, 4th edn. Thousand Oaks, CA: Sage.

Seidl, D. (2007), 'General strategy concepts and the ecology of strategy discourses: a systemic-discursive perspective', *Organization Studies*, 28/2: 197–218.

Seidl, D., MacIntosh, R., and MacLean, D. (2006), *Strategy Workshops and Strategic Change: Toward a Theory of Endogenous Strategic Change*, Business Research Paper no. 2006–8. Munich School of Management.

Seidl, D., MacLean, D., and MacIntosh, R. (2011), 'Rules of suspension: a rules-based explanation of strategy workshops in strategy process', paper presented at seventy-first annual meeting of the Academy of Management, San Antonio, Texas, 15 August.

Singh, K., Ang, S. H., and Leong, S. M. (2003), 'Increasing replication for knowledge accumulation in strategy research', *Journal of Management*, 29/4: 533–49.

Smets, M., Jarzabkowski, P., Burke, G., and Spee, P. (forthcoming), 'Reinsurance trading in Lloyd's of London: balancing conflicting-yet-complementary logics in practice', *Academy of Management Journal*.

Spee, P., and Jarzabkowski, P. (2011), 'Strategic planning as communicative process', *Organization Studies*, 32/9: 1217–45.

Star, S. L., and Griesemer, J. R. (1989), 'Institutional ecology, translations, and boundary objects: amateurs and professionals in Berkeley's Museum of Vertebrate Zoology, 1907–39', *Social Studies of Science*, 19/3: 387–420.

Stenfors, S., Tanner, L., Syrjänen, M., Seppälä, T., and Haapalinna, I. (2007), 'Executive views concerning decision support tools', *European Journal of Operational Research*, 181/2: 929–38.

Stensaker, I., and Falkenberg, J. (2007), 'Making sense of different responses to corporate change', *Human Relations*, 60/1: 137–77.

Stronz, M. M. (2005), 'Strategic learning in the context of strategy implementation: a case study of implementers in action', doctoral thesis. New York: Teachers College, Columbia University.

Thornton, P. H., Ocasio, W., and Lounsbury, M. (2012), *The Institutional Logics Perspective: A New Approach to Culture, Structure, and Process*. Oxford University Press.

Tsang, E. W., and Kwan, K.-M. (1999), 'Replication and theory development in organizational science: a critical realist perspective', *Academy of Management Review*, 24/4: 759–80.

Vaara, E., and Whittington, R. (2012), 'Strategy-as-practice: taking social practices seriously', *Academy of Management Annals*, 6/1: 285–336.

Van Aaken, D., Koob, C., Rost, K., and Seidl, D. (2013), 'Ausgestaltung und Erfolg von Strategieworkshops: eine empirische Analyse', *Zeitschrift für betriebswirtschaftliche Forschung*, 65/7: 588–616.

Van de Ven, A. H., and Poole, M. S. (2005), 'Alternative approaches for studying organizational change', *Organization Studies*, 26/9: 1377–404.

Volberda, H. W. (2004), 'Crisis in strategy: fragmentation, integration or synthesis', *European Management Review*, 1/1: 35–42.

Wenger, E. (1998), *Communities of Practice: Learning, Meaning, and Identity*. Cambridge University Press.

Whittington, R. (2006), 'Completing the practice turn in strategy research', *Organization Studies*, 27/5: 613–34.

Whittington, R., Jarzabkowski, P., Mayer, M., Mounoud, E., Nahapiet, J., and Rouleau, L. (2003), 'Taking strategy seriously: responsibility and reform for an important social practice', *Journal of Management Inquiry*, 12/4: 396–409.

Zald, M. N. (1995), 'Progress and cumulation in the human sciences after the fall', *Sociological Forum*, 10/3: 455–79.

7 Practical relevance of practice-based research on strategy

VIOLETTA SPLITTER and DAVID SEIDL

The practical relevance of research is of great concern to strategy scholars. Indeed, the lack of practical relevance that traditional strategy research was widely perceived to have was one of the main factors that spurred the practice-based approach to strategy (Jarzabkowski and Whittington 2008; Johnson, Melin and Whittington 2003; Whittington *et al.* 2003). According to some of the proponents of the strategy-as-practice approach, the preoccupation with 'what people do in strategy' is the key to increasing the practical relevance of strategy research (Whittington 2006). Nevertheless, we are just beginning to understand in more detail how and in what way a practice-based approach to strategy can produce practically relevant knowledge – that is, can make a difference to management practice (Nicolai and Seidl 2010).

Traditionally, the relevance gap has been seen as resulting either from obstacles in the transfer of scientific knowledge to management practice or from problems in the production of scientific knowledge itself (for an overview of the literature, see Bartunek and Rynes 2014). In response to the former we find various suggestions for improving the mode of communication between academics and practitioners (Beer 2001), and in response to the latter there are calls for more collaborative forms of research (Gibbons *et al.* 1994; Van de Ven 2007) and alternative research designs (Lawler 1999). While these arguments are well rehearsed, practice-based management scholars have offered a new take on the relevance debate by examining the particular ontological and epistemological conditions for generating practically relevant knowledge in research. Practice-based scholars apply practice theory to examine the relation of the practices of management practitioners with those of management researchers. As Jarzabkowski, Mohrman and Scherer (2010: 8)

put it: 'Academics are also practitioners – of scholarly pursuit. Their practices. . .reflect their interests and occur within an institutional setting that they shape and from which they derive meaning.' A common argument (Sandberg and Tsoukas 2011; Splitter and Seidl 2011) is that, although researchers and managers are practitioners, they operate in two distinct areas of practice that function according to two different modes of reasoning: the logic of management research and the logic of management practice. As a consequence, managers and researchers differ in their perceptions of the world, limiting their mutual understanding and hence the potential impact of research. Practice-based scholars argue that only by reflecting the logic of management practice in the research process itself can researchers overcome the fundamental divide between management research and practice.

In this chapter we bring together different studies that draw on a practice-based perspective to examine the practical relevance of management research in general and strategy-as-practice research in particular. Although these studies agree that practice-based research has to be grounded in the logic of management practice to be practically relevant, they have provided different suggestions on how this can be achieved. Two of the studies focus on the ways in which scientific knowledge is produced (Sandberg and Tsoukas 2011; Splitter and Seidl 2011), while another focuses more on the way in which scientific knowledge is transferred from management research to management practice (Jarzabkowski and Wilson 2006). More specifically: the first study examines the process through which management scholars can capture the object of their research and develop theories based on practical rationality; the second study provides a framework that enables researchers to reflect on their own role in that process; and the third study investigates the process through which scientific knowledge is dissociated from and adapted to practice. In turn, the insights from investigating this process inform the development of theories built on the logic of management practice.

The remainder of this chapter is structured into five sections. In the next section we outline the social differences between strategy research and strategy practice, which stem from the scientific and the practical modes of reasoning that underlie each area. Following that, we review three approaches for capturing the logic of management practice, and then go on to discuss in which ways strategy-as-practice research can be expected to be relevant to practice. We conclude the chapter with a summary of its contributions and directions for future research.

The social differences between strategy research and strategy practice as a challenge to practical relevance

Scholars within the tradition of strategy as practice tend to focus either on how the differences between strategy research and strategy practice impact the production of knowledge (Sandberg and Tsoukas 2011; Splitter and Seidl 2011) or on how these differences impact the use of knowledge (Jarzabkowski and Wilson 2006). Although these authors draw on different practice-theoretical perspectives (such as those of Heidegger, Bourdieu and Aristotle), they share the assumption that the practices employed by strategy scholars and strategy practitioners are *socially different* and that the knowledge inherent in these practices is epistemologically different (see Table 7.1).

The difference between strategy research and strategy practice, as two distinct social contexts, has been elaborated by Splitter and Seidl (2011). They draw particularly on the theory of Pierre Bourdieu, who, more than any other practice theorist, has sought to grasp the social distinction between science and practice. Bourdieu (2002) speaks of the spheres of research and management practice as belonging to different 'social fields', in

the sense that these fields differ in their social structure, which is shaped by different interests and assumptions and different forms and structures of capital. Because of these structural differences, actors in each field face different possibilities and constraints while they carry out their socially shaped activities. In the academic field of strategy research, for example, scholars share an interest in publishing articles in academic journals. This interest inevitably has an impact on their practices such as the production of scientific knowledge. Similarly, in the economic field of management practice, for example, the development of a competitive advantage might guide many managers' practices.

Given that the same interests and forms of capital guide the practices of actors in a particular field, these actors also share the same assumptions on what is of value in that field. Bourdieu (1998) calls the axiomatic assumptions that shape the practices of the members of a field 'doxa'. These unconsciously shared valuations render the practices of other actors in the field meaningful and appropriate. In that sense, *doxa* guides the way in which the members of a field interpret 'the world by excluding any practice that would go against the taken-for-granted assumptions' (Splitter and Seidl 2011: 104). As a result of *doxa*, the structure of a field, and, by extension, the possibilities and constraints that actors face when enacting their practices, are conceived as natural and self-evident.

In the academic field of strategy in particular, *doxa* guides the judgements that scholars form about what is considered rigorous research. Thus, in this academic field *doxa* determines the way in which scholars evaluate the practices of other scholars as appropriate or otherwise. Analogously, managerial practices enacted in the economic field receive their specific meanings and intelligibility from being enacted in that particular field. Consequently, *research* practices that comply with the interests, capital and *doxa* that shape the structure of this field are likely to be recognized by strategy scholars as appropriate and relevant. By contrast, research practices are unlikely to be recognized as such by members of the academic field of strategy *practice* because they do not comply with the interests, capital and *doxa* that shape the structure of the economic field of management practice. 'This implies that research focusing on practical relevance rather than academic relevance addresses actors outside the field' (Splitter and Seidl 2011: 105).

Another difference between strategy research and strategy practice lies in what Bourdieu (2002) terms 'skholé'. *Skholé* is the 'time liberated from practical occupations and preoccupations of the world [that makes] a relation to the world possible that is liberated from practical urgencies' (Bourdieu 2000: 10). Thus, in contrast to actors in other fields, particularly in the economic field of management practice, academics engaged in management research are freed from time pressure and pressure to act. According to Bourdieu (1988), it is this *skholé* that allows researchers to conduct their studies, and, in a sense, makes science possible at all. Nevertheless, *skholé* also leads to researchers observing the practitioners' world differently from how practitioners see it themselves. Knowledge produced through strategy research is thus associated with a specific mode of observation that Bourdieu (1975) calls the 'scholastic view'. The scholastic view implies a distance between research and practice that results from the social condition of *skholé*. Bourdieu and Wacquant (1992: 78) define the scholastic view as 'an abstraction of the world to think about the world'. In other words, the scholastic view is a social distance that originates in the difference between the social conditions of the academic field and those of praxis. This view tends to emphasize the timelessness and generality of knowledge and entails the neutralization of practical urgencies. Thus, strategy research that is based on the scholastic view

> tends to be directed at universality and timelessness, which erases many conditions that are necessary to practical enactment…, [whereas] knowledge based on practical experience tends to emphasize immediacy and applicability in a specific context and is ordinarily more focused in time and space than is academic scholarship   (Splitter and Seidl 2011: 105).

Strategy scholars, for example, use the term 'strategy' in a universal and rigorous way, which does not necessarily resonate with the experiential, contextual and evaluative way in which the same term is used by strategy practitioners (Grand,

Rüegg-Stürm and von Arx 2010; Paroutis and Heracleous 2010). As a consequence, the scholastic distance between strategy research and strategy practice results largely in knowledge that is not practically relevant to strategy practitioners. Paradoxically, the scholastic distance is a necessary condition for the production of scientific knowledge and at the same time opposed to management practice. Thus, according to the practice-based approach, practices in the academic field of strategy research and the economic field of strategy practice are structured differently and, as a result of the scholastic view, the practices that are applied in the academic field of strategy research produce scientific knowledge that is detached from strategy practice.

In a similar vein, Sandberg and Tsoukas (2011) argue that scientific rationality forces management scholars to impose a scientific logic on management practice the underlying logic of which is, however, fundamentally different. The authors state that scientific rationality is based on three assumptions that underpin the development of theory in organization and management research. First, scientific rationality is based on the assumption that the world is constituted by distinct entities with distinct properties. The second assumption, which stems from the first, is that in science the basic form of producing knowledge is the epistemological relation between subject and object. The third assumption is that the epistemological relation between subject and object constitutes the logic of management practice. These assumptions are inherent in the perspective of 'normal science' (Langley 2010), which regards knowledge based on scientific rationality and developed through scientific rigour as superior to the knowledge that practitioners produce. The perspective of 'normal science' assumes that management practices – such as strategy practices – can be substantially improved if they are based on scientific rationality. Thus, the more rigorous the description of these practices, the better the chances for practitioners to improve their actions.

Sandberg and Tsoukas (2011) mention three particular problems that are associated with scientific rationality. First, knowledge based on scientific rationality prevents researchers from comprehending management practice because it is disconnected from the 'meaningful totality into which practitioners are immersed' (Sandberg and Tsoukas 2011: 341). Second, scientific rationality ignores the 'situational uniqueness that is characteristic of the tasks practitioners do'; and, third, it construes time differently from the way in which it is 'experienced by practitioners' (341). Thus, in the case of scientific rationality, as in the case of *skholé*, knowledge is generated through the detachment of scholars from management practice and through the disconnection of knowledge from its social context, as it is based on the assumption 'that people are detached, contemplative, and theoretical rather that they are involved, concerned and practical' (Weick 2005: 467).

Sandberg and Tsoukas (2011) drew on the existential ontology of Martin Heidegger to explore further the differences underlying scientific and practical rationality. They argue that the scholastic view, as an ontology that underlies scientific rationality, 'assumes disconnection – namely, that we, as sentient beings, are initially separated from the world to which we subsequently become contingently connected' (Sandberg and Tsoukas 2011: 343). In contrast to the scholastic view, they propose a view based on the notion of 'being-in-the-world'. From this perspective, human beings are never 'separated but always already entwined with others and things in specific sociomaterial practice worlds, such as teaching, nursing, managing, and so on' (343). In this sense, 'entwinement' can be seen as the primary mode of existence, and 'being' is understood as existing as part of a totality that comprises other beings and things. Consequently, something can neither *be* nor *be understood* outside or apart from this totality: being entwined with the world makes it possible for something 'to be at all, to be intelligible as something' (344).

In the context of management practice, the underlying logic is not constituted by scientific rationality but by the 'entwinement of ourselves, others, and things in a relational whole, in the sense that we are always already engaged in specific socio-material practices' (Sandberg and Tsoukas 2011: 345). This is true both for the practitioners and the scholars themselves. Consequently, strategy scholars can be seen as practitioners of scholarship who are entwined with the sociomaterial practice of *researching* strategy, whereas strategy practitioners are entwined with the specific sociomaterial practice of *doing* strategy. In this sense, the notion of entwinement differs in essence from scientific rationality and contrasts with the scholastic view. The entwinement of strategy scholars and practitioners entails the enactment of practices in different meaningful totalities, however, namely the totality of management research and the totality of management practice. As a consequence, strategy scholars are at risk of basing their research on scientific rationality, which is disconnected from management practice.

In line with the premise of entwinement as the basic form of knowledge production, Jarzabkowski and Wilson (2006) examined the contextual and intuitive nature of the knowledge that is inherent in management practice, which has important implications for how scientific knowledge on strategy can be utilized and applied. They point out that scientific knowledge on strategy is typically regarded as a set of robust concepts that are used to guide rational strategic action. When scholars describe contextual conditions as the objective reality and provide prescriptions for action, they draw on a representational epistemology, which assumes that knowledge is used in a rational and optimized – rather than in a contextual and intuitive – manner. From this perspective, 'any practical use of strategy knowledge other than direct instrumental application in accordance with contextual conditions is regarded as a matter of deviance, deliberate distortion or corruption' (Jarzabkowski and Wilson 2006: 360). Consequently, the representational perspective on the use of knowledge invalidates the contextual and evaluative conditions under which knowledge is used.

In order to show that strategy practitioners do not instrumentally apply and use strategy knowledge, Jarzabkowski and Wilson drew on a practice perspective informed by Aristotle, which defines knowledge use as 'practical-evaluative wisdom' (Jarzabkowski and Wilson 2006: 360). Practical-evaluative wisdom enables strategy practitioners to deal with the particular contingencies of real-life situations by fashioning knowledge to situational demands. From a practice perspective, practitioners do not use scientific knowledge linearly and

Table 7.1 Overview of practice-based approaches

	Theorizing through practical rationality	Participant objectivation	Dissociation process
Study	Sandberg and Tsoukas (2011)	Splitter and Seidl (2011)	Jarzabkowski and Wilson (2006)
Source	Heidegger	Bourdieu	Aristotle
Focus	Knowledge production	Knowledge production	Knowledge transfer
Critique	Scientific rationality (knowledge detached from time and context)	Unawareness of scholastic view (social distance to practice)	Misperception of the practitioners' use of academic knowledge
Implications	Capture the meaningful totality and situational uniqueness of management practices	Reflect on and control social constraints of scientific knowledge production	Grasp the contextual and intuitive nature of knowledge use by practitioners; no scientific determination of tool use
Technique	Search for entwinement and breakdowns	Integration of the social distance between the researcher and the object of study into the analysis	Consideration of the dissociation process in scientific knowledge production

unidirectionally but adapt it to the needs of practical situations. In this sense, strategy practitioners do not objectively possess strategy knowledge; it is part of the 'social practices in which strategic actors participate in order to communicate and construct meanings about strategy, furthering their ends in ways that are intelligible to others' (Jarzabkowski and Wilson 2006: 360). Thus, practitioners adopt existing scientific knowledge in their strategizing practices, 'adapting it to their own purposes with little concern for its theoretical origins or purposes' (360). This implies that scientific knowledge on strategy is not used as strategy scholars intend it to be used but, instead, becomes contextualized and embedded in the practitioners' strategizing practices. In this sense, the way in which practitioners use scientific knowledge follows the logic of management practice rather than the logic of science, as representational epistemology assumes.

To summarize, in this section we have described three distinct approaches to explaining the differences between research and practice from a practice-theoretical perspective. All three approaches concur that, because strategy research and strategy practice constitute different social fields, which differ in their social structures, beliefs and interests, the

practices enacted in each field are also structured differently. Because of what Bourdieu (2002) terms *skholé*, the knowledge that is inherent in practices enacted in the academic field of strategy research is detached from the logic of management practice. This detachment is mirrored in scientific rationality and results in knowledge that is disconnected from context, time and, generally, from the meaningful totality in which managers' practices are immersed. Consequently, knowledge that follows the logic of scientific rationality and is based on representational epistemology does not take into account the contexts in which knowledge is meant to be used, which limits its ability to be practically relevant.

Implications for strategy-as-practice research

In this section, we review the various ways in which practice-based scholars have proposed to capture the logic of management practice. While Sandberg and Tsoukas (2011) and Splitter and Seidl (2011) focused on how knowledge is produced, Jarzabkowski and Wilson (2006) concentrated on the transfer of knowledge from research to management practice. Drawing on these works, we propose three different ways of increasing the practical relevance of strategy research. The first proposal (Sandberg and Tsoukas 2011) addresses the question of how strategy scholars can capture the object of research and develop theories based on practical rationality. The second proposal (Splitter and Seidl 2011) relies on the concept of 'participant objectivation', which is a specific kind of reflexivity on the role of the researcher in the process of capturing the object of research. Finally, the third proposal (Jarzabkowski and Wilson 2006) outlines how scholars should reflect on the process through which strategy theory is transferred to strategy practice in a way that increases the practical relevance of the former.

Moving from theories of scientific rationality to theories of practical rationality

To overcome the limitations that theories of scientific rationality impose on research, Sandberg and Tsoukas (2011) suggest that scholars should shift to theories based on practical rationality. To this end, they have introduced a framework for the development of these theories, pointing out that this framework would enable management scholars to capture the logic of management practice. According to them, practical rationality offers a coherent onto-epistemological framework for generating what they call 'practical rationality theories' – theories that capture essential aspects of the logic of management practice, by exploring how organizational practices are constituted and enacted by actors. This framework involves two interrelated strategies that allow researchers to access the logic of management practice.

The first research strategy entails 'a shift from entities as the point of departure to entwinement' (Sandberg and Tsoukas 2011: 340). This entwinement strategy requires taking a sociomaterial practice as a starting point, investigating the activities that are involved to understand how this practice is accomplished and exploring the specific characteristics or identity of the focal practice, as well as how it relates to other practices. An example of a sociomaterial practice that illustrates the entwinement strategy is teaching (Schatzki 2005; Sandberg

and Tsoukas 2011). Teaching forms a relational totality that consists of particular activities, such as lecturing, interacting with students and mentoring, and the use of certain tools, such as textbooks, whiteboards and software (e.g. Power-Point), which are defined by the way in which they are utilized in specific activities and in reference to other tools. These activities and tools are entwined and together form the totality of the teaching practice, which orients its practitioners towards achieving certain ends and defines various methods of teaching, as well as what matters in teaching. Thus, the elements of the teaching practice provide the practitioners of teaching with guidance on what matters and on how and when certain tools are to be used. The example of teaching shows that the entwinement strategy directs the attention of scholars to how relational totalities are accomplished and enables them to capture 'the distinct and unreflexive ways in which people routinely act while entwined with others and tools' (Sandberg and Tsoukas 2011: 344). In the field of management in particular, the entwinement strategy would therefore allow management scholars to capture the relational whole of specific practices and how they are entwined with the specific sociomaterial totality of management practice.

The second research strategy involves focusing the research attention on temporary breakdowns, such as interruptions in the way practitioners routinely operate. The purpose of the research strategy to search for breakdowns is to 'let the practice reveal itself through the moments it temporarily breaks down, namely, the moments when things do not work as anticipated' (Sandberg and Tsoukas 2011: 347). In other words, the strategy that focuses on breakdowns enables management scholars to shed light on the significance of the taken-for-granted distinctions that practitioners cannot articulate while they deploy the practice. If a temporary breakdown in the flow of practitioners' action occurs, practitioners temporarily step back from what they routinely do and reflect on how they actually accomplish their work. In these moments the logic of practice comes to the fore, because the relational whole in which the practices are embedded becomes momentarily manifest. The second research strategy thus relies on exploring how practitioners respond to unintended consequences and become aware of the possibility of different practices, when their flow of action is disrupted. Exploring these aspects enables scholars to grasp what is significant to practitioners and, therefore, to grasp the logic underpinning their sociomaterial practice.

Taking again the example of teaching, Sandberg and Tsoukas (2011) show that a lecturer who delivers a lecture to a class of students is immersed in this practice in the sense that he/she fulfils the task of teaching without being specifically aware of the layout of the room, the presentation of the material (such as a PowerPoint slideshow), the behaviour of the class, and so on. Only when an interruption occurs – for example, when there is a technical problem with PowerPoint – will the lecturer shift from being immersed in the practice of teaching to the mode of reflection, which involves, for example, finding out what has caused the problem and fixing it. Because of this breakdown, the lecturer momentarily pays explicit attention to specific aspects of Power-Point – such as the projector and the connection between laptop and projector. In other words, the specific relational whole, and the entwinement of the people and objects involved in teaching, become apparent, which allows the researcher to grasp the logic underlying the sociomaterial practice of teaching.

While theories of scientific rationality retain the scholastic view, theories of practical rationality can overcome this view by prompting researchers to investigate entwinement and breakdowns in the context of management practice. Theories of practical rationality aim to capture the logic of practice by providing an account of management practice as it is enacted, and thus embedded, in a relational whole. By capturing the logic of management practice, theories of practical rationality are therefore more likely to be practically relevant. Sandberg and Tsoukas (2011) suggest that management research that is built on practical rationality is more connected to management practice because it brings researchers closer to management practice as it is experienced by practitioners, rather than by researchers.

Employing 'participant objectivation'

The second approach to overcoming the problems that result from the scholastic distance between theorists and practitioners involves a specific kind of reflexivity that Bourdieu (1978; 1990; 2003) refers to as 'participant objectivation'. Splitter and Seidl (2011) expand on this concept to explore how strategy researchers can produce practically relevant knowledge about strategy practice.

Participant objectivation incorporates in the research study an analysis of the researcher's subjective relation to the object of study. This enables researchers to reflect on the scholastic view and acknowledge how it influences their scientific, taken-for-granted reasoning about the object they study. Bourdieu (2000: 50) argues that participant objectivation equips scholars with

> a scientific thought that is aware of itself and its limits to be capable of thinking practice without destroying its object. It is thus to understand what kind of understanding the scholastic thought has of this practical understanding and the difference between practical and scientific knowledge.

Reflexivity in the form of participant objectivation focuses on two interrelated aspects: first, the role of the researcher in the investigation – specifically, the social conditions that determine his/her own research practices. Second, the analysis of the object of research – specifically, the practical conditions that determine how the social practices under study are examined. Participant objectivation enables strategy scholars to consider the distinction between their inevitably scholastic view and the practical view of strategists to their research. This enables them to overcome the potential bias towards the object of research that may result from an unreflexive scholastic view. In this sense, participant objectivation mainly consists of a 'process of objectivation of the subject of objectivation' (Bourdieu 1988: 67).

To illustrate the concept of participant objectivation, we turn to Bourdieu's own ethnographic work on kinship relations in Kabylia, Algeria (Bourdieu 1976). The excerpt below sketches why Bourdieu applied the concept of participant objectivation to conduct this study:

I realized very early on that, in my fieldwork in Kabylia, I was constantly drawing on my experience of the Béarn society of my childhood, both to understand the practices that I was observing and to defend myself against the interpretations that I spontaneously formed of them or that my informants gave me (Bourdieu 2003: 288).

Implicitly, Bourdieu drew comparisons between his experiences in his home town, Béarn, in France and his observations of the Algerian peasantry. In other words, he realized that his subjective relation to the Kabyle society biased his ethnographic observations, leading him to examine his subject from a scholastic viewpoint. In order to analyse the bias that stemmed from the scholastic distance between his position as French researcher and the Kabyle society, he transferred his research experiences made in Kabylia to Béarn. Applying a multi-sited ethnography, Bourdieu went back to Béarn and, as in Kabylia, conducted first-hand observations and wrote field-diaries, transferring methodically the conceptual schemes on which he based his analysis and the conclusions he drew from his empirical results from one place to the other. In this manner, he was able to identify the social differences between how he comprehended the object of his study and how his informants did.

Bourdieu cross-referenced the field data he collected in Kabylia and Béarn and questioned the processes through which he produced and interpreted both sets by employing the same instruments of observation and pursuing the same questions in both communities. Participant objectivation was based on how he, as the researcher, related to the sites, not on how each site related to the other. Participant objectivation led him to become reflexively aware and to methodologically control the 'social unconscious' that he was investigating ethnographically in Kabylia, as well as of the unseen effects of his ethnographic research, such as 'the artificial de-temporalization and totalizing effects of the genealogical charts [used] to capture kinship relations that are never grasped by agents in such totality and simultaneity' (Bourdieu 1990: 162). In this way, Bourdieu was able to grasp not only the object (the kinship system) but also the subject of objectivation – himself – and his

position in the Béarn society. Thus, participant objectivation made visible the social determinants that were inherent in his scholastic view and unconsciously oriented his scientific choices.

Even though this is an extreme illustration of participant objectivation in the field of anthropology, this principle can also be applied in the field of strategy as practice. In the latter context, the reflexive process of participant objectivation consists in objectifying the subjective relation between academics and the practices they study. This relation must be subjected to the same social analysis as the management practices themselves. In other words, scholars first need to analyse the objective structures and conditions underlying their academic field in order to analyse subsequently how they, as researchers, relate to the practice of strategists. Analysing the subjective relation between researcher and object of study makes it possible to identify the social boundaries within which knowledge is produced and the 'decisive choices (of topic, method, theory, etc.) that this relation entails' (Splitter and Seidl 2011: 110). The theoretical and methodological choices that determine how a scholar will study the practice of strategists are indicative of how the structures of the academic field and the subjective relation between researcher and object influence the knowledge that is produced from studying the practice of strategists.

Bourdieu (2000; 2004; Bourdieu and Wacquant 1992) further elaborates that reflexivity in the form of participant objectivation can be properly realized only if it becomes a generally shared principle of social research. He therefore calls for an institutionalization of 'reflexivity as the common law of the field, which would thus become characterized by a sociological critique of all by all that would intensify the effects of the epistemological critique of all by all' (Bourdieu 2004: 91).

To summarize, Splitter and Seidl (2011) argue that reflexivity in the form of participant objectivation is the basis for rigorous research on the grounds that it enables researchers to control the constraints that the social relation between researcher and object of study place on scientific knowledge production. In other words, it enables the researcher 'to construct scientific objects into which the relation of the researcher to the object is not unconsciously projected' (Splitter and Seidl 2011: 111). Taking into account the scholastic distance between the practical and scientific modes of knowledge production in the analysis of strategy research allows scholars to grasp the logic of management practice. If researchers fail to engage reflexively with the scholastic view, they will remain unaware of their social boundaries that this view places on scientific knowledge production, and, as a consequence, their research results are not likely to be of practical relevance to strategy practitioners. In this sense, 'reflexivity through participant objectivation is crucial to any scientific study of the activities of strategists that aims to be relevant not only academically but also practically' (Splitter and Seidl 2011: 111).

Dissociation and bricolage of strategy knowledge

In contrast to Sandberg and Tsoukas (2011) and Splitter and Seidl (2011), Jarzabkowski and Wilson (2006) concentrated on the transfer of knowledge between strategy scholars and practitioners. They argue that scholars transform theoretical knowledge into strategy tools that practitioners then use within their own context. They describe the process through which theoretical knowledge becomes transformed into applied knowledge in a practical context as a 'dissociation process'. On this basis, they argue that reflecting on and understanding the practical logic underlying the dissociation process can lead scholars to redesign scientific knowledge in order to make it more practically relevant.

According to Jarzabkowski and Wilson (2006), the dissociation process through which theoretical knowledge is converted into practically applicable knowledge comprises two steps. The first step involves simplifying theoretical knowledge into 'artefacts', such as strategy tools, that become disseminated into management practice in various ways – for example, through management consultants or MBA courses. Most schools of strategy theory, such as the 'positioning school' (Porter 1979) and the 'capability-building school' (Barney 1991; Prahalad and Hamel 1990; Teece, Pisano and Shuen 1997), have produced tools of this kind. Examples include Porter's five forces

and the Boston Consulting Group portfolio matrix, which are attributed to the positioning school, and the resource-based view framework and the concept of dynamic capabilities, which originate in capability-building theory.

As Jarzabkowski and Wilson (2006) point out, however, managers and strategists do not apply directly in their professional practice the knowledge 'artefacts' that strategy research makes available to them; this requires a second step in the dissociation process, in which strategy practitioners experiment with, modify and apply these artefacts to the context of strategy practice. In this part of the dissociation process, strategy practitioners may use a knowledge artefact, partly or wholly, in ways that deviate from the purpose for which researchers originally designed it. Jarzabkowski and Wilson (2006) define the process through which practitioners adapt artefacts for a scientifically unanticipated purpose as 'bricolage' (Lévi-Strauss 1966). The *bricolage* of strategy artefacts describes the process through which

> actors produce their own intentful activities from the artefacts that structure everyday activity. Bricolage involves taking existing tools and fashioning them to an individual's own ends, without particular regard for either the most appropriate tool for a task or for the original purpose of the tool to be used (Jarzabkowski and Wilson 2006: 360).

To illustrate the second phase of the dissociation process, Jarzabkowski and Wilson draw on Chesley and Wenger's (1999) account of how a company integrated the 'balanced scorecard' tool in its strategy. Chesley and Wenger (1999) show that, by contextualizing and adapting the balanced scorecard, which was initially designed to assess performance, the company set in motion strategic conversation and change. In the process of implementing the balanced scorecard, it was adapted to fit the organizational context, and its contextual use was the spur to strategic conversations about organizational change. By fitting the tool to the organizational context, it provided a language with which the organization could discuss strategy.

> Quite literally, the framework gave them something to talk about in a common language

and in an organization where it had long been felt that textbook organizational solutions did not work in management practice. Modifying the framework provided a legitimacy previously absent and this legitimacy then facilitated discussions about performance and change (Jarzabkowski and Wilson 2006: 361).

This example of *bricolage* illustrates how, in this case, the use of a particular tool – the balanced scorecard – deviated from assessing performance and how this enabled actors to produce their own intentful activities, which included strategic conversation about change.

In this sense, Jarzabkowski and Wilson (2006) argue that strategy artefacts are typically dissociated from the theoretical research in which they originated when strategy practitioners adapt and apply them for purposes other than those for which they were conceived. Thus, in the context of strategy, *bricolage* describes the process through which practitioners innovatively use existing, easily accessible and adjustable tools rather than acquire new knowledge. The above shows that, in the second phase of the dissociation process, practitioners do not misuse or abuse scientific strategy knowledge but use it according to the logic of practice. This is effected by highly skilled and experienced practitioners, who can adapt strategy tools to their situated contexts and thus endow them with new meanings and purposes (Wright, Paroutis and Blettner 2013).

Jarzabkowski and Wilson (2006) argue that capturing the practical logic inherent in the dissociation process described above would enable strategy scholars to enhance the practical relevance of their research. The enhanced practical understanding of how an artefact that has originated in scientific strategy research is used will help researchers better understand its nature and potential, and thereby benefit the field of research from which this artefact arose. In other words, understanding how practitioners engage in *bricolage* creates a feedback loop into strategy research, in the sense that when practitioners use and modify theoretical knowledge artefacts they provide researchers with knowledge that enables them to address practical organizational problems.

Forms of practical relevance of practice-based strategy research

Building on the tradition of strategy as practice, we have outlined three ways in which strategy researchers can capture the logic of management practice. We argue that applying the suggested approaches will help scholars produce research that is relevant and can make a difference to strategy practice. In the following, we briefly discuss what kinds of practical relevance can be expected from practice-based scholarship.

Researchers investigating the practical relevance of scientific knowledge typically distinguish between three types of relevance (Knorr 1976; Pelz 1978; Astley and Zammuto 1992; Nicolai and Seidl 2010). They speak of *instrumental relevance* when scientific results provide guidelines for action. The classical example is the technological rule that follows the formula 'if you want to achieve Y in situation Z, then perform something like action X' (Nicolai and Seidl 2010: 1267). They speak of *conceptual relevance* when scientific results change the ways in which practitioners perceive or construe their problem situation. Finally, they speak of *legitimizing* or *symbolic relevance* when scientific results provide symbolic resources for justifying chosen courses of action.

Against the background of our characterization of strategy research and strategy practice as different social fields, it is fairly clear that the results of strategy-as-practice research are unlikely to be of direct instrumental relevance to practitioners, in the sense of providing guidelines for action. We have seen that, on account of their scholastic view, researchers are inevitably distanced from the world as experienced by the practitioner. Hence, scientific knowledge, even if it is based on the logic of practice and participant objectivation, does not put researchers into a position to enact strategy practices – not least because they lack the necessary practical skills (Chia and Holt 2006). Strategy-as-practice researchers, like all management researchers, are therefore not in a particularly strong position for offering practitioners instrumental advice of what to do.

Even though strategy-as-practice research might not offer instrumentally 'actionable knowledge'

(Jarzabkowski and Wilson 2006), however, it can still be conceptually relevant. It may provide practitioners with conceptual tools based on in-depth empirical studies in situated contexts (Langley 2010) that will enable them to broaden their understanding of concrete situations. 'In other words, strategy research can enable practitioners to improve their concrete work practices through a better understanding of the logic of management practice that underlies their activities' (Splitter and Seidl 2011: 112). There are three distinct forms in which strategy-as-practice research can be of conceptual relevance to strategy practice. First, strategy research can uncover contingencies and make the practitioners become aware of 'new or alternative routes of action' (Nicolai and Seidl 2010: 1270). A practice-based perspective on strategy allows scholars to lay bare the practical rationality of the management practices they observe. In this sense, strategy research can identify managerial practices and the particular conditions under which they are enacted. In turn, this enables scholars to describe the possibilities that enacting these practices opens to practitioners and the limitations that they face. Strategy research that is built on practical rationality 'lets practice manifest itself through outlining the relational whole in which practice is routinely taking place, which practitioners are normally unaware of and what was previously opaque in their routine practices' (Sandberg and Tsoukas 2011: 353). Second, practice-based research might point out causal relationships and unknown side effects that strategy practitioners are not aware of. The development of frameworks that grasp the meaningful totality in which practitioners are immersed is also likely to lay bare the causal relationships underlying the logic of management practice. If practitioners become aware of these causal relationships they will gain a better understanding of the problem situation they have to tackle, given that usually they are aware only of some of the causal relationships that affect their practices. Third, strategy-as-practice research may provide managers with linguistic constructs through concepts and tools (Jarzabkowsi and Wilson 2006) that enable them 'to look at their organizational practices in a different light and, based on that, be able to create new ways of performing and enacting their practices' (Sandberg and Tsoukas 2011: 355). Linguistic constructs may thus change the way practitioners think and talk about their practices and problem situations. Interestingly, it is exactly the distance from the concrete management practice, preventing strategy-as-practice researchers from producing instrumentally relevant knowledge, that puts them in a particularly strong position for offering practitioners novel ways of understanding their problem situations.

Finally, like all management research, the output of strategy-as-practice research may also be of legitimizing or symbolic relevance to practitioners. As Astley and Zammuto (1992: 452) point out: 'Managers often point to theoretical models or research findings to justify courses of action.' strategy-as-practice research may offer rhetorical devices, such as symbolic labels, that might be used in legitimizing particular managerial decisions. After all, strategy-as-practice research has given rise to many new labels, such as 'inductive versus deductive strategy making' (Regnér 2003), 'strategic episodes' (Hendry and Seidl 2003) and 'strategy without design' (Chia and Holt 2009), that can be used for 'buttress[ing] the scientific appearance' (Whitley 1995: 63) of an argument. To the extent that strategy-as-practice research is or will be explicitly based on theories of practical rationality rather than scientific rationality, however, it is likely to lose some of its scientific appearance and, hence, some of its potential for being used by practitioners for symbolic purposes.

In sum, in the field of strategy as practice, scholars can actively create practically relevant knowledge mostly in the form of conceptual knowledge. Conceptual knowledge poses particular challenges with respect to relevance, however, relating mainly to the degree to which practitioners are willing to engage with that kind of knowledge (Nicolai and Seidl 2010). First, whereas the aim of instrumental knowledge is to simplify the problem situation (by providing guidelines for action), the purpose of conceptual knowledge is to reveal the complexity of a given situation by indicating the causal relationships between the various elements of the problem situation, as well as alternative actions for tackling it. This means that practitioners have to deal with a higher degree of complexity, however, of which they were previously unaware. Second, in order to grasp fully the potential of the conceptual knowledge that pertains to a particular situation, practitioners must have at least some rudimentary understanding of the theoretical context within which the scientific knowledge was produced. In order to apply novel concepts or theoretical frameworks to their specific contexts and thus comprehend a specific situation better, strategy practitioners need to understand how and why these concepts and frameworks work. Nevertheless, as Seidl (2007) argues, even if practitioners have a limited understanding of the conceptual foundation of the artefacts they use, these artefacts may still broaden the understanding of the problem situation through 'productive misunderstandings' that can help practitioners grasp better a problem situation.

Future directions and conclusion

In this chapter we have reviewed practice-based studies that examine the ontological and epistemological conditions for producing research that proves relevant to management practice. Drawing on these works, we have shown that researchers inevitably adopt a scholastic point of view, namely a mode of reasoning that is detached from strategy practice. The scholastic view leads many scholars to produce knowledge built on scientific rationality, which makes it impossible to capture directly the logic of strategy practice and hampers the possibilities of cross-fertilization between the fields of research and practice. Scholars can increase the practical relevance of their research, however, by developing theories based on practical logic. We have outlined three approaches to capturing the logic of management practice: (1) the development of practical rationality theories; (2) the application of 'participant objectivation'; and (3) consideration of the dissociation process. We argue that, if strategy-as-practice research builds on these insights, it can prove a particularly fruitful approach to generate knowledge that is of conceptual relevance to strategy practice.

All the studies we have considered in this chapter provide insights into how practically relevant knowledge can be produced and used, and may even provoke a 'societal shift towards better everyday strategizing practice, empowered by more effective practices and a deeper pool of skilled practitioners' (Whittington 2006: 629). At the same time, they also raise new questions, relating in particular to three potential areas of research.

The first area is that of empirical research. Currently there is scant empirical evidence on the practical relevance of scientific research on strategy. With few notable exceptions, mostly in the tradition of classroom experiments, such as the studies by Jarzabkowski *et al.* (2013) and Wright, Paroutis and Blettner (2013), there are hardly any empirical studies on how scientific knowledge on strategy is applied in strategy practice. Thus, a potential area for future research would be to examine how practitioners use scientific knowledge on strategy, for instance by investigating how practitioners adapt scientific knowledge to their strategizing practices, and what happens to scientific knowledge when practitioners apply it.

The second area that future research could investigate both empirically and theoretically is the extent to which scholars can implement the research practices that derive from each of the three proposed approaches to research that we discussed earlier, the aim of which is to capture the logic of management practice. These include the suggestion that researchers should reflect on their role in the process of research by applying participant objectivation and the idea of developing direct feedback loops between research and practice based on practitioners' *bricolage* of strategy tools. In this context, researchers could explore how research practices can be combined with the conventions of the system in which research is conducted and published so that they capture the logic of practice, or the conditions under which these research practices can be implemented.

Finally, a still under-represented issue in current SAP research is the role of education as an intermediary between research and management practice. Although there are two practice-based studies by Vaara and Faÿ (2011; 2012) that illustrate the important role of business schools in the general process of educating prospective practitioners, future research could investigate more closely the specific role of education in disseminating strategy research.

References

Astley, W. G., and Zammuto, R. F. (1992), 'Organization science, managers, and language games', *Organization Science*, 3/4: 443–60.

Barney, J. (1991), 'Firm resources and sustained competitive advantage', *Journal of Management*, 17/1: 99–120.

Bartunek, J. M., and Rynes, S. L. (2014), 'Academics and practitioners are alike and unlike: the paradoxes of academic–practitioner relationships', *Journal of Management*, 40/5: 1181–201.

Beer, M. (2001), 'Why management research findings are unimplementable: an action science perspective', *Reflections*, 2/3: 58–65.

Bourdieu, P. (1975), 'The specificity of the scientific field and the social conditions of the progress of reason', *Social Science Information*, 14/6: 19–47.

(1976), *Entwurf einer Theorie der Praxis: Auf der ethnologischen Grundlage der kabylischen Gesellschaft*. Frankfurt: Suhrkamp Verlag.

(1978), 'Sur l'objectivation participante: réponse à quelques objections', *Actes de la recherche en sciences sociales*, 23: 67–9.

(1988), *Homo Academicus*. Redwood City, CA: Stanford University Press.

(1990), *The Logic of Practice*. Redwood City, CA: Stanford University Press.

(1998), *Practical Reason: On the Theory of Action*. Redwood City, CA: Stanford University Press.

(2000), *Pascalian Meditations*. Redwood City, CA: Stanford University Press.

(2002), *La domination masculine*. Paris: Éditions du Seuil.

(2003), 'Participant objectivation', *Journal of the Royal Anthropological Institute*, 9/2: 281–94.

(2004), *Science of Science and Reflexivity*. Cambridge: Polity.

Bourdieu, P., and Wacquant, L. (1992), *An Invitation to Reflexive Sociology*. University of Chicago Press.

Chesley, J. A., and Wenger, M. S. (1999), 'Transforming an organization: using models to foster a strategic conversation', *California Management Review*, 41/3: 54–73.

Chia, R., and Holt, R. (2006), 'Strategy as practical coping: a Heideggerian perspective', *Organization Studies*, 27/5: 635–55.

(2009), *Strategy without Design: The Silent Efficacy of Indirect Action*. Cambridge University Press.

Gibbons, M., Limoges, C., Nowotny, H., Schwartzman, S., Scott, P., and Trow, M. (1994), *The New Production of Knowledge: The Dynamics of Science and Research in Contemporary Societies*. London: Sage.

Grand, S., Rüegg-Stürm, J., and von Arx, W. (2010), 'Constructivist epistemologies in strategy as practice research', in Golsorkhi, D., Rouleau, L., Seidl, D., and Vaara, E. (eds.), *Cambridge Handbook of Strategy as Practice*: 63–78. Cambridge University Press.

Hendry, J., and Seidl, D. (2003), 'The structure and significance of strategic episodes: social systems theory and the routine practices of strategic change', *Journal of Management Studies*, 40/1: 175–96.

Jarzabkowski, P., Giulietti, M., Oliveira, B., and Amoo, N. (2013), '"We don't need no education" – or do we? Management education and alumni adoption of strategy tools', *Journal of Management Inquiry*, 22/1: 4–24.

Jarzabkowski, P., Mohrman, S. A., and Scherer, A. G. (2010), 'Organization studies as applied science: the generation and use of academic knowledge about organizations: introduction to the special issue', *Organization Studies*, 31/9–10: 1189–207.

Jarzabkowski, P., and Whittington, R. (2008), 'Directions for a troubled discipline: strategy research, teaching, and practice – introduction to the dialog', *Journal of Management Inquiry*, 17/4: 266–8.

Jarzabkowski, P., and Wilson, D. C. (2006), 'Actionable strategy knowledge', *European Management Journal*, 24/5: 348–67.

Johnson, G., Melin, L., and Whittington, R. (2003), 'Guest editors' introduction: micro strategy and strategizing: towards an activity-based view', *Journal of Management Studies*, 40/1: 3–22.

Knorr, D. (1980), 'Effect of recovery methods on yield, quality and functional properties of potato protein concentrates', *Journal of Food Science*, 45/5: 1183–6.

Knorr, K. D. (1976), *Policy-Makers Use of Social Science Knowledge: Symbolic or Instrumental?*, Research Memorandum no. 103. Vienna: Institute for Advanced Studies.

Langley, A. (ed.) (2010), *The Challenge of Developing Cumulative Knowledge about Strategy as Practice*. Cambridge University Press.

Lawler, E. E. (1999), *Doing Research that Is Useful for Theory and Practice*. Lexington, MA: Lexington Books.

Lévi-Strauss, C. (1966), *The Savage Mind*. University of Chicago Press.

Nicolai, A., and Seidl, D. (2010), 'That's relevant! Different forms of practical relevance in management science', *Organization Studies*, 31/9–10: 1257–85.

Paroutis, S., and Heracleous, L. (2010), 'First-order strategy discourse: the strategy meaning-making process in practice', paper presented at Strategic Management Society Finland special conference 'Intersections of strategy processes and practices', Helsinki, 19 March.

Pelz, D. C. (1978), 'Some expanded perspectives on use of social science in public policy', in Yinger, M. J., and Cutler, S. J. (eds.), *Major Social Issues: A Multidisciplinary View*: 346–57. New York: Free Press.

Porter, M. E. (1979), 'How competitive forces shape strategy', *Harvard Business Review*, 57/2: 137–45.

Prahalad, C. K., and Hamel, G. (1990), 'The core competence of the corporation', *Harvard Business Review*, 68/3: 79–91.

Regnér, P. (2003), 'Strategy creation in the periphery: inductive versus deductive strategy making', *Journal of Management Studies*, 40/1: 57–82.

Sandberg, J., and Tsoukas, H. (2011), 'Grasping the logic of practice: theorizing through practical rationality', *Academy of Management Review*, 36/2: 338–60.

Schatzki, T. R. (2005), 'Peripheral vision: the sites of organizations', *Organization Studies*, 26/3: 465–84.

Seidl, D. (2007), 'General strategy concepts and the ecology of strategy discourses: a systemic-discursive perspective', *Organization Studies*, 28/2: 197–218.

Splitter, V., and Seidl, D. (2011), 'Does practice-based research on strategy lead to practically relevant knowledge? Implications of a Bourdieusian perspective', *Journal of Applied Behavioral Science*, 47/1: 98–120.

Teece, D. J., Pisano, G., and Shuen, A. (1997), 'Dynamic capabilities and strategic management', *Strategic Mangement Journal*, 18/7: 509–33.

Vaara, E., and Faÿ, E. (2011), 'How can a Bourdieusian perspective aid analysis of MBA education?', *Academy of Management Learning and Education*, 10/1: 27–39.

(2012), 'Reproduction and change on the global scale: a Bourdieusian perspective on management education', *Journal of Management Studies*, 49/6: 1023–51.

Van de Ven, A. H. (2007) *Engaged Scholarship: A Guide for Organizational and Social Research*. Oxford University Press.

Weick, K. E. (2005), 'Theory and practice in the real world', in Tsoukas, H., and Knudsen, C. (eds.), *The Oxford Handbook of Organization Theory*: 453–7. Oxford University Press.

Whitley, R. (1995), 'Academic knowledge and work jurisdiction in management', *Organization Studies*, 16/1: 81–105.

Whittington, R. (2006), 'Completing the practice turn in strategy research', *Organization Studies*, 27/5: 613–34.

Whittington, R., Jarzabkowski, P., Mayer, M., Mounoud, E., Nahapiet, J., and Rouleau, L. (2003), 'Taking strategy seriously: responsibility and reform for an important social practice', *Journal of Management Inquiry*, 12/4: 396–409.

Wright, R. P., Paroutis, S., and Blettner, D. P. (2013), 'How useful are the strategic tools we teach in business schools?', *Journal of Management Studies*, 50/1: 92–125.

PART II

Theoretical Resources: Social Theory

Giddens, structuration theory and strategy as practice

RICHARD WHITTINGTON

Introduction

Anthony Giddens' (1984) structuration theory has an obvious appeal for strategy-as-practice researchers. Of course, Giddens is a practice theorist himself; for him, understanding people's activity is the central purpose of social analysis. Giddens makes a direct appeal, therefore, offering concepts of agency, structure and structuration that have intrinsic importance to practice research. His conception of human agency affirms that people's activity matters: practice needs studying because it makes a difference to outcomes. At the same time, his notion of social structure allows for both constraint and enablement: to understand activity, we must attend to institutional embeddedness. And the concept of structuration brings together structure and agency to give them flow – continuity, but also the possibility of structural change.

All these features of structuration theory are attractive to SAP researchers in themselves. Giddens has an indirect appeal as well, however, for his central concepts can help connect strategy as practice to other streams of organizational research too. The structurationist sense of flow builds a bridge to the important process tradition in organization theory, which has long drawn on structuration theory to analyse change over time (Pettigrew 1985; Floyd *et al.* 2011; Langley 2009). The importance of people's activity complements the growing appreciation of the role of individuals in the emergent micro-foundations stream of strategy research (Powell, Lovallo and Fox 2011; Barney and Felin 2013). Finally, and constituting an important theme in this chapter, structuration theory's concern for institutional embeddedness offers an obvious platform for recent efforts to encourage strategy as practice and institutional

theory to work together (Suddaby, Seidl and Lê 2013; Vaara and Whittington 2012).

My task in this chapter should be an easy one, therefore. In exploring the various ways in which Giddens' structuration theory may contribute to strategy-as-practice research, I shall be pushing at many open doors. Structuration theory is not easy to apply empirically, however, and there are alternative approaches that can do more or less similar kinds of job. My advocacy of structuration theory will not be monomaniac. Accordingly, I intend to investigate how management researchers have already tried to apply structuration theory in empirical research, including within the SAP tradition. I also compare structuration theory with two quite close alternatives, both similarly concerned for the relationship between structure and agency: the practice-theoretic approach of Pierre Bourdieu and the critical realist approach associated with Roy Bhaskar and Margaret Archer. I argue that, while each has its merits, those strategy-as-practice researchers already using structuration theory are at risk of conceding too much ground to these rival theoretical traditions. While for followers of Bourdieu and Bhaskar constraints loom large, structurationist-inspired researchers have tended to neglect Giddens' own emphasis on social structural context, as something that both constrains and enables.

It is this appreciation of social structural context that provides my main theme in this chapter. An important opportunity for SAP researchers is to exploit structuration theory more completely in order to understand the larger social structures, or institutions, in which strategy takes place and of which strategy is itself a part. Such an understanding can thereby connect strategy-as-practice researchers to institutional theory, at the same time as reinforcing the resistance of micro-foundational researchers to reductionism and extending the range of process scholars beyond the merely organizational. Structuration theory mandates full-spectrum research: the wide-angled analysis of institutions, as well as the microscopic study of praxis.

My approach in this chapter will be mostly practical. By and large, I leave aside the theoretical debate about the fundamental rights and wrongs of structuration theory (see, for example, Parker 2000; O'Boyle 2013). This chapter is more in the spirit of a users' guide. Accordingly, the next section introduces structuration theory's key concepts, notably *social practice, social systems, agency, structures, rules, resources, duality, structuration, institutions* and both *institutional analysis* and *analysis of strategic conduct*. The chapter goes on to consider structuration theory's advantages and disadvantages by comparison with the rival theoretical approaches of Bourdieu and Bhaskar, indicating circumstances in which structuration theory may be more applicable. It continues by reviewing some key empirical operationalizations of structuration theory both generally in the management literature and specifically in the strategy-as-practice tradition. This review brings out some common themes, many with considerable ongoing potential, but also raises the striking neglect of the strategy field as an institution in and of itself. For a structurationist approach to practice, the institution of strategy is just as much natural territory as the analysis of conduct. The chapter concludes by reaffirming the continuing and part-exploited value of structuration theory to researchers of strategy practice.

An outline of structuration theory

Giddens developed structuration theory as a sociology lecturer and later professor at the University of Cambridge. He was also co-founder of the successful social sciences publisher Polity; director of the London School of Economics between 1997 and 2003; and, during the 1990s and the first decade of this century, an influential political thinker, pioneer of the 'third way' associated with reformist politicians Tony Blair and Bill Clinton.

These practical involvements are relevant because – a point that I shall return to – Giddens is not just an armchair theorist but somebody who actively intervenes in the world, engaging in issues of major change (Stones 2005).

Structuration theory specifically was developed in a series of books that began with Giddens' *New Rules of Sociological Method* (1976), continued through his *Central Problems of Social Theory* (1979) and culminated in the most extended and systematic statement, in which he outlines his theory of structuration: *The Constitution of Society* (1984). The leitmotif of these books was an endeavour to overcome the traditional dualisms of social theory. In place of such divides as between voluntarism and determinism, individualism and structuralism and micro and macro, structuration theory offers a bridge, consistent with Giddens' conciliatory 'third way' thinking in politics.

The central span of this structurationist bridge is 'practice'. Giddens begins *The Constitution of Society* by placing practice right at the heart of his concerns: 'The basic domain of the social sciences, according to the theory of structuration, is neither the experience of the individual actor, nor any form of societal totality, but social practices ordered through time and space' (Giddens 1984: 2). Contemporary commentators on practice theory (such as Schatztki 2001; Reckwitz 2002; Denis, Langley and Rouleau 2007; Caldwell 2012; Nicolini 2012) accordingly nominate Giddens as a leading practice theorist, alongside Pierre Bourdieu and Michel Foucault. For structuration theory, though, the social practice concept is particularly useful for its bridging role. Thus, practice is obviously about activity, but through this lens such activity is neither merely individual nor simply voluntary. For example, religious practices are shared rather than idiosyncratic, and they constrain as much as they inspire. The practice concept links the micro and the macro likewise. A snatch of play on the football pitch is both a local moment of practice and the expression of institutionalized sporting rules, formal and informal, that are accepted worldwide.

Giddens (1976: 81) himself defines *social practice* as an 'ongoing series of practical activities'. This definition carries with it both the sense of regularity and continuity and a respect for the day-to-day work involved in getting ordinary but necessary things done. Regular activities bring together people into *social systems*, which are reproduced over time through continued inter-action. These social systems exist at various levels – a particular national society, an industry, an organization or a strategy project team, for example. For Giddens (1984), it is important that these systems do not bind their members into some kind of deterministic homeostatic loop. Rather, systems are typically somewhat overlapping, con-tradictory and precarious. As employees, family members and citizens, most of us participate in several kinds of social system: work, home and polity. We are constantly struggling between the divergent demands of these social systems, and we are rarely as good as we would like to be at managing any of them. Although somehow our collective interactions are usually enough to keep them going, these systems suffer plenty of local failures, and none is likely to have sufficient empire over us to enforce complete obedience. One day work gets priority over family, the next day the other way round.

Indeed, it is this participation in plural social systems that underwrites the human potential for *agency*. System contradictions pose sometimes awkward, sometimes opportune choices for our conduct: work late or just go home? For Giddens (1984: 9–10), it is important to recognize the potential for agency in just about everyone, by virtue of their participation in multiple social systems (domestic, economic, political, and so on). Agency here is the capacity to do otherwise: to follow one system of practices and to refuse another; thus, to work late is to prioritize the eco-nomic system over the domestic one. Such agency makes a difference to the world, in small ways or large, as it contributes to the reproduction or neg-ation of each particular system. Choosing to go home may not only protect one's own family life; in some tiny way, it contributes to the preservation of the family as a general system within society at large. In this sense, everybody has some sort of social power.

With this recognition of distributed power, Gid-dens expresses a fundamental respect for human potential. There is a dignity to Giddens' character-ization of the person. Certainly, people may have unconscious motivations; yes, they may not be able to account fully for their actions; and of course such actions are liable to have unintended conse-quences. Nevertheless, Giddens (1984) insists that people typically have high levels of 'practical con-sciousness'. Practical consciousness exceeds dis-cursive consciousness, the ability actually to articulate the motives for activity. Thus, although they may be unclear and they often make mistakes, people are more knowledgeable about their prac-tice than they can actually tell, and they constantly monitor and adjust this practice in order to achieve their purposes. It is this semi-conscious practicality that allows actors to make choices that may finally be effective.

The potential effectiveness of human agency is what makes people's activity worth close and penetrating observation: not wholly predictable, and variably skilled, people make a difference to the world through their choices, refusals or fail-ures. From a Giddensian point of view, simple social position is an unreliable predictor of actions and outcomes. To return to the organizational domain, the analyst should not assume that man-agers are exhaustively defined by their class pos-ition in society or their hierarchical position in the organization; family, moral or political concerns may be implicated as well. The family business patriarch (or matriarch) has more at stake than just profit. Nor should they expect a smooth translation of managerial tasks into action: managers can be either more or less skilful – or dedicated – in carrying out their roles. Managers may be dis-tracted, half-hearted, self-interested or simply not fully competent. As such, their activities need to be understood in their particularity, and it is important to study motives and interpretations intimately from the inside, not just remotely from without.

Agency is more than a matter of individual will and skill, of course. For Giddens, agency is enhanced by control over *resources*; it is exercised through the following, or rejection, of *rules*. These rules and resources are the structural properties of social systems, in which *structures* are rela-tively enduring and general principles of system ordering. In structuration theory, rules have a wide meaning, to include not just those that are legislated in some sense ('The strategic plan must be approved by November') but also less formal routines, habits, procedures or conventions ('We usually do a SWOT [strengths, weaknesses, opportunities and threats] analysis; SWOT analysis means looking at strengths and weaknesses; of course we put it on a flip chart'). Resources, on the other hand, are of two types, allocative and authoritative. Allocative resources involve command over objects and other material phenomena; authoritative resources concern command over people. Strategy, of course, is all about resources – both the material resources that are the subject of strategy and the authoritative resources that grant decision-making power over these resources. For Giddens (1984), people have more capacity for agency the more structural resources they hold and the more plural the rules they are able to negotiate. Resources give power; plurality affords discretion. Thus, Giddens is able at once to resist individualism and to reject the 'hard' or deterministic notions of social structure previously prominent in the social sciences: structures are not inimical to agency, but essential to it.

Giddens (1984) highlights three characteristic forms of interaction in which this agency is performed: communication, the exercise of power and sanction (see Figure 8.1). These three forms of interaction are analytically associated with three corresponding structural dimensions of social systems-signification, domination and legitimization. Signification refers to a system's discursive and symbolic order – that is, rules governing the types of talk, jargon and image that predominate (see also Vaara, this volume). Legitimization refers to the regime of normatively sanctioned institutions; these rules extend from formal legal constraints and obligations to the kinds of unwritten codes that are embodied in an organization's particular culture. Finally, the dimension of domination concerns material and allocative resources; these concern political and economic institutions, most obviously the state or the firm. It can be readily seen that these three dimensions connect structuration theory directly with issues of discourse, power and institutional legitimacy that are prominent throughout organization and management theory.

The middle part of Figure 8.1 refers to 'modalities', the means by which structural dimensions are expressed in action. Thus, in communicating, people draw on interpretive schemes that are linked to structures of signification; in exercising power, they draw on what Giddens calls 'facilities', for example rights defined by the dimension of domination such as those pertaining to organizational position or ownership; and, in sanctioning, they draw on norms of appropriate behaviour embedded in the structures of legitimization. To illustrate, a manager's action may be shaped by the strong norm of improving organizational performance; it may simultaneously be guided by an interpretive scheme that trusts in the efficacy of 'strategy' as a means to achieve that objective; finally, it will be empowered by facilities such as a sufficiently senior position within the organizational hierarchy. As the horizontal double-headed arrows in

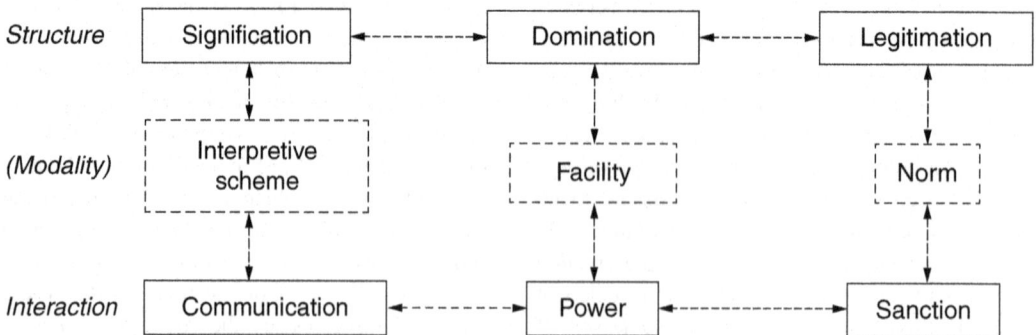

Figure 8.1 Forms of interaction in structuration theory
Source: Giddens (1984: 29, fig. 2). Used with permission from Polity Press and University of California Press.

Figure 8.1 imply, however, the three dimensions are analytic distinctions that do not rule out inter-weaving in practice. A theme that is very important for Giddens is reciprocity; for example, norms that analytically belong to the dimension of legitimiza-tion can also, by the very giving of legitimacy, reinforce the facilities that originate in the dimen-sion of domination. Thus, managerial powers gain from the fact of their legitimacy.

This regard for reciprocity takes us to Giddens' (1984) key notion of the the 'duality of structure'. Through this *duality* he means to replace the trad-itional dualism (opposition) between structure and agency, by an assertion of their mutual depend-ence: '[T]he structural properties of a system are both the medium and the outcome of the practices they recursively organise' (Giddens 1984: 25). In other words, these structural properties are essen-tial to action, at the same time as being produced or reproduced by this action. Structure does not have just the sense of constraint implied by social theor-ies that emphasize ideological hegemony and the unequal distribution of resources. Structure is also enabling, as it furnishes both the resources that make action possible and the rules that guide it. Managers are powerful agents by virtue of their control over allocative and authoritative resources and their command of the rules by which to apply them effectively. Their power is both enhanced and inhibited by norms of appropriate conduct, as more or less shared by colleagues and subordinates within their system.

The concept of *structuration* embodies this mutual dependence of structure and agency. The neologism adds to the static word 'structure' a sense of action over time: structuration implies an active historical process. Structuration happens as agents draw on the various rules and resources of their systems; as they do so, they either reproduce or amend the structural principles that organized their activities in the first place. Thus, structuration theory admits structural continuity while allowing for deliberate innovation and change. Structures typically work like language: at the core, sufficient stability to allow the effective storing of know-ledge over time; at the margins, the creation of new words and usages to accommodate changing needs and circumstances. Managers, then, can be

seen as constantly drawing on past arrangements as they repeat, tinker with, bend or challenge what worked for them previously. Returning to Figure 8.1, the vertical double-headed arrows reflect both the 'downward' influences of structure on action and the 'upward' influences of action on structure.

An important implication of structuration, there-fore, is that structures are not fixed or given. Of course, there is typically a good deal of continuity in the arrangement of structural rules and resources within society. Giddens (1984) describes the rela-tively enduring structural properties of systems as *institutions*, which tend to confront each individual as solid and apart (see Balogun, Beech and John-son, this volume). At the highest level, the capital-ist system is an institution, its structural properties stretching over time and space in a way far beyond isolated efforts at change. Ultimately, however, Giddens insists that structures exist only as they are instantiated in action or as people retain them in their memories. In the eyes of critics and rivals (such as Archer 1995), this formulation seems to give structures an ephemeral and immaterial char-acter: the past has only weak influence over the present, and resources are somewhat virtual. Gid-dens' formulation also points to important truths, however. Rules that are forgotten have no pur-chase; there is little value to resources unless rights over them are recognized; left unused, rules and resources soon fall into desuetude. The structural properties of a system are ultimately only repro-duced, therefore, to the extent that its members continue to draw on them in action.

The methodological implications of duality and structuration may seem dauntingly holistic. Strictly, duality implies equal attention to both structure and agency, while structuration charges us to understand the past at the same time as engaging intimately with the present. Despite his theoretical orientation, however, Giddens (1984: 281–354) is sensitive enough to practicalities to provide a thorough and realistic discussion of structuration theory's implications for empirical research. Most important here is his concept of 'methodological bracketing', whereby the researcher can concentrate on one theme while putting the rest on hold. In particular, Giddens

(1979; 1984) proposes a distinction between the *analysis of strategic conduct*, the means by which actors draw on their structural rules and resources in their social activities, and *institutional analysis*, which suspends interest in conduct for the understanding of institutional context across space and time. Strategic conduct analysis typically calls on anthropological or ethnographic modes of 'thick description'; it might apply, for instance, to the study of a group of strategists at work on the creation of strategy in a particular organization. Institutional analysis, with its larger horizon, is more likely to draw on a range of macro-sociological approaches, including the historical and the quantitative; this would be relevant to understanding the spread of particular strategy practices, such as strategy consulting, over time and across different sectors or countries. In the interests of practicality, it is quite legitimate for the researcher to focus on one or the other, rather than risk being overwhelmed in the attempt to grasp the whole. What is critical, though, is that the researcher should explicitly recognize this bracketing, and acknowledge the place of what is being left out. In summarizing the separation of the analysis of conduct and the analysis of institutions, Giddens (1979: 80) insists: 'It is quite essential to see that this is only a methodological bracketing: these are not two sides of a dualism, they express a duality, the duality of structure.'

Attractions and alternatives

Structuration theory offers strategy-as-practice researchers several attractive elements. I stress three: attention to micro-sociological detail; a sensitivity to institutional context; and openness to change. Nonetheless, as this section will explore, there are some powerful rival perspectives available as well.

To start with, Giddens endorses a fascination with the details of everyday life. Practice is at the centre of his theory, and he respects the skills – the practical consciousness – that people need simply to go on. A favourite reference for Giddens (1984) is Erving Goffman, whose micro-sociology reveals the wonderful accomplishment involved in taken-for-granted social encounters. From a structuration point of view, how managers simply get through apparently ordinary and routine encounters is a perfectly legitimate object of study, and their successes and failures can make a difference, small or large, to what follows afterwards. In Giddens' (1984) methodological terms, this micro-sociological detail is all rich stuff for the analysis of strategic conduct. Structuration theory is ready to appreciate the minute skills with which a strategist performs his/her job – even down to the artful manipulation of a PowerPoint or the apt choice of words in a strategic conversation (Samra-Frederiks 2003; Kaplan 2011).

At the same time, of course, the duality of structure opposes a wholly micro perspective. Giddens (1979: 81) is explicitly critical of Goffman for his neglect of institutions, of history and of structural transformation. For structuration theory, the fascination of ordinary activities lies in part with how they express larger structural principles. Structuration theory's second attractive feature, therefore, is its intimate connection of the micro and the macro, conduct and institutions. Everyday decisions about the inclusion or exclusion of different employees in the strategy process either reinforce or amend established social and organizational hierarchies. Even the minutest instance of strategizing expresses, in its aspiration to shape the future, the power of the firm in contemporary capitalism. A complete understanding of micro-instances of practice requires, therefore, acknowledgement of the structural principles that enable and constrain that practice; equally, the full significance of such instances may stretch far beyond the micro-moment. In short, Giddens will not let us forget that activity is institutionally situated. Structuration theory constantly asks: what made that possible; why did that *not* happen; and how does that reproduce or change what is possible in the future? From this point of view, the triumph in the strategy debate of particular managers may be attributable not simply to the technical appropriateness of their proposal but to their mastery of legitimate strategy discourse, their hierarchical position, their relationship to capital or their social status in terms, for example, of gender or ethnicity (see Rouleau 2005; Whittington 1989). At some point, institutional analysis is necessary to complete the understanding of strategic conduct.

While insisting on the power of larger structural principles, structuration theory always admits their ultimate pliability. Giddens is on the side of the political reformers, after all. The third attractive feature that I wish to highlight here, therefore, is that structuration theory allows for innovation and change. Structural principles are only relatively enduring, with the struggles of the everyday liable to amend them. In the classic Chandlerian firm from the middle of the twentieth century, strategy was the preserve of top management; formulation was separate from implementation (Chandler 1962). Today, in many large Western organizations at least, middle managers appear to be winning greater inclusion in the strategy process, as their command over legitimate strategy discourse increases, new electronic technologies facilitate participation and they accept for themselves greater performance responsibilities (Knights and Morgan 1991; Floyd and Lane 2000; Whittington, Basak-Yakis and Cailluet 2011). This structural change is not legislated for at a single stroke, however. From a structuration theory perspective, the emerging principle of middle management inclusion is the outcome of countless individual endeavours to learn new skills, to respond to new technological opportunities and to accept new forms of accountability. Every engagement by middle managers in the strategy process of their organizations is at once an expression of this structural change and, insofar as they are effective, an extension of it. Hard work, multiplied by many times, can make structural change happen.

Some see this structural pliability as going too far (Parker 2000; Reed 2005; O' Boyle 2013). For many critics, alternative theoretical approaches, such as the practice theory of Bourdieu or the realist theory of Bhaskar and Archer, are more persuasive. Both these approaches share structuration theory's recognition of the production of structure by human actors, but they give greater weight to continuity or constraint. It is worth drawing the contrasts in order to understand the sphere in which structuration theory is particularly apt.

As described by Gomez, in this volume, Bourdieu (1990) too advances a theoretical account of constrained human agency. For him, the role of structural rules and resources are played, first, by habitus, the ingrained dispositions that guide day-to-day activity; and, second, by notions of capital (social and symbolic, as well as material). While capital defines the sphere of possibility, and habitus shapes its understanding, they do not constrain outcomes absolutely. Capital and habitus may be relatively set, but these structural conditions are determinant only in the sense of a hand of cards: once the hand is dealt, the cards are fixed, yet the outcomes of the game are still finally shaped by the skill of the players as the game unfolds. The prior distribution of the cards sets limits, but a good player can squeeze out extra tricks from quite unpromising hands. In this Bourdieusian view, then, people are like card-players, seizing chances in the flow of the game, often through intuition as much as reason. For Bourdieu, agency is largely opportunistic.

The critical realist tradition also proposes a 'pivotal' role for practice (Bhaskar 1989; Archer 2000: 154–90; see also Vaara, this volume). Although structures are ultimately derived from human action, however, they are 'harder' in critical realism because – it is claimed – they go both deeper and further back. Structural depth refers to structures' foundational role for action – something that is not directly accessible to scientific observation but that can be retrospectively inferred from outcomes. For example, career success may owe something to the skills of individuals, largely visible, but it also relies on underlying structures (class, patriarchy or whatever) that are less immediately open to view; these structures reveal themselves by the fact that, in many societies, so many successful managers turn out to be male and well-born. To understand causality in careers, the analyst has to dig deeper than just skilful individuals. Structures go further back in the sense that they are preconditions for action, instead of being instantiated in that action. Structures come first: the career successes of today derive from the distribution of resources in the past. This harder sense of structure encourages Archer (1995) in particular to assert a stark dualism between action and structure, as against the conciliatory 'duality' of Giddens. For her, the sharp separation of action and structure, and the placing of structure first, helps us to appreciate the hierarchical distribution of opportunities for action, the delay and costs involved in structural transformation and the likely need for collective rather than individual struggle to win change that is against the interests of those starting higher up the hierarchy. In critical realism, agency is not easy.

Both the practice theory of Bourdieu and the critical realism of Bhaskar and Archer have their attractions, and, indeed, have been applied empirically in strategy research (respectively by, for example, Oakes, Townley and Cooper 1998; and Whittington 1989). Here my object is to consider their practical value for research rather than their fundamental theoretical merits and demerits. Bourdieu, an anthropologist of traditional societies and analyst of the 'société bloquée' that was postwar France, is conservative in his expectations. Distributions of capital are so fixed, and habitus so engrained, that by and large the most one can expect of agents is improvisatory skill within tight margins of discretion. A Bourdieusian perspective would probably be particularly illuminating, therefore, in the study of strategy episodes when structural change is both unsought and unlikely, but opportune interventions can still make a difference within certain boundaries. Such episodes might be a tough strategic negotiation, or the competitive 'selling' of a strategic issue to top management, when success or failure would depend in part on how well the actors played the hands they were dealt. On the other hand, a critical realist approach, with its origins in radical politics, might be better for the analysis of structural obduracy in the face of repeated endeavours at change. As radicals have found often enough, structures can be pretty deep-rooted. Critical realism's hard understanding of structures, and its appreciation of hierarchical power and interests, might be particularly insightful in a case in which, for example, middle managers were trying but failing to influence change in an organization's strategy or processes.

This is not to say that structuration theory is oblivious either to deep-rooted constraints or to deft opportunism: Giddens is certainly alive to the skill of the agent, and his structures are a good deal more substantial than critical realists give him

credit for (King 2010; Stones 2005: 54–5; Whittington 1992). It is merely to allow that there are circumstances in which Bourdieusian conservativism, or hard realism, may have special things to offer. Nonetheless, in contemporary organizations, structuration theory will be relevant widely enough: most organizations today are undergoing constant change, and for many 'empowerment' is at least a rhetoric, and often a (qualified) reality. Structuration theory has real purchase when circumstances are plural and fluid, when firms enjoy oligopolistic powers of discretion or when middle managers – or others – are confident and knowledgeable enough to exploit their powers. The world offers plenty of scope for Giddensian agency. The task of the next section, then, is to explore some existing applications of structuration theory, both within organization studies generally and within the domain of strategy as practice in particular.

Structuration theory in practice

To some extent the basic idea of structuration has become a conventional wisdom of organization studies, as it is now of sociology more widely (Parker 2000). The early use of structuration theory in management studies to challenge traditional representations of organizational structure as objective and somehow 'real' (for example, Ranson, Hinings and Greeenwood 1980) hardly seems radical now. As some of Giddens' key insights have become absorbed into the taken-for-granted category, structuration theory might easily have faded from the literature's bibliographies. Novelty or exoticism would no longer be sufficient to justify the trouble of citation.

In fact, Giddens is now the fifth most cited author within the social sciences, ahead of Freud and Marx (O'Boyle 2013). His work continues to be a source of debate and inspiration in the management and organizational literature, with frequent reviews in different specialisms (for example, Thompson 2012; Heracleous 2013). In the management and organization literature, Giddens' citations are on a steadily upwards trend. Thus, a Google Scholar search in journals with 'Management' or 'Organization' in their titles and with both the words 'Giddens' and 'structuration' produces ninety-two citations in 2000, 112 in 2005 and 156 in 2012. It might be that the application of structuration theory is often somewhat lopsided (as I argue later), tending to focus at the micro-level of strategic conduct rather than institutional analysis (Whittington 1992; Pozzebon 2004). Nevertheless, it is clear that Giddens remains an important resource for management scholars – indeed, never more so.

This continued use of Giddens has been particularly reinforced by the turn to practice in management studies (Chia and MacKay 2007; Whittington 2006). This section, therefore, examines in some depth two particularly exemplary applications of structuration theory within the practice-orientated organization literature in general, before reviewing some significant pieces within the strategy-as-practice literature in particular.

My focus here is on the articles of Orlikowski (2000) and Feldman (2004). There are plenty of other prominent and influential articles in organization theory that could provide guidance and inspiration in applying structuration theory (such as Barley 1986; Heracleous and Barrett 2001; Boudreau and Robey 2005; Pentland and Feldman 2007; Berends, van Burg and van Raaij 2011). I choose Orlikowski (2000) and Feldman (2004) in particular, however, both because they exemplify relevant themes and because they have made particularly effective use of diagrams to highlight key features of structuration theory. These two articles deserve closer study than presented here, but significant issues of structure, agency and method can nonetheless be brought out.

In her article 'Using technology and constituting structures', Orlikowski (2000) draws on structuration theory to examine the usage of information technology in organizations. Her focus is particularly on Lotus Notes – a software package purporting to promote collaborative working and knowledge-sharing – in a consultancy and a software house. Orlikowski (2000: 408, emphasis in original) takes a 'practice lens' in order to emphasize how 'we often conflate two aspects of technology: the technology as *artefact* (the bundle of material and symbolic properties packaged in some socially recognizable form, e.g. hardware,

software, technique) and the *use* of technology, or what people actually do with the technological artefact in their recurrent, situated practices'. Drawing on ethnographic shadowing and interview methods, she reveals a mixture of limited, personal and sometimes improvisatory usage of this purportedly collaborative technology.

For her, structuration theory helps us to understand the improvisatory nature of 'technology-in-practice' because of its insistence that structural principles are not fixed and objective, but only instantiated in practice. In this case, the structures of Lotus Notes technology are emergent in action rather than being inherent and somehow determinant. For example, the customer support specialists in Orlikowski's software house made improvisatory use of Lotus Notes for their Incident Tracking Support System (ITSS). As in Figure 8.2, within a structural context of a cooperative culture, a team incentive structure and a departmental learning orientation, the support specialists were able to express their agency to experiment with new ways of working. In this they were assisted by Lotus Notes' technological facilities, the departments' norms of team play and quality, and a shared interpretive scheme that was optimistic about technology in general and the potential of Lotus Notes in particular. Instead of just using Lotus Notes as prescribed, the support specialists developed new practices, such as entering calls into the ITSS database retrospectively rather than simultaneously and browsing through colleagues' call records in order build up practical knowledge. Structuration theory's respect for human agency thereby alerts the analyst to the possibility of discovering in use technological capacities that were not originally designed.

A second empirical study making very explicit empirical use of Giddens is Feldman's (2004) article on organizational processes in a university's halls of residence. Feldman spent four years engaged in 1,750 hours of observation, participation and conversation, as well as gathering 10,000 e-mails. Her theme in the article is 'how changes in the internal processes of an organization can take one kind of resource and recreate it as a different resource' (Feldman 2004: 295). She writes that taking a social practice theory perspective helped

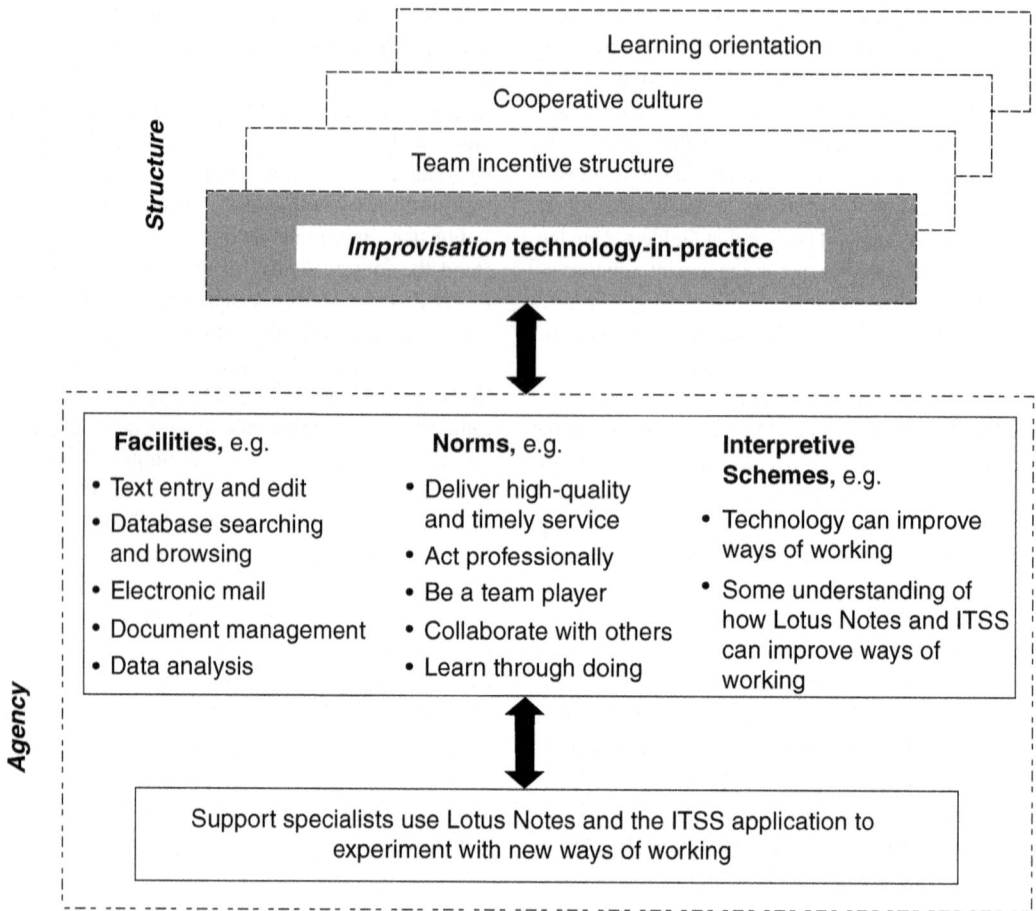

Figure 8.2 A structurationist *view on technology-in-practice*
Source: Reprinted permission, Orlikowski (2000: 420, fig. 9). Copyright 2000, the Institute for Operations Research and the Management Sciences (INFORMS), 5521 Research Park Drive, Suite 200, Catonsville, MD 21228, USA.

her to understand how these internal processes connect the earlier resources with the later ones – in other words, to understand change over time. The key change here was the centralization of the hiring and training of hall staff, with implications for the building directors (BDs) in charge of each residential hall.

Feldman (2004) takes specifically a structurationist perspective on the relationships between resources, rules (which she calls 'schema') and actions, with each tending to reproduce the others. She demonstrates these relationships by comparing the responses to incidents of student bulimia before

and after the centralization of the recruitment and training processes of hall staff. Figure 8.3, taken from her article, has effectively three columns: the first, on the left-hand side, shows the theoretical relationship, with the typical structurationist cycle of reproduction; the second is the empirical relationship *before* the change in process; the third, on the right-hand side, shows the relationship *after* the centralization. Although the empirical resource categories remain the same – networks, authority, trust, and so on, indicated in the bottom oblongs – they change their nature with the introduction of the new hiring and training practices. Hall staff

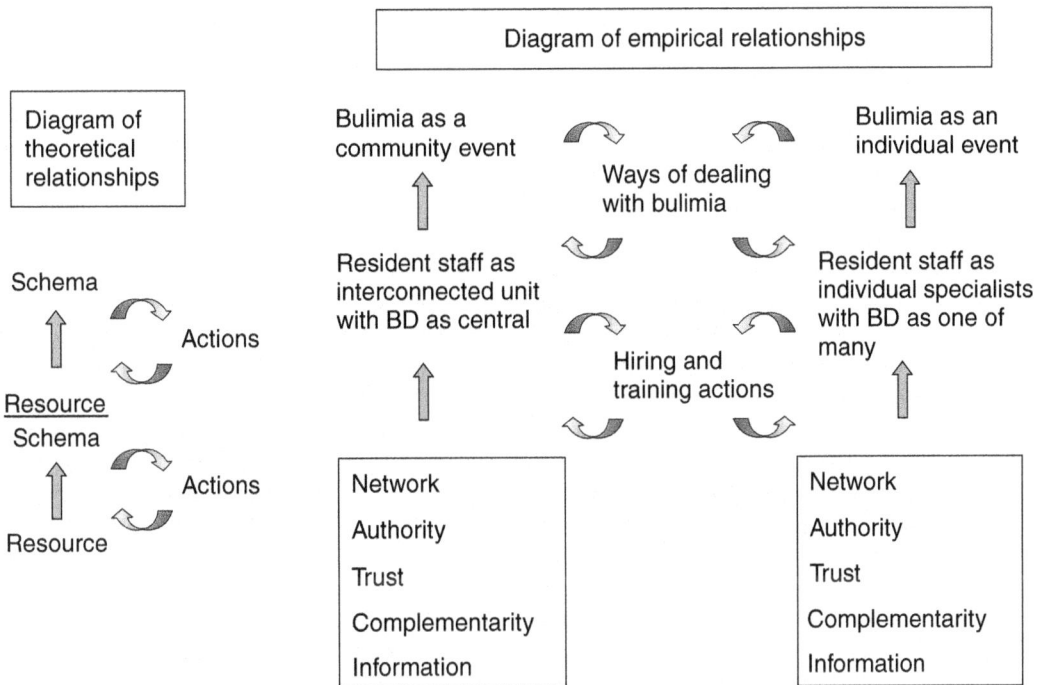

Figure 8.3 A structurationist *view on organizational practices in a student hall*
Source: Printed by Permission, Feldman (2004: 300, fig. 2). Copyright (2004), the Institute for Operations Research and the Management Sciences (INFORMS), 5521 Research Park Drive, Suite 200, Catonsville, MD 21228, USA.

become more fragmented, and the BDs lose their earlier central status. The result is that the schema for dealing with bulimia, and the actual responses (actions), become less communitarian, more individual. The circular loops in the figure convey the sense that resources reinforce schema; schema shape actions; and actions call forth more of the original resources. For example, acceptance of the new, more specialized responsibilities entrenched hiring preferences for more 'professional' staff, who in turn naturally tended to favour more individualistic responses. This circularity tends towards embedding patterns of response, despite the university's building directors' increasing frustration with the situation.

These two Giddensian studies offer an interesting contrast as well as some shared themes. First of all, the studies show how the structurationist framework can accommodate very different empirical patterns of behaviour: Orlikowski (2000)

stresses improvisation, while Feldman (2004) chooses – in this article – to highlight reinforcement. Thus, the structurationist framework can handle both creativity and circularity, agency and structure. Important similarities lie in these authors' recognition of structural context, however, and the intensity of the research method. Orlikowski (2000) and Feldman (2004) alike emphasize the structure of the prevailing resources, schema, norms and facilities. These are set up before the analysis of action, recognized as preconditions for what actually happens. Both authors are also impressive in terms of their empirical commitment: Orlikowski conducted work-shadowing; Feldman engaged in four years of observation. These authors take seriously the structurationist mandate to study practice from the inside.

It is easy to imagine extensions of these two structurationist studies into the domain of strategy as practice. Orlikowski's (2000) sensitivity to the improvisatory way in which people use Lotus Notes could be translated into a study of how strategists actually use standard strategy tools, such as Porter's five forces or even simple SWOT analysis. Orlikowski's insights suggest that usage is unlikely to be precisely 'by the book', but that actors will nonetheless find new and creative applications for them – perhaps, for instance, in internal communications or organizational politics. Feldman's (2004) emphasis on circular reinforcement is suggestive too. Her broad framework might, for example, be applied to studying the introduction of a new strategic planning system, opening up its various effects, functional and dysfunctional, intended and unintended.

The emerging strategy-as-practice literature has in fact already taken up aspects of Giddens and structuration theory. Table 8.1 summarizes ten empirical studies in leading American and European journals that have made use of Giddensian notions in fairly substantive fashion, while relating themselves broadly to the SAP tradition. These are chosen as representative rather than absolutely comprehensive, and some of these authors have used Giddens elsewhere as well (for example, Jarzabkowski and Wilson 2002; Mantere and Vaara 2008). Reviewing these reveals at least three common themes.

The most striking theme that emerges from the ten articles summarized in Table 8.1 is the strong emphasis on middle manager activity: Balogun and Johnson (2005) insist on middle manager interpretation and resistance; Fauré and Rouleau (2011) consider the negotiations between accountants and site managers; Howard-Grenville (2007), Kaplan (2008) and Rouleau (2005) concern themselves with middle managers' activity around particular strategy projects or initiatives; Mantere (2008) and Paroutis and Pettigrew (2007) focus on the roles of middle managers in the strategy process. There is an interesting combination in the article by Paroutis and Heracleous (2013), which examines both top- and middle-level management accounts of strategy. Of course, middle managerial activity is rich ground for strategy as practice, interested as it is in uncovering the significance of the everyday in strategy. But structuration theory reinforces this tendency to look beyond top management because of its emphasis on

agency – the capacity of nearly everybody to make a difference. From a structuration theory point of view, middle managers can be expected to exercise a crucial shaping role in strategy not only through their creative improvisation in the implementation of strategy but also through their deliberate and potentially skilful attempts at upwards influence. As Balogun and Johnson (2005) and Kaplan (2008) show, top managers – the conventional guardians of strategy – cannot expect to exert effective control because of the distribution of power and the indeterminateness of structural rules and resources.

A second theme is the commitment to intense and intimate research engagement, in line with the endeavours of Orlikowski (2000) and Feldman (2004). For Paroutis and Heracleous (2013), Giddens provides the motivation for sticking close to the data, allowing meaning to emerge from managerial discourse as directly as possible. Ethnographic or observational methods are used by Fauré and Rouleau (2011), Howard-Grenville (2007), Jarzabkowski (2008), Kaplan (2008) and Rouleau (2005). Balogun and Johnson (2005) are innovative in also using a diary method, their research subjects recording regularly their own thoughts and impressions as their organizations changed over time. The remainder rely more on interviewing, but in all cases involve many participants and avoid simple closed questions. The commitment to local understanding is underlined by the typical focus on a very limited number of organizations, typically just one. Mantere (2008) is exceptional in spanning twelve organizations, but his concern is with managers in general rather than the fate or characteristics of particular organizations. Paroutis and Heracleous (2013) offer an intriguing way forward, in combining interviews in eleven organizations with an in-depth case study: here they are able to establish a general institutional template as context for the situational specificity of their main case. In one way or another, all these studies use methods appropriate to the analysis of strategic conduct (Giddens 1984), attempting to grasp actors' activities, their own understandings, their achievements and their skills.

The final column of Table 8.1 points to a third theme: the reliance on additional sources of theory.

Table 8.1 Giddens in the study of strategy practice

Authors	Subject	Key methods	Structuration theory use	Additional theories
Balogun and Johnson (2005), *Organization Studies*	Unintended outcomes and middle manager interpretation of change strategies	Case study: diaries and review meetings	Agency, meanings and the dialectic of control	Sensemaking
Fauré and Rouleau (2011), *Accounting, Organizations and Society*	Micro-practices of calculation used in budgeting conversations	Case study: interviews and ethnographic observation	Agents' social competence; reproduction and unintended consequences	Communication theory
Howard-Grenville (2007) *Organization Science*	Middle manager issue-selling over time	Case study: ethnographic participant observation	Norms, routines and schemas reproduced through practice	Organizational politics and resourcing
Jarzabkowski (2008), *Academy of Management Journal*	Types of strategizing behaviour and their effects	Comparative case studies: interviews and observation	Structure and agency; recursivity and change	Institutional theory
Kaplan (2008), *Organization Science*	Middle managers' framing contests round rival projects	Observation, interviews and documents	Power as indeterminate and enacted by skilful actors	Goffmanesque frame theory
Mantere (2008), *Journal of Management Studies*	Middle managers' expectations regarding strategy	Large interview data set across twelve organizations	Agency and knowledgeability	Middle manager roles
Paroutis and Pettigrew (2007), *Human Relations*	Strategy teams' activity in centre and periphery	Case study: interviews	Routinized nature of practice and the knowledgeability of agents	Strategy process
Paroutis and Heracleous (2013), *Strategic Management Journal*	The institutional work of changing strategy discourse over time	Case study: interviews	Discourse as enabling and constraining; keeping close to the data	Institutional theory
Rouleau (2005), *Journal of Management Studies*	Middle managers interpreting and selling change	Case study: ethnography	Discursive and practical consciousness; social structures	Sensemaking and sensegiving
Salvato (2003), *Journal of Management Studies*	Micro-strategies in innovation and design	Comparative case studies: interviews	Agency in using and adapting firm routines	Dynamic capabilities

For Giddens (1984), structuration theory is more of a broad orientation or sensitizing device than a precise theory in itself. Structuration theory points the researcher towards certain types of phenomena, such as agency, as seen in many of these papers. Structuration theory rarely has much to say about how these phenomena are likely to behave in particular circumstances, however; nor, as a theory of society in general, does it offer many concepts for organizations in particular. Accordingly, all these ten articles draw upon other kinds of theory, mostly widely employed in organizational studies already: for example, Salvato (2003) relates to dynamic capabilities theory, Balogun and Johnson (2005) and Rouleau (2005) resort to the sensemaking tradition of Weick (1995), while Jarzabkowski (2008) and Paroutis and Heracleous (2013) use institutional theory. Typically, these theories provide additional conceptual language, such as sensemaking or framing, or point to strategy-specific phenomena, such as issue-selling or innovative design. Generally these ten articles do not use these additional theories to develop propositions about phenomena in different circumstances – though, as I shall argue in a moment, structuration theory would not exclude this option.

So far, then, structuration theory has been predominantly useful to strategy-as-practice researchers in directing attention towards middle managers, rather than just the top managers typical in strategy research. It has also inspired a commitment to the intimate research methodologies characteristic of the analysis of strategic conduct. At the same time, these researchers have not relied upon structuration theory alone: quite often, they have anchored themselves theoretically in the mainstream by drawing upon theoretical traditions that are already well recognized within organization studies in general. There are, then, common threads across the ten articles in Table 8.1; this commonality also points to opportunities.

Opportunities for structurationist research

We can treat structuration theory fairly pragmatically, as just one resource for strategy-as-practice researchers, and its value determined according to the task in hand (Johnson *et al.* 2007). So far, SAP researchers have clearly found it useful for the analysis of strategic conduct, especially for understanding the agency of middle management. This is a rich seam for research, and there is both scope and need for more. Middle managers are a large population, and their skills and futures are fundamental to the mission of the business schools in which most strategy-as-practice researchers are employed. We have only begun to understand their predicament with regard to strategy, and in our MBA classes and executive education courses we have an audience eager to learn more. But here I shall point to three more kinds of research opportunity, two of which are logical extensions, while the third is a more radical departure from prevailing streams of SAP research.

The first extension builds on the existing strategy-as-practice strength with regard to middle managers. Just as structuration theory has helped us to appreciate the role of those outside the top management team, so could it help to uncover other relatively neglected groups of actors in strategy work. Obvious examples of under-researched groups include strategy consultants, strategy gurus and strategic planners (for some suggestive exceptions, see Sturdy, Schwarz and Spicer 2006; and Greatbatch and Clark 2002). Such consultants, gurus and planners are typically in advisory roles rather than decision-making ones, but the structurationist respect for agency would predict an influence for them considerably greater than formally allowed, and probably exercised in subtle ways. Another neglected group, often frustrated consumers of strategy, are lower-level employees (Mantere 2005; Mantere and Vaara 2008). An agency-sensitive perspective would propose for such employees a degree of discretion that required their practical understanding of strategy for effective implementation, at the same time as predicting considerable scope for resistance and reinterpretation. A structurationist approach to the practice of strategy would highlight the likely importance of communications, buy-in and unexpected initiatives and contradictions right down the organizational hierarchy.

A second extension of existing tendencies is to exploit more fully the mid-range theoretical resources (such as sensemaking, contingency theory, and the like) that are already being used in strategy-as-practice work in order to develop more propositional forms of research. A good deal of SAP research so far has been revelatory in nature, uncovering the previously unremarked. This is often fascinating, and consistent with practice theory's ambition to 'exoticise the domestic' (Bourdieu 1988: xi). Now that the practice perspective has exposed the phenomena, however, there is increasing scope for deriving from these mid-range theories formal research propositions about variation in these phenomena or their effects. Such propositional research might take, for example, the form of investigating the theoretically indicated conditions under which some kinds of conduct or outcome are more likely than others. As a simple illustration, some kind of contingency-theoretic framework could motivate propositions about the conditions under which strategy tools are more relied upon in strategy-making activity or less. The methodological implication of this kind of approach is typically careful theoretical sampling aiming for structured comparison, such as one set of cases or episodes in which the conditions are present, compared with another set in which the conditions are absent. This kind of move beyond revelatory research towards propositional research promises big pay-offs both in terms of practical guidance and academic publication. Propositions can provide the basis for practical guidelines (for example, this practice is more effective under these conditions than those), and they are the favoured method of many North American journals.

A more radical departure would be to go beyond the analysis of strategic conduct that has prevailed so far and seize the area of enormous but neglected opportunity highlighted by Giddens' (1984) methodological dichotomy, namely institutional analysis. This is thoroughly consistent with Suddaby, Seidl and Lê's (2013) call for strategy-as-practice research to recognize more fully the institutional context in which strategizing is set. Structuration theory's commitment to duality clearly indicates unfinished business for strategy as practice, and there is certainly a large empirical gap to fill. As Paroutis and Heracleous (2013) indicate, strategy is an institution in itself. Strategy has its own tools and language (SWOT, core competence, and so on), its professional societies (the Association of Strategic Planning, the Society of Competitive Intelligence Professionals, the Strategic Planning Society), its learned society (the Strategic Management Society), its authorities and gurus (Porter, Hamel, and so on), its specialized journals (the *Harvard Business Review*, the *Strategic Management Journal*, and so on), its recognized educational and career tracks (business schools and leading strategic consultancies) and both full-time professional practitioners (strategic planners, consultants, analysts) and part-timers – the ordinary managers who get sucked in at various levels to make, communicate or implement strategy. Strategy thus constitutes a field, or social system, with

its own structural rules (norms of practice) and resources (authority), upon which its members draw in their day-to-day activities. The strategic conduct that has been so richly observed by previous strategy-as-practice researchers relies in part on strategy's rules and resources, and this same conduct contributes to their reproduction, sometimes their transformation. To work on strategy is typically to know the right tools and language, to have gone through appropriate educational and career tracks and to borrow the authority of legitimate strategic practice. In general, analysts of conduct notice these rules and resources only locally and fleetingly as they are instantiated, alongside all the other kinds of rule and resource, in particular moments of strategizing.

The opportunity for SAP researchers now is to analyse the institution of strategy more systematically as an institutional field in its own right (Knights and Morgan 1991; Hendry 2000). Such institutional analysis would not only inform research into strategic conduct; it would support the regulation and reform of the strategy field itself. The strategy field is prolific of ideas ('stick-to-the-knitting', 'network effects', and so on); these ideas sometimes sweep around the world economies, penetrating new sectors, such as the public sector, and new countries, such as reform economies, with little product testing (Ghemawat 2002). It is not clear that the strategy field's leading bodies (its professional organizations, its learned society and its educational institutions) are adequate yet to the task of regulation (Whittington *et al.* 2003; Whittington 2012). The 'new economy' strategies of the dot.com and Enron era around the turn of the century, and later the 'financial supermarket' diversification strategies of companies such as Citigroup, were offered little critical scrutiny by the strategy field. In retrospect, we now all recognize their fatal flaws. Unlike the accounting profession and the financial markets, however, the strategy field left its economic, professional and educational apparatus largely untouched when these new strategies' enormous failings were finally revealed. For Giddens, both the theorist of duality and a political reformer, this reluctance to reflect on and modify strategy as an institution would seem strangely half-hearted.

There are two clear routes forward for the institutional analysis of strategy. The first is to develop a macro-understanding of the field as a whole, and its evolution over time. Strategy deserves the same kind of historical and sociological analysis that for the other professions – such as medicine, law or social work – have long been routine (for example, Abbott 1988). Here key questions would include how the boundaries of strategy have been defined and managed, the kinds of language that have been used to describe it (from long-range planning to business model engineering), the ways in which knowledge and technologies have been produced and disseminated and the nature and the extent of its membership (both full-time and part-time). Particularly important for informing the analysis of strategic conduct would be understanding the variety and force of strategy's rules and resources in different kinds of contexts. Strategy was born in the United States, but we know little systematically about how its practices translate into on-the-ground praxis in very different contexts, such as Chinese state-owned enterprises or Gulf State business fiefdoms. Important for institutional regulation and reform, on the other hand, would be understanding of how the field of strategy, and its effects, evolve over time. For example, the formalization of strategy attributed to the 1960s and 1970s may have played a large part in undermining US competitiveness (Hayes and Abernathy 1980); by their own accounts at least, it took the combined efforts of iconic managers such as Jack Welch and rhetorical gurus such as Mintzberg and Pascale finally to relax it (Mintzberg 1994; Pascale 1990; Welch 2001). Ghemawat (2002) highlights similarly damaging consequences from the 'new economy' strategies of the dot.com boom, with its overexcited talk of disruption, network effects and increasing returns. By scrutinizing the ways in which strategy as a field may have had dysfunctional consequences in the past, and how the field has previously corrected itself, we can become both more alert to the field's dangers today and more sophisticated in dealing with them.

The second route forward is to better understand the particular products of the strategy field, both its practices and its practitioners. There is an important shift implied here, from the focus on the particular and local common in the analysis of strategic conduct to the more general patterns and trends of institutional analysis. With regard to strategy practices, the analysis of strategic conduct will tend to show that they are typically improvised and reinterpreted in particular moments of praxis, so that their core characteristics are only unreliably deduced from particular instances of use. Strategy practices need, therefore, to be approached also from 'above', to understand them generically as well as locally. For example, the analytical tools of strategy, such as the BCG matrix, are usually well understood conceptually but not very well in terms of what they tend to mean in practice (particular kinds of data-gathering, representation and political negotiation, for example). It is as if pharmacists knew only the chemistry of a particular pill but not its practical usage and effects. In terms of practitioners, the need is for a better grasp of the kinds of people who typically engage in strategy in particular kinds of decisions, organisations, sectors and even countries. Given the heavy focus on middle managers in the analysis of strategic conduct, an important contextual question is the extent to which middle managers are now involved in strategy generally and under what conditions. To fully appreciate a middle manager's success or failure in an episode of strategic conduct, it is necessary to understand how routine and legitimate that middle manager's intervention was in that particular type of context. These kinds of institutional analysis of practices and practitioners lend themselves to the survey and statistical approaches common within the new institutional theory tradition within organization studies (Scott 2000).

This institutional analysis is not, of course, fundamentally separate from the analysis of strategic conduct: as in Gidden's (1984) duality, to focus on the institutional level is merely an expedient but ultimately provisional bracketing. In the end, the goal is to bring conduct and institutions together so that they can be more completely understood as the mutually constitutive phenomena they are. Institutional analysis is necessary to appreciate the potentialities and constraints, skill and clumsiness, involved in particular moments of strategic conduct. In turn, strategic conduct analysis can help us understand how strategy's institutions can themselves be changed, by professional bodies and educational providers especially, but also by the sheer effort of managers in general.

Conclusion

This chapter has introduced structuration theory, underlining the power of its concepts of agency, structure and structuration over time. It has also highlighted several possible implications for strategy-as-practice researchers. In particular, the chapter has identified the work of Orlikowski (2000) and Feldman (2004) as offering inspiring models from outside the strategy discipline in terms of their careful focus on people's activity, studied intimately through ethnographic methods. The chapter has also reviewed ten studies in the strategy-as-practice field in which Giddens' ideas have particularly supported the close examination of middle manager conduct, revealing the scope for constrained agency deep within organizations and the potential limits to the power of those at the top. Given the audiences for SAP researchers, this stream of work has strong potential, especially as it develops more propositional forms of knowledge and extends its reach to others outside the very top of organizations, such as consultants and other employees.

I have also pointed to the potential of structuration theory to make connections to other streams of research, however, both contributing to them and learning from them. Above all, I have underlined the value of understanding strategy as a societal institution in and of itself. Here there are possible contributions both to micro-foundational and process streams of strategy research. With regard to micro-foundations (Barney and Felin 2013), an understanding of strategy practitioners as embedded in their institutional contexts can help guard against individualistic reductionism. The micro-foundational view rightly recognizes the inter-relatedness of micro-level actors and macro-level phenomena. Nevertheless, a structurationist sensitivity to institutions would reinforce understanding of how individual actors do not simply interact with societal contexts but are inseparable expressions of those contexts. Jack or Jill may be

individuals, yet their identities are essentially social: they are managers, consultants, planners or whatever, and thus infused with capabilities and expectations that are societal in origins, not just personal. Giddens' (1984) notion of methodological bracketing reminds us that considering individuals as 'micro', or focusing on 'micro to macro' links, is to make merely methodological moves, sometimes convenient but always incomplete. In this respect, SAP researchers can contribute to the micro-foundational view by emphasizing a sociological as well as a psychological characterization of individual actors.

The structurationist perspective can at the same time link to the process tradition in organization theory (Langley and Tsoukas 2011), especially to its concern for change over time. As we have seen, strategy-as-practice has been productive of rich ethnographic accounts of strategy processes, providing deep insights into what is going on 'inside the process'. There has been a natural synergy between practice and process traditions here. Where SAP researchers can still make a further distinctive contribution, however, is to draw in more of what is going on outside the processes – the external changes in societal rules and resources that influence strategizing in particular firms. Still exemplary in this respect is Oakes, Townley and Cooper's (1998) study of how the rise of new conceptions of strategy in Canadian public sector discourse impacted the strategizing processes in particular museums. Changes in museum strategizing could be understood only in the light of wider changes in Canadian society.

Finally, there is the potential of structuration theory to prompt research on strategy as an institution. So far strategy-as-practice research has focused largely on activity or conduct; there has been little on the general characteristics of strategy as an institutionalized set of rules and resources that, alongside others, enable and constrain this conduct. This is anomalous theoretically, for Giddens insists that focus on either one of conduct or institution should be merely a matter of methodological bracketing, provisional and self-conscious. His duality of structure implies that the analysis of strategy activity is incomplete without a thorough understanding of institutional context, of which strategy as a field must necessarily be an important part. Neglect of strategy as institution falls short also in policy terms, for the strategy field is an influential and inventive one, constantly spinning out new ideas, sometimes (as perhaps during the high tide of formal planning during the 1960s and 1970s, or the dot.com era of the 1990s) with widely damaging consequences. Giddens the reformer would be concerned that the strategy field is not very good at regulating itself – indeed, that it lacks sufficient systematic knowledge of its own internal workings even to try to do so more effectively. It is worthwhile investing in an institutional analysis of strategy. After all, the merit of structuration theory, vis-à-vis more fatalistic theoretical rivals such as those of Bourdieu and Bhaskar, is its confidence in our human capacity to change institutions for the better. With the 'practical' so strongly implied in our field's title, making practice better should surely be a central part of our research endeavour.

References

Abbott, A. (1988), *The System of the Professions: An Essay on the Expert Division of Labor.* University of Chicago Press.

Archer, M. (1995), *Realist Social Theory.* Cambridge University Press.

(2000), *Being Human: The Problem of Agency.* Cambridge University Press.

Balogun, J., and Johnson, G. (2005), 'From intended strategies to unintended outcomes: the impact of change recipient sensemaking', *Organization Studies*, 26/11: 1573–601.

Barley, S. R. (1986), 'Technology as an occasion for structuring: evidence from observations of CT scanners and the social order of radiology departments', *Administrative Science Quarterly*, 31/1: 78–108.

Barney, J., and Felin, T. (2013), 'What are micro-foundations?', *Academy of Management Perspectives*, 27/2:138–55.

Berends, H., van Burg, E., and van Raaij, E. M. (2011), 'Contacts and contracts: cross-level network dynamics in the development of an aircraft material', *Organization Science*, 22/4: 940–60.

Bhaskar, R. (1989), *Reclaiming Reality: A Critical Realist Introduction to Contemporary Philosophy.* London: Verso.

Boudreau, M. C., and Robey, D. (2005), 'Enacting integrated information technology: a human agency perspective', *Organization Science*, 16/1: 3–18.

Bourdieu, P. (1988), *Homo Academicus.* Redwood City, CA: Stanford University Press.

(1990), *The Logic of Practice.* Cambridge: Polity.

Caldwell, R. (2012), 'Reclaiming agency, recovering change? An exploration of the practice theory of Theodore Schatzki', *Journal for the Theory of Social Behaviour*, 42/3: 283–303.

Chandler, A. D. (1962), *Strategy and Structure: Chapters in the History of the American Industrial Enterprise.* Cambridge, MA: MIT Press.

Chia, R., and MacKay, B. (2007), 'Post-processual challenges for the emerging strategy-as-practice perspective: discovering strategy in the logic of practice', *Human Relations*, 60/1: 217–42.

Denis, J.-L., Langley, A., and Rouleau, L. (2007), 'Strategizing in pluralistic contexts: rethinking theoretical frames', *Human Relations*, 60/1: 179–215.

Fauré, B., and Rouleau, L. (2011), 'The strategic competence of accountants and middle managers in budget making', *Accounting, Organizations and Society*, 36/3: 167–82.

Feldman, M. S. (2004), 'Resources in emerging structures and processes of change', *Organization Science*, 15/3: 295–309.

Floyd, S. W., and Lane, P. (2000), 'Strategizing throughout the organization: management role conflict and strategic renewal', *Academy of Management Review*, 25/1: 154–77.

Floyd, S. W., Cornelissen, M. W., Wright, M., and Delios, A. (2011), 'Processes and practices of strategizing and organizing: review, development, and the role of bridging and umbrella constructs', *Journal of Management Studies*, 48/5: 933–52.

Ghemawat, P. (2002), 'Competition and business strategy in historical perspective', *Business History Review*, 76/1: 37–74.

Giddens, A. (1976), *New Rules of Sociological Method.* London: Hutchinson.

(1979), *Central Problems of Social Theory.* London: Macmillan.

(1984), *The Constitution of Society.* Cambridge: Polity.

Greatbatch, D., and Clark, T. (2002), 'Laughing with the gurus', *Business Strategy Review*, 13/3: 10–18.

Hayes, R. H., and Abernathy, W. (1980), 'Managing our way to economic decline', *Harvard Business Review*, 58/4: 67–77.

Hendry, J. (2000), 'Strategic decision making, discourse and strategy as social practice', *Journal of Management Studies*, 37/7: 955–78.

Heracleous, L. (2013), 'The employment of structuration theory in organizational discourse: exploring methodological challenges', *Management Communication Quarterly*, 27/4: 599–606.

Heracleous, L., and Barrett, M. (2001), 'Organizational change as discourse: communicative actions and deep structures in the context of information technology implementation', *Academy of Management Journal*, 44/4: 755–78.

Howard-Grenville, J. A. (2007), 'Developing issue-selling effectiveness over time: issue selling as resourcing', *Organization Science*, 18/4: 560–77.

Jarzabkowski, P. (2008), 'Shaping strategy as a structuration process'. *Academy of Management Journal*, 51/4: 621–50.

Jarzabkowski, P., and Wilson, D. C. (2002), 'Top teams and strategy in a UK university', *Journal of Management Studies*, 39/3: 355–81.

Johnson, G., Langley, A., Melin, L., and Whittington, R. (2007), *Strategy as Practice: Research Directions and Resources*. Cambridge University Press.

Kaplan, S. (2008), 'Framing contests: strategy making under uncertainty', *Organization Science*, 19/5: 729–52.

—— (2011), 'Strategy and PowerPoint: an inquiry into the epistemic culture and machinery of strategy making', *Organization Science*, 22/2: 320–46.

King, A. (2010), 'The odd couple: Margaret Archer, Anthony Giddens and British social theory', *British Journal of Sociology*, 61/S1: 253–60.

Knights, D., and Morgan, G. (1991), 'Corporate strategy, organizations, and subjectivity: a critique', *Organization Studies*, 12/2: 251–73.

Langley, A. (2009), 'Studying processes in and around organizations', in Buchanan, D. A., and Bryman, A. (eds.), *The Sage Handbook of Organizational Research Methods*: 409–29. London: Sage.

Mantere, S. (2005), 'Strategic practices as enablers and disablers of championing activity', *Strategic Organization*, 3/2: 157–84.

—— (2008), 'Role expectations and middle manager strategic agency', *Journal of Management Studies*, 45/2: 294–316.

Mantere, S., and Vaara, E. (2008), 'On the problem of participation in strategy: a critical discursive perspective', *Organization Science*, 19/2: 341–58.

Mintzberg, H. (1994), *The Rise and Fall of Strategic Planning*. Englewood Cliffs, NJ: Prentice Hall.

Nicolini, D. (2012), *Practice Theory, Work, and Organization: An Introduction*. Oxford University Press.

Oakes, L. S., Townley, B., and Cooper, D. J. (1998), 'Business planning as pedagogy: language and control in a changing institutional field', *Administrative Science Quarterly*, 43/2: 257–92.

O'Boyle, B. (2013), 'Reproducing the social structure: a Marxist critique of Anthony Giddens's structuration methodology', *Cambridge Journal of Economics*, 37/5: 1019–33.

Orlikowski, W. J. (2000), 'Using technology and constituting structures: a practice lens for studying technology in organizations', *Organization Science*, 11/4: 404–28.

Parker, J. (2000), *Structuration*. Milton Keynes: Open University Press.

Paroutis, S., and Heracleous, L. (2013), 'Discourse revisited: dimensions and employment of first-order strategy discourse during institutional adoption', *Strategic Management Journal*, 34/8: 935–56.

Paroutis, S., and Pettigrew, A. M. (2007), 'Strategizing in the multi-business firm: strategy teams at multiple levels and over time', *Human Relations*, 60/1: 99–135.

Pascale, R. T. (1990), *Managing on the Edge: How Successful Companies Use Conflict to Stay Ahead*. New York: Simon & Schuster.

Pentland, B. T., and Feldman, M. S. (2007), 'Narrative networks: patterns of technology and organization', *Organization Science*, 18/5: 781–95.

Pettigrew, A. M. (1985), *The Awakening Giant: Continuity and Change in Imperial Chemical Industries*. Oxford: Blackwell.

Pozzebon, M. (2004), 'The influence of a structurationist view on strategic management research', *Journal of Management Studies*, 41/2: 247–72.

Powell, T. C., Lovallo, D., and Fox, C. (2011), 'Behavioral strategy', *Strategic Management Journal*, 32/13: 1369–86.

Ranson, S., Hinings, B., and Greenwood, R. (1980), 'The structuring of organizational structures', *Administrative Science Quarterly*, 25/1: 1–17.

Reckwitz, A. (2002), 'Toward a theory of social practices: a development in culturalist theorizing', *European Journal of Social Theory*, 5/2: 243–63.

Reed, M. (2005), 'Reflections on the realist "turn" in organization and management studies', *Journal of Management Studies*, 42/8: 1621–44.

Rouleau, L. (2005), 'Micro-practices of strategic sensemaking and sensegiving: how middle managers interpret and sell change every day', *Journal of Management Studies*, 42/7: 1413–41.

Salvato, C. (2003), 'The role of micro-strategies in the engineering of firm evolution', *Journal of Management Studies*, 40/1: 83–108.

Samra-Fredericks, D. (2003), 'Strategizing as lived experience and strategists' everyday efforts to shape strategic direction', *Journal of Management Studies*, 40/1: 141–74.

Schatzki, T. R. (2001), 'Introduction: practice theory', in Schatzki, T. R., Knorr Cetina, K., and von Savigny, E. (eds.), *The Practice Turn in Contemporary Theory*: 1–14. London: Routledge.

Scott, W. R. (2000), *Institutions and Organizations*. London: Sage.

Stones, R. (2005), *Structuration Theory*. Basingstoke: Palgrave Macmillan.

Sturdy, A., Schwarz, M., and Spicer, A. (2006), 'Guess who's coming to dinner? Structures and the use of liminality in strategic management consultancy', *Human Relations*, 59/7: 929–60.

Suddaby, R., Seidl, D., and Lê, J. (2013), 'Strategy-as-practice meets neo-institutional theory', *Strategic Organization*, 11/3: 329–44.

Thompson, M. (2012), 'People, practice, and technology: restoring Giddens' broader philosophy to the study of information systems', *Information and Organization*, 22/3: 188–207.

Vaara, E., and Whittington, R. (2012), 'Strategy-as-practice: taking social practices seriously', *Academy of Management Annals*, 6/1: 285–336.

Weick, K. E. (1995), *Sensemaking in Organizations*. Thousand Oaks, CA: Sage.

Welch, J. (2001), *Jack: What I've Learned Leading a Great Company and Great People*. London: Headline.

Whittington, R. (1989), *Corporate Strategies in Recession and Recovery: Social Structures and Strategic Choice*. London: Unwin Hyman.

(1992), 'Putting Giddens into action: social systems and managerial agency', *Journal of Management Studies*, 29/6: 693–712.

(2006), 'Completing the practice turn in strategy research', *Organization Studies*, 26/4: 613–34.

(2012), 'Big strategy/small strategy', *Strategic Organization*, 10/3: 263–8.

Whittington, R., Basak-Yakis, B., and Cailluet, L. (2011), 'Opening strategy: evolution of a precarious profession', *British Journal of Management*, 22/3: 531–44.

Whittington, R., Jarzabkowski, P., Mayer, M., Mounoud, E., Nahapiet, J., and Rouleau, L. (2003), 'Taking strategy seriously: responsibility and reform for an important social practice', *Journal of Management Inquiry*, 12/4: 396–409.

CHAPTER 9

An activity theory approach to strategy as practice

PAULA JARZABKOWSKI and CAROLA WOLF

This chapter introduces activity theory as an approach for studying strategy as practice. Activity theory conceptualizes the ongoing construction of activity as a product of activity systems, comprising the actor, the community with which that actor interacts and those symbolic and material tools that mediate between actors, their community and their pursuit of activity. The focus on the mediating role of tools and cultural artefacts in human activity seems especially promising for advancing the strategy-as-practice agenda, for example as a theoretical resource for the growing interest in socio-materiality and the role of tools and artefacts in (strategy) practice (for example, Balogun *et al.* 2014; Lanzara 2009; Nicolini 2009; Spee and Jarzabkowski 2009; Stetsenko 2005). Despite its potential, in a recent review Vaara and Whittington (2012) identified only three strategy-as-practice articles explicitly applying an activity theory lens. In the wider area of practice-based studies in organizations, activity theory has been slightly more popular (for example, Blackler 1993; 1995; Blackler, Crump and McDonald 2000; Engeström, Kerosuo and Kajamaa 2007; Groleau 2006; Holt 2008; Miettinen and Virkkunen 2005). It still lags behind its potential, however, primarily because of its origins as a social psychology theory developed in Russia with little initial recognition outside the Russian context, particularly in the area of strategy and organization theory, until recently (Miettinen, Samra-Fredericks and Yanow 2009). This chapter explores activity theory as a resource for studying strategy as practice as it is socially accomplished by individuals in interaction with their wider social group and the artefacts of interaction. In particular, activity theory's focus on actors as social individuals provides a conceptual basis for studying the core question in strategy-as-practice research: what strategy practitioners *do*.

The chapter is structured in three parts. First, an overview of activity theory is provided. Second, activity theory as a practice-based approach to studying organizational action is introduced and an activity system conceptual framework is developed. Third, the elements of the activity system are explained in more detail and explicitly linked to each of the core SAP concepts: practitioners, practices and praxis. In doing so, links are made to existing strategy-as-practice research, with brief empirical examples of topics that might be addressed using activity theory. Throughout the chapter, we introduce key authors in the development of activity theory and its use in management and adjacent disciplinary fields, as further resources for those wishing to make greater use of activity theory.

Background to activity theory

Context and core concepts of activity theory

This section provides a brief overview of the foundations of activity theory before discussing elements that are particularly applicable to the strategy-as-practice agenda. Russian cultural historical activity theory (CHAT), which is grounded in a Marxist tradition, was developed by Lev Vygotsky (1978) to explain the development of human consciousness. In particular, Vygotsky wanted to avoid representations of the mind as separate from the social context in which consciousness develops. Hence, his theory is inherently social, accounting for human consciousness as it develops in interaction with a collectively evolving cultural and historical context. 'The individual could no longer be understood without his or her cultural means; and the society could no longer be understood without the agency of individuals who use and produce artifacts' (Engeström 2001: 134). Engeström refers to these origins as the first generation of activity theory, followed by two further generations expanding Vygotsky's original ideas (for example, Engeström 1996; 2001).

Vygotsky's students and colleagues, particularly Leontiev (1978), developed a second generation of activity theory (Engeström 1996) by proposing activity as the unit of analysis in which to examine human consciousness, thereby moving beyond the individual focus of Vygotsky's model. In activity, individuals interact with the wider cultural and historical context in which they are engaged, so developing consciousness in an overtly social way that is both conditioned by and responsive to the wider collective of which they are part. While individuals are shaped by the collective with which they interact, this is not deterministic, as individuals both learn how to act from and also contribute to the evolving cultural and historical context. Engeström (1987; 1990) has been a key figure in the development of activity theory within the education and learning field, as well as taking it more widely into the study of organizations. Based on Vygotsky's original model and Leontiev's shift of focus beyond the individual, one of Engeström's main contributions has been helping to elaborate whole activity systems as the unit of analysis in which an activity occurs (see Kaptelinin and Nardi 2006: 137–43; Miettinen, Samra-Fredericks and Yanow 2009). The activity system concept provides an integrative framework, encompassing the interactions that take place between individuals, the cultural and historical context of their activity, and the various tools and technologies that mediate that activity. Engeström's (1987; 1993) approach elaborates activity theory by identifying specific elements of the activity system, such as the social structuring mechanisms of roles, the division of labour, tools and the implicit and explicit rules through which individuals interact as they construct activity, in particular the activity of learning.

Activity theory as a learning theory emphasizes the dynamic, continuously unfolding activity of learning and the role of mediation, which Engeström (2001: 137) casts as an alternative to traditional learning theories:

Standard theories of learning are focused on processes where a subject (traditionally an individual, more recently possibly also an organization) acquires some identifiable knowledge or skills in such a way that a corresponding, relatively lasting change in the behaviour of the subject may be observed. [...] The problem is that much of the most intriguing kinds of learning in work organizations violates this presupposition. People and organizations are all the time learning something that is not stable, not even defined or understood ahead of time.

Engeström (1987) thus focuses on collective transformations rather than individual learning, proposing an interactional perspective on the joint creation of knowledge and new (organizational) practices. Such transformations are grounded in resolving contradictions in the activity system (see also Engeström 2000; 2001; Engeström, Kerosuo and Kajamaa 2007; Kerosuo 2011). Based on the principles of Marxist dialectics, internal contradictions (Ilyenkov 1977; 1982) are identified as a key driver of change (for example, Engeström 1987; 2000; Engeström and Sannino 2011) in an activity system. Contradictions arise as the historical aspects of the activity system come into tension with new elements, such as new technologies, or as new rules of conduct emerge. These elements provoke disturbances within the historical accumulation of activity and so generate 'concrete innovative actions' (Engeström 2000: 309), which constitute learning and transformation. This process of emergence can arise not only in interaction within the activity system but through the interactions between activity systems, particularly as subjects and the various tools of mediation often span multiple activity systems. Engeström (1996; 2001) thus identifies a third generation of activity theory that moves beyond the analysis of separate activity systems towards exploring interactions within multiple activity systems. Blackler, Crump and McDonald (2000), for example, apply such an extension of the unit of analysis in their study of a network of different strategy development groups, each comprising a different activity system, within a single organization.

In sum, activity theory premises that psychological development is a social process arising from an individual's interactions within particular historical and cultural contexts (Vygotsky 1978). Interaction provides an interpretive basis from which individuals attribute meaning to their own and others' actions (Vygotsky 1978; Wertsch 1985). This interaction is profoundly located within practical activity, being the daily work in which actors engage (Kozulin 1999; Leontiev 1978). In this activity, we may study *how* – through what means – individuals interact with others and are enabled to partake in the collective activity of a community. In activity theory, practical activity is mediated through the technical and psychological tools that individuals draw upon to interact with each other (Wertsch 1985). Vygotsky (1978) was concerned with psychological tools, such as algebraic symbols, schemes, diagrams, maps and mechanical drawings, as well as the acquisition and use of language, through which actors invoke meaning and which mediate between their own subjective consciousness and the activity they perform in a community. The point of such tools is that they are oriented towards activity. They come into use to mediate the practical activity that is constructed between actors (Kozulin 1999). The analysis of activity and its transformation must therefore consider 'the presence of (a) manufactured objects and concepts that mediate the interaction between individuals and concepts; (b) traditions, rituals, and rules that mediate the interaction between individuals and the community; and (c) the division of labour that mediates the interaction between the community and the actions of its members' (Gherardi and Nicolini 2001: 49).

The contribution of activity theory to understanding organizational practices

Activity theory has been further elaborated in fields as diverse as work psychology, cognitive science, communication theory and information technology (see, for example, Engeström, Miettinen and Punamäki 1999; Nardi 1996a), in ways that are pertinent to understanding organizational practices (see Table 9.1). For example, Engeström's activity system approach to analysing collective activity has been found useful in organization studies, in

which there is often an interest in studying how individuals coordinate their actions within the collective activity of a group, unit, division or organization. Aspects of Engeström's activity system model have been used by those organization theory scholars who examine organizational learning, contradictions and paradoxes associated with organizational and strategic change (for example, Adler 2005; Blackler 1993; 1995; Engeström, Kerosuo and Kajamaa 2007; Jarzabkowski 2003; 2005; Jarzabkowski and Balogun 2009; Kerosuo 2011; Prenkert 2006). In particular, activity theory provides avenues for understanding how learning and collective transformation can be brought about by 'accumulated developmental contradictions within and between activity systems' (Engeström 2000: 308–9), so encouraging us to explore these triggers of change in organizational practice (Gherardi and Nicolini 2001).

Activity theory complements other practice-based approaches to learning because of its focus on the collective accomplishment of organizational learning (for example, Engeström 2000; Gherardi and Nicolini 2001; Nicolini, Gherardi and Yanow 2003), with learning being approached 'not as something that takes place in the mind but as something produced and reproduced in the social relations of individuals when they participate in society' (Gherardi and Nicolini 2001: 47). Like the activity theory approach, learning is about participating in specific practices, typically within a community of practice (for example, Brown and Duguid 1991; Lave and Wenger 1991; Wenger 1998). For instance, Lave and Wenger (1991) illustrate the way that newcomers learn through participation how to construct themselves as members of a community, even as their participation reconstructs that community.

While an activity system approach focuses attention on the activity arising from the system, it need not exclude individual activity (for example, Malopinsky 2008), but this is, rather, a matter of foreground and background. In other words, a focus on the individual is always sensitive to the collective practices and social interactions of the system in which the individual acts. Activity theory thus complements other social theories of practice, because of its positioning of practice as a

Table 9.1 Exemplars of studying organizational practices through an activity theory lens

Study	Conceptual focus	Contribution
Blackler and Regan (2009)	The transformation of practices and the role of intentionality and agency	The authors draw on practice theory and, more specifically, activity theory to analyse the reorganization of social services in order to expand the knowledge on collective intentionality and distributed agency, allowing for a dynamic perspective on teams and communities of practice that deals with the uncertainties and contradictions that actors are exposed to in modern work environments.
Blackler, Crump and McDonald (1999)	The development and change of organizational practices	The article uses activity theory as a lens to study organizational learning, more specifically to analyse changes in the design practices of a high-technology company; it traces the attempted change strategy and the emerging outcomes.
Blackler, Crump and McDonald (2000)	The cooperation of multiple members and parts of the organization in strategy-making	This is a comparative case study of three strategy development teams analysing practices in a high-technology company with a focus on the integration and cooperation of multiple activity systems in an organization.
Engeström (2001)	The transformation of organizational practices and the collaboration and coordination of different groups of actors	The article uses third-generation activity theory and its focus on the interaction of multiple activity systems to study expansive learning in a Finnish hospital in order to advance knowledge on inter-organizational learning.
Engeström, Kerosuo and Kajamaa (2007)	The transformation of organizational practices	The authors compare the change of organizational practices in two municipal health centres in Finland to analyse different types of discontinuity of organizational change, namely mundane and directional organizational change.
Foot (2002)	The role of objects and goal orientation	The author elaborates on the notion of objects in cultural-historical activity theory and analyses the formation of the Russian Network for Ethnological Monitoring as an illustrative case of the formation of objects, demonstrating how participants perceive and engage with this object.
Holt (2008)	The recognition and implementation of entrepreneurial opportunities	The author draws on existing studies and data from a longitudinal study of UK entrepreneurs; this study uses activity theory to analyse the social embeddedness of creating entrepreneurial opportunities and transforming them into businesses.
Jarratt and Stiles (2010)	The practitioners' interpretation and application of strategic tools	The authors apply an activity theory framework to study executive engagement with specific strategic tools and methodologies; they identify three models of strategizing activity and associated behaviour (routinized, reflective and imposed practice) dependent upon the executives' interpretation of the operating environment.
Jarzabkowski (2003)	How strategic practices mediate stability and change in strategy-making in the interaction between top managers and their organizations	This is a comparative study of how the strategy practices of direction-setting, resource allocation, and monitoring and control either distribute shared interpretations or mediate between contested interpretations of strategy in ways that have consequences for strategic change or stability.
Jarzabkowski and Balogun (2009)	Strategic planning as mediator between the different interests and power of top and middle managers in different divisions within a multinational organization	This study across multiple divisions and levels of the firm shows how a strategic planning process that is issued by top managers is the source of contradictions and contestation across a multinational; the planning process is modified to better account for and mediate between different interests and power, so showing how mediating tools are 'retooled' as they mediate between subject positions.
Lanzara (2009)	The role of artefact mediation for changes in practice	This is an in-depth case study analysing the introduction of courtroom video recording to study the role of artefact mediation in changes of organizational practice, exploring the disruptive effects caused by new artefacts and the reshaping of practice through engagement with the new medium.

Table 9.1 (*cont.*)

Study	Conceptual focus	Contribution
Miettinen and Virkkunen (2005)	The mediating role of artefacts in changing and creating practices	The authors draw on the concept of epistemic object and activity theory to study occupational health and safety inspectors in their effort to establish a new instrument for planning inspection activities in order to analyse the role of artefacts for changes of human practice (or sets of routines) and how new practices are supported by specific tools and procedures.
Nicolini (2009)	Understanding and theorizing organizational practice	The author develops a theoretical framework to address the multidimensionality of work practices and discuss dimensions of the framework, drawing on an empirical study of telemedicine; understanding practice necessitates a zooming in on practice and zooming out of practice realized by applying multiple theoretical perspectives, including activity theory.
Prenkert (2006)	Sources of transformation of organizational practices and tools to manage change	This article uses a case study of the introduction of an inter-organizational information system to analyse the management of paradoxical organizational practice; it develops activity system analysis as a tool to identify elements of organizational practice and paradoxes, actively managing dialectical change processes resulting from paradoxes in organizations.

profoundly social human activity (see, for example, Miettinen, Samra-Fredericks and Yanow 2009; Miettinen, Paavola and Pohjola 2012). The activity system approach, therefore, is particularly apposite to the study of strategy as practice because it enables a study of strategy practitioners that also pays attention to the strategy practices that they draw upon and the strategy praxis in which they are engaged.

An activity system framework for studying practitioners, practices and praxis

This section presents an activity system model, Figure 9.1, that shows how activity systems concepts can inform the strategy-as-practice research agenda, particularly the interrelated study of strategy practitioners, strategy praxis and strategy practices as the three central pillars of the practice of strategy (for example, Jarzabkowski 2005; Whittington 2006; Vaara and Whittington 2012). Diagrammatic representations of activity systems that model similar concepts but also interpret some different elements may be found in other studies (such as those of Blackler, Crump and McDonald 2000; Engeström 1993; Kaptelinin and Nardi 2006).

The subject is the individual or group of actors who form the focal point for analysis. Any group of actors might be positioned as the subject, depending upon whether their contributions to activity are central to the research. In Figure 9.1, strategy practitioners (A) are conceptualized as the subject: those actors who do strategy and through whose eyes strategy-as-practice researchers wish to understand and interpret strategy. Activity theory does not predispose any particular actor to be a strategy practitioner but, rather, provides a way of analysing activity from the perspective of an actor that has been designated as a strategy practitioner in any particular study. For example, strategy practitioner subjects have variously been identified as strategy development groups (Blackler, Crump and McDonald 1999; 2000), top managers (Jarzabkowski 2003; 2005) and divisional managers (Jarzabkowski and Balogun 2009). The subject nature of the practitioner is important, as it emphasizes the SAP concern to understand strategy work by analysing the way that a particular actor or group of actors does that work. Activity theory avoids the reductionism and marginalization of the social that can arise from an excessive focus on the individual, however (Archer 1982; Dawe 1970; Lockwood 1964). The subject's 'doing' of strategy is

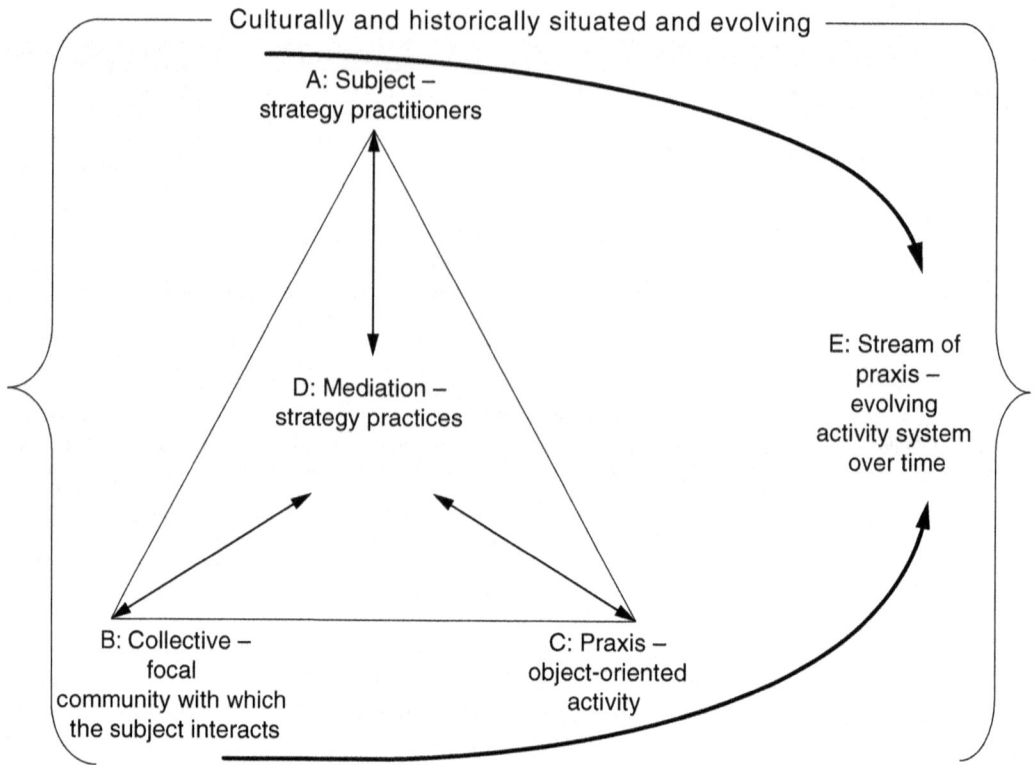

Figure 9.1 An activity framework for studying strategy-as-practice questions

always understood in relation to the collective (B), comprising those other actors with whom they interact in the pursuit of goal-directed activity.

Activity is both goal-oriented, in that it is directed towards a practical outcome (Kozulin 1999), and also shared (Leontiev 1978). Different subjects input their individual actions into the ongoing activity of the system. Subjects (A in Figure 9.1) thus associate with a collective (B) in constructing goal-oriented activity (C). Activity is a long-duration concept: a flow of activity over time (E), as indicated by the curved arrows in Figure 9.1, which imply that the system is not static but is in a constant state of becoming. While activity may be studied at any point in time, it is continuously being constructed in, and also constructing, the interactions between subjects and their community. Hence, activity is best thought of in dynamic terms as a stream or flow of activity. We propose that this concept of continuously

flowing goal-oriented activity is valuable for understanding strategy praxis and how it evolves over time. In particular, activity is a useful level of analysis because it separates the tightly interwoven interactions between actors and their community, directing attention to the strategy praxis that is accomplished in these interactions (see also Blackler 1993; Jarzabkowski 2005).

As illustrated in Figure 9.1, an activity system framework also explains the mediation (D) of interactions between subjects, the collective and their shared activity. Mediation is a distinctive concept in activity theory that explains how individual actors, the community and their shared endeavours are integrated in the pursuit of activity. Mediation occurs through various practices, such as strategy artefacts (e.g. spreadsheets, PowerPoint, whiteboards), strategy processes (e.g. planning and budgeting processes) and strategy language (e.g. competitive advantage, value creation), that enable interaction between actors and their community (Engeström 1993). Such practices are situated, meaning that they reflect both the cultural and historical properties of the wider society in which they are embedded, and also the local interpretations of those practices as artefacts for action. Practices of mediation both lend meaning to and are imbued with meaning by the situation in which they are used. They enable interaction between the participants in the activity system and mediate shifting dynamics of influence in the construction of goal-directed activity. Mediation thus provides a means of understanding how diverse actors' actions are rendered mutually intelligible and collective, to the extent that shared activity can take place (Leontiev 1978; Suchman 1987; Turner 1994).

An activity system is not particular to one type of analytic unit, such as an organization or a group. Rather, it provides a conceptual framework for placing boundaries around the focal subject, collective and activity in any particular set of interactions in order to study their dynamics as a system. Existing studies have identified whole organizations (Blackler 1993; 1995; Jarzabkowski 2003; 2005; Jarzabkowski and Balogun 2009; Spender 1995), strategy development groups (Blackler, Crump and McDonald 2000), virtual learning communities (Walker 2004) and doctor–patient interactions (Engeström 1993) as activity systems. The activity system depicted in Figure 9.1 may thus be used to study strategy-as-practice phenomena and research questions at varying levels (see Jarzabkowski and Spee 2009). Conceptualizing strategy as practice within an activity system enables us to generate an interdependent view, understanding how the actions in one part of the system affect actions in another part, with these interdependencies mediated by the practices. As an integrative conceptual framework, activity theory is insightful because of its theoretical premise that the study of one part of an activity system necessarily incorporates other parts of the activity system. The following sections locate each element of Figure 9.1 within the theoretical resources provided by activity theory and explain how these resources can inform the study of practitioners, practices and praxis.

Strategy practitioners: a subject in interaction with the collective

Strategy as practice is focused primarily upon strategy as something that *people do* (Jarzabkowski 2004). Furthermore, the strategy-as-practice research agenda aims to take existing strategy research beyond its dominant focus on top managers by bringing a wide range of actors to centre stage (see, for example, Ezzamel and Willmott 2008; Jarzabkowski, Balogun and Sedil 2007; Johnson, Melin and Whittington 2003; Johnson *et al.* 2007; Laine and Vaara 2007; Mantere 2005; 2008; Mantere and Vaara 2008; McCabe 2010; Whittington 2006). This has led to broad definitions of who might be considered a strategy practitioner: 'Strategy's practitioners are defined widely, to include both those directly involved in making strategy – most prominently managers and consultants – and those with indirect influence – the policy-makers, the media, the gurus and the business schools who shape legitimate praxis and practices' (Jarzabkowski and Whittington 2008: 101–2). Such broad definitions enable the study of what different types of strategy practitioners do. Studying what people do is not only an empirical question but also an ontological question, based on whether individual doing is conceptualized as a solo, primarily cognitive, activity or as an interactive, primarily social, activity (Turner 1994). Activity theory brings three important features to the study of what people do.

First, activity theory conceptualizes individual doing as engaging in activities with a wider social group (Vygotsky 1978), also known as the collective or the community (Engeström 1993; Leontiev 1978). 'Doing' as an individual in isolation is not possible. Even when individuals act alone, they do so with consideration of the social group, drawing upon the social practices of that group. As illustrated in Figure 9.1, in activity theory the social nature of doing is captured by conceptualizing the individual as the *subject*. It is through this subject's intentions and actions that activity may be understood. Activity is always collective, however, inasmuch as, even in acting alone, an individual relates to the collective and draws upon the tools and symbols of that collective. For example, when strategy practitioners work alone to develop a spreadsheet or think about strategy in the car while driving home, it is impossible to do these actions without drawing upon collective cultural and historical precepts. Through culturally and historically embedded practices – the strategy language of competitive advantage and barriers to entry, strategy concepts such as growth and market value added, and strategy tools such as planning cycles and spreadsheets – practitioners bring into being their solo strategizing actions. These strategizing actions draw upon and contribute to the cultural and historical practices of the wider social group, even if the spreadsheet or strategy thoughts are constructed in isolation.

Conceptualizing the strategy practitioner as a subject interacting within an activity system (see Figure 9.1) provides a social basis for analysing what strategists do within a particular group, division or organization. In other words, it conceptualizes doing as located within a specific context, known as an activity system, in which particular types of doing may be better understood. For example, Jarzabkowski (2005; 2008) found that top managers in three universities were each pursuing four similar streams of strategic activity; research, teaching, commercial income and size and scope. Their ways of doing these similar streams of activity varied in accordance with the different cultural and historical practices of the activity systems that comprised the universities, however. The strategy practitioner is thus always a subject interacting with a wider collective, and this situatedness is important in studying what strategists do.

Second, activity theory incorporates intentionality into the subject (Kaptelinin and Nardi 2006). Although individuals draw upon and contribute to cultural and historical practices, they are not simply pawns of the collective. Rather, they have motives and desires that they impute to their actions. Intention is thus inherent in action, even when such intentions may be latent rather than immediately apparent to the actor. Intent is particularly important for understanding what constitutes a strategist as a competent practitioner, as it goes beyond what strategists do to how they interpret their doings and their aspirations in doing, whether

these are ultimately realized or not. Additionally, intent allows us to examine and compare different actors – consultants, middle managers, top managers, non-executive directors and others – as strategy practitioners with different motives and desires, even when they interact with the same collective in pursuing strategy. For example, Blackler, Crump and McDonald (2000) studied three different strategy development groups within the same high-tech company, comparing their interactions with the organizational activity system about the same strategy. Different subject groups had varied intentions and attributed different motives to their actions, with tensions emerging from the subjects' varying perspectives on the success of their actions and the organization's strategic activity. These differences in subjects' intentions provide a basis for identifying variation in engagement and outcomes for strategy participants, even within the same activity system.

Third, an activity theory perspective on the actor as a social subject provides an ontological basis for studying what strategists do – that is, it goes beyond the empirical cataloguing of their actions into a social analysis of these actions. Studying what strategy practitioners do might well result in a long list of things 'done', such as making a telephone call, writing, typing, talking to an associate, going to a meeting, examining a report, drinking coffee, putting numbers in a spreadsheet, and so forth. The amount of time allocated to each of these actions could also be analysed, deriving a categorization of things that strategy practitioners do and for how long. This list will indeed describe what strategy practitioners do, but it will not be very insightful about doing strategy work or about being a strategist. It will become much more informative if we know who the focal community is that the practitioner telephones, writes to, talks with, meets, examines a report from, develops a spreadsheet for and why these particular actions are important in this context. Furthermore, we may study variations in the intentions attributed to those same actions when the practitioner interacts with a different focal community, such as shareholders, board members, subordinates, consultants or peers. Simply put, it is not enough to know that practitioners prepare spreadsheets as part of what they do but, rather, to know the purpose of the spreadsheet in this activity system, at whom it is directed and what motivations the strategist attributes to his or her actions. When an activity theory lens is applied, analysing what the strategy practitioner does becomes an ontological question about the social nature of doing. Such analysis allows us to understand how what people do constructs them as strategic actors.

Recent advances in strategy process and practice-based studies have emphasized a wider definition of the actors who contribute to strategy-making beyond a top-management-centred view on strategy (for example, Wolf and Floyd forthcoming). As the circle of participants in strategy-making widens beyond top managers (for example, Floyd and Wooldridge 1992; 1997; Mantere and Vaara 2008; Rouleau and Balogun 2011), so strategy-as-practice scholars have explored how the nature of strategy as a profession has changed over time (Whittington, Cailluet and Yakis-Douglas 2011). One key question in this agenda is how (future) managers are trained and educated to fulfil strategic roles, given that, despite its central role in propagating the use of strategy tools (for example, Jarzabkowski *et al.* 2013; Wright, Paroutis and Blettner 2013), management education is often considered to fall short in preparing students to become successful actors in actual strategy praxis (Whittington 2006: 626). The strong tradition of activity theory in educational research provides valuable insights into understanding the education of strategists, and how they use strategy tools and technologies they have learned in accomplishing particular activities (Jarzabkowski and Kaplan 2015). Such uses are innately social and connected to the stream of activity that may be mediated by the use of a particular tool, such as Porter's five forces or a SWOT analysis. For example, Spee and Jarzabkowski (2009: 224) highlight that 'tools are not necessarily applied instrumentally, and that their use is shaped both by social and political dynamics between actors and by a strategy tool's design properties'.

The education of (future) managers with strategic responsibilities, therefore, involves enabling these managers to experience strategy 'tools-in-use' rather than assuming that textbook uses apply to strategy practice (Jarzabkowski and Kaplan

2015). The central role of tool mediation in activity theory enables us to focus on how games or play can be integrated into strategy-teaching and how the use of such tools can enhance experience-based learning (for example, Engeström, Miettinen and Punamäki 1999). In the educational field, for example, scholars have demonstrated how games, such as board games, and other forms of play can enhance learning processes (Holzman 2009: chap. 3, 45–66; Luk 2013; Smith 2006). Games themselves can be analysed as activity systems 'in which the general and shared object of the actors is the state of the game, which they attempt to control with the help of certain tools and within certain rules, in order to win the game' (Engeström 2000: 302–3). Based on this research tradition, practice-based studies on the training and education of strategists could draw on activity theory to explore how games and play (Jacobs and Heracleous 2007) can enhance learning and advance understanding about the role of creativity-enhancing tools and their contribution to creativity in strategic planning processes (for example, Wolf and Floyd forthcoming).

Strategy practices as mediators

The strategy-as-practice research agenda is also concerned with the practices of strategy-making (for example, Jarzabkowski 2003; 2004; Jarzabkowski, Balogun and Seidl 2007; Whittington 2003; 2006). There is little consistency, however, in the definitions of the practices that have been employed by scholars within the strategy-as-practice field (Jarzabkowski and Spee 2009). This is perhaps not surprising, given the various philosophical and theoretical underpinnings of practices (Schatzki, Knorr Cetina and von Savigny 2001). Activity theory provides some valuable concepts for analysing strategy practices. In particular, as illustrated in Figure 9.1, activity theory may be used to conceptualize strategy practices as mediators within an activity system. They mediate between any given subject group, their focal community and the strategic activity in which the community is engaged. Mediation is an aspect of activity theory that increasingly has been drawn upon to look at problems of coordination and shared activity in organizations and in strategy processes (for example, Adler 2005; Blackler 1993; 1995; Blackler, Crump and McDonald 2000; Foot 2002; Jarzabkowski 2003; 2005; Jarzabkowski and Balogun 2009; Miettinen and Virkkunen 2005; Spender 1995). In these studies, the organization, or one of its parts, is conceptualized as an activity system in which common activity is accomplished through mediation. This section explains the principles of mediation and how it may be drawn upon to conceptualize the role of strategy practices in doing strategy.

Human actions and interactions are mediated: 'Activity theory casts the relationship between people and tools as one of mediation; tools mediate between people and the world' (Kaptelinin and Nardi 2006: 10). Mediating tools or mechanisms can take social, physical and cognitive forms, such as operating procedures, heuristics, scripts, routines and languages (Omicini and Ossowski 2004). Mediation suggests that, despite their potentially different perspectives and interests, actors are able to integrate their actions in the pursuit of shared activity (Engeström 1993; Kozulin 1999). Activity theory does not conceptualize these mechanisms as primarily the instruments of any particular constituent, however, such as senior managers. Rather, different constituents may appropriate the same mechanisms in order to mediate between their varied purposes and interests (Rabardel and Beguin 2005). Furthermore, mediators are not neutral but have historical and cultural baggage that can both constrain and enable action and interaction. Mediating mechanisms thus incorporate longer-duration aspects of interaction between actors, so that mediation is not simply part of the moment but is also part of the wider collective activity. We now explain how the concept of mediation supports the analysis of three aspects of strategy practices: their role in socially accomplishing strategic activity; how practices are themselves altered as part of the evolving activity of the activity system; and how they mediate between different subjects within an activity system.

Mediation is a valuable concept for examining how particular practices that coordinate strategic activity, such as planning procedures and resource allocation mechanisms, shape the evolving strategic activity of an organization (Blackler 1993; 1995; Blackler, Crump and McDonald 2000; Jarzabkowski 2005; Jarzabkowski and Balogun 2009; Miettinen and Virkkunen 2005). Classical strategy process studies, such as those of Burgelman (1983; 1996), have shown that senior managers may establish such mechanisms in order to guide and control the actions of others in the organization towards specific strategies. Far from these mechanisms being the property of senior managers, however, or, indeed, having an inherent meaning that exists outside any particular group of actors, different actors may appropriate them to shape strategy according to their own intentions (Jarzabkowski 2005). Indeed, Burgelman found that Intel's shift from being a memory chip company in a failing market to a leading microprocessor company was attributable to the way that middle managers appropriated the resource allocation rule of 'Maximize margin per wafer' to reallocate manufacturing line capacity. This use of the resource allocation mechanism shifted the company strategy towards microprocessors, even as senior managers continued to invest in memory chips as the core Intel strategy. While the resource allocation rule remained constant over time because of the cultural and historical premises of it as a strategic control mechanism at Intel, the meanings attributed to it, and the actions taken by different players as they drew upon it, changed the activity of the organization. Hence, as Jarzabkowski (2005) suggests, strategy practices, such as resource allocation models, do not simply coordinate and control strategic activity but, rather, mediate between different actors in accomplishing an evolving stream of strategic activity over time.

In accommodating different actors, the mediating mechanism may itself come to adopt new cultural and historical meanings: 'Tools evolve during the development of an activity, and they carry the cultural and social knowledge and experiences of the people who invented and modified them in order to solve certain problems' (Malopinsky 2008: 60). While strategy practices are culturally and historically located, such that their origins are institutionalized (Whittington 2006), the activity-theoretic premise is that they are also continually evolving as they are drawn upon and modified to accommodate different actors' positions. For example, Jarzabkowski and Balogun (2009) show how strategic planning templates and associated brand campaigns in a multinational, Brandco, evolved from a uniform campaign designed by top managers to a more flexible campaign that could accommodate the different interests and strategic activities of operating companies in markets both small and large. These modifications to the planning procedure arose from efforts by actors in different operating companies to socially accomplish the planning procedure within the situated demands of their own market places. While strategic planning has a 'general' or cross-contextual character when it is introduced, these institutionalized properties come into tension with the locally situated actions of different subjects (Miettinen and Virkkunen 2005). Thus, different subjects, from their local perspectives, continuously interact with the planning mechanism, fashioning it to their ends, even as they are fashioned by it: 'Accordingly, the activity-theoretical approach regards retooling, the shared creation of artefacts used as means of reflecting and practical transformation of activity, as a key to changing practices' (Miettinen and Virkkunen 2005: 443). Jarzabkowski and Balogun (2009) draw on activity theory to explain how and why strategic planning retained a generalized set of steps that characterized it as a planning mechanism even as it was being modified to account for managers in large and small markets as different subjects.

Discourse, which is often integral to such planning processes and tools, is classified as another important mediator of activity (Engeström and Sannino 2011; Holman 2000; Wells 2002; 2007) that is highly resonant with the strategy-as-practice research agenda (for an overview, see Balogun et al. 2014). Discursive studies on strategy enhance our understanding of how strategy practitioners interpret and, indeed, use the concept of strategy (Paroutis and Heracleous 2013), shed light on managers' participation in strategy-making (Mantere and Vaara 2008) and explain how actors engage with specific practices such as strategic planning and related outcomes (for example, Abdallah and Langley 2014; Vaara, Sorsa and Pälli

2010). In particular, recent works emphasize the role of discourse in mediating other critical elements of strategic activity associated with sensemaking, power and sociomateriality (for example, Balogun, Jarzabkowski and Vaara 2011; Balogun et al. 2014; Ezzamel and Willmott 2008; Laine and Vaara 2007; McCabe 2010; Vaara, Sorsa and Pälli. 2010). Positioning discourse, with its deep social, historical and cultural roots, at the centre of strategic activity enables us to scale our level of analysis up or down, from the micro-episodes of specific strategy workshops and meetings (for example, Jarzabkowski and Seidl 2008) to the institutional realm (for example, Suddaby, Seidl and Lê 2013).

Discourse is often at the heart of 'manifestations of contradictions' within activity systems (Engeström and Sannino 2011: 369), so helping to bring to the foreground the power dynamics involved in mediation that have commonly been underplayed in activity theory (Blackler, Crump and McDonald 2000). These authors suggest that scholars examine power as an ongoing product and medium of the retooling process, as new ways of relating and new activities emerge around the reactions to and modifications of the mediating mechanism. For example, Balogun, Jarzabkowski and Vaara's (2011) study illustrates how the evolution of a planning procedure in a multinational also facilitated evolving relationships between the key subjects involved in planning. Actors in the different operating companies evolved from being disengaged with or resistant to a common multinational strategy to being interdependent subjects comprising strategy formulators (top managers), strategy implementers (actors in small markets) and strategy translators (actors in large markets). These evolving relationships were mediated through discursive struggles over the retooling of the planning procedure, with the different subject groups gaining new voices as they began to understand their own activity in relation to others and to the common strategic activity of Brandco. Much organizational research that draws on activity theory has examined the process of mediation but has paid less attention to its implications for how and why subjects come to accommodate each other in pursuing common activity. The evolution and modification of mediating practices to account for the intentions of different subjects (Malopinsky 2008; Miettinen and Virkkunen 2005) is also associated with the evolution and modification of social relationships and power dynamics between these subjects; the practices mediate between subjects within an activity system, even as they mediate the activity in which the system engages.

Focusing on those strategy practices that mediate between different actors as subjects within an activity system offers potential insights into inclusive strategizing. Past research has emphasized the positive performance effects of including middle managers in strategy processes (for example, Floyd and Wooldridge 1992; 1997; Ketokivi and Castañer 2004). The inclusion of middle managers in strategy-making is dependent on how well organizational contexts support or impede middle management participation, however (Rouleau and Balogun 2011). Mantere (2008: 304), for example, identifies eight enablers that encourage middle managers in pursuing their strategic roles, including enablers such as top managers responding to feedback ('responsiveness'), reacting to new ideas and supporting them ('refereeing') and inviting middle managers' participation in formal strategy processes ('inclusion'). An activity theory perspective can help identify and elaborate upon those mediating tools that support such enablers and facilitate communication between top and lower level management in strategy-making. For example, information systems research provides insight into how technological communication tools and social software enhance inclusiveness in decision-making (Haefliger et al. 2011; Hasan and Pfaff 2012; Stieger et al. 2012; Whittington 2014). Such research explains how technological tools can be designed to facilitate participation and interaction among multiple strategic actors.

Activity theory is particularly pertinent for furthering the study of technologically mediated strategizing. Activity theory has been drawn on in the field of human and computer interaction in two ways. First, activity theory underpins much of the literature on the situated interactions between technology and people, exploring human–computer interaction (for example, Kaptelinin and Nardi 2006; Nardi 1996a). Second, the way that computing systems enable collaborative working across distributed actors – that is, people who may not be co-located or who may be working in parallel – has been analysed using activity theory concepts of cognition as social activity that is distributed across multiple actors in interaction. Thus, activity theory has been used to aid the design of technologies to better account for the human operator's activity, as well as to understand how distributed technological systems work in human situations (Frawley 1997). For example, activity theory has shed light on the subjective experiences of actors using a technology, how that technology mediates their interaction with others who may be distributed across time and space (such as virtual communities or parallel processing) and how it enables or constrains their collective activity (Omicini and Ossowski 2004; Walker 2004). These aspects of activity theory have also informed a vein of work on distributed cognition (for example, Hutchins 1995; Nardi 1996b) that has, in its turn, informed practice-based studies of coordination and collaboration in organizations (for example, Nardi 2005; Orlikowski 2002) that can also be insightful for studies of how technology mediates strategy-making.

Technologically enabled strategizing need not stop with the inclusion of middle and lower-level management but could potentially reach beyond organizational borders. For example, despite discussions on open innovation, the strategic role of external stakeholders remains understudied (Chesbrough and Appleyard 2007; Whittington, Cailluet and Yakis-Douglas 2011). Equally, inter-organizational collaboration in strategy-making generates increasing interest in SAP research. Studying the interaction between multiple activity systems (Engeström 2001) could further enhance our understanding of intra-organizational communication (for example, Blackler, Crump and McDonald 1999; 2000; Stieger et al. 2012) or the inclusion of outside parties, including customers or suppliers in strategy-making (for example, Chesbrough and Appleyard 2007; Haefliger et al. 2011). Furthermore, with a growing interest in understanding how technology can facilitate the inclusion of (external) stakeholders (for example, Haefliger *et al.* 2011), activity theory provides a framework for systematically analysing the role of technology in these mediation processes (for example, Allen, Karanasios and Slavova 2011; Allen *et al.* 2013), such as how specific technologies such as wikis can enhance wider participation and inclusion of knowledge workers in organizational transformations (Hasan and Pfaff 2012).

This section has explained the concept of mediation as it relates to strategy practices and the way that they shape the evolving strategic activity of an activity system; the relationships between subjects in an activity system; and how activity itself shapes the strategy practices. A few studies in the strategy and organization field (see Table 9.1) have used activity theory to look at mechanisms that coordinate strategic activity, such as planning procedures and administrative systems (for example, Blackler 1993; 1995; Jarzabkowski 2003; 2005; Jarzabkowski and Balogun 2009). Activity theory provides a richer repertoire of possibilities for identifying strategy practices, however, which may take social, physical and cognitive forms (Kozulin 1999; Vygotsky 1978), such as operating procedures, heuristics, scripts, routines and languages (Omicini and Ossowski 2004). Future research that draws upon activity theory could undertake more detailed examinations of how various strategy practices, such as meetings, spreadsheets, decision rules, particular forms of speech and types of technology, mediate the interactions between actors in an activity system, and how this mediation socially accomplishes an evolving stream of strategic activity.

Strategy praxis: object and collective activity

Praxis refers to the stream of activity in which strategy is accomplished over time, which might be explored at different levels depending upon the specific research focus. For example, praxis might be studied at the institutional level as a particular type of widely diffused activity, such as merger and acquisition behaviour within an industry, or at the micro-level of a particular individual or group of individuals engaged in decision-making activity

about a merger or acquisition. Various theoretical and research agenda papers in strategy as practice have conceptualized praxis at three different levels: micro, meso and macro (for example, Jarzabkowski 2004; Jarzabkowski, Balogun and Seidl 2007; Jarzabkowski and Spee 2009; Johnson *et al.* 2007; Whittington 2006). Activity theory lends itself well to the study of praxis at different levels through the concepts of goal-directed and collective activity.

Activity theory focuses upon practical or goal-directed activity. Practical activity provides a focus for interaction; people interact in order to do something (Kozulin 1999; Leontiev 1978), meaning that their activity is oriented towards an outcome or object. The object is a distinctive concept in activity theory. It refers to the higher-order motive or desire to which practical activity is directed (Kaptelinin and Nardi 2006; Engeström and Blackler 2005). It is a more comprehensive concept than an objective, which implies a shorter-term, attainable accomplishment that motivates a specific task. Object is a more visionary concept, which might be thought of as a broad goal orientation that motivates a stream of practical activity comprising many smaller actions. For example, a university may have a strategic object of being an elite research institution at which its various actors direct their activity. That activity is made up of a complex of actions, such as writing papers, submitting grant applications, supervising doctoral students, conducting experiments, running conferences, and so forth. Each of these actions has an objective that is important to the goal but is not the goal and, at times, may bear little apparent relationship to the goal. For example, attending a colleague's research seminar or reading a doctoral student's chapter are actions with immediate objectives that are no longer directly related to the goal. Rather, these actions are part of a complex of actions undertaken within the activity system as part of the goal-oriented activity that is directed at the object of becoming an elite research institution.

Such activity is collective (Leontiev 1978). It is accomplished through the input of multiple actors, each of whom may conceptualize the object somewhat differently. A stream of activity is invested with meaning and purpose through the historically and culturally situated understandings of the different actors who contribute to that activity over time (Jarzabkowski 2005; Spender 1995). In the above example, different subjects' perspectives on and interests in the same object of securing elite research institution status may be similar but not the same. Academics may want international recognition from their peers, and their subjective interests can be facilitated by the object of an elite research institution, as opportunities to do top research and attain recognition are enabled by the institutional context. Vice-chancellors or rectors want to run institutions that have access to the best financial and human resources, which is enabled by the object of an elite research institution. Students want to be taught by leading academics and attain degrees that have high status in the labour market, which is enabled by the object of an elite research institution. While all subjects share the same broad object, an elite research institution, the goal-oriented activity of each and their cultural and historical expectations about the object may be quite different, and even in contradiction with each other (Jarzabkowski 2005; Sillince, Jarzabkowski and Shaw 2012). For example, academics may want to publish more papers, while vice-chancellors may want more large research grants, and students may want more teaching time with top professors. All these motives that can be attributed to the object are part of its collective pursuit, so that the object itself is not stable. Rather, the goal-directedness of activity is continuously being accomplished through the interactions and contests between actors. This is a key feature of activity system analysis: examining how a collective output is accomplished through interactions and contests between actors, which modify the orientation both of the activity and of the actors engaged in it (Engeström and Blackler 2005; Foot 2002).

Collective activity is thus purposive or object-oriented activity accomplished through a complex of actions over time. Object-oriented activity is of long duration, being historically and culturally situated, although it is not immutable and evolves over time as the complex of actions are reproduced and reconstructed according to the motives and desires of different parties. As Engeström and Blackler (2005: 310) note, '[O]bjects are constructed by actors as they make sense, name, stabilize, represent and enact foci for their actions and activities. [Nonetheless, it would] be a mistake to assume that objects are constructed arbitrarily on the spot; objects have histories and built-in affordances, they resist and "bite back".' These concepts are valuable for understanding strategy praxis at different levels. For example, it is possible to study the strategic object of an organization and analyse how different strategy groups reconstruct that organizational object, even as they interpret and contribute to it (for example, Blackler, Crump and McDonald 2000), or how one group of actors, such as top managers, respond to the evolving organizational object in their own construction of it (for example, Jarzabkowski 2005; Jarzabkowski and Balogun 2009). If an organization is to achieve some collective strategic activity, this will consist partly of given intentions and partly of emergent features of each subject's own activities, motives and intents.

Furthermore, activity theory may be used to examine contradictions between objects. While most strategy literature deals with strategy as a single construct, examining how organizations pursue or fail to pursue a single strategy, organizations are complex and hence likely to be pursuing multiple objects simultaneously, some of which may be in contradiction (Denis, Langley and Rouleau 2007), such as the object of resource efficiency alongside patient care in hospitals (Denis, Lamothe and Langley 2001) or of exploiting existing assets alongside exploring new opportunities that may cannibalize these assets (Smith 2014). In activity theory, this complexity arises from the multiple cultural and historical layers in which the organization is embedded, which give rise to contradictions between objects (Engeström 1987; 1990). For example, Blackler and Regan (2009) show how changes in the institutional environment arising from a shift in public policy create contradictions within the strategic object during the reorganization of family and child support services. Hence, the activity system is always embedded in multiple and contradictory cultural and historical events that both shape and are shaped by what occurs within the system. There have been few studies of contradictions between different objects within an activity system, however, or conflicts within any specific object as it undergoes change. Activity theory offers an opportunity for more complex analysis of the conflicts between strategies in organizations. In particular, it provides a theoretical lens for studying strategizing within pluralistic contexts that are beset by complex and contradictory goals, which has become an increasingly relevant area for strategy-as-practice research (for example, Denis, Langley and Rouleau 2007; Jarzabkowski and Fenton 2006; Jarzabkowski, Lê and Van de Ven 2013).

Although these concepts of object and collective activity have been used in strategy-as-practice research only to look at organization-level strategy praxis, other studies have examined micro-phenomena, such as the object of a doctor–patient interaction (Engeström 1993). Future SAP studies might also adopt these concepts to examine the strategy praxis of more micro-activity systems, such as a particular strategy workshop or meeting. The activity system framework (Figure 9.1) would also be valuable to study strategy praxis at the industry level. For example, strategic alliances could be conceptualized as an object comprising a complex interplay of competitive and collaborative interactions by different state, regulatory and organizational actors, each of whom have different objects in achieving alliance as an industry standard (for example, de Rond and Bouchiki 2004; Vaara, Kleymann and Seristö 2004). Importantly, the framework provided in this chapter enables a focus upon strategy as a stream of praxis accomplished over time through the interactions between participants in an activity system. Strategy evolves over time as it is contested and differently interpreted by participants, rather than being a single event or objective to be measured for its returns to one party or at one point in time.

Conclusion

This chapter has presented an activity theory approach to the study of strategy as practice. In doing so, it has developed an activity theory framework for analysis and explained how specific activity theory

concepts can illuminate existing questions and topics for strategy-as-practice research.

In summary, the application of an activity theory lens can further enhance the study of strategy practices, the actors involved in strategy and the praxis of strategy in at least three ways. First, it does so by providing a framework to study individual strategy actors, in order to answer questions such as how practitioners learn to be strategy actors; how strategy practitioners are socialized into a strategy-making community of practice; and how material, technological or discursive practices can mediate participation in strategy-making, among others. Second, by offering a perspective on collective strategizing and the interaction of strategy practitioners in different human activity systems inside and outside the organization, activity theory enables us to elaborate on questions such as how people work skilfully together; how their interactions are aligned through different mediating practices, such as tools, technologies and discourses; and how we can better understand the nature of agency and intent as it is distributed across an activity system in strategy-making (Blackler and Regan 2009; Schatzki 2002). Finally, an activity theory framework allows us to focus on the stream of activity within which strategy praxis is constructed and unfolds over time. While we have long focused on understanding how strategy emerges as a pattern in a stream of actions (for example, Mintzberg and Waters 1985), the exploration of strategy emergence remains an evergreen issue, indicating our need for methodologies that place activity at the heart of analysis.

References

Abdallah, C., and Langley, A. (2014), 'The double edge of ambiguity in strategic planning', *Journal of Management Studies*, 51/2: 235–64.

Adler, P. (2005), 'The evolving object of software development', *Organization*, 12/3: 401–35.

Allen, D., Brown, A., Karanasios, S., and Norman, A. (2013), 'How should technology-mediated organizational change be explained? A comparison of the contributions of critical realism and activity theory', *MIS Quarterly*, 37/3: 835–54.

Allen, D., Karanasios, S., and Slavova, M. (2011), 'Working with activity theory: context, technology, and information behavior', *Journal of the American Society for Information Science and Technology*, 62/4: 776–88.

Archer, M. S. (1982), 'Morphogenesis versus structuration: on combining structure and action', *British Journal of Sociology*, 33/4: 455–83.

Balogun, J., Jacobs, C. D., Jarzabkowski, P., Mantere, S., and Vaara, E. (2014), 'Placing strategy discourse in context: sociomateriality, sensemaking, and power', *Journal of Management Studies*, 51/2: 175–201.

Balogun, J., Jarzabkowski, P., and Vaara, E. (2011), 'Selling, resistance and reconciliation: a critical discursive approach to subsidiary role evolution in MNEs', *Journal of International Business*, 42/6: 765–86.

Blackler, F. (1993), 'Knowledge and the theory of organizations: organizations as activity systems and the reframing of management', *Journal of Management Studies*, 30/6: 863–84.

— (1995), 'Knowledge, knowledge work and organizations: an overview and interpretation', *Organization Studies*, 16/6: 1021–46.

Blackler, F., Crump, N., and McDonald, S. (1999), 'Managing experts and competing through innovation: an activity theoretical analysis', *Organization*, 6/1: 5–31.

— (2000), 'Organizing processes in complex activity networks', *Organization*, 7/2: 277–300.

Blackler, F., and Regan, S. (2009), 'Intentionality, agency, change: practice theory and management', *Management Learning*, 40/2: 161–76.

Brown, J. S., and Duguid, P. (1991), 'Organizational learning and communities-of-practice: toward a unified view of working, learning, and innovation', *Organization Science*, 2/1: 40–57.

Burgelman, R. A. (1983), 'Corporate entrepreneurship and strategic management: insights from a process study', *Management Science*, 29/12: 1349–64.

— (1996), 'A process model of strategic business exit: implications for an evolutionary perspective on strategy', *Strategic Management Journal*, 17/S1: 193–214.

Chesbrough, H. W., and Appleyard, M. M. (2007), 'Open innovation and strategy', *California Management Review*, 50/1: 57–76.

Dawe, E. (1970), 'The two sociologies', *British Journal of Sociology*, 21/2: 207–18.

Denis, J. L., Lamothe, L., and Langley, A. (2001), 'The dynamics of collective leadership and strategic change in pluralistic organizations',

Academy of Management Journal, 44/4: 809–37.

Denis, J.-L., Langley, A., and Rouleau, L. (2007), 'Strategizing in pluralistic contexts: rethinking theoretical frames', *Human Relations*, 60/1: 179–215.

De Rond, M., and Bouchiki, H. (2004), 'On the dialectics of strategic alliances', *Organization Science*, 15/1: 56–69.

Engeström, Y. (1987), *Learning by Expanding: An Activity-Theoretical Approach to Developmental Research*. Helsinki: Orienta-Konsultit.

— (1990), *Learning, Working and Imagining: Twelve Studies in Activity Theory*. Helsinki: Orienta-Konsultit.

— (1993), 'Developmental studies of work as a testbench of activity theory: the case of primary care medical practice', in Chaiklin, S., and Lave, J. (eds.), *Understanding Practice: Perspectives on Activity and Context*: 64–103. Cambridge University Press.

— (1996), 'Developmental work research as educational research', *Nordisk Pedagogik: Journal of Nordic Educational Research*, 16/5: 131–43.

— (2000), 'Activity theory and the social construction of knowledge: a story of four umpires', *Organization*, 7/2: 301–10.

— (2001), 'Expansive learning at work: toward an activity theoretical reconceptualization', *Journal of Education and Work*, 14/1: 133–56.

Engeström, Y., and Blackler, F. (2005), 'On the life of the object', *Organization*, 12/3: 307–30.

Engeström, Y., Kerosuo, H., and Kajamaa, A. (2007), 'Beyond discontinuity: expansive organizational learning remembered', *Management Learning*, 38/3: 319–36.

Engeström, Y., Miettinen, M., and Punamäki, R.-L. (eds.) (1999), *Perspectives on Activity Theory*. Cambridge University Press.

Engeström, Y., and Sannino, A. (2011), 'Discursive manifestations of contradictions in organizational change efforts: a methodological framework', *Journal of Organizational Change Management*, 24/3: 368–87.

Ezzamel, M., and Willmott, H. (2008), 'Strategy as discourse in a global retailer: a supplement to rationalist and interpretive accounts', *Organization Studies*, 29/2: 191–217.

Floyd, S. W., and Wooldridge, B. (1992), 'Middle management involvement in strategy and its association with strategic type: a research note', *Strategic Management Journal*, 13/S1: 153–67.

(1997), 'Middle management's strategic influence and organizational performance', *Journal of Management Studies*, 34/3: 465–85.

Foot, K. A. (2002), 'Pursuing an evolving object: a case study in object formation and identification', *Mind, Culture, and Activity*, 9/2: 56–83.

Frawley, W. (1997), *Vygotsky and Cognitive Science: Language and the Unification of the Social and Computational Mind*. Cambridge, MA: Harvard University Press.

Gherardi, S., and Nicolini, D. (2001) 'The sociological foundation of organizational learning', in Dierkes, M., Berthoin Antal, A., Child, J., and Nonaka, I. (eds.), *Handbook of Organizational Learning and Knowledge*: 35–60. Oxford University Press.

Groleau, C. (2006), 'One phenomenon, two lenses: understanding collective action from the perspective of coorientation and activity theories', in Cooren, F., Taylor, J. R., and Van Every, E. J. (eds.), *Communication as Organizing*: 157–180. Mahwah, NJ: Lawrence Erlbaum.

Haefliger, S., Monteiro, E., Foray, D., and von Krogh, G. (2011), 'Social software and strategy', *Long Range Planning*, 44/5: 297–316.

Hasan, H., and Pfaff, C. (2012), 'An activity-theory analysis of corporate wikis', *Information Technology and People*, 25/4: 423–37.

Holman, D. (2000), 'A dialogical approach to skill and skilled activity', *Human Relations*, 53/7: 957–80.

Holt, R. (2008), 'Using activity theory to understand entrepreneurial opportunity', *Mind, Culture, and Activity*, 15/1: 52–70.

Holzman, L. (2009), *Vygotsky at Work and Play*. New York: Routledge.

Hutchins, E. (1995), *Cognition in the Wild*. Cambridge, MA: MIT Press.

Ilyenkov, E. V. (1977), *Dialectical Logic: Essays on Its History and Theory*. Moscow: Progress.

(1982), *The Dialectics of the Abstract and the Concrete in Marx's Capital*. Moscow: Progress.

Jacobs, C. D., and Heracleous, L. (2007), 'Strategizing through playful design', *Journal of Business Strategy*, 28/4: 75–80.

Jarratt, D., and Stiles, D. (2010), 'How are methodologies and tools framing managers' strategizing practice in competitive strategy development?', *British Journal of Management*, 21/1: 28–43.

Jarzabkwoski, P. (2003) 'Strategic practices: an activity theory perspective on continuity and change', *Journal of Management Studies*, 40/1: 23–55.

(2004), 'Strategy-as-practice: recursiveness, adaptation and practices-in-use', *Organization Studies*, 25/4: 529–60.

(2005), *Strategy as Practice: An Activity-Based View*. London: Sage.

(2008), 'Shaping strategy as a structuration process', *Academy of Management Journal*, 51/4: 621–50.

Jarzabkowski, P., and Balogun, J. (2009), 'The practice and process of delivering integration through strategic planning', *Journal of Management Studies*, 46/8: 1255–88.

Jarzabkowski, P., Balogun, J., and Seidl, D. (2007), 'Strategizing: the challenges of a practice perspective', *Human Relations*, 60/1: 5–27.

Jarzabkowski, P., and Fenton, E. (2006), 'Strategizing and organizing in pluralistic contexts', *Long Range Planning*, 39/6: 631–48.

Jarzabkowski, P., Giulietti, M., Oliveira, B., and Amoo, N. (2013), '"We don't need no education" – or do we? Management education and alumni adoption of strategy tools', *Journal of Management Inquiry*, 22/1: 452–72.

Jarzabkowski, P., and Kaplan, S. (2015), 'Strategy tools-in-use: a framework for understanding "technologies of rationality" in practice', *Strategic Management Journal*, 36/4: 537–58.

Jarzabkowski, P., Lê, J., and Van de Ven, A. H. (2013), 'Responding to competing strategic demands: how organizing, belonging and performing paradoxes co-evolve', *Strategic Organization*, 11/3: 245–80.

Jarzabkowski, P., and Seidl, D. (2008), 'The role of meetings in the social practice of strategy', *Organization Studies*, 29/11: 1391–426.

Jarzabkowski, P., and Spee, P. (2009), 'Strategy-as-practice: a review and future directions for the field', *International Journal of Management Reviews*, 11/1: 69–95.

Jarzabkowski, P., and Whittington, R. (2008), 'Hard to disagree, mostly', *Strategic Organization*, 6/1: 101–6.

Johnson, G., Langley, A., Melin, L., and Whittington, R. (2007), *Strategy as Practice: Research Directions and Resources*. Cambridge University Press.

Johnson, G., Melin, L., and Whittington, R. (2003), 'Guest editors' introduction: micro strategy and strategizing: towards an activity-based view', *Journal of Management Studies*, 40/1: 3–22.

Kaptelinin, V., and Nardi, B. (2006), *Acting with Technology: Activity Theory and Interaction Design*. Cambridge, MA: MIT Press.

Kerosuo, H. (2011), 'Caught between a rock and a hard place: from individually experienced double binds to collaborative change in surgery', *Journal of Change Management*, 24/3: 388–99.

Ketokivi, M., and Castañer, X. (2004), 'Strategic planning as an integrative device', *Administrative Science Quarterly*, 49/3: 337–65.

Kozulin, A. (1999), *Vygotsky's Psychology: A Biography of Ideas*. Cambridge, MA: Harvard University Press.

Laine, P.-M., and Vaara, E. (2007), 'Struggling over subjectivity: a discursive analysis of strategic development in an engineering group', *Human Relations*, 60/1: 29–58.

Lanzara, G. F. (2009), 'Reshaping practice across media: material mediation, medium specificity and practical knowledge in judicial work', *Organization*, 30/12: 1369–90.

Lave, J., and Wenger, E. (1991), *Situated Learning: Legitimate Peripheral Participation*. Cambridge University Press.

Leontiev, A. N. (1978), *Activity, Consciousness and Personality*. Englewood Cliffs, NJ: Prentice Hall.

Lockwood, D. (1964), 'Social integration and system integration', in Zollschan, G. K., and Hirsch, H. W. (eds.), *Explorations in Social Change*: 244–57. Boston: Houghton Mifflin.

Luk, J. C. M. (2013), 'Forms of participation and semiotic mediation in board games for second language learning', *Pedagogies: An International Journal*, 8/4: 352–68.

Malopinsky, L. (2008), 'Facilitating organizational change: the use of activity theory as a framework for social construction of strategy knowledge', unpublished PhD thesis. Indianapolis: Indiana University.

Mantere, S. (2005), 'Strategic practices as enablers and disablers of championing activity', *Strategic Organization*, 3/2: 157–84.

(2008), 'Role expectations and middle manager strategic agency', *Journal of Management Studies*, 45/2: 294–316.

Mantere, S., and Vaara, E. (2008), 'On the problem of participation in strategy: a critical discursive perspective', *Organization Science*, 19/2: 341–58.

McCabe, D. (2010), 'Strategy-as-power: ambiguity, contradiction and the exercise of power in a UK building society', *Organization*, 17/2: 151–75.

Miettinen, R., Paavola, S., and Pohjola, S. (2012), 'From habituality to change: contribution of activity theory and pragmatism to practice theories', *Journal for the Theory of Social Behaviour*, 42/3: 345–60.

Miettinen, R., Samra-Fredericks, D., and Yanow, D. (2009), 'Re-turn to practice: an introductory essay', *Organization Studies*, 30/12: 1309–27.

Miettinen, R., and Virkkunen, J. (2005), 'Epistemic objects, artifacts and organizational change', *Organization*, 12/3: 437–56.

Mintzberg, H., and Waters, J. A. (1985), 'Of strategies, deliberate and emergent', *Strategic Management Journal*, 6/3: 257–72.

Nardi, B. A. (ed.) (1996a), *Context and Consciousness: Activity Theory and Human–Computer Interaction*. Cambridge, MA: MIT Press.

Nardi, B. A. (1996b), 'Studying context: a comparison of activity theory, situated action models, and distributed cognition', in *Context and Consciousness: Activity Theory and Human–Computer Interaction*: 69–102. Cambridge, MA: MIT Press.

(2005), 'Objects of desire: power and passion in collaborative activity', *Mind, Culture, and Activity*, 12/1: 37–51.

Nicolini, D. (2009), 'Zooming in and out: studying practices by switching theoretical lenses and trailing connections', *Organization*, 30/12: 1391–418.

Nicolini, D., Gherardi, S., and Yanow, D. (eds.) (2003), *Knowing in Organizations: A Practice-Based Approach*. Armonk, NY: M. E. Sharpe.

Omicini, A., and Ossowski, S. (2004), 'Coordination and collaboration activities in cooperative information systems', *International Journal of Cooperative Information Systems*, 13/1: 1–7.

Orlikowski, W. J. (2002), 'Knowing in practice: enacting a collective capability in distributed organizing', *Organization Science*, 13/3: 249–73.

Paroutis, S., and Heracleous, L. (2013), 'Discourse revisited: dimensions and employment of first-order strategy discourse during institutional adoption', *Strategic Management Journal*, 34/8: 935–56.

Prenkert, F. (2006), 'A theory of organizing informed by activity theory: the locus of paradox, sources of change, and challenge to management', *Journal of Organizational Change Management*, 19/4: 471–90.

Rabardel, P., and Beguin, P. (2005), 'Instrument mediated activity: from subject development to anthropocentric design', *Theoretical Issues in Ergonomics Science*, 6/5: 429–61.

Rouleau, L., and Balogun, J. (2011), 'Middle managers, strategic sensemaking, and discursive competence', *Journal of Management Studies*, 48/5: 953–83.

Schatzki, T. R. (2002), *The Site of the Social: A Philosophical Account of the Constitution of Social Life and Change*. University Park: Pennsylvania State University Press.

Schatzki, T. R., Knorr Cetina, K., and von Savigny, E. (eds.) (2001), *The Practice Turn in Contemporary Theory*. London: Routledge.

Sillince, J., Jarzabkowski, P., and Shaw, D. (2012), 'Shaping strategic action through the rhetorical construction and exploitation of ambiguity', *Organization Science*, 23/3: 630–50.

Smith, H. (2006), 'Playing to learn: a qualitative analysis of bilingual pupil–pupil talk during board game play', *Language and Education*, 20/5: 415–37.

Smith, W. K. (2014), 'Dynamic decision making: a model of senior leaders managing strategic paradoxes', *Academy of Management Journal*, 57/6: 1592–623.

Spee, P., and Jarzabkowski, P. (2009), 'Strategy tools as boundary objects', *Strategic Organization*, 7/2: 223–32.

Spender, J.-C. (1995), 'Organizations are activity systems, not merely systems of thought', in Shrivastava, P., and Stubbart, C. (eds.), *Advances in Strategic Management: Challenges within the Mainstream*, vol. B: 153–74. Greenwich, CT: JAI Press.

Stetsenko, A. (2005), 'Activity as object-related: resolving the dichotomy of individual and collective planes of activity', *Mind, Culture, and Activity*, 12/1: 70–88.

Stieger, D., Matzler, K., Chatterjee, S., and Ladstätter-Fussenegger, F. (2012), Democratizing strategy: how crowdsourcing can be used for strategy dialogues', *California Management Review*, 54/4: 1–26.

Suchman, L. (1987), *Plans and Situated Actions*. Cambridge University Press.

Suddaby, R., Seidl, D., and Lê, J. (2013), 'Strategy-as-practice meets neo-institutional theory', *Strategic Organization*, 11/3: 329–44.

Turner, S. (1994), *The Social Theory of Practices*. Cambridge: Polity.

Vaara, E., Kleymann, B., and Seristö, H. (2004), 'Strategies as discursive constructions: the case of airline alliances', *Journal of Management Studies*, 41/1: 1–35.

Vaara, E., Sorsa, V., and Pälli, P. (2010), 'On the force potential of strategy texts: a critical discourse analysis of a strategic plan and its power effects in a city organization', *Organization*, 17/6: 685–702.

Vaara, E., and Whittington, R. (2012), 'Strategy-as-practice: taking social practices seriously', *Academy of Management Annals*, 6/1: 285–336.

Vygotsky, L. (1978), *Mind in Society: The Development of Higher Psychological Processes*. Cambridge, MA: Harvard University Press.

Walker, K. (2004), 'Activity systems and conflict resolution in an online professional communication course', *Business Communication Quarterly*, 67/2: 182–97.

Wells, G. (2002), 'The role of dialogue in activity theory', *Mind, Culture, and Activity*, 9/1: 43–66,

(2007), 'The mediating role of discoursing in activity', *Mind, Culture, and Activity*, 14/3: 160–77.

Wenger, E. (1998), *Communities of Practice. Learning, Meaning, and Identity*. Cambridge University Press.

Wertsch, J. (1985), *Vygotsky and the Social Formation of the Mind*. Cambridge, MA: Harvard University Press.

Whittington, R. (2003), 'The work of strategizing and organizing: for a practice perspective', *Strategic Organization*, 1/1: 119–27.

(2006), 'Completing the practice turn in strategy research', *Organization Studies*, 27/5: 613–34.

(2014), 'Information systems strategy and strategy-as-practice: a joint agenda', *Journal of Strategic Information Systems*, 23/1: 87–91.

Whittington, R., Cailluet, L., and Yakis-Douglas, B. (2011), 'Opening strategy: evolution of a precarious profession', *British Journal of Management*, 22/3: 531–44.

Wolf, C., and Floyd, S. W. (forthcoming), 'Strategic planning research: toward a theory-driven agenda', *Journal of Management*.

Wright, R. P., Paroutis, S., and Blettner, D. P. (2013), 'How useful are the strategic tools we teach in business schools?', *Journal of Management Studies*, 50/1: 92–125.

A Bourdieusian perspective on strategizing

CHAPTER 10

MARIE-LÉANDRE GOMEZ

The firm is not a homogeneous entity that can be treated as a rational subject – the 'entrepreneur' or the 'management' – oriented towards a single, unified objective. It is determined (or guided) in its 'choice' not only by its position in the structure of the field of production, but also by its internal structure, which, as a product of all its earlier history, still orients its present... Its strategies are determined through innumerable decisions, small and large, ordinary and extraordinary, which are, in every case, the product of the relationship between, on the one hand, interests and dispositions associated with positions in relations of force within the firm and, on the other, capacities to make those interests or dispositions count, capacities which also depend on the weight of the different agents concerned in the structure, and hence on the volume and structure of their capital.

Bourdieu (2005: 69)

Introduction

With the spread of strategy-as-practice research (see introduction, this volume; Heracleous and Jacobs 2011; Vaara and Whittington 2012), the focus has been on how strategy is actually performed in organizations. Strategy is more than something written in a strategic plan (Whittington and Cailluet 2008) or just relying on top management decision-making. SAP researchers have built upon major social theories (Sandberg and Tsoukas 2011; Seidl and Whittington 2014; Vaara and Whittington 2012) to define practice from different perspectives, but mostly emphasizing that practice is a human activity in relation with a strong social context. It is no surprise that the ideas of the French sociologist Pierre Bourdieu (1930–2002) have been used from the very beginning of strategy-as-practice research in some seminal works,

such as those by Jarzabkowski (2005), Whittington (2006) and Chia and Holt (2006). In nearly ten years Bourdieu's work has spread among strategy-as-practice studies. It has mostly been used to study how strategy emerges and becomes established in the actions of individuals and institutions (Chia and Holt 2006; 2009); to explore how strategizing bridges the relationship between the micro levels of human activity and the macro levels of social and institutional context (Gomez and Bouty 2011); to investigate strategists, as legitimate entrepreneurs (De Clercq and Voronov 2009) or corporate elites (MacLean, Harvey and Chia 2010); and how strategic practices and discourses maintain domination from corporate management (Laine and Vaara 2007; Kerr and Robinson 2012). Bourdieu's frame has also inspired the search of relevance for research in strategy (Sandberg and Tsoukas 2011; Splitter and Seidl 2011). Nevertheless, Bourdieu's work has long been underutilized, as noted by Chia (2004: 30): '[A]dvocates of practice-based approaches to strategy research may have underestimated the radical implications of the work of practice social theorists such as Bourdieu...who they rely upon to justify this turn to practice.'

The aim of this chapter is to expose how Bourdieu's theory of practice contributes to a better understanding of strategizing and can advance research on strategy. In the first section, I present the core elements of Bourdieu's theory, with the concepts of field, capital and habitus. In the second section, I discuss how this framework can contribute to advancing the strategy-as-practice research agenda by overcoming the dichotomies that shape but constrain research in strategy: the micro/macro antagonism, the opposition between structure and agency and the dilemma between planning and emergence in strategy. In the third section, I examine how Bourdieu's praxeology broadens our view of strategy. Strategizing appears as a subtle fit between the trajectory of agents and the field, and Bourdieu's frame opens new perspectives on the study of practitioners, with the need to account for the symbolic violence that is exerted in strategy as a practice, and it also helps to reframe the role of academics. Finally, I address some problematic issues that have been raised about practitioners' reflexivity and determinism.

Bourdieu's framework: a relational and dispositional system

Practice is a central concern in Bourdieu's work. It is the concept he uses to account for social life. By 'practice', he means 'concrete human activity' (Bourdieu 1990b: 13). In his structural constructivist epistemology (Bourdieu and Wacquant 1992: 11), concrete human activity always takes place in the social world, even for very basic activities: what people eat and, most of all, the way they eat; the sport they like, and the way they practise it; or their political opinions, and the way they express them. All human activities are conditioned by the social world people live in, and their social position in this social world (Bourdieu 1998). Bourdieu hardly uses the word 'practice' itself, however, nor does he formally define it. He mostly refers to the 'economy of practice', or 'the practical sense' to explain our immediate relation with the social world in which we are embedded. With the concepts of habitus, capital and field (but also many other secondary ones, such as 'doxa' or 'illusio', which cannot be detailed in this chapter), Bourdieu draws a theory of practice that is particularly rich and exhaustive: a 'shared sociological treasure', as qualified by Lahire (2001).

Bourdieu was trained as a philosopher, worked as an ethnologist and rapidly turned to the still emerging and non-dominant discipline that sociology was in the late 1950s. In his 'theory of practice', Bourdieu has either built from major intellectuals or has positioned his ideas against them: he rereads Weber's sociology of the religious fact and the role of symbolic power through the lens of the structuralism of Levi-Strauss to draw his conception of 'field' (Bourdieu 2000:

172–9), but at the same time he denies Weber's precept that legitimacy acknowledgement is a free and conscious act (Bourdieu 1990b: 63); he criticizes the ignorance of Foucault and the structuralists for the active dimension of symbolic production and the ability of agents to grasp opportunities; he draws on Marx's view of praxis from the 'Theses on Feuerbach' (Bourdieu 2000: 136) and his vision of a conflicting social world, but he deplores his determinism, his incapacity to conceive agency and the overall primacy of economic factors upon symbolic and cultural elements (Bourdieu 1990a: 41). In the meanwhile, he rejects the over-reflexivity of Garfinkel and Giddens. He also mobilizes the phenomenology of Husserl, Heidegger and Merleau-Ponty (Bourdieu 1990a) and builds upon Pascal to reject the traditional dichotomies between body and mind, understanding and apprehending, subject and object. Wittgenstein, Bachelard and Durkheim are major sources for his work, too (Calhoun 2003). Bourdieu's approach on the social world is particularly fertile, capitalizing on major intellectual influences to build its own coherent and systemic framework to comprehend social life. By so doing, it provides a fruitful toolkit to conceptualize strategy and strategizing, including the metaphor of game, the notions of the field and capital, and habitus.

The metaphor of game

Bourdieu frequently uses the metaphor of game to characterize his sense of social life and to show the interconnectedness of habitus, field, capital and practice (Bourdieu 1990a: 66; Bourdieu and Wacquant 1992: 98; Bourdieu 2000: 151). Players oppose one another, sometimes with ferocity: the game is a space for struggles to conquer the goals that are at stake. Players elaborate strategies in order to reinforce their positions and their gains (Bourdieu and Wacquant 1992: 98–9). These strategies and the struggles underlie the match. The stakes that motivate participants are particular to every game. Players are subsumed in the game, they are taken by the game. They feel that they are taking part in a larger system – not only the team and the match, but also the game itself. Every match is different, and players develop new strategies, new forms of actions, according to the position they occupy in the team. The forces attached to the players depend on their various strengths and weapons, and on their position in the playground. The one who plays as a defender will not have the same possibilities as the one playing as a striker. In the same way, players from a team at the top of the league will not develop the same strategies as those in an aspiring one.

Players act according to their feel for the game, the field and the rules, and by anticipating their co-players and opponents' actions. During a match the actions of players cannot be constrained to a simple application of the rules of the game, nor to rational and reflexive analysis of the situation, which would suppose a clear separation between action and thinking. The players use the way they integrated and interpreted the rules and their possibilities for action. It is a state of belief that characterizes the players' relation with the rules. They learned various possible actions through the game and training. In every match, however, they will face new situations, during which they will not just use their knowledge but also restructure it. They possess a 'sense of the game' that is the result of initial predispositions, training and practice, through which they integrated the rules. The player 'exactly knows what he has to do...without need to know what he does. Neither automaton, nor rational actor' (Bourdieu 2002: 74).

Social spaces as fields, capital as resources and stakes

The game is an example of a *field*, a microcosm among the numerous ones that exist in our social world. Every field is relatively autonomous. It is built, structured and organized through time and space. It is ruled by its own stakes and specific interests (Bourdieu 1990a). If photographed at a given moment, the field is a field of forces, a field of struggles – even those presented as disinterested, such as science, the arts or academia (Bourdieu and Wacquant 1992). Analysing the structure of the field reveals 'the state of the forces between agents or institutions engaged in struggle' to dominate the field (Bourdieu and Wacquant 1992: 77). Participants in a field are qualified as *agents*, because

they are 'neither a subject confronting the world as an object in a relation of pure knowledge, nor completely shaped by a "milieu" exerting a form of mechanical causality' (Bourdieu 2000: 150). Organizations constitute fields that are included in larger fields, such as industries, competitive markets, economy and society (Bourdieu 2005: 205, 217). As such, organizations are at one and the same time agents, involved in the field of their competitive environment, and a field in its own right, where individuals – taken as agents – evolve.

Agents' positions in the field are largely influenced by the capital they possess. Capital is both a resource and a stake; it is a key asset for the players. The possession of capital not only ensures a dominant position in the field but also provides more opportunities for action, and creates the conditions for increasing capital in the future. Bourdieu distinguishes various forms of capital, and each field favours different sorts of capital. 'Just as the relative value of cards changes with each game, the hierarchy of the different species of capital...varies across the various fields' (Bourdieu and Wacquant 1992: 98). Economic capital is composed by financial resources and material resources. Cultural capital includes cultural goods (paintings, books), cultural knowledge, qualifications and elements embodied through habitus, such as mastering language, cultural and social codes (Bourdieu 1979). Social capital comprises networks and social relations (Bourdieu 2002: 56). Within a company as a field (Bourdieu 2005), the capital of individuals as agents can be analysed in terms of bureaucratic capital (linked to responsibilities, action domain, hierarchical level and seniority); financial capital (the control of direct and indirect financial resources that agents can mobilize through their budget); technological capital (possessing expertise or a specific skill); organizational capital (the capacity to master procedures and formal rules); social capital (involvement in networks); and informational capital (privileged access to knowledge). For an organization, we can analyse forms of corporate capital (Bourdieu 2005: 194) that contribute to the building of success factors for the company.

The value granted to the various forms of capital varies among fields, and with time. Within some fields, such as industrial and trading sectors, economic capital will be the most prestigious, whereas, in other ones, other forms of capital, such as cultural capital, will be more valued. This social recognition of capital leads to symbolic effects that are forms of symbolic capital. Symbolic capital is the form of capital that is most valued in a given field. All sorts of capital are potentially symbolic capital, according to the meaning bestowed within a specific field (Bourdieu 2000: 240). The prestige and hierarchy in social order resulting from the distribution of symbolic capital appears natural and taken for granted by most agents in the field because it has been integrated into their habitus.

The positions of agents in the field can be established with the volume and structure of capital they possess. Their social positions constrain and condition practices but do not determine them. Agents may have different personal perspectives on practice: even with similar positions and trajectories in the field, two agents will not necessarily do the same thing. One may appear audacious and take some risks, whereas another one may appear conservative. Personal dispositions – habitus – are fundamental in order to account for practice.

Habitus as the driver for practice

Agents' practices rest on habitus. Habitus is the system of dispositions for action that are socially constituted (Bourdieu 1990a; Bourdieu and Wacquant 1992: 98). It is a set of schemes of perceptions, appreciations and beliefs (Bourdieu 1977: 95) of what to do or not to do, what is good or bad, in relation to a probable future. It is a repertory of dispositions, acquired in practice, and which allows practice.

The construction of the habitus is a long-lasting process. It is the product of a trajectory: the habitus is the result of experience, and it is influenced by the different environments the agent goes through. Hence, a specific field will influence the habitus of its members through the integration of its rules. Habitus is the result of inculcation but also an appropriation of the field's 'doxa', the taken-for-granted assumptions on the way things work in the field. *Doxa* is a belief in the legitimacy of the game and its stakes. As a matter of fact, the habitus is

both personal and social. It is personal because it is developed through the particular experience of the agent. It is linked to the personal initial dispositions of the agents, their particular experiences in the field. It is social, because it is highly linked to the context of the field and the agent's position inside this field. It is 'the social embodied' (Bourdieu and Wacquant 1992: 127), a 'socialized subjectivity' (Bourdieu 2005: 211). Its schemes of perceptions and appreciation (systems of preferences, tastes, beliefs) are the product of collective and individual history. Then, the habitus shapes practices, being a 'modus operandi'. We don't need to rationalize to act; the habitus drives our actions in an immediate, non-mediated way.

Habitus functions as 'structured and structuring dispositions' (Bourdieu 1990a: 52). As a structured disposition, it is the product of the interpretation of past experience and learning, which allows repetition of action. As a structuring disposition, it is an art of inventing, which allows improvisation in the particular context of a new practice. Bourdieu insists on the creative, active, inventive capacity of agents (Bourdieu 1990a: 55) while stating that their environment, experience and history are major influences. It 'makes possible the achievement of infinitely diversified tasks' (Bourdieu 1977: 95). In a permanent interaction, habitus shapes practice, but in turn is restructured and transformed through practice.

The concepts of field, capital and habitus are integrated in Bourdieu's theory of practice, and form a system (Golsorkhi and Huault 2006; Emirbayer and Johnson 2008). They are completely interrelated and interact in a dynamic way, affecting one another; their combination is necessary to obtain a complete picture of practices. As Bourdieu (1990a: 56) puts it: '[Practices] can therefore only be accounted for by relating the social conditions in which the habitus that generated them was constituted, to the social conditions in which it is implemented.'

Advancing strategy-as-practice research by overcoming dichotomies

Bourdieu's theory not only provides a toolkit to analyse the practices of strategizing. It also helps to overcome some dichotomies that strategy-as-practice research has criticized and proposed going beyond (Jarzabkowski, Balogun and Seidl 2007; Whittington 2006). As stated by Wacquant:

> Bourdieu refuses to establish sharp demarcations between the external and the internal, the conscious and the unconscious, the bodily and the discursive. [He] seeks to capture the intentionality without intention, the knowledge without cognitive intent, the prereflective, infraconscious mastery that agents acquire of their social world by way of durable immersion within it...and which defines properly human social practice (Bourdieu and Wacquant 1992: 19–20).

Linking the micro and macro levels of strategy

Strategy research has developed around the opposition between the micro and macro levels, with 'micro' referring to individual or intra-organizational aspects and 'macro' to the external environment, with researchers adopting either a micro or macro perspective on strategy. Strategic process studies have advanced research on micro phenomena by considering the role of individual actions in strategizing (Van de Ven 1992) and change (Mintzberg and Westley 1992), and by focusing on 'the sequences of incidents, activities, and actions unfolding over time' (Pettigrew 1992: 7). In the same perspective, and proclaiming affiliation with strategy process research (Johnson, Melin and Whittington 2003), the practice-based approach to strategizing has primarily focused on the micro level. Pioneers in strategy as practice called for more 'micro-activity-based approaches' (Wilson and Jarzabkowski 2004: 14), and to study strategy as practice as a subunit used to describe what people do: activities (Orlikowski 2002), episodes (Hendry and Seidl 2003; Maitlis and Lawrence 2003) or core micro-strategies (Salvato 2003). These works have contributed to a better understanding of what happens at the micro level in strategizing.

By focusing only on individuals' action, however, this micro-centred approach has all but lost the link between micro and macro that is inherent in a practice-based approach (Chia and MacKay

2007), and the explanatory and analytical strengths of theories of practice, which are particularly powerful in accounting for the individual within the collective: 'Fascination with the detailed understanding of local praxis can produce what we term "micro-isolationism"' (Seidl and Whittington 2014: 2). A growing number of authors call for better bridging between the micro and macro levels of practices, especially in strategy research (Carter, Clegg and Kornberger 2008; Golsorkhi 2006; Nicolini 2012; Vaara and Whittington 2012; Whittington 2007). Seidl and Whittington (2014) suggest that a Bourdieusian perspective is one of the opportunities to enlarge the ontological views in strategy-as-practice research. Effectively, Bourdieu's focal point is 'neither the individual...nor groups...but the relation between two realizations of historical actions, in bodies and things' (Bourdieu and Wacquant 1992: 126). This ontological complicity between the agent and the field helps to solve the micro/macro opposition, treating agents as social individuals. Their practice relies on both their position in the field and their personal experience, thoughts and dispositions, also built in the social world.

In parallel, institutionalist scholars deplore the overly macro perspective of institutional studies, focusing on the legitimization and the diffusion of practices without considering either their origins or the people using them. For this reason, Battilana, Leca and Boxenbaum (2009), Czarniawska-Joerges and Sevon (1996) and Lounsbury and Crumley (2007) have called for a better understanding of who the initiators of new strategies are and how strategies emerge. As suggested by Lounsbury and Crumley (2007: 1007), '[T]here is an opportunity to expand intra-organizational practice research in a way that better appreciates the relationship between organizational and institutional dynamics.' The institutional work perspective tries to reconcile the micro and macro levels of analysis (Lawrence, Suddaby and Leca 2009). The study of institutional work maintains a fascination with the relationship between institutions and action. It also maintains as central the structurationist notion that all action is embedded in institutional structures, which it simultaneously produces, reproduces and transforms (Lawrence,

Suddaby and Leca 2011: 52). In contrast with practice, the concept of work explicitly implies some intentionality and efforts. Nevertheless, recent analysis of institutional work resonates with a practice-based approach to strategizing (Battilana, Leca and Boxenbaum 2009), and could enrich SAP research, as shown by Smets, Morris and Greenwood (2012). These authors propose a 'practice-driven' model of institutional change, which connects practice, organization and field. They have analysed the change in a law firm and traced how institutional change arose from a concatenation of multi-level mechanisms such as situated improvising, or normative network reorganizing.

Overcoming the dichotomy between agency and structure

The second dichotomy that shapes the literature on strategy opposes the freedom of agency and the determinism of structures. On the one hand, strategy appears to be a voluntarist approach in which the freedom of firms and managers is overemphasized (Mintzberg and Lampel 1999). On the other hand, strategy can be viewed as overly conditioned by the structures of the industry. The ecology of population approach considers the strength of the environment's inertial structures (Hannan and Freeman 1984) and concludes that companies can survive only if they possess characteristics that match the environment (Carroll 1988). Even the competitive group approach considers the weight of the environment, stating that strategy success depends on the strategic group in which a company is located (Reger and Huff 1993).

How to consider simultaneously agents' capacity to orientate their lives and the weight of social structures in which they are embedded? This question has been a permanent challenge in Bourdieu's work. He has repeatedly exposed the problems of structuralism, which denies the capacity of agents to escape their social destiny, and of pure agency. Bourdieu does not deny structures and agency, but he accepts neither their opposition, nor their division. For Bourdieu, 'objectivism and subjectivism, mechanicalism and finalism, structural necessity and individual agency are false

antinomies. Each of these paired opposites reinforces the other; all collude in obfuscating the anthropological truth of human practice' (Bourdieu and Wacquant 1992: 10).

Bourdieu's theory explicitly proposes to overcome the opposition between agency and structure (Bourdieu 1990a) and establishes a strong relation between these concepts. They coexist, and mirror and permeate each other in a genetical way: the former is the embodiment of the latter. There exists a correspondence between the social structures and the personal, mental structures, through the relation between field and habitus. The structures of the field are projected on agents through their relative habitus and capital developed in the field. 'Cumulative exposure to certain social conditions instills individuals an ensemble of durable and transposable dispositions that internalize the necessities of the extant social environment, inscribing inside the organism the patterned inertia and constraints of external reality' (Bourdieu and Wacquant 1992: 13). At the same time, agents keep trying to avoid the determinants of the structure through their habitus and increase in capital. This system allows a better capture of the dynamics and the complexity of organizational life. As summarized by Özbilgin and Tatti (2005: 867–8), Bourdieu's praxeology 'allows for a reading of the interplay among individual choices, capacity and strategies with structural conditions in a way that is true to organizations reality's relational and dynamic properties'.

Escaping planning versus emergence dilemma

Planning versus emergence represents the third opposition that characterizes strategy research and that strategy-as-practice research proposes to escape from (Rasche and Chia 2009). Research has long overemphasized the intentionality of strategy and the reflexive ability of decision-makers, as, for example, in studies of strategic planning (Ansoff 1965) and core competence (Prahalad and Hamel 1994). Strategy is mostly considered as the product of a deliberate top-down design process. As Chia and Holt (2009: 23) state, 'Attributing authorship of strategic decisions solely to autonomous, consciously choosing, intentional agents understates the ever-present moderating effects that invisible historical and cultural forces immanent in situations have on the eventual choices made.' In contrast, some other approaches, such as complexity, consider that strategy is based on emergence, and self-organizing behaviours (Stacey 1995). They are positioned against the rational choice paradigm. For Thietart and Forgues (1995), organizations, when they are facing counteracting forces, can even develop chaotic strategies, with no possibility of observing similar reactions and similar results. From chaos, new stabilities then emerge. This perspective does not help us understand the coherence that can be found in strategizing, and to relate the organization to its field.

Bourdieu's praxeology offers a different understanding of strategy. Owing to the complicity between habitus and field that drives practice, 'the most effective strategies are those which, being the product of dispositions shaped by the immediate necessity of the field, tend to adjust themselves spontaneously to that necessity, without express intention or calculation' (Bourdieu 2000: 138). In the double relation of habitus and field, agents produce reasonable strategies and not rational ones. Bourdieu uses the word 'strategy', but advises that in his perspective this is not rational reasoning. The principle of strategy is not a calculation, a conscious search for specific profit maximization (Bourdieu 1984). It is based on the practical sense, which largely bypasses cognitive structures, is registered in one's body and enables one to act 'as one should' (Bourdieu 2000: 139). Being involved in the field, agents develop both thoughts and perceptions that help them to immediately distinguish between the feasible and the unfeasible: 'Far from being posited in an explicit, conscious project, the strategies suggested by habitus [function] as a "feel for the game" aim' (Bourdieu and Wacquant 1992: 128).

Implications of Bourdieu's theory of practice for strategizing and strategy research

Bourdieu's theory of practice sheds an original light on action, agency and actors, and it has aided

strategy research in the following ways: proposing a new approach to what strategizing consists of; analysing who strategists are, as entrepreneurs or as business elites; and comprehending symbolic violence in strategic practices. Bourdieu's approach also calls for a rethink of the position of academics with regard to society. In the following section, I elaborate on these issues.

Towards a refined approach on strategizing

Chia and Holt (2006; 2009) have largely mobilized Bourdieu's frame, in conjunction with Heidegger, to explain how strategy emerges, 'takes shape and infuses itself in everyday actions of individuals and institutions' (Chia and Holt 2009: xi). They propose that strategy-making ought to be conceived as a process of 'wayfinding', which is opposed to navigating (Chia and Holt 2009: 159). Navigating exemplifies the more classical understanding of strategy-making: the strategist (captain), using established maps or models to read and analyse the environment (analysis), determines his or her own strategic capabilities and priorities (position, timeframe, resources, etc.), sets a target destination accordingly (strategic goal) and then steers the ship accordingly to its preset destination (execution). For the pioneers themselves, though, who did not have the benefit of pre-existing maps, navigation involves 'wayfinding': finding one's way among unexplored oceans, 'reaching out into the unknown and developing an incomplete but practically sufficient comprehension of the situation in order to cope effectively with it' (Chia and Holt 2009: 159).

The infusion of strategizing in mundane practical actions is also highlighted by Gomez and Bouty, who have shown that 'the nature of strategy-making should be conceived as an ebb and flow between a calculative and voluntary vision on the one hand, and an unplanned emergence on the other' (Gomez and Bouty 2011: 935). As such, strategizing is a voluntary process, but not necessarily as usually understood: intentionality is not a prerequisite for an articulated strategy. Habitus produces reasonable strategies, not rational ones, and practitioners should not be overemphasized as reflexive actors. Nevertheless, 'without being rational, ...agents are reasonable'

(Bourdieu and Wacquant 1992: 129), and they adopt strategies that match with their resources and expectations, at the encounter of their own trajectory and the field's evolution. Agents are able to strategize through a series of moves that are 'organized as strategies without being the product of a genuine strategic intention' (Bourdieu 1977: 73). As a consequence, 'the world is comprehensible, immediately endowed with meaning' (Bourdieu 2000: 135), so that 'strategic outcomes do not presuppose deliberate prior planning or intention'. As Bourdieu summarizes it: '[P]eople are not fools... [T]hey know how to read the future that fits them, which is made for them and for which they are made...through practical anticipation' (Bourdieu and Wacquant, 1992: 130). In this perspective, Gomez and Bouty (2011) analysed how an influential practice initially emerged, with an empirical study in the field of haute cuisine. Mobilizing the institutional entrepreneur's habitus and his position in terms of capital, they show how this new practice developed locally within a strong 'complicity' relationship between this chef and the field of haute cuisine, exemplifying the encounter between two histories: the history of haute cuisine, and the chef's personal history in this field.

Strategists as entrepreneurs and business elites

The second stream of SAP research mobilizing Bourdieu focuses on the analysis of the strategist. SAP research first highlighted the key role of middle managers in strategizing (Laine and Vaara 2007; Mantere 2005; Rouleau 2005). More recent Bourdieusian studies have focused on entrepreneurs and elites, however, which had previously received more attention from traditional strategic approaches than from strategy as practice. Whereas research in strategy has long studied business elites through their sociodemographic characteristics, or leadership attributes, Bourdieu's framework shines an insightful light on strategic leaders through legitimacy and field domination. In particular, De Clercq and Voronov (2009) have tackled the issue of entrepreneurs' legitimacy in their field. They show that the success of entrepreneurs relies on

their legitimacy. Newcomers entering a field are not automatically considered as entrepreneurs by the various stakeholders. Legitimacy is obtained by enacting a variety of field-prescribed rituals that entrepreneurs are expected to perform, and their ability to be perceived as legitimate field players is shaped by their access to cultural and symbolic capital. Stringfellow, Shaw and Maclean (2014) have shown that, in a mature industry, heterodoxic entrepreneurs, diverging from the social norms, have more difficulties building legitimacy and access to resources in a venture-capital process.

In another vein, Bourdieu's framework helps explain why power and resources are held by a small group of dominant agents constituting an elite. Accordingly, MacLean, Harvey and Chia (2010) analysed French and British corporate elites trajectories. They underline that the power is unevenly distributed among the dominant, being highly concentrated in the hands of a small number of dominant agents within corporate business. They note the ascension of a small minority of corporate agents to dominance and the subsequent accession of a select few to the power elite. They show the importance of accumulating cultural capital in the early years of a career, and during the process of ascension; in the meanwhile, the mobilization of social capital (connections to others providing support and opportunities) increases symbolic capital. These dynamics are crucial for eventual accession to the field of power and the power elite. Focusing more specifically on British business elites, Maclean, Harvey and Chia (2012) show that reflexive practices play a key role in elite strategies, particularly for those who came from non-privileged classes. Focusing on French top-tier business elite, MacLean, Harvey and Kling (2014) elaborate on different processes. They highlight the crucial role of external networks and social origins. Higher-status agents benefit from mutual recognition that enhances their likelihood of co-option to the extra-corporate networks. Social origin still exerts an enduring influence on selection dynamics that inform the processes of reproduction in the corporate elite and society at large.

In addition to these insightful perspectives on elites and entrepreneurs, Bourdieu's framework is particularly appropriate for the study of dominated agents and the dynamics of domination. More focus on middle managers, and on 'bottom-line' workers, could advance our understanding of resistance and compliance from dominated agents, and reproduction in strategizing. Moreover, the analysis of domination could shed light on what happens with women and gender issues in strategizing as well.

Comprehending symbolic violence in strategizing

The least developed stream of studies addresses symbolic violence in strategizing, in particular in terms of highlighting the critical role and impact of strategic practices and tools on people, organizations and fields. This might be because it deals with power and domination issues in the field, and reveals the symbolic violence that is exerted upon dominated agents. Symbolic violence is a key concern in Bourdieu's analysis, as it is the main way social power is expressed. In most of our social worlds, the forces exerted by dominant agents in order to keep on dominating the field are non-physical, taken for granted, unconscious and mostly symbolic. They nonetheless encompass what Bourdieu terms 'symbolic violence'. Symbolic violence is 'the violence which is exercised upon a social agent with his or her complicity' to ensure and enforce dominating practices (Bourdieu and Wacquant 1992: 167). 'The established order, with its relations of domination, its rights and prerogatives, privileges and injustices, ultimately perpetuates itself so easily [including at the organizational level] that the most intolerable conditions of existence can so often be perceived as acceptable and even natural' (Bourdieu 1998: 1, quoted by Emirbayer and Johnson 2008). These common and taken-for-granted beliefs are socially and historically constructed. They contribute to maintaining the social structures and the hierarchies between dominant and dominated agents without exercising physical violence.

So far, little research has investigated the impact of strategic practices over agents, which would reveal the struggles for power and forms of symbolic violence in strategizing. In their seminal work, Oakes, Townley and Cooper (1998) show how business planning exerts various forms of control over the organization and its members. By performing and announcing the coming changes in strategy, it is, of course, coercive; but business planning also exercises a more subtle form of control through language: it provides legitimate forms of discourses and arguments, and sanctions others: '[B]usiness planning excluded certain ideas as unthinkable, such as not being businesslike, efficient, customer-oriented, and revenue-seeking, while also proposing a vision of the organization as a business, subject to instrumental reasoning' (Oakes, Townley and Cooper 1998: 271). Using Bourdieu's work, they show that the introduction of business planning affected the distribution of positions in the field and modified the symbolic and cultural capitals. They consider business planning to exert a form of symbolic violence – the violence exerted upon agents with their complicity (Bourdieu and Wacquant, 1992: 167). The power of naming and categorizing represents a strong mode of domination, and, in any field, there are some struggles to gain this power (Bourdieu 1984).

Although not explicitly drawing on Bourdieu, the role of discourses has also been analysed by Laine and Vaara (2007). They outline the specific role of discourse by dominating and dominated agents. They argue that strategic discourses are a space for struggles, 'a dialectical battle between competing groups' (Laine and Vaara 2007: 30), between corporate management and more dominated agents, such as middle managers or project managers. Kerr and Robinson (2012) have, in turn, outlined the consequences of the globalization of the Scottish bank industry and the first impacts of the crisis. Through the lens of symbolic and economic violence, they outline the strategies followed by the Scottish banking elite to maintain their position within their own organization and, at the same time, within a field becoming transorganizational.

Other topics could be studied from this perspective as well. One area appears particularly important nowadays: the consequences of financialization in strategizing could be analysed from a Bourdieusian perspective, focusing on symbolic violence dynamics. It would unveil the impact of the progressive spread of financial tools and financial valuation practices (Boltanski and Chiapello 2005; Morales and Pezet 2012).

A different posture for researchers in strategy?

The lack of relevance of strategy research has regularly been pointed out (Hambrick 2005; Patent, Chia and Burt 2014). Sandberg and Tsoukas (2011: 239) point out that research has been disconnected from managerial concerns so far because their rationalities are not compatible: '[T]he scientific rationality framework prevents researchers from developing theories that capture "the logic of practice".' Vaara and Durand (2012) recommend, among other points, placing agency in context, to focus on practices that enable and constrain strategy-making and to provide critical analysis of underlying beliefs and norms. These guidelines speak in favour of a Bourdieusian approach in strategizing. In the same vein, Golsorkhi *et al.* (2009) have called for greater responsibility on the part of scholars and the development of Bourdieusian studies in organizations. More generally, a better understanding of the field of education, particularly the MBA market field, would help academics to enhance their perspectives on both teaching and research, their relationships and the tensions with which they live. Vaara and Faÿ (2011) call for the use of Bourdieu's frame to analyse our own field of education; in particular, it would capture the various dominant forces: 'Bourdieu's framework helps us to better comprehend how both accreditation and widespread ranking tend to standardize and homogenize and thus impede comprehensive change' (Vaara and Faÿ 2011: 39).

Nevertheless, building on Bourdieu, Splitter and Seidl (2011) have warned about the 'scholastic view' of researchers: 'scholastic view' refers to 'an abstraction of the world to think about the world' (Bourdieu and Wacquant, 1992: 78), the particular point of view resulting from the researcher's detached position towards the object of

research, originating from the differences between the social conditions of the academic field and those of the managerial field. The scholastic view creates the distance necessary for the researcher to develop scientific knowledge, but, at the same time, it ignores the practical urgencies of managers, and thus makes scientific knowledge irrelevant for practitioners. Splitter and Seidl (2011) recommend researchers to engage in 'participant objectivation', a particular form of reflexivity that, according to Bourdieu, is the only way to produce valid scientific knowledge that may also prove relevant to practitioners. Participant objectivation requires 'objectivizing the researcher's subjective relation to his or her object of research' (Splitter and Seidl 2011: 108). These authors give a warning to strategy-as-practice researchers who tend to promote a simple form of reflexivity by examining their own research practices, whereas participant objectivation would also imply accounting for the underlying objective structures of the academic field, meaning analysing 'the relation of researchers to strategists' practices' (111).

Thus, adopting a Bourdieusian perspective on strategy means more than producing more relevant research. With the *eternel retour* of rationality in management practices and research (Cabantous and Gond 2011), research on strategizing needs to unveil the 'form *par excellence* of symbolic violence, the power which…is exerciced through rational communication" (Bourdieu 2000: 83). This form of communication is particularly widespread in strategic practices, and scholars need to position themselves with regard to their role in society. As Bourdieu warns us,

> The social sciences, which alone can unmask and counter the completely new strategies of domination which they sometimes help to inspire and to arm, will more than ever have to choose which side they are on: either they place their rational instruments of knowledge at the service of ever more rationalized domination, or they rationally analyse domination and more especially the contribution which rational knowledge can make to de facto monopolization of the profits of universal reason (Bourdieu 2000: 83–4).

Problematic issues and key concerns

Is the practitioner unreflexive? Core differences with Giddens

Whereas strategy research mostly postulates that practitioners analyse their actions and are able to objectify their doings, Bourdieu rejects this form of reflexivity. This does not mean that he denies the will of, and some ability on the part of, agents to inquire about their position and their practice (Bourdieu and Wacquant 1992: 72). He nevertheless claims that reflexivity is strongly bounded. Agents have a non-mediated relation with practice: they are taken by the game, and they take the rules for granted. In order to discover the structures of the field and that they are not objective but socially constructed, agents generally need the intervention of external members such as sociologists. Researchers encounter the same difficult with reflexivity as practising the 'scientific game', and are bounded by scholastic bias. Despite the fact that agents cannot describe the nature of the structure of the field, however, dominated agents have a strong sense of their domination and the symbolic violence that is exerted upon them (Bourdieu 2000). This difficult, almost impossible, reflexivity of practitioners is a key difference between Bourdieu and Giddens. For Giddens, social actors are reflexive and monitor the flow of actions and structural conditions; they adapt their actions to their evolving understandings. Bourdieu strongly rejects this form of reflexivity.

Bourdieu's theory of practice and Giddens' structuration theory are frequently compared, particularly in strategy-as-practice research (Jarzabkowski 2005; Rasche and Chia 2009; Seidl and Whittington 2014), in which they are referred to equally. Both scholars acknowledge a close relationship between individual agency and social structures (De Clercq and Voronov 2009; Nicolini 2012). For Schatzki (1997), both even 'overintellectualize practices and actions'. In Giddens' structuration theory, structure and agency are a duality that cannot be conceived of apart from one another: there is no agency without structures that shape motives into actions, but there can be no structures independent of the routines that create

them. Structure consists in the rules and resources that give similar social practices a systemic form. A social system is a set of reproduced social practices and relations between actors. Actors continually develop routines that give them a sense of security and that enable them to deal efficiently with their social lives. Giddens emphasizes that actors have power to shape their own actions but that the consequences of actions are often unintended. According to Giddens, structure can be constraining no actors, but structures can also enable actors to do things they would not otherwise be able to do. Indeed, Giddens considers that structuralists overemphasize structural constraints. This is a major difference from Bourdieu, who acknowledges the possibilities of escaping one's dominated destiny, but considers this to be difficult, and grants a much more conditioning role to the structures of the field.

An overdeterministic view of social life?

One of the most pre-eminent critiques that have been raised with regard to Bourdieu's work is the overestimation of the determinism of social structures, leaving little space to human agents for escaping their destiny and transforming the field (Mutch 2007). This critique is particularly problematic for strategy as practice: is strategy determined by the social structures of the field, with a weak role of agents, for whom changing the rules of the game and the trajectory of their organization would be almost impossible?

Bourdieu explicitly rejected such a deterministic view (Bourdieu and Wacquant 1992: 135–6). He insisted on the generative capacity of habitus and its creative capacity (Bourdieu 1990a: 55; Bourdieu and Wacquant 1992: 122). The structures of the field condition the habitus, but this is not inexorable (Bourdieu 2000: 64). If the practical sense is the most frequent principle, agents can also develop strategic calculations, 'objectively oriented lines of action' (Bourdieu and Wacquant, 1992,: 129), in order to maximize their gains in capital. For DeClercq and Voronov, 'Bourdieu acknowledges the strategic nature of agents' behaviour, which is not simply governed or constrained by rules but rather should be seen in light of their positions in the field' (DeClercq and Voronov 2009: 818). As such, Bourdieu's theory of practice is relevant for thinking about change. His overall intellectual project was indeed to make explicit the nature and the rules of the social games he studied (such as education, voting and housing), so that agents could reconsider them instead of taking them for granted and complying to these rules, and thus stop contributing to the reproduction of a social order that led to their own domination. He considered that, with this knowledge, agents would be more able to change their destiny, even acknowledging the difficulties that would be faced.

As stated by MacLean, Harvey and Chia (2010), Bourdieu suggests, moreover, that movement can occur within structures of domination; there is potential for change, usually incremental, resulting from strategy and agency. In propagating a legitimate vision of the social order, those in dominant positions never entirely succeed in establishing a monopoly. Within any field, subordinate organizations and agents strive to find ways to neutralize the advantages of the dominant, and at times discover ways to destabilize dominant rivals with 'subversion strategies' (Emirbayer and Williams 2005: 693). Symbolic struggles, Bourdieu argues, possess a degree of autonomy from the structures in which they are embedded, and he does acknowledge the gradual transformation of the dominant system over time (Bourdieu 1998: 336–9). Bourdieu's frame remains one of the most structuralist, however, and thus deterministic in its approaches to practice (Rasche and Chia 2009; Schatzki 2005).

Conclusion

The use of Bourdieu's theory of practice has already contributed to advances in strategy-as-practice research. Bourdieu's frame helps to overturn simple descriptions of stages and actions in strategizing. It is particularly adapted to the study of strategizing in contexts of strategic changes in order to depict what happens when strategic changes occur and how these changes modify the forces ruling the field (Bourdieu 2005), or how dominant agents develop strategies to maintain their power over the field. With a dynamic and relational approach to human activity, the field/habitus/practice system highlights the complexity of strategizing and the interconnectedness of the micro and macro levels, agency and structure, and deliberate and emergent strategies. This framework emphasizes the complex but fascinating relations between the individuals, their trajectory and their environment; their degree of freedom and the weight of structural constraints, rationalization and non-reflexivity in practice; and collective and collaborative work and symbolic struggles. These insights open up wide avenues in strategy research, to provide a better account of what really happens and is at stake in organizations. As Bourdieu puts it:

> Investigating how decisions come to be taken remain more or less meaningless so long as they confine themselves to the merely phenomenal manifestations of the exercise of power, that is to say, to discourse and interactions, ignoring the structure of relations of forces between the institutions and the agents (Bourdieu 2005: 69–70).

This perspective engages researchers to analyse more deeply the symbolic violence exerted upon agents during strategizing processes. Although the need for criticality has been pointed (Nicolini 2012; Seidl and Whittington 2014; Vaara and Whittington 2012), research in strategy has so far seldom brought to light the violence in these struggles. Agents involved in strategizing are indeed actually engaged in harsh competition, with sanctions and rewards essential. Bourdieu's work has been mobilized to study entrepreneur legitimacy (De Clercq and Voronov 2009) and corporate elites (MacLean, Harvey and Chia 2010). Similarly, research could fruitfully investigate middle managers and how they react to dominant forces: how they comply, how they resist and how they develop alternative strategies, but also the suffering related to the pressure and the inability to escape from these forces. Furthermore, one key current issue deals with the financialization of strategizing. More research is needed to account for the impact of financiancialization, with the spread of financial practices, tools, valuation and professionals in strategizing.

Following the example of Bourdieu, who studied so-called 'disinterested' fields (Bourdieu 2000) such as academia, sports and artistic fields, SAP researchers could investigate strategizing in fields such as business schools and universities, academic research, creative industries and hospitals. These fields are facing major changes; they have long been left to one side by research in strategy, and a Bourdieusian approach could help to account for the change that is occurring, and relating it to the people and organizations making things happen, and those being subjected to these changes and society at large.

References

Ansoff, I. (1965), *Corporate Strategy*. New York: McGraw-Hill.

Battilana, J., Leca, B., and Boxenbaum, E. (2009), 'How actors change institutions: towards a theory of institutional entrepreneurship', *Academy of Management Annals*, 3/1: 65–107.

Boltanski, L., and Chiapello, E. (2005), *The New Spirit of Capitalism*. London: Verso.

Bourdieu, P. (1977), *Outline of a Theory of Practice*. Cambridge University Press.

(1979), 'Les trois états du capital culturel', *Actes de la Recherche en Sciences Sociales*, 30: 3–6.

(1984), *Distinction: A Social Critique of the Judgement of Taste*. London: Routledge & Kegan Paul.

(1990a), *The Logic of Practice*. Cambridge: Polity.

(1990b), *In Other Words: Essay towards a Reflexive Sociology*. Cambridge: Polity.

(1998), *Practical Reason*. Redwood City, CA: Stanford University Press.

(2000), *Pascalian Meditations*. Cambridge: Polity.

(2002), *Questions de sociologie*. Paris: Éditions de Minuit.

(2005), *The Social Structures of the Economy*. Cambridge: Polity.

Bourdieu, P., and Wacquant, L. (1992), *An Invitation to Reflexive Sociology*. Cambridge: Polity.

Cabantous, L., and Gond, J.-P. (2011), 'Rational decision making as performative praxis: explaining rationality's *éternel retour*', *Organization Science*, 22/3: 573–86.

Calhoun, C. (2003), 'Pierre Bourdieu', in Ritzer, G. (ed.), *The Blackwell Companion to Major Classical Social Theorists*: 274–309. Malden, MA: Blackwell.

Carroll, G. R. (1988), *Ecological Models of Organizations*. Cambridge, MA: Ballinger.

Carter, C., Clegg, S., and Kornberger, M. (2008), 'Strategy as practice?', *Strategic Organization*, 6/1: 83–99.

Chia, R. (2004), 'Strategy-as-practice: reflections on the research agenda', *European Management Review*, 1/1: 29–34.

Chia, R., and Holt, R. (2006), 'Strategy as practical coping: a Heideggerian perspective', *Organization Studies*, 27/5: 635–55.

(2009), *Strategy without Design: The Silent Efficacy of Indirect Action*. Cambridge University Press.

Chia, R., and MacKay, B. (2007), 'Post-processual challenges for the emerging strategy-as-practice perspective: discovering strategy in the logic of practice', *Human Relations*, 60/1: 217–42.

Czarniawska-Joerges, B., and Sevon, G. (1996), *Translating Organizational Change*. Berlin: Walter de Gruyter.

De Clercq, D., and Voronov, M. (2009), 'Toward a practice perspective of entrepreneurship: entrepreneurial legitimacy as habitus', *International Small Business Journal*, 27/4: 395–419.

Emirbayer, M., and Johnson, V. (2008), 'Bourdieu and organizational analysis', *Theory and Society*, 37/1: 1–44.

Emirbayer, M., and Williams, E. (2005), 'Bourdieu and social work', *Social Service Review*, 79/4: 689–724.

Golsorkhi, D. (2006), *La fabrique de la stratégie: Une perspective multidimensionnelle*. Paris: Vuibert.

Golsorkhi, D., and Huault, I. (2006), 'Pierre Bourdieu: critique et réflexivité comme attitude analytique', *Revue Française de Gestion*, 165: 15–34.

Golsorkhi, D., Leca, B., Lounsbury, M., and Ramirez, C. (2009), 'Analysing, accounting for and unmasking domination: on our role as scholars of practice, practitioners of social science and public intellectuals', *Organization*, 16/6: 779–97.

Gomez, M.-L., and Bouty, I. (2011), 'The emergence of an influential practice: food for thought', *Organization Studies*, 32/7: 921–40.

Hambrick, D. C. (2005), 'What if the academy actually mattered?', *Academy of Management Review*, 19/1: 11–16.

Hannan, M. T., and Freeman, J. (1984), 'Structural inertia and organizational change', *American Sociological Review*, 49/2: 149–64.

Hendry, J., and Seidl, D. (2003), 'The structure and significance of strategic episodes: social systems theory and the routine practices of strategic change', *Journal of Management Studies*, 40/1: 175–96.

Heracleous, L., and Jacobs, C. D. (2011), *Crafting Strategy: Embodied Metaphors in Practice*. Cambridge University Press.

Jarzabkowski, P. (2005), *Strategy as Practice: An Activity-Based Approach*. London: Sage.

Jarzabkowski, P., Balogun, J., and Seidl, D. (2007), 'Strategizing: the challenges of a practice perspective', *Human Relations*, 60/1: 5–27.

Johnson, G., Melin, L., and Whittington, R. (2003), 'Guest editors' introduction: micro strategy and strategizing: towards an activity-based view', *Journal of Management Studies*, 40/1: 3–22.

Kerr, R., and Robinson, S. (2012), 'From symbolic violence to economic violence: the globalizing of the Scottish banking elite', *Organization Studies*, 33/2: 247–66.

Lahire, B. (2001), *Le travail sociologique de Pierre Bourdieu: Dettes et critiques*. Paris: Éditions La Découverte.

Laine, P.-M., and Vaara, E. (2007), 'Struggling over subjectivity: a discursive analysis of strategic development in an engineering group', *Human Relations*, 60/1: 29–58.

Lawrence, T. B., Suddaby, R., and Leca, B. (2009), *Institutional Work: Actors and Agency in Institutional Studies of Organizations*. Cambridge University Press.

(2011), 'Institutional work: refocusing institutional studies of organization', *Journal of Management Inquiry*, 20/1: 52–8.

Lounsbury, M., and Crumley, E. T. (2007), 'New practice creation: an institutional perspective on innovation', *Organization Studies*, 28/7: 993–1012.

MacLean, M., Harvey, C., and Chia, R. (2010), 'Dominant corporate agents and the power elite in France and Britain', *Organization Studies*, 31/3: 327–48.

MacLean, M., Harvey, C., and Chia, R. (2012), 'Reflexive practice and the making of elite business careers', *Management Learning*, 43/4: 385–404.

MacLean, M., Harvey, C., and Kling, G. (2014), 'Pathways to power: class, hyper-agency and the French corporate elite', *Organization Studies*, 35/6: 825–55.

Maitlis, S., and Lawrence, T. B. (2003), 'Orchestral manoeuvres in the dark: understanding failure in organizational strategizing', *Journal of Management Studies*, 40/1: 109–39.

Mantere, S. (2005), 'Strategic practices as enablers and disablers of championing activity', *Strategic Organization*, 3/2: 157–84.

Mintzberg, H., and Lampel, J. (1999), 'Reflecting on the strategy process', *Sloan Management Review*, 40/3: 21–30.

Mintzberg, H., and Westley, F. (1992), 'Cycles of organizational change', *Strategic Management Journal*, 13/S2: 39–59.

Morales, J., and Pezet, A. (2012), 'Financialization through hybridization: the subtle power of financial controlling', in Huault, I., and Richard, C. (eds.), *Finance: The Discreet Regulator: How Financial Activities Shape and Transform the World*: 19–39. London: Palgrave Macmillan.

Mutch, A. (2007), 'Reflexivity and the institutional entrepreneur: a historical exploration', *Organization Studies*, 28/7: 1123–40.

Nicolini, D. (2012), *Practice Theory, Work, and Organization: An Introduction*. Oxford University Press.

Oakes, L. S., Townley, B., and Cooper, D. J. (1998), 'Business planning as pedagogy: language and control in a changing institutional field', *Administrative Science Quarterly*, 43/2: 257–92.

Orlikowski, W. J. (2002), 'Knowing in practice: enacting a collective capability in distributed organizing', *Organization Science*, 13/3: 249–73.

Özbilgin, M., and Tatti, A. (2005), 'Book review essay: understanding Bourdieu's contribution to organization and management studies', *Academy of Management Review*, 30/4: 855–77.

Patent, S., Chia, R., and Burt, G. (2014), 'Relevance or "relevate"? How university business schools can add value through reflexively learning from strategic partnerships with business', *Management Learning*, 45/3: 267–88.

Pettigrew, A. M. (1992), 'The character and significance of strategy process research', *Strategic Management Journal*, 13/S2: 5–16.

Prahalad, C. K., and Hamel, G. (1994), *Competing for the Future*. Cambridge, MA: Harvard Business School Press.

Rasche, R., and Chia, R. (2009), 'Researching strategy practices: a genealogical social theory perspective', *Organization Studies*, 30/7: 713–34.

Reger, R. K., and Huff, A. S. (1993), 'Strategic groups: a cognitive perspective', *Strategic Management Journal*, 14/2: 103–23.

Rouleau, L. (2005), 'Micro-practices of strategic sensemaking and sensegiving: how middle managers interpret and sell change every day', *Journal of Management Studies*, 42/7: 1413–41.

Salvato, C. (2003), 'The role of micro-strategies in the engineering of firm evolution', *Journal of Management Studies*, 40/1: 83–108.

Sandberg, J., and Tsoukas, H. (2011), 'Grasping the logic of practice: theorizing through practical rationality', *Academy of Management Review*, 36/2: 338–60.

Schatzki, T. R. (1997), 'Practices and actions: a Wittgensteinian critique of Bourdieu and Giddens', *Philosophy of the Social Sciences*, 27/3: 283–308.

Schatzki, T. R. (2005), 'Peripheral vision: the sites of organizations', *Organization Studies*, 26/3: 465–84.

Seidl, D., and Whittington, R. (2014), 'Enlarging the strategy-as-practice research agenda: towards taller and flatter ontologies', *Organization Studies*, 35/10: 1407–31.

Smets, M., Morris, T., and Greenwood, R. (2012), 'From practice to field: a multilevel model of practice-driven institutional change', *Academy of Management Journal*, 55/4: 877–904.

Splitter, V., and Seidl, D. (2011), 'Does practice-based research on strategy lead to practically relevant knowledge? Implications of a Bourdieusian perspective', *Journal of Applied Behavioral Science*, 47/1: 98–120.

Stacey, R. D. (1995), 'The science of complexity: an alternative perspective for strategic change processes', *Strategic Management Journal*, 16/6: 477–95.

Stringfellow, L., Shaw, E., and Maclean, M. (2014), 'Apostasy versus legitimacy: relational dynamics and routes to resource acquisition in entrepreneurial ventures', *International Small Business Journal*, 32/5: 571–92.

Thietart, R.-A., and Forgues, B. (1995), 'Chaos theory and organization', *Organization Science*, 6/1: 19–31.

Vaara, E., and Durand, R. (2012), 'How to make strategy research connect with broader issues that matter?', *Strategic Organization*, 10/3: 248–55.

Vaara, E., and Faÿ, E. (2011), 'How can a Bourdieusian perspective aid the analysis of MBA education?', *Academy of Management Learning and Education*, 10/1: 27–39.

Vaara, E., and Whittington, R. (2012), 'Strategy as practice: taking social practices seriously', *Academy of Management Annals*, 6/1: 285–336.

Van de Ven, A. H. (1992), 'Suggestions for studying strategy process: a research note', *Strategic Management Journal*, 13/S1: 169–88.

Whittington, R. (2006), 'Completing the practice turn in strategy research', *Organization Studies*, 27/5: 613–34.

(2007), 'Strategy practice and strategy process: family differences and the sociological eye', *Organization Studies*, 28/10: 1575–86.

Whittington, R., and Cailluet, L. (2008), 'The crafts of strategy: special issue introduction', *Long Range Planning*, 41/3: 241–7.

Wilson, D. C., and Jarzabkowski, P. (2004), 'Thinking and acting strategically: new challenges for interrogating strategy', *European Management Review*, 1/1: 14–20.

An economies-of-worth perspective on strategy as practice: justification, valuation and critique in the practice of strategy

JEAN-PASCAL GOND, BERNARD LECA and CHARLOTTE CLOUTIER

Introduction[1]

How do individuals justify their viewpoints during public disputes? What practices do they mobilize to so do? How do they proceed to evaluate whether a state of affairs is fair or unfair? The term 'economies-of-worth' – sometimes also called 'French pragmatist sociology' or the 'School of Conventions' – describes a set of French sociological works that address these questions. These works, described by Baert and Carreira da Silva (2010: 43) as 'the most important post-Bourdieu treatise in French sociology' (see also Stark 2000), focus on the competences of actors to reach agreements in mundane situations of disputes (Boltanski 2012 [1990]; 2013; Boltanski and Thévenot 2006 [1991]; Thévenot 2007). They do so in particular by building a comprehensive framework to analyse how social actors evaluate the worth of things and beings across multiple social spheres, establish equivalences between them and, in so doing, forge agreements that enable collective action (Boltanski and Thévenot 2006 [1991]). Initially, these works sought to distance themselves from the critical sociology of Karl Marx or Pierre Bourdieu, notably by refusing to explain social relations by means of structures, power or violence but, rather, by means of actors' *practices* (Boltanski 2012 [1990]; Cochoy 2000). Such practices are broadly defined

to include the discursive, cognitive and material resources that actors deliberately mobilize in specific social situations. As such, they are consistent with most definitions currently in use in strategy-as-practice studies (for example, Reckwitz 2002; Schatzki, Knorr Cetina and von Savigny 2001). Among the diversity of social practices that fit this description, however, economies-of-worth scholars have paid particular attention to the practices of *justification, valuation* and *critique,* which they deem to be essential for solving disputes or dealing with injustice in everyday social life.

Such a focus makes the economies-of-worth framework a fitting perspective to advance current research in strategy as practice. Despite a growing body of studies elucidating different aspects of the practice of strategy, surprisingly little is known of the normative, evaluative and critical practices that underlie the making of strategy (Seidl and Whittington 2014; Vaara and Whittington 2012; Whittington 2006). This comes as a surprise given that strategy practitioners spend a great deal of their time justifying (Hendry 2000), evaluating (Simons 1995) and defending their strategic decisions in the wake of criticisms from staff, board members, analysts and other stakeholders (Whittington *et al.* 2003). Furthermore, in theorizing the relationships between multiple forms of worth and actors' everyday situated action (Cloutier and Langley 2013), not only can the economies-of-worth framework support studies of strategy-making in pluralistic contexts (Denis, Langley and Rouleau 2007), it can also help address recurrent calls by strategy-as-practice

[1] We thank Damon Golsorkhi, Thibault Daudigeos, Charles Kirschbaum and Gazi Islam for their helpful comments on a prior version of this chapter.

scholars for bridging micro-level praxis with larger social phenomena (Seidl and Whittington 2014; Whittington 2006). As such, the economies-of-worth framework offers a relevant and interesting lens through which to advance our understanding of strategy as a social practice.

Thus far, relatively little strategy-as-practice research has deliberately built on the economies-of-worth framework. This lack of engagement is surprising given the natural fit of this stream of research with a situated social practice perspective (Annisette and Richardson 2011; Bénatouïl 1999; Silber 2003) and the growing attention that strategy scholars are paying to institutional pluralism (Kraatz and Block 2008) and organizational hybridity (Battilana and Lee 2014). This situation may be explained by the strategy community's lack of exposure to these works and by the combination of this perspective with concepts from institutional theory in prior empirical studies (for example, McInerney 2008; Patriotta, Gond and Schultz 2011; Ramirez 2013) that may have blurred its distinctive flavour and specific potential (Brandl et al. 2014; Cloutier and Langley 2013; Daudigeos and Valiorgue 2010; Diaz-Bone 2014; Gond and Leca 2012).

In this chapter, we provide a short introduction to the economies-of-worth framework and discuss its particular relevance for studying the practice of strategy. Focusing on the framework developed by Boltanski and Thévenot (2006 [1991]; 1987), our aim is to specify what makes this stream of research specific and distinctive from other perspectives, such as Bourdieu's sociology or institutional logics, and to present its potential and value added for investigating new areas of research in strategy such as justification, valuation and critique. The chapter is organized as follows. First, we provide an historical account of the emergence of the economies-of-worth framework, and then we introduce its key concepts, including *order of worth*, *worlds*, *critique*, *test*, and *compromise*. Next we show how the framework has been used by strategic management scholars to investigate problems of justification in pluralistic contexts, rhetorical strategies of justification and the resolution of inter-organizational conflicts. A third section opens perspectives for better integrating the economies-of-worth framework with strategy-as-practice

research. The chapter concludes by reaffirming the potential distinctive contribution of French pragmatist sociology for strategy-as-practice researchers.

The emergence of economies of worth

From critical sociology to the sociology of critical capacities

Economies of worth originated in an attempt to address a paradox inherent to the 'critical intention' of French classical sociology and critical sociology, both inspired by the works of Pierre Bourdieu. The intent of Bourdieu's sociology (see, for example, Bourdieu 1986; Bourdieu and Passeron 1977 [1970]) was to unveil the structures of domination at work in society in order to favour the emancipation of agents (Golsorkhi et al. 2006). This project aligns with French classical sociology's willingness to uncover the 'illusion' of actors' self-perceptions of their social reality by providing them with a more 'accurate' representation of the actual social order in which they live (Durkheim 1993 [1937]), which is made apparent by 'professional sociologists' thanks to their 'objective' methods of inquiry (Boltanski 2012 [1990]). Following this approach, sociological knowledge is itself 'critical,' as it aims to provide actors with the knowledge they need to understand their own social situations.

This perspective creates an important blind spot, however, as it fails to clarify its own normative standpoint:

> [I]t has the defect of revealing inequalities, described as so many injustices, *without clarifying the position of justice on the basis of which they can be defined as such* (Boltanski 2012: 26 [1990: 58], emphasis added).

It also tends to assume that sociologists have a capacity to understand injustice that, to some extent, is denied to laypeople. Nevertheless, prior empirical work conducted by Boltanski, Thévenot and others on the ordinary practices of 'denunciation' (when individuals denounce or complain that a particular way of being or doing in social life is not 'right' or acceptable) suggested that laypeople – not only sociologists – also have critical capacities of their own (Boltanski and Thévenot 1983; 1989; Boltanski, Darré and Schiltz 1984). The sociology of critical capacities used in ordinary contexts of disputes can address the blind spot of critical sociology by revealing the underlying mechanisms inherent to all types of critical activity in society. It can also uncover the value scale or principles of equivalence that are tacitly used by critical sociologists when they criticize various aspects of the existing social order (Boltanski 2012 [1990]; Cochoy 2000). Such a shift in perspective involves a shift from a 'critical sociology' to a 'sociology of critical capacities' (Boltanski and Thévenot 1999).

Consequently, building on Chomsky (1975) and Habermas (1984), Boltanski (2012 [1990]) suggests that ordinary people share a set of common competences that allows them to engage in justification work or critique and, by so doing, denounce what they view as unfair or protest that the values they believe in are not being respected (Boltanski, Darré and Schiltz 1984). To specify this point, Boltanski and Thévenot adopt as an axiom the idea of a 'common humanity', which states that all social actors 'belong to humanity on the same basis' (Boltanski and Thévenot 2006: 74). On this basis, actors can mobilize justifications based on multiple grounds, each of which grants them 'more agency' than is typically assumed in the Bourdieusian model of habitus (see, for example, Cochoy 2000) or in the institutional logics framework (see, for example, Pernkopf-Konhäusner 2014). Although this axiom is restrictive – it excludes social contexts within which human beings would see their humanity denied, such as slavery, even though such situations are obviously relevant to the social analysis of justice (see Godechot 2009: 195) – it has the virtue of enhancing actors' agency by pointing to the existence of an autonomous sense of justice and possible indignation shared by all human beings.

A second consequence of this positioning is that, from this perspective, 'critical' or 'Bourdieusian' scholars no longer hold the monopoly over lucidity and critical capacity (Boltanski 2012 [1990]). Thus, the role of these scholars is not to 'free' social actors from Bourdieu's 'biographical illusion' (Bourdieu 1986) but, rather, to account for the diversity of social actors' justifications and the multiple forms of critiques they voice. In so doing, they are able to uncover the underlying principles at stake in the process of denunciation articulated by critical sociology (Boltanski 2013). Accordingly, the position of professional sociologists and of laypersons becomes 'symmetric' in the analysis: from this perspective, both categories of actors have critical capacities.

Third, the ambition of the economies-of-worth perspective is not only to account for agents' justifications and the logics underlying them but also to clarify what allows for these critiques to be heard by others and to produce social effects (Boltanski and Thévenot 1999). Inspired by the early developments of actor–network theory (see, for example, Boltanski and Thévenot 2006 [1991]: 20), the economies-of-worth framework offers insights into the elements that might favour or improve the deployment of critical capacities (and thus agency), notably by considering the role of objects or material artefacts in critical activities and by focusing on the specific 'social situations' or 'critical moments' when critique takes place, rather than focusing solely on actors' cognitive capacities (Boltanski 2012 [1990]; Boltanski and Thévenot 2006 [1991]).

Fourth, and finally, there is no intention within the economies-of-worth perspective to offer an overall framework for understanding social interactions. Consequently, it can be combined with other approaches such as actor–network theory or ethnomethodology (see, for example, Blondeau and Cevin 2004; Thévenot 1984). As an analytical framework, the economies-of-worth framework is meant to be combined with other approaches so as to better unveil actors' critical competences and the multiple regimes of action that they use when engaging in critique (for example, Denis, Langley and Rouleau 2007).

Capturing actors' competences within and across regimes

The overall aim of the economies-of-worth framework is thus to study how actors use their competences in situated actions (Boltanski 2012 [1990]; Boltanski and Thévenot 1999; Boxenbaum 2014; Thévenot 2001; 2006 [1991]). To account for the logic behind the behaviours of actors, Boltanski and Thévenot (2006 [1991]) refer to the notion of *regime* (in French, *régime*). Consistent with their emphasis on actors' competences, Boltanski and Thévenot's intention here is to account for the multiple modes of action that actors need to be competent in, in order to evolve within complex, pluralistic contexts (Pernkopf-Konhäusner 2014). As Thévenot (2006: 6) puts it:

> She too (the actor) is confronted by a plurality of models, not these of the social theorist, but those that laypersons usually use to comprehend events in terms action, to understand what others do, or to reassess one's own behaviour. For the subject of action, plurality isn't about classification, it is about one's connection to the world. Indeed, a person's integrity as well as his integration within a community depends on his ability to compose with such plurality.

In so doing, the goal of Boltanski and Thévenot is to move beyond the description of practices and account for the logics on which actors rely to 'coordinate' their actions, notably by capturing the specific competences involved in achieving coordination (Boltanski 2012 [1990]; Thévenot 2006; 2007). While the list of such regimes continues to grow, researchers have already identified several of them on the basis of various criteria (Thévenot 2010). Boltanski (2012: 68–78 [1990: 129–47]) has defined four different regimes of action depending on whether a regime involves a dispute or not, and whether it is possible to justify action through a system of equivalence. Table 11.1 provides an overview of this typology of regimes of action.

For example, the regime of 'peace in agape' refers to situations in which actors are ready to give without expecting anything in return, and can be exemplified by two people in love with each other. Principles of equivalence are of no use in such contexts, as 'counting' activities can hardly help establish the sincerity of love. Equivalence is not an issue either in the regime of 'dispute in violence', because, when a dispute occurs, dialogue is impossible and actors resort to violence to solve their conflict. In contrast with these two situations, principles of equivalence are central in Boltanski's two other regimes of action. The regime of 'peace in fairness' refers to situations in which actors behave routinely. While rules are not questioned, actors will be careful to ensure that everyone behaves in an appropriate way. Routines embed principles of equivalence, and hence ensure the fair distribution of objects and status among people: respecting routines suffices for maintaining peace, and following them is regarded as appropriate behaviour. Finally, the regime of 'dispute in justice' refers to situations in which a dispute occurs between actors who can argue about justice or fairness without resorting to violence. In such situations, actors must publicly justify their claims and engage in dialogue in order to arrive at some form of resolution. To do so, they will rely either tacitly or explicitly on existing conventions or principles of equivalence to evaluate the situation and solve their dispute. According to Boltanski and Thévenot, actors can easily shift from one regime of action to another in their daily activities.

The last regime, 'dispute in justice', offers the best opportunity to apprehend the full set of principles of equivalence that actors are likely to

Table 11.1 Boltanski's four regimes of action

		Nature of the relationships between actors	
		Dispute	Peace
Possibility of justifying action through a system of equivalence	Yes	**Justice** Disputes can refer to existing principles of equivalence to be solved	**Fairness** Peace between actors is ensured through a fair distribution of things
	No	**Violence** Disputes occur without any form of justification	**Love (Agapè)** Peace results from the freely agreed submission of actors to each other

Source: Matrix developed from Boltanski (2012: 68–78 [1990: 129–47]).

mobilize in order to justify their action, as, in this context, actors have to formulate and articulate their rationales to justify the pursuit or interruption of a course of action. The broader research programme of French pragmatist sociology led by Boltanski and Thévenot in the late 1980s was aimed precisely at empirically uncovering these multiples forms of justification, by studying in a variety of contexts how actors justified what they thought was fair and unfair (Boltanski 2012 [1990]; Thévenot 1989). A first mapping of possible justifications (Boltanski and Thévenot 1987) was subsequently developed on the basis of eleven empirical studies later published in a collection edited by the authors entitled *Justesse et justice dans le travail* (Boltanski and Thévenot 1989; for an overview of these studies, see Jagd 2011: 348). This book complemented earlier works of this research team about denunciations (Boltanski, Darré and Schiltz 1984) and was used by Boltanski (2012 [1990]) to elaborate additional conceptual elements of what would form the economies-of-worth framework. The consolidated version of the economies-of-worth framework appears in the book *On Justification: Economies of Worth* (Boltanski and Thévenot 2006 [1991]), which was first published in French in 1991, then translated into English in 2006. We rely on this seminal book to present the core elements of the economies-of-worth framework.

The economies-of-worth framework

As discussed above, the economies-of-worth framework captures the 'grammars of justification' mobilized by actors in real-life contexts and builds on an axiom of 'common humanity', according to which there is a shared sense of justice among human beings. Under the constraint of justification, people, in order to be heard, have to ground their statements in what others consider is a legitimate worth. For Boltanski and Thévenot (2006 [1991]), there is a 'limited plurality' of principles that can be used to establish such a legitimate worth during a dispute. The aim of the economies-of-worth framework is to capture this 'limited plurality' in orders of worth and provide a set of core concepts to explain how they are mobilized by actors on a day-to-day basis.

Orders of worth and common worlds

Orders of worth correspond to higher-order principles that can be mobilized by actors to justify their claims. Because orders of worth point to specific representations of the common good, they play the role of ultimate principles of justification on which actors can agree. One can find a plurality of definitions of the common good across social spheres, however, and, accordingly, there is a plurality of orders of worth. According to Boltanski and Thévenot (2006 [1991]), several 'common worlds' organized around specific orders of worth can be distinguished. Specifically, their original framework distinguishes between six 'common worlds' ('cities' or 'polities', depending on how the French word *cité* is translated), each of which is related to a different order of worth: the *civic* world, the world of *fame*, the *market* world, the *industrial* world, the *domestic* world and the *inspired* world. To describe the principles of equivalence upon which these common worlds are organized, the authors rely on a systematic analysis of classical works of political philosophy, as these texts 'clarified and formalized' the competences that people mobilize in disputes in order to reach a form of social equilibrium. Table 11.2 provides a brief description of each of these six common worlds.

This list of six worlds proposed by Boltanski and Thévenot was never meant to be exhaustive, and other worlds have been identified subsequently. For instance, Lafaye and Thévenot (1993) and Thévenot, Moody and Lafaye (2000) have proposed the *green* world as an additional 'common world', and Boltanski and Chiapello (2005 [1999: 154–89]) have proposed a *projective* (or *project*) world, to reflect the 'new spirit of capitalism'. Table 11.3 presents a consolidated overview of these eight worlds. In line with Boltanski and Thévenot's (2006 [1991]) original framework, each of these eight worlds specifies how legitimacy is assessed in each world, what tests demonstrate actors' worth, the types of objects and actors populating it and the world's relationship with time and space. The orders of worth inherent to each world can be best observed when usual interactions or social coordination are disrupted – that is, during moments that Boltanski and Thévenot (2006 [1991]) have called 'critical moments'.

Table 11.2 Summary description of the common worlds

Common worlds	Descriptions
Civic	The realm of duty and solidarity. In this world, what is valued is that which is united, representative, legal, official and free. Individuals in this world accede to worth by freely joining and being part of a collective; their individual will subordinated to the general will – that which seeks the common good, the good of all. Leaders are elected and valued because they represent the aspirations of the masses. To place individual interests ahead of collective interests is panacea in this world. One for all, and all for one.
Industrial	The realm of measures and efficiency. In this world, what is valued is precise, functional, professional, productive, efficient and useful. A world in which technological objects and scientific methods take centre stage. Optimization and progress are noble pursuits. All forms of 'waste' are frowned upon. Actors in this world are professional, hard-working, focused and thorough. Perfection is to be found in the optimally functioning system (whether mechanical, technological or human).
Market	The realm of money and the market. In this world, what is valued is rare, expensive, valuable and profitable. The law of the market prevails, and actors deemed worthy are those who know how to take advantage of it and reap its rewards, such as wealth. Wealth is an end, and individuals with dignity in this world are 'detached from the chains of belonging and liberated from the weight of hierarchies'. This gives them the ability to judge market opportunities objectively and unemotionally, and thus 'win'.
Domestic	The realm of the 'family', in its symbolic sense. In this world, what is valued is that which is firm, loyal, selfless and trustworthy. Hierarchy and tradition play central roles. Superiors are informed and wise, and must care and nurture those who are lower in the hierarchy. Great importance is attached to one's upbringing, as upbringing and good manners reflect where one 'comes from'. The priority of actors in this world is on preserving, protecting and nurturing the unit (family, guild, group, etc.) to which one belongs, as, without this unit, one is nothing.
Inspirational	The realm of creativity and 'art'. In this world, what is most valued is that which is passionate, emergent, spontaneous and inspired. The creative journey, with its ups and downs, its moments of elation and its subsequent feelings of doubt and suffering, is what life 'is all about': an adventure, an endless horizon of mystery and a discovery. The journey is the end, not the means. Moments of 'genius' are unpredictable and unexpected: they appear in flashes and sparks. Actors in this world are repulsed by habit and shun routines. They dream, imagine, take risks and 'live'.
Fame	The realm of fame and popularity. In this world, what is valued is that which is visible, famous, influential, fashionable and recognized. The worth of actors is determined by the opinion of others. To be banal, unknown or forgotten is shameful. An 'undiscovered' genius is a contradiction, as a genius must be known to be considered so. Any and all means for achieving fame and recognition are sought after and legitimate.

Source: From Cloutier and Langley (2013), after Boltanski and Thévenot (2006 [1991]).

Critique and critical moments

A regime of justification will be mobilized by actors in contexts of disputes. Thus, in order to observe how actors justify their positions, one must focus on the 'critical moments' in a dispute, when actors criticize each other. Indeed, differences in organizational actors' justifications are often identifiable by means of the *critiques* that each addresses to the other in such situations. These will often take the form of reasons that each partner gives to explain why a particular course of action is not acceptable (Boltanski and Thévenot 2006 [1991]) or why particular evaluative criteria are not appropriate for assessing a task or a decision (Lamont 2012). For example, a CEO arguing that investments in green technology (*green world*) should not be pursued because they do not contribute to increasing shareholder value is critiquing the view that business decisions should be made on any basis other than the market (*market world*). A theatre director crashing his car into the front doors of the French presidential palace to denounce cuts in the public subsidies he receives seeks to remind politicians that artistic activities may have some intrinsic worth (*inspired world*) that cannot be captured solely by the financial success of a cultural establishment (*market world*).

Test of worth

In the desire to resolve a dispute, actors may choose to subject a decision or an action to a *test*, in order to determine whether or to what extent it

Table 11.3 Consolidated overview of eight 'worlds' according to the economies-of-worth framework

'Common worlds'	Market	Industrial	Civic	Domestic	Inspired	Fame	Green*	Project**
Mode of evaluation (worth)	Price, cost	Technical efficiency	Collective welfare	Esteem, reputation	Grace, singularity, creativeness	Renown, fame	Environmental friendliness	Connection, flexibility, adaptability
Test	Market competitiveness	Competence, reliability, planning	Equality and solidarity	Trustworthiness	Passion, enthusiasm	Popularity, audience, recognition	Sustainability, renewability	Transition from one project to another
Form of relevant proof	Monetary	Measurable criteria, statistics	Formal, official	Oral, exemplary, personally warranted	Emotional involvement and expression	Semiotic	Ecological ecosystem	Reputation
Qualified objects	Freely circulating market good or service	Infrastructure, project, technical object, method, plan	Rules and regulations, fundamental rights, welfare policies	Patrimony, locale, heritage	Emotionally invested body or item, the sublime	Sign, media	Pristine wilderness, healthy environment, natural habitat	Project, networks
Qualified human beings	Customers, consumers, merchants, sellers	Engineers, professionals, experts	Equal citizens, solidarity unions	Authorities	Creative beings, artists	Celebrities	Environmentalists, ecologists	High-social-capital, adaptable individuals
Time formation	Short-term, flexibility	Long-term planned future	Perennial	Customary part	Eschatological, revolutionary, visionary moment	Vogue, trend	Future generations	Time of the project
Space formation	Globalization	Cartesian space	Detachment	Local, proximal anchoring	Presence	Communication network	Planet ecosystem	Network

Source: Adapted from Boltanski and Thévenot (2006: 159–211),
* Thévenot, Moody and Lafaye (2000: 241),
** Boltanski and Chiapello (1999: 161–92).

meets the criteria for determining worthiness within a given world (Dansou and Langley 2012). Such tests are not necessarily done explicitly, but are reflected in the rhetorical arguments that one actor might address to another in an effort to convince the other that he/she is 'right' (Boltanski and Thévenot 2006 [1991]). If the test criteria are met, then the decision or proposed course of action is deemed worthy within that world, and the dispute is resolved. If not, actors may propose applying a different test, based on criteria stemming from a different world, or they may propose a different course of action, and re-subject it to the same test. This process might be pursued until an agreement is reached, or actors may give up and choose to walk away and leave their dispute unresolved (in which case flare-ups may recur in the future).

Tests may also apply to specific persons. Indeed, as a spokesperson for a particular world, a specific actor may also be subject to a test in order to determine whether he/she is 'worthy' enough to represent the interests of a given world in a dispute. These nuances are interesting as they allow for considerable analytical richness when applied to empirical data. For example, certain large multinational corporations (MNCs) have begun to hire former non-governmental organization (NGO) executives to handle relations with environmental or community stakeholders. A spokesperson with such a background may (or so the company hopes) be deemed more worthy in the eyes of these stakeholders as compared to a public relations professional with no prior relations in the field. Stakeholders will probably subject the hiring decision to a test of worth of their own in order to decide whether they endorse the decision (by accepting to work with the person or not, for example).

Device

According to Boltanski and Thevenot (2006: 12 [1991]), the establishment of a proof in the context of a test of worth does not rely only on actors' cognitive engagement:

> Proofs oriented toward the sense of what is just have in common with scientific proofs the fact that they both rely not only on mental states, in the form of convictions or beliefs, but also on stable

and coherent arrangements, and thus on objects subject to general assessment.

Accordingly, objects may be used to evaluate worth on a variety of criteria, and, once agreement on criteria has been reached, these may be sealed by means of a *device* (in French – *dispositif*), which usually takes some material form (such as a protocol, an award, a form (to fill), a dedicated space, etc.). Hence, the purpose of objects within the economies-of-worth framework is both to support the *evaluation of various types of worth* in a context of disputes and to provide a *device* to bind actors together in some concrete way by triggering a change in practice, which over time might become institutionalized and embedded into new routines (D'Adderio 2008; 2010; Leonardi and Barley 2008).

The search for a compromise and the matrix of critiques

The recognition and definition of a variety of common worlds highlights the complexity of reaching agreements in situations of dispute that involve a plurality of worlds and associated orders of worth. The search for a compromise will be considerably facilitated if actors agree to resolve their dispute within one common world, and hence rely on the principles of equivalence and tests of worth structuring that particular world to do so. In such contexts, criticisms can still exist, but they will generally focus on whether the material device used to conduct the test is appropriate, or revolve around denouncing biases related to the implicit presence of criteria from another world affecting the test being conducted. Despite these, however, an agreement can usually be reached by removing any ambiguity in the test and making it as pure as possible.

The outcomes of situations in which actors fail to agree on which world is most appropriate for resolving a dispute are far less certain. In such situations, actors cannot rely on the well-established principle of equivalence of one world for doing so but, rather, have to develop a new or specific test of worth that mixes principles of equivalence from two or more worlds. The agreement thus reached is often complex and less stable, as it can easily be denounced from the perspective of the other worlds involved.

To clarify these situations and study how common worlds conflict with each other, Boltanski and Thévenot (2006: 237–73 [1991: 291–334]) have developed a 'matrix of critiques', in which they systematically analyse how each of the six common worlds might criticize the other five. For instance, corporate lobbying activities that make perfect sense from a market world perspective (for example, accessing new markets for genetically modified organisms – GMOs) or an industrial world perspective (such as being allowed to develop new GMOs) can be criticized from a civic world perspective (for instance, pro-GMO lobbying being denounced as an anti-democratic practice). Similarly, government subsidies granted to artistic organizations for civic reasons (*civic world*) (such as the 'cultural exception' argument for supporting French cinema) can be denounced by private entities that are not funded by the state on the basis that such subsidies distort competition (*market world*). Although Boltanski and Thévenot's matrix suggests that the types of critiques addressed by one world to another are relatively predictable, the question of whether one type of criticism will dominate in a given interaction remains an empirical question.

Distinctiveness of the economies-of-worth perspective

Overall, the economies-of-worth framework provides a coherent set of concepts to account for the processes whereby actors justify their viewpoints and engage in collective action. Despite a specific focus on justification as a set of activities involving the critical capacities of actors, frequently asked questions about the framework relate to its distinctiveness in contrast with other approaches, such as Bourdieu's critical sociology or the institutional logics perspective. Our account of the historical emergence of the economies-of-worth framework makes it clear how this perspective specifically addresses the blind spot arising from the normative foundations of critical activity within Bourdieu's sociology. As already discussed, by addressing this gap the economies-of-worth framework clearly

departs from critical sociology. By focusing on how laypeople in ordinary contexts of disputes engage with a plurality of orders of worth, Boltanski and Thévenot provide actors with more agency than Bourdieu does. In particular, the economies-of-worth framework accounts for the capacities that actors have to mobilize orders of worth from multiple common worlds. The social competences related to justification are regarded as common to all human beings – whatever their 'habitus' or status may be. Another distinctive element is the downtuning of power in the economies-of-worth framework. The omission of power as an explanatory mechanism is deliberate. By its very construction, the economies-of-worth framework avoids the question of *power relations* in order to focus on *how justification and agreement are collectively achieved in specific institutional spheres*:

> While the existence of power relations clearly has to be acknowledged, it was important for me [in the economies-of-worth framework] to show that, in certain situations, people can reach justifiable and universalizable agreements that are capable of holding up in the face of denunciations that characterize them as mere power relations disguised as relation of justice (Boltanski, 2012: 41 [1990: 83]).

Bracketing power was thus a necessary step to clarify the normative basis of critical sociology and make the critical activities of actors explicit. This being said, Boltanski (2011 [2009]; 2013) has shown that the sociology of actors' critical capacity, as captured by the economies-of-worth framework, can be combined with critical sociology to understand how and when actors' power comes into play, notably by studying whether and how they immunize themselves from the imperatives of justification. Although this position has recently been critically discussed by CMS scholars (see, for example, Parker 2013; Willmott 2013), it remains an original perspective for studying pragmatically whether and how actors' critical activities produce social effects, hence moving critical management studies beyond their 'anti-performative' stance (Fournier and Grey 2000).

The relationship between the economies-of-worth framework and the institutional logics perspective is somewhat less explicit, however. Despite obvious

Table 11.4 Comparison of assumptions between institutional logics and the economies-of-worth frameworks

	Friedland and Alford	Boltanski and Thévenot
Label	Logics.	'Worlds' or 'orders of worth' (terms are used alternately).
Definition	Organizing principles of the central institutions of the capitalist West that shape individual preferences and organizational interests and that help frame collective action.	Ordering principles based on shared definitions of the 'common good' that people establish for the purpose of assessing themselves and one another; they enable collective action.
Assumptions about change	Shifts between logics may occur when a field evolves; stability is the result of actors seeking to conform to or realign with dominant logics.	Stability is negotiated locally on an ongoing basis by competent actors in public debates over what is legitimate or not.
Domain-specificity	Assumes that, in certain domains, certain logics tend to prevail (e.g. each logic parses to a specific domain).	'Worlds' refer to accepted definitions of the common good that can apply to any domain.
Mutual exclusivity	Logics are mutually exclusive; can sometimes be interdependent, and multiple logics can coexist, although it is expected that one or at most two logics will dominate in a given field.	Worlds not seen as interdependent, but multiple worlds can coexist in the form of arrangements or compromises.
Level of analysis	Primary focus is at field level (higher-order logics are instantiated at the level of the field).	Primary focus is at the level of wider society.
Term used for defining what is acceptable	Legitimacy or appropriateness – defined as 'Yes' or 'No'; beliefs, practices, etc. are either legitimate or not legitimate.	Worthiness – can be assessed by degrees; beliefs, practices, actors, objects can be more or less legitimate depending on certain criteria.
Agency of actors	Limited; logics are usually taken for granted.	Considerable; social actors can draw on worlds strategically to suit their purpose.

Source: Cloutier and Langley (2013: 11).

similarities and potential complementarities (Brandl *et al.* 2014; Cloutier and Langley 2013; Daudigeos and Valiorgue 2010; Gond and Leca 2012), the epistemological and ontological stances of each approach are quite different. Table 11.4 summarizes some of these key differences.

For example, within the economies-of-worth framework, conflict and change are normal (Gond and Leca 2012). Stability, when it is achieved, is by definition temporary, whereas, within the institutional logics perspective, stability is the norm, and change is the exception. The assumption of agency within the economies-of-worth framework is thus much more pronounced than it is within the institutional logics perspective (Boxenbaum 2014; Pernkopf-Konhäusner 2014). The economies-of-worth framework also views social interactions as more fluid and changeable than is the case for institutional logics or for Bourdieu's sociology, as explained by Friedland (2009: 29, emphasis added):

Boltanski and Thévenot's conventions of equivalence, and the material, embodied practices through which they are enacted, *are intentionally conceptualized so as to be transposable across institutional domains.*

Finally, 'worthiness' within the economies-of-worth framework (the equivalent of which is 'legitimacy' within the institutional logics perspective) can be measured and granted in degrees, which is not usually the case for legitimacy (Deephouse and Suchman 2008).

The distinctive theoretical flavour of the economies-of-worth framework, with its focus on situated actions, actors' social competences and specific categories of practices that pertain to justification, denunciation and the search for socially acceptable agreement, thus makes it a particularly relevant perspective for the study of strategy as practice.

Economies of worth *in practice*

Although the ideas underlying the economies-of-worth framework have been discussed in the French-speaking sociological, organizational and management communities (for example, Jagd 2011; Livian and Herreros 1994), the almost fifteen-year wait for the translation of the economies of worth foundational book into English after its original publication certainly slowed its appropriation by English-speaking research communities (Brandl *et al.* 2014; Cloutier and Langley 2013; Daudigeos and Valiorgue 2010; Gond and Leca 2012; Rasheed, Moursli and Priem 2010). On account of its 'pragmatist' orientation, it was picked up relatively early by French-Canadian scholars working in the strategy-as-practice field (for example, Mesny, Roch, Langley, Rouleau, etc.), mainly as a means of exploring strategizing processes in pluralistic contexts. Other management and strategy scholars have mobilized the economies-of-worth framework to analyse strategic or inter-organizational dynamics that are relevant to strategy-as-practice scholarship, even though they may not have been explicitly anchored in this stream of research. We review these three perspectives in turn, focusing in each case on a couple of key illustrative studies.

Strategizing in pluralistic contexts

According to certain scholars, organizations, in order to have a clear view of the goals they must pursue, require the presence of a dominant logic (Prahalad and Bettis 1986) or coalition (Fligstein 1990). From this perspective, pluralism is viewed as problematic, as it is thought to inevitably trigger either conflict (for example, Ezzamel 1994) or inertia (for example, Westphal and Bednar 2005). Pluralism is frequent in organizations, however, and may be increasingly so, particularly as organizations become more complex (Kraatz and Block 2008). How are decisions about goals, performance metrics or stakeholder concerns addressed in such contexts?

In a 2007 article, Denis, Langley and Rouleau (2007) discuss at length how the economies-of-worth framework might be useful for exploring strategizing activities in pluralistic contexts. In particular, they suggest that the economies-of-worth framework can be helpful to view and analyse strategy-making as a dynamic process of negotiating an agreement and coordinating action within a perspective in which strategy is viewed less as the outcome of top management decisions and more as both a compromise between various orders of worth and the outcome of a process of valuation:

> Because individuals in an organization will not always identify with similar worlds and because a single individual may identify with multiple worlds, the invention and negotiation of conventions becomes critical to ensure coordination and cooperation (Denis, Langley and Rouleau 2007: 192).

The authors also argue that the economies-of-worth framework invites scholars to view *strategists as 'critics'* who think critically about the accepted orders of worth prevailing within their organization and who can see opportunities to frame their strategies in ways that are coherent with them, facilitating their acceptance and implementation. Conversely, strategists might introduce a new order of worth into a debate over strategy in order to alter organizational dynamics. Finally, they suggest that the economies-of-worth framework makes it possible to explore how *performance provides legitimacy.* In other words, the legitimacy of potential strategists to take part in the elaboration of an organization's strategy depends on those actors' capacity to demonstrate their 'worth' within the worlds most valued by the organization or their ability to mobilize alternative orders of worth in the process of strategy evaluation. Through these processes, the importance of specific worlds within the organization is reaffirmed.

To date, a handful of strategy-as-practice researchers have built on these ideas, some using the economies-of-worth framework and others not. For example, in a study that could have used the framework, Abdallah (2007) analyses the production of strategy as a process whereby a compromise between different worlds (creative and market) is negotiated through discourse in order to accommodate constituencies with different values. Daigle and Rouleau (2010), for their part, undertook a similar study, also in an arts organization, but this time using the economies-of-worth framework, which allowed them to see how organizational actors, in the production of strategic documents, managed to accommodate, through micro-compromises in the text itself, opposing artistic (inspired) and financial (market) objectives. What these and other studies show is that pluralism and actors' competences engaged in the formation of compromises may be more important and central to strategizing than traditional top-down approaches imply (Denis, Langley and Rouleau 2007; Jarzabkowski and Fenton 2006; Jarzabkowski, Sillince and Shaw 2010).

Finally, the economies-of-worth framework has been used to suggest that intra-organizational pluralism can be a potential source of strategic strength by enabling innovation and enhancing creativity. For example, building on the economies-of-worth framework, Stark (2009) coined the term 'heterarchy' to describe an organizational design that is specific to organizations that seek to generate, rather than suppress, perplexing situations. Actors in these types of organizations recognize the legitimacy of plural rather than singular conceptions of what is worthy on the premise that ambiguity between different orders of worth favours creativity and innovation (Girard and Stark 2002). Based on his research, Stark argues that pluralistic organizations constitute unstable but highly adaptable organizations.

As a whole, these pioneering works have demonstrated the value added of the economies-of-worth framework for unpacking the complex process of coordination involved in strategizing, investigating whether and how multiple orders of worth are balanced, maintained or altered within organizations and evaluating the impact of strategic pluralism organizational outcomes such as innovation. Future studies of pluralistic strategizing could advance these perspectives by considering a broader range of orders of worth with which to investigate the tensions and paradoxes inherent in managing the more normative aspects of strategy. Such studies could also focus on 'hybrid' organizational contexts, such as social enterprises (Battilana and Lee 2014), for which a plurality of justification modes are routinely mobilized (Mair, Battilana and Cardenas 2012). By so doing, such studies shift researchers' analytical lens from within to outside organizational borders, allowing them to consider a broader range of outcomes produced by specific approaches to the strategic management of pluralistic contexts.

Rhetorical strategies of justification

A second stream of research that has engaged with the economies-of-worth framework has focused on the *strategic management of external legitimacy through the mobilization of appropriate 'orders of worth'*. Controversies involving the emergence of critiques from a plurality of stakeholders are particularly useful to help uncover the rhetorical processes whereby organizations engage in 'justification work', because it is usually in public contexts that actors are subjected to an imperative of justification (Patriotta, Gond and Schultz 2011; Ramirez 2013; Taupin 2012). Patriotta, Gond and Schultz (2011), for example, investigated how Vattefall, a German energy group, managed its moral legitimacy by engaging in justification work after an incident at one of its nuclear power plants. The hypersensitivity of Germans to the topics of environmentalism and nuclear energy fuelled an intense controversy over the issue that lasted several months and that engaged a vast set of stakeholders (such as environmentalist activists, politicians and journalists). The study's findings show how the corporation progressively diversified the number of orders of worth it mobilized – beyond the market and industrial worlds – in order to maintain its legitimacy in the wake of the criticisms it received, which were grounded in the civic, green and domestic worlds. Through its 'justification work', the focal organization could develop robust justifications to restore public agreement in its activities and thus maintain its licence to operate its remaining power plants.

Similarly, Ramirez (2013) and Taupin (2012) have both deepened the analysis of the role played by discursive practices in the maintenance or repair of legitimacy in the context of a crisis, while mobilizing even more elements of the original economies-of-worth framework. For example, by highlighting the central role of an 'experience of perceived injustice' as a triggering factor that pushes actors to engage in justification work, Ramirez (2013) comes back to an essential insight of Boltanski and Thévenot (2006 [1991]). His study shows in particular how the members of the British audit profession engaged in institutional work to repair their worth after having been heavily criticized for their lack of accountability. Focusing on the recent post-2008 crisis of the financial credit rating industry, Taupin (2012) documents the discursive changes in the industry over a ten-year period (2000–2010). His study uncovers the mechanisms and practices that serve to maintain the legitimacy of a whole industry despite continuing controversy. These include confirming the existence of prior regulation, qualifying objects according to concepts of regulation and adopting a 'circular rhetoric' that immunizes them from critique. Taupin's analysis usefully complements prior work by showing how difficult it is to reconcile several orders of worth in a meaningful way, notably in contexts that call for regulative reforms.

Although these three studies are positioned mainly in institutional theory rather than strategy as practice, they show nevertheless how the economies-of-worth framework can help shed light on the discursive micro-strategies that organizational actors might mobilize to maintain or repair their legitimacy when it is challenged, and hence informs works aimed at uncovering how strategizing impacts the day-to-day management of organizational legitimacy. These works tend to be over-focused on the discursive dimensions of the economies-of-worth framework, however, while neglecting the materiality of justification practices. In moving one step closer to the original axioms and conceptualization of practice proposed by the economies-of-worth framework, future research in this stream of study might consolidate and expand these insights by moving beyond the context of the written press to consider the various forums through which organizational actors can seek to build robust justification, such as trials, live press interventions and public hearings. While remaining 'public spaces', such contexts make it possible to consider the materiality of different justifications and their embodiment by specific spokespersons and not others.

Justification across organizations: strategizing partnerships

A third stream of organizational research that overlaps with strategy-as-practice study focuses on strategizing in the context of inter-organizational relationships. Because different organizations may belong to distinct social spheres and hence have different comprehensions of what is worthy, cross-sectoral partnerships often lead to conflictual relations. Consequently, such partnerships are particularly appropriate for investigating the critical

moments when distinct 'common worlds' clash (Jagd 2011). Mesny and Mailhot (2007), for example, investigated the case of an industry–university research partnership in which the market and industrial orders of worth dominated the justification discourse of the corporate partners, whereas the 'inspired world' and to some extent the 'civic' and 'domestic' orders of worth dominated that of academics. Most of the controversies that emerged were managed through two specific compromises. The first engaged the inspirational and market/industrial orders of worth by developing new concepts such as the notion of 'creative markets' (Mesny and Maillot 2007: 219–20). The second combined the world of fame and the civic world by describing the partnership in advertising material as a collective effort between academic and industry to 'promote innovation and socio-economic development' (220–1).

Cloutier (2009) and Cloutier and Langley (forthcoming) focus on partnerships between non-profit organizations and their funders to investigate how cooperation is achieved between organizations that mobilize quite different notions of worth to justify their actions. Thanks to a rich longitudinal data set, she identifies different types of compromise that partners negotiated to maintain cooperation. This study clarifies the material aspects of compromise and evaluates their robustness, on the basis of specific organizational contingencies and how orders of worth are combined.

Although these studies have highlighted the potential of the economies-of-worth framework to investigate the practices underlying cross-sectoral collaborations, much can still be done to understand how practices of justification are mobilized over time to stabilize or maintain alliances across organizations and over time. In particular, the role of materiality in sealing and solidifying strategic alliances by establishing robust forms of compromise could be further theorized.

As a whole, our brief review of prior research considering strategic practice and the economies-of-worth framework suggests that, even though pioneering studies have established the framework's potential for advancing several lines of thought within the strategy-as-practice domain, including within (pluralistic strategy-making), outside (rhetorical strategizing) and across organizational contexts (strategizing partnerships), such work is still in its infancy, and numerous follow-up studies are needed to further and better integrate strategy as practice and the economies-of-worth framework. Despite the above advances, there is still much to be gained by treating the economies-of-worth framework as a theoretical resource to help advance the strategy-as-practice research agenda. The value added of the economies-of-worth framework for strategy-as-practice scholars may also lie in further exploiting its focus on the specific practices of justification, critique and valuation in strategizing that have been neglected in prior works on strategy.

Uncovering new domains for studying strategy as practice

In our view, the economies-of-worth framework can help extend existing strategy-as-practice research by focusing on neglected dimensions of strategizing work (*justification as practice*), on the one hand, and by inviting a cross-fertilization of some of its insights with recent works in economic sociology (*valuation as practice*) or critical management studies (*critique as practice*), on the other.

Justification as practice

Much of the day-to-day work of strategists is of a rhetorical nature (Hyland 1998; Jarzabkowski and Sillince 2007). Strategists spend a considerable amount of time communicating (Mintzberg 1971) and justifying their strategies, and convincing others that these are indeed the ones the organization should follow (Mantere 2005; Spee and Jarzabkowski 2011). In other words, strategists' role is not only to define what strategic direction an organization should take but to also justify to others, including employees, board members, shareholders and other stakeholders, that such is also the *right* strategic direction to take under the circumstances – a task that is not always easy, as an organization's various stakeholders may not agree on what the organization's main strategic orientation is or should be (Cornelissen, Holt and

Zundel 2011; Ketokivi and Castañer 2004; Mantere and Sillince 2007; Pitt 2001).

One explanation for this is that organizations routinely have to juggle priorities that are not always compatible (Karpik 1972), such as those underlying innovation (inspired world), manufacturing processes (industrial world), profit-making (market world) and environmental responsibility (green world). Within this frame, an interesting question becomes: *under such circumstances, how do strategists, in practice, achieve strategic coherence* (Laurila and Lilja 2002; Nath and Sudharsham 1994)? Because it offers conceptual tools for understanding the source of such conflicts and how they might be resolved, the economies-of-worth framework provides an interesting lens through which to make sense of these dynamics. In this vein, strategy-as-practice studies that have used discursive or narrative approaches for analysing the work of strategists could be reanalysed for deeper insights using the economies-of-worth framework. For example, a study by Vaara and Tienari (2011) that looks at how organizational actors mobilized different narrative constructions of identities and interests (globalist, nationalist and Nordic) in the case of the cross-border merger of a financial services group is a case in point. Different ante-narratives are identified, some of which served to legitimize the merger and some of which served to resist it. Although the study helps uncover the different narratives and their unfolding over time, it does not show how the embedded tensions in them were resolved by actors. Given that the mergers did go through, some sort of resolution of differences must have been achieved, but how they came about is less clear. The economies-of-worth framework could help explain these processes, as it provides a grammar of justification that can be used to unpack the process whereby actors create equivalences between distinct approaches to the worth that prevails within the new entity.

Conversely, studies might also consider *how organizational actors become aware of the worlds to which organizational members might be responsive* and study *how they use them reflexively to persuade other actors to follow a particular course of action*. This can be the case internally, such as when actors try to advance or defend a particular agenda within an organization (greater or less focus on sustainability issues, for example), or, more broadly, at the level of the field. An example of the latter can be found in a study undertaken by McInerney (2008) that mobilizes the economies-of-worth framework. In his study of the shaping of the non-profit technology assistance field in the United States, various actors with stakes in the outcomes used position, context and charisma to advance different narratives and justifications on how work in the field 'ought to be done' in their efforts to shape the field to their advantage. Here justifications are approached in an instrumental manner and viewed as a potentially strategic tool to support institutional work. Although such a strategic approach to the economies-of-worth framework departs significantly from Boltanski and Thévenot's (2006 [1991]) initial approach, it is nevertheless fitting to analyse how strategy might be redefined. Similar analyses can be undertaken on topics such as how actors justify the maintenance of a corporate social responsibility strategy during an economic downturn, or the non-closure of an underperforming factory for political or social reasons, for example.

Valuation as practice

A second direction for advancing strategy-as-practice research points to the clarification of the formats, roles and uses of the principles of equivalence mobilized by actors to evaluate a given strategy's worth. Central to the economies-of-worth framework are the criteria used for evaluating worth and the problems related to the commensuration of multiple types of worth that may facilitate or prevent the formation of a consensus between actors. Organizational scholars have recently engaged with a growing stream of research on the social practice of valuation (Lamont 2012) by relying on the economies-of-worth framework, sometimes in combination with other concepts aiming at capturing how actors construct equivalences (see, for example, Callon and Muniesa 2005; Espeland and Stevens 1998; Karpik 2010). For instance, Reinecke (2010) investigated how multiple orders of worth were involved in the social construction of what a 'fair price' is in the Fair Trade industry, and

Huault and Rainelli (2011) highlight how forms of 'resistance to commensuration' made it difficult to reach an agreement on a single evaluation metric in the process of constructing a market for weather risk. Both studies show how the economies-of-worth framework can help theorize the dynamics at play in the construction of valuation devices, notably by uncovering the forms of worth that are at stake in such processes.

These insights are particularly relevant for analysing the role played by metrics and calculative devices in the doing of strategy. It is generally accepted that corporate leaders must strive to reconcile the claims of multiple stakeholders, which may reflect distinct types of worth. At the same time, to pilot or deploy their chosen strategy within the organization, they adopt management control systems that tend to focus managers' attention on a single or a limited set of metrics (Boussard 2001; Simons 1995). *How, then, are multiple forms of worth embedded within a given commensuration process? How do calculative devices support the building of strategies that value specific types of worth?* Future strategy-as-practice research could address these questions by investigating how agreements and disagreements emerge around the metrics used to evaluate or deploy organizational strategy.

In this vein, scholars theorizing the relationship between strategy-making and accounting practices might find inspiration in an emerging stream of studies that uses the economies-of-worth framework to uncover how multiple orders of worth are mobilized through accounting practice and devices (Annisette and Richardson 2011; Annisette and Trivedi 2013). Building again on the concept of heterarchy (Stark 2009), future research could also seek to uncover the practices that sustain the construction of calculative compromises between orders of worth within organizations and show how such practices reflect and affect corporate strategic positioning.

Finally, the economies-of-worth framework might be used to help explain why similar firms evolving in a given industry adapt differently to their competitive environment. The prevalence of profit as a motive might vary between firms (market criteria of worth having to coexist with civic or green criteria of worth), resulting in varied strategic responses to competitive demands. For example, Moursli and Cobbaut (2006) used the framework to show how organizational actors in respite care organizations applied different criteria of worth to define the notion of 'quality' care, which led to different types of service offerings across establishments within the industry (an establishment that 'feels like home', for example, as opposed to one that is 'highly efficient'). Similar studies in different industries or fields might uncover different dynamics and other types of emergent forms.

Critique as practice

By exploring criticism as a practical activity, the economies-of-worth framework can contribute to broadening the scope of strategy-as-practice research, notably by considering *how organizational forms other than corporations 'strategize'*. strategy-as-practice scholars may wish to extend their inquiries beyond organizations to social movements, in order to study the strategic practices of activists who challenge society's established order and related structures of domination. The economies-of-worth framework offers useful insights that complement the social movement approach currently used in organizational analysis (de Bakker *et al.* 2013; Tilly 2004; Zald and Berger 1978), particularly in situations of dispute in which actors must find a solution to their conflict without resorting to violence. In addition, different directions have been suggested about *how actors might use pragmatist sociology to criticize and challenge existing institutions*. Heinich (1998), for example, suggests that the economies-of-worth framework be used to investigate how mediation between contradictory interests is managed, and in practice, how consensus is achieved or reorganized. Thévenot (2006) goes one step further by recalling that the economies-of-worth framework was developed first and foremost to analyse a single regime, that of justice. He insists that other regimes should also be valued, but that the domination of capitalism in today's society tends to reduce their importance. For example, the 'agapè' regime of love and giving is dismissed as irrational by capitalist ideology. Consequently, Thévenot

suggests that promoting other regimes, based on different principles of equivalence, can be a way to radically question capitalism. This view echoes ongoing research that shows how capitalist ideas are progressively infiltrating an ever-growing number of spheres of social life that previously had been sheltered from them (for example, Zelizer 2005).

Boltanski (2011 [2009]), on the other hand, suggests that pragmatist sociology can also help actors *question transgressions made by the dominant worlds they refer to*. Such questioning is a mild form of criticism, however, as it usually leads to reform rather than to radical change. To overcome this, Boltanski (2011 [2009]) suggests that critics need to develop a 'meta critique', which can be elaborated by combining the economies-of-worth framework with critical sociology, from which it initially departed. While the economies-of-worth framework can help actors structure and publicize their critiques, critical sociology can help them consider alternative possibilities. Critical sociology unveils existing structures of domination and questions the prevailing consensus and the institutions that support them, which are usually taken for granted by actors (Boltanski 2011 [2009]).

These different suggestions move beyond grand critical discourses to offer a practice-based approach that shows how critical thinking can have practical effects. From a research perspective, such a move could potentially bridge practice-based approaches with the emerging research agenda on 'critical performativity' – defined as 'active and subversive intervention into managerial discourses and practices' (Spicer, Alvesson and Kärreman 2009: 538). Studying the practices underlying the making of strategy by actors and organizations seeking to radically transform corporate behaviour can significantly expand the scope of research undertaken by strategy-as-practice scholars and open up new perspectives through cross-fertilization with critically oriented scholars.

Conclusion

In sum, although a growing number of management studies have engaged with the economies-of-worth framework, surprisingly little is known about the underlying assumptions and context of emergence of this promising perspective and its relevance to strategy-as-practice scholarship. The aim of this chapter has therefore been to advance this burgeoning area of inquiry by providing an overview of the economies-of-worth framework, discussing its assumptions and origins, reviewing prior management studies that have used this framework and discussing its potential to advance current theorization of strategy as practice. Our review of prior research suggested that, despite the demonstrated potential of the economies-of-worth framework to understand the complex process of strategizing in pluralistic contexts, to analyse the rhetorical strategies of justification mobilized by organizations and to investigate strategizing as an inter-organizational phenomenon, its use within the strategy-as-practice domain is still emergent. Further cross-fertilization of the strategy-as-practice and economies-of-worth perspectives requires the study of strategizing empirically in hybrid organizational contexts, considering the material dimensions of justification and enlarging the scope of cross-sectoral collaborations currently under study.

In our view, 'taking strategy seriously' (Whittington et al. 2003; Whittington 2006) as a social practice also involves paying more attention to the normative/societal, evaluative and critical dimensions inherent to strategy-making. The economies-of-worth framework offers a timely and relevant perspective to address these three challenges by offering researchers the opportunity to empirically investigate 'justification as practice', 'valuation as practice' and 'criticism as practice'. We have outlined a research agenda along these three lines of research by focusing on how managers and executives justify their strategy in front of multiple publics, by unpacking the metrics developed and used by strategy practitioners to measure and assess the 'worth' of their strategies and by studying how actors who promote social critique themselves 'strategize' and critically engage with strategy-makers within and across organizations.

Delivering on this agenda could significantly expand current strategy-as-practice lines of inquiry and enable its cross-fertilization with business and society, economic sociology and critical management studies. At a time when strategy-as-practice scholars are concerned with 'micro-isolationism' – defined as the tendency to explain local activities in their own terms – and are in search of new theoretical perspectives to address this issue and shift the ontological lens of the field (Seidl and Whittington 2014), a consolidated practice-focused economies-of-worth framework could dynamically bridge local activities of justification, valuation and critique to the societally anchored higher orders of worth. Consequently, such a framework offers a welcome and relevant remedy for overcoming such 'micro-isolationism', notably through its unique and distinctive combination of insights from actor–network theory with the social sensitivity of a pragmatic approach to critique.

References

Abdallah, C. (2007), 'Production et appropriation du discours stratégique dans une organisation artistique', *Revue Française de Gestion*, 174: 61–76.

Annisette, M., and Richardson, A. (2011), 'Justification and accounting: applying sociology of worth to accounting research', *Accounting, Auditing and Accountability Journal*, 24/2: 229–49.

Annisette, M., and Trivedi, V. U. (2013), 'Globalization, paradox and the (un)making of identities: immigrant chartered accountants of India in Canada', *Accounting, Organizations and Society*, 38/1: 1–29.

Baert, P., and Carreira da Silva, F. (2010), *Social Theory in the Twentieth Century and Beyond*, 2nd edn. Cambridge: Polity.

Battilana, J., and Lee, M. (2014), 'Advancing research on hybrid organizing', *Academy of Management Annals*, 8/1: 397–441.

Bénatouïl, T. (1999), 'A tale of two sociologies: the critical and pragmatic stance in contemporary French sociology', *European Journal of Social Theory*, 2/3: 379–96.

Blondeau, C., and Sevin, J.-C. (2004), 'Entretien avec Luc Boltanski, une sociologie toujours mise à l'épreuve', ethnographiques, www.ethnographiques.org/2004/Blondeau,Sevin.

Boltanski, L. (2011 [2009]), *On Critique: A Sociology of Emancipation*. Cambridge: Polity.

(2012 [1990]), *Love and Justice as Competences.* Cambridge: Polity.

(2013), 'A journey through French-style critique', in du Gay, P., and Morgan, G. (eds.), *New Spirits of Capitalism? Crises, Justifications, and Dynamics*: 43–59. Oxford University Press.

Boltanski, L., and Chiapello, E. (2005 [1999]), *The New Spirit of Capitalism.* London: Verso.

Boltanski, L., Darré, Y., and Schiltz, M.-A. (1984), 'La dénonciation', *Actes de la Recherche and Sciences Sociales*, 51: 1–40.

Boltanski, L., and Thévenot, L. (1983), 'Finding one's way in social space: a study based on games', *Social Science Information*, 22/4–5: 631–80.

(1987), *Les économies de la grandeur.* Paris: Presses Universitaires de France.

(1989), *Justesse et justice dans le travail*, Paris: Presses Universitaires de France.

(1999), 'The sociology of critical capacity', *European Journal of Social Theory*, 2/3: 359–77.

(2006 [1991]), *On Justification: Economies of Worth.* Princeton University Press.

Bourdieu, P. (1986), 'L'illusion biographique', *Actes de la Recherche en Sciences Sociales*, 62–63: 69–72.

Bourdieu, P., and Passeron, J.-C. (1977 [1970]), *Reproduction in Education, Society and Culture.* London: Sage.

Boussard, V. (2001), 'Quand les règles s'incarnent: l'exemple des indicateurs prégnants', *Sociologie du Travail*, 43/4: 533–51.

Boxenbaum, E. (2014), 'Toward a situated stance in organizational institutionalism: contributions from French pragmatist sociology theory', *Journal of Management Inquiry*, 23/3: 319–23.

Brandl, J., Daudigeos, T., Edwards, T., and Pernkopf-Konhäuser, K. (2014), 'Why French pragmatism matters to organizational institutionalism', *Journal of Management Inquiry*, 23/3: 314–18.

Callon, M., and Muniesa, F. (2005), 'Economics markets as calculative devices', *Organization Studies*, 26/8: 1129–250.

Chomsky, N. (1975), *Reflections on Language.* New York: Pantheon Books.

Cloutier, C. (2009), 'Managing opportunity, managing power and managing difference: how non-profits strategically manage their relations with funders', PhD thesis. HEC Montreal.

Cloutier, C., and Langley, A. (2013), 'The logics of institutional logics: insights from French pragmatist sociology', *Journal of Management Inquiry*, 22/4: 360–80.

(forthcoming), 'Negotiating the moral aspects of purpose in single and cross-sector collaborations', *Journal of Business Ethics.*

Cochoy, F. (2000), 'L'économie des conventions comme dépassement des sociologies antérieures', in *Histoire et Reconstruction de la Sociologie*: chap. 13. University of Toulouse II – Le Mirail.

Cornelissen, J., Holt, R., and Zundel, M. (2011), 'The role of analogy and metaphor in the framing and legitimization of strategic change', *Organization Studies*, 32/2: 1701–16.

D'Adderio, L. (2008), 'The performativity of routines: theorising the influence of artefacts and distributed agencies on routine dynamics', *Research Policy*, 37/5: 769–89.

(2010), 'Artefacts at the centre of routines: performing the material turn in routine theory', *Journal of Institutional Economics*, 7/2: 197–230.

Daigle, P., and Rouleau, L. (2010), 'Strategic plans in arts organizations: a compromising tool between artistic and managerial values', *International Journal of Arts Management*, 12/3: 13–30.

Dansou, K., and Langley, A. (2012), 'Institutional work and the notion of test', *M@n@gement*, 15/5: 502–27.

Daudigeos, T., and Valiorgue, B. (2010), *'Convention Theory': Is There a French School of Organizational Institutionalism?*, RMT Working Paper no. 10–04. Grenoble École de Management.

De Bakker, F. G., den Hond, F., King, B., and Weber, K. (2013), 'Social movements, civil society and corporations: taking stock and looking ahead', *Organization Studies*, 34/5–6: 573–93.

Deephouse, D. L., and Suchman, M. (2008), 'Legitimacy in organizational institutionalism', in Greenwood, R., Oliver, C., Sahlin, K., and Suddaby, R. (eds.), *The Sage Handbook of Organizational Institutionalism*: 49–77. Thousand Oaks, CA: Sage.

Denis, J.-L., Langley, A., and Rouleau, L. (2007), 'Strategizing in pluralistic contexts: rethinking theoretical frames', *Human Relations*, 60/1: 179–215.

Diaz-Bone, R. (2014), 'Methodological positioning and perspectives: comparing economies of convention with the institutional logics approach', *Journal of Management Inquiry*, 23/3: 324–7.

Durkheim, É. (1993 [1937]), *Les règles de la méthode sociologique.* Paris: Presses Unitaires de France.

Espeland, W. N., and Stevens, M. L. (1998), 'Commensuration as a social process', *Annual Review of Sociology*, 24: 313–43.

Ezzamel, M. (1994), 'Organizational change and accounting: understanding the budgeting system in its organizational context', *Organization Studies*, 15/2: 213–40.

Fligstein, N. (1990), *The Transformation of Corporate Control*. Cambridge, MA: Harvard University Press.

Fournier, V., and Grey, R. (2000), '"At the critical moment": conditions and prospects for critical management studies', *Human Relations*, 53/1: 7–32.

Friedland, R. (2009), 'The endless fields of Pierre Bourdieu', *Organization*, 16/6: 1–31.

Girard, M., and Stark, D. (2002), 'Distributing intelligence and organizing diversity in new media projects', *Environment and Planning A*, 34/11: 1927–49.

Godechot, O. (2009), 'Book review: *On Justification: Economies of Worth*', *Cultural Sociology*, 3/1: 193–5.

Golsorkhi, D., Leca, B., Lounsbury, M., and Ramirez, C. (2009), 'Analysing, accounting for and unmasking domination: on our role as scholars of practice, practitioners of social science and public intellectuals', *Organization*, 16/6: 779–97.

Gond, J.-P., and Leca, B. (2012), *Theorizing Change in Pluralistic Institutional Contexts: What Can Economies of Worth and New-Institutionalism Learn from Each Other?*, LEM Working Paper no. 2012–15. University of Lille 1.

Habermas, J. (1984), *The Theory of Communicative Action*. Cambridge: Polity.

Heinich, N. (1998), *Ce que l'art fait à la sociologie*. Paris: Minuit.

Hendry, J. (2000), 'Strategic decision making, discourse, and strategy as social practice', *Journal of Management Studies*, 37/7: 955–77.

Huault, I., and Rainelli, H. (2011), 'A market for weather risk? Conflicting metrics, attempts at compromise and limits to commensuration', *Organization Studies*, 32/10: 1395–419.

Hyland, K. (1998), 'Exploring corporate rhetoric: metadiscourse in the CEO's letter', *Journal of Business Communication*, 35/2: 224–44.

Jagd, S. (2011), 'Pragmatic sociology and competing orders of worth in organizations', *European Journal of Social Theory*, 14/3: 343–59.

Jarzabkowski, P., and Fenton, E. (2006), 'Strategizing and organizing in pluralistic contexts', *Long Range Planning*, 39/6: 631–48.

Jarzabkowski, P., and Sillince, J. (2007), 'A rhetoric-in-context approach to building commitment to multiple strategic goals', *Organization Studies*, 28/11: 1639–65.

Jarzabkowski, P., Sillince, J., and Shaw, D. (2010), 'Strategic ambiguity as a rhetorical resource for enabling multiple interests', *Human Relations*, 63/2: 219–48.

Karpik, L. (1972), 'Les politiques et les logiques d'action de la grande entreprise industrielle', *Sociologie du Travail*, 14/1: 82–105.

    (2010), *Valuing the Unique: The Economies of Singularities*. Princeton University Press.

Ketokivi, M., and Castañer, X. (2004), 'Strategic planning as an integrative device', *Administrative Science Quarterly*, 49/3: 337–65.

Kraatz, M. S., and Block, E. S. (2008), 'Organizational implications of institutional pluralism', in Greenwood, R., Oliver, C., Sahlin, K., and Suddaby, R. (eds.), *The Sage Handbook of Organizational Institutionalism*: 243–75. Thousand Oaks, CA: Sage.

Lafaye, C., and Thévenot, L. (1993), 'Une justification écologique? Conflit dans l'aménagement de la nature', *Revue Française de Sociologie*, 34/4: 495–524.

Lamont, M. (2012), 'Toward a comparative sociology of valuation and evaluation', *Annual Review of Sociology*, 38: 201–21.

Laurila, J., and Lilja, K. (2002), 'The dominance of firm-level competitive pressures over functional-level institutional pressures: the case of Finnish-based forest industry firms', *Organization Studies*, 23/4: 571–87.

Leonardi, P. M., and Barley, S. R. (2008), 'Materiality and change: challenges to building better theory about technology and organizing', *Information and Organization*, 18/3: 159–76.

Livian, Y. F., and Herreros, G. (1994), 'L'apport des économies de la grandeur: une nouvelle grille d'analyse des organisations?', *Revue Française de Gestion*, 101: 43–59.

Mair, J., Battilana, J., and Cardenas, J. (2012), 'Organizing for society: a typology of social entrepreneuring models', *Journal of Business Ethics*, 111/3: 353–73

Mantere, S. (2005), 'Strategic practices as enablers and disablers of championing activity', *Strategic Organization*, 3/2: 157–84.

Mantere, S., and Sillince, J. (2007), 'Strategic intent as a rhetorical device', *Scandinavian Journal of Management*, 23/4: 406–24.

McInerney, P. B. (2008), 'Showdown at Kykuit: field configuring events as loci for conventionalizing accounts', *Journal of Management Studies*, 45/6: 1089–116.

Mesny, A., and Mailhot, C. (2007), 'The difficult search for compromises in a Canadian industry/university research partnership', *Canadian Journal of Sociology*, 32/2: 203–26.

Mintzberg, H. (1971), 'Managerial work: analysis from observation', *Management Science*, 18/2: 97–110.

Moursli, A.-C., and Cobbaut, R. (2006), 'Analyse de la co-existence d'organismes non-lucratives, lucratives et publiques dans le secteur des maisons de repos', in Eymard-Duvernay, F. (ed.), L'économie des conventions: Méthodes et résultats, vol. II, Développements: 351–65. Paris: Éditions La Découverte.

Nath, D., and Sudharsham, D. (1994), 'Measuring strategy coherence through patterns of strategic choices', *Strategic Management Journal*, 15/1: 43–63.

Parker, M. (2013), 'Beyond justification', in du Gay, P., and Morgan, G. (eds.), *New Spirits of Capitalism? Crises, Justifications, and Dynamics*: 124–41. Oxford University Press.

Patriotta, G., Gond, J.-P., and Schultz, F. (2011), 'Maintaining legitimacy: controversies, orders of worth and public justifications', *Journal of Management Studies*, 48/8: 1804–36.

Pernkopf-Konhäusner, K. (2014), 'The competent actor: bridging institutional logics and French pragmatist sociology', *Journal of Management Inquiry*, 23/3: 333–7.

Pitt, M. (2001), 'In pursuit of change: managerial constructions of strategic intent', *Strategic Change*, 10/1: 5–21.

Prahalad, C. K., and Bettis, R. A. (1986), 'The dominant logic: a new linkage between diversity and performance', *Strategic Management Journal*, 7/6: 485–501.

Ramirez, C. (2013), '"We are being pilloried for something, we did not even know we had done wrong!" Quality control and orders of worth in the British audit profession', *Journal of Management Studies*, 50/5: 845–69.

Rasheed, A., Moursli, A.-C., and Priem, R. L. (2010), 'Stimulating theory creation through isolation, confrontation and integration: the case of French convention theory', paper presented at the annual Academy of Management meeting, Montreal, 8 August.

Reckwitz, A. (2002), 'Toward a theory of social practices: a development in culturalist theorizing', *European Journal of Social Theory*, 5/2: 243–63.

Reinecke, J. (2010), 'Beyond a subjective theory of value and towards a "fair price": an organizational perspective on fairtrade minimum price setting', *Organization*, 17/5: 563–81.

Schatzki, T. R., Knorr Cetina, K., and von Savigny, E. (eds.) (2001), *The Practice Turn in Contemporary Theory*. London: Routledge.

Seidl, D., and Whittington, R. (2014), 'Enlarging the strategy-as-practice research agenda: towards taller and flatter ontologies', *Organization Studies*, 35/10: 1407–21.

Silber, I. F. (2003), 'Pragmatic sociology as cultural sociology: beyond repertoire theory?', *European Journal of Social Theory*, 6/4: 427–49.

Simons, R. A. (1995), *Levers of Control: How Managers Use Innovative Control Systems to Drive Strategic Renewal*. Cambridge, MA: Harvard Business School Press.

Spee, P., and Jarzabkowski, P. (2011), 'Strategic planning as communicative process', *Organization Studies*, 32/9: 1217–45.

Spicer, A., Alvesson, M., and Kärreman, D. (2009), 'Critical performativity: the unfinished business of critical management studies', *Human Relations*, 62/4: 537–60.

Stark, D. (2000), *For a Sociology of Worth*, working paper. New York: Center on Organizational Innovation, Columbia University.

(2009), *The Sense of Dissonance: Accounts of Worth in Economic Life*. Princeton University Press.

Taupin, B. (2012), 'The more things change… Institutional maintenance as justification work in the credit rating industry', *M@n@gement*, 15/5: 528–62.

Thévenot, L. (1984), 'Rules and implements: investment in forms', *Social Science Information*, 23/1: 1–45.

(1989), 'Équilibre et rationalité dans un univers complexe', *Revue Économique*, 40/2: 147–97.

(2001), 'Pragmatic regimes governing the engagement with the world', in Schatzki, T. R., Knorr Cetina, K., and von Savigny, E. (eds.), *The Practice Turn in Contemporary Theory*: 56–73. London: Routledge.

(2006), *L'action au pluriel: Sociologie des régimes d'engagement*. Paris: Éditions La Découverte.

(2007), 'The plurality of cognitive formats and engagements: moving between the familiar and the public', *European Journal of Social Theory*, 10/3: 409–23.

(2010), 'Autorità e poteri alla prova della critica: l'oppressione del governo orientato all'obiettivo', *Rassegna Italiana di Sociología*, 4: 627–60.

Thévenot, L., Moody, M., and Lafaye, C. (2000), 'Forms of valuing nature: arguments and modes of justification in environmental disputes', in Lamont, M., and Thévenot, L. (eds.), *Rethinking Comparative Cultural Sociology: Polities and Repertoires of Evaluation in France and the United States*: 229–72. Cambridge University Press.

Tilly, C. (2004), *Social Movements, 1768–2004*. Boulder, CO: Paradigm.

Vaara, E., and Tienari, J. (2011), 'On the narrative construction of multinational corporations: an antenarrative analysis of legitimation and resistance in a cross-border merger', *Organization Science*, 22/2: 370–90.

Vaara, E., and Whittington, R. (2012), 'Strategy-as-practice: taking social practices seriously', *Academy of Management Annals*, 6/1: 285–336.

Westphal, J. D., and Bednar, M. (2005), 'Pluralistic ignorance in corporate boards and firms' strategic persistence in response to low firm performance', *Administrative Science Quarterly*, 50/2: 262–98.

Whittington, R. (2006), 'Completing the practice turn in strategy research', *Organization Studies*, 27/5: 613–34.

Whittington, R., Jarzabkowski, P., Mayer, M., Mounoud, E., Nahapiet, J., and Rouleau, L. (2003), 'Taking strategy seriously: responsibility and reform for an important social practice', *Journal of Management Inquiry*, 12/4: 396–409.

Willmott, H. (2013), 'Spirited away: when political economy becomes culturalized', in du Gay, P., and Morgan, G. (eds.), *New Spirits of Capitalism? Crises, Justifications, and Dynamics*: 98–123. Oxford University Press.

Zald, M. N., and Berger, M. A. (1978), 'Social movements in organizations: coup d'état, insurgency, and mass movements', *American Journal of Sociology*, 83/4: 823–61.

Zelizer, V. (2005), *The Purchase of Intimacy*. Princeton University Press.

A Wittgensteinian perspective on strategizing

SAKU MANTERE

Introduction

In this chapter, I explore the potential the work of the philosopher Ludwig Wittgenstein has to contribute to strategy-as-practice scholarship. For many, Wittgenstein was the most influential philosopher of the twentieth century. His realization that the only satisfactory way to understand language was to understand the social life it enables provided a basis for what was to become the practice turn in social sciences. His work has informed a diverse set of social theorists, from Giddens (1984) to Bourdieu (1977) and Lyotard (1986), all of whom build on Wittgenstein's elaborate inquiry into the ontology of language as a social phenomenon that is rooted in practice. Like these theorists, I shall focus on the concept of the *language game*, the central theme running through the 'late and middle periods' in Wittgenstein's thought. I argue that the language game is a useful concept in making sense of strategy practice in a theoretical as well as a methodological sense.

While Wittgenstein's work has not been utilized to a great extent within the extant body of work on strategy as practice (but see Seidl 2007; Mantere 2013), at least two groups of scholars have used his concepts in their work within management and strategic management scholarship. The first group focuses on meta-theoretical concerns, as these researchers have found Wittgenstein's work on language games useful in studying the methodology, philosophy and ideology of the management sciences. A particular area of interest is the relationship between management scholars and practitioners (Astley and Zammuto 1992; Beyer 1992; Donaldson 1995). This scholarship characteristically uses the language game concept to examine the knowledge interest in management scholarship – that is, the issue of whether the task of management scholarship is to explain or understand phenomena, help managers or emancipate the oppressed (Rao and Pasmore 1989). Hassard (1988) uses language games to seek a solution to the challenge of paradigm incommensurability in the management sciences. Seidl (2007) examines the processes through which strategy labels give rise to a variety of organization-specific strategy concepts within organizational discourses. Holt and Mueller (2011) draw on the normative powers of language games in an effort to resolve methodological misunderstandings between critical realist and social constructionist organizational scholars.

The second group of scholars has applied the concept of the language game to a theoretical (as opposed to meta-theoretical) purpose. Language games have enriched understanding on within various focal topic areas such as organizational knowledge (Chia and Holt 2008; Tsoukas and Vladimirou 2001), competitive advantage (Powell 2001; Rindova, Becerra and Contardo 2004), organizational dialogue (Beech 2008; Shotter 2008) and strategy as an organizational phenomenon (Mantere 2013).

In this chapter, I argue that language games have the potential to help us make sense of three major issues within the strategy-as-practice agenda. First, language games shed more light on the discursive struggles endemic to the practice of strategy (Laine and Vaara 2007; Mantere and Vaara 2008). Strategy work, both in academic and in practical domains, is characterized by pursuits of defining 'rules for the game' built on collective agreement. Nevertheless, the forging of such agreement is an inherently political affair. Strategy language has profound implications for the strategic organizations that it influences. As has been illustrated by authors who have studied strategy from a discursive angle (for example, Barry and Elmes 1997a; Ezzamel and Willmott 2008; Hardy, Palmer and Phillips 2000; Knights and Morgan 1991; Laine and Vaara 2007; Mantere and Vaara 2008), the way we use the language of strategy – or, indeed, the way the language uses us – is also intimately tied to how we practise it. A prominent example of the tangled webs of the linguistic and non-linguistic aspects in strategy practice is Oakes, Towley and Cooper's (1998) account of the radical transformation of values within the administration of the provincial museums and cultural heritage sites in Alberta, Canada, following the introduction of a strategic planning system. Even though other thinkers already prominent in organization studies, such as Foucault, have built on the view that discourse is connected to a non-linguistic reality (see, for example, Ezzamel and Willmott 2008), Wittgenstein's use of the concept 'game' brings particular insight into this phenomenon. When we play a particular strategy language game, we are committing ourselves to a set of (discursive or non-discursive) activity patterns and dispositions. A game can be played only if the players adhere to a particular set of rules. We are inclined to persuade, or even to force, others to agree to them so that *our* game may continue.

Second, Wittgenstein's work sheds new light on the ways in which strategy can be viewed at different levels of analysis. Language games are connected to each other through intricate network relations, which Wittgenstein terms 'family resemblance'. Family resemblance accounts for the ways in which strategy practices are interlinked across field, network, organizational and micro levels. Importantly, strategy is understandable at such different levels through the work of 'linguistic experts', who are responsible for maintaining the rules of proper use for strategy terms at these levels (Mantere 2013). Third, language games are understandable in the context of what Wittgenstein calls 'forms of life', a non-linguistic foundation. Such a notion of 'life', used to characterize the non-linguistic background of social practice, can direct our attention to a number of important yet often neglected aspects of strategy practice.

Language games

The Austrian-born philosopher Ludwig Wittgenstein appears to have been a characteristically volatile thinker. He experienced a number of revolutions in his philosophy. The best known of these revolutions took place between his early period, realized in *Tractatus Logico-Philosophicus* (Wittgenstein 2001 [1921]), and the subsequent middle and late periods, which came to fruition in the *Philosophical Investigations*, which were published posthumously (Wittgenstein 1953 [1951]).

During his early period Wittgenstein focused on building what he called the picture theory of language. In this view, language was conceived through its capacity to represent the world. Concepts find correlates in classes of objects in the world; the term 'professor', for instance, is a label for a class of individuals. In the picture theory of language, the use of logical syntax enables the composition of words into propositions, which correspond to states of affairs in the real world, just as pictures depict specific situations. For instance, the proposition 'Professor Eero Vaara went disco dancing on New Year's Eve' depicts a lively picture of a certain state of affairs. Logical syntax composes constituent concepts into a proposition, the truth value of which can be ascertained. Thus, by studying language we study reality, as 'the limits of language mean the limits of my world' (Wittgenstein 2001 [1921]: §5.6). After having explicated the picture theory of language in his early masterpiece *Tractatus Logico-Philosophicus*, Wittgenstein felt he had solved the problems of philosophy, thus making the pursuit of philosophical problems unnecessary. He subsequently pursued the careers of elementary schoolteacher, architect and gardener (Monk 1990).

Wittengenstein did return to philosophy, however. He reappeared in Cambridge in 1929 – an event that inspired John Maynard Keynes to express the following sentiment: 'Well, God has arrived. I met him on the 5.15 train' (Monk 1990). Wittgenstein had begun to realize that the picture theory of language may not have been a satisfactory account after all when one looked at how language was *practised* by language users. Although language was used to represent states of affairs, it was also used to do many other things. Our ability to describe Professor Vaara's performative activities is one thing, but the picture theory does not account for what happens should Professor Vaara state 'I order my entire research team to go disco dancing to celebrate the acceptance of our paper in *Organization Studies*', nor when the bouncer of the nightclub declares 'I *deny* you entry into the club because of the way you are dressed'. *Ordering* and *denying* are just two examples of the innumerable purposes for which language is used beyond stating and describing.

Hence, if one is to make sense of the nature of language, one needs to look at the many varieties of practice when language is used. Instead of the view of language as a picture of reality, dominant in his early writings, in his middle- and late-period work Wittgenstein roots language in social practice, in the variety of ways language is used by all sorts of communities. As such, Wittgenstein is one of the founding fathers of the practice turn in social science (Schatzki 1997; 2001).

In *Philosophical Investigations*, Wittgenstein demonstrates the limited scope of his early picture view of language by introducing a simple social context in which language would serve such a function. He introduces us to a 'tribe' of bricklayers. Language supports the role structure between the tribe's masters and apprentices in their building activity.

> Let us imagine a language...The language is meant to serve for communication between a builder A and an assistant B. A is building with building-stones; there are blocks, pillars, slabs and beams. B has to pass the stones, and that in the order in which A needs them. For this purpose they use a language consisting of the words 'block', 'pillar', 'slab', 'beam'. A calls them out; ...B brings the stone which he has learnt to bring at such-and-such a call. [...] Conceive this as a complete primitive language (Wittgenstein 1953 [1951]: §2).
> We could imagine that the language of §2 was the whole language of A and B; even the whole language of a tribe. The children are brought up to perform these actions, to use these words as they do so, and to react in this way to the words of others. An important part of the training will consist in the teacher's pointing to the objects, directing the child's attention to them, and at the same time uttering a word; for instance, the word 'slab' as he points to that shape (§6).
> We can also think of the whole process of using words in as one of those games by means of which children learn their native language. I will call these games 'language-games' and will sometimes speak of a primitive language as a language-game.
> And the processes of naming the stones and of repeating words after someone might also be called language-games. Think of much of the use words in games like ring-a-ring-a-roses.
> I shall also call the whole, consisting of language and the actions into which it is woven, the 'language-game' (§7).

Wittgenstein's example demonstrates, on the one hand, how language games are embedded in social practice, and on the other hand how narrow the conception is of language based on pure representation. Language is 'woven into action', and people do much more than merely denote things with language. In their various social settings, our natural languages serve a number of purposes. Instead of a picture of a world, language is, in Wittgenstein's terminology,

> a tool-box: there is a hammer, pliers, a saw, a screw-driver, a ruler, a glue-pot, glue, nails and screw. [...] The functions of words are as diverse as the functions of these objects (Wittgenstein 1953 [1951]: §11).

For Wittgenstein, language games were a method of conducting philosophical inquiry as well as constituting an ontological building block. He introduces and analyses simple language games, such as the one in the bricklayer example, to focus attention on what he regards as important aspects of language; he seeks to make sense of various fundamental philosophical questions, concerning, for instance, meaning, the mind and mathematics. Wittgenstein anticipated a critique about his choice to focus on simple language games. Some readers may argue that the analysis of simple language games does not really represent our language; the analysis does not deal with all its complexity. 'But how would one define a "complete language"?' Wittgenstein asks. Was language 'complete' before the inclusion of the vocabulary of quantum physics, for instance? He offers a compelling metaphor of language as an ancient city:

[A]sk yourself whether our language is complete; whether it was so before the symbolism of chemistry and the notation of the infinitesimal calculus were incorporated in it; for these are, so to speak, suburbs of our language. (And how many houses or streets does it take before a town begins to be a town?) Our language can be seen as an ancient city: a maze of little streets and squares, of old and new houses, and of houses with additions from various periods; and this surrounded by a multitude of new boroughs with straight regular streets and uniform houses   (Wittgenstein 1953 [1951]: §18).

The example shows that, for Wittgenstein, language is dynamic, evolving. As it is used in numerous aspects of life, language contains a dazzling variety of different arenas for human life and interaction. Some of its aspects are chaotic, some ordered. Consider, on the one hand, the language game played by a lover, wooing an object of desire; and, on the other hand, the language game played by a chemist, who uses the periodic table to work with a complex chemical equation. Language bends to both purposes, as we can imagine it will bend to numerous purposes yet undiscovered. This is the reason, Wittgenstein reminds us, why language is never 'complete'.

Some rules need to be observed: language games and discursive struggles

In his case study in telecommunications firms, Regnér (2003) shows how strategy work may be radically different between organizational centres and peripheries. He writes:

The findings show a twofold character of strategy creation, including fundamental different strategy activities in the periphery and centre, reflecting their diverse location and social embeddedness. Strategy making in the periphery was *inductive*, including externally oriented and exploratory strategy activities like trial and error, informal noticing, experiments and the use of heuristics. In contrast, strategy making in the centre was more *deductive* involving an industry and exploitation

focus, and activities like planning, analysis, formal intelligence and the use of standard routines (Regnér 2003: 57, emphasis in original).

Organizations are not singular language games with respect to their strategy concepts. Even if Regnér does not talk of language per se, the activities that he discusses – planning, analysis, trial and error, experiments – mainly take place in language. Regnér's example should be enough to convince us that few organizations can be characterized as single language games.

Strategy work is a plural domain over which Wittgenstein's work can fuel novel research. It is particularly relevant for research focused on strategy discourse as an arena of discursive struggle (for example, Hardy, Palmer and Phillips 2000; Laine and Vaara 2007; Mantere and Vaara 2008, Dameron and Torset 2014). This literature seeks to understand the fact that strategy discourses are employed by various stakeholders in promoting particular realities within an organization. Focusing on particular arenas of agreement and disagreement over the use of language, for instance, furthers the agenda of studying the discursive struggles in the practice of strategy. The study of conflicting language games would help us unravel the behavioural commitments that specific conceptual arrangements within an organization involve, as well as how such behavioural arrangements are contested through discursive practice.

Does Wittgenstein leave room for contestation or contradiction between different language games? Games typically involve agreement over the rules that must be followed to be playable at all. Does the metaphor of a game imply a conflict-free view of social life? Wittgenstein does argue that '[language users] agree in the *language* they use. That is not agreement in opinions but in form of life' (*Philosophical Investigations*: §241, emphasis in original). One might draw a conclusion from the notion of 'agreement' that Wittgenstein regards language games as essentially non-contestable.

Wittgenstein's argument does not imply non-contestability, however. Consider the following passage (Wittgenstein 1969 [1951]):

Is it wrong for me to be guided in my actions by the propositions of physics? Am I to say I have no good ground for doing so? Isn't precisely this what we call a 'good ground' (608)?

Supposing we met people who did not regard that as a telling reason. Now, how do we imagine this? Instead of the physicist, they consult an oracle. (And for that we consider them primitive.) Is it wrong for them to consult an oracle and be guided by it? [..] If we call this 'wrong' aren't we using our language-game as a base from which to combat theirs (609)?

And are we right or wrong to combat it? Of course there are all sorts of slogans which will be used to support our proceedings (610).

Where two principles really do meet which cannot be reconciled with one another, then each man declares the other a fool and heretic (611).

I said I would 'combat' the other man, – but wouldn't I give him reasons? Certainly; but how far do they go? At the end of reasons comes persuasion (think what happens when missionaries convert natives) (612).

Wittgenstein here shows a contrast between two language games in terms of what is regarded as a 'good ground': one a modern form of life, based on natural science; the other a pre-modern one, based on the use of an oracle consulted in determining matters of course. When practitioners of the two language games argue about matters of course, we see that each one supports a different rationality. In order to work, each rationality needs to rely on the rules of its own language game. When such rules conflict, we reach the end of rationality. Contesting the language game is to contest the form of life upon which it is founded. Contesting language games from the outside is a matter of persuasion, not of reasoning.

The notion of 'agreement' is important, not because it suggests non-conflict but because it reminds us that language use always involves *some* language game, which is founded on *some* form of life. Consider the following example:

I recently hosted a strategy seminar for a group of corporate communications and HR officials at a large, multinational firm. At a certain point, a junior consultant stated that he wanted to 'have a say in our strategy'. 'Are you saying that you want to be *empowered*?' asked a senior communications manager. 'No, I don't bloody wanna be *empowered*', retorted the junior consultant; 'I said

I wanna have a say in our strategy!' The junior consultant was clearly agitated.

I remember being puzzled at first. Was 'empowerment' not about 'having a say'? It appeared that there was an implicit struggle about whether to play a specific language game, however. It appeared that, in the organization in question, 'empowerment' was involved in a language game, which, while allowing non-senior individuals limited agency, also reaffirmed a form of life in which managers decided who was to have agency and who was not.

How does one go about analysing a language game such as this? One interpretation of the surprising reaction of the junior consultant when faced by the challenge of reinterpreting his need as 'being empowered' would be to read the question 'Are you saying that you want to be empowered?' as 'Would you like your superiors/ me to empower you?'. The rules of empowerment, applied like this in the 'empowerment' language game, may involve a number of conditions that limit the extent of agency for those empowered or of the reciprocal behaviours anticipated in gratitude for being empowered.

The example should illustrate that language games, and seemingly innocent words that play a role in language games, are indeed 'woven into action', as Wittgenstein suggests, in everyday contexts. It also illustrates that language games are challenged. While at first glance 'being empowered' and 'having a say' might be regarded as synonyms according to the rules of some management science language games, there is a fundamental difference in subjectivity in the rules of the language games within the example corporation. 'Having a say' involves having agency or being a subject, whereas 'being empowered' implies 'being empowered by X', who in our case company is a senior manager.

In a paper written with Eero Vaara (Mantere and Vaara 2008), we looked at connections between strategy language and *participation*. We witnessed multiple struggles over participation, with discursive practices impeding and facilitating the agency of different players. I now briefly draw upon our analysis of one of our case organizations (Mantere and Vaara 2008: 348, emphasis in original):

In Organization 2, a large telecommunications firm, strategy-making was seen as a 'serious business', open only to a selected group of people. Well-known international consultants were used to facilitate the top management team in its strategy work. Access to strategy documentation, even to those documents found in the company intranet, was limited to people at the top managerial echelons. In their discourse, strategy was typically envisioned as a 'direction' set by the top management team, aided by the consultants. A top management team member explained this as follows:

> This is the *order of things* in my mind: First top management defines a vision, a desired end state, which is then pursued... Strategy is then formed into a kind of a set of operative activities leading to the desired end state. (TMT member)

The organization consisted of a large workforce of expert personnel. While some of them had internalized the top-down approach to strategy, others were frustrated. Some of them openly questioned the non-participatory nature of strategy work.

> Our information policy [withholding information] is almost hysterical. I cannot say that I know these [strategy documents] very well. I got promoted recently and only then was I allowed access to these documents in the intranet. You don't get much information if you don't have sufficient *rank and insignia*... This was the first time I got to know where we are going as an organization. (Marketing manager)

To channel their frustration, some organizational members used cynicism to ridicule the organization's strategy work:

> I used to work in a smaller firm where people could participate in strategic planning. In my new role in this large firm, I have had to teach myself that planning is none of my business. They want to maintain a very small *inner circle* in this organization, and once a year, in a *huge spectacle*, to present it all in one *spectacular* slide. (Sales support manager)

The quotations from individual interviews already illustrate the contradictory language games played by top and middle managers. The top manager in the example refers to an 'order of things' for strategy work, making use of a religious metaphor that promotes the naturalization of followership and obedience. The quotations from the middle manager contain resistance to the order of things through the use of a similar metaphoric domain. 'Inner circle', another metaphor with a religious clang, is used to challenge the naturalization of the hegemonic practices of strategy-making. The military metaphor 'rank and insignia' is used in a very similar way. The notion that language games are woven into action, that they are built on a non-linguistic foundation, is particularly evident in the accounts of the two middle managers. The 'order of things' is evident in a large array of social arrangements, such as limited access below a specific organizational level to strategy documents in the company intranet, and strategy workshops that are one-man 'spectacles'.

Below, I have transcribed a new segment from a discussion within a group of middle managers in a strategy seminar in 'organization 2'. The segment appears to be a constructive debate between the middle managers about the rules of applying the label 'strategy.' Middle managers have direct access to the practices of the operational personnel as well as the top managers, and thus can be seen as mediators between multiple language games. Organizational strategy appears strikingly different from the standpoint of these two realities.

Consequently, glimpses of at least two contrasted forms of life can be seen in the tension between two language games. The first, which I call the 'operational language game', approaches strategy as a policy that guides everyday work. The second language game, which I call the 'general management language game', conceives strategy as a set of choices at the organizational level. These two correspond to the organizational realities perceived by the operative staff, on the one hand, and the top management, on the other. The staff experience the organization from the reality of operations whereas the everyday task of a general manager is to think about the organization as an integrated whole.

I have chosen a sequence of seven lines of dialogue, which illustrate the tension between the two language games. I report and discuss each line of dialogue in the order that they were stated. The dialogue is launched when, faced with the challenge of defining what the label 'strategy' means for him, middle manager 1 (M1) responds [1] by stating a problem that he sees as endemic to organization 2:

> [1] M1: I think that, here at [organization 2], we have a need, an absence, a problem: that there are plenty of fine strategies but they don't seem linked to people's work or departments. . .

The dialogue starts with M1 implicitly stating the premise of the operational language game: strategy is something that has an impact in the lives of the operational staff. The problem he observes is that strategy does not play a role in everyday activities, as it is not 'linked' to them. M2 continues, playing the same game:

> [2] M2: It is also dangerous when implementing strategies like these, because the contradictions between the actual work to be done and the lofty thoughts behind these strategies become apparent when you examine them. We are still in the relatively satisfactory position that, whether we did things one way or another, we have always been able to explain how it was an appropriate ICT strategy of some kind.

M2 notes [2] that the problem that M1 stated is dangerous. Organization 2 had experienced an affluent stage of growth in a rather benevolent market environment, which M2 refers to as a 'relatively satisfactory position'. His worry is that, if strategies do not affect operations, any operational activities can be justified as 'strategic' in post hoc rationalization. Instead, strategy *should* guide the normative role of guiding operations. This means that unsuccessful strategy work is characterized by 'loftiness' or not being 'linked to people's work or departments'. Unsuccessful strategy appears tautological, alien or even absurd, as it is separated from the everyday work context. In the next comment [3], however, we witness a third middle manager adopt a wholly different stance towards strategy, offering a new set of rules:

> [3] M3: I feel that strategy is just like you said, making choices, and I think our strategies are of the kind that no clear choices have been made.

M3 offers a generic definition for the label 'strategy'. Instead of discussing the effects that strategy

should have at the operational level, M3 portrays strategy in abstract terms. Strategy is making 'clear choices'. The choices she refers to as 'our strategies' would not appear to be operational level choices but choices that affect the organization at large. Indeed, this is what strategy means in the life of the general management: making choices for the organization.

In response to M3's definition, we see middle managers fluctuating between the operational and general management language games, trying to come to grips with the label 'strategy'. M1 tries [4] to return the discussion to the rules of the operational language game, and attempts to reduce the notion of 'choice' to an operational, normative notion of 'what to do':

> [4] M1: At least none were made in which it was defined what not to do. The strategies embrace the whole world. . .but they don't say anything about what we are not meant to do, what sorts of things we don't want to get into.

M1 continues [4] to seek 'strategy' from the viewpoint of operations. Choices are characterized by their normative powers, in their ability to guide 'what to do' or 'what not to do'. Surprisingly, we next [5] see M3 backing away from the general management language game:

> [5] M3: So they are not pointing us in a certain direction – so what? I think strategy is in actuality born only when things get done.

M3 seems to begin a new argument in [5], exploring a new tentative definition for strategy as something 'born only when things get done'. She questions the notion that strategy should be 'pointing us in a certain direction' to have a normative effect on operations. The two definitions offered by M3 for strategy in [3] and [5] do not seem to support each other, as 'making choices' at the organizational level hardly seems necessary to 'getting things done', which seems like an operational expression. M2 seeks to resolve this ambiguity [6], trying to push the discussion back into the general management language game:

> [6] M2: Yeah, and then you have to register all sorts of things that would have needed to be done

anyway. It is non-strategy work, in any case. Everyone is looking for profitable growth, there are no companies out there that want to cut back at a loss of profitability. Sure, the customer is valuable, and this can create a certain ambience for the company, but that a company works towards growth is not really a choice, it is stating the obvious.

Even if M2 starts with a 'yeah', he seems to oppose M3's definition of strategy, characterizing 'getting things done' as 'non-strategy work'. He notes that all operations are striving for profitability. This is 'non-strategy work'. He pushes the operative language game into the corner, noting that '[e]veryone is looking for profitable growth'. M2 appears to argue that strategy is to not do what every other company is doing. Strategy is something other than 'stating the obvious'. Consequently, an analytical discussion should treat strategy and operations as separate issues. To be strategic, an organization needs to be different from 'everyone'. This represents a general management view on strategy. The unit of analysis is the organization in relation to other organizations.

M3 does not back away. She continues [7] by toying with the notion of disbanding the general management language game altogether, suggesting that all strategy may be about eliminating non-profitable activities.

[7] M3: Yes, so then profitable growth should be expressed strategically in a way that eliminates all non-profitable activities. [...] Perhaps [strategy] is that indeed, but we just don't dare to say it. Or what it actually means.

M3 defines strategy simply as profitable operations [7]. This notion seems trivial while playing the general management language, yet it is not trivial at all while playing the operational language game.

We can use Wittgenstein's work on language games to tease out two central aspects to strategy practice from the transcript. First, it reinforces the notion that, in organization 2, strategy practice forms a network consisting of number of language games. Strategy talk is embedded in non-linguistic foundation, in routinized conceptions about what strategy means in terms of how it is lived and practised. The language games people promote are not used only to promote particular forms of life but also to contest other forms of life. Importantly, as we have seen Wittgenstein argue in his example about missionary work, the two strategy language games seem to contain localized rationalities that are incompatible with each other. The general management and the operational language games are used to portray each other's foundations as absurd, in the manner that a meteorologist might portray the foundations of a rain dance as 'superstition', and vice versa.

Second, strategy practice is characterized by the pursuit of agreement. The middle managers spend a great deal of effort trying to persuade each other about the correct meaning of the label 'strategy'. They are trying to forge agreement while playing a number of competing language games. Nevertheless, the language games on which they are drawing are built on competing rationalities. In [3], M3 toys with the general management rationality, only to find herself arguing in favour of the operational rationality [5], almost contradicting her initial sentiment. 'I feel that strategy is just like you said, making choices, and I think our strategies are of the kind that no clear choices have been made' is contrasted with the sentiment that 'profitable growth should be expressed strategically in a way that eliminates all non-profitable activities. [...] Perhaps [strategy] is that indeed, but we just don't dare say it.'

Language games thus highlight a key aspect in our language use: *some* language games, some sets of rules, are needed. In strategy practice in particular, which is often an arena for crucial decisions – mergers, spin-offs, corporate restructurings, layoffs, acquisitions, market entries and exits – the collective need for agreement is to be expected. People need to figure out the rules, as a lot is at stake. We also see, however, the way in which different language games reflect the local rationalities of the forms of life upon which they are founded. Wittgenstein's example of the differences between the practices of consulting an oracle or a physics expert in finding 'good grounds' showed us that, when language games come into contradiction, we reach the end of reason and enter the realm of persuasion.

Family resemblance and strategy at different levels

Language games are a powerful methodological lens for focusing on meaningful units of analysis in the search for strategy practices. A key criterion for drawing the borders on a particular language game is agreement over the proper use of concepts in determining matters of course. Wittgenstein argues that people agree in the language they use. Situations in which we see disagreement over the use of language are particularly fruitful for this inquiry, as we can see the outlines of competing rationalities when they are contrasted with each other. It must be kept in mind, however, that any way we choose to draw the borders of a specific language game is essentially contestable (Holt and Mueller 2011) whenever we choose to talk about the language game of a specific organization, the language game of its management team, that of a specific business unit within the organization, and so on.

Language games are intertwined and interconnected as a network. As noted above, its borders are open for dispute and change over time, as Wittgenstein would seem to suggest to us through his example of language as an ancient city. As social contexts interlink with each other, language games form networks. Wittgenstein presents language games as linked together in a complex set of interrelations that he calls *family resemblance*:

> Instead of producing something common to all that we call language, I am saying that these phenomena have no one thing in common which makes us use the same word for all, but that they are related to one another in many different ways (Wittgenstein 1953 [1951]: §65).

> I can think of no better expression to characterize these similarities than 'family resemblances'; for the various resemblances between members of a family: build, features, colour of eyes, gait, temperament, etc. etc. overlap and cries-cross in the same way. And I shall say: 'games' form a family (§67).

As resemblance is carried through membership in a family, areas of agreement and disagreement extend over a network of what could be called *the strategy language game*. Family members resemble each other in a number of ways, yet rarely can it be argued that a single characteristic is definitive for a family. Instead of a single characteristic, family membership is characterized by a number of characteristics that are shared in a network-like fashion. Correspondingly, language games are not reducible to a single set of behaviours. Instead, language games form a virtually boundless network.

The network view of language games has been used by organizational scholars to contest oversimplified demarcations between forms of life and language games. Importantly, Mauws and Phillips (1995) have suggested a network view in their account of the relationship between academic and practitioner language games. Astley and Zammuto (1992) caused a stir (see Beyer 1992; Donaldson 1995; Mauws and Phillips 1995) by arguing that managerial discourse and scholarly discourse on organizations are separate language games with different rules, objectives and underlying assumptions. Hence, Astley and Zammuto (1992) argue that 'organizational scientists should be viewed not as engineers offering technical advice to managers but as providers of conceptual and symbolic language for use in organizational discourse'. Mauws and Phillips (1995) criticize Astley and Zammuto's argument that practitioners and academics play according to different language games. They contest the existence of a non-problematic way of drawing the border where one language game ends and another begins. Instead, they argue, we should see both discourses – practical and academic (however we might plot them out) – as embedded in a network of interconnected language games.

Strategic management can be understood at very different levels of analysis (Vaara 2010; Balogun *et al.* 2014). On the one hand, it is something that people do in organizations. This viewpoint regards strategic management as work. On the other hand, strategic management is an industry (Whittington 2006), a discipline (Knights and Morgan 1991) or an ideology (Shrivastava 1986) that has a life of its own at the institutional level of analysis, beyond the particular organizations in which it is encountered. Indeed, the relation between institutional field practices, organizational actions and intra-organizational activities has been pointed out as a key part of the strategy as practice agenda (see Johnson *et al.* 2007: fig. 1.1).

The concept of family resemblance allows us to conceive linkages between language games at different levels of analysis: from the level of strategy as a discipline (Knights and Morgan 1991) to organization-level strategy narratives (Barry and Elmes 1997a) to more micro-level linguistic interactions within the organization (Samra-Fredericks 2003). Language games are founded on agreement, and their dynamics can be seen as struggles for agreement. The discipline of strategic management as an institutional field is characterized by the pursuit of agreement over what its key concepts mean. If 'agreeing over language' was not important, the history of the entire field would not be filled with battles between different factions in strategic management. Consider, for instance the following debates.

- Ansoff's (1991) and Mintzberg's (1990; 1991) heated exchange on whether strategic management is about planning or learning.
- Barry and Elmes' (1997a; 1997b) and Ireland and Hitt's (1997) debate on whether strategy is a form of fiction – in other words, whether narrativity is inherent to strategic management as a phenomenon (as Barry and Elmes suggest) or whether it is relevant only to 'implementation' (as Ireland and Hitt suggest).
- Porter's (1996) complaint that we have started to confuse strategic management with operational effectiveness.

Different scholarly practices are enabled by language games when strategy is regarded as 'fiction' (Barry and Elmes 1997a), 'a distinctive market position' (Porter 1996) or 'pattern in a stream of actions' (Mintzberg 1978). When a particular kind of agreement wins over others, scholars playing a particular language game need to proceed in their study of their topic in a particular manner. Indeed, discussion across strategy schools is often difficult. This might well be the case because authors across schools are playing different language games – as well as trying to persuade and bully each other to accept a particular rule set as a basis for accepted behaviour. To make matters more complicated, the institutional field of strategic management does not only consist of academics. Whittington *et al.* (2003) have shown us the multidisciplinary nature of strategy discourse, as various players such as consultants, practitioners, academics and politicians have a stake in how strategic management evolves as an institution.

Language games can help make better sense of the dynamic between the institutional and organizational level of strategic management. The first account of the adoption of institutional strategy language by organizations was given by Seidl (2007), who explores how strategy concepts are transformed in their adoption across organizations. Marrying the notion of language games with Luhmann's notion of organizations as systems, he argues (Seidl 2007: 197) that 'no transfer of strategy concepts across different discourses is possible. Instead, every single strategy discourse can merely construct its own discourse-specific concepts. Different discourses, however, draw on the same strategy labels, which leads to "productive misunderstandings."'

The key to Seidl's argument is that strategy concepts are not adopted as such; they are reinvented within organizational language games, where they are applied as playing new roles. In other words, even if organizational practitioners might use a term such as 'core competence', which is the exact label used by Hamel and Prahalad (1994), the concept of core competence will have an organization-specific meaning. The Wittgensteinian explanation for this is that the concept meaning is regarded as rule-following behaviour with respect to the agreed-upon rules within a specific language game. Hence, it is important to draw a clear distinction between the label used and the content of the concept as a set of rules within a particular language game.

We often mistakenly take it for granted that the labels used in institutional discourse, such as 'core competence', 'implementation', 'strategy process', 'strategy renewal', 'participation in strategy', 'empowerment' and 'industry', retain their concept meaning when they play a part in different organizational language games. Instead of a concept being transferred across from an institutional domain into an organization, a new concept is recreated in each instance to fill the meaning of a label. When it is discovered that the new labels do not really fit the current dominant language games, and as contradictions are discovered, new meaning is constructed that enriches the language games through 'productive misunderstanding' (Seidl 2007).

Seidl's paper bridges the gap between the institutional and organizational levels of analysis in strategy as practice as it discusses how labels from the institutional level meet the organizational level. But can an organization itself be conceived as a single language game? My previous 'being empowered' example demonstrates that intra-organizational language games may be contested. Hence, one may suspect that multiple strategic management language games exist within an organization.

In addition to devoting our attention to discursive struggles, serious attention should also be devoted to how different organizational language games *support* each other through relations of family resemblance. Specifically, family resemblance could be used to further the agenda set by Seidl (2007) in the study of the transfers of language between the institutional and organizational levels of analysis. Organizational language games are connected with their environments in various different ways (Mauws and Phillips 1995), which the concept of family resemblance could elucidate. While Seidl's focus has been on the uniqueness of organization-specific strategy concepts that appear under common labels, family resemblance could be a way of understanding the commonalities between them. Family resemblance could also inform empirical work on how different discursive practices at different levels interact and intertwine in organizational strategy practice.

Strategy and organizational life

The notion of a form of life as a non-linguistic foundation for a language game also presents an intriguing conceptualization of sociomateriality in strategizing. The topic of sociomateriality is highlighted as one of the key questions of

contemporary strategy scholarship. Vaara and Whittington (2012: 32) (see also Balogun et al. 2014) note that 'research into strategy praxis needs to go beyond discourse to consider how the material, in the form of both bodies and artifacts, is used to accomplish strategy work'. While Wittgenstein's work on family resemblances allows us to draw connections between multiple levels, his work also allows us to peer into the very micro level, into the subjective experience of strategy as a form of life, and how this subjective experience is built in the interaction between discursive and non-discursive aspects. Wittgenstein argues that language games are always embedded in non-linguistic activity (Glock 1996). He calls this non-linguistic foundation of language 'a form of life', and notes that Wittgenstein (1976 [1937], quoted by Glock 1996) says:

> [I]t is characteristic of our language that the foundation on which it grows consists in steady forms of life, regular activity. Its function is determined *above all* by the action which it accompanies.

Language enables and regulates social activity, and our words became meaningful against a form of life. Wittgenstein regarded forms of life as a stable, non-linguistic foundation upon which language games are built. Indeed, forms of life can be defined as 'the set of [behavioural] responses in which we agree and the way they interweave with our activities' (Kripke 1982).

In the context of organization studies, Hassard (1988) builds on Wittgenstein's work to suggest that there exists a 'language game of everyday life', through which members of different scientific paradigms may interact. This would seem to be a transcendental reading of language games (Glock 1996), however, which does not find support in Wittgenstein's work. Even though Wittgenstein argued that language games are founded on forms of life, this does not mean that they can be reduced to some non-linguistic, ontological bedrock. The Wittgenstein of the middle and late periods emphasized that language is built on social context, which is in no way universal to all human conduct. Different language games are built on a dazzling variety of social contexts. Wittgenstein regarded language games as 'anthropological' in nature, founded on specific, situated contexts instead of some fundamental 'human nature' (Glock 1996).

Shotter has suggested that the tendency to focus on the 'small, concrete and idiosyncratic details' (Shotter 2005): 113) of organizational life is the most promising aspect for management studies in Wittgenstein's method in his late period. Focusing on how language games are woven into action helps us attend to the 'embodied, living meetings' (118) that characterize organizations, instead of treating organizations as abstract, objectified systems. The recognition that strategy is a lived experience (Samra-Fredericks 2003; 2005) is embedded in the very notion of strategy-as-practice scholarship, which views strategy as something people do in organizations – not something that organizations have (Whittington 2006). Indeed, a few scholars have already worked on strategy practice as a lived experience within the SAP community. Highly original results have been provided by Samra-Fredericks (2003; 2005), who has elucidated the potential of strategy rhetoric to steer everyday life by concentrating on significant 'strips' of everyday interaction. A recent, parallel development is the work of Chia and Holt (2006), who explore a view of strategy as 'practical coping'. They use Heidegger's phenomenological work to further our understanding of strategy as a lived experience consisting of human interaction, arguing that 'the dominant "building" mode of strategizing that configures actors (whether individual or organizational) as distinct entities deliberately engaging in purposeful strategic activities derives from a more basic "dwelling" mode in which strategy emerges nondeliberately through everyday practical coping' (Chia and Holt 2006: 635).

None of the scholars working on the 'lived' aspects of Wittgenstein's work have extended his ideas to an exploration of sociomateriality, however. For future studies, this would seem to be a natural direction. Things and bodies have consequences. In their sensemaking during the episodes leading to the shooting of the Brazilian electrician Jean Charles de Menezes (Cornelissen, Mantere and Vaara 2014), for instance, the police officers used the material clue of being given hollow-point bullets, intended for the effective killing of their

target, to fill out a gap in the ambiguous orders they received.

As illustrated in Wittgenstein's bricklaying example, language games are intertwined with material objects. The use of strategy concepts requires rule-following behaviour, and such behaviour requires the use of material objects (Mantere 2013); just consider much of strategy work without a computer running PowerPoint, a projector, screen, a physical room (Kaplan 2011). Equally, the human body is a crucial tool in such strategic rule-following (Küpers, Mantere and Statler 2013). Students of strategy can peer into sociomateriality by seeking to understand which rule-following organizational strategy discourses elicit, and understanding the role of objects and bodies in the functioning of such rule-following.

Conclusion

The study of Wittgenstein constitutes a discourse of its own in the study of Western philosophy. In this chapter, I have not participated in the philosophical debates around Wittgenstein's work, or tried to conduct an exegesis of what Wittgenstein 'really meant' in one text or the other. Rather, I have aimed to tease out insights from Wittgenstein's work that are relevant to the study of strategy as practice. I have employed the concept of 'language game', and the associated concepts of 'family resemblance' and 'form of life', to elaborate on three major domains within strategy-as-practice research. This chapter has been an early reflection in what I hope might become a Wittgensteinian stream of thought within the SAP agenda. I hope that I have managed to convince the reader that Wittgenstein should be considered alongside thinkers such as Giddens, Bourdieu, de Certeau, Luhmann, Heidegger and Foucault, who have already informed and inspired our work.

References

Ansoff, H. I. (1991), 'Critique of Henry Mintzberg's "The design school: reconsidering the basic premises of strategic management"', *Strategic Management Journal*, 12/6: 449–61.

Astley, W. G., and Zammuto, R. F. (1992), 'Organization science, managers and language games', *Organization Science*, 3/4: 443–60.

Balogun, J., Jacobs, C. D., Jarzabkowski, P., Mantere, S., and Vaara, E. (2014), 'Placing strategy discourse in context: sociomateriality, sensemaking, and power', *Journal of Management Studies*, 51/2: 175–201.

Barry, D., and Elmes, M. (1997a), 'Strategy retold: toward a narrative view of strategy discourse', *Academy of Management Review*, 22/2: 429–52.

(1997b), 'On paradigms and narratives: Barry and Elmes's response', *Academy of Management Review*, 22/4: 847–9.

Beech, N. (2008), 'On the nature of dialogic identity work', *Organization*, 15/1: 51–74.

Beyer, J. M. (1992), 'Metaphors, misunderstandings and mischief: a commentary', *Organization Science*, 3/4: 467–74.

Bourdieu, P. (1977), *Outline of a Theory of Practice*. Cambridge University Press.

Chia, R., and Holt, R. (2006), 'Strategy as practical coping: a Heideggerian perspective', *Organization Studies*, 27/5: 635–55.

(2008), 'On managerial knowledge', *Management Learning*, 39/2: 141–58.

Cornelissen, J., Mantere, S., and Vaara, E. (2014). 'The contraction of meaning: the combined effect of communication, emotion and materiality on sensemaking in the Stockwell shooting', *Journal of Management Studies*, 51/5: 699–736.

Dameron, S., and Torset, C. (2014), 'The discursive construction of strategists' subjectivities: towards a paradox lens on strategy', *Journal of Management Studies*, 51/2: 291–319.

Donaldson, L. (1995), 'The Weick stuff: managing beyond games', *Organization Science*, 3/4: 461–6.

Ezzamel, M., and Willmott, H. (2008), 'Strategy as discourse in a global retailer: a supplement to rationalist and interpretive accounts', *Organization Studies*, 29/2: 191–217.

Giddens, A. (1984), *The Constitution of Society*. Cambridge: Polity.

Glock, H. (1996), *A Wittgenstein Dictionary*. Oxford: Blackwell.

Hamel, G., and Prahalad, C. K. (1994), *Competing for the Future*. Cambridge, MA: Harvard Business School Press.

Hardy, C., Palmer, I., and Phillips, N. (2000), 'Discourse as a strategic resource', *Human Relations*, 53/9: 1227–48.

Hassard, J. (1988), 'Overcoming hermeticism in organization theory: an alternative to paradigm incommensurability', *Human Relations*, 41/3: 247–59.

Holt, R., and Mueller, F. (2011), 'Wittgenstein, Heidegger and drawing lines in organization studies', *Organization Studies*, 32/1: 67–84.

Ireland, D. R., and Hitt, M. A. (1997), '"Strategy-as-story": clarifications and enhancements to Barry and Elmes' arguments', *Academy of Management Review*, 22/4: 844–7.

Johnson, G., Langley, A., Melin, L., and Whittington, R. (2007), *Strategy as Practice: Research Directions and Resources*. Cambridge University Press.

Kaplan, S. (2011), 'Strategy and PowerPoint: an inquiry into the epistemic culture and machinery of strategy making', *Organization Science*, 22/2: 320–46.

Knights, D., and Morgan, G. (1991), 'Corporate strategy, organizations, and subjectivity: a critique', *Organization Studies*, 12/2: 251–73.

Kripke, S. (1982), *Wittgenstein on Rules and Private Language*. Cambridge, MA: Harvard University Press.

Küpers, W., Mantere, S., and Statler, M. (2013), 'Strategy as storytelling: a phenomenological collaboration', *Journal of Management Inquiry*, 22/1: 83–100.

Laine, P., and Vaara, E. (2007), 'Struggling over subjectivity: a discursive analysis of strategic development in an engineering group', *Human Relations*, 60/1: 29–58.

Lyotard, J.-F. (1986), *The Postmodern Condition: A Report on Knowledge*. Manchester University Press.

Mantere, S. (2013), 'What is organizational strategy? A language-based view', *Journal of Management Studies*, 50/8: 1408–26.

Mantere, S., and Vaara, E. (2008), 'On the problem of participation in strategy: a critical discursive perspective', *Organization Science*, 19/2: 341–58.

Mauws, M. K., and Phillips, N. (1995), 'Understanding language games', *Organization Science*, 6/3: 322–34.

Mintzberg, H. (1978), 'Patterns of strategy formation', *Management Science*, 24/9: 934–48.

(1990), 'The design school: reconsidering the basic premises of strategic management', *Strategic Management Journal*, 11/3: 171–95.

(1991), 'Learning 1, planning 0: reply to Igor Ansoff', *Strategic Management Journal*, 12/6: 463–66.

Monk, R. (1990), *Ludwig Wittgenstein: The Duty of Genius*. New York: Penguin Books.

Oakes, L. S., Townley, B., and Cooper, D. J. (1998), 'Business planning as pedagogy: language and control in a changing institutional field', *Administrative Science Quarterly*, 43/2: 257–92.

Porter, M. E. (1996), 'What is strategy?', *Harvard Business Review*, 74/6: 61–78.

Powell, T. C. (2001), 'Competitive advantage: logical and philosophical considerations', *Strategic Management Journal*, 22/9: 875–88.

Rao, M. V. H., and Pasmore, W. A. (1989), 'Knowledge and interests in organization studies: a conflict of interpretations', *Organization Studies*, 10/2: 225–39.

Regnér, P. (2003), 'Strategy creation in the periphery: inductive versus deductive strategy making', *Journal of Management Studies*, 40/1: 57–82.

Rindova, V. P., Becerra, M., and Contardo, I. (2004), 'Enacting competitive wars: competitive activity, language games and market consequences', *Academy of Management Review*, 29/4: 670–86.

Samra-Fredericks, D. (2003), 'Strategizing as lived experience and strategists' everyday efforts to shape strategic direction', *Journal of Management Studies*, 40/1: 141–74.

(2005), 'Strategic practice, "discourse" and the everyday interactional constitution of "power effects"', *Organization*, 12/6: 803–41.

Schatzki, T. R. (1997), 'Practices and actions; a Wittgensteinian critique of Bourdieu and Giddens', *Philosophy of the Social Sciences*, 27/3: 283–308.

Schatzki, T. R. (2001), 'Introduction: practice theory', in Schatzki, T. R., Knorr Cetina, K., and von Savigny, E. (eds.), *The Practice Turn in Contemporary Theory*: 1–14. London: Routledge.

Seidl, D. (2007), 'General strategy concepts and the ecology of strategy discourses: a systemic-discursive perspective', *Organization Studies*, 28/2: 197–218.

Shotter, J. (2005), '"Inside the moment of managing": Wittgenstein and the everyday dynamics of our expressive-responsive activities', *Organization Studies*, 26/1: 113–35.

(2008), 'Dialogism and polyphony in organizing theorizing in organization studies: action guiding anticipations and the continuous creation of novelty', *Organization Studies*, 29/4: 501–24.

Shrivastava, P. (1986), 'Is strategic management ideological?', *Journal of Management*, 12/3: 363–77.

Tsoukas, H., and Vladimirou, E. (2001), 'What is organizational knowledge?', *Journal of Management Studies*, 38/7: 973–93.

Vaara, E. (2010), 'Taking the linguistic turn seriously: strategy as a multifaceted and inter-discursive phenomenon', in Baum, J. A. C., and Lampel, J. (eds.), *Advances in Strategic Management*, vol. XXVII, *The Globalization of Strategy Research*: 29–50. Bingley, UK: Emerald.

Vaara, E., and Whittington, R. (2012), 'Strategy-as-practice: taking social practices seriously', *Academy of Management Annals*, 6/1: 285–336.

Whittington, R. (2006), 'Completing the practice turn in strategy research', *Organization Studies*, 27/5: 613–34.

Whittington, R., Jarzabkowski, P., Mayer, M., Mounoud, E., Nahapiet, J., and Rouleau, L. (2003), 'Taking strategy seriously: responsibility and reform for an important social practice', *Journal of Management Inquiry*, 12/5: 396–409.

Wittgenstein, L. (1953 [1951]), *Philosophical Investigations*. Oxford: Blackwell.

(1969 [1951]), *On Certainty*. Oxford: Blackwell.

(1976 [1937]), 'Cause and effect: intuitive awareness', *Philosophia*, 6/3–4: 409–25.

(2001 [1921]), *Tractatus Logico-Philosophicus*. London: Routledge.

A Foucauldian perspective on strategic practice: strategy as the art of (un)folding

FLORENCE ALLARD-POESI

Strategic management defines itself as the art, or science, of governing an organization with the aim of implementing intentions. In this way, strategic management presents itself as an exercise of will that includes the capacity to influence, to *fold or have folded*, the actions of other organizational members.[1] This concept, which is dominant in strategic management, deserves to be further qualified, however. Following the example of other management practices, strategic management can be seen as a social practice (Whittington 2002), involving rules and working standards that serve to restrict the actions of the subject-strategist and limit the field of possible action (Schatzki 2001). It contains vocabulary, discourses and meanings that, at least partially, define the list of problems and possible solutions envisaged by the strategist (Vaara 2010). It relies on material artefacts (pictures, maps, spreadsheets, etc.) that help managers to carry on their everyday activities (Jarzabowski, Spee and Smets 2013).

Departing from a conception of strategy as something organizations have or do not have, the strategy-as-practice approach views strategy as an activity that individuals accomplish as they interact in both a physical and social context (Whittington 2002; Rouleau 2005). As a social practice, strategizing is animated by the dialectic tension between the *singularity* of the here and now of all activity and the generality and *recurrence* of the routines, norms, rules, techniques and tools on which all practice relies; between the uniqueness of the activity in the situation, that which we call *the practice* or *praxis*, and the repetition of the sociocultural artefacts,

usually called *practices*, by which the strategic activity is actually realized (see Whittington 2002: 4; Jarzabowski and Spee 2009). This dialectical conception of strategy draws attention to the enabling – as well as potentially constraining – aspects of all social practices (see Giddens 1993).

As currently developed, however, SAP research continues to retain the idea of the strategist as a deliberate, competent and sometimes all-powerful *bricoleur* (Allard-Poesi 2006). This stream of research continues to assume that, despite an apparent similarity among 'pre-packaged' strategic practices, managers are still able to recreate practices and adapt them to their particular demands and specific context (see Jarzabowksi 2003; Vaara and Whittington 2012): '[Practices] do not impose rigid constraints, but instead enable iteration and adaptation' (Jarzabowski and Spee 2009: 14).

Drawing on Foucault's work, some researchers distance themselves from this powerful, almost heroic concept of the strategic practitioner to develop a critical analysis of strategy (for example, Ezzamel and Willmott 2008; 2010; Laine and Vaara 2007; McCabe 2010; Mantere and Vaara 2008). They mostly rely on Knights and Morgan's (1991; 1995) seminal work and define strategy as a discourse – that is 'a set of ideas and practices which condition our ways of relating to, and acting upon, particular phenomenon' (Knights and Morgan 1991: 253). In this perspective, strategy is understood as what Foucault (1991: 61) calls a 'discursive formation', or 'body of knowledge' (*savoir*: Foucault 1969) – that is, a 'limited practical domain...which [has] [its] boundaries, [its] rules of formation, [its] conditions of existence', and that defines 'what is actually said' (Foucault 1969: 63).

---

[1] This concept does not exclude the emergent, unpredictable part of collective actions.

While strategy as discursive formation is marked by a wide variety of statements, concepts and theories (Mantere and Vaara 2008; Vaara and Whittington 2012), this variety remains limited by a number of rules (Foucault 1969: 1991) that make certain statements read as 'strategic', while excluding others. The task of the researcher, then, is to define these 'rules of statements', which render specific statements possible (and others not) and which create a specific discursive formation (or 'reading system': Lilley 2001: 69).

Foucault (1969; 1991) insists that a discursive formation is not exclusively defined by the 'things said'. Discourse forms knowledge, or *savoir*, to the extent that it is governed by specific rules of statements, *and* because it is related to what he calls 'extra-discursive formations'. These designate the material conditions that make a specific discursive formation possible, in particular 'the criteria used to designate those who received by law the right to hold a [medical] discourse' (that is, who has the right to talk about strategy?), the 'scale of observation', which helps designate the object of discourse (that is, where and how does one look?) and the 'mode of recording, preserving, accumulating, diffusing and teaching... discourse' (Foucault 1991: 67). In this perspective, strategy, as a body of knowledge, cannot be reduced to its discursive expression (that is, the things said). It is a *specific assemblage* (or diagram: Foucault 1969) between 'seeing and saying' (Lilley 2001), between what Deleuze (1988: 49) calls 'the visible and the articulable', so that the 'things said' at a given time point depend both on the particular rules of statements of the time *and* the material conditions that make certain things able 'to come to our attention' (Lilley 2001: 71).

Following this concept of strategy as a *savoir*, three lines of analysis can be developed. First, strategy may be viewed as embodied in a set of *discursive and material social practices* that actualize and reproduce its discourses, constituting in this way a *'power-knowledge' system*. Using Foucault's genealogy as analytical framework (Foucault 2001b [1978]; see also Foucault 1975; 1976), the first section of this chapter outlines the historical, contextual and accidental character of strategic discourses.

Second, strategy may be seen as a *discursive formation* governed by a set of *rules of statements* that managers have to follow if they want to act as strategists. Following Foucault's archeological analysis (see Foucault 1969; 1971), the task of the researcher is to uncover these rules and appreciate their 'power-effect' in the organization (second section).

Finally, following Foucault's last works on the techniques of selves (Foucault 2001c [1983]; 2001f [1988]) and the history of sexuality (Foucault 1984a; 1984b), some researchers consider that strategic practices frame, if not inscribe, the subjectivity of the managers, who, in this way, become 'strategists'. In my view, however, strategic practices cannot be considered as techniques of selves, as they do not imply work on oneself in order to create a specific subjectivity but, rather, involve the strategist's elaboration of a project. In this sense, strategic management is similar to a monitoring technique in which the strategist is led to '*unfold*' himself (Deleuze 1988: 110): to reveal one's intentions, say what is hidden and 'objectify' one's subjectivity in order to enter into the relationships of knowledge and power. This is the subject of the third section.

In summary, the critical approach developed in this chapter distances itself from the idea of adaptability (which is prevalent in the current strategy-as-practice approach) by noting the inscriptions that strategic practices leave on the practitioners and their behaviour. Strategic practices are seen more as techniques of control at a distance through which strategists are led to reveal their intentions. The connection made here between the Foucauldian perspective and the current approach(es) to strategy as practice reveals a contrasting conception of strategy, strategists and their volition, thus paving the way for new areas of research.

Genealogical practices

Genealogy of strategic practices

Developed by Foucault in *Surveiller et punir* (*Discipline and Punish*: Foucault 1975), genealogical analysis relies on the idea that a practice or political technique, such as imprisonment, takes it meaning and dynamic as an element in a larger field of power techniques that aim to influence individuals' behaviour. In this perspective, the emergence and transformation of a social practice, and the knowledge connected with it, are analysed as resulting from the transformation of previous practices, from the appearance of rival practices and, finally, from the connection of some of these new practices to an existing diagram of practices – that is, a complex assemblage of discursive and material practices that define what can be done and said in a particular domain (medicine, for instance) at a given time (Foucault 1969). Punishment via imprisonment, for example, is understood as an extension, or expression, of a much larger group of disciplinary techniques elaborated in the school, factory or army – techniques whose purpose is to control populations and to maximize individual and collective efficiency.

It is through this genealogical reading that Knights and Morgan (1991; 1995) analyse the emergence and diffusion of strategic practices. The authors (1991: 254) note that strategic discourse took off in the United States after World War II. Since the 1930s the discipline has benefited, as with most managerial innovations, from the practice of collaboration between business schools and the business world, as well as from the existence of powerful professional groups. Strategic practices and ideas did not immediately find their place, however. Management practices were initially turned towards the organization and supervision of production and not towards clients, markets or the competition. There are numerous reasons for this. In particular, the domination of an entrepreneurial ideology with the notion of the invisible hand promoted 'inspired leaders' as opposed to rational ones and made the idea of planning a difficult one. In addition, the domination of large market-controlling conglomerates left only the unoccupied niches to small enterprises, thereby limiting strategic moves.

At the end of World War II some planning of the relationship between corporations and their markets became essential. The gradual modification of ownership structures and the appearance of the managerial firm forced managers to report their

activities and results to the stakeholders. The rapid internationalization of American firms, along with the concomitant appearance of multi-divisional firms, further exacerbated the difficulties of control with which these firms were confronted. Different subsidiary and business unit managers were required to report to top management on their activities and results – an obligation that, according to Knights and Morgan (1991; 1995), in turn promoted auditing practices, reporting procedures and financial advisers. Hoskin, Macve and Stone (2006) show that strategic practices relied heavily on accounting and reporting techniques that had been developed during the nineteenth century. While strategic discourse was, of course, not yet inevitable, Knights and Morgan (1991) emphasize how its rise was facilitated by strategy's previous success and progress within the military domain, as well as the influence of academic authors such as Igor Ansoff.

Genealogical analysis of the emergence and diffusion of strategic practices clearly distinguishes itself here from the concepts developed in the mainstream strategy-as-practice approach. Underlining the lack of empirical research on the institutionalization of strategic practices, Vaara and Whittington (2012), following Jarzabowski and Spee (2009), suggest taking inspiration from institutional theories. In a macro-institutional perspective (see Whittington 2002; Johnson, Melin and Whittington 2003; Jarzabkowski 2004), the adoption and diffusion of strategic practices is seen *as a necessity* for the organization (as opposed to the result of the fortuitous interlinking between prior transformations and new ideas): organizations adopt certain structures and forms (organizational templates: DiMaggio and Powell 1983: 27), programmes and policies (Greenwood, Suddaby and Hinings 2002) or particular ways of carrying out a function (Kostova and Roth 2002) in order to meet external expectations and pressures. If one follows the institutional work approach, the investigation will be on how particular actors are able to introduce and transform prevailing practices in a field or on a larger scale.

By contrast, the genealogical perspective developed by Knights and Morgan underlines that strategic practices are neither 'necessities' nor the result of the actions of one particular actor but, rather, the result of *prior changes* in practice and discourses as well as *chance occurrence*. Genea- logical analysis also encourages us to consider strategic practices as belonging to a larger arena of power techniques – techniques that may orient and influence the meanings and aims of strategic practices.

To be governed at a distance

The analyses of Knights and Morgan suggest that the success of strategic practices cannot be fully understood without taking into account the econ- omy of control they imply. Strategic practices are fundamentally related to techniques of control at a distance – a control that, as Hoskin, Macve and Stone's (2006) analysis shows, relies on and pre- supposes (both logically and historically) modern accounting techniques. In fact, these accounting techniques define a 'field of visibility' (Brighenti 2007) that is necessary to carry out strategic prac- tices: they organize time and space (Carmora, Ezzamel and Gutiérrez 2002; Quattrone and Hopper 2005), allowing one to see, localize, meas- ure and calculate activities, individuals and their results, to track and detect waste and to correct inadequate behaviours (Miller and O'Leary 1987).

Ezzamel, Willmott and Worthington (2008) show that the strategic priority given now to the creation of value for the stockholder is accompan- ied by a proliferation of numbers and accounting calculations. They permit the precise evaluation of activities, justify strategic moves (recentring, exter- nalization, cost reduction plans) and render indi- viduals responsible for fixed objectives. Similarly, Cuganesan, Dunford and Palmer (2012) outline how the introduction of new management account- ing practices oriented towards the quantification of human resources and their allocation to specific programs contribute to, if not determine, the defin- ition of the strategic priorities of a public agency formed to fight serious and organized crimes.

Foucault's (1975) attention to the details of the material aspects of discipline leads us to further investigate the role of material artefacts and related techniques in strategic practices. While Alvesson and Kärreman (2011: 1131) have criticized the so-called 'Foucauldian studies' for their 'inability to account for how and why certain discourses tend to stick while others don't', I contend that con- sidering strategic practices as a set of discourse and related techniques of visibility might explain why certain strategic practices are able to gain a foot- hold while others are not: if strategic practices comprise both discourse and related material prac- tices, their relative 'grip' on individual behaviours and organizational practices may be due to their coupling or uncoupling to one another. For instance, Gordon, Clegg and Kornberger (2009) have demonstrated how a programme aimed at introducing increased democracy and empower- ment in a police service, even though accompanied by a discourse about the imperative of change in police ethics, failed, and reporting practices remained unchanged and continued to reproduce existing power relationships.

Such an approach to strategic practices as related to techniques of visibility also sheds light on the disciplinary aspects of strategy. SAP research usu- ally defines the micro-practices of strategists as the flexible and creative adaptation of strategic tools, languages and techniques (see Vaara and Whitting- ton 2012: 12–14 for a review) and remains attached to the conceptualization of the manager as, within certain limits, 'all-powerful' (Allard- Poesi 2006; 2009). By contrast, Foucauldian stud- ies suggest that these managerial micro-moves and apparent 'freedom' are framed, if not formed, by strategic discourse and the techniques of visibility that accompany them.

Looked at from this angle, strategic practice appears less as a rupture with the disciplinary model described by Foucault (1975) and more as an economic change in terms of its target and method of application. In fact, strategic practices share a number of traits with the disciplinary model described by Foucault (see also Hoskin, Macve and Stone 2006; Hopper and Macintosh 1998):

Strategy supposes *hierarchical supervision* in terms of what operational workers bring to middle man- agers, who, in turn, report to top management who then report to the stockholders (see Roberts *et al.* 2006).

Strategic discourse also relies on *comparison with certain norms* (specifically, sector results) as well as with the results originally targeted. It is particularly through these fine-grained metrics and 'normalizing sanctions' that the success, relative failure or change in the enterprise and in the organizational members' behaviour can be seen and sanctioned (McKinlay and Starkey 1998; Ezzamel and Willmott 2008).

- Finally, the *examination techniques* employed by managers, stakeholders, fund managers and credit rating agencies momentarily link (each month, trimester, year) the techniques of supervision with normalizing sanctions during collective encounters at which the results obtained are carefully examined. These encounters, resembling the oral exam sessions used in school as described by Foucault (1975), have not been confined to the organization. Roberts *et al.* (2006: 283) show how fund and executive manager meetings closely resemble examination sessions: executives and top managers anticipate investor wants and carefully prepare their answers, their gestures and their behaviours so as to 'make the organization attractive'. The meetings may be understood as 'ritual subjection to the values of shareholders' (284).

In a number of ways, strategic practices also depart from the disciplinary model Foucault describes.

- First, the techniques of control deployed in the organization after World War II relied on a *complex set of reporting techniques* (internal audits, dual reporting) and not only on the direct and physical surveillance of the disciplinary model. The way of looking at activities and people in organizations, increasingly mediated by a complex set of information technologies such as enterprise resource planning systems, became depersonalized, mainly indirect (Hopper and Macintosh 1998) and polycentric (Brighenti 2007). It is therefore in the name of visibility and of a greater understanding of corporate activities that expert consultants in new technologies and managers justified the continuing implementation of information systems that were steadily more reliable, more reactive, more precise and more powerful (Quattrone and Hopper 2005; 2006). It is equally in the name of this same visibility that the strategic processes themselves became 'technologized' through the implementation of standardized approaches such as the balanced scorecard (BSC: see Mantere and Vaara 2008) or the proliferation of fine-grained accounting metrics and calculations (Ezzamel, Willmott and Worthington 2008).

Second, while in the disciplinary model, it is the minutiae of attitudes and behaviours (see McKinlay 2002) that constitute the target of surveillance, the techniques of surveillance accompanying strategic discourse focus on the *results of their performance*. This implies that surveillance is intermittent (as opposed to continuous) and that it transcends the traditional frontiers and time limits of the organization (as opposed to remaining within the walls of the factory). Executive managers must certainly meet the requirements of the investors, but 'the conduct of fund managers is itself formed within a field of visibility of league tables comparing quarterly fund performance' (Roberts *et al.* 2006: 282). This trait echoes Hoskin, Macve and Stone's (2006: 24) concept of strategy: '[T]he horizons [of strategy] transcend[ed] immediate operational concerns associated with the annihilation of the enemy, to extend continuously into an indefinite future, and extensively over all conceivable space' (for a similar analysis, see Kornberger and Clegg 2011).

Finally, strategy relies on techniques of visibility in which it is up to the strategist to *make him-/herself known* by declaring intentions and expected results; it is the strategist who will report the obtained results; it is up to the strategist to describe, through control procedures, what tools he/she has used to self-monitor. 'It is the managers who must give an account of themselves to the fund managers' (Roberts *et al.* 2006: 290). While the disciplinary model described by Foucault (and the panoptic framework that served as his model: Foucault 1975) has someone watching someone who is him-/herself being watched, the gaze is, above all, brought onto the *strategist*, his/her activities and results. This characteristic of the control process is not specific to top managers. Since the last quarter of the twentieth century it has also concerned middle and operation managers, as 'a negotiative conception of management [was] substituted for one based on the crude imposition of standards' (Miller and O'Leary 1987: 257). The main instrument of this visibility is the budget, through which managers specified their expectations regarding future performance of their activities. Ezzamel *et al.* (2007) show that this process extends beyond private sector firms. The implementation of the 'Local Management of Schools' programme in the United Kingdom, which was aimed at transforming each school into a 'locally managed and accountable' entity, led 'school managers and head teachers to *represent* their schools in convenient economic terms' (Ezzamel *et al.* 2007: 154, emphasis added). Schools were asked to detail their aims and objectives in order to provide the basis for 'constructing budget plans indicating the intended use of resources to achieve these goals' (164).

What appears critical, then, is the extent to which the organization, its managers and its members communicate the truth about themselves – which is not at all the same as being revealed through the eyes of others.[2]

In sum, the Foucauldian perspective underlines how techniques of visibility and related material practices take part in the machinery of strategic practices and of their power effects. In order to appreciate this performative aspect further, recent research has focused on the discursive dimensions of strategic practices (Foucault 1991).

Strategic practices as a body of knowledge

Strategic practices as discourse

Strategic discourse as a 'discursive formation' is marked by a wide variety of statements, concepts and theories – a variety that we may refer to as *strategic discourses*. Vaara (2010) and Mantere and Vaara (2008) have shown how other bodies of knowledge and discourses (military, financial and even spiritual) influence strategic practices and discourses in organizations. If one follows Foucault's analysis, this variety would be seen as limited by a number of rules (Foucault 1969; 1991) that make certain statements read as 'strategic', while excluding others. The task of the researcher, then, is to define these 'rules of statements' that render specific statements possible (and others not) and that create a specific discursive formation (or

'reading system': Lilley 2001: 69); this unity we may refer to as *strategic* or *strategy discourse*.

While the archaeology of strategic discourse – that is, the definition of the rules of statements that condition strategic discourse – remains to be looked at, critical discursive research converges to see strategy as ruled by the following. First, strategic discourse is oriented both towards the internal organization and to its 'external' environment (competitors, customers, markets: Knights and Morgan 1995: 198, 206; Vaara, Kleymann and Seristö 2004: 25), which is perceived as changing and potentially hostile. Second, in this context, strategy is concerned with the organization's future – a future that includes improved competitiveness and efficiency (Oakes,Townley and Cooper 1998: 276; Samra-Fredericks 2003: 149–50), rendering organizational change imperative (Knights and Morgan 1995: 206; Oakes, Townley and Cooper 1998: 276; Samra-Fredericks 2003: 149–50). Third, strategic discourse is dominated by an instrumental rationality in which economic ends and 'facts' both dictate the adequate course of action (Ezzamel and Willmott 2008: 205; 2010: 79; Samra-Fredericks 2005: 823).

In summary, strategic discourse conveys a sense of order and naturality (in SWOT analysis, for instance: Oakes, Townley and Cooper 1998) that 'encourages a self-disciplined commitment to the rational objectives and projects of [the] organization' (Knights and Morgan 1995: 212) from top management as well as from operating personnel (see Mantere and Vaara 2008: 348–9). This sense of naturality and instrumentality gives strategic discourse tremendous power and legitimacy in the organization. In an in-depth analysis of the strategic plan of the city of Lahti, Finland, Vaara, Sorsa and Pälli (2010) show how it tends to prioritize consensus, to make strategic priorities imperative and to cancel any dissent and debate, giving the strategic plan a power force potential. Investigating the power effects of a strategic change discourse over time in a building company, McCabe (2009) demonstrates that the ambiguity of strategic discourse contributes to the adhesion of organizational members at the beginning of the process. Even though, later on, contradictions and equivocality can generate dissent and distance from some

---

[2] The model described here relies on self-revelation, which appears, finally, closer to the 'pastoral' power model as described by Foucault (1984a) than to the disciplinary model. As for the Christian examination of conscience, it involves the description of desires, not as a method of self-questioning but as a method of control.

staff and managers confronted with redundancies and excessive workload, the ambiguity also encourages actions and initiatives from other managers who strive to enact the strategic change.

This research provides invaluable insights into the power effects of strategic discourse, but it remains uncertain whether these characteristics (ambiguity, naturality, instrumentality) are specific to strategic discourse or are also shared by other modern discourse (see Townley 2002; 2005 for similar conclusions for human resource management discourse).

Strategic practices as a (limited) will to influence

Lilley underlines that strategic discourses tend to gravitate around the notion of strategic intent (Lilley 2001). As pointed out by Knights and Morgan (1991), to be a strategist is to take risks, be an agent of change, be responsible and, above all, to have plans, intentions and objectives to achieve. This intent justifies strategic action, possible organizational changes and even, as the study by Mantere and Vaara (2008) shows, the degree of participation of the organization's members in its elaboration.

Lilley (2001: 73–5) also notes the tendency of strategic discourse to proliferate, investing in new fields and objects, such as corporate strategy, business strategy, information systems strategy and marketing strategy. Certain areas of management are 'saved' from strategic discourse, however, because the discourse will retain those objects that it may want to, and can, influence and exclude others. This is why certain sectors, while being regulated for a long time, have only recently been affected by strategic discourse: the banking sector (Knights and Morgan 1995), for instance; and more recently, via the progressive implementation of new public management, education (Ezzamel et al. 2007), cities (Kornberger and Clegg 2011; Vaara, Sorsa and Pälli 2010) and public agencies (Cuganesan, Dunford and Palmer 2012).

The formation of strategic discourse is also distinguished by its irregular and episodic character (Hendry and Seidl 2003). Ensconced in specific rituals, and often limited to a group of privileged

actors, the intentionality that strategic discourse brings is not a practical intentionality linked to the continuation of activity but is, instead, an *abstract, formalized intentionality,* detached from daily practices, operations and contexts; this trait is heavily used by consultants and strategists when they want to silence dissenting voices (see Kornberger and Clegg 2011).

This analysis of strategic practices as a field of knowledge decisively departs from the idea of a flexible strategic practice, adaptable and adapted to the context and purposes of the actors, that is prevalent in the currently dominant strategy-as-practice approach. Empirical research in strategy as practice (for reviews, see Vaara and Whittington 2012; Jarzabkowski and Spee 2009) underlines the continuous adaptation of strategic practices to their micro-context (which includes the relationships between individuals, and the set of tools, vocabulary and supports at their disposal) as well as the transformations that the practices themselves exercise on organizational context (Tsoukas and Chia 2002).

As individuals can cut themselves off from daily practice with strategic episodes, and yet at the same time be integrated in multiple social systems and their associated practices, they are capable of reconstructing and adapting their strategizing to their interests and problems of the moment (Hendry and Seidl 2003). In fact, many scholars see strategic practices as a set of resources allowing managers to create a particular strategic practice. Taking inspiration from Giddens (1991: 80), Whittington (1992: 696) considers that the diversity of social systems and activities in modern societies offers individuals an increased capacity to choose their lifestyles and identities. Participating in a multiplicity of social systems (political, domestic, professional, etc.), individuals are liable to import rules and resources to an organization, and to question and transform the existing system of practices (Hung and Whittington 1997). In a closely related perspective, Jarzabkowski (2003), following Engeström's activity theory (Engeström 1987, cited by Blackler 1993), emphasizes how managers take advantage of the inherent contradictions of the different dimensions of a concrete activity to destabilize the activity system and thus introduce the impetus for change.

Departing from this perspective, the Foucauldian analysis of strategic practices as a body of knowledge shows that, while strategic discourse and practices may be quite diverse, it does not necessarily imply that they are created by free, all-powerful individuals. Strategic practices obey a specific regime that has an established set of rules and parameters – a regime that excludes, at the same time, other 'worlds of possibilities' (Calàs and Smircich 1988: 206, quoted by Linstead and Brewis 2007: 359). As discourse, strategic practices obey rules of statements that are marked by instrumental rationality, naturality and abstract intentionality. Strategic practices are also related to a system of visibility that restricts and influences what strategic practices can accomplish. In sum, strategic practices clearly frame the range of possible actions and the ways in which we see the organization and its environment. This leads us to question its consequences for our lives as subjects.

The strategist 'unfolded': say what you want

The strategist subject: 'Say what you want'

The Foucauldian concept of practices considers the practitioner as a subject constituted through the discursive and non-discursive practices that he/she accomplishes. The notion of subject may be understood in two different ways in the Foucauldian approach to strategic practices.

On the one hand, the subject can be taken as equivalent to *subjectivity* – that is, a set of 'psychic dispositions', an ensemble of assumptions, beliefs, aspirations (Chan 2000: 1060) and meanings (Knights and Morgan 1991: 254). Subject, in this perspective, encapsulates both behavioural (corporeal) and psychic (interiority) dimensions. It is this extensive concept of subject that is embraced by Knights and Morgan (1991: 254) when they write that 'discourses are at one level internal to the subject, providing the basis on which subjectivity itself is constructed'. It is also this concept that is referred to by Miller (1987: 2) when he states that 'power acts indirectly on the interior of the person. . . [It] attempts to invest the individual with a series of personal objectives and ambitions.' This assumes not only that strategic discourse is used to influence how one should act and see oneself in specific circumstances but that it succeeds in its attempts to do so. Following this approach, some researchers emphasize that strategic practices inscribe the practitioners' subjectivity and contribute to the building of their identity as strategist. This identity implies mastering, at least in part, one's environment and future (Knights and Morgan 1991); it is the ability to be autonomous, responsible, capable of taking risks and being an agent of change (Oakes, Townley and Cooper 1998; Knights and McCabe 2003); to have plans, designs and intentions (Lilley 2001); to take distance from daily operations and reflect rationally on the issues at stake; to be firm, resolute and proactive (Samra-Fredericks 2005) – in sum, to be 'powerful'.

In my view, assimilating the Foucauldian notion of subject to that of subjectivity is questionable for at least two reasons. First, this conception cannot distinguish itself from the dominant view of strategist in most strategy-as-practice research. In fact, the two versions envisage the strategist as a *bricoleur* strategist who does what he/she wants within the limit of the means and resources at his/her disposal. The two versions also understand strategists as capable of manipulating the material, social and symbolic resources at their disposal (Hung and Whittington 1997; Rouleau 2005; Rouleau and Balogun 2010), of taking advantage of the resources' inherent contradictions and diversity in order to transform, or adapt, these resources to their own purposes (Jarzabkowski 2003). Second, this extensive conceptualization of the subject accords too much power to discourse (see Alvesson and Kärreman 2011) and reads Foucault's work as structuralist, which is doubtful (Foucault 2001d [1983]). Foucault warns us against such a powerful conception of discourse when he states that 'discourse is not a place where subjectivity irrupts', only a place of subject positions and functions (Foucault 1991: 58).

By '*subject*', Foucault means one who acts in accordance with the rules and norms of a discursive formation and, in this way, endorses a particular role and occupies a specific '*subject position*'

(Foucault 1991). While excluding subjectivity, the word 'subject' entails two meanings: "subject to someone else by control and dependence, and being tied to one's own identity by a conscience or self-knowledge" (Foucault 1982: 212). Discursive and extra-discursive practices are understood here as mechanisms of subjection (*assujettissement*), the dual process of subjugation (or subordination) and subjectivation – that is, the promotion of a specific definition of who one is and how one should act (Chan 2000: 1063–4), but not how one actually thinks.

The researcher's task, then, is to 'map the role and operations exhausted by different "discoursing subjects"' (Foucault 1991: 62), as these reveal the means and resources that subjects may use to achieve a better position in the discursive field. 'The moment came to consider these facts of discourse no longer simply in their linguistic dimension, but in a sense. . .like games, strategic games of action and relation, question and answer, domination and evasion, as well as struggle' (Foucault 2001a [1974]: 1407). This perspective, developed in *Archaeology of Knowledge* (Foucault: 1969) and *Discipline and Punish* (Foucault: 1975), is what Knights and Willmott argue for when they stress that 'who we are and what we are (i.e. our social identity) is confirmed and sustained through our positioning in practices which reflect and reproduce prevailing power-knowledge relations' (Knights and Willmott 1989: 550). It is this concept that is adopted by Samra-Frederick (2003: 2005), Laine and Vaara (2007) and Mantere and Vaara (2008) when they investigate the discursive practices of strategists and the resulting interactional order.

In this sense, strategic discourses have performative power but are not 'all-powerful'. In fact, recent empirical studies outline the conditions and limits of the strategic force potential (Vaara, Sorsa and Pälli 2010; McCabe 2009). For instance, Laine and Vaara (2007) show that, even if strategic discourses are aimed at gaining control, they can also give rise to resistance as they undermine the position of particular members, who will develop alternative strategic discourses to re-establish their legitimacy and position themselves as 'strategic actors'.

While bringing insight into the power of strategy, this stream of research focuses on strategy as discourse and tends to neglect the material dimensions of strategic practices previously underlined. To reiterate, Foucault (1975) urges us to pay attention to the concrete dimensions of strategic practices and techniques that shape people's conduct and relationships, and through which we are constituted as 'subjects'. While strategic discourse promotes independence, self-control and free will, strategic practices rely on techniques of visibility that imply that the strategist 'makes him-/herself known' by declaring intentions and expected results. In doing so, the strategist is liable to see his/her desires 'captured' in a field of visibility and recast within the categories and terms of techniques and 'significant others' belonging to that field.

In sum, a Foucauldian analysis of strategic practices suggests that the techniques of visibility, which make strategic discourse possible, greatly contribute to the fabric of the strategist-subject – a contribution that countervails the idea of autonomy and free will that strategic discourse express. Outlining the 'double-edged sword' aspect of strategic practices, my analysis calls for complementing critical discursive approaches with methods that investigate the techniques of visibility and control surrounding strategic discourse. It also suggests reconsidering the possibilities of resistance in organizations.

Subjectivity as resistance

For Foucault (2001f [1988]: 1604), resistance supposes the exercise of practices of self-transformation by which the subject, relying on social practices, tries to transform himself (see also Foucault 2001e [1984]; Townley 1995). In ancient Greece, these techniques of self required that one has listened to, and assimilated, the lessons of the masters or the ancient texts.[3] The constitution of self also supposes at the same time *significant work on self* as a means of freedom, as only a free

---

[3] The Grecian techniques of self were aimed at managing this area of power present in all relations and were thus akin to a form of government.

person can dominate others (his/her children, his/her partner). It is only by using the 'personal' rules that he/she has acquired through self-work that he/she will be able to create a *personal subjectivity*. This work on self supposes that the individual will actively engage with others and the world, analyse his/her personal reactions and ensure that these reactions respect the principles of order (Townley 1995).

Deleuze (1988: 104, 107–8) highlights the fact that, for Foucault, subjectivity is created by *'fold-ings'*: the inside of thought being a fold from the 'outside' (relationships of power and knowledge). This subjective fold is not a sign or a reflection of the outside. It is a specific derivative that takes a sort of independence from forces of power and knowledge, to the extent that the individual is capable of bending these forces by using techniques and work on self. The capacity to fold in outside forces in order to create oneself as an independent being assumes irreducible freedom. In other words, the *resistance comes first*, and is not exclusively (as works by Knights 2002 and others indicate) a consequence of practices of knowledge and power, of their diversity, of their contradictions and of the 'multiple identities' they allow. Moreover, it is this resistance and this liberty that allow the constitution of personal subjectivity.

Given this perspective, resistance must be distinguished from the various discursive battles that take place among organizational members as they all claim a strategist's position and its associated identity (see Laine and Vaara 2007). Resistance must also be distinguished from the disengagement, passivity, cynicism or irony that may be observed as people encounter difficulties while enacting the various (and sometimes contradicting) injunctions of strategic discourses (see Knights and McCabe 2003; Knights 2002; McCabe 2009).

Foucault's conception of subjectivity must also be differentiated from the dominant strategy-as-practice approach (see also Townley 1995; Linstead and Brewis 2007). As opposed to an existing 'self' or subjectivity waiting to be revealed, excavated and eventually transformed, Foucault invites us to envisage the self as a kind of 'work-in-progress' as one actively engages with others and the world. To resist, in this perspective, necessarily

assumes working with, and questioning, these subjectivities that are 'given' to us through strategic practices. It is a struggle, then, not only with individualizing practices of control but, equally, against those practices 'that consist of attaching each individual to a well-known and well-learned identity, determined once and for all' (Deleuze 1988: 113).

In my view, strategic practices cannot give rise to resistance; they do not assume the intensification of the subject's relationship to self that the Foucauldian conception of resistance implies. It is not concerned with working on oneself so that one becomes an autonomous person (a free citizen, in ancient Greece). Rather, it implies working on a project, and then revealing what one wants to accomplish. While working on oneself may help to constitute the independent 'subject' by the changes that the work requires, strategic practices imply an *'unfolding'* of self, bringing forth the subjectivity in order to be better seen. The transformation of strategic diagnostic tools clearly illustrates this 'unfolding': a sort of ironing out of subjectivity. The matrices developed by McKinsey in the 1960s had managers translate into specific criteria what was, for them, the appeal of a sector – a translation through which they expressed their intentions (turnover, profit and growth, for example). More recently, the tools developed by the same (Copeland 2000) push the strategist to translate his/her intentions into specific criteria, with portfolio value as a terminal objective, along with a series of concrete steps to reach it.

Perhaps strategic practices do participate in the constitution of forms of subjectivity, but I believe that they aim, above all, to bring light to subjects' subjective 'folds' and desires. As such, strategic practices appear poorly equipped to create a form of resistance.

Conclusion

Foucauldian analysis invites us to envisage strategic practices as a body of knowledge that is a specific set of discursive practices and practices of visibility. These strategic practices appear to be governed by rules of influence and intent that will be limited by what we can 'see'. Being inscribed within a larger field of power, strategic practices emerge as a complex series of changes that take part in the modern enterprise's techniques of control at a distance. In this way, these strategic practices *diverge from the model of disciplinary supervision* that Foucault (1975) describes. It is, in effect, up to those who are being supervised to show that they are supervising themselves using adequate procedures, and it is up to them to make themselves seen by revealing their intentions and results. In this sense, strategic management is similar to a monitoring technique in which the strategist is led to an *'unfolding'* of self (Deleuze 1988: 110): to reveal one's intentions, say what is hidden, 'objectify' one's subjectivity, in order – once again – to enter into the relationships of knowledge and power.

Looked at from this angle, strategic practices resemble the modern techniques of governmentality that Rose speaks of. As other modern techniques of self, strategic practices suppose that the strategist-subject 'makes the feelings, wishes and emotions of the self visible to itself' (Rose 1999: 228). Strategy, then, would not be an art of folding (or leading) others, nor even self-folding (submitting to the control of others), but more of a personal unfolding: bringing to the surface, and objectifying, desires and intentions in order to be better 'seen' (Rose 1999), and to be caught up in the relations of knowledge and power (Deleuze 1988); becoming, through self-revelation and self-control, a blank surface upon which other intentions and other projects can be inscribed.

This Foucauldian perspective opens up new areas of research for the study of strategy as practice. First, one may question how strategists manage the empowering/disempowering effects of strategic practices: how do they maintain the 'free will' attached to strategic discourse while at the same time meeting the requirements of others' desires when entering a field of visibility? Different responses to these issues might be hypothesized: making the others' desires one's own (see Roberts *et al.* 2006); maintaining both 'desires' even if one runs the risk of following contradictory courses of actions (see Lüscher and Lewis 2008); pursuing the others' requirements (such as financial performance) while recasting one's own

objectives in domains that others do not consider as important (corporate image, marketing actions towards end customers, for instance); or ignoring or resisting others' desires (and running the risk of losing support from 'significant others'). While, in theory, all answers are possible, the characteristics of the field of visibility in which the organization and the strategist are embedded are certainly determinant in the 'desires' that will be expressed and followed.

Second, this invites us to investigate the 'topography' of the field of visibility that serves to condition strategic discourse and its consequences for organizational actions and practices: Who looks at the organization? Using what techniques and criteria? What are the consequences on the strategies pursued and the management practices adopted by the firm? It is self-evident here that the more dependent the organization is on external stakeholders, the more 'visible' their strategies should be. This may explain why firms tend to redefine activities around their 'core business' and/or restructure their corporate body (merging or outsourcing: see Roberts *et al.* 2006). Conversely, one may hypothesize that actions of resistance are more liable to take place either in the organizations that have not yet been colonized by strategic discourse or, as mentioned earlier, outside the organization. In my view, studying the forms and evolution of such initiatives would be of great interest for strategy research.

Third, the perspective outlined here urges us to investigate the role of information technology in the development of strategic discourse – a dimension that, with a few exceptions (such as Leclerc-Vandelannoitte, 2011; Mantere and Vaara 2008; Jarzabwoski, Spee and Smets 2013), is rarely taken into account. In particular, this analysis encourages us to more closely study, and identify, which characteristics of the mechanisms of visibility give actors the feeling that they are in better control of strategic processes, and to investigate their consequences on strategic decisions and practices. What place is taken today by methods such as the BSC, which promises managers better control over strategic processes and measures of performance? What are the effects of information systems (enterprise resource planning, business intelligence, for example) on strategic discourse and behaviour? These systems, with all their complexity and shifting character, have the tendency to 'get away' from their designers; they create 'blind spots' and 'trading zones' (Mouritsen and Dechow 2005), or collapse traditional time-space dichotomies, rendering control diffused and off-centred, with action at a distance becoming problematic (Quattrone and Hopper 2005). It appears crucial to study their modalities of functioning and their coupling/uncoupling with strategic discourse in order to appreciate the power effects of strategic practices. These research issues call for complementing our critical discursive approaches with methods that specifically seek to characterize the techniques of visibility and control surrounding strategic discourse (see Jarzabkwoski, Spee and Smets 2013 for an example).

Finally, the differences between the Foucauldian perspective of strategy and the prevailing strategy-as-practice approach as discussed here can be usefully mobilized to question their respective foundations. The notion of free will or intentionality appears as an important line of demarcation. Although certainly a structuring element, this notion has been the object of a limited number of research studies, as if it is assumed that intention exists and does not need to be questioned (see also Ruef 2003: 247). After the (socio)cognitive approach, which questioned how managers and their teams 'think', we became interested in what they 'do' and who they 'are', but have avoided the question of what they 'want'. This could very well be a unique opportunity to question the notion of strategic intent. Whether managers do what they want, or they are, and want, what they do, remains unexplored.

In sum, Foucault's perspective invites us to question the conditions and 'limits' of the performative effects of strategic practices. Of course, these suggestions do not exhaust all avenues for future research. They are meant to be seen as an invitation to strategy researchers to work more closely with colleagues from other disciplines (accounting, information systems and human resources management, or HRM, in particular) so as to better see and appreciate the 'power effects' of strategy.

References

Allard-Poesi, F. (2006), 'La stratégie comme pratique (s): ce que faire de la stratégie veut dire', in Golsorkhi, D. (ed.), *La fabrique de la stratégie: Une perspective multidimensionnelle*: 27–47. Paris: Vuibert.

(2009), 'La stratégie comme art de se déplier', in Golsorkhi, D., Huault, I., and Leca, B. (eds.), *Les études critiques en management: Une perspective française*: 163–84. Laval: Eska.

Alvesson, M., and Kärreman, D. (2011), 'Decolonializing discourse: critical reflections on organizational discourse analysis', *Human Relations*, 64/9: 1121–46.

Blackler, F. (1993), 'Knowledge and the theory of organizations: organizations as activity systems and the reframing of management', *Journal of Management Studies*, 30/6: 863–84.

Brighenti, A. (2007), 'Visibility: a category for the social sciences', *Current Sociology*, 55/3: 323–42.

Calàs, M., and Smircich, L. (1988), 'Reading leadership as a form of cultural analysis', in Hunt, J. G., Baliga, R. D., Dachler, H. P., and Schriesheim, C. A. (eds.), *Emerging Leadership Vistas*: 201–26. Lexington, MA: Lexington Books.

Carmora S., Ezzamel, M., and Gutiérrez, F. (2002), 'The relationship between accounting and spatial practices in the factory', *Accounting, Organizations and Society*, 27/3: 239–74.

Chan, A. (2000), 'Redirecting critique in postmodern organization studies: the perspective of Foucault', *Organization Studies*, 21/6: 1059–75.

Copeland, T. E. (2000), *Valuation: Measuring and Managing the Value of Companies*, 3rd edn. Hoboken, NJ: John Wiley.

Cuganesan, S., Dunford, R., and Palmer, I. 2012. 'Strategic management accounting and strategy practices within a public sector agency', *Management Accounting Research*, 23/4: 245–60.

Deleuze, G. (1988), *Foucault*. Minneapolis: University of Minnesota Press.

DiMaggio, P., and Powell, W. (1983), 'The iron cage revisited: institutional isomorphism and collective rationality in organizational fields', *American Sociological Review*, 48/2: 147–60.

Engeström, Y. (1987), *Learning by Expanding: An Activity-Theoretical Approach to Developmental Research*. Helsinki: Orienta-Nonsultit.

Ezzamel, M., Robson, K., Stapleton, P., and McLean, C. (2007), 'Discourse and institutional change: "giving accounts" and accountability', *Management Accounting Research*, 18/2: 150–71.

Ezzamel, M., and Willmott, H. (2008), 'Strategy as discourse in a global retailer: a supplement to rationalist and interpretive accounts', *Organization Studies*, 29/2: 191–217.

(2010), 'Strategy and strategizing: a post-structuralist perspective', in Baum, J. A. C., and Lampel, J. (eds.), *Advances in Strategic Management*, vol. XXVII, *The Globalization of Strategy Research*: 75–109. Bingley, UK: Emerald.

Ezzamel, M., Willmott, H., and Worthington, F. 2008. 'Manufacturing shareholder value: the role of accounting in organizational transformation', *Accounting, Organizations and Society*, 33/2–3: 107–40.

Foucault, M. (1969), *L'archéologie du savoir*. Paris: Gallimard.

(1971), *L'ordre du discours*. Paris: Gallimard.

(1975), *Surveiller et punir: Naissance de la prison*. Paris: Gallimard.

(1976), *Histoire de la sexualité*, vol. I, *La volonté de savoir*. Paris: Gallimard.

(1982), 'The subject and power', in Dreyfus, H. L., and Rabinow, P. (eds.), *Michel Foucault: Beyond Structuralism and Hermeneutics*: 208–26. University of Chicago Press.

(1984a), *Histoire de la sexualité*, vol. II, *L'usage des plaisirs*. Paris: Gallimard.

(1984b), *Histoire de la sexualité*, vol. III, *Le souci de soi*. Paris: Gallimard.

(1991), 'Politics and the study of discourse', in Burchell, G., Gordon, C., and Miller, P. (eds.), *The Foucault Effect: Studies in Governmentality*: 53–72. University of Chicago Press.

(2001a [1974]), 'La vérité et les formes juridiques', in Defert, D., and Ewald, F. (eds.), *Michel Foucault: Dits et écrits*, vol. II, *1976–1988*: 1406–514. Paris: Gallimard.

(2001b [1978]), 'La "gouvernementalité", cours du Collège de France, 1977–1978, "Sécurité, territoire et population", 4ième leçon, 1er février 1978', in Defert, D., and Ewald, F. (eds.), *Michel Foucault: Dits et écrits*, vol. II, *1976–1988*: 635–57. Paris: Gallimard.

(2001c [1983]), '"L'écriture de soi", corps écrit, 5: l'autoportrait', in Defert, D., and Ewald, F. (eds.), *Michel Foucault: Dits et écrits*, vol. II, *1976–1988*: 1234–49. Paris: Gallimard.

(2001d [1983]), '"Structuralisme et poststructuralisme"; entretien avec G. Raulet', in Defert, D., and Ewald, F. (eds.), *Michel Foucault: Dits et écrits*, vol. II, *1976–1988*: 1250–76. Paris: Gallimard.

(2001e [1984]), 'L'éthique du souci de soi comme pratique de la liberté; entretien avec H. Becker, R. Fornet-Betancourt et A. Gomez-Müller', in Defert, D., and Ewald, F. (eds.), *Michel Foucault: Dits et écrits*, vol. II, *1976–1988*: 1527–48. Paris: Gallimard.

(2001f [1988]), 'Technologies of the self', in Defert, D., and Ewald, F. (eds.), *Michel Foucault: Dits et écrits*, vol. II, *1976–1988*: 1602–32. Paris: Gallimard.

Giddens, A. (1991), *Modernity and Self-Identity*. Cambridge: Polity.

(1993), *New Rules of Sociological Method: A Positive Critique of Interpretive Sociologies*, 2nd edn. Oxford: Polity.

Gordon, R., Clegg, S., and Kornberger, M. (2009), 'Embedded ethics: discourse and power in the New South Wales Police Service', *Organization Studies*, 30/1, 73–99.

Greenwood, R., Suddaby, R., and Hinings, C. (2002), 'Theorizing change: the role of professional associations in the transformation of institutionalized fields', *Academy of Management Journal*, 45/1: 58–80.

Hendry, J., and Seidl, D. (2003), 'The structure and significance of strategic episodes: social systems theory and the routine practices of strategic change', *Journal of Management Studies*, 40/1: 175–96.

Hopper, T., and Macintosh, N. (1998), 'Management accounting numbers: freedom or prison – Geenen versus Foucault', in McKinlay, A., and Starkey, K. (eds.), *Foucault, Management and Organization Theory*: 126–50. London: Sage.

Hoskin, K., Macve, R., and Stone, J. (2006), 'Accounting and strategy: towards understanding the historical genesis of modern business and military strategy', in Bhimani, A. (ed.), *Contemporary Issues in Management Accounting*: 165–90. Oxford University Press.

Hung, S.-C., and Whittington, R. (1997), 'Strategy and institutions: a pluralistic account of strategies in the Taiwanese computing industry', *Organization Studies*, 18/4: 551–75.

Jarzabkowski, P. (2003), 'Strategic practices: an activity theory perspective on continuity and change', *Journal of Management Studies*, 40/1: 28–55.

(2004), 'Strategy as practice: recursiveness, adaptation, and practices-in-use', *Organization Studies*, 25/4: 529–60.

Jarzabkowski, P., and Spee, P. (2009), 'Strategy-as-practice: a review and future directions for the field', *International Journal of Management Reviews*, 11/1: 69–95.

Jarzabkowski, P., Spee, P., and Smets, M. (2013), 'Material artifacts: practices for doing strategy with "stuff"', *European Management Journal*, 31/1: 41–54.

Johnson, G., Melin, L., and Whittington, R. 2003. 'Guest editors' introduction: micro strategy and strategizing: towards an activity-based view', *Journal of Management Studies*, 40/1: 3–22.

Knights, D. (2002), 'Writing organizational analysis into Foucault', *Organization*, 9/4: 575–93.

Knights, D., and McCabe, D. (2003), 'Governing through teamwork: reconstituting subjectivity in a call center', *Journal of Management Studies*, 40/7: 1587–619.

Knights, D., and Morgan, G. (1991), 'Corporate strategy, organizations, and subjectivity: a critique', *Organization Studies*, 12/2: 251–73.

(1995), 'Strategic management, financial services and information technology', *Journal of Management Studies*, 32/2: 191–214.

Knights, D., and Willmott, H. (1989), 'Power and subjectivity at work: from degradation to subjugation in social relations', *Sociology*, 23/4: 535–58.

Kornberger, M., and Clegg, S. (2011), 'Strategy as performative practice: the case of Sydney 2030', *Strategic Organization*, 9/2: 136–62.

Kostova, T., and Roth, K. (2002), 'Adoption of an organizational practice by subsidiaries of multinational corporations: institutional and relational effects', *Academy of Management Journal*, 45/1: 213–33.

Laine, P.-M., and Vaara, E. (2007), 'Struggling over subjectivity: a discursive analysis of strategic development in an engineering group', *Human Relations*, 60/1: 29–58.

Leclercq-Vandelannoitte, A. (2011), 'Organization as discursive constructions: a Foucauldian approach', *Organization Studies*, 32/9: 1247–71.

Lilley, S. (2001), 'The language of strategy', in Westwood, R., and Linstead, S. (eds.), *The Language of Organization*: 66–88. London: Sage.

Linstead, S., and Brewis, J. (2007), 'Passion, knowledge and motivation: ontologies of desire', *Organization*, 14/3: 351–71.

Lüscher, L. S., and Lewis, M. W. (2008), 'Organizational change and managerial sensemaking: working through paradox', *Academy of Management Journal*, 51/2: 221–40.

Mantere, S., and Vaara, E. (2008), 'On the problem of participation in strategy: a critical discursive perspective', *Organization Science*, 19/2: 341–58.

McCabe, D. (2010), 'Strategy-as-power: ambiguity, contradiction and the exercice of power in a UK building society', *Organization*, 17/2: 151–75.

McKinlay, A. (2002), '"Dead selves": the birth of the modern career', *Organization*, 9/4: 595–614.

McKinlay, A., and Starkey, K. (1998), '"The velvety grip": managing managers in the modern corporation', in *Foucault, Management and Organization Theory*: 111–25. London: Sage.

Miller, P. (1987), *Domination and Power*. London: Routledge.

Miller, P., and O'Leary, T. (1987), 'Accounting and the construction of the governable person', *Accounting, Organizations and Society*, 12/3: 235–65.

Mouritsen, J., and Dechow, N., (2005), 'Enterprise resource planning systems, management control and the quest for integration', *Accounting, Organizations and Society*, 30/7–8: 691–733.

Oakes, L. S., Townley, B., and Cooper, D. J. (1998), 'Business planning as pedagogy: language and control in a changing institutional field', *Administrative Science Quarterly*, 43/2: 257–92.

Quattrone, P., and Hopper, T. (2005), 'A "time–space odyssey": management control systems in two multinational organisations', *Accounting, Organizations and Society*, 30/7–8: 735–64.

(2006), 'What is IT? SAP, accounting and visibility in a multinational organisation', *Information and Organization*, 16/3: 212–50.

Roberts, J., Sanderson, P., Barker, R., and Hendry, J. (2006), 'In the mirror of the market: the disciplinary effects of company/fund managers meetings', *Accounting, Organizations and Society*, 31/3: 277–94.

Rose, N. (1999), *Governing the Soul: The Shaping of the Private Self*, 2nd edn. London: Free Association Books.

Rouleau, L. (2005), 'Micro-practices of strategic sensemaking and sensegiving: how middle managers interpret and sell change every day', *Journal of Management Studies*, 42/7: 1413–41.

Rouleau, L., and Balogun, J. (2010), 'Middle managers, strategic sensemaking, and discursive competence', *Journal of Management Studies*, 48/5: 953–83.

Ruef, M. (2003), 'A sociological perspective on strategic organization', *Strategic Organization*, 2/1: 241–51.

Samra-Fredericks, D. (2003), 'Strategizing as lived experience and strategists' everyday efforts to shape strategic directions', *Journal of Management Studies*, 40/1: 141–74.

—— (2005), 'Strategic practice, "discourse" and the everyday interactional constitution of "power effects"', *Organization*, 12/6: 803–41.

Schatzki, T. R. (2001), 'Practice mind-ed orders', in Schatzki, T.R., Knorr Cetina, K., and von Savigny, E. (eds.), *The Practice Turn in Contemporary Theory*: 42–55. London: Routledge.

Townley, B. (1995), '"Know thyself": self-awareness, self-formation and managing', *Organization*, 2/2: 271–89.

—— (2002), 'Managing with modernity', *Organization*, 9/4: 549–73.

—— (2005), 'Théorie des organisations: la place du sujet', in Hatchuel, A., Pezet, E., Starkey, K., and Lenay, O. (eds.), *Gouvernement, organisations et gestion: L'héritage de Michel Foucault*: 63–91. Presses de l'Université Laval.

Tsoukas, H., and Chia, R. (2002), 'On organizational becoming: rethinking organizational change', *Organization Science*, 13/5: 567–82.

Vaara, E. (2010), 'Taking the linguistic turn seriously: strategy as a multifaceted and interdiscursive phenomenon', in Baum, J. A. C., and Lampel, J. (eds.), *Advances in Strategic Management*, vol. XXVII, *The Globalization of Strategy Research*: 29–50. Bingley, UK: Emerald.

Vaara, E., Kleymann, B., and Seristö, H. (2004), 'Strategies as discursive constructions: the case of airline alliances', *Journal of Management Studies*, 41/1: 1–35.

Vaara, E., Sorsa, V., and Pälli, P. (2010), 'On the force potential of strategy texts: a critical discourse analysis of a strategic plan and its power effects in a city organization', *Organization*, 17/6: 685–702.

Vaara, E., and Whittington, R. (2012), 'Strategy-as-practice: taking social practices seriously', *Academy of Management Annals*, 6/1: 285–336.

Whittington, R. (1992), 'Putting Giddens into action: social systems and managerial agency', *Journal of Management Studies*, 29/6: 693–712.

—— (2002), *Practice Perspectives on Strategy: Unifying and Developing a Field*, working paper. Saïd Business School, University of Oxford.

A narrative approach to strategy as practice: strategy-making from texts and narratives

VALÉRIE-INÈS DE LA VILLE and ELÉONORE MOUNOUD

The narrativizing of practices is a textual 'way of operating', having its own procedures and tactics. [...] Shouldn't we recognize its scientific legitimacy by assuming that instead of being a remainder that cannot be, or has not yet been, eliminated from discourse, narrativity has a necessary function in it, and that a theory of narration is indissociable from a theory of practices, as its condition as well as its production.

De Certeau (1988: 78)

Introduction

The strategy-as-practice approach requires a close and detailed scrutiny of practitioners' activities. Such a micro-level approach enables us to depart from the conventional perspective and delve 'inside the process to examine intimately the kind of work that is actually being done' (Whittington and Cailluet 2008: 244), to study in more detail 'individual' rather than 'organizational' performance (Samra-Fredericks 2003). Moving attention away from macro-processes towards various aspects of the minutiae of strategy-making has changed the discourse used by researchers to explain how strategy is conceived, explained and communicated (Whittington 2007; Vaara and Whittington 2012). In practice, strategizing is essentially considered as micro-processes – that is, the actual activities carried out by individuals within their organized contexts: '[S]trategy is something that *people do*' (Jarzabkowski and Whittington 2008: 282, emphasis added).

Although social practice theory tends to emphasize the tacit and informal dimensions of practices and praxis, SAP research has focused on 'the work,

the workers and tools of strategy' (Jarzabkowski and Whittington 2008: 285), leading to the privileging of explicit practices, especially on operating procedures and standards (Jarzabkowski 2004; 2005), norms of appropriate strategic behaviour set by industry recipes (Spender 1989) and legitimizing discourses (Barry and Elmes 1997). Furthermore, while social practice theory advocates 'agency' for everyone in everyday life, strategy-as-practice research pays attention mainly to special events (Hendry and Seidl 2003) and top management (Samra-Fredericks 2003). Thus, the approach's achievement has been largely a change in the method of observing strategic management, and not the basic categories of thought (Jarzabkowki, Balogun and Seidl 2007; Johnson *et al.* 2007; Whittington 2011). So far, strategy-as-practice research has mainly focused on the visible part of the iceberg: people, events and explicit tools. The actual practice in itself, which 'involves a constant parsing out of the individual, the local and the societal' (Whittington 2011: 185), has not yet been sufficiently investigated. Thus, Vaara and Whittington (2012: 2) underline the 'need to go further in the analyses of social practices to unleash the full potential of this perspective'.

Focusing on micro-activities raises the subsequent problem of linking individual actions to macro-outcomes. Making a 'practice turn' in strategy research requires not only knitting together 'micro-practices' and 'macro-outcomes' but also avoiding being caught in the trap of considering practices as just something people do. Practices are construed as social skills that have been culturally acquired, hence unconsciously absorbed and embodied. This compels us to take the dynamic and emerging fields of practices as the starting point for analysis, thereby getting by with the usual macro/micro distinction. Schatzki (2005) proposes that we should view practices as relational sites in which events, entities and meanings compose one another. Chia and MacKay (2007) call for shifting the focus of analysis 'from individual strategists to the historically and culturally transmitted fields of practice'. Gherardi emphasizes that 'theories of practice view actions as 'taking place' or 'happening', as being performed 'through a network of connections-in-actions, as life-work and dwelling' (Gherardi 2009: 115). The main challenge, then, is to overcome the prevalent individualistic focus on micro-level managerial activities and roles, which leaves a mass of larger social issues melting into the under-theorized, all-encompassing category of 'context' (Tsoukas 1994; Willmott 1997). Vaara and Whittington (2012: 2) thus identify the importance of recognizing the macro-institutional nature of practices as one of the five directions to be followed by SAP research.

Following the Heideggerian view, Chia and Holt (2006) argue that the dominant 'building' mode of strategy-making, in which actors are distinct entities deliberately engaging in purposeful strategic activities, is actually derived from a more basic 'dwelling' mode in which strategy-making emerges non-deliberately through everyday practical 'coping'. Practical 'coping' is rooted in social practices. Social practices are identity-forming and strategy-setting activities. They provide individuals with resources to interpret and improvise their role; they shape the scope and the extent of their exploratory activities and initiatives to cope with the ongoing flow of organizational development (Chia and Holt 2006). Mundane practical 'coping' can produce unexpected and strategically important outcomes, as shown in the famous example of Honda's success in the United States (Pascale 1984), in Regnér's (2003) uncovering of local improvisation at the periphery of corporate reach, in de La Ville's (2006) work on emerging technological strategies in a start-up and in Rouleau's (2005) analysis of strategy formation in everyday interactions. These studies show the importance of recognizing how much of strategy formation is rooted in the non-deliberate practical action of

'coping' that escapes the logic of planned and intentional action. For Sandberg and Tsoukas (2011), the challenge of grasping practice is to escape the modern scientific rationality that pervades management theoretical frameworks, and to elaborate the premises of an alternative practical rationality that considers entwinement as the cornerstone of existence. Entwinement means that being and doing become intelligible when included in a relational scheme articulating concomitantly the 'embodied other' and a specific 'sociomaterial' world. Moreover, Feldman and Orlikowski (2011) point out the conceptual creativity needed to elaborate a language as well as a logic that tolerate ambiguity and adequately express the dynamic, recurrent and relational nature of everyday practices.

This chapter builds upon the distinction between the 'building' and the 'dwelling' modes in order to introduce a narrative approach to strategy as practice (de La Ville and Mounoud 2003; Fenton and Langley 2011; Brown and Thompson 2013). We contend that strategy-as-practice research is still mainly imbued with the conceptual categories of the dominant 'building' mode. We argue that the integration of the 'dwelling' mode into strategy formation, as well as the combination of the 'building' and the 'dwelling' modes in strategy-making, are the key challenges for research in this area. Nevertheless, 'practices are difficult to access, observe, measure or represent because they are hidden tacit, and often linguistically inexpressible in propositional terms' (Gherardi 2009:116). As much of the actual doing of strategy takes place through talks, stories and texts, we therefore feel the need for a narrative approach to strategy as practice. This approach relates strategy-making to producing and using texts and narratives, and also provides the conceptual and methodological means to deal with the challenges mentioned above. We aim at taking into account not only the production of texts and talks but also their consumption; a narrative approach enables strategy research to engage more deeply in the 'practice turn' and to develop a 'certain research sensibility to the unspoken, the inarticulate and even the often unconscious aspects of strategy-making' (Chia and MacKay 2007; see also Raelin 2007).

This chapter is organized in four sections. The first section describes the various perspectives on narratives brought into strategy research. Beyond the overall functionalist interest in good stories, it shows the importance of texts in strategy and management. The second section, on the basis of the work of Paul Ricœur, develops the implications of this very notion of text. The third section follows Michel de Certeau's analysis of practices to identify a narrative way of forming strategy. In line with Chia and Holt's (2006) view, we consider producing texts as the dominant 'building' mode of strategy-making. This mode is actually derived from a more basic 'dwelling' mode, in which strategy formation emerges through reading texts and producing daily narratives. The last section draws the implications of our conceptual framework of 'strategy-making from texts and narratives', which is based upon the dynamics of reading and writing 'texts'. This offers a perspective in which all organizational actors may participate in strategy formation when producing and consuming texts and narratives, thus engaging in a *bricolage* of strategy.

Narratives in strategy research

Since the publication of Barry and Elmes' (1997) article on the narrative aspects of strategic discourses, it has been generally accepted that strategy – organizational strategies and theories of strategy alike – consists of stories told by key people, generally leaders, to other people such as shareholders, members of the organization and other stakeholders. This work has highlighted the double nature of strategy – narrative production and process of narration – by which various stories about strategic choices are connected, tested, reinforced or weakened. It has also emphasized the fictive nature of strategy narratives and linked strategic change processes to the romantic genre, the adventure novel of ordeal and to realistic fiction (Vaara and Reff Pedersen 2013). With a certain degree of irony, the authors underline the epic, even hagiographic, character of the strategic discourses of leaders. For example, the promotion of neo-Schumpeterian heroes in entrepreneurial

strategies created a heroic drift in many research accounts of new venture founding (de La Ville 2006).

Why are stories and narratives so interesting? The basic function of a story is to organize a series of events and actors into a common, acceptable and comprehensible temporal framework. By reorganizing events in a temporal framework, stories preserve and build the continuity of actions. The perception of the stakes of the present situation enables us to reorganize past events into a story. Restructuring a group of relationships creates retrospective senses, hence enabling further action. This faculty of generating sense has led researchers to become interested in stories told within organizations. Stories may not only present themselves as *whole* stories with a coherent plot and a definitive structure, such as 'grand narratives' do, but also encompass *small* stories constructed by individuals in everyday life as well as story fragments or antenarratives (Boje 2001), and even gossip (Gabriel 2000). This focus on 'small stories' (Georgakopolou 2007) constructed in interaction defines the new narrative turn moving from narratives as text to narrative as practice.

Stories and storytelling have now pervaded management, strategy and marketing research (Boyce 1996; Salmon 2007) and have put in the forefront a new array of consultants and gurus. Good stories are hence considered an effective factor in implementing strategic ideas. Strategy formulation involves a narrative production of an integrative story that enables the leaders to reorganize past events according to a plausible and desirable logic. What is at stake is the capacity of stories to construct a persuasive and stimulating message to facilitate memorization and training or to persuade stakeholders of the relevance of a strategy. Leaders need to be good storytellers – that is, be able to tell convincing stories that must be both coherent to gain credibility and stimulating to facilitate their reception and implementation. 'Thus a literature has developed around the promoting of storytelling as a formalized practice or management technique in itself'(Fenton and Langley 2011: 1179).

In a functionalist view, the construction of a good story supposes an overall intentionality, and

so does not take into account unintentional phenomena such as improvisations or routine activities. Thus, the functionalistic view of strategic
stories fails to capture the complexity of strategic
processes and practices. It prevents us from
widening the field of analysis to include the ordinary narratives of mid- to low-level organizational
members in relationship with the higher-level
'visionary' strategy produced by senior executives.
Is the intrinsic quality of a good story able to
dissolve the integrative difficulties inherent in the
strategic exercise, however? Moreover, can the
integrative strategic narrative be considered
effective without including the interpretations of
people to whom it is addressed? To escape this
oversimplistic view of managerialist storytelling,
we need to develop our understanding of the
narrative perspectives on strategy research.

The interest of social scientists in narratives is
grounded in the way people organize knowledge in
their daily life. It is suggested that people organize
their experience in the form of scripts about goal-
based events that include people, places and
events, and that these scripts are recounted in the
form of stories. On the one hand, it has become
generally accepted that narrative is a universal
form in which people construct, represent and
share experience (Bruner 1990). On the other hand,
experience shows how deep cultural narratives are,
how powerful socializing agents stories are and,
conversely, how much they reveal about the
values, beliefs and thought processes of a given
culture or community.

Bruner (1986), among others, has argued that it
is difficult to distinguish between the stories children learn and the stories they build from their
direct experience and knowledge. The narrative
ability to create stories develops during childhood
through reminiscing and engaging in symbolic
play (Engel 1995). Narratives do not merely
convey fantasies or the representation of unusual
feelings or experiences but also provide a fundamental intra- and interpersonal process, through
which children make sense of themselves in the
world. Storytelling is a deep social activity and a
powerful private activity. Children tell stories
when alone, they tell stories that have private
meanings and they use stories as much for their

internal thoughts and feelings as they do to communicate. What researchers have learned so far is
that children invent stories in much the same way
as they create play scenarios: with the pleasure of
creativity. It is important to keep in mind that the
form and content of children's stories are tied to
the context in which they are told and the purpose
for which they are told (Engel 2005).

For Barbara Czarniawska, there are three different modes of mobilizing narratives: it is possible
for the researcher to build explanations out of
'narratives from the field', to build his/her own
'narrative in the field' and even to define 'organizing as narration' (Czarniawska 1997: 25). Building
on Czarniawska's distinction, we identify three
narrative perspectives in strategy research that we
detail in the next section. The first one is the
interactional perspective, developed in relation to
communication studies, which defines strategic
narratives as meta-conversations; in the second
perspective, strategy is portrayed by researchers
as a story of domination in organizations; and, in
the third, organizations and strategies are seen as
narration.

Strategic narratives as meta-conversations

The interactional perspective highlights the vital
importance of communication in organizational
life in general and strategy formation in particular.
For followers of this approach (Giroux 1998; Taylor and Robichaud 2004; Robichaud, Giroux and
Taylor 2004; Fenton and Langley 2011), ordinary
activities develop through conversations, which
constitute coherent discursive units in themselves.
Giroux describes this process as a 'chain of conversations' spread out in time and space. She considers a dialogical mode of production of strategy,
'through a polyphonic vision of the community
where several voices are heard, and where the
heteroglossia (the simultaneous presence of several
languages) is accepted' (Giroux 1998: 7, our translation). The formulation of strategy is then conceived as a narrative process that organizes
polyphony. The concept of polyphony recognizes
the coexistence, interaction and mutual definition
of various voices and logics. In this polyphonic
process, strategy formulation is never controlled

by one single author, so it is particularly complex. Strategy is worked out gradually by negotiation within a 'meta-conversation' (Giroux and Demers 1997) dedicated to strategy formation, and leads to the drafting of a strategic text.

This proposition is based on the analytical distinction between the two dimensions of discourse as text (what is said) and conversation (what is accomplished in the saying): 'Conversation refers, in other words, to the interactive, situated "eventfulness" of language use; text refers to the semiotic artefact (oral or written) produced in the use of language, which may persist as a trace and record of past conversations' (Robichaud, Giroux and Taylor 2004); a meta-conversation is then defined as 'a conversation that embeds, recursively, another conversation'. The meta-conversation simultaneously incorporates and reconstructs the local discussions within the organization into an encompassing conversation, in which the identity of the organization as a whole is continuously regenerated. The process at work is the production of a meta-narrative that enfolds and transcends the narratives of the different communities comprising the organization.

Taylor and Robichaud (2004) suggest that, for organizational members to interact, they must construct a shared language, embodied in a text that enables them to cooperate. This begins with everyday conversation with mutual interaction, which is a prerequisite of organized activity. The resulting narratives constitute secondary productions, which formalize the interpretations constructed in conversation and carry them towards future actions. Not only does the text produced retain the traces of the original conversations, it frames subsequent actions by offering interpretive frameworks for the sensemaking of ongoing events. This view relates the concept of text to that of the framework of interaction, which is inspired by Erving Goffman and has previously been used in analysing strategy formation (de La Ville 2001).

Strategic narratives as discourse of domination

Narratives express identities (Czarniawska 1997; Rhodes and Brown 2005) and are part of the identity work performed in organizations 'as people locate themselves and others in various roles through the stories they tell' (Fenton and Langley 2011: 1180). When it comes to strategy, individual narratives of practitioners and broader strategy narratives are both analysed as power/knowledge claims or discourses. Inspired by the work of Foucault (mainly 1971; 1976), the critical organizational discourse perspective (Vaara 2002; Phillips and Hardy 2002; Fairclough 2005) focuses on discourses as linguistically mediated constructions of social realities. Discourses are important means through which beliefs, values and norms are reproduced, and at times transformed, in social life (Fairclough 2003). This perspective is one of the various approaches to discourse analysis (van Dijk 1997), and to organizational discourse analysis in particular (Hardy and Philips 2004; Grant et al. 2004).

These studies highlight the disciplining power of discourses on the ordinary practices of organization members, stemming from their capacity to impose and legitimize certain interpretative frameworks at the expense of others. Foucault warns that it is a question 'of no longer treating the discourses as sets of signs (of meaningful elements which refer to contents or representations), but as practices which systematically form the objects about which they speak' (Foucault 1976). Discourses should be considered 'surreptitious objectivations' (*objectivations subreptices*): they appear to be built by induction and serve to describe the world, but in fact they actually constitute the world. More generally, the language used on a daily basis within an organization is itself a bearer of logics of domination, which direct ordinary interactions and activities and legitimize power relations (Hardy 2004).

Strategy discourse is thus considered to be a complex set of meanings constituting this body of knowledge (Knights and Morgan 1991), as well as a part of the complex set of social practices formulating strategy as an organizational practice. Moreover, the work of Vaara and colleagues (Vaara 2002; Mantere and Vaara 2008) enables us to identify how specific conceptions of strategy work are reproduced and justified in organizational strategy formation. The idea that strategy includes a disciplining dimension emphasizes the importance of the stakes of power and legitimization invoked in the strategic exercise. Mantere and Vaara's (2008) analysis shows that strategy as practice involves alternative and even competing discourses that have fundamentally different kinds of implications for participation in strategy work.

Critical theorists (Alvesson and Deetz 2000; Putnam and Cooren 2004; Gherardi 2009) offer a distinctive point of view on key documents, such as regulations, procedures and memorandums. Discourses are selected, perpetuated and subsumed in texts, which are registered, preserved and memorized in accordance with the disciplinary function of the organization. These texts do not result from interaction between organization members; rather, they influence strategy formulation by virtue of their structured and permanent character, which enables organizations to survive (McPhee 2004). Discourses and texts mobilize mechanisms of domination based on legitimized rationality and the invoked scientific nature of the discipline. They result in practices of monitoring and controlling, but also aim at influencing the subjectivity and identity of organization members. Hardy and Phillips (2004) highlight how certain actors are able to mobilize economic, cultural and social capital to legitimize their power. From this point of view, the very notion of discourse includes domination and is opposed to the ordinary, fragmentary, situational narratives being built during the course of the everyday activities of organization members and bearing the stamp of subjectivity and of emotion.

Organizations and strategies as narration

The third view is grounded in the claim made by McIntyre (1988) that 'it is useful to think of an enacted narrative as the most typical form of social life' (cited by Czarniawska 2002). Its initiator, Czarniawska (1997), has a deep interest in the daily activities of the organization members, which result in the creation of the organization itself. She identifies two types of conversations: those allowing for the confrontation of personal experience or actions between two parties, and those manufacturing texts beyond the personal experience of the individual by imposing standards of behaviour and decision. This coexistence results in

fierce competition between the 'stronger' order – that of the official discourse, which reinforces institutional domination by controlling interpretations – and the 'weaker' order – that of the ordinary narratives, which try to make sense of daily activities. Her work suggests an ironic stance with regard to the impact of strategists, as she finds strategy to be a relatively artificial discursive construction, far removed from the realities experienced by organization members and geared to institutional concerns for domination and justification. Without any impact on the future of organizations and with no control over its daily activities, strategy appears in her descriptions to be a kind of meaningless ritual (de La Ville and Mounoud 2003). The severity of this assessment is partly explained by Czarniawska's focus on public organizations, in which the distance between official discourses and actual practices might be particularly perceptible.

In Czarniawska's view, everyday life within the organization takes shape through ordinary narratives in which individuals select events, organize temporalities, typify key characters, build identity relationships, structure their experience and construct and transform their interpretations. Drawing on Bruner's point that 'there is an availability, or a predisposition to organise experience in narrative form by building intrigues' (Bruner 1990), we assume that the continuity of existence may be understood by recounting this same existence – a narrative process of fashioning one another's identities. Through the spoken word, exchanged and retained among themselves, organization members construct and perpetuate their identities and their organized activity. Language, speech, plot production, mere stories and ordinary narrations are experienced as inherent to organizing itself. The construction of activities, knowledge and identities is thus structured in and through a complex interlacing of narrative processes, which is always spontaneous, related to unforeseen events and socially organized (Czarniawska 1998).

In the two following sections, we develop our view of strategy as narration, including narrative production and the process of narration, in which the future is created through a collective narrative that is dispersed and fragmented, being the subject of partial developments, major transformations and inscriptions perpetuated in texts. Strategy-making, when considered as directing the future and leading organization members to comply with this direction, results partly in the production of texts (McPhee 2004; Putnam and Cooren 2004; Fenton and Langley 2011). Nevertheless, not all texts can be qualified as 'strategic', nor is strategy formation confined to the processes of creating or monitoring the effects of 'strategic' texts. We consider first the implications of this production of texts.

Strategy formation as producing texts

Strategic texts constitute forms of mediation, in and through which organizational actors reflexively understand their situations, give meaning to their actions and anticipate their futures. Produced strategic texts thus have a double relation with the context (the preceding texts with which they interact) and the situation (the mundane organizational activities and practices to which they relate and help organize).

Texts organize relationships of intertextuality and polyphony

The production of a strategic text relies on a group of scriptural prerequisites. To be described as 'strategic', the text must bring together appropriate standards, rules and criteria that explicitly connect it to the discipline of management and to various genres relevant to strategy, such as management reports, business plans, development plans, refocusing plans, asset redeployment plans, etc. Processes of institutionalization accompany and support the production of strategic texts while differentiating them from other textual productions. MBA programmes, specialized academic courses, consulting firms and trade associations legitimize strategists and increase their influence. Strategic activity is seen through textual productions that communicate to shareholders the relevance of the strategic project and the strategic team's control. For example, Vaara, Sorsa and Pälli (2010) identify five central discursive features that could be conceived as distinctive features of the strategy genre, while Cornut, Giroux and Langley (2012) examine the particular features of the strategic plan

genre of communication. They argue that these discursive features have important implications for the textual agency of strategic plans and their performative effects. They identify their impact on power relations and their ideological implications.

The notion of 'intertextuality' allows us to appreciate writing as a permanently creative flux, integrating previous standards and conventions in order to produce texts that are likely to be readable, understandable and recognizable by an audience. It has been described by Julia Kristeva (1980: 69) as a reaction to the tendency to analyse texts as discrete and closed units, the meaningfulness of which lay in their internal structure. Drawing on the dialogue perspective proposed by Mikhail Bakhtin (1968) in literary theory, she contends that texts become meaningful if they are considered as a fragment relating to former texts. Shared codes allow both the writer and the reader to recognize, situate and appreciate the text in the continuum of literary production. It is worth noting that this post-structuralist perspective considers that every text is under the dominance of previous texts, which impose a universe of codes in relation to which it will be read and understood by certain audiences. This suggests a drastic shift in the method of analysing reading and writing by focusing the effort on studying the process of structuration through which the text comes into being. By questioning the romantic roots that lead to the invention of the notion of 'authorship', this perspective lays special emphasis on the fact that writers are compelled to use pre-existing concepts and conventions to communicate with an audience. Their individual creative skills are socially founded in shared language and scriptural conventions. This is why Roland Barthes defines text as a tissue of quotations, a creative art consisting in weaving together former codes, references and genres (Barthes 1974).

Strategic texts are embedded in intertextual relations in multiple ways. First, they are related to pre-existent strategic texts within an organization and the settings in which they have been produced. Second, they are governed by discursive orders based on strategic management as a discipline (Hardy 2004). Third, they are imbued with the constitutive values of the institutional environment in which they are embedded. Knights and Morgan

(1991) argue that the rise of strategy was linked to the historical emergence of managerial capitalism in postwar Western industries. In a documented essay, Whittington, Cailluet and Yakis-Douglas (2011) depict the progressive structuring of strategy since the 1950s as the emergence of a precarious professional field, including corporate elites, strategic planners, consultancy companies, academics and middle managers, that is shaped permanently by changing organizational, societal, cultural and technological forces. For Whittington *et al.* (2003), we should investigate the role of strategic consultants and business schools in promoting particular kinds of strategic practices. Strategy inevitably includes an ideological dimension, because it reproduces the inequalities of the capitalist society, extends Western managerial structures and presents the objectives of dominant elites as universal goals. Therefore, we definitely need to keep a critical eye on the institutional field of strategic management and the behaviour it promotes (Vaara and Whittington 2012). Being institutionally inscribed, strategic texts propose worlds that include a disciplining function founded both on legitimized scriptural standards and on institutionalized value systems.

Because they present a proposal for a relation with the world, strategic texts cannot ignore the multiplicity of voices, actions and narratives within the organization (Giroux and Demers 1997). The very production of strategic texts organizes a polyphonic relationship among voices, which always remain singular and develop autonomously, but answer one another, oppose one another and contribute to proposing new worlds (O'Connor 2000; Hardy 2004). Strategy formation proceeds from the application of strategic practices, going beyond the order of discourse and conversation to integrate a body of knowledge into explicit activities and tacit tactics. Furthermore, the ordinary practices of managers and the texts that underlie them, through the resistance that they express, continually nourish the inventiveness of the organizational actions and form an ongoing, emerging and vital part of the strategic activity. Either these practices are gradually recognized, named and defined so as to be integrated into the strategic text or they remain invisible or external (perhaps because they occur outside official channels). Thus, strategic texts operate a selection and organization of mundane organizational narratives.

Texts draw upon a large range of codes and social norms that allow them to be assigned to a particular genre. Genres are situated and evolving conventions that enable us to classify texts and outline their relationship with each other. Literary theorists have demonstrated that the definition of genres is quite fluid and relates to ongoing changes and social renegotiations, leading to a permanent blurring of borders and a constant mitigation of their distinctive characteristics (Bakhtin 1968; Barthes 1974; Kristeva 1980).

We are fully aware that such a brief presentation of the notions of 'intertextuality' and 'polyphony' borrowed from cultural studies and literary analysis is a risky undertaking. Nevertheless, in the context of this chapter, we aim at transposing this notion into a managerial perspective, in an attempt to offer some insights on how the creativity hidden in mundane organizational activities can be embodied in strategy.

Texts call for reading

To analyse the dynamics of texts, we draw on Paul Ricœur, for whom the concept of 'text' covers a limited category of signs: those that comprise a form of fossilization comparable with that produced by writing (Ricœur 1991), which allows the conservation and the linearization of the conversation. When writing is added to a previous statement, it modifies the relationship with the utterances, which Ricœur calls the 'ostensive reference' – that is, the object with which one expresses oneself. Writing creates a different relationship from that of face-to-face conversation: the reader is absent from the writing and the author from the reading. The text is thus the product of a simultaneous eclipsing of the reader and the author. In this view, the nature of the text is underlined. Because of its fossilization into a medium, because of the lack of association between the intention of the author and the intention of the text, because of the use of 'non-ostensive' references and the substitution of unknown readers for a visible listener, the text must be differentiated from a face-to-face or situated discourse.

Consequently, 'the text awaits and calls for reading' (Ricœur 1991). Ricœur distinguishes two ways of understanding reading: to explain and to interpret. 'To explain is to bring out the structure, i.e. the internal relations of dependence, which constitute the static of the text. To interpret is to follow the path of thought opened up by the text and to start heading towards the orientation of the text' (Ricœur 1991). This dualism suggests a dialectic in the activity of reading, as movement between these two activities produces comprehension. The open nature of the text is made salient: references are offered to propose a 'world' and build a new meaning. Reading is possible because text is not closed in on itself; it is open to other things. Reading is thus a creative activity that prolongs the creation of writing. As stated by Ricœur (1991), '[T]o read is, in any hypothesis, to conjoin a new discourse to the discourse of the text.'

Strategic texts are characterized by their ambiguity; their significance is unresolved, as for any text, because the distance caused by its written form is open to alternative readings and constructions depending on the situations of readers. While interpreting strategic texts, organizational actors propose their relations with the world. This process of appropriation, which takes place in the narrative register (as we show in the next section), is complex, dense, emergent and dynamic.

We have underlined the 'building' mode of strategy formation as producing strategic texts. It is important to keep in mind that these texts are themselves embedded in a 'context' of previous texts and are derived from the polyphony of situated narratives. It is now possible to envisage the more basic 'dwelling' mode of strategy formation, the everyday practical 'coping' with the rules and texts of the organization. The relationship of this 'dwelling' mode with the 'building' one is similar to that of reading with writing.

Narratives as practical coping with strategic texts

The creativity of reading, put forward by Ricœur, is shared by Michel de Certeau, who argues for a greater emphasis on the activity of reading to oppose the excessive importance placed on writing in contemporary society – a society that he finds 'increasingly written, organized by the capacity to modify things and to reform the structures through scriptural models (scientific, economic, political), and gradually transformed into combined "texts" (administrative, urban, industrial, etc.)'. He strives to show that reading is not a passive activity; it modifies its object, reinvents beyond the intention of the text and builds a different 'world', which belongs to the reader, in place of the author, 'to make the text liveable'. Readers carry out 'a reappropriation of the other's text: he poaches there, he is transported there, he becomes plural there' (de Certeau 1988).

Reading as consuming texts

According to de Certeau, everyday life is distinctive from other practices of existence because it is repetitive and unconscious. An interesting point is the distinction he makes between the concepts of strategy and tactics. De Certeau links 'strategies' with institutions and structures of power, while 'tactics' are utilized by individuals to create space for themselves in environments defined by strategies. For example, he describes 'the city' as a 'concept', generated by the strategic manoeuvring of governments, corporations and other institutional bodies, which produce things such as maps that describe the city as a unified whole experienced by someone looking down from high above. By contrast, a walker on the street moves in ways that are tactical and never fully determined by the plans of organizing bodies. He/she may take short cuts or meander aimlessly, rather than following the utilitarian layout of the grid of streets. This concretely illustrates de Certeau's assertion that everyday life works by a process of poaching on the territory of others, recombining the rules and products that already exist in culture in a way that is influenced, but never wholly determined, by those rules and products.

For de Certeau, consumption supposes the acceptance of an offer of products, but not a passive one. Consumers are active; they take pleasure in consuming, and consider themselves free and creative in doing so. Under the apparent banality of ordinary gestures and routine actions lurks an extraordinary creativity often ignored by theory. Individuals show a great capacity for 'making do'. They exhibit inventiveness in terms of shrewd ploys and stratagems to work out their own way of doing things, whether it is cooking, strolling through a town, shopping or whatever. When analysed superficially, certain routine behaviours reveal a form of submission. On close scrutiny, they reveal ongoing experimentations filled with resistance and creativity. The relationship between reading and writing is of a comparable nature: texts, just like the goods offered on the market, are produced by manufacturers who offer them to consumers – the readers – who decide upon their significance and use them in their own ways.

De Certeau's analysis of consumption is oriented towards the ordinary practices of consumers, who are defined as 'users of goods imposed upon them by producers'. Indeed, in offering products to consumers, producers assume a position of domination, against which consumers resist by developing inventive attitudes and practices. By mirroring consumption and reading, de Certeau reveals the two sides of consumption. On the one hand, consuming entails a form of acceptance of an imposed offer of goods. On the other, consumers are neither passive nor docile; they experience freedom, creativity and pleasure – just as readers do. Commenting on empirical investigations of several situational social practices such as reading, talking, dwelling, cooking, wandering around, etc., de Certeau explores scientific literature in order to clarify the purpose of his theoretical undertaking:

> It may be supposed that these operations – multiform and fragmentary, relative to situations and details, insinuated into and concealed...within devices, whose mode of usage they constitute, and thus lacking their own ideologies or institutions – conform to certain rules. In other words, there must be a logic of these practices (de Certeau 1988: xv).

Narrativity in strategy formation

Thus, strategy-making can be understood as a permanent creative process including not only what strategists produce/write, such as texts, budgets, plans, matrices, charts and strategies, but also the ways in which organization members consume/read these productions. This conceptual framework leads us to question how organizational actors read – that is, use and transform – strategic texts in their daily activities.

Reading takes place through the mobilization of innumerable fragmentary, instantaneous, opportunistic tactics (de La Ville and Mounoud 2001a). 'These tactics also demonstrate the degree to which intelligence is inseparable from the struggles and the daily pleasures which it articulates... Because of its intangible nature, a tactic depends on time and remains vigilant to catch any possibilities of profit. It does not keep what it gains. It is necessary for it to play constantly with the events to transfer them into opportunities' (de Certeau 1988). Being incapable of capitalizing voluntarily on their achievements to control temporality and the course of events, these tactics, which are peculiar to the art of reading, may produce tangible and sometimes irreversible strategic effects, such as delays in implementation, side-tracking from the main objectives, operational diversions, more or less continuous symbolic rejections or the subversion of authority.

Daily practice expresses creativity, a capacity 'to put up with', to subvert imposed rules and create room for manoeuvre. Practice includes the subconscious part of creativity, seen in clever devices and inventions. This creativity is also evident in attempts to negotiate meanings of actions and events among organization members – that is, in ordinary and everyday narratives. The narrative register indeed enables the practical art to express itself, to experiment, to improvise and to resist the domination of a disciplining totality envisaged by some strategic texts.

Adopting this view provides a new way of looking at practice, because it enables us to accept strategic discourses as a production and an offer of a (cultural) good: a text. Thus, we might be able to suggest new ways of explaining how people read, use and transform this particular cultural product. Linstead and Grafton-Small (1992) contrast the production of corporate culture with the creative consumption of organizational culture by organization members. To use this conception it is necessary to supplement the analysis of the discourse of strategy (representation) and of the time spent attending strategic meetings (behaviour) with a study of what middle managers and employees actually 'make' or 'do' during that time and how they use these discourses. With their 'making' or 'doing' being devious and dispersed, it remains difficult for the researcher to analyse. In organizations, employees and managers do not adopt, adhere to or share the 'strategic' vision or intent of their 'charismatic leaders'. In their everyday activities, they actively interpret, criticize, learn and experiment with possible attitudes and microdecisions in order to implement or resist the multiple implications of strategic changes imposed on them. This reading – or consumption – of strategic texts constitutes a second-order production, which de Certeau calls a 'fabrication' – that is, a narrative that is added to the intention of strategic texts.

This conceptualization makes it possible to comprehend the complexity and the creativity of strategy formation and to reconsider the problematic bond between the 'emergent' and the 'deliberate'. On the one hand, processes of institutionalization accompany and support the emergence of integrative organizational discourses that become strategic texts. On the other, innumerable readings ensue in a disorderly way, gradually giving shape to a multiplicity of tactics that constitute strategic practice.

Implications for research

As summed up in Table 14.1, we have defined strategy formation as the interplay between producing/writing strategic texts and consuming/reading them, so producing daily narratives. Thus, a narrative approach results in three levels of analysis. First, the writing of strategic texts implies the use of standards, which authorize the inscription of the texts in one of the strategic genres (Vaara and Reff Pedersen 2013). Strategic texts thus (re)produce the dominant discourse of strategy. Strategic genres are crafted by the institutional 'ruling order'. Strategic practices are defined, legitimized and spread mainly by academics and consultants,

Table 14.1 Strategy-making from texts and narratives

Consumption/production interplay	
Ruling order	Consuming social practices; producing strategic practices as dominant discourses (discipline)
Strategic texts	Consuming dominant discourses (intertextuality); consuming everyday narratives (polyphony); producing strategic texts (strategic genre)
Unruly practice: narratives	Consuming strategic texts (practical coping: resistance, *bricolage*, emplotment); producing everyday narratives (games, recipes, tales)

because of the (questionable) professionalization and industrialization of strategic management. Second, strategic texts proceed from multi-level multi-actor processes, creating a 'complex mosaic of stories' (Fenton and Langley 2011) through the selection and polyphonic organization of mundane organizational narratives. Third, strategy formation also includes the creative reading of strategic texts, producing unpremeditated tactics for resisting their domination. The consumption of strategy can be seen at managerial level, in the activities of top and middle managers enrolled in participating in strategic episodes (Suominen and Mantere 2010) – but not only. For example, Abdallah and Langley (2014) show how various forms of ambiguity in strategic texts generate different forms of consumption among organization members.

Our main claim is that more research on the consumption side of strategy-making is needed. Reading practices revealed by narratives can be reconstructed by the researcher from qualitative inquiry based upon observations and conventional unstructured and semi-structured interviews. De Certeau and Ricœur help us in defining what we should be looking for. De Certeau identifies three places in which this practical creativity of ordinary accounts can be seen: the 'games' that formalize the organizing rules of 'actions', the 'game recipes' that teach the practices available and the 'tales and legends' that expose the available good and evil tricks. This aspect of consumption, because of its dispersion, surreptitiousness and deviousness, evades the eye of the researcher and the managers alike, and both have to develop the ability to recognize it, to give room and voice to it and to incorporate part of it in strategic texts. Thus, a narrative perspective needs to collect *in vivo* narratives and can barely rely on documentary and interview materials. The collection of individual narratives from organizational members through in-depth interviewing seems to be a particularly promising method for understanding how people make sense of what they are doing and how they relate their own individual identities and trajectories to that of the organizations. Strategy research needs to give a stronger emphasis to an ethnographic approach directed towards uncovering the contextual and hidden characteristics of strategy-making, however (Rasche and Chia 2009).

The concept of plot developed by Paul Ricœur helps us to bring to light the various narratives produced while organizational members consume strategic texts. Ricœur (1984) builds his concept of 'emplotment' (*mise en intrigue*) around Aristotle's sentence that 'the plot is the imitation of the action – for by plot, I here mean the arrangement of the incidents' (*Poetics*, part VI). For Ricœur, the narrative, defined as 'emplotment', combines the Aristotelian concepts of *mimesis* (imitation) and *muthos* (arrangement of the incidents): 'For me, this guideline is plot, insofar as it is a synthesis of the heterogenous. Plot, in effect, "comprehends", in one intelligible whole, circumstances, goals, interactions, and unintended results' (Ricœur 1984: 142). The semantic innovation of narrative consists in the invention of a plot, which is also a work of synthesis. Through the plot, objectives, causes and incidents are brought together under the temporal unity of an action that is complete and forms a whole.

The narrative perspective gives way to examination of the consumption/production interplay across three levels of analysis, as shown in Table 14.1. Consumption is first because nothing happen in a vacuum; even the production of strategic texts, at the top and in the name of the organization, is a *bricolage*.

The consumption of dominant discourses and strategic practices can be tracked within the management fashion framework (Abrahamson 1996; Sturdy 2004). Corbett and Mounoud (2011) have

developed such an analysis. Their study encompasses the ruling order and the direction conveyed in the official discourse, as well as a political view focusing on the instrumental use of strategies to secure power. Strategies are adopted not just because of their supposed effectiveness but, rather, because they 'provide a potentially comforting sense of order and identity and/or control' (Sturdy 2004). Strategies are related to the language devices and tricks used by management gurus and other suppliers of ideas to convince the somewhat naïve manager. Focusing on daily narratives allows them to grasp all the contradictions and tensions brought by strategy in the daily activity. In turn, they show how individuals are able to play with the texts. Practice is the singular art of coping through combination, inventiveness and 'Do it yourself!' techniques – that is, 'a way of thinking invested in a way of acting...which cannot be dissociated from an art of using' (de Certeau 1988).

The consumption of strategic texts can also be traced, even if it is not explicit, in research on middle managers. Following the seminal work of Floyd and Wooldridge (2000), there is a growing interest in their role and participation in strategy formation (Rouleau 2005; Fauré and Rouleau 2011; Rouleau and Balogun 2011). Through a fine-grained study of daily conversations held by accountants in order to set up a budgeting control procedure in a construction firm, Fauré and Rouleau (2011) analyse how accountants and middle managers engage in various forms of discretionary tactics aimed at redefining their respective accountabilities within the new context of a strategic partnership imposed on them. The mutual tactic aimed at reducing the gap between forecasts and actual achievements consisted of putting forward the acceptability of numbers for the new partner rather than strictly applying the procedures that make budgetary control reliable. These tactics sometimes led to smoothed figures and clandestine and dilatory arrangements, justified by the need to render some figures plausible within this new way of setting up budgets required by the partnership strategy. Thus, research has drifted away from top management teams, helping to anchor it in daily practices. Rouleau and Balogun (2011) studied the way middle managers enact the strategic roles allocated to them. They identify two situated, but interlinked, discursive activities, critical to this accomplishment. If language use is key, it has to be combined with an ability to devise a setting in which to perform the language by drawing on contextually relevant verbal, symbolic and sociocultural systems. Their final conclusion is that 'this in turn suggests that we need to teach strategy differently, taking a more discursive and less analytical approach', in line with the work of Jazarbkowski and Whittington (2008) and Raelin (2007).

Conclusion

Drawing from the narrative perspective in organization studies and building on previous work on narrative approaches to strategy (de La Ville and Mounoud 2003; Fenton and Langley 2011; Brown and Thompson 2013), we define a research agenda for a narrative approach to strategy as practice. In this view, researchers should address the strategic role of mundane stories and narratives that give meaning to daily experiences and acknowledge the relationships that these mundane narratives have with texts produced by dominant stakeholders. More precisely, we consider the fundamental role of reading as a process of consumption, and thus comprehension, of texts. Therefore, we propose a model for strategy formation that builds on how strategic texts are created recursively, starting from the mundane narratives that influence daily practices (de La Ville and Mounoud 2001b), interacting with previous texts and using standards that help them to be recognized as strategic. Strategic texts are thus involved in a double relationship with the context (the body of the preceding texts to which it relates) and with the situation (the ordinary activities it accounts for and helps organize).

Our framework highlights the mediation role of strategic texts between institutional contexts and organizational situations and clarifies the processes involved in strategic textual productions. We consider strategic documents that organizations produce, such as written plans, to be texts. Thus, they

may be considered as 'being read' by organization members. Understanding strategy-making based on reading and writing is useful in order to unfold the complexities of strategy formation. Strategy-making has much to do with the capacity to master the skills of discussion. The practice aspect of strategy-making appears to be immersed in the narration of human experience, however. As a major consequence, a narrative perspective cannot rely on documentary and interview materials, and asks for ethnographic fieldwork.

Strategy formation brings into play complex processes of interaction between organizational productions of contrasting nature. It may be understood by using the text as a model of 'judicious' or sensible action. The latter 'becomes a subject of science on the condition that a kind of objectivity equivalent to the fossilization of the discourse through writing exists' (Ricœur 1991). Ricœur thus equates ordinary action with speech and conversation; action is also a representation anchored in the present, with a structure resembling that of speech acts and utterances. Conversely, the judicious action, associated with strategic action, perpetuates itself, leaves traces and becomes memorable. An action leaves its mark when it contributes to the emergence of significant configurations. A process of recording transforms it into a 'document' or 'archive' of organizational action, which brings it closer to the textual form and distinguishes it from the conversation. The judicious action results from emancipation with regard to the initial context and develops meanings that can be actualized or completed under new and different circumstances.

Consequently, the analysis of strategy formation must not be centred only on the conversations or the interactions described as 'strategic'. Strategy-making should be considered as the combination of the production of texts and their creative consumption in daily activities. This practical coping can be traced in the various forms of *bricolage*, resistance, imitation and emplotment that people engage in. We need to look for the places where this practical creativity of ordinary accounts can be seen, which de Certeau identified as the games, the game recipes that teach the practices, and the tales. Consumption can be understood as the dominated production of second-order narratives. The descending order of the dominant discourse of strategy and the ascending order of the resisting narrative constitute two realms of strategy-making, and strategic texts are their point of intersection and articulation. This meeting shows the complexity of strategy formation – that is, an ongoing process of becoming, through which the practice of strategy is brought into being at every instant of organizational life (Langley *et al.* 2013: 5). The context dominates and informs the strategic text because it provides the rules for it to form itself. In return, the strategic text, fuelled by ordinary accounts of organization members' practices, is subject to creative readings and resistant consumption. 'Human action is open to whoever can read' (Ricœur 1991). Through this double role of mediation, the strategic text may gather meaning and become effective.

References

Abdallah, C., and Langley, A. (2014), 'The double edge of ambiguity in strategic planning', *Journal of Management Studies*, 51/2: 235–64.

Abrahamson, E. (1996), 'Management fashion', *Academy of Management Review*, 2/1: 254–85.

Alvesson, M., and Deetz, S. (2000), *Doing Critical Research Management*. London: Sage.

Bakhtin, M. (1968), *Rabelais and His World*. Cambridge, MA: MIT Press.

Barry, D., and Elmes, M. (1997), 'Strategy retold: toward a narrative view of strategic discourse', *Academy of Management Review*, 22/2: 429–52.

Barthes, R. (1974), *S/Z: An Essay*. London: Cape.

Boje, D. M. (2001), *Narrative Methods for Organizational and Communication Research*. London: Sage.

Boyce, M. (1996), 'Organizational story and storytelling: a critical review', *Journal of Organizational Change*, 9/5: 5–26.

Brown, A. D., and Thompson, E. R. (2013), 'A narrative approach to strategy-as-practice', *Business History*, 55/7: 1143–67.

Bruner, J. S. (1986), *Actual Minds, Possible Worlds*. Cambridge, MA: Harvard University Press.

(1990), *Acts of Meaning*. Cambridge, MA: Harvard University Press.

Chia, R., and Holt, R. (2006), 'Strategy as practical coping: a Heideggerian perspective', *Organization Studies*, 27/5: 635–55.

Chia, R., and MacKay, B. (2007), 'Post-processual challenges for the emerging strategy-as-practice perspective: discovering strategy in the logic of practice', *Human Relations*, 60/1: 217–42.

Corbett, I., and Mounoud, E. (2011), 'Looping the loop: the consumption and production of knowledge management ideas and practices', *Management Learning*, 42/2: 165–81.

Cornut, F., Giroux, H., and Langley, A. (2012), 'The strategic plan as a genre', *Discourse and Communication*, 6/1: 21–54.

Czarniawska, B. (1997), *Narrating the Organization: Dramas of Institutional Identity*. University of Chicago Press.

(1998), *A Narrative Approach to Organization Studies*. Thousand Oaks, CA: Sage.

(2002), 'Interviews and organisational narratives', in Gubrium, J. F., and Holstein, J. (eds.), *Handbook of Interviewing*: 733–49. Thousand Oaks, CA: Sage.

De Certeau, M. (1988), *The Practice of Everyday Life*. Berkeley: University of California Press.

De La Ville, V. I. (2001), 'L'actualisation collective des pratiques stratégiques', in Drisse (ed.), *Le management stratégique en représentations*: 113–48. Paris: Ellipses.

(2006), 'Collective learning processes in high tech firms: enablers and barriers to the innovation process', in Bernasconi, M., Harris, S., and Monsted, M. (eds.), *High Tech Start-Up: Creation and Development of Technology Based Firms*: 69–85. London: Routledge.

De La Ville, V. I., and Mounoud, E. (2001a), 'The tactics of strategising: a very ordinary perspective', paper presented at the European Institute for Advanced Studies in Management workshop 'Micro-strategy and strategising', Brussels, 1 February.

De La Ville, V. I., and Mounoud, E. (2001b), 'Narrating the practice of "strategy": in search of a genre…', paper presented at the seventeenth European Group for Organisation Studies colloquium, Lyon, 7 July.

(2003), 'Between discourse and narration: how can strategy be a practice?', in Czarniawska, B., and Gagliardi, P. (eds.), *Narratives We Organise By*: 95–113. Amsterdam: John Benjamins.

Engel, S. (1995), *The Stories Children Tell*. New York: W. H. Freeman.

(2005), 'Narrative analysis of children's experience', in Greene, S., and Hogan, D. (eds.), *Researching Children's Experience: Methods and Approaches*: 199–216. London: Sage.

Fairclough, N. (2003), *Analyzing Discourse: Textual Analysis for Social Research*. London: Routledge.

—— (2005), 'Critical discourse analysis, organizational discourse, and organizational change', *Organization Studies*, 26/6: 915–39.

Fauré, B., and Rouleau, L. (2011), 'The strategic competence of accountants and middle managers in budget making', *Accounting, Organizations and Society*, 36/3: 167–82.

Feldman, M. S., and Orlikowski, W. J. (2011), 'Theorizing practice and practicing theory', *Organization Science*, 22/5: 1240–53.

Fenton, C., and Langley, A. (2011), 'Strategy as practice and the narrative turn', *Organization Studies*, 32/9: 1171–96.

Floyd, S. W., and Wooldridge, B. (2000), *Building Strategy from the Middle: Reconceptualizing Strategy Process*. Thousand Oaks, CA: Sage.

Foucault, M. (1971), *L'ordre du discours*. Paris: Gallimard.

—— (1976), *The Archaeology of Knowledge*. New York: Harper & Row.

Gabriel, Y. (2000), *Storytelling in Organizations: Facts, Fictions, and Fantasies*. Oxford University Press.

Georgakopoulou, A. (2007), *Small Stories, Interaction and Identities*. Amsterdam: John Benjamins.

Gherardi, S. (2009), 'The critical power of the "practice lens"', *Management Learning*, 40/2: 115–28.

Giroux, N. (1998), 'La communication dans la mise en œuvre du changement', *Management International*, 3/1: 1–14.

Giroux, N., and Demers, C. (1997), 'Communication organisationnelle et stratégie', *Management International*, 2/2: 17–32.

Grant, D., Hardy, C., Oswick, C., and Putnam, L. L. (eds.) (2004), *Handbook of Organizational Discourse*. London: Sage.

Hardy, C. (2004), 'Scaling up and bearing down in discourse analysis: questions regarding textual agencies and their context', *Organization*, 11/3: 415–25.

Hardy, C., and Philips, N. (2004), 'Discourse and power', in Grant, D., Hardy, C., Oswick, C., and Putnam, L. L. (eds.), *Handbook of Organizational Discourse*: 299–316. London: Sage.

Hendry, J., and Seidl, D. (2003), 'The structure and significance of strategic episodes: social systems theory and the routine practices of strategic change', *Journal of Management Studies*, 40/1: 175–96.

Jarzabkowski, P. (2004), 'Strategy as practice: recursiveness, adaptation and practices-in-use', *Organization Studies*, 25/4: 529–60.

—— (2005), *Strategy as Practice: An Activity-Based Approach*. London: Sage.

Jarzabkowski, P., Balogun, J., and Seidl, D. (2007), 'Strategizing: the challenges of a practice perspective', *Human Relations*, 60/1: 5–27.

Jarzabkowski, P., and Whittington, R. (2008), 'A strategy-as-practice approach to strategy research and education', *Journal of Management Inquiry*, 17/4: 282–6.

Johnson, G., Langley, A., Melin, L., and Whittington, R. (2007), *Strategy as Practice: Research Directions and Resources*. Cambridge University Press.

Knights, D., and Morgan, G. (1991), 'Corporate strategy, organizations, and subjectivity: a critique', *Organization Studies*, 12/2: 251–73.

Kristeva, J. (1980), *Desire in Language: A Semiotic Approach to Literature and Art*. New York: Columbia University Press.

Langley, A., Smallman, C., Tsoukas, H., and Van de Ven, A. H. (2013), 'Process studies of change in organization and management: unveiling temporality, activity and flow', *Academy of Management Journal*, 56/1: 1–13.

Linstead, S., and Grafton-Small, R. (1992), 'On reading organizational culture', *Organization Studies*, 13/3: 331–55.

Mantere, S., and Vaara, E. (2008), 'On the problem of participation in strategy: a critical discursive perspective', *Organization Science*, 19/2: 341–58.

McIntyre, A. (1988), *Whose Justice? Which Rationality?* London: Duckworth.

McPhee, R. (2004), 'Text, agency and organization in the light of structuration theory', *Organisation*, 11/3: 355–71.

O'Connor, E. (2000), 'Plotting the organization: the embedded narrative as a construct for studying change', *Journal of Applied Behavioral Sciences*, 36/2: 174–92.

Pascale, R. T. (1984), 'Perspectives on strategy: the real story behind Honda's success', *California Management Review*, 26/3: 47–72.

Phillips, N., and Hardy, C. (2002), *Discourse Analysis: Investigating Processes of Social Construction*. London: Sage.

Putnam, L. L., and Cooren, F. (2004), 'Alternative perspectives on the role of text and agency in constituting organizations', *Organization*, 11/3: 323–33.

Raelin, J. A. (2007), 'Towards an epistemology of practice', *Academy of Management Learning and Education*, 6/4: 495–519.

Rasche, A., and Chia, R. (2009), 'Researching strategy practices: a genealogical social theory perspective', *Organization Studies*, 30/7: 713–34.

Regnér, P. (2003), 'Strategy creation in the periphery: inductive versus deductive strategy making', *Journal of Management Studies*, 40/1: 57–82.

Rhodes, C., and Brown, A. D. (2005), 'Narrative, organization and research', *International Journal of Management Reviews*, 7/1: 167–88.

Ricœur, P. (1984), *Time and Narrative*, 3 vols. University of Chicago Press.

(1991), *From Text to Action: Essays in Hermeneutics*, vol. II. Evanston, IL: Northwestern University Press.

Robichaud, D., Giroux, H., and Taylor, J. R. (2004), 'The meta-conversation: the recursive property of language as the key to organizing', *Academy of Management Review*, 29/4: 1–18.

Rouleau, L. (2005), 'Micro-practices of strategic sensemaking and sensegiving: how middle managers interpret and sell change every day', *Journal of Management Studies*, 42/7: 1413–41.

Rouleau, L., and Balogun, J. (2011), 'Middle managers, strategic sensemaking and discursive competence', *Journal of Management Studies*, 48/5: 953–83.

Salmon, C. (2007), *Storytelling: La machine à fabriquer des histoires et à formater les esprits*. Paris: Éditions La Découverte.

Samra-Fredericks, D. (2003), 'Strategizing as lived experience and strategists' everyday efforts to shape strategic direction', *Journal of Management Studies*, 40/1: 141–74.

Sandberg, J., and Tsoukas, H. (2011), 'Grasping the logic of practice: theorizing through practical activity', *Academy of Management Review*, 36/2: 338–60.

Schatzki, T. R. (2005), 'The sites of organizations', *Organization Studies*, 26/3: 465–84.

Spender, J. C. (1989), *Industrial Recipes*. Oxford: Blackwell.

Sturdy, A. (2004), 'The adoption of management ideas and practices: theoretical perspectives and possibilities', *Management Learning*, 35/2: 155–79.

Suominen, K., and Mantere, S. (2010) 'Consuming strategy: the art and practice of managers' everyday strategy usage', in Baum, J. A. C., and Lampel, J. (eds.), *Advances in Strategic Management*, vol. XXVII, *The Globalization of Strategy Research*: 211–45. Bingley, UK: Emerald.

Taylor, J. R., and Robichaud, D. (2004), 'Finding the organization in the communication: discourse as action and sensemaking', *Organization*, 11/3: 395–413.

Tsoukas, H. (1994), 'What is management? An outline of a metatheory', *British Journal of Management*, 5/4: 289–301.

Vaara, E. (2002), 'On the discursive construction of success/failure in narrative of post-merger integration', *Organization Studies*, 23/2: 211–48.

Vaara, E., and Reff Pedersen, A. (2013), 'Strategy and chronotopes: a Bakhtinian perspective on the construction of strategy narratives', *M@n@gement*, 16/5: 593–604.

Vaara, E., and Whittington, R. (2012), 'Strategy-as-practice: taking social practices seriously', *Academy of Management Annals*, 6/1: 285–336.

Vaara, E., Sorsa, V., and Pälli, P. (2010), 'On the force potential of strategy texts: a critical discourse analysis of a strategic plan and its power effects in a city organization', *Organization*, 17/6: 685–702.

Van Dijk, T. A. (1997), *Discourse as Social Interaction*. London: Sage.

Whittington, R., Jarzabkowski, P., Mayer, M., Mounoud, E., Nahapiet, J., and Rouleau, L. (2003), 'Taking strategy seriously: responsibility and reform for an important social practice', *Journal of Management Inquiry*, 12/4: 396–409.

Whittington, R. (2007), 'Strategy practice and strategy process: family differences and the sociological eye', *Organisation Studies*, 28/10: 1575–86.

Whittington, R. (2011), 'The practice turn in organization research: towards a disciplined transdisciplinarity', *Accounting, Organizations and Society*, 36/3: 183–6.

Whittington, R., and Cailluet, L. (2008), 'The crafts of strategy: special issue introduction by the guest editors', *Long Range Planning*, 41/3: 241–7.

Whittington, R., Cailluet, L., and Yakis-Douglas, B. (2011), 'Opening strategy: evolution of a precarious profession', *British Journal of Management*, 22/3: 531–44.

Willmott, H. (1997), 'Rethinking management and managerial work: capitalism, control and subjectivity', *Human Relations*, 50/11: 1329–40.

Actor–network theory and strategy as practice

CHRISTOPHER S. CHAPMAN, WAI FONG CHUA and
HABIB MAHAMA

Introduction

The aim of the chapter is to show how actor–
network theorizing can contribute to our understanding of strategy as practice. Practice theorization offers a broad church, with many partially
overlapping sets of interests and concerns, as discussed in the collection of writings found in *The
Practice Turn in Contemporary Theory* (Schatzki,
Knorr Cetina and von Savigny 2001). In this chapter we seek to show the variety of points of contact
between the sensitivities making up a strategy-as-
practice research agenda and those arising from
actor–network theory as one particular part of this
broader set of theories. Through such an engagement, we find opportunities for SAP research to
pursue its agenda and to address a range of critiques that it has faced from those frustrated that its
progress so far has not been as great as hoped.

In setting itself a core agenda, the strategy-as-
practice approach questions the view that 'strategy
is something organizations have', with a view to
shifting to consideration of 'strategy as something
people do in organizations' (Whittington 2006).
Pursuing such an agenda has radical implications,
questioning as it does the notion of strategy as a
legitimate resource at the hands of top management. By making practice central to understanding
strategy, this literature suggests that the locus of
strategizing is dispersed (for anyone participating
in the organization has the potential to engage in
strategizing) and the instantiation of strategy may
follow a complex, non-linear and less determinate

The authors gratefully acknowledge the insightful and
constructive comments and questions on earlier versions of
this chapter from the editors of the handbook together with
Professor Martin Kornberger and Professor Jan Mouritsen.

trajectory involving the interplay of multiple conflicting logics.

Among all of the development and debate around
the strategy-as-practice agenda, we trace some particular criticisms that have been made (namely Araujo and Easton 1996; Whittington 2006; Rasche
and Chia 2009). We focus our discussion around
these, since we find that they are helpful as a way to
reiterate and develop central aspects of the agenda
of SAP research. More importantly, given the focus
of this chapter, we find that these criticisms can be
directly addressed through the adoption of elements
of actor–network theorizing into strategy-as-practice research. Overall, then, we present these criticisms not as judgement of the quality or intentions
of the field. Rather, we see them as comments made
about particular subsets of studies that serve a
useful purpose as conceptual tools to further
strengthen and develop the field. With this caveat
on the role of these criticisms in this chapter firmly
in mind, we now briefly rehearse them.

First, criticism has been made of a tendency to
focus on describing observable patterns of strategic
behaviour, consistent routines or coherent clusters
of activities rather than engaging with how these
observable patterns come to exist (Araujo and
Easton 1996; Rasche and Chia 2009). In other
words, there has been concern that, instead of
dealing with practice per se, there has been a focus
on the ostensible patterned consistency of strategic
activities. On this, Rasche and Chia (2009: 721)
argue that 'focusing on ostensible strategic activities may increase the amount of phenomenon that
can be investigated but it may tell us little about
how such activities cumulatively amount to strategy practices'.

Second, the criticism has been made that it is a
risk to adopt a narrow focus on the firm as a locus

266 Chapman, Chua and Mahama

of strategic activity. In other words, research has tended to conceptualize the firm as the centre from which strategy emerges, becomes developed and is then implemented, to act on what Araujo and Easton (1996) refer to as the 'hostile and faceless environment'. Araujo and Easton (1996) argue that the analytical distinction between the firm and the environment is unhelpful if we are to understand practices of strategizing. This is because conceptualizing the firm as the locus of strategic activities can lead researchers to narrowly isolate and investigate the 'micro-level managerial activity and roles, leaving larger social forces on one side in an un-theorized category of "context"' (Whittington 2006: 616–17). The notion of strategy, in principle, implies the effacing of this distinction. This makes the theorization of how the inside (firm) and outside (environment) co-produce and collectively enact strategy a matter of central importance.

Third, the concern has been raised of a tendency to ignore the role of material objects and attribute agency only to 'strategic individuals'. This is because much current research associates strategy with the agency of people. Limiting agency to only intentional human actors limits what we can understand about strategy as practice; a more sophisticated concept of agency is of value here. On this, Araujo and Easton (1996: 368) call for research to 'dissociate the notion of strategy from well-articulated, prior intentions', as 'intentions follow actions or are articulated retrospectively after actions are taken'. Dissociating strategy from intentionality will allow for the agency of material objects to be accounted for in strategy practices, leading to the study of how, in the performing of strategy, agency is distributed between humans and material objects. It should also allow a greater consideration of non-linear patterns of influence and agency.

In considering these three critiques, we find considerable potential for research informed by actor–network theory to promote research in strategy as practice that seizes the opportunities that the critics feel are being missed. In order to elaborate this premise, in the sections that follow we first review the origins of actor–network theory and outline some of its foundational principles. We

then explore how these principles have been drawn on to develop a broad literature that fruitfully develops our understanding of strategy as practice. In reviewing these studies, we will trace the various streams of preoccupations that have emerged in actor–network theorizing over time. We conclude with a brief discussion of a recently emerging strand of thinking around collective experimentation and elaborate the promise this shows for further developing our understanding of strategy as practice.

Sketching the conceptual origins of actor–network theory

Actor–network theory has its origins in the laboratory studies conducted by Bruno Latour, Michel Callon and others at the École des Mines du Paris (Callon, Law and Rip 1986). The central theme of their studies was to understand what scientists do in practice, with a specific focus on the agency through which scientific knowledge is produced, rejected and/or reproduced. This early work produced some important theoretical insights.

First, the work of the scientist is constructed socially, and the social does not reside in human beings alone but in networks in which the social and material are 'jumbled together' (to form socio-technical networks). To understand what leads to scientific truth claims, there was a need to follow the scientist to the places where science work is carried out (such as the laboratory). It was these insights that led to actor–network theory's focus on practice as a central issue in understanding phenomena, and laid the foundation for the publication of works on science in action (Latour 1987) and science as practice and culture (Pickering 1992).

Second, there are no predetermined (or predeterminable) driving forces behind conduct or practices, and no entity (human or technological) has absolute essence. In other words, you do not start examining practices with the presumption that those practices would be explained by some predetermined factors. Rather, you start with the practice and then discover explanatory factors as the practice is being conducted and observed. In addition, by indicating that no entity has absolute essence, actor–network theory takes the view that, on their own, and in isolation, entities are unable to act. Entities acquire their form, existence and influence on others when viewed in relation to other entities with which they interact. Here, actor–network theory advocates a relational view, or what has come to be known as relational materiality.

The third insight, that what appears real (such as observed patterns in strategic activities), is a discursive formation, which emphasizes the role of discourse and textual material in making things appear real. Through discourse, people render real what they believe the situation to be, more so than on the basis of some objective and independent reality.

Building on these foundational insights, actor–network theory has grown and developed through the elaboration and discussion of a number of foundational principles, which we argue have direct relevance for the development of the strategy-as-practice agenda. These are the principles of generalized symmetry, recursivity and radical indeterminacy.

The principle of generalized symmetry

By the principle of generalized symmetry, actor–network theorists argue that (1) 'everything' deserves explanation and (2) everything that is to be explained should be approached in the same way (Law 1994). The principle of generalized symmetry was developed from David Bloor's (1982; 1991) notion of symmetry, which was one of the core tenets of his 'strong programme'.[1] Bloor and his colleagues working on the sociology of scientific knowledge were critical of the asymmetrical treatment of science (nature) and society or the privileging of science over society in work

undertaken in the traditional sociology of science. This traditional stream of research sought to analyse phenomena by assigning scientific explanations to what appears to be 'truthful', 'rational', 'right' or 'successful' and sociological explanations to those that have been distorted from the 'true path of reason' (Latour 1987). This work concentrated on the social aspects (distortions), since for its proponents the scientific or technical aspects are taken as given a priori.

Bloor and his colleagues deplored the asymmetrical treatment of scientific knowledge and social analysis and proposed that the same methods of analysis be applied to the study of scientific knowledge and social processes, since both are generated by the same kind of factors (Law 1994). In this respect, they maintained that the same explanations need to be offered to any knowledge whether it is considered rational or irrational, right or wrong, successful or unsuccessful, truthful or untruthful. They contended that sociological explanations can be applied to scientific knowledge notwithstanding the degree of rationality. Thus, 'scientific achievements held to be correct should be just as amenable to sociological analysis as those thought to be wrong' (Latour and Woolgar 1986: 23–4). Actor–network theorists took this notion of symmetry to radical levels through the principle of generalized symmetry. In addition to the symmetrical explanations of science (natural) and society (social), the principle of generalized symmetry is applied to human and non-human actants,[2] and the inside/outside divide.

The actor–network theory notion of agency and sociality moves away from a human-centred approach to an approach that has no specific centre. Law (1992: 383, emphasis in original) states:

> Let me be clear. Actor–network theory is analytically radical in part because it treads on a set of ethical, epistemological, and ontological toes. In particular, it does not celebrate the idea that there is a difference in kind between people on one hand, and objects on the other. It denies that people are *necessarily* special.

---

[1] The strong programme was devised to address methodological rather than substantive issues from the sociological investigation of scientific knowledge (Bloor 1991). Bloor proposes four tenets in the strong programme: causality (conditions that bring about belief or states of knowledge); impartiality (with respect to truth and falsity, rationality and irrationality, success or failure); symmetry (the same type of cause would explain both true and false beliefs); and reflexivity (its patterns of explanation would have to be applied to sociology itself).

[2] Actants, in actor–network theory, refer to human and non-human actors that acquire their form and capacity to act by virtue of their relations with other actors.

The actor–network theory view is that agency is not simply a human property (because human beings are intentional) but may also reside in material objects in a patterned network of relations (Law 1992). Almost all the interactions between humans are mediated through objects of one kind or the other, and hence these objects also participate in the social. Writing on how human interactions are mediated through material objects, Law (1992: 382) notes, for example,

> I am standing on a stage. The students face me, behind serried ranks of desks, with paper and pens. They are writing notes. They can see me, and they can hear me. But they can also see transparencies that I put in the overhead projector. So the projector, like the shape of the room, participates in the shaping of our interaction. It mediates our communication and it does this asymmetrically, amplifying what I say without giving students much of a chance to answer back (Thompson, 1990). In another world it might, of course, be different. The students might storm the podium and take control of the overhead projector. Or they might, as they do if I lecture badly, simply ignore me. But they don't, and while they don't the projector participates in our social relations: it helps to define the lecturer–student relationships. It is a part of the social. It operates on them to influence the way in which they act.

This broader definition of agency and sociality requires that the human and non-human actants participating in shaping interactions and effects should be treated symmetrically. Treating human and non-human actants symmetrically does not imply extending intentionality to objects and mechanism to people, however (Callon and Latour 1992), as intentionality is not a precondition for the exercise of agency or for participation in the social. Analytically, it implies that we need to investigate how the human and the non-human interact or combine to generate specific effects, and hence the generalized symmetry principle analytically effaces the distinction between them by focusing on the agency through which they simultaneously produce and reproduce action.

The inside/outside divide (that is, the firm/environment divide) in the investigation of scientific knowledge is also avoided by the principle of generalized symmetry. Latour (1987) argues that scientists (who constitute the inside) are not in any way insulated from the external economic and political environment. The scientists, through their production of scientific knowledge, affect the way politicians, policy-makers, statisticians and economists go about their everyday life, and these outsiders equally shape and influence the work of the scientists. The scientific insider draws his/her resources from the outside, and so the relation between the inside and the outside is vital in understanding scientific knowledge. Writing on the isolation of the inside from the outside, Latour (1987: 152, emphasis in original) argues:

> The first lesson to be drawn from this unfortunate example [of an isolated specialist] is that there is a direct relationship between the size of the outside recruitment of resources and the amount of work that can be done on the inside. [. . .] The second lesson from this example is that an *isolated* specialist is a contradiction in terms. Either you are isolated and very quickly stop being a specialist, or you remain a specialist but this means you are not isolated.

Latour (1987) argues that there is a positive feedback loop between the inside, where science resides, and the outside, where other scientists have to go. He states:

> It is because of this feedback that, if you get inside a laboratory, you see no public relations, no politics, no ethical problems, no class struggle, no lawyers; you see science isolated from society. But this isolation exists only in so far as other scientists are constantly busy recruiting investors, interesting and convincing people. The pure scientists are like helpless nestlings while the adults are busy building the nest and feeding them. It is because West or the boss are so active outside that the microkids or the collaborator are so entrenched inside pure science. If we separate this inside and this outside aspect, our travel through technoscience would become entirely impossible (Latour 1987: 156).

The inside and the outside work in a relationship to generate effects that come to exist as scientific knowledge. Actor–network theory proposes that, for analytical purposes, the inside/outside divide needs to be avoided, so that we can study how their linkages produce scientific knowledge.

Thus, by proposing generalized symmetry, actor–network theory seeks to avoid the a priori distinction between nature and society, human and non-human actants, inside and outside. It sees them as effects generated in the process of network-building and claims that these elements interact in a patterned network of relations. Actor–network theorists argue for free association between these elements, and that there should be no arbitrary limit on the extent to which the elements explain or interact with each other. These elements should be allowed to associate freely without any definite boundary between them (Keys 1998).

The principle of generalized symmetry has implications for studying strategy as practice. First, by effacing the a priori distinction between the firm (as the locus of strategic control) and the environment (on which strategy acts), as well as human and material objects, actor–network theory focuses theoretical and empirical attention on how they are assembled into what comes to be known as strategy. For instance, Latour would argue that we should study strategy by focusing on what is held together (the association and strategic activities) as strategy, not what holds (the firm) strategy together (Latour 1986). What is held together is an outcome of heterogeneous engineering involving the entanglement of the inside and outside as well as the social and material (Orlikowski 2007; Goodman 2001); and there are mutual exchange properties among these elements, through a series of associations, to the extent that their individual identities become less important (Schneider *et al.* 2010; Goodman 2001). In other words, in seeking to understand strategy as practice, we have to discard the individual identities of entities (firm, environment, top management, social, technical, etc.) and focus analytical attention on the collective outcomes/effects of their interactions (Latour 1993).

The principle of recursivity

Actor–network theory views a network of relationships as a recursive process rather than a free-standing structure (Law 1994). The network is considered both as the medium and the outcome of interactions, and it recursively and precariously generates and reproduces itself in further interactions (Law 1992; 1994). This implies that no network or its constituent elements is permanently stable, complete or final, and hence that stability cannot be taken for granted. Further, as heterogeneity is introduced into the network by virtue of the diversity of its component elements, network activities are precarious, incomplete and contestable. The elements associated with the network gain their spatial integrity by virtue of the nodes and relays they occupy/perform in the relations, and so they are constantly engaged in struggles to define and redefine their positions relative to others (Law 1992). Networks of relations are considered sites of struggle, resistance and negotiations, and, through these, relations are constantly in a state of change. This state of change is both a medium and an outcome of stabilizing the relationships held together by the network. Rather than wish these away, the actor–network theory position is that they require explanation, and must be explained if research is to contribute to knowledge.

The actor–network theory view is that networks of relations are constantly in flux; accordingly, the core focus of research is to explore how the relations between its elements get performed, become stable and durable, albeit temporarily (Law 1999). This implies that we do not start the study of a network by assuming its structural properties or patterns and expecting these structural properties or patterns to predetermine practical action. Thus, for example, we do not begin to analyse strategy as practice by hypothesizing that planning departments that are highly centralized would tend to yield strategic plans that take less time to formulate but have a lower acceptance rate among the organization's rank and file. Instead, practices create and enact these patterns and relations – that is, rather than seeking to explain only ostensible patterns in relationships, they draw our attention to their performative character. Performativity relates to how the fragments are fitted together to form stable and durable relations. In actor–network theory, it is assumed that elements are performed in, by and through the relations within which they are located. The question explored by actor–network theorists, therefore, is (Law 1999: 4): 'How is it that things get performed (and perform themselves) into relations that are relatively stable and stay in place?' Another question (Law 1992) is: why is it that some networks are much more performed than others are? Thus, actor–network theorists are interested in the performative character of relations and the elements constituted into those relations. Law (1992: 386) summarizes the core of the theory this way:

> This, then, is the core of the actor–network approach: a concern with how actors and organizations mobilize, juxtapose, and hold together the bits and pieces out of which they are composed; how they are sometimes able to prevent those bits and pieces from following their own inclinations and making off; and how they manage, as a result, to conceal for a time the process of translation itself and so turn a network from heterogeneous set of bits and pieces each with its own inclinations, into something that passes as a punctualized actor.

In this respect, actor–network theory directs our attention to the array of practical activities through which strategy practices emerge and by which they are enacted. The types of research questions that could become of interest might be how strategic planning workshops 'actually' work; how non-human actants such as PowerPoint slides or financial numbers have agency; and how ideas about 'best practice' strategy maps travel through time and distance to influence how people do their jobs. In stressing the emergent and enacted character of strategy, actor–network theory insists that these phenomena 'exist only in the doing of them' (Callon 2004).

The principle of radical indeterminacy

Actor–network theorists contend that interests are multiple and indeterminate (Callon and Law 1982; Law 1994; Kayatekin 1998). This is in sharp contrast to the treatment of interests in economics and in some sociological writings, and raises questions about the underlying logic of strategizing. In economic theory (and other related theories), each actor category is implicitly assumed to be homogeneous with respect to interests (Soderbaum 1993: 401), and hence only one interest is assumed to be relevant. Actor–network theorists consider such unitary account of interests as narrow and

limiting. Latour and Woolgar (1986), for instance, note that such unitary accounts (in the context of science and technology) limit the range of phenomena that can be studied about the processes through which scientific knowledge is constituted and disseminated. Theorists within the actor–network tradition argue that each actant is associated with many and varied interests, and so researchers should be talking of multiple interests rather than single interest. They therefore adopt a much broader, all-inclusive approach by allowing all possible variables to be included in any investigation of scientific knowledge, with no interest explanation to be privileged over others.

Moreover, actor–network theorists reject the theoretical imputation of interests to actants by researchers, such as the imputation of economic interests by strategy researchers. As Callon and Law (1982: 621) note, actor–network theory is 'not concerned with the general explanatory[3] form of interest explanations' but is interested in the attribution and transformation of interests by actants. Interests are not to be seen as background factors to be imputed by analysts. Rather, they are brought to the foreground as attributes assigned by actants to themselves and those they interact with. Actor–network theorists hold the view that actants are constantly exploring the potential presence or absence of interests in their work and the work of others, as each part of their networks is constantly being contested by these actants. This also implies that interests are not static but dynamic and fluid; they change as new data become available, or when new challenges emerge, and the form that future interests may take is not determinate. Thus, in actor–network theory, interests are not only multiple but indeterminate.

Tracing actor–network principles in the development of strategy-as-practice research

In the previous section we outlined the fundamental principles underlying the development and interests of actor–network theory. In discussion of

---

[3] The imputation of interests to actants by analysts and researchers

the literature[4] that follows we made inevitable choices for inclusion and exclusion based on our aim to demonstrate particular lines of development that relate to actor–network theorizing and that, we feel, hold some promise for the development of strategy-as-practice research.

We are not the first to see the linkages here, of course. Back in 2006 Steen, Coopmans and Whyte sought to stimulate debate about the potential of actor–network theory for strategy research. The intent of Steen, Coopmans and Whyte (2006) was to disrupt the dichotomy between structure and agency and to refocus research attention towards the complex interdependent relationships between these analytical categories. For them, managers do not simply operate within structures but also participate in (re)creating these structures. They call for emphasis on 'the myriad of traceable processes by which a variety of actors connect together', as it is those processes that give birth to both structures and agencies (Steen, Coopmans and Whyte 2006: 307). To do this, they argue that actor–network theory offers potential or theorizing stability (structure) and strategic change (agency) simultaneously. In the section that follows we briefly trace the developments made by some of the relatively few studies that heeded this early call.

Cabantous, Gond and Johnson-Cramer (2010) conceptualize rational decision-making as a form of strategy and then focus on examining the practices by which such decisions are made within the organization. They argue that rationality should not be treated as a property that organizations have but, rather, as an outcome of purposive practical activity, and that organizational actors' choice of such activity is influenced by rational choice theory. Drawing on actor–network theory notions of performativity and calculability, they argue that rational decision-making involves a theory and a set of material devices that are constitutive of (and constituted by) the theory's core assumptions. By performativity, they imply that theory does not simply describe practices but constructs and enacts the practices it describes. Rational decisions, they

argue, involve making practice fit theory – a process that relies heavily on the agency of calculative devices.

The empirical analysis by Cabantous, Gond and Johnson-Cramer (2010), which is based on work by decision analysts, reveals that rational decision-making is a three-stage process of the performativity of rational choice theory. First, the analyst engages in practices of making the organizational context fit the principles of rational choice theory. These practices rely mainly on social interaction and the construction of a network of allies to facilitate the enactment of a decision context that is consistent with the assumptions of rational choice theory. Second, he or she translates decision parameters into numbers and transforms the decision context into a micro-world in which numbers thrive. Finally, the analyst relies on calculations to mobilize entities, previously quantified, to enable rational decisions to be made in a manner consistent with theory. In summary, the study emphasizes the role of theory in shaping actors' reality, language and practices; it also reveals the central role of material devices in the social construction of rational decision-making.

By examining the interaction between decision analysts, rational decision theory and the material devices that inhabit (and activate) the core assumptions of rational decision theory, Cabantous, Gond and Johnson-Cramer (2010) shift away from a human-centred approach to studying decision-making to an approach that focuses on interactions of both human and material devices. This is consistent with the principle of generalized symmetry.

While the actor–network theory concept of generalized symmetry is evident in Cabantous, Gond and Johnson-Cramer's (2010) study, a way to further this analysis from an actor–network theory perspective would be to give consideration to the non-linear and recursive processes of decision-making. This way, we might learn about the struggles and controversies associated with performing rational choice theory in practice. Moreover, it would allow us to question (as does Chua 1995) the rationality of the processes of making decisions; rational choice theory prescribes a patterned approach to decision-making, and whether that pattern has been followed would be

---

[4] Space constraints mean that this is a necessarily partial selection on our part.

revealed if attention is paid to the actor–network principles of recursivity. From an actor–network theory perspective, empirically determining how rational choice theory inserts itself in decision-making, and imputing influence (or essence) to the theory *ex ante*, forecloses the possible roles of other decision-making theories (and interests) and therefore limits the range of phenomena that could be examined in the study.

Giraudeau (2008) draws on actor–network theory to examine the role of artefacts in strategic planning. He focuses on strategic plans, as particular types of artefacts, and how they contribute not just to the programming of predetermined strategies but also to the emergence of new strategies. He argues that material objects act – that is, they construct the logic of action, and may do so either as intermediaries (transporting information/control without modification) or mediators (transforming the meaning and significance of the information/control being transported). In this empirical study of Renault's investment strategy, he found that plans provided visual and textual representation of the contexts and strategies that enhanced strategic imagination, thereby creating conditions in which the formulation of new strategy was possible. He also found that plans may constrain innovative strategy.

Giraudeau (2008), in considering material objects as actors, transcends the human/non-human actor divide and focuses on how, through interactions, they bring strategy into being. This is consistent with the principle of generalized symmetry, as it privileges neither human actors nor material objects. Furthermore, and in consonance with the principles of recursivity, the analysis does not presuppose any essence for plans but, rather, focuses on the possibilities offered for the discovery of surprising and interesting uses of plans. A challenge that might have been interesting would have been to allow more for multiple and changing interests to have been accounted for in a manner consistent with the principle of radical indeterminacy.

The studies by Cabantous, Gond and Johnson-Cramer (2010) and Giraudeau (2008) both highlight the importance of material objects in strategy practices. The premise that actor–network theorizing has both conceptual and practical potential to develop strategy-as-practice research is strong, therefore. In terms of helping to elaborate and take stock of this potential in greater detail, however, we find that there are rather more studies in the field of accounting that have drawn on actor–network theory in order to explore how accounting as an object inserts itself in organizational process, how it exercises agency, and the effects generated as accounting interacts with other entities. We therefore briefly overview this literature in the remainder of this section, since not just the theorization but also the overlapping interests in control and direction through calculations and management tools make the interface between accounting and strategizing a particularly fruitful one.

The study by Preston, Cooper and Coombs (1992) is one of the earlier ones to examine the emergence and exercise of agency of material devices such as accounting. Drawing on the actor–network theory notion of fabrication, they studied how management budgeting systems were assembled and enacted in specific UK hospitals. Consistent with principle of recursivity, these researchers moved away from a presumption that management budgeting (and accounting, generally) is a well-defined technical system that unproblematically inserts itself into organizations in predefined ways. Doing so enabled them to avoid the simplicity of describing observable ostensive patterns associated with the implementation of management budgeting initiatives. It allowed them to focus their attention on how these patterns come about, become (or are) embedded in organizations, and the effects they generate as they interact with other organizational practices. In particular, in seeking to explain how management budgets take hold (or not) in the hospitals they studied, they did not start with a study of a ready-made management budget; rather, they started with the activities (and the associated competing logics) of fabricating the budgets. They found that, instead of being a technology ready-made for a well-defined purpose, management budgeting systems were rather fabricated, with loose characteristics, purposes and uses.

These findings about how the management budgets were fabricated are a useful starting point in understanding the agency of budgets. More specifically, Preston, Cooper and Coombs (1992) show that the capacity of any technology or system to act depends, to a large extent, on how it is fabricated and assembled and the networks of action in which it is a part. These findings have implications for studying strategy as practice. Rather than starting with a ready-made strategy, they call for study of how the strategy is fabricated in the first instance, as the activities of fabricating a strategy may explain why that strategy may or may not be successful.

Chua (1995) draws on actor–network theory notions of fabrication, inscriptions and expertise to explore the sociotechnical linkages and practices that enabled 'new' accounting numbers to be fabricated, deployed and sustained for several years. Influenced by the principle of generalized symmetry, Chua (1995) accounts for not just intentional human acts but also the agency of material objects, and how the human and the material objects are jumbled together in a network of relations that sought to create and enact particular accounting numbers in three Australian hospitals. Her findings challenged conventional understanding of accounting in organizations. By studying the processes of experimenting with accounting numbers, she found that what came to be articulated as the 'new' accounting technology did not emerge due to 'rational economic reasons'. Rather, the new accounting emerged because an uncertain faith was able to tie together diverse and shifting interests in an actor network. Here, Chua's (1995) work highlights the indeterminacy of accounting technologies and the practices and outcomes to which they are oriented.

In this study, accounting numbers did not become usable facts because they faithfully represented reality, but they were, rather, outcomes of historical interest that were tied together. In other words, 'the numbers generated were consistent/ factual enough to hold together diverse purposes' (Chua 1995: 138), and the interests so tied together in turn sustained those accounting numbers for several years. Like the study by Preston, Cooper and Coombs (1992), this study provides useful insights about how we may study strategy as practice. It highlights the fact that everyday rules of

managing social life matter if we are to understand practices of strategizing. Such rules may help explain (1) how competing logics in the making up of strategy are negotiated and settled; (2) why certain strategies are sustained much longer than others; (3) how people pragmatically make choices to resolve the dilemmas posed by information gaps; (4) the agency of seemingly weak inscriptions that become strong because of the presence of metrological chains; and (5) the role of experts within and outside the organization in the emergence and enactment of strategy.

Briers and Chua (2001) offer some insights about how an actor–network theory approach effaces the analytical distinction between the firm (inside) and the environment (outside). This allows the exploration of the co-production and enactment of strategy in practice, consistent with the principle of generalized symmetry. Their study provides an example of how change is precipitated by a heterogeneous network of local (within the firm) and global (outside the firm) actors (including machines, boundary objects and other material objects). In seeking to explain accounting and organizational change, they explored how local organizational discourse and practices were influenced by and influenced global ideas and practices (such as activity-based-costing) and the consequences of that for organizational practices of accounting.

Following this network in action allowed the researchers to understand the uneven nature of change and to reconceptualize what, in practice, constitutes successful or unsuccessful accounting change. Like Chua (1995), they found that successful change is not necessarily about what is right but is more about what holds diverse things and people together.[5] Their study rejects a simple rational economic account of change and draws our attention to the diverse confluences of organizational and extra-organizational origins of change. In other

---

[5] For an intriguing recent study that develops this point, see Dambrin and Robson (2011); these authors study the development and implications of a performance measurement system in which direct measurement was impossible, given the particular rules governing arrangements for pharmaceutical sales in France.

words, they highlight the indeterminacy of the processes and outcomes of change. This study suggests a way forward for understanding strategy as practice. In particular, it emphasizes that the origin of strategic change may lie beyond the firm, thereby necessitating exploration of how the local and the global participate in the emergence and enacting of strategy. It also argues against a focus on the more ostensive patterns of strategizing by highlighting the fragile, temporal and uneven nature of organizational practices.

Chua and Mahama (2007) examine the role of network ties in the construction and the agency of accounting numbers. They draw on actor–network theory notions of relational materiality (as articulated by the principle of generalized symmetry) and fragility (in consonance with the principle of recursivity) to conceptualize accounting technologies and numbers as interdependent actants, and sought to explore how accounting numbers come to acquire their existence, form, meaning and influence in a network of relationships. They engaged with the processes of experimenting with accounting numbers in inter-firm alliances, and highlight the challenges of translating and representing the relevant dimensions of performance in terms of numbers. They explain these challenges with reference to the composition of, and mode of relating within, the complex network of inter-organizational relationships the accounting numbers are meant to represent and on which they are meant to act.

In particular, the distribution of relationships among actants and the strength of the ties these actants forged were material in explaining the success or failure of accounting. On this basis, Chua and Mahama (2007) argue that accounting is not merely a form of technical control, nor can it be said to be exclusively social. They argue that research should move beyond dichotomizing control into technical and social and, instead, focus on how accounting draws on both the social and the technical to generate effects. Their study also challenges the notion that accounting generates order. In practice, accounting may also serve as a conduit for disorder, in that one cannot predetermine the effects of accounting; accounting numbers may be drawn upon to serve multiple and changing interests.

This study provides at least three leads for SAP research. First, that network ties matter if we are to understand how strategy emerges and becomes instantiated in practice. Second, in practice there is no clear analytical distinction between the social and the technical; accordingly, the analytical focus in strategy-as-practice research should be on how strategy is both a social and a technical practice. Third, it also challenges the taken-for-granted notion that strategy creates orderly organizational practices as they become translated into operation. In practice, strategy may create both order and disorder.

Skærbæk and Tryggestad (2010) explicitly engage with strategy by examining the possible roles of accounting devices in the structuring, (re) formulation and implementation of strategy. Drawing on the actor–network theory notion of framing and overflowing, they found that the coming into being of any particular strategy and strategic action is closely linked to a stream of calculative devices such as accounting. By this, and consistent with the principle of generalized symmetry, they draw the attention of accounting and strategy researchers alike to the role of material objects beyond the passive role (as mere tools in the hands of strategists) traditionally ascribed to these devices.

In contract to Cabantous, Gond and Johnson-Cramer (2010), Skærbæk and Tryggestad (2010) started with no general assumption or predetermination of what constituted strategy, strategic actors or the path dependence of strategy implementation. Rather, they followed the everyday practices of strategizing, and this led to at least two interesting findings. First, managers are not key strategic actors by virtue of the location in the organizational hierarchy. Key strategic actors may not necessarily be those occupying the executive suite in the organization; they could be located in unexpected places within and outside the organization. This raises questions about what actually constitutes the strategic centre of an organization, and also draws the attention of strategy-as-practice researchers to the dispersed origins of strategy and the dangers of focusing on a specific group of managers for studying strategy.

Second, Skærbæk and Tryggestad (2010) highlight the importance of accounting for the agency of material objects in the formulation and implementation of strategy in practice. They show through their ethnographic study that strategy, rather than flowing from the intentional human actors, was successively being adapted to and mutually constituted by accounting devices. In other words, strategy was continuously being reformulated towards that which was in consonance with accounting rubrics and outcomes. This raises an important issue about the specific roles of calculative agencies in strategy as practice, namely whether they serve strategy, create strategy or both. Actor–network theorizing holds much promise for dealing with this issue.

Building on Robson's (1991; 1992) earlier work on accounting as inscription device, Qu and Cooper (2011) examine the influence of particular modes of consultant–client interaction in the processes of assembling a balanced scorecard. While Robson (1991; 1992) studied accounting inscriptions and their specific roles in change and control at a distance, Qu and Cooper (2011) investigated how these inscriptions were produced. They provide empirical evidence of how inscription-building created a platform for negotiating the contours of a balanced scorecard in a consultant–client interaction and explain the emergent balanced scorecard as a co-production. Conceptually, co-production is at the core of the principle of generalized symmetry, which calls for the effacing of the separation of outside/inside, technical/social and human/non-human actors. The focus is, rather, on the interaction between and among these forces and the effects that they generate. This notion of co-production is relevant to strategy research as it highlights the role of organizational outsiders (specifically, consultants) in the creation and enactment of strategy. The corporate landscape is now awash with various types of strategy consultants laying claim to particular expertise.

As these consultants interact with organizations, they shape the strategic activities of these organizations in significant ways. This further reinforces the idea that an actor–network theory approach, as adopted by Qu and Cooper (2011), may be a useful starting point for understanding the origins of strategy, its path dependence and its effects. This is particularly so because the accounting technology they studied (the balanced scorecard) is generally held as a tool for representing and enacting strategy.

Strategizing as collective experimentation and calculation

In this chapter we have sought to show how actor–network theory presents many opportunities for developing our understanding of strategy as practice through the application of its theoretical insights to the study of strategy in the making. As the preceding overview of studies indicates, actor–network theory comprises a range of theoretical streams, to the extent that Law (1992) describes it as 'diasporic'. It *is* diasporic, in that it transforms itself with time and across space, but all the parts are partially connected. In our view, a strand of thinking that has emerged very recently, relating to what Caliskan and Callon (2009) refer to as an economization process, is particularly apt for theorizing strategy as practice. In particular, Callon's (2009) notion of collective experimentation resonates with the practices of making up and performing strategy. In this section, we present this notion of collective experimentation and show how it can be drawn upon to theorize and empirically investigate strategy practices.

In an actor–network theory sense, no one can be entirely sure in advance of the form and material arrangement needed to establish and perform strategy (Callon, Lascoumes and Barthe 2009). This is because strategy is an outcome of processes of experimentation that draw together multiple actors into a hybrid forum and take place at varying local sites. Strategy as practice may therefore be theorized as a collective experimentation with matters of concern. Matters of concern are the issues and questions (such as concerns with cost, competition, new markets, customer satisfaction, shareholder value, etc.) for which existing organizational arrangements are incapable of providing satisfactory solutions and stability. When matters of concern are identified, they trigger uncertainty about existing forms of organizing and create the conditions in which it is possible for actors to engage in strategizing activities. Consequently, to understand how strategy emerges and becomes enacted, it is imperative to begin with the underlying matters of concern.

Matters of concern do not emerge naturally, neither are they predeterminable. They are outcomes of problematizations – a 'gradual process of fragmentation and division of issues into joint formulations of a set of different problems which in a sense, at least partially, are substitutive for the initial issue' (Callon, Lascoumes and Barthe 2009: 543). Callon, Lascoumes and Barthe argue that the dynamics of problematization is a complex process that is neither completely consensual nor total. In the problematization process, the initial issues of concern are taken up by multiple actors, who interpret them on the basis of their idiosyncrasies and translate then into well-developed problems for which strategizing becomes a necessity. For Callon, Lascoumes and Barthe (2009), such problematization processes lead to the constitution of a network whose content and extensions evolve in relation to the translations that are attempted between problems.

It is these processes of problematizing matters of concern that strategy-as-practice researchers need to follow in order to uncover the complex origins of strategy and to account for observed strategizing activities. This will shift attention away from exploring ostensible consistency in patterns of strategic activities, not because these patterns are unimportant but because their relevance lies in the multilateral negotiations and contestations that gave them birth.

When issues are problematized and transformed into matters of concern, hybrid forums are constituted whose tasks are to find solutions to these concerns. They are hybrid forums 'because they are open spaces where groups can come together to discuss technical options involving the collective, hybrid because the groups involved and the spokesperson claiming to represent them are heterogeneous, including experts, politicians, technicians and laypersons who consider themselves involved' (Callon, Lascoumes and Barthe 2009: 18). The concept of hybrid forums shifts attention away from the narrow focus on the firm as a locus of strategic activities, as it dissolves the distinction between actors inside and those outside the organization. These hybrid forums engage in collective experimentation with the matters of concern, resulting in some form of strategy – a temporary one. Here, matters of concern are transformed into a system of calculable questions, and the complexities of the world are compressed into two-dimensional models of competitors, bargaining power, industry regulations, ethical considerations and market reactions, among others.

Strategy-as-practice research might fruitfully engage with the processes by which the complex relations between the firm and its environment are transported and transformed into experimental models that allow actors to engage in strategizing activities. SAP research might also investigate how transpositions occur while maintaining equivalences with the 'real' world. It is here that research will start to uncover the struggles that attend strategy-making in practice.

Transportation and transformation require calculative agencies. These agencies help mobilize the world so that it might be subjected to a series of experimentation. Using theoretical ideas from actor–network theory, accounting researchers have long recognized the role of calculative agencies in the crafting of strategy and control. Much of the emphasis on calculation has been on accounting inscriptions/devices that frame particular strategic options as viable, profitable and/or feasible and others as invalid and/or unprofitable. Tools such as the balanced scorecard, the preparations of documents for an initial public offering, budgets, Gantt charts, human resource maps, etc. are all argued to act in conjunction with other human actors in the crafting of strategy. Like other studies in the organizational studies literature, the emphasis is on accounts as actants that frame the possible and probable, and, in some cases, transform and reframe extant conceptualizations.

Strategy-as-practice researchers may advance our knowledge by investigating the role of these calculative agencies in the collective experimentation that characterizes the making up and performing of strategy. By doing so, SAP researchers will be addressing the criticism that research within the area ignores the role of material objects. These material objects (such as calculative agencies) are powerful mainly because they say nothing explicit, and, because they say nothing explicit, they 'encourage, solicit and prepare the articulation of propositions' (Callon, Lascoumes and Barthe 2009: 54) and allow for identities to be assigned, relations to be established and strategic actions to be imputed.

The actor–network theory view is that, because experimental processes in general (and calculative agencies in particular) are exclusionary, the very entities that are excluded in experimentation processes may pose challenges to the successful reproduction (or implementation) of the experimental model, for those entities will still be present out there and will continue to maintain relations with the entities included in the experimental model, and thus influence the capacity of the models to act. Strategy-as-practice research will benefit from engaging closely with the struggles to reproduce strategies and to account for the role of the other entities that were initially excluded in the collective experimentation, because the challenges faced in reproducing the experimental models may become sources of new matters of concern, leading to another cycle of experimentation and strategizing. Strategizing is a never-ending process of experimentation.

An example of a strategy research study that could have benefited from theorizing using the notion of experimentation is that of Denis et al. (2011). They focus on the processes and practices of formulating a viable strategic orientation for three large teaching hospitals. This was characterized by a continuous process of making, unmaking and remaking decisions – a phenomenon that Denis et al. (2011) refer to as 'escalating indecision'. The cumulative episodes of decision-making described in the paper could have been richly theorized with the actor–network theory notion of experimentation with matters of concern. The matter of concern here was the quest to reorientate the hospital system through mergers into large teaching hospitals. There were no ready-made solutions, just an ensemble of a diverse set of actors who were to negotiate, through a series of strategic decisions, the material form of the merged entity. The decision episodes associated with the development of the merger principles and protocol and the reproduction of the protocol in practice resonate with the notion of compressing the complex world into a model that inhabits assumptions about the functional form of the merged entity. Using the actor–network theorizing as explained above would have revealed the problematization, simplification, summarization and translations that occurred and the specific agency exercised by each of the actors (human and material).

Another strategy research study that could have drawn on the notion of experimentation is that of Gunn and Williams (2007). They focus on the use of 'strategic tools' in organization and examine their research question through a survey of the actors involved in strategy practices ('strategists'). They identified particular types of tools used in practice and clustered these tools based on the groups of actors who used them in strategy work. While this allows them to identify who uses particular types of strategic tool, more could have been uncovered in the study if the authors had theorized their research problem and design using the concept of experimentation. For instance, the notion of experimentation would have guided the research towards understanding the matters of concern that led to strategizing and would have revealed how agency was attributed to specific tools, leading to some of these tools being labelled as strategic and others not. We argue that these tools do not come with ready-made solutions but, rather, they become articulated and acquire their essence as part of the process of experimenting with matters of concerns. In other words, rather than taking the tools as given, the notion of experimentation would have focused analytical attention on how the tools emerged and became strategic, how these tools exercise agency in the strategic management of the organization and the effects they generate when they insert themselves (or become inserted) in organizations.

Concluding thoughts

In this chapter we have outlined an argument as to why research drawing on actor–network theorizing may engage with strategy-as-practice studies to focus empirical attention on the performative aspects of doing strategy. We argue that this approach offers a direct and effective way to exploit opportunities highlighted by various critics of SAP research, who felt that more could be done to further its agenda.

We first set out some of the foundational principles of actor–network theory: the principle of generalized symmetry, the principle of recursivity and the principle of radical indeterminacy. We then discussed a variety of empirical studies of strategy as practice that had taken up the opportunity to apply actor–network theorizing, highlighting not just when this had been strong but also when there were further steps that might have been taken from an actor–network theory perspective. We complemented this discussion with an elaboration of how a range of studies focused on accounting further informed the potential of actor–network theory in research on strategy as practice – both through their detailed engagement with actor–network theory and with their focus on how calculative practices might be understood as strategic.

Having set this out in the extant empirical literature, we went on to emphasize that, as with practice theory more generally, actor–network theory is more diasporic than it is a highly programmed field of activity. In bringing our discussion to a conclusion, we chose a recently emerging strand of interest within this diaspora relating to the role of collective experimentation and calculation as a final set of ideas that offer much potential to researchers wishing to further develop our understanding of strategy as practice.

In taking on this remit for the chapter, we are sensitive to the irony of treating actor–network theory in such a programmatic fashion. In discussing the nature and impact of actor–network theorizing, we have sought to demonstrate how its evolution demonstrates an openness and fluidity that is fitting to its own preoccupations and to the further development of the strategy-as-practice agenda.

In drawing to a conclusion here, we offer a final caveat concerning the pitfalls of black-boxing actor–network theory itself. In setting out this chapter as an offering of opportunity to the SAP community, it is appropriate that we also emphasize that the opportunity offered represents a significant intellectual struggle. Although the foundational principles of actor–network theory are

simple to set out (just as the guiding principles underlying strategy as practice are), the intellectual discipline required in execution to live up to them is considerable (indicating another similarity with the strategy-as-practice agenda).

Those who might find in this chapter sufficient points of interest to wish to read further would be well served in delving a little into the parts of the actor–network literature that have engaged in critical self-reflection on the gap between its intentions and their realization in practice. Latour (2004) offers a lament for the relative absence of a radical critical edge to actor–network theory studies despite this being a key initiating concern. This concern for the difficulty of the extant actor–network theory literature in addressing questions of power also forms a part of the critical self-reflection of Alcadipani and Hassard (2010). Happily, in framing and composing their critique of actor–network theory, these authors end by offering an argument as to how their concerns can be addressed. In similar vein, in this chapter we began with the rehearsal of some criticisms of strategy as practice. We did so, however, in order to show that actor–network theory offers clear and compelling reasons for confidence that these criticisms are not fundamentally threatening to the strategy-as-practice agenda but, rather, that they help to elaborate challenges that can and should be worked on with the help of actor–network theorizing.

References

Alcadipani, R., and Hassard, J. (2010), 'Actor–network theory, organizations and critique: towards a politics of organizing', *Organization*, 17/4: 419–35.

Araujo, L., and Easton, G. (1996), 'Strategy: where is the pattern?', *Organization*, 3/3: 361–83.

Bloor, D. (1982), 'Wittgenstein and Mannheim on the sociology of mathematics', in Collins, H. M. (ed.), *Sociology of Scientific Knowledge: A Source Book*: 39–57. Bath University Press.

(1991), *Knowledge and Social Imagery*, 2nd edn. University of Chicago Press.

Briers, M., and Chua, W. F. (2001), 'The role of actor–networks and boundary objects in management accounting change: a field study of an implementation of activity-based costing', *Accounting, Organizations and Society*, 26/3: 237–69.

Cabantous, L., Gond, J.-P., and Johnson-Cramer, M. (2010), 'Decision theory as practice: crafting rationality in organizations', *Organization Studies*, 31/11: 1531–66.

Caliskan, K., and Callon, M. (2009), 'Economization, part 1: shifting attention from the economy towards processes of economization', *Economy and Society*, 38/3: 369–98.

Callon, M. (2004), 'Europe wrestling with technology', *Economy and Society*, 33/1: 121–34.

(2009), 'Civilizing markets: carbon trading between in vitro and in vivo experiments', *Accounting, Organizations and Society*, 34/3–4: 535–48.

Callon, M., Lascoumes, P., and Barthe, Y. (2009), *Acting in an Uncertain World: An Essay on Technical Democracy*. Cambridge, MA: MIT Press.

Callon, M., and Latour, B. (1992), 'Don't throw the baby out with the Bath school! A reply to Collins and Yearley', in Pickering, A. (ed.), *Science as Practice and Culture*: 345–68. University of Chicago Press.

Callon, M., and Law, J. (1982), 'On interests and their transformation: enrolment and counter-enrolment', *Social Studies of Science*, 12/4: 615–25.

Callon, M., Law, J., and Rip, A. (1986), *Mapping the Dynamics of Science and Technology: Sociology of Science in the Real World*. Basingstoke: Macmillan.

Chua, W. F. (1995), 'Experts, networks and inscriptions in the fabrication of accounting images: a story of representation of three public hospitals', *Accounting, Organizations and Society*, 20/2–3: 111–45.

Chua, W. F., and Mahama, H. (2007), 'The effect of network ties on accounting controls in a supply alliance: field study evidence', *Contemporary Accounting Research*, 24/1: 47–86.

Dambrin, C., and Robson, K. (2011), 'Tracing performance in the pharmaceutical industry: ambivalence, opacity and the performativity of flawed measures', *Accounting, Organizations and Society*, 36/7: 428–55.

Denis, J.-L., Dompierre, G., Langley, A., and Rouleau, L. (2011), 'Escalating indecision: between reification and strategic ambiguity', *Organization Science*, 22/1: 225–44.

Giraudeau, M. (2008), 'The draft of strategy: opening up plans and their uses', *Long Range Planning*, 41/3: 291–306.

Goodman, D. (2001), 'Ontology matters: the relational materiality of nature and agro-food studies', *Sociologia Ruralis*, 41/2: 182–200.

Gunn, R., and Williams, W. (2007), 'Strategic tools: an empirical investigation into strategy in practice in the UK', *Strategic Change*, 16/5: 201–16.

Kayatekin, S. A. (1998), 'Observations on some theories of current agrarian change', *Review of African Political Economy*, 25: 207–19.

Keys, P. (1998), 'OR as technology revisited', *Journal of the Operational Research Society*, 49/2: 99–108.

Latour, B. (1986), 'The powers of association', in Law, J. (ed.), *Power, Action and Belief: A New Sociology of Knowledge?*: 264–80. London: Routledge & Kegan Paul.

(1987), *Science in Action: How to Follow Scientists and Engineers through Society*. Cambridge, MA: Harvard University Press.

(1993), *We Have Never Been Modern*. Brighton: Harvester Wheatsheaf.

(2004), 'Why has critique run out of steam? From matters of fact to matters of concern', *Critical Inquiry*, 30/2: 225–48.

Latour, B., and Woolgar, S. (1986), *Laboratory Life: The Construction of Scientific Facts*. Princeton University Press.

Law, J. (1992), 'Notes on the theory of the actor–network: ordering, strategy and heterogeneity', *Systems Practice*, 5/4: 379–93.

(1994), *Organizing Modernity*. Oxford: Blackwell.

(1999), 'After ANT: complexity, naming and topology', in Law, J., and Hassard, J. (eds.), *Actor Network Theory and After*: 1–14. Oxford: Blackwell.

Orlikowski, W. J. (2007), 'Sociomaterial practices: exploring technology at work', *Organization Studies*, 28/9: 1435–48.

Pickering, A. (ed.) (1992), *Science as Practice and Culture*. University of Chicago Press.

Preston, A. M., Cooper, D. J., and Coombs, R. W. (1992), 'Fabricating budgets: a study of the production of management budgeting in the National Health Service', *Accounting, Organizations and Society*, 17/7: 561–93.

Qu, S. Q., and Cooper, D. J. (2011), 'The role of inscriptions in producing a balanced scorecard', *Accounting, Organizations and Society*, 36/6: 344–62.

Rasche, A., and Chia, R. (2009), 'Researching strategy practices: a genealogical social theory perspective', *Organization Studies*, 30/7: 713–34.

Robson, K. (1991), 'On the arenas of accounting change: the process of translation', *Accounting, Organizations and Society*, 16/5–6: 547–70.

(1992), 'Accounting numbers as "inscription": action at a distance and the development of accounting', *Accounting, Organizations and Society*, 17/7: 685–708.

Schatzki, T. R., Knorr Cetina, K., and von Savigny, E. (eds.) (2001), *The Practice Turn in Contemporary Theory*. London: Routledge.

Schneider, F., Steiger, D., Ledermann, T., Fry, P., and Rist, S. (2010), 'No-tillage farming: co-creation of innovation through network building', *Land Degradation and Development*, 23/3: 242–55.

Skærbæk, P., and Tryggestad, K. (2010), 'The role of accounting devices in performing strategy', *Accounting, Organizations and Society*, 35/5: 108–24.

Soderbaum, P. (1993), 'Values, markets, and environmental policy: an actor–network approach', *Journal of Economic Issues*, 27/2: 387–408.

Steen, J., Coopmans, S., and Whyte, J. (2006), 'Structure and agency? Actor–network theory and strategic organization', *Strategic Organization*, 4/3: 303–12.

Whittington, R. (2006), 'Completing the practice turn in strategy research', *Organization Studies*, 27/5: 613–34.

PART III

Theoretical Resources: Organization and Management Theories

An institutional perspective on strategy as practice

MICHAEL SMETS, ROYSTON GREENWOOD and MICHAEL LOUNSBURY

Introduction

Institutional scholars have recently started to reach out to strategy-as-practice concepts to better conceptualize institutional landscapes and the ways in which organizations construct and navigate them in practice. Specifically, they seek to engage SAP scholarship in order to enhance their theorizing of institutional logics (Thornton, Ocasio and Lounsbury 2012), 'institutional complexity' (Greenwood et al. 2011) and 'institutional work' (Lawrence and Suddaby 2006) and their understanding of the 'micro-foundations' of institutions (Powell and Colyvas 2008). Simultaneously, strategy-as-practice scholars have begun to look beyond the intra-organizational activities that have traditionally pre-occupied them and to work at their stronger context-ualization in the broader social orders that have been the hallmark of institutional research (Vaara and Whittington 2012; Whittington, in this volume).

This rapprochement may appear unsurprising, given that both theoretical strands share common roots in the seminal works of Bourdieu (1977; 1990) and Giddens (1984). Much like siblings separated at birth, however, institutional and practice theories have gone on distinct journeys, char-acterized by different foci on the structure–agency spectrum and levels of analysis. While institutional scholarship through the 1990s often gave primacy to structure, stability and the macro-level contexts that condition organizations (DiMaggio and Powell 1983; Greenwood et al. 2008; Scott 1987), strategy-as-practice scholars have empha-sized agency, potential for change and the collect-ive activities of individuals inside organizations (Chia and Holt 2009; Jarzabkowski 2005; Jarzab-kowski and Wolf, in this volume). This history makes the recent re-engagement noteworthy and

means that, much like reunited siblings with differ-ent views of the world, they can open each other's eyes to new phenomena and start looking at famil-iar phenomena in new ways.

The metaphorical notion of estrangement, reunion and mutual enrichment drives the structure of this chapter. In the second section we briefly trace the evolution of institutional theory to under-stand where and why it lost touch with practice theory and which issues have recently motivated it to reach out for re-engagement. The third sec-tion then outlines shared concerns and concepts over which institutional and strategy-as-practice scholars can connect and strike up fruitful conver-sations. The fourth section sketches the nascent insights that have recently emerged from some of those conversations. Finally, the conclusion sum-marizes the mutual benefits to be gained from blending institutional and SAP scholarship and outlines yet under-explored areas as avenues for future research.

Overview of evolution of institutional theory

Institutional theory is today 'perhaps the dominant approach to understanding organizations' (Green-wood et al. 2008: 2). It arose in the late 1970s in response to 'structural contingency theory', which argues that organizational structures should align with the exigencies of the organization's tasks and technical context (for example, Lawrence and Lorsch 1967; Van de Ven, Ganco and Hinings 2013). Structural arrangements would, accord-ingly, vary significantly with specific 'technical' contingencies, such as organizational size, com-plexity and uncertainty.

Meyer and Rowan (1977) observed that, within any given sector, organizations used similar rather than different arrangements, however, and explain this similarity with the influence of the social and cultural context in which organizations are embedded. Organizations, they propose, face 'powerful institutional rules' (Meyer and Rowan 1977: 343) that define appropriate – 'legitimate' – forms of organizing, which render organizations in the same context more similar and stable.

Institutional stability

The core thesis of institutional theory embedded in early formulations, therefore, is that organizations conform to social expectations because doing so provides legitimacy, a perception that an organization – its purposes and arrangements – are appropriate and socially acceptable. Such social approval, in turn, provides access to material and symbolic resources that support organizational survival, suggesting that organizations must heed their social as much as their technical context. In their foundational pieces, Tolbert and Zucker (1983) propose that early adopters of management practices probably do so for technical reasons, whereas later adopters are motivated by institutional reasons, and DiMaggio and Powell (1983) specify the pressures by which institutional expectations are conveyed and organizational similarities produced: *mimetic*, in which organizations observe and copy others; *normative*, whereby firms comply because of ethical obligation; and *coercive*, in which organizations conform to the regulations of powerful organizations such as the state.

Much early work gave particular attention to confirming Meyer and Rowan's (1977) original thesis that organizations adopt arrangements that have little apparent technical merit and nuance the mechanisms by which these arrangements diffuse (for a review, see Greenwood *et al.* 2008). The common theme of this work was that organizations operate within an 'institutional' context of norms, beliefs and expectations that is subconsciously reproduced or policed by an infrastructure of agencies such as the state or the professions. Thus, organizations 'are not free-floating islands of

rationality or units of political expediency; instead they are seriously constrained by social expectation and the properties of legitimacy' (Greenwood, Jennings and Hinings 2015), and institutionalized structures persist 'over long periods of time without further justification or elaboration, and are highly resistant to change' (Zucker 1987: 446). Distinctly cognitivist positions that alternatives to such institutionalized rules, norms and structures are 'literally unthinkable' (Zucker 1983: 25) produced increasing dissatisfaction with institutionalists' inability to conceptualize change.

Institutional change

Therefore, prompted by DiMaggio (1988) and others (for example, Greenwood and Hinings 1996; Hirsch and Lounsbury 1997), the weight of institutional research gradually shifted towards explaining how institutional arrangements evolve and change. Making sense of the sprawling literature on institutional change is difficult, but two questions have attracted especial attention: where and how do actors gain the reflexivity to imagine institutional alternatives and initiate change, and how are new ideas successfully 'theorized'?

Reflexivity

The earliest approach portrays institutional change as a result of exogenous 'jolts' (Meyer 1982). Jolts from outside the field undermine taken-for-granted institutions and enable actors to reflect and consider previously 'unthinkable' alternatives. A prominent example is Thornton's (2002) account of the higher education publishing industry, which was shaken by the entry of large enterprises and then reconstructed around the market-oriented logic they brought with them. Likewise, Lounsbury (2002) documents how new forms of investing and organizing arose outside the centre of the finance industry. These trends are echoed in various studies that have illustrated that, when jolts occur, reflexivity is particularly likely among 'peripheral players' (for example, Battilana, Leca and Boxenbaum 2009; Leblebici *et al.* 1991), who are often disadvantaged by existing arrangements and therefore more motivated to become 'institutional entrepreneurs' (DiMaggio, 1988: 14) and reshape them according to their interests.

A second explanation of change proposes that reflexivity occurs not as a consequence of shocks to a field but from tensions within it (Greenwood and Suddaby 2006; Seo and Creed 2002). Central to this argument is the concept of 'institutional logics', which, as Thornton and Ocasio (2008) and Thornton, Ocasio and Lounsbury (2012) argue, has become a core tenet of institutional theorizing since the turn of the millennium. Broadly, institutional logics are defined as the symbolic and material elements that comprise a field's 'organizing principles' (Friedland and Alford 1991: 248) or simply its 'rules of the game' (Thornton and Ocasio 2008: 112). Logics provide individuals and organizations with systems of meaning and criteria by which to understand the roles, identities and appropriate social behaviours involved in social exchange. Importantly, modern society comprises a 'plurality' of logics (Kraatz and Block 2008), the relative influence of which varies from field to field. When competing logics, such as family, community, religion, state, market, profession or corporation (Thornton, Ocasio and Lounsbury 2012), impose conflicting demands on a field and its incumbent organizations, they cause the aforementioned endogenous tensions. Such 'institutional complexity' (Greenwood *et al.* 2011) is particularly likely to be experienced by organizations at the interstices of different logics. As Greenwood and Suddaby (2006) have established, those interstitial positions can be occupied by central players in a field, such as elite accounting firms, in their case. These organizations, once they become aware of institutional alternatives and motivated to pursue them, can then, in contrast to their peripheral peers, leverage their status, size and visibility to change existing, and 'theorize' new, institutional arrangements.

Theorization

Notably, institutional change agents have not only to discover an institutional alternative to suit their own preferences but also to convince their peers

that this alternative has merit for the entire field. 'Theorization' (Strang and Meyer 1993) is the process by which that merit is constructed and new practices legitimized. It is, essentially, a political struggle in which the appropriateness of existing and alternative templates of behaviour is contested (Greenwood, Suddaby and Hinings 2002; Suddaby and Greenwood 2005). Possible theorizing agents range from professional associations to critics, journalists or social movements (for a review, see Schneiberg and Lounsbury 2008). The relative attention different agents command depends on their ability to deploy resources, such as cultural, political or financial, and formal regulatory authority and establish their 'discursive legitimacy' – that is, their recognized right to exercise 'voice' in the situation (Hardy and Phillips 1998).

Much recent work has examined *how* theorization is accomplished and focused especially on the use of language or 'discourse', because it makes 'certain ways of thinking and acting possible, and others impossible or costly' (Phillips, Lawrence and Hardy 2004: 638). These are acts of cultural entrepreneurship (Lounsbury and Glynn 2001). It is therefore a critical skill for successful institutional entrepreneurs to 'craft a compelling message advocating for change' (Etzion and Ferraro 2010: 1092). For instance, Lounsbury (2001) shows how a viable recycling infrastructure emerged only once activists had re-theorized recycling as a *for-profit* service, thus legitimizing recycling by connecting it with the market logic of critical players. Likewise, the discursive analogy of financial reporting successfully associated an environmental sustainability 'audit' with an already legitimate market-based practice and thereby facilitated its adoption by corporations (Etzion and Ferraro 2010).

Successful theorization is not simply linguistic gymnastics, however. It has a profound, yet too often neglected, political dimension. As Maguire, Hardy and Lawrence (2004: 671; see also Schneiberg and Lounsbury 2008) remind us, institutional change is not simply the outcome of discursive struggles – that is, of appeals to higher-order values and ideals – but of 'political struggles...fuelled by the mobilization of challenges around competitive projects and logics'. Hence, theorization involves not simply rhetorical skill but the spelling out of the political implications, such as the political costs of not supporting change.

Institutional work

'Institutional work' research has sought to broaden the institutional change research agenda to examine how a wider variety of actors contribute to the creation, alteration or maintenance of institutions (Lawrence, Leca and Zilber 2013; Lawrence, Suddaby and Leca 2009a; 2011). The institutional work agenda seeks 'to redirect attention from institutions per se to the "purposive action" by which they are accomplished' (Lawrence and Suddaby 2006: 217). By doing so, this strand of literature has produced an antidote to the simplified images either of relatively dis-embedded and 'hypermuscular' institutional entrepreneurs (Lawrence, Suddaby and Leca 2009b: 1) or of mindless institutional reproduction (Delbridge and Edwards 2008; Smets and Jarzabkowski 2013) that previously dominated the institutional entrepreneurship literature. Likewise, the practices driving institutional processes have become much clearer, thanks to studies of, for example, the 'boundary work' required in renegotiating forestry practices (Zietsma and Lawrence 2010), the role of rules and rituals in maintaining institutions (Dacin, Munir and Tracey 2010) or the 'repair work' required after public challenges to an organization's legitimacy (Patriotta, Gond and Schultz 2011).

The sense in which this work has embraced core tenets of practice theory and penetrated to the 'micro-level routines' (Lawrence and Suddaby 2006: 247) of institutional agency is less clear, however. So far, it appears that the institutional work literature has primarily produced a more micro perspective, in the sense of providing a more granular view on the practices that drive broader institutional processes. With few exceptions, however (for example, Dacin, Munir and Tracey 2010; Lounsbury 2001; Smets and Jarzabkowski 2013; Zilber, 2002), these practices are performed by

organizations (Gawer and Phillips 2013) or field-level entities (for example, Helfen and Sydow 2013; Micelotta and Washington 2013). The extent to which institutional work has penetrated to the micro *level*, exploring the practices by which individuals accomplish institutions, has remained limited. Furthermore, between the relatively macro-level research sites and its original definition as '*purposive* action...*aimed at* creating, maintaining and disrupting institutions' (Lawrence and Suddaby 2006: 215, emphasis added), the institutional work concept has retained strong overtones of projective agency (Emirbayer and Mische 1998) and planned change. By focusing on field-level purposive action, *institutional* work remains detached from individuals' *practical* work – that is, their efforts to accomplish the everyday tasks of their job. Therefore, we argue, to fully realize its promise of providing 'a broader vision of agency in relationship to institutions' (Lawrence, Suddaby and Leca 2009b: 1), institutional work should take *work* more seriously and more fully engage the practice-theoretical legacy it claims (Kaghan and Lounsbury 2011).

Institutional logics and complexity

The institutional logics perspective has become the dominant strand of contemporary institutional theorizing, focusing on developing micro-foundations to reorient institutional analysis towards the study of heterogeneity and change as ongoing (Lounsbury and Boxenbaum 2013; Thornton, Ocasio and Lounsbury 2012). As part of this effort, there have been explicit efforts to engage practice theory. Building on the early statement by Friedland and Alford (1991), this perspective has been extremely generative, producing a stream of articles across top journals in sociology and management, and has become a central focus for researchers submitting to the Organization and Management Theory Division of the Academy of Management (Lounsbury and Beckman 2015).

The study of 'institutional complexity', focusing on the sources and consequences of multiple, often competing, logics, has provided a particularly fruitful area for research at the interface of logics and practice. It is striking to note that institutional work scholarship has sought limited engagement with research on institutional logics. This is perplexing, insofar as the encounter of 'incompatible prescriptions from multiple institutional logics' (Greenwood *et al.* 2011: 317) – which is the definitional characteristic of institutional complexity – enables, even requires, actors to engage in institutional creation, maintenance or disruption – in short, to engage in institutional work (Smets and Jarzabkowski 2013).

As outlined above, the previously underappreciated variety and interaction of coexisting institutional logics originally gained prominence when scholars discovered that they can motivate and enable institutional change. Here, institutional complexity was considered a transitory state from which one logic would emerge to dominate another subsequent period of stability. Since then, however, it has been recognized that many organizations, by their very nature, are institutionally complex because of the 'jurisdictional overlap' of competing logics that naturally govern their structures and practices (Thornton, Ocasio and Lounsbury 2012: 57). These organizations, including hospitals (Denis, Lamothe and Langley 2001; Reay and Hinings 2009), universities (Sauermann and Stephan 2013; Townley 1997) and social enterprises (Battilana and Dorado 2010; Jay 2013; Pache and Santos 2013b; Tracey, Phillips and Jarvis 2011), have to permanently manage 'constellations' of two or more competing logics (Goodrick and Reay 2011; for broader overviews, see Greenwood, Magàn Diaz and Céspedes Lorente 2010; Greenwood *et al.* 2011; Kraatz and Block 2008).

Following the intellectual legacy that institutional demands compromise technically efficient operations, institutional complexity was initially considered externally imposed and problematic. Accordingly, documented organizational responses have been predominantly defensive, seeking to 'reduce institutional complexity by neutralizing opposing pressures' (Raaijmakers *et al.* 2015: 85), avoid stigma (Carberry and King 2012) or buffer against institutional enforcement (for example, Greenwood and Suddaby 2006; Smets, Morris and Greenwood 2012). Alternatively, when

conflicting demands are not just externally imposed but internally 'represented' (Pache and Santos 2010) by organizational members, organizations have to complement their focus on managing external legitimacy threats with efforts to minimize internal conflict, typically by compartmentalizing competing logics in different locales, units or processes (for example, Jarzabkowski, Lê and Van de Ven 2013; Lounsbury 2007). Simply put, if institutional logics constitute the 'rules of the game', then institutional complexity resembles an organization playing 'in two or more games at the same time' (Kraatz and Block 2008: 2). Ensuring that different games are played in different places makes sense, because playing by the rules of one 'game' breaks the rules of another.

Perplexingly, then, the recent past has seen the rise of 'hybrid' organizations, most notably among social enterprises, that voluntarily incorporate competing logics (for a review, see Battilana and Lee 2014). This trend suggests that institutional complexity may be beneficial by, for instance, bolstering impact-oriented activities by tapping into separate sources of expertise, legitimacy or funding (for example, Jay 2013; Pache and Santos 2013b). As institutional theorists have largely emphasized conflicts between competing logics, however, we know surprisingly little about how such benefits are reaped. So far, suggestions include the integration of compartmentalized logics by senior managers or the blending of competing demands into a hybrid logic or practice (Battilana and Dorado 2010; Smets, Morris and Greenwood 2012). Both approaches carry distinct risks, however, such as insufficient integration, mission drift or the neglect of one constituent logic (Battilana and Dorado 2010; Jay 2013), and both have remained under-specified at the individual level. While we know how organizations can structurally facilitate the accommodation of institutional complexity, we know very little about the individuals who inhabit these structures and the ways in which they employ them. The nascent understanding of individual-level responses to institutional complexity (for example, McPherson and Sauder 2013; Pache and Santos 2013a) is surprising, however, given the increasing prevalence of individuals working across institutional divides

(Jarzabkowski, Lê and Van de Ven 2013; Smets, Morris and Greenwood 2012). In fact, in most complex organizations, conflicting prescriptions collide in everyday operations, and institutional complexity must be managed continuously. Here, the 'institutional work' of accomplishing institutions in the throes of practical work is particularly relevant, and, we argue, practice-theoretical approaches to institutions offer a powerful conceptual toolkit for understanding these situations.

Reaching out for a helping hand

As the above overview suggests, the journey of institutional theory so far suggests areas where practice and strategy-as-practice scholars could significantly contribute. Broadly, these areas concern the predominant emphasis upon macro social structures, especially at the level of the field; the coarse conceptualization of agency; and the almost binary approach to coexisting logics as conflicting or compatible in situations of institutional complexity.

Thus far, arguments about institutional change, work and complexity have focused on the macro social or organizational levels. For instance, the exogenous shocks or endogenous contradictions that have been associated with institutional change are located at the level of the field; the resultant complexities are, with the exceptions noted above, largely addressed through organizational structures or practices (for reviews, see Greenwood et al. 2011; Pache and Santos 2010). Moreover, institutional work is often accomplished by organizational or field-level actors, which has kept the concept of institutional work detached from practical work, defined as actors' everyday occupational tasks and activities (Kaghan and Lounsbury 2011; Smets and Jarzabkowski 2013).

These trends are not entirely surprising given that the primary focus of institutional analysis is the relationship between organizations and their socio-cultural context. As Greenwood, Hinings and Whetten (2014) have pointed out, though, the emphasis of institutional theorizing may have become overly concerned with detailing and elaborating field-level mechanisms and processes, to

the neglect of attending to the interface of organizations and the field and, perhaps in particular, to the mechanisms and processes that occur *within* an organization. Not surprisingly, there are calls for burrowing into the 'micro-foundations' of institutional processes (Kaghan and Lounsbury 2011; Lounsbury 2008; Powell and Colyvas 2008). As Barley (2008: 510) prosaically puts it:

> Institutions and actors meet in the throes of everyday life. In this sense, as the British might say, everyday life is institutional theory's coalface; it is where the rubber meets the road of reality. For over 30 years, the coalface has lain largely idle while institutionalists have sought their fortunes in the cities of macro-social theory. As a result, there is plenty of coal left to mine. What we need are more miners.

The second assumption – usually implicit – bubbling under recent work on institutional work and change is the central importance of motivated agency. While we have learned that exogenous shocks and endogenous contradictions can undermine existing institutional arrangements and sharpen actors' awareness of institutional alternatives, we know relatively little about how they transform their awareness into action. Predominantly, existing studies presume that actors encounter alternative institutional arrangements, select a favourable option and purposively push for its advancement (Greenwood et al. 2011; Greenwood and Suddaby 2006; Seo and Creed 2002). As Smets and Jarzabkowski (2013: 1283) point out, however, this approach 'fails to consider the process through which new complexities are experienced and responses developed, rather than selected', especially when novel complexities highlight the inadequacies of current arrangements but do not offer a suitable 'ready-to-wear' alternative. They therefore echo calls for a broader and more nuanced perspective on agency (Battilana and D'Aunno 2009; Lawrence, Suddaby and Leca 2009b; 2011) to develop a better understanding of how new institutional arrangements may emerge and how 'different modes of agency unfold as actors develop and realize their interests in particular institutional settings' (Smets and Jarzabkowski 2013: 1283).

Lastly, with a few exceptions (such as Goodrick and Reay 2011; Greenwood *et al.* 2010; Pache and Santos 2013b; Sauermann and Stephan 2013), institutional scholars have predominantly portrayed coexisting logics as binary: either compatible or contradictory. Our understanding of institutional work, complexity and change would therefore benefit from studies that 'delve deeper into the dynamic patterns of complexity' (Greenwood *et al.* 2011: 334) and uncover how, in their everyday practice, actors can construct logics as more or less compatible, or even reap complementarities between seemingly conflicting logics (Smets *et al.* 2015).

In summary, current scholarship on institutional work, complexity and change would benefit from more granular and nuanced conceptualizations of micro- and individual-level dynamics, agency and the relationships between coexisting logics. We contend, and develop below, that the 'practice perspective' (for example, Bourdieu 1977; 1990; Jarzabkowski 2005; Schatzki 2001; Whittington 1996) is a timely reply to the calls for understanding the micro-processes of (de)-institutionalization, institutional work and institutional complexity, and is one that avoids the oversimplified image of hypermuscular, projective agency.

How to connect strategy-as-practice and institutional scholarship

Given that strategy-as-practice and institutional perspectives have been estranged, what are the common interests and related concepts that motivate scholars from both camps to reach out to the other (for example, Hallett 2010; Lounsbury and Crumley 2007; Smets, Morris and Greenwood 2012; Thornton, Ocasio and Lounsbury 2012; Vaara and Whittington 2012; Whittington 2006; Whittington, in this volume)? First, and most intuitively, practice theory directly addresses persistent calls for exploration of the 'micro-foundations' of institutional processes. It does so by directing attention to how people engage in 'doing' their work and how, in so doing, they experience and shape the social structures that have traditionally preoccupied institutional theorists. In this context,

the conceptual toolkit of strategy as practice neatly complements that of institutional scholars and could help connect the 'macro-worlds' of institutions to the 'micro-worlds' of the individuals within them (Kaghan and Lounsbury 2011: 75; see also Whittington 2006). The differentiation of practice, praxis and practitioners (Jarzabkowski, Balogun and Seidl 2007; Suddaby, Seidl and Lê 2013; Whittington 2006) adds much-needed granularity and conceptual clarity to the currently somewhat loose use of 'practice' in institutional scholarship. In particular, strategy as practice offers a promising conceptual toolkit for probing more deeply into the micro-foundations of institutions, by drawing attention to the activities of individuals (Jarzabkowski 2005; Jarzabkowski and Wolf, in this volume) and to the tools, methodologies and materials they employ in their everyday actions and interactions (Jarzabkowski, Spee and Smets 2013; Lê and Spee, this volume; Orlikowski 2010; Seidl, and Guérard, this volume; Spee and Jarzabkowski 2009; 2011; Streeck, Goodwin and LeBaron 2011).

The second factor motivating a mutual reaching out is that, even though exploring institutional micro-foundations has merit in its own right, it is particularly salient with regard to the now dominant concept of institutional 'logics' (Thornton, Ocasio and Lounsbury 2012). In order to demonstrate the power of logics, it is necessary to show how they matter 'in action' – that is, how they are experienced, enacted and adapted in people's everyday lives (Lounsbury 2007; Lounsbury and Boxenbaum 2013; McPherson and Sauder 2013; Smets *et al.* 2015; Smets, Morris and Greenwood 2012; Zietsma and Lawrence 2010). The institutional logics concept opens broad avenues for connecting institutional and practice scholarship, because logics are expressed in '*material practices*, assumptions, values, beliefs and rules' (Thornton 2004: 69, emphasis added). In this sense, institutional logics are akin to the 'shared' or 'general' understandings studied by practice theorists (Schatzki 2002; 2006). Both infuse bundles of otherwise trivial activities with 'thematic coherence', order and meaning, turning them into a recognizable and legitimate practice (Smets, Morris and Greenwood 2012: 879; see also Lounsbury and Crumley 2007; Smets *et al.* 2015).

The mutual benefit for both theory strands lies in the attention to broader cultural frameworks – that is, to institutional (rather than organizational) logics, on the one hand, and to the instantiation of these logics in everyday praxis, on the other. Thus, closing the gap between institutions and actions and attending more closely to the structuration of social orders *in action* (Chia and Holt 2009; Grand, Rüegg-Stürm and von Arx, in this volume; Vaara and Whittington 2012) holds significant potential for advancing our understanding of institutional change and work.

Lastly, SAP scholars share the institutionalists' concern with pluralistic or complex settings in which competing demands need to be managed or accommodated (Denis, Langley and Rouleau 2007; Jarzabkowski, Lê and Van de Ven 2013; Jarzabkowski, Matthiesen and Van de Ven 2009; Zilber 2011). This interest forms a natural beachhead for discussions of institutional complexity. Practice theory offers the conceptual toolkit to discover how institutional complexity is 'part of the ordinary, everyday nature of work, rather than exceptional phenomena' (Jarzabkowski, Matthiesen and Van de Ven 2009: 289; see also Smets *et al.* 2015). Just as institutional logics are enacted in practice, their incompatibilities are problematized in practitioners' engagement in everyday practice (Smets and Jarzabkowski 2013; Smets, Morris and Greenwood 2012). In this sense, a strategy-as-practice toolkit attends not only to how institutional complexity is accommodated but also to how it is initially constructed in praxis. Particularly helpful, here, is the practice theorist's sensitivity to how people 'go on' in the face of complexity and tension (Chia and Holt 2009; Giddens 1984), as well as their relational ontology (Emirbayer 1997; Hosking 2011; Mutch, Delbridge and Ventresca 2006), thus providing a useful corrective to the binary approach to coexisting logics that largely dominates current discussions of institutional complexity.

Blending institutional and practice perspectives: a review and research agenda

In this section, we review some early insights that have emerged at the intersection of institutional and practice scholarship. Specifically, we point out the potential for a more nuanced understanding of the role of individuals, the nature of agency and the relationality of logics, much of which is – despite those recent advances – still untapped.

Probing more deeply: studying individuals at work

Several studies have recently taken institutional 'work' literally and, drawing more heavily on a practice-theoretical toolkit, studied the mundane activities of individuals at work – and their institutional ramifications (Jarzabkowski, Matthiesen and Van de Ven 2009; Jarzabkowski *et al.* 2013; Pache and Santos 2013b; Zietsma and Lawrence 2010). Smets, with Jarzabkowski (2013) and with Morris and Greenwood (2012), for instance, studied the everyday work of banking lawyers in a newly merged global law firm to understand how their transactions create clashes between incompatible professional logics, how lawyers improvise around those incompatibilities and how their improvisations eventually congeal in a new hybrid practice. Doing so takes seriously the role of individuals as 'carriers of institutions' (Zilber 2002: 234) and 'reconnects the construction of institutionally complex settings to the actions and interactions of the individuals who inhabit them' (Smets and Jarzabkowski 2013: 1279).

This shift in level of analysis opens up several promising new perspectives on issues of institutional change, work and complexity. First, it takes seriously March's (1981: 564) call to resist the 'search for drama', be it in studies of institutional change, work or complexity. Practice theorists' characteristic attention to the mundane actions and interactions of individuals is sensitive to the ways in which the social order of 'general understandings' or 'institutional logics' is accomplished by everyday people as part of their everyday work, not just by the 'hypermuscular' institutional entrepreneurs who have dominated earlier studies (Lawrence, Suddaby and Leca 2009: 1). On the one hand, this sensitizes institutional scholars to a new class of relevant actors: 'individuals at the front line' (Reay, Golden-Biddle and Germann

2006: 979). As Smets and colleagues (2015) have recently confirmed in their study of reinsurance underwriters in Lloyd's of London, in contrast to the dominant position in the literature, it need not be '*leaders* who are able to understand...requirements of constituencies of multiple logics' (Greenwood *et al.* 2011: 356, emphasis added). Instead, ordinary people doing ordinary work may manage institutional complexity, or engage in institutional work to maintain or change the institutions they inhabit. On the other hand, where these individuals are yoked together by the exigencies of their work, the noise and conflict typically associated with the institutionalization of new practices is likely to be muted (Lounsbury and Crumley 2007; Zilber 2002) and theorization more 'unobtrusive' (Smets, Morris and Greenwood 2012: 895) than earlier studies, as reviewed above, have found. New ways of working diffuse through the private networks of those engaged in the practice and therefore may do so without attracting the attention of change opponents.

Second, a practice perspective can help discover new origins, and the earliest moments of institutional change, as well as new mechanisms by which it unfolds. For instance, Smets, Morris and Greenwood (2012) found that changes to the professional logic of German lawyers emerged from their daily interactions with their English counterparts on cross-border banking transactions, in which incompatible norms of professional conduct collided. Initially, lawyers tried to improvise around these incompatibilities; not to challenge any institutional infrastructures, but simply to 'get the deal done' (Smets, Morris and Greenwood 2012: 887). It was only later, when their improvisations congealed into organizational guidelines and, eventually, new institutional norms, that their actions assumed the more 'purposive' flavour of institutional work (Smets and Jarzabkowski 2013). Studies that attend to research sites only once such 'purposive' institutional work has commenced, 'drama' erupted or a new institutional vision taken shape are likely to miss these earliest moments and mundane origins of change. A practice perspective that is more attuned to the emergence of change from practical work and improvisation (Chia and Holt 2009; Chia and MacKay 2007; Feldman

2000; Orlikowski 1996) promises a more complete and granular understanding of institutional change, however, from its origins in the exigencies of everyday work to experimentation with possible institutional alternatives (Smets and Jarzabkowski 2013) and the field-level embedding of the chosen option. At the same time, connecting the two theories offers practice scholars opportunities to apply their existing insights on how individuals 'invent, slip into, or learn new ways of interpreting and experiencing the world' (Orlikowski 2002: 253) to the institutional ramifications and consequences of those experiences.

Third, aiming a practice lens at individual actors can advance discussions of institutional complexity, because an increasing number of practitioners, such as professionals, physicians and academics (Grey 2003; Heimer 1999; McPherson and Sauder 2013; Reay and Hinings 2009; Sauermann and Stephan 2013), regularly work across institutional logics. Importantly, they may face unpredictable changes in the salience of the different demands they face. For instance, Heimer (1999) found that neonatal intensive care physicians need to balance the competing demands of medicine, family and the law every time they attend to a newborn in a critical condition. The balance they strike may be different every time, however, depending on the nature of the case at hand. In these situations, structural organization-level responses to institutional complexity are likely to fail, as they cement a relatively static balance between competing demands (for example, Dunn and Jones 2010; Pache and Santos 2013b). Accordingly, institutionalists have called for greater attention to 'situationism', defined as 'the influence of the immediate situation's characteristics – in time and place – on individual behavior, [as it] accounts for inconsistencies of individual behavior across situations' (Thornton, Ocasio and Lounsbury 2012: 80). Practice theory can help address this call through its sensitivity to people's 'practical understanding' (Schatzki 2006: 1864) – that is, their personal, tacit 'feel' for how to perform competently, even in a particular, complex situation in which different logics collide. Hence, while institutionalists have commonly emphasized the 'embeddedness' of individuals in 'logics', practice theorists offer a more balanced view in which a logic, or 'general understanding', is complemented by a 'practical understanding' that allows individuals to skilfully navigate situations in which different general understandings appear pertinent.

The profound insight at this intersection of institutional and practice theory is that individuals, and not just organizations, can 'carry' multiple logics. Institutionalists have pointed to this ability (for example, Delmestri 2006; DiMaggio 1997; Pache and Santos 2013a), but it is the practice perspective that reveals how individuals can *do* so in practice. Zilber (2011), for instance, shows how participants at an industry conference used language and situational cues to switch between logics and promote different discourses. More recently, Smets and colleagues (2015) have developed a process model of three interrelated mechanisms, labelled 'segmenting', 'bridging' and 'demarcating', which allow individuals to balance conflicting logics in a state of dynamic tension in which they fruitfully feed off each other – a dynamic we discuss in greater detail below. Rather than the organization developing structures and practices to differentiate and integrate competing logics, individuals use their practical understanding to 'not only know *how* to enact multiple logics, but also *where* and *when*' (Smets *et al.* 2015, emphasis in original), iteratively separating and combining them according to their relative salience in a specific situation.

Lastly, attention to individual actors and to the situatedness of their actions not only reveals new mechanisms of managing complexity but also discovers more instances of complexity. If we accept that institutional complexity is a normal and permanent state for many organizations, then we should study them under normal conditions and not, as institutionalists have done to date, only during moments of upheaval and crisis. As Smets, Morris and Greenwood (2012: 892, emphasis in original) highlight, '[I]t is not the existence of institutional complexity per se that precipitates change, but the *novelty* of this complexity.' The permanent balancing of competing logics, and hence the absence of change, should therefore be studied during times of apparent stability, when complexities are no longer novel, but possibly

'settled' (Rao and Kenney 2008) in routines that allow individuals to continuously 'go on' in the face of complexity (Giddens 1984). The practice perspective, in this sense, is particularly suited for the study of such 'institutionalized complexity' (Smets *et al.* 2015), because it is attuned to the accommodation of complexity in less notable, yet effortful, routines, rather than overtly strategic responses (Chia and Holt 2009; Smets and Jarzabkowski 2013). Paradoxically, though, as no 'drama' will alert scholars to these situations, spotting the instances in which competing logics are routinely balanced may be particularly difficult, and, similarly, so too might be the generation of new insights into the practical management of complexity (Jarzabkowski *et al.* 2013).

Taking institutional 'work' literally: refining notions of agency and intentionality

In the recent past Emirbayer and Mische's (1998) differentiation of iterative, projective and practical-evaluative dimensions of agency has informed the institutional conceptualization of agency (for example, Battilana and D'Aunno 2009; Seo and Creed 2002). So far, however, the literature has remained dominated by the iterative dimension, underpinning institutional reproduction, and the projective dimension, which drives institutional entrepreneurship or creation through the purposive pursuit of a desirable future institutional state (Battilana and D'Aunno 2009; Lawrence, Suddaby and Leca 2009b). This is perplexing, as, arguably, the practical-evaluative dimension, which allows actors to exercise judgement and 'get things done' in the here and now (Smets, Morris and Greenwood 2012; Tsoukas and Cummings 1997), should be particularly relevant in discussions of institutional complexity. To date, however, it has received relatively little attention. A more comprehensive adoption of Emirbayer and Mische's (1998) framework and increased attention to practical-evaluative agency would not only help with the discovery of the earliest moments of change, as discussed above. It would also reveal the dynamic interaction, and changing order of dominance, between different dimensions of agency.

As Smets and Jarzabkowski (2013) argue, the encounter of conflicting institutional demands at work need not automatically activate projective agency, which is what some would seem to suggest (Lawrence, Suddaby and Leca 2009b; Seo and Creed 2002), because this presupposes the existence of a 'ready-to-wear' solution. Instead, they suggest, individuals progress through a stage of practical-evaluative experimentation with alternative institutional arrangements from which they develop the preferred solution, which they subsequently pursue through 'purposive' institutional work. Notably, as highlighted by the practice perspective, the experimentation from which a preferred institutional arrangement is developed is not driven by the future-oriented nature of projective agency but, primarily, by the need to resolve present issues in the moment. This is intuitive, insofar as 'most individuals are not grand entrepreneurs, but practical people doing practical work to get a job done' (Smets and Jarzabkowski 2013: 1304). The critical role of practical-evaluative agency is likely to be overlooked when institutional studies shy away from studying the 'coalface' of everyday work. This is why we advocate that studies of institutional work take 'work' more literally, and strategy-as-practice scholars apply their established conceptual toolkit in order to enhance the nuance and granularity of our understanding of these micro-level institutional dynamics.

An important positive side effect of refining our understanding of agency is a correspondingly closer look at intentionality (Lawrence, Suddaby and Leca 2009b; Tsoukas, in this volume). Notably, the practical-evaluative experimentations we discussed above remain focused on accomplishing work in the moment. They lack the intention of changing institutional arrangements and are, therefore, not 'purposive' in the narrow sense of being *'aimed at* creating, maintaining, and disrupting institutions' (Lawrence and Suddaby 2006: 217; emphasis added). While these actions are not intentional in this narrow sense, however, it seems wrong to deem them as unintentional, because they are firmly aimed at accomplishing practical work –

a motivation for change more systematically acknowledged in the practice literature (Feldman 2000; Kellogg, Orlikowski and Yates 2006; Orlikowski 1996). Smets and Jarzabkowski (2013), therefore, suggest the need to transcend dichotomies of (un)intentional institutional work by more clearly examining the object of the intentionality. Specifying that object is important not only for understanding the original motivation for initiating change, irrespective of its outcome, but also for understanding its unfolding, because the intention of accomplishing work coordinates dispersed change agents. Improvisations that may emerge in an uncoordinated fashion, yet with the intention of addressing the same issue, do not accumulate entirely 'accidentally' (Plowman *et al.* 2007), nor are they explicitly orchestrated by a planned strategy or 'institutional design' (Hargrave and Van de Ven 2006: 867). Instead, they are implicitly coordinated by the 'heedful interrelating of practitioners doing work' (Dorado 2005: 396). Hence, taking 'work' seriously not only gives the institutionalist more nuanced insights into the nature of intentionality in institutional work but also offers strategy scholars an important complement to existing notions of emergent and planned change that considers practice as an important mode of coordination.

Looking at others: refining notions of relationality in institutional research

Despite the above-listed advances in our understanding of intentionality, which a practice perspective on institutional dynamics offers, 'the self (and intentionality) cannot be understood without reference to the particular "others" in which the acting individual is embedded' (Kaghan and Lounsbury 2011: 75). So far, however, institutionalists have painted a black and white picture of those 'others', especially in discussions of institutional complexity. Nevertheless, practice-theoretical understandings of relationality and the active construction of 'others' (Emirbayer 1997; Hosking 2011; Mutch, Delbridge and Ventresca 2006) provide the conceptual toolkit to paint a more colourful and dynamic picture of how, in practitioners' engagement with complex institutional environments, 'constellations' of coexisting logics are constructed as more or less compatible (Goodrick and Reay 2011; Greenwood, Magàn Diaz and Céspedes Lorente 2010; Reay and Hinings 2009). Specifically, closer attention to these practice-theoretical concepts promises key insights regarding the dynamic construction of institutional complexity and of the possible benefits that can be obtained from it.

First, a practice focus corrects simplistic ideas that certain logics – or, at least, some of their elements (Pache and Santos 2013b; Sauermann and Stephan 2013) – are intrinsically compatible or conflicting. Instead, they are constructed as such through practitioners' skilful praxis. In their study of cross-border transactions in a global law firm, Smets and Jarzabkowski (2013), for instance, show how English and German banking lawyers constructed their respective conflicting professional logics as 'strange' at first, but then reconstructed them as 'contradictory', 'compatible' and, eventually, complementary. Conversely, some studies of social enterprises document how they successfully bridged seemingly conflicting logics of for-profit work and social impact, but later slipped back into a more conflictual rendering of both logics, leading to profound change or the organization's demise (Jay 2013; Tracey, Phillips and Jarvis 2011). Most recently, in their model of balancing mechanisms, Smets and colleagues (2015: 30 emphasis in original) conclude that 'degrees of conflict or complementarity not only depend on *what* aspects of logics clash (Pache and Santos 2010; 2013b), but also on *how* they are situationally brought together in practice'. Nascent insights into such skilful practical combination warrants further elaborations that 'delve deeper into the dynamic patterns of complexity' (Greenwood *et al.* 2011: 334).

Second, these elaborations are particularly warranted because the reconstruction of conflicting logics as compatible, or even complementary, appears of great value to scholars of institutions, practice and strategy. A while ago Kraatz and Block (2008: 8) conjectured that the ability to operate constructively across institutional logics can produce multiplicative legitimacy benefits and allow organizations 'to forge identities which

are uniquely their own'. Since then a nascent understanding has emerged about how conflicting logics and their constituent practices can positively feed off each other to generate performance-enhancing complementarities (for example, Ansari, Wijen and Gray 2013; Jay 2013). Smets *et al.* (2015) are the most recent to elaborate how the balancing of 'conflicting-yet-complementary' logics can occur in practice. One obvious application of their analysis is the ambidexterity literature, as ambidexterity relies on complementarities between exploitation and exploration (March 1991), arguably two conflicting logics of learning (Greenwood *et al.* 2011; Tushman and O'Reilly 1996). Blending insights from debates in strategy as practice and institutional complexity holds good promise for advancing these discussions with an understanding of how institutional complexity can be leveraged in practice (Jarzabkowski *et al.* 2013).

Conclusion

Without exception, the nascent insights generated from the blending of institutional and practice theory require further testing and elaboration. Hence, we call for research that probes more deeply into all the dynamics described above. Beyond this, however, we want to draw particular attention to one area that, somewhat counter-intuitively, appears in particular need of attention. Until relatively recently institutionalists have focused on field-level phenomena and black-boxed what goes on inside organizations; strategy-as-practice scholars, by contrast, have done the opposite, and looked inside that black box (Lounsbury and Crumley 2007). Surprisingly, despite the recent coming together of these two perspectives, few scholars appear to be looking *at* the box. More precisely, organizations and their specific properties filter, mute or amplify interactions between the levels of institutions and praxis (Battilana and Dorado 2010; Pache and Santos 2010; 2013b; Smets *et al.* 2015 Smets, Morris and Greenwood 2012). The ways in which they do so are often relegated to boundary conditions of broader mechanisms, however. Rarely do they occupy the centre stage of institutional or SAP analysis. Three facets, we argue, merit particular attention.

First, we need to be sensitive to what organizations do – that is, what problems they address and what business they are in – because the practice in which coexisting logics come together matters for the degree of conflict, compatibility or complementarity that practitioners experience (Smets *et al.* 2015). In short, the same two logics may appear more conflicting in the context of one practice than another. Logics of science and commerce, for instance, are easily constructed as complementary in industrial science, but not in academic science (Sauermann and Stephan 2013). Likewise, professional and commercial logics are more compatible in business services to large corporations (Greenwood and Suddaby 2006; Smets, Morris and Greenwood, 2012) than, for instance, in medical services (Reay and Hinings 2009). More attention should be paid to the interactions between the logics that come together, the nature of the work in which they do, and the practices individuals use to construct their relationality.

Second, we need to better understand the mediating role of organizational properties such as size, reputation, internationalization, organizational form or mode of governance at play in mediating the experience and resolution of institutional complexity, and enabling the institutional work this involves. We know, for instance, that such properties can buffer from external institutional pressures (Dorado 2005; Greenwood and Suddaby 2006), provide physical or organizational spaces that practitioners can use to shield themselves from scrutiny or interference (Anand, Gardner and Morris 2007; Kellogg 2009; Smets *et al.* 2015) or help coordinate dispersed improvisations to congeal into recognizable new practices (Smets, Morris and Greenwood 2012).

Lastly, we see promising avenues for future research in the more prominent acknowledgement of the artefacts and materials that practitioners use in how institutions are created, maintained and changed. As institutionalists grow more accustomed to penetrating to the micro-level practices in which logics are enacted and adapted, their logical next step should be to also attend to the 'stuff' involved in these practices (Jarzabkowski, Spee and Smets 2013; Orlikowski and Scott 2008), because the context of practice is 'not only institutional but also mundanely material' (Jarzabkowski *et al.* 2013: 367). The pursuit of these avenues for research can generate insights that connect individual, organizational and institutional levels of analysis into compelling multi-level models of how everyday praxis is shaped by the broader institutional frameworks in which it is embedded, and how practical efforts to accomplish work can congeal and radiate to the level of the field to reshape the institutional infrastructure in which they are embedded (Smets, Morris and Greenwood 2012).

References

Anand, N., Gardner, H., and Morris, T. (2007), 'Knowledge based innovation: emergence and embedding of new practice areas in management consulting firms', *Academy of Management Journal*, 50/2: 406–28.

Ansari, S., Wijen, F., and Gray, B. (2013), 'Constructing a climate change logic: an institutional perspective on the "tragedy of the commons"', *Organization Science*, 24/4: 1014–40.

Barley, S. R. (2008), 'Coalface institutionalism', in Greenwood, R., Oliver, C., Sahlin, K., and Suddaby, R. (eds.), *The Sage Handbook of Organizational Institutionalism*: 490–515. London: Sage.

Battilana, J., and D'Aunno, T. (2009), 'Institutional work and the paradox of embedded agency', in Lawrence, T., Suddaby, R., and Leca, B. (eds.), *Institutional Work: Actors and Agency in Institutional Studies of Organizations*: 31–58. Cambridge University Press.

Battilana, J., and Dorado, S. (2010), 'Building sustainable hybrid organizations: the case of commercial microfinance organizations', *Academy of Management Journal*, 53/6: 1419–40.

Battilana, J., Leca, B., and Boxenbaum, E. (2009), 'How actors change institutions: towards a theory of institutional entrepreneurship', *Academy of Management Annals*, 3/1: 65–107.

Battilana, J., and Lee, M. (2014), 'Advancing research on hybrid organizing: insights from the study of social enterprises', *Academy of Management Annals*, 8/1: 397–441.

Bourdieu, P. (1977), *Outline of a Theory of Practice*. Cambridge University Press.

—— (1990), *The Logic of Practice*. Cambridge: Polity.

Carberry, E. J., and King, B. G. (2012), 'Defensive practice adoption in the face of organizational stigma: impression management and the diffusion of stock option expensing', *Journal of Management Studies*, 49/7: 1137–67.

Chia, R., and Holt, R. (2009), *Strategy without Design: The Silent Efficacy of Indirect Action*. Cambridge University Press.

Chia, R., and MacKay, B. (2007), 'Post-processual challenges for the emerging strategy-as-practice perspective: discovering strategy in the logic of practice', *Human Relations*, 60/1: 217–42.

Dacin, M. T., Munir, K., and Tracey, P. (2010), 'Formal dining at Cambridge colleges: linking ritual performance and institutional maintenance', *Academy of Management Journal*, 53/6: 1393–418.

Delbridge, R., and Edwards, T. (2008), 'Challenging conventions: roles and processes during nonisomorphic institutional change', *Human Relations*, 61/3: 299–325.

Delmestri, G. (2006), 'Streams of inconsistent institutional influences: middle managers as carriers of multiple identities', *Human Relations*, 59/11: 1515–41.

Denis, J.-L., Lamothe, L., and Langley, A. (2001), 'The dynamics of collective leadership and strategic change in pluralistic organizations', *Academy of Management Journal*, 44/4: 809–37.

Denis, J.-L., Langley, A., and Rouleau, L. (2007), 'Strategizing in pluralistic contexts: rethinking theoretical frames', *Human Relations*, 60/1: 179–215.

DiMaggio, P. (1988), 'Interest and agency in institutional theory', in Zucker, L. G. (ed.), *Institutional Patterns and Organizations: Culture and Environment*: 3–21. Cambridge, MA: Ballinger.

—— (1997), 'Culture and cognition', *Annual Review of Sociology*, 23: 263–87.

DiMaggio, P., and Powell, W. (1983), 'The iron cage revisited: institutional isomorphism and collective rationality in organizational fields', *American Sociological Review*, 48/2: 147–60.

Dorado, S. (2005), 'Institutional entrepreneurship, partaking and convening', *Organization Studies*, 26/3: 385–414.

Dunn, M. B., and Jones, C. (2010), 'Institutional logics and institutional pluralism: the contestation of care and science logics in medical education, 1967–2005', *Administrative Science Quarterly*, 55/1: 114–49.

Emirbayer, M. (1997), 'Manifesto for a relational sociology', *American Journal of Sociology*, 103/2: 281–317.

Emirbayer, M., and Mische, A. (1998), 'What is agency?', *American Journal of Sociology*, 103/4: 962–1023.

Etzion, D., and Ferraro, F. (2010), 'The role of analogy in the institutionalization of sustainability reporting', *Organization Science*, 21/5: 1092–107.

Feldman, M. S. (2000), 'Organizational routines as a source of continuous change', *Organization Science*, 11/6: 611–29.

Friedland, R., and Alford, R. R. (1991), 'Bringing society back in: symbols, practices and institutional contradictions', in Powell, W., and DiMaggio, P. (eds.), *The New Institutionalism in Organizational Analysis*: 232–63. University of Chicago Press.

Gawer, A., and Phillips, N. (2013), 'Institutional work as logics shift: the case of Intel's transformation to platform leader', *Organization Studies*, 34/8: 1035–71.

Giddens, A. (1984), *The Constitution of Society*. Cambridge: Polity.

Goodrick, E., and Reay, T. (2011), 'Constellations of institutional logics', *Work and Occupations*, 38/3: 372–416.

Greenwood, R., and Hinings, C. R. (1996), 'Understanding radical organizational change: bringing together the old and the new institutionalism', *Academy of Management Review*, 21/4: 1022–54.

Greenwood, R., Hinings, C. R., and Whetten, D. A. (2014), 'Rethinking institutions and organizations', *Journal of Management Studies*, 51/7: 1206–20.

Greenwood, R., Jennings, P. D., and Hinings, C. R. (2015), 'Sustainability and organizational change: an institutional perspective', in Henderson, R., Gulati, R., and Tushman, M. (eds.), *Leading Sustainable Change: An Organizational Perspective*: 323–55. Oxford University Press.

Greenwood, R., Magàn Diaz, A., Li, S., and Céspedes Lorente, J. (2010), 'The multiplicity of institutional logics and the heterogeneity of organizational responses', *Organization Science*, 21/2: 521–39.

Greenwood, R., Oliver, C., Sahlin, K., and Suddaby, R. (2008), 'Introduction', in *The Sage Handbook of Organizational Institutionalism*: 1–46. London: Sage.

Greenwood, R., Raynard, M., Kodeih, F., Micellota, E., and Lounsbury, M. (2011), 'Institutional complexity and organizational responses', *Academy of Management Annals*, 5/1: 1–55.

Greenwood, R., and Suddaby, R. (2006), 'Institutional entrepreneurship in mature fields: the big five accounting firms', *Academy of Management Journal*, 49/1: 27–48.

Greenwood, R., Suddaby, R., and Hinings, C. R. (2002), 'Theorizing change: the role of professional associations in the transformation of institutionalized fields', *Academy of Management Journal*, 45/1: 58–80.

Grey, C. (2003), 'The real world of Enron's auditors', *Organization*, 10/3: 572–6.

Hallett, T. (2010), 'The myth incarnate: recoupling processes, turmoil, and inhabited institutions in an urban elementary school', *American Sociological Review*, 75/1: 52–74.

Hardy, C., and Phillips, N. (1998), 'Strategies of engagement: lessons from the critical examination of collaboration and conflict in an interorganizational domain', *Organization Science*, 9/2: 217–30.

Hargrave, T. J., and Van de Ven, A. H. (2006), 'A collective action model of institutional innovation', *Academy of Management Review*, 31/4: 864–88.

Heimer, C. A. (1999), 'Competing institutions: law, medicine, and family in neonatal intensive care', *Law and Society Review*, 33/1: 17–66.

Helfen, M., and Sydow, J. (2013), 'Negotiating as institutional work: the case of labour standards and international framework agreements', *Organization Studies*, 34/8: 1073–98.

Hirsch, P. M., and Lounsbury, M. (1997), 'Putting the organization back into organization theory', *Journal of Management Inquiry*, 6/1: 79–88.

Hosking, D. M. (2011), 'Telling tales of relations: appreciating relational constructionism', *Organization Studies*, 32/1: 47–65.

Jarzabkowski, P. (2005), *Strategy as Practice: An Activity-Based Approach*. London: Sage.

Jarzabkowski, P., Balogun, J., and Seidl, D. (2007), 'Strategizing: the challenges of a practice perspective', *Human Relations*, 60/1: 5–27.

Jarzabkowski, P., Lê, J., and Van de Ven, A. H. (2013), 'Responding to competing strategic demands: how organizing, belonging, and performing paradoxes coevolve', *Strategic Organization*, 11/3: 245–80.

Jarzabkowski, P., Matthiesen, J., and Van de Ven, A. H. (2009), 'Doing which work? A practice approach to institutional pluralism', in Lawrence, T. B., Suddaby, R., and Leca, B. (eds.), *Institutional Work: Actors and Agency in Institutional Studies of Organizations*: 284–316. Cambridge University Press.

Jarzabkowski, P., Smets, M., Bednarek, R., Burke, G., and Spee, P. (2013), 'Institutional ambidexterity: leveraging institutional complexity in practice', in Lounsbury, M., and Boxenbaum, E. (eds.), Research in the Sociology of Organizations, vol. XXXIX, Institutional Logics in Action, part B: 37–61. Bingley, UK: Emerald.

Jarzabkowski, P., Spee, P., and Smets, M. (2013), 'Material artifacts: practices for doing strategy with "stuff"', *European Management Journal*, 31/1: 41–54.

Jay, J. (2013), 'Navigating paradox as a mechanism of change and innovation in hybrid organizations', *Academy of Management Journal*, 56/1: 137–59.

Kaghan, W., and Lounsbury, M. (2011), 'Institutions and work', *Journal of Management Inquiry*, 20/1: 73–81.

Kellogg, K. C. (2009), 'Operating room: relational spaces and microinstitutional change in surgery', *American Journal of Sociology*, 115/3: 657–711.

Kellogg, K. C., Orlikowski, W. J., and Yates, J. (2006), 'Life in the trading zone: structuring coordination across boundaries in postbureaucratic organizations', *Organization Science*, 17/1: 22–44.

Kraatz, M. S., and Block, E. (2008), 'Organizational implications of institutional pluralism', in Greenwood, R., Oliver, C., Sahlin, K., and Suddaby, R. (eds.), *The Sage Handbook of Organizational Institutionalism*: 243–75. London: Sage.

Lawrence, P. R., and Lorsch, J. W. (1967), *Organization and Environment: Managing Differentiation and Integration*. Boston: Harvard Business School Press.

Lawrence, T. B., Leca, B., and Zilber, T. B. (2013), 'Institutional work: current research, new directions and overlooked issues', *Organization Studies*, 34/8: 1023–33.

Lawrence, T. B., and Suddaby, R. (2006), 'Institutions and institutional work', in Clegg, S.,

Hardy, C., Lawrence, T. B., and Nord, W. R. (eds.), *The Sage Handbook of Organization Studies*, 2nd edn: 215–53. London: Sage.

Lawrence, T. B., Suddaby, R., and Leca, B. (eds.) (2009a), *Institutional Work: Actors and Agency in Institutional Studies of Organizations*. Cambridge University Press.

—— (2009b), 'Introduction: theorizing and studying institutional work', in *Institutional Work: Actors and Agency in Institutional Studies of Organizations*: 1–28. Cambridge University Press.

—— (2011), 'Institutional work: refocusing institutional studies of organization', *Journal of Management Inquiry*, 20/1: 52–8.

Leblebici, H., Salancik, G. R., Copay, A., and King, T. (1991), 'Institutional change and the transformation of interorganizational fields: an organizational history of the US radio broadcasting industry', *Administrative Science Quarterly*, 36/3: 333–63.

Lounsbury, M. (2001), 'Institutional sources of practice variation: staffing college and university recycling programs', *Administrative Science Quarterly*, 46/1: 29–56.

—— (2002), 'Institutional transformation and status mobility: the professionalization of the field of finance', *Academy of Management Journal*, 45/1: 255–66.

—— (2007), 'A tale of two cities: competing logics and practice variation in the professionalizing of mutual funds', *Academy of Management Journal*, 50/2: 289–307.

—— (2008), 'Institutional rationality and practice variation: new directions in the institutional analysis of practice', *Accounting, Organizations and Society*, 33/4–5: 349–61.

Lounsbury, M., and Beckman, C. (2015), 'Celebrating organization theory', *Journal of Management Studies*, 52/2: 288–308.

Lounsbury, M., and Boxenbaum, E. (eds.) (2013), *Research in the Sociology of Organizations*, vol. XXXIX, *Institutional Logics in Action*, 2 parts. Bingley, UK: Emerald.

Lounsbury, M., and Crumley, E. T. (2007), 'New practice creation: an institutional perspective on innovation', *Organization Studies*, 28/7: 993–1012.

Lounsbury, M., and Glynn, M. A. (2001), 'Cultural entrepreneurship: stories, legitimacy, and the acquisition of resources', *Strategic Management Journal*, 22/6–7: 545–64.

Maguire, S., Hardy, C., and Lawrence, T. (2004), 'Institutional entrepreneurship in emerging fields: HIV/AIDS treatment advocacy in Canada', *Academy of Management Journal*, 47/5: 657–79.

March, J. G. (1981), 'Footnotes to organizational change', *Administrative Science Quarterly*, 26/4: 563–77.

—— (1991), 'Exploration and exploitation in organizational learning', *Organization Science*, 2/1: 71–87.

McPherson, C. M., and Sauder, M. (2013), 'Logics in action: managing institutional complexity in a drug court', *Administrative Science Quarterly*, 58/2: 165–96.

Meyer, A. D. (1982), 'Adapting to environmental jolts', *Administrative Science Quarterly*, 27/4: 515–37.

Meyer, J. W., and Rowan, B. (1977), 'Institutionalized organizations: formal structure as myth and ceremony', *American Journal of Sociology*, 83/2: 340–63.

Micelotta, E. R., and Washington, M. (2013), 'Institutions and maintenance: the repair work of Italian professions', *Organization Studies*, 34/8: 1137–70.

Mutch, A., Delbridge, R., and Ventresca, M. (2006), 'Situating organizational action: the relational sociology of organizations', *Organization*, 13/5: 607–25.

Orlikowski, W. J. (1996), 'Improvising organizational transformation over time: a situated change perspective', *Information Systems Research*, 7/1: 63–92.

—— (2002), 'Knowing in practice: enacting a collective capability in distributed organizing', *Organization Science*, 13/3: 249–73.

—— (2010), 'The sociomateriality of organisational life: considering technology in management research', *Cambridge Journal of Economics*, 34/1: 125–41.

Orlikowski, W. J., and Scott, S. V. (2008), 'Sociomateriality: challenging the separation of technology, work and organization', *Academy of Management Annals*, 2/1: 433–74.

Pache, A.-C., and Santos, F. (2010), 'When worlds collide: the internal dynamics of organizational responses to conflicting institutional demands', *Academy of Management Review*, 35/3: 455–76.

—— (2013a), 'Embedded in hybrid contexts: how individuals in organizations respond to competing institutional logics', in Lounsbury, M., and Boxenbaum, E. (eds.), *Research in the Sociology of Organizations*, vol. XXXIX, *Institutional Logics in Action*, Part B: 3–35. Bingley, UK: Emerald.

(2013b), 'Inside the hybrid organization: selective coupling as a response to conflicting institutional logics', *Academy of Management Journal*, 56/4: 972–1001.

Patriotta, G., Gond, J.-P., and Schultz, F. (2011), 'Maintaining legitimacy: controversies, orders of worth, and public justifications', *Journal of Management Studies*, 48/8: 1804–36.

Phillips, N., Lawrence, T. B., and Hardy, C. (2004), 'Discourse and institutions', *Academy of Management Review*, 29/4: 635–52.

Plowman, D. A., Baker, L. T., Beck, T. E., Kulkarni, M., Solansky, S. T., and Travis, D. V. (2007), 'Radical change accidentally: the emergence and amplification of small change', *Academy of Management Journal*, 50/3: 515–43.

Powell, W. W., and Colyvas, J. A. (2008), 'Micro-foundations of institutional theory', in Greenwood, R., Oliver, C., Sahlin, K., and Suddaby, R. (eds.), *The Sage Handbook of Organizational Institutionalism*: 276–98. London: Sage.

Raaijmakers, A., Vermeulen, P., Meeus, M., and Zietsma, C. (2015), 'I need time! Exploring pathways to compliance under institutional complexity', *Academy of Management Journal*, 58/1: 85–110.

Rao, H., and Kenney, M. (2008), 'New forms as settlements', in Greenwood, R., Oliver, C., Sahlin, K., and Suddaby, R. (eds.), *The Sage Handbook of Organizational Institutionalism*: 352–70. London: Sage.

Reay, T., Golden-Biddle, K., and Germann, K. (2006), 'Legitimizing a new role: small wins and microprocesses of change', *Academy of Management Journal*, 49/5: 977–98.

Reay, T., and Hinings, C. R. (2009), 'Managing the rivalry of competing institutional logics', *Organization Studies*, 30/6: 629–52.

Sauermann, H., and Stephan, P. (2013), 'Conflicting logics? A multidimensional view of industrial and academic science', *Organization Science*, 24/3: 889–909.

Schatzki, T. R. (2001), 'Introduction: practice theory', in Schatzki, T. R., Knorr Cetina, K., and von Savigny, E. (eds.), *The Practice Turn in Contemporary Theory*: 1–14. London: Routledge.

(2002), *The Site of the Social: A Philosophical Account of the Constitution of Social Life and Change*. University Park: Pennsylvania State University Press.

(2006), 'On organizations as they happen', *Organization Studies*, 27/12: 1863–73.

Schneiberg, M., and Lounsbury, M. (2008), 'Social movements and institutional analysis', in Greenwood, R., Oliver, C., Sahlin, K., and Suddaby, R. (eds.), *The Sage Handbook of Organizational Institutionalism*: 650–72. London: Sage.

Scott, W. R. (1987), 'The adolescence of institutional theory', *Administrative Science Quarterly*, 32/4: 493–512.

Seo, M. G., and Creed, W. E. D. (2002), 'Institutional contradictions, praxis, and institutional change: a dialectical perspective', *Academy of Management Review*, 27/2: 222–47.

Smets, M., and Jarzabkowski, P. (2013), 'Reconstructing institutional complexity in practice: a relational model of institutional work and complexity', *Human Relations*, 66/10: 1279–309.

Smets, M., Jarzabkowski, P., Spee, P., and Burke, G. (2015), 'Reinsurance trading in Lloyd's of London: balancing conflicting-yet-complementary logics in practice', *Academy of Management Journal*, 58/3: 1–39.

Smets, M., Morris, T., and Greenwood, R. (2012), 'From practice to field: a multilevel model of practice-driven institutional change', *Academy of Management Journal*, 55/4: 877–904.

Spee, P., and Jarzabkowski, P. (2009), 'Strategy tools as boundary objects', *Strategic Organization*, 7/2: 223–32.

(2011), 'Strategic planning as communicative process', *Organization Studies*, 32/9: 1217–45.

Strang, D., and Meyer, J. W. (1993), 'Institutional conditions for diffusion', *Theory and Society*, 22/4: 487–511.

Streeck, J., Goodwin, C., and LeBaron, C. (2011), *Embodied Interaction: Language and Body in the Material World*. Cambridge University Press.

Suddaby, R., and Greenwood, R. (2005), 'Rhetorical strategies of legitimacy', *Administrative Science Quarterly*, 50/1: 35–67.

Suddaby, R., Seidl, D., and Lê, J. (2013), 'Strategy-as-practice meets neo-institutional theory', *Strategic Organization*, 11/3: 329–44.

Thornton, P. H. (2002), 'The rise of the corporation in a craft industry: conflict and conformity in institutional logics', *Academy of Management Journal*, 45/1: 81–101.

(2004), *Markets from Culture: Institutional Logics and Organizational Decisions in Higher Educational Publishing*. Redwood City, CA: Stanford University Press.

Thornton, P. H., and Ocasio, W. (2008), 'Institutional logics', in Greenwood, R., Oliver, C., Sahlin, K., and Suddaby, R. (eds.), *The Sage Handbook of Organizational Institutionalism*: 99–129. London: Sage.

Thornton, P. H., Ocasio, W., and Lounsbury, M. (2012), *The Institutional Logics Perspective: A New Approach to Culture, Structure, and Process*. Oxford University Press.

Tolbert, P. S., and Zucker, L. G. (1983), 'Institutional sources of change in the formal structure of organizations: the diffusion of civil service reform, 1880–1935', *Administrative Science Quarterly*, 28/1: 22–39.

Townley, B. (1997), 'The institutional logic of performance appraisal', *Organization Studies*, 18/2: 261–85.

Tracey, P., Phillips, N., and Jarvis, O. (2011), 'Bridging institutional entrepreneurship and the creation of new organizational forms: a multi-level model', *Organization Science*, 22/1: 60–80.

Tsoukas, H., and Cummings, S. (1997), 'Marginalization and recovery: the emergence of Aristotelian themes in organization studies', *Organization Studies*, 18/4: 655–83.

Tushman, M. L., and O'Reilly, C. A. (1996), 'Ambidextrous organizations: managing evolutionary and revolutionary change', *California Management Review*, 38/4: 8–30.

Vaara, E., and Whittington, R. (2012), 'Strategy-as-practice: taking social practices seriously', *Academy of Management Annals*, 6/1: 1–52.

Van de Ven, A., Ganco, M., and Hinings, C. R. (2013), 'Returning to the frontier of contingency theory of organizational and institutional design', *Academy of Management Annals*, 7/1: 393–440.

Whittington, R. (1996), 'Strategy as practice', *Long Range Planning*, 29/5: 731–5.

(2006), 'Completing the practice turn in strategy research', *Organization Studies*, 27/5: 613–34.

Zietsma, C., and Lawrence, T. B. (2010), 'Institutional work in the transformation of an organizational field: the interplay of boundary work and practice work', *Administrative Science Quarterly*, 55/2: 189–221.

Zilber, T. B. (2002), 'Institutionalization as an interplay between actions, meanings, and actors: the case of a rape crisis center in Israel', *Academy of Management Journal*, 45/1: 234–54.

(2011), 'Institutional multiplicity in practice: a tale of two high-tech conferences in Israel', *Organization Science*, 22/6: 1539–59.

Zucker, L. G. (1983), 'Organizations as institutions', in Bacharach, S. B. (ed.), *Research in the Sociology of Organizations*: 1–47. Greenwich, CT: JAI Press.

(1987), 'Institutional theories of organization', *Annual Review of Sociology*, 13/1: 443–64.

Relating strategy as practice to the resource-based view, capabilities perspectives and the micro-foundations approach

PATRICK REGNÉR

Introduction

Although strategy-as-practice research has thrived during the last decade, the resource-based view (RBV: Barney 1991; Peteraf 1993; Wernerfelt 1984) and capabilities perspectives (Dosi, Nelson and Winter 2000; Eisenhardt and Martin 2000; Winter 2003) have continued to dominate mainstream strategic management research. Recent work has also started to show an increased interest in the micro aspects of strategy, emphasizing micro-foundations as essential in understanding organizational capabilities and resources and their origins (Abell, Felin and Foss 2008; Felin and Foss 2005; Gavetti 2005; Teece 2007). There have been repeated calls for examinations at the intersection between these research directions and SAP research (Jarzabkowski and Kaplan 2010; Johnson et al. 2007; Johnson, Melin and Whittington 2003; Regnér 2012; Vaara and Whittington 2012), but surprisingly little of this nature has materialized so far, with a few exceptions (for example, Ambrosini 2003; Ambrosini, Bowman and Burton-Taylor 2007; Kaplan 2008; Regnér 2003; 2008; Salvato 2003; 2009).

This chapter examines the intersection between strategy as practice and perspectives that have dominated strategy content research during the last couple of decades. Specifically, it examines differences and commonalities, potential relationships and synergies between strategy as practice and the RBV, capabilities perspectives and the micro-foundations approach. It further investigates extant strategy-as-practice research at this intersection

and identifies potential future research opportunities. What can possibly be gained from investigating this intersection? There are four points that are of particular importance. First, besides underlining the importance of strategy practices and activities generally for strategic management, it may provide insights into how practices, praxis and practitioners underlie resources and capabilities that maintain competitive advantage. If we accept that there is a relationship between what managers do and strategy content and outcomes, a key issue is determining how practices both enable and impede managers in their strategy praxis concerning resources and capabilities. By linking strategy as practice to resource-based, capabilities and micro-foundations research, it is thus possible to demonstrate the prominence of practices, social contexts and interactions for strategy. This is, of course, in contrast to extant assumptions in these strategy content research areas that often primarily emphasize rational top managers and individuals. The link to the resource-based and capabilities views may thus strengthen the main theoretical traits of the SAP approach and consolidate it.

Second, linking strategy as practice to resource and capabilities views promises to show not only how practices, praxis and practitioners underlie resources and capabilities but also how these, in turn, influence the former. New insights might be gained as the resource and capability embeddedness of strategy actors and activities are taken into consideration. The organizational technologies, competences and/or knowledge that provide for

competitive advantage may shape and form strategizing. Hence, in the same way that strategy practices are embedded in broader institutional
contexts, they are embedded in broad organizational technologies and capabilities.

Third, by linking strategy as practice with the
RBV and capabilities perspectives and micro-
foundations approach, we can advance our understanding of strategy more generally and possibly
contribute to a more integrated strategic management view. Indeed, just over ten years ago, when
the *Journal of Management Studies'* very first
special issue on micro-strategy and strategizing
was produced, it highlighted how this new
approach could potentially contribute to developing strategic management theory at the intersection
with the RBV (Johnson, Melin and Whittington
2003). The explanatory power of examining the
relationship between micro-activities and resources
was underlined as a primary motive for the
approach, with the aim of bridging the artificial
divide between strategy content and process. If
we continue to pursue this, the end result may be
much more profound than providing another angle
on the RBV. In fact, by employing a practice lens
that links micro descriptions and explications
of strategizing and more macro organizational
resources and capabilities, it might be possible to
shed new light on old truths in strategic management. Inconsistencies in research that lead to the
collapse of reigning theories and paradigms are
almost always observed by scholars from disciplines other than those traditionally dominating the
field (Kuhn 1970). In brief, the strategy-as-practice
approach, which is based on social theory and
sociology, may be able to develop strategic management theory in more fundamental ways than
first anticipated.

Finally, clearly linking strategy practices and
activities with strategy content and outcomes may
be of benefit to managerial practice, which is a
significant aspect that has sometimes been overlooked in strategy as practice (Langley in this
volume; Regnér 2011; Splitter and Seidl in this
volume).

The gist of this chapter is pragmatic and generative. It is pragmatic in the sense that it does not
delve into all epistemological and ontological

considerations and discrepancies concerning
the various strategic management views and
approaches discussed. It is generative in not only
reviewing extant research but in trying to highlight
possible linkages between the various streams of
research and in pointing to potential avenues for
future research at their intersection. The examination will make use of the common strategy-as-
practice framework including practices, praxis and
practitioners (Whittington 2006). *Practices* refer to
tools and shared behavioural procedures, including
norms and cognitive procedures, that are organizationally specific (they also operate on the institutional level – practices of larger organizational
fields). People draw on practices in their *praxis* –
that is, what they actually do in relation to strategy,
including formulating and implementing strategy.
Finally, *practitioners* are people developing,
shaping and executing strategy, and they come in
many forms, including top, middle and line managers as well as external experts and other actors.

In the next section I first present a very brief
overview of the resource-based, capabilities
and micro-foundations perspectives. The section
following this includes a review of extant empirical
strategy-as-practice research at the intersection
with these research approaches. The fourth part of
the chapter discusses the discrepancies and commonalities between strategy as practice and these
perspectives and approaches. In the fifth section
research opportunities and potential contributions
of SAP research at the intersection with the RBV,
capabilities perspectives and micro-foundations
approach are examined. Finally, I conclude and
discuss how strategy as practice might possibly
contribute to a more complete understanding of
strategy.

The resource-based view, capabilities perspectives and micro-foundations approach

There have been several calls to link strategy as
practice more closely to the 'mainstream' strategy
literature (Jarzabkowski and Kaplan 2010). The
resource-based and capabilities views have often
been at the centre of these calls (Johnson, Melin

and Whittington 2003; Johnson *et al.* 2007; Regnér 2008), and more recently the linkages to the micro-foundations approach have been emphasized (Regnér 2012; Vaara and Whittington 2012). In brief, these calls show that strategy as practice is underutilized in understanding resources, capabilities and their micro-foundations, and vice versa. Figure 17.1 displays an exploded map of strategic management and various parts of the strategy field, which can help explain where research is lacking in this respect. The figure illustrates various parts of the strategy field and their relationships. It differentiates between the micro (activities/praxis) and macro (institutional field practices) levels of strategy, with the middle level (organizational actions) representing the orthodoxy of strategic management discipline, including the separation between 'strategy content' and 'strategy process'. While Johnson *et al.*'s (2007) interest is strategy as practice at the lower level of micro-activities in the figure, they emphasize how the doing of strategy straddles all three levels and both strategy content and processes. So far, however, strategy as practice has mostly covered a lot of ground in the lower right side of the figure – that is, actors' activities and their relationship to organizational strategy processes. Less emphasis has been paid to the lower left corner: actors' activities in relation to strategy content and organizational-level strategies.

The resource-based and capabilities views, which have become central in strategy content research during the last couple of decades, operate at the level of the firm and organization (the middle box on the left in Figure 17.1; the example given by Johnson *et al.* 2007 is 'diversification', but could just as well be 'resource and capability configuration'). The aim of these perspectives is to explain heterogeneity between organizations and how one organization may triumph over others and gain competitive advantage on the basis of its idiosyncratic resources and capabilities (this resource and capability approach to strategy is presented in most textbooks, such as that by Johnson *et al.* 2014). The RBV thus argues that competitive advantage and superior performance by an organization are explained by the distinctiveness of its resources and capabilities (Peteraf 1993;

Wernerfelt 1984). To achieve sustained competitive advantage these need to be valuable, rare, imperfectly imitable and not substitutable (Barney 1991). Imperfect imitability is a central tenet of the RBV (Barney 1986a; 2001), and can be explained by various factors. One primary reason why resources can be costly to imitate may be their specialization, sophistication and/or complexity (Kogut and Zander 1992; Rivkin 2000; Rumelt 1984; Winter 1987). More subtle reasons are unique historical conditions that may put an organization on a path-dependent trajectory that followers cannot later attain (Barney 1991; Dierickx and Cool 1989; Lippman and Rumelt 1982) and causal ambiguity, which implies that the relationship between an organization's resources and capabilities and its sustained competitive advantage is imperfectly understood by the focal organization itself and, above all, by its competitors (Barney 1986a; Lippman and Rumelt 1982; Reed and Defillippi 1990; Rumelt 1984; Szulanski 1996). How to develop the desired resources and capabilities in the short to medium term is thus simply not clear for competitors. Another foundation for imitation impediments is social complexity, which implies that resources and capabilities involve extremely complex social phenomena, including organizational culture, social interrelationships, traditions, trust and reputation, which competitors are unable to systematically imitate and manage (Barney 1991).

The RBV can be described as the 'High Church' version of the resource-based and capabilities views (Levinthal 1995), and has often relied on rational choice and equilibrium assumptions (for example, Barney 1986a; 1991; Peteraf 1993; Wernerfelt 1984). In contrast, the 'Low Church' capabilities version (Dosi, Nelson and Winter 2000; Winter 1988; 2003; Zollo and Winter 2002) relies rather more on evolutionary economics (Nelson and Winter 1982) and behavioural traditions (Cyert and March 1963). Capabilities are defined in terms of high-level routines or a collection of routines (Winter 2003), and the focus of this research is on how organizations develop, maintain and advance their capabilities. This version has less confidence than many RBV scholars and traditional economists in the view that strategic decision-makers

Content   **Process**

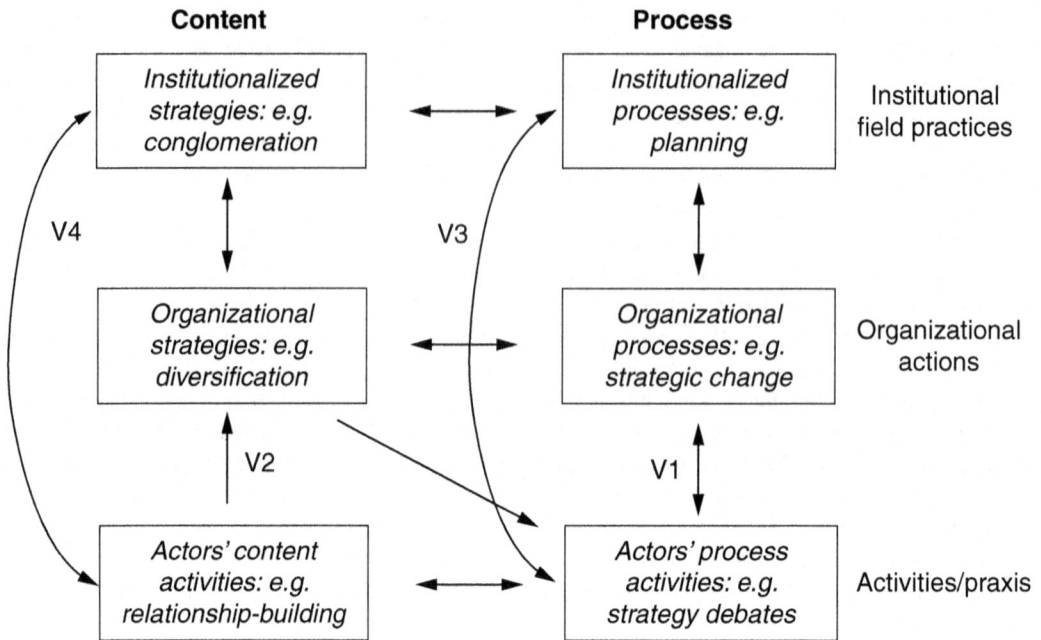

Figure 17.1 An exploded map of strategic management
Source: Johnson *et al.* (2007).

and organizations can smoothly adapt their resources and capabilities to changing environmental conditions (Dosi, Nelson and Winter 2000). Instead, the emphasis is often on initial conditions and the path dependence of resources and capabilities; once an organization is formed on the basis of certain capabilities it is difficult to change and adapt, even if changes in the environment should require this.

The difficulty to adapt is captured in the division of capabilities into *ordinary* and *dynamic* capabilities (Winter 2003). Ordinary capabilities allow organizations to be successful and earn a living now, but they may not be enough to provide for long-term survival and competitive advantage in the future if the environment changes. Dynamic capabilities, in contrast, are capabilities directed at environmental change with a capacity to create, extend or modify capabilities (Helfat *et al.* 2007; Teece 2007; Teece, Pisano and Shuen 1997). These capabilities are of particular interest for strategy as practice, since strategy analysis and planning are examples of dynamic capability – as

are product development and innovation, forming and integrating alliances, etc. (Eisenhardt and Martin 2000). Finally, it should be noted that the resource and capabilities views are not without critics, and several scholars have emphasized the risk of tautology in them and their lack of specificity and dynamics (Bromiley and Papenhausen 2003; Kraaijenbrink, Spender and Groen 2010; Priem and Butler 2001). Interestingly, one research path in the resource and capabilities tradition comes rather close to acknowledging the importance of social contexts and interactions between people in strategy, similarly to strategy as practice. Indeed, the very essence of the knowledge-based view of the firm (Grant 1996; Kogut and Zander 1992; 1996; Nonaka and Takeuchi 1995; Spender 1996; Zander and Kogut 1995) is that firms represent social knowledge of coordination and learning. In the following I sometimes refer to the diverse variants of resource and capabilities perspectives as a single approach, since the dividing line between them is far from precise. Likewise, the distinction between resources and capabilities is not always clear; some treat both as variations of resources (Barney 1991), while others make a distinction within which 'capabilities' refer to an organization's capacity to deploy resources (Amit andSchoemaker 1993; Makadok 2001).

Parts of resource and capabilities research have recently started to open up to possible explanations at the actor level, including potential micro/macro explications. Capability views have thus begun to incorporate more aspects in terms of actors, intentionality and agency (Becker *et al.* 2005; Gavetti, Levinthal and Ocasio 2007; Teece 2007), and some scholars of the RBV have likewise initiated an emphasis on the micro (Alvarez and Barney 2008; Barney 2001). In particular, a micro-foundations approach has emerged as a reaction to what is seen as an exaggerated focus on organizational and collective-level capabilities (Felin and Foss 2005). It is argued that the capabilities construct denies any role of the individual and that strategy is, instead, rooted in individual action and interaction (Abell, Felin and Foss 2008; Foss 2011). The focus is on how individuals and their interactions aggregate to form collective effects and organizational capabilities, resources and routines (Barney and Felin 2013). In a related and emerging stream of research, the focus is on 'behavioural strategy', including cognitive and psychological explanations, with an emphasis on managerial judgements and their limits (Powell, Lovallo and Fox 2011). In the context of Figure 17.1, the micro-foundations approach highlights relationship V2 ('vertical relationship no. 2'), and how individual decisions and activities and individuals in interactions aggregate to form capabilities.

Interestingly, the focus on micro-foundations started out as an approach that primarily emphasized the individual and largely rejected the role of structures, institutions and social context, but its more recent interpretations have initiated some acknowledgement of these factors (Barney and Felin 2013; Felin *et al.* 2012). Some researchers have therefore indicated a departure from the heavy emphasis on the individual and acknowledged that other factors, including processes, structures and social interactions, may be of some significance. There is as yet no coherent view or

theory of micro-foundations, however (Barney and Felin 2013); like strategy as practice, it tends to be an approach with an interest in the micro aspects of strategy. It has also been criticized for exaggerated reductionism, specifically because it often excludes social relations and interactions (Hodgson 2012; Hodgson and Knudsen 2011) and fails to consider that capabilities develop over long time periods that often go beyond individual tenures in organizations, and even lifetimes (Winter 2012).

Strategy-as-practice research at the intersection with contemporary strategy content research streams

Strategy-as-practice research has only recently started to address the window of opportunity at the intersection with the RBV, organizational capabilities perspectives and micro-foundations approach. Despite the surge in SAP research during the last decade, surprisingly few articles explicitly examine organizational capabilities or resources. Nevertheless, Table 17.1 summarizes six representative articles at this intersection. This empirical work has an explicit focus on how certain practices and/or praxis and/or practitioners underpin resources, capabilities and technologies. The articles were chosen for illustrative purposes, and there may be other articles of relevance. For example, there are several studies on strategy as practice that at least partly relate to organizational capabilities, but, even though these seemingly play an important role, they are rarely made explicit.

The studies in Table 17.1 examine a variety of issues related to capabilities, resources and technologies, but they share four common themes: a focus on strategy praxis and outcomes, multiple practitioners and practices, similar methodological approaches and a reliance on a diversity of theories. First, they all share a focus on strategy *praxis* or *activities* and their relationship to strategy and organizational *outcomes* (Table 17.1, columns 2 and 3). The outcomes in the articles refer to competitive advantage (Ambrosini 2003), renewed (Salvato 2003; 2009) or novel capabilities (Regnér 2003), successful or less successful service outcomes (Ambrosini, Bowman and Burton-Taylor

2007), and technology investment decisions (Kaplan 2008). The studies investigate praxis or activities that underlie competitive-advantage-generating resources and capabilities (Ambrosini 2003; Ambrosini, Bowman and Burton-Taylor 2007), activities that underlie dynamic capabilities, and activities that otherwise contribute to capability renewal (Kaplan 2008; Regnér 2003; Salvato 2003; 2009). Ambrosini (2003) and Ambrosini, Bowman and Burton-Taylor (2007) most clearly establish a relationship between specific activities and strategy outcomes, including competitive advantage. Their studies examine various forms of praxis (tacit managerial activities, coordination activities, etc.) and demonstrate how the activities underlie resources and generate certain strategy outcomes and competitive advantage. Interestingly, some of the studies that examine strategizing show that activities that influence capability development do not necessarily involve traditional and formal strategy activities such as analyzing, planning, etc. Instead, a rather diverse set of activities are described as relevant to capability development. For example, Salvato (2003; 2009) examined how different types of day-to-day activities and experimentation at lower organizational levels, together with top management activities, contribute to capability renewal and change. Likewise, Regnér (2003) highlights how peripheral inductive strategy activities, including experimental and trial and error activities, contribute to the creation of new strategies and capabilities while central deductive activities rather promote extant capabilities.

The varieties of praxis or activities in the studies suggest a second common theme, including distributed strategy-making and *multiple practitioners*, drawing on a *varied set of practices* (Table 17.1, columns 2 and 3). For example, Ambrosini, Bowman and Burton-Taylor (2007), in their fine-grained analysis of what underpins resources, examined numerous practitioners at several organizational levels and observed clear differences between both practices and related outcomes in the two divisions they investigated. Notably, practices that are not always considered 'strategic' in the traditional sense (strategic analysis, planning, etc.) may still have significant

consequences for strategy outcomes. For example, Salvato (2003; 2009) highlights the importance of design practices and I emphasize (Regnér 2003) the significance of innovation practices. These latter findings thus support other strategy-as-practice studies that consider strategy as something immanent in purposive action that draws on broader tendencies and predispositions, rather than strategy as individual (top management) purposeful action only (Chia and Holt 2006; Chia and Rasche, in this volume). Sensemaking and cognitive frames have figured prominently in several studies on strategy as practice (Balogun and Johnson 2004; Rouleau 2005), and Kaplan's (2008) study, summarized in Table 17.1, demonstrates the importance of framing practices in technology investment decisions. The study explicates how diverse actors engage in political framing contests to legitimize their own cognitive frames. Consequently, it shows the significance of how technologies and capabilities are situated in cognitive frames, and thus are in the eyes of the beholder.

A third important commonality of the studies is the use of similar *methodological approaches* (Table 17.1, column 4). They all include ethnographic and observational methods combined with interviews and archival data, and most of them use a comparative case study design. Based on these methods, the scholars meticulously worked back from the various strategy outcomes (resources, capabilities, strategies, decisions, etc.) and traced relevant actors and the minutiae of their activities. These intimate, in-depth and fine-grained investigations were therefore focused on how particulars of strategy activities and actors' actual work underlie strategy outcomes. Some of the studies also examined interactions between actors (Ambrosini, Bowman and Burton-Taylor 2007; Kaplan 2008) and cognitive structures (Ambrosini 2003; Kaplan 2008; Regnér 2003). Most of them also include examinations of a broad set of actors at several organizational levels (and, in some cases, external actors), in contrast to the focus on top management and individuals in mainstream strategy research. In brief, the focus on situated actors, their specific micro-activities, their interactions and their sensemaking, and thus an emphasis on a relational totality of strategy, is in sharp contrast to the emphasis

Table 17.1 Research at the intersection between strategy-as-practice and resource-based capabilities and micro-foundations research

Authors	Focus	Findings	Main methods	Main theoretical base
Ambrosini (2003)	Activities underpinning tacit routines and organizational performance	• Tacit activities and routines as determinants of competitive advantage	Case studies: six organizations • Interviews • Causal/cognitive mapping	• RBV • Organizational routines • Psychology
Regnér (2003)	Strategy activities and cognitive structures in the centre versus periphery	• Establishing a link between activities and capabilities: inductive activities in the periphery supporting new capabilities and deductive activities in the centre supporting extant capabilities	Comparative case studies: four multinational corporations • Interviews • Observation • Documents	• Practice theory • Capability and dynamic capability view
Salvato (2003)	Activities, routines and resources in strategic initiatives	• Dynamic capabilities as based on the repeated combination of stable core micro-strategies involving routines, activities and resources, which generate new strategic initiatives	Comparative case studies: two multinational corporations • Interviews • Observation • Documents	• Capability and dynamic capability view • Giddens' structuration theory
Ambrosini, Bowman and Burton-Taylor (2007)	Inter-team coordination activities	• Establishing a link between practices and service outcomes: specific managerial activities, physical location and interactions as determinants of competitive advantage	Comparative case study: two divisions in a large public financial service company • Interviews • Observation • Documents	• Practice theory • RBV
Kaplan (2008)	Technology strategy initiatives and cognitive frame differences	• Various actors engaging in political framing practices and contests to make their strategy views and technologies resonate and gain active support	Case study: two projects in an R&D group within a multi-divisional corporation • Ethnography/ Observation • Interviews • Documents	• Practice theory • Goffman's frame theory • Social movement theory
Salvato (2009)	Day-to-day activities in capability development	• Mindful ordinary activities and local experimentation as central to organizational renewal and new capabilities	Case study: tracking product innovation processes in a multinational corporation • Interviews • Observation • Archival documents	• Capability and dynamic capability view • Organizational routines

on aggregate strategies, capabilities, resources, etc. in traditional research.

A final common theme among the studies is their reliance on *several and diverse theories* (Table 17.1, column 5). Naturally, general practice theories, including structuration theory, play an important role in these studies, but they also rely on a whole set of other theoretical traditions. Resource-based and capabilities-based views, of course, play principal roles. Ambrosini (2003) and Ambrosini, Bowman and Burton-Taylor (2007) take the RBV as their point of departure when examining the activities underlying resources that provide competitive advantage. Salvato (2003; 2009) draws on the capabilities and dynamic capabilities views, as does Regnér (2003). Ambrosini (2003) and Salvato (2003; 2009) also build on organizational routine theories and studies that emphasize routine change (Feldman 2000; Feldman and Pentland 2003; see also Feldman in this volume). Interestingly, Ambrosini (2003) also employs various theories from psychology. This has so far been unusual in the SAP approach, given its sociological base, even though sensemaking and cognitive structures, which have figured in several studies (for example, Kaplan 2008), of course have roots in psychology. Finally, Table 17.1 also shows that Kaplan (2008) uses Goffman's frame theory, which is more familiar to strategy as practice, and she also draws on social movement theory. The latter may be particularly useful when analysing how individuals' activities and interactions aggregate to form capabilities.

Differences and similarities between strategy as practice and the mainstream strategy research streams

While SAP research at the intersection with the RBV, capabilities perspectives and the microfoundations approach is exciting and shows a lot of promise, the review above also confirms that it has been rather limited to date. One reason may be the clear and distinct differences between strategy as practice and these views and approaches. The dissimilarities between the research streams relate both to epistemological and ontological discrepancies, which are apparent from several chapters in this handbook (see, for example, Chapters 1–4). Most fundamentally, strategy as practice's emphasis on a mutual constitution and relational totality of practices as routinized behaviour interconnected to mental and bodily activities, things, tools and emotions (Reckwitz 2002) differs completely from the Cartesian tradition including dualisms, which the other views and approaches rely on. Although the specifics of the ontological differences are not detailed and reiterated here, it can be observed that the distinctions between

strategy as practice and the other research streams include level of analysis, primary interests, root disciplines and outcome focus (see Regnér 2008), as outlined below.

First, strategy as practice emphasizes practices, praxis and practitioners on the level of actors while the RBV and capabilities perspectives centre on organization-level resources, capabilities and routines. Micro-foundations research shares the focus on actors or practitioners with strategy as practice, however, but primarily emphasizes individuals and does not emphasize practices and the shared understandings and interactions they rely on. Second, the key interest of strategy as practice is strategizing as a social practice, building on social theory. The interest of the RBV and capabilities perspectives, in contrast, is strategy as a means to achieve competitive advantage, building on mainstream and evolutionary economics. This points to the third, and perhaps most fundamental, difference between the diverse research streams: concerns with strategy outcome. Strategy-as-practice research has not primarily been concerned with outcome, and when it has the focus has been on the performance of practices, procedures, tools, workshops, discourses, etc. rather than organizational or firm-level performance (Guérard, Langley and Seidl 2013). This is in contrast with the RBV and the capabilities perspectives, which emphasize outcomes, and micro-foundations research, which instead has capabilities as an outcome variable. Other differences between the research streams include methodological approaches and a rather larger focus on non-profit organizations in SAP research.

In their stronger forms, the differences between the strategy-as-practice and the other research streams are very distinct, and translations of strategy concepts from one area to the other may be rather difficult (Seidl 2007). For example, in some micro-foundations approach methods, the sole point of departure is the individual, including a primary focus on rational and utility-maximizing agents and how their actions determine macro outcomes (Foss 2011; Felin and Foss 2005; 2011; for a critical evaluation, see Hodgson 2012). This is in sharp contrast to strategy as practice, of course, which starts with historical and extant practices and how they constrain or enable actors, often based on structuration theory (Giddens 1984; see Whittington, this volume). The divergence is most clear when making comparisons with strategy-as-practice interpretations that fully draw on a practice philosophy in which the solitary focus is on practice as the basic unit, with no independently existing elements and no dichotomy between the micro and macro whatsoever (see Orlikowski, this volume). In these strong forms the research streams might even be considered as incommensurable, with few possibilities of any reconciliation. Despite these conflicting assumptions, however, several comparable interests and characteristics are evident in the diverse research streams' weaker forms. In fact, some recent reviews (Barney and Felin 2013; Vaara and Whittington 2012) even suggest that they have much in common and that there may be synergies between them.

The strategy-as-practice and capabilities perspectives both emphasize practices and routines in continuous processes; the importance of historical and localized contexts; the behavioural traits of organizational members; strategy as situational; and path dependence, with limited change capacities (Regnér 2008). Strategy as practice also overlaps with the knowledge-based view in terms of the emphasis on social interactions, as indicated earlier (Grant 1996; Kogut and Zander 1992; 1996). While the emphasis in the capabilities perspective and the knowledge-based view is on the organizational level, however, and thus a collection of whole routines and collective knowledge, strategy as practice is more concerned with the inner workings of capabilities, routines and knowledge (Parmigiani and Howard-Grenville 2011). This takes us to the micro, and an emphasis on the individual level and human agency, which implies a close affinity with the micro-foundations approach. There is a clear resemblance in this respect between these two latter strategy research areas, as observed in both strategy-as-practice (Floyd and Sputtek 2011; Regnér 2012) and micro-foundations research (Barney and Felin 2013), as illustrated by the following quotations:

> SAP's attention to micro-level praxis suggests an obvious affinity as well with the current interest in Micro-Foundations in strategy research... (Vaara and Whittington 2012: 320).

> The strategy-as-practice area shares a broad affinity with the microfoundations program in that it seeks to more carefully delve into the actual micro activities, behaviors, and processes of strategy and organization... (Barney and Felin 2013: 145).

In sum, despite some fundamental differences in assumptions, strategy-as-practice research shares an emphasis on shared routines and practices with the capabilities view; the importance of social interactions with the knowledge-based view; and a focus on the micro, including actors, their interactions and their agency, with the micro-foundations approach.

Research opportunities

Despite important differences in assumptions the discussion above shows that there are several potential overlaps between strategy as practice and the RBV, the capabilities perspectives and the micro-foundations approach. In fact, it has been proposed that strategy as practice is in a unique position to connect the micro with the macro, to bridge structure and agency and to broaden the range of outcomes to encompass resources and capabilities (Vaara and Whittington 2012). This type of research could potentially contribute to capabilities and RBV research at the level of the firm and organization (Figure 17.1, middle left box and arrows). Moreover, it might develop strategy-as-practice research on the content side (Figure 17.1, lower left box and V2) and, hence, contribute to micro-foundations research, including actors and interactions underpinning capabilities. Furthermore, such research could also strengthen extant SAP research (Figure 17.1, primarily lower right box and arrows).

There are two principal research paths at the intersection between strategy as practice and the RBV, capabilities perspectives and micro-foundations approach that offer promising future research opportunities. First, strategy-as-practice research can examine how micro processes and content activities (Figure 17.1, lower right and left boxes) both relate to organization-level strategies, including resource and capability configurations and allocations (middle left box). Most extant SAP research at the intersection with the RBV and capabilities perspectives belongs to this principal research path. The second principal research path has attracted less attention so far and is based on an incorporation of resources and capabilities (Figure 17.1, middle left box) and micro-foundations (lower left box) into strategy-as-practice approaches, which may change how strategy practices, praxis and practitioners (lower right box and arrows) are examined and interpreted. Both these principal research paths are discussed below.

The first principal research path can be illustrated by a range of relations (or, indeed, 'foundations') of strategy that capabilities perspectives and the micro-foundations approach tend to leave out. Both overlook a fundamental aspect that is at the centre of strategy as practice: seeing strategy as something people do in specific social contexts. Social context and interactions enable and constrain actors' strategy activities in various ways and may have significant consequences for what, and how, capabilities emerge. The arrows surrounding the lower left part of Figure 17.1 all indicate that micro-strategy activities are not isolated but depend on various social contexts and interactions. Regardless of whether our interests lie in the characteristics of capabilities or their micro origins, we need to consider the social context of strategizing and relations between people. Hence, there are interactional consequences of actors in a social context; individuals may strategize differently depending on the setting, which can influence strategy outcomes, organizational capabilities and – in the end – competitive advantage. Organization-level resource and capability configurations may thus be contingent on particular activities aimed at forming them (Figure 17.1, lower left box and V2), but also more indirectly on strategy praxis (Figure 17.1, lower right box and lower double arrow).

The second principal research path implies that strategy as practice may benefit from incorporating fundamental aspects of the RBV, capabilities perspectives and micro-foundations approach into examinations of strategy practices, praxis and practitioners. Often the basic characteristics of resources and capabilities (Figure 17.1, middle left box) are ignored when strategy practices are examined. These may be important, however, as practices and praxis are embedded in certain resources and capabilities (such as technologies, competences and knowledge) and may be contingent on these (diagonal arrow in the lower part of Figure 17.1). More generally, it is essential to determine the ways in which strategy practices indeed are *strategic* at all, by explaining how strategy procedures, workshops, tools, etc. directly relate to and/or aim at developing or changing resources or capabilities (and/or competitive positions) – something that SAP research sometimes tends to leave out. This suggests broadening the range of outcomes to also incorporate organization-level performance. Finally, the institutionalization of the resource and capabilities perspectives and techniques per se in academia and in practice is also of interest to strategy-as-practice research.

On the basis of both principal research paths above, it is possible to identify several promising future research avenues at the intersection between strategy as practice and the RBV, capabilities perspectives and micro-foundations approach. I will limit my discussion to five main themes and opportunities, however. The first two themes concentrate on the first principal research path: how micro-process and content activities relate to organization-level resources and capabilities. The final three themes focus on the second principal research path: how practices, praxis and practitioners are embedded in resources and capabilities, and how these can be incorporated into extant strategy-as-practice research.

Micro-process and content activities and resources and capabilities

First, there are numerous interesting research opportunities in the examination of micro-processes and content activities and their association with organization-level outcomes, including resources, capabilities, decisions, etc. In fact, this has been described as 'an open window of opportunity' (Vaara and Whittington 2012: 321) for strategy-as-practice scholars interested in how the micro relates to organization-level resources and capabilities. Specifically, and in relation to micro-foundations, it offers an opportunity to reach beyond the individual-centric focus in this research to also include the role of social contexts and interactions as underlying capabilities and resources (Regnér 2014). A fundamental question here is how practices, practitioners and praxis contribute to and shape capability creation, acquisition and combination. This can be investigated by working backwards from the resultant capabilities, decisions, etc. and then identifying the particular practices, practitioners and praxis involved; alternatively, one can examine how the resources, capabilities, decisions, etc. evolve in real time by examining the former. Both these approaches have been used in the studies mentioned in Table 17.1. Future studies can, for example, explore how particular strategy practices embedded in certain social contexts relate to specific strategy outcomes (capabilities, resources, decisions, knowledge, etc.). This may provide an understanding of how social contexts shape behaviour, outcomes and performance. One can examine how various practitioners and their interactions in diverse sections of an organization or in different organizations influence strategy outcomes. This could possibly also include scrutiny of the fine-grained specifics of the processes and mechanisms involved in these interactions; for example, how various forms of discourses, negotiations and politicking relate to certain organization-level outcomes.

A second area within the first principal research path above that offers promising research opportunities relates to what was most new in the RBV (Barney 2001): inimitability. While physical and technological imitation difficulties are of importance, including resource and capability specializations, as well as sophistication and/or complexity (Kogut and Zander 1992; Rivkin 2000; Winter 1987), other barriers to imitation are even more important (Barney 1991). These include causal ambiguity (Lippman and Rumelt 1982), unique historical conditions and social complexity (Barney 1991). They have seldom been untangled, but strategy-as-practice research holds out the possibility of sorting out the details of these processes and mechanisms. Although extant research in

behavioural strategy and micro-foundations has started to look into psychological explanations in this respect (Gavetti 2005; 2012; Hodgkinson and Healey 2011), organizational contexts and social interactions also need to be taken into consideration (Winter 2011). Clearly, strategy practices and practitioners, and the norms and culture entangled with them, contribute to the social complexity of resources and capabilities and may thus afford inimitability (Regnér 2010), which is also recognized in the RBV (Barney 1986b). For example, strategy-as-practice research can disentangle the interactions and tacitness that contribute to inimitability and competitive advantage (for example, Ambrosini 2003; Ambrosini, Bowman and Burton-Taylor 2007). Strategy practices may also include norms that are socially complex and thus difficult to understand and follow for competitors outside a specific organizational or institutional context, and they may therefore contribute to inimitability (Jonsson and Regnér 2009). SAP research could potentially also move beyond these observations of institutional and normative barriers to imitation and unpack their fine-grained details. For example, it could discern exactly how the practices and shared norms are entangled and why they confer inimitability. Finally, a careful examination of the micro-practices and foundations underlying strategy could perhaps separate out how capabilities become idiosyncratic, valuable and inimitable as they are transposed when organizations apply generalized strategy practices in different ways (see Vaara and Whittington 2012).

Resources and capabilities and practices, praxis and practitioners

The second principal research path discussed above offers three other interesting research opportunities. Hence, a third research opportunity includes an examination of the extent to which, and how, strategy practices and praxis are embedded in certain resources and capability frames and interpretations, with possible consequences for the qualities of the former. Strategists are thus not only entwined in and carriers of particular strategy practices, they are also embedded in socio-material resource and capability practices, including certain assumptions, standards, tools, norms, activities, etc. This opens up interesting research opportunities as to how the use and understanding of strategy procedures, tools, techniques, etc. may be dependent on particular cognitive frames tied to specific resources and capabilities (see Eggers and Kaplan 2009; 2013). Yet another possible research area when examining frames and sense-making is to examine closely how they could contribute, as part of social practices or capabilities, to various biases in strategic decision-making (see Vaara and Whittington 2012). This would offer an alternative to the primary focus on individual cognitive biases in extant micro-foundations and strategy behaviour work.

A fourth important research avenue, also based on the second principal research path discussed above, suggests incorporating fundamental aspects of the RBV and capabilities views and micro-foundations into strategy as practice. It implies an exploitation of the link to organizational and strategy outcomes commonly used in strategy content perspectives. This does not suggest an abandonment of strategy as practice's concerns with other outcomes, but including organization-level outcomes may reveal hitherto uncovered details of strategy practices. First, the degree to which successful organizations and firms simply have more resources for more extensive and elaborate strategy practices, including strategic planning processes, tools, workshops, etc., and vice versa, could be examined. This might shed light on the common assumption that more (and presumably better) strategy practices result in improved strategy outcomes. Another approach in this vein would be to investigate the basic characteristics of strategy practices and their connection to strategy outcome, such as examining how – and possibly why – extensive, deliberate and formalized strategizing does not always materialize into intended strategy outcomes and better performance (for example, improved and inimitable resources and capabilities), which is far from uncommon. In fact, an examination of the minutiae of the strategy practices and their application in praxis that do not produce intended strategy outcomes and improved resources and

capabilities could possibly result in more practical advice from SAP research – something that is really needed (Splitter and Seidl, in this volume). Of course, examining the opposite would also be highly interesting – that is, the extent to which more emergent forms of strategizing may be more successful (see Vaara and Whittington 2012). In fact, although it is widely acknowledged that strategy is often recognized only retrospectively (Burgelman 1983; Weick 1995) and can emerge non-deliberately through everyday practical coping (Chia and Holt 2006; Chia and Rasche, in this volume), surprisingly little strategy-as-practice research has accumulated around this (for an exception, see Regnér 2003). In sum, examining how strategy practice and praxis differ between organizations and firms with different success rates may be highly informative.

A final research opportunity at the intersection of strategy as practice and resource and capabilities perspectives within the second principal research path above is a more general examination of why these perspectives and the analytics and tools involved (resource/capability analysis, VRIO framework,[1] etc.) have become dominant in strategic management. Besides relating to institutionalized actions on the organizational level (Figure 17.1, middle boxes), this would take us to the upper boxes of institutional field practices in Figure 17.1 (V3 and V4 arrows). Reviews have emphasized the promise of analysing strategy as an institution in itself (Vaara and Whittington 2012; Whittington, in this volume), and of course the RBV and organizational capabilities perspectives are by now well established and institutionalized not just in academia but in practice. For example, one research opportunity in this vein lies in tracing how the institutionalized mantra of 'Focus on core competences' has changed strategy practices and praxis not only for corporate- and business-level strategy within organizations but also within business school research and education and among consultants. This type of examination

---

[1] VRIO refers to the criteria for sustained competitive advantage in terms of resources and capabilities: value, rarity, inimitability and support by the organization (Barney 1997).

could, for example, include investigations of changes in planning, analytics, tools, workshops and discourses. The shift in strategy focus also facilitates investigation into exactly how practices and praxis are mutually constitutive and how the role of practitioners may have shifted. In brief, investigating the change from a primary external and industry focus to an internal and resource/capability focus offers ample opportunities to explore how the social and material influence strategy.

Conclusion

This chapter has provided a review of extant research and potential research opportunities at the intersection of strategy as practice and resource-based, capabilities and micro-foundations research. It has demonstrated how strategy-as-practice research can be strengthened by pursuing these opportunities and how they potentially can contribute to a more integrative view of strategy. The chapter reviewed six studies that have started to examine the intersection between SAP research and the strategy content research streams. In addition, the differences and similarities between these and strategy as practice were examined. Finally, two principal paths for research at this intersection were discussed: examining how micro-processes and content activities relate to organization-level resources and capabilities; and examining how practices, praxis and practitioners are embedded in resources and capabilities.

Several research opportunities within the two principal research paths were examined. First, by examining practices, praxis and practitioners and illuminating and explicating how they underlie capabilities, strategy-as-practice research can contribute to questions raised in the micro-foundations approach, but with an emphasis on social interactions and contexts. It was further shown how strategy-as-practice research might describe and clarify the social complexities that may provide for inimitability in capabilities and resources, including interactions between people in strategy practices and praxis. Another promising research approach includes examinations of how strategy

praxis and practices, and the shared practical understandings on which they rely, may be affected by organizations' extant resource and capability configurations and by activities that are directly aimed at developing resources and capabilities. In other words, the embeddedness of strategy practices and praxis in certain resource and capability configurations may influence them, and so may activities directed at developing resources and capabilities. Strategy-as-practice research can also contribute by investigating the extent to which strategy practices and praxis are contingent on organizational performance and success. Finally, the institutionalization of resource and capability theories, frameworks, tools and analysis is itself ripe for investigation in the strategy-as-practice field.

In brief, this chapter shows that, despite some fundamental discrepancies between strategy as practice and the RBV, capabilities perspectives and micro-foundations research, these research streams are not primarily in competition but are, rather, complementary modes of investigating strategy. Strategy as practice can contribute descriptions and examinations of what underlies capabilities (or, indeed, their 'foundations'), including social contexts and the interactions of strategizing; it may also be further developed by incorporating questions of how strategy practices and praxis may be embedded in certain resource and capability configurations. Research at this intersection may also contribute to a more complete and integrative view of strategy that finally bridges its content, process and practice aspects, which have too long been separated in strategic management research.

References

Abell, P., Felin, T., and Foss, N. J. (2008), 'Building micro-foundations for the routines, capabilities, and performance links', *Managerial and Decision Economics*, 29/6: 489–502.

Alvarez, S. A. and Barney, J. (2008), 'Opportunities, organizations, and entrepreneurship', *Strategic Entrepreneurship Journal*, 2/4: 265–7.

Ambrosini, V. (2003), *Tacit and Ambiguous Resources as Sources of Competitive Advantage*. London: Palgrave.

Ambrosini, V., Bowman, C., and Burton-Taylor, S. B. (2007), 'Inter-team coordination activities as a source of customer satisfaction', *Human Relations*, 60/1: 59–98.

Amit, R., and Schoemaker, P. J. (1993), 'Strategic assets and organizational rent', *Strategic Management Journal*, 14/1: 33–46.

Balogun, J., and Johnson, G. (2004), 'Organizational restructuring and middle manager sensemaking', *Academy of Management Journal*, 47/4: 523–49.

Barney, J. (1986a), 'Strategic factor markets: expectations, luck, and business strategy', *Management Science*, 32/10: 1231–41.

(1986b), 'Organizational culture: can it be a source of sustained competitive advantage?', *Academy of Management Review*, 11/3: 656–65.

(1991), 'Firm resources and sustained competitive advantage', *Journal of Management*, 17/1: 99–120.

(1997), *Gaining and Sustaining Competitive Advantage*. Reading, MA: Addison-Wesley.

(2001), 'Resource-based theories of competitive advantage: a ten-year retrospective on the resource-based view', *Journal of Management*, 27/6: 643–50.

Barney, J., and Felin, T. (2013), 'What are microfoundations?', *Academy of Management Perspectives*, 27/2: 138–55.

Becker, M. C., Lazaric, N., Nelson, R. R., and Winter, S. G. (2005), 'Applying organizational routines in understanding organizational change', *Industrial and Corporate Change*, 14/5: 775–91.

Bromiley, P., and Papenhausen, C. (2003), 'Assumptions of rationality and equilibrium in strategy research: the limits of traditional economic analysis', *Strategic Organization*, 1/4: 413–38.

Burgelman, R. A. (1983), 'A process model of internal corporate venturing in the diversified major firm', *Administrative Science Quarterly*, 28/2: 223–44.

Chia, R., and Holt, R. (2006), 'Strategy as practical coping: a Heideggerian perspective', *Organization Studies*, 27/5: 635–55.

Cyert, R. M., and March, J. G. (1963), *A Behavioral Theory of the Firm*. Englewood Cliffs, NJ: Prentice Hall.

Dierickx, I., and Cool, K. (1989), 'Asset stock accumulation and sustainability of competitive advantage', *Management Science*, 35/12: 1504–11.

Dosi, G., Nelson, R. R., and Winter, S. G. (eds.) (2000), *The Nature and Dynamics of Organizational Capabilities*. Oxford University Press.

Eggers, J. P., and Kaplan, S. (2009), 'Cognition and renewal: comparing CEO and organizational effects on incumbent adaptation to technical change', *Organization Science*, 20/2: 461–77.

(2013), 'Cognition and capabilities: a multi-level perspective', *Academy of Management Annals*, 7/1: 295–340.

Eisenhardt, K. M., and Martin, J. A. (2000), 'Dynamic capabilities: what are they?', *Strategic Management Journal*, 21/10–11: 1105–21.

Feldman, M. S. (2000), 'Organizational routines as a source of continuous change', *Organization Science*, 11/6: 611–29.

Feldman, M. S., and Pentland, B. T. (2003), 'Reconceptualizing organizational routines as a source of flexibility and change', *Administrative Science Quarterly*, 39/3: 484–510.

Felin, T., and Foss, N. J. (2005), 'Strategic organization: a field in search of microfoundations', *Strategic Organization*, 3/4: 441–55.

(2011), 'The endogenous origins of experience, routines, and organizational capabilities: the poverty of stimulus', *Journal of Institutional Economics*, 7/2: 231–56.

Felin, T., Foss, N. J., Heimeriks, K. H., and Madsen, T. L. (2012), 'Microfoundations of routines and capabilities: individuals, processes, and structure', *Journal of Management Studies*, 49/8: 1351–74.

Floyd, S. W., and Sputtek, R. (2011), 'Rediscovering the individual in strategy: methodological challenges, strategies, and prospects', in Bergh, D. D., and Ketchen, D. J. (eds.), *Research Methodology in Strategy and Management*, vol. VI, *Building Methodological Bridges*: 3–30. Bingley, UK: Emerald.

Foss, N. J. (2011), 'Invited editorial: why microfoundations for resource-based theory are needed and what they may look like', *Journal of Management*, 37/5 1413–28.

Gavetti, G. (2005), 'Cognition and hierarchy: rethinking microfoundations of capabilities development', *Organization Science*, 16/6: 599–617.

(2012), 'Toward a behavioral theory of strategy', *Organization Science*, 23/1: 267–85.

Gavetti, G., Levinthal, D., and Ocasio, W. (2007), 'Perspective – neo-Carnegie: the Carnegie School's past, present, and reconstructing for the future', *Organization Science*, 18/3: 523–36.

Giddens, A. (1984), *The Constitution of Society*. Cambridge: Polity.

Grant, B. (1996), 'Toward a knowledge-based view of the firm', *Strategic Management Journal*, 17/S1: 109–22.

Guérard, S., Langley, A., and Seidl, D. (2013), 'Rethinking the concept of performance in strategy research: towards a performativity perspective', *M@n@gement*, 16/5: 566–78.

Helfat, C., Finkelstein, S., Mitchell, W., Peteraf, M., Singh, H., and Winter, S. G. (2007), *Dynamic Capabilities: Understanding Strategic Change in Organizations*. Oxford: Blackwell.

Hodgkinson, G. P., and Healey, M. P. (2011), 'Psychological foundations of dynamic capabilities: reflexion and reflection in strategic management', *Strategic Management Journal*, 32/13: 1500–16.

Hodgson, G. M. (2012), 'The mirage of microfoundations', *Journal of Management Studies*, 49/8: 1389–94.

Hodgson, G. M., and Knudsen, T. (2011), 'Poverty of stimulus and absence of cause: some questions for Felin and Foss', *Journal of Institutional Economics*, 7/2: 295–8.

Jarzabkowski, P., and Kaplan, S. (2010), 'Taking "strategy-as-practice" across the Atlantic', in Baum, J. A. C., and Lampel, J. (eds.), *Advances in Strategic Management*, vol. XXVII, *The Globalization of Strategy Research*: 51–71. Bingley, UK: Emerald.

Johnson, G., Langley, A., Melin, L., and Whittington, R. (2007), *The Practice of Strategy: Research Directions and Resources*. Cambridge University Press.

Johnson, G., Melin, L., and Whittington, R. (2003), 'Guest editors' introduction: micro strategy and strategizing: towards an activity-based view', *Journal of Management Studies*, 40/1: 3–22.

Johnson, G., Whittington, R., Scholes, K., Angwin, D., and Regnér, P. (2014), *Exploring Strategy: Text and Cases*, 10th edn. London: Pearson.

Jonsson, S., and Regnér, P. (2009), 'Normative barriers to imitation: social complexity of core competences in a mutual fund industry', *Strategic Management Journal*, 30/5: 517–36.

Kaplan, S. (2008), 'Framing contests: strategy making under uncertainty', *Organization Science*, 19/5: 729–52.

Kogut, B., and Zander, U. (1992), 'Knowledge of the firm, combinative capabilities, and the replication of technology', *Organization Science*, 3/3: 383–97.

Kogut, B., and Zander, U. (1996), 'What firms do? Coordination, identity, and learning', *Organization Science*, 7/5: 502–18.

Kraaijenbrink, J., Spender, J.-C., and Groen, A. J. (2010), 'The resource-based view: a review and assessment of its critiques', *Journal of Management*, 36/1: 349–72.

Kuhn, T. S. (1970), *The Structure of Scientific Revolutions*, 2nd edn. University of Chicago Press.

Levinthal, D. (1995), 'Strategic management and the exploration of diversity', in Montgomery, C. A. (ed.), *Resource-Based and Evolutionary Theories of the Firm*: 19–42. Dordrecht: Kluwer Academic.

Lippman, S. A., and Rumelt, R. P. (1982), 'Uncertain imitability: an analysis of interfirm differences in efficiency under competition', *Bell Journal of Economics*, 13/2: 418–38.

Makadok, R. (2001), 'Toward a synthesis of the resource-based and dynamic-capability views of rent creation', *Strategic Management Journal*, 22/5: 387–401.

Nelson, R. R., and Winter, S. G. (1982), *An Evolutionary Theory of Economic Change*. Cambridge, MA: Belknap Press.

Nonaka, I., and Takeuchi, H. (1995), *The Knowledge-Creating Company*. Oxford University Press.

Parmigiani, A., and Howard-Grenville, J. (2011), 'Routines revisited: exploring the capabilities and practice perspectives', *Academy of Management Annals*, 5/1: 413–53.

Peteraf, M. (1993), 'The cornerstones of competitive advantage: a resource-based view', *Strategic Management Journal*, 14/3: 179–91.

Powell, T., Lovallo, D., and Fox, C. (2011), 'Behavioral strategy', *Strategic Management Journal*, 32/13: 1369–86.

Priem, R. L., and Butler, J. E. (2001), 'Is the resource-based view a useful perspective for strategic management research?', *Academy of Management Review*, 26/1: 22–40.

Reckwitz, A. (2002), 'Toward a theory of social practices: a development in culturalist theorizing', *European Journal of Social Theory*, 5/2: 243–63.

Reed, R., and Defillippi, R. J. (1990), 'Causal ambiguity, barriers to imitation and sustainable competitive advantage', *Academy of Management Review*, 15/1, 88–102.

Regnér, P. (2003), 'Strategy creation in the periphery: inductive versus deductive strategy making', *Journal of Management Studies*, 40/1: 57–82.

(2008), 'Strategy-as-practice and dynamic capabilities: steps towards a more dynamic view of strategy', *Human Relations*, 61/4: 565–88.

(2010), 'Strategy process research and the RBV: social barriers to imitation', in Mazzola, P., and

Kellermanns, F. W. (eds.), *Handbook of Research on Strategy Process*: 90–108. Cheltenham: Edward Elgar.

— (2011), 'Book review of *Cambridge Handbook of Strategy as Practice*', *Management*, 14/2: 157–76.

— (2012), 'Strategy as practice: untangling the emergence of competitive positions', in Dagnino, G. B. (ed.), *Handbook of Research on Competitive Strategy*: 182–200. Cheltenham: Edward Elgar.

— (2014), 'Strategy-as-practice and micro-foundations', online seminar, Henry Stewart Talks, http://hstalks.com/main/view_talk.php?t=2724&r=693&c=250.

Rivkin, J. W. (2000), 'Imitation of complex strategies', *Management Science*, 46/6: 824–44.

Rouleau, L. (2005), 'Micro-practices of strategic sensemaking and sensegiving: how middle managers interpret and sell change every day', *Journal of Management Studies*, 42/7: 1413–41.

Rumelt, R. P. (1984), 'Towards a strategic theory of the firm', in Lamb, R. B. (ed.), *Competitive Strategic Management*: 556–70. Englewood Cliffs, NJ: Prentice Hall.

Salvato, C. (2003), 'The role of micro-strategies in the engineering of firm evolution', *Journal of Management Studies*, 40/1: 83–108.

— (2009), 'Capabilities unveiled: the role of ordinary activities in the evolution of product development processes', *Organization Science*, 20/2: 384–409.

Seidl, D. (2007), 'General strategy concepts and the ecology of strategy discourses: a systemic-discursive perspective', *Organization Studies*, 28/2: 197–218.

Spender, J. C. (1996), 'Making knowledge the basis of a dynamic theory of the firm', *Strategic Management Journal*, 17/S1: 45–62.

Szulanski, G. (1996), 'Exploring internal stickiness: impediments to the transfer of best practice within the firm', *Strategic Management Journal*, 17/S2: 27–43.

Teece, D. J. (2007), 'Explicating dynamic capabilities: nature and microfoundations', *Strategic Management Journal*, 28/13: 1319–50.

Teece, D. J., Pisano, G., and Shuen, A. (1997), 'Dynamic capabilities and strategic management', *Strategic Management Journal*, 18/7: 509–33.

Vaara, E., and Whittington, R. (2012), 'Strategy-as-practice: taking social practices seriously', *Academy of Management Annals*, 6/1: 285–336.

Weick, K. E. (1995), *Sensemaking in Organizations*. Thousand Oaks, CA: Sage.

Wernerfelt, B. (1984), 'A resource-based view of the firm', *Strategic Management Journal*, 5/2: 171–80.

Whittington, R. (2006), 'Completing the practice turn in strategy research', *Organization Studies*, 27/5: 613–34.

Winter, S. G. (1987), 'Knowledge and competence as strategic assets', in Teece, D. J. (ed.), *The Competitive Advantage: Strategies for Industrial Innovation and Renewal*: 159–84. New York: Harper & Row.

— (1988), 'On Coase, competence, and the corporation', *Journal of Law, Economics, and Organization*, 4/1: 163–80.

— (2003), 'Understanding dynamic capabilities', *Strategic Management Journal*, 24/10: 991–5.

— (2011), 'Problems at the foundations? Comments on Felin and Foss', *Journal of Institutional Economics*, 7/2: 257–77.

— (2012), 'Capabilities: their origins and ancestry', *Journal of Management Studies*, 49/8: 1402–6.

Zander, U., and Kogut, B. (1995), 'Knowledge and the speed of the transfer and imitation of organizational capabilities: an empirical test', *Organization Science*, 6/1: 76–92.

Zollo, M., and Winter, S. G. (2002), 'Deliberate learning and the evolution of dynamic capabilities', *Organization Science*, 13/3: 339–51.

Theory of routine dynamics and connections to strategy as practice

MARTHA S. FELDMAN

Introduction

Recent research in the fields of both routines and strategy has used practice theory to focus attention on the dynamic and generative processes that result in strategy and routines and that have previously been studied as relatively static entities (Jarzabkowski 2005; Feldman and Orlikowski 2011; Whittington, this volume). Strategy as practice and the theory of routine dynamics are, thus, distinct but related theories of organizing. In this chapter I discuss similarities and synergies between the study of routines as dynamic processes and the study of strategy as practice. I focus particular attention on the emergent and mutually constituted nature of these organizational processes. I argue that these characteristics make the a priori identification of analytical entities difficult and misleading. As a result, definitions of routines and strategy, or of processes that constitute them, need to be developed in the context of specific empirical settings and specific research questions.

This chapter is written from the perspective of routines and seeks to identify some of the ways in which routine dynamics can contribute to strategy-as-practice research. The theory of routine dynamics is not only a compatible theory but also a useful tool for the study of strategy as practice. Accordingly, I begin the chapter with a description of routine dynamics. In the second section I discuss the connections between routine dynamics and strategy as practice. The third section explores challenges that research in routine dynamics and strategy as practice have in common, specifically the issue of identifying relevant action and enacted patterns and issues of multiplicity, or the 'problem' of identifying a singular routine or strategy. The fourth section presents studies of routine dynamics

that contribute to strategy as practice and that show how strategies emerge through routines. Methodological implications are summarized briefly in the conclusion.

Theory of routine dynamics

In recent years a theory of routines has developed through the work of many scholars. The foundational work was provided by Martha Feldman and Brian Pentland, each working independently and, later, jointly. Pentland's work developed the idea of routines as effortful accomplishments (Pentland and Reuter 1994). Feldman's work built on this idea and pointed out that routines were not only effortful but also emergent (Feldman, 2000). Together, the two have proposed a reconceptualization of routines as dynamic and generative (Feldman and Pentland 2003). This theory of routine dynamics argues that routines consist of both performative and ostensive aspects, that performative and ostensive aspects are mutually constitutive and that routines always entail both.

Organizational routines are 'repetitive, recognizable patterns of interdependent actions carried out by multiple actors' (Feldman and Pentland 2003: 95). This definition is based on and compatible with the research on routines since the 1940s (for example, Stene 1940), including work based on the behavioural theory of the firm (Cyert and March 1963) and on evolutionary economics (Nelson and Winter 1982) and discussions of recurrent action patterns (Cohen et al. 1996). This definition helps us to see the importance of studying both specific actions and recognizable patterns.

Specific actions make up the performative aspects of routines. When we talk about the performative aspect, we are focused on the specific actions taken in specific times and places by specific people or sometimes machines. The initial definition of the performative aspect stated that the actions are taken by people (Feldman and Pentland 2003: 95). Influenced by interest in sociomateriality and Latour's focus on non-human actants, this formulation broadened to include objects as capable of action (D'Adderio 2008; 2011; Pentland and Feldman 2008; Pentland, Haerem and Hillison 2011; Pentland *et al.* 2012). Computers are one of the most accessible examples of objects that act, but garbage trucks (Turner and Rindova 2012), pricing models (Zbaracki and Bergen 2010) or communities (D'Adderio 2014) may also act.

Action is sometimes understood to imply intentionality, autonomy and control, as in rational action (Joas 1996). This is not the meaning I use here. Indeed, such a meaning misses much of the potential in action for creativity (Joas 1996). Instead, by 'action', I am referring to the 'doings and sayings' (since sayings are a form of doings) that make up practices (Schatzki 2012: 15). Such actions are situated (Suchman 2007) and may be more or less mindful (Levinthal and Rerup 2006). Action taken in routines is often directed towards accomplishing a task, but the many structures created and recreated through the actions – or, indeed, through the routines – may not be intended, foreseen or perceived (Giddens 1984; Bourdieu 1990). This way of conceptualizing action eschews the separation of mind and body. Thus, action in routines is embodied, but being embodied does not imply being mindless or on autopilot.

Recognizable patterns comprise the ostensive aspect of routines. The ostensive aspect is the routine in principle or the patterns that are created and recreated through the specific actions taken in specific times and places (Feldman 2000; Feldman and Pentland 2003). It is made up of enacted patterns. In other words, the ostensive aspect is an abstraction or an interpretation of what the actions add up to (Dionysiou and Tsoukas 2013). While it is possible to describe in writing a moment in the development of such patterns, it is a mistake to equate the ostensive aspect with formal procedures such as standard operating procedures (Pentland and Feldman 2008). Ostensive aspects are more

stable than performances but less stable than written or formal procedures, because they are, in fact, created and recreated through performance. As performances vary, ostensive patterns change.

While 'the routine in principle' could be confused with something that exists only as an idea or a routine that is not enacted, this is not the meaning used in this theory, and it is one of the reasons for using the term 'ostensive'. Merriam-Webster defines 'ostensive' as 'of, relating to, or constituting definition by *exemplifying* the thing or quality being defined' (emphasis added).[1] Wittgenstein uses colour (for example, red or blue) as an example of an ostensive definition (Wittgenstein 2001 [1951]). While there is a scientific definition of blue (for example, a range of light wavelengths), on an everyday basis we know the colour blue through the various blues (or objects coloured blue) that exemplify blue. In other words, there are things *we can point to* that make up the pattern that we recognize as blue. Performances are what we can point to that make up the ostensive patterns. Ostensive aspects, therefore, always have performances as a referent (see also Latour 1986; Sevon 1996).

Another complication associated with the ostensive aspect is that there are many patterns that are enacted as people enact routines. Enacting a routine involves performing some actions, usually in sequence. A hiring routine, for instance, may involve advertising a position, **applying**, reviewing applications, **waiting to hear back**, notifying applicants, *interviewing*, **waiting to hear back**, making an offer and **responding to the offer**. Note that, in this list, many actions (those in bold font) are from the perspective of the hiring person or organization and other actions (those in regular font) are from the perspective of the person applying. Interviewing is a pattern that could be described from either of these points of view. Thus, we already have at least two patterns that are part of the ostensive aspect.

This description of a routine is pretty abstract, however. There are many ways of advertising or interviewing, of applying or waiting. Hiring

---

[1] See www.merriam-webster.com/dictionary/ostensive.

routines can be enacted in ways that are alienating and intimidating or in ways that create patterns of organizational membership and begin the training process (Feldman 2000). Budgeting routines can be enacted in ways that enhance coordination across units or exacerbate conflict across units (Feldman 2003). Pricing can be enacted in ways that promote organizational truces or that encourage truces to collapse (Zbaracki and Bergen 2010). Garbage collection can be enacted in ways that increase or decrease coordination with customers (Turner and Rindova 2012). Replicating a production process can be enacted in ways that produce more alignment or more improvement (D'Adderio 2014). For any routine, therefore, there are many possible patterns that comprise the ostensive aspect.

The existence of many possible patterns raises the reasonable question: what is *the* routine? (As I point out below, there is an analogous question about strategy.) The short answer is that this question cannot be answered a priori, and that answering it a priori has often led people to mistake a standard operating procedure or espoused routine for enacted routines. It is often convenient for communication, however, whether for research or for practice, to identify routines in relation to a task such as hiring or budgeting or pricing, and to identify some of the steps that may be involved in accomplishing or pursuing such tasks. An alternative approach is more experiential. From this perspective, routines are the experience of 'I (or we) can do it again'. The people who are 'doing it again' identify what is being done, and the patterns of action they identify comprise the routine. One version of this experiential approach has been articulated as arising from a process of mutual role-taking that produces a shared understanding of what we are doing (Dionysiou and Tsoukas 2013).

This issue of multiple patterns shows that the identification of routine cannot be separated from actions that people (or machines) take and that create and recreate patterns. Neither a performance nor a pattern is a routine. (Hence, there are no performative routines or ostensive routines.) While people (or machines) can certainly take action independent of a specific pattern, patterns in the ostensive aspect are enacted or made of actions,

and we cannot know whether an action is part of the performative aspect of a routine without connecting it to one or more patterns that are part of the ostensive aspect of a routine. Routines are always comprised of both performances and patterns. Thus, the mutually constitutive relationship of performative and ostensive is central to this practice-based theory of routines.

Mutual constitution

The relationship of performative and ostensive aspects is a relationship of mutual constitution. It is analogous to a relationship of agency and structure. In much of social science, relationships of agency and structure or individual and institution, for instance, have been theorized as contrasting or dualistic ontologies (Suchman 2007; Lave 1988; Nicolini 2012). In a practice ontology, however, these are not dualistic but mutually constitutive. This ontological relationship is most starkly described by Giddens but is also central to practice theory as articulated by Bourdieu (Feldman and Orlikowski 2011). Giddens (1984), for instance, refers to structure as both medium and outcome. Structure is a medium for agentic action and the outcome of agentic action. In other words, we cannot take action without operating within structures and without producing and reproducing them.

Mutual constitution is central to a practice ontology and differs from either a linear feedback relationship, in which two independent entities influence one another, or a dualistic relationship, in which entities have oppositional ontologies (Feldman and Orlikowski 2011). In relations of mutual constitution, separation is an analytical convenience, and what appear to be separate entities cannot exist independently of one another. To use an example other than from organizations, the wind and the wind blowing are not separate things. The wind is only wind as it blows (Elias 1978, cited by Emirbayer 1997). Michel's work based on an ethnographic study of investment banks provides an organizational example. She demonstrates the mutual constitution of person and organization by showing that otherwise similar people experienced being (ontology as shown through their experience of time, of causality, of language and of personhood) very differently through the practices they enacted in the two different banks (Michel 2014). This study also shows how these practices and routines constituted different orientations to organizational change – an important strategic outcome.

This relationship of mutual constitution is particularly important to understanding the dynamic nature of routines. The mutual constitution of performances and patterns (or performative and ostensive aspects) generates both apparent stability and more or less change. In other words, stability and change in routines are generated through the acting and re-enacting of routines, including the variations, modifications and alterations that are intrinsic to the enacting (Feldman 2000; Feldman and Pentland 2003). By seeing that the same relationship creates both stability and change, we see that stability and change are also mutually constituted (Tsoukas and Chia 2002; Farjoun 2010).

The relationship of mutual constitution is also fundamental to the relation between routines and strategy. This relation is explored in the following section. Here I note simply that it is, in large part, the relation between actions and patterns that has made both routines and strategy attractive to scholars of practice. Embedded in the very idea of routine or strategy is the idea of patterns that are enacted.

Routine dynamics and strategy as practice

Strategy as practice focuses on the 'doing' of strategy through both formal and informal practices (Whittington 1996; Jarzabkowski 2005; Johnson et al. 2007; Golsorkhi et al. 2010; Vaara and Whittington 2012). Strategy as practice, like routine dynamics, is based on practice theory (Jarzabkowski 2005; Whittington 2010, Vaara and Whittington, 2012).

Strategy as practice includes the study of activities that are consciously and intentionally associated with developing and implementing organizational strategy, as well as the study of activities that contribute to the emergence of strategy (Jarzabkowski, Balogun and Seidl 2007; Vaara and Whittington 2012). While avoiding

methodological individualism, strategy as practice focuses attention on the roles of actors (Vaara and Whittington 2012) and the specifically human nature of the actors who enact strategy (Jarzabkowski, Balogun and Seidl 2007; Jarzabkowski and Spee 2009). Strategy as practice may be studied from the micro, meso or macro perspective, though to date most of the studies are oriented to the micro or meso level (Jarzabkowski and Spee 2009).

Organizational routines are implicated in strategy as practice in at least three ways. First, strategizing, like any organizational process, is enacted through routines. Formal strategic practices have been the focus of many studies of strategy as practice (Golsorkhi et al. 2010). Although not all of these would qualify as routines, many of them do. There are, for example, routines for strategy workshops (Hendry and Seidl 2003) and strategy meetings (Jarzabkowski and Seidl 2008). Moreover, a myriad of formal administrative routines affect the strategizing process (Jarzabkowski 2003; 2005).

Second, routines and strategy can both be understood as emergent, enacted practices. While traditional understandings of routines and strategy have located both the phenomena in written formulations and the decisions of upper-level management, the practice turn in each area has focused attention on enactment. Routines and strategies that exist only on paper are empty formalizations, and specific actions taken constitute what routines and strategies are in practice. Hendry, Kiel and Nicholson (2010), for instance, shows that the specific practices of boards produce different kinds of oversight. Similarly, Sonenshein (2013) shows that a strategy of fostering creativity in the context of a retail franchise involves the enactment of specific practices enacted by the managers and sales people.

Third, strategy and routines are recursively related. Just as action and pattern are mutually constituted, so are strategies and routines (Hendry and Seidl 2003; Salvato 2003). Strategy constrains routines and, *at the same time*, the routines constrained by strategy produce the strategy that constrain them. As a result of this mutual constitution of strategy and routines, understanding the nature of routines is useful for understanding the practices of strategy. Understanding the dynamics of routines and how they contribute to stability and change are particularly important for seeing how the routines implicated in strategy practices contribute to the stability and change of organizational strategies.

Salvato, for instance, shows that strategic evolution results from the repetition of 'bundles of micro-activities' executed by people at the lower as well as the upper levels of an organization. These micro-activities, of which routines are a significant part, constitute core micro-strategies subject to managerial guidance through the introduction of new variations and their selective retention (Salvato 2003).

Some routines (for example, the strategy meeting) are communication episodes that are particularly significant in the production of strategy. These can be analysed according to the Luhmannian evolutionary model, in which the 'communicative system generates random mutations and then "selects" changes from these' (Hendry and Seidl 2003: 180). As Hendry and Seidl argue, seeing these routines as Luhmannian episodes alerts us to the importance of how they are initiated and whether the initiation allows for strategic reflection, how they are ended and whether the ending allows for strategic outcomes to be integrated without disrupting other routines that are central to stability, and whether they are conducted in ways that allow for structural generativity.

Routines also contribute to organizational schema (Rerup and Feldman 2011), and the management of schema change is an important part of strategic sensemaking (Balogun and Johnson 2004; 2005). Empirical studies of strategic change have shown the importance of this relationship between routines and schema (Rouleau 2005; Jarzabkowski, Lê and Feldman 2012). Rouleau, for instance, analysed routines (and conversations) in the implementation of a strategic change, and shows how middle managers used routines (and conversations) to position both sensemaking and sensegiving when a clothing company expanded its lines of fashion. As she describes it, 'The focus is on the way managers – not only top management but middle and lower teams and by extension every organizational member – provide information and influence people around them by modifying their daily routines and adjusting their discourse to the new strategic orientation' (Rouleau 2005: 1433).

Similarly, Jarzabkowski, Lê and Feldman (2012) describe how cycles of routines were essential to the reconstruction of end-to-end management in a British utility when that critical strategic capability was disrupted as the result of a regulatory change. They show that the effort to enact routines enabled people first to identify what was missing and then to experiment with ways of filling the void. Later cycles of routine enactment provided ways of testing the new elements and stabilizing them into new schemas of how to accomplish the work.

Challenges in routines theory and strategy as practice

The similarity in theoretical foundation means that strategy as practice and routines theory share some similar challenges. In the following, I discuss the challenge of identifying actions and patterns, as well as the related challenge of multiplicity, some of the forms these challenges take and some ways that scholars, particularly scholars of routines, have dealt with them. Relations of mutual constitution are intrinsic to the challenges discussed below. As Emirbayer comments in his manifesto for a relational sociology, 'When beginning with ramifying webs of relations rather than substances, it becomes notoriously difficult to justify the empirical boundaries that one draws' (Emirbayer 1997: 304). Indeed, mutual constitution implies continuous constitution and the consequent difficulty in a priori identification of entities, even for the purposes of analysis.

Identifying actions and patterns

A central issue for both strategy as practice and routines theory is identifying relevant actions. In routines theory, this is the performative aspect. While the performative aspect of routines is easier to define and to grasp than the ostensive aspect, specific actions taken at specific times and places are often missing in organizational research on either routines or strategy. This may be partly a consequence of the need to summarize and generalize and fit empirical studies into thirty-page journal articles, but it is also because taking action and enactment seriously open up a great deal of complexity. In the earlier part of this chapter I identified action as not necessarily intentional and established that the actions considered to be part of a routine might differ depending on point of view and also on the patterns being enacted. Potentially, any action could be part of a routine. If routines are practices with the potential to change as they are enacted, rather than stable and inertial entities, how do you know that an action is part of a routine?

Strategy may have an even broader range of actions that could potentially be considered strategic. A review of strategy-as-practice research shows that actions taken by top managers (Jarzabkowski 2005; 2010), by middle managers (Whittington 2010) and by any of the people who work in organizations (Johnson et al. 2007: 7) are considered relevant. Jarzabkowski and Spee (2009) suggest that strategy as practice may also be concerned with the actions of people outside organizations. Actions taken by any of these groups could take many different forms.

Strategy as practice brings into the field of strategy research what are sometimes referred to as 'micro-activities' (Johnson, Melin and Whittington 2003: 3, cited by Johnson et al. 2007) or as 'micro-level social activities, processes and practices' (Golshorski et al. 2010: 1). In other words, strategy as practice, like routines research, is concerned with the specific actions taken in specific times and places; and, as with routines research, it is in the bounding of these actions as relevant to enacting strategy that complications emerge.

Johnson et al. (2007: 7) specify that they are talking about 'what people do in relation to strategy' and highlight, in particular, board meetings and strategy awaydays. In other words, strategy as practice is constrained to being related to something strategic. What does it mean to be strategic, though? Is 'strategic' defined by something external to practices such that some practices are strategic and others are not? Is it possible that strategy

is really what is produced by the accumulated actions of people acting in and through an organization? Or is strategy related to reinforcement or change in the direction of specified (and intentional) organizational action?

The logic of mutual constitution suggests that actions and patterns cannot be defined or identified independently of one another. They are mutually constituted. For routines, this means that a routine cannot be identified as performative or ostensive, but must consist of both actions and enacted patterns. As a result, a routine cannot be defined a priori but only as it is enacted. Following the same logic, what is strategic cannot be defined a priori but must be justified in the context of a specific organization and the specific questions being explored through research.

Without denying this complexity, routines researchers have found that a definition of action that provides some on-the-ground criteria has been useful. Thus, most routines research identifies specific *observable* actions that are identified either by the people who take the actions or by others as related to accomplishing a task, such as hiring or training an employee (Feldman 2000; Rerup and Feldman 2011), setting the price of a product (Zbaracki and Bergen 2010), collecting garbage (Turner and Rindova 2012) or developing a new product (Salvato 2009) or technology (Howard-Grenville 2005). Such a definition makes it possible to use observations of what people are doing and their descriptions of the way they work to build routines from actions.

Critics will argue that identifying the relevance of action in relation to accomplishing a task is smuggling intention in as an explanatory variable. Chia and his co-authors claim that placing primacy on the prior strategic intent of actions rests on a presumption of methodological individualism and the concomitant micro/macro distinction (Chia and Holt 2006; 2009; Chia and McKay 2007). The problem with these presumptions is the implication that individuals are entities that are independent of their contexts (Michel 2014). This implication leads to misunderstandings about the nature of practice and the relationship to strategy. In particular, it suggests that strategy explains practice rather than strategy being 'a *discernible pattern* emerging in a stream of actions' (Chia and McKay 2007: 224, emphasis in original). In the latter formulation the identification of strategy is a pattern lifted out of or excerpted from ongoing practices rather than the cause of these practices.

Chia and Holt address this problem by distinguishing between purposive and purposeful action. 'A purposive creation has its centre of gravity in itself; one that is goal oriented (i.e., purposeful) has its centre external to itself; the worth of one resides in being, that of the other in its result' (Chia and Holt 2009: 110). While earlier formulations of purposiveness rested on notions of mindlessness (for example, Chia and McKay 2007: 235), this formulation is consistent with Schatzki's notion that action often has 'intentional directedness' (Schatzki 2012: 15) without suggesting that cognitive representations either determine actions or explain outcomes. Indeed, Chia and Holt (2009: 111) argue that 'local absorbed purposive actions may often give rise unexpectedly to more systemic outcomes that were never intended on the part of the actors themselves'.

In research on routines, this internal centre of gravity has been discussed as endogenous change or how routines change through their enactment (Feldman 2000; Pentland, Haerem and Hillison 2011.) While people may be oriented to hiring or training or budgeting or pricing, their actions may change largely in orientation to a wide range of enacted patterns they are endogenously creating and recreating, or what Mark Johnson refers to as 'aesthetics' (Johnson 2007: 89).[2] As a result, the ostensive patterns are not defined only as they relate to tasks but also to a broad range of patterns that are enacted as people orient to tasks. For example, in my research on university housing, building directors enacted a damage assessment routine through a series of actions that produced a

professional identity pattern of landlord rather than their preferred professional identity of educator. The ostensive pattern of landlord was sufficiently distasteful that they reconfigured a routine that efficiently assessed damage and recouped the cost of these damages for a routine that took a great deal more of their time to accomplish the same ends (Feldman 2003; Sandberg and Tsoukas 2011).

Thus, related to the challenge of relevant action is the challenge of identifying patterns. The term 'ostensive aspect' in the theory of routines serves as a mid-range concept (Merton 1968) that provides a way of abstracting while remaining connected to the empirical context. It allows one to distinguish routines from written rules or formal instantiations – the standard operating procedures or espoused routines that are often mistaken for, and mask, the enacted routine. It also provides a way of talking about the multiplicity of enacted patterns.

To my knowledge, there is no equivalent to the ostensive aspects in strategy as practice. While in some ways similar (and both deriving from Wittgenstein), language games, as discussed by Mantere (2010), appear to have a broader analytical scope. The concept is used to discuss several different relationships: (1) that words may mean very different things in different organizations and to different people within the same organization (for example, what does empowerment mean?); (2) how words take on meaning in context (for example, how do people negotiate the meaning of strategy?); and (3) what patterns are created through strategic action (for example, is inclusion or exclusion created?). The concept of ostensive aspects is more limited than the concept of language games, relating most closely to the third relationship – the patterns created through strategic action.

While it is not an easy concept, the notion of 'ostensive' does provide a way of talking about patterns that are produced through action, as opposed to imagined, intended or mandated patterns. In strategy as practice such a concept could provide a basis for discussions about what makes the patterns strategic and what counts as strategic action. It would also help establish that what is strategic and that what counts as strategic action have to be defined on a case-by-case basis.

---

[2] Johnson defines aesthetics as the following: 'By the term "aesthetics" I do not mean merely the philosophy of art and beauty; rather, I regard aesthetics as concerning everything that goes into our ability to grasp the meaning and significance of any aspect of our experience, and so it involves form and structure, the qualities that define a situation, our felt sense of the meaning of things, our rhythmic engagement with our surroundings, our emotional interactions and on and on.'

Multiplicity

Taking seriously the idea that routines and strategies are emergent and dependent upon the specific actions taken over time creates another challenge beyond the issue of the identification of actions and patterns. I refer to this challenge here as multiplicity, but it could also be called heterogeneity or dispersion. What if the actions taken can add up to many different patterns? What if many different combinations of actions can produce the same pattern? If routines are not the same as the written formulation, then how do we know what *the* routine is? If strategy is not what top managers say it is, then how do we know what *the* strategy is?

A good example of multiplicity in organizational routines has emerged from studies of microfinance organizations (Canales 2011; 2014). Microfinance involves lending small amounts of money to people who do not have access to more traditional bank loans. Microfinance lending uses social rather than material collateral and takes the bank to the people rather than assuming people will come to the bank. Loan officers in microfinance perform many of the same tasks as in traditional banks, such as approving loans and accounting for repayment.

Canales has found that loan officer routines can be enacted in two different ways within the same organization (and guided by the same rules). He refers to these as 'the letter of the law' and 'the spirit of the law'. 'Spirit of the law' loan officers enact routines of moneylending through a holistic approach that does not separate the business interactions from the personal and familial relations of the person receiving the loan. They help the loan recipient solve problems and build networks. 'Spirit of the law' loan officers tend to extend deadlines when the recipient has experienced problems, such as weather conditions or health problems, that make it difficult to repay. 'Letter of the law' loan officers enact routines of moneylending by limiting their engagement to transactions directly related to the loan. They do not provide advice or engage in problem-solving, and they do enforce deadlines for repayment strictly.

Though Canales does not use the language of performative and ostensive, 'letter of the law' and 'spirit of the law' are ostensive patterns of the moneylending routine. They are enacted through the specific performances of specific loan officers as they lend money to specific people at specific times and places. These ostensive patterns are distinct from, though not entirely independent of, the written rules and regulations of the microfinance organizations. In this case, the multiplicity is multiple patterns created by different people enacting the same routine in different ways.

Multiplicity may also occur as the same people enact the same routine in different ways. Salvato (2009), for instance, found that ways of enacting the routine for new product development mirrored closely the standard operating procedure only about 40 per cent of the time in the design firm he studied (Alessi). He refers to this kind of multiplicity as dispersion. Unlike the microfinance example, the multiplicity is not individual interpretations of the new product development routine, but is related to the situated nature of each project. Salvato (2009: 393) refers to these as 'everyday experimental activities performed by internal or external agents'. What is significant here is not just that the routine is performed differently for different projects but that the organization consistently produces creativity through enacting these situated multiple versions of product development.

Grand (2012) provides a somewhat different perspective on multiplicity in routine enactment. He examines a high-fashion fabric-manufacturing firm that has been at the forefront of its field for decades (Jakob Schläpfer). This firm consistently produces different outcomes by enacting the same routines. Grand identified six creativity routines, including a routine for connecting to the past as well as a routine for moving on, which Grand refers to as the emptying routine. The analysis shows that, while the routines are not all equally active at the same time, their consistent presence and interactive nature is important to the creative work of the firm. The multiplicity here is multiple – in the variety of routines, in the different ways they come together and in the creative outcomes.

Thus, we have different forms of multiplicity. There are individual orientations and interpretations of the same routine, as reflected in the Canales research. Empirically, this is probably the most common form of multiplicity, at least as reflected in current research. These differences may be based upon temporal orientation (Howard-Grenville 2005), position in the supply chain (Zbaracki and Bergen 2010), organizational role (Feldman 2003, Turner and Rindova 2012) or professional or organizational culture (D'Adderio 2014). We also have the same routines combining to produce different outcomes over time, however, as in the case of Grand's (2012) research, and organizations that have 'a routine' that is regularly innovated, as in Salvato's research.

Scholars have begun to address the issue of multiplicity as it relates to routines. Dionysiou and Tsoukas (2013) have proposed a process based on symbolic interaction dynamics. They suggest that individual role-taking is an important mechanism in creating the patterns that constitute the ostensive aspect of routines. Individuals experience the routine relationally, and 'each participant abstracts and generalizes, not simply from personal understandings and actions but from understandings and actions that have been jointly, intersubjectively established' (Dionysiou and Tsoukas 2013: 191). This process allows for both a core of shared experience and a periphery of more idiosyncratic experiences. Others have proposed patterning as the general process through which ostensive patterns are created (Feldman et al. 2013). These proposals are concerned both with the experience of enacting a routine and with how people enacting routines know what they are doing, as opposed to identifying patterns from an external perspective. While it is possible to observe actions from the outside and to impute patterns to these actions, these approaches suggest that we may be able to learn a great deal about the potentiality of actions within organizations by taking seriously the patterns as experienced by those enacting them. The patterns people experience as they enact them are important guides to the actions that make sense to take when adjustments need to be made to continue a pattern or when new patterns need to be enacted (Jarzabkowski, Lê and Feldman 2012).

Routine dynamics as contribution to strategy as practice

Although it has long been clear that strategic decisions affect how routines are designed, the research in routine dynamics supports SAP research by focusing on the reverse: the effects of the actions and patterns of routines on the organizational capabilities and firm strategies (Salvato and Rerup 2011). Scholars working from routines up to strategy have suggested a number of ways in which strategies emerge through routines.

Rerup and Feldman (2011), for instance, have pointed out that, as problems in enacting routines arise and are resolved, the resolutions can have implications for and raise serious questions relevant to organizational schemata, or what we might call the ostensive aspect of the organizational strategy. In the case of their research, they show how resolving problems enacting routines that were consistent with an espoused organizational schema characterized by an either/or orientation (for example, either entrepreneurial or bureaucratic; either like a family or professional) pushed the organization towards an enacted schema characterized by a both/and orientation (both entrepreneurial and bureaucratic; both family-like and professional). Thus, this research shows a dynamic interplay between the enacted routines (what it is possible to do) and the enacted organizational schemata or emergent strategy (what kind of organization this is and how it operates).

Canales' research on microfinance provides another example of the relationship between the way routines are enacted and organizational strategy (Canales 2014). He argues that the way loan officers enact moneylending adds up to the strategy for the organization. If all (or most) loan officers enact the routines of moneylending in similar ways (either 'letter of the law' or 'spirit of the law'), the strategy of the organization is defined by that pattern. When microfinance organizations have loan officers who enact different moneylending routines, however, the emergent strategy depends on how these routines relate to one another. Canales has found that organizational structures that encourage 'letter of the law' and 'spirit of the law' loan officers to engage with and take into consideration one another's concerns are more successful at the organizational or branch level, because 'spirit of the law' loan officers are required to take into consideration the accounting issue while 'letter of the law' officers are required to take into consideration the more 'human' issues. This emergent strategy takes advantage of the strengths of each approach. Of course, strategies can also emerge in which one way of enacting the lending routines dominates and that do not combine the strengths of each approach.

While strategies may emerge without intervention by management, management can play an important role in taking advantage of the various ways that routines can be enacted. Salvato (2009) found that multiplicity or dispersion arose naturally through the 'everyday experimental activities performed by internal or external agents' (Salvato 2009: 393), but that in many of the cases he studied (22 per cent) management took action to incorporate and combine these adaptations in ways that were beneficial to the creative potential of the organization.

Grand observed management practices that even more systematically combined the many actions and patterns involved in creativity routines (Grand 2012). He proposes that strategic management consists of the enactment of pragmatic engagement regimes that are oriented both normatively (to some kind of good) and practically (to some kind of reality). The different orientations allow pragmatic engagement regimes to enable managers to scale up and down continuously between the specific and the general. Grand identified four engagement regimes in the fabric-manufacturing firm. The connections between the creativity routines discussed earlier are not simply temporal or sequential but are woven together through engagement regimes, each of which picks up some of the strands of the creativity routines. In this way the multiplicity of enacted performances add up not only to the performance of routines but also to strategic capabilities.

Through Grand's theorizing, strategic management becomes a fully dynamic activity connecting the micro (enacted performances of people in organizations) and the macro (strategic regimes). Strategic capabilities are not conceived as bundles of routines. The black box of the routine is fully open and the engagement regimes perform the important function of weaving together performances that the routines make available. Thus, routines perform tasks and also make available a multiplicity of potential capacities. Strategy is related to routines, but is neither in control of routines nor simply the accumulation of routines. Management activity is organized through the engagement regimes, which create connections between the multiplicity of performances enacted through routines and the multiplicity of strategy potentialities.

Conclusion

Research on routine dynamics and research on strategy as practice share a common theoretical foundation. As a result, they share many of the same conceptual challenges. These challenges arise not from inconsistencies in the theoretical foundation but from expectations borne of more static orientations in which the focus of study can be identified as if it were independent. The mutual constitution of actions and patterns in both routines and strategy creates opportunities for expanding our capacity to understand the dynamic nature of these organizational phenomena and the ways they are enacted.

These theoretical challenges have methodological implications, which I have hinted at throughout the discussion. Theories that are based on the independence of entities support methodological expectations that entities can be defined independently of their relationality. Theories of practice, by contrast, entail relationality (Feldman and Orlikowki 2011; Nicolini 2012; Schtazki 2012). As described by Emirbayer (1997), relationality requires us to identify our focus of analysis in situ rather than a priori. This approach to analysis is exemplified in the work on knowing in practice (Lave 1988; Orlikowski 2002; Nicolini, Gherardi and Yanow 2003; Gherardi 2006), in work on resourcing (Feldman 2004; Howard-Grenville

2007; Feldman and Quick 2009; Feldman and Worline 2012; Sonenshein 2014; Dittrich and Seidl 2014) and in some recent work on sociomateriality (Orlikowski 2007; Orlikowski and Scott 2008; D'Adderio 2014).

What the practice approach entails is defining terms as they are enacted in relation to specific empirical contexts as well as specific research questions. In routines research this means, for instance, that neither the performative nor the ostensive aspect of routines is defined a priori. In strategy research, what makes action strategic, for example, would be defined relationally. This approach entails the active engagement of the researcher in identifying analytical features of routines and strategies and explaining the choices made in relation to the empirical context and the research question. This does not preclude the possibility of comparing routines or strategies across organizational contexts, but it does require the researcher to explain why the comparison is valid for the research at hand.

As research continues, there are many opportunities for developing the connections between the dynamics of routines and strategy as practice. As the examples in this chapter show, we have much to gain by marrying these compatible approaches. The theorizing in both fields is relatively young, but there is much potential for cross-fertilization and mutual learning.

References

Balogun, J., and Johnson, G. (2004), 'Organizational restructuring and middle manager sensemaking', *Academy of Management Journal*, 47/4: 523–49.

Balogun, J. (2005), 'From intended strategies to unintended outcomes: the impact of change recipient sensemaking', *Organization Studies*, 26/11: 1573–601.

Bourdieu, P. (1990), *The Logic of Practice*. Cambridge: Polity.

Canales, R. (2011), 'Rule bending, sociological citizenship, and organizational contestation in microfinance', *Regulation and Governance*, 5/1: 90–117.

Canales, R. (2014), 'Weaving straw into gold: managing organizational tensions between standardization and flexibility in microfinance', *Organization Science*, 25/1: 1–28.

Chia, R., and Holt, R. (2006), 'Strategy as practical coping: a Heideggerian perspective', *Organization Studies*, 27/5: 635–55.

(2009), *Strategy without Design: The Silent Efficacy of Indirect Action*. Cambridge University Press:

Chia, R., and MacKay, B. (2007), 'Post-processual challenges for the emerging strategy-as-practice perspective: discovering strategy in the logic of practice', *Human Relations*, 60/1: 217–42.

Cohen, M. D., Burkhart, R., Dosi, G., Egidi, M., Marengo, L., Warglien, M., and Winter, S. G. (1996), 'Contemporary issues in research on routines and other recurring action patterns of organizations', *Industrial and Corporate Change*, 5/3: 653–98.

Cyert, R. M., and March, J. G. (1963), *A Behavioral Theory of the Firm*. Englewood Cliffs, NJ: Prentice Hall.

D'Adderio, L. (2008), 'The performativity of routines: theorising the influence of artefacts and distributed agencies on routines dynamics', *Research Policy*, 37/5: 769–89.

(2011), 'Artifacts at the centre of routines: performing the material turn in routines theory', *Journal of Institutional Economics*, 7/S2: 197–230.

(2014), 'The replication dilemma unravelled: how organizations balance multiple goals in routine transfer', *Organization Science*, 25/5: 1325–50.

Dionysiou, D., and Tsoukas, H. (2013), 'Understanding the (re)creation of routines from within: a symbolic interactionist perspective', *Academy of Management Review*, 38/2: 181–205.

Dittrich, K., and Seidl, D. (2014), 'Resourcing routine change: how resources contribute to routine dynamics', paper presented at the sixth 'International symposium on process organization studies', Rhodes, 20 June.

Elias, N. (1978), *What Is Sociology?* New York: Columbia University Press.

Emirbayer, M. (1997), 'Manifesto for a relational sociology', *American Journal of Sociology*, 103/2: 281–317.

Farjoun, M. (2010), 'Beyond dualism: stability and change as a duality', *Academy of Management Review*, 35/2: 202–25.

Feldman, M. S. (2000), 'Organizational routines as a source of continuous change', *Organization Science*, 11/6: 611–29.

(2003), 'A performative perspective on stability and change in organizational routines', *Industrial and Corporate Change*, 12/4: 727–52.

(2004), 'Resources in emerging structures and processes of change', *Organization Science*, 15/3: 295–309.

Feldman, M. S., and Orlikowski, W. J. (2011), 'Theorizing practice and practicing theory', *Organization Science*, 22/5: 1240–53.

Feldman, M. S., and Pentland, B. T. (2003), 'Reconceptualizing organizational routines as a source of flexibility and change', *Administrative Science Quarterly*, 48/1: 94–118.

Feldman, M. S., and Quick, K. S. (2009), 'Generating resources and energizing frameworks through inclusive public management', *International Public Management Journal*, 12/2: 137–71.

Feldman, M. S., and Worline, M. W. (2012), 'Resources, resourcing, and ampliative cycles in organizations', in Cameron, K., and Spreitzer, G. (eds.), *The Oxford Handbook of Positive Organizational Scholarship*: 629–41. New York: Oxford University Press.

Feldman, M. S., Worline, M. W., Baker, N., and Lowerson, V. (2013), 'Routines, disruption and the temporalities of continuity', paper presented at the twenty-ninth European Group for Organizational Studies colloquium, Montreal, 4 July.

Gherardi, S. (2006), *Organizational Knowledge: The Texture of Workplace Learning*. Oxford: Blackwell.

Giddens, A. (1984), *The Constitution of Society*. Cambridge: Polity.

Golsorkhi, D., Rouleau, L., Seidl, D., and Vaara, E. (2010), 'Introduction: what is strategy as practice?', in *Cambridge Handbook of Strategy as Practice*: 1–20. Cambridge University Press.

Grand, S. (2012), 'Routines, strategies and management: engaging for recurrent creation "at the edge"', *Habilitation manuscript*. University of St. Gallen, Switzerland.

Hendry, K. P., Kiel, G. C., and Nicholson, G. (2010), 'How boards strategise: a strategy as practice view', *Long Range Planning*, 43/1: 33–56.

Hendry, J., and Seidl, D. (2003), 'The structure and significance of strategic episodes: social systems theory and the routine practices of strategic change', *Journal of Management Studies*, 40/1: 175–96.

Howard-Grenville, J. A. (2005), 'The persistence of flexible organizational routines: the role of agency and organizational context', *Organization Science*, 16/6: 618–36.

(2007), 'Developing issue-selling effectiveness over time: issue selling as resourcing', *Organization Science*, 18/4: 560–77.

Jarzabkowski, P. (2003), 'Strategic practices: an activity theory perspective on continuity and change', *Journal of Management Studies*, 40/1: 23–55.

Jarzabkowski, P. (2005), *Strategy as Practice: An Activity-Based Approach*. London: Sage.

(2010), 'An activity-theory approach to strategy as practice', in Golshorski, D., Rouleau, L., Seidl, D., and Vaara, E. (eds.), *Cambridge Handbook of Strategy as Practice*: 127–40. Cambridge University Press.

Jarzabkowski, P., Balogun, J., and Seidl, D. (2007), 'Strategizing: the challenges of a practice perspective', *Human Relations*, 60/1: 5–27.

Jarzabkowski, P., Lê, J., and Feldman, M. S. (2012), 'Toward a theory of coordinating: creating coordinating mechanisms in practice', *Organization Science*, 23/4: 907–27.

Jarzabkowski, P., and Seidl, D. (2008), 'The role of meetings in the social practice of strategy', *Organization Studies*, 29/11: 1391–426.

Jarzabkowski, P., and Spee, P. (2009), 'Strategy-as-practice: a review and future directions for the field', *International Journal of Management Reviews*, 11/1: 69–95.

Joas, H. (1996), *The Creativity of Action*. University of Chicago Press.

Johnson, G., Melin, L., and Whittington, R. (2003), 'Guest editors' introduction: micro strategy and strategizing: towards an activity-based view', *Journal of Management Studies*, 40/1: 3–22.

Johnson, G., Langley, A., Melin, L., and Whittington, R. (2007), *Strategy as Practice: Research Directions and Resources*. Cambridge University Press.

Johnson, M. (2007), '"The stone that was cast out shall become the cornerstone": the bodily aesthetics of human meaning', *Journal of Visual Art Practice*, 6/2: 89–103.

Latour, B. (1986), 'The powers of association', in Law, J. (ed.), *Power, Action and Belief: A New Sociology of Knowledge?*: 264–80. London: Routledge & Kegan Paul.

Lave, J. (1988), *Cognition in Practice*. Cambridge University Press.

Levinthal, D. A., and Rerup, C. (2006), 'Crossing an apparent chasm: bridging mindful and less mindful perspectives on organizational learning', *Organization Science*, 17/4: 502–13.

Mantere, S. (2010), 'A Wittgensteinian perspective on strategizing', in Golshorski, D., Rouleau, L., Seidl, D., and Vaara, E. (eds.), *Cambridge Handbook of Strategy as Practice*: 155–67. Cambridge University Press.

Merton, R. K. (1968), *Social Theory and Social Structure*. New York: Free Press.

Michel, A. (2014), 'The mutual constitution of persons and organizations: an ontological perspective on organizational change', *Organization Science*, 25/4: 1082–110.

Nelson, R. R., and Winter, S. G. (1982), *An Evolutionary Theory of Economic Change*. Cambridge, MA: Belknap Press.

Nicolini, D. (2012), *Practice Theory, Work, and Organization: An Introduction*. Oxford University Press.

Nicolini, D., Gherardi, S., and Yanow, D. (eds.) (2003), *Knowing in Organizations: A Practice-Based Approach*. Armonk, NY: M. E. Sharpe.

Orlikowski, W. J. (2002), 'Knowing in practice: enacting a collective capability in distributed organizing', *Organization Science*, 13/3: 249–73.

(2007), 'Sociomaterial practices: exploring technology at work', *Organization Studies*, 28/9: 1435–48.

Orlikowski, W. J., and Scott, S. V. (2008), 'Sociomateriality: challenging the separation of technology, work and organization', *Academy of Management Annals*, 2/1: 433–74.

Pentland, B. T., and Feldman, M. S. (2008), 'Designing routines: on the folly of designing artifacts, while hoping for patterns of action', *Information and Organization*, 18/4: 235–50.

Pentland, B. T., Feldman, M. S., Lui, P., and Becker, M. (2012), 'Dynamics of organizational routines: a generative model', *Journal of Management Studies*, 49/8: 1484–508.

Pentland, B. T., Haerem, T., and Hillison, D. (2011), 'The (n)ever changing world: stability and change in organizational routines', *Organization Science*, 22/6: 1369–83.

Pentland, B. T., and Reuter, H. H. (1994), 'Organizational routines as grammars of action', *Administrative Science Quarterly*, 39/3: 484–510.

Rerup, C., and Feldman, M. S. (2011), 'Routines as a source of change in organizational schemata: the role of trial-and-error learning', *Academy of Management Journal*, 54/3: 577–610.

Rouleau, L. (2005), 'Micro-practices of strategic sensemaking and sensegiving: how middle managers interpret and sell change every day', *Journal of Management Studies*, 42/7: 1413–41.

Salvato, C. (2003), 'The role of micro-strategies in the engineering of firm evolution', *Journal of Management Studies*, 40/1: 83–108.

(2009), 'Capabilities unveiled: the role of ordinary activities in the evolution of product development processes', *Organization Science*, 20/2: 384–409.

Salvato, C., and Rerup, C. (2011), 'Beyond collective entities: multilevel research on organizational routines and capabilities', *Journal of Management*, 37/2: 468–90.

Sandberg, J., and Tsoukas, H. (2011), 'Grasping the logic of practice: theorizing through practical rationality', *Academy of Management Review*, 36/2: 338–60.

Schatzki, T. R. (2012), 'Primer on practice', in Higgs, J., Barnett, R., Billett, S., Hutchings, M., and Trede, F. (eds.), *Practice-Based Education*: 13–26. Rotterdam: Sense.

Sevón, G. (1996), 'Organizational imitation in identity transformation', in Czarniawska, B, and Sevón, G. (eds.), *Translating Organizational Change*: 49–68. Berlin: Walter de Gruyter.

Sonenshein, S. (2014), 'How organizations foster the creative use of resources', *Academy of Management Journal*, 57/3: 814–48.

Stene, E. (1940), 'An approach to a science of administration', *American Political Science Review*, 34/6: 1124–37.

Suchman, L. (2007), *Human–Machine Reconfigurations: Plans and Situated Actions*, 2nd edn. Cambridge University Press.

Tsoukas, H., and Chia, R. (2002), 'On organizational becoming: rethinking organizational change', *Organization Science*, 13/5: 567–82.

Turner, S. F., and Rindova, V. (2012), 'A balancing act: how organizations pursue consistency in routine functioning in the face of ongoing change', *Organization Science*, 23/1: 24–46.

Vaara, E., and Whittington, R. (2012), 'Strategy-as-practice: taking social practices seriously',

Academy of Management Annals, 6/1: 285–336.

Whittington, R. (2006), 'Completing the practice turn in strategy research', *Organization Studies*, 27/5: 613–34.

—— (2010), 'Giddens, structuration theory and strategy as practice', in Golsorkhi, D., Rouleau, L., Seidl, D., and Vaara, E. (eds.), *Cambridge Handbook of Strategy as Practice*: 109–26. Cambridge University Press.

Wittgenstein, L. (2001 [1951]), *Philosophical Investigations*, 3rd edn. Oxford: Blackwell.

Zbaracki, M. J., and Bergen, M. (2010), 'When truces collapse: a longitudinal study of price-adjustment routines', *Organization Science*, 21/5: 955–72.

Identity work as a strategic practice

DAVID OLIVER

CHAPTER 19

Introduction

Identity is a powerful, motivating force in organizations today. Originating as an individual-level construct in the field of psychology, identity has long been used to explain behaviour and enhance self-understanding by offering a personal frame of reference that legitimizes decision-making and enables the formation of stable relationships with others. It has also been extended to the collective and organizational levels, where it can provide an (evolving) sense of structure and continuity over time. Whether explicitly or not, questions related to identity – at all levels of analysis – frequently underlie a great deal of organizational strategizing, making identity a theoretical construct worthy of examination by strategy-as-practice scholars.

Identity is derived from the Latin word 'idem', meaning 'the same' (Abend 1974). As such, it includes an implicit historical and retrospective element, in that understanding what remains the same requires looking backward in time. While at first glance this may appear to distinguish identity from strategy's inherent future orientation, the two concepts share a number of important characteristics. Each involves a struggle to achieve some kind of balance between similarity and uniqueness, or 'optimal distinctiveness' (Brewer 1991; Deephouse 1999). Each contributes to a perception of coherence and stability in organizations, which is often used to frame decisions and actions. Furthermore, both identity and strategy have undergone something of a transformation of late, with strategy's recent 'practice turn' (Whittington 2006) mirrored by an growing interest in 'process' studies in the organizational literature on identity (Schultz et al. 2012).

This chapter develops the perspective of identity as a form of strategic practice. Building largely on processual studies of identity, it proposes that identity work integrating different levels of analysis

and temporal orientations enables and constrains strategy work, and can itself constitute a strategic practice. The chapter is organized into four main parts. It begins by providing a (necessarily brief) overview of key studies in the vast fields of identity and identification in the organization literature, categorized by level of analysis: individual, collective and organizational. It then reviews existing work linking identity with strategy, and organizes this into three perspectives: identity as strategic resource, identity as a lens or framing device and identity as a form of work. The third section builds on process identity studies to develop the perspective of identity work as a form of strategic practice operating across temporal orientations and levels of analysis. It thus directly addresses identity's *mutually shaping* relationship with strategy practice (Chia and MacKay 2007; Oliver and Bürgi 2005; Sillince and Simpson 2010) and praxis (Johnson, Balogun and Beech 2010). The chapter concludes with some proposed avenues for future research.

Three levels of identity in organizational studies

Individual identity

Originating in the fields of psychology and psychoanalysis, the notion of individual identity has been used to describe how an individual develops a self-image, or mental model, of him-/herself (Erikson 1968). Defined as an 'inner sense of sameness' and 'continuity of character' (Maitlis and Christianson 2014), identity integrates our various structures and substructures, enabling us to act on our environments as a unified entity (van Tonder and Lessing 2003). Identity therefore involves inward-directed sensemaking (Pratt 2003) concerning self-referential meaning, exemplified by the response to questions such as 'Who am I?' and 'Who are we?'. Our identities as individuals evolve through environmental interactions as well as introspection/analysis, however, and so identity also has a distinctively relational aspect. We need to know who we are not in order to know who we are, and thus we cannot form an identity without reference to other entities. Interest in identity has grown as questions of meaning have been perceived as increasingly salient, in part because of the growing number of identity options and changes that individuals (and organizations) face in an increasingly interconnected world.

Individual identities are constructed in large part through processes of 'identity work', a sociological concept initially developed to explain ways in which homeless people generate identities providing self-worth (Snow and Anderson 1987). Along with identity negotiation and repair, identity work has its origins in symbolic interactionism (Blumer 1969), which largely treats identity work as an individual activity. Sociological theories of the 'self', however, describe a whole entity – including its various socially ascribed identities – as an integrative whole (Pratt and Kraatz 2009). Individuals socially construct their own 'selfhood' through interactions with others throughout their lives (Jenkins 1996), in ways that are culturally situated and based on discursively constructed expectations or 'ideal selves' (Wieland 2010). When one's sense of self is challenged (that is, through 'sensebreaking'), identity exploration is encouraged as a means of filling the resulting meaning void (Pratt 2000). Thus, the self can both stimulate and constrain identity work conducted at the individual level.

Social and collective identity and identification

Although it originated as an individual construct, identity also clearly influences and is influenced by groups and collectives, including organizations. Indeed, identity's integrative and generative qualities appear to travel relatively easily across levels of analysis (Albert, Ashforth and Dutton 2000). The ways in which the identity of social groups influence individual identities is studied through

social identity theory, which focuses on 'that part of an individual's self-concept which derives from his knowledge of his membership of a social group (or groups) together with the value and emotional significance attached to that membership' (Tajfel 1978). According to social identity theory, individuals *identify* with collectives (such as demographic groups, professions or organizations) in cognitive, affective and evaluative ways (Tajfel and Turner 1985). These in-groups are then positively differentiated in comparison with out-groups on some valued dimension, and internalized in the individual – contributing to their sense of self (Turner 1982). Social identity gets at a sense of 'we' or 'us', and focuses on the distinctive features of a group. This process can involve identification with a jointly produced 'story world', which creates commonality among community members while differentiating them from outsiders (Fiol and Romanelli 2012).

Organizational theorists have taken a particular interest in the *social* processes through which collective and organizational identities are negotiated and renegotiated. 'Collective identity' has been studied in the context of teams, organizations and other social groupings, and refers to elements of identity shared by various group members (Pratt 2003). Like individual identity's focus on one's distinctive features, collective identity is 'the self, defined in group terms, as different and distinct from a specific out-group' (Hogg, van Knippenberg and Rast 2012). Studies in the organizational literature have found that having a collectively shared identity can increase motivation in work groups, and the ability of leaders to communicate and create a sense of shared identity may make them more effective (Ellemers, De Gilder and Haslam 2004). A strong team identity has also been linked to higher team performance (Lembke and Wilson 1998), lowered conflict and improved cooperation (Jehn, Northcraft and Neale 1999), more effective handling of critical incidents (Oliver and Roos 2003) and reduced shirking (Eckel and Grossman 2005). Social identity theory further suggests that people tend to select activities congruent with salient aspects of their identities, at both individual and organizational levels (Ashforth and Mael 1989).

Organizational identity

Identity at the organizational level of analysis has attracted a great deal of scholarly attention over the past three decades. Albert and Whetten (1985) initially defined organizational identity in terms of a set of claims related to an organization's *central* character, *distinctiveness* and temporal *continuity* – a definition that guided scholarship for many years. The organizational identity field has evolved to encompass a plurality of perspectives spanning a variety of ontological and epistemological viewpoints, however, giving rise to a multiplicity of research methodologies and designs (Corley *et al.* 2006).

Organizational identity has inspired attention in an age of growing pressure for stakeholder involvement, globalization, outsourcing, strategic alliances, use of 'external' contractors, cross-functional teams and the 'collapse' of internal/external organizational boundaries (Hatch and Schultz 1997). New organizational structures focusing on teams and projects can create a plurality of objectives and processes that heightens organizational complexity (Denis, Langley and Rouleau 2007), with some of these changes threatening the ability of organizations to perpetuate themselves through repositories of organizational history and method (Albert, Ashforth and Dutton 2000). These changes have stimulated interest in internalized cognitive structures, or 'rudders', of what the organization stands for, in the heads and hearts of its members (Albert, Ashforth and Dutton 2000). The ability of organizations to inspire identification among members, or 'the perception of oneness or belongingness to some human aggregate' (Ashforth and Mael 1989), can strengthen in-group cooperation within that organization (Dutton, Dukerich and Harquail 1994). The strength of an employee's identification can be shaped by images of his/her organization, or the collective identity stories that people tell and write to each other in the organization (Brown 2006).

The notion of organizational identity has also sparked a number of controversies, however, concerning its ontological and epistemological nature (Whetten and Godfrey 1998; Cornelissen 2002; Gioia, Schultz and Corley 2002). An important ontological debate has focused on whether organizational identity consists of *institutionalized*

claims or *shared perceptions* among members (Whetten and Mackey 2002) (sometimes referred to as 'top-down' versus 'bottom-up' approaches). On the one hand, organizations are unique among other collectives in that they are social actors, and identities are categorical self-descriptions used by social actors to satisfy their identity requirements. Reflecting institution theory, some identity scholars consider organizational identity to be a set of institutionalized claims that exist irrespective of the individual organizational members of the organization (Whetten 2006). Institutions supply a set of possible legitimate identity elements with which to construct, give meaning to and legitimize identities and identity symbols, and organizations engage in institutional *bricolage* in incorporating these cultural meanings, values, sentiments and rules into their identity claims (Glynn 2008).

On the other hand, social constructionists argue that organizational members – through social interaction – collectively build a shared understanding of who their organization is. This bottom-up 'meanings-based' approach to identity indicates that, 'although identity is influenced by the social context, individuals and organizations experience it as a deeply personal phenomenon' (Gioia *et al.* 2013: 173). As one form of social identity, organizational identity is a fact of life constructed by, and relevant to, many organizational members (Haslam, Postmes and Ellemers 2003). Organizational members of various levels and on various occasions (re)negotiate a description of their organizations as they engage in sensemaking 'self' and 'other' (Clegg, Rhodes and Kornberger 2007). Some scholars have tried to integrate these two perspectives, proposing that individuals enact identities and organizations encourage this enactment through sensebreaking and sensegiving, thus making it both a top-down and a bottom-up process (Ashforth, Harrison and Corley 2008).

Identity as strategic resource, lens or work?

In the strategy literature, identity has been characterized variously as a strategic resource or asset potentially underlying a firm's competitive advantage

Table 19.1 Three perspectives on the role of identity for strategy

Strategy focus	Identity focus	Temporal orientation	Implication of identity for strategy
Content	Attributes	Past	Identity as resource
Process	Frame	Past and present	Identity as lens
Practice	Process	Past, present and future	Identity as work

(Whetten and Mackey 2002), as a lens through which evaluations are made and decisions framed about internal resources, competences and environmental factors (Dutton and Dukerich 1991) and as a form of work that enables and constrains strategy (Oliver and Bürgi 2005) (see Table 19.1). Each of the three perspectives connects most closely to one of three focuses of strategy research (content, process and practice), as well as bearing slightly different temporal orientations. It is important to note that not all identity strategy research fits neatly into just one of these perspectives, and at times more than one is mobilized – sometimes in the same study. While all three hold potential interest for SAP scholars, however, it is the third perspective – 'identity as work' – involving elements of practice and/or process, that bears the clearest connection to the strategy-as-practice field.

Identity as a resource

The first identity perspective broadly focuses on the detection of identity attributes in an individual, group or organization. Consistent with the field of strategy content, this perspective focuses on identifying attributes that may constitute organizational resources, which in turn can be integrated into an organization's strategy in order to develop and sustain a competitive advantage. This perspective has attracted particular attention among scholars working with the resource-based view of the firm, in which organizational identity has been described as a 'classic, socially complex resource' (Barney, speaking in Reger *et al.* 1998) that may ultimately become a source of competitive advantage (Barney and Stewart 2000).

According to the identity-as-resource perspective, a widely shared and durable organizational identity can be considered a strength if it provides a firm with confidence to weather threats, although it may become a weakness if it leads to hubris, myopia and inertia. It is a firm's distinctive attributes in a

particular environmental context (in resource-based language, its 'heterogeneity') that should be identified and managed in order to create competitive advantage. In a further extension of this argument, Sillince (2006) draws a parallel between organizational identity and the classic VRIN resource framework (Barney 1991), proposing that an attractive organizational identity may be thought of as a *valuable* resource, that identity distinctiveness relates to *rareness*, centrality relates to *inimitability* and enduringness relates to *non-substitutability*. The implication is that organizational identity is something that can be evaluated, measured and controlled.

The notion that organizational identity should be managed in this way dates back to initial functionalist studies of the construct, which sought to identify mechanisms used by organizational leaders and strategists to articulate and change identity – in view, for example, of externally imposed organizational categories (Elsbach and Kramer 1996). The strategic implication for identity in this perspective is that it is a resource to be managed – or 'regulated', in the language of identity scholars – in part to influence and control employee identification (Alvesson and Willmott 2002). Strategic management of an organization's identity is also vital to ensuring coherence between strategic choices, with Ravasi and Phillips (2011) finding that leaders at Bang & Olufsen reassessed, refocused and tuned identity claims in order to make identity-consistent strategic investments. The temporal orientation of this perspective is largely on the past. Managing the history of an organization is one way managers can attempt to substantively regulate organizational identity (Suddaby, Foster and Trank 2010).

Identity as a lens

The second perspective relates more to identity's role in the strategy development process. Under this perspective, identity acts as a frame influencing how organizational members perceive and interpret their environment, and consequentially develop strategic agendas (Dutton and Penner 1993). This identity perspective shares a great deal with cognitive approaches to strategy development (Porac, Thomas and Baden-Fuller 1989), as well as many facets of the process stream of strategy research (for example, Pettigrew 1985). Identity serves both to constrain the generation of strategic options and to influence how organizations see new strategic opportunities (Gustafson, speaking in Reger *et al.* 1998). From a strategic standpoint, an individual's beliefs about an organization's identity act as a lens shaping his/her perception of an issue's legitimacy, its importance and the feasibility of any resolution, which can also influence collective action by top management. Identity beliefs can influence which resources an organization considers to be 'strategic' (Ravasi and Phillips 2011). Organizational identity claims as articulated by stakeholders may take the form of 'stylized narratives' about an organization's 'soul', or essence, without which organizations may be ambivalent about making strategic choices (Ashforth and Mael 1996).

The lens perspective has also been found to apply at different levels of analysis. Social identity frames have been found to act as enablers of coordinated action among people in ways that lead to new knowledge creation practices in multinational corporations (Regnér and Zander 2011). Firm-level strategies may also be influenced by the extent to which organizations identify themselves as members of a higher-level 'strategic group identity', with identification particularly strong to groups that include high-status firms (Peteraf and Shanley 1997). Strategic considerations may also influence an organization's 'identity domain', or the cognitive competitive space that holds psychological value for a firm's management (Livengood and Reger 2010).

The main temporal orientations of this identity perspective relate to the past and present. Thus, while any attempt at strategic change is likely to be influenced by identity (Nag, Corley and Gioia 2007), an organizational identity lens becomes particularly salient in moments of significant strategic change, including mergers and acquisitions. For example, during an acquisition, multiple and varied interpretations of organizational identities past and present may enable an organization to recapture past elements of distinction in the face of current pressures for standardization (Chreim 2007). The strength of organizational identification – in addition to cultural compatibility and strategic combination potential – might be evaluated when deciding the extent to which a merger or acquisition should be organizationally integrated, particularly in mergers of 'equals' in which the assumption of equality itself tends to reinforce pre-existing identities (Zaheer, Schomaker and Genc 2003).

Identity as work

The third identity perspective presents the greatest theoretical opportunities for strategy-as-practice scholars. It builds on the growing interest in identity's dynamic or *processual* aspects (Clegg, Rhodes and Kornberger 2007), while emphasizing social practice involving different levels of analysis, and generally extending across past, present and future notions of identity. This is the notion of identity as *work*.

On an individual level, the identity work of CEOs has been found to influence their own praxis, and have a significant impact on strategic organizational changes (Johnson, Balogun and Beech 2010). CEOs are also part of broader collective and organizational identities, however, and the mutually constitutive nature of identity work means that, as individuals construct their own identities, they are also influencing these higher-level identities in which they participate. Identity work can therefore be part of a larger group process involving indexes of the self that evoke meaning to others (Schwalbe and Mason-Schrock 1996), and provide a form of reflexive continuity across time and space (Giddens 1991). Thus, in addition to their personal identity work, organizational members participate in identity work to actively construct the various social identities that influence how they live their lives (Watson 2008). Drawing on sociological and social movement literatures, Langley *et al.* (2012) have proposed the notion of 'group identity work' – identity work that is a group accomplishment – and found it to be highly salient in understanding strategizing processes in the context of a merger. At the organizational identity level of analysis, these forms of identity work have been defined as 'people being engaged in forming, repairing, maintaining, strengthening or revising the constructions that are productive of a sense of coherence and distinctiveness' (Sveningsson and Alvesson 2003). Processual studies of organizational identity development refocus attention on how organizational identity is constructed through identity work, and how it is negotiated, affirmed, contested and maintained as an ongoing accomplishment (Schultz et al. 2012).

Identity work can have both active and passive forms (Wieland 2010). Active identity work occurs when individuals are aware of their self-constructions, while passive identity work occurs through more routine processes (Watson 2008). Active identity work has thus far been privileged in the organization studies literature, though more recent work has examined how identity work can be limited and controlled by organizational routines (Brown and Lewis 2011). For example, managerial control of employee identity work has been found to be an increasingly salient element of the employment relationship (Alvesson and Willmott 2002).

The identity-as-work perspective draws on past, present, and future temporal orientations, as one's desired future identity (on varying levels of analysis) is dynamically informed by one's historical and present circumstances. This perspective therefore draws heavily on a processual view of identity. The next section briefly discusses developments in the process school of identity research, as well as introducing some methodological considerations potentially of interest to SAP scholars.

Processual identity approaches and methods

Rather than focusing on stable and essentialist conceptions of identity, process scholars are more inclined to explore the complex processes that are involved in its constitution, including its relational and associative nature as an outcome of collective interactions. Processual approaches to identity tend to problematize essentialist claims, considering them to be, at best, stabilizing moments in an ongoing process of identity formation and re-formation (Ybema et al. 2009). Grounded in social constructionist theories of knowledge (Berger and Luckmann 1966), this research seeks to explore some of identity's 'flow' qualities (Gioia and Patvardhan 2012).

At the individual level of analysis, the identity dynamics of the lived experiences of strategists have been explored in the context of strategic change, with Beech and Johnson (2005) finding that individual identity issues can have a significant impact on the strategy of firms involved in a CEO succession. On the organizational level, process studies attend in particular to how identity is formed and constructed in an organizational context (Cornelissen, Haslam and Balmer 2007), through such lenses as discourse (Hardy, Lawrence and Grant 2005), performance (Clegg, Rhodes and Kornberger 2007) or narration (Brown 2006). Studies from a process perspective have examined such themes as identity tensions (Fiol 2002), fluidity (Gioia, Schultz and Corley 2000), paradox (Pratt and Foreman 2000) and other means by which an organizational sense of 'self' with some form of distinctive continuity across space and/or time is developed (for example, Clegg, Kornberger and Rhodes 2005). In this light, process work on organizational identity has come to reflect a deeper refocusing that has occurred within the study of individual identity, whereby interest has shifted from the singular and fixed 'self' to a working and active self-concept influenced by social circumstances (Markus and Wurf 1987).

An important conversation in the organizational identity process field concerns more temporal issues related to organizational identity's continuity. While most scholars initially focused on organizational identity's more stable or 'essential' aspects at a point in time (for example, Elsbach and Kramer 1996), process scholarship has tended to focus on more 'dynamic' aspects of identity. Rather than an objective, enduring characteristic of an organization, organizational identity has been considered a 'temporary, context-sensitive and evolving set of constructions' (Alvesson, Ashcraft and Thomas 2008: 6). Gioia, Schultz and Corley (2000) propose that organizational identity is an 'adaptively instable' product of social interactions and intersubjective negotiations of meanings between organizational members, while others recommend replacing so-called 'enduring' aspects of organizational identity with 'having continuity' (Gioia *et al.*, 2013).

Process-oriented scholars of organizational identity have studied ways in which it is produced, modified and reified within and through communicative interaction (Hardy, Lawrence and Grant 2005; Taylor and Van Every 1993). A particularly popular means of examining organizational-identity-related discourse has been through the analysis of organizational narratives (Humphreys and Brown 2002; Chreim 2005). A narrative view of organizational identity relaxes many of the previously held realist/essentialist assumptions in suggesting that collective identities do not necessarily need to be fully shared, continuous, consistent or enduring. It conceives of these aspects as primarily empirical aspects requiring examination, such as the extent to which narrative convergence in a specific organization might exist and how and whether it relates to identity (Brown 2006).

Because of their performative ability to associate particular concepts with material references to (re) create desired objects, such as a sense of self (Hardy, Palmer and Phillips 2000), narratives are a particularly effective form of organizational identity talk (Brown, 2006; Chreim 2005; Humphreys and Brown 2002). These studies build on the assumption that organizational members come to understand the identities of their organizations through the narratives they construct to situate themselves in space and time. Processes of narratively constructing organizational identities can take place in the context of informal interactions, in formal structures such as work groups or departments, as well as in workshops, meetings and briefings, including through the use of material objects (Oliver and Roos 2007). Specific performances or constructions of organizational identity are deemed appropriate, or not, by organizational actors within relevant contexts for decisions and actions.

Identity work as a strategic practice

A key implication of the identity-as-work perspective for the field of strategy is that, more than serving as a resource or a lens, identity work – on various levels of analysis and over various time scales – has a reciprocal or *co-constitutive* relationship with strategy. Identity may be enacted and expressed through strategy, as well as being inferred, modified or affirmed *from* strategy (Oliver and Bürgi 2005). As with Giddens' structuration practices (Giddens 1984), organizational identity can simultaneously evoke prior meanings and create conditions for new ones, in a recursive relationship between process and outcomes (Oliver and Bürgi 2005). Organizational identity inheres in work practices, especially in the ways that members use knowledge, with Orlikowski (2002: 257) arguing that 'actively and recurrently producing a distinctive and shared...identity' can itself be thought of as an organizational practice. Thus, instead of focusing on identity processes as somehow separate from individuals and organizations, they should be regarded as integrated in a strategic context (Chia and MacKay 2007).

Identity may therefore be considered an element of strategizing, while strategizing processes contribute to the formulation of an organization's identity. As Glynn observes: '[C]onflicts of strategic definition and resolution can stem from conflicts over identity' (Glynn 2000: 295). Organizational identity beliefs potentially serve as a wellspring for strategy, while elements of a firm's strategic objectives influence its identity. Recent extensions of the definition of organizational identity beyond 'who we are as an organization' to also include 'what we *do* as a collective' (Nag, Corley and Gioia 2007), and activities and beliefs about 'what' we stand for and 'why' a firm is successful (Livengood and Reger 2010), support this closer connection to strategy.

In beginning to connect the notions of identity work with strategy work, it is important to acknowledge an implicit temporal distinction. Sillince and Simpson (2010) have proposed that identity work consists of the retrospective reformulation of meaning attributed to past events, while strategy work is prospective reimagination of alternative futures. This may involve the creation of a cognitive distance between the perception of the current and the ideal desired identity – an 'identity gap' (Reger *et al.* 1994) – as part of efforts to effect identity, and possibly strategic, change. An identity gap can also be created between a perceived historical or current organizational identity and a shared 'desired organizational identity' – the environmental-assessment-matched response to the question 'Who *should* we be as an organization?' (Rughase 2006). So-called 'future identities' would appear to share many characteristics with vision/mission or strategic intent in the strategy literature.

Identity work can be particularly critical in the strategic context of mergers and acquisitions. In their study of organizational identity during a merger, Clark *et al.* (2010) found that a 'transitional identity' can be used to allow historical identities to be temporarily suspended, by creating a balance between ambiguity and a projected and shared future identity. As such, senior managers might engage in sensegiving via image management in order to overcome sources of inertia in the previously existing identities, and improve the chances of merger success (Clark *et al.* 2010). Their identity work can also involve nurturing *situated* organizational identifications with changing organizational identities grounded in enduring values and outcomes, rather than in outdated or rigid organizational attributes (Fiol 2001).

Future directions

This chapter has explored a number of ways that identity and identification have been employed in a strategy context, and has proposed the notion of identity work as a strategic practice. To further develop these and other identity strategy themes, this chapter identifies five themes with the potential to generate useful research questions for future study. These include identity emergence, identity across levels of analysis, identity and time, identity talk and identity and materiality.

Identity emergence

One context in which identity work intensively influences strategic practices is in the creation of new organizations. As with the field of strategy of practice, in which the 'emergence' of strategy has been identified as an important future research direction (Vaara and Whittington 2012), the emergence and formation of identity also holds promise as a rich topic of study (Gioia *et al.* 2013). In temporal terms, new organizations have no history, and so the identity work involved in their development most closely pertains to present and future activities.

In their study of 'iterative' organizations – ones in which the structure and activities of the organization are episodic in nature and organizational identity construction is repeated indefinitely – Foreman and Parent (2008) detail the important, interrelated roles played by activities, key individuals and cultural elements. In their focus on the precursors of identity, Fiol and Romanelli (2012) propose that the ability to develop enthusiastic new story worlds may be of critical importance to the emergence of new collective identities. In their study of a new college, Gioia *et al.* (2010) found that identity construction passed through eight sequential stages, and that the social constructionist and social actor views of organizational identity are both needed and complementary to this process. Organizational identity development has also been linked to broader field-level identities (Barry and Elmes 1997). All these findings would benefit from additional study. For example, drawing on long-standing strategic questions, what is the comparative role of founders, competitors and other stakeholders during the creation of new organizations? What is the nature of their identity work, and how does it occur?

Identity across levels of analysis

The strategy-as-practice domain attempts to integrate across levels of analysis – a factor distinguishing it from the field of strategy process (Chia and MacKay 2007; Vaara and Whittington 2012). Inspiration for further inter-level studies may be drawn from similar integration attempts in the identity literature (Cornelissen, Haslam and Balmer 2007). Most of the organizational literature on identity at the individual level of analysis has focused on the CEO and top management team. It may be useful at this time to explore inter-level identity work as these individuals attempt to influence middle management, external strategy consultants or other individuals elsewhere in the organization who 'consume' and perhaps influence the strategic direction of the firm. Future research could work to connect the 'How?', the 'What?' and the 'Why?' of organizational identity formation (Gioia *et al.* 2013) in a strategic context.

As strategy work can occur on corporate, firm and operational levels, the relationships between different levels of identity (or 'self') merit further scholarly attention, particularly in cases in which identities are 'nested' (Ashforth, Rogers and Corley 2011). Studies of *professional* identity may also be relevant, to the extent that professionals have traditionally been found to be highly defined by what they do (Pratt, Rockmann and Kaufmann 2006). How do organizational members reconcile their team, departmental and organizational identities in formulating or executing strategy? As with the SAP literature, the ability to connect micro-level identity construction phenomena to macro-level process models is critical to shedding light on many of these questions.

Identity and time

If one accepts that organizational identity (like strategy) is socially constructed, produced and reproduced through interactions among organizational members and other stakeholders (Scott and Lane 2000), then we also need more insight into the nature of this construction process in existing firms over time. In what ways might an organization's future strategy lead to identity construction or change? In promising early work on this question, Langley *et al.* (2012) have identified distinct patterns in identity work when group identities were renegotiated in the context of a merger.

Other questions relate to exploring how historical organizational identity claims and understandings can be mobilized and evoked to present a strategically attractive future. For example, Schultz and Hernes (2013) show how organizational memories were used in the LEGO company to develop identity in the present – and future – as the company moved from a 'mass market producer

of play materials' to a 'premium idea-based company dedicated to systematic creativity'. The implicit importance of temporality in discussions of both identity and strategy – beyond simple evocations of the past identities and future strategies – calls for additional longitudinal studies of identity practices, processes and dynamics.

Identity talk

As the strategy-as-practice field has long been influenced by narrative (Barry and Elmes 1997; Fenton and Langley 2011), identity has also been described as the ability to integrate external events into an ongoing story of self – to keep a particular narrative going (Giddens 1991). On the organizational level, it has been proposed that identity work is largely a rhetorical exercise linked to strategy (Sillince and Simpson 2010). For example, rhetoric about resources and competitive advantage may heavily influence and help sustain organizational identities (Sillince 2006).

In what ways might language and communicative action be used to articulate a potential 'identity gap' (Reger *et al.* 1994) to motivate a parallel 'strategy gap' for an organization? What forms of 'identity talk' are particularly relevant to the development of an organization's strategy? Beech and Johnson (2005) have used narrative analysis to study identity work in a time of strategic change. To what extent can *narrating* an organization be considered a strategic practice for engaging in organizational identity work? Discourse analysis in its various forms has also attracted attention as a means of studying identity work (Hardy, Lawrence and Grant 2005), paving the way for further studies in a more strategic context.

Identity and materiality

Further questions relate to the importance of materiality and embodiment. Materiality is clearly important in understanding strategizing practices (Vaara and Whittington 2012). Can the use of material objects help us better understand the more tacit elements of organizational identity, which may have a lasting impact on a firm's strategy (Oliver and Roos 2007)? To what extent might other materials influence interwoven identity and strategy practices? What role might embodied cognition (Harquail and King 2010) or 'embodied metaphors' play in this process (Heracleous and Jacobs 2008)?

Other potential research topics relating to strategy's influence on identity practices include the use of identity 'referents' (Hardy, Lawrence and Grant 2005), or targets of comparison. Foreman and Parent (2008) identified operational (such as activities-based), personnel (such as key individuals) and spatial (such as local culture and history) referents in iterative organizations, but much more work may be done here. In addition, 'negative referents' (Gioia *et al.* 2010), or 'identity foils' (Ashforth and Johnson 2001), may also be relevant to processes of organizational *disidentification* – that is, we define ourselves and our organizations by what they are *not*. How do these processes work in a strategic context?

Conclusion

Although identity and strategy emerge from different research traditions and temporal orientations, they share many characteristics that highlight the potential for fruitful cross-fertilization between them. Each can be the source of organizational coherence and stability, and yet each has also experienced a turn towards process and/or practice by scholars in recent years. This chapter attempts to introduce and organize the organizational literature on identity for use by strategy-as-practice scholars. In particular, the growing literature on identity processes presents a great deal of potential, as it provides the basis for understanding the implications of identity work as a form of strategic practice.

While notions of identity are frequently employed in the course of strategizing activities and practices, we need further research to help illustrate the nature of this phenomenon. Some potential sources of research questions for future interest among SAP scholars include identity emergence as well as issues related to level of analysis, time, talk and materiality. Methodologically, scholars in each of the two fields have great scope for inspiring each other. Both wrestle with

challenges related to connecting micro- to macro-phenomena over time, and with questions related to the use of narrative and discourse analysis, among others. It is hoped that further interactions between the two fields will lead to a deepening of our understanding of the role each plays in contemporary organizations.

References

Abend, S. A. (1974), 'Problems of identity: theoretical and clinical applications', *Psychoanalytic Quarterly*, 43/4: 606–37.

Albert, S., Ashforth, B. E., and Dutton, J. E. (2000), 'Organizational identity and identification: charting new waters and building new bridges', *Academy of Management Review*, 25/1: 13–17.

Albert, S., and Whetten, D. A. (1985), 'Organizational identity', in Cummings, L. L., and Staw, B. M. (eds.), *Research in Organizational Behavior*, vol. VII: 263–95. Greenwich, CT: JAI Press.

Alvesson, M., Ashcraft, K. L., and Thomas, R. (2008), 'Identity matters: reflections on the construction of identity scholarship in organization studies', *Organization*, 15/1: 5–28.

Alvesson, M., and Willmott, H. (2002), 'Identity regulation as organizational control: producing the appropriate individual', *Journal of Management Studies*, 39/5: 619–44.

Ashforth, B. E., Harrison, S. H., and Corley, K. G. (2008), 'Identification in organizations: an examination of four fundamental questions', *Journal of Management*, 34/3: 325–74.

Ashforth, B. E., and Johnson, S. A. (2001), 'Which hat to wear? The relative salience of multiple identities in organizational contexts', in Hogg, M. A., and Terry, D. J. (eds.), *Social Identity Processes in Organizational Contexts*: 31–48. Philadelphia: Psychology Press.

Ashforth, B. E., and Mael, F. (1989), 'Social identity theory and the organization', *Academy of Management Review*, 14/1: 20–39.

(1996), 'Organizational identity and strategy as a context for the individual', in Baum, J. A. C., and Dutton, J. E. (eds.), *Advances in Strategic Management*, vol. XIII, *The Embeddedness of Strategy*: 19–64. Bingley, UK: Emerald.

Ashforth, B. E., Rogers, K. M., and Corley, K. G. (2011), 'Identity in organizations: exploring cross-level dynamics', *Organization Science*, 22/5: 1144–56.

Barney, J. (1991), 'Firm resources and sustained competitive advantage', *Journal of Management*, 17/1: 99–120.

Barney, J., and Stewart, A. C. (2000), 'Organizational identity as moral philosophy: competitive implications for diversified companies', in Schultz, M., Hatch, M. J., and Holten Larsen, M. (eds.), *The Expressive Organization: Linking Identity, Reputation, and the Corporate Brand*: 36–47. Oxford University Press.

Barry, D., and Elmes, M. (1997), 'Strategy retold: toward a narrative view of strategic discourse', *Academy of Management Review*, 22/2: 429–52.

Beech, N., and Johnson, P. (2005), 'Discourses of disrupted identities in the practice of strategic change', *Journal of Organizational Change Management*, 18/1: 31–47.

Berger, P. L., and Luckmann, T. (1966), *The Social Construction of Reality: A Treatise in the Sociology of Knowledge*. Garden City, NY: Anchor Books.

Blumer, H. (1969), *Symbolic Interactionism*. Englewood Cliffs, NJ: Prentice Hall.

Brewer, M. B. (1991), 'The social self: on being the same and different at the same time', *Journal of Personality and Social Psychology Bulletin*, 17/5: 475–82.

Brown, A. D. (2006), 'A narrative approach to collective identities', *Journal of Management Studies*, 43/4: 731–53.

Brown, A. D., and Lewis, M. A. (2011), 'Identities, discipline and routines', *Organization Studies*, 32/7: 871–95.

Chia, R., and MacKay, B. (2007), 'Post-processual challenges for the emerging strategy-as-practice perspective: discovering strategy in the logic of practice', *Human Relations*, 60/1: 217–42.

Chreim, S. (2005), 'The continuity–change duality in narrative texts of organizational identity', *Journal of Management Studies*, 42/3: 567–93.

—— (2007), 'Social and temporal influences on interpretations of organizational identity and acquisition integration', *Journal of Applied Behavioral Science*, 43/4: 449–80.

Clark, S. M., Gioia, D. A., Ketchen, D. J., and Thomas, J. B. (2010), 'Transitional identity as a facilitator of organizational identity change during a merger', *Administrative Science Quarterly*, 55/3: 397–438.

Clegg, S., Kornberger, M., and Rhodes, C. (2005), 'Learning/becoming/doing', *Organization*, 12/2: 147–67.

Clegg, S., Rhodes, C., and Kornberger, M. (2007), 'Desperately seeking legitimacy: organizational identity and emerging industries', *Organization Studies*, 28/4: 495–513.

Corley, K. G., Harquail, C. V., Pratt, M. G., Glynn, M. A., Fiol, C. M., and Hatch, M. J. (2006), 'Guiding organizational identity through aged adolescence', *Journal of Management Inquiry*, 15/2: 85–99.

Cornelissen, J. (2002), 'On the "organizational identity" metaphor', *British Journal of Management*, 13/3: 259–68.

Cornelissen, J., Haslam, S. A., and Balmer, J. M. T. (2007), 'Social identity, organizational identity and corporate identity: towards an integrated understanding of processes, patternings and products', *British Journal of Management*, 18/S1: 1–16.

Deephouse, D. L. (1999), 'To be different, or to be the same: it's a question (and theory) of strategic balance', *Strategic Management Journal*, 20/2: 147–66.

Denis, J.-L., Langley, A., and Rouleau, L. (2007), 'Strategizing in pluralistic contexts: rethinking theoretical frames', *Human Relations*, 60/1: 179–215.

Dutton, J. E., and Dukerich, J. M. (1991), 'Keeping an eye on the mirror: image and identity in organizational adaptation', *Academy of Management Journal*, 34/3: 517–54.

Dutton, J. E., Dukerich, J. M., and Harquail, C. V. (1994), 'Organizational images and member identification', *Administrative Science Quarterly*, 39/2: 239–63.

Dutton, J. E., and Penner, W. (1993), 'The importance of organizational identity for strategic agenda building', in Hendry, J., Johnson, G., and Newton, J. (eds.), *Strategic Thinking: Leadership and the Management of Change*: 89–113. Chichester, UK: John Wiley.

Eckel, C., and Grossman, P. (2005), 'Managing diversity by creating team identity', *Journal of Economic Behavior and Organization*, 58/3: 371–92.

Ellemers, N., De Gilder, D., and Haslam, S. A. (2004), 'Motivating individuals and groups at work: a social identity perspective on leadership and group performance', *Academy of Management Review*, 29/3: 459–78.

Elsbach, K. D., and Kramer, R. M. (1996), 'Members' responses to organizational identity threats: encountering and countering the

Business Week rankings', *Administrative Science Quarterly*, 41/3: 442–76.

Erikson, E. H. (1968), *Identity, Youth and Crisis*. New York: W. W. Norton.

Fenton, C., and Langley, A. (2011), 'Strategy as practice and the narrative turn', *Organization Studies*, 32/9: 1171–96.

Fiol, C. M. (2001), 'Revisiting an identity-based view of sustainable competitive advantage', *Journal of Management*, 27/6: 691–9.

—— (2002), 'Capitalizing on paradox: the role of language in transforming organizational identities', *Organization Science*, 13/6: 653–66.

Fiol, C. M., and Romanelli, E. (2012), 'Before identity: the emergence of new organizational forms', *Organization Science*, 23/3: 597–611.

Foreman, P. O., and Parent, M. M. (2008), 'The process of organizational identity construction in iterative organizations', *Corporate Reputation Review*, 11/3: 222–44.

Giddens, A. (1984), *The Constitution of Society*. Cambridge: Polity.

—— (1991), *Modernity and Self-Identity: Self and Society in the Late Modern Age*. Cambridge: Polity.

Gioia, D. A., and Patvardhan, S. D. (2012), 'Identity as process and flow', in Schultz, M., Maguire, S., Langley, A., and Tsoukas, H. (eds.), *Constructing Identity in and around Organizations*: 50–62. Oxford University Press.

Gioia, D. A., Patvardhan, S. D., Hamilton, A. L., and Corley, K. G. (2013), 'Organizational identity formation and change', *Academy of Management Annals*, 7/1: 123–93.

Gioia, D. A., Price, K. N., Hamilton, A. L., and Thomas, J. B. (2010), 'Forging an identity: an insider–outsider study of processes involved in the formation of organizational identity', *Administrative Science Quarterly*, 55/1: 1–46.

Gioia, D. A., Schultz, M., and Corley, K. G. (2000), 'Organizational identity, image, and adaptive instability', *Academy of Management Review*, 25/1: 63–81.

—— (2002), 'On celebrating the organizational identity metaphor: a rejoinder to Cornelissen', *British Journal of Management*, 13/3: 269–75.

Glynn, M. A. (2000), 'When cymbals become symbols: conflict over organizational identity within a symphony orchestra', *Organization Science*, 11/3: 285–98.

—— (2008), 'Beyond constraint: how institutions enable identities', in Greenwood, R., Oliver, C., Sahlin, K., and Suddaby, R. (eds.), *The Sage Handbook of Organizational Institutionalism*: 413–30. Thousand Oaks, CA: Sage.

Hardy, C., Lawrence, T., and Grant, D. (2005), 'Discourse and collaboration: the role of conversations and collective identity', *Academy of Management Review*, 30/1: 58–77.

Hardy, C., Palmer, I., and Phillips, N. (2000), 'Discourse as a strategic resource', *Human Relations*, 53/9: 1227–48.

Harquail, C. V., and King, A. (2010), 'Construing organizational identity: the role of embodied cognition', *Organization Studies*, 31/12: 1619–48.

Haslam, S. A., Postmes, T., and Ellemers, N. (2003), 'More than a metaphor: organizational identity makes organizational life possible', *British Journal of Management*, 14/4: 357–69.

Hatch, M. J., and Schultz, M. (1997), 'Relations between organizational culture, identity and image', *European Journal of Marketing*, 31/5–6: 356–65.

Heracleous, L., and Jacobs, C. D. (2008), 'Understanding organizations through embodied metaphors', *Organization Studies*, 29/1: 45–78.

Hogg, M. A., van Knippenberg, D., and Rast, D. E. (2012), 'Intergroup leadership in organizations: leading across group and organizational boundaries', *Academy of Management Review*, 37/2: 232–55.

Humphreys, M., and Brown, A. (2002), 'Narratives of organizational identity and identification: a case study of hegemony and resistance', *Organization Studies*, 23/3: 421–47.

Jehn, K., Northcraft, G., and Neale, M. (1999), 'Why differences make a difference: a field study of diversity, conflict and performance in workgroups', *Administrative Science Quarterly*, 44/4: 741–63.

Jenkins, R. (1996), *Social Identity*. London: Routledge.

Johnson, P., Balogun, J., and Beech, N. (2010), 'Researching strategists and their identity in practice', in Golsorkhi, D., Rouleau, L., Seidl, D., and Vaara, E. (eds.), *Cambridge Handbook of Strategy as Practice*: 243–57. Cambridge University Press.

Langley, A., Golden-Biddle, K., Reay, T., Denis, J.-L., Hébert, Y., Lamothe, L., and Gervais, J. (2012), 'Identity struggles in merging organizations: renegotiating the sameness–difference dialectic', *Journal of Applied Behavioral Science*, 48/2: 135–67.

Lembke, S., and Wilson, G. (1998), 'Putting the "team" into teamwork: alternative theoretical contributions for contemporary management practice', *Human Relations*, 51/7: 927–44.

Livengood, R. S., and Reger, R. K. (2010), 'That's our turf! Identity domains and competitive dynamics', *Academy of Management Review*, 35/1: 48–66.

Maitlis, S., and Christianson, M. (2014), 'Sensemaking in organizations: taking stock and moving forward', *Academy of Management Annals*, 8/1: 57–125.

Markus, H., and Wurf, E. (1987), 'The dynamic self-concept: a social psychological perspective', *Annual Review of Psychology*, 38: 299–337.

Nag, R., Corley, K. G., and Gioia, D. A. (2007), 'The intersection of organizational identity, knowledge, and practice: attempting strategic change via knowledge grafting', *Academy of Management Journal*, 50/4: 821–47.

Oliver, D., and Bürgi, P. (2005), 'Organizational identity as a strategic practice', paper presented at the fourth 'International critical management studies' conference, Cambridge, 6 July.

Oliver, D., and Roos, J. (2003), 'Dealing with the unexpected: critical incidents in the LEGO Mindstorms team', *Human Relations*, 56/9: 1057–82.

— (2007), 'Beyond text: constructing organizational identity multimodally', *British Journal of Management*, 18/4: 342–58.

Orlikowski, W. J. (2002), 'Knowing in practice: enacting a collective capability in distributed organizing', *Organization Science*, 13/3: 249–73.

Peteraf, M., and Shanley, M. (1997), 'Getting to know you: a theory of strategic group identity', *Strategic Management Journal*, 18/S1: 165–86.

Pettigrew, A. M. (1985), *The Awakening Giant: Continuity and Change in Imperial Chemical Industries*. Oxford: Blackwell.

Porac, J. F., Thomas, H., and Baden-Fuller, C. (1989), 'Competitive groups as cognitive communities: the case of Scottish knitwear manufacturers', *Journal of Management Studies*, 26/4: 397–416.

Pratt, M. G. (2000), 'The good, the bad, and the ambivalent: managing identification among Amway distributors', *Administrative Science Quarterly*, 45/3: 456–93.

— (2003), 'Disentangling collective identities', in Polzer, J. T. (ed.), *Identity Issues in Groups*: 161–88. London: Elsevier.

Pratt, M. G., and Foreman, P. (2000), 'Classifying managerial responses to multiple organizational identities', *Academy of Management Review*, 25/1: 18–42.

Pratt, M. G., and Kraatz, M. S. (2009), 'E pluribus unum: multiple identities and the organizational self', in Dutton, J. E., and Morgan Roberts, L. (eds.), *Exploring Positive Identities in Organizations*: 385–410. Mahwah, NJ: Lawrence Erlbaum.

Pratt, M. G., Rockmann, K. W., and Kaufmann, J. B. (2006), 'Constructing professional identity: the role of work and identity learning among medical residents', *Academy of Management Journal*, 49/2: 235–62.

Ravasi, D., and Phillips, N. (2011), 'Strategies of alignment: organizational identity management and strategic change at Bang & Olufsen', *Strategic Organization*, 9/2: 103–35.

Reger, R. K., Barney, J., Bunderson, J., Foreman, P. O., Gustafson, L. T., Huff, A. S., Martins, L., Sarason, Y., and Stimpert, J. (1998), 'A strategy conversation on the topic of organizational identity', in Whetten, D. A., and Godfrey, P. (eds.), *Identity in Organizations: Building Theory through Conversations*: 99–169. Thousand Oaks, CA: Sage.

Reger, R. K., Gustafson, L. T., Demarie, S. M., and Mullane, J. V. (1994), 'Reframing the organization: why implementing total quality is easier said than done', *Academy of Management Review*, 19/3: 565–84.

Regnér, P., and Zander, U. (2011), 'Knowledge and strategy creation in multinational companies', *Management International Review*, 51/6: 821–50.

Rughase, O. G. (2006), *Identity and Strategy: How Individual Visions Enable the Design of a Market Strategy that Works*. Cheltenham: Edward Elgar.

Schultz, M., and Hernes, T. (2013), 'A temporal perspective on organizational identity', *Organization Science*, 24/1: 1–21.

Schultz, M., Maguire, S., Langley, A., and Tsoukas, H. (eds.) (2012), *Constructing Identity in and around Organizations*. Oxford University Press.

Schwalbe, M. L., and Mason-Schrock, D. (1996), 'Identity work as group process', in Markovsky, B., Lovaglia, M. J., and Simon, R. (eds.), *Advances in Group Processes*, vol. XIII: 115–50. Bingley, UK: Emerald.

Scott, S. G., and Lane, V. R. (2000), 'A stakeholder approach to organizational identity', *Academy of Management Review*, 25/1: 43–62.

Sillince, J. (2006), 'Resources and organizational identities: the role of rhetoric in the creation of competitive advantage', *Management Communication Quarterly*, 20/2: 186–212.

Sillince, J., and Simpson, B. (2010), 'The strategy and identity relationship: towards a processual understanding', in Baum, J. A. C., and Lampel, J. (eds.), *Advances in Strategic Management*, vol. XXVII, *The Globalization of Strategy Research*: 111–43. Bingley, UK: Emerald.

Snow, D. A., and Anderson, L. (1987), 'Identity work among the homeless: the verbal construction and avowal of personal identities', *American Journal of Sociology*, 92/6: 1336–71.

Suddaby, R., Foster, W. M., and Trank, C. Q. (2010), 'Rhetorical history as a source of competitive advantage', in Baum, J. A. C., and Lampel, J. (eds.), *Advances in Strategic Management*, vol. XXVII, *The Globalization of Strategy Research*: 147–73. Bingley, UK: Emerald.

Sveningsson, S., and Alvesson, M. (2003), 'Managing managerial identities: organizational fragmentation, discourse and identity struggle', *Human Relations*, 56/10: 1163–93.

Tajfel, H. (1978), 'Social categorization, social identity and social comparison', in *Differention between Social Groups: Studies in the Social Psychology of Intergroup Relations*: 61–76. London: Academic Press.

Tajfel, H., and Turner, J. C. (1985), 'The social identity theory of intergroup behavior', in Worchel, S., and Austin, W. G. (eds.), *Psychology of Intergroup Relations*, 2nd edn: 7–24. Chicago: Nelson-Hall.

Taylor, J. R., and Van Every, E. J. (1993), *The Vulnerable Fortress: Bureaucratic Organization and Management in the Information Age*. University of Toronto Press.

Turner, J. C. (1982), 'Towards a cognitive redefinition of the social group', in Tajfel, H. (ed.), *Social Identity and Inter-Group Relations*: 15–40. Cambridge University Press.

Vaara, E., and Whittington, R. (2012), 'Strategy-as-practice: taking social practices seriously', *Academy of Management Annals*, 6/1: 285–336.

Van Tonder, C. L., and Lessing, B. C. (2003), 'From identity to organisational identity: evolution of a concept', *South African Journal of Industrial Psychology*, 29/2: 20–8.

Watson, T. J. (2008), 'Managing identity: identity work, personal predicaments and structural circumstances', *Organization*, 15/1: 121–43.

Whetten, D. A. (2006), 'Albert and Whetten revisited: strengthening the concept of organizational identity', *Journal of Management Inquiry*, 15/3: 219–34.

Whetten, D. A., and Godfrey, P. (eds.) (1998), *Identity in Organizations: Developing Theory through Conversations*. Thousand Oaks, CA: Sage.

Whetten, D. A., and Mackey, A. (2002), 'A social actor conception of organizational identity and its implications for the study of organizational reputation', *Business and Society*, 41/4: 393–414.

Whittington, R. (2006), 'Completing the practice turn in strategy research', *Organization Studies*, 27/5: 613–34.

Wieland, S. M. B. (2010), 'Ideal selves as resources for the situated practice of identity', *Management Communication Quarterly*, 24/4: 503–28.

Ybema, S., Keenoy, T., Oswick, C., Beverungen, A., Ellis, N., and Sabelis, I. (2009), 'Articulating identities', *Human Relations*, 62/3: 299–322.

Zaheer, S., Schomaker, M., and Genc, M. (2003), 'Identity versus culture in mergers of equals', *European Management Journal*, 21/2: 185–91.

Sensemaking in strategy as practice: a phenomenon or a perspective?

JOEP CORNELISSEN and HENRI SCHILDT[1]

Given the broad interest of strategy-as-practice scholars in the situated emergence of strategy from the actual actions, choices, cognitions, language and emotions of actors within organizations, it is inevitable that the literature has intersected with the sensemaking literature that has emerged around Karl Weick's work. Sensemaking has long been the dominant theoretical approach to meaning and interpretation in mainstream organization studies, including topics such as decision-making (Maitlis 2005), behaviours during crises (Weick 1993) and organizational change (Gioia *et al.* 1994). Sensemaking in fact provides a range of resources for theorizing, as it is less of a theory than a broad umbrella construct encompassing and synthesizing a range of observations and approaches from social theory, sociology and social psychology (Weick 1979).

In recent years, the concept of sensemaking has been regularly invoked and used as part of SAP research in empirical and theoretical work alike. Indeed, sensemaking has become such a central plank in the study of strategy practice that it is frequently mentioned as a theoretical foundation of the field (Balogun *et al.* 2014). In this chapter we review the various ways in which sensemaking is used in SAP research and elaborate its future potential to advance how we understand and research strategy practices, praxis and practitioners.

Our review of past strategy-as-practice research suggests that sensemaking was, and continues to be, used in a largely perfunctory manner alongside other theoretical sources, such as structuration and practice theory in SAP research, although the appropriation of the sensemaking literature has grown in prominence in recent years. We also find

that the use of sensemaking is more varied than that of most other concepts – and is thus defined in somewhat different ways across SAP studies. In the broadest sense, scholars use the term 'sensemaking' to refer to a category of empirically observable practices, mostly relating to instances of individual thought and group conversations relating to strategy (Balogun *et al.* 2014). In other cases, scholars appropriate the sensemaking literature more explicitly to capture the interplay of interpretations and action as enactment (see Porac, Thomas and Baden-Fuller 1989).

Consistent with the sensemaking literature overall, strategy-as-practice scholars typically invoke sensemaking as an umbrella theoretical perspective rather than as a predictive theory in support of specific hypotheses, propositions, theoretical mechanisms or focal constructs of interest (Weick 1995; Maitlis and Christianson 2014). The wide-ranging and ambitious breadth of the original sensemaking literature (see Weick 1995) aligns well with the original remit of SAP research being primarily methodological and phenomenon-driven. Sensemaking provides, in effect, a rich smorgasbord of theoretical constructs and models that furnish a basic theoretical vocabulary and rough coordinates for focusing on particular phenomena and describing and explaining these in empirical study (Balogun 2006; Jarzabowski 2003; Rouleau 2005). Its basic vocabulary also connects with other theoretical constructs and traditions that have somewhat similar social constructionist and sociocognitive underpinnings, such as discourse (Balogun *et al.* 2014; Mantere and Vaara 2008), framing (Kaplan 2008) and managerial and organizational cognition (Kaplan 2011a). Its broad scope and these interconnections with a range of topics and constructs generally explain the broad appeal of sensemaking across SAP research – and, indeed, management and organization studies more generally.

[1] Both authors have contributed equally to this chapter. We appreciate the feedback from the editors of this volume on earlier versions of this text.

345

Nevertheless, by using sensemaking theory only, or even largely, as a broad umbrella term for an interpretive research approach or for marking empirical observations around thinking and talking related to strategy, we argue that strategy-as-practice researchers are also missing a trick. In fact, we argue that moving beyond the application of sensemaking as a typology or umbrella construct – and thus largely as a guidepost or as a precursor to theory – would instead lead to an increase in the specificity of theoretical claims, and thereby to more precise explanations of the subject matter. In line with this aspiration, we will elaborate specific avenues for theory development that are consistent with the broader theory of sensemaking and that, we think, suit the level of analysis of SAP research. In elaborating these suggestions, we also argue that the concept of sensemaking itself needs to be conceptualized and defined in more precise ways in order to make sure that its theoretical claims are parsimonious and logically coherent and have sufficient operational mileage for empirical research. This may be accomplished for SAP research by relating more specifically to empirical findings in prior sensemaking studies and by connecting more explicitly to particular aspects of sensemaking, such as the original works in sociology and psychology that Weick's (1995) work draws on.

The chapter is structured as follows. We start with a brief introduction to the theory of sensemaking in management and organization theory. We follow this introduction with a summative review of how the theory has been used in strategy-as-practice research. We then highlight common themes and areas of interest in SAP research that have made use of sensemaking. We end the chapter with a number of formative suggestions for SAP researchers to make the most of sensemaking as a theoretical resource.

Core ideas of sensemaking: cognitive frames, enactment and conceptual tensions

Sensemaking represents a body of theory and methodological observations originally articulated by Weick (1979; 1995). It incorporates a number

of key assumptions for studying organizations and organizing, most important among them the concern with human cognition conceived as *cognitive frames* or schemas, and the process of *enactment*, which implies a recursive interaction between actions and interpretations (Weick 1979; 1995). Although sensemaking also incorporates a number of additional elements, such as an evolutionary framework (the enactment, selection, retention cycle) and a strong emphasis on post hoc rationalizations (linking to cognitive dissonance theory), we elaborate cognitive frames and enactment in particular, since they have proved to be the most durable influence (see, for example, Weick, Sutcliffe and Obstfeld 2005).

Cognitive frames

The focus on cognitive frames is premised on the notion that individuals in organizations attend to cues available in the organization and its environment selectively and compress them into much less detailed cognitive frames (also known as *mental models* and schemas: see, for example, Kaplan 2011a). Because such compressed frames guide perceptions, inferences and behaviour (for example, Weick 1995; Weick, Sutcliffe and Obstfeld 2005), actors' cognitive frames, which shape how the environment is understood, often explain their behaviours better than the actors' actual environment. In crisis situations, selective attention and simplified interpretations of the environment in fact often create frames that can lead to behaviours that appear, in hindsight, to be myopic and counterproductive (Weick 1993).

In common with many interpretive approaches, sensemaking examines the relationship between observations and interpretations, seeking to theorize why there is in fact regularity in the way people form interpretations and meaning in organizations (Maitlis and Sonenshein 2010; Maitlis and Christianson 2014). Building on laboratory research in cognitive psychology, sensemaking researchers have also examined how the framing or definition of situations in organizations through words drive perception and the 'extraction of cues' in real time (for example, Cornelissen, Mantere and

Vaara 2014; Maitlis and Sonenshein 2010; Snook 2000; Weick 1993; 1995). Activating a specific cognitive frame creates expectations about important aspects of the context or circumstance, and the individuals to attend to and elaborate on the default or prototypical scenario suggested by this cognitive frame, making perceptions dependent on salient references (see Kahneman 2003: 459).

It is useful to contrast sensemaking as a cognitive perspective to the range of other interpretive approaches that preceded it and that have developed concurrently in sociology. Arguably the most distinguishing factor of sensemaking studies has been its embrace of an ontology that recognizes 'real' material circumstances. In contrast to other social constructivist perspectives, sensemaking studies typically assume that frames are formed as imperfect descriptions of some underlying reality that the researcher has a privileged perspective on (typically through hindsight: for example, Weick 1988; 1993). Thus, while most discourse scholars, for example, would not argue that one way to construct the reality is superior to another, Weick (1993) clearly outlines specific interpretations of a crisis situation as wrong or faulty, categorizing such situations as the 'breaking down' of sensemaking. Suggesting that plausibility trumps accuracy as the criterion for interpretations, Weick (1995) implies a definite reality to make interpretations more or less accurate – something that some of the more constructivist interpretative perspectives do not suggest (for example, Rorty 1989). Although Burrell and Morgan (1979: 266) have criticized Weick's 'ontological oscillation' between the objective view of the researcher and a subjective view of the actors studied, Weick (1995) embraces 'eclecticism', suggesting that there is great value in comparing how researchers armed with the benefit of hindsight and with access to their research subjects interpret a reality.[2]

Despite these original assumptions in the literature, the focus of the more recent sensemaking literature has shifted to more social constructivist

interpretive approaches. Indeed, most researchers following Weick, including the vast majority of strategy-as-practice researchers, have ignored the semi-realist focus on the interpretation of an 'objective' physical or social reality (for example, Daft and Weick 1984). Instead, the term 'sensemaking' tends to be closely aligned with generic interpretive traditions in sociology as the formation of shared understandings (such as visions of an organization's future) with no clear correspondence to any objective external 'facts' (Cornelissen 2012; Corley and Gioia 2004; Gioia and Chittipeddi 1991). Whereas initial formulations by Weick (1995) emphasized sensemaking as a specifically *cognitive* and *retrospective* activity in which actual events and physical reality are interpreted, Weick's own more recent work has similarly shifted to a focus on the *discursive* and *prospective* aspects of sensemaking (Weick, Sutcliffe and Obstfeld 2005).

Enactment

Another key plank of sensemaking is the idea of environmental enactment (Weick 1979). This construct was introduced on the back of connections with cognitive dissonance theory (Festinger 1957), to develop the idea of retrospective rationalizations, and with it the notion of biological enaction and self-organizing systems (Varela 1979). The concept of enactment captures the idea that managers create, or 'enact', their organizational environments by shaping them through their actions and selectively interpreting the results. At its most basic form, 'enactment' captures the active experimentation through which an organization takes actions in order to generate feedback and learn (Daft and Weick 1984). In more complex situations, organizational enactment represents self-fulfilling prophecies whereby (arbitrary) assumptions made by the organization lead it to act in ways that shape its environment towards those assumptions (Weick 1995).

The classic study of the myopic enactment of strategies in the Scottish knitwear community of Hawick by Porac, Thomas and Baden-Fuller (1989) provides the most widely used example.

---

[2] This eclecticism probably follows from Weick's background as an experimental psychologist, wherein subjects' interpretations are seen in the light of the 'correct' answers originally designed into the experiment by the researcher.

Their exemplary analysis demonstrates the way in which cognition and behaviours became tied together, with beliefs about the competition guiding decisions and behaviours and, simultaneously, being reinforced by the actions that were taken. In this way, interpretations are self-fulfilling, because the managers enact the very environment they believe to exist in the first place and continue to reproduce it. The construct of enactment, as part of sensemaking, suggests that an environment is constructed and enacted by actors rather than being a wholly separate external reality that individual agents simply 'cope' with. The key advantage of the enactment perspective is that it provides the potential for a processual analysis that moves beyond isolated snapshots of cognitions or behaviours to the coevolution of actors and the environments they inhabit (Cornelissen, Mantere and Vaara 2014; Porac, Thomas and Baden-Fuller 2011; Kaplan 2011a).

Tensions in organizational sensemaking literature

In addition to the broad range of ideas in Weick's work, sensemaking has been applied to issues ranging from situated coping with crisis (Weick 1988) to organizational coordination (Weick and Roberts 1993) and the management of change (Gioia and Chittipeddi 1991). This widespread use has, perhaps not surprisingly, created several tensions between alternative uses of the concept. These uses are not really contradictions but, rather, variations in the way sensemaking is approached and understood. The tensions we highlight here reflect the methodological and theoretical choices of scholars who use the sensemaking perspective, and as such they also represent opportunities for strategy-as-practice scholars to bridge across insights from the somewhat disconnected contributions in the literature.

Action-related frame application versus discursive frame construction

The organizational sensemaking literature has commonly focused on the highly situated 'activation', or inducement, of cognitive frames in the heads of individuals and their relationship to perceptions, interpretations and actions in real time (Whiteman and Cooper 2011), often when immediate action is required (Weick 1993). In such a situated context, sensemaking involves individuals assigning environmental cues to a prior cognitive frame, or schema (Starbuck and Milliken 1988; Weick 1995), which enables them to 'comprehend, understand, explain, attribute, extrapolate, and predict' (Starbuck and Milliken 1988: 51). The activity of matching stimuli or cues to a cognitive frame points to the retrospective nature of much sensemaking activity, as well as the effect that an activated frame has on interpretation and experience (Weick, Sutcliffe and Obstfeld 2005). Once invoked, frames, as part of sensemaking, impart organizing structure and may have a strong hold over individuals' interpretations and actions in context. In other words, activating a cognitive frame creates expectations about important aspects of the context or circumstance by directing individuals to elaborate on the default or prototypical scenario in a manner suggested by the frame (see Tannen 1979; Cornelissen and Werner 2014).

In contrast, a more recent part of the literature focuses on processes of meaning construction in and through the exchange of language, or any other symbolic signification processes that take place over longer time periods (Maitlis and Christianson 2014). This literature focuses on how individuals and groups in organizations collectively construct a 'sense' of complex or abstract issues such as organizational changes (Corley and Gioia 2004; Gioia and Chittipeddi 1991). Here, the interpretation is not established through the selective yet largely mechanistic application of a pre-existing cognitive frame but, rather, often entails the joint construction of an entirely new frame in interactions between individuals in groups or larger organizations (Maitlis and Christianson 2014). This alternative reading of sensemaking implies a shift away from individuals to groups and organizations, and from sensemaking as accessing or retrieving cognition (from a largely cognitive psychological perspective) to sensemaking as a social construction or joint accomplishment. In other words, the latter stream of work draws on more social constructionist commitments (Morgan, Frost and Pondy 1983), in which language and symbolic interactions take centre stage in sensemaking.

Abstracted discourse and frames versus materiality and situated cognition

The strong social constructionist emphasis in the sensemaking literature not only complements the cognitive psychological focus in Weick's initial work (1979) but also challenges the assumption that language simply triggers or prompts the retrieval of frames and frame-based meaning and expectations from memory. Rather, words and expressions used in a specific context may *construct* frames and expectations (see, for example, Cornelissen 2012; Quinn and Worline 2008). One of the main insights in recent sensemaking studies is the observation that more generally the bodily actions of individuals, including verbal speech, do not simply express previously formed mental concepts or broader cognitive frames (Cornelissen and Clarke 2010). In contrast, bodily practices, such as bodily gesturing and physical social interaction, should be seen as part and parcel of the very activity in which concepts and conceptualizations are formed (Cornelissen, Mantere and Vaara 2014; Maitlis and Sonenshein 2010; Stigliani and Ravasi 2012; Whiteman and Cooper 2011).

Illustrating the potential inherent in a more situated and embodied approach to sensemaking, recent studies have elaborated how individuals form conceptualizations (that is, make sense) through physically grasping, holding or manipulating material objects (Stigliani and Ravasi 2012; Whiteman and Cooper 2011). Interpretations are in effect constructed through interaction with material objects, and based on the sensations and ideas that such interactions afford (Whiteman and Cooper 2011). Furthermore, when such embodied acts are taking place in a social context, the physical manipulation of objects may be exploited to cue meaning to others, in essence providing a 'scaffolding' around which new meanings are collectively constructed (Kendon 2004). Stigliana and Ravasi (2012), for example, demonstrate how designers shared visuals and artefacts that grounded common imagery for new products and that allowed them to collectively

elaborate and build up new emergent ideas. In this process, individuals, while communicating and interacting with one another, do not need to share, or even have access to, the same knowledge (Whiteman and Cooper 2011). Instead, in such ongoing processes of communication, individuals generally exploit the built-up 'common ground' between them – in the form, for example, of a redrawn visual diagram (Bechky 2003). The common ground provides a resource for constructing collective understanding and for deriving pragmatic inferences that guide action (Clark 1996; Goffman 1974).

Summary

The various strands of the sensemaking literature considered above are all consistent with the notion of sensemaking as frame-based meaning construction – that is, the formation, abandonment and changing of beliefs coherently grouped as part of frames. In what we consider to be the most interesting studies in the sensemaking tradition, the focus has shifted away from existing cognitive frames and their effects at the individual level to the joint creation and active use of frame-based meanings within organizations and industries. In other words, the more recent and interesting sensemaking literature shifts attention to instances of fram*ing* in real-time communication, elaborating how sensemaking combines language, cognition, behaviours and material contexts. This emphasis away from a strictly cognitive to a more social constructionist reading of sensemaking chimes well with a broader shift of the strategy field away from considering strategic cognition and mental models in isolation (Kaplan 2011a) towards areas of research such as strategy as practice, which embed cognition and action in ongoing material and symbolic acts of individual managers within groups and cultures in which strategy is collectively created, made and done (Rasche and Chia 2009).

The use of sensemaking in strategy-as-practice research

The previous section described the broad contours of sensemaking in mainstream management and organization studies more generally. In this section we move from this broader introduction of sensemaking to a more specific review of how it has been invoked and used as part of SAP research. To do so, we started with automated searches within the Social Sciences Citation Index. We began by searching for articles that mentioned both 'sensemaking' and 'strategy' as part of their title, abstract or keywords. We then filtered the articles to focus primarily on papers in which 'strategy' and 'practice' were mentioned. These two steps led to a set of fifty-six articles, which includes studies that are specifically labelled as strategy as practice and studies that focus on sensemaking/giving and strategic change, as well as more general work on managerial and organizational cognition. We read through all these articles, and list the most prominent studies in Table 20.1.

Table 20.1 provides a systematic overview of the reviewed strategy-as-practice studies and their use of sensemaking. As indicated by the table, many studies on sensemaking focus on various issues that individuals and groups in organization interpret or evaluate, such as the extent of political conflict (Mueller *et al.* 2013). The most central and generic focus of SAP sensemaking research, however, has been on the formation of alignment within (Jarzabkowski and Seidl 2008; Kaplan 2008) and between (Rouleau 2005) different levels of organizational hierarchy. We now highlight a number of observations related to our review and reading of these studies.

Perhaps the most striking observation we made based on our detailed reading of these articles was the common use of sensemaking not as a theory or perspective but as a shorthand or label for an empirical phenomenon. 'Sensemaking' in strategy-as-practice studies often simply marks instances of thinking and talking in organizations through which individuals and groups reach conclusions concerning some ambiguous or novel strategic issue. By studying such instances of thinking and talking in organizations, SAP scholarship on sensemaking has drawn attention to a number of important topics, which we summarize briefly: the role of the past and the future in strategy formation, and how leaders influence employees, as 'followers', through sensegiving practices.

Sensemaking as empirical phenomena of thinking and talking

A close reading of the literature revealed that, rather than a theoretical perspective, strategy as practice predominantly appropriates sensemaking as a broad umbrella construct or as designating empirically situated practices (Das and Kumar 2010; Fenton and Langley 2011). An early example in the SAP tradition is provided by Pye (2002), who offers up sensemaking as the most apt theoretical perspective for explaining how and why directors of large corporate firms may have shifted in their thinking about how to 'run' an organization. The accounts of these directors are not directly analysed or explained with sensemaking constructs, however, and as a result the use of sensemaking in this study remains rather ambiguous. Whereas the Pye (2002) study perhaps pre-dates the initial emergence of the SAP community, a number of studies that are specifically labelled as strategy as practice similarly offer up sensemaking as a broad theoretical perspective or framework for SAP research (Balogun 2006; Balogun *et al.* 2014).

Other examples of sensemaking as a category of empirical processes include micro-studies of sensemaking as situated instances of thinking and talking by managers and employees within organizations (Balogun *et al.* 2005; Rouleau 2005; Rouleau and Balogun 2011; Liu and Maitlis 2014; Kwon, Clarke and Wodak 2014). Rouleau and Balogun (2011), for example, present a rich set of empirical cases of how middle managers used their skills in language and communication to persuade employees to support and enact a change. Their analysis follows a pragmatic rhetorical tradition, in that they detail how managers set the scene, target and engage certain individuals and frame the change in a very skilful manner. Other examples in this vein are recent studies of 'talk' in meetings, and how specific discursive turns or expressions may pragmatically influence others, and in turn create a consensus, common ground or resolution around a set of strategic issues or decisions (Kwon, Clarke and Wodak 2014; Liu and Maitlis 2014).

It is also perhaps somewhat worrying that, for most   strategy-as-practice   research   papers

Table 20.1 Selected studies bridging the strategy-as-practice approach and sensemaking

Study	Research question/aim	Use of sensemaking	Other theoretical sources	Research design	Key findings and implications
Bogner and Barr (2000)	How do managers make sense of hypercompetitive environments, and how does their sensemaking lead to actions and the potential formation of new industry recipes?	Central construct: 'adaptive sensemaking'	Cognitive frames, mental models	Theoretical paper	Sensemaking is viewed as conscious act of rethinking industry circumstances and as a cognitive disposition to anticipate and respond to change. Sensemaking is fostered through cognitive diversity in decision-making teams.
Pye (2002)	How do directors suggest they 'run' organizations, and how have such explanatory accounts changed over time?	Central explanation	-	58 interviews with directors of large UK plcs in 1987–1989 and 1998–2000	Accounts of good governance and strategy have become more similar over time, in part based on language associated with successive corporate governance codes. Sensemaking is offered as best possible explanation of strategists' thinking and discourse, over and beyond other discourse, sociological and institutional explanations.
Jarzabkowski (2003)	How are specific strategic practices implicated in sustaining or changing patterns of strategic activity over time?	Citations	Activity systems, structuration theory	Comparative case study design of the strategy process in three UK universities (open-ended interviews and observations of meetings)	Strategic practices tie actors and structures together, and may be based on inherent contradictions that surface, occasioning change. Analysis of activity systems is limited to assumptions about continuity and change → need for alternative frameworks (Jarzabkowski 2005; 2008).
Rouleau (2005)	What are the micro-practices of sensemaking and sensegiving through which middle managers try to initiate and effect change?	Fundamental theoretical frame	No: specific literature on middle managers and strategic change	Ethnography, mainly participative observations of a strategic change of reorienting the clothing lines of the firm	The change process involves iterative conversations around translating the new orientation into new routine products. Discourse, or language, is essential to create new shared understanding and bridge client expectations; middle managers' role is to translate and codify changes into new routines.
Balogun (2006)	How do individual- and group-level sensemaking processes impact the effectiveness of a strategic change initiative?	Fundamental theoretical frame	No: specific literature on middle managers and strategic change	Diary study of 26 middle managers across three divisions in a privatized utility company undergoing change	Employees interpret activities and events that they cannot understand on the basis of past schemas, which in turn may trigger a chain of interpretations that can have positive or negative consequences.

Table 20.1 (*cont.*)

Study	Research question/aim	Use of sensemaking	Other theoretical sources	Research design	Key findings and implications
					Sensemaking is seen as a broad intersubjective, communicative template for studying change; sensemaking episodes are interlinked and lead to (unforeseen) organizational consequences.
Bean and Hamilton (2006)	How do employees in remote and distributed workplaces make sense of a major change?	Fundamental theoretical frame	No	Observations and interviews with employees of a telecommunications company following a downsizing and move to a flexible project management structure for the entire organization	Leaders are framed through metaphors and catchphrases in support of the change, with some employees adapting their sensemaking and others actively questioning or resisting the change – yet the lack of physical boundaries inhibited sensemaking to converge and stabilize among employees.
Maitlis and Lawrence (2007)	What are the conditions that trigger and enable stakeholder and leader sensegiving?	Central theoretical frame	No; literature on strategic change	Interviews and observations of change processes in three symphony orchestras	Sensemaking is seen as a broad intersubjective, communicative template for studying change; variation in leader sensegiving and in compliant and resistant forms of employee sensemaking. Leader sensegiving around the change was triggered by whether issues were salient and the environment complex, and stakeholders doubted the competence of these leaders; and enabled by their issue related expertise and discursive competence.
Kaplan (2008)	How do power and framing together influence decision-making about the strategic direction of a firm?	Citations	Cognitive frames	Ethnography of a communication technology company	The discursive ability of leaders is crucial in order to frame the nature of a strategic change and shift the sensemaking of employees in a desired direction. Sensemaking and sensegiving interconnected in framing contests between managers on the strategic direction of the firm. Frames are both cognitive and symbolic; which frames won in the end and informed the decision depended on the skilful way in which certain actors used frames to mediate and bridge between competing views and interests.
Jarzabkowski and Seidl (2008)	How are strategy meetings involved in stabilizing existing strategic orientations or in	Citations	No; literature on strategy as practice	Comparative study of 51 meetings in three UK universities	The conventional script of meetings (initiation, conduct, termination) together with specific actions of the chairperson and participants open up or restrict strategy discussions.

Table 20.1 (cont)

Study	Research question/aim	Use of sensemaking	Other theoretical sources	Research design	Key findings and implications
	instigating and sustaining a change in strategic orientations?			(observations of meetings)	Free discussions that open up during meetings are important to initiate variations on a particular strategy.
Sonenshein (2009)	How do ethical issues emerge in organizations, and how, based on their emergence, do employees make sense of them?	Central explanation	Issue-selling	Case study (including survey and interviews) of employees of a retailing firm going through a strategic change process	Employees raise ethical issues concerning the change (or, alternatively, shift to the majority opinion and status quo) triggered by broken promises, contrast or discrepancies. Triggers (such as broken promises or contrast with the past) for sensemaking raised ambiguity and active occasion of sensemaking during a change.
Rasche and Chia (2009)	'[T]he meaning and significance of the term "social practice" and its relation to strategy-as-practice research'	Interpretation: the formation of meaning based on embodied background knowledge of the actors	Practice theories (neo-structuralist and neo-interpretative)	Conceptual	'[S]ocial practices in general and strategy practices in particular can be approached from either a neo-structuralist and/or neo-interpretative perspective.'
Das and Kumar (2010)	How are alliances interpreted by partners from different countries? How do these interpretations shape behaviours?	Interpretation: application of frames to understand alliance progress. Enactment: frame choice influences the evolution of the alliance	Cognitive frames; strategic alliance literature; international business (national cultures)	Conceptual paper	'Sensemaking of chaos' – a view in which unexpected events need to be explained and managed – versus 'sensemaking in chaos', in which the unexpected is the operating norm and potentially 'transformative'.
McCabe (2010)	'[H]ow ambiguity infuses the exercise of power in both intentional and unintentional ways'	Interpretation: the formation of meaning, subject to power	Critical theory, power	Case study of an organization, 17 interviews + various documents	Power is distributed among managers and non-managers in strategy practice; ambiguity can both increase and decrease power.
Rouleau and Balogun (2011)	What discursive activities do middle managers use to make sense of a change and to involve others in the broader change effort?	Fundamental theoretical frame	No: specific literature on middle managers and strategic change	Secondary reading of the interview data from the research projects reported by Rouleau (2010) and Balogun et al. (2005)	The discursive ability of middle managers is central to translating a change into action; such ability does not only relate to skills in language use and conversational skills but also to performative acts of setting the scene (knowing who to target, which people t bring together, etc.)

Table 20.1 (*cont.*)

Study	Research question/aim	Use of sensemaking	Other theoretical sources	Research design	Key findings and implications
					The sensegiving of middle managers is more likely to be effective in finding broad support for a change when it uses language and communication format that skilfully mediates between different interests and brings groups of people together.
Fenton and Langley (2011)	What is the contribution of the narrative perspective to strategy as practice?	Peripheral: sensemaking broadly captures the formation of strategy but remains implicit	Narrative theory	Conceptual	Narratives influence sensemaking through praxis (making sense of strategies through narratives), practices (narratives as inputs to sensemaking), actors (by defining identities), texts and 'narrative infrastructure'.
Leonardi, Tsedal and Neeley (2012)	'[L]earn why managers often communicate the same message through different media'	Interpretation: the formation of consensus concerning the implications of a discrepant event to the organization	Communications	Ethnographic field notes from a case company	Managers with positional power communicate once and then follow up if the message doesn't sink in. Managers without positional power communicate multiple times to enrol recipients into interpretive process
Vuori and Virtaharju (2012)	How can emotional arousal be used to enhance the adoption of new beliefs through sensegiving?	Focus on sensegiving and sensemaking as the interactive discussions in which the beliefs promoted by managers are accepted	Emotions	Survey + interviews + observations	*'The basic idea is that sense-receivers will adopt new strong beliefs if a sensegiver first focuses on increasing their level of emotional arousal, and only then associates that arousal with a desired way of understanding the organization and its situation.'*
Küpers, Mantere and Statler (2013)	Complement cognitive sensemaking by examining strategizing from the embodied perspective as narration at the outskirts of the organization	Interpretation: particularly middle manager evaluation of top management's communicated strategy	Narrative theory/ storytelling; embodied practice approaches	Action research (workshop)	Narrative practices related to middle management strategizing: struggles over 'hot' words; desacralization of strategy; rituals of self-sacrifice.
Kaplan and Orlikowski (2013)	When does sensemaking involving the past, present and future (temporal work) lead to acceptable conclusions? When do sensemaking outcomes	Interpretation: synonymous to 'temporal work', the practices (mainly discussions) through which mutually	Cognitive frames	Qualitative single company case	Sensemaking about the future often works through analogies.

Consensus is particularly difficult to create with regard to the future. |

Table 20.1 (cont.)

Study	Research question/aim	Use of sensemaking	Other theoretical sources	Research design	Key findings and implications
	lead to change versus stability?	acceptable assumptions, beliefs and conclusions are reached			Sensemaking (involving the past, present and future) is successful when the outcomes are coherent, plausible, and politically acceptable.
Stigliani and Ravasi (2012)	Accounting for the interplay between conversational and material practices in the transition from individual to collective sensemaking	Interpretation and creation: projective and future-oriented generation and evaluation of new ideas, including individual cognition, conversations and the material props	'Material turn'	Qualitative, single company case	Develop a model with four stages of 'macro-level sensemaking' linked to micro-level practices. Four stages are: noticing and bracketing; articulating; elaborating; and influence.
Mueller et al. (2013)	How do top management teams make sense of organizational politics and what are the implications for change?	The creation of discursive accounts that provide shared meaning (explanations/stories) of organizational reality (here, politics)	Power	Ethnomethodology, case study of a multinational	Power and politics are not independent factors exogenous to talk but also organizational interpretations that emerge from collective and individual sensemaking.
Balogun et al. (2014)	What theoretical domains and realms of analysis affect our understanding of strategic discourse in context?	Central explanation	Power and sociomateriality	Theoretical paper	Discursive research on strategy as practice to connect with research on other aspects of strategy, such as material practices, thoughts and action. Strategy as practice needs to have a firmer theoretical base in traditions such as sensemaking to gain more theoretical traction (and to offset a purely discursive perspective).

investigating sensemaking as an empirical phenomenon, little or no difference would result from
replacing the term 'sensemaking' with the collo-
quial phrase 'thinking and talking'. For example,
in a study by Kaplan and Orlikowski (2013), when
actors 'make sense' of strategy they think and talk
about it. The outcome of 'sensemaking' is predominantly the endorsement or rejection of certain
propositional beliefs (often called *interpretations*
or *meanings*) that emerge from talking and thinking, either individually or in groups (for example,
Maitlis 2005). Given such empirical focus, what do
actors in organizations think and talk about when
they 'make sense'? While there is no single answer
to this among the SAP studies we reviewed, almost
all instances identify sensemaking as concerning
something ambiguous, typically the identity or
strategy of the organization (Gioia and Thomas
1996) or events that are taking place in its environment (Nigam and Ocasio 2010). At times sensemaking can be about future products (Stigliani and
Ravasi 2012), the environment of the organization
(Porac, Thomas and Baden-Fuller 1989), strategic
changes (Balogun 2005) or specific issues, problems or events (Maitlis 2005; Sonenshein 2009).
With a focus on the ambiguous and atypical, sensemaking tends to be invoked in the papers we
reviewed as an episodic response to particular situations in which meaning has to be constructed or
sense regained, as opposed to seeing sensemaking
as a continuous and basic feature of organizational
cognition and behaviour (Weick, Sutcliffe and
Obstfeld 2005).

Given this phenomenon-based approach to sensemaking, the use of sensemaking by strategy-as-
practice scholars is often also influenced by other
theories that they use or (implicitly) subscribe to.
For example, scholars who take a strong practice
theory approach to sensemaking will see it less as a
deliberate activity and more as a habitual routine
driven by actors' macro-cultural backgrounds
(Rasche and Chia 2009). Indeed, from neo-
structural and strong practice approaches, the outcome of sensemaking episodes (that is, how actors
think and talk about various circumstances) is predominantly defined by the background and
embodied habitus of the actors (Rasche and Chia
2009) – which is quite distinct from many of

Weick's conceptions (for example, Weick 1993).
In contrast, when actors take a narrative approach
to sensemaking (Fenton and Langley 2011), the
outcomes of sensemaking are seen as more intrinsically connected to the crafting of narratives (see
also Boje 1991). Again, when Fenton and Langley
(2011) suggest that the conclusions that actors in
organizations reach are linked to the 'narrative
infrastructure' and 'metaconversations' that shape
the talking and thinking around strategy, sensemaking is conceived and theorized from a perspective that is quite distinct from Weick's (1979)
original social psychological approach.

Recognizing explicitly that 'sensemaking' as it
is used in current strategy-as-practice articles represents largely the empirical phenomenon of
talking and thinking might appear at first to
devalue the research tradition. We think that such
a usage also helps to demystify sensemaking in a
positive way, however, drawing attention to the
value of studying thinking and talking from a
naturalistic and situated perspective without an
overly strong guiding theoretical commitment.
The concept of sensemaking has, arguably, helped
legitimize the ambitious efforts of SAP scholars to
explore the antecedents and consequences of thinking and talking collectively about strategy. Indeed,
one could argue that there is hardly a more central
question in strategy practice than when, why, how
and with what consequences individuals and
groups think and talk about ambiguous issues
around strategy.

The future and the past

The focus on sensemaking has also attuned recent
strategy-as-practice research to the role of the past,
the present and the future in the creation and communication of strategies. Following sociological
and narrative theorists (for example, Emirbayer
and Mische 1998; Ricœur 1984), Kaplan and Orlikowski (2013) draw attention to the fact that interpretations formed through thinking and talking
tend to always relate to the past, the present and
the future. In doing so, they provide an empirical
study that takes the future-oriented aspect of sensemaking seriously (Weick, Sutcliffe and Obstfeld

2005) and shows how interpretations of the past are vital not only for organizational identity work (for example, Ravasi and Schultz 2006) but also for the formulation of strategic forecasts. While Kaplan and Orlikowski offer the new term 'temporal work' to depict sensemaking that is sensitive to the past and the future, essentially *all* strategy-related sensemaking includes some form of temporal work (see Gioia and Chittipeddi 1991; Gioia *et al.* 1994).

Specifically, uncertainty and the ability of actors to reach an acceptable interpretation under conditions of ambiguity and competing interpretations is a central problem in strategy practice (Kaplan and Orlikowski 2013). Given the inherent uncertainty of the future and the ambiguity of any evidence that may back interpretations of future events and outcomes, it is often hard for managers to reach a consensus that can act as a basis for deliberate decisions and actions. Without some shared understanding of the future, however, no plans or decisions can be made. Nevertheless, an unfounded commitment to an expected future can also lead to potentially disastrous decisions (Porac, Thomas and Baden-Fuller 1989; 2011). We note in existing work in strategy as practice and sensemaking more generally that there are different ways of conceptualizing prospective, or future-oriented, notions of sensemaking. One way in which prospective sensemaking has been defined is in reference to retrospective sensemaking, the suggestion being that individuals are not automatically and recursively tied to any prior cognitive frames or beliefs but can also construct through creative leaps or by learning, from others, new sets of beliefs (Cornelissen and Clarke 2010; Gioia and Mehra 1996; Stigliani and Ravasi 2012). 'Prospective' in this sense thus refers to extending prior beliefs into a new set of understandings.

Another definition of future or prospective sensemaking involves narrative accounts of individuals that clearly foreground a time dimension and suggest where events may be heading (Fenton and Langley 2011). Here, the future is conceptualized as an integral part of individuals' sensemaking, with the narrative form compressing a complex set of circumstances and cause-and-effect relationships into a neat narrative sequence (see also

Garud, Schildt and Lant 2014). Finally, the approach of Kaplan and Orlikowski (2013) suggests the need for more processual or longitudinal analyses that describe how sensemaking may shift over time, regardless of whether the thinking and talking of individuals clearly incorporate references to the future. Future work in strategy as practice may follow in this direction, and may even opt to extend analyses of strategy into a process tradition that extends beyond specific events or episodes that are assumed to mark and 'capture' strategy in very specific and circumscribed ways (Chia and Holt 2006; Schultz and Hernes 2013; Holt and Cornelissen 2014).

Sensegiving practices

Although a number of sensemaking studies have focused on how sense is created in a bottom-up manner between individuals with similar (professional) backgrounds and roughly positioned at the same level of hierarchy (Stigliani and Ravasi 2012; Quinn and Worline 2008), a significant body of research on strategy as practice has focused specifically on how leaders or managers at higher levels in an organization may direct and guide the collective sensemaking of others within that organization (Balogun 2005; Maitlis 2005; Maitlis and Lawrence 2007; Mantere, Schildt and Sillince 2012; Rouleau 2005). Gioia and Chittipeddi (1991) describe such strategic acts of persuasion and communication as 'sensegiving' aimed at influencing 'the sensemaking and meaning construction of others toward a preferred redefinition of organizational reality' (Gioia and Chittipeddi 1991: 442). This initial work on sensegiving highlighted the importance of leaders or managers strategically using certain keywords, slogans, catchphrases and metaphors in conceptualizing a change or strategic initiative and in directing employees and other stakeholders in their sensemaking of that change or initiative (Gioia and Chittipeddi 1991; Gioia *et al.* 1994). In these studies, Gioia and his colleagues, for example, point out how the president of a US state university used clever metaphorical phrases and idioms (such as 'world-class') to initiate a change and to direct senior members of the university and other stake-holders in their own interpretations and ways of implementing the change.

Subsequent research on sensegiving has explored the mechanics of communication between different layers of an organization (for example, Balogun and Johnson 2004; Maitlis 2005), as well as the 'discursive ability', or communication skills, of leaders and managers to conceptually frame a strategic decision or change and to gain support for their views (Maitlis and Lawrence 2007; Rouleau and Balogun 2011). To be successful, sensegiving must often be preceded by organizational sensebreaking – efforts through which managers try to make their subordinates reject or give up beliefs and commitments that constitute the existing cognitive frame (Mantere, Schildt and Sillince 2012; Pratt 2000). A key emphasis in many of these studies is that individual managers or leaders can, by virtue of their hierarchical position and discursive skills, shape and direct the interpretations of organizational members and other stakeholders towards a new set of interpretive frames (for example, Fiss and Zajac 2006; Gioia and Chittipeddi 1991; Maitlis and Lawrence 2007; Mantere, Schildt and Sillince 2012). As Fiss and Zajac (2006: 1174) suggest, '[B]y framing strategic change and thereby articulating a specific version of reality, organizations may secure both the understanding and support of key stakeholders for their new strategic orientation, because it shapes how people notice and interpret what is going on, influencing the strategic choices that they subsequently make.'

Researchers have provided evidence that leaders indeed gain 'followers' for their strategy depending on how they communicate with them (Maitlis and Lawrence 2007; Mantere, Schildt and Sillince 2012; Rouleau and Balogun 2011). Even so, the implicit premise is also one of an asymmetry based on hierarchical power differences: members of the organization are cast as passive agents whose basic role is to respond (or not) to the manager's efforts, when sense is literally 'given' to them. Recent work has not so much questioned this assumption as pointed to the largely neglected issue of power and politics in sensemaking (Maitlis and Sonenshein 2010; Maitlis and Christianson

2014; McCabe 2010). The question of who is able to give sense and define a common reality requires a stronger theorization of power and politics as part of sensemaking, including how it may be exercised through the wielding of discourses, resources or 'soft' power by leaders or senior managers, but equally by middle managers and other employees in the organization. Sensegiving therefore provides a natural focus in studies of strategy practices (Bean and Hamilton 2006; Gioia and Chittipeddi 1991; Maitlis and Lawrence 2007; Rouleau and Balogun 2011). In addition, moving beyond a focus on the content of communications, recent work in strategy as practice has also started to focus on issues such as emotions in sensegiving (Vuori and Virtaharju 2012), finding that the increase of emotional arousal by leaders facilitates the acceptance of new beliefs by followers.

Future research opportunities

We envisage sensemaking remaining a central topic in strategy-as-practice research. The current literature on sensemaking and SAP research is rich and varied and features a range of topics and themes. In this chapter we have summarized a number of overarching themes that cut across the literature, and in doing so have attempted to highlight the dominant ways in which sensemaking has been used and invoked in strategy-as-practice research. We have also discussed the use of sensemaking in SAP research against the background of how the sensemaking concept has been used in the management and organizational literature more generally.

On the basis of this discussion, we believe that future research can take two alternative paths. First, it is possible that sensemaking remains a broad umbrella construct or shorthand code for attending to empirical instances of thinking and talking in organizations, with the focus being on elaborating antecedents and consequences for how individuals in organizations reach certain conclusions. Sensemaking may then remain a helpful term (albeit jargon) for conveying what is studied. Should this first path be chosen, we envisage SAP research on sensemaking drawing more heavily on other explicit theories (such as around identity, discourse or rhetoric) that help provide structure to their empirical examinations. Second, strategy-as-practice researchers can, alternatively, become more accurate in their appropriation of sensemaking, synthesizing sub-streams of empirical sensemaking studies and focusing on particular aspects, such as the selective application of cognitive frames or longitudinal enactment processes. Since sensemaking is already fragmented, to the extent that any single study cannot cover all the bases of sensemaking theory (Maitlis and Christianson 2014), researchers may opt to commit themselves to a specific fragment of sensemaking research more explicitly, and in doing so may increase the coherence and specificity of their terminology.

While these two paths, as general directions, apply to SAP research on sensemaking, by the same token they also apply to sensemaking research more generally. As Cornelissen and Clarke (2010: 553) comment:

> Over the past fifteen years, sensemaking has become an increasingly popular umbrella construct (Hirsch & Levin, 1999) that has usurped divergent theoretical principles around, for example, cognitive dissonance, the autonomic nervous system, behavioral enactment, social identity, behavioral routines, emotions, speech acts, and escalation of commitment (e.g., Weick, 1995; Weick et al., 2005). Integration of these principles into a single construct is laudable, but it lacks specificity and provides broad, rather than specific, guidance to empirical research.

For sensemaking to remain useful to management researchers, we believe that it is necessary for researchers to use and specify the concept in theoretically specific ways that allow them to explore certain knowledge claims and form their findings into a coherent whole. While researchers may not want to give up on the breadth associated with the concept, using it in an empirical context necessitates specific acts of translation or a focus on specific constructs, such as enactment or cognitive frames. In the rest of this section we discuss specific opportunities related to temporality, materiality and sensegiving in strategy-as-practice research and the role that a sensemaking lens might play in exploring these topics.

Temporality and sensemaking

In terms of specific research agendas for SAP research, temporality represents one of the most vital areas for further research. Strategy is inherently about the past (how the organization has become what it is), the present (what the organization and its environment currently are) and the future (what the organization can become and in what environment it must operate). Few approaches to strategy, besides sensemaking, have managed to even recognize these tensions, however (though see the work on organizational identity by Ravasi and Schultz 2006; Schultz and Hernes 2013). Ontologically and epistemologically, management researchers have typically struggled with conceptualizing and studying time, in part because of their methodological grounding in variance approaches to research (Langley 1999). Strategy-as-practice research is one area of research that clearly recognizes this challenge and offers real opportunities for stronger theorizations of time within strategy practices and outcomes. It is also fair to say, however, that it has not come that far in doing so. Future research on the future (pardon the pun) would therefore do well, we think, to identify and borrow other theoretical tools from domains such as narrative theory and the sociology of expectations to grapple with this pregnant domain (for example, Garud, Schildt and Lant 2014). Sensemaking theory constitutes one set of viable resources that SAP researchers may use for this purpose, although, when they use it, they may want to give sensemaking concepts a more distinct future-oriented and processual dimension (Stigliani and Ravasi 2012).

Materiality and sensemaking

Another research agenda involves expanding sensemaking research from cognition and discourse to various 'material' elements, such as physical and virtual artefacts, drawings and embodied settings (Stigliani and Ravasi 2012; Whiteman and Cooper 2011). In their classic studies, Porac, Thomas and Baden-Fuller (1989; 2011) have already highlighted how the beliefs of knitwear manufacturers were built up on the basis of communal notions of identity and material practices such as pricing, procurement and positioning in a market. These tight links between cognition and materiality in turn led to biased perceptions, constrained alternative conceptualizations and directed actions in a contained and repetitive cycle. The result, in their study, was that actors in the knitwear industry were not able to redefine their competitive space and basis of competition, despite the warning signals. Porac, Thomas and Baden-Fulle (2011: 652) have recently concluded that 'perhaps [the] most important observation coming out of the Scottish study' is that 'the cognitive and material aspects of the knitwear industry (indeed, all industries) are thickly interwoven. It seems to us that it is this intermingling that makes strategic imagination, innovation, and new ways of acting so difficult, and the downward spiral of mature businesses so problematic.'

While perhaps less dramatic in terms of consequences, a range of strategy-as-practice studies have focused on traditional strategy objects, such as PowerPoint slides, figures and diagrams, and how these mediate processes of sensemaking, or thinking and talking (Kaplan 2011b). There is also increasingly a broader sociomaterial focus in SAP research (Balogun *et al.* 2014), which embeds strategizing individuals in specific material contexts such as meetings and strategy workshops (Jarzabkowski and Seidl 2008), and focuses on how specific tools (analytical diagrams, software) and objects (flip charts, Post-it notes), together with those contexts, mediate the sensemaking that takes place. The latter focus suggests a move that we think is particularly useful, namely adding more analytical layers to the otherwise predominant focus of sensemaking as purely symbolic processes of language use and cognition – a reduction that, as we noted, became prevalent some years ago but is not reflective of the breadth of the original sensemaking concept.

A richer analytical approach such as this that attends to materiality is not without its challenges, however. For one, it requires 'multi-modal' analysis, whereby researchers develop and apply protocols towards analysing other modes of sensemaking and communication, such as visual diagrams and behavioural gestures, alongside speech. Such multi-modal approaches are quickly

becoming mainstream within the social sciences, however (perhaps marking a new 'turn' in scholarship and methods), and SAP research may well be one of the first communities that introduce and mainstream such approaches into strategy and management and organization studies more generally.

Sensegiving and sensemaking

A final suggestion for further research would be to advance our understanding of sensegiving practices, and how and when managers manage to gain broad-based support for strategies or strategic changes. Current strategy-as-practice research on sensegiving is starting to explore other dynamics of communication and meaning construction besides the mentioned presupposed asymmetrical influence model, in which sense is literally 'given', or handed over by managers to employees (Bean and Hamilton 2006). Rouleau and Balogun (2011), for example, detail the conversational dynamics between middle managers and employees that are crucial to the construction of joint meanings, and for those meanings to stick. Kaplan (2008) demonstrates how sensegiving and sensemaking overlap and interact in framing contests between managers, as they strategically try to win over others in the organization to support a strategic direction or change. Framing, Kaplan suggests, is both symbolic and cognitive (Goffman 1974) and involves mediating between joint interests and different understandings (Cornelissen 2012), rather than simply subscribing to a linear model of the one party convincing the other of their views and interests. In other words, although such a linear focus may characterize some contexts of strategic change (Gioia and Chittipeddi 1991), the assumption within SAP work of strategy practices being distributed and done across levels in the organization would suggest a move away from this classic premise in future sensegiving research. Such a move may be facilitated by a focus on more distributed and dialogic models of communication, rather than the linear transmission model assumed by traditional sensegiving research. Aided by such models, SAP research may then explore how, through specific communication processes across the organization (involving multiple individuals and layers), a new joint sense of a strategy is being constructed and also supported. In addition, future research on sensegiving may also benefit from a greater focus on emotional arousal and affect besides a focus on persuasive forms of language and communication, and may make effective use of experiments and other approaches utilizing larger data sets that help more convincingly conclude when and why sensegivers can successfully shape recipients' beliefs (see Vuori and Virtaharju 2012). While most sensegiving research in a SAP context is done within the natural settings of organizations, there is, we think, scope for behavioural field and laboratory experiments that specifically focus in on specific predictions around sensegiving, such as the role of emotional arousal in influencing the sensemaking of members of the organization, or the use of certain visionary language or narratives in instigating a change in meaning. Doing so would combine broad sets of observations gathered directly in natural settings with more predictive experimentation aimed at formalizing and strengthening theoretical predictions.

Conclusion

When we began writing this chapter, we considered sensemaking to be a broad umbrella construct that captures a rich theoretical perspective initiated by Weick. Through a close reading of actual studies from the strategy-as-practice perspective, however, we concluded that sensemaking in this tradition could often be more aptly characterized as a label for a set of empirical phenomena rather than as a theoretical perspective. A minority of empirical studies on sensemaking actively draw on prior research findings or theoretical ideas on sensemaking in prior SAP studies, with most studies instead invoking sensemaking as a label or shorthand code for the thinking and talking that is studied through qualitative methods and analysed in the light of other substantive theories, such as narrative theory or sociomaterial approaches.

We argue that the sensemaking literature offers more explicit theoretical ideas, however, including attending to cognitive frames and enactment processes, and thus encourage SAP scholars to draw upon those ideas more explicitly in the future. Based on a review of both the strategy-as-practice and sensemaking literatures, we suggest temporality and materiality to be the most interesting emerging domains at the intersection of the two research traditions. Not only are temporality and materiality emerging hot topics among sensemaking scholars, but they are also topics of central importance to strategy scholarship more generally. While the role of the discursively constructed futures and various material artefacts in strategy work have remained virtually unacknowledged outside the SAP and sensemaking traditions, the two topics warrant far broader attention in the near future.

References

Balogun, J. (2006), 'Managing change: steering a course between intended strategies and unanticipated outcomes', *Long Range Planning*, 39/1: 29–49.

Balogun, J., Gleadle, P., Hope Hailey, V., and Willmott, H. (2005), 'Managing change across boundaries: boundary-shaking practices', *British Journal of Management*, 16/4: 261–78.

Balogun, J., Jacobs, C. D., Jarzabkowski, P., Mantere, S., and Vaara, E. (2014), 'Placing strategy discourse in context: sociomateriality, sensemaking, and power', *Journal of Management Studies*, 51/2: 175–201.

Balogun, J., and Johnson, G. (2004), 'Organizational restructuring and middle manager sensemaking', *Academy of Management Journal*, 47/4: 523–49.

Bean, C. J., and Hamilton, F. E. (2006), 'Leader framing and follower sensemaking: response to downsizing in the brave new workplace', *Human Relations*, 59/3: 321–49.

Bechky, B. A. (2003), 'Sharing meaning across occupational communities: the transformation of knowledge on a production floor', *Organization Science*, 14/3: 312–30.

Bogner, W. C., and Barr, P. S. (2000), 'Making sense in hypercompetitive environments: a cognitive explanation for the persistence of high velocity competition', *Organization Science*, 11/2: 212–26.

Boje, D. M. (1991), 'The storytelling organization: a study of story performance', *Administrative Science Quarterly*, 36/1: 106–28.

Burrell, G., and Morgan, G. (1979), *Sociological Paradigms and Organisational Analysis*. London: Heinemann.

Chia, R., and Holt, R. (2006), 'Strategy as practical coping: a Heideggerian perspective', *Organization Studies*, 27/5: 635–55.

Clark, H. H. (1996), *Using Language*. Cambridge University Press.

Corley, K. G., and Gioia, D. A. (2004), 'Identity ambiguity and change in the wake of a corporate spin-off', *Administrative Science Quarterly*, 49/2: 173–208.

Cornelissen, J. (2012),'Sensemaking under pressure: the influence of professional roles and social accountability on the creation of sense', *Organization Science*, 23/1: 118–37.

Cornelissen, J., and Clarke, J. S. (2010), 'Imagining and rationalizing opportunities: inductive reasoning, and the creation and justification of new ventures', *Academy of Management Review*, 35/4: 539–57.

Cornelissen, J., Mantere, S., and Vaara, E. (2014), 'The contraction of meaning: the combined effect of communication, emotions and materiality on sensemaking in the Stockwell shooting', *Journal of Management Studies*, 51/5: 699–736.

Cornelissen, J., and Werner, M. D. (2014), 'Putting framing in perspective: a review of framing and frame analysis across the management and organizational literature', *Academy of Management Annals*, 8/1: 181–235.

Daft, R. L., and Weick, K. E. (1984), 'Toward a model of organizations as interpretation systems', *Academy of Management Review*, 9/2: 284–95.

Das, K., and Kumar, R. (2010), 'Interpartner sensemaking in strategic alliances: managing cultural differences and internal tensions', *Management Decision*, 48/1: 17–36.

Emirbayer, M., and Mische, A. (1998), 'What is agency?', *American Journal of Sociology*, 103/4: 962–1023.

Fenton, C., and Langley, A. (2011), 'Strategy as practice and the narrative turn', *Organization Studies*, 32/9: 1171–96.

Festinger, L. (1957), *A Theory of Cognitive Dissonance*. Evanston, IL: Row, Peterson.

Fiss, P. C., and Zajac, E. J. (2006), 'The symbolic management of strategic change: sensegiving via framing and decoupling', *Academy of Management Journal*, 49/6: 1173–93.

Garud, R., Schildt, H. A., and Lant, T. (2014), 'Entrepreneurial storytelling, future expectations, and the paradox of legitimacy', *Organization Science*, 25/5: 1479–92.

Gioia, D. A., and Chittipeddi, K. (1991), 'Sensemaking and sensegiving in strategic change initiation', *Strategic Management Journal*, 12/6: 433–48.

Gioia, D. A., and Mehra, A. (1996), 'Review of Karl E. Weick's *Sensemaking in Organizations*', *Academy of Management Review*, 21/4: 1226–30.

Gioia, D. A., and Thomas, J. B. (1996), 'Identity, image and issue interpretation: sensemaking during strategic change in academia', *Administrative Science Quarterly*, 41/3: 370–403.

Gioia, D. A., Thomas, J. B., Clark, S. M., and Chittipeddi, K. (1994), 'Symbolism and strategic change in academia: the dynamics of sensemaking and influence', *Organization Science*, 5/3: 363–83.

Goffman, E. (1974), *Frame Analysis: An Essay on the Organization of Experience*. Boston: North Eastern University Press.

Hirsch, P. M., and Levin, D. Z. (1999), 'Umbrella advocates versus validity police: a life-cycle model', *Organization Science*, 10/2: 199–212.

Holt, R., and Cornelissen, J. (2014), 'Sensemaking revisited', *Management Learning*, 45/5: 525–39.

Jarzabkowski, P. (2003), 'Strategic practices: an activity theory perspective on continuity and change', *Journal of Management Studies*, 40/1: 23–55.

(2005), *Strategy as Practice: An Activity-Based View*. London: Sage.

(2008), 'Shaping strategy as a structuration process', *Academy of Management Journal*, 51/4: 621–50.

Jarzabkowski, P., and Seidl, D. (2008), 'The role of strategy meetings in the social practice of strategy', *Organization Studies*, 29/11: 1391–426.

Kahneman, D. (2003), 'Maps of bounded rationality: a perspective on intuitive judgment and choice', in Frangsmyr, T. (ed.), *Les Prix Nobel 2002*: 449–89. Stockholm: Nobel Foundation.

Kaplan, S. (2008), 'Framing contests: strategy making under uncertainty', *Organization Science*, 19/5: 729–52.

(2011a), 'Research in cognition and strategy: reflections on two decades of progress and a look to the future', *Journal of Management Studies*, 48/3: 665–95.

(2011b), 'Strategy and PowerPoint: an inquiry into the epistemic culture and machinery of strategy making', *Organization Science*, 22/2: 320–46.

Kaplan, S., and Orlikowski, W. J. (2013), 'Temporal work in strategy making', *Organization Science*, 24/4: 965–95.

Kendon, A. (2004), *Gesture: Visible Action as Utterance*. Cambridge University Press.

Küpers, W., Mantere, S., and Statler, M. (2013), 'Strategy as storytelling: a phenomenological exploration of embodied narrative practice', *Journal of Management Inquiry*, 22/1: 83–100.

Kwon, W., Clarke, I., and Wodak, R. (2014), 'Micro-level discursive strategies for constructing shared views around strategic issues in team meetings', *Journal of Management Studies*, 51/2: 265–90.

Langley, A. (1999), 'Strategies for theorizing from process data', *Academy of Management Review*, 24/4: 691–710.

Leonardi, P. M., Tsedal, B., and Neeley, E. G. (2012), 'How managers use multiple media: discrepant events, power, and timing in redundant communication', *Organization Science*, 23/1: 98–117.

Liu, F., and Maitlis, S. (2014), 'Emotional dynamics and strategizing processes: a study of strategic conversations in top team meetings', *Journal of Management Studies*, 51/2: 202–34.

Maitlis, S. (2005), 'The social processes of organizational sensemaking', *Academy of Management Journal*, 48/1: 21–49.

Maitlis, S., and Christianson, M. (2014), 'Sensemaking in organizations: taking stock and moving forward', *Academy of Management Annals*, 8/1: 57–125.

Maitlis, S., and Lawrence, T. (2007), 'Triggers and enablers of sensegiving in organizations', *Academy of Management Journal*, 50/1: 57–84.

Maitlis, S., and Sonenshein, S. (2010), 'Sensemaking in crisis and change: inspiration and insights from Weick (1988)', *Journal of Management Studies*, 47/3: 551–80.

Mantere, S., Schildt, H. A., and Sillince, J. (2012), 'Reversal of strategic change', *Academy of Management Journal*, 55/1: 172–96.

Mantere, S., and Vaara, E. (2008), 'On the problem of participation in strategy: a critical discursive perspective', *Organization Science*, 19/2: 341–58.

McCabe, D. (2010), 'Strategy-as-power: ambiguity, contradiction and the exercise of power in a UK building society', *Organization*, 17/2: 151–75.

Morgan, G., Frost, P., and Pondy, L. R. (1983), 'Organizational symbolism', in Pondy, L. R., Frost, P., Morgan, G., and Dandridge, T. (eds.), *Organizational Symbolism*: 3–35. Greenwich, CT: JAI Press.

Mueller, F., Whittle, A., Gilchrist, A., and Lenney, P. (2013), 'Politics and strategy practice: ethnomethodologically-informed discourse analysis perspective', *Business History*, 55/7: 1168–99.

Nigam, A., and Ocasio, W. (2010), 'Event attention, environmental sensemaking, and change in institutional logics: an inductive analysis of the effects of public attention to Clinton's health care reform initiative', *Organization Science*, 21/4: 823–41.

Porac, J. F., Thomas, H., and Baden-Fuller, C. (1989), 'Competitive groups as cognitive communities: the case of Scottish knitwear manufacturers', *Journal of Management Studies*, 26/4: 397–416.

(2011), 'Competitive groups as cognitive communities: the case of Scottish knitwear manufacturers revisited', *Journal of Management Studies*, 48/3: 646–64.

Pratt, M. G. (2000), 'The good, the bad, and the ambivalent: managing identification among Amway distributors', *Administrative Science Quarterly*, 45/3: 456–93.

Pye, A. J. (2002), 'The changing power of "explanations": directors, academics and their sensemaking from 1989 to 2000', *Journal of Management Studies*, 39/7: 907–26.

Quinn, R., and Worline, M. C. (2008), 'Enabling courageous collective action: conversations from United Airlines flight 93', *Organization Science*, 19/4, 497–516.

Rasche, A., and Chia, R. (2009), 'Researching strategy practices: a genealogical social theory perspective', *Organization Studies*, 30/7: 713–34.

Ravasi, D., and Schultz, M. (2006), 'Responding to organizational identity threats: exploring the role of organizational culture', *Academy of Management Journal*, 49/3: 433–58.

Ricœur, P. (1984), *Time and Narrative*, 3 vols. University of Chicago Press.

Rorty, R. (1989), *Contingency, Irony, and Solidarity*. Cambridge University Press.

Rouleau, L. (2005), 'Micro-practices of strategic sensemaking and sensegiving: how middle managers interpret and sell change every day', *Journal of Management Studies*, 42/7: 1413–41.

Rouleau, L., and Balogun, J. (2011), 'Middle managers, strategic sensemaking and discursive competence', *Journal of Management Studies*, 48/5: 953–83.

Schultz, M., and Hernes, T. (2013), 'A temporal perspective on organizational identity', *Organization Science*, 24/1: 1–21.

Snook, S. A. (2000), *Friendly Fire: The Accidental Shootdown of US Black Hawks over Northern Iraq*. Princeton University Press.

Sonenshein, S. (2009), 'Emergence of ethical issues during strategic change implementation', *Organization Science*, 20/1: 223–39

Starbuck, W., and Milliken, F. (1988), 'Executive perceptual filters: what they notice and how they make sense', in Hambrick, D. C. (ed.), *The Executive Effect: Concepts and Methods for Studying Top Managers*: 35–65. Greenwich, CT: JAI Press.

Stigliani, I., and Ravasi, D. (2012), 'Organizing thoughts and connecting brains: material practices and the transition from individual to group-level prospective sensemaking', *Academy of Management Journal*, 55/5:1232–59.

Tannen, D. (1979), 'What's in a frame? Surface evidence for underlying expectations', in Freedle, R. O. (ed.), *New Directions in Discourse Processing*: 137–81. Norwood, NJ: Ablex.

Varela, F. (1979), *Principles of Biological Autonomy*. Amsterdam: Elsevier North.

Vuori, T., and Virtaharju, J. (2012), 'On the role of emotional arousal in sensegiving', *Journal of Organizational Change Management*, 25/1: 48–66.

Weick, K. E. (1979), *The Social Psychology of Organizing*, 2nd edn. New York: McGraw-Hill.

(1988), 'Enacted sensemaking in crisis situations', *Journal of Management Studies*, 25/4: 305–17.

(1993), 'The collapse of sensemaking in organizations: the Mann Gulch disaster', *Administrative Science Quarterly*, 38/4: 628–52.

(1995), *Sensemaking in Organizations*. Thousand Oaks, CA: Sage.

Weick, K. E., and Roberts, K. H. (1993), 'Collective mind in organizations: heedful interrelating on flight decks', *Administrative Science Quarterly*, 38/3: 357–81.

Weick, K. E., Sutcliffe, K. M., and Obstfeld, D. (2005), 'Organizing and the process of sensemaking', *Organization Science*, 16/4: 409–21.

Whiteman, G., and Cooper, W. H. (2011), 'Ecological sensemaking', *Academy of Management Journal*, 54/5: 889–911.

The communicative constitution of strategy-making: exploring fleeting moments of strategy

FRANÇOIS COOREN, NICOLAS BENCHERKI, MATHIEU CHAPUT and CONSUELO VÁSQUEZ

Practice-based approaches in management scholarship and organizational communication studies have in the past mainly evolved along parallel trajectories. Nonetheless, their epistemological and ontological stances – mostly influenced by a pragmatic positioning – and their shared concern for ordinary day-to-day (organizational) practices make them complementary trends of literature that would benefit from a more systematic and engaged dialogue (for similar arguments, see Fenton and Langley 2011; Spee and Jarzabkowski 2011; Vásquez, Sergi and Cordelier 2013). Accordingly, this chapter is a first attempt to put together two bodies of literature, the strategy-as-practice and the communicative constitution of organization approaches – stemming, respectively, from practice-based studies and organizational communication – in order to explore the role of talk and text in strategy-making.

Let us first note that we engage in this dialogue as communication scholars interested in understanding processes of organizing by acknowledging the constitutive force of communication (Putnam and Nicotera 2009). We therefore take a particular point of view for studying organization, more broadly, and here, strategy-making, which is deeply informed by the three following premises: (1) to always start from (rather than arriving at) communication as the motto of every inquiry; (2) to take a broad definition of communication that acknowledges the material and social world in which it takes place; and (3) to account for the many kinds of languages, not only spoken and written, that participate in constituting organization and organizing (Cooren, Taylor and Van Every 2006; see also Cooren *et al.* 2011).

Applied to the study of strategy and strategy-making, this implies that we should not begin by looking at strategy as originating in the individual and his/her situation and then, subsequently, asking how it gets *transmitted* in communication. From a communicational approach, we focus on strategy – what it is, what it does – and we question the constitutive role of communication in this being and acting. We also extend this questioning to other forms of communication that do not pertain solely to human activity; texts, objects, architectural elements, as we will argue, also 'communicate', and thus take part in the making of strategy. Finally, while accounting for the key role of language as talk and text, we do not exclude other modes of communication, such as paralinguistic or non-human modalities, that can also allow us to fully explore how communication constitutes strategy.

We propose in this chapter to focus on what we coin *fleeting moments of strategy*, which are moments when *matters of concerns* are presented, discussed, questioned and/or accepted in order to collectively decide how to go about them. The conceptual and methodological toolbox we develop in this chapter allows us to define these *matters of concerns* and to explore how they are consequential for strategy-making – that is, 'for the way an organization defines and appropriates value' (Jarzabkowski 2008: 370). This subtle (and yet radical) shift of orientation – from practitioners only to communication in all its forms – is one that, we believe, is worthwhile taking, as it can offer interesting alternatives to go beyond human action, broadening the analysis to other agents, or 'web of practices' (Vaara and Whittington 2012: 310).

In what follows we first position our approach with regard to the SAP literature, engaging more specifically with the discursive perspective on talk and text, which has also acknowledged the central role of communication in the making of strategy. Second, we further develop the communicational approach we propose in this chapter. We then illustrate with empirical material, taken from the second author's fieldwork, how to analyse *fleeting moments of strategy-making* through the construction of *matter of concerns*. Finally, we conclude with a discussion on the contributions of this approach to strategy as practice, considering here practice both as the object of scholarly study of strategy and as the actual practice of strategic actors.

Revisiting talk and text in strategy as practice through a communicational lens

In the last decade strategy as practice has become increasingly widespread in management and organization studies (see Jarzabkowski 2005; Johnson *et al.* 2007; Whittington 2006). Inscribed in the so-called practice turn (Reckwitz 2002; Rouse 2007; Schatzki, Knorr Cetina and von Savigny 2001), this research acknowledges the importance of studying strategy as situated and socially accomplished activities, shifting from a static and possessive view of strategy (something that an organization *has*) to a processual and performative definition of strategizing (something that organizational actors *do*). Hence, strategy as practice is concerned with the doing/making of strategy: who does it, how it is done and what implication this has for shaping processes of organizing (Jarzabkowski 2005).

There have been many propositions to define strategy as practice and its correlated terms, such as 'strategy', 'strategizing', 'strategic' and so forth (Golsorkhi *et al.* 2010; Jarzabkowski 2005; Johnson *et al.* 2007; Whittington 2003; 2006). In this chapter, following Vaara and Whittington, we define (general) practices as the 'accepted ways of doing things, embodied and materially mediated, that are shared between actors and routinized over time' (Vaara and Whittington 2012: 287), and we use the term 'strategy-making' as a generic term to describe the collection of activities that take part in the

constitution of organizational strategies, which includes 'more or less deliberate strategy formulation, the organizing work involved in the implementation of strategies and all other activities that lead to the emergence of organizational strategies, conscious or not' (287). We particularly engage with this idea of 'the emergence of organizational strategies', which is a shared concern in the strategy-as-practice scholarship for understanding how strategy is constituted through the live experienced and day-to-day efforts of organizational actors (Hendry and Seidl 2003), be they deliberated (that is, strategic planning: Jarzabkowski 2003; Vaara, Sorsa and Pälli 2010) or not (that is, emergent strategy: Regnér 2003; Samra-Fredericks 2003).

To do so, as introduced previously, we propose to take a communicational approach as a means of unpacking these collective, heterogeneous and interactional practices through which strategy-making unfolds. According to this approach, communication is not 'simply one of the many factors involved in organizing, and it cannot be merely the vehicle for the expression of pre-existing "realities"; rather, it is the means by which organizations are established, composed, designed, and sustained' (Cooren *et al.* 2011: 1150). As such, organizations (and we will argue, in this chapter, the same applies to strategy) essentially *consist of* processes of communication.

The argument that strategy *is* a communicative achievement has not yet been explicitly developed in the strategy-as-practice literature. A recent exception is Spee and Jarzabkowski's (2011) article, which draws upon the organizational communication literature to study strategic planning as a communicative process, described as the interpenetration of talk and text. The article shows that communication is not an a posteriori activity for 'communicating' the strategic plan but, rather, 'something that is integral to the planning process itself' (Spee and Jarzabkowski 2011: 1238; for a similar argument, see Clarke, Kwon and Wodak 2012; Kwon, Clarke and Wodak 2009; Samra-Fredericks 2005; 2010; Whittle *et al.* 2014; Wodak, Kwon and Clarke 2011). We must, of course, acknowledge that the idea that processes or activities of communication have a key role in the making of strategy is not completely new (even though the word 'communication' is rarely mobilized in this literature). In the past various kinds of discursive approaches have nourished the strategy-as-practice literature by defining strategy as discursive constructions (for example, Hardy, Palmer and Phillips 2000; Knights and Morgan 1991; Mantere and Vaara 2008; Vaara, Kleymann and Seristö 2004). More specifically, these approaches have examined strategy-making as processes in which talk and/or text are used to achieve strategic ends; they include studies of rhetoric (for example, Jarzabkowski, Sillince and Shaw 2010; Denis *et al.* 2011), narratives (for example, Boje 2008; Fenton and Langley 2011; Vaara and Tienari 2011), sensemaking (for example, Balogun and Johnson 2005; Stensaker and Falkenberg 2007) and conversation (for example, Hoon 2007; Liu and Maitlis 2014; Samra-Fredericks 2003; 2005; 2010).

This trend of literature has greatly contributed in showing that strategy-making involves a large amount of talk and text, such as meetings, memos and presentations, and that their outcomes are also discursive (for example, strategic plans and Power-Point presentations: see Suominen and Mantere 2010). We believe it has tended to overemphasize the role of practitioners, however (how *they* mobilize talk and text for communicating and shaping strategy), which has led to a subject-centred understanding of strategy and strategy-making and to what we regard as a reductive definition of communication as a linguistic *resource* for strategy-making – one that implies that communication is an activity restricted to humans (see, for instance, Wodak, Kwon and Clarke 2011).

In their recent overview of SAP literature, Vaara and Whittington (2012: 310) highlight the need for a more 'nuanced understanding of strategic agency as taking place in a web of practices'. While recognizing the achievements of this stream of research in moving away from an exclusive focus on individuals and their actions towards considering the enabling and constraining effects of social practices, they argue for broadening the analysis of agency. To take one step further in this direction, we believe that there is a need to adopt a relational view of agency (Robichaud 2006; see also Peirce's relational ontology: Peirce 1965 [1934]; 1992 [1898]; Houser and Kloesel 1992), which allows for de-centring (strategic)

practices by defining agency as a 'situationally embedded connection of connections between heterogeneous entities' (Robichaud 2006: 102).[1]

The communicational approach we put forth in this chapter engages in such a direction by adopting a broad conception of what communication means. In a nutshell (we develop this argument further in the next section), we propose to consider communication as *the establishment of a link, connection or relationship through something* (Cooren 2000), whereby who or what 'communicates' can be associated with individuals, certainly, but can also refer to objects, architectural elements and even more abstracts forms of agents, such as emotions, ideas, principles or values (Cooren 2010). Taking this approach implies a reconsideration of the role of materiality in strategy-making (Vaara and Whittington 2012). In other words, this means focusing on how, through the imbrication of talk and text, multiple and heterogeneous agents contribute to the making of strategy.

Exploring matters of concern: a communicational toolbox for studying strategy-making

What, therefore, does it mean to claim that communication is constitutive of strategy? In order to respond to this question, we first need to answer the question 'What is communication?'. As mentioned previously, this implies that we adopt a very broad conception of what communication means. Defining communication as *the establishment of a link, connection or relationship through something* (Cooren 2000) allows us to refer to multiple and diverse situations in which *what* establishes the relationship can be as concrete as an artefact or an architectural element or as abstract as coldness, rigidity, openness and warmth. Furthermore, we also realize that *communication has no absolute point of origin* (Latour 1996). For instance, saying 'This official announcement is communicating

---

[1] This relational approach also echoes what is today called relationism or relational sociology (see Crossley 2010; Dépelteau 2008; Dépelteau and Powell 2013; Donati 2010; Powell and Dépelteau 2013).

Table 21.1 Key aspects of a CCO perspective on strategy-making

What to identify in conversations	*Matters of concern/interest* = what seems to recurrently, routinely and persistently **animate** the participants
How to identify matters of concern/interest	• What is *positioned* in the conversation as *repeatedly leading human participants to do what they do* • What the participants *invoke/convoke/evoke* in their conversations to explain/justify/legitimize/account for their positions or actions • The matters that appear to matter to define what should be done
How to name a matter of concern/interest	• Everything *in the name of which* a given strategic move appears to be proposed • All the elements that are supposed to *count, matter* or *make a difference* in a given situation
What these matters of concern/interest do	• They *participate in* and *stand under* the co-formulation of any strategy • They bring with them their own *weight* or *value* to *define* or *dictate* what should or should not be strategically done
Examples of matters of concern/interest	• Principles • Facts • Ideals • Documents • Values • Graphs • Objectives • Hearsay

important pieces of information to the employees' is *one way* of describing what might be happening, but one could just as well have said 'Management is communicating important pieces of information to the employees', 'The company is communicating important pieces of information to the employees' or even 'These important pieces of information are communicating bad news to the employees'.

What or who is communicating to whom or what through what or whom is always a matter of *selection* in a chain of agency (Cooren 2006) – a selection that analysts can certainly decide to do, but that participants also do in the way they account for what is happening. Furthermore, according to the premise we adopt in this chapter, which argues for the *communicative constitution of reality* (Cooren 2012), anything or anyone, in order to be and act, has to be *communicated into being and acting*. For instance, an organization exists and functions through all the beings or agents that/who are deemed to re-present, materialize or embody *it*, making it present (again) to us – a presence that sometimes can be negotiated or questioned. These beings or agents can be as varied as websites, spokespersons, buildings, contracts, mission statements, values, products, employees or operations (Brummans, Cooren and Chaput 2009; Chaput, Brummans and Cooren 2011).

The question now becomes, therefore: how can we study *strategy* and *strategy-making* according to this perspective, and to what extent can this

approach not only cohere with but also contribute to the way SAP scholars conceive of these practices? Table 21.1 provides what we consider essential aspects of a CCO perspective on strategy-making. First, we should note that this communicational approach seems a priori a very good candidate to analyse practices conceived as the 'accepted ways of doing things, embodied and materially mediated, that are shared between actors and routinized over time' (Vaara and Whittington 2012: 287). Studying practices indeed involves the analysis of instituted, established and repeated forms of doing, which implies that we never leave the terra firma of interaction in order to identify them (Cooren 2006).

The idea of the repetition, recurrence and stabilization of specific forms of doing also implies that we conceive of human agents as *led* or *animated* by specific habits, procedures, values or routines, which function as the *third party* (Taylor and Van Every 2011) communicating or expressing itself through these practices. Studying practices from a communicational approach thus consists of unfolding *what* seems to recurrently, routinely and persistently *animate* the actors. In terms of methodology, we privilege an ethnographic approach, supported by the use of a video camera, to better understand what animates the actors and to deeply describe how they collectively negotiate these *matters of concerns* in practice. Analytically speaking, this will mean observing what is positioned as *repeatedly leading actors to do what they do* – that is, what they invoke, convoke or evoke in their talks and writings to explain, justify, legitimize or account for their positions or actions and those of others.

In the case of strategy-making conceived as a practice, this implies identifying all the various forms of agency that are iteratively convoked/invoked/evoked by participants to co-construct, more or less deliberately and consciously, a strategy. In concrete terms, what this means is describing in talks, texts and actions *everything in the name of which a given move appears to be proposed* – that is, all the things that are supposed to *count*, *matter* or *make a difference* in a given situation, and that are key for the way an 'organization defines and appropriates value' (Jarzabkowski, 2008: 370). These *matters of concern* (Latour 2008) or *matters of interest* are, by definition, what is supposed to animate the actors when they defend or evaluate a position, account for or 'disalign' from an action, or justify or oppose an objective.

These *matters* thus constitute what literally and figuratively participates in and stands under the co-formulation of a strategy. Strategizing can therefore be conceived as weighing, pondering, calculating or evaluating *what* in a given situation *dictates* a certain move in order to fulfil a given objective. As we see, and in keeping with the communicational approach we propose, human beings are not the only ones who perform this activity, since *it involves the staging, in the discussion, of various matters of concerns that bring with them their own weight or value to define or indicate what should or should not be done.*

Furthermore (and this is crucial for fully embracing this approach), at no point do we – as analysts and participants – leave the terra firma of interaction (Cooren 2006). Analysing strategizing from this perspective consists of unfolding the 'web of agencies' that comes to stand under or substantiate it, whether these agencies are not just principles, ideals, values or objectives but also facts, documents, graphs, tables or hearsay. The world of strategy is thus a world in which many matters can come to make a difference, knowing that all these matters (of concern and interest) will constitute the third parties that produce iteration, repetition or recurrence. If strategy is indeed a *practice*, it means that there are specific ways of strategizing and that a detailed study of these practices will lead us to identify what iteratively appears to count, make a difference or matter to the participants.

How can one observe, record and reflect on *fleeting moments of strategy* in the daily practical achievements of organizational agents, as this notion strongly implies a temporary, almost slippery, potentially improvised and highly contingent character? Since, as we argue throughout this chapter, strategy emerges in communication, we rely on the use of a video camera as an observational device to enable researchers to capture full segments of interactions held within organizational settings. As we show in this section, the monitoring of a meeting with this technology can provide a detailed archive of planned discussions on this issue, as we illustrate with our first excerpt, or *how agents talk about strategy*. In addition, the inconspicuous use of a video camera can reveal those instants when strategy is practised in an 'unannounced' fashion, which is highlighted in the second excerpt, or *how agents talk strategically* (even when strategy is not brought up formally as an item on the agenda listing).

What difference does a video camera make? Notwithstanding the ethical concerns linked to the privacy and comfort of the observees (notably discussed by Pink 2001; 2006), delegating the observational duties to a recording device provides unparalleled *in situ* access to what agents say and do, as well as the material conditions in which these events occur. It is worth noting that the use of a video camera does not necessarily mean that we focus especially on the behavioural aspects of the conversations we study; rather, it is more a way to record an interaction as exhaustively and richly as possible. This richness/exhaustiveness then allows us to be more confident in the way we analyse interactions, even if these analyses do not necessarily concentrate on the non-verbal aspects of what is performed by the participants.

How, finally, does one operate the transition from audio-visual recordings to (finite) texts? While this ethnographically inspired approach offers a certain degree of freedom in the way to select and analyse observations, we repeatedly scrutinized the extensive recordings provided by the second author of this chapter, attempting to bracket together *fleeting moments of strategy* that emanated from the continuous flow of recorded interactions. The use of specific keywords (strategy, strategic planning, etc.), as well as the evocation of *matters of concerns* by the agents (such as 'What's going on here?', 'What is to be done?', 'How do we (re)act?'), oriented our search. The selected excerpts were then transcribed according to the conventions of conversation analysis (ten Have 1999; see also Appendix I). Finally, collaborative analyses of the selected data were conducted and reviewed over time by all four authors of us, in order to reach a shared understanding of what was being displayed by the observed agents with regard to the communicative constitution of strategy-making. In the next section we illustrate how this conceptual framework can be put to work in the analysis of an empirical case of strategy-making.

The communicative constitution of matters of concern in strategy-making

The two excerpts we put forward for analysis in this chapter are taken from the same meeting of the board of directors of a tenants' association in an underprivileged and multicultural district in Montreal. The sequence took place a few months after the group had received a request from the Gauthier Foundation,[2] its main funding agency, to develop a strategic plan for the next five years. It is also important to note that the meeting took place shortly after city elections had been held.

The meeting brings together Charles and Diane, respectively the director and the assistant director of the group, with other members of the board. The latter are volunteers, but also representatives of other organizations. Many of them used to work at the tenants' association or to be interns, either as lawyers, architects or social workers. Michael is the chairman of the board, which means that he contributes to the preparation of the minutes and the agenda.

As Latour (2005) points out, any starting point for a research is (or should be) as good as any other. This is why we chose, as our first excerpt,

a conversation that clearly addresses the strategic planning effort demanded by the funding agency. Since this conversation is labelled by participants themselves as having to do with 'strategy', we may hope to learn something about the way they deploy this notion in practice. In contrast, the second excerpt, which emerges from a conversation that follows the first, does not have to do, as such, with strategic planning. We show that it features many of the characteristics that are regularly considered to define strategy and strategy-making, however. In particular, it displays a sense of urgency, calculation and immediate relevance – all factors associated with an orientation towards the future.

Both these excerpts (which were translated from French to English) can be seen as *fleeting moments of strategy*, as they are temporal and more or less deliberative moments when matters of concerns are being constructed, and – more importantly – when they are presented (and more or less accepted) as being consequential for the organization. Therefore, an analysis of these excerpts will scrutinize (1) which matters raise concerns for the participants, (2) how these matters are justified as deserving attention (and why some weigh more than others), (3) which agencies are invoked, evoked or convoked in support of the various matters of concern and finally (4) how these are regarded as consequential (or not) for the organization.

First excerpt: speaking strategically about not being strategic

158	DIANE	Gauthier, strategic planning,
159		when I saw the agenda we did,
160		eh (1.0) Because it's [Michael
161		who did the minutes (we
162		completely forgot that).
163	CHARLES	[Well, I
164		gave you, I think, a part of it,
165		but it's not over. It's true it
166		stayed unfinished, if we want
167		to do it.
168	DIANE	And we went on holidays (a
169		little), we kind of forgot all that.
170	CHARLES	There are all kinds of things.
171		It may not be as urgent as we
172		thought. Because...
173	DIANE	She did not call us back!

174 CHARLES   She did not call us back [and, uh
175 DIANE   [I called
176   her and she did not even return
177   my calls.
178 CHARLES   No. There is- there is (1.0)
179   There wasn't, as such (.) uh (.)
180   an emergency. Uh, let's say
181   that it isn't a priority. It will be
182   something we'll keep doing but.
183   uh, during the winter, let's say,
184   with the Gauthier Foundation,
185   there, it will be part of the
186   follow-up on things we'll
187   present. But that's because…
188   There are many things that
189   came up, uh…, since then. We
190   haven't had contact with her
191   and, uh…
192 DIANE   Again, I've… For the Christmas
193   party, I sent her an invitation.
194 CHARLES   Yeah.
195 DIANE   And we haven't had any return-
196   nothing. (1.0)
197 Eli   (And so it)
198 CHARLES   But let's say that we're not in
199   danger with the Gauthier
200   Foundation. And, uh, it's only
201   an attempt to improve our
202   financial situation, which we
203   will be able to pursue during…
204 DIANE   There's maybe the government
205   agency that ((inaudible, laugh))
206   (.)
207 CHARLES   Let's say, to summarize in a
208   simple, simple, simple, simple
209   way, the Gauthier Foundation
210   is not worrying at the moment.
211 DIANE   Okay
212 JOAN   So, uh…
213 DIANE   And we have a three-year
214   contract, so, they will come
215   back about this probably
216   perhaps like next year, we
217   should [for next year…
218 CHARLES   [Yeah, but, during
219   winter I want to finalize what I
220   began; I will communicate
221   again with her, to update her on
222   the cases, you know…
223 DIANE   And, if we do it during the
224   coming year, the events will be

225   for the next year, so we will be
226   more able to (low voice,
227   inaudible)
228 ELI   Regarding the activities?
229 DIANE   Yeah,
230 ELI   Did we do something regarding
231   the municipal elections?

What does this episode tells us in terms of strategy and strategy-making? First, we need to acknowledge who or what appears to count or matter, at least for Diane and Charles, as they are doing most of the talking in this sequence. With everyone looking and commenting on the agenda, Diane raises her voice and says: 'Gauthier, strategic planning, when I saw the agenda we did, eh (1.0). Because it's Michael who did the minutes…' (lines 158–161). As she says that, she is looking at a sheet in front of her, implying that she is reading the new topic from the agenda. Her intervention introduces a matter of concern, the need to talk about strategic planning, although it would be more accurate to note that it is also, or even mostly, the agenda that reminds everyone of this concern.

Given the discouraged tone she uses and the fact that it is Michael, and not her, who, she said, set the agenda, she expresses a sort of disaffiliation in this regard, as if she were saying: the agenda says that we should now speak about strategic planning, but this is not really something I would like to talk about. The fact that, prior to Diane's intervention, everyone is orienting to the agenda (or the minutes) could otherwise be read as a commitment from the participants to follow the order of discussion that was prepared for them (and *by* them, at the previous meeting). The strategic planning exercise is thus supposed to become (again) a 'matter of concern' because of its prior inscription in this document, even though Diane's reading of that item could cast some doubt regarding its (strategic) value at the time being.

How, then, can we determine if 'strategic planning' constitutes a matter of concern for the meeting's participants? By looking for what is supposed to *count*, *matter* or *make a difference* – that is, all the things that are potentially animating the participants in what they say or do. Here, in response to Diane's intervention, Charles offers his colleagues an up-to-date status, marking its incompleteness while hinting at the possibility for them to act on this matter: '[B]ut it's not over. It's true it stayed unfinished, *if we want to do it*' (lines 165–167, emphasis added). This last assertion confirms that a matter of concern, or a certain calculation, is at stake here: they could decide to do it, but they could also decide not to do it, depending on how they weigh or evaluate the situation.

The conversation then turns towards weighing what should support their action, or absence of it. Diane's answers evokes bad timing to account for why this question remained unfinished, as they 'went on holidays (a little)', and they 'kind of forgot all that' (lines 168–169). Charles is prone to discard this possible lack of reactivity on their part, however, adding: 'It may not be as urgent as we thought. Because…' (lines 171–172). So, while the agenda positions strategic planning as a topic of discussion – that is, as something that is supposed to deserve their attention, interest or concern – we see Charles mitigating its importance, implying that it might not matter as much as they think. In a good case of how matters of concern are communicatively co-constructed, Diane substantiates her collaborator's justification by marking as significant the lack of response on the part of their funding agency.

The fact that the Gauthier Foundation representative failed to call them back, evoked by Diane and further confirmed by Charles, here appears to play a big role in their co-definition of the situation. This absence is indeed supposed to substantiate the position that strategic planning be considered by the group as not an urgent matter at this point. It thus dictates, according to them, that they do not grant the status of priority to this plan, as this lack of urgency is also shared by their outside collaborators. Although Charles never really clarifies all the other things that might substantiate this position, he also specifies several times that he would continue working on it during the coming months ('It will be something we'll keep doing but, uh, during the winter, let's say, with the Gauthier Foundation, there, it will be part of the follow-up on things we'll present' (lines 181–187)). While remaining unspecified, these various things still add up to *weigh in* for an absence of urgency regarding the question of the strategic plan.

Being strategic in this case thus consists, for Charles, in keeping working on this plan while not urging this matter – a move that is substantiated, for instance, when he specifies that doing this exercise will better their financial situation. While Diane's interventions could be read as invitations to 'drop the ball', Charles' several moves to mark his commitments to work on the plan could be read as attempts to mark the relative importance of this matter. To support his claims, and reassure his associates, Charles summarizes the situation by saying: 'But let's say that we're not in danger with the Gauthier Foundation. And, uh, it's only an attempt to improve our financial situation, which we will be able to pursue during…' (lines 198–203).

He thus offers a way to read the whole situation to the people around the table. While the lack of response on the part of their funding agency could look suspicious, or at least equivocal, he tells them that the global lack of concern for the strategic plan – that is, Charles and Diane's lack of concern, based on the funding agency's apparent lack of concern – does not put their organization in danger. This conclusion is presented as the way he weighs, ponders or evaluates the situation. To prove or illustrate the lack of danger, the whole exercise is also presented in positive terms and not in terms of constraints and injunctions (lines 200–202). This is something they will keep working on, but not right now (lines 202–203).

There is therefore *strategizing*, to the extent that we see him weighing the pros and cons of waiting and seeing. According to his reading, some of the aspects of the situation indicate, demonstrate or show that they can put strategy on the back-burner (the funding agency's apathy, for instance) while others require, demand or dictate that they keep working on it (the simple fact that they were requested to do so by the funding agency). Strategizing, according to our analysis, could thus be depicted as evaluating, pondering of weighing what a given situation dictates, requires or demands in terms of intervention. What is noteworthy, however, is that *this weighing/pondering/ evaluating does not originate only from the human participants but also from the situation itself, expressing itself through various aspects.*

While the funding agency's apathy indicates that it could wait, the fact that the strategic plan was requested shows that there are grounds to worry a little. Weighing, pondering or evaluating, a key aspect of strategizing, is therefore possible only through the voicing of various matters that present, actualize or stage themselves to the participants. Although some of them might lend their weight to a given position or action, others might lend theirs to an opposing one. If strategizing is the product of a co-construction through a given conversation, such a co-construction can take place only through the matters (of concern) that substantiate it through this discussion. These matters, therefore, are what literally and figuratively participate in and stand under the co-formulation of a strategy.

The matter is closed by Eli's complete change of topic. Eli's move comes in continuation with Diane's intervention – that is, he does not wait for a downtime in the conversation. The change of topic and its acceptance by all participants may be read as a dismissal of the topic by most participants and their satisfaction with its postponing. In addition to the initial heteronomous constitution of the topic as a matter of concern – and its labelling as 'strategic' – through the agenda, the downplaying of the importance of the topic indicates that, while the Gauthier Foundation may call the requested exercise 'strategic planning', it does not appear to be strategic to the participants. This shows that the 'strategic' character of strategic planning is actively renegotiated – and that, paradoxically, participants exhibit a fair amount of strategy in doing so. The discussion is pretty much a highly strategic and sophisticated justification of a lack of interest in, and action for, strategic planning. Hence, the strategic dimension of a given stake is not (only) intrinsic but also has to be discursively performed in practice.

Second excerpt: how can we know we are being strategic until we see what we said?

The second excerpt shortly follows the first one during the meeting. When Eli changes topic, he asks a question about the municipal elections and the organization's involvement in the local ridings. After a relatively brief discussion on various topics, a conversation about some of the district's

upcoming construction projects emerges. This conversation could be looked at as a long monologue by Charles. We show, however, that it is, in fact, co-constructed – and, more specifically, that the uncovering of its 'strategic' dimension is the product of this co-construction.

The relevance of this excerpt lies in the transition from an ill-defined matter of concern to a set of clear matters. In other words, contrary to some understandings of strategy, the participants do not begin with a well-defined 'picture of the destination' (Kaplan and Norton 2001: 74). The constitution of matters of concern is exactly what is at stake. While conventional ideas on strategy speak of a vision, here we are a step back, in what may be described as a situation of 'strategic myopia', and we witness the moment when participants are gradually gaining focus on the situation. This is achieved not because of the intrinsically 'strategic' value of these matters of concern but, rather, communicatively: through the evolution of the conversation and, in particular, through the interplay of the various discussants and what matters to them. The value of these matters of concern is confirmed when they are related to the organization's funding and, ultimately, its survival.

The following summary of the conversation highlights the moments when the topic is gradually widened and its strategic aspect discovered (the full transcript of the conversation is presented in Appendix II).

(1) Charles begins by discussing a local housing project and the way it was presented at a borough meeting. (2) The conversation then evolves more broadly towards a discussion of the way housing projects are decided by various committees in the borough. (3) This, in turn, leads to the recognition that all members of these committees are controlled by the borough's elected officials, which means that, once elected, the officials can pretty much do whatever they want. Additionally, the community organizations that could oppose questionable projects are too afraid to intervene, because they depend on the borough for their funding and activities. (4) This diagnosis entails that the tenants' association is isolated and outnumbered in its opposition to some projects. This means that the organization needs to find new

people to support its struggle, which leads Charles to invite the board members to help him personally with this task. (5) Finally, it is stressed that, if the borough can reshape the district, it also means that the population will change and gentrify, which ultimately will lead the organization to lose funding, as its grants are based on the local low-income demographics.

As we see, we move from an anecdote about a particular borough meeting to, finally, a claim about the very survival of the organization given the gentrification of the district. When Charles is describing the borough meeting, the identification of a clear matter of concern appears to be puzzling for his interlocutors. In other words, they have problems figuring out why this should matter to them and the association. This passage from Charles' concerns to theirs is made possible by various interventions. For example, Brenda asks him (lines 67–68) what they should think of all of this, which leads Charles to speak in more normative terms, qualifying some of the city borough representatives' interventions as being 'lies' and the consultation process as being a 'request' (which in the original French has disparaging overtones). He also invokes the various plans and versions thereof, which he examined, as so many elements supporting his claim. At the very least, board members should be concerned because city officials are not saying the truth.

The elaboration of matters of concern continues as other board members intervene in Charles' account to support it or to ask for clarifications. Supporting Charles' account is, for instance, what Joan does when she completes Charles' sentence (line 145) to say that the members of the urban planning committee will do what the elected officials want, or when she starts saying that the project will go on no matter what – which Charles confirms by saying: 'They will do what they want' (line 172). Joan also leads Charles to clarify his ideas when she asks whether there are people who are interested by the situation he is describing – that is, the borough's elected officials controlling the urban-planning process (line 175).

This leads Charles to broaden the scene and to cast his story in terms of a struggle between the organization and the borough. He admits that 'not enough' people are interested, and that those who

should be – the district's other community organizations – are 'under influence'. Later in the conversation Diane supports Charles' depiction of the other organizations as being dependent on the borough by providing concrete example of such cases. In other words, what is at stake is not only the borough's ability to conduct bogus consultations and control the committees in charge of urban planning but also the balance of power between the borough and the organization, which is left alone fighting for social justice and democracy. The borough clearly has the upper hand, since it also controls the other community organizations, which should have been the tenants' associations' partners.

The interactional evolution of Charles' story is consequential not only for the gradual discovery of a matter of concern, which shows to the participants (and to us) that the organization might be in relative isolation with respect to the borough, but also in linking this issue back to the organization's own stakes. The first way in which the diagnosis of the association's lack of support is of relevance is that *it literally draws a programme of action*. Having presented the situation, Charles indeed points out: 'Okay, but that's the way it is. I say we need to have new people. That's important. We have a problem in the district, we're missing intellectuals. When I say intellectuals, I mean, y'know, people who, y'know…, who are interested by causes and who are ready to discuss' (lines 195–203).

In other words, the situation that Charles has just depicted is presented as what leads him to draw this specific conclusion, which is another way to say that this situation dictates or requires, according to him, that some action be taken regarding the involvement of intellectuals in this battle. As we see, it is *not only* Charles who says that intellectuals should be involved *but also*, and indirectly, the situation itself (the lies, the isolation, the dependence) he has been depicting. All these matters of concern point, according to him, to the necessity of doing something. The obvious and urgent character of this programme of action is visible in interaction and communication, thanks to the other participants' interventions and to the rapid pace of turn in the talks from this point onwards.

The issue is brought closer to home when Joan asks 'So, our conclusion is?' (line 252). To this,

Charles answers 'It's not going very well', which triggers a reformulation of the need to get people involved, but also to get members of the board (that is, the very people participating in the discussion) to stick behind him. As we see, the co-construction of a programme of action is made possible through the various interventions that are made around the table, in that they lead Charles to voice what they should do – which is another way to say that he is led to voice what the situation dictates. Voicing what they should do is indeed possible because various matters of the situation are presented as leading them to this conclusion.

Following this, the conversation – with Diane's contribution – moves to the fact that the very 'face and image' of the district are at stake. They are being changed given the borough's ability to control any kind of opposition. Charles follows on Diane's input to say that the population is being replaced by new, richer inhabitants. The hubbub that follows indicates that this matter appears to be relevant to participants (see Jefferson 1972). In other words, it catches their interest; it preoccupies them. Charles then insists that the replacement of the district's population by a wealthier class of people will distort the data on which are decided 'the money we get, the grants, the interests that we have' (lines 318–320). He therefore completes the circle and links back what started as an apparently innocuous anecdote to the very funding and survival of the organization.

Through the evolution of the story, but also through other participants' interventions, we see that an initially confused sense of concerns continuously evolves, thanks to requests for clarification and supporting comments, towards a clear set of issues, including the city's control of the planning process, the isolation of the association, the districts' changing population and the association's funding. The latter element, which has a direct impact on the association's survival, is supposed to show how the organization is directly impacted by the issues that are raised, and completes the progression from an initial anecdote to the organization's own values, including the way it values a series of matters of concern.

When Joan starts saying, with an interrogative tone, 'So we...' (line 406), Charles completes it by saying that 'we need to talk about this' and to get people interested. This may be seen as the initiation of an action plan on the basis of the conversation. The conversation about an action plan is ended, however, when Michael, who is presiding over the meeting, suggests that the conversation is drifting away from what was intended on the agenda. Interestingly, he identifies this conversation about the changes in the district as having to do with a board members' retreat that is supposed to take place sometime later, which implies that *he recognizes that the conversation has drifted towards strategic issues that are broader than the agenda item being discussed*. The agenda that triggered, in the first excerpt, the conversation about strategy is also what allows the recognition of the current conversation as strategic, bringing it to an end.

This second conversation shows that a conversation that is not identified initially as strategic can reveal itself to have a strategic dimension. This discovery is a collective achievement, given that it is the interaction between participants and their contribution to the evolution of a narrative – in particular by requesting clarification over the meaning of elements of the story – that helps situate it in broader contexts and connect it with issues that matter to the organization. In other words, participants collectively constitute issues as 'matters of concern', and actions present themselves as being required (that is, find new followers) on the basis of these constitutions.

Discussion

This chapter has outlined a communication approach to strategy, as an attempt to bridge the growing bodies of literature on the communicative constitution of organization and strategy as practice. It has provided conceptual and methodological guidance in how to conceive of communication beyond the classical model of transmission and its focus on individual human agents, favouring instead a constitutive view of communication, which is seen as the linkage or connection between agents through something, with the connecting and connected agents not exclusively limited to human beings. In addition, this extended view of communication is posited as generative of numerous organizational phenomena, leading us to conceive of strategy-making as communication episodes *in which specific matters of concerns lend their weights to various courses of action.*

Furthermore, we have proposed speaking of *fleeting moments of strategy*, to highlight how collective endeavours are progressively born as *effects* of the contributions, and therefore do not exist prior to the practices that generate them. Accordingly, the theoretical and empirical outcomes of this chapter supplement previous work arguing for an understanding of strategy as practice as a communication process (Spee and Jarzabkowski 2011). To speak of fleeting moments of strategy thus implies close observation of how strategy emerges from communication, but this notion also serves to stress the contextually built, volatile, timely, situated and sometimes partly improvised dimension of strategic activities. To qualify strategy as emerging out of communication does not restrict the use of such approach to 'purely emergent' instances, as opposed to deliberate ones (to employ Mintzberg and Waters' 1985 terminology), but this nonetheless invites analysts to seek out strategy-making beyond the formal forums in which planning is set to occur.

To illustrate the fleeting character of strategy in the never-ending flow of communication, we examined two interaction sequences occurring during a community organization's meeting. We showed how strategic planning could be purposefully eschewed by organizational members, despite being inscribed on the meeting's agenda, as specific matters provided good (strategic) reasons to argue for a seeming lack of concern, or urgency, for that item. Simultaneously, strategic reflections can appear unexpectedly, and be stated retrospectively, as when a trivial anecdote about a public meeting triggered a co-constructed account evaluating the borough's political landscape, ultimately culminating in a David-versus-Goliath type of story in which action became imperative to protect tenants' rights and ensure the organization's survival.

While borrowing extensively from the literature on strategy as practice, we have attempted to define the communicative accomplishment of strategy in a novel manner, consisting in picturing such activity as the expression, co-construction and negotiation of specific *matters of concern*, or matters of interest.

Making use of a term originating from science studies (see Latour 2004; 2008), we propose that strategy, understood as a practice, derives from interactions aiming to *define what matters or counts in specific situations* and weigh, ponder or evaluate *what these matters dictate, require or demand* in order to know what to do. In contrast with mainstream research on strategic planning, and its focus on rational calculations of individuals, our approach simultaneously assigns a central role to the 'living beings whose emotions, motivations and actions shape strategy' (Jarzabkowski 2008: 364), while de-centring those beings by adding new members in the 'plenum of agency' (Cooren 2006) that constitutes organizational realities and actions.

Consequently, mobilizing our version of the CCO approach amounts to singling out *which matters matter* – that is, to track down all that is valued, devalued or evaluated during interactions, with strategy as practice encompassing the 'accomplished flow of activity that is consequential for the way an organization defines and appropriates value' (Jarzabkowski 2008: 370). While not limiting ourselves to any single type of communicative utterances, genre or competence, we assign a particular importance to discussions regarding, specifically, what is judged and shows itself as important, meaningful, significant or troublesome – in other words, as matters of concern or interest. Therefore, this view of strategic activities implies a search for motives, accounts, justifications and explanations that people incessantly invoke, convoke or evoke in the elaboration of matters of concern, as a never-ending quest to answer the question 'What is to be done?'.

The illustrations analysed above offer some evidence for such a line of thought on communicative understandings of strategy. In the first excerpt, lacklustre interest in proceeding with strategic planning is overtly justified by an apparent reciprocal lack of interest from outside collaborators, as well as by the absence of close deadlines, which literally *devalue* this matter as an urgent concern to be addressed at the current time. With the second one, we can trace down a series of concerns (about the consultation process, the municipal plan changes, the lack of reliable allies and the need to recruit new partners), which end up *valuing* the

Table 21.2 How a CCO perspective responds to Vaara and Whittington's (2012) research agenda

Research agenda for strategy as practice	How a CCO approach responds to this agenda
Define how agency is constituted in a web of practices	• Extension of communication beyond human agents • Agents = anyone or anything that *makes a difference* or *counts* in a given situation (e.g. matters of concern) • An agent lends its weight to a given course of action over another
Pay attention to the macro-institutional nature of practices	• We never leave the firm ground of interactions • The *there* and the *then* necessarily require to be *made present* in the *here* and the *now* of interaction flows
Account for emergence in strategy-making	• Strategizing invariably emerges from the *interplay of various agents in communication* • Strategy-making may occur during interactions that are not labelled as deliberately strategic
Recognize more accurately the role of materiality	• *Materiality* = the state of what *stands under* something else (matters of concern/interest = what stand under these concerns or interests) • Materiality expresses itself in interaction through matters of concern/interest
Envisage critical analysis	• What voices (do not) matter in strategizing? • What matters (do not) matter in strategizing?

necessity to address the very funding and survival of the association. Overall, in accordance with the premises of CCO scholarship (Cooren *et al.* 2011), communication represents the very breeding ground in which strategically inclined interactions are susceptible to occur, and in which matters of concern value and devalue each other.

In this broader sense, a focus on communication processes and their outcomes certainly promises a valuable contribution to any comprehensive study of strategy as practice. Can we be more specific, though, when highlighting the added value of a communication approach to that growing body of literature? We can certainly benefit, in this attempt, by acknowledging the directions for future research recently sketched out by Vaara and Whittington (2012). In their work, the authors name five concerns that could be constructively addressed by scholars devoted to strategy as practice. These directions are: (1) to further emphasize how agency is constituted in a web of practices; (2) to pay attention to the macro-institutional nature of practices; (3) to account for emergence in strategy-making; (4) to recognize more accurately the role of materiality; and (5) to envisage critical analysis. While it would certainly seem presumptuous of us to position the CCO approach as the 'catch-all solution' to each of these directions, we can still assert, quite humbly, that a communicational

perspective could provide elements to emulate regarding most of these concerns (see Table 21.2).

Broadening what is entitled by the term 'agency' equates, for Vaara and Whittington, with moving away from methodological individualism, the latter promoting a 'focus on individuals and their actions and behaviors without regarding the enabling and constraining effects of social practices' (Vaara and Whittington 2012: 310). Building upon the principle of symmetry between agents of heterogeneous nature (Callon 1986), the communication approach depicted in this chapter rightfully argues for an extension of communication beyond individual agents (as noted by prior examples), substituting it with a view encompassing as agents anyone or anything that makes a difference in a given situation, lending its weight to a given course of action over another (Cooren 2010). Communication itself thus becomes a web in which various things and/or people get linked, attached or connected together as part of an iterative process, and potentially stabilized, for instance through an agenda inscribing a specific item to be discussed during an upcoming meeting.

Conceived in this alternative manner, agency can be rethought with multiple agents observed as making a difference. Subsequently, once we begin unfolding the interactions using the analytical vocabulary of the CCO approach, we note that the range of agents grows considerably to include, in addition to human beings such as Charles and Diane, documents such as modified municipal plans and agendas, sites such as parks and streets, entities the likes of funding organisms and boroughs administration, objectives such as financial security, and emotions such as indignation. While one could legitimately argue that a majority of these agents were made present through the talk of a single few individuals, it would be equally true to claim that unfolding the conversation in such a manner enables one to provide a richer portrayal of the matters of concerns displayed during this particular meeting, and a better understanding of the respective weight of these agents in the outcome of strategy-making.

The second direction established by Vaara and Whittington (2012) stresses the need of linking micro-activities to macro-level institutional phenomena. Here again, a communication approach may contribute to future research based on the simple yet compelling assumption that we never leave the firm ground of interactions. To state it differently, what occurs at different times, or in different locations, the *there* and the *then*, necessarily requires to be made present in the *here* and the *now* of interaction flows (Vásquez 2013). This also puts much importance on the role of various entities: through the use of charts, forms, websites, regulations and directives, practitioners and analysts alike are able to trace down the implications of numerous agents (political, economical, strategic, etc.) in the due course of their discussions of matters of concern.

Especially relevant here would be the relative weight of the physically absent in the outcome of the matters of concern at hand: the lady from the funding agency who does not return calls and flexible deadlines in the first scenario, the not-so-transparent officials and complacent community organizations in the second one. This conceptual shift seems especially advantageous, as it does not imply any type of gap (theoretically useful, but empirically non-existent) between the micro and macro orders of reality (Latour 2005). Despite the abandonment of this micro/macro divide, analytical shifts between the predominantly local (turns of talk, for instance) and societal concerns (issues of contracts, ethics, allies and the like) can nonetheless be operated through writing, for example by zooming in and out between different theoretical

and empirical concerns (Nicolini 2009), or, alternatively, by observing how participants themselves come to modify the lens with which to analyse matters of concern.

Here, the co-constructed account on the transformations of the boroughs offers a brilliant illustration of the successive *circumferences* of scene – a notion employed by Burke (1945) to refer to the rhetorical boundaries 'one must draw around an act in order to interpret it' (Anderson 2007: 44). While we cannot really elaborate on this point here, one could decide to explore how this ability to draw persuasive circumferences can contribute to the baggage of rhetorical skills displayed by practitioners, just like the astute use of words (Samra-Fredericks 2003), emotions (Samra-Fredericks 2004), exploitation of ambiguity (Sillince, Jarzabkowski and Shaw 2012), storytelling (Boje 2008) or the reframing of accounts (Sillince and Mueller 2007).

The third and fourth directions proposed by Vaara and Whittington (2012) attend, respectively, to the place of emergence and materiality, and direct our attention towards the potential contribution of a communication perspective on the methodological level. Regarding emergence, the CCO approach will instruct that strategizing invariably emerges from the interplay of various agents in communication (Taylor and Van Every 2000). This, in turn, invites analysts to observe actual instances of organizational interactions, instead of relying on alternative research strategies involving interviews or questionnaires. Students of strategy as practice rightfully echo this preference for the situated experience of organizational actors, since methods other than direct observation overlook the very substance of strategy-making (Johnson *et al.* 2007).

What, then, is to be observed? As our examples illustrate, studies of interactions during meetings provide considerable access to the matters of concerns that express and weigh themselves in the day-to-day life of organizations. As such, meetings are usually identified as decisive sites in which many organizational activities are created, transformed and shattered (Schwartzman 1989; Tracy and Dimock 2004). This, obviously, includes strategy-making (Jarzablowski and Seidl 2008). One lesson to be learned from our analysis, however, is that strategy-making may occur during interactions that are not labelled as deliberately strategic; as we have stated repeatedly, formal instances devoted to strategic planning may culminate in talking about strategy without necessarily talking strategically, and at other times something approaching a strategic plan may be improvised from seemingly mundane moments of talk.

From this particular vantage point, therefore, strategy may be lurking around any corner, and be found where unexpected, inviting analysts to preserve a flexible and reflexive attitude towards their object of study, and raising another question in the process: how are we to observe the communication work involved in strategy as practice? We need to acknowledge that, without direct access to that community organization's meeting, and without the inconspicuous use of a video camera, pretty much all the empirical evidence displayed in this chapter to support our views would have vanished. This strongly underlines the importance of video-recording samples of organizational life, principally for students of practice and communication.

Despite some limitations (such as risks of obtrusive presence, selectivity in the choice of plans), this technique of data collection renders accessible layers of interactions that could hardly be observed by any other means, including bodily movements and gazes, silences and fluctuations in voice tones, and the manipulation of documents and other artefacts. It also enables more collaborative forms of scholarly analysis, which researchers, and even practitioners, can join to discuss what occurs during specific moments of interaction in organizational settings (Cooren *et al.* 2007). Those are some of the reasons justifying a greater use of audio-visual recordings in the study of strategy as practice, in which such an approach is only starting to blossom (see Liu 2013; Stronz 2005).

Finally, while the CCO perspective introduced in this chapter does not necessarily share the basic assumptions of critical theory (for a discussion, see Cooren, Taylor and Van Every 2006; Taylor and Van Every 2000), conceiving of strategy as various matters of concerns collectively weighing each other could stimulate some interesting investigations regarding issues of voice and representation, matters of inclusions and exclusions and how specific agents become entitled to speak and act in the name of specific matters. On a broader level, the close-up, detailed analysis of interaction episodes in organizational settings could help uncovering the taken-for-granted assumptions at work during strategy-making, as well as the various (f)actors that enable or constrain it, although this path has yet to be explored. Aside from that prospective research direction, we could also reflect on the ways that organizational communication could, in turn, benefit from the strategy-as-practice literature. If only for practical reasons, however, it would seem wiser to emulate Charles and Diane by postponing this matter of concern for another time.

Appendix I – Transcription conventions

• Brackets indicate that the encased portions of the utterances are produced simultaneously. Left-hand brackets designate the beginning of simultaneity, whereas right-hand brackets mark its end.

BOB: I wish [he was on time].
KATHY: [He is always] late.

Bob and Kathy, respectively, say 'he was on time' and 'He is always' at the same time.

• Underlining indicates that the speaker is emphasizing this specific portion of the utterance.

BOB: I cannot stand him.

Bob is emphasizing the word 'stand'.

• Equal signs indicate that there is no time elapsed between two utterances.

BOB: He's a very nice guy=
KATHY: =and so considerate towards them.

When Bob finishes with 'guy', Kathy starts her turn right away by saying 'and'. There is no interval between the two turns.

• A period in parentheses indicate a very short pause (less than one-tenth of a second).

KATHY: So we could, (.) you know.

The pause between 'could' and 'you know' is almost imperceptible.

• Numbers in parentheses indicate intervals in the stream of talk. These intervals (indicated in seconds and tenth of seconds) can be identified within an utterance or between utterances.

BOB: How do you change that?

(2.5)

ERIC: How do you change what?

This indicates that 2.5 seconds elapse between the completion of Bob's turn and the beginning of Eric's turn.

- Double parentheses indicate that what is encased is a description of what is happening during the interaction. What is enclosed is not a transcription.

MARK: Honestly.
((Harry's cellphone rings))

- Hyphens indicate that the prior syllable has been cut off short.

BOB: He is so biz-he is so strange.

Bob is about to say 'bizarre' but stops and rephrases his assessment.

- Repeated colons indicate prolongation of the immediately preceding sound. The length of the colon row denotes the length of the prolongation.

KATHY: He is so::: tired.

The pronunciation of the word 'so' is prolonged by Kathy.

- Repeated 'x's mean that it is impossible to work out what the person is saying.

BOB: So far as I can see [xx].
KATHY: [He is useless].

Kathy's comment 'He is useless' drowns out what Bob is saying.

Note: For more details on these transcribing conventions, see Van Dijk (1997: 312–14), as well as Atkinson and Heritage (1984: ix–xvi).

Source: Based on Gail Jefferson's (1984) transcription techniques.

Appendix II – Transcription of the board of directors' discussion on urban planning

1		
2	C:	The meeting of the assembly, uh, of the
3		borough council of, uh, the beginning of
4		December – I don't remember the date.
5	D:	Fifteen or sixteen… Fifteen sixteen?
6	C:	Uh, six, seven, I believe. And it says
7		that, there are people who reacted –
8		there is a person who is named, for
9		example – anyway, who reacts, who
10		says that, 'Listen, you keep carrying
11		out projects while there is a
12		consultation; what's this story, is
13		that consultation serious or not?'
14		And, uh, the borough mayor says,
15		uh, what's told in the newspaper,
16		'Well, we do not want to delay,
17		uh, the projects because of the
18		consultation.' And the director of
19		urban planning says, uh, 'Anyway, uh,
20		the consultation is not on the projects,
21		on the buildings, and related stuff, but
22		on the parks and the streets.'
23	J:	Uh?
24	E:	The what?
25	B:	The parks and the streets.
26	C:	The parks, 'parcos' and the streets.
27	J:	Parques.
28	C:	Parques – of course, of course, that's it.
29		((Laughs))
30	E:	Okay.
31	C:	Isn't that a huge enough? So, what we
32		need-Because I want to put that on
33		paper, but, uh, in any case, (1.0) they
34		approved – it was the, uh, the seventh-
35		the seventh at nigh- no, Monday, yes,
36		the eleventh, the eleventh – they
37		approved another project that will be
38		next to the Staples. The first phase –
39		there will be four phases and uh,
40		anyways, to make a long story short, in
41		the plans, we see quite well that the
42		streets, Elizabeth Street, according to
43		the plan that was released last June, but
44		which theoretically should only be a
45		proposal. If we do a consultation, logic
46		would be that we should still be able to
47		change the proposal, but, uh, in that
48		plan it was indicated, in June, that
49		Elizabeth would not be continued North
50		of Madison Avenue, meaning that

51		Elizabeth Street would get up to
52		Madison.
53	B:	Uh uh.
54	C:	It stops there; you go either east or west.
55	B:	Like Applewood.
56	C:	What?
57	B:	Applewood Street.
58	C:	Yes, Applewood is closed. In other words
59		the whole triangle [is closed].
60	B:	[will be closed].
61	C:	And the whole triangle, there are only
62		bicycle lanes and walking paths. There
63		are no more cars in there, or in any case
64		they are not real streets anyways. That's
65		what we can guess in the June plan. It's
66		not completely obvious but
67	B:	What should we think? What should we
68		think of all this?
69	C:	I'm getting to what I want to say. The
70		plan that was adopted on Monday
71		builds on what was in the June plan.
72		I examined the plans. The street, in the
73		plan, is closed. So, when the director of
74		planning says that the streets are part,
75		are the object of consultation, that's also
76		a lie. It's a lie to say that the
77		consultation is not about the projects
78		because it was said that it was on the
79		projects. He says it's only the streets
80		and the parks, but I can see that this
81		street will become in part a place where
82		buildings will be erected and partly
83		parks. It's lies. The consultation, there,
84		it was an operation to attempt to fool
85		everyone. Me, there, when the guy came,
86		the first question that I asked him, I
87		asked him if the law required him to go
88		through with the consultation he was
89		doing. Because, I was, what I knew,
90		was that if the law forced him to do that,
91		then it meant there was a clear
92		framework he had to respect and that he
93		had to stop everything – for example,
94		take into account what is suggested
95		during the consultation and change
96		afterwards if needed. He said, 'No, the
97		law doesn't force us.' So, it's an opera,

98	it's a request from the borough, here,
99	to do a consultation. The process began
100	since 2005, I want, I want to continue,
101	I want to produce another document, or
102	other documents, I want to show that
103	there was, that there was this regulation
104	in 2005, in 2006, in 2007… And they
105	were setting all the bases to orient
106	towards a specific direction. All of a
107	sudden, hop! In 2009 there is a
108	consultation – come on! Everything's
109	there, everything is going towards the
110	thing, and there is a consultation and
111	things keep going like before.
112	I've had a meeting, there, last week.
113	I went to a meeting, a short meeting that
114	wasn't about this, but the planning
115	director was there; y'know, I can see in
116	the discourse he held that they are going
117	in that direction. What I want to say is
118	that their plan is like I thought; (.) there
119	is a plan, they apply it and nobody can
120	stop them. The consultation, it's a sham,
121	and the system allows them to function
122	the way they want. Because I was
123	mention…, mentioning it already. There
124	are two regulations that allow them to
125	act in all freedom. It's the regulation on
126	demolition and the regulation on the
127	construction of particular projects. The
128	two regulations are built the same way.
129	And both regulations, what you need,
130	quickly, there, there are two levels.
131	Okay? The first level, there is a decision
132	that's taken, and then there's an appeal.
133	The first level, okay, it consists of, it
134	consists of what? It consists of…
135	There's a committee that takes the
136	decision. The committee – it is, uh, it's
137	insulting for people's intelligence – the
138	committee is made up of the urban
139	planning advisory committee. Each
140	borough, each city in Quebec, has an
141	urban planning advisory committee.
142	They are people who are chosen by the
143	elected officials because, uh, they are
144	people who will say=

145 J: =What they want=
146 C: =exactly what they want them to say. So
147   they choose them on purpose. So, the
148   urban planning advisory committee, it
149   has its own meeting, its own dynamic, it
150   does its own things, but, also, it can be
151   used to be part of the committee of the
152   regulation on the construction of
153   particular projects. So it's there, and
154   there's on top of that an elected official,
155   who to this point, at least what I saw, it
156   has been the borough mayor. So there is
157   the urban planning committee chosen
158   by the elected officials, uh, a group of
159   yes-men and of yes-women, plus the
160   mayor, who are the first level. And the
161   decision they take, you can appeal from
162   it. Where? In front of the committee
163   on, er… the borough committee!
164   Again the elected officials! The elected
165   officials are at both levels! In both
166   cases! They're dying of laughter. They
167   control the whole process. A and B!
168   Impossible. They can destroy the city,
169   demolish the city, rebuild the city; there
170   is no one who can stop them.
171 J: So, to sum up, they will do the project.
172 C: They will do what they want. S::: S::: I
173   will produce a small document to
174   explain this, we've got to get this out=
175 J: =There are people who are interested?
176 C: =It makes no sense. So, this – I am glad you
177   are asking the question. We need… I tell
178   myself… I am thinking about all this,
179   and I say, one, the thing that [xx
180 J: [But the
181   answer is yes or no? Or…
182 C: Not enough. The people who are
183   interested by this are under influence=
184 J: =Hum, hum=
185 C: =For the most part. They are under the
186   influence, they are afraid for their grants,
187   so they have a hypocritical discourse.
188   Or they shut their- or they manage to be
189   on the side of the administration.
190 B: Who are you talking about?
191 C: Of all the other community

192   organizations.
193 B: Okay.
194 C: Except us. And I'm not saying that to
195   brag about us. Okay, but that's the way
196   it is. I say we need to have new people.
197   That's important. We have a problem in
198   the district; we're missing intellectuals.
199   When I say 'intellectuals' I mean,
200   y'know, people who y'know,
201   (inaudible)
202 C: Who are interested by causes and who
203   are ready to discuss.
204 B: (consultation?)
205 C: Yes, a bit. This kind of people. We
206   would need these people, but
207   immigrants, maybe, of all origins.
208   That's one thing we would need. And
209   we would need, I, there – I can't, there's
210   one thing that's very clear. I cannot hold
211   the fight by myself and I don't want to
212   hold a fight by myself.
213 J: But that's what I mean.
214 C: And I want to feel that there are other
215   people than myself. It's senseless to do
216   it alone, because they will say it's just
217   him who's whining. And I know it leads
218   nowhere.
219 J: Hence my question!
220 C: No, there is no one else.
221 D: Because.
222 C: We've got mostly people on the other
223   side.
224 D: It's because people=
225 B: =(inaudible)
226 D: It's because people oppose… The way
227   it goes, a bit… They do not agree, but,
228   as Charles says, they use some double
229   talk, everything is a bit (1) they say one
230   thing and its opposite in the same
231   sentence, as does Mister We-know-
232   who. There a bit of that… ((laughs))
233   (inaudible)
234 C: And it's not better with some other
235   groups who are doing, in my opinion.
236   Anyways, the groups – there, there,
237   that's another chapter – both groups
238   who work in the district, that's there's,

239 there's only one thing that's of interest
240 to them: it's doing projects. So, that the
241 city gives them projects, the rest, there,
242 they will=
243 J: =(inaudible)=
244 C: =never go beyond that.
245 D: But that's all the groups, isn't it?
246 (inaudible)
247 C: Yes, all the groups. But they are, those
248 that are here, on top of that, they fight
249 together. Or at least there's a game,
250 there's quite an ambiguous game that's
251 going on, at the moment. (1.0)
252 J: So, our conclusion is?
253 C: It's not going very well.
254 J: It's not going very well. But if we don't
255 have, if we don't attract a new follower…
256 C: I was looking forward to telling you
257 about this because I felt that, at least, we
258 need the board of directors to feel a bit
259 interested, and I personally need to feel
260 that you, it interests you, and that you
261 will be thinking about this. Because I
262 know it's not an imminent threat in the
263 next three weeks everyone will lose
264 their dwelling.
265 (inaudible)
266 C: But we've got enough experience and
267 we have all read enough to know that
268 sooner or later there are things coming.
269 D: Because what's going on, is that the city
270 is doing is transforming. Well, I say the
271 city,
272 J: I understand.
273 D: The city administration is changing
274 the face and the image of the city as it is,
275 the construction, I mean, without
276 consultation, without saying anything,
277 doing it all on the sly. All of a sudden
278 the small buildings become housing
279 towers. Without there having ever been
280 any debate on that=
281 L: =Yeah, yeah=
282 D: =Without any discussion, without it
283 being public. It's done one project at a
284 time, and all of a sudden we end up
285 with…

286 C: Yes. That's what's coming.
287 ((hubbub))
288 C: But look, what we know.
289 D: (Long term) they are also saying that's
290 it's on twenty years.
291 C: What we know at the moment. Three
292 thousand apartments on Beechtree.
293 Eight thousand on Western. That's
294 eleven thousand.
295 (inaudible)
296 C: I say, at least two thousand on Central.
297 Maybe more, but at least two thousand.
298 So we're at thirteen thousand
299 apartments. Thirteen thousand
300 apartments, there's fifteen percent of
301 social housing, eighty-five percent of
302 condos. Okay? So that means that,
303 we've got approximately, out of thirteen
304 thousand apartments, two thousand
305 social housing and eleven thousand
306 condos. Multiply that by two persons
307 and a half, two people, two people
308 and a half, there, we' just grown the
309 population of the district of twenty-five,
310 thirty thousand residents with income
311 that's more I mean, their income it's
312 fifty thousand and upward. So, keep in
313 mind the outlook of the district just
314 changed. Because the statistics=
315 ((side conversations, small comments))
316 C: =That we've got in the district, forget
317 that, it's all changed, it will create a
318 distortion. The statistics that decide the
319 money we get, the grants, the interest
320 that we have, the distortion that this
321 mass will produce in the district, il will
322 mess up the whole thing. And keep in
323 mind that those people attend shops that
324 no one… and you know very well how
325 gentrification works.
326 B: Well yes.
327 (1.5)
328 M: Yes.
329 C: I am especially. I am- I mention a
330 small detail in passing. Comments like
331 those of that guy, for example, who says
332 that uh he is he does, anyways, I don't

333   want to get into that, but I take just a
334   few seconds, he says uh "The City
335   should not create ghettos, uh neither
336   rich people ghettos or ghettos for the
337   poor." It's an absolutely dumb opinion.
338   I know why he does this. He wants to
339   give the impression that he is critical,
340   while he gives a critique that has no
341   effect in reality.
342 J: Hum.
343 D: Saying one thing and its opposite.
344 C: Exactly. It's not a ghetto. It's exactly
345   the opposite. A ghetto is something
346   that's closed. That's something that's
347   open, that will eat up the rest of the
348   district. We need the opposite.
349 M: (covered)
350 C: Because the other thing we need to
351   understand and that's worrying, is what
352   will happen with Eli- With the
353   Applewood subway station.
354 J: Hum.
355 C: This, listen, the urban plan, look, the
356   urban plan, it does-
357 J: Beechtree?
358 C: Uh?
359 L: Yeah.
360 J: Beechtree (inaudible)
361 C: Yeah. The urban plan, no, it announces
362   two things, the urban plan of two
363   thousand four. It announces Beechtree,
364   and Central. These are the two projects
365   in the district, the two sectors in the
366   district that need to be developed.
367   What's coming up is Central.
368   Inevitably, because they did the first, the
369   other one is coming up. But apparently,
370   in two thousand five, sorry in two
371   thousand ten, meaning the fifth year, uh,
372   because they, they, in any case, this
373   year, they're talking of updating it, of
374   revising it, of taking a new look at it.
375   I asked the question, the other day, when
376   I went to the meeting, I asked the
377   director of urban planning. Indeed, it's
378   coming up, he didn't give any details,
379   but it's coming up. What will be in

380   there? I examined closely, I mean, the
381   the the (1.5) the zoning and what
382   the plans have in store, there's nothing,
383   nothing in terms of zoning change, in
384   terms of renovations, in terms of
385   changes for the surroundings of the
386   Applewood station. It doesn't mean it's
387   not going to happen at some point.
388   Because it does say in in their
389   documents that they're thinking about
390   it. It will come at some point. And that,
391   it means demolishing apartments to
392   build a different type of apartments.
393   This one is different. Because on
394   Central it would be about doing pretty
395   much the same thing than on Beechtree-
396   Madison, that is to say take
397   commercial-industrial, and instead put
398   some residential. That doesn't disturb
399   the residential. Where they will be
400   major changes, is around the
401   Applewood station, meaning they're
402   demolishing existing housing to build
403   other types of units for a different class
404   of people. So, anyways, I'm mentioning
405   this.
406 J: So we-
407 C: But, I, what we need- I am suggesting
408   this, we need to talk about this. We need
409   to find a way to get people in the district
410   interested, in order to get a group
411   together.
412 D: I just want to mention that (inaudible),
413   something he said the other time at the
414   housing committee made me jump.
415   Because we were talking about this a
416   bit, we (opposed) something. He said,
417   "Oh, well, I am not against the district
418   getting richer."=
419 C: =He's saying anything=
420 D: =I said, me neither, on the condition
421   that it's the people from the district who
422   get richer.
423 B: Well yes, that's it.
424 L: Well yes (inaudible)
425 B: (inaudible)
426 D: That's, that's

427 C: That's what I don't like with his speech
428   (inaudible)
429   ((hubbub))
430 D: You see the attitude.
431 C: It's someone who says anything, the
432   only thing that interests him is that
433   ROMEL gets more projects. He is ready
434   to kill the district as long as his
435   organization has projects.
436   ((hubbub))
437 C: It's not a thought through approach.
438 M: I propose that we move on to something
439   else and that this item, we talk about it
440   exactly during our orientation congress.
441   That way... Because now we're kind of
442   doing the orientation congress.
443   ((laughs))
444 D: So, did we determine a date for the
445   orientation congress?
446 M: Yeah, that's it.
447   (19:20)

References

Anderson, D. (2007), *Identity's Strategy: Rhetorical Selves in Conversion*. Columbia: University of South Carolina Press.

Atkinson, J. M., and Heritage, J. (eds.) (1984), *Structures of Social Action: Studies in Conversation Analysis*. Cambridge University Press.

Balogun, J., and Johnson, G. (2005), 'From intended strategies to unintended outcomes: the impact of change recipient sensemaking', *Organization Studies*, 26/11: 1573–601.

Boje, D. M. (2008). *Storytelling Organizations*. London: Sage.

Brummans, B., Cooren, F., and Chaput, M. (2009), 'Discourse, communication, and organisational ontology', in Bargiela-Chiappini, F. (ed.), *The Handbook of Business Discourse*: 53–65. Edinburgh University Press.

Burke, K. (1945), *A Grammar of Motives*. Berkeley: University of California Press.

Callon, M. (1986), 'Some elements of a sociology of translation: domestication of the scallops and the fishermen of St Brieuc Bay', in Law, J. (ed.), *Power, Action and Belief: A New Sociology of Knowledge?*: 196–223. London: Routledge & Kegan Paul.

Chaput, M., Brummans, B., and Cooren, F. (2011), 'The role of organizational identification in the communicative constitution of an organization: a study of consubstantialization in a young political party', *Management Communication Quarterly*, 25/2: 252–82.

Clarke, I., Kwon, W., and Wodak, R. (2012), 'A context-sensitive approach to analysing talk in strategy meetings', *British Journal of Management*, 23/4: 455–73.

Cooren, F. (2000), *The Organizing Property of Communication*. Amsterdam: John Benjamins.

(2006), 'The organizational world as a plenum of agencies', in Cooren, F., Taylor, J. R., and Van Every, E. J. (eds.), *Communication as Organizing: Practical Approaches to Research into the Dynamic of Text and Conversation*: 81–100. Mahwah, NJ: Lawrence Erlbaum.

(2010), *Action and Agency in Dialogue: Passion, Incarnation and Ventriloquism*. Amsterdam: John Benjamins.

(2012), 'Communication theory at the center: ventriloquism and the communicative constitution of reality', *Journal of Communication*, 62/1: 1–20.

Cooren, F., Kuhn, T. R., Cornelissen, J., and Clark, T. (2011), 'Communication organizing and organization: an overview and introduction to the special issue', *Organization Studies*, 32/9: 1149–70.

Cooren, F., Matte, F., Taylor, J. R., and Vásquez, C. (2007), 'A humanitarian organization in action: organizational discourse as an immutable mobile', *Discourse and Communication*, 1/2: 153–90.

Cooren, F., Taylor, J. R., and Van Every, E. J. (eds.) (2006), *Communication as Organizing: Practical Approaches to Research into the Dynamic of Text and Conversation*. Mahwah, NJ: Lawrence Erlbaum.

Crossley, N. (2010), *Towards Relational Sociology*. London: Taylor & Francis.

Denis, J.-L., Dompierre, G., Langley, A., and Rouleau, L. (2011), 'Escalating indecision: between reification and strategic ambiguity', *Organization Science*, 22/1: 225–44.

Dépelteau, F. (2008), 'Relational thinking: a critique of co-deterministic theories of structure and agency', *Sociological Theory*, 26/1: 51–73.

Dépelteau, F., and Powell, C. (eds.) (2013), *Applying Relational Sociology: Relations, Networks, and Society*. New York: Palgrave Macmillan.

Donati, P. (2011), *Relational Sociology: A New Paradigm for the Social Sciences*. Abingdon: Routledge.

Fenton, C., and Langley, A. (2011), 'Strategy as practice and the narrative turn', *Organization Studies*, 32/9: 1171–96.

Golsorkhi, D., Rouleau, L., Seidl, D., and Vaara, E. (eds.) (2010), *Cambridge Handbook of Strategy as Practice*. Cambridge University Press.

Hardy, C., Palmer, I., and Phillips, N. (2000), 'Discourse as a strategic resource', *Human Relations*, 53/9: 1227–48.

Hendry, J., and Seidl, D. (2003), 'The structure and significance of strategic episodes: social systems theory and the routine practices of strategic change', *Journal of Management Studies*, 40/1: 175–96.

Hoon, C. (2007), 'Committees as strategic practice: the role of strategic conversation in a public administration', *Human Relations*, 60/6: 921–52.

Houser, N., and Kloesel, C. (eds.) (1992). The Essential Peirce: Selected Philosophical Writings, vol. 1, 1867–1893. Bloomington: Indiana University Press.

Jarzabkowski, P. (2003), 'Strategic practices: an activity theory perspective on continuity and change', *Journal of Management Studies*, 40/1: 23–55.

(2005), *Strategy as Practice: An Activity-Based Approach*. London: Sage.

(2008), 'Strategy as practice', in Barry, D., and Hansen, H. (eds.), *The Sage Handbook of New Approaches in Management and Organization*: 364–78. London: Sage.

Jarzabkowski, P., and Seidl, D. (2008), 'The role of meetings in the social practice of strategy', *Organization Studies*, 29/11: 1391–426.

Jarzabkowski, P., Sillince, J., and Shaw, D. (2010), 'Strategic ambiguity as a rhetorical resource for enabling multiple interests', *Human Relations*, 63/2: 219–48.

Jefferson, G. (1972), 'Side sequences', in Sudnow, D. (ed.), *Studies in Social Interaction*: 294–338. New York: Free Press.

Johnson, G., Langley, A., Melin, L., and Whittington, R. (2007), *Strategy as Practice: Research Directions and Resources*. Cambridge University Press.

Knights, D., and Morgan, G. (1991), 'Corporate strategy, organizations, and subjectivity: a critique', *Organization Studies*, 12/2: 251–73.

Kwon, W., Clarke, I., and Wodak, R. (2009), 'Organizational decision-making, discourse, and power: integrating across contexts and scales', *Discourse and Communication*, 3/3: 273–302.

Latour, B. (1996), 'On interobjectivity', *Mind, Culture, and Activity*, 3/4: 228–45.

(2004), 'Why has critique run out of steam? From matters of fact to matters of concern', *Critical Inquiry*, 30/2: 225–48.

(2005), *Reassembling the Social: An Introduction to Actor–Network-Theory*. Oxford University Press.

(2008), *What Is the Style of Matters of Concern?* Assen, Netherlands: Royal Van Gorcum.

Liu, F. (2013), 'Emotion and strategizing: exploring emotional dynamics and senior team strategizing in meetings', unpublished PhD dissertation. Vancouver: University of British Columbia.

Liu, F., and Maitlis, S. (2014), 'Emotional dynamics and strategizing processes: a study of strategic conversations in top team meetings', *Journal of Management Studies*, 51/2: 202–34.

Mantere, S., and Vaara, E. (2008), 'On the problem of participation in strategy: a critical discursive perspective', *Organization Science*, 19/2: 341–58.

Mintzberg, H., and Waters, J. A. (1985), 'Of strategies, deliberate and emergent', *Strategic Management Journal*, 6/3: 257–72.

Nicolini, D. (2009), 'Zooming in and out: studying practices by switching theoretical lenses and trailing connections', *Organization Studies*, 30/12: 1391–418.

Peirce, C. S. (1965 [1934]), *Collected Papers*, vol. V, *Pragmatism and Pragmaticism*. Cambridge, MA: Belknap Press.

(1992 [1898]), *Reasoning and the Logic of Things*, ed. Ketner, K. L. Cambridge, MA: Harvard University Press.

Pink, S. (2001), *Doing Visual Ethnography*. London: Sage.

(2006), *The Future of Visual Anthropology: Engaging the Senses*. Abingdon: Routledge.

Powell, C., and Dépelteau, F. (eds.) (2013), *Conceptualizing Relational Sociology: Ontological and Theoretical Issues*. New York: Palgrave Macmillan.

Putnam, L. L., and Nicotera, A. M. (2009), *Building Theories of Organization: The Constitutive Role of Communication*. New York: Routledge.

Reckwitz, A. (2002), 'Toward a theory of social practices: a development in culturalist theorizing', *European Journal of Social Theory*, 5/2: 243–63.

Regnér, P. (2003), 'Strategy creation in the periphery: inductive versus deductive strategy making', *Journal of Management Studies*, 40/1: 57–82.

Robichaud, R. (2006), 'Steps toward a relational view of agency', in Cooren, F., Taylor, J. R., and Van Every, E. J. (eds.), *Communication as Organizing: Practical Approaches to Research into the Dynamic of Text and Conversation*: 101–14. Mahwah, NY: Lawrence Erlbaum.

Rouse, J. (2007), 'Practice philosophy', in Turner, S., and Risjord, M. (eds.), *Handbook of the Philosophy of Science,* vol. XV, *Philosophy of Anthropology and Sociology*: 630–81. London: Elsevier.

Samra-Fredericks, D. (2003), 'Strategizing as lived experience and strategists' everyday efforts to shape strategic direction', *Journal of Management Studies*, 40/1: 141–74.

(2004), 'Managerial elites making rhetorical and linguistic "moves" for a moving (emotional) display', *Human Relations*, 57/9: 1103–43.

(2005), 'Strategic practice, "discourse" and the everyday interactional constitution of "power effects"', *Organization*, 12/6: 803–41.

(2010), Researching everyday practice: the ethnomethodological contribution', in Golsorkhi, D., Rouleau, L. Seidl, D., and Vaara, E. (eds.), *Cambridge Handbook of Strategy as Practice*: 230–42. Cambridge University Press.

Schatzki, T. R., Knorr Cetina, K., and von Savigny, E. (eds.) (2001), *The Practice Turn in Contemporary Theory*. London: Routledge.

Schwartzman, H. B. (1989), *The Meeting: Gatherings in Organizations and Communities*. New York: Plenum Press.

Sillince, J., and Mueller, F. (2007), 'Switching strategic perspective: the reframing of accounts of responsibility', *Organization Studies*, 28/2: 155–76.

Sillince, J., Jarzabkowski, P., and Shaw, D. (2012), 'Shaping strategic action through the rhetorical construction and exploitation of ambiguity', *Organization Science*, 23/3: 630–50.

Spee, P., and Jarzabkowski, P. (2011), 'Strategic planning as communicative process', *Organization Studies*, 32/9: 1217–45.

Stensaker, I., and Falkenberg, J. (2007), 'Making sense of different responses to corporate change', *Human Relations*, 60/1: 137–78.

Stronz, M. (2005), 'Strategic learning in the context of strategy implementation: a case study of implementers in action', unpublished PhD dissertation. New York: Columbia University.

Suominen, K., and Mantere, S. (2010), 'Consuming strategy: the art and practice of managers' everyday strategy usage', in Baum, J. A. C., and Lampel, J. (eds.), *Advances in Strategic Management*, vol. XXVII, *The Globalization of Strategy Research*: 211–45. Bingley, UK: Emerald.

Taylor, J. R., and Van Every, E. J. (2000), *The Emergent Organization: Communication as Its Site and Surface*. Mahwah, NJ: Lawrence Erlbaum.

(2011), *The Situated Organization: Case Studies in the Pragmatics of Communication Research*. New York: Routledge.

Ten Have, P. (1999), *Doing Conversation Analysis: A Practical Guide*. Thousand Oaks, CA: Sage.

Tracy, K., and Dimock, A. (2004), 'Meetings: discursive sites for building and fragmenting community', in Kalbfleisch, P. J. (ed.), *Communication Yearbook 28*: 127–65. Mahwah, NJ: Lawrence Erlbaum.

Vaara, E., Kleymann, B., and Seristö, H. (2004), 'Strategies as discursive constructions: the case of airline alliances', *Journal of Management Studies*, 41/1: 1–35.

Vaara, E., Sorsa, V., and Pälli, P. (2010), 'On the force potential of strategy texts: a critical discourse analysis of a strategic plan and its power effects in a city organization', *Organization*, 17/6: 685–702.

Vaara, E., and Tienari, J. (2011), 'On the narrative construction of multinational corporations: an antenarrative analysis of legitimation and resistance in a cross-border merger', *Organization Science*, 22/2: 370–90.

Vaara, E., and Whittington, R. (2012), 'Strategy-as-practice: taking social practices seriously', *Academy of Management Annals*, 6/1: 285–336.

Van Dijk, T. A. (ed.) (1997), *Discourse Studies: A Multidiscilpinary Introduction*, vol. I, *Discourse as Structure and Process*. London: Sage.

Vásquez, C. (2013), 'Spacing organization (or how to be here and there at the same time)', in Robichaud, D., and Cooren, F. (eds.), *Organization and Organizing: Materiality, Agency and Discourse*: 127–49. New York: Routledge.

Vásquez, C., Sergi, V., and Cordelier, B. (2013), 'From being branded to doing branding: studying representation practices from a communication-centered approach', *Scandinavian Journal of Management*, 29/2: 125–36.

Whittington, R. (2003), 'The work of strategizing and organizing: for a practice perspective', *Strategic Organization*, 1/1: 119–27.

(2006), 'Completing the practice turn in strategy research', *Organization Studies*, 27/5: 613–34.

Whittle, A., Housley, W., Gilchrist, A., Lenney, P., and Mueller, F. (2014), 'Power, politics, and organizational communication: an ethnomethodological perspective', in Cooren, F., Vaara, E., Langley, A., and Tsoukas, H. (eds.), *Language and Communication at Work: Discourse, Narrativity, and Organizing*: 71–94. Oxford University Press.

Wodak, R., Kwon, W., and Clarke, I. (2011), '"Getting people on board": discursive leadership for consensus building in team meetings', *Discourse and Society*, 22/5: 592–644.

Analytical frames for studying power in strategy as practice and beyond

STEWART CLEGG and MARTIN KORNBERGER

[Strategy] is the art of creating power.

Freedman (2013: xii)

Introduction

This chapter provides a systematic reflection on how power can be used as an analytical framework to study strategy. Such an endeavour faces the difficulty of having to deal with two rather large bookshelves: one collects those authors who share a concern with power, albeit that they might not use the term 'strategy'; on the other shelves, the writers on strategy often tend to have a more implicit than explicit interest in theories of power. To make things even more difficult, the two bookshelves are usually placed in different parts of libraries. Philosophers, sociologists, political scientists, organization theorists and others may well be interested in power but business school professors study strategy in overwhelmingly economic terms with competition conceived as warfare by other means. It is ironical that, for all the forceful imagery of strategy writing, often drawing on military metaphors, there is a dearth of explicit accounts of power relations and strategy. The irony attaches to the fact that strategy is so consciously aimed at changing power relations – in the market, in the organization, or vis-à-vis government regulators; it speaks of 'forces' and (value) 'chains', of competition and advantages, but, strangely, it neglects issues of power. We find Lawrence Freedman's introductory quote one of the most apt definitions of strategy, as it alludes to the important fact that power is dynamically created in specific contexts, and that it is power that makes it possible to accomplish an objective. For Freedman (2013), strategy is the 'central political art', as it is concerned with getting more out of a situation than the

balance of power would initially suggest. It is in this sense that strategy is concerned with the creation of power. Perhaps it is telling that Freedman is a professor of war studies (and thus his books are located on yet another shelf in the libraries).

In this chapter we will roam and range in the library, moving from one shelf to another, following ideas and mobilizing authors, resulting in the following structure. First we review some of the key texts of the strategy-as-practice literature that deals with power. We frame analysis by discussing the relation between power and (1) 'strategy' as noun, (2) 'strategizing' as verb and (3) making things strategic ('strategic' as adjective). Such a simple heuristic device will enable us to emphasize the different agents, mechanisms and effects that can guide the study of power and strategy. We conclude our chapter with a brief reflection on further research opportunities that follow from our analysis.

Reviewing strategy as practice and power

It is strategy as practice's big accomplishment to have scholars connect the two bookshelves and established first a trickle, then a flow, of communication across disciplinary boundaries (for an overview, see Vaara and Whittington 2012). As result, there are a number of contributions to the strategy-as-practice literature that make the point that strategy and power relations are necessarily coterminous. We now briefly review some of the most significant of recent empirical accounts, all of which find some direction from Knights and Morgan's (1991) embryonic paper, developing the critical strand of SAP research with an interest in power relations (for early accounts, see Ezzamel and Willmott 2004; 2008; Hendry 2000; Lilley

2001). Drawing on Foucault, the novel idea put forward by Knights and Morgan was to suggest that strategy discourses exercise power: it is various strategy discourses that constitute subject positions and delineate the space in which the manager emerges as a strategic actor. Strategy was defined as a set of (discursive) practices that had to be analysed with regard to their power effects on the organization, the environment and those doing the strategizing. Knights and Morgan put special emphasis on the identity of the strategist, who, in their view, represents a new form of subjectivity that stands in contrast to that of the bureaucrat, the planner and other much-criticized embodiments of 'organization man' (Whyte 2013).

The focus on discourse has provided fertile soil for the study of strategy. For instance, Phillips, Sewell and Jaynes (2008: 772) argue that discourse, including that of strategy, is 'continually and recursively acting on individual meaning making through the operation of text'. When strategists engage in discursive practices – that is, when they write or speak as strategists – they engage simultaneously in a political activity in which they are involved in 'a struggle for power in and around organizations that seeks to determine the nature of concepts and subject positions and to control how the resulting objects are understood and treated' (Phillips, Sewell and Jaynes 2008: 773; see also Hardy and Thomas 2014). In the same vein, Fenton and Langley (2011: 3) argue that '[s]trategy narratives select and prioritize – indeed, this is their ostensible managerial purpose. However, as they achieve this, they also implicitly express, construct and reproduce legitimate power structures, organizational roles, and ideologies (Mumby, 1987).' In an empirical application, Vaara, Sorsa and Pälli (2010) analyse how the strategy discourse shaped the city administration of Lahti, in Finland. They argue that strategy documents serve several purposes: '[T]hey communicate negotiated meanings, legitimate ways of thinking and action and de-legitimate others, produce consent but may also trigger resistance, and have all kinds of political and ideological effects, some more apparent than others' (Vaara, Sorsa and Pälli 2010: 686). Likewise, Eriksson and Lehtimäki (2001: 202) suggest understanding 'strategy rhetoric as a cultural product on which the strategy-makers draw, because the rhetoric is regarded as effective and convincing... [It] is taken as self-evident and legitimate, and is used without questioning the presumptions on which it is built.' These studies share a concern with how the discursive practices of strategizing not only express and legitimize power relations but also constitute and 'create' power, to use Freedman's phrase: strategy represents the instrument that allows us to speak on behalf of others, including people, shareholders, the future or the environment. Collecting these voices in the strategy discourse, the strategist amplifies his/her power and influence.

On a more micro-discursive level, Samra-Fredricks (2005) offers ethnographies of strategists at work by audio-recording their naturally occurring talk-based interactive routines. Strongly influenced by ethnomethodological conversation analysis, she carefully investigated how order is produced in and from everyday talk. Strategic practice is reconceptualized in terms of four forms of knowledge, which 'make up' the validity claims of truthfulness, correctness, sincerity and intelligibility that any 'discourse' must make to be taken seriously by would-be rational actors. Samra-Fredericks analyses the talk in use by people, organizationally, in doing strategy as her empirical material, noting that such strategy talk assumes 'much symbolic significance and material consequentiality when skilfully spoken/deployed and combined with other features at the right time and in the "correct" way' (Samra-Frericks 2005: 828).

Building on both Knights and Morgan (1991) and Samra-Fredericks (2005), McCabe (2010) seeks to supplement accounts of the doing of strategy with those of doing power and stratification. Necessarily, a critique of the conventional organization theory power literature is made as being overly managerial; instead, a relational Foucauldian analysis of power is called for. Unlike Samra-Fredericks' sole focus on talk, the discursive materials drawn on also include written documents from within the organization in question. Strategy is analysed as 'a manifestation of the managerial claim to power' (McCabe 2010: 172). Similarly, Laine and Vaara (2007) analyse strategy discourses as a form of top management mobilization in the struggle for control in the organization. From their perspective, strategy seeks to establish hegemony by creating coherence and consensus among organization members. What happens, however, is that these attempts at control work as occasions for discursive and other forms of resistance, especially by middle managers, who develop alternative but coupled strategy discourses that provide them with room to manoeuvre in controversial situations. Strategy seeks to impose corporate identity, which is often resisted – in this case, especially by project engineers who have quite distinct notions of identity. Organizational discourse then becomes seen as a battlefield on which competing groups struggle to assert strategy as they see it. Specific discourses, taken to be strategy by their progenitors, create subject positions for those whom they envisage, configure and constitute as objects of strategy. These others have ideas of their own to draw on, however, as well as discursive capabilities that enable them to do so. Hence, the struggles over strategy become, inevitably, struggles over diverse identity claims: discourses around strategizing involve battles over agency and identity, as Laine and Vaara (2007) demonstrate. Frequently, as in the case considered, these play out in ways that the originators of the formal strategies never envisaged or anticipated.

Strategy therefore represents a form of change, directed or not, intended or not. Change threatens the balance of power and provokes resistance; in fact, resistance is a constitutive element of power relations (Foucault 1982). Thomas, Sargent and Hardy (2011) show how organizational becoming in which strategic meaning is negotiated occurs in and through organizational talk targeted towards organizational change. While they establish that resistance to such strategy talk often ensues, they see such resistance as being potentially generative dialogue, in which resistance can be a positive form of power as well as more oppositional and inhibiting of innovation (see Courpasson, Dany and Clegg 2012).

In sum, what we can learn from reviewing some of the most important studies on strategy as practice and power relations is that the use of language is central to the analysis of strategy in practice, whether as written text, formal discourse or situated talk. As we have seen, from the 1990s onwards a steadily growing body of literature reflected this insight, advocating the study of strategy as narrative, using the tools of discourse analysis to dissect power effects. The underlying assumption of this stream of research is that strategies are narratives and 'pedagogic devices' that, through their language, format how organizations are imagined, what their key properties are and how they should be managed (Oakes, Townley and Cooper 1998). Strategy exercises what Bourdieu (1977) labels symbolic power: through its aesthetics (think of the often evoked 'big pictures' that strategists produce, literally, as images: Kornberger 2012) it constructs social order.

No doubt, discourse is central to the exercise of power; but an analytics focused on discursive power does not exhaust the ways in which power might operate in practice. In order to systematically explore complementary analytical strategies, we have organized our chapter through the following heuristic: the relation between power and (1) 'strategy' as noun, (2) 'strategizing' as verb and (3) making things strategic ('strategic' as adjective). Using the distinction between noun, verb and adjective, we can propose a sketch that tabulates the differences implied (see Table 22.1). As the table indicates, each perspective focuses on different elements of the strategy-as-practice mix. Next, we discuss the distinctions between them in more detail.

Strategy: the noun

Strategy, power and interests

Some early strategy writers who were engaged with what were, in their day, current debates about power relations did appreciate the linkages between strategy and power. One of the best cases in point is Andrew Pettigrew, who writes on power and strategic decision-making:

> [D]ecision-making is a political process in which outcomes are a function of the balancing of various power vectors. The processing of demands and the generation of support are the principle components of the general political structure through which

Table 22.1 Summary of analytical framework to study power and strategy, strategizing and making things strategic

	Key concepts	Theoretical inspirations	Who has agency in the strategy process	Locus of strategizing
Strategy	Decision-making, non-decision-making and interests	Political science, sociology (Bachrach and Baratz, Lukes and others)	Top management	Headquarters
Strategizing	Practice, discourse and technology	Philosophy, anthropology sociology (Foucault, Wittgenstein and practice theorists)	Top management and others (mainly middle managers)	Organization, including practices, routines, rituals and technologies
Making things strategic	Visualization, valuation and mobilization	Social studies of science, (actor) network theory, new economic sociology, anthropology of markets, accounting	Human and non-human actors; collective action	Networks, devices and obligatory passage points

power is wielded. The final decisional outcome will evolve out of the processes of power mobilisation attempted by each party in support of its demand (Pettigrew 1973).

Here, decision-making represents the link between the strategist, on the one hand, and power, on the other hand. In the moment of decision-making both collide. Pettigrew's (1985) historical account of change at ICI, the major British chemical company, illustrates this collision. Dissatisfied with the simple linearity of existing accounts of strategy as a matter of 'formulation', 'implementation' and 'process', Pettigrew drew on his background as an anthropologist and sociologist to study strategic decision-making as a process deeply embedded in the context of the firm in which it occurs. From this perspective, the idea that strategy is first formulated and then what is formulated is implemented in a linear fashion is misjudged; in practice, the two stages meld together, informing each other as a process that elapses through time. What makes decision-making strategic is not the announcement of something as strategic or not so much as the extent to which a strategic direction unfolds over time. We should not expect it to do so evenly or linearly; instead, there will be missteps, some forwards and some backwards, that become glossed as demonstrating historical continuities over time. Those glosses that prevail are those with the most clout; it is power relations and political struggles

that provide narrative consistency by means of accounts that reflect the outcomes of these relations and struggles. ICI attempted to change its strategy, structure, technology and organizational culture over the period from 1960 to 1983. Pettigrew collected both comparative and longitudinal data from four of ICI's largest divisions and from the corporate headquarters. The change process was, indeed, unlike textbook depictions: divisions were not interested in the changes that they saw being imposed on them; they contested them, creating not so much an unfolding dynamic strategy as one marked frequently by inertia and failure to connect in ways that were planned. Plans do not make strategies; politics do. Radical change produces radical resistance and slow absorption of the changes planned.

Pettigrew's work was a useful corrective to some earlier views of strategic choice, which Child (1972) had pioneered. These views assumed that organizational elites were able to make strategic choices that would shape the determinants of contingency theory: the environment, technology and size of the firm. Although Child's views were correct in critiquing the determinism of earlier contingency views of design, if only because organizational design is not an adaptive response to structural contingencies over which there is no choice, the perspective that he brought to bear stands corrected by Pettigrew. Organizational elites might make choices strategically but the process whereby these choices may or may not be enacted is a complex and highly political process, the micro-management of which is crucial to the strategic outcomes.

Both Pettigrew and Child focused on decision-making as the locus of strategy; what both overlooked is that there is also non-decision-making, through which power might be exercised. Non-decision-making, as introduced into the literature by Bachrach and Baratz (1962), follows this logic: actors with vested interests in particular arenas of power seek to make issues disappear or frame them in such a way that they fall outside people's agendas. To the extent that they are successful, these actors bound other actors' rationality. Following Bachrach and Baratz, choices have to be scrutinized critically, as they might conceal more than they presumably offer: to choose between green energy and other, less sustainable sources of energy might be a choice; yet what this choice conceals is the more difficult discussion about the need to slow down energy usage, change consumption patterns and perhaps discard the imperative of continuous economic growth. A version of the same empirical logic is clearly at play also in Flyvbjerg's (1998) analysis of the different strategies of power relations evident in the municipality of Aalborg, Denmark, as a ten-year struggle to produce an integrated bus station and transport hub unfolded in a process in which agents representing cyclists, motorists, local businessmen and –women, councillors, the media and academic researchers became enrolled. Their interests and access to differential resources patterned the logic of the various actors' strategies. Power relations proved to be the authors of strategy; as we have said elsewhere (Carter, Clegg and Kornberger 2008b), policy follows politics, much as Machiavelli (1995 [1513]) stipulated.

From hidden preferences to 'real' interests?

For Bachrach and Baratz (1962), there were two faces of power: the seen and the unseen; decision-making and non-decision-making; the worlds of issues and non-issues. A few years later Lukes (1974) remade their two faces of power as a two-dimensional model to which he added a third dimension. At the core of the third dimension of power was a conception of power working against the interests of actors.

The notion of interests and of power as a set of practices that serve to occlude interests is potent. It was at the base of Marcuse's (1964) influential model of one-dimensional man, in which he draws heavily on Packard's (1957) *The Hidden Persuaders*. Such a view of strategy could be easily elaborated: strategy would assert itself by systematically developing a false sense of what actors' interests are in order to sell them products that they neither need nor really want. Marketing strategy that builds market share for products based on other than authentic interests is the well-known case in point: power works through making people believe that it is in their own best interest to buy the latest mobile phone or pair of jeans. Power, according to Lukes, works best when people internalize power's interests to the point that they believe it to be their own desires and choices.

Tempting as this line is, it is difficult to hold. First, it assumes that actors have preferences that are, albeit inauthentic, nonetheless coherent and stable; this resembles the image of the *Homo oeconomicus* – an atomistic, calculative, rational actor, just with an inverse mathematical sign. A considerable amount of organization theory research that has its roots in Simon's (1955) notion of 'bounded rationality' has criticized the idea of stable preferences that guide rational actors' decision-making processes. Second, the assumption that actors have interests that they do not know but that some other can and does know assumes that someone – the theoretician or the strategist – has some insight into what the 'real' interests of the person are. Conceptually, the latter condition reveals the roots of this perspective in the worldview of Marxism, especially the Leninist variant (inherited and inherent in, one may want to add, some strands of critical management studies), in which stipulative definition of the real interest of whole biopolitical categories of 'workers', 'peasants', 'kulaks', intellectuals', etc. could be assumed. To tell the other what his/her real interests are against his/her preferences, however they are shaped or however mistaken one thinks them to be, is a profoundly undemocratic act; it assumes that the other does not know his/her own mind and that one does.

Analytically, this leaves power researchers in a difficult position: when the people they study claim that they do what they do because of their choice, the theory diagnoses this as a sure sign of strong power being exercised. Hence, the researcher has to dismiss what informants tell him/her and bracket what they say as false consciousness or something along those lines. Indeed, a great deal of critical research on fields such as strategy entails implicit conspiracy logic, in which subjects of strategy misrecognize their interests because they have been systematically duped into being sold something that they do not really need. By contrast, the ways that subjects constitute their interests are fluid, viscous and liquid. What we can say is that strategy is oriented towards constituting, framing, shaping, channelling and changing subjects' preferences, and to the extent that it is able to do so then it necessarily affects interests. Perhaps the easiest way to think of this is in terms of political strategy: selling state-owned housing to the people who rent them creates consumers whose life interest in shelter is now tied to the fate of those institutions that lend them mortgages, those employers who pay them wages to service the mortgage, and those members of their families who depend on these mortgages and that employment for their shelter. Given the different framing of their interests now as members of a property-owning democracy rather than renters dependent on a state bureaucracy, there is a reasonable probability that the preferences they exhibit at the ballot box might reflect this new order of interests; Conservative politicians such as Margaret Thatcher clearly thought so. Interests are fixed neither by structural relations in the broader society, however, nor by abstract theoretical determination. They are a result of countless interpellations, of signifiers that float hither and thither, of competing fragments of narrative through which to grasp a life, its chances, choices and consequences as memory collects, recollects and projects its unfolding.

Strategizing: the verb

At the core of the strategy-as-practice perspective is the premise that strategy analysis has to take social practices 'seriously' (Vaara and Whittington 2012). It assumes that strategy work 'relies on organizational and other practices that significantly affect both the process and the outcome of resulting strategies' (Vaara and Whittington 2012: 286). It is opposed to an approach in which individuals or groups are sources and targets of strategic decision-making determined by stable interests, and hence the unit of analysis. Thus, it shifts the focus away from the earlier dimensional approaches that lace through power analysis from Marcuse (1964) to Lukes (1974).

As the above review of the SAP literature and power has demonstrated, strategy and power should be analysed through discourse: strategy offers techniques of speaking, of thinking and of seeing the world in specific ways, constituting certain phenomena as objects and subjects of strategy and vesting them with various powers as an effect of strategy discourse. Strategy discourse not only fashions the subjects through which it speaks, it also configures objects so that they become a target for strategic interventions. As Knights and Morgan put it, '[S]trategy is actively involved in the constitution, or re-definition, of problems in advance of offering itself as a solution to them' (Knights and Morgan, 1991: 270). In this and other Foucault-inspired critical readings of strategy, it is the talk and practice of strategy that becomes equipped with agency (see Ezzamel and Willmott 2008; McCabe 2010; Laine and Vaara 2007; Thomas, Sargent and Hardy 2011). Strategy is not so much a tool of those in power as it is a form of framing of talk and texts that does something both to those in power and those being governed.

As a linguistic genre (see Pälli, Vaara and Sorsa 2009), strategy is powerful because it has become taken for granted as a way of framing the world in which we live. It is not just discourse that makes strategy a powerful force; inextricably intertwined with it are practices, routines and rituals that perform strategy. In a study of strategy-making in the city of Sydney, we have attempted to illustrate how the seemingly mundane practices of strategizing constitute the space, time, objects and subjects of strategy (Kornberger and Clegg 2011). For instance, through the minute organization of interaction with external stakeholders, the strategists attempted to 'lift stakeholders' thinking', which resulted in a discourse that was depoliticized and recast as focused on the 'big picture' – a literal projection of the future that bracketed the interests and concerns expressed in the here and now. In addition to a focus on discourse and practices, an innovative strand of technology-oriented research analyses the power effects of strategy processes. In a study on the epistemic culture of strategy-making, Kaplan (2011) analyses how a particular technology – in her case, PowerPoint – formatted people's thoughts about strategic issues. PowerPoint, Kaplan argues, affords collaboration between individuals through providing space for discussions and integration of ideas, while simultaneously acting as cartographic practice that frames ideas, creating technologically bounded rationalities. In turn, these 'collaborative and cartographic practices shaped the strategic choices and actions' in the case study organization she researched (Kaplan 2011: 320). PowerPoint, with its logical sequencing, its stepwise progression and its formats for expressing ideas, imposes a tacit linearity and causally one-directional rationality on the most sophisticated and the most mundane expression. Indeed, once ideas have been formatted in PowerPoint it is almost impossible to distinguish the mundane from the sublime, because the provenance and complexity of ideas effectively disappears; everything is made mundane.

PowerPoint frames the relation between cognition, on the one hand, and power, on the other (Kaplan 2008). Frames are schemes of interpretation (Goffman 1974) that, in the context of strategizing, legitimize certain perspectives, highlight particular threats, stress certain internal resources and allow for discursively creating cause/effect relationships (Kaplan 2008; Benford and Snow 2000). Framing is the strategic practice that relates the exercise of power to the work of imagination: that which is a strategically relevant idea will have to pass through the frame, which conditions categories of relevance and significance. The exercise of power is intrinsically related to knowledge, and the creation of knowledge relies on power (to fix, to categorize, to keep stable, etc.) in order to be able to flow (Foucault 1982).

Another way of thinking about power/knowledge relations is to say that power must fix appropriate standing conditions for knowledge to be apparent; think of the massive infrastructure of CERN, the European Organization for Nuclear Research, in Switzerland, and the billions of euros spent in creating the standing conditions in which the Higgs boson elementary particle, initially theorized in 1964, had its discovery announced at CERN in July 2012. New knowledge confirming the existence of a particle that had, to that point, existed only propositionally now entered the socially constructed world of science and everyday knowledge; but it was able to do so only because of the power assembled as CERN, funded and organized through the auspices of twenty European Union member states, which had created the Large Hadron Collider. Such knowledge demands dedicated strategy and considerable deployment of power to be possible. Strategy works through practices and technologies, even those as rare, exotic – indeed, unique – as the Large Hadron Collider. Power was in play, working through the practices, technologies and discourses that flowed in and through the collider, its scientific community, the funding bodies, administrators, managers and media advisers that clustered around it. Discourses are always in play; they will invariably be politically contested; they will play an important legitimizing role; they do not have explanatory monopoly; they require assemblage with many other forms of practice – with people, capabilities, technologies and things.

This brings us to some of the concerns that a practice-based power analysis of strategizing poses (for a more detailed critique, see Carter, Clegg and Kornberger 2008a). First, strategy is equipped with agency, but it remains unclear how this agency exercises power. For instance, Vaara, Sorsa and Pälli (2010: 691) claim: '[T]he strategy document became a textual agent, an actor that had the capacity to produce action form a distance.' Although this is a nice analytical point, the empirical narrative of Vaara, Sorsa and Pälli's study seems to indicate a more traditional picture: the actors in the quotes they provide are politicians, city board members, and members of the city administration. Much SAP research still assumes the manager in the cockpit; in fact, this might be part of strategy as practice's heritage, in which a 'closeness' to practice and managers has been enshrined (see Whittington 1996).

A second point addresses the realpolitik of strategy as practice's mutual constitution of strategizing and subjectivity. In most practice accounts, strategy discourse and a myriad of strategy practices construct 'prospective narratives that both constrain and enable actors in their future activity but that never completely determine it' (Fenton and Langley 2011: 16). In other words, there is a recursive relation between strategy and actors. The stronger version of strategy as practice – the one that takes practices (perhaps too) seriously – needs to explain how strategy achieves at least some level of consistency and direction. The 'institutional logic' of Vaara, Sorsa and Pälli's text is not an actor's categorical device; it is very much an imposition of an academically strategic discourse onto the categories that the members typically deploy. In some respects it says more about the analytical strategy of the researchers than it does about that of those being analysed. Ascribed 'institutional logics' such as new public management, post-bureaucratic practices and, more generally, neoliberal ideologies provide the (assumed) pattern that allows the 'strategic id' to behave as if it had its own teleology. Such an 'as if' assumption is important, for if strategy did not represent something seeking to be consistent and directional it would hardly be possible to analyse it. As a result, most work that analyses the verb 'strategizing' as power has lingering above or underneath it a rather large noun – some kind of third-dimensional power, be it domination, performance, managerialism or something else.

Making things strategic: strategy as an adjective

Through the lens of strategy as practice, the world of headquarters, strategy meetings and retreats produces a picture of shifting alliances in which a complex web of practices, discourses and technologies lead to intended and unintended consequences that can only momentarily be disciplined

through the relentless labour of strategizing. Practice approaches shift power analysis through focusing on the doing of strategy: practices assume a life on their own; strategy affords certain futures through its technologies. The suspicion is that practices perform futures, sometimes in line with, sometimes against, those who deploy them in the name of what is still assumed to be their interests.

An alternative analytical approach to grasping the relation between power and strategy would be to study neither those doing strategy nor the practices they enact (or which enact them) but to look more closely at how things *become* strategic in the first place. This assumes that strategy is not a thing (with strategy as practice) and that strategy is not a practice (against strategy as practice) consisting of rituals and routines exercised by strategists. Rather, strategy is most powerful when seen as an adjective – as something that exercises power through its ability to attach itself to people, objects, ideas and events.

Take the example of the global financial crisis – not the recent one, but the one from 1928/9 described by Galbraith (1975 [1954]) so magisterially. He analyses the role of a minute little object and its massive impact on the emergence of the crisis: the stock market ticker. The ticker was an object that should merely represent movements and prices at the exchange; like a thermostat, it was designed to take the temperature of the market. What in fact the ticker did, however, was to cause the acceleration of the crisis. When stock prices spiralled downwards in October 1929 an unprecedented amount of people decided to sell. Usually the ticker would tell them the going price; because of the firestorm sales, though, the ticker increasingly lagged behind the declining values, encouraging a further stampede of selling on the back of fear. Because the ticker dropped behind actual prices, it triggered people's worst scenarios; the machine designed to report reality had turned into a mechanism that created a frightful doomsday picture, which, in the manner of a self-fulfilling prophecy, became true because people believed it to be so (Galbraith 1975 [1954]; see also Preda 2006). The point is simple: what had been thought to act as a device, representing only the present reality, turned out to produce another reality (Mackenzie 2006).

In this sense, the device had become a *strategic* actor in, and cause of, the crisis. Note that the ticker did not figure prominently in any rational strategist's interest-guided analysis (if at all, perhaps only as source of information); it was also not part of strategy practices; but it did exercise devastating power, which doubtlessly qualifies it as something that deserves the label 'strategic'. If we take such emergent strategic (perhaps even non-human) actors seriously, we have to ask not only what their power is but also how they become powerful. What powers attach themselves to objects (ideas, people, technologies, events) so that they have significant strategic effects, and how do they do it?

Mechanism for making things strategic: an attachment theory of strategic power

Fortunately, there is a growing body of literature that studies assemblages of human and non-human actors, how they organize and are organized across networks and how they exercise strategic power effects. The literature is usually summarized under the acronym ANT, for actor–network theory (Law and Hassard 1999; Latour 2005), including related fields such that the study of science and technology (originally focused on laboratories from which ANT eventually escaped), the social studies of finance and various strands of the 'new' new economic sociology and anthropology of markets literature (for an overview, see McFall and Ossandón 2014).

Callon and Law (1997) articulated their concern with strategy early on, arguing that it is this combination of artefacts, technologies, social organization and people that creates the possibility of strategic action. To attribute strategic action to one person – such as a captain on a ship – is possible (in the case of an accident, for instance) but misleading, '[b]ecause the capacity for strategy is an affect of a more or less stable arrangement of materials' (Callon and Law 1997: 7). Strategic action is always a 'collective property': 'All action is collective since it is distributed; what varies are the mechanisms for attributing the source of action' (Çalışkan and Callon 2010: 10).

ANT's network approach to strategizing has started to be used more widely in strategy as practice and related fields. For instance, in Kaplan's already quoted study (2011), explicit reference is made to ANT and science and technology studies (STS), arguing that PowerPoint as a technology should be analysed as exercising a significant influence on the strategy process, if not as having agency. Whittle and Mueller (2010) explore the construction and legitimization of strategic ideas in their ethnographic study of the role of management accounting systems. Both studies (Whittle and Mueller 2010; Kaplan 2011) focus on the constitutive role of technology in strategizing; the authors argue that technology and, perhaps more generally, artefacts and their materiality have a significant impact on the supposedly Cartesian mind of the strategist. In reality, senior managers do not practise strategy. Rather, strategy has to be understood as collective action, as a corollary of network action. Power resides not in people, nor in practices (alone), but in networks' ability to *make things strategic*. What holds these networks together is not just people but also technology, artefacts and a myriad of other devices (Callon, Millo and Muniesa 2007).

We can develop this idea further by following a little frog. Building on ANT, Tryggestad, Justesen and Mouritsen (2013) tell the story of how frogs were translated from being 'non-existent' into strategic actors in a construction project. They studied a developer who had acquired land and planned to build residential dwellings on it. Since time is of the essence in development projects, the firm was ready to start planning and constructing as soon as the ink on the purchasing agreement dried. Waterholes were then discovered on the site, however, and soon its residents – 500 protected moor frogs – were identified. The project came to a halt. The frogs – hitherto leading blameless and anonymous semi-aquatic lives, in obscurity other than for a few amphibian specialists – became a contested object, with several spokespersons claiming to know what was in the frogs' best interests and to speak for them. Such was the articulation of the frogs' interests that the development firm hired their own frog experts as consultants, who worked on determining means whereby the frogs could coexist with the construction workers and trucks, and all the noise and habitat destruction that these would create. That meant learning to adapt to the cyclical time of the frogs' lives (as opposed to the linear time of project manager's charts) and constructing frog protection devices, such as corridors through which they could move without being bulldozed. The story has a happy ending, when the frogs themselves became strategic protagonists in the marketing campaign to sell the finished buildings; who would not want to live in a natural idyll with protected moor frogs? Our point: the frog had become a strategic actor, in that it shaped the future significantly. It was neither practices nor interests that explain the process, however. How can we explain the process through which frogs became strategic and powerful? What are the mechanisms that make things strategic?

Visualization

First, strategic power needs to attach itself to something as jumpy as a frog, as mechanical as a ticker or as massive as the Large Hadron Collider; there needs to be a materiality through which power flows for it to become strategic. Each of these things became and functioned as obligatory passage points through which meaning, power and knowledge flowed and were condensed (Clegg 1989). As obligatory passage points, their materiality becomes an object of strategic contestation. We can see this clearly with the moor frogs, by returning to Tryggestad, Justesen and Mouritsen (2013). Far from being just a frog, the little creature became the contested object of strategic power. Quite small-scale and local questions came into play. Did the waterholes represent a natural habitat or were they just large puddles that could be bulldozed? Were the frogs a rare species or just one of the many animals that had to give way as the construction work commenced? Once it was accepted that they could – and did – bring the construction machinery to a halt, who could speak on behalf of them and suggest a safe cohabitation strategy for them? An epistemic machine sprang into action, based on environmental sciences and equipped with measuring tools, to track the life course of the frogs and ensure they would survive. The frog underwent a series of translations, from being just an animal to becoming a protected species, gaining significance as a valuable part of the ecosystem, until finally ending up on the cover of the sales brochure for the newly built housing, thus making the frog an active marketing agent. In short, the frogs became objects of visualization strategies that rendered them tangible and hence manageable. The strategic power that the frog exercised was conditioned by the many attempts to turn it into an epistemic object that could be counted and counted on. It is these techniques of visualization, these technologies of accounting, through which the frog took on strategic significance.

Tryggestad, Justesen and Mouritsen's frogs are but one example of how something becomes strategic; there are a plethora of other examples that illustrate the importance of materialization and visualization for making things strategic. Think of rankings and their strategic importance. Espeland and Sauder (2007) argue that rankings are devices that do not simply describe their objects but actively shape them through their representations. Rankings make commensurable what was idiosyncratic beforehand, and, through this operation, they create categories and relations between entities that were previously unrelated. Kornberger and Carter (2010) studied city rankings, and speculate that they provide the a priori condition for competition between cities to take place; how else could cities understand competition if they were not quite literally arranged on a (league) table next to each other, reduced to a few characteristics that make them similar? The point is that such rankings are visualizations of relations, and without such visualizations the rankings would not exercise strategic power. Rankings order and hierarchize; they distribute a heterogeneous population into bands (the top ten, the top forty-five journals, etc.); and they summarize their results in simple, seductive formats that can easily be reproduced by newspapers, enacted in meetings and enrolled in strategies. In other words, it is through visualization techniques that rankings can travel, spread globally and exercise their power locally. Their aesthetics is the precondition for their contagious effects. Indeed, as Pollock and D'Adderio (2012) argue, rankings and other valuation mechanisms have to be analysed as aesthetic devices that exercise their power because they model, illustrate, draw, rank and map their objects. Hats for restaurants, letters for credit ratings, stars for Amazon sellers' reliability; all these strategic powers are exercised through strong, if simplifying, visualization.

Analytically, an attachment theory of strategic power will study these visualizations and materializations not as an afterthought but as integral elements of power. In doing so, it will address traditional strategy's myopia in terms of focusing on the mind and its models as disembodied, abstract cognition.

Valuation

Second, there needs to be an account, some form of rationalizing mechanism, that makes valuable that which has been made visible. The frog has to be 'rare', the ticker has to be a 'sign' of something, the ranking has to be legitimate to become a strategic force, the Higgs boson particle has to be known in theory before it can exist in practice. What is made visible has to be 'figured out' (Miller 2008): it has taken on a *Gestalt* that communicates its inner logic, meaning and value. Such 'figuring out' is contingent on references to a variety of 'gods' (Friedland 2009) – such as efficiency, truth, nature, democracy. Ironically, against the protestations of the CERN scientists, the Higgs boson particle became known as the 'God particle', because of the imagination of Lederman (1993). In both valuation and visualization terms Lederman was doing the scientists a favour that they did not appreciate. The term 'God particle' is much more iconic than 'Higgs boson'; even if one knows not what that means, at least everyone has some idea about who God might be. The moor frogs became valuable when they jumped onto the list of protected species; God particles make the complexity of theoretical physics' experiments tangible to a lay public; rankings are powerful because they claim to bring competition and market efficiency to domains in which prices are not adequate indicators of value.

Let us use example of rankings to explore how things are being made valuable in detail. First and foremost, rankings are forms of (e)valuation that result from calculative practices (Miller 2001; see also Lamont 2012). Indicators are defined,

measures taken and numbers added up to assign precise locations on league tables, indicating the relative position of the ranked object, its status and its worth. Hence, value is nothing pre-existing but something that is ushered into being through the act of valuation. This analysis follows Dewey (1939; see also Muniesa 2011), who speaks of a 'flank movement' with which he moved from the question of value to a processual view of studying valuation as an 'activity of ranking, an act that involves comparison' (Dewey 1939: 5). To assume value to be an essential characteristic of a thing would equate to 'calling the ball struck in baseball, a hit or a foul' (Dewey, quoted by Muniesa 2011: 25); of course, it is not the ball that is valuable, but the apparatus around it that makes it mean something. Players, judges and coaches, audience, media, sponsors and a myriad of other network actors, as well as material and symbolic elements such as the lines drawn on the playing field, conventions and rules, league tables to track performances, tournaments to establish winners, etc. – all these elements conspire when the ball touches the ground and give that serendipitous moment meaning beyond its occurrence. The 'flank movement' shifts attention from the ball to the network of elements and the evaluative infrastructure that make it valuable.[1]

The study of strategic power implies dissecting how valuation as a process constitutes the value of objects in the first place. It means deconstructing calculative practices and evaluative infrastructures with the aim of showing how they construct value through their operations. In the final analysis, it means asking how legitimization takes place: which ranking can claim to tell the truth about university education, and legitimize those who act upon it? Why are moor frogs more valuable than other species that may disappear as a consequence of construction work, and how and why can some speak (and who will these be?) on behalf of the frogs? In so doing, the focus on valuation corrects a second myopia of traditional strategy research: it folds the social into the economical and the macro into the micro by making 'the distance between

---

[1] This paragraph is a direct reference to Kornberger *et al.* (2015).

value and its measure collapse in an analytically constructive manner' (Muniesa 2011: 24).

Mobilization

In order to become strategic, things need to enter circuits of power (Clegg 1989). Such circuits can be described as networks through which initially non-significant elements become strategic powers. Networks are the medium in which the strategic power of things is configured. Think of commercial strategic battles (such as the fight by German car manufacturers against an EU-wide regulation of carbon emission standards for cars) that flow through networks of media in order to shape public opinion. Or take social movements that exercise their power through communication networks that are faster and more robust and reach more widely than those of their corporate targets (Weber, Rao and Thomas 2009).

Strategic network power can be analysed on two levels: the material-technological level (Galloway and Thacker 2007) and the sociopolitical level (Castells 2009). First, let us look at the relation of material technology and power. Inspired by Deleuze's short essay on the control society (1992), Galloway and Thacker (Galloway and Thacker 2007; Galloway 2012) remind us that networks are not liberating per se; rather, they 'exercise novel forms of control that operate at a level that is anonymous and non-human, which is to say material' (Galloway and Thacker 2007: 5). They do so through 'protocols', Galloway and Thacker suggest; the notion of the protocol applies to analysis of the power effects of networks, in which 'power relations are in the process of being transformed in a way that is resonant with the flexibility and constraints of information technology' (Thacker 2004: xix). Protocols refer to power structures that are embedded in technology; protocol is the apparatus that facilitates the functioning of networks and provides the 'logic that governs how things are done within that apparatus' (Galloway and Thacker 2007: 29). Protocol manages flows within networks; it regulates access and manages relationships between distributed network elements. 'Protocols,' Galloway and Thacker (2004: 8) write, 'are all the conventional rules and standards that govern relationships within networks.'

A protocol is purely process-based: it does not contain any 'substance' on its own; it exists only to make things happen. Therein lies its particular power, which derives from its technological function: it is based on code, which in turn is a form of text that exists merely to be executed. In contrast to the law or other codes that exercise power, protocol cannot be spoken, nor does it allow for interpretation; protocol is concerned only with performing its operations.

Analysing strategic power includes an analysis of material network control because it is through protocol and its codes that events and ideas are formatted and edited. As Neff and Stark (2004: 186) remark pointedly, if 'architecture is politics set in stone, then information architecture is politics in code'. Protocol is the architecture that defines the conditions for something to be able to travel through networks, and hence to potentially mobilize others. In this sense, interface design in social networks and sharing functions on websites are of strategic importance: Facebook's 'like' button can make or break a cause, and a hashtag on Twitter can provoke considerable controversy (also known as 'shitstroms'). Analytically, it is important to keep in mind that dissemination strategies represent mobilization potential; they are forms of governance designed to create strategic objects.

Inextricably linked to the material-technological power of networks is their sociopolitical dimension, analysed by Castells (2009). He argues that the self is a network composition connected to a world of networks; familiar metaphors constitute our sensemaking, constructing socially available narrative frames. Communication between people then occurs through communication networks, which range from face-to-face communication, as the most immediate, to those that are laced globally as multiple, overlapping, open and sociospatially interactive systems comprising interconnected nodes. It is the nodes of the networks that configure power relations, which operate as obligatory passage points. Power relations therefore have a structural architecture, expressed in terms of spatial and temporal orderings, focused on the creation of value conceived in terms of various rationalities that are also an expression of power. In recent times, however, with the rise of digital technologies, the most important communication channels have become digital mass self-communication networks, operating through social-networking channels. These channels are increasingly plural in their messages, customers and products but increasingly concentrated in their ownership. These and other communication networks exercise power, as they represent the obligatory point of passage through which an idea must pass in order to mobilize collective action and hence become strategic.

The focus on networks corrects a third myopia of traditional strategy research: it moves the analytical focus from the strategist as author and actor towards an analysis of the possibility of collective action, distributed cognition and mobilization in networks.

Concluding reflection

An attachment theory of strategic power focuses on three key moments that guide its analysis: visualization, valuation and mobilization. It studies the material conditions for things to become strategic, the processes through which values are attributed to them and the networks through which they travel and mobilize others. It is a theory of events, objects and things becoming strategic. It extends strategy-as-practice research in important ways, by bringing in collectives of humans and non-humans as strategic actors and extending the locus of strategizing from the organizational practices to networks, devices and technologies. Were an attachment theory of strategic power to have a location proper it would have to be in the fluidity of networks. Most importantly, the attachment theory of strategic power contributes towards understanding how collective action (on organization, movement, field and societal level) emerges; as Becker writes in a wonderful paper on collective action in the art world (1974), conventions work as the art worlds' organizing principle. Importantly, conventions have to be understood against current institutional theory: not as norms but in the etymological sense of 'con-venere' (like a convener of a meeting, event or conference), as bringing materials and ideas, spaces and times, people and events together as an assemblage that coheres. An attachment theory of strategy would dissect these conventions and analyse how its heterogeneous elements are visualized, valued and equipped to travel the world, unfolding their powers.

The analytical challenge of this approach is evident: if strategy as practice was in danger of losing its object (what is *not* a strategic practice, anyway?), then this danger becomes the modus vivendi of an attachment theory of strategy. Frogs, tickers, rankings, the 'like' button – everything can become a strategic power. If it is assumed that 'strategic' is but a floating signifier, then the task of the analyst will be to understand under which precise conditions this signifier becomes attached to an historical idea, event, object, even a person or a group, making it powerful.

For the future the research agenda is pregnant with possibilities, as strategy in practice is further explored in terms of adjectival, noun and verb contingencies. From the ethnomethodological accounts of Samra-Fredericks, inspiration may be drawn for careful analysis of how organization members make sense of and do strategy in everyday talk; from research such as McCabe's there are possibilities for textual analysis of formal documents; Laine and Vaara demonstrate the uses to which interview data taken not as interpretive insights but as a depiction of languages in use can be put; from studies such as those of Thomas, Sargent and Hardy the real-time analysis of strategy workshops can be developed further; and from analysis such as that of Ezzamel and Willmott there are many affordances with what we have termed an attachment approach in which the devices used to secure specific effects can be analysed in their particulars.

Our analysis suggests the importance of studying processes of visualization, valuation and mobilization in order to understand how things become strategic. In concluding, we argue that strategy-as-practice research should engage with the panoply of methods, approaches and complementary theoretical positions available, so as to advance empirical knowledge of strategy's power in action – as verb, noun and adjective. No one of them is the right, 'royal' road to understanding; just as strategy is multifaceted, so should be its interpretations.

References

Bachrach, P., and Baratz, M. S. (1962), 'Two faces of power', *American Political Science Review*, 56/4: 947–52.

Becker, H. S. (1974), 'Art as collective action', *American Sociological Review*, 39/6: 767–76.

Benford, R. D., and Snow, D. A. (2000), 'Framing processes and social movements: an overview and assessment', *Annual Review of Sociology*, 26: 611–39.

Bourdieu, P. (1977), *Outline of a Theory of Practice*. Cambridge University Press.

Çalışkan, K., and Callon, M. (2010), 'Economization, part 2: a research programme for the study of markets', *Economy and Society*, 39/1: 1–32.

Callon, M., and Law, J. (1997), 'After the individual in society: lessons in collectivity from science, technology and society', *Canadian Journal of Sociology*, 22/2: 165–82.

Callon, M., Millo, Y., and Muniesa, F. (2007), *Market Devices*. Malden, MA: Blackwell.

Carter, C., Clegg, S., and Kornberger, M. (2008a), 'Strategy as practice', *Strategic Organization*, 6/1: 83–99.

—— (2008b), *A Very Short, Fairly Interesting and Reasonably Cheap Book about Studying Strategy*. London: Sage.

Castells, M. (2009), *Communication Power*. Oxford University Press.

Child, J. (1972), 'Organizational structure, environment and performance: the role of strategic choice', *Sociology*, 6/1: 1–22

Clegg, S. (1989), *Frameworks of Power*. London: Sage.

Courpasson, D., Dany, F., and Clegg, S. (2012), 'Resisters at work: generating productive resistance in the workplace', *Organization Science*, 23/3: 801–19.

Deleuze, G. (1992), 'Postscript on the societies of control', *October*, 59/Winter: 3–7.

Dewey, J. (1939), *A Theory of Valuation*. University of Chicago Press.

Eriksson, P., and Lehtimäki, H. (2001), 'Strategy rhetoric in city management: how the presumptions of classic strategic management live on?', *Scandinavian Journal of Management*, 17/2: 201–23.

Espeland, W. N., and Sauder, M. (2007), 'Rankings and reactivity: how public measures recreate social worlds 1', *American Journal of Sociology*, 113/1: 1–40.

Ezzamel, M., and Willmott, H. (2004), 'Rethinking strategy: contemporary perspectives and debates', *European Management Review*, 1/1: 43–8.

Ezzamel, M., and Willmott, H.(2008), 'Strategy as discourse in a global retailer: a supplement to rationalist and interpretive accounts', *Organization Studies*, 29/2: 191–217.

Fenton, C., and Langley, A. (2011), 'Strategy as practice and the narrative turn', *Organization Studies*, 32/9: 1171–96.

Flyvbjerg, B. (1998), *Rationality and Power: Democracy in Practice*. University of Chicago Press.

Foucault, M. (1982), 'The subject and power', in Dreyfus, H. L., and Rabinow, P. (eds.), *Michel Foucault: Beyond Structuralism and Hermeneutics*: 208–26. University of Chicago Press.

Freedman, L. (2013), *Strategy: A History*. Oxford University Press.

Friedland, R. (2009), 'Institution, practice, and ontology: toward a religious sociology', *Research in the Sociology of Organizations*, 27/1: 45–83.

Galbraith, J. K. (1975 [1954]), *The Great Crash 1929*. London: Penguin Books.

Galloway, A. R. (2012), *The Interface Effect*. Cambridge: Polity.

Galloway, A. R., and Thacker, E. (2004), 'Protocol, control, and networks', *Grey Room*, 17: 6–29.

—— (2007), *The Exploit: A Theory of Networks*. Minneapolis: University of Minnesota Press.

Goffman, E. (1974), *Frame Analysis: An Essay on the Organization of Experience*. Cambridge, MA: Harvard University Press.

Hardy, C., and Thomas, R. (2014), 'Strategy, discourse and practice: the intensification of power', *Journal of Management Studies*, 51/2: 320–48.

Hendry, J. (2000), 'Strategic decision-making, discourse, and strategy as social practice', *Journal of Management Studies*, 37/7: 955–77.

Kaplan, S. (2008), 'Framing contests: strategy making under uncertainty', *Organization Science*, 19/5: 729–52.

—— (2011), 'Strategy and PowerPoint: an inquiry into the epistemic culture and machinery of strategy making', *Organization Science*, 22/2: 320–46.

Knights, D., and Morgan, G. (1991), 'Corporate strategy, organizations, and subjectivity: a critique', *Organization Studies*, 12/2: 251–73.

Kornberger, M. (2012), 'Governing the city: from planning to urban strategy', *Theory, Culture and Society*, 29/2: 84–106.

Kornberger, M., and Carter, C. (2010), 'Manufacturing competition: how accounting practices shape strategy making in cities', *Accounting, Auditing and Accountability Journal*, 23/3: 325–49.

Kornberger, M., and Clegg, S. (2011), 'Strategy as performative practice: the case of Sydney 2030', *Strategic Organization*, 9/2: 136–62.

Kornberger, M., Justesen, L., Koed Madsen, A., and Mouritsen, J. (eds.) (2015), *Making Things Valuable*. Oxford University Press.

Laine, P.-M., and Vaara, E. (2007), 'Struggling over subjectivity: a discursive analysis of strategic development in an engineering group', *Human Relations*, 60/1: 29–58.

Lamont, M. (2012), 'Toward a comparative sociology of valuation and evaluation', *Sociology*, 38/1: 201–21.

Latour, B. (2005), *Reassembling the Social: An Introduction to Actor–Network-Theory*. Oxford University Press.

Law, J., and Hassard, J. (eds.) (1999), *Actor Network Theory and After*. Oxford: Blackwell.

Lederman, L. (1993), *The God Particle: If the Universe Is the Answer, What Is the Question?* New York: Delta.

Lilley, S. (2001), 'The language of strategy', in Westwood, R., and Linstead, S. (eds.), *The Language of Organization*: 66–89. London: Sage.

Lukes, S. (1974), *Power: A Radical View*. London: Macmillan

Machiavelli, N. (1995 [1513]), *The Prince*, ed. Milner, S. J. London: Everyman.

MacKenzie, D. (2006), *An Engine, Not a Camera: How Financial Models Shape the Markets*. Cambridge, MA: MIT Press.

Marcuse, H. (1964), *One-Dimensional Man: Studies in the Ideology of Advanced Industrial Society*. London: Routledge.

McCabe, D. (2010), 'Strategy-as-power: ambiguity, contradiction and the exercise of power in a UK building society', *Organization*, 17/2: 151–75.

McFall, L., and Ossandón, J. (2014), 'What's new in the *"new*, new economic sociology" and should organization studies care?', in Adler, P., du Gay, P., Morgan, G., and Reed, M. (eds.), *Oxford Handbook of Sociology, Social Theory, and Organization Studies: Contemporary Currents*: 510–33. Oxford University Press.

Miller, P. (2001), 'Governing by numbers: why calculative practices matter', *Social Research*, 68/2: 379–96.

(2008), 'Figuring out organizations', paper presented at Nobel symposium 'Foundations of organizations', Saltsjöbaden, Sweden, 28 August.

Mumby, D. K. (1987), 'The political function of narrative in organizations', *Communication Monographs*, 54/2: 113–27.

Muniesa, F. (2011), 'A flank movement in the understanding of valuation', *Sociological Review*, 59/S2: 24–38.

Neff, G., and Stark, D. (2004), 'Permanently beta', in Howard, P. N., and Jones, S. (eds.), *Society Online: The Internet in Context*, 173–88. Thousand Oaks, CA: Sage.

Oakes, L. S., Townley, B., and Cooper, D. J. (1998), 'Business planning as pedagogy: language and control in a changing institutional field', *Administrative Science Quarterly*, 43/2: 257–92.

Packard, V. O. (1957), *The Hidden Persuaders*. New York: D. McKay.

Pälli, P., Vaara, E., and Sorsa, V (2009), 'Strategy as text and discursive practice: a genre-based approach to strategizing in city administration', *Discourse and Communication*, 3/3: 303–18.

Pettigrew, A. M. (1973), *The Politics of Organizational Decision-Making*. London: Tavistock.

(1985), *The Awakening Giant: Continuity and Change in Imperial Chemical Industries*. Oxford: Blackwell.

Phillips, N., Sewell, G., and Jaynes, S. (2008), 'Applying critical discourse analysis in strategic management research', *Organizational Research Methods*, 11/4: 770–89.

Pollock, N., and D'Adderio, L. (2012), 'Give me a two-by-two matrix and I will create the market: rankings, graphic visualisations and sociomateriality', *Accounting, Organizations and Society*, 37/8: 565–84.

Preda, A. (2006), 'Socio-technical agency in financial markets', *Social Studies of Science*, 36/5: 753–82.

Samra-Fredericks, D. (2005), 'Strategic practice, "discourse" and the everyday interactional constitution of "power effects"', *Organization*, 12/6: 803–41.

Simon, H. A. (1955), 'A behavioral model of rational choice', *Quarterly Journal of Economics*, 69/1: 99–118.

Thacker, E. (2004), 'Foreword: protocol is as protocol does', in Galloway, A. R. (ed.), *Protocol: How Control Exists after Decentralization*: xxiii–xxii. Cambridge, MA: MIT Press.

Thomas, R., Sargent, L., and Hardy, C. (2011), 'Managing organizational change: negotiating meaning and power–resistance relations', *Organization Science*, 22/1: 22–41.

Tryggestad, K., Justesen, L., and Mouritsen, J. (2013), 'Project temporalities: how frogs can become stakeholders', *International Journal of Managing Projects in Business*, 6/1: 69–87.

Vaara, E., Sorsa, V., and Pälli, P. (2010), 'On the force potential of strategy texts: a critical discourse analysis of a strategic plan and its power effects in a city organization', *Organization*, 17/6: 685–702.

Vaara, E., and Whittington, R. (2012), 'Strategy-as-practice: taking social practices seriously', *Academy of Management Annals*, 6/1: 285–336.

Weber, K., Rao, H., and Thomas, L. G. (2009), 'From streets to suites: how the anti-biotech movement affected German pharmaceutical firms', *American Sociological Review*, 74/1: 106–27.

Whittington, R. (1996), 'Strategy as practice', *Long Range Planning*, 29/5: 731–5.

Whittle, A., and Mueller, F. (2010), 'Strategy, enrolment and accounting: the politics of strategic ideas', *Accounting, Auditing and Accountability Journal*, 23/5: 626–46.

Whyte, W. H. (2013), *The Organization Man*. Philadelphia: University of Pennsylvania Press.

A critical perspective on strategy as practice

MARTIN BLOM and MATS ALVESSON

Introduction

During the last two decades the strategy-as-practice perspective has emerged, from what is often claimed to be a growing discontent with much of current, mainstream strategy research. In particular, the fact that human actors and their actions in strategy research have been lost to sight has been acknowledged (Jarzabkowski, Balogun and Seidl 2007; Jarzabkowski and Spee 2009). Sometimes the perspective is said to contribute with a 'sociological eye' (Whittington 2007) on strategy and strategists, as opposed (or, at least, as a complement) to mainstream, mainly North-American-inspired strategic management research, with its reductionist, economics-based assumptions about firms and industries. The ambition is to move away from the abstract statistical analysis of performance effects and instead, in the tradition of process-oriented strategy scholars such as Mintzberg (1973) and Pettigrew (1973), open up the 'black box' of strategy work (Golsorkhi et al. 2010). Foundational works, such as those by Balogun and Johnson (2004), Hendry (2000), Jarzabkowski (2003; 2004; 2005), Johnson, Melin and Whittington (2003) and Whittington (1996; 2004), have ignited (but also framed) an impressive research activity during the last ten years. Strong research groups focusing on strategy as practice have emerged during this period, especially in the United Kingdom, Canada and Finland; an SAP online community (the Strategy as Practice International Network) has been established; and numerous papers have been presented at major conferences (many of which have been published later in prestigious journals). In other words, much has been achieved; as always, though, it is important to be (self-)critical and reflect upon a growing, popular and seemingly successful body of

knowledge (Alvesson and Deetz 2000) such as strategy as practice.

The purpose of this chapter is twofold: (1) to review and comment on strategy as practice from a critical perspective; and (2) to suggest how a critical perspective – and, in particular, critical management studies (CMS) – can be leveraged in a future research agenda. The structure of the chapter will follow this logic. After this short introduction, we continue by illuminating what we (and others) see as problems, shortcomings or pitfalls with current SAP research. This is partly done from a CMS perspective. We then continue with a section that briefly outlines critical management studies, and in particular how it can be further incorporated in SAP research. A summary section concludes the chapter.

A critical perspective on strategy as practice

First, and especially given the title and the nature of this section, we would like to emphasize that, from an overall perspective, we sympathize with the major aims and ambitions of strategy as practice, such as the important and justified 'sociological eye' (Whittington 2007), and perhaps even more so an ethnographic eye on strategic management (which usually gives a more reflexive perspective than that provided by the never-ending stream of narrow firm-performance-related research), the ideal of close encounter with the objects of study (for example, Balogun, Huff and Johnson 2003) and the wish to have some impact on how strategy actually is practised (Golsorkhi *et al.* 2010: 13).

Of course, we are not the first to direct a critical perspective on strategy as practice.

Methodological concerns have been raised by, for example, Venkateswaran and Prabhu (2010). More fundamental (but still intra-paradigmatic) criticisms against strategy as practice have previously been formulated by Chia and MacKay (2007) and, perhaps in particular, by Carter, Clegg and Kornberger (2008a; 2008b). Their critique includes strategy as practice's reluctance or inability to break away from orthodox strategic management research (in particular, the resource-based view) and associated managerial interests, the over-eclectic and confusing use of the term 'practice' (see also the chapters by Orlikowski and Tsoukas in this book) and limited advances in relation to previous process-oriented strategy research (see also Chia and MacKay 2007; Ezzamel and Willmott 2004; Whittington 2007). Furthermore, Carter, Clegg and Kornberger (2008a; 2008b) call for a more critical perspective on the practice of strategy that more clearly takes issues such as power and identity into account. In line with this, they also wish for a more 'philosophically and sociologically challenging notion of both strategy and practice' (Carter, Clegg and Kornberger 2008a: 91). We will come back to this critique later in the chapter.

The critique provided above seems to have had some effect on the field. In the first edition of this handbook (2010), there is a clear indication that 'the point is taken': 'This critique [referring primarily to Carter and colleagues] served as a key motivator for the expansion and development of the strategy as practice research agenda in this handbook' (Golsorkhi et al. 2010: 4). In this chapter we examine the possible effects of (parts of) this criticism. Our purpose is, obviously, not just to repeat previous critique, but it would be hard not to discuss and refer to parts of it. Here it is also important to note that neither of us as authors of this chapter would label ourselves as specialized 'SAP scholars'; therefore, we think it is fair to say that we, at least partly, provide an external view and critique on the field. We think this brings certain qualities, as insiders tend to have particular blinders and interests in preserving basic assumptions, as well as keeping some 'truths' unshaken.

Ambivalent relationship to mainstream research

Even if SAP research often positions itself as an alternative to mainstream strategic management research, with its 'focus on the effects of strategies on performance' and 'micro-economic approach and...methodological preoccupation with statistical analysis' (Golsorkhi et al. 2010: 1), it still seems fair to characterize strategy as practice's relationship with mainstream research as ambivalent (something that has also been pointed out previously by Carter, Clegg and Kornberger 2008b). In recent years it seems at least as if 'diplomatic relations' have been established with regard to mainstream research, with strategy as practice being rewarded with some form of 'diplomatic recognition', as a possibly odd but legitimate part of strategic management research. Strategy as practice has for a long time had its own standing working group at the European Group for Organizational Studies,[1] but it now also has an established 'interest group' in the more mainstream-oriented Strategic Management Society ('Strategy practice') as well as in the Academy of Management ('Strategizing activities and practice'). This is not just a coincidence, of course, but an outcome of hard work and a determined resolve to establish and promote the field. In spite of previous critics' call for a more defiant and challenging relationship to mainstream research, there are influential SAP researchers who, on the contrary, advocate and seek a closer and more harmonic relationship. Golsorkhi et al. (2010: 12) write that strategy as practice must not be isolated. There are even authors who suggest that strategy as practice is or might become complementary to and compatible with the dominant (not to say hegemonic) resource-based view (Johnson, Melin and Whittington 2003; Johnson et al. 2007; Regnér 2008).

'Why, therefore, this outstretched hand towards mainstream research?' one might ask. There are genuine intentions and ambitions in terms of 'bridging' strategy as practice with previous and contemporary theories on strategy, strategizing and

[1] This standing working group has, in fact, now ended; see www.egosnet.org/swgs/current_swgs.

strategic management. There is also an understandable desire to publish SAP research in established and highly ranked journals. In order to do this, it is often necessary to refer and relate to – or even 'speak to' – strategic management scholars outside the core SAP group. In some cases this 'dialogue' can, of course, be imposed by orthodox editors and/or reviewers, but it can also be opportunistically emphasized in order to improve the chances of publication by trying to appeal to a larger audience – an audience that many SAP researchers would perhaps like to be recognized and taken seriously by.

It is often a productive intellectual endeavour to reach out to other domains in order to broaden the relevance of one's research (Alvesson and Sandberg 2014), but it might also be important to ask oneself *what* domains it is appropriate to address. Even if it might be career-promoting for the individual to publish in mainstream journals and thereby, in the best-case scenario, be quoted and referred to by more established, mainstream researchers, it might come at a cost. Many mainstream management journals' emphasis on 'scientific rigour', in combination with a desire for conformity so as to fit more mainstream editors/reviewers, might serve as an 'intellectual straitjacket' (Carter, Clegg and Kornberger 2008b: 102) on strategy as practice (as well as other alternative fields or research programmes aiming to question established traditions and truths).

The risk of uninhibited (and paradigmatically inconsistent, according to, for example, Carter, Clegg and Kornberger 2008a) fraternization with mainstream strategic management research should not be exaggerated in the case of strategy as practice, however. At least until recently, the danger of intellectual 'inbreeding' via a rather narrow self-citing network (Clegg 2011) of a few dominating names and research groups has seemed to pose a more important threat to the field. The fact that SAP research is still so dominated (in terms of publications, references/citations, management tracking at conferences and so forth) by a handful of productive individuals might fuel some of the negative characteristics of so-called 'box research' (Alvesson and Sandberg 2014), including a silo mentality, intra-group communication,

'nitty-gritty' debates and an unquestioning attitude to one's own – as well as the foundational texts' – explicit or implicit assumptions.

In a partial defence of SAP researchers, it could be argued that they have always been willing to look 'outside the box' for theoretical ideas and useful concepts (more on this in the next section). Whittington (2006) includes most leading sociologists as important inspirations for strategy as practice. Borrowing established concepts from other fields and traditions has a long and solid history within strategy as practice. A more urgent question, perhaps, is where to relate the results and contributions. It is easy to get the impression that the main audience seems to be other SAP specialists within the same tribe (unless, as mentioned above, someone is bold enough to relate to the resource-based view or another mainstream strategic management perspective).

One could argue that many of the more influential SAP texts have been published in prestigious but generalist journals such as *Human Relations*, *Organizational Studies*, *Journal of Management Studies*, *Academy of Management Journal* and so forth. This is true. Potentially, these journals reach a rather varied, global audience of management and organization scholars. The problem is that academics, even the readers (mainstream or not) of these journals, still tend to be instrumental and read what seems to be relevant for their specific box(es). Besides, a problem that is to some extent magnified with many so-called 'A' journals is the presentation of results and contributions. Strategy as practice is, of course, not immune or an exception here. Compliance with formats and norms under the banners of 'rigour' and 'focus' tends to 'domesticize' bold claims, creativity, imagination and broader and/or practical relevance (Bartunek, Rynes and Ireland 2006; Clark and Wright 2009; Courpasson 2013; Gabriel 2010), turning scholars (and enthusiastic SAP researchers?) into 'academic journal technicians' (Alvesson and Sandberg 2013). The space, format and requirements of many journals are particularly problematic given the often espoused ambition to present rich, close-up empirical studies of how practitioners strategize. This book and, for instance, those by Johnson *et al.* (2007) and Jarzabkowski (2005) are, however, examples of encouraging exceptions to the journal-publishing norm so dominant in contemporary social science.

Regardless of publication outlet, the question is: is mainstream, orthodox strategic management a (or even *the* most) relevant 'box' (Alvesson and Sandberg 2014) to relate SAP research to? Perhaps it is (see, for example, Regnér 2008; 2011; compare Carter, Clegg and Kornberger 2008a; 2008b). Regardless of the answer to this question, it is vital to reflexively ask ourselves: *'Why?'*

Philosophy envy

If mainstream strategic management research is suffering from 'physics envy' (Bennis and O'Toole 2005; Flyvbjerg 2001), with its obsession with cause and effects, abstract regression, rigour and methodological procedures (busy producing managerial 'science fiction': Clegg 2011: 1587), strategy as practice, with its eclectic view on theories and method, cannot be said to fall into the same trap. Instead, SAP research might run the risk of another 'siren song': philosophy envy.

When we write 'philosophy' here, we unorthodoxly also include the grand social theorists and/or sociologists referred to in Part II in this book. Perhaps this soft spot for the big names in social science is understandable. Early strategy-as-practice work was very much a reaction to abstract, conceptual or quantitative, database-generated research at firm or industry level, and the aim was to take the actual strategy work conducted by those who claimed to work with 'strategy' seriously (Whittington 1996). Being close to the empirical phenomena at hand was (and, to a large extent, still is) regarded as a virtue, often with ethnomethodological approaches as ideal (Samra-Fredericks 2010). Ezzamel and Willmott (2004), as well as Carter, Clegg and Kornberger (2008a), note, however, that descending into the details of strategic management techniques significantly reduces the ability to analyse, for example, power and politics. By looking with fresh eyes on the 'tribe' of strategists, their rituals (strategic planning procedures, strategy workshops, strategy meetings and so forth) and artefacts (PowerPoint, Excel, flip charts, whiteboards, etc.), the risk of coming across

as a somewhat low-abstract, down-to-basics empiricist is evident. Indeed, SAP research often focuses empirically on 'the micro-level social activities, processes and practices that characterize organizational strategy and strategizing' (Golsorkhi *et al.* 2010: 1), or what Carter, Clegg and Kornberger (2008b: 98) refer to as the 'nitty-gritty details of strategy formation'. It is perhaps not that surprising – with this critique in mind (see, for example, Carter, Clegg and Kornberger 2008a; Ezzamel and Willmott 2004) – that SAP scholars wish to rise above this and say something rather generic, philosophically informed and theoretically advanced by 'drawing on' the big names in social science. We fully agree that it is good to strive for intellectual text production, and when it comes to strategy and strategizing as well, but this can also be taken too far, as an over-reaction to previous criticism.

As indicated in the previous section, we consider 'box-breaking' research (Alvesson and Sandberg 2014) as something usually beneficial and worth aiming at, but, beside the critical question of *what* other box(es) (mainstream strategic management, practice theory, structuration theory, activity theory, discourse theory, sensemaking theory and so forth) to connect to, there are also other risks or considerations that need to be taken into account.

The first risk is associated with the rather eclectic and frequent usage of the 'big names' and well-developed theories in social science – something also pointed out by, for instance, Carter, Clegg and Kornberger (2008b: 106, emphasis in original):

> The recruitment of scholars as diverse as Bourdieu (1977, 1990), de Certeau (1984), Foucault (1977), Giddens (1984) and Schatzki et al. (2001) to strategy as practice ones again raises the question of what is its *distinctive* contribution.

One might here, of course, also add Heidegger, Vygotsky and Wittgenstein – as suggested in Part II of this book – to the list of influential names and intellectual authorities that SAP researchers try to lean on.

'What is the problem, then?' one might ask. In addition to the risks of inconsistency, fragmentation and confusion within the strategy-as-practice field as a consequence of this 'promiscuous' (Carter, Clegg and Kornberger 2008b: 105) usage of theories and scholars, there is a risk that the grand names and theories will actually blind the researcher and – based on their influence, reach and clout in terms of explanatory power – to some extent prevent (instead of enable) new insights and theories on strategy and strategizing. New theories in management and organization studies (strategic management included) are rare, as a consequence of the significant level of importation and domestication of theories from other fields within social science (Oswick, Fleming and Hanlon 2011). Strategy as practice seems to score highly in this regard, as indicated by Part II as well as the introduction to this book. As a result,

> efforts within the discipline are focused on domesticating existing theories rather than generating new ones. This is detrimental, because in addition to the lack of new theories, the domestication process typically involves streamlining and/or modifying the original theory in order to fit the problems or conceptual tasks of OMT [organization and management theory], and the original nuance is often sacrificed to fit the indigenous field's concerns (Oswick, Fleming and Hanlon 2011: 328).

We see here a risk of research results along the lines of 'Aha, Foucault is applicable also on strategizing middle managers!', with limited contribution to or development of the borrowed supporting theory and a rather marginal advancement of our understanding of strategy and strategizing. We do not advocate an introspective (re)turn to orthodox, in-box theory. Reaching out to other domains in order to offer new, creative and useful understandings and/or problematizations of strategy and strategy work can often be a productive 'strategy' (Alvesson and Kärreman 2007; Alvesson and Sandberg 2014). Furthermore, there are also the arguments that one should stand on the shoulders of giants and not try to reinvent the wheel. Sometimes, though, perhaps we *should* try to reinvent the wheel – in this case a revealing and useful theory on strategy and strategizing. One comparable and inspirational example could be Mintzberg and Waters' (1985) notion of deliberate, emergent

and realized strategies – a theory on the strategy process with high impact both on theoretical and practical understandings of strategy and strategy work. This does not need to be done in splendid isolation; all research is, by definition, to a greater or lesser extent an act of intercontextual borrowing, since there are 'always foundational antecedents prefiguring and shaping the formulation of a specific theory' (Oswick, Fleming and Hanlon 2011: 318). As Oswick, Fleming and Hanlon point out, however, instead of just importing grand theories from other areas we also need to consider the possibility of a less unilateral stream of thinking, with skilful conceptual 'blending', which might also be able to generate some 'export' of theories and concepts from strategy-as-practice research to other areas. The risk is otherwise evident that future 'SAP theory' will continue to be created *outside* the SAP domain.

Another risk associated with using borrowed abstract theories in order to make sense of the praxis, practices and practitioners (Jarzabkowski 2005; Jarzabkowski, Balogun and Seidl 2007; Whittington 2006) of strategy is that we might lose the interest and attention of the latter category: the practitioners. Is this a problem? Some would surely claim that we primarily publish for an audience of scholars with similar interests and theoretical repertoires to our owns (hence, only other 'SAPpers' can review, comment and appreciate the theoretical/scientific value of abstract texts produced by other SAP researchers). There are SAP researchers who emphasize the importance of practical impact and relevance, however, describing their task as 'to advance our theoretical understanding in a way that has practical relevance for managers and other organizational members' (Golsorkhi *et al.* 2010: 1), striving for 'a societal shift towards better everyday strategizing praxis, empowered by more effective practices and a deeper pool of skilled practitioners' (Whittington 2006: 629). Others, such as Regnér (2011), recognize the lack of dialogue with practitioners as a shortcoming. The problem is to some extent already recognised among SAP scholars: 'Practice research should be accessible to practitioners. Increasingly sophisticated theoretical analysis runs the risk of becoming alienated from the problems and challenges of the practitioners' (Golsorkhi *et al.* 2010: 13). Here, both the level of abstraction associated with many of the 'borrowed' favourite theories and the (sometimes encouraged) fragmentation of theories might contribute to a situation in which strategy as practice as a research community 'finds itself handicapped in its efforts to penetrate society with its message' (March 2005: 10).

Vagueness and grandiosity

As with all non-trivial concepts, the exact meaning of strategy (in practice) is seldom clear, and often varies considerably. This is difficult to avoid, but less vagueness would probably benefit the strategy-as-practice literature. Without wanting to characterize all SAP studies as lacking in this respect, we now point to some common shortcomings. Sometimes the meaning and definition of 'practice' is a topic of discussion with some serious efforts at clarification (see, for example, Rouleau 2013, and the chapters by Orlikowski, Chia and Rasche as well as Tsoukas in this book), but the meaning of strategy is typically left unexplored and is treated as a self-evident given, or only as a first-order empirical construct. Jarzabkowski and Spee (2009: 90) find 'a lack of consistent theoretical and, in particular, empirical use of the term practices'. We would say the same about 'strategy', and find this even more unclear and varied in terms of its theoretical and empirical use – or, as Rouleau (2013: 561) puts it, 'While strategy-as-practice researchers have adopted a diversity of views about the practice notion, the view of strategy has not really been questioned. The debate around what strategy is still matters!' Jarzabkowski, Balogun and Seidl (2007: 7–8) define strategy, from a strategy-as-practice perspective, 'as a situated, socially accomplished activity, while strategizing comprises those actions, interactions and negotiations of multiple actors and the situated practices that they draw upon in accomplishing that activity'. The definition is repeated by, for instance, Jarzabkowski and Seidl (2008) and Jarzabkowski and Spee (2009), but if one did not know that it was about strategy it would be impossible to guess what the definition is supposed to refer to. The definition could

equally well fit, for example, operative work, leadership, health care or teamwork.

What SAP researchers treat as strategy is sometimes rather far-fetched. Rouleau (2005) studied salespeople in the fashion industry explaining for retailers a new collection being part of what was referred to as a new strategy. While one can perhaps refer to this as implementing a strategy and thus a part of the latter, such a generous scope for strategy as practice means that almost everything going on in organizations could be included in 'strategy', including service workers smiling as part of a strategy for increased customer satisfaction or lecturers lowering demands in courses as part of a university expansion strategy. A smile or the replacement of a book with a simpler one could then be addressed as strategy as practice. Jarzabkowski and Seidl (2008) studied what were referred to as strategy meetings in universities. The meetings were strategic according to interviewed top managers, who claimed that they were consequential for the organization as a whole. The empirical theme that received most attention by the researchers was whether university top management should have control over some journals published and owned by departments. Whether this affected the organization as a whole is uncertain. It could be linked to a strategic reorientation in order to make the university more commercial, but it is not self-evidently something 'strategic'. That it was addressed by senior people is not necessarily a convincing argument in itself. The paper claims to be about strategy meetings, which is certainly not incorrect, but most of the descriptions and analysis focus on issues such as agenda-setting, free or constrained discussions, stabilizing and destabilizing elements could presumably be used for understanding formal meetings in general and not necessarily only, or primarily, strategic issues or meetings.

The domain (strategy as practice) and labels (strategy/strategic management) might be serving here as protective barriers, such that those researchers considered to be within this specialized and protected area can do their work in a fairly undisturbed way, claiming expertise, uniqueness and novelty, and only be assessed by others sharing this specific orientation (Alvesson and

Sandberg 2014). The insiders can thereby claim their peculiarity towards, for example, the broader organization studies field, while, in terms of the content of many studies, being closer to the latter than, say, mainstream strategic management (even if we recognize that the distinction between strategy and organization studies is, to a significant degree, arbitrary). This type of immunization strategy – protecting studies behind the label of strategy as practice and getting reviewers who have signed up for this sub-specialism – is not uncommon, but nor is it unproblematic.

Generally, strategy work in a more delimited sense might, from an empirical perspective, be relatively rare and often difficult to access for researchers. As a consequence, many SAP researchers may be said to study organizations/ managers in practice more than strategy as or in practice. Why use strategy vocabulary, however, even if it is questionable whether 'strategy' is at hand and when other labels seem more motivated? Part of the answer lies in the flair around having 'strategy' as a signifier. In a society characterized by widespread dreams of grandiosity (Alvesson 2013) – that is, ambitions to boost status and identity less through practices, competence and performance than by window-dressing, discourse and fantasies about one's own significance and remarkability in relation to more modest others – doing 'strategy' or 'strategic' things provides a powerful means to increase the relative importance and status of an individual, organization or profession.

A management consulting firm studied by Blom and Lundgren (2013) had four divisions, and the one labelled 'Strategic Services' (later just 'Strategy') earned more prestige, paid higher salaries and had higher entry requirements compared to the other three divisions, which provided other kinds of management advice/services (namely services not sold and delivered under the banner of 'strategy' and/or 'strategic'). Another example is human resource managers' aspirations to do more strategic work (Alvesson 2013: 163, emphasis added): 'New and more worthy tasks were in the offing... As personnel *strategists*, they should follow up and monitor comprehensive and long-term issues, be members of the company's top management group, etc.' One of the personnel managers (or HR manager, with the new, more grand terminology) described his working day in the following way:

> I may say that I seldom manage to do what I would like to do in my role as a personnel manager. [chuckles]. It is like most of us, actually, but I would really like to work strategically, looking to the future, working with the managers more than we do (Alvesson 2013: 163).

It is perhaps not that surprising that a category of co-workers feeling marginalized and too far away from prestige and power (here associated with strategic management) should want to be taken more seriously by doing more strategy together with corporate management. Similar aspirations can also be found among other staff/support functions such as procurement, distribution, marketing, communications and finance (Alvesson 2013: 164; see also Chalmers 2001). The same pattern – strategy as some kind of guiding star for what one *ought* to do – is also found, however, among those one would expect actually to have overall responsibility for corporate strategy: boards of directors. Tricker (2012: 191–3) shows that directors typically would like to spend half their time on 'strategy formulation', but, when he followed them to see how they actually *did* spend their time, they seemed to spend only approximately a quarter of their time on this. Instead, they spend almost two-thirds of their time on past- and present-focused activities, such as 'accountability issues' and the 'monitoring and supervision' of management. Not even the highest corporate echelons are immune to the normative pressure of being seen as strategic and practising strategy. The switch to grander labels can also be found among management scholars, who have dropped less grandiose labels such as 'managerial' work, 'small business', 'personnel administration' and 'planning' in favour of 'leadership', 'entrepreneurship', 'HRM' (or even 'strategic HRM') and 'strategic management'. As one North American colleague told one of us, he thought it was great to have a chair in strategy, as it was much better paid than if it had been in the area of, and labelled as, organization studies. (Most SAP people, like this person, would probably see him as an 'organization studies' person much more than one in strategic management – except for the many occasions when there is a pay-off from being into 'strategy'.)

'What, then, is the problem (for strategy as practice)?' one might ask. Should not we just allow people to fantasize and perhaps inflate their import-ance by labelling what they do as 'strategy'/'stra-tegic'/'strategy work'? Who are we, as researchers, to tell people that what they do at work should not be regarded as strategizing? From the very dawn of the strategy-as-practice endeavour there has been an explicit ambition to take seriously the talk, meanings and work by practitioners (Whittington 1996). This ideal sits very well with the idea of being 'close' to the strategy practitioners, which often justifies both an ethnomethodological (Samra-Fredericks 2010) and an overall construct-ivist approach (Grand, Rüegg-Stürm and von Arx 2010). To be 'close-with' (Johnson, Balogun and Beech 2010) how people talk about, make sense of and practise 'strategy' has, for many SAP research-ers, served as a guiding star during the last two decades. These ideals and orientations often justify research characterized by an emic approach (Head-land, Pike and Harris 1990), with a rather inductive relationship to empirical data.

One problem with this is, of course, that local definitions and understandings of strategy are hard to relate to results from previous research, based on other (most probably different) conceptions of strategy (see the chapter written by Langley in this book for a further discussion on this challenge). Dependent on which 'strategic episode' (Hendry and Seidl 2003) is singled out for analysis, very different views on strategy/strategizing are likely to come out, exposing a possibly endless number of language games (Pondy 1978) and personal mean-ings. How actors try to construct 'strategy' in everyday life is indeed both interesting and rele-vant, and one could say that we can never control the signifier and that it is good to address strategy in a variety of ways, even if we then run the risk of turning everyone into 'strategists' and almost everything into 'strategizing'. The risks of losing analytical precision and that having excessively broad categories prevents rather than enables intel-lectual dialogue need to be considered, however.

As scholars (strategy-as-practice specialists or not), we are not immune to the societal tendencies

of grandiosity. Most of us would probably like to study and write about things that are regarded as important by peers and key stakeholders (as well as ourselves, of course), and get proper recognition for it. Strategic management and other forms of strat-egy work probably achieve a relatively high score here; studying how people deal with strategic issues must almost, by definition, be important. In addition to this, and as indicated earlier in this chapter and in Part II of this book, there is also an inclination to 'draw upon' the grand names of social theory, soci-ology and philosophy. Again, this can, of course, sometimes easily be justified on the basis of the concepts' explanatory power and ability to reveal something new and important regarding strategy work. There is also the risk, though, that we use the grand theories more as a routine (others seem to do it and get published, therefore one tries to do the same) and as a way to demonstrate how philosoph-ically informed and sophisticated our research is (perhaps as a reaction to its sometimes rather down-to-earth, mundane empirical nature?) – or, as Carter, Clegg and Kornberger (2008b: 106) scep-tically remark, 'We are not convinced that the insights from these authors [referring to names such as Bourdieu, de Certeau, Foucault, Giddens and Schatzki] have been used in other than a highly ornamental way.' By looking only at how success-ful SAP researchers have been to date when it comes to publishing texts based on various grand social theories, it may very well be a useful strategy also for the future, when SAP researchers can carry on evoking 'heavily branded social theory and con-tinue to accumulate all the currently fashionable names under its roof' (Carter, Clegg and Kornber-ger 2008b: 110). The question is: how much impact will this have on our understanding of strategy and strategy work (not to mention the practitioners and actual praxis 'out there') outside the narrow circle of readers of a few career-boosting scientific journals?

A critical perspective within strategy as practice

Until now we have discussed strategy as practice from a critical perspective and highlighted what we (and others) see as problematic characteristics or important choices/trade-offs. It is now time to turn to seeing how a critical perspective, that of critical management studies, can be used productively *within* the SAP agenda (though the demarcation is not so strict, and CMS-inspired strategy as practice will include some critique of 'conventional' strategy-as-practice thinking, as indicated above). In order to do this, we first need to very briefly outline some important characteristics usually associated with CMS.

Constituting critical management studies

Very much like strategy as practice, the critical management studies discipline is characterized by various lines of thinking and intellectual traditions. In the centre, however, is a questioning of authority and the relevance of mainstream thinking and practice (Alvesson and Deetz 2000), and its concern is with 'the study *of*, and sometimes *against*, management rather than with the development of techniques or legitimations *for* management' (Alvesson, Bridgman and Willmott 2009: 1, emphasis in original). A key assumption here is that 'dominant theories and practices of management and organization systematically favour some (elite) groups an/or interests at the expense of those who are disadvantaged by them; and that this systematic inequality or interest-partiality is ultimately damaging for the emancipatory prospects of all groups' (Alvesson, Bridgman and Willmott 2009: 7). An explicit interest in knowledge production that enables emancipation (Habermas 1972 [1968]) is therefore often the norm. Fournier and Grey (2000) point to three key characteristics of CMS: denaturalization (questioning what is taken for granted); non-performativity (a focus on aspects other than functionalism, effectiveness and output in a narrow sense – something we come back to later when discussing a possible research agenda); and reflexivity (the capacity to recognize all accounts of organization and management as mediated by the particular tradition of their authors).

It is perhaps too general, however, to say something distinct about CMS. Alvesson (2008) has outlined the more specific concerns of CMS as follows.

(1) A critical questioning of ideologies, institutions, interests and identities that are assessed to be dominant, harmful and under-challenged through negations, deconstructions, revoicing or defamiliarization.
(2) Aiming to inspire social reform in the presumed interest of the majority and/or non-privileged, as well as resistance/emancipation from ideologies, institutions and identities that lock people in unreflective and reproduced ideas, intentions and practices (with some appreciation of the constraints of the work and life situations of people – including managers – in the contemporary organizational world).

Often, but not always, class, race and/or gender are used as lenses in order to identify and define underprivileged interests. Many versions of CMS also point out how dominant institutions and discourses bring about more general negative effects, such as consumerism and environmental harm, conformism and uncritical, unimaginative thinking, creating dependences and problematic identity projects (for example, followers to leaders, clients to experts and brand lovers with fetishist addictions to specific brands).

Given the broad, inclusive and heterogeneous body of work associated with critical thinking, it should come as no surprise that there are tensions and some 'tribe-ism' within CMS. One such is the classical tension between critical scholars who subscribe to critical realism and those who lean towards a more poststructuralist orientation (Contu and Willmott 2005; Jones 2009; Reed 2009). Another is the debate on (critical) performativity and how (if) to engage in dialogue with managers (Fournier and Grey 2000; Spicer, Alvesson and Kärreman 2009; Wickert and Schaefer 2015).

Partly related to the tensions described above are the (external and internal) criticisms that have been raised against CMS. One such critique is the tendency to a 'one-eyed hypercriticism' that fails to recognize possible productive, functional and socially positive outcomes from management, organizations and capitalism (Alvesson and Deetz 2000). Surely, though, not all aspects of modern society are dark and gloomy, even if they are what CMS scholars usually focus on. Global poverty reduction, increased gender equality, productive managerial efforts to reduce negative environmental effects, satisfaction at work, improved working conditions and so forth seldom get much space in CMS texts. Related to this as well is the tendency to criticize without offering or suggesting any alternatives to the status quo. Sometimes this 'non-performativity' is even regarded as a virtue and a deliberate, useful form of denaturalization (Fournier and Gray 2000). The CMS discipline has also been criticized for being a rather detached, elitist armchair project. Alvesson and Willmott (1996: 83) write that its output sometimes has been 'interpreted as the work of a disgruntled group of intellectuals whose privileged class background has impeded their identification with the interests of working people'. In short: an intellectual elite that makes a career for itself by – in an abstract and publishable way – describing non-privileged groups' 'true interests' and how management and/ or 'the system' are manipulating them. One can further question if it makes sense to treat 'managers' as one coherent, privileged group with a shared common interest (bracketing together *all* corporate managers from the CEO down to the first line team lead – perhaps fifteen hierarchical levels down the pyramid) and view all their prerogatives and privileges as unjust and illegitimate, as is often routinely done in many CMS texts. Whether managers really share the interests of capital/shareholders and should be regarded as their loyal 'tools' is also debatable (Berle and Means 1932; Donaldson and Davis 1991; Mace 1971). Sympathy with the managerial class is a sensitive topic, especially among 'CMS purists': 'Any measure of sympathy for managers and other elites may be interpreted as a loss of nerve that renders CMS needlessly vulnerable to absorption within the progressive mainstream and thus disables its critical edge' (Alvesson, Bridgman and Willmott 2009).

Nevertheless, in spite of these possible problems with critical management studies, we see the potential of a more CMS-informed research agenda for future strategy-as-practice endeavours (see also McCabe 2010; Rouleau 2013; Whittington and Vaara 2012). A first and necessary step would be to reflect on and decide how to relate to the problems/challenges outlined in the first part of this

chapter. In particular, the relationship with mainstream strategy thinking needs to be considered. A key task of CMS is to question dominant, orthodox, mainstream thinking. To accept the underlying assumptions and claims in, for example, RBV or transaction cost economics and try to harmonize SAP research with this will typically not result in interesting critical research. Therefore, for strategy-as-practice students considering doing critical research, or upgrading the questioning element in their studies, the relationship with mainstream strategic management research needs to be carefully considered. In addition, the often well-intended, inclusive, emic-inspired view on strategy needs to be questioned. Strategy as a signifier should not be taken for granted but, rather, critically scrutinized. Is it really the most appropriate signifier for what we are studying? As discussed above, 'strategy' sounds impressive, but it may have rhetorical rather than representational value.

Even if we assume that the issues above are sorted out in a CMS-oriented direction, there might still be some perceived barriers for the average SAP-researcher interested in doing CMS-inspired work. The discipline, with its emancipatory aim, is very often explicitly and overtly political in its nature; many associate it with a leftish political agenda and/or more or less radical social movements. This is not completely wrong (even if there exist exceptions within the CMS tradition), and might, of course, turn some enthusiastic strategy researchers (not comfortable with this political orientation) off. It is important to recognize, however, that CMS can *also* be used in order to scrutinize any idea or practice found to be problematic: dominant so-called 'progressive ideologies', the intentions and behaviour of social movements, the conduct of unions and so on. Political correctness and naïve ideas of democracy being a blessing in complex organizations can be fruitful themes for critical analysis. Furthermore, some arguments and motives within CMS can be found in and justified by such diverse authorities as Marxist writings *and* official messages from the Vatican, making the political dimension more complex than often assumed. One could even say that critical studies targeting the 'usual suspects' – patriarchy, managerialism, bureaucracy, new (or old) public management and so forth – in pre-packaged, for-mulaic ways run against the spirit of critical thinking.

Towards a CMS-informed research agenda

The first point to make is that strategic management, as a body of knowledge as well as organizational practice, *needs* to be studied from a critical perspective. Strategy is almost by definition forward-oriented, and hence implies future, potentially long-lasting power effects. Shrivastava (1986) was an early observer of the ideological character of strategic management, claiming that strategy discourse helps legitimize existing power structures and resource inequalities (see also Knights and Morgan 1991). Strategic management is usually conceived in terms of 'mobilizing resources in ways that strengthen the focal organization's command of its environment and/or weaken the position of competitors' (Alvesson and Willmott 1996: 129), indicating a need to identify those on the losing end, which could potentially include groups of employees, suppliers, customers, the public and the environment. Levy, Alvesson and Willmott (2003: 104–5) also make a passionate call for critical analysis:

> Strategic management deserves critical investigation because it has assumed a dominance in managerial discourse and become a model for decision processes in a wide range of organizations beyond the private sector. Strategy is privileged as a field of management theory and managerial practice. Strategy pundits and makers make claim to expertise, insight and authority that reproduce and legitimate organizational inequalities. Strategy frames and legitimizes managers' practices as they strive to advance a company's market position, defend against regulatory or social threats, and secure control amidst challenges from labour, stockholders or other stakeholders. When management practitioners and scholars proclaim the primacy of strategy, Critical Theorists need to subject the field to close scrutiny.

How, then, can strategy as practice and critical management studies be integrated in a fruitful way? Below we outline five potential critical research endeavours or themes that, to some

degree, build on previous strategy-as-practice studies with a 'critical flavour' but also add some new – and perhaps more radical – questions and contributions in relation to previous SAP literature. This is, of course, just one out of many ways to sketch a critical research agenda for strategy as practice, and CMS purists may accuse it of not being critical/radical enough. We believe, however, that it provides a useful way of linking the two disciplines that continues to build on the work in this direction that has already been carried out. It also draws on 'parallel' critical studies done in other comparable areas within management and organization studies, such as leadership. These studies might serve as inspiration/and or foundation for further SAP work in this direction. The five themes are summarized in Table 23.1.

Strategy as power

Strategy and strategic management often tend to be viewed and described as mainly neutral, plural, productive and positive activities. This is very much the case in mainstream literature, of course, but it also seems to have characterized a major part of the strategy-as-practice research agenda to date (Hardy and Thomas 2014; Laine and Vaara 2007; McCabe 2010). A first and necessary step in order to tread a more critical path is therefore to recognize the political character of strategic management and strategizing – that is, strategy as power (McCabe 2010; Phillips and Dar 2009). This has been done to some extent within earlier works by, for example, Mintzberg (1985), Pettigrew (1973; 1977) and Pfeffer (1992), but not in the fundamental way suggested by more CMS-oriented strategy scholars (for example, Ezzamel and Willmott 2008; Levy, Alvesson and Willmott 2003; Knights and Morgan 1990; 1991; McCabe 2010). On the basis of these earlier writings on strategy and power, it becomes clear that one aspect of strategizing is how different organizations, groups within organizations, individual managers and so forth compete for influence and resources (Pfeffer and Salancik 1978). 'Strategy' can here be viewed as a battlefield: all groups compete for the 'goodies' associated with 'strategy'.

One basic aspect of analysis for SAP scholars interested in doing critical research would

Table 23.1 A critical research agenda

Themes	Examples of research questions	Examples of relevant studies
Strategy as power	- Ideological foundations for strategic management as a knowledge field? - Who/what is promoted/disadvantaged by strategic management as practice? - What are the power effects within/outside the focal organization?	Ezzamel and Willmott (2008); Hardy and Thomas (2014); Laine and Vaara (2007); Levy, Alvesson and Willmott (2003); Knights and Morgan (1991; 1995); McCabe (2010); Shrivastava (1986)
Diffusion of strategic management	- Contradictions, inconsistencies and ambiguities in relation to claims of 'strategy work'? - Robustness of identities as 'strategists'? - 'Stickiness' of strategic management discourses? - Strategizing as a ceremonial identity boost for middle managers?	Alvesson and Kärreman (2011)*; Balogun and Johnson (2004; 2005); Mantere and Vaara (2008); Rouleau (2005); Samra-Fredricks (2005); Thomas, Sargent and Hardy (2011)
Ir- and non-rationalities of strategic management	- Deviations from the rationalistic claims of strategic management? - How is the tension between ex ante and ex post strategizing handled?	Balogun and Johnson (2005); Kärreman and Alvesson (2001)*; Mintzberg and Waters (1985)
The consequences and performativity of strategic management	- What are the unintended or intended negative effects of strategic management? - What are the social and ecological effects? - How can these effects be mitigated or changed/improved from a broader societal perspective?	Alvesson and Kärreman (2011)*; Knights and Morgan (1991); Newton (2009); Spicer, Alvesson and Kärreman (2009)*
Anti-strategerialism	- What aspects or organizational reality are hidden as a consequence of the ubiquitous usage of the signifier 'strategy'? - Do we need strategy and strategic management at all (in practice and as a scholarly discipline)? - What other vocabulary could be used instead? - What would be the consequences for the lived reality at work?	Alvesson and Sveningsson (2003; 2012)*; Gemmill & Oakley (1992)*

Note: * = a study not labelled as being about strategy/strategic management but that might still serve as a useful example and/or inspiration.

therefore be to try to identify privileged groups (winners) and non-privileged groups (losers) in relation to strategizing and strategic management. Which business units will gain or end up on the losing end as a consequence of a new corporate strategy? Will increased competitive advantage for one Western multinational enterprise obliterate competing firms in the developing world? Will a new sourcing strategy squeeze suppliers upstream in the supply chain? How does a new customer segmentation strategy constitute, and possibly discriminate, different groups of consumers? Which voices will be included (and listened to) in the strategizing process?

Focusing *only* on these 'sectoral interests' increases the risk of trivializing the political dimension of strategic management (Alvesson and Willmott 1995), however, and failing to recognize 'how managers' practical reasoning about corporate strategy is conditioned by politico-economic structures that extend well beyond the boundaries of any particular organizational sector' (Alvesson and Willmott 1996: 132). Therefore, it is important to recognize and include the historical, ideological and socio-economic forces that shape the very conditions for strategizing in the analysis (Levy, Alvesson and Willmott 2003; Phillips and Dar 2009). CMS encourage a broader view than those advocated by students of explicit or easily detected forms of power and politics.

Examples of research questions include the following.

- What are the ideological foundations for and/or tensions within strategic management as a field of knowledge?
- Which ideologies, institutions, interests and identities are promoted and disadvantaged by strategic management as practice?
- What are the power effects of strategizing processes – within as well as outside the focal organization?

These themes to some extent encourage broader concerns than specific activities studied through detailed observations, but the challenge for strategy as practice would be to relate practice and process both to inputs (such as ideological foundations) and to outcomes (power effects), which are sometimes traceable in observable practices, but sometimes hidden or implicit in these.

Diffusion of strategic management

More than twenty years ago Knights and Morgan (1991: abstract) described how corporate strategy had penetrated corporate life, serving as

> a mechanism of power that transforms individuals into particular kinds of subjects who secure a sense of well-being through participation in strategic practices... It touches on the very sense of what it is to be human as well as having effects that readily legitimize prevailing relations of inequality and privilege in contemporary organizations and institutions.

Several critical studies of strategic management have focused on how it is regarded as a privilege for the higher echelons of the corporate hierarchy, and how it serves the naturalization, legitimization and maintenance of their domination and prerogatives (Alvesson and Willmott 1995; 1996; Knights and Morgan 1990; 1991; Shrivastava 1986).

In more recent years, however, there have been studies emphasizing the dispersed nature of strategizing, showing how it is also a concern and activity of middle managers (Balogun and Johnson 2004; 2005; Rouleau 2005). This can be seen as

neutral, or even as progressive; but there is considerable ambiguity here that is worth investigating. A key issue is: to what extent are middle managers 'really' doing 'strategy'? Behind the claims, there are perhaps the contemporary eagerness to make as much as possible appear impressive and a loose usage of favourable labels (Alvesson 2013). The truth claims of middle managers doing strategy work may call for systematic, critical scrutiny. A good research question from a CMS perspective could be: how is this construction produced? Another question – going in the opposite direction – could be: if/when there is such a radical dispersion of strategizing, what does it mean (a classical inquiry within strategy as practice, but posed here from an explicitly critical perspective)? What is the nature of the involvement, the concerns and activities? Full responsibility, the production of plans, consultation, the selective application and refinement of 'strategies'? Or (to return to the previous question) are they mainly encouraged to use strategy vocabulary and then view themselves in another, more appealing way? Is there perhaps a 'strategy deception', whereby middle level managers are *led* to believe – or talk themselves into believing – that the use of strategy talk or fantasizing means that they are really taking part in the significant transformation and shaping of the organization and its future?

Of course, there are probably enormous variations here, from the distribution of strategy work – in which local and/or bottom-up initiatives have substantial and far-reaching effects – to the actual 'strategy' being mere ceremonial. A CMS take on strategy as practice would then encourage the view or assumption of the latter, such that research would focus on the lack of substance in activities framed as strategy. Whether subjects 'really' buy into these ('back stage' as well), and how they play a role in defining them or whether such definitions are shaky and fragmented, would be important to try to understand, giving the flooding of working life with strategy (as talk).

As previously discussed, doing – or giving the impression of doing – strategy can be seen as a means to protect or increase one's influence, prestige and well-being (see also Laine and Vaara 2007; Mantere and Vaara 2008). It is often regarded as a premium label, fully in line with, for example, 'leadership' as being more prestigious/ important than mere management, planning, administration, coordination, control and so on (Blom and Alvesson 2014). We want to be confirmed, associated with something prestigious, and to distance ourselves from what is regarded as mundane or trivial, and as a consequence we tend to load an increasing number of phenomena with strong, positive, exaggerated meaning to generate attractiveness, success and distance from the paltriness and mediocrity of everyday life (Alvesson 2013: 9).

Having said that, it is important to acknowledge many SAP researchers' ambitions to make strategic management somewhat less solemn, important and grand – strategy with a small 's'. For example, Samra-Fredericks (2003; 2005) and Laine and Vaara (2007) have studied and scrutinized the mundane, everyday outcomes of strategy discourse in great detail. Again, though, we would like to sound a warning about the vagueness/grandiosity trap (as described in a previous section) in taking this too far. There is often a mixed message in terms of critical exploration and debunking, on the one hand, and the labelling of this as strategy as practice, on the other. Close-up studies very often give a different picture from distanced – and often superficial – studies, in which a conventional, nice 'surface' tends to be reproduced. This can threaten the dominant view of organizations as characterized by semi-rational decision-making, arrangements, strategies, leadership and so forth. Often, however, the latter vocabulary is used, reproduced and, thus, reinforced. Managers (middle, senior, top) claim that they are doing strategy work. Researchers are then involved in the acceptance, co-construction or reinforcement of a specific view of managers. Here SAP researchers are in a similar risky situation to that of students of leadership, entrepreneurship, etc. A way of moving beyond this would be to more carefully – and, when motivated, sceptically – follow the ways in which middle managers and others construct themselves as being involved in strategy, critically examining these constructions. This is quite different from simply accepting the accounts made by managers portraying their activities as strategies or of strategic importance.

Examples of such research questions would include the following.

- When and how do people in organizations claim to be doing strategy work? What are the contradictions, inconsistencies and ambiguities involved in this?
- Do the identity constructions involved in managers as strategists hold water – that is, stand up to a 'reality test' – or are the construction efforts undermined by experiences, activities or 'anti-stories', making it difficult to uphold the strategy discourse? Here it is important to also investigate the 'strategists' outside these settings, when this identity stands the best chance of being expressed and confirmed. Does the strategic management discourse 'stick' or is it invoked only in specific, and perhaps uncommon, situations?
- Are middle managers as 'strategists' trying to associate themselves more closely with top management, making the symbolic and perhaps also substantive distance from their subordinates more distinctive?

Ir- and non-rationalities of strategic management

According to Mintzberg (2004), the education of MBAs means the insertion of a systematic form of non-rationality, or even irrationality, into companies: MBAs assuming and acting as if they can develop companies without having any deeper understanding of the business than what they have acquired mainly through reports, financial and other quantitative data and the use of strategic management models. This does not necessary contribute to a sound economy, Mintzberg argues. A CMS/SAP research interest could therefore include studies based on the assumption of business often being difficult to rationally operate and that non-rationalities prevail. This is perhaps not so remarkable, but management (and their apologists in business schools) often assume and pretend (sincerely believe in?) a superior form of analytical rationality. This is the basic form of managerial legitimization, which may be quite thin and threatened by exposure, including within management groups themselves.

From a conventional point of view, this should perhaps not be taken too far; maybe strategy/strategic management *should* emphasize the 'rational'; otherwise it might lose much of its relevance as a signifier. Nevertheless, much analysis, idea generation, reality construction and decision-making includes heavy doses of narcissism, hubris, 'garbage can' dynamics, group-thinking, adherence to traditions and institutionalized paths, following of fashions and so forth. The many examples of mergers or organizational change initiatives that fail indicate the limitations of strategic management in terms of being a primarily rational type of activity.

An interesting example of strategic management concerns the emergent nature of much business. A CEO of an IT consultancy firm we studied remarked that 'strategy sometimes depends on whom you are sitting next to on the flight'. Sometimes this may lead to a project that can expand and form part of the organization without much strategy work pointing out this route. Mintzberg's (and others') view of strategy as a pattern of behaviour gives a rather negative view of the subject matter and diverges from most understandings of strategy. How do managers relate to this, though? Presumably most believe they are, and claim to be, forward-looking when they are engaged in strategic management, not trying to do strategy retrospectively. How do they struggle to preserve a view of themselves as doing strategy in the contexts of emergence, 'garbage can' decision-making and the role of chance in large sections of business life?

Examples of research questions would include the following.

- As a presumably rational activity, strategic management gives legitimization to corporate management functions at various hierarchical levels. Perhaps, however, there are basic divergences from the ideal. If so, what is the nature of these?
- How do managers preserve a view of strategizing as a rational activity in light of all the irregularities characterizing corporate life?
- What are the practices for dealing with the tension between a priori and ex post 'strategy'? What are the relationships between these? How

is strategy invented and reinvented? (Inevitably, this calls for longitudinal studies.)

The consequences and performativity of strategic management

Strategy is often understood in terms of its business-related outcomes. Critical management studies introduce a broader set of criteria. What are the social (material and non-material) and ecological consequences of strategic management? This is a matter of trying to investigate and discuss not only the intended but also the unintended consequences (Balogun and Johnson 2005) of strategic management outside the spheres of effectiveness and profit-making. The material effects involve not just corporate financial performance but also power relations in the market place and in society. Mergers and acquisitions may increase corporate power and create dependence on the part of suppliers, customers, local communities and so forth. Strategic changes may influence employment and work conditions (Phillips and Dar 2009).

Many, if not most, companies are in the business of creating significant negative environmental effects to a greater or lesser extent, though this is seldom directly brought out in strategy-as-practice studies. Internationalization and the outsourcing of production may be far from environmentally neutral. Putting this under the radar of a CMS/SAP approach would raise more awareness of what is sometimes not explicitly addressed in strategy work (Newton 2009). A simple example could be the internationalization of higher education, which often means that foreign students (and their visiting professors) will fly relatively frequently between their home countries and their 'internationalized' universities, with an obviously negative carbon footprint effect.

Strategizing means the subjectification of managers and other employees, either as strategists, supposed to comply with strategic-management-related knowledge and seeing themselves as specific types of subjects, or as subordinates to strategists, defined as subjects implementing what the strategists have decided upon. This is not, as mentioned before and emphasized by Knights and

Morgan (1991) and others, neutral, but instead means a specific formation and regulation of people at work. The subordination of subjects to a strategic management regime is, of course, not necessarily, or even mainly, problematic in terms of constraints – there is a clear empowerment element as well – but it is important to draw attention to the potentially negative side. The colonization of strategy talk may exercise a strong disciplinary and normalizing effect on (senior and middle?) managers. Not doing strategy is seen as a deviation, a source of inferiority, shame and guilt. The eagerness of SAP and other 'strategy advocates' to portray corporate life as (mainly) about strategies and strategy work contributes to this normalization, and the effects of such models and vocabularies on the formation of managers and corporate relations could be explored in depth.

Here it may make sense to move away from a narrow interest on discourse, on what is talked about in specific meetings about 'strategy', and investigate how this is related to specific material consequences, as well as people's understandings and social relations outside specific 'strategic episodes'. Some critical work takes the centrality of discourse as self-evident (Ezzamel and Willmott 2008; Knights and Morgan 1991). It is arguable that there has been too much focus on discourse in critical strategy as practice to date. Perhaps the extra-discursive also needs to be carefully considered (Alvesson and Kärreman 2011; Fairclough 2005).

Related to the potential outcomes (whether intended or unintended) of strategy processes is the matter of critical performativity – that is, the outcome of critical strategy research (Spicer, Alvesson and Kärreman 2009). If strategy-as-practice researchers seriously want to have an impact on how strategy is not only talked about but thought about and practised 'out there', perhaps more researchers need to be slightly more explicitly normative (again). The risk otherwise is that that role will be taken over by management consultants, gurus, financial analysts, business journals or other tradesmen in knowledge, who would gladly fill the empty space left by strategy/management/organization scholars preoccupied by the abstract domestication of theories, trying to make

it in the global publication game, being more interested in the details of discourse and its internal effects on discourse users than broader issues of corporate development and effects 'out there', on employees, other social interests and the environment. Moreover, a strong focus on the details of conversations and other micro-issues could lead to limited interest from people outside the restricted number of other sub-specialists, interested in, say, conversation analysis methods or the application of Foucauldian ideas. Here a more open, reflexive and assumption-questioning attitude often lacks presence in favour of a gap-spotting, 'add to the literature' approach, in which far too much is taken for given and assumptions and vocabularies are uncritically reproduced and applied.

Examples of research questions would include the following.

- What are the unintended or intended negative effects of strategic management?
- What are the social and ecological effects?
- How can these effects be mitigated or changed/ improved from a broader societal perspective?

Anti-strategerialism

A radical approach would be to see the entire idea of 'strategy' and 'strategic management' as basically problematic. Of course, consideration of the broader picture, goal-setting and planning are most probably still necessary activities, but this does not necessarily call for the large-scale use of the strategy/strategic management vocabulary. Do we need strategy and strategic management at all (in practice and as a scholarly discipline)?

One very radical view here could mean challenging the entire notion of strategic management (and strategy as practice as well?) and view the idea of strategic management as a strange notion, being a key ingredient in the contemporary expansion of management into a colonizing force that needs to be fundamentally challenged rather than being a target for minor questioning, confirmation and reproduction. Perhaps a less all-embracing and categorical view, and more adapted to the specific field of strategic management, would be to take an 'anti-strategerialism' position. This would be similar to anti-managerialism – that is, wanting to reduce rather than expand a particular, dominating discourse, mindset and practice. Good management/organizations could work without emphasizing the strategist and strategizing. Trying to describe what is happening in organizations could be done without the use of the framework and vocabulary. Would this not make the SAP researcher unemployed, though? Not necessarily. One could still carry out studies of organizations and carefully, but sceptically (and perhaps ironically, or even cynically), follow the discourse of strategy in use – that is, in explicit talk or managerial claims that something is about strategy. The approach would then not limit itself to discourse, however – to the too easy acceptance and reproduction of the inclination to use this sometimes self-flattering and ego-boosting representation. The trick would be to avoid reductionist, self-contained discursivism and more broadly investigate the doings and outcomes of managerial work and 'strategy', with a focus on those (many?) cases in which organizational and managerial practice fall short of living up to the ideal – and pretentiousness, confirmation and comfort – of strategy talk. It would also be necessary to critically explore contradictions and discrepancies in organizations, and explore the often not so grandiose nature of the latter. This could, in many cases, mean a demystification of management and an undermining of managerial privilege. Management studies do indeed need to resist the reinforcement of grandiose managerialism – a favourite project for 'pop' management authors, consultants, managers, academic teachers and researchers eager to make students, practitioners and themselves happy through all the favoured grandiose representations of strategy and strategic management (HRM, branding, purchasing, etc.), leadership, knowledge work and so on (Alvesson 2013). Aiming for sensitive representations often leads to demystification. A more open and ironic take on strategy would here be beneficial.

Critical research could then expose strategic management (as a knowledge field and practice) and supplement existing work with an 'anti-strategerialism' research agenda. This could be formulated as 'SIF' (strategy in fantasy) or 'SIPP' (strategy in the PowerPoint presentation). Such

anti-strategerialism could then add to these parts of critical management studies that are basically sceptical to management, leadership and human resources management as a fundamentally substantive and 'good-doing' type of project (see, for example, Alvesson and Sveningsson 2003; 2012).

To repeat, as with all the points suggested in this chapter, we are *not* suggesting categorical position-taking but a careful consideration of a range of possibilities to be used when assessed to be appropriate in terms of empirical justification and positive intellectual effect. Strategic management may materially drive the world, it may be a key force in the exercise of power and/or the creation of wealth (and other substantive outcomes, from increased/limited local control, unemployment, increased/decreased ecological damage), but it may also be fairly marginal in these respects, and a broader study may indicate that strategy as practice is best (or, at least, well and interestingly) conceptualized as SIF or SIPP. This would necessitate avoiding the discourse narrowness of many SAP studies, risking overemphasizing the importance of managers labelling what they do as 'strategy' and/or the significance of meeting or planning activities with sometimes very limited, if any, consequences for practices outside the small rituals and ceremonies that managers engage in.

An interesting example here could be the comparison of studies by Samra-Fredericks (2005) and Foley (2010), both addressing the purchasing of a new IT system. The former does rigorous and painstaking conversation analysis of meetings, in which everything that is framed by the researcher as strategy as practice (see also Phillips and Dar 2009) is investigated in detail. It all appears rather serious. Foley (2010) refers to himself being part of a committee deciding upon the issue. After much intensive work, with the ambition of processing as much information as possible and making a rational decision, the committee members finally became overwhelmed and exhausted by all the information overload, and decided to buy the IT system sold by the most appealing and persuasive salesperson. Strategy is not even mentioned in the account.

A counter-argument to the taken-for-granted nature (among many, and influential, groups) of the importance of strategy is offered by Wallander (2003), former CEO of one of Sweden's largest banks and chairman of several large companies, and widely seen as a reflective, innovative, academically minded senior executive. He writes that visions and strategy talk in board meetings often made him feel sleepy. He generally found these abstract and disconnected from what one specifically should deal with. Rather than long-term objectives and plans, it appeared to him to be preferable just to realize that things always change and to be alert when needed. This would be in line with at least a preparedness to consider an 'anti-strategerialism' point of view and resist its colonizing effects. The task then, for CMS-informed SAP research would be to be less uptight about strategy and look at how this notion may be camouflaging things going on that are somewhat removed from what is claimed. This project could draw some inspiration from the one by Alvesson and Sveningsson (2003), published with the title 'The great disappearing act: difficulties in doing "leadership"', in which managers' claims to leadership appeared to reflect wishful thinking and (self-)impression management rather than their actual practices.

Examples of research questions would include the following.

- Do managers and executives really work with strategy in a more specific, advanced sense? Or are they mainly masquerading as being involved in strategic management? If so, at least part of the time, how is the trick done?
- In other words, how are corporate and managerial reality, full of operative, administrative, and ad hoc activities, being hidden in favour of constructions of strategy and strategizing? How are subjects dealing with all the ambiguities and contradictions involved?
- Do we need strategy and strategic management – that is, framing functions and activities in these terms – at all (in practice and as a scholarly discipline)?
- What other signifiers would be appropriate in order to make sense of the activities? What would be the consequences for the lived realities at work (for managers and non-managers) of avoiding/reducing strategy talk?

The suggested themes described above are summarized in Table 23.1.

Each of the themes described above allows for various levels of criticality; for example, a 'light' CMS approach would be to question taken-for-granted assumptions, blind spots, contradictions and so forth, while a more radical stance would be to generate completely new, alternative understandings/practices (critical performativity) in line with the emancipatory aims of the CMS tradition. This approach allows each interested SAP researcher to choose his/her critical engagement both in terms of target (the five themes) and degree of criticality and radicalism.

Of course, these themes are not mutually exclusive, nor collectively exhaustive, but our intention is not to suggest a fully coherent framework. Instead, we offer a plurality of themes for rethinking conventional strategic management as well as strategy as practice. Various themes may be more or less fruitful to investigate depending on specific empirical circumstances. Sometimes strategy does lead to substantial outcomes, sometimes little beyond managerial ritualism.

Summary

In this chapter, the task has been to scrutinize strategy as practice critically, and to suggest a more critically oriented research agenda. We have emphasized what we (and in some cases other critics before us) see as problematic features and deliberately refrained from looking at the bright side of things. We have revisited some challenges and issues that had previously been highlighted by other critics. One such issue concerns strategy as practice's relationship to mainstream, orthodox strategic management. Here we underline the importance of understanding *why* SAP researchers want to have this (regarded by some as limiting or even extra-paradigmatic) 'dialogue'. We also elaborate further on the issue of the eclectic – sometimes perhaps even 'promiscuous' and 'ornamental' (Carter, Clegg and Kornberger 2008b) – use of the grand names of social science within elements of SAP research. Besides the risk of inconsistency, fragmentation and confusion within the strategy-as-practice field, there is a risk that the grand names and theories actually will blind the researcher and – based on their influence, reach and force in terms of explanatory power – to some extent prevent new insights and theories on strategy and strategizing. There is thus a risk that future 'SAP theory' will continue to be created *outside* the SAP domain, and its often high level of abstraction might make strategy as practice's explicit ambition to have an impact on the praxis, practices and practitioners hard to live up to.

We sound a warning about the tendencies of overusing and inflating the signifier and discourse of strategy. It is often unclear how and why this term is used and whether it is the best way to frame a study. Finally, and related to this point, we also warn about what we see as tendencies of grandiosity, especially among a common object of study within strategy as practice – the 'strategists' – since doing 'strategy' or 'strategic' things provides a powerful means to increase the relative importance and status of an individual, organization or profession. Strategy as a signifier can hence be understood as a 'premium label' that affects status, prestige, power and privileges, fuelling frequent usage with increasingly stretched meanings. This is something we as scholars need to reflexively consider, rather than uncritically reproduce grandiose claims of self-appointed 'strategists' or impose the label 'strategy' on anything studied by SAP researchers. Formulas such as 'I am a SAPper and therefore what I study is strategy' or 'The people I study say that this is about strategy and therefore it is (or could/should be treated as such)' need to be questioned and problematized. A parallel would be if a power researcher or a gender researcher studied episodes of power or gendering only if the individuals concerned told the researcher that they were about power or gender. A critical exploration of claims to strategy/strategy work and the explosion of the use of the signifier would be welcome within the strategy-as-practice field.

Furthermore, we have suggested five themes for CMS-inspired SAP research. These themes range from inquiries into the power effects of strategy/strategic management to counter-assumptions on the rationality and substantiality of strategy/

strategic management and a fundamental questioning of the whole discipline – do we need strategy/strategic management at all (in practice and as a scholarly discipline)?

Finally, our judgement is that strategy as practice as a research field still has significant potential to contribute to our understanding of strategy and strategy work. The basic ambition is good, and in-depth studies are very important. The response to the challenges and research opportunities discussed above will help to specify how the field transforms itself in the next step of 'maturity'. In sum, we think that more strategy-as-practice scholars should aim (or at least hope) for a radical contribution that will affect *both* our theoretical understanding of strategy/strategy work *and* how strategy is talked about, thought about and practised 'out there'. This might imply fewer but more ambitious contributions/publications, as well as alternative publication outlets. It could also involve less conformist and more CMS-oriented research questions and lines of interpretations. Such an ambition and research orientation will – at least partly – deal with most of the issues, pitfalls and challenges we have outlined in this chapter.

References

Alvesson, M. (2008), 'The future of critical management studies', in Barry, D., and Hansen, H. (eds.), *The Sage Handbook of New Approaches in Management and Organization*: 13–30. London: Sage.

(2013), *The Triumph of Emptiness*. Oxford University Press.

Alvesson, M., Bridgman, T., and Willmott, H. (2009), 'Introduction', in *The Oxford Handbook of Critical Management Studies*: 1–26. Oxford University Press.

Alvesson, M., and Deetz, S. (2000), *Doing Critical Management Research*. London: Sage.

Alvesson, M., and Kärreman, D. (2007), 'Constructing mystery: empirical matters in theory development', *Academy of Management Review*, 32/4: 1265–81.

(2011), 'Decolonializing discourse: critical reflections on organizational discourse analysis', *Human Relations*, 64/9: 1121–46.

Alvesson, M., and Sandberg, J. (2013), *Constructing Research Questions*. London: Sage.

(2014), 'Habitat and habitus: boxed-in versus box-breaking research', *Organization Studies*, 35/7: 967–87.

Alvesson, M., and Sveningsson, S. (2003), 'The great disappearing act: difficulties in doing "leadership"', *Leadership Quarterly*, 14/3: 359–81.

(2012), 'Un- and repacking leadership: context, relations, constructions and politics', in Uhl-Bien, M., and Ospina, S. (eds.), *Advancing Relational Leadership Theory: A Conversation among Perspectives*: 203–26. New York: Information Age.

Alvesson, M., and Willmott, H. (1995), 'Strategic management as domination and emancipation: from planning to process to communication and praxis', in Shrivastava, P., and Stubbart, C. (eds.), *Advances in Strategic Management*, vol. XI: 85–112. Greenwich, CT: JAI Press.

(1996), *Making Sense of Management: A Critical Introduction*. London: Sage.

Balogun, J., Huff, A. S., and Johnson, P. (2003), 'Three responses to the methodological challenges of studying strategizing', *Journal of Management Studies*, 40/1: 197–224.

Balogun, J., and Johnson, G. (2004), 'Organizational restructuring and middle manager sensemaking', *Academy of Management Journal*, 47/4: 523–49.

(2005), 'From intended strategies to unintended outcomes: the impact of change recipient sensemaking', *Organization Studies*, 26/11: 1573–601.

Bartunek, J. M, Rynes, S. L., and Ireland, D. R. (2006), 'What makes management research interesting, and why does it matter?', *Academy of Management Journal*, 49/1: 9–15.

Bennis, W., and O'Toole, J. (2005), 'How business schools lost their way', *Harvard Business Review*, 83/5: 96–104.

Berle, A., and Means, G. C. (1932), *The Modern Corporation and Private Property*. New York: Macmillan.

Blom, M., and Alvesson, M. (2014), 'All-inclusive and all good: the hegemonic ambiguity of leadership', paper presented at thirtieth European Group for Organizational Studies colloquium, Rotterdam, 3 July.

Blom, M., and Lundgren, M. (2013), 'Strategy consultants doing strategy: how status and visibility affect strategizing', *African Journal of Business Management*, 7/14: 1144–60.

Bourdieu, P. (1977), *Outline of a Theory of Practice*. Cambridge University Press.

(1990), *The Logic of Practice*. Cambridge: Polity.

Carter, C., Clegg, S., and Kornberger, M. (2008a), 'Strategy as practice?', *Strategic Organization*, 6/1: 83–99.

(2008b), *A Very Short, Fairly Interesting and Reasonably Cheap Book about Studying Strategy*. London: Sage.

Chalmers, L. V. (2001), *Marketing Masculinities: Gender and Management Politics in Marketing Work*. Westport, CT: Greenwood Press.

Chia, R., and MacKay, B. (2007), 'Post-processual challenges for the emerging strategy-as-practice perspective: discovering strategy in the logic of practice', *Human Relations*, 60/1: 217–42.

Clark, T., and Wright, M. (2009), 'So, farewell then… Reflections on editing the Journal of Management Studies', *Journal of Management Studies*, 46/1: 1–9.

Clegg, S. (2011), 'Book review: *Cambridge Handbook of Strategy as Practice*', *Organization Studies*, 32/11: 1587–9.

Contu, A., and Willmott, H. (2005), 'You spin me around: the realist turn in organization and management studies', *Journal of Management Studies*, 42/8: 1645–62.

Courpasson, D. (2013), 'On the erosion of "passionate scholarship"', *Organization Studies*, 34/9: 1243–9.

De Certeau, M. (1984), *The Practice of Everyday Life*. Berkeley: University of California Press.

Donaldson, L., and Davis, H. L. (1991), 'Stewardship theory or agency theory: CEO governance and shareholder returns', *Australian Journal of Management*, 16/1: 49–64.

Ezzamel, M., and Willmott, H. (2004), 'Rethinking strategy: contemporary perspectives and debates', *European Management Review*, 1/1: 43–8.

(2008), 'Strategy as discourse in a global retailer: a supplement to rationalist and interpretive accounts', *Organization Studies*, 29/2: 191–217.

Fairclough, N. (2005), 'Peripheral vision: discourse analysis in organization studies: the case for critical realism', *Organization Studies*, 26/6: 915–39.

Flyvbjerg, B. (2001), *Making Social Sciences Matter: Why Social Inquiry Fails and How It Can Succeed Again*. Cambridge University Press.

Foley, M. (2010), *The Age of Absurdity*. London: Simon & Schuster.

Foucault, M. (1977), *Discipline and Punish: The Birth of the Prison*. New York: Pantheon Books.

Fournier, V., and Grey, C. (2000), 'At the critical moment: conditions and prospects for critical management studies', *Human Relations*, 53/1: 7–32.

Gabriel, Y. (2010), 'Organization studies: a space for ideas, identities and agonies', *Organization Studies*, 31/6: 757–75.

Gemmill, G., and Oakley, J. (1992), 'Leadership: an alienating social myth?', *Human Relations*, 45/2: 113–29.

Giddens, A. (1984), *The Constitution of Society*. Cambridge: Polity.

Golsorkhi, D., Rouleau, L., Seidl, D., and Vaara, E. (2010), 'Introduction: what is strategy as practice?', in *Cambridge Handbook of Strategy as Practice*: 1–20. Cambridge University Press.

Grand, S., Rüegg-Stürm, J., and von Arx, W. (2010), 'Constructivist epistemologies in strategy as practice research', in Golsorkhi, D., Rouleau, L., Seidl, D., and Vaara, E. (eds.), *Cambridge Handbook of Strategy as Practice*: 63–78. Cambridge University Press.

Habermas, J. (1972 [1968]), *Knowledge and Human Interests*. New York: Beacon Press.

Hardy, C., and Thomas, R. (2014), 'Strategy, discourse and practice: the intensification of power', *Journal of Management Studies*, 51/2: 320–48.

Headland, T., Pike, K., and Harris, M. (eds.) (1990), *Emics and Etics: The Insider/Outsider Debate*. Newbury Park, CA: Sage

Hendry, J. (2000), 'Strategic decision making, discourse, and strategy as social practice', *Journal of Management Studies*, 37/7: 955–77.

Hendry, J., and Seidl, D. (2003), 'The structure and significance of strategic episodes: social systems theory and the routine practices of strategic change', *Journal of Management Studies*, 40/1: 175–96.

Jarzabkowski, P. (2003), 'Strategic practices: an activity theory perspective on continuity and change', *Journal of Management Studies*, 40/1: 23–55.

(2004), 'Strategy as practice: recursiveness, adaptation, and practices-in-use', *Organization Studies*, 25/4: 529–60.

(2005), *Strategy as Practice: An Activity-Based Approach*. London: Sage.

Jarzabkowski, P., Balogun, J., and Seidl, D. (2007), 'Strategizing: the challenges of a practice perspective', *Human Relations*, 60/1: 5–27.

Jarzabkowski, P., and Seidl, D. (2008), 'The role of meetings in the social practice of strategy', *Organization Studies*, 29/11: 1391–426.

Jarzabkowski, P., and Spee, P. (2009), 'Strategy-as-practice: a review and future directions for the field', *International Journal of Management Reviews*, 11/1: 69–95.

Jefferson, G. (1984), 'On stepwise transition from talk about a trouble to inappropriately next-positioned matters', in Atkinson, J. M., and Heritage, J. (eds.), *Structures of Social Action: Studies of Conversation Analysis*: 191–222. Cambridge University Press.

Johnson, P., Balogun, J., and Beech, N. (2010), 'Researching strategists and their identity in practice: building "close-with" relationships', in Golsorkhi, D., Rouleau, L., Seidl, D., and Vaara, E. (eds.), *Cambridge Handbook of Strategy as Practice*: 243–57. Cambridge University Press.

Johnson, G., Langley, A., Melin, L., and Whittington, R. (2007), *Strategy as Practice: Research Directions and Resources*. Cambridge University Press.

Johnson, G., Melin, L., and Whittington, R. (2003), 'Guest editor's introduction: micro strategy and strategizing: towards an activity-based view', *Journal of Management Studies*, 40/1: 3–22.

Jones, C. (2009), 'Poststructuralism in critical management studies', in Alvesson, M., Bridgman, T., and Willmott, H. (eds.), *The Oxford Handbook of Critical Management Studies*: 76–98. Oxford University Press.

Kärreman, D., and Alvesson, M. (2001), 'Making newsmakers: conversational identity at work', *Organization Studies*, 22/1: 59–89.

Knights, D., and Morgan, G. (1990), 'The concept of strategy in sociology: a note of dissent', *Sociology*, 24/3: 475–83.

(1991), 'Corporate strategy, organizations, and subjectivity: a critique', *Organization Studies*, 12/2: 251–73.

(1995), 'Strategy under the microscope: strategic management and IT in financial services', *Journal of Management Studies*, 32/2: 191–214.

Laine, P.-M., and Vaara, E. (2007), 'Struggling over subjectivity: a discursive analysis of strategic development in an engineering group', *Human Relations*, 60/1: 29–58.

Levy, D., Alvesson, M., and Willmott, H. (2003), 'Critical approaches to strategic management', in Alvesson, M., and Willmott, H. (eds.), *Studying Management Critically*: 92–111. London: Sage.

Mace, M. L. (1971), *Directors: Myth and Reality*. Cambridge, MA: Harvard University Press.

Mantere, S., and Vaara, E. (2008), 'On the problem of participation in strategy: a critical discourse perspective', *Organization Science*, 19/2: 341–58.

March, J. (2005), 'Parochialism in the evolution of a research community: the case of organization studies', *Management and Organization Review*, 1/1: 5–22.

McCabe, D. (2010), 'Strategy-as-power: ambiguity, contradiction and the exercise of power in a UK building society', *Organization*, 17/2: 151–75.

Mintzberg, H. (1973), *The Nature of Managerial Work*. New York: Harper & Row.

 (1985), 'The organization as a political arena', *Journal of Management Studies*, 22/2: 133–54.

 (2004), *Managers Not MBAs: A Hard Look at the Soft Practice of Managing and Management Development*. San Francisco: Berrett-Koehler.

Mintzberg, H., and Waters, J. A. (1985), 'Of strategies, deliberate and emergent', *Strategic Management Journal*, 6/3: 257–72.

Newton, T. (2009), 'Organizations and the natural environment', in Alvesson, M., Bridgman, T., and Willmott, H. (eds.), *The Oxford Handbook of Critical Management Studies*: 125–43. Oxford University Press.

Oswick, C., Fleming, P., and Hanlon, G. (2011), 'From borrowing to blending: rethinking the processes of organizational theory building', *Academy of Management Review*, 36/2: 318–37.

Pettigrew, A. M. (1973), *The Politics of Organizational Decision-Making*. London: Tavistock.

 (1977), 'Strategy formulation as a political process', *International Studies in Management and Organization*, 7/2: 78–87.

Pfeffer, J. (1992), 'Understanding power in organizations', *California Management Review*, 35/1: 29–50.

Pfeffer, J., and Salancik, G. (1978), *The External Control of Organizations: A Resource Dependence Perspective*. New York: Harper & Row.

Phillips, N., and Dar, S. (2009), 'Strategy', in Alvesson, M., Bridgman, T., and Willmott, H. (eds.), *The Oxford Handbook of Critical Management Studies*: 414–32. Oxford University Press.

Pondy, L. (1978), 'Leadership as a language game', in McCall, J., and Lombardo, M. (eds.), *Leadership: Where Else Can We Go?*: 87–99. Durham, NC: Duke University Press.

Reed, M. (2009), 'Critical realism in critical management studies', in Alvesson, M., Bridgman, T., and Willmott, H. (eds.), *The Oxford Handbook*

of Critical Management Studies: 52–75. Oxford University Press.

Regnér, P. (2008), 'Strategy-as-practice and dynamic capabilities: steps towards a dynamic view of strategy', *Human Relations*, 61/4: 565–88.

 (2011), 'Book review: *Cambridge Handbook of Strategy as Practice*', *M@n@gement*, 14/2: 157–76.

Rouleau, L. (2005), 'Micro-practices of strategic sensemaking and sensegiving: how middle managers interpret and sell change every day', *Journal of Management Studies*, 42/7: 1413–41.

 (2013), 'Strategy-as-practice at a crossroads', *M@n@gement*, 16/5: 547–65.

Samra-Fredericks, D. (2003), 'Strategizing as lived experience and strategists' everyday efforts to shape strategic direction', *Journal of Management Studies*, 40/1: 141–74.

 (2005), 'Strategic practice, "discourse" and the everyday interactional constitution of "power effects"', *Organization*, 12/6: 803–41.

 (2010, 'Researching everyday practice: the ethnomethodological contribution', in Golsorkhi, D., Rouleau, L., Seidl, D., and Vaara, E. (eds.), *Cambridge Handbook of Strategy as Practice*: 79–90. Cambridge University Press.

Schatzki, T. R., Knorr Cetina, K., and von Savigny, E. (eds.) (2001), *The Practice Turn in Contemporary Theory*. London: Routledge.

Shrivastava, P. (1986), 'Is strategic management ideological?', *Journal of Management*, 12/3: 363–77.

Spicer, A., Alvesson, M., and Kärreman, D. (2009), 'Critical performativity: the unfinished business of critical management studies', *Human Relations*, 62/4: 537–60.

Thomas, R., Sargent, L., and Hardy, C. (2011), 'Managing organizational change: negotiating meaning and power–resistance relations', *Organization Science*, 22/1: 22–41.

Tricker, B. (2012), *Corporate Governance: Principles, Policies, and Practices*. Oxford University Press.

Venkateswaran, R., and Prabhu, G. (2010), 'Taking stock of research methods in strategy-as-practice', *Electronic Journal of Business Research Methods*, 8/2: 156–62.

Wallander, J. (2003), *Decentralisation – Why and How to Make It Work: The Handelsbanken Case*. Stockholm: SNS.

Whittington, R. (1996), 'Strategy as practice', *Long Range Planning*, 29/5: 731–5.

(2004), 'Strategy after modernism: recovering practice', *European Management Review*, 1/1: 62–8.

(2006), 'Completing the practice turn in strategy research', *Organization Studies*, 27/5: 613–34.

(2007), 'Strategy practice and strategy process: family differences and the sociological eye', *Organizational Studies*, 28/10: 1575–86.

Whittington, R., and Vaara, E. (2012), 'Strategy-as-practice: taking social practices seriously', *Academy of Management Annals*, 6/1: 285–336.

Wickert, C., and Schaefer, S. (2015), 'Towards a progressive understanding of performativity in critical management studies', *Human Relations*, 68/1: 107–30.

PART IV

Methodological Resources

Using ethnography in strategy-as-practice research

ANN L. CUNLIFFE

Introduction

When we think of ethnography we surely go back to those classic organizational ethnographies, which generated rich, in-depth and fascinating insights into various aspects of organizational life: Elton Mayo's famous Hawthorne studies (Roethlisberger and Dickson 1956); Melville Dalton's (1959) study of power and politics in management, which he observed while working as a manager in a US factory; Elliot Jacques' (1951) collaborative field study of worker and management relationships, with a research team of eight people at the UK Glacier Metal Company; Trist and Bamforth's (1951) two-year study of the longwall coal mining method technology, social organization, work conditions and group processes (Bamforth himself had been a miner); Walker and Guest's (1952) study of assembly line work; and W. F. Whyte's (1948) study of interactions and work practices in a Chicago restaurant.

More recently, who can forget that John Van Maanen's (1991) study of Disneyland's organization culture and work practices ended when he was fired for a 'Mickey Mouse offense' (his hair was too long) after three years working as a ride operator? Or the subtle challenge to the control and authority of a director in Tony Watson's (1994) ethnography of management in a UK plant, as executives rearranged their seating so that the director was unable to sit in his 'normal' seat? And Bud Goodall's (2005) poignant comment in his narrative ethnography of his discovery that his father, unknown to Bud, had been a CIA agent: 'A narrative inheritance touches everything, one way or another, in our lives' (Goodall 2005: 503). He also makes the observation that stories from the past not only help us explain stories of the present but that embedded in such stories are

dialectical tensions of identity, relationships and culture.

Such rich stories and detailed observations are the stuff of ethnography. 'Ethnographers describe, principally in writing, how the people of some place and time perceive the world and how they act in it' (Ingold 2008: 90), and they do so on the basis of prolonged immersion in a research site, getting to know people and how they live their lives. It is not just description, though; there is, of course, a purpose: by examining often taken-for-granted practices and perceptions, we can discover new and often unanticipated processes and relationships and offer theoretical insights into the situations under study (for example, culture, strategy, work practices, identity, etc.). 'What you see when you read a good ethnography is a text carefully dotted through with interpretive insights about organizational life, the ethnographer's and participants' ways of sense making that connect with the reader and cause him or her to "see differently"' (Cunliffe 2010: 229).

Ethnography therefore resonates strongly with strategy as practice, which is based on the assumption that strategy is an everyday social practice that is carried out by people in their actions, interactions, texts and conversations. Indeed, Balogan, Huff and Johnson (2003: 197) argue that we need to 'understand how everyday behavior in organizations creates strategic choices and consequences', on micro levels as well as macro levels of analysis. While they do not advocate ethnography especially, they do advocate research designs that focus on 'deep data-gathering', variety, context and longitudinal studies – which is the stuff of ethnography. In addition, if we take Whittington's (2006) conceptualization of strategy as practice as exploring the relationship between the macro and micro levels of organization and between practice, practitioners and praxis, then the connections between strategy as practice and ethnography come sharply into focus – as does the value of an ethnographic methodology to strategy-as-practice researchers. Ethnographers and SAP scholars are concerned alike with these relationships, as well as with emerging actions and interactions, sensemaking, stakeholder perceptions and/or multiple interpretations, thoughts and interpretations, the interplay of social and material, thick versus thin description, relevance and so on. As Rasche and Chia (2009: 726) argue, strategy-as-practice scholars need to utilize ethnographic approaches 'not merely as an interpreter of actor meanings and intentions but [to be] highly attuned to the minute, often unnoticed and seemingly insignificant, moves, mannerisms and dispositions of the strategist him- or her-self'. In other words, ethnography connects with practice through its emphasis on particularizing data by noticing details of interactions, actions and conversations – as in the examples at the beginning of the chapter – and, to notice such detail, we need to gather first-hand experiential data.

Given these connections, what possibilities does ethnography offer to strategy-as-practice researchers? In order to answer this question, I will give a brief overview of key considerations in ethnography. In doing so, I note relevant ethnographic studies that are illustrative and may be of interest. I then address an issue that I believe is an important precursor to any form of research, ethnographic or otherwise – that is, understanding the ontology underpinning our work and its influence on our research practice. I frame these issues in relation to our understanding and study of practice.

Key considerations in ethnography

It is not my intention in this chapter to give a historical overview of ethnography; this has been done elsewhere (see Cunliffe 2010; Locke 2011; Zicker and Carter 2010). Instead, I begin by focusing on some key considerations in ethnography in relation to its potential for research in the strategy-as-practice field.

Ethnography as methodology

Ethnography, I suggest, is a methodology, not a method. Broadly speaking, methodology relates to the choices made about how to carry out research: the knowledge paradigm and practices that underpin the study, the research site, how the researcher will engage (or not) with respondents, what constitutes 'data', and how they will be collected and analysed. Methods, as we will see in the following section, are the techniques by which data are collected and analysed. What, then are the key characteristics of this methodology?

My first brush with ethnography (although I didn't realize it at the time) was US sociologist Donald Roy's (1959) *Banana Time*. Roy had worked in a New York garment factory, studying how a group of operatives who were isolated from other employees and engaged in routine work 'toughed out' a twelve-hour day, six days a week. I recall being fascinated by the social processes Roy observed, the (ironically!) ritualistic conversational themes and activities that operatives engaged in throughout the day to deal with the monotony of their work. For example, every day Ike stole and ate Sammy's banana – hence 'banana time' – and yet, every day, Sammy still brought in a banana. His main conclusion was that such regularized informal interactions in a group's subculture were a big source of job satisfaction. His story and detailed examples make the concepts come alive for the reader.

Roy's study is typical of the ethnographic methodology of the 1950s that was based on the Chicago school, a group of sociologists including Whyte, Goffman and Becker who studied the everyday interactions in urban life using ethnography. These scholars emphasized that fieldwork, participant observation and native interpretations were crucial to understanding the empirical world (Becker, Hughes and Strauss 1961; Blumer 1954). Only by studying people in their everyday activities can we grasp the complexity, intricacy and mundanity (commonplace activities) of organizational life (see Atkinson *et al.* 2007; Ybema *et al.* 2009). The focus is therefore very much on practical activities, interactions and practices, and it is this that makes it of particular relevance to studies of strategy in practice.

Broadly speaking, ethnographies are about the following (Cunliffe 2010).

- *Culture:* situated interactions, cultural artefacts, symbols, stories and texts.
- *Context and temporality*: studying people in their naturally occurring settings and over a period of time to discover how meanings, actions, practices, organizing, etc., emerge. Samra-Fredericks' (2003) ethnographic study of senior managers and directors in a manufacturing organization not only vividly drew attention to the need to study strategizing as lived experience in a particular context, it also highlighted the value of ethnography in exploring a fine-grained analysis of how – in this context – one strategist was able to shape strategic direction through his relational-rhetorical skill.
- *Sociality and meanings:* how people live their lives, do their work and interact with others – that is, relationships between people, groups, context and culture. Rouleau and Balogun (2011) emphasize the importance of understanding the interrelated nature of the relational, political and discursive dimensions of strategic sensemaking and change – and it is here that ethnographic studies could enhance current work by providing in-depth data of the micro-practices involved in sensemaking and strategic influencing.
- *Thick description* (Geertz 1973): detailed descriptions and interpretations of local understandings, as opposed to 'thin' descriptions, incorporating generalized findings, factual statements and coded or statistical data. Watson (2011) argues that, despite the fact that ethnography requires researchers to gain a high level of access, spend long hours in the field and be emotionally resilient, it is essential to the strategy-as-practice research agenda because it helps us get close to the work, interactions, actions and identities of strategists in particular organizations.

As these characteristics imply, most ethnographies focus on a single site or organization as a means of capturing micro-practices, and this is both a strength and a foundation for one of the main criticisms of ethnography: how can insights from a single site be generalized across, and made relevant to, other contexts? I explore this issue below.

The logic of ethnography

> What I heard at first, before I started to listen, was a stream of disconnected bits of communication which did not make much sense... What I saw at first, before I began to observe, was occasional flurries of horseplay...
>
> Roy (1959: 161)

In contrast to positivism's logic of validation, which is based on a hypothetico-deductive methodology in which theory generates hypotheses that are then tested through data, ethnography utilizes a logic of discovery (Locke 2011). A logic of discovery means carrying out research without preconceived models or frameworks, and being open to any surprises we may experience in the field and working with them to develop new ideas, concepts and/or explanations (Agar 2010). What does 'being open to surprise' mean, though? Roy's comment above highlights an important element; it means that ethnographers first notice occurrences and comments without an immediate evaluation (Kostera 2007): looking at the details, noticing what goes on around us in an unmediated and unfiltered way. Thus, ethnographers record what at first may seem unimportant and without reason, with the idea that, over time, meanings may become clearer, connections and interpretations made, as we get a better sense of the whole context. This is a fundamental characteristic of the logic of discovery. In her ethnographic study of how cognitive frames influence strategy-making in a communications technology firm, Kaplan (2008) looked specifically for surprises or 'breakdowns' using observation, interviews and documents.

Within this logic, ethnographic work is often based on abduction (Van Maanen, Sorensen and Mitchell 2007) rather than deduction (testing theory) and induction (generalizing theory from data). Abduction focuses on the interplay of experience, literature and ideas to generate new understandings and insights about the specific practices under study. Ethnographers do not begin with a specific theory or plan that they apply; rather, they begin with the questions 'How do

I start to study this issue?', 'Who do I speak with next?' and 'What do I do next?' (Agar 2010). In other words, they are open to the 'new or unacknowledged behaviors and processes that have important implications for organizational life' (Locke 2011: 614), and search a repertoire of theories to explain them. In doing so, they play data through theories and theories through data to form new interpretations. Abduction therefore offers a useful way of generating theory for strategy-as-practice scholars because it offers a way of addressing Whittington's (2006) call to examine the relationship between practitioners, practice and praxis.

In answering Agar's questions, it is often helpful to think about your 'sampling strategy'. Tracy (2013: 136–7) identifies at least three strategies:

> Typical instances – the selection of people and events representative of normal practices and processes. This has the advantage of giving a sense of 'normal' practices and behaviours, but may mean that the researcher does not consider the surprises or breakdowns that can lead to learning and change.
>
> Maximum variation and extreme instances – where a researcher talks to people with differing positions and views, and/or attends unique events to develop alternative perspectives and new insights. Examples might include studying employees who criticize or refuse to adopt a strategic initiative or how managers deal with a strategic crisis. This form of sampling can lead to the discovery of data that challenges existing theories.
>
> Critical instance – the selection of key events and/or problems that have an practical impact in some way. The identification of critical incidents may not lead to information about the norm, but can help illustrate activities that are important and how such events are dealt with.

Within these approaches an ethnographer might also use snowball sampling, whereby he/she talks to new people on the basis of recommendations from existing research participants. While this can maximize access, it also needs to be monitored to ensure that an unintended outcome is not an unrepresentative sample of close colleagues but, rather, that the study comprises a diverse sample of participants.

Positioning the ethnographer

A key consideration in ethnographic work is the relationship between the ethnographer and other research participants. As already noted, in contrast to positivist methodologies, in which the researcher is the neutral expert observer, the Chicago school advocates participant observation, in which ethnographers work in the context they are studying, observing and getting to know their respondents. While this allows for in-depth first-hand experience, it can lead to complications, some of which, as Roy found, are physical. As he noted, 'Before the end of the first day, Monotony was joined by his twin brother, Fatigue. I got tired. My legs ached, and my feet hurt. Early in the afternoon I discovered a tall stool and moved it up to my machine to "take a load off my feet." But the superintendent dropped in to see how I was "doing" and promptly informed me that "we don't sit down on this job"' (Roy 1959: 160). In this example, the researcher's experience itself provides data about organizational practices!

The ethnographer may also face emotional challenges. Butcher (2013) struggled with emotional attachment and a 'longing to belong' to the group of machine shop workers he was studying, having been an apprentice engineer in a similar organization, only to find that he belonged *to* the group as a guest, but was never *in* the group. Deep engagement with our research participants means we can run the risk of becoming too involved beyond our role. I am reminded of Russell's (2005) agonizing decision about whether to continue to support a very troubled student as she was leaving her field research in a school.

In contrast, Goodall positioned himself and his experience as the source of data and insights. His *narrative ethnography* consists of 'narratives shaped out of a writer's personal experiences within a culture and addressed to academic and public audiences' (Goodall 2000: 9). He argues that personal stories are also collective stories because we live and work in a dialectical relationship with our social, cultural, historical and linguistic circumstances, commenting that narrative ethnographers are 'never not working'.[1] Narrative ethnography is

---

[1] See www.hlgoodall.com (accessed 26 August 2013).

a form of auto-ethnography that requires careful crafting to bring out the broader relevance.

In positioning themselves in their research, ethnographers inevitably have to think about their relationships with people in the research site – relationships that may shift across time as they encounter different people and situations. Based on her fieldwork experience, Geetha Karunanayake and I have proposed four "hyphen-spaces"[2] of ethnographer–research participant relationships (Cunliffe and Karunanayake 2013).

Insider–outsiderness Is the ethnographer native to the organization and does he/she have an ongoing role there? An instance of insiderness might be a strategist writing about his/her experiences, incorporating literature and theoretical observations in the account.

Sameness–difference Is the ethnographer similar to members of the organization in terms of gender, ethnicity, cultural values, language, etc.?

Engagement–distance Is the ethnographer engaged with participants in their activities and are participants actively engaged in the research process? An engaged relationship occurs when researchers and strategists partner to co-produce research and, possibly, changes in practice.

Political activism–active neutrality To what extent is the ethnographer involved in participant agendas for action and change?

These relationships influence, and are influenced by, the methodology and knowledge paradigm or problematic we work from, and may need to be reassessed and renegotiated. As ethnographers and researchers studying practice, we also need to be reflexively aware of the potential ethical and identity-related tensions and dilemmas that may emerge in these spaces for both ourselves and our research participants. For example, if we see or experience bullying or illegal activities during our fieldwork, do we have a responsibility to act? It is

also important to consider what impact our presence in the field may have for our research participants – on their relationships and position, or the attitudes of colleagues in their organization. In their account of research co-produced between academic and practitioner, Orr and Bennett (2012: 434) talk about Bennett's research being 'a source of baffled amusement' to a practitioner colleague.

Methods to generate thick descriptions

As previously stated, methods are the techniques by which data are collected and analysed, and it is important to note that the methods used should be consistent with the research questions and the type of data that need to be collected to answer these questions. Within ethnography a range of methods are often used in order to obtain data that provide an in-depth understanding, and possibly multiple interpretations (see below), of lived experience. Methods include: participant observation, text and discourse analysis, conversation analysis, grounded theory, narrative analysis (see, for example, Fenton and Langley 2011), interviews (structured to unstructured), informal conversations, observation and/or recording of meetings and activities, shadowing (see Czarniawka 2007), film (for example, Erkama and Vaara 2010), diary studies and action research (see Heron and Reason 2006). We will look at examples of studies using such methods from different knowledge paradigms or problematics in the following section. In addition, Part IV of the handbook incorporates a range of methods, many of which are relevant to ethnography. Here I point to two examples of studies that use different methods to generate thick descriptions of experience. The first illustrates the range of methods that can be used within an ethnographic study. The second utilizes the rather unusual method of a storytelling workshop.

Fauré and Rouleau's (2011) ethnographic study exploring how accountants and middle managers enact their knowledge of strategy in their conversations around numbers used in-depth interviews, observations of meetings, site visits and daily activities, and external and internal company documents as sources of data. The use of a range of

---

[2] 'Hyphen-spaces' emphasize the emergent, multiple and agentic spaces of possibility created in the relationships between researchers and research participants. In such spaces, influence is mutual, multiple meanings are articulated and identities are worked out in different ways.

methods is important in gathering data about how accountants and managers negotiated and achieved a mutual understanding in their daily activities. Fauré and Rouleau analyse the data using a form of conversation analysis and document analysis. In doing so, they are examining how respondents performed 'strategic competence'.

Based on a phenomenological narrative approach, Küpers, Mantere and Statler (2013) utilized a storytelling workshop they designed for members of an organization. During the workshop they asked participants to tell stories of the company's strategy around the narrative genres of comic, tragic and epic. From this they identify three storytelling practices: struggling for ownership, desacralizing strategy and a ritual of self-sacrifice. Although this is not part of an ethnographic study, storytelling workshops could well be used as a method within strategy-as-practice research, especially if the purpose of the research involves impact and organizational change. This example also illustrates the importance of context in ethnographic research – that stories and practices change both within and across different organizations.

To summarize, given the focus of SAP researchers on *how* and *why* strategy comes into being or is performed, then the methods used need to capture not just observable micro-practices but the tacit knowledge held by strategists that may influence their actions. This means engaging in longitudinal, in-depth fieldwork and using multiple methods and forms of data collection to gather the particularized and comprehensive details required for a thick description of practice. This approach to fieldwork is also necessary in gathering data to illustrate and explain the emergent and fluid nature of strategy-making – explanations that quick snapshot surveys or interviews do not provide.

The use of different methods and data sources provides a means of exploring the multiple perspectives often embedded in lived experience. In-depth interviews and practitioner diaries can be a way of surfacing espoused theories, differing views and the intentions of practitioners. Observations and recordings of meetings and everyday conversations can help identify 'theories-in-use' (Argyris and Schön 1974); the communicative

and interactional practices used in creating meaning; and the tacit knowledge held by practitioners, which may be seen in their actions yet remains unarticulated. Text and discourse analytic methods offer a way of connecting and exploring how 'formalized' products such as strategic plans emerge from, and are enacted in, everyday micro-practices.

Theorizing: connections and possibilities

An important methodological issue in ethnography is how 'to systematize the procedure by which we move from an appreciation of ethnographic detail to concepts useful in addressing problems' (Becker 1963: 191). Theorizing from extensive and multiple sources of data is not easy and, of course, depends on what we see as 'good theory'. Van Maanen, Sorensen and Mitchell (2007) argue that our understanding of what theory is is not well defined or commonly understood. What is theory? Theory could be a guess, conjecture, hypothesis, proposition and/or a model. It is also seen as a law, the relationship between variables and an account of a social process. I argue later that how we define theory depends on the problematic we work from, but here I address some general issues in theorizing from ethnographic data.

Deductive theorizing is rare in ethnographic work; inductive and abductive theorizing is more prevalent. As such, there is less emphasis on the linear relationships and causal mechanisms of positivist theory and more on 'narrative reasoning' (Ashkanasy 2013) or 'imaginative understandings' (Charmaz 2007), aiming to show patterns and broad connections. Charmaz (2007: 135, emphasis in original), although talking specifically about grounded theory, highlights what I believe to be integral in theorizing practice from ethnographic data when she writes about '*seeing* possibilities, *establishing* connections, and *asking* questions'.

Theorizing based on induction often follows a bottom-up (theorizing from data) rather than a top-down (theorizing from the literature) approach, although Shepherd and Sutcliffe (2011) do propose an inductive top-down form. Inductive theorizing involves a process of coding, categorizing or identifying themes in the data, developing claims based on these and then turning the claims into concepts by comparing them with existing theories (see Tracy 2013). In their study of how ambiguity occurs during multiple strategizing activities, while using a longitudinal case study method rather than ethnography, Aggerholm, Asmuß and Thomsen (2012) show how actors' multiple meanings around a strategic theme turn into a strategy document, which is then translated and interpreted in different ways. They follow a bottom-up approach, collecting data through participant observation, video recordings and interviews, and then thematically analyse and code the content as a means of theorizing the strategy process as three 'situated contexts': authoring comes first, followed by a translation phase and an interpretation phase. In this inductive process, *theoretical sensitivity* (Glaser 1978) is an important feature: developing the insight to recognize and understand what is important in the field. Generally speaking, this means immersing oneself in the data and being open to what respondents find meaningful and significant.

Abduction is often seen as the heart of ethnography, especially in disciplines such as anthropology and sociology (Agar 2010). It is neither a bottom-up nor a top-down way of theorizing but a way of connecting context, meaning and everyday practices with existing and new ideas. It involves developing new ideas, theories, explanations and solutions from the close examination of a particular context or case, but in a suppositional way, in the sense that these are 'theories' about what is possible, not about what is representational or predictive (Locke, Golden-Biddle and Feldman 2008). Vaara, Sorsa and Pälli's (2010) critical discourse analysis of the official strategic plan in a Finnish city uses an abductive approach, going 'back and forth between our theoretical ideas and empirical analyses to create an increasingly elaborate understanding of the various discursive features that seemed to explain the power effects of the strategic plan' (Vaara, Sorsa and Pälli's 2010: 690). This process of theorizing involves making connections and using our imagination to develop possible explanations.

Generalizability – or writing 'convincing' ethnographic accounts

A perennial criticism of ethnography is that it is dependent on the ethnographer – his/her theories, perceptions and biases. Consequently, ethnographies are not replicable or generalizable, because not only will different ethnographers see the same context in different ways but the details are particular to the context. This criticism could also be extended to the study of strategic practice within a particular organizational context. In this section I offer four ways of addressing 'generalizability' within ethnographic research.

First, it is important to note that ethnographers think about 'generalization' in a different way from positivist and 'scientific' researchers. Whereas, with the latter, generalization is typically seen as being *across* contexts and case, within ethnography generalizations are made *within* contexts (Tracy 2010). Generalizing within contexts can be seen in two ways: (1) that instances and small details, such as the specific strategic practices of managers within one organization, can be placed in relation to broader theories and concepts; and (2) specific practices from one group of strategists may *resonate* with strategists in other organizations. Thus, for ethnographers, the purpose is not to develop abstract theoretical generalizations but to create insights from within a context that resonate in other contexts – both practical and theoretical. So, for example, the 'strategic micropractices of calculation' identified by Fauré and Rouleau (2011) as being used in a French construction company could well resonate with accountants and middle managers in other companies, and they connect their notion of strategic competence with broader concepts such as structuration theory and pedagogic action. In this way, theory and practice can both be enhanced.

Another way of addressing generalizability is critical cultural anthropologist George Marcus's (1995) idea of multi-sited or mobile ethnographies – 'multiple sites of observation and participation that cross-cut dichotomies such as the local and the global' (Marcus 1995: 95). A multi-sited research methodology examines the flow of meanings, discourses and narratives; the formation and relationships in and between cultural logics, economies and practices; and systemic forms of domination and resistance, within and across sites. An example of when a multi-sited ethnography would be particularly appropriate would be when studies of environmental sustainability are involved. Multi-sited ethnography is not just about things being understood similarly or differently across different sites (Neyland 2008); it is also about following something – a practice or process – across time and space: 'Strategies of quite literally following connections, associations, and putative relationships are thus at the very heart of designing multi-sited ethnographic research' (Marcus 1995: 97). Such connections may relate to participants, an object (text), a discourse or metaphor, plots and stories, a life/biography and even a conflict about particular issues. Orr's (1996) study of Xerox technicians is one such example; he followed the technicians as they visited various clients in different organizations. Another is Hannerz's (2003) following of foreign news correspondents as they travelled continents to report news – examining translocal issues of collaboration and competition; how news moved between agencies, electronically and in print; and relationships between correspondents and editors back home. Multi-sited ethnography could be used by strategy-as-practice researchers in different ways, such as to follow a strategist as he/she moves around an organization in an effort to develop support for a strategic initiative or shape his/her identity as a strategist.

Marcus (1995) argues that multi-sited research tests the limits of ethnography because it is about connecting local knowledges with 'world systems' – which are *not* portrayed as total, fixed representations but, instead, mapped as emerging relationships between sites. Peltonen (2007) suggests that one area of study that lends itself to multi-sited ethnography is international management. In his study of the lived experience of middle managers in MNCs, he connects their individual experiences of restructuring, mobile careers, family stress, being on call twenty-four hours a day, etc. with the macro-level market-driven characteristics of global capitalism – that is, the 'human consequences of global capitalism' (Peltonen 2007: 355). In doing so, he offers a way of linking local and global practices. Such an approach could be used to study strategic practice in multinational organizations.

Another way of linking micro and macro and the local with the global within multi-sited ethnography is Davide Nicolini's (2009) double movement of 'zooming in' and 'zooming out' on practice. This requires the use of various theoretical lenses and perspectives (zooming in), then zooming out to follow the connections between the practice being studied and the broader practices in which they are situated, or the translocal effects of the immediate practice – for example, historical, cultural and structural practices and changes. In this way, we begin to understand the societal/ organizational effects of situated practices – and vice versa. Zooming 'in' and 'out' therefore offers a way of studying the relationship between practices and strategy-making in one organization and how this might relate to broader professional, industry or cultural practices.

Finally, in a now classic article, Karen Golden-Biddle and Karen Locke (1993) argue that, in ethnographic work, the question is not how results from an ethnographic study of one research site can be generalized to others but how ethnographers can convince readers that their work is credible and rigorous. They argue that ethnographic texts 'convince' if they meet the following three criteria.

(1) *Authenticity:* this shows that the ethnographer has been there and grasped the 'life world' of participants. Research accounts can convey the vitality and detail of everyday life by gathering and analysing data in a disciplined way. In a strategy-as-practice context, this means using the language that strategists use and being able to describe and explain their actions, conversations and relationships in ways that show the ethnographer understands the context in which they are spoken and their impact. It may also mean using multiple methods of data collection. In Vaara, Sorsa and Pälli's (2010) ethnographic study of strategic planning in a Finnish city, they drew on thematic interviews, media texts, individual diaries and e-mails to carry out a critical discourse analysis of the city's strategic plan. This enabled them to give

specific quotes, examples and details to illustrate the power of strategy documents. Other indicators of authenticity may be images and visual examples (videos, photographs, etc.).

(2) *Plausibility:* The story makes sense, the connection between the descriptive and conceptual is explained, potentially problematic assertions are made sensible and a distinctive contribution is made. As a result, the practices identified are connected to theories in a meaningful and persuasive way. Samra-Fredericks (2003) carefully situates her analysis of the real-time interactions of strategists in an ethnomethodological perspective by identifying the 'mundane knowledge' and 'reasoning procedures' they used. Her fine-gained analysis connects the specific comments of strategists with six features of talk that draw on linguistic, conversation and rhetorical traditions; the analysis of the empirical data is consistent with the philosophical and theoretical position taken. This coherent story, supported by evidence, enables her to achieve her goal of drawing attention to the need to study strategic practice 'as lived'.

(3) *Criticality:* the text causes the reader to question taken-for-granted assumptions, through form and rhetorical style. A number of the texts cited in the introduction to this chapter exemplify this aspect. A more contemporary study by Watson (2009) is thought-provoking in using a manager's autobiography to connect his personal identity work with broader historical, cultural and social issues. The rhetorical style of the paper, along with its content, captures attention and causes the reader to think about identity differently.

These are useful guidelines for writing and for justifying ethnographic accounts, and they make sense given that ethnographies are about rich, thick descriptions and interpretations of processes, practices or phenomena situated in particular contexts. In other words, the key question is not 'Is this work generalizable?' but 'Do the insights generated in this context resonate in other contexts?'.

Having given an overview of key considerations in ethnography, I now address some deeper fundamental issues relating to the knowledge paradigms or problematics underpinning research, with specific reference to the study of practice. Understanding how the knowledge problematic we work from influences our research design is important in ensuring that we engage in consistent and rigorous research. In doing so, I refer to illustrative studies from the strategy-as-practice field.

The ontology of practice and implications for ethnography

'Practice' is a construct or a lens through which we study everyday life, and, as such, its meaning is contested (Geiger 2009). I want to suggest that what we see as practice and how we study practices depends on our ontological assumptions. This means asking fundamental ontological and epistemological questions prior to research.

- What is the ontological nature of practice?
- What does 'good' knowledge about practice look like?
- What are the implications for research design?
- Practice is for whom and by whom?

Elsewhere (Cunliffe 2011), in trying to answer these questions from a general organization studies perspective, I have articulated three knowledge problematics that underpin our research: objectivism, subjectivism and intersubjectivism. Each problematic is based on ontological and epistemological assumptions that each have their own internal logic that influences how we view our topic of research, what we see as 'data', how we collect, interpret and theorize from these data and how we write our research accounts. I briefly outline each problematic in Table 24.1 before going on to examine the implications for studying practice.

Studying practice from the objectivist problematic

For researchers working within an objectivist problematic, practice is an object of study – a phenomenon that can be observed and understood from outside the practice. The characteristics of a practice and/or process, routines, norms, stages and types are identified to form the basis of a factual

Table 24.1 Three problematics

	Objectivism	Subjectivism	Intersubjectivism
Ontology	A real concrete social reality existing independently from us. Humans as socialized into that reality.	Realities socially constructed in the interactions, discursive practices, language use and conversations of people. Humans as actors and interpreters, shaping and shaped by understandings of 'realities'.	Shared, unique and contested understandings of social 'realities' created between people in and across moments of time and space. Humans embedded in relationships with others at many levels.
Epistemology	Search for structures, laws, systems, rules, behavioural patterns, categories, processes, roles, generalized identities and relationships between elements.	Knowledge and knowing occurring in the mundane and indexical activities of people.	A knowing in situ from within the moment of interaction and conversation. Meanings and understanding created fleetingly between people.
Practice	Practice is studied as an object or phenomenon – abstracted from the context, situated interactions and intentions of people. Generalizable characteristics, models and theories of practice can be identified.	Practice is embedded in the actions, interactions and conversations of people in a particular context. We need to understand the actors' intentions and interpretations and study how they talk about their experience in order to generate interpretive insights.	Practice is complexly interwoven in responsive relationships between people, in which meanings, actions and our sense of what is going on shifts in and through time and across relationships. Insights and transitory understanding are shaped between people.

Source: Based on Cunliffe (2011).

account and knowledge that can be generalized and replicated across contexts. Objectivist studies can be both big-data and small-data studies, so, while the latter may involve a study of micro-practices, the key differentiator in relation to other problematics lies in what is seen as 'data', and how the data are treated. For example, from an objectivist problematic, actions, activities and forms of language may be identified in a specific context or practice, but treated as 'stand-alone' or unconnected to the people performing them. The Van Maanen ethnography of Disneyland mentioned earlier is, as he says himself, 'an old-fashioned realist ethnography that tells of a culture' (Van Maanen 1991: 58) in which he studies the socialization processes, the type of work culture and the emotional and stage management practices that went on behind the scenes at Disneyland.

In their review of the field, Vaara and Whittington (2012) imply that most studies of strategies as practices are from an objectivist perspective, whether structuration, sociomaterial or discursive. In other words, while the focus is on practices, language and/or activities, these are addressed as phenomena – objects abstracted from the intentions, emotions and interpretations of the

strategists themselves. Heimeriks, Schijven and Gates (2012) provide an example of such research in their study of the risk management practices, knowledge transfer practices and integration practices relating to learning in the context of post-acquisition integration processes. They used survey and interview data from executives to test hypotheses and develop generalizations and predictions about how these practices do and should operate. Dependent, independent and control variables are identified and measured, and excerpts from interviews are used to substantiate theoretical postulates. Relationships in each hypothesis are graphed. Practice is therefore extracted and abstracted from the doing. This can been seen in statements such as this: 'Our core argument is that the rigidity that codification entails needs to be counteracted by higher-order routines [that] manifest themselves in an array of concrete organizational practices' (Heimeriks, Schijven and Gates 2012: 704).

Lee and Myers (2004) utilized critical ethnography to study enterprise integration in an Asia-Pacific organization. During an intensive year of fieldwork one author interviewed, observed, attended meetings, engaged in informal conversations and gathered data from the company intranet, annual reports, e-mails and newspaper articles. Lee and Myers (2004: 372) conclude that corporate strategy 'can be contested terrain' with dominant coalitions and varied political agendas. They analyse the data from a critical, but nevertheless objectivist, problematic.

Paroutis and Pettigrew's (2007) inductive study of the practices of strategy teams in a multi-business firm was also carried out from an objectivist problematic. They studied 'the duality of recursiveness and adaptation' by interviewing managers and examining strategy documents, coding data using NVivo 2. As a result, they identify seven categories of practice, along with the activities comprising each practice. They also offer a first-order factual account of the development of a new strategy-planning process using excerpts from interviews to illustrate practices and processes. They then offer a 2 X 2 conceptual matrix, a 'diagnostic tool' (Paroutis and Pettigrew 2007: 131) to map the seven strategizing practices in relation to recursiveness and adaptation within and/or across strategy teams.

While focusing on managers' formal and informal strategic conversations and interactions – which might imply a subjectivist ontology – Hoon's (2007) longitudinal case study aims to 'examine the mechanisms of redefining the strategic context of strategy implementation' (Hoon 2007: 927). The purpose of the research was objectivist in that it 'was concerned with understanding the logic behind unfolding activities which represent the underlying generative mechanisms that explain how and why observed activities occur' (930). Data were collected using semi-structured interviews, observation of formal and informal meetings, memos written by managers, and a review of documents, then coded and categorized into activity types.

The key indicators in these objectivist studies are terms such as 'categories', 'mechanisms', 'processes', 'coding' and 'hypotheses'. From an objectivist problematic, the focus lies on the properties or types of practices in the context studied, with human intentions and interpretations taken out, and the identification of properties and practices that can be generalized to other contexts.

Indeed, in his ethnographic study of telemedicine practices, Nicolini (2011) is explicit that his intention was 'to substitute the dominant belief that subjects are the ultimate source of meaning and knowledge with the view that knowledge and meaning reside in a nexus of practices' (Nicolini 2011: 603). In other words, practice is the *object* of study, not the *subjective* interpretations around people's practices.

Studying practices from a subjectivist problematic

> [M]an is an animal suspended in webs of significance he himself has spun, I take culture to be those webs, and the analysis of it to be therefore not an experimental science in search of law but an interpretive one in search of meaning.
>
> Geertz (1973: 3)

While objectivists view strategy as some*thing out there* that can be studied as an independent entity, subjectivists see strategizing evolving in the meanings and activities of organization members (for example, Ezzamel and Wilmott 2008; Jarzabkowski 2005). *Within* a subjectivist problematic, people have a reflexive relationship with the world around them, meaning that they both constitute and are constituted by their surroundings – a broadly social constructionist perspective (Cunliffe 2008). Practices are therefore enacted by people in particular places, times and situations, and their understanding of these practices emerges from, and influences, their practices – rather like Escher's lithograph of two hands drawing each other. To understand people's practices, we therefore need to ask research participants what it is that they are doing and why. A key difference with objectivism is that subjectivist research is concerned with the meanings that the actors themselves give to their practices, rather than the researcher's meaning. In addition, my use of the term 'practices' here, compared to the 'practice' of objectivism, is to emphasize – deliberately – the fluidity, the differing interpretations and the different forms of practice *as people engage in the practice*. Subjectivist research often focuses on the micro-practices and interpretations of people and how these play out in particular contexts.

For example, in their study of strategic planning practices in three multi-generational firms, Nordqvist and Melin (2010) used open-question interviews, observations of meetings and casual conversations to develop case descriptions and 'tell the story'. They talk about who the actors are, what they do, and their different interpretations: 'The group CEO prefers to use the white board to draw pictures of his overall visions. A board member says, "It is exciting to see him draw and move the different boxes... However, several top managers and other employees in LT say they lack a more formal and systematic strategic planning process"' (Nordqvist and Melin 2010: 19). This example highlights key elements of a subjectivist research methodology, which may incorporate stories and narratives of practice from the practitioner's perspective, different interpretations, excerpts from conversations and open interviews. Subjectivist accounts may also include photographs, film, researcher field notes, and excerpts from practitioner diaries and accounts.

Laine and Vaara (2007) used participant observation, company documents, semi-structured interviews and an abductive analytic to examine the discourses and discursive practices around strategic development. They look at how the language used by corporate management, managers and engineers made sense of and constructed strategy, and their and others' identities, in multiple ways. Working from a subjectivist perspective, their concern is for actors' interpretations and mobilization of discourses.

Finally, Samra-Fredericks' (2003) study of strategists at work utilized an ethnomethodological approach that is based on social constructionism but takes what I would call a 'to the right' conservative view (see Cunliffe 2011). As she says, 'Ethnomethodology's basic principles are consistent (epistemologically and ontologically) with the tenets of social constructionism (Berger and Luckmann, 1967). It is where everyday talk may "presume an objective world of facts 'out there'", yet close analysis of the ways members apprehend that world reveals their own collaborative social construction of those facts' (Samra-Fredericks 2003: 147). In other words, the ontological assumption is that a commonly understood objectified social and organizational reality is constructed subjectively by people. She uses conversation analysis to study the detailed linguistic mechanics of conversations, as a means of drawing attention to how strategists create strategic direction in their conversations. This is not written from the perspective of the strategists, however, nor does it incorporate their interpretations.

The key indicators of subjectivist ethnographies are terms such as 'making sense', 'actors' interpretations', 'conversations', 'multiple interpretations', 'intentions', 'knowing' and 'practising'.

Engaging in practices within an intersubjective problematic

An intersubjective ontology differs from subjectivism in that it is not about individual subjects and their interpretations and actions ('I's) but about 'we-ness' – that we are always 'selves-in-relation-to-others' (Ricœur 1992; Merleau-Ponty 1964 [1960]). Our practices and understandings of such practices are shaped *between us* (intentionally and otherwise), in situ, in our relationally responsive interactions and conversations (Shotter 2008). The implications of this problematic for our practices is that:

- no one person is in control; we are always responding to and anticipating an 'other' (person, situation, event, practice...);
- we may have similar and different understandings;
- our practices are never given or final, but 'transformed in what is created' in the moment (Bakhtin 1986 [1953]: 120); and
- research itself is also a practice, and, as such, researchers and practitioners are an integral and reflexive part of sensemaking.

In other words, we begin to think about how we can work *with* practitioners to share knowledge/knowing and meanings/understandings *between us* about a particular practice. Working within an intersubjective problematic involves collaborative research in which the practices of researching and strategizing combine in making sense of how strategizing occurs.

Participatory action research offers one way of working from an intersubjective problematic because all research participants share 'in the way research is conceptualized, practiced, and brought to bear on the life-world. It means ownership, that is, responsible agency in the production of knowledge and improvement of practice' (McTaggart 1997: 28). From a participatory action research perspective, academics and practitioners are *together* responsible for knowledge production and improving practice; 'research' is therefore a collaborative endeavour in which ideas and information are shared.

I cannot find an example of a strategy-as-practice study carried out from this problematic. The Küpers, Mantere and Statler (2013) article mentioned previously is perhaps the nearest, though the workshop is taken out of the lived organizational experience of participants. Interestingly, in organization studies we often exhort managers to be 'participative', and yet we are rarely collaborative ourselves in our research. Most examples of research within an inter-subjective problematic are in community studies, education and health. Within our discipline, Peter Reason and John Heron have worked on this approach to action research consistently. Indeed, Reason (2006) argues that action research is inherently concerned with practice, and highlights its intersubjective and 'responsible' nature: 'The focus on practical purposes draws attention to the moral dimension of action research—that it is inquiry in the pursuit of worthwhile purposes, for the flourishing of persons, communities, and the ecology of which we are all a part' (Reason 2006: 188).

Future possibilities

> Contemporary organizing is increasingly understood to be complex, dynamic, distributed, mobile, transient, and unprecedented, and as such needs approaches that will help us theorize these kinds of novel, indeterminant, and emergent phenomena.
>
> Feldman and Orlikowski (2011: 1240)

Ethnography is a way of studying the complex and dynamic relationships that occur in organizational life. As such, it is a methodology of relevance to the strategy-as-practice field. In particular, the multiple methods that can be used in ethnographic

fieldwork facilitate the possibility of studying actions, interactions, intentions and practices around strategizing as it happens. Because the ethnographer is embedded in the field, connections can be identified between organizational, group and individual practices, as well as focusing on an under-researched area: the identity work of strategists.

I suggest that much of the work in the SAP field in general is from an objectivist problematic, with few subjectivist (especially those taking a more interpretivist perspective) and intersubjectivist studies. Working from these two latter problematics, and using an ethnographic methodology, can offer new insights into our understanding of the relational and reflexive (Cunliffe 2014; Cunliffe and Eriksen 2011) nature of strategizing as an emerging and lived experience. In particular, intersubjectivist research, in which researchers and organizational participants work together to make meaning, may offer fruitful insights for theorizing strategy as practice and practising theorizing in strategizing in different ways. Within this problematic, the use of action research and collaborative and co-constructed methods within an overarching ethnographic methodology has much to offer.

While the value of such approaches are acknowledged as important in narrowing the academic/ practice gap (for example, Balogun, Huff and Johnson 2003; Splitter and Seidel 2011; Vaara and Whittington 2012), academics are faced with increasing pressures to publish a specified number of articles in 'top' journals with narrow views of qualitative research. This encourages the use of short-term, relatively easy-to-apply methods that often result in thin descriptions and coded abstractions of practice. As Vaara and Whittington (2012) state, however, the challenges facing strategy-as-practice researchers relate to getting close to practitioners, being able to apply complex social theories and studying taken-for-granted micro-practices in such a way that we can also understand the macro-level consequences. They conclude that 'the rewards of meeting these challenges are great' (Vaara and Whittington 2012: 325). I suggest that ethnography offers an opportunity to meet these challenges head-on and develop socially robust knowledge that is of relevance to practitioners.

References

Agar, M. (2010), 'On the ethnographic part of the mix: a multi-genre tale of the field', *Organizational Research Methods*, 13/2: 286–303.

Aggerholm, H. K., Asmuß, B., and Thomsen, C. (2012), 'The role of recontextualization in the multivocal, ambiguous process of strategizing', *Journal of Management Inquiry*, 21/4: 413–28.

Argyris, C., and Schön, D. (1974), *Theory in Practice: Increasing Professional Effectiveness*. San Francisco: Jossey-Bass.

Ashkanasy, N. (2013), 'Editors' comments: internationalizing theory: how "fusion theory" emanates from down under', *Academy of Management Review*, 38/1: 1–5.

Atkinson, P., Coffey, A., Delamont, S., Lofland, J., and Lofland, L. (eds.) (2007), *Handbook of Ethnography*. London: Sage.

Bakhtin, M. M. (1986 [1953]) *Speech Genres and Other Late Essays*, ed. Emerson, C., and Holquist, M. Austin: University of Texas Press.

Balogun, J., Huff, A. S., and Johnson, P. (2003), 'Three responses to the methodological challenges of studying strategizing', *Journal of Management Studies*, 40/1: 197–224.

Becker, H. S. (1963), *Outsiders: Studies in the Sociology of Deviance*. New York: Free Press.

Becker, H. S., Hughes, E. C., and Strauss, A. L. (1961), *Boys in White: Student Culture in Medical School*. University of Chicago Press.

Berger, P. L., and Luckmann, T. (1967), *The Social Construction of Reality: A Treatise in the Sociology of Knowledge*. London: Penguin Books.

Blumer, H. (1954), 'What is wrong with social theory?', *American Sociological Review*, 19/1: 3–10.

Butcher, T. (2013), 'Longing to belong', *Qualitative Research in Organizations and Management*, 18/3: 242–57.

Charmaz, K. (2007), *Constructing Grounded Theory: A Practical Guide through Qualitative Analysis*. London: Sage.

Cunliffe, A. L. (2008), 'Orientations to social constructionism: relationally-responsive social constructionism and its implications for knowledge and learning', *Management Learning*, 39/2: 123–39.

— (2010), 'Retelling tales of the field: in search of organizational ethnography 20 years on', *Organizational Research Methods*, 13/2: 224–39.

— (2011), 'Crafting qualitative research: Morgan and Smircich 30 years on', *Organizational Research Methods*, 14/4: 647–73.

— (2014), *A Very Short, Fairly Interesting and Reasonably Cheap Book about Management*, 2nd edn. London: Sage.

Cunliffe, A. L., and Eriksen, M. (2011), 'Relational leadership', *Human Relations*, 64/11: 1425–49.

Cunliffe, A. L., and Karunanayake, G. (2013), 'Working within hyphen-spaces in ethnographic research: implications for research identities and practice', *Organizational Research Methods*, 16/3: 364–92.

Czarniawska, B. (2007), *Shadowing and Other Techniques for Doing Fieldwork in Modern Societies*. Malmo: Liber.

Dalton, M. (1959), *Men Who Manage: Fusions of Feeling and Theory in Administration*. New York: John Wiley.

Erkama, N., and Vaara, E. (2010), 'Struggles over legitimacy in global organizational restructuring: a rhetorical perspective on legitimation strategies and dynamics in a shutdown case', *Organization Studies*, 31/7: 813–39.

Ezzamel, M., and Wilmott, H. (2008), 'Strategy as discourse in a global retailer: a supplement to rationalist and interpretive accounts', *Organization Studies*, 29/2: 191–217.

Fauré, B., and Rouleau, L. (2011), 'The strategic competence of accountants and middle managers in budget making', *Accounting, Organizations and Society*, 36/3: 167–82.

Feldman, M. S., and Orlikowski, W. J. (2011), 'Theorizing practice and practicing theory', *Organization Science*, 22/5: 1240–53.

Fenton, C., and Langley, A. (2011), 'Strategy as practice and the narrative turn', *Organization Studies*, 32/9: 1171–96.

Geertz, C. (1973), *Thick Description: Toward an Interpretive Theory of Culture*. New York: Basic Books.

Geiger, D. (2009), 'Revisiting the concept of practice: toward an argumentative understanding of practicing', *Management Learning*, 40/2: 129–44.

Glaser, B. G. (1978), *Theoretical Sensitivity: Advances in the Methodology of Grounded Theory*. Mill Valley, CA: Sociology Press.

Golden-Biddle, K., and Locke, K. (1993), 'Appealing work: how ethnographic texts convince', *Organization Science*, 4/1: 1–22.

Goodall, Jr H. L., (2000), *Writing the New Ethnography*. Lanham, MD: Altamira Press.

(2005), 'Narrative inheritance: a nuclear family with toxic secrets', *Qualitative Inquiry*, 11/4: 492–513.

Hannerz, U. (2003), 'Being there…and there…and there! Reflections on multi-site ethnography', *Ethnography*, 4/2: 201–16.

Heimeriks, K. H., Schijven, M., and Gates, S. (2012), 'Manifestations of higher-order routines: the underlying mechanisms of deliberate learning in the context of post-acquisition integration', *Academy of Management Journal*, 55/3: 703–26.

Heron, J., and Reason, P. (2006), 'The practice of co-operative inquiry: research "with" rather than "on" people', in Reason, P., and Bradbury, H. (eds.), *Handbook of Action Research: Participative Inquiry and Practice*: 144–54. London: Sage.

Hoon, C. (2007), 'Committees as strategic practice: the role of strategic conversation in a public administration', *Human Relations*, 60/6: 921–52.

Ingold, T. (2008), 'Anthropology is *not* ethnography', *Proceedings of the British Academy*, 154: 69–92.

Jacques, E. (1951), *The Changing Culture of a Factory*. London: Tavistock.

Jarzabowski, P. (2005), *Strategy as Practice: An Activity-Based Approach*. London: Sage.

Kaplan, S. (2008), 'Framing contests: strategy making under uncertainty', *Organization Science*, 19/5: 729–52.

Kostera, M. (2007), *Organizational Ethnography: Methods and Inspirations*. Lund: Studentlitteratur AB.

Küpers, W., Mantere, S., and Statler, M. (2013), 'Strategy as storytelling: a phenomenological collaboration', *Journal of Management Inquiry*, 22/1: 83–100.

Laine, P.-M., and Vaara, E. (2007), 'Struggling over subjectivity: a discursive analysis of strategic development in an engineering group', *Human Relations*, 60/1: 29–58.

Lee, J. C., and Myers, M. D. (2004), 'Dominant actors, political agendas, and strategic shifts over time: a critical ethnography of an enterprise systems implementation', *Journal of Strategic Information Systems*, 13/4: 355–74.

Locke, K. (2011), 'Field research practice in management and organization studies: reclaiming its tradition of discovery', *Academy of Management Annals*, 5/1: 613–52.

Locke, K., Golden-Biddle, K., and Feldman, M. S. (2008), 'Making doubt generative: rethinking the role of doubt in the research process', *Organization Science*, 19/6: 907–18.

Marcus, G. E. (1995), 'Ethnography in/of the world system: the emergence of multi-sited ethnography', *Annual Review of Anthropology*, 24: 95–117.

McTaggart, R. (ed.) (1997), *Participatory Action Research: International Contexts and Consequences*. Albany, NY: SUNY Press.

Merleau-Ponty, M. (1964 [1960]), *Signs*. Evanston, IL: Northwestern University Press.

Neyland, D. (2008), *Organizational Ethnography*. London: Sage.

Nicolini, D. (2009), 'Zooming in and out: studying practices by switching theoretical lenses and trailing connections', *Organization*, 30/12: 1391–418.

Nicolini, D (2011), 'Insights from the field of telemedicine', *Organization Science*, 22/3: 602–20.

Nordqvist, M., and Melin, L. (2010), 'The promise of the strategy as practice perspective for family business strategy research', *Journal of Family Business Strategy*, 1/1: 15–25.

Orr, J. E. (1996), *Talking about Machines: An Ethnography of a Modern Job*. Ithaca, NY: ILR Press.

Orr, K., and Bennett, M. (2012), 'Down and out at the British Library and other dens of co-production', *Management Learning*, 43/4: 427–42.

Paroutis, S., and Pettigrew, A. M. (2007), 'Strategizing in the multi-business firm: strategy teams at multiple levels and over time', *Human Relations*, 60/1: 99–135.

Peltonen, T. (2007), 'In the middle of managers: occupational communities, global ethnography and the multinationals', *Ethnography*, 8/3: 346–60.

Rasche, A., and Chia, R. (2009), 'Researching strategy practices: a genealogical social theory perspective', *Organization Studies*, 30/7: 713–34.

Reason, P. (2006), 'Choice and quality in action research practice', *Journal of Management Inquiry*, 15/2: 187–203.

Ricœur, P. (1992), *Oneself as Another*. University of Chicago Press.

Roethlisberger, F. J., and Dickson, W. J. (1956), *Management and the Worker*. Cambridge, MA: Harvard University Press.

Rouleau, L., and Balogun, J. (2011), 'Middle managers, strategic sensemaking, and discursive competence', *Journal of Management Studies*, 48/5: 953–83.

Roy, D. (1959), '"Banana time": job satisfaction and informal interaction', *Human Organization*, 18/4: 158–68.

Russell, L. (2005), 'It's a question of trust: balancing the relationship between students and teachers in ethnographic fieldwork', *Qualitative Research*, 5/2: 181–99.

Samra-Fredericks, D. (2003), 'Strategizing as lived experience and strategists' everyday efforts to shape strategic direction', *Journal of Management Studies*, 40/1: 141–74.

Shepherd, D. A., and Sutcliffe, K. M. (2011), 'Inductive top-down theorizing: a source of new theories of organization', *Academy of Management Review*, 36/2: 361–80.

Shotter, J. (2008), *Conversational Realities Revisited: Life, Language, Body and World*. Taos, NM: Taos Institute.

Splitter, V., and Seidl, D. (2011), 'Does practice-based research on strategy lead to practically relevant knowledge? Implications of a Bourdieusian perspective', *Journal of Applied Behavioral Science*, 47/1: 98–120.

Tracy, S. J. (2010), 'Qualitative quality: eight "big tent" criteria for excellent qualitative research', *Qualitative Inquiry*, 16/10: 837–51.

(2013), *Qualitative Research Methods: Collecting Evidence, Crafting Analysis, Communicating Impact*. Chichester, UK: Wiley-Blackwell.

Trist, E. L., and Bamforth, K. W. (1951), 'Some social and psychological consequences of the longwall method of coal-getting', *Human Relations*, 4/1: 3–38.

Vaara, E., Sorsa, V., and Pälli, P. (2010), 'On the force potential of strategy texts: a critical discourse analysis of a strategic plan and its power effects in a city organization', *Organization*, 17/6: 685–702.

Vaara, E., and Whittington, R. (2012), 'Strategy-as-practice: taking social practices seriously', *Academy of Management Annals*, 6/1: 285–336.

Van Maanen, J. (1991), 'The smile factory: work at Disneyland', in Frost, P. J., Moore, L. F., Louis, M. R., Lundberg, C. C., and Martin, J. (eds.), *Reframing Organizational Culture*: 58–76. Newbury Park, CA: Sage.

Van Maanen, J., Sorensen, J. B., and Mitchell, T. R. (2007), 'The interplay between theory and method', *Academy of Management Review*, 32/4: 1145–54.

Walker, C. R., and Guest, R. H. (1952), *The Man on the Assembly Line*. Cambridge, MA: Harvard University Press.

Watson, T. J. (1994), *In Search of Management: Culture, Chaos and Control in Managerial Work*. London: Routledge.

(2009), 'Narrative, life story and manager identity: a case study in autobiographical identity work', *Human Relations*, 62/3: 425–52.

(2011), 'Ethnography, reality, and truth: the vital need for studies of "how things work" in organizations and management', *Journal of Management Studies*, 48/1: 202–17.

Whittington, R. (2006), 'Completing the practice turn in strategy research', *Organization Studies*, 27/5: 613–34.

Whyte, W. F. (1948), *Human Relations in the Restaurant Industry*. New York: McGraw-Hill.

Ybema, S., Yanow, D., Wels, H., and Kamsteeg, F. (2009), 'Studying everyday organizational life', in *Organizational Ethnography: Studying the Complexities of Everyday Life*: 1–20. London: Sage.

Zicker, M. J., and Carter, N. T. (2010), 'Reconnecting with the spirit of workplace ethnography: a historical review', *Organizational Research Methods*, 13/2: 304–19.

Researching strategists and their identity in practice: building 'close-with' relationships

JULIA BALOGUN, NIC BEECH and PHYL JOHNSON

Introduction

The strategy-as-practice field has, from its inception, had an interest in innovative research methodology (Balogun, Huff and Johnson 2003). This interest was driven principally by the recognition that empirical studies of strategy as practice faced contradictory pressures to, on the one hand, gain the necessary depth of data yet, on the other, possess sufficient breadth to enable theorizing on the basis of 'praxis, practices and practitioners' (Whittington 2006a). The challenge is to collect data that drill deep enough to meet the micro-challenge of the SAP agenda in terms of detail on strategic activity (Johnson, Melin and Whittington 2003) but also to enable a sufficient understanding of the linkages between that detail of action and 'higher'-level outcomes in order to address the 'So what?' question and theorize beyond the specifics of the particular context under study (Balogun, Jarzabkowski and Seidl 2007; Jarzabkowski, Balogun and Seidl 2007; Whittington 2007).

This chapter contributes to the developing methodological dialogue (Balogun, Huff and Johnson 2003; Denis, Langley and Rouleau 2007; Langley 2007; Hodgkinson and Clarke 2007; Vaara and Whittington 2012) in the SAP field. To do so, it builds on the argument advanced by Balogun, Huff and Johnson (2003: 197) that strategy-as-practice 'research can not advance significantly without reconceptualising frequently taken-for-granted assumptions about the way to do research and the way we engage organizational participants'. Whereas existing reflections on the methodological challenges for strategy as practice are typically inclusive, however (that is, addressing challenges that pertain to praxis, practices and practitioners), this

chapter adopts a more exclusive approach. While maintaining the position that strategizing occurs at the nexus of praxis, practices and practitioner activity and to study one aspect means in some way to study all, it privileges study of the practitioner. Empirical SAP research has tended to focus on praxis and practices, or practitioners and the practices they draw on, with much less research focusing on practitioners and their praxis. Existing work demonstrates the important, yet often overlooked, impact of strategists' identities on their strategizing activity (for example, Balogun et al. 2014; Beech and Johnson 2005; Johnson, Balogun and Beech 2006; Rouleau 2003; Suominen and Mantere 2010; Fenton and Langley 2011): understanding how strategists shape strategizing activity through *who they are*. This chapter argues, therefore, that the strategy-as-practice field needs to recognize the importance of identity, and that this has significant methodological implications if SAP researchers are to adequately study the linkages between strategy practitioners and their strategy work. It demands a 'close-with' relationship between the researcher and his/her research subjects that moves beyond the 'close-to' relationship originally called for by Balogun, Huff and Johnson (2003) and that, as an approach, can also contribute more generally to an understanding of how to meet the 'drilling down' and 'So what?' challenges of this field. Thus, the purpose of this chapter is to explicate a methodology that enables exploration of the interconnectedness of strategists' identities and their praxis and to consider the research implications that this raises.

The first part of the chapter offers a brief summary of the developing methodological dialogue within the strategy-as-practice field. It then builds an argument for the particular foci of the chapter on practitioners and their identity, drawing on an empirical vignette that illustrates the impact of strategists' identity on their work. The second part of the chapter examines the particular challenges of studying practitioners' identity in SAP-oriented work through a more in-depth consideration of what is meant by 'identity'. It builds an argument for moving to a 'close-with' relationship with research subjects. From this, the chapter develops ground rules for research seeking to jointly explore strategists' identity and their strategic work. It concludes with methodological recommendations based on this analysis.

Researching strategy as practice

The first issue on strategy as practice in the *Journal of Management Studies* (Johnson, Melin and Whittington 2003) called for research that focuses on the work of the strategist with the aim of understanding the everyday processes, practices and activities involved in the making and doing of strategy. The aim was to redress the balance in strategy research, which since the 1980s had been influenced increasingly by the research traditions of microeconomics. As a result, most research in the field avoids the exploration of the *doing* of strategy as a human activity. Consistent with the broader return to practice in many areas of management research, strategy as practice seeks to re-engage with the strategic practitioner. It is concerned with 'strategizing', and how strategists think, talk, act and feel, but also with the tools and technologies created and/or employed by strategists (be it five forces analysis, Post-it notes, specialized planning and analysis software or workshops and awaydays) and the impact of this activity on strategic outcomes (Whittington 2003; 2006a).

This focus on re-engagement with the strategic practitioner carries with it implications for research and research methods. Balogun, Huff and Johnson (2003) argue that the need to be 'close to' strategic practice and the practitioner, and to be able to trace actions through to outcomes, requires a reconceptualization of the way we do research and the way we engage with organizational participants. In particular, they argue that, if researchers want to get 'close to' the practitioner, they need to draw the practitioner

in, and that this in turn demands that they do research that is relevant. Ethnographic approaches and case studies are attractive (and now common in the field) since there is a need to collect data on strategists and their practices within context; this provides the depth. The relevance criterion remains, however, and changing research contexts – such as large, multinational and highly diversified change-orientated organizational settings – increasingly require complementary methods providing more breadth and flexibility. In targeting a *general* SAP audience, Balogun, Huff and Johnson (2003) advocate that any research approach should (1) provide evidence that is broad and deep through data that are contextual, longitudinal, collected at multiple levels and facilitate comparison across sites; (2) elicit the commitment of informants because it is interesting and maybe enjoyable; (3) make effective use of research time because of the large and varied amount of data required; (4) anchor the questions being asked in the organizational reality – that is, be relevant; and (5) go beyond research 'feedback' in order to contribute to organizational needs and provide informants with useful insights.

This approach is, in fact, highly suggestive of an action research approach (Eden and Huxham 1996), or insider/outsider research (Bartunek, 2008), in which the researcher and the research participant walk the research path together (Calori 2002). Collaboration with those inside the organization can be fruitful in meeting many of these five guidelines for strategizing research since, by their nature, collaborative projects are contextual and, once an insider is engaged, the relationship is often longitudinal. Greater real-time involvement is not a panacea in itself, however. Focusing on three methods in particular to enable a greater breadth and depth of data – interactive discussion groups, self-reporting and practitioner research – Balogun, Huff and Johnson also argue that there is a skill extension agenda for researchers:

> The complications of our research sites mean that individual researchers, even groups of researchers, cannot count on gaining an insider's perspective on their own. In order to do excellent and insightful research, researchers need to be project managers, skilled negotiators, trainers, co-workers and collaborators as well as writers, methodologists, analysts and theorists. Our argument, in sum, is

that the logic of strategising requires that we re-conceive our basic identities as researchers (Balogun, Huff and Johnson 2003: 220).

Langley and Abdallah (2011) similarly argue that in-depth and largely qualitative data are central to the development of the strategy-as-practice per-spective. In their view, this is a direct result of the nature of the phenomenon itself: dynamic, complex and involving intense human interaction and the need to get close to the phenomenon. They argue for observation to capture the experience of *doing* strategy, but also for interviews and other forms of interaction with research participants to understand the *interpretations* that people place on these activ-ities, and, in addition to both of these, for careful attention to be paid to collecting strategizing arte-facts – for example, a flip chart when emerging from a strategy workshop. These criteria point to a focus on a small number of organizations being studied in depth. They then move on, however, to argue that within this there are research choices and dilemmas for the SAP researcher. These are to do with epi-stemological choices and research strategies; sam-pling and research design; access and data collection; and analysis and theorizing. Moreover, in the consideration of these, they echo the issues raised by Balogun, Huff and Johnson (2003), namely the frequent need by researchers engaged in getting access to study that which is often a commercially or culturally sensitive phenomenon (such as strategizing and strategic change), and the need to engage in a trade-off between close proxim-ity to the practice of strategy (and potentially direct) involvement and the independence usually expected from academic researchers. In other words, if the strategy-as-practice field acknowledges strategists as both subjects and experts, how do SAP researchers map and maintain a boundary that has high-utility outcomes for both parties?

Overall, therefore, although there is no suggestion that there is no *one best way* to do strategy-as-prac-tice research, there is a general acceptance within the SAP field that the phenomena of interest to the researcher, the researcher's theoretical and onto-logical perspectives and preferences (and what researcher is able to offer to the strategist all?), *do* and *should* affect the approach taken. Never-theless, there is another less explicit but possibly

equi-present shared assumption (that is unmet) at play in the contemporary SAP debate: it is generally agreed that getting close to strategic practitioners and their practices is a requirement (Johnson *et al*. 2007). Moreover, it seems intuitively obvious that the more intimate the data sought from strategists, the closer the relationship needs to be. Thus, if the phenomenon of interest is more about the strategic practitioner, and aspects of the practitioner such as his/her iden-tity, then this closeness may in turn mitigate against the breadth requirement advocated by Balogun, Huff and Johnson (2003). This raises an alternative research challenge that is less about enabling breadth and depth and more about getting greater depth than has been typically required by any strategizing research. This is certainly the case for research that adopts an identity lens.

Researching strategizing and identity

The importance of identity

Recent reviews of empirical research (Balogun, Jarzabkowski and Seidl 2007; Jarzabkowksi, Balo-gun and Seidl 2007) against the three strategy-as-practice areas (practitioners, praxis and practice: Whittington 2006a) and methodological commen-taries (Denis, Langley and Rouleau 2007) have found that research typically keeps only two of these three areas in focus at any one time. There is a tendency to focus on praxis and practices, or practitioners and the practices they draw on, with much less research focusing on practitioners and their praxis. Consequently, the understanding of how strategists shape strategizing activity through *who they are* is underdeveloped.

For some strategists this link is obvious. For example, Neal's Yard sells organic skin and body care and natural remedies. The founder, Romy Jen-kins, was a pioneer of natural and organic products, and so it is not surprising that the business she founded has a mission to transform lives through empowering people to live by the principles of natural health. Equally, it is not surprising that the entrepreneur who has taken the business over from her, Peter Kindersley, is an organic farmer. With the exception of the study by Rouleau (2003), however, who explores the impact of gender on strategists

Box 25.1   Practitioners and their praxis: illustrating the impact of identity

On his entry in the firm, this CEO had a personal agenda for change. His image in the business community had been one where leadership results and strategic outcomes were achieved via 'alpha-male' management; in large part he was hired to perform this role. As a result a series of challenges in his private life, however, his strongly held personal goal was to develop towards a more transformational style of leadership. His strategic goal was to push the firm through a strategic change focused on differentiated growth requiring a new culture: to move from comfortable to edgy.

As he used executive coaching to enable himself to move towards a transformational and empathic style of leadership, he was simultaneously implementing his programme of strategic change to shift the firm's position in the market place, to double the volume of business and to move to a more competitive product line. This involved a significant organizational development agenda, including: changing organizational structure, making redundancies, altering the format of the top management team, initiating an externally focused talent management strategy (that is, making big hires from competitors) and implementing a performance management system impacting reward. As the changes under way in the firm touched and impacted on the employees, the CEO's own identity work to shift to a more benign style of leading was largely rejected; he was frequently re-typecast as a bully and tempted back into aggressive outbursts.

A resolution was achieved over time, as signals of strategic success incrementally emerged, his effortful (and increasingly reflexively aware) identity work

continued and pockets of acceptance of the strategic/cultural change spread, and all this merged into a consensual position. The CEO-orientated narratives present in the firm at this consensual point in time finally cast him as a mature coach leading a changed and high-performing firm.

The marked narrative pattern during the change period was of an iterative and negotiated nature, however. The CEO's attempts to push on with his own self-actualization at times fell on deaf ears, depending on the sensemaking of employees' groups with regard to the strategic change. If the change was impacting on groups within the organization, while they moved through resistance to acceptance, the CEO had to be the villain even if his behaviour was congruent with an empathic, coaching leadership style.

Interestingly, this process also occurred in reverse. For example, a seemingly delayed acceptance of a change-congruent initiative would draw an exaggeratedly aggressive behaviour pattern from the CEO. Equally, enthusiastic employee response to strategic success, which placed the CEO in the role of organizational hero for his employees, triggered such an anxiety response from him that he performed a self-sabotage. This forced his employees to re-narrate him in an identity position closer to one he felt comfortable with at that stage of his personal development.

There were multiple examples like this of the interrelationship of the CEO's identity work, the identity projected on him and visible signals of strategic change.

---

and their work, there is little research that attempts to explore the impact of strategists' (multiple/changing) identity on their strategy work and therefore strategic outcomes. Beech and Johnson (2005) show that there is a strong link between the identity of strategists and their strategy-making activities, however, through their focus on the identity work during the change of a CEO (see Box 25.1). It highlights the impact of a strategist's identity on his/her praxis, and how, through time, a reciprocal interaction develops between the CEO's identity work and his own praxis: identity shapes praxis,

yet the praxis also shapes his identity, and ultimately strategic change at an organizational level.[1]

'Praxis' is a term whose use has developed over a considerable time in sociopolitical theory. A brief insight into this development is important here, because it shows why there is a strong link between identity and praxis and highlights certain

---

[1] It is important to note that these events played out over a six-year period and have multiple layers of complexity as well as multiple actors and outcomes. We mean to summarize only one vein of analytic interpretation here.

methodological issues. In Aristotelian terms praxis is the actions of free men in the political-ethical community (Steffy and Grimes 1986), whereas in Marxist usage it constitutes conscious agential action in resistance to alienating socio-economic conditions (Margolis 1989). Graham-Hill and Grimes (2001) emphasize the significance of meaningfulness in praxis. Action taken to improve the political-ethical community or to resist an alienating context can be agential only if there is deliberate intention to move towards a particular goal, and this goal orientation, together with a community of language users (Wittgenstein 1958 [1951]), is what renders praxis meaningful. In short, the actors have a 'local theory' (Silverman 1970) of what they are doing, what it means and why they are doing it. Hence, praxis is the interdependence and integration of theory and practice (Zuber-Skerritt 2001) in a meaningful way within a social context.

Praxis is, therefore, intrinsically linked to identity, and thus identity can provide a route to understanding praxis. People's purposes, enactment of roles and the meanings they construct within their linguistic communities are fundamental both to how they identify themselves and to their praxis. The question for researchers, however, is: how is it possible to understand the praxis of others? This, it is argued below, is not as straightforward as interviewing strategists about the meaning of their action, nor can it be simply observational research. Rather, it requires an approach that goes beyond talking *to* or observing strategists: to being *with* them. This implies a co-inhabitation of a set of meanings and an exploration of intended and unintended, conscious and unconscious actions and consequences.

This '*with*' line of argument suggests that a focus on practitioners and their praxis requires a *far greater knowledge* of, and therefore *far greater proximity* to, practitioners than that typically achieved in SAP research. Therefore, it is perhaps unsurprising that the research to date exhibits a lack of focus on the practitioners and their praxis. Achieving such proximity, both in task and rapport, is no easy matter. Hambrick (2007) has restated this belief, while a special issue of the *Academy of Management Journal* (August 2007)

acts almost as a confessional for the lack of research that is genuinely close to practice. The challenge is to be not just 'close to' practitioners, and able to observe what they do, but also '*close with*' practitioners, in a relationship that enables the researcher to share practitioners' worldviews and experiences (Van de Ven 2007). Along with the exceptional experiences that are commonly reported in research, there is a need to focus on the everyday and mundane (Ybema *et al.* 2009; Yanow 2009). This takes us close to the Schutzian researcher/researched as 'we' advocated by Calori (2002) as the highest-utility research relationship in management research.

Thus, while other routes to studying practitioners, such as cognition (Hodgkinson and Clarke 2007), have merit, these approaches typically do not discuss or meet the 'close-with' criterion, and as such lack some of the power we believe can come from the identity approach, with its direct connection to the felt experience of self-knowing (McLeod 1997; Cooper 2003) on the part of the strategist. Although much progress has been made, there is still some distance to go (Jarzabkowski, Mohrman and Scherer 2010). To appreciate the methodological challenge of an identity approach, however, we first need to extend our understanding of identity.

Uncovering and identifying identity

Identity has been associated traditionally with individual people, organizations, social groups and artefacts such as products and brands (Parker 2007). The traditional conception is that identity is that which is stable and distinctive over time (Ford and Ford 1994). As a result, one is able to recognize the person in different circumstances, places and times. Social and collective identities have been a focus of research in organization studies for some time (Ashforth and Mael 1989). Many studies of social identity have focused on stability (Gioia and Thomas 1996), though there is now an increasing interest in the dynamics of identities as they impact on organizational members' interpretations of themselves, others and their social situation. Here the concern is with such interpretations as they impact on the actions strategists undertake in strategy-making, and how such actions are subsequently fitted into the self-conception of the strategists.

Identity is regarded as both a product of and a producer of action and interpretation (Pullen and Linstead 2005). In other words, this conception of identity is neither simply that strategists do what they do because of who they are nor that who they are is a result of what they do. Rather, the understanding is that people's identities as strategists develop through interaction, success, failure and being recognized as strategists. Doing strategy and being a strategist are not regarded as a dichotomy but as interlinked. In strategy as practice this is regarded as being integrated with praxis, as actions relate to the 'local theories' that strategists have of how they could improve the situation and the meanings that underlie the theory–action intersect. One (increasingly prominent) way of researching identity as interconnected doing and being is through focusing on activities that, although they perform an organizational function, also establish, maintain or defend an identity. While strategists and leaders are carrying out their everyday practice they are simultaneously enacting an identity of strategist (Sveningsson and Larsson 2006) within the political constraints and possibilities that such identities impose (Thomas and Davies 2005). The 'identity work' literature is typified by a dynamic and social construction perspective on identity. Identity work is defined by Sveningsson and Alvesson (2003: 1165) as the processes of

> forming, repairing, maintaining, strengthening or revising the constructions that are productive of a sense of coherence and distinctiveness.

One significant aspect of identity work is the narratives that people produce and retell in organizations. Narrative methods for use in strategy as practice more generally are covered in depth by Rouleau (see Chapter 26 in this volume), who explains the relationship between life stories and narratives of practice. Here, although through a slightly different angle from Rouleau (this volume), this chapter still promotes and uses narrative analysis as a way of getting 'close with' the meanings, interpretations and actions of strategists as they link identity and praxis.

The way that people narrate the story of their strategy-making practice intrinsically links the 'What?', the 'How?' and the 'Who?' of strategy practice. Narratives can be analysed to inform the practitioner–praxis foci identified in this chapter as they highlight the objects and actions to which the strategist directs attention, but, in addition, narratives also serve to 'announce and enact who they are' (Creed and Scully 2000: 391). Narrating an experience means that the *practitioner* (storyteller) has to cast the self and others in roles and account for the limits and possibilities of these roles. Narrative practices are a form of identity work, as they construct and represent characters as having particular identities, and then make sense of events on the basis of those identities. Hence, if the sensemaking is coherent it reinforces the perceptions of the validity of those identity attributions.

Equally, narrative analysis can offer insight into *praxis*, or the local theories embedded (sometimes unwittingly) in the everyday practice of strategists. Narrative analysis seeks to uncover the causal attributions implicit within stories, and these relate to attributed agency (Beech and Sims 2007). For example, in the way a strategist relates events, is strategy formed in response to 'the market' or is the strategist the primary agent in decision-making? There is also often attribution of responsibility (Gabriel 2004), in which praise or blame is allocated to objects and agents. Therefore, a narrative will typically contain implicit informal theories about how causation operates, who has agency and where responsibility lies in the situation. These informal theories are part of praxis, as they are 'always already' 'written into' practice (Zuber-Skerritt 2001). For example, when causation is regarded as residing in the context rather than in the strategic actors, a reactive response to market forces would be the natural outcome.

Narrative analysis therefore offers a framework for deconstructing experience with strategists in a way that uncovers the interconnectedness between identity construction, praxis and practice. This is not necessarily an easy or comfortable process, however, and it leaves questions as to how these narratives are accessed. Interrogating and revealing deep assumptions and informal theories about why things are as they are can strike at the heart of a person's overt self-identity. It is this need to uncover such narratives that points to the need for more in-depth relationships with practitioners than has previously been suggested.

Moving to 'close-with' relationships to access identity

The implication of Erving Goffman's perspective on action and interaction in relationships (Goffman 1959; 1961) is that there is always a degree of distance between people, and this in turn has implications for doing identity research. In the research relationship there is a necessary distance between the researcher and the actor in the organization (or research participant). Each has a role and each has role expectations of the self and other, and interaction between them is framed by the setting. For example, if the research participant is responding to a request to be interviewed about strategy processes, he/she is likely to privilege examples he/she sees as 'strategic' and to construct a narrative of the self as strategist. The implication of this is that the interview is a setting for a performance, and the nature of the performance is mediated by the sensemaking that the actor brings to the performance (Alvesson and Deetz 2000).

As such, when researching links between strategists and their identity, it is necessary to access multiple performances, which in turn requires a more participatory approach to data-gathering (Kärreman and Alvesson 2004), creating a 'close-with' relationship in multiple times and spaces. For example, the researcher could observe decision-making meetings or potentially take an active role as a facilitator (Broadfoot, Deetz and Anderson 2004), but also precede and then follow up on the observed action with one-to-one discussions to build a more complete picture of the two-way linkages between the strategists involved and their actions. The research question is not: what are the 'real strategy' and the 'real strategist' like behind the performance? The questions are: who is the actor being when he/she performs strategy-making? And what are the implications of who they are being for what they do, and vice versa?

These questions lead to three areas of methodological consideration (see Figure 25.1) that we, as

authors, believe are central to the 'close-with' research approach advocated here as key to researching in the practitioner–praxis space. These are developed in the last section of this chapter and are illustrated using the empirical work discussed in Box 25.1.

Building 'close-with' relationships to study strategists and their identity

Design principles for 'close-with' relationships

This chapter has argued that central questions in the practitioner–praxis research space are: who is the actor being when he/she performs strategy-making? And what are the implications of who they are being for what they do, and vice versa? In order to develop insightful answers to these questions it is necessary to develop a degree of closeness *with* the practitioner that allows the researcher to deconstruct the performance from more than one perspective (Boje 2001). Accordingly, the researcher needs to be able to enter into the performance and see it from the perspective of different actors. There are some forms of data-gathering that are more likely to render this aim possible than others. Broadly, there are three principles or ground rules (see Figure 25.1) that research that seeks to examine the relationship between actors' identities and their practices needs to follow.

First, a *longitudinal engagement* is necessary, as this allows the researcher to perceive the performance(s) over time and in different circumstances such that the consistencies and variances in the way the strategist *is* during different phases of strategy-making, and in the company of different people, can be observed. Second, it is desirable to gather data from *more than one type* of performance. For example, observations of different types of meetings, combined with observation of communication to others about the outcome of these meetings and interviews about the meetings and communication, offer the researcher the chance to observe how the actor constructs versions of the self in these different settings. Third, the researcher

Design principles		
Longitudinal engagement	More than one performance	Access to back stage

Data collection		
Emergence: going fishing	Qualitative and relationship-based multi-faceted design: primary and secondary sources	Close-with relationships

Pillars of practice				
Legitimacy researcher	Relationship/ trust-building	Positive growth and actualization orientation	Reflective practice	Drawing inferences

Figure 25.1 Practitioners and their praxis: illustrating the impact of identity

needs to gain 'back-stage' (Goffman 1961) access to the actors through one-to-one meetings to gain appreciation of their personal perspectives separate to the researcher's observations before, during and after different performances. Dependent on the skills of the researcher, this could take the form of one-to-one informal conversations, or coaching sessions in which the researcher and the strategist are not restricted to either the strategy-making agenda or the formal research agenda. Even in such back-stage interactions performance is still occurring (in a sense, one performs 'the real me'), but this performance adds another layer of richness to the multi-performance perspective.

These three design principles have implications for data collection (see Figure 25.1). It is the access to the back stage that, more than anything, creates the need for the 'close-with' relationship. Gathering data from more than one type of performance requires a predominantly qualitative approach with a multifaceted design drawing on both primary and secondary sources of data. Finally, the longitudinal

design also involves allowing for the tracking and emergence of changing issues. These implications are discussed in the following section.

Data collection: applying design principles

This section outlines how the data for the CEO illustration (see Box 25.1) were collected to demonstrate the links from design principles to data collection, and how this creates research that is both 'close to' and 'close with' the practitioner. The next section then extends this example to distil some general pillars of practice for those wanting to work closely with strategic practitioners.

More than one type of performance

This research consisted of longitudinal action research spanning six years, and had a *multifaceted design*. All the primary data were qualitative and existed in the forms of visual and audio recordings, observational field notes, case notes from therapy sessions, diarized reflections of the researcher and written outputs from consultancy interventions – for example, e-mail communications, reports, flip charts and action plans. Secondary data were widely available in the firm once relationships had been established. Primary and secondary data collection opportunities alike were episodic and opportunistic and coincided with the firm's use of the researcher as a paid consultant.

In this research design, the data were very much the *outcomes* of the primary research activity, which was to be *in relationship* with a series of significantly agentic individuals involved in the firm's strategic change. This follows on from the fundamental assumption underpinning the researcher's professional psychotherapeutic practice (Rogers 1961)[2] – that is, the *relationship* is the therapy, not the diagnosis or other interventions that the therapist may make. The analogy here would be that the relationship is the method, not the interviewing or the videoing of meetings.

Accessing back-stage performance: close-with relationships

The research was fundamentally based on a foundation of multiple 'close-with' relationships[3] between the researcher and the aforementioned agentic organizational members, and, in each of these relationships, there was a win-win possibility present for both parties. The primary relationship was that of *therapist–client* between the researcher and the CEO. The secondary set of relationships were those of *consultant–clients* between the researcher and the top management community. The tertiary relationships were based on the shared activity of *collaborative reflective interpreters*, which took place with the researcher and the CEO and the researcher and the HR directors of the firm – in other words, they made sense of their interpretations together. This last relationship marks the transition from coach/therapist/consultant relationship to trusted adviser status that is referred to as being crucial for high-impact intervention (Maister 1997; Wasylyshyn 2003; 2005).

A therapeutic relationship is not essential, however. Similar data could have been collected from one-to-one conversations with research participants in circumstances in which the researcher has worked to build a relationship of trust between him-/herself and the research participants. The issue is the nature of the relationship developed between the researcher and the researched. It is this relationship requirement in particular that extends the research from a 'close-to' to a 'close-with' relationship.

Longitudinal: attitude to emergence 'going fishing'

The journey towards this set of close-with research relationships began with the primary client (the CEO) and his need to be in a relationship with the researcher (that is, it was his problem), as he was able to articulate it at the time of first contact. For him, his problem was the firm's management population and, more specifically, his top team, which was in need of development in order to improve its performance. Adopting a positive attitude to emergence, however, allowed two other interpretations to emerge, be espoused and then in turn create touch points for relationships to build beyond the primary client. In this case, a 'fishing' meeting with the company chairman allowed him to articulate that the CEO was the problem, and a 'fishing trip' to a top team meeting allowed the team to articulate that the senior managers and the organizational culture were the problem. This allowed the top team members to begin their *client–consultant* relationship to solve their problem (the senior managers and the culture) and the CEO to form his *client–therapist* relationship to solve the chairman's problem (him) as well as his own (his team).

Having a positive attitude to the emergence of opportunities and the creation of touch points to relationship-building can result in wasted or unproductive fishing trips from which nothing emerges. This can be mitigated, but ultimately it is an unavoidable part of this style of management research. This echoes the views of Denis, Langley and Rouleau (2007) that the researcher's attitude to ambiguity and surprise is an important mediator of how successful research of this kind turns out to be.

---

[2] Rogerian person-centred therapy.
[3] Calori (2002: 877) refers to 'we-relationships' that allow for the 'true understanding of human beings'.

Pillars of practice for 'close-with' relationships

In order to first build and then maintain the types of multiple 'close-with' relationships described in the illustrative research context used here, several general pillars of *professional research practice* need to be under active management.

Legitimacy

This issue is illustrated by the exchange of articles between Whittington (2006b) and Hodgkinson and Wright (2006). The position of the management academic as a legitimate relationship partner for senior managers is not always straightforward. In the illustration presented here (see Box 25.1), it was very clearly the responsibility of the management academic to have a *legitimate* offering in terms of the actualization of the individuals worked with or their strategic goals, and, moreover, to be skilled in the execution of that offering. In this case, the grounds for legitimacy were professional qualification: the practice of and continuing professional development as a psychotherapist alongside several years of mentored consultancy practice in the organizational development arena.

While not all academics will have legitimacy stemming from a professional qualification such as that of a therapist, there are other practices they should be able to draw on or develop from their academic practice so as to provide legitimacy. These include, for example, their knowledge of managerial practice in areas such as strategy formulation and strategic change, executive development and workshop facilitation skills. In order to work in a close-with relationship with a practitioner, in which the strategic practitioner gains value from open dialogue with the academic, and vice versa, an academic must expect to offer some expertise that furnishes legitimacy, or there is no basis for a relationship. For a close-with relationship, this legitimacy will need to extend far beyond the commonplace quid pro quo of access for feedback.

Relationship-building with trust

Trust is needed to facilitate a research relationship. In the example discussed here, this was actively and explicitly worked on by the researcher and accepted – by the commitment of time and patience – as a significant part of the building of the 'close-with' relationship. Clearly, anonymity was a large part of this, while confidentiality was not necessarily always needed. As an example, the early part of relationship-building is almost always all about the purposeful negotiation and testing of trust by both parties, irrespective of the espoused purpose of their meeting. This is true even in less intensive data-gathering methodologies, such as focus groups (Balogun, Huff and Johnson 2003) or interviews, in which there is a desire for those researched to be completely open. In the example here, trustworthiness was continually tested by the subtle pushing of boundaries, as well as by overt challenges to the researcher, such as 'Well, I suppose that you've already been told this, haven't you?' and 'I guess you are primarily working for the CEO here, and so I have to watch what I say to you, don't I?'.

Researchers effectively have to prove themselves by honouring any commitments they make to confidentiality, anonymity and/or Chinese walls, and therefore accept their role in occasionally having difficult conversations. For therapists, this is part of their professional practice, but it should also be part of the professional research practice of all management academics wanting to build close-with relationships. Researchers must also be alert to inadvertently breaking their commitments, by, for example, realizing that repeating verbatim what certain individuals say, even if they are not named, could give away who said what by the words used and the phraseology. This requires an awareness of organizational politics, high levels of intrapersonal empathy and a recognition that research-based close-with relationships are typically not the same as consultancy relationships. 'Close-with' researchers therefore ought to be asking difficult and complicated questions but in professional and safe ways.

'To invoice or not to invoice' is a question that arises from any discussion of trust in the building of 'close-with' relationships. To be in a relationship as a consulting academic ought to mean the expectation on the client's part of an invoice for professional services. While the presence of an invoice creates one form of legitimacy, however, it disrupts another: the right to ask difficult and – to the client, at least – potentially non-relevant questions as a professional researcher. Access is often granted free in exchange for academics providing something of use, however, and this usually creates the sense for researchers of being under no obligation to respond to pressure to break commitments they have made to individuals. Our suggestion is the careful consideration of the counter-point, which is the potential impact on the legitimacy element of the 'close-with' relationship when making this decision.

Positive growth and actualization orientation

The third pillar of practice illustrated by the notion of 'close-with' research is the strict necessity that any interventions made by researchers must be *orientated* to *positive growth* and *actualization*. In the research described here, for example, there was a primary concern for the development of the clients and the clients' organization (Wasylyshyn 2003; 2005), akin to the medical practitioner's 'First do no harm' principle. Ultimately, the researcher has to be interested in the practitioner and his/her organization for its own sake as well as for research outcomes: to care about managers. Calori talks about needing to enjoy the time and commitment offered when working with practitioners (Calori 2002: 878). This need for an interest in managers as practitioners and as individuals might not be apparent in early relationships, but, as relationships develop, researchers must expect that the practitioners with whom they are engaging will want to use some of the time they spend with the researcher to reflect on and develop their own practice. The researcher must enter into such relationships recognizing and expecting this. There should be an element of mutual growth and learning, however, although the learning might not be around the same issue. While, for practitioners, the learning will almost inevitably be around their personal practice and growth, for the researcher the learning might be around generic practice, or theoretically informed insights about the phenomenon of study.

Researchers must also recognize the risk involved in this type of research, as some relationships do not work out and therefore do not deliver.

This is alluded to above by the reference to 'fishing trips'. Another research site similar to the one presented in Box 25.1 was being researched in a similar way in the same time period by the same researcher. The CEO–therapist relationship simply did not gel. No 'close-with' relationship emerged to obtain the depth of data needed to theorize about the CEO's identity work and strategic change. It would not have had a positive outcome for the CEO for the relationship to be pursued, so the opportunity was passed over to another colleague. In this way, it can be seen that, sometimes, potentially high-value research opportunities have to get turned down as well as accepted.

Reflective practice

The research design just described reads, rightly, as a complex psycho-social political scenario. It is not at all straightforward (again we point to the exchange between Whittington 2006b and Hodgkinson and Wright 2006), and, for this reason, it requires execution that includes *reflective practice* on the part of the researcher. For instance, being in multiple 'close-with' relationships and in multiple roles within the same context requires the researcher to be very aware of the nature, purpose and, therefore, *boundaries* of each of those relationships. This is connected to the trust issue raised above.

Active reflection and boundary management are, in fact, the catalysts for action. In other words, being aware of a boundary or principle allows for any decisions around what is sayable and doable to be well taken. Reflective practice was achieved in the research setting discussed here using professionally required therapeutic supervision, consultancy mentoring and academic co-author dialogue. A further level of reflective practice was used in the analytic interpretation of events. In this way, researchers write themselves into their own analysis (Roos 2004). Reflective practice is thus a generic requirement of researchers working in close-with relationships.

Drawing inferences to meet the 'So what?' challenge

As with any collaborative research (Balogun, Huff and Johnson 2003), there is an onus on the researcher to move beyond reflection and link back to theory to address the 'So what?' question. This is partly aided through reflective practice by the researcher, but it is also about how data analysis is used to draw inferences from the data collected – and, in the case of research conducted through 'close-with' relationships, this will, of course, be inductive theory-building. The linkage previously discussed between narratives and identity provides one means of analysis, since the analysis stage can draw conclusions together through narrative. *Narrative analysis* (Boje 2001; Gabriel 2000) is therefore one means to this end. The stories that strategists tell of strategy-making (and its social environs) are constructed from *identity positions*, and have implications for the construction of identities.

This analysis is complicated by the fact that one of the significances of the identity positions is that they entail certain legitimacies (Alvesson and Willmott 2002). For example, in particular settings 'voice' will be granted to, and acknowledged in, certain identities. We see this in Box 25.1. At the outset of the story the board regarded the role and issue identities of the CEO as legitimate, which gave him the space to push through certain actions. They were less prepared for the personal identity as it emerged. The more empathetic self would probably be acceptable outside the workplace, but, once it had started to impact within work, a conflict of legitimacy arose. It is complex analyses such as these, however, that enable the researcher to draw inferences against existing studies in identity and strategy as practice to develop understanding about how 'who strategists are' affects what they do, and vice-versa.

In conclusion: lessons of 'close-with' relationships for strategy-as-practice research

The chapter has focused on exploring how to advance innovation in SAP research methods by considering in greater depth how to research the strategic practitioner. The central argument is that an identity perspective can enable researchers to study better the links between strategic practitioners and their praxis, and that this in turn

necessitates a close-with relationship with research participants, and therefore a certain methodological approach. While the particular methodological approach described here is a therapeutic relationship, this chapter is not arguing that this is the only approach that can be used to study strategic practitioners more closely, or that this is the only way of getting at practitioner identity. Rather, this example is used to derive a generic methodological approach to accesses identity through narratives captured from longitudinal engagement, multiple performances and back-stage access to the strategic practitioner as a person separate from his/her organizational role identity in a researcher–researched close-with relationship. More generally, if the strategy-as-practice field is to extend the study of strategic practitioners and their praxis, this requires a closeness of relationship that is more typical than it has been in SAP research to date.

Furthermore, this chapter argues that these conclusions are a logical extension of much that is written about methods for strategy-as-practice research. Figure 25.1 proposes a linked set of criteria that SAP research needs to meet if it is to genuinely achieve Calori's highest-utility management research. There are two particularly important aspects to the illustration we have drawn on to develop this figure that should be noted, however: (1) the creative insight on method it provides and (2) the extent to which reflexive rigour is required to deliver this style of work.

This chapter has also drawn on a particular illustration of praxis in and around a strategic change, but, equally, the identity approach can be used for the in-depth exploration of strategy work, such as strategy workshops and awaydays or boardroom strategic debates and decision-making. The focus could be on a single strategist involved in this work, such as the CEO, or multiple strategists. Similarly, the identity lens can be used to study those strategic practitioners who sit outside top management teams, such as middle managers, and their strategy work in the strategy-making process.

It is also important to reconnect the conclusions to the discussion in the first part of the chapter, and offer reflections that are more widely digestible to the strategy-as-practice community. The research agenda under discussion in this chapter has been the better understanding of *practitioners* in their *praxis of strategy-making*. As we argued earlier, fundamentally, the praxis and the person mutually implicate each other, and so one cannot be understood fully without the other. The discussion has focused on research efforts that seek to hold both the practitioner and his/her praxis in focus at the same time. Clearly, this would lead to criticism of more distant forms of research per se. Over and above this, however, the chapter is also arguing for a mindset shift, to move SAP research from a concern with the production of research that is close to practice to one that prioritizes being '*close with*' practice. The significant point in this chapter is the profound importance of relationship-building activity and the end result of making an impact.

In order to deliver 'close-with' relationship-orientated research that does deliver practitioner impact, some or all of the following lessons must be learned within the strategy-as-practice community. First, there is a need to critique, develop and extend our identities as researchers. In order to be in a 'close-with' relationship there must be more substance to a researcher's engagement than his/her research questions. Such demands may be beyond the capabilities of a doctoral student, but the challenge for those working in the field is to pay personal and professional development attention to this point throughout an academic career.

Second, there is a shift in terms of our attitude to the linearity of the research process. It certainly needs to be longitudinal, but also, because of its relationship-centricity, this type of work follows diffuse lines of causality in the collection and analysis of data, is erratic as opposed to consistent in terms of activity and almost certainly moves forwards and backwards in time. This requires long-term relationships, which is both demanding and potentially in contradiction to the pressures that academics face to get in, get data, get out and publish. The former pushes academics more towards an approach reminiscent of a 'smash and grab' raid.

This leads to the third and final point: there is a need for moral and ethical reflection by researchers active in this area. In other words, if there is not a genuine interest in and concern for the management practitioners and their practices under exploration, then the research opportunity should not be taken. Note that each of the three lessons is fundamentally about the researcher as the research tool, and not about a set of methods and techniques. The SAP community now faces the challenge of how to facilitate this form of slow-paced researcher development in today's high-demand, high-expectation, high-paced academic environment. We are not arguing that this is necessary for all types of strategy-as-practice research, but it is more likely to be true for those in the field who want to place the practitioner as central to their research agenda, as opposed to practices or praxis.

References

Alvesson, M., and Deetz, S. (2000), *Doing Critical Management Research*. London: Sage.

Alvesson, M., and Willmott, H. (2002), 'Identity regulation as organizational control: producing the appropriate individual', *Journal of Management Studies*, 39/5: 619–44.

Ashforth, B. E, and Mael, F. (1989), 'Social identity theory and the organization', *Academy of Management Review*, 14/1: 20–39.

Balogun, J., Huff, A. S., and Johnson, P. (2003), 'Three responses to the methodological challenges of studying strategizing', *Journal of Management Studies*, 40/1: 197–224.

Balogun, J., Jacobs, C. D., Jarzabkowski, P., Mantere, S., and Vaara, E. (2014), 'Placing strategy discourse in context: sociomateriality, sensemaking, and power', *Journal of Management Studies*, 51/2: 175–201.

Balogun, J., Jarzabkowski, P., and Seidl, D. (2007), 'Strategy as practice perspective', in Jenkins, M., Ambrosini, V., and Collier, N. (eds.), *Advanced Strategic Management: A Multi-Perspective Approach*: 196–214. London: Palgrave Macmillan.

Balogun, J., Johnson, P., and Beech, N. (2006), 'Unlocking interlocking cycles of strategy practice and identity work', paper presented at British Academy of Management conference, Belfast, 14 September.

Bartunek, J. (2008), 'Insider/outsider team research: the development of the approach and its meanings', in Shani, A., Adler, N., Mohrman, A., Pasmore, A., and Stymne, B. (eds.), *Handbook of Collaborative Management Research*: 73–91. Thousand Oaks, CA: Sage.

Beech, N., and Johnson, P. (2005), 'Discourses of disrupted identities in the practice of strategic change: the mayor, the street-fighter and the insider-out', *Journal of Organizational Change Management*, 18/1: 31–47.

Beech, N., and Sims, D. (2007), 'Narrative methods for identity research', in Pullen, A., Beech, N., and Sims, D. (eds.), *Exploring Identity: Concepts and Methods*: 288–301. Basingstoke: Palgrave Macmillan.

Boje, D. M. (2001), *Narrative Methods for Organizational and Communication Research*. London: Sage.

Broadfoot, K., Deetz, S., and Anderson, D. (2004), 'Multi-levelled, multi-method approaches to organizational discourse', in Grant, D., Hardy, C., Oswick, C., and Putnam, L. L. (eds.), *Organizational Discourse*: 193–211. London: Sage.

Calori, R. (2002), 'Essai: real time/real space research: connecting action and reflection in organization studies', *Organization Studies*, 23/6: 877–83.

Cooper, M. (2003), *Existential Therapies*. London: Sage.

Creed, W. E., and Scully, M. A. (2000), 'Songs of ourselves: employees' deployment of social identity in workplace encounters', *Journal of Management Inquiry*, 9/4: 391–412.

Denis, J.-L., Langley, A., and Rouleau, L. (2007), 'Strategizing in pluralistic contexts: rethinking theoretical frames', *Human Relations*, 60/1: 179–215.

Eden, C., and Huxham, C. (1996), 'Action research for management research', *British Journal of Management*, 7/1: 75–86.

Fenton, C., and Langley, A. (2011), 'Strategy as practice and the narrative turn', *Organization Studies*, 32/9: 1171–96.

Ford, J. D., and Ford, L. W. (1994), 'Logics of identity, contradiction and attraction in change', *Academy of Management Review*, 19/4: 756–86.

Gabriel, Y. (2000), *Storytelling in Organizations: Facts, Fictions, Fantasies*. Oxford University Press.

(2004), 'Narratives, stories and texts', in Grant, D., Hardy, C., Oswick, C., and Putnam, L. L. (eds.), *The Sage Handbook of Organizational Discourse*: 61–78. London: Sage.

Gioia, D. A., and Thomas, J. B. (1996), 'Identity, image and issue interpretation: sensemaking during strategic change in academia', *Administrative Science Quarterly*, 41/3: 370–403.

Goffman, E. (1959), *The Presentation of Self in Everyday Life*. London: Penguin Books.

(1961), *Encounters: Two Studies in the Sociology of Interaction*. Indianapolis: Bobbs-Merrill.

Graham-Hill, S., and Grimes, A. J. (2001), 'Dramatism as method: the promise of praxis', *Journal of Organizational Change Management*, 14/3: 280–94.

Hambrick, D. C. (2007), 'Upper echelons theory: an update', *Academy of Management Review*, 32/2: 334–43.

Hodgkinson, G. P., and Clarke, I. (2007), 'Conceptual note: exploring the cognitive significance of organizational strategizing: a dual-process framework and research agenda', *Human Relations*, 60/1: 243–55.

Hodgkinson, G. P., and Wright, G. (2006), 'Neither completing the practice turn, nor enriching the process tradition: secondary misinterpretations of a case analysis reconsidered', *Organization Studies*, 27/12: 1895–901.

Jarzabkowski, P., Balogun, J., and Seidl, D. (2007), 'Strategizing: the challenge of a practice perspective', *Human Relations*, 60/1: 5–27.

Jarzabkowski, P., Mohrman, S., and Scherer, A. (2010), 'Organization studies as applied science: the generation and use of academic knowledge about organizations: introduction to the special issue', *Organization Studies*, 31/9–10: 1189–207.

Johnson, G., Melin, L., and Whittington, R. (2003), 'Guest editors' introduction: micro strategy and strategizing: towards an activity-based view', *Journal of Management Studies*, 40/1: 3–22.

Johnson, G., Whittington, R., Melin, L., and Langley, A. (2007), *Strategy as Practice: Research Directions and Resources*. Cambridge University Press.

Kärreman, D., and Alvesson, M. (2004), 'Cages in tandem: management control, social identity and identification in a knowledge-intensive firm', *Organization*, 11/1: 149–75.

Langley, A. (2007), 'Process thinking in strategic organization', *Strategic Organization*, 5/3: 271–82.

Langley, A., and Abdallah, C. (2011), 'Templates and turns in qualitative studies of strategy and management', in Bergh, D. D., and Ketchen, D. J. (eds.), *Research Methodology in Strategy and Management*, vol. VI, *Building Methodological Bridges*: 201–35. Bingley, UK: Emerald.

Maister, D. (1997), *Managing the Professional Service Firm*. New York. Free Press.

Margolis, J. (1989), 'The novelty of Marx's theory of praxis', *Journal for the Theory of Social Behaviour*, 19/4: 367–88.

McLeod, J. (1997), *Narrative and Psychotherapy*. London: Sage.

Parker, M. (2007), 'Identification: organizations and structuralisms', in Pullen, A., Beech, N., and Sims, D. (eds.), *Exploring Identity: Concepts and Methods*: 61–82. Basingstoke: Palgrave Macmillan.

Pullen, A., and Linstead, S. (2005), 'Introduction: organizing identity', in *Organization and Identity*: 1–17. London: Routledge.

Rogers, C. R. (1961), 'A process conception of psychotherapy', in *On Becoming a Person: A Therapist's View of Psychotherapy*: 125–62. Boston: Houghton Mifflin.

Roos, J. (2004), 'I matter: remaining the first author in strategy research', in Floyd, S., Roos, J., Kellerman, F., and Jacobs, C. D. (eds.), *Innovating Strategy Processes*: 252–62. Oxford: Blackwell.

Rouleau, L. (2003), 'Micro-strategy as gendered practice: resisting strategic change through the family metaphor', paper presented at the nineteenth European Group for Organization Studies colloquium, Copenhagen, 5 July.

Silverman, D. (1993), *Interpreting Qualitative Data: Methods for Analysing Talk, Text and Interaction*. London: Sage.

Silverman, L. H. (1970), 'Further experimental studies of dynamic propositions in psychoanalysis: on the function and meaning of regressive thinking', *Journal of the American Psychoanalytic Asociation*, 18/1: 102–24.

Steffy, B. D., and Grimes, A. J. (1986), 'A critical theory of organization science', *Academy of Management Review*, 11/2: 322–36.

Suominen, K., and Mantere, S. (2010), 'Consuming strategy: the art and practice of managers' everyday strategy use', in Baum, J. A. C., and Lampel, J. (eds.), *Advances in Strategic Management*, vol. XXVII, *The Globalization of Strategy Research*: 211–45. Bingley, UK: Emerald.

Sveningsson, S., and Alvesson, M. (2003), 'Managing managerial identities: organizational fragmentation, discourse and identity struggle', *Human Relations*, 56/10: 1163–93.

Sveningsson, S, and Larsson, M. (2006), 'Fantasies of leadership: identity work', *Leadership*, 2/2: 203–24.

Thomas, R., and Davies, A. (2005), 'Theorizing the micro-politics of resistance: new public management and managerial identities in the UK public services', *Organization Studies*, 26/5: 683–706.

Vaara, E., and Whittington, R. (2012), 'Strategy-as-practice: taking social practices seriously', *Academy of Management Annals*, 6/1: 285–336.

Van de Ven, A. (2007), *Engaged Scholarship: A Guide for Organizational and Social Research*. Oxford University Press.

Wasylyshyn, K. (2003), 'Executive coaching: an outcome study', *Consulting Psychology Journal: Practice and Research*, 55/2: 94–106.

—— (2005), 'The reluctant president', *Consulting Psychology Journal: Practice and Research*, 57/1: 57–70.

Whittington, R. (2003), 'The work of strategizing and organizing: for a practice perspective', *Strategic Organization*, 1/1: 119–27.

—— (2006a), 'Completing the practice turn in strategy research', *Organization Studies*, 27/5: 613–34.

—— (2006b), 'Learning more from failure: practice and process', *Organization Studies*, 27/12: 1903–6.

—— (2007), 'Research that makes a difference, one way or another', in Johnson, G., Langley, A., Melin, L., and Whittington, R. (eds.), *Strategy as Practice: Research Directions and Resources*: 218–21. Cambridge University Press.

Wittgenstein, L. (1958 [1951]), *Philosophical Investigations*, 2nd edn. Oxford: Blackwell.

Ybema, S., Yanow, D., Wels, H., and Kamsteeg, F. (2009), 'Studying everyday organizational life', in *Ethnography and Organizations: Studying the Complexities of Everyday Organizational Life*: 1–20. London: Sage.

Zuber-Skerritt, O. (2001), 'Action learning and action research: paradigm, praxis and programs', in Sankara, S., Dick, B., and Passfield, R. (eds.), *Effective Change Management through Action Research and Action Learning: Concepts, Perspectives, Processes and Applications*: 1–20. Lismore, Australia: Southern Cross University Press.

Studying strategizing through biographical methods: narratives of practices and life trajectories of practitioners

LINDA ROULEAU

Despite efforts to develop innovative and new research methods for studying strategizing, most strategy-as-practice research has been based on longitudinal case studies drawing on interviews, observations and documents (Vaara and Whittington 2012). While these methods provide a complex set of historical and contextual data that are obviously necessary for understanding practices, they tend to concentrate on the organizational level, thus leaving unclear the way managers and others draw on their explicit and tacit knowledge when they are strategizing. Nonetheless, the essence of strategist agency cannot be separated from strategists' life experience and their social, professional and/or managerial identity (Tengblad 2012). Therefore, there is a need to develop interest in methods offering the possibility to better understand who strategists are and how they define themselves, how they make sense of the strategy and how they position themselves within their organization and external networks.

Biographical methods constitute a set of pertinent narrative methods of inquiry for carrying out in-depth studies of strategizing practices (Fenton and Langley 2011). With the aim of understanding the subjective essence of a person's life or part of that life, biographical research focuses on individuals, who are asked to narrate their experiences and provide their own accounts of the significant change they have gone through over time (Goodley et al. 2004). To better understand the practices and skills individuals use when they are strategizing, biographical methods constitute a relevant methodological option offering multiple variants

(biography, life story, autobiography, life history and so on) that can be used in complementary ways with ethnographic, participative and visual qualitative methods of inquiry (Merrill and West 2009).

This chapter proposes to study strategizing by collecting data through a specific kind of biographical method, namely narratives of practices. Narratives of practices are specific life stories that focus on work experience and professional trajectories (Bertaux 1981). As with any biographical method, narratives of practices, or work life stories, allow the researcher to dig into the 'life-world' of strategists, whether they are managers or not, in order to capture the taken-for-granted streams of routines, events, interactions and knowledge that constitute their practices (Küpers, Mantere and Statler 2013). For example, Gerstrøm (2013) draws on a variant of this method in her doctoral thesis to study how managers defend, protect and adapt their identity when dealing with financial crisis. Gialdini (2013) has studied the changes in the financial brokerage activities over time by asking brokers to narrate their life story at work. These recent strategy-as-practice studies show how, in telling their own stories of what they have gone through, managers and brokers bring together beliefs, events and a sense of self to express their lived experience of the major strategic change faced by their organization and their industry.

To explore the opportunities and challenges that narratives of practices as life stories at work can offer to SAP researchers, the chapter is divided into four parts. First, it provides an overview of what narratives of practices are. Second, the chapter explains why narratives of practices constitute a relevant methodology for gaining an in-depth look into the world of practitioners who are strategizing. Third, it draws on some illustrative data extracted from a previous study involving middle managers dealing with the restructuring of their organization. Fourth, the chapter concludes by discussing the challenges of using narratives of practices to study strategizing.

Narratives of practices as life stories at work

Adopting the strategy-as-practice perspective in research involves using methodological tools to understand how managers and others strategize in the course of their day-to-day activities. All biographical methods, such as life stories (Lambright and Quinn 2011), autobiographies (Watson 2009), collective life stories (Lieblich 2013), self-report methods (Spowart and Nairn 2014) and so on, meet this requirement in two ways. First, biographical methods provide a sequential account of the interactional stream of experience that allows the researcher to capture what has been said and done by the practitioner who is telling his/her story. Second, biographical methods give the practitioners the ability to tell in their own words what their 'theories-in-use' are (Koliba and Lathrop 2007). By recounting what works and what does not, they draw on their knowledge and experience to generate narrative accounts of what is relevant in their practice.

In management, the reconstruction of the life stories of successful executives and entrepreneurs (Iacocca, Sloan, Jobs and others) has been, and still is, widely exploited. Indeed, when successful senior executives or entrepreneurs tell their stories, a part of those accounts is of a public nature and contributes to maintaining specific visions and interests that can secure the corporate image with the multiple stakeholders (Schoenberger 2001). Since the end of the 1980s, however, the genre has been undergoing a renewal. Biographical methods are gaining in importance, and several authors working in different sub-fields of management are adopting it (Sims 1993; Kimberley and

Bouchikhi 1995; Kisfalvi 2000; Cohen and Mallon 2001; Shamir and Eilam 2005; Cohen 2006; Crowley-Henry and Weir 2007; Díaz García and Welter 2013; Lambright and Quinn 2011).

This chapter proposes to look at narratives of practices, a specific biographical method for studying how practitioners are strategizing. As Bertaux (1981) explains, a narrative of practices is in some ways a life story focused on one part of this life, either professional, political, parental, communitarian or other. For example, Davids (2011) reconstitutes through documents and interviews a Mexican female politician's life story in order to demonstrate the micro-dynamics on which her political agency was based. In doing so, Davids is drawing on the political life story of this woman or the 'narrative of practices' of this politician. In fact, narratives of practices that focus on strategist or managerial life story are close to what have been called life stories at work or career life stories (Valkevaara 2002). Narratives of practices are centred on the practitioners' strategic change account, emphasizing its embeddedness in their whole work trajectory.

With the narrative turn in management and organization studies, we are seeing the terms 'narrative' and 'practice' used together more and more often. The term 'narrative-based practice' refers to the narratives related to specific forms of professional practice, such as nursing, social work and even manager (Robson 2013). The term 'narrative practices' has to do with how individuals work with and use their stories in order to construct their identity and/or make sense of what is happening (Gubrium 2010). In some ways, narratives 'of' practices help to integrate these two views. In this chapter, the term 'narratives *of* practices' is used as a generic expression to refer to a research method in which practitioners are invited to make their personal account of strategic events while situating it in their whole managerial and organizational career. Following Watson (2009), narratives of practices correspond in some ways to the autobiographical strategy work that individuals perform when asked to recount their own trajectory. The difference is that, in narratives of practices, the narrators have to pay specific attention to the strategic change they are experiencing when recounting their professional story.

Each narrative of practices is the result of the temporal schema structuring the trajectories of the individuals who are telling their stories (Bertaux and Kohli 1984). First, every narrative of practices has a beginning, a development and an end. As with any story, a narrative of practices is a sequential account of events structured around a plot involving different characters. Through the accounts that practitioners give of the strategic change they are narrating, they also share a part of their experience in which their 'stocks of knowledge' reside. Second, this story needs to be inscribed in their socioprofessional trajectory. Individuals are not just strategists, managers, consultants and so on; they are, first and foremost, social actors. Therefore, there is a need to know their own story of their past (how they became a strategist or manager) and how they situate themselves in relation to their future in order to understand how and why they act in specific ways. It is the embeddedness of the strategic change's story in their own individual life story at work that makes narratives of practices a specific biographical research method for studying how managers and others are strategizing and which set of knowledge and skills they draw on when doing strategic change.

Time is also important in narratives of practices, at the level of the relations between the researcher and the practitioner who is telling his/her story. Narratives of practices result from the construction through time of a relationship between a researcher (the narratee) and a practitioner (the narrator) telling his/her work story. In fact, the production of narratives of practices, like any variant of the biographical method, involves several meetings with the narrator (Merrill and West 2009). This has two advantages. On one hand, it establishes a deeper relationship with the practitioner, on whom the wealth of the data that are collected depends. On the other hand, the practitioner who is telling his/her story has the chance to reflect on what he/she said and to prepare for the next interview, usually being aware of the theme in advance. These multiple encounters also give the researcher the chance to return to certain points that remain obscure. Narratives of practices are, in fact, the result of a narrative co-construction whose authenticity and consistency – two of the three fundamental criteria

of the biographical method, according to Atkinson (1998), the third being the integrity of the researcher – depend on the bonds of trust, the way the researcher and the subject engage each other in this narrative process. In this sense, the narrating is an event in the practitioner's work life as it is part of the construction of that life (Essers and Benschop 2007). It is the same for the researcher too; the hearing is both about the life told and constitutive of it and of the researcher's life. The story as it is told influences both the practitioner and the researcher.

Even though narratives of practices are centred on individuals, this does not mean that managers and others are considered perfect rational agents, as the neoliberal ideology claims. Rather, narratives of practices are about the subjective interpretation of what happens at work. Indeed, the narrators' stories are subject to reinterpretations every time they are retold. Moreover, when practitioners are telling their life story at work, they try to encapsulate it in a coherent and structured account in order to make sense of it to themselves and to the researcher. According to Bertaux and Delcroix (2000), even though there is a distance between work life as it is experienced and work life as it is told, the subjective account that practitioners give cannot be separated from the way they live their work. The way managers and others live their work influences the way they talk about it. Therefore, narratives of practices provide an 'experiential truth' of the narrator's work life; and it is this experiential truth, more than the complete and accurate real account of events, that the SAP researcher is looking for when he/she is using narratives of practices as a research method.

Given the subjective nature of narratives of practices, it might seem that they constitute an acontextual research method, since they are based on gathering information from personal interpretations. When practitioners recount their stories, however, these stories are necessarily rooted – explicitly or not – in different levels of reality (Chamberlayne and Spano 2000). In fact, in the narrative act, the individuals who tell their stories do so by positioning themselves in their sociohistorical context (Cederberg 2014). Throughout their account, practitioners will refer to the organizational and societal context, the structure of the industrial sector they work in and/or the socio-professional category they belong to. They do so by evoking meaningful scripts and templates or some working rules they think are appropriate to the situation they are talking about. This allows the researcher to capture the contextual dimension, which is, consciously or not, part of the narratives of practices. Of course, the researcher needs to be aware of the contextual discourses that are available to the narrators and that allow them to render their story acceptable both for themselves and for the researcher.

As for the biographical method in general, narratives of practices are used to promote reflexive thought, or even the individuals' empowerment vis-à-vis their professional practices (Suárez-Ortega 2013). By telling their own stories to someone else, the practitioners contribute to clarifying their interpretation of events, and this review of their experience allows them to take a step back from their action. Narrating one's own life story at work constitutes a reflexive act that changes the self and changes life (Rouleau 2003). Part of the reality construction occurs in the meaning that people develop while speaking. As an act of reflecting on oneself, narrating one's own work experience procures a sense of personal satisfaction and might help in taking actions in the future.

In addition to these distinctive features, it must be added that biographical methods, like narratives of practices, offer multiple possibilities for collecting and analysing data (Eide 2012). The research design can take a variety of forms and fit into broader mixed-methods procedures (von der Lippe 2010). Several researchers use the ethnographic research and the life story approach conjointly. This is what Cohen (2006) did, for example, when he combined two methodological approaches, multi-sites ethnography and multi-generation life story interviews, to study the patterns of knowledge transmission between workers in a globalization context. In addition, the data from the biographical method can also be used as secondary data. In the paper I wrote with Balogun on middle managers, we drew on two narratives of practices of successful middle managers, produced for purposes other than those of the paper, to propose a

framework showing how they discursively accomplished their sensemaking activities (Rouleau and Balogun 2011). Although, most of the time, biographical data are gathered individually, they can also be amassed collectively. For example, Lieblich (2013) collected groups of autobiographical writings of women. Biographical methods such as narratives of practices and other variants can also be the object of structural analyses that draw on quantitative analytical methods involving content analysis and co-occurrence analysis (Atkinson 1998). Finally, the biographical method can even be used in the framework of comparative research approaches at the international level. This was the case with the SOSTRIS ('Social Strategies in Risk Societies') project, the objective of which was to understand global social transformations by taking into account the diversity and the complexity of individual trajectories (Chamberlayne and Spano 2000). This project brought together researchers from seven European countries (the United Kingdom, France, Germany, Greece, Italy, Spain and Sweden), all using the biographical method (Centre for Biography in Social Policy, Sociology Department, East London University).

Narratives of practices and strategizing

Until now few strategy-as-practice researchers have integrated biographical methods in their research, even though many studies have recognized the interest of using them (Fenton and Langley 2011; Küpers, Mantere and Statler 2013; Voronov, De Clercq and Hinings 2013; Landry 2011). Balogun (2003) and Hope (2010) have used semi-structured diaries that, as a self-reporting method, are a variant of the biographical method (see also Balogun and Johnson 2004). As mentioned in the introduction, two theses on practitioners from the financial sector have innovated in paying specific attention to the life trajectories of their informants. Other researchers have studied practitioners at lower levels involved in major strategic change in order to understand the transformations in their skills and competences (Arnaud 2009; Vaidyanathan 2012).

As the strategy-as-practice perspective is at a crossroads (Rouleau 2013), there is a need to strengthen our commitment to the view of practice as knowledge, and biographical methods offer a privileged path in this direction. Put differently, if we want to understand 'what people do when they are strategizing', there is a need to base our research on methods that allow us to access to the multiple forms of knowledge people draw on in their situated activity (Fauré and Rouleau 2011). By being focused on the individuals who are telling their stories, narratives of practices provide a privileged access to practitioners who represent the distinctive level of analysis of the SAP perspective. This section explains why narratives of practices constitute a relevant and innovative methodology for understanding how managers and others are strategizing.

The strategy-as-practice perspective invites researchers to conceive strategy as any social practice contextually embedded in a set of cultural, political and institutional relations (Vaara and Whittington 2012). Because managers and others tell their story using social frames and conventions that seem appropriate to the cultural and organizational norms of their situation (Díaz García and Welter 2011), narratives of practices allow the researcher to understand the situated, discursive and interactional nature of the strategy formation. Biographical methods such as narratives of practices are interested in the 'practical' accomplishment of social actors able to engage in the production of organizational life, and therefore adopt a position that recognizes the skills and competences of individuals as well as their social embeddedness (Crowley-Henry and Weir 2007). By inscribing the strategic change account in the practitioner's professional or working trajectory, drawing on narratives of practices allows us to understand how strategy is accomplished and performed in social relationships and affiliations that go beyond the managerial end purposes of the strategy.

Strategizing is done on a daily basis at the boundary of organizational activities – that is, where the practitioners meet people (clients, partners, suppliers, etc.) from their environment (Teulier and Rouleau 2013). Therefore, the SAP perspective aims to understand how managers mobilize the explicit and tacit knowledge relative to their firm's positioning in its environment. As 'reflective practitioners', to use Schon's (1987) term, when managers tell their stories they will also reveal a part of the linguistic and relational skills they used in the course of their action. In addition, through their stories, they will say what tools and models they used to exercise their capacity for action. By recounting events – what they did concretely – the practitioners reveal part of the stock of interpretive procedures they draw on when they are relating to others (Atkinson 1998). Through the choice of events that they decide to recount or not to recount, they partly reveal the shared knowledge in which their practices are entrenched (Goodley et al. 2004).

Finally, strategy-as-practice researchers are interested in investigating a larger range of practitioners than top managers in strategy formation (Johnson, Melin and Whittington 2003; Balogun, Huff and Johnson 2003; Jarzabkowski, Balogun and Seidl 2007). In the social sciences, biographical methods are recognized for their capacities to give a voice to people (for example, immigrants, farmers, tradespersons and so on) who are generally excluded from the official history – the history that was interpreted in favour of the interests of the dominant classes. In the same way, narratives of practices enable us to give back a voice not only to middle and lower managers but also to all the actors belonging to the various subgroups inside or around the organization who are generally not considered in traditional strategy research (Denis, Langley and Rouleau 2010).

Overall, narratives of practices are both sufficiently rich and complex to be able to analyse in detail how practitioners are strategizing. It is a methodological approach that, as Table 26.1 shows, adequately meets the five criteria that Balogun, Huff and Johnson (2003) have selected for identifying appropriate methods for research on strategizing. The narrative of practices is a research method that allows the collection of complex data focused on questions of concern to managers and that maximizes researchers' time and resources. As well as being a very undemanding method for the organization and providing access to high-quality

Table 26.1 Narratives of practices according to Balogun, Huff and Johnson's (2003) criteria

Method requirements for strategizing research	How narratives of practices meet these criteria
Provide broad and deep data collection	Data based on a temporal schema Data embedded in a context Data that can be compared Data that can be gathered from individuals belonging to all hierarchical levels
Elicit full and willing commitment from informants	Very undemanding method for the organization Satisfying method for participants
Make the most effective use of researchers' time	Data collection time concentrated during meetings Analysis develops from meeting to meeting Permit collection of a wide range of empirical evidence (practices, events, discourses, representations, etc.)
Anchor the questions being asked in the organizational realities	Sensitive to organizational issues Take into account what interests the narrator
Provide useful results	Permit participants to take stock of their actions Permit participants to think about their professional trajectory Favour the development of a relationship of trust with the researcher that can lead to subsequent collaborations

interpretative data, it allows researchers to gather a wide range of empirical evidence to reveal strategy formation at the micro level. In addition, narratives of practices encourage practitioners to be reflexive, and at the same time require a more intense form of commitment on the part of researchers – elements that Balogun, Huff and Johnson (2003) identify as being very important criteria for selecting methods for SAP research. Of course, the full potential of this research method depends in the last instance on the researchers' skills at entering into contact

with the practitioner who is telling his/her story, establishing a relation of trust and considering themselves as partners in the research rather than outside observers.

Middle managers' narratives of practices

In order to convince readers of the relevance and usefulness of narratives of practices for studying strategizing, this section presents some results of a study based on this variant of biographical methods. The research aim was to study the role of middle managers who had experienced an organizational restructuring. In the next few lines I first show how the data were collected and ana-lysed. Then the case of Mary is used to present four sets of practices underlying different types of knowledge that middle managers draw on to deal with a restructuring.

The middle managers I met were recruited through 'expert opinion' (personal contacts, an MBA class and an arrangement with a firm spe-cializing in executive career management). To facilitate the aggregation of data, each participant was asked to suggest some names of people who had gone through the same restructuring, thereby producing what Bertaux (1981) has called 'clus-ters' of narratives of practices. These micro-groups were needed in order to grasp a part of the contextual complexity in which their action took place. While the cross-referencing of the events provided an outline of the context, the different ways of recounting the events revealed the meaning each middle manager gave to them. Fifty-eight narratives of practices with middle managers working in the private (twenty-three), public (eighteen) and non-profit (seventeen) sectors were gathered in order to better under-stand how the middle managers were experien-cing or had experienced the restructuring of their organization.

As mentioned above, it is usual to meet the narrator several times when researching through narratives of practices. In this study, the narratives of practices were gathered from at least three meet-ings with each practitioner. From the beginning the middle managers were informed of the objective of each of the meetings, which allowed them to think about the next meeting and prepare their accounts. In the first meeting, the managers narrated their career path from their schooling to their first experiences of managing to when they were hired for their current job. This meeting allowed them to recall how they became middle managers and what the most notable experiences were in their own trajectory to becoming the middle manager they now are. The second meeting focused on the present, and was entirely given over to the role they played in the restructuring and how they saw and made sense of the events surrounding it. The third meeting dealt mainly with their career forecast – that is, their own future as well as the future of the company after the restructuring. This projection into the future after having recounted their past and their present is a good way to learn what managing means for them and how they see their role. In general, the meetings lasted from ninety minutes to two hours. In several cases, more than three meetings were held, because the stories related to the restructurings sometimes required more time. In most cases, the meetings took place during the restructuring and were spread out over four months.

In this way, approximately 300 hours of narratives were collected. To facilitate the data transcription step and to reduce the costs, I proceeded in two stages: first, the best narratives of practices (fifteen) were transcribed in full, and then syntheses or mini-cases of the other narratives were written. Even though there are multiple ways of analysing data from biographical methods (Kaźmierska 2014), I proceeded in two steps: (1) by coding the information on the basis of factual categories relevant to the narrator (for example, events in the restructuring, consequences of the restructuring on the middle manager's work, activities and formal roles carried out by the middle managers); and (2) by extensively analysing the narratives of practices. This step involved first bringing out the representations and meanings given to the restructuring – such as ability to act on the situation, search for legitimacy, interpretations of the changes – in the middle managers' narratives. Next, a repertory of activities and representations was constructed for each narrative. It

was then possible to depict the general sense of each narrative while identifying some contradictions between the first and the second or third narratives. These contradictions conveyed by the narrators acted as discursive revealers of their changing identity (Wengraf 2000). Working with these contradictions helped to depict the changes in the ways they accomplished and made sense of their roles throughout the organizational restructuring.

The repertory of activities and representations was also helpful for investigating the practices and knowledge they drew on in the restructuring. For example, four broad sets of practices were identified. Each of them is founded on a specific type of knowledge (Figure 26.1). These practices can be stated as follows: (1) approaching the restructuring as a life crisis (individual knowledge); (2) convincing others (socio-organizational knowledge); (3) mobilizing networks (relational knowledge); and (4) dealing with unintended consequences (professional knowledge and technical knowledge). In order to illustrate these practices, the case of Mary is presented. Mary was a nurse, and she had been working in the same health care organization for twenty-five years, where she had held the position of director of nursing in the long-term care department. With the restructuring, she became coordinator of nursing in the day surgery unit, and was also in charge of patient services.

Approaching the restructuring as a life crisis (individual knowledge)

The difficulty with restructurings is that middle managers find themselves at the centre of a set of contradictory tensions that destabilize the way things are usually done. In Mary's case, she was collegially managing her team-mates. With the restructuring she became the coordinator of a unit resulting from the merger of two teams with different cultural backgrounds. Suddenly, and through no desire of her own, she found herself at the head of a recomposed team whose operating rules were not clear and were somewhat conflicting. While she was still 'grieving' her forced transfer, she was asked to implement a new beneficiary service philosophy. Tensions were high in the merged

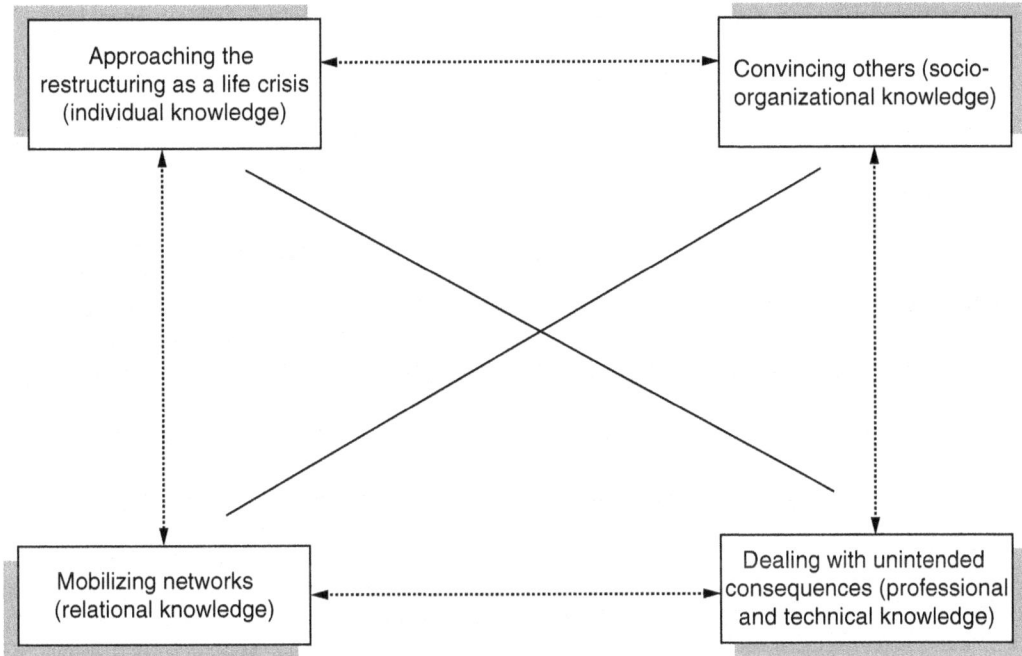

Figure 26.1 Practices of middle managers in organizational restructuring (underlying types of knowledge)

team, especially since the reorganization called into question the nursing profession. Thus, this middle manager found herself immersed in a situation that she knew would be difficult to solve in the short term.

Based on all the narratives of practices obtained in this study, it seems that some managers who were wrestling with such dilemmas came through better than others. The difference partly resided in their ability to use the stock of knowledge they had stored up in the course of their prior individual experiences. In fact, those who acted as if they were dealing with another 'life crisis' seemed to come through much better than the others. Having already experienced difficult situations, they drew upon difficult key past events in their lives to act and react to the ambiguity provoked by the restructurings.

In the narratives of practices analysed, several middle managers mentioned having lived through major life crisis events – such as the death of a father, a divorce or the illness of a loved one – that to a greater or lesser degree contributed to orienting their professional trajectory. When in their initial meeting middle managers mentioned

having experienced a major life crisis event, the subsequent interview on the restructuring took a narrative form similar to the one used in the preceding interview to recount that difficult time. This was observed in 75 per cent of cases in which middle managers had mentioned such an event in the first interview. In other words, the narrators symbolically positioned their narrative as if the restructuring was nothing but another 'life crisis'. For example, if they had experienced the previous challenge as a 'victim', they also positioned themselves as a victim in their narrative of the restructuring. In contrast, if they had played a central role in a personal life crisis situation, their narrative of the restructuring was that of a hero.

In Mary's case, she became responsible for her family at a very young age, and this seems to have determined her professional trajectory. She says:

> I am the eldest in a family of six children; my parents divorced when I was quite young. At fourteen, I took over the role of mother of the family, since my mother was at work. I had to take care of the others; it was the beginning of my apprenticeship. [. . .] Since the age of fourteen I've

always worked to pay for my studies, to be independent. I had to take on my responsibilities at a young age. That's how I became a nurse. It's also why I've always been very methodical, planning to organize the future. It's difficult to take care of others if you're not able to take care of yourself.

Therefore, the central plot in her narrative of practices concerning her professional life is based on motherhood. It is also in these terms that she talks about the restructuring:

> We used to be like a little family, and suddenly everything changed. I was a stranger to half the girls. We didn't see things the same way. I had to live with them. We had to learn to respect each other. It was long, and I had a hard time, but now things are better. Maybe we're becoming a blended family.

In telling how she approaches her work throughout the restructuring, this middle manager draws on metaphors and conventions that are meaningful for her (family, motherhood, respect, and so on), and by so doing she is also expressing what she means when talking about work, restructuring and life in general. For her, strategizing has to be accomplished through symbols and activities that are meaningful to her and that guide her in life – that is to say, through her practical knowledge of what life is.

Convincing others (socio-organizational knowledge)

In a restructuring, communicating the new strategy – the new direction the company is taking – poses a difficult problem for a number of middle managers. In fact, in a restructuring, middle managers are called upon daily to translate the new direction in terms that can be understood by their colleagues, and even by the people with whom they are in contact outside the organization. Thus, middle managers have to create meaning by using the 'right words' and by creating effective images of the change that will allow them to capture the attention of the other, and if necessary influence the person with whom they are interacting (Rouleau and Balogun 2011). Rather than talking in

strategic terms, they have to use ordinary language and shared meaning to effectively translate the main issues. According to one middle manager, 'There are several ways to present a change; you have to choose the one that you think will please, and that will be the most credible to the person you are talking to.'

For several middle managers, this skill depends in part on their ability to make their comments fit into the socio-organizational codes that will make sense for the other. For example, using the seduction mode when addressing women, creating enthusiasm and magic when speaking to journalists, playing on nationalistic feeling to persuade investors to promote economic development by investing in small firms are all ways to draw on social codes during day-to-day interactions and encounters to convince the other that there are certain elements of the change that are positive in the long term.

In the restructuring, Mary has to convince the nurses with whom she is working to tell their patients that day surgery is as good as, and even preferable to, in-hospital convalescence, when they know that their patients prefer to stay in the hospital. This is not an obvious situation, since the nurses themselves are convinced that the new rule is a budgetary prerogative rather than the result of a real concern for patients. So, she says:

> I know what they think. I can't change that. What I say to my girls is: 'Let's give them [the administration] a chance. But we won't change the way we give care. In this hospital, we always said that care was important; what counts in the end is how we do it – what happens on the floor.'

This comment shows that Mary is a compromising person. She tries to convince the nurses by drawing on their team spirit and her relationships with them ('my girls'). In so doing, she is drawing on her practical knowledge of the social codes that constitute them as a team. By evoking the hospital culture and reassuring them about their autonomy in their job, however, she is referring to organizational codes, and she positions herself as a protector of their professional identity, thus reaffirming that, despite the message she conveys to adopt the new rules, she is mainly on their side.

Mobilizing networks (relational knowledge)

In a restructuring, the social network – the strong ties as much as the weak ties – constitutes a first-order resource. This network arises from an exchange negotiated among several people, such as colleagues, subordinates and people from outside the company. This negotiated exchange takes the following form: 'I am doing such and such for you but you owe me one.' This is the way to thwart or to use the formal rules of the organization or to create flexible ties between structural interfaces that otherwise would never encounter each other.

In the restructuring, Mary has to adapt to a different care logic, and she has to use her own networks in order to be able to rebuild a new team spirit. In this vein, Mary relates:

> With the restructuring, I often felt at a disadvantage. I had always worked in long-term care, so, working in day surgery – in the beginning I wasn't sure; it was another world. I was lucky I wasn't alone; when I had a problem, a girl who I did not understand and with whom I had difficulty, I knew who to see to find a way to work with her or to protect myself. In general, when I have a problem, I go see the people I know; I learn a lot from them.

In a restructuring, it is these internal and external networks that allow middle managers to adequately play their strategic role. When these networks are destabilized for a period, they take on an even more critical importance. In the same way, the long-standing knowledge of the day-to-day anecdotes and rumours about the organization that are central to the organization's cultural cement constitute indispensable practical knowledge to advance a priority file, and, of course, to ensure that the work is done on time. The appropriate use of one's network at the right time can be as helpful as the practical knowledge indispensable for activating it.

Dealing with unintended consequences (professional knowledge and technical knowledge)

Even though they may have been very carefully planned, restructurings almost always entail a set of unexpected consequences (technical problems, changes in customers' habits, etc.). These often degenerate into conjunctural crises that have the effect of brutally emphasizing the failures and the contingencies of the ongoing restructuring. These crises can also be intensified by uncontrollable events that occur simultaneously in the environment, such as holiday periods or disastrous climate conditions, thus creating emergency situations that enormously complicate the course of the change.

During these difficult periods management cannot always act effectively, since it is itself undergoing reorganization. It is often the middle managers who have been in the organization for some time who are left to solve the problems. Their professional and technical knowledge as well as their work and organizational experience sometimes enable them to pinpoint a technical detail that can make all the difference. This situation is what happens to Mary, and this is how she tells the story:

> One day there was a fire in the chronic care wing. Files were missing; they were overwhelmed. The new director didn't know what to do. It was a free-for-all in the unit. I said: 'I'll go. I did it for twenty-five years, I know several of the patients, I'll get it running again; it won't take too long.' Not everyone agreed, but it really helped them; it enabled them to avoid problems. The DG thanked me several times.

In this quote, we can see that, because Mary has worked in long-term care for many years, she is able to efficiently deal with the situation. Moreover, when experienced middle managers are able to resolve a crisis in the course of the restructuring, as Mary does, they become the 'heroes of the day' with senior management. So, for a moment, they receive some recognition from their superiors while they are paying the costs of the ongoing restructuring.

This dual dynamic of negation/recognition impacts their identity as middle managers – that is to say, the way they position themselves in relation to their subordinates and superiors. For example, in her narrative of practices, Mary demonstrates that, while she was previously focused on the well-being of the patient, her new responsibilities lead her to define herself through her ability to control and dispatch the work throughout her team. Despite the fact that this identity change seems to be difficult (as was also the case for most of the other middle managers I met), she nonetheless supports the restructuring by drawing on her knowledge through the set of practices described above.

Challenges of using narratives of practices

The use of narratives of practices to better understand the transformation of middle managers' role and identity in restructurings illustrates that it is a method that offers multiple possibilities for exploring how strategizing is accomplished in practice. By being reflexive, by requiring greater closeness between practitioners and researchers and by producing complex and in-depth data, narratives of practices, like any variant of biographical methods, constitute an innovative methodological option for strategy-as-practice researchers. Nevertheless, three major challenges await researchers who use narratives of practices to study strategizing. These challenges have to do with sampling, data collection and data analysis.

The first challenge related to the use of narratives of practices – and, more largely, to biographical methods in general – concerns choosing the people to be invited to tell their stories (Goodley et al. 2004; von der Lippe 2010). Researchers have to find people who possess the basic characteristics they are looking for and who have something to say. This becomes more complicated when researchers are considering using narratives of practices in a perspective recognizing that strategy is not uniquely the domain of top managers. While everyone has an interesting story to tell, not everyone has the same ability to narrate his/her own story and step back from the events that mark the life of an organization. For example, researchers must avoid practitioners who merely recount one event after another and who might use this experience as a platform they would not otherwise have. Even though narratives of practices facilitate access to data, since they are based first and foremost on the individual's goodwill rather than the organization's, it is nonetheless risky to use the narratives of practices approach with practitioners whose narrative skills cannot be evaluated beforehand. Thus, researchers may find it pertinent to pair this method with other data collection procedures in order to increase the quality of the narratives of practices – for example, organizational ethnography, collective interview, personal documents, shadowing, phone diaries. It must be remembered that, in terms of narratives of practices, it is not so much the number of narratives but, rather, the depth of the data collected that counts (Merrill and West 2009).

The second challenge is linked to the fact that narratives of practices are reflective discourses that are retrospectively performed (Suárez-Ortega 2013). By nature, narratives of practices are based on the key stages of the person's life story at work (von der Lippe 2010). Apart from a few cues from the researchers at the start to ask the narrators to tell a segment of their story, it is preferable to leave people free to organize their discourse as they choose. Incidentally, the story produced is not, strictly speaking, at the level of the practical conscience, so researchers must make sure to guide their narrators to relate what they said and what they did rather than let them wander and reflect on their actions. In other words, researchers constantly have to bring the narrators back to their actions: what they did and what they said (Goodley et al. 2004). Narrators will always have a tendency to rationalize their action and, for the sake of social desirability vis-à-vis their interviewers – who are linked to business schools or universities – to use established and proven management models. Here, vigilance is indispensable, and I emphasize once again that researchers have the responsibility to regularly bring the narrators' story back to the level of facts: what happened, what was said. This is the only way to ensure privileged access to the practical knowledge that the individuals drew upon when they strategized. This access will then depend on the researchers' data analysis strategies (Robson 2013). For instance, researchers will have to find ways to bring out the manner in which the narrators deployed their tacit competence, such as by constantly comparing and contrasting the themes that emerge from the whole framework of the story in order to interpret the hidden meanings of that story.

The third challenge concerns the fact that narratives of practices are first and foremost a biographical method in which individuals plot and make sense of their own story (Fillis 2006). Thus, the contextual dimension, though always present in the narrative, is not always apparent to the person who is outside the story being told. Researchers must provide themselves with the analytic means to locate and bring out the contextual elements contained in the narrations (Cederberg 2014; Díaz García and Welter 2013). This obviously requires the researchers to have a profound preliminary knowledge of these contextual elements. To facilitate the task, they can conduct some collective narratives of practices, or they can plan to cross-reference the narratives during data analysis. Finally, it is important to triangulate the data gathered in order to reinforce the researchers' knowledge of the context in which the stories they are examining were produced so that they can meet this challenge, which is typical of all the variants of the biographical method (Eide 2012).

These challenges are far from being unsolvable (Fillis 2006); but they do require creativity, rigour and the researchers' profound involvement in the design research (Robson 2013). Among other things, triangulation of the data sources allows the researcher to cope with these challenges (Eide 2012). For example, official records may facilitate a good sampling, help the researcher to refocus the interview when necessary and corroborate information (Robson 2013). Finally, the researcher should never forget that the quality of the data collected through narratives of practices depends on the authenticity of the relationships lived and experienced with the practitioner (Lieblich 2013). In other words, what is told, heard and interpreted in narratives of practices arises out of the intersubjective connection between the researcher and the practitioner. Such relationships might be impeded by psychological processes such as identification from the practitioner to the researcher or transference from the researcher to the practitioner (Suárez-Ortega 2013). Even though the researcher is never fully protected from orienting the story and interpreting it through his/her own unconscious representations and desires, it is necessary to design the research in ways that will allow him/her to introspectively distance him-/herself from the whole process.

Conclusion

This chapter has looked at narratives of practices as thematic life stories focused on work experience. It argues that narratives of practices provide a complex set of interpretive data relevant to better understanding how practitioners strategize through their daily activities. By looking at data collected from a previous study involving middle managers dealing with a restructuring, this chapter illustrates how they draw on their knowledge in order to accomplish their strategic role. As with any methodological tools, narratives of practices comprise some strengths and weaknesses, which will now be discussed.

The first strength of the narratives of practices technique as a methodology for studying strategizing is that it really enters into the subjective account of what managers and others 'do'. The second is that it provides fertile data that can be used by strategy-as-practice researchers to develop typologies of practices and skills deployed by managers, to formulate propositions and even to propose theoretical models of strategizing. The third strength is that the wealth and the depth of the data gathered are such that they can serve to explore multiple research questions around strategizing. While I was studying the transformation of middle managers' role in organizational restructuring, these data might also have been used to look at other themes and advance a large set of organizational concepts. Finally, this method is particularly useful for exploring problems and questions for which data might be difficult to obtain. For example, given that restructurings generally occur in a conflictual context, the use of narratives of practices has greatly facilitated access to data.

The major criticisms of narratives of practices are that they make generalizing difficult and that the quality of the data depends on the depth of the relationships between the researcher and the subject. As stated earlier, another weakness is the difficulty of selecting and finding a good storyteller. Finally, as with any other qualitative study, they generally provide an abundance of data, which need to be carefully and relevantly reduced and coded for analytic headway to be made in order to really contribute to advancing research on strategy as practice.

Like any research method, narratives of practices are more suitable for advancing some agendas than others. Here, two main SAP research perspectives might be considered. First, narratives of practices might be relevant for research concerned with the knowledge, skills and emotions used by managers when they are strategizing. For example, strategic leadership, the role of practitioners in strategic innovation and work identity in strategic change might be very convenient topics to be explored through narratives of practices. Second, given that biographical methods have been used for researching people traditionally marginalized by researchers, narratives of practices might also be a good way to explore how practitioners who are not generally associated with strategy research contribute to the making of strategy. Beyond middle managers, it might be interesting to use narratives of practices to look at how consultants, lower managers, boundary workers and institutional entrepreneurs strategize in their daily activities.

In short, for the researcher, studying strategizing through narratives of practices is an enriching experience, while, for the subject, narrating one's own story can be an insightful and empowering one. When I conducted narratives of practices with middle managers, several of them testified to the reflective benefits they gained from the exercise. Managers rarely have the opportunity to talk about themselves, what they do, who they are and what they think, and this is even truer in a restructuring. Some of them called me after the meetings in order to let me know that this experience was the beginning of a period of reflection that led them elsewhere in their career.

References

Arnaud, N. (2009), 'The communicational making of a relation-specific skill: contributions based on the analysis of a conversation to strategy-as-practice and resource-based view perspectives', paper presented at the twenty-fifth European Group for Organization Studies colloquium. Barcelona, 2 July.

Atkinson, R. (1998), *The Life Story Interview*. London: Sage.

Balogun, J. (2003), 'From blaming the middle to harnessing its potential: creating change intermediaries', *British Journal of Management*, 14/1: 69–83.

Balogun, J., Huff, A. S., and Johnson, P. (2003), 'Three responses to the methodological challenges of studying strategizing', *Journal of Management Studies*, 40/1: 197–224.

Balogun, J., and Johnson, G. (2004), 'Organizational restructuring and middle managers', *Academy of Management Journal*, 47/4: 523–49.

Bertaux, D. (1981), *Biography and Society: The Life Story Approach in the Social Sciences*. London: Sage.

Bertaux, D., and Delcroix, C. (2000), 'Case histories of families and social processes: enriching sociology', in Chamberlayne, P., Bornat, J., and Wengraf, T. (eds.), *The Turn to Biographical Methods in Social Science*: 71–89. London: Routledge.

Bertaux, D., and Kohli, M. (1984), 'The life story approach: a continental view', *Annual Review of Sociology*, 10: 215–37.

Cederberg, M. (2014), 'Public discourses and migrant stories of integration and inequality: language and power in biographical narratives', *Sociology*, 48/1: 133–49.

Chamberlayne, P., and Spano, A. (2000), 'Modernisation as lived experience: contrasting case studies from the SOSTRIS project', in Chamberlayne, P., Bornat, J., and Wengraf, T. (eds.), *The Turn to Biographical Methods in Social Science*: 321–36. London: Routledge.

Cohen, L., and Mallon, M. (2001), 'My brilliant career? Using stories as a methodological tool in careers research', *International Studies of Management and Organization*, 31/3: 48–68.

Cohen, P. (2006), 'Re-doing the knowledge: labour, learning and life story in transit', *Journal of Education and Work*, 19/2: 109–20.

Crowley-Henry, M., and Weir, D. (2007), 'The international protean career: four women's narratives', *Journal of Organizational Change Management*, 20/2: 245–58.

Davids, T. (2011), 'The micro dynamics of agency: repetition and subversion in a Mexican right-wing female politician's life story', *Journal of European Women's Studies*, 18/2: 155–68.

Denis, J.-L., Langley, A., and Rouleau, L. (2010), 'The practice of leadership in the messy world of organizations', *Leadership*, 6/1: 67–88.

Díaz García, C., and Welter, F. (2013), 'Gender identities and practices: interpreting women entrepreneurs' narratives', *International Small Business Journal*, 31/4: 384–404.

Eide, A. K. (2012), 'Life stories: beyond construction', *Journal of Critical Realism*, 11/2: 139–62.

Essers, C., and Benschop, Y. (2007), 'Enterprising identities: female entrepreneurs of Moroccan or of Turkish origin in the Netherlands', *Organization Studies*, 28/1: 49–69.

Fauré, B., and Rouleau, L. (2011), 'The strategic competence of accountants and middle managers in budget making', *Accounting, Organization and Society*, 36/3: 167–82.

Fenton, C., and Langley, A. (2011), 'Strategy as practice and the narrative turn', *Organization Studies*, 32/9: 1171–96.

Fillis, I. (2006), 'A biographical approach to researching entrepreneurship in the smaller firm', *Management Decision*, 44/2: 198–212.

Gerstrøm, A. (2013), 'World disruption: how bankers reconstruct the financial crisis', PhD thesis. Aarhus University, Denmark.

Gialdini, L. (2013), 'L'agir stratégique dans l'intermédiation financière de type brokerage: un essai de modélisation selon la perspective strategy as practice', PhD thesis. Grenoble: École des Sciences de la Gestion.

Goodley, D., Lawthom, R., Clough, P., and Moore, M. (2004), *Researching Life Stories: Method, Theory, Analysis in a Biographical Age*. London: Routledge.

Gubrium, J. F. (2010), 'Another turn to narrative practice', *Narrative Inquiry*, 20/2: 387–91.

Hope, O. (2010), 'The politics of middle management sensemaking and sensegiving', *Journal of Change Management*, 10/2: 195–215.

Jarzabkowski, P., Balogun, J., and Seidl, D. (2007), 'Strategizing: the challenges of a practice perspective', *Human Relations*, 60/1: 5–27.

Johnson, G., Melin, L., and Whittington, R. (2003), 'Guest editors' introduction: micro strategy and strategizing: towards an activity-based-view', *Journal of Management Studies*, 40/1: 3–22.

Kaźmierska, K. (2014), 'Analyzing biographical data: different approaches of doing biographical research', *Qualitative Sociology Review*, 10/1: 6–17.

Kimberley, J. R., and Bouchikhi, H. (1995), 'The dynamics of organizational development and change: how the past shapes the present and constrains the future', *Organization Science*, 6/1: 9–19.

Kisfalvi, V. (2000), 'The threat of failure, the perils of success and CEO character: sources of strategic persistence', *Organization Studies*, 21/3: 611–40.

Koliba, C., and Lathrop, J. (2007), 'Inquiry as intervention: employing action research to surface intersubjective theories-in-use and support an organization's capacity to learn', *Administration and Society*, 39/1: 51–76.

Küpers, W., Mantere, S., and Statler, M. (2013), 'Strategy as storytelling: a phenomenological collaboration', *Journal of Management Inquiry*, 22/1: 83–100.

Lambright, W. H., and Quinn, M. M. (2011), 'Understanding leadership in public administration: the biographical approach', *Public Administration Review*, 71/5: 782–90.

Landry, P. (2011), 'A conceptual framework for studying succession in artistic and administrative leadership in the cultural sector', *International Journal of Arts Management*, 13/2: 44–58.

Lieblich, A. (2013), 'Healing plots: writing and reading in life-stories groups', *Qualitative Inquiry*, 19/1: 46–52.

Merrill, B., and West, L. (2009), *Using Biographical Methods in Social Research*. London: Sage.

Robson, I. (2013), 'Women's leadership as narrative practice: identifying "tent making", "dancing" and "orchestrating" in UK Early Years services', *Gender in Management: An International Journal*, 28/6: 338–58.

Rouleau, L. (2003), 'La méthode biographique', in Giordano, Y. (ed.), *Conduire un projet de recherche*: 134–71. Paris: Management & Société.
(2013), 'Strategy-as-practice research at a crossroads', *M@n@gement*, 16/5: 547–65.

Rouleau, L., and Balogun, J. (2011), 'Middle managers, strategic sensemaking, and discursive competence', *Journal of Management Studies*, 48/5: 953–83.

Schoenberger, E. (2001), 'Corporate autobiographies: the narrative strategies of corporate strategists', *Journal of Economic Geography*, 1/3: 277–98.

Schon, D. A. (1987), *Educating the Reflective Practitioner*. San Francisco: Jossey-Bass.

Shamir, B., and Eilam, G. (2005), 'What's your story? A life-stories approach to authentic leadership development', *The Leadership Quarterly*, 16/3: 395–417.

Sims, D. (1993), 'The formation of top managers: a discourse analysis of five managerial autobiographies', *British Journal of Management*, 4/1: 57–69.

Spowart, L., and Nairn, K. (2014), '(Re)performing emotions in diary-interviews', *Qualitative Research*, 14/3: 327–40.

Suárez-Ortega, M. (2013), 'Performance, reflexivity, and learning through biographical-narrative research', *Qualitative Inquiry*, 19/3: 189–200.

Tengblad, S. (2012), *The Work of Managers: Towards a Practice Theory of Management*. Oxford University Press.

Teulier, R., and Rouleau, L. (2013), 'Middle managers' sensemaking and interorganizational change initiation: translation spaces and editing practices', *Journal of Change Management*, 13/3: 308–37.

Vaara, E., and Whittington, R. (2012), 'Strategy-as-practice: taking social practices seriously', *Academy of Management Annals*, 6/1: 285–336.

Vaidyanathan, B. (2012), 'Professionalism "from below": mobilization potential in Indian call centres', *Work, Employment and Society*, 26/2: 211–17.

Valkevaara, T. (2002), 'Exploring the construction of professional expertise in HRM: analysis of four HR developers' work histories and career stories', *Journal of European Industrial Training*, 26/2–4: 183–96.

Von der Lippe, H. (2010), 'Motivation and selection processes in a biographical transition: a psychological mixed method study on the transition into fatherhood', *Journal of Mixed Methods Research*, 4/3: 199–221.

Voronov, M., De Clercq, D., and Hinings, C. R. (2013), 'Institutional complexity and logic engagement: an investigation of Ontario fine wine', *Human Relations*, 66/12: 1563–96.

Watson, T. J. (2009), 'Narrative, life story and manager identity: a case study in autobiographical identity work', *Human Relations*, 62/3: 425–52.

Wengraf, T. (2000), 'Uncovering the general from within the particular: from contingencies to typologies in the understanding of cases', in Chamberlayne, P., Bornat, J., and Wengraf, T. (eds.), *The Turn to Biographical Methods in Social Science*: 140–64. London: Routledge.

Researching everyday practice: the ethnomethodological contribution

DALVIR SAMRA-FREDERICKS

The studies of work [Garfinkel] inspires [...] [examine] the detailed and specifiable process of producing orders based on shared methods, trust, competence and attention.

Rawls (2008: 702)

Introduction

Harold Garfinkel originally coined the term 'ethnomethodology' in the 1950s to capture his central interest in (for us, organizational) members' 'folk' or everyday taken-for-granted methods (also called practices) or practical reasoning procedures for accomplishing a social order that constitutes sense. Garfinkel (1974: 16) later commented that 'ethno' referred, 'somehow or other, to the availability to a member of common-sense knowledge of his society as common-sense knowledge of the whatever'. While Garfinkel's 'daunting prose' (Silverman 2000: 138) may deter us from reading him first-hand, others, such as Heritage (1984), have offered accessible summaries of his work. Garfinkel's ethnomethodological stance was also subsequently taken up in a unique way by Harvey Sacks (see Jefferson 1992; see also Silverman 1998) and colleagues in the late 1960s, establishing conversation analysis. Under the auspices of the 'missing what', both Garfinkel and Sacks argued that social scientists were missing out the observable and reportable 'work' – in other words, the everyday ordinary activities of members whereby they make accountable and visible those entities we call, for example, 'welfare agencies', hospitals, factories, courtrooms, families and various other kinds of organizations/ bureaucracies.

In quite diffuse ways, ethnomethodological thinking and ideas have seeped into the management and organization studies field through the work of Weick (1995: 11) and Giddens (1984; see Boden 1991). More recently the social theorist and philosopher Theodore Schatzki (2005: 479) – when detailing the parameters of a practice turn in social theory – has also contended that his 'site ontology' is 'clearly allied with a variety of micro-oriented approaches to social life, for example, ethnomethodology'. When turning to the more general substantive 'topic' in this chapter – strategy work – ethnomethodology has also been briefly referred to by Knights and Morgan (1991) in their Foucauldian-based appraisal/critique of corporate strategy and the inherent constitution of subjectivity and other 'power effects'. If we narrow our attention further onto *this handbook's* substantive topic – the doing of strategy as practice, or strategizing – then EM's potential contribution has also been explicitly voiced by Clegg, Carter and Kornberger (2004) and Clark (2004), and more recently by Balogun *et al.*(2014):

> Strategy should be considered empirically in terms of ethnomethodology: an analysis of those things actually done by the actors themselves *in situ* as the doing of strategy (Clegg, Carter and Kornberger 2004: 27).

Empirical studies drawing upon EM to study strategy as practice remain rare, however. This also applies to CA, as Greatbatch and Clark (2012; Greatbatch 2009) also observe. Nonetheless, recognition of EM/CA's contribution in terms of generating insight into this domain of activity continues to grow, with others often citing the research published earlier (Samra-Fredericks 2003a; 2004; 2005b), such as strategy-as-practice researchers (for example, Liu and Maitlis 2014) and more broadly in organization studies the study by Dick and Collings (2014). While ambitious, it is the task of this chapter to indicate why EM/CA is relevant and what it requires of the researcher. To do so, this chapter offers a selective incursion into the EM/CA canon and deliberately sets aside the diversity of EM/CA (see, for example, Maynard and Clayman 1991; 2003; Turner 1974: 7) as well as the controversies and debates these traditions have instigated (touched upon by Rawls 2008; Samra-Fredericks 2004a).

The chapter is structured as follows. Relevant aspects of Garfinkel's EM and Sacks' CA are briefly noted and followed by the reproduction of two snippets of transcribed interaction from two studies. They indicate what this intellectual infrastructure offers, and convey – in the concluding section – the sorts of issues and challenges EM/CA raise for the SAP researcher.

What are ethnomethodology and conversation analysis?

Ethnomethodology

The ethos that animates ethnomethodological studies of work arises from Garfinkel's (1967) distinctive stance on social order. The intellectual influences upon Garfinkel include phenomenology and the works of Husserl and Schutz in the 1940s. The lesson from phenomenology, however, was to 'transform everyday categories and objects into activities that constitute them'. So, rather than being a concern for consciousness, it was, for Garfinkel, a concern with 'embodied activity' and the everyday 'practical production' of world-making 'accounts in the detail of concrete talk and behaviour that participants co-produce' (Maynard 2003: 11–12). Substituting 'world-making' with 'strategy-making', we begin to see what strategy-as-practice researchers would examine in the work of strategists – namely, co-produced embodied activity, concrete talk and behaviour that constitutes social order and sense. Long-standing problems or issues and topics across philosophy and sociology also came to be treated by Garfinkel as members' situated accomplishments – for example, problems such as efforts to render a 'theory of action, the nature of intersubjectivity and the social constitution of

knowledge' (Heritage 1984: 3) or topics such as trust, reasoning, knowledge, meaning, order, morals, methods, language and competence. Studies of members' everyday and naturally occurring social interactions are *the* starting point for illuminating such 'foundational sociological issues' (Button 1991; Heritage 1984: 7–36; Maynard and Clayman 2003; Samra-Fredericks and Bargiela-Chiappini 2008).

For EM researchers, the central 'fact production in flight' (as Garfinkel says: Boden 1994: 46) is social order, which is accomplished through those complex arrays of taken-for-granted *methods and reasoning procedures*. This focus on methods and reasoning procedures (and inferential practices) is also one we could more simply express as 'unearthing everyday skills' (Silverman 2000: 138); this immediately marks out one important connection to strategy as practice: interests in the skills for accomplishing strategic effectiveness. If we were to also substitute – or, rather, parse – this notion of social order in the light of strategy-as-practice interests, then attention would turn to the ways that 'organization' and the phenomenon we call 'strategy' are accomplished as members draw upon particular methods and reasoning procedures. In so doing, of course, members also integrally accomplish particular social-moral, economic and legal configurations, as well as a 'situated identity'. Further, as the ethnomethodologist Egon Bittner (1974 [1965]: 75) contends, it is an approach in which

> the meaning of the concept [organization or strategy, etc.], and of all of the terms and determinations that are subsumed under it, must be discovered by studying their use in real scenes of action by persons whose competence to use them is socially sanctioned.

Garfinkel's proposal, then, was to look at what people are 'really and actually' doing *as they do* what they do, and to discover in those actions the 'structures of practical action' and the ways they come to make 'sense' (Boden 1994: 44–5). EM's particular notion of 'sense' may also add to another growing area of interest within the SAP field – that is, sensemaking (Gioia and Chittipeddi 1991; see also Balogun and Johnson 2005). When conceptualizing the practice of strategy as a socially situated accomplishment in which 'sense' is done, members' practical reasoning or use of 'ethno' methods during interactional sequences is placed centre stage. It is also a move that extends close study not only of the ways members stabilize a social order or 'organization' (or 'institutions' such as science or medicine) but also of the ways they bring forth objects or phenomena such as the strategy document and 'markets'/environment (Samra-Fredericks 2005a; 2010).

This summary also begins to indicate that a particular orientation or set of methodological commitments characterizes the EM-influenced strategy-as-practice researcher. Of these, language *is* a form of social action and sequential order *is* pivotal for yielding mutual intelligibility, or 'sense' or meaning. Clearly, it is uncontentious to assert that, when we get close to (strategy) practitioners, often all they do all day and every day is talk – something that Mintzberg's (1973) classic study first highlighted. Sacks and his colleagues' development of CA has shown just how skilled the work of talking for world-building is. Heritage later explicitly added (Heritage 1997) that, through doing so, we talk an array of institutions 'into being'.

Conversation analysis

Influenced by the ethnomethodological enterprise in the 1960s, Sacks (see Jefferson 1992; Garfinkel and Sacks 1970) set out to study the '*social organization* of mind, culture and interaction' (Schegloff 1992: xii, emphasis added) and founded conversation analysis, also later termed 'talk-in-interaction' (for example, Psathas 1995). It is premised upon recording talk-in-interaction and generating transcripts employing a detailed notation system arising from the original efforts of Jefferson. Following Garfinkel's EM, CA also rests first and foremost on the study of the sequential procedures of talk for reality construction (Sacks 1972; Jefferson 1992; see also Boden 1994; Boden and Zimmerman 1991; Drew and Heritage 1992; Heritage 1997; Silverman 1998). This has often meant beginning with the 'hallmark' of CA, namely the turn-taking system. In CA, such

practices or methods are shown to be basic to human sociality (Schegloff 1992). Indeed, while studies of turn-taking are studies of the ways that speakers negotiate interruptions and do repairs, or how conversations are opened or closed, they are also studies of the practices for accomplishing a social order. The inherent need for commitment and reciprocity also lays support for the point that sequence relevancies 'turn out to be moral relevancies' (Rawls 1989: 165). This is something CA scholars advance from fine-grained studies of 'adjacency pairs' and/or 'dis-preferreds' (Sacks 1987 [1973]; Sacks, Schegloff and Jefferson 1974; Sacks and Schegloff 1979; Pomerantz 1984). In CA, context is also not assumed or taken as a 'given' but, instead, a dynamic creation 'expressed in and through the sequential organization of interaction' (Heritage 2004: 223).

There are two other major developments arising from Sacks' seminal work (see Jefferson 1992) and further establishing vibrant sub-fields of study. One is studies of membership categorization devices (MCDs), which explicitly deal with a sociology of knowledge. In earlier work I mentioned the MCD of 'accountant' and the activities its deployment performed in terms of displacing the knowledge of another board member and consolidating the view that he lacked 'strategic thinking' (Samra-Fredericks 2003). The second development has crystallized into the 'institutional talk' programme and is particularly relevant here since it moves beyond the original CA focus on the 'social institution *of* interaction' to studies of the 'management of social institutions *in* interaction' (Heritage 2004: 222–3, emphasis in original). When dealing with institutionality *in* talk, how institutions such as business, law, medicine, education, government/ state bureaucracies and so on are accomplished is centralized. Such studies also acknowledge that 'institutional realities exist "in" and as documents, buildings, legal arrangements, and so on' (Heritage 2004: 223).

In studies of institutionality in talk-in-interaction, the focus, again, is on *how* – that is, the methods or practical reasoning procedures through which, for example, diagnosis, instruction, decision, advice and counselling are done, turn by turn, and *made* meaningful and consequential *during inter*action. As one useful starting point, Heritage (1997; see also 2004) has identified 'six basic places to probe the institutionality of inter-action' once we have audio-/video-recorded natur-ally occurring interaction. They are: turn-taking organization; the overall structural organization of the interaction; sequence organization; turn design; lexical choice; and epistemological and other forms of asymmetry. I am conscious of space here, but these are briefly touched upon where possible, alongside other relevant features in the next section. In this next section, two illustrative extracts will be reproduced to begin to indicate EM/CA's potential relevance and contribution. In particular, the way EM/CA offers one route for explicating the intricate skills, inferential practices or ethnomethods members use, as well as how members learn to strategize, is outlined. The cru-cial question for me has always been 'How is that done?' (Lynch and Bogen 1994: 93), and I begin with a brief outline of my research approach. A summary of just five key issues and challenges around doing this form of research is then offered in the concluding section.

Some background

Like 'workplace studies' (Luff, Hindmarsh and Heath 2000; Hindmarsh and Heath 2000), my research has drawn on EM and CA in an effort to grasp the 'real-time' richness and complexity of the work members do as they do it among each other. Elevating the 'How?' question, the research also adopted social science 'methods' based upon Garfinkel's stance (later summed up by Maynard and Clayman 2003: 175–6) that we 'follow the animal' – or, in my case, senior managers formally tasked with shaping strategic direction. I have characterized my field 'method' as a form of work-shadowing or non-participant observation in which, over six- to twelve-month periods and across different realized 'spaces', I have followed and thus observed but also, crucially, audio-recorded members' talk-in-interaction. In some cases, this included video-recordings too (for a more detailed account, see Samra-Fredericks 2004b). Through doing so, analyses of the situated

and interactionally coordinated ways members also use embodied resources such as 'gaze' and gesture to accomplish their work can be scrutinized as well (Samra-Fredericks 2010; see also Llewellyn and Hindmarsh 2010).

These recordings offer a means for a repeated and slow-motion fine-grained study of members' talk, bodily movements and coordinated use of various tools and technologies. Alongside the vis-ible material 'world' of documents, whiteboard screens, computer displays and so on, elusive methods and sequentially derived reasoning pro-cedures for object construction also come within analytical purview. The video-recordings have also assisted transcript generation when three or more individuals spoke in fast succession as well as enabling gesture or gaze to be noted in the tran-scripts. The audio-recordings are repeatedly listened to first and then transcriptions of the sort reproduced here are eventually generated. It is important to note that these transcripts vary from CA orthodoxy since pauses, for example, are not timed to tenths of a second. Two further points need to be made as part of an effort to maintain anonymity and confidentiality. First, the reproduc-tion of video stills in written research accounts is not undertaken because of concerns around identi-fying the speakers/company. Second, there are no references to members' names, the products, ser-vices, financial details, technology and so forth included in the transcripts. There is, instead, a [square] bracket noting a broad description therein. I now turn to the two illustrative extracts.

Two illustrative extracts

First illustrative example

Having entered 'the field' to simply see 'how things are done', what *transpired* in one study of senior managers shaping strategic direction across a twelve-month period (Samra-Fredericks 2003) was that I was able to undertake a detailed analy-sis of their accomplishment of two 'facts' – a weakness in strategic thinking in the executive team and an 'organizational weakness' in IT cap-ability. By backtracking and through fine-grained analysis of their talk-in-interactions, the ways one member (strategist A in the transcripts, and SA in the chapter text) influenced strategic direction and assembled a form of interpersonal effectiveness were traced. Part of this analysis drew on the CA tradition and moved on to identifying six features/skills constituting such effectiveness in terms of an ability to: speak forms of knowledge; mitigate and observe the protocols of human interaction (the moral order); question and query; display appropriate emotion; deploy metaphors; and, finally, put history 'to work'. The point was also made, however, that only through combining these features at a particular point in time–space *and* given those particular others present, engaged in that specific task, was a form of 'effectiveness' accomplished.

The following is one of four extracts that were selected; it enables me here to concisely illustrate one of those features and SA's 'store' of ethno-methods. This was his use of questions – deployed at the 'right' time and in the 'right' way. This was shown to assist his constitution of those two 'facts' in terms of the weakness. The extract is just one minor move in a series that accomplished such 'big' outcomes – a point returned to in the concluding comments section.

Returning to Heritage's six places to probe the institutionality of talk – here, 'lexical choices' in terms of 'policy', 'company', 'mainframe', 'internal department', 'PCs' suggest that we are dealing with – and constituting – 'organization' and strategy work/strategizing. There was also an epistemological asymmetry, which crystallized as each turn was *sequentially* – and, arguably, skil-fully – taken. It is here that the use of questions became central. Questions are from that collection that Sacks and colleagues have termed 'adjacency pairs', since most often a question prompts an answer in the next/adjacent turn (or there is an insertion sequence, which 'holds off' an immediate answer but seeks to clarify, etc.). The ability to lodge questions and queries inserts the speaker into the split-second ebb and flow of interaction. Fur-ther, as studies of institutional talk have demon-strated, they can also curb or constrain the action possibilities of another. The latter was found to be something SA consistently did and was allied with his use of 'ethnomethods' (Garfinkel 1967) such as *knowing* when and *how to* 'let pass, gloss and question' (Turner 1988).

Empirical studies across the field of CA/insti-tutional talk programme and pragmatics have shown that the use of this basic linguistic resource

Extract 1 (simplified transcription conventions are presented in the Appendix)

		[[interrupts]
	MD	[but that's not policy =
	STRATEGIST A	= What I was trying to get at =
	STRATEGIST B	= Well, of course it isn't, but =
5	STRATEGIST A	= but what I was trying to drive is, but what is [the policy?
	MD	[hang on [name
		of strategist C], just let me go in a second =
	STRATEGIST A	= and that's the question that I asked of yourself and
		[name of strategist C]: what is the company policy?
10	STRATEGIST B	Yes.
	STRATEGIST A	Now you defined it for me as (.) Company-wide activity should
		utilize the mainframe
	STRATEGIST B	Yes =
	STRATEGIST A	= specific internal departments' special needs can utilize PCs.
15	STRATEGIST B	Yes.
	STRATEGIST A	Having *accepted* that as the policy, (.) I'm saying we ain't
		working to the policy.
	STRATEGIST C	[He's right
	STRATEGIST B	[interrupts

is a powerful mode of interpersonal control (for example, Harris 1995; Molotch and Boden 1985). Often, certain members are *expected* to ask the questions while others *should* provide answers, and through meeting these expectations they constitute the membership categories of magistrate/defendant, teacher/pupil, doctor/patient, etc. together with settings such as courtrooms, classrooms and doctors' surgeries. Institutional representatives have been shown to deprive others of this most fundamental architecture of social structure and reflexively constitute that institutionality in and through such methods. These kinds of empirical studies also reveal just what is meant by the 'constraining and enabling' features that 'social structure' affords members (Giddens 1984). In this light, EM/CA studies can also easily move onto examining the everyday, mundane exercise of power and can contribute to critical studies of strategy/management, as shown elsewhere (Samra-Fredericks 2005b; see also Whittle *et al.* 2013).

Extract 1 is one concise illustration of SA's employment of series of questions as queries traced across a number of interactional moments. They bear a striking similarity to courtroom questioning, in which 'reasonableness' is conveyed while also curbing another's possibilities for a counter-move. In these ways, the question was deemed to be skilfully utilized by SA to deprive another (SB, here) of the means to configure a social reality even when the contextual norms were not tightly prescribed as in courtroom interaction. Like prosecutors in a courtroom, however, SA's questions, queries and statements were presented in such a way that a minimal response was deemed necessary (Dillon 1990). Here, SB was positioned to supply a minimal answer, 'Yes' (lines 10, 13 and 15), and was deprived of this basic resource to ask a corresponding question or to elaborate. Further, as in courtroom contexts (Dillon 1990), questions were 'chained together' to follow a line of reasoning or lead to a 'particular position' (Boden 1994: 124). In other words, bits and pieces of information were sequentially pieced together to *mean* something in particular. Each question and answer on its own is arguably innocent, but, when chained or 'sequenced' in this fashion (and

adopting *this* 'turn-taking organization'), then inferences are drawn and consequences followed. Here, through this *sequencing*, the inferential 'work' accomplished a 'fact' or reality that policy was not being implemented. Moreover, what was also realized – or inferred – was an asymmetry of knowledge that, through subsequent and similar kinds of turns taken across time–space, enabled SA to constitute the 'sense' that SB lacked strategic capability. In sum, this extract offers us a glimpse of one fleeting moment that, nevertheless, accomplished such 'bigger' outcomes, piece by piece, turn by turn.

What was also simultaneously and interactionally accomplished in the space of seconds was something we could 'label' as a political and morally laden appraisal of another's competence. SB was positioned to be a part of the problem of non-implementation, while at the same time SA preserved a sense of reasonableness as he utilized the context (including others). Overall, then, through *this* chaining of questions/queries, timed to perfection, and given *this* lexeme selection, he gained 'far more "readability"' than a memo or report'; indeed, he acquired a 'great deal of interactional "value" packed into a fleeting moment of talk' (Boden 1994: 113). It was a 'minor move', which *began* to lay a 'sense' of what *had* happened and seemingly *continued* to happen, and, as a minor move *laminated* onto the next, and the next and so on, that 'fact' – a weakness in strategic thinking on SB's part – crystallized.

The issue of minor moves and 'big' accomplishments is discussed further in the concluding section, but we can note in passing here that what is also simultaneously accomplished is an 'identified actor' – here, 'the strategist'. He/she too is a sequential achievement (Garfinkel 2006 [1948]; Rawls 2008), and, in the second illustrative extract, a situated identity in terms of a more knowledgeable strategist inducting another into the art of strategizing is glimpsed. One important point here is that, within CA, the analytical constraint is that we 'describe how the participants themselves orient to and make relevant specific social identities within their interactions on a moment-by-moment basis' (Greatbatch 2009: 486, and citing Schegloff 1987; 1992; 1997).

Second illustrative example

This second illustrative extract is drawn from a different study in which one core task the members were engaged in was developing – writing – the annual strategy document (greater detail available from Samra-Fredericks 2005a; 2010). Retaining the broad question 'How is that done?', this second study's empirical materials – unexpectedly – provided an answer to the question 'How do strategists learn to strategize?'. The reproduced extract provides a glimpse of how a member instructed another to *learn* to see as a strategist as they do the 'work' of constructing one core object of knowledge – the market. Given this chapter's objectives, however, the full nature and scope of their talk-in-interaction to do this work is set aside: we need only note that this was *the first* formal occasion on which a depiction of their market was deemed to be consolidating.

Strategist 1 (S1 in chapter text) is the more senior strategist (a director of strategy) in a large UK company, with strategist 2 (S2) being a senior manager in finance. Here, they are approximately an hour into a meeting aiming to refine the draft strategy document.

While I purposefully set aside their embodied choreography in terms of gaze and page turns (see Goodwin 1994; Hindmarsh and Heath 2000) to focus on the vocal components, it is important to note that the indexical properties of 'this' (line 1), 'that one' or 'that' (lines 2, 5, 9, 13, 14, 15, 18), 'there' (lines 10, 12, 14) and 'here's' (line 18) were resolved because of a physical closeness. In other words, S2 was close enough to 'see' what S1 was referring to in the document before them (detailed by Samra-Fredericks 2010). On another, *more* fundamental level, object construction hinged on the sequential unravelling of a particular 'this' and 'that'. So, through *these sequence* orders and given the *lexemes* selected and a shared understanding of the broad task – that is, assessing 'environment' and writing the annual strategy document – they came to construct their core 'object of knowledge', the market, in a particular way (line 18). At line 18, S1 arrives at a juncture that makes explicit the inferential work carried across the prior turns. S2's 'Yes' (line 17) had latched onto S1's prior turn and may have assisted the swift and uncontested move from the 'if' (as possibilities) *to* one that now 'says' it *is* consolidating (line 18). Further, given *this sequential* 'social organization of

Extract 2

	STRATEGIST 1	So we really need to make this, (.) something *like that one* needs to be about the economic downturn and impact on market structure.
	STRATEGIST 2	Um.
		[brief silence as both read]
5	STRATEGIST 1	What did you say on that? (.) You said... (.) When you say [name of division], do you mean [group name]?
	STRATEGIST 2	Er, yeah, [name of company], and the organization,
		the external market.
	STRATEGIST 1	I'd think I'd call that 'recent trends' [quietly speaks as reads],
10		'survival' [reads], it's another bit that goes in there. I think you've got it somewhere else but the, urm, the dirt-cheap asset prices need to go in there.
	STRATEGIST 2	Yeah, I've got that in the main body of the report, and the competition, but, yeah, we can put that in there as well.
15	STRATEGIST 1	I think it's part of the, (.) if you made that into market structure =
	STRATEGIST 2	= Yes =
	STRATEGIST 1	= What that says is, (.) here's a big consolidation piece [inaudible three words]. It's (.) consolidation [as he writes].

referring' to the range of 'thats' (lines 2, 5, 9, 13, 14, 15, 18), and allied with the selection of particular lexemes that classify phenomena, 'the words' themselves become clearer in terms of meaning *this* and not that.

Heritage (1997) refers to lexical choices as one of six places to probe the institutionality of talk, as they furnish the distinctions that characterize and constitute fields of activity – here, 'strategic management'. Therefore, a cursory glance beginning at line 2 immediately points to two major phenomena: 'economic downturn' and 'market structure'. Subsequently, we journey through the vocabulary of strategy, also pointing to the institutional relevancies and character of this encounter given both our and their common-sense knowledges: 'external markets', 'recent trends', 'survival', 'dirt-cheap asset prices', 'competition', 'market structure' and 'consolidation'. These words characterize a recognizable discursive field of activity we call strategizing. It is also where *the* core distinctions revolve around the market (Knights and Morgan 1991), itself a pivotal element in 'environment' (with other elements being stakeholders such as government, shareholders, the local community, etc.). S1, in selecting *these words*, in *this way*, in *this order*, met background expectancies (a pattern or 'logic-in-use'), which assert that, when 'economic downturns' 'impact on market structure' (line 3) and are *coded* ('I'd call that. . .') under 'recent trends' (line 9), and then linked to 'dirt-cheap asset prices' (lines 11–12) alongside information on 'competition' (line 14), they highlight or generate a particular reality in terms of a market – here, as a 'big consolidation piece' (line 18). Notably, too, it is the relationship between the items that constitutes the information for those competent enough to read it (Rawls 2008; Heath and Luff 2000).

Thus, when 'recent trends', 'distressed assets' (the latter not reproduced here) and so forth are sequentially ordered in this way (and textualized), then it seems that the only recognizable or mutually intelligible object is that of a 'market' consolidating.

Recalling the specific character of reflexivity in EM, in which what is said is always taken in relation to the last – that is, it reflects back on the last (see Boden 1994: 46) – attending to the reflexive sequential chain means that we can begin to detail the ways S1 and S2 constituted the basic order of sensemaking here (Rawls 2008). Crucially, no word is clear on its own. Further, it is through such selection and combining of lexemes *and* given the sequential order properties that they inherently rendered 'object[s] as independent of the experience or perception of any one individual' (Smith 1996: 187, cited by Hindmarsh and Heath 2000: 529). They concretized epiphenomena as objects seemingly 'out there'. In this case, the object is a market consolidating, albeit momentarily stabilized here. While this is one minor move, however, it was a move *in a series* that 'fixed' this description as each next move laminated onto the next and the next.

What was also simultaneously accomplished through such talk-in-interaction was the instruction of S2 into the art of strategizing – or, to add precision, into the subtleties of the sequential relationships enabling him to also begin to make inferences appropriate to his profession and 'see' accordingly. The ethnomethodologist Charles Goodwin (1994: 606) has empirically demonstrated the ways a member acquires 'professional vision', defined as a profession or community of practice's 'socially organizing ways of seeing and understanding events that are answerable to the distinctive interests of a particular social group'. From having recorded and transcribed S1 and colleagues' talk-in-interaction, the 'details' for the assembly of such a 'vision' and the ways others subtly acquire it (and, hence, do the work of strategizing) become available (Samra-Fredericks 2005a; 2010). While there is limited space to detail all aspects of this realized dynamic, briefly, the CA notion of 'turn design' – also mentioned by Heritage as one of his 'six places' – sensitizes us to the ways particular turns are designed to select particular next actions. So, for example, at line 9, when S1 uses the phrase 'I'd think I'd call that' (and then, seconds later, 'I would call that', 'I'd call that' and 'I'd make that': see Samra-Fredericks 2010), he invites particular kinds of responses. S1's usage could not also be simply categorized as a mannerism in terms of his way of speaking (substantiated from analysis across a range of settings) and given the sequential order properties here.

When taking account of *where* these phrases were spoken and *what* the talk dealt with, they *occasioned* 'learning on the job'. In other words, S1 was subtly instructing S2 to 'see' what he 'sees'. Through this turn design, he also inherently switched 'positions' and, basically, said: 'If I were you I would do X or Y', as well as inviting S2 in his next turn to do agreeing, or clarifying or querying and so on. Moreover, these phrases also simultaneously handled particular interactional contingencies given that S1 was amending or appraising S2's work: S2 had drafted *this* current version of the annual strategy document. Simply, S1 also did mitigation through this usage and thereby preserved established relational webs as he continued to do both 'the work' and 'instruct' another. If we attend to the ways a speaker/practitioner such as S1 subtly marks out his/her knowledge through ostensibly trivial linguistic forms such as 'I'd call that', and when combined with scrutiny of lexeme use, sequential order properties and so on, we begin to see just *how* instruction is done and, correspondingly, how another learns the practice in situ. One last point is that knowledge of other senior colleagues also tempered *what* and *how* they wrote what they did in the strategy plan (elaborated by Samra-Fredericks 2010).

Concluding comments

Further commentary on the kinds of detailed analysis of the range of methods and reasoning procedures across the two illustrative extracts is beyond the remit of this chapter. Nevertheless, I hope that the brief outline here begins to indicate just what EM/CA can offer to those SAP researchers interested in advancing our understanding of everyday strategy practice. It does demand a particular orientation to the 'world' and phenomena such that, for example, in the second study we move beyond conceptualizing the strategy plan as a 'thing' (object) and/or a 'given' feature of organizational settings today. Instead, we attend to the ways it is intricately accomplished *during human-talk-based processes* and how, as part of this, members routinely stabilize – and without a 'pause' – those 'big' objects such as the 'market' into something

known or knowable. As Suchman (1987: 57) asserts, the 'outstanding question for social science…is not whether social facts are objectively grounded, but how that objective grounding is accomplished'. The first study pursued this in terms of two organizational weaknesses, the second in terms of the 'fact' of a market consolidating. I add, of course, that only when each minor move laminates onto the next and the next do such 'facts' or this object – market/environment – not only become mutually intelligible but also seemingly come to exist independently of the experience of individuals.

While space constraints have also prevented detailed commentary on another inherent accomplishment, it remains important to note that, as they talked in this fashion, they also simultaneously realized tied subjective identities as strategists (Knights and Morgan 1991; Samra-Fredericks 2005b) or, in EM terms, an identified actor (Rawls 2008). Like the question posed by Garfinkel (see Hill and Crittenden 1968; reproduced in Garfinkel 1974: 15) about the jurors in his seminal study – 'What makes them jurors?' – the question for me has been: what makes them 'strategists'? As Greatbatch (2009: 486) further adds, CA also carefully 'distinguishes between discourse identities, such as questioner-answerer', and the intricate, often simultaneous, rendering of 'larger social/organizational identities…such as sex, ethnicity and occupational role, which derive from wider societal and institutional formations'. Hence, alongside the current growing interest in strategists' identity work, EM/CA also provides one insightful route available to strategy-as-practice researchers if the interest is in the question: which skills and knowledge furnish manager/leader/strategist effectiveness as they do X or Y tasks? *How* do they learn to do the work, in situ? *How* are particular 'outcomes' constituted? And so on and so forth. We must also acknowledge a range of challenges and issues for the SAP researcher, however; just five are noted next.

First, there are practical challenges: getting access to organizational members doing their work, especially when what they talk about can be highly market-sensitive, means that negotiations can be protracted. For example, in the 2003 study, negotiations for access began in early 1987, with entry eventually granted in the early 1990s. Then, having accessed such rich empirical materials over a period of time, I was faced with finding and investing a lot of time to listen to/view the recordings again and again, and then transcribe and undertake the kinds of detailed analysis glimpsed here (see Samra-Fredericks 2004b). This can be prohibitive too.

The second challenge is also practical: while the time invested in fieldwork and analysis can be immense, the selection of just a few illustrative extracts and the allied compression of the fine-grained, wide-ranging analysis into a standard-length journal article is difficult to achieve. It also raises questions such as: on what basis are the extracts reproduced in written accounts selected? In light of the practical problem of space constraints, it simply makes sense to reproduce those extracts that concisely illustrate as many of the focal analytical features as possible. Space restrictions may also result in a partial account, as, for example, in the 2003 study, when I focused upon SA's accomplishments. Hence, the fine-grained analysis of SB's responses, which also assisted the constitution of situated identities and those 'facts', was set aside. So, too, only six features were discussed. These are all issues the strategy-as-practice researcher will face. If the interest is in 'how' practitioners/strategists do the work they do as they do it, however, then they are worth grappling with as best we can.

The third issue and challenge concerns the requirement within EM for 'unique adequacy' in order to do the analysis. It brings to our attention a difficult and perhaps contentious issue, since it seemingly challenges us to acquire the competence of the member in order to be able to describe what they do/see. Because 'objects' are not just there but need to be mutually orientated to (Rawls 2008), then what we describe as researchers may not be what a member 'sees'. This may point to forms of collaborative research with practitioners who do the work while also recognizing that asking them can be insufficient because much of what they do is so taken for granted. Indeed, I have yet to come across a practitioner who reported to me that sitting close to his/her colleague was crucial for effective

task completion, or that his/her employment of 'well' or 'but' – mitigating disagreement and thus maintaining relations – was something they used on X or Y occasions. This is what they use and do, however, and through doing so constitute effectiveness. As Rawls (2008: 716) adds, because we find that 'the details of practices are not recoverable from accounts', if we pose questions during interviews then all sorts of methodological issues arise alongside the more fundamental 'charge' that we have not actually accessed the phenomenon – here, strategic practice.

What, then, can an observer/researcher do? One point of relief is that, if we are attending to basic everyday skills (methods, knowledges and so on), as Silverman suggests, we do have a starting 'adequacy'. What is also relevant and of assistance is the CA stipulation to demonstrate where in the transcripts members are orientating to phenomena claimed by the researcher. This acutely holds us 'in check'. This latter issue has also given rise to debates around remaining 'transcript-intrinsic', however (see Samra-Fredericks 2004a), with others such as Moerman (1988; 1992; see also Alvesson and Kärreman 2000) arguing for the need to combine CA with ethnography. There are no neat answers (Perakyla 2004; see also Greatbatch and Clark 2012: 455), but CA and allied approaches do demand a form of discipline that constantly returns the researcher (me) to a crucial question: on what basis am I advancing this analytical claim? CA in particular is a 'data-driven methodology' (Greatbatch 2009: 496)

Linked to this is the fourth challenge and issue. While sticking close to what is observable or visibly orientated to by the speakers *in* the transcript is one hallmark of 'pure' CA, we do face a challenge if the phenomena are more elusive – such as claims that class or race is 'present' and consequential as two people talk, for example – *and/or* if the phenomena span time-space, as was the case for me (for instance, the constitution of the two mentioned weaknesses). One practical resolution that also adheres to the EM/CA theoretical stance is the *chronological* reproduction of fragments of transcripts (for example, four in the 2003 study) that also concisely illustrate and substantiate the theoretical claims concerning the linkages between strategists' talk-in-interaction and the 'outcomes'. In other words, each strip of interaction is conceptualized as *one* layer or 'minor move' *in a succession*, laminating to produce plausible 'facts' about those 'organizational weaknesses'. Boden (1994) offered me the two key concepts here: the notions of 'minor moves' and 'laminate'.

As reported in the original 2003 study, lamination encapsulated the important concepts of process, time, interaction and outcome. Process and time have been recognized as key issues for empirical research within strategic management, and, generally speaking, outcomes are what everyone is interested in and are available for easy expression after the 'event'. But the real-time interaction in and through which such 'outcomes' are accomplished has been routinely ignored. Only through placing interaction centre stage can the 'How?' question be answered. What also seeps through here is that the EM/CA traditions defy attempts to carve up the world into micro, meso or macro. So, while strategy-as-practice scholars may grapple with this in a number of, quite often still insightful, ways and attempt a visual representation of the 'linkages both across realms and between elements of strategy work' (Balogun *et al.* 2014: 184), I agree with Boden's (1994: 3, emphasis added) opening words: that it is an

> irony of language, in my view, and a consequential one at that, that we have come to call [a flexible web of patterned relations] 'structure': . . .few terms are more quickly concretized and reified into a nearly immovable and insuperable object. . . In the study of *organizations especially*, scholarship has become highly fragmented by virtue of a near obsession with so-called 'levels of analysis'. Driven almost entirely by considerations that are rooted in methodological constraints rather then empirical evidence, quite a number of talented researchers critique or ignore each other's findings and theories based on essentially socially constructed, if methodologically tidy, distinctions that are features of data sets and statistical convention rather than properties of the real world.

Boden also cites the philosopher Maurice Merleau-Ponty, who suggested that social science is engaged in a 'retrospective illusion' in which, for example, sociologists, 'having invented structure. . ., take it to be the preexisting condition of our research'.

It is, instead, a part of the sociologist/researcher's common-sense knowledge (a resource) that builds this discipline. As Boden (1994: 5, emphasis in original) has incisively added, the 'tiniest local moment of human intercourse contains *within* and *through* it the essence of society and vice versa' (see volume 29, issue 5, of *Organization Studies*).

Finally, there is perhaps an even bigger challenge in light of the orthodoxy that Boden critiques and that Garfinkel's EM issued to social scientists. This has recently been summed up by Rawls (2008: 725, emphasis in original), who asserts that the EM endeavour is one in which

> no details can be reduced in the name of theoretical clarity. It is *theoretical clarity that must serve the interests of the details*. Not positivist, not post-modern, not realist or idealist, not micro or macro – it is a new kind of theory – a different kind of theory – challenging the terms of conventional theoretical debate.

EM and CA studies of work (the institutional talk programme) demonstrate that 'contingent details are theoretically significant'. As glimpsed here, these traditions invite us to access the still elusive nature of a practice being done that inherently and sequentially accomplishes 'objects' and social (organizational) order. Only then can the skilled – methodical – and knowledgeable ways members do so be detailed. Their sequential use of particular words and classifications, methods for mitigation, gaze, sequentially ordered referrals to indexicals and 'this-and-that' and so on and so forth is a form of moment-by-moment management of contingent detail for displays of a 'mutually recognizable' order. In my case, and without doubt, the 'fact' of a market consolidating was an 'accomplishment of details' that 'exhibit[ed] order properties in their sequencing' (Rawls 2008). Tiny details such as the taking of turns, mitigating through 'well', question use, the selection and location of words, etc. do, nevertheless, constitute 'big' phenomena. We also come to see why prescription is *not* forthcoming – given the details and complexity we deal with. Importantly and paradoxically, though, we retain relevance for practitioners. Examples of studies delivering practical relevance are not hard to find in the EM/CA canon. For instance, Xerox PARC and other EM-informed centres of research have been funded by large corporations because they see the value and contribution of fine-grained ethnomethodologically informed ethnographic studies that maintain the ordered intricacies of practices.

For me, having previously worked in private- and public-sector organizations, the absence of details in the literature that I later read as a 'student' was curious. One of these was Pettigrew's (1985) impressive study of 'continuity and change' at ICI; it rightly remains a landmark study, but it also elicited that pivotal question: *how?* I wanted to 'see' Harvey-Jones in action – or, more accurately, during *inter-action*. Which methods/skills and forms of knowledges were mobilized by him during his talk-in-interaction with the various members/consultants, so that they all *saw* the contours of the same object (the environment) that way? EM and allied approaches such as CA offer 'this prize' (Rawls 2008), and, more recently too, it was heartening to find that in a ten-year review of 198 qualitative articles published in five of our major journals that one of the articles singled out by Bluhm *et al.* (2011: 1878–9) is the 2003 publication I have drawn upon here for the first illustration. They state that it 'most stands out for its contribution to the progress of qualitative methods in management research…on everyday strategizing…, pushing the boundaries…and providing a model for others to do the same'. I very much hope that others will take up a conversation with aspects of these traditions, and, like me, come to be dazzled by what we all do – *and* do in such utterly taken-for-granted ways.

Appendix – Transcription symbols (simplified)

[signals interruption

[words in brackets] substitute referrals to names of people, financial figures, products, etc. *or* the transcriber is unsure of word spoken, noted as (inaudible X words)

E::longated sound
= signals immediate latching on
Italic signals emphasis
underlining signals rising intonation

Where text is placed in single quotation marks *within* an utterance, it signals that the speaker was reading out what was written down in the text before him/her.

NB: transcription of pauses departs from the conventions of CA and here are noted as either:
(.) signalling a pause of less than a second;
Or, (brief pause), signalling a pause of more than a second but less than two seconds.

References

Alvesson, M., and Kärreman, D. (2000), 'Taking the linguistic turn in organizational research', *Journal of Applied Behavioral Science*, 36/2: 136–58.

Balogun, J., Jacobs, C. D., Jarzabkowski, P., Mantere, S., and Vaara, E (2014), 'Placing strategy discourse in context: sociomateriality, sensemaking, and power', *Journal of Management Studies*, 51/2: 175–201.

Balogun, J., and Johnson, G. (2005), 'From intended strategies to unintended outcomes: the impact of change recipient sensemaking', *Organization Studies*, 26/11: 1573–602.

Bittner, E. (1974 [1965]), 'The concept of organization', in Turner, R. (ed.), *Ethnomethodology: Selected Readings*: 69–81. Harmondsworth, UK: Penguin Books.

Bluhm, D. J., Harman, W., Lee, T. W., and Mitchell, T. R. (2011), 'Qualitative research in management: a decade of progress', *Journal of Management Studies*, 48/8: 1866–91.

Boden, D. (1991), 'The world as it happens: ethnomethodology and conversation analysis', in Ritzer, G. (ed.), *Frontiers of Social Theory: The New Synthesis*: 185–213. New York: Columbia University Press.

(1994), *The Business of Talk*. Cambridge: Polity.

Boden, D., and Zimmerman, D. H. (eds.) (1991), *Talk and Social Structure: Studies in Ethnomethodology and Conversation Analysis*. Cambridge: Polity.

Button, G. (ed.) (1991), *Ethnomethodology and the Human Sciences*. Cambridge University Press.

Clark, T. (2004), 'Strategy viewed from a management fashion perspective', *European Management Review*, 1/1: 105–11.

Clegg, S., Carter, C., and Kornberger, M. (2004), 'Get up, I feel like being a strategy machine', *European Management Review*, 1/1: 21–6.

Dick, P., and Collings, D. G. (2014), 'Discipline and punish? Strategy discourse, senior manager subjectivity and contradictory power effects', *Human Relations*, 67/12: 1513–36.

Dillon, J. T. (1990), *The Practice of Questioning*. London: Routledge.

Drew, P., and Heritage, J. (eds.) (1992), *Talk at Work: Interaction in Institutional Settings*. Cambridge University Press.

Garfinkel, H. (1967), *Studies in Ethnomethodology*. Upper Saddle River, NJ: Prentice Hall.

(1974), 'The origins of the term "ethnomethodology"', in Turner, R. (ed.), *Ethnomethodology: Selected Readings*: 96–101. Harmondsworth, UK: Penguin Books.

(2006 [1948]) *Seeing Sociologically: The Routine Grounds of Social Action*. Boulder, CO: Paradigm.

Garfinkel, H., and Sacks, H. (1970), 'On formal structures of practical actions', in McKinney, J. D., and Tiryakian, E. A. (eds.), *Theoretical Sociology*: 337–66. New York: Appleton-Century Crofts.

Giddens, A. (1984), *The Constitution of Society*. Cambridge: Polity.

Gioia, D. A., and Chittipeddi, K. (1991), 'Sensemaking and sensegiving in strategic change initiation', *Strategic Management Journal*, 12/6: 433–48.

Goodwin, C. (1994), 'Professional vision', *American Anthropologist*, 96/3: 606–33.

Greatbatch, D. (2009), 'Conversation analysis in organizational research', in Buchanan, D. A., and Bryman, A. (eds.), *The Sage Handbook of Organizational Research Methods*: 484–99. London: Sage.

Greatbatch, D., and Clark, T. (2012), 'Conversation analysis in management research', in Symon, G., and Cassell, C. (eds.), *Qualitative Organizational Research: Core Methods and Current Challenges*: 451–72. London: Sage.

Harris, S. (1995), 'Pragmatics and power', *Journal of Pragmatics*, 23/2: 117–35.

Heath, C., and Luff, P. (2000), *Technology in Action*. Cambridge University Press.

Heritage, J. (1984), *Garfinkel and Ethnomethodology*. Cambridge: Polity.

(1997), 'Conversation analysis and institutional talk: analysing data', in Silverman, D. (ed.), *Qualitative Research: Theory, Method and Practice*: 161–82. London: Sage.

(2004), 'Conversation analysis and institutional talk: analyzing data', in Silverman, D. (ed.), *Qualitative Research: Theory, Method and Practice*, 2nd edn: 222–45. London: Sage.

Hill, R. J., and Crittenden, K. S. (eds.) (1968), *Proceedings of the Purdue Symposium on Ethnomethodology*, Institute Monograph no. 1. West Lafayette, IN: Purdue Research Foundation.

Hindmarsh, J., and Heath, C. (2000), 'Sharing the tools of the trade: the interactional constitution of workplace objects', *Journal of Contemporary Ethnography*, 29/5: 523–62.

Jefferson, G. (ed.) (1992), *Harvey Sacks: Lectures on Conversation*, 2 vols. Malden, MA: Blackwell.

Knights, D., and Morgan, G. (1991), 'Corporate strategy, organizations, and subjectivity: a critique', *Organization Studies*, 12/2: 251–73.

Liu, F., and Maitlis, S. (2014), 'Emotional dynamics and strategizing processes: a study of strategic conversations in top team meetings', *Journal of Management Studies*, 51/2: 202–34.

Llewellyn, N., and Hindmarsh, J. (eds.) (2010), *Organization, Interaction and Practice*. Cambridge University Press.

Luff, P., Hindmarsh, J., and Heath, C. (2000), *Workplace Studies: Recovering Work Practice and Informing System Design*. Cambridge University Press.

Lynch, M., and Bogen, D. (1994), 'Harvey Sacks' primitive natural science', *Theory, Culture and Society*, 11/4: 65–104.

Maynard, D. W. (2003), *Bad News, Good News: Conversational Order in Everyday Talk and Clinical Settings*. University of Chicago Press.

Maynard, D. W., and Clayman, S. E. (1991), 'The diversity of ethnomethodology', *Annual Review of Sociology*, 17: 385–418.

(2003), 'Ethnomethodology and conversation analysis', in Reynolds, L. T., and Herman-Kinney, N. J. (eds.), *Handbook of Symbolic Interactionism*: 173–204. Lanham, MD: Alta Mira Press.

Mintzberg, H. (1973), *The Nature of Managerial Work*. New York: Harper & Row.

Moerman, M. (1988), *Talking Culture*. Philadelphia: University of Pennsylvania Press.

(1992), 'Life after CA: an ethnographer's autobiography', in Watson, G., and Seiler, R. M. (eds.), *Text in Context*: 20–34. Newbury Park, CA: Sage.

Molotch, H. L., and Boden, D. (1985), 'Talking social structure: discourse, domination and the Watergate hearings', *American Sociological Review*, 50/3: 273–88.

Perakyla, A. (2004), 'Conversation analysis', in Seale, C., Gobo, G., Gubrium, J. F., and Silverman, D. (eds.), *Qualitative Research Practice*: 165–79. London: Sage.

Pettigrew, A. M. (1985), *The Awakening Giant: Continuity and Change in Imperial Chemical Industries*. Oxford: Blackwell.

Pomerantz, A. (1984), 'Agreeing and disagreeing with assessments: some features of preferred/ dispreferred turn shapes', in Atkinson, M. J., and Heritage, J. (eds.), *Structures of Social Action: Studies in Conversation Analysis*: 57–101. Cambridge University Press.

Psathas, G. (1995), *Conversation Analysis: The Study of Talk-in-Interaction*. Newbury Park, CA: Sage.

Rawls, A. W. (1989), 'Language, self and social order: a re-evaluation of Goffman and Sacks', *Human Studies*, 12/1: 147–72.

(2008), 'Harold Garfinkel, ethnomethodology and workplace studies', *Organization Studies*, 29/5: 701–32.

Sacks, H. (1972), 'An initial investigation of the usability of conversational data for doing sociology', in Sudnow, D. (ed.), *Studies in Social Interaction*: 31–74. New York: Free Press.

(1987 [1973]), 'On the preferences for agreement and contiguity in sequences in conversation', in Button, G., and Lee, J. R. E. (eds.), *Talk and Social Organization*: 54–69. Clevedon, UK: Multilingual Matters.

Sacks, H., and Schegloff, E. (1979), 'Two preferences in the organization of reference to persons to conversation and their interaction', in Psathas, G. (ed.), *Everyday Language: Studies in Ethnomethodology*: 15–21. New York: Irvington.

Sacks, H., Schegloff, E., and Jefferson, G. (1974), 'A simplest systematics for the organizations of turn-taking for conversation', *Language*, 50/4: 696–735.

Samra-Fredericks, D. (2003), 'Strategizing as lived experience and strategists' everyday efforts to shape strategic direction', *Journal of Management Studies*, 40/1: 141–74.

(2004a), 'Understanding the production of "strategy" and "organization" through talk amongst managerial elites', *Culture and Organization*, 10/2: 125–41.

(2004b), 'Talk-in-interaction', in Symon, G., and Cassell, C. (eds.), *Qualitative Methods and Analysis in Organisational Research*: 214–27. London: Sage.

(2005a), 'Understanding our world as it happens', paper presented to the first 'Organization Studies Summer Workshop', Santorini, Greece, 13 June.

(2005b), 'Strategic practice, "discourse" and the everyday interactional constitution of "power effects"', *Organization*, 12/6: 803–41.

(2010), 'The interactional accomplishment of a strategic plan', in Llewellyn, N., and Hindmarsh, J. (eds.), *Organization, Interaction and Practice*: 198–217. Cambridge University Press.

Samra-Fredericks, D., and Bargiela-Chiappini, F. (2008), 'Introduction to the symposium on the foundations of organizing: the contribution from Garfinkel, Goffman and Sacks', *Organization Studies*, 29/5: 653–75.

Schatzki, T. R. (2005), 'The site of organizations', *Organization Studies*, 26/3: 465–84.

Schegloff, E. (1987), 'Between macro and micro: contexts and other connections', in Alexander, J. C., Giesen, G., Munch, R., and Smelser, N. J. (eds.), *The Micro–Macro Link*: 207–36. Berkeley: University of California Press.

(1992), 'Introduction', in Jefferson, G. (ed.), *Harvey Sacks: Lectures on Conversation*, vol I: ix–lxii. Malden, MA: Blackwell.

(1997), 'Whose text? Whose context?', *Discourse and Society*, 8/2: 165–87.

Silverman, D. (1998), *Harvey Sacks, Social Science and Conversation Analysis*. Cambridge: Polity.

(2000), 'Routine pleasures: the aesthetics of the mundane', in Linstead, S., and Hopfl, H. (eds.), *The Aesthetics of Organization*: 130–53. London: Sage.

Smith, D. E. (1996), 'Telling the truth after postmodernism', *Symbolic Interaction*, 19/3: 171–202.

Suchman, L. (1987), *Plans and Situated Actions: The Problem of Human–Machine Communication*. Cambridge University Press.

Turner, J. H. (1988), *A Theory of Social Interaction*. Redwood City, CA: Stanford University Press.

Turner, R. (ed.) (1974), 'Introduction', in *Ethnomethodology: Selected Readings*: 7–12. Harmondsworth, UK: Penguin Books.

Weick, K. (1995), *Sensemaking in Organizations*. Thousand Oaks, CA: Sage.

Whittle, A., Housley, W., Gilchrist, A., Mueller, F., and Lenney, P. (2013), 'Power, politics and organizational communication: an ethnomethodological perspective', in Cooren, F., Vaara, E., Langley, A., and Tsoukas, H. (eds.), *Language and Communication at Work: Discourse, Narrativity, and Organizing*: 71–94. Oxford University Press.

Critical discourse analysis as methodology in strategy-as-practice research

EERO VAARA

Introduction

In recent years scholars have started to pay attention to the discursive aspects of strategizing (Knights and Morgan 1991; Hendry 2000; Samra-Fredericks 2005; Seidl 2007; Balogun *et al.* 2014). These studies have highlighted the underlying assumptions of strategy as a body of knowledge (Knights and Morgan 1991), the central role of narratives and other discourse forms in organizations (Barry and Elmes 1997), the importance of rhetorical skills in strategizing (Samra-Fredericks 2003; 2005) and the implications that specific conceptions of strategy have on identity and power (Ezzamel and Willmott 2008; Mantere and Vaara 2008; McCabe 2010). This stream of research can be understood as part of the more general interest in the social and organization practices around strategy, although some scholars have argued that the strategy-as-practice movement has not been able to incorporate or develop original critical discursive perspectives on strategy (Clegg, Carter and Kornberger 2004; Carter, Clegg and Kornberger 2008). In the following I take a broad perspective and focus on the issue of how we can better understand the discursive aspects of strategy and strategizing from a critical angle. My intention is to try to refrain from constructing barriers between SAP studies and critical discursive analyses, as such barriers would do a disservice both to the development of strategy as practice and to the promotion of critical analysis of strategy as discourse and practice.

The purpose of this chapter is to explain how critical discourse analysis can serve to further our understanding of strategy and strategizing. CDA is a methodological approach that allows one to examine the constitutive role that discourses play in contemporary society. Its origins lie in applied linguistics (Fairclough 2003; van Dijk 1998; Wodak and Meyer 2002), and this is why it emphasizes the central role of texts and their analysis more than other approaches – such as Foucauldian and other post-structuralist methodologies – in discourse analysis. Unlike some other linguistic methods, however, CDA underlines the linkage between discursive and other social practices, thus not reducing everything to discourse, as is the danger with some relativist forms of discourse analysis. In brief, I argue that it is precisely through such an approach that we can better map out and understand the role of discursive practices in the micro-level processes and activities constituting strategies and strategizing in contemporary organizations. This is not to say that CDA would be the only fruitful methodology but to try to explain how it can be used in the analysis of some of the most central but still poorly understood issues in strategizing.

Lately, we have seen examples of strategy studies explicitly drawing on CDA (Balogun, Jarzabkowski and Vaara 2011; Hardy, Palmer and Phillips 2000; Hodge and Coronado 2006; Laine and Vaara 2007; Mantere and Vaara 2008; Kwon, Clarke and Wodak 2009; 2014). There are also papers that have focused on the use of CDA in studies of strategic management (Phillips, Sewell and Jaynes 2008; Vaara 2010). Nevertheless, there is a need to spell out in a concrete manner what exactly CDA can mean and tease out in terms of a better understanding of social and discursive practices constituting strategy and strategizing in and around contemporary organizations. In particular, I argue that CDA can advance our understanding of: (1) the central role of formal strategy texts; (2) the use of discursive practices in strategy conversations; (3) the discursive construction of conceptions of strategy and subjectivity in organizational strategizing; (4) the processes of legitimization in and through strategy discourse; and (5) the ideological underpinnings of strategy discourse as a body of knowledge and praxis. At the same time, attention must be focused on the methods used in such analysis. My position here is that CDA can be conducted in various ways but that a close reading of specific texts is a crucial requirement of such analysis.

The rest of this chapter is organized as follows. I next provide an outline of CDA as a methodological approach to studying strategy as practice. Then I explain how CDA can help to better understand the central role of formal strategy texts with selected examples of studies applying discursive approaches in various ways. This is followed by an example of the close reading of specific texts that is a crucial distinctive feature of CDA research. The conclusion summarizes the main points and emphasizes key issues in the application of CDA.

Critical discourse analysis: an overview

Critical discourse analysis is a methodological approach that allows one to examine the constitutive role that discourses play in contemporary society. Its origins lie in applied linguistics, and it has been developed by scholars such as Norman Fairclough, Teun van Dijk, Theo van Leeuwen and Ruth Wodak. In recent years it has been applied in various ways across the social and human sciences. Foucauldian and other post-structuralist approaches are at times also considered critical discursive analyses, though their epistemological assumptions are distinctively different. While these differences should be underlined, there is a linkage between the approaches, as, for example, Fairclough's work draws on Foucault's ideas. Rather than forming one coherent whole, however, there are different traditions in CDA. For example, Fairclough and Wodak (1997: 262–8) distinguish between French discourse analysis, critical linguistics, social

semiotics, sociocultural change and change in discourse, sociocognitive studies, the discourse-historical method, reading analysis and the Duisburg school. As the label of 'CDA' is at times linked exclusively with Fairclough and his colleagues' work, it has also been proposed that we should move towards using a broader notion of critical discourse studies (CDS) instead of CDA.

Like all discursive approaches, CDA sees discourse as both socially conditioned and socially constitutive. It is this latter 'constructive' or 'performative' effect of discourse that makes it a central object of study for social science. Accordingly, language not only reflects 'reality' but is the very means of constructing and reproducing the world as we experience it.

CDA implies seeing discourses as part of social practice, however. This means that, unlike some more relativist approaches, CDA scholars share a viewpoint according to which not everything is reducible to discourse. In a sense, discourses are particular 'moments' among others in the complex social processes constituting the world. Accordingly, CDA scholars usually emphasize the dialectics of (social) structure and discourse; discourses are, in this sense, both the products of structures and the producers of structures. These dialectics are especially salient in Fairclough's work, in which discourse is seen to have effects on social structures, as well as being determined by them, and so contributes to social continuity and social change (see, for example, Fairclough 1989; 1997; 2003).

What is most distinctive in CDA is its in-built critical stance. In simple terms, CDA aims at revealing taken-for-granted assumptions in social, societal, political and economic spheres, and examines power relationships between various kinds of discourses and actors (van Dijk 1998; Fairclough 1989: 2003). In a sense, CDA attempts to make visible social phenomena that often pass unnoticed. Importantly, in CDA, discourses are not seen as neutral in terms of their ideological content but a major locus of ideology. Fairclough goes as far as stating that 'ideology is pervasively present in language' and 'that fact ought to mean that the ideological nature of language should be one of the major themes of modern social science' (Fairclough 1989: 2). In discourse analysis of this kind, the concept of ideology is usually a broad one. Fairclough (1989) sees ideologies as 'common-sense' assumptions that treat specific ideas and power relations as natural. Van Dijk views ideology as the 'basis of the social representations shared by members of a group' (van Dijk 1998: 8). This view is different from the classical Marxist emphasis on 'false consciousness' and closer to post-structuralist (Laclau and Mouffe 1985) or culturalist (for example, Chiapello 2003) conceptions of ideology. In this view, rather than one 'ideology', the focus is on alternative or competing ideologies linked with or mediated by specific discourses.

Methodologically, CDA scholars point out that one cannot understand specific texts and discourses without considering the social context in question. Fairclough (2003) argues that discourses should, ideally, be analysed simultaneously at textual (micro-level textual elements), discursive practice (the production and interpretation of texts) and social practice (the situational and institutional context) levels, which is theoretically helpful but empirically very difficult to achieve. The discourse-historical method of Wodak (for example, Wodak *et al.* 1999), in turn, emphasizes the importance of the historical dimension in such analysis by maintaining that the emergence of specific discourses always takes place in a particular sociohistorical context.

All CDA scholars also underline the importance of intertextuality – that is, seeing specific texts or communications as parts of longer chains of texts. In simple terms, this means that the meaning created in a particular discursive act can hardly be understood without a consideration of what is 'common knowledge' or what has been said beforehand. This issue of intertextuality is also related to the broader question of interdiscursivity – that is, how specific discourse and genres are interlinked and constitute particular 'orders-of-discourse' – ensembles of relationships between discourses in particular social contexts. These orders-of-discourse can be seen as the discursive reflections of social order, and thus help us to understand the discursive aspects of social structures (Fairclough 1989; 2003).

Overall, organizational discourse analysis – including its more critical versions – has focused less on the textual micro-elements and more on the linkages between discourse use and organizational action (for example, Phillips and Hardy 2002; Mumby 2004). This is an understandable perspective, given the underlying interest in organizational processes; yet it is important to analyse textual elements in sufficient detail to be able to understand their subtle effects in the broader context (see also Fairclough 2005). In fact, a particularly appealing, but at the same time challenging, goal in CDA studies is to be able to place a specific discursive event into the broader interdiscursive context, and thus be able to exemplify more general tendencies through specific texts. The level of analysis must obviously depend on the research question and design, however.

What, then, are suitable empirical materials for CDA? In principle, any kind of textual material (documents, speeches, conversations, media texts, etc.) is useful for critical discursive inquiry. Such analysis can also include other modes of semiosis, however. Thus, for instance, visual representations in the form of pictures, symbols and so forth can turn out to be important in the critical analysis of discourses in particular contexts.

In-built in CDA is the idea that its nature depends on the application, and that particular ideas have to be refined according to the context. Furthermore, such an analysis therefore often becomes interdisciplinary. In fact, some CDA scholars argue that the essence of CDA is to combine methods of linguistic analysis with social theories and subject-specific understanding (Fairclough 2005).

How can CDA be used to advance our knowledge of the discursive and other social practices constituting strategy and strategizing in contemporary organizations? In the following I argue that CDA can advance our understanding of the central role of formal strategy texts, the use of discursive practices in strategy conversations, the discursive construction of conceptions of strategy and subjectivity in organizational strategizing, the processes of legitimization in and through strategy discourse, and the ideological underpinnings of strategy discourse as a body of knowledge and praxis. This is not intended as an exclusive list of important topics but a serious attempt to spell out important research topics that can be elucidated by CDA.

A CDA approach to strategy and strategizing

The central role of formal strategy texts

From a CDA approach, it is natural to start with the central role of strategy documents in strategizing. Such texts are crystallizations of strategic thought and often play a crucial role as 'official' strategies legitimizing or delegitimizing specific actions. Further, strategy documents are a genre of their own, reproducing specific kinds of practices in and around organizational decision-making. With few exceptions (Eriksson and Lehtimäki 2001), this topic has received little attention, however, which may be partially explained by a deficiency of useful methods such as CDA.

A rare example is, nevertheless, provided by Hodge and Coronado (2006). They examine the role of strategy documents from a CDA perspective. They focus on the Mexican government's Plan-Puebla-Panama, which is a historically significant policy document dealing with the south-east region of the country. They analysed the various discursive and ideological elements of this document, and illustrate how discourse on economic reform involved a 'complex' of global capitalist and nationalist discourses and ideologies that was used to promote the opening up of Mexican markets to multinational companies based outside Mexico. Their analysis also shows that the form and vocabulary of the document reproduced corporate rhetoric, and thus had a fundamental impact on the discursive and ideological struggles in Mexican society.

Another example comes from my own research (Pälli, Vaara and Sorsa, 2009; Vaara, Sorsa and Pälli 2010), examining the role of strategy documents in the city of Lahti. In our analysis, we focus on the city's official strategy document of 2005. The document is in many ways a typical strategic plan comprising a SWOT analysis, mission and vision statements, strategic objectives, critical success factors and scorecards that examine the operation of the city organization and its development. This strategic plan was the first of its kind, however, and it had a fundamental impact on decision-making in this city organization, and on crucial choices concerning its services and management. Our analysis shows that a proper understanding of the effects of strategy texts requires an analysis of the more general characteristics of strategy as genre as well as the specific discursive choices in the text in question. As a result of our own inductive analysis, we have identified five central discursive features of this plan: self-authorization (representing the document as a discursive text with frequent explicit references to its importance); special terminology (shared and specified lexicon known by strategy specialists); discursive innovation (new articulations that crystallized key strategic ideas); forced consensus (an expressed need to reach some degree of unanimity or alignment for the strategic plan); and deonticity (the obligatory and imperative nature of the plan). We argue that these discursive features are not trivial characteristics; they have important implications for the textual agency of strategic plans, their performative effects and their impact on power relations, and they have ideological implications. While the specific characteristics and effects are likely to vary depending on the context, we maintain that these features can, with due caution, be generalized and conceived as distinctive features of strategy as genre.

Although not explicitly drawing on CDA, other studies have significantly added to this stream of research. In particular, Kornberger and Clegg (2011) studied strategic planning in Sydney, and elucidate the power dynamics in the production of the strategic plan and its performative effects. Cornut, Giroux and Langley (2012) have in turn further elaborated on the genre of strategy text, and highlight their characteristic features, as well as the implications for the production and consumption of texts. While these examples illuminate some of the most important features of strategy documents as well as their effects, more work is required to better understand the role of individual strategy texts and, more generally, the genre of strategy texts. Such analysis should, ideally, combine detailed examination of the linguistic features of these texts with a social analysis of the processes of production and consumption in the specific setting in question.

The use of discursive practices and strategies in strategy conversations

Apart from specific strategy texts, CDA can be applied to analyses of strategy discourse in organizations. Such an analysis can focus on the content on strategy discourse and various kinds of struggles around specific strategies. For instance, Samra-Fredericks has drawn from ethnomethodology and conversation analysis and highlighted key rhetorical and discursive aspects of strategy-making (Samra-Fredericks 2003; 2004a; 2005). Aggerholm, Asmuß and Thomsen (2012) have focused on ambiguity and multivocality in strategy conversations.

Kwon, Clarke and Wodak (2009: 2014; Wodak, Kwon and Clarke 2011) have, in turn, explicitly used CDA in their studies of strategy meetings. In particular, Wodak, Kwon and Clarke (2011) identify five discursive strategies – bonding, encouraging, directing, modulating and re/committing – that were used by a chair to create consensus around a strategic idea. Bonding serves the discursive construction of the group identity needed to achieve consensus; encouraging stimulates the participation of others to be active and creative; directing means bringing the discussion towards closure and resolution by reducing the equivocality of ideas; regulating focuses attention on specific external environmental issues; and re/committing implies moving from a consensual understanding towards a commitment to action. In another paper (Kwon, Clarke and Wodak 2014), the same authors explore the more general discursive strategies that team members use to create shared views. These include re/defining, equalizing, simplifying, legitimizing and reconciling. Re/defining means developing and expressing relevant new information and viewpoints on the issue at hand; equalizing involves encouraging participation by relaxing protocols and power structures; simplifying means reducing the complexity of competing definitions by narrowing down understanding; legitimizing implies justifying underlying assumptions and building up the credibility of particular views; and reconciling means enabling alignment by different means. These studies not only elaborate on these discursive strategies but also provide rich examples of the linguistic devices used with these strategies, such as narratives and metaphors.

On the whole, however, there is a need to go further in the analysis of strategy meetings, the conversations in them, the discursive practices and strategies used and, in particular, the linguistic micro-level processes and functions involved. It is also important to examine how these discursive practices are linked with emotional expressions, bodily gestures and other social and sociomaterial practices (see also chapter 32, by Seidl and Guérard).

The construction of strategy and subjectivity in organizational discourse

CDA can also be used to examine underlying issues, such as conceptions of strategy and their implications for subjectivity and the identity of various organizational actors. CDA of this kind can thus elucidate the construction of organizational power relationships and more general power structures in organizational strategizing.

Some prior studies on strategy discourse have highlighted these issues. In particular, Samra-Fredericks (2003; 2004a; 2004b) has taken a conversation analysis perspective on strategy talk. Although her work has been distinctively ethnographic in orientation and used methods such as conversation analysis (see her chapter in this handbook), this research can also have implications for the critical discourse analysis of subjectivity in strategy talk. Central in this approach that she calls 'lived experience' are the constant micro-level processes, practices and functions that constitute conceptions of strategy and organizational relationships in social interaction. In her analysis, she focuses on the specific rhetorical skills that strategists use to persuade and convince others – and to construct a subjectivity as strategists. These include the ability to speak forms of knowledge, mitigate and observe the protocols of human interaction, question and query, display appropriate emotion, deploy metaphors and put history to 'work'. The essential point in such analysis is that it is through mundane speech acts and various micro-level practices that particular ideas are promoted and others downplayed, and specific voices heard or marginalized. She (Samra-Fredericks 2005) has later shown that Habermas's theory of communicative action and ethnomethodological theories can pave the way for fine-grained analysis of the everyday interactional constitution of organizational power relations in strategizing.

Explicit CDA studies have been rare, however. An exception is provided by Laine and Vaara (2007). In brief, our analysis shows how subjectivity and power relations are constructed in an engineering organization. We report three examples of competing ways of making sense of and giving sense to strategic development, with specific subjectification tendencies. First, we demonstrate how corporate management can mobilize and appropriate a specific kind of strategy discourse to attempt to gain control of the organization, which tends to reproduce managerial hegemony, but also to trigger discursive and other forms of resistance. Second, we illustrate how middle managers resist this hegemony by initiating a strategy discourse of their own to create room for manoeuvre in controversial situations. Third, we show how project engineers can distance themselves from management-initiated strategy discourses to maintain a viable identity despite all kinds of pressures.

Another example of CDA focusing on subjectivity and power is provided by Mantere and Vaara (2008) (see also chapter 12, by Mantere, in this handbook). Our analysis focuses on the discursive construction of strategizing in twelve Nordic-based professional organizations to better understand the problem of participation – or, more accurately, the lack of it – in contemporary organizations. In our analysis, we followed a CDA approach to examine how managers and other organizational members made sense of and gave sense to strategy work. We concentrated on interviews, but also used other sources of data to map out discursive practices that characterized strategizing in these organizations. We distinguish three central discourses that seemed to systematically reproduce non-participatory approaches: mystification (the obfuscation of organizational decisions through various discursive means); disciplining (the use of disciplinary techniques to constrain action); and technologization (the imposition of a technological system to govern the activities of individuals as

resources). We also identify three discourses that explicitly promote participation, however: self-actualization (discourse that focuses attention on the ability of people as individuals to outline and define objectives for themselves in strategy processes); dialogization (discourse integrating top-down and bottom-up approaches to strategizing); and concretization (discourse that seeks to establish clear processes and practices in and through strategizing). This analysis has helped us to understand how non-participatory approaches are legitimized and naturalized in organizational contexts, and also how alternative discourses may be mobilized to promote participation.

Although not explicitly CDA, other studies have thereafter advanced our understanding of subjectivity and power in strategy. By drawing on Foucauldian discourse analysis, Ezzamel and Willmott (2008) have shown how top managers and organizational members alike use strategy discourses to resist the change imposed upon them. McCabe (2010) has elaborated on various forms of discursive resistance and the implications on subjectivity and power. Dameron and Torset (2014) have, in turn, focused on the tensions in strategy work, and they distinguish between three forms of strategists' subjectivities: mystifying subjectivity, technical subjectivity and social subjectivity. Finally, by drawing on Foucauldian ideas, Hardy and Thomas (2014) focus on the intensification of power in strategy work – involving both the promotion of specific ideas and resistance to them. They identify and elaborate on discourses that employ specific sociomaterial and discursive intensification practices. These include tailoring, packaging, scheduling, bulking up, holding to account and associating.

These studies provide examples of the various kinds of discursive constructions and their implications for strategizing and, more generally, for the subjectivity and power relations of organizational actors. They show how a careful analysis of specific interview and other texts can be combined with other methods of data. They also highlight the difficulties of having to select specific textual examples among many others, however, and the challenges in reporting only glimpses of detailed analyses in articles of tight space constraints.

The discursive legitimization of strategies

CDA can also assist in the analysis of the legitimizing and naturalizing effects of particular strategy discourses. This means focusing attention on the discursive practices and strategies that legitimize and naturalize specific social practices, but not others. It is important to emphasize that legitimization not only deals with the specific phenomenon, action or practice in question but is also linked with the power position of the actors (van Leeuwen and Wodak 1999). For example, the legitimization of specific strategic ideas taken by a corporation also legitimizes the power position and leadership of the corporate management and the strategists in question.

Hardy, Palmer and Phillips (2000) provide an example of how CDA can be applied to better understand such legitimization processes in particular organizational contexts. They illustrate how the use of specific strategic statements involves circuits of activity, performativity and connectivity. First, in circuits of activity, specific discursive statements are introduced to evoke particular meanings. Second, such discursive actions must intersect with circuits of performativity. This happens when the discourses make sense to other actors. Third, when these two circuits intersect, connectivity occurs. This means that specific 'discursive statements' 'take'. They illustrate this process by a study of a Palestinian NGO in which a specific kind of discourse finally 'took' and legitimized particular organizational changes.

Vaara, Kleymann and Seristö (2004), in turn, studied the discursive practices through which specific strategies such as airline alliances are legitimized and naturalized. By drawing on CDA (Fairclough 1997), we focus on the discursive practices involved in the legitimization and naturalization of specific kinds of strategies in an industrial field. The case in point was the emergence and institutionalization of 'strategic alliances' as the appropriate strategies in the airline industry. The analysis reveals specific discursive practices that seem to be often used when legitimizing specific strategies such as airline alliances. These discursive practices included the problematization of traditional strategies, rationalization,

the objectification and factualization of alliance benefits, the fixation of ambiguous independence concerns, the reframing of cooperation problems as 'implementation' issues and the normalization of alliance strategies.

Despite these analyses, it seems that we have only begun to map out and understand the myriad processes through which specific strategies are legitimized and naturalized. What these examples illustrate is that such legitimization analysis needs to take into consideration both the production and consumption of discourses, which is not easy to tackle in any empirical research project (Hardy and Phillips 2004). The example of Hardy, Palmer and Phillips (2000) shows how the tracking down of discursive statements can be combined with contextual analysis focusing on the actions of specific individuals and groups. The study of Vaara, Kleymann and Seristö (2004) in turn demonstrates how the analysis of legitimization can comprise various types of textual data, including company documents, interviews and media texts. Future studies of organizational strategizing could also focus on media texts, which appears to be a particularly fruitful way to make use of CDA (Vaara and Tienari 2008). I will come back to this issue in the example of CDA below.

The ideological underpinnings of strategy discourse

Prior studies have helped us to better understand strategy as a body of knowledge and its ideological underpinnings. Such analysis covers the discipline of strategy, including not just its academic (spread, for example, by business schools) but also professional (spread, for instance, by consultants) and popular (spread, for example, by the media) versions (Whittington 2006). Shrivastava (1986) provided one of the first critical analyses of strategy as a body of knowledge. Although not focusing on the discursive aspects, his Giddens-inspired analysis highlights specific problematic features that seem to characterize strategy as a discipline. In particular, he distinguishes and elaborates on in-built ideological elements such as the undetermination of action norms, the universalization of specific (sectional) interests, the denial of conflict and contradiction, the idealization of specific sectional interests and the naturalization of the status quo. The major difficulty with such tendencies is that they are an inherent part of this body of knowledge – so much so, in fact, that they most often pass unnoticed.

To uncover these ideological elements, others have then worked on specific theoretical perspectives. Most notably, by drawing on Foucault (1973; 1980), Knights and Morgan (1991) took a genealogical perspective to strategy discourse (as a body of knowledge). They trace the roots of this discourse in post-war American capitalism and emphasize that the advance of this discourse was not a 'necessity' but a result of a number of specific developments. In their analysis, Knights and Morgan focus on 'the way in which individuals are transformed into subjects whose sense of meaning and reality becomes tied to their participation in the discourse and practice of strategy' (Knights and Morgan 1991: 252). They specifically argue that strategy discourse provides managers with a rationalization of their successes and failures, that it sustains and enhances the prerogatives of management and negates alternative perspectives on organizations, that it generates a sense of security for managers, that it sustains gendered masculinity, that it demonstrates managerial rationality, that it facilitates and legitimizes the exercise of power and that it constitutes subjectivities for organizational members, who secure their sense of reality by participation in this discourse.

Their analysis has inspired others to engage in critical reflection on strategy discourse. For example, Levy, Alvesson and Willmott (2003) propose a critical-theory-inspired perspective to go further in the exploration and analysis of the hegemonic nature of strategy discourse and associated practices. In particular, they draw on Gramsci's (1971) analysis of hegemony. In this view, organizational structures and management practices are inherently political. Ideology then 'works as a force that stabilizes and reproduces social relations while masking and distorting these same structures and processes' (Levy, Alvesson and Willmott 2003: 93). This view implies that strategy discourse is part of the continuous reconstruction of the hegemonic relationships in contemporary organizations, particularly in corporations. The important insight here is that, by believing in and adopting the strategy discourse, the disadvantaged actors accept and reproduce their subordination – without being aware of it.

Others have taken specific kinds of poststructuralist perspective on strategy discourse. Lilley (2001) has provided a Deleuzian analysis of strategy discourse. He argues that we can only identify 'strategy' when we see it, and speak of it when we seek to create or transform it, because we can draw upon a specific set of techniques that allows us to turn the concept of strategy into a 'thing' that we can represent in words and/or pictures. As a result, what we nowadays see or construct as strategy is not something natural but rather particular, resulting from the specific historically determined practices and techniques that govern our cognition and discourse. Grandy and Mills (2004) offer another interesting analysis of strategy discourse. By drawing on Baudrillard's ideas, they argue that we have reached a stage of third-order simulacra – that is, our strategy discourse has attained a level of presentation that is hyper-real. In a sense, the strategy discipline and its various models and practices have started to live a life of their own that is disconnected from the (other) reality. Still others have thereafter focused attention on the academic discourse itself. In particular, Thomas, Wilson and Leeds (2013) have argued that we have only started to understand the historical canonization and institutionalization of strategic management as a discipline and practice.

Although these analyses have greatly advanced our understanding of the ideological underpinnings and power implications of strategy discourse, they can be complemented with CDA. In other words, CDA can assist in systematic analyses of how strategy discourse has evolved, how it has been spread, what kinds of underlying assumptions are ingrained in specific strategy texts and how these texts and discourses have constructed and reproduced specific kinds of ideological assumptions, identities and power relations. The methodological point is that the prior studies have remained at an abstract level and not provided clear textual examples of the discourses analysed. To be clear, this is not a problem from the point of view of the specific tradition in question, but it does mean that there is a great deal of room for more text-oriented micro-level analyses that could, on the one hand, illustrate and validate the insights of prior analyses of this body of knowledge and, on the other, make use of established methods and examples of conducting similar kinds of analysis in other areas (for example, Fairclough 2003).

How to conduct CDA? An example of a media text

As should be clear by now, CDA is a methodology that can be applied in various ways. The tradition in applied linguistics has been to focus on the close reading of specific texts. In the context of strategy research, however, critical discourse analysis is likely to raise more questions concerning the selection of texts and the generalizability of findings than when applied in linguistics. Consequently, there is a need to proceed in stages such as the following (see also Vaara and Tienari 2004).

- *Definition of the research questions that reflect the critical orientation.* As exemplified in the previous sections, CDA focuses on issues and concerns of social and societal importance that require critical scrutiny.
- *Overall analysis of the textual material leading to a selection of 'samples' of texts.* CDA can focus on a larger number of texts or only on one text, but the selection of the sample needs to be made very carefully.
- *Close reading of specific texts.* This phase is crucial in CDA, as the objective is to provide concrete illustrations at the textual micro level.
- *Elaboration on findings and their generalizability.* After a close reading of a text, the key findings should be elaborated on and placed in their wider context.

It should be emphasized, however, that CDA is in its very nature 'abductive' – that is, the research involves constant refinement of theoretical ideas with an increasingly accurate understanding of the empirical phenomena (Locke, Golden-Biddle and Feldman 2008). As Wodak

puts it: 'A constant movement back and forth between theory and empirical data is necessary' (Wodak 2004: 200). Figure 28.1 provides a simplified view of the typical stages in CDA research.

The close reading of texts is the crucial distinctive feature of CDA research. In the following I exemplify this close reading by an analysis of a media text that was originally published by Vaara and Tienari (2008). In our analysis, we focus on the discursive legitimization of a shutdown decision in the media. As discussed above, the discursive legitimization of specific strategies is an important but still under-researched area in strategy as practice. Although such close reading can be conducted in various ways, it is important to focus attention on the representativeness of the text in terms of its genre and particular characteristics. Our analysis focuses on a typical media text that helped us to uncover and exemplify how the media make sense of such strategic decisions.

In such close reading, it is also vital to employ specific theoretical models and ideas as guiding principles in the analysis. We used the theoretical model developed by van Leeuwen and Wodak (1999), in which they distinguish authorization, rationalization, moral evaluation and mythopoesis as typical discursive legitimization strategies.[1] While such close reading is, by its very nature, interpretive and subjective, specified theoretical starting points help to structure the analysis and ascertain that the analysis captures essential aspects of the phenomenon in question. This is not to say that all CDA applications in strategy-as-practice research should use specific linguistic theories, but that it is important to be able to move beyond the most apparent surface level of the texts, to be able to identify and elaborate on the key discursive and social practices in question.

The case in question is the shutdown of a long-standing marine engine factory in the city of Turku, Finland, carried out by Wärtsila Group in 2004 and 2005. The company's decision created a huge debate in Finland around their strategy and

[1] We thus focus on the discursive construction of 'organizational strategies' that are legitimized by 'discursive legitimization strategies' (sometimes called 'practices').

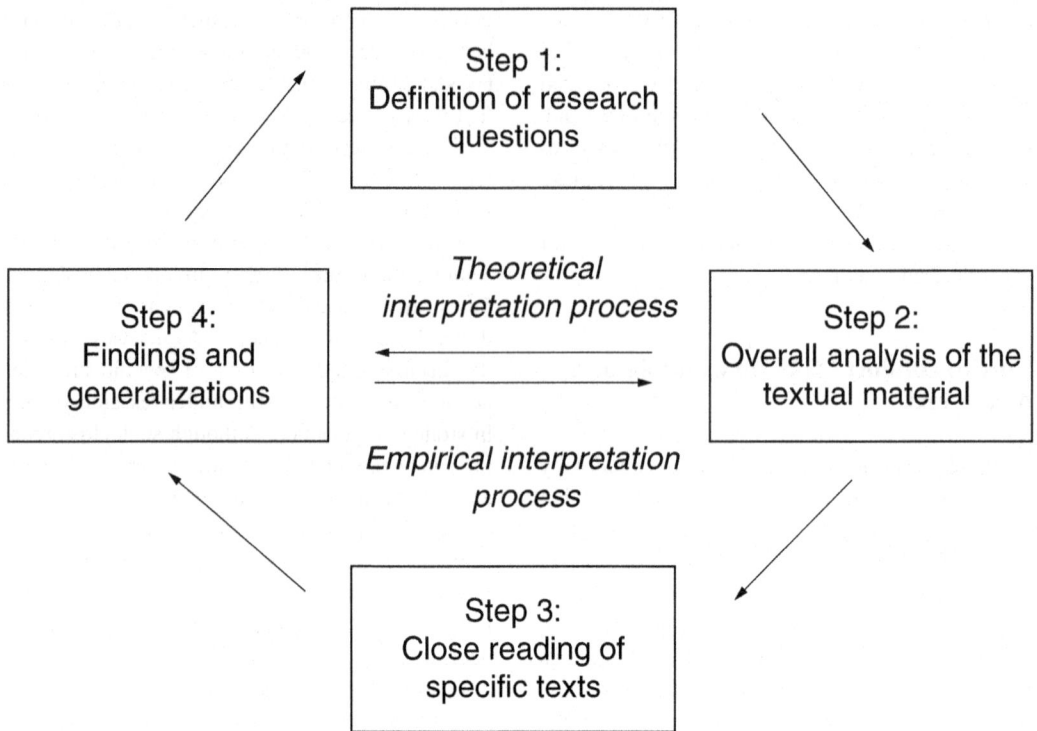

Figure 28.1 Critical discourse analysis as abduction
Source: Modification of a figure presented by Vaara and Tienari (2004).

the overall legitimacy of such decisions. The following text illustrates how the shutdown was initially presented in the leading Finnish daily newspaper, *Helsingin Sanomat*, which can be seen as an opinion leader in the Finnish media. This reporting created a specific sense of legitimacy around the controversial decision and set the tone for the subsequent public discussion (*Helsingin Sanomat*, 15 January 2004).

Wärtsilä moves its engine manufacturing to Italy
  480 people lose their jobs, 200 maintenance men remain in Turku
  Capacity is cut to improve profitability

The engine manufacturer Wärtsilä will shut down its long-standing factory in Turku and move its production to Trieste, Italy. Of the 680 employees in Turku, 480 will lose their jobs. A couple of hundred people will retain their jobs in diesel engine maintenance service. About 130 of those

who are going to lose their jobs will have an opportunity for early retirement; 350 employees will be dismissed. Production will be transferred to Italy in the fall.

The CEO of Wärtsilä, Ole Johansson, says that engine production in Vaasa [another Finnish city] will continue as before. There are 1,600 employees in Vaasa and about 1,200 in Trieste. Vaasa is the technology and R&D center for the entire Wärtsilä Group.

According to Johansson, the shutdown is not due to a lack of competitiveness in Turku. He says that the multinational has only bad alternatives since overcapacity has to be cut because of weak demand. This shutdown will, according to Johansson, secure full employment in Vaasa and Trieste.

The shutdown is part of Wärtsilä's restructuring program, which was started last September. The group will reduce its workforce by a total of 1,100 people. On Wednesday it was announced that a total of 70 people would be made redundant in Norway and Holland. Johansson   shutdown of the Turku factory would affect 'a few dozen jobs' with subcontractors in the Turku region.

Johansson argues that concentration of large engine production at Trieste is justified because the factory is Wärtsilä's largest. Concentration will create flexibility for changes in demand. While two different engine types are manufactured in Turku, several are made in Trieste, including those made in Turku.

When demand is strong, a factory like Turku is effective, but it becomes problematic when the market slows down. Last year people in Turku faced temporary layoffs. Trieste does not require large investments, as is the case in Turku, where more production capacity is needed. Trieste also has direct access to natural gas, which is needed for testing gas engines.

This solution will significantly increase the profitability of the 'multinational corporation', Johansson estimates. The share price of the corporation increased after the shutdown news. According to Johansson, restructuring production will generate annual savings of approximately 60 million euros, which will affect earnings from 2005 onwards.

This news report is a typical example of a discursive struggle over shutdowns. The genre of the focal text is business news, but the text is also an approving commentary on the 'official' information given by Wärtsilä's corporate communications. The text thus represents a hybrid genre, typical of contemporary media (Fairclough 1995; van Dijk 1990). On the whole, global capitalist discourse is the dominant discourse used; it provides the primary framework to make sense of the controversial decision. Several legitimization strategies are used. To a large extent, the text rests on the *authorization* provided by CEO Ole Johansson. The involvement of the CEO lends credibility to the evidence provided, most clearly shown in his speech acts. The journalist composing and editing the text also uses other means of authorization, however. Importantly, the reference to the increase in share price serves as a particularly powerful legitimization strategy. In a sense, the 'market' acts as the ultimate authority in contemporary global capitalism.

Various *rationalization* strategies are also used. Financial rationalization plays an accentuated role: the shutdown is legitimized by references to profitability improvement and annual savings. This is the case even though the CEO admits that the 'competitiveness' of the unit is not a problem per se. This is one of the most striking features of this text: the improvement of future profitability, rather than current problems, is the main reason given for the shutdown. In this sense the text deals with 'imaginaries' (Fairclough and Thomas 2004) or 'futurological prediction' (Fairclough 2003). The modality of the text is a significant part of the rationalization. For example, the claim that 'over-capacity has to be cut' is portrayed as an obligation in terms of the future success of the MNC, leaving no room for alternative scenarios.

Defining the Wärtsilä Group as an MNC makes all the difference in the text. This framing legitimizes the shutdown by appealing to the effect it will have on the overall profitability of the corporation. This is a key theme in the text, and it is explicitly spelled out in the final comment of the CEO: 'This solution will significantly increase the profitability of the multinational corporation.' From other media texts published – for example, in the local newspaper – we learn that this is in stark contrast to the view held by people in Turku, who saw the factory (and the company itself) as an integral part of the shipbuilding tradition in the Turku region from the late eighteenth century. From this perspective, shutting down the unit – especially since it was profitable – did not make any sense. 'Over-capacity' is a particularly interesting rationalization theme in the text. It nominalizes a state of affairs accepted as fact. It also involves discursive 'technologization' (Fairclough 1995: 91–111), in the sense that grasping the issue at hand ('overcapacity') is difficult without detailed knowledge of the industry dynamics. What happened in the previous year – the 'temporary layoffs' – is also used as evidence here. Other rationalizations include pointing out that the unit in Trieste is larger than the one in Turku, that the Trieste unit allows for a better concentration of production and that it provides more access to necessary natural resources. 'Concentration' and 'flexibility' are interesting themes in this respect. They are often used by decision-makers in MNCs to create a positive sense of the prospects for reorganizing production across national borders.

Moralization strategies are also used in the text. While the beginning of the text effectively raises doubts concerning the moral basis of the shutdown decision by pointing to dramatic job losses, the latter part of the text echoes the official corporate view. An important part of legitimization is that the eventual unemployment of the workers in Turku is necessary so that workers in Vaasa and Trieste will have 'full employment'. As a linguistic detail, the verb 'secure' is used as a particularly forceful confirmation. The reference to Vaasa is crucial from a nationalistic Finnish perspective, since it justifies the layoffs in one location by the 'fact' that this will allow the other unit in Finland to survive. Taking up the layoffs in other countries (Norway and the Netherlands) then serves as a justification of processual fairness. The significance of job losses elsewhere in the Turku region, for example, in relation to the MNC's subcontractors is played down (only 'a few dozen jobs' will be lost). It is the apparent inevitability of the situation, however ('[we have] only bad alternatives'), that serves as the overarching moralization strategy in the text.

Finally, there are interesting *mythopoetical* elements in the text. There is a restructuring programme already under way in the MNC, and the shutdown decision is an essential part of this programme. The restructuring programme can be seen as a euphemism for layoffs, and its narrative construction makes it a self-justifying structure. The shutdown becomes a strategic – not a haphazard – one-off decision. This attaches an additional sense of inevitability to this particular decision.

We can thus see how particular discursive legitimization strategies are used to legitimize a specific organizational strategy with significant social and material consequences: the transfer of production and loss of jobs. The point is that media texts such as this one are a key part of complex discursive processes through which particular organizational strategies – and not others – are legitimized.

Methodologically, such close reading of a specific text can be the essence of the analysis. Depending on the empirical research design, however, it might also be useful to combine examples from multiple texts and other observations to provide a more complete analysis of the phenomenon in question.

Conclusion

I have argued in this chapter that CDA has a great deal to offer to strategy-as-practice research because it provides means to critically analyse contemporary social problems by targeted linguistic analysis (Fairclough 2003). This is why it can and should be applied to SAP research. There are also specific reasons for advocating its use at this point in time. On the one hand, we still know little of the role of language in strategy and strategizing. Although the discursive aspects of strategy have received increasing attention in prior studies (Laine and Vaara 2007; Mantere and Vaara 2008; Phillips, Sewell and Jaynes 2008), these analyses are still rare and have relatively little weight in the overall body of strategy research. CDA is one, though not of course the only, methodology that can assist in developing better understanding of the central discursive processes and practices as well as their implications. On the other hand, strategy research in general and strategy-as-practice studies in particular have been criticized for a lack of critical analyses (Carter, Clegg and Kornberger 2008). CDA is an approach that can partly help to remedy this state of affairs.

CDA is no panacea, however. The applications of CDA in general and in management research in particular have been criticized for a lack of rigour and detail in the actual linguistic analyses. Moreover, students of CDA have at times been accused of making self-serving selections of texts and distorted interpretations. CDA invites the researcher to take a stand on issues – more so than in conventional analyses. This should not be misinterpreted as an opportunity to produce any kind of critical comment based on one's convictions or general observations. On the contrary, it is necessary to make sure that one's own interpretations are based on careful textual evidence and logical argumentation.

This chapter has provided some ideas as to what such analysis can entail. I have outlined particularly important topics that deserve special attention. These include the central role of formal strategy texts, the use of discursive practices in strategy conversations, the discursive construction of conceptions of strategy and subjectivity in organizational strategizing, legitimization in and through strategy discourse and the ideological underpinnings of strategy discourse as a body of knowledge and praxis. What I have sketched here can be seen as a preliminary research agenda that, it is to be hoped, will inspire more fine-grained empirical analyses. This list of topics is by no means exhaustive, however, and there are many other questions that warrant attention in the future. Future studies can take many directions, ranging from detailed linguistic analysis of the particular features of strategy texts to a broader analysis of the production and consumption of strategy research.

While a critical discourse analysis methodology can accommodate various theoretical perspectives and empirical methods, I wish to conclude by emphasizing its three key requirements. First, the critical orientation must be taken seriously, which should be shown throughout the analysis from the initial formulation of the research questions to the final conclusions. The point is to focus on issues and concerns that require critical analysis in the strategy domain. Not all discourse analysis is or needs to be critical, but then it should not be called CDA. Second, CDA must include a detailed analysis of texts that provide the empirical basis for the key arguments to be made. This most often requires the close reading of specific texts that can provide concrete illustrations of the focal phenomena at the textual micro level. Third, these texts must then also be placed in their social contexts. I believe that it is through such analysis that we can best understand the linkage between discursive and other organizational practices in strategizing and the social and societal consequences of strategy discourse.

References

Aggerholm, H. K., Asmuß, B., and Thomsen, C. (2012), 'The role of recontextualization in the multivocal, ambiguous process of strategizing', *Journal of Management Inquiry*, 21/4: 413–28.

Barry, D., and Elmes, M. (1997), 'Strategy retold: toward a narrative view of strategic discourse', *Academy of Management Review*, 22/2: 429–52.

Balogun, J., Jacobs, C. D., Jarzabkowski, P., Mantere, S., and Vaara, E. (2014), 'Placing strategy discourse in context: sociomateriality, sensemaking, and power', *Journal of Management Studies*, 51/2: 175–201.

Balogun, J., Jarzabkowski, P., and Vaara, E. (2011), 'Selling, resistance and reconciliation: a critical discursive approach to subsidiary role evolution in MNCs', *Journal of International Business Studies*, 42/6: 765–86.

Carter, C., Clegg, S., and Kornberger, M. (2008), 'Strategy as practice?', *Strategic Organization*, 6/1: 83–99.

Chiapello, E. (2003), 'Reconciling the two principal meanings of the notion of ideology: the example of the concept of the "spirit of capitalism"', *European Journal of Social Theory*, 6/2: 155–71.

Clegg, S., Carter, C., and Kornberger, M. (2004), 'Get up, I feel like being a strategy machine', *European Management Review*, 1/1: 21–8.

Cornut, F., Giroux, H., and Langley, A. (2012), 'The strategic plan as a genre', *Discourse and Communication*, 6/1: 21–54.

Dameron, S., and Torset, C. (2014), 'The discursive construction of strategists' subjectivities: towards a paradox lens on strategy', *Journal of Management Studies*, 51/2: 291–319.

Eriksson, P., and Lehtimäki, H. (2001), 'Strategy rhetoric in city management: how the central presumptions of strategic management live on?', *Scandinavian Journal of Management*, 17/2: 201–23.

Ezzamel, M., and Willmott, H. (2008), 'Strategy as discourse in a global retailer: a supplement to rationalist and interpretive accounts', *Organization Studies*, 29/2: 191–217.

Fairclough, N. (1989), *Language and Power*. London: Longman.

(1995), *Media Discourse*. London: Edward Arnold.

(1997), *Critical Discourse Analysis: The Critical Study of Language*. London: Longman.

(2003), *Analyzing Discourse: Textual Analysis for Social Research*. London: Routledge.

(2005), 'Discourse analysis in organization studies: the case for critical realism', *Organization Studies*, 26/6: 915–39.

Fairclough, N., and Thomas, P. (2004), 'The discourse of globalization and the globalization of discourse', in Grant, D., Hardy, C., Oswick, C., and Putnam, L. L. (eds.), *The Sage Handbook of Organizational Discourse*: 379–96. London: Sage.

Fairclough, N., and Wodak, R. (1997), 'Critical discourse analysis', in van Dijk, T. (ed.), *Discourse as Social Interaction*: 258–84. London: Sage.

Foucault, M. (1973), *The Order of Things: The Archaeology of Human Sciences*. New York: Vintage Books.

Foucault, M. (1980), *Power/Knowledge: Selected Interviews and Other Writings 1972–1977*, ed. Gordon, C. New York: Pantheon Books.

Gramsci, A. (1971), *Selections from the Prison Notebooks*, eds. Nowell Smith, G., and. Hoare, Q. New York: International.

Grandy, G., and Mills, A. J. (2004), 'Strategy as simulacra? A radical reflexive look at the discipline and practice of strategy', *Journal of Management Studies*, 41/7: 1153–70.

Hardy, C., Palmer, I., and Phillips, N. (2000), 'Discourse as a strategic resource', *Human Relations*, 53/9: 1227–48.

Hardy, C., and Phillips, N. (2004), 'Discourse and power', in Grant, D., Hardy, C., Oswick, C., and Putnam, L. L. (eds.), *Handbook of Organizational Discourse*: 299–316. London: Sage.

Hardy, C., and Thomas, R. (2014), 'Strategy, discourse and practice: the intensification of power', *Journal of Management Studies*, 51/2: 320–48.

Hendry, J. (2000), 'Strategic decision making, discourse, and strategy as social practice', *Journal of Management Studies*, 37/7: 955–77.

Hodge, B., and Coronado, G. (2006), 'Mexico Inc.? Discourse analysis and the triumph of managerialism', *Organization*, 13/4: 529–47.

Knights, D., and Morgan, G. (1991), 'Corporate strategy, organizations, and subjectivity: a critique', *Organization Studies*, 12/2: 251–73.

Kornberger, M., and Clegg, S. (2011), 'Strategy as performative practice: the case of Sydney 2030', *Strategic Organization*, 9/2: 136–62.

Kwon, W., Clarke, I., and Wodak, R. (2009), 'Organizational decision-making, discourse, and power: integrating across contexts and scales', *Discourse and Communication*, 3/3: 273–302.

—— (2014), 'Micro-level discursive strategies for constructing shared views around strategic issues in team meetings', *Journal of Management Studies*, 51/2: 265–90.

Laclau, E., and Mouffe, C. (1985), *Hegemony and Socialist Strategy*. London: Verso.

Laine, P.-M., and Vaara, E. (2007), 'Struggling over subjectivity: a discursive analysis of strategic development in an engineering group', *Human Relations*, 60/1: 29–58.

Levy, D. L., Alvesson, M., and Willmott, H. (2003), 'Critical approaches to strategic management', in Alvesson, M., and Willmott, H. (eds.), *Studying Management Critically*: 92–109. London: Sage.

Lilley, S. (2001), 'The language of strategy', in Westwood, R., and Linstead, S. (eds.), *The Language of Organization*: 66–88. London: Sage.

Locke, K., Golden-Biddle, K., and Feldman, M. S. (2008), 'Making doubt generative: rethinking the role of doubt in the research process', *Organization Science*, 19/6: 907–19.

Mantere, S., and Vaara, E. (2008), 'On the problem of participation in strategy: a critical discursive perspective', *Organization Science*, 19/2: 341–58.

McCabe, D. (2010), 'Strategy-as-power: ambiguity, contradiction and the exercise of power in a UK building society', *Organization*, 17/2: 151–75.

Mumby, D. (2004), 'Discourse, power and ideology: unpacking the critical approach', in Grant, D., Hardy, C., Oswick, C., and Putnam, L. L. (eds.), *The Sage Handbook of Organizational Discourse*: 237–58. London: Sage.

Pälli, P., Vaara, E., and Sorsa, V. (2009), 'Strategy as text and discursive practice: a genre-based approach to strategizing in city administration', *Discourse and Communication*, 3/3: 303–18.

Phillips, N., and Hardy, C. (2002), *Discourse Analysis: Investigating Processes of Social Construction*. Thousand Oaks, CA: Sage.

Phillips, N., Sewell, G., and Jaynes, S. (2008), 'Applying critical discourse analysis in strategic management research', *Organizational Research Methods*, 11/4: 770–89.

Samra-Fredericks, D. (2003), 'Strategizing as lived experience and strategists' everyday efforts to shape strategic direction', *Journal of Management Studies*, 40/1: 141–74.

—— (2004a), 'Understanding the production of "strategy" and "organization" through talk amongst managerial elites', *Culture and Organization*, 10/2: 125–41.

—— (2004b), 'Managerial elites making rhetorical and linguistic "moves" for a moving (emotional) display', *Human Relations*, 57/9: 1103–43.

—— (2005), 'Strategic practice, "discourse" and the everyday interactional constitution of "power effects"', *Organization*, 12/6: 803–41.

Seidl, D. (2007), 'General strategy concepts and the ecology of strategy discourses: a systemic-discursive perspective', *Organization Studies*, 28/2: 197–218.

Shrivastava, P. (1986), 'Is strategic management ideological?', *Journal of Management*, 12/3: 363–77.

Thomas, P., Wilson, J., and Leeds, O. (2013), 'Constructing "the history of strategic management":

a critical analysis of the academic discourse', *Business History*, 55/7: 1119–42.

Vaara, E. (2010), 'Taking the linguistic turn seriously: strategy as multifaceted and interdiscursive phenomenon', *Advances in Strategic Management*, 27/1: 29–50.

Vaara, E., Kleymann, B., and Seristö, H. (2004), 'Strategies as discursive constructions: the case of airline alliances', *Journal of Management Studies*, 41/1: 1–35.

Vaara, E., Sorsa, V., and Pälli, P. (2010), 'On the force potential of strategy texts: a critical discourse analysis of a strategic plan and its power effects in a city organization', *Organization*, 17/6: 685–702.

Vaara, E., and Tienari, J. (2004), 'Critical discourse analysis as a methodology for international business studies', in Piekkari, R., and Welch, C. (eds.), *Handbook of Qualitative Research Methods for International Business*: 342–59. Cheltenham: Edward Elgar.

(2008), 'A discursive perspective on legitimation strategies in MNCs', *Academy of Management Review*, 33/4: 985–93.

Van Dijk, T. (1990), *News as Discourse*. Hillsdale, NJ: Lawrence Erlbaum.

(1998), *Ideology: A Multidisciplinary Approach*. London: Sage.

Van Leeuwen, T., and Wodak, R. (1999), 'Legitimizing immigration control: a discourse-historical perspective', *Discourse Studies*, 1/1: 83–118.

Whittington, R. (2006), 'Completing the practice turn in strategy research', *Organization Studies*, 27/5: 613–34.

Wodak, R. (2004), 'Critical discourse analysis', in Seale, C., Gubrium, J. F., and Silverman, D. (eds.), *Qualitative Research Practice*: 197–213. London: Sage.

Wodak, R., de Cillia, R., Reisigl, M., and Liebhart, K. (1999), *The Discursive Construction of National Identity*. Edinburgh University Press.

Wodak, R., Kwon, W., and Clarke, I. (2011), '"Getting people on board": discursive leadership for consensus building in team meetings', *Discourse and Society*, 22/5: 592–644.

Wodak, R., and Meyer, M. (2002), *Methods of Critical Discourse Analysis*. London: Sage.

Studying strategy as practice through historical methods

MONA ERICSON, LEIF MELIN and ANDREW POPP

Introduction

This chapter is about why and how historical methods are suitable for studies of strategy as practice with its focus on activities that characterize strategy and strategizing, for which the umbrella term 'strategy-making' is often used (Vaara and Whittington 2012). The ambition is to bring clarity to how we can approach strategy-as-practice research from a historical perspective. By introducing and elaborating different categories of historical methods, the chapter offers specific insights into how to use such methods.

Strategy-as-practice research contributes by providing important insights into practice, praxis, and the role and identity of practitioners, using a variety of methods (Jarzabkowski and Spee 2009: Vaara and Whittington 2012). Although some studies do incorporate the notion of history, the interest in historical method is limited. Kaplan and Orlikowski's (2013) study of a dynamic set of strategy-making practices reveals, through the development of chronologies, that managers negotiate and resolve differences in interpretations of the past, present and future. The influence of history on present strategic activity is also apparent in studies of sociocultural codes (Rouleau 2005), the sedimentation of social praxis into practices of replicating routines (Campbell-Hunt 2007) and with regard to an organization's predisposition to act path-dependently (Jarzabkowski 2004). Drawing on Bourdieu (1990), scholars direct attention to practice in relation to habitus – that is, the agent's predisposition to act in a certain way in a field, which denotes a social world, such as an industry or a market. History is mentioned in connection with habitus and field. The construction of habitus and field implies long-lasting processes, conditioned by environment, experience and history

(Gomez 2010; Gomez and Bouty 2011). Without explicitly referring to history or a historical method, Whittington, Cailluet and Yakis-Douglas (2011) provide a long view of strategy professionals, in-house strategic planners and external strategy consultants. The long view is based on an analysis of advertisements for these professionals in *The New York Times* between 1960 and 2000. It should also be acknowledged that studies implicitly account for history through a focus on the emergent character of strategy practice (for example, Balogun and Johnson 2004; Dougherty 2004; Giraudeau 2008; Hendry, Kiel and Nicholson 2010; Jørgensen and Messner 2010; Stensaker and Falkenberg 2007). With a concern for language and discourse, SAP scholars further indicate that history does play a role (Clarke, Kwon and Wodak 2012). Through a narrative act, the researcher captures a sociohistorical dimension (Rouleau 2010).

The above-mentioned studies are all examples of promising work, but we need to push the development of practice-based research further, elevating the dimension of history through the application of suitable methods. The study of strategy has its own history, one in which the work of historians and the use of historical methods have been a central influence. So far, however, there has been little dialogue between historians and strategy-as-practice scholars. Historians have not shown themselves strongly aware of the practice stream but it is also the case that the 'living role of history has so far been missing in the strategy as practice literature' (Ericson and Melin 2010: 326).

This chapter is organized as follows. First we direct our attention to business historians and their relationship with strategy scholarship. This section includes an examination of the sources used in business history research, the ways in which they are used and the theoretical frameworks within which they are deployed. As pointed out, historians are inductive, source-driven researchers; as a result, their methods are largely shaped by their sources. Next we map how we might begin to reconcile history and strategy as practice through method. The following section presents and elaborates four different categories of historical methods suitable for the study of strategy as practice. These categories refer to written sources and narratives, micro-history, ego documents and lived experience. The concluding section of the chapter reflects on these categories, their challenges and their limits. It also comments on the meaning and implications of a historical approach within a strategy-as-practice perspective.

The use of historical methods in traditional strategy research

All strategies, being enacted amid the flow of time, not only *have* a history but unfold history through a practice associated with a past (Ericson and Melin 2010). Historians tell stories about strategies in very particular ways, however. Lipartito (1995: 5–6) contends that business historians have barely begun to notice a 'simple temporal fact', namely that, in 'undertaking action, especially creative, innovative actions, organizations must project themselves into the future, beyond what is readily known'. In this vision, even rationality becomes a temporally relative term, a 'function of when a decision is taken' (Lipartito 1995: 17). This matters, as mainstream strategy studies owe a considerable debt to business historians, who constitute probably the largest community of scholars to have considered strategy from explicitly historical perspectives.

The emergent discipline of business history is closely related to the development of the case method, according to which strategy is framed as something made through isolated moments of intentional decision-making that provide a critical turning point in a chronological narrative flow of events. The narrative leads up to the moment of a strategic decision, ushering in the future, shaped by the strategic decision taken. Moreover, strategy is

done by identifiable, often elite, agents, who are operating within the context of organizational structure and environmental constraints. As McKenna (2009: 231) notes, case writers must remain confident in their ability to impute 'strategic intentionality from historical outcomes'.

The relationship between business history and case study as a method was cemented by the dominant influence over both business history and strategy studies exerted by Alfred Chandler, professor at Harvard Business School (McKenna 2006). Chandler's influence over the study of strategy was strengthened, for example, in the work of Rumelt (1974) and, more recently, Whittington and Mayer (2000), who maintain that many of the world's largest corporations, founded in the nineteenth century, can serve as a reference point for Chandler-influenced research on strategy and structure. Their work has led to the gradual refinement of the so-called strategy–structure–ownership–performance (SSOP) nexus. Papers on strategy and structure continue to appear in core business history journals, and in 2011 *Business History* dedicated a special issue to the application of the SSOP model to the European corporation. Colli, Iversen and de Jong (2011: 9) conclude that the model has been 'successful in mapping the evolution of corporate structures in response to changing strategies'.

Thus, the writing of business history on strategy has very specific characteristics that need to be carefully identified. Central has been the strategy–structure nexus. Chandler (1962) argues that strategy leads structure in a dynamic, unidirectional pattern of change. Temporality is not problematized in this view of strategy: time is irreversible, and chains of cause and effect proceed in a path-dependent fashion. McGovern and McLean (2013: 453) claim that, at a certain point in the history of the studied firm, a '"path of competence development" had been set'. At the same time, the focus on strategy as the outcome of decision promotes a particular view of managerial agency. As McKinlay (2013: 141) argues, business history is subject to a 'centripetal pull…towards managerial decision-making as the decisive agent'.

Chandler's influence over subsequent business historical studies of strategy has been called a 'compelling foundational narrative' (Scranton

2008: 427). Very few business historians have looked to other later streams in strategy studies for theoretical lenses. Kipping and Cailluet's (2010) deployment of Mintzberg's (1989) emergent perspective on a historical case is almost unique. Kipping and Cailluet (2010: 103) frame their study by using the strategy and structure duality and conclude that 'the company always found a way to direct its own course'.

As argued above, the dominant approach to studying strategy from a historical perspective can and should be subject to critique. Adorisio and Mutch (2013: 106) regard business history as 'rather a conservative discipline', while also lamenting the 'presentism' of much management and organization studies. Bell and Taylor (2013: 133) contend that the business history 'community remains characterized by methodological detachment and epistemological disengagement'. Schwarzkopf (2012: 2), a business historian, complains about the 'extraordinary survival of the epistemological position of realism' within the discipline. Undoubtedly, apart from work relating to the concept of routine (Jones 2002), the closest business history has come to a practice-based perspective is in the work of Lipartito (2013).

Noting the discipline's reliance on functional models derived from economics, Lipartito (1995) makes a plea for taking the role of culture much more seriously. He explicitly relates culture to practice, whereby culture is seen as 'a system of values, ideas, and beliefs which constitute a mental apparatus for grasping reality' (Lipartito 1995: 2). Worth mentioning also is Boyce's (2010) study of multi-generational epistolary conventions in a shipping firm, pronouncing an understanding of business culture that relates to business leaders' reality. He finds that familial epistolary conventions changed over the generations, speculating that the distancing of the later generations from the day-to-day detail of operations had to do with the control over events exercised by large corporations.

As indicated in this section, there are several reasons why business historians have neglected practice when studying strategy. The first reason is epistemological; the high wall that historians, according to Bell and Taylor (2013), build around

their own practices. Another is a bias, inherited from Chandler (1962), that is relatively unconcerned with the 'day-to-day practices we call "business"' (Lipartito 2008: 432). A further reason is methodological: specifically, the nature of the sources and their use, particularly the use of corporate archives.

Challenges of traditional historical methods

Historical work builds on careful attention to a variety of sources, assessing the authenticity, representativeness and relevance of a source. Textual sources, especially documentary ones, are privileged but, increasingly, historians admit to using oral sources, images and other representations, such as fiction, artefacts and ephemera (Tosh 2010). Business history relies heavily on the business archive, as 'archival records are a constitutive element of business historical research, and such research, in turn, is fundamental for a holistic understanding of the role of enterprise in modern capitalist societies' (Schwarzkopf 2012: 1). It limits itself to aspects and entities of history that have an archive. Moreover, practices simply do not find themselves recorded in corporate archives. Until very recently business historians tended to naturalize the archive, refusing to problematize its contents, organization or use, as further articulated by McKinlay (2013: 141, emphasis in original):

Naturally, business historians, especially those following Alfred Chandler, have concentrated on accounting and directors' papers, the better to reconstruct the dynamics of strategic decision-making and the design of organizational structures. 'Strategy' *then* 'structure' was not just a Chandlerian epigram, a hypothesis from which to start and a conclusion to be reached, but was also an echo of the natural hierarchy of the archive.

Corporate archives are very particular entities in their content and organization, such that the 'order of the business archive reflects and constitutes *modern* power' (McKinlay 2013: 141, emphasis in original). A particular retrospective understanding of the firm is written into them over time, as cumulative decisions are taken as to what to include and preserve, and what to exclude, and thus often to destroy. They tend to concentrate on 'official' documentation, beginning with accounting and ownership data followed by the minutes of the board of directors, and other high-level boards and committees. High-level correspondence, internal and external, between executives and other offices may survive, after careful 'weeding', along with contracts and some personnel records. Photographs, technical plans, creative designs, press clippings, advertising materials and memoirs are all considered little better than ephemera; their survival should normally be considered a matter of chance rather than of design. At the same time, it should be noted that the vast majority of firms never leave behind any meaningful archival trace and are, in a sense, unrecoverable.

The cumulative effect of this building of the archives is to silently shape the histories that can be written. Schwarzkopf (2012) points out the interesting case of a leading British advertising agency that was effectively wiped from historical memory when all its records were destroyed in the late 1960s after its merger with an American firm. Now the history of advertising is dominated by the history of the 'winners'. Even when they exist, though, the records contain many silences. When attempting to write the history of the strategy and growth of one particular firm, McGovern and McLean (2013: 456) discover that 'no clearly articulated strategy was described in board meeting minutes'. From a strategy-as-practice perspective, this might be considered a somewhat naïve expectation. Even if researchers maintain a belief that strategy is a result of the conscious decisions of executives, however, then such records as minute books can be deeply disappointing.

When we begin to work historically we discover that the experiential dimensions to organizational practice, and their relation to action and process, lie yet another remove deeper in the 'lostness' of time past. Decker's (2013: 157) note that 'archives that allow the researcher to reconstruct the embedded rules of knowledge production are quite rare for business historians' is a considerable understatement. At the same time, business historians often display considerable faith in the 'assuredness of

strategic plans and diagrams of corporate structures' (McKinlay 2013: 150).

If the content of the archive itself constrains strategy studies from a historical perspective, so do the attitudes of many historians. The archive is a site of power; the silences are not just mere accidents resulting from the haphazard erosion of the past. Silences reflect the choices of those who have the power to make them. We have to be profoundly careful about conceptualizing archives as the 'memory of an organization' (Decker 2013: 160). Business history rarely acknowledges this process of silencing, and tends to naturalize the archive as a relatively complete and objective representation of the 'reality' of the firm's history, though debate about the status of the archive is becoming more frequent (Decker 2013; Fellman and Popp 2013; Kobrak and Schneider 2011; Schwarzkopf 2012). Furthermore, a wider range of sources and traces than is typically found in the corporate archive is finding its way into the practices of some business historians (for example, French and Popp 2010). Nonetheless, the archive remains a largely unrecognized complex of problems, especially in a strategy-as-practice perspective.

Thus, in summation, the challenges involved in a closer integration of a historical perspective into strategy-as-practice research are considerable. Despite their interest in the inherently processual nature of practice, practice scholars are not always attuned to thinking historically, and, contrary to business historians, they may even lack sensitivity to context. Business historians are rarely theoretically inclined to go looking for fine-grained practices, and, in any case, these fine-grained practices are seldom captured in the sources on which business historians typically rely. Therefore, if the corporate archive is silent on much of what goes on inside a firm, it is perhaps most silent on that which interests the strategy-as-practice researcher. Examples are the vast majority of formal meetings below the highest echelons; all informal meetings on every echelon, such as gatherings in corridors, coffee breaks, evenings in the pub; and even what most employees, managers and operatives alike, actually do from day to day: when they turn up, when they leave, the tasks they perform in between and *how* they go about performing them. Nor does the archive record how people feel about, interpret and react to the experience of work and organizational life, nor the tacit, unwritten codes that shape organizational life and lie submerged under the organizational charts that represent the firm.

Methods for studying strategy as practice historically: four categories

From the preceding reviews it can be seen that we face epistemological, conceptual and methodological challenges. Our purpose here is not to solve these different challenges but to put the emphasis on the outlining and use of historical methods. It seems evident that business historians and strategy practice scholars overlap in their interest in strategizing in the process of time and that a dialogue is thus worthwhile. Encouragingly, some business historians are beginning to engage explicitly with, for example, process theory (Popp and Holt 2012) and narrativization (Hansen 2012). Nonetheless, it is clear that we lack methods designed specifically for studies of the history of strategy practice. This section attempts to narrow the implied gap by attending to four categories of historical methods. It draws extensively on our own work, as this enables us to provide insights into the genesis and operation of the methods.

The first category relates to written sources and narratives, re-examining relatively 'conventional' sources with a different eye on and an attention to the omissions and silences, interpretively focused on the deconstruction of what it is the source might be expected to tell us. The second category concerns microhistory and is derived from the increasingly influential microhistorical approach, which has been described as a 'method of clues'. The third category dedicates interest to so-called ego documents, including letters, diaries, memoirs, wills and similar documents expressive of personal desires and values. The first three categories all revolve about both a particular type of sources and ways of reading and interpreting them. The emphasis on sources as the foundation of our suggested methodological approaches to studying strategy as practice historically reflects both history's instinct for the inductive and the paucity of

the traces of practice in conventional business history sources. Finally, the fourth category refers to lived experience, which is perhaps the most challenging of the categories we are suggesting here. Lived experience refers to an existential mode of 'being-in-the-world' that entails the dialogical way individuals relate to each other and to the cultural past (Gadamer 1989).

Rereading conventional sources and narratives

The first category of historical methods is based on the rereading of accepted accounts or reading differently conventional sources. Exemplary here is McKenna's (2009) deconstruction of a Harvard teaching case focused on the Honda motorcycle company. Much history writing falls quite naturally into a narrative pattern. Narratives have a powerful naturalizing force. In particular, narratives and narrativizing appear to allow time its true role, as understood in common-sense terms: life lived forwards. Perhaps as a result, unsurprisingly, narratives dominate the framing of most studies of strategizing through the vast majority of business history and beyond. In terms of the effect of these processes on our scholarship, it can subtly lead us to see strategy as a deliberative, motive force, and, moreover, one initiated and directed by identifiable, often elite agents within the context of organizational structure and environmental constraints. We need to be cautious, however, as these naturalizing effects occlude and close down just as much as they expose. In fact, McKenna (2009: 221) demonstrates in the textual and intellectual unpacking of the chosen Harvard case how 'the successive accumulation of artifacts has made each subsequent round of analysis ever more dependent on previous interpretations'. No matter how distant the text became from the world it sought to describe and explain, the case writers remained confident of their ability to impute 'strategic intentionality from the historical outcomes' (McKenna 2009: 231).

McKenna did something easy to describe but difficult to do well. He simply reversed and ran backwards the stages by which a series of narratives accumulated around the famous strategy case.

In doing so, he exposed to the light the mechanics of how this totemic object lesson in strategizing became 'particularly over-determined' and 'how the original problem came to be buried under a series of didactic mementos created by each succeeding generation' (McKenna 2009: 220). As those mementos accumulate, the certainty increases that only one explanation is right. This method might be usefully applied to many different kinds of texts, such as commemorative company histories. It is akin to a piece of literary detective work, and might be particularly appropriate for scholars already familiar with notions of language as a constitutive factor in a social phenomenon such as practices of strategy.

In contrast, the study by one of us, Popp (2001), emerged from work with some very conventional business history sources, utilizing a series of auditors' reports to explore family and firm culture, and its impact on strategy formation, at prestige pottery manufacturer Minton and Sons. These reports ran in sequence for a number of years, from a period in the late nineteenth century during which the firm was facing severe pressures. This made them valuable. Moreover, they were in some cases quite extensive, being almost closer to a consultant's report than a typical auditor's report and including recommendations that represented potentially very significant shifts in the firm's operations. Thus, they contained a great deal of very useful factual information, as well as discussion of the firm's existing strategies. They would undoubtedly have helped flesh out a conventional narrative of how the firm survived that period in its history. They had more to give, however. First, it was not clear why they even existed. The firm was not a publicly listed company at the time and was under no legal obligation to employ an external auditor. This insight depended on the historian's typical contextual knowledge, in this case of British company law. Two questions arose then: why had the reports been commissioned, and how were they received?

This is a very clear example of a method whereby a historian will arrive at his/her research question from the source. The reports themselves were unable to answer either question, however. Elsewhere in the archive, though, there was found a brief and apparently inconsequential internal memorandum. In fact, this scrap, the only traceable reaction by senior managers to the auditors, provided a critical statement of the firm's strategic thinking – if we can call it that – at this vital juncture. The memo utterly rejected the auditors' recommendations, and did so not on the basis of a forensic analysis but through appeal to the firm's history, prestige and values (this was a family firm). Suddenly we gain a new understanding of strategy formation taking place in a deeply inchoate manner from deep, almost subterranean wells of culture. Methodologically, the insight derives from bringing into dialogue the two sources; practically, it emerges from an attentive, alert reading of the sources that notices that the dialogue is possible.

Microhistory

In the above example, the singular memorandum existed as part of a very large and quite typical corporate archive, and it acted as the key that unlocked the solution to a problem. Our second category, microhistory, starts from a focus on micro-scale moments and events, suggesting an obvious affinity with the interest of strategy as practice in the quotidian. In contrast to the example of the memorandum given above, its clues are not only small but also typically isolated and unusual. Moreover, they act not as end points but beginnings, spurring the research question that is to be pursued. Microhistory emphasizes the duality of sources as exceptional/normal. Simply to work with very small, odd, anomalous or fragmented pieces of evidence is not enough, however. Microhistory focuses on the so-called double movement between the micro and macro levels (suggesting another contrast with the memorandum example, which was focused on solving a particular problem). Thus, there is a deliberate, repeated and ongoing shifting in focus between the particular and the general, echoing the importance of differing contexts as emphasized in the strategy-as-practice perspective (Johnson *et al.* 2007; Vaara and Whittington 2012). The 'movement from one level or sphere is qualitative, and generates new information' (Peltonen 2001: 357). This movement throws light in unexpected ways, through surprise dichotomies and affinities. Illustrative here is Holt and Popp's study (2013) of leadership succession strategy at the family firm Wedgwood and Sons in the late eighteenth century. The entire study revolves around a single letter written by founder Josiah Wedgwood to his son Jos (Josiah II) acknowledging the latter's desire not to leave the business. It is a remarkable document: deeply felt, displaying great sensitivity and very difficult to make sense of in the context of Josiah's life as a highly driven and successful entrepreneur who had expressed an explicit desire that his sons inherit his business.

Making sense of this documentary source required both a very deep and careful reading of the letter itself and, simultaneously, lifting our eyes from it to explore not only Josiah's wider correspondence but also the wider social, political and religious milieu. Read thus, the letter opened a wide window on the normally submerged topic of emotions in family business and their relationship to strategy formation emerging out of the depths of interpersonal relations. What first appears to be a very deliberate, conscious process of strategic decision-making is revealed through the microhistorian's double movement as the working out of long-run and often hidden or implicit modes of being, practices, with a specific organizational-familial setting. At the end of their study the authors conclude: 'The moment of succession was not a singular event; it sprang from a welter of symbolic, material and institutional arrangements gathered by Josiah and his family, and it projected all manner of possibility as purposes and relations were (re)worked amongst members' (Holt and Popp 2013: 14).

Microhistory can struggle to build a stable edifice on mundane sources, however. The wider connections built up cannot be mere allusions or similes; they need to be rooted in deep contextual knowledge. If so, microhistory is possible from the most mundane of sources, such as a single anonymously sent postcard, as its starting point for interpretation (Popp forthcoming). Organizational life, routines, processes and practices generate billions of documents and other artefacts. The vast majority of these are truly banal; a few, though, possess great potential. The keys to good

microhistory as a method include, on the one hand, care, precision and exactitude and, on the other, imagination, intuition and creativity.

Ego documents

Mention of letters also gestures towards the third category of historical methods, namely ego documents. Fulbrook and Rublack (2010: 263) define an ego document as one 'providing an account of, or privileged information about, the "self" who produced it'. They can also be referred to as self narratives or testimonies to the self. Fulbrook and Rublack (2010: 263) note that they allow us to focus on what 'might conveniently be summarized as..."structures and subjectivities"'. Letters are exemplary ego documents (as Josiah Wedgwood's letter referred to above). Apart from letters, ego documents could include diaries, memoirs, wills and other documents expressive of personal desires, priorities and values.

Popp (2012) and Popp and Holt (2012; 2013) draw on a large collection of ego documents: more than 200 personal letters exchanged between members of one business family over a period of more than four decades. At the core of the collection are more than 100 letters between a married couple engaged in an entrepreneurial enterprise, with approaching a half of those dating from the two-year period of their courtship. Utilizing these letters to understand the couple's motivations, values and experiences as entrepreneurs demanded immersion in the codes of romantic correspondence prevalent in their society at the time at which they wrote. Given the mass of both primary and secondary material necessary to reach this understanding, this was a slow process for which there was no short cut. Instead, the researchers had to (literally) live with the material.

Much as of what we might think of as strategy practice might be located in and experienced by the self. As Fulbrook and Rublack (2010) warn, however, ego documents can be very problematic sources with which to work. Their potential drawback lies in what is also their very strength: the apparent immediacy and authenticity of the access they give to the self. As social selves, though, we very rarely, if ever, write purely from the essential, internal self. Rather, even when we are writing with no audience in mind at all, as in a private diary, we write in ways mediated through codes, usages and shared languages. We draw on repertoires of expression adopted from elsewhere, relapsing often into cliché and convention. Understanding these shared linguistic threads and conventions is, in methodological terms, the key to opening up the ego document to interpretation and analysis.

Lived experience

Ego documents could also provide access to what is commonly termed 'lived experience', the fourth and final method category for incorporating a historical perspective in strategy-as-practice studies that we wish to present here. Lived experience, a phenomenological concept first offered by Dilthey (1985), refers to the pre-reflective dimensions of human existence. In accordance with the dwelling mode, grounded in Heidegger's phenomenological thinking, lived experience associates with an understanding and interpretation that propose a movement in the sense of feeling one's way through a world that is itself in motion (Chia 2004; Chia and Holt 2006; Chia and Rasche 2010). Applying a Heideggerian perspective on strategy as practice, Tsoukas (2010) adds that non-deliberate spontaneous acting is practical coping embedded within a broader sociomaterial context.

Influenced by the work of Heidegger, Gadamer (1989), from a philosophical hermeneutical perspective, further elaborates the notion of lived experience in association with 'hermeneutical situatedness', which refers to the individual's existential connections with the world. This means that the lived experience category gives primacy to interpretive studies, accentuating a dialogical openness to experience as dependent on historical grounding. Accordingly, this method category is not made up of methods that assist us in describing lived experience *of* history. Lived experience does not imply an enduring residue of specific moments in a human being's life. Lived experience refers to an ongoing integrative life process with which the practitioner entwines, hermeneutically situated – as

represented by 'horizon'. Horizon refers to an individual's standpoint and current understanding of a matter, and is always in motion (Gadamer 1989).

Lived experience implicates a qualitative method that is realized through techniques such as protocol-writing, interviewing and observation. Protocol-writing is the generating of original descriptive text of a person's experience. Such a text avoids causal explanations and generalizations, presenting practice as lived through – 'from the inside, as it were; almost like a state of mind' (Van Manen 1990: 64). From a lived-experience perspective, we are then not interested in the practitioner's subjective experiences. Instead, we try to understand what it is the practitioner does as an aspect of the practitioner's life, remaining oriented to the question of what it is like and what it means to be involved in strategy practice. As researchers we need to remember that lived experience questions are meaning questions and that lived experience 'can never be grasped in its full richness and depth since lived experience implicates the totality of life' (Van Manen 1990: 36).

Interviewing, in the form of dialogue and conversation, could also help us to stay close to experience as lived, serving as a means for exploring experiential narrative material. Narrative entails a communicative structure that corresponds to people's ways of experiencing life (Demers, Giroux and Chreim 2003). Through the words the practitioners use when telling about their here-and-now involvement, practice opens up to a historical dimension. It comes alive in practitioners' present efforts to keep in force a cultural past intrinsically linked to practice (Ericson 2014). As pointed out by Ericson (2007) and Ericson and Melin (2010), the dialogical, conversational form of interviewing opens up to a historical-grounding understanding of strategy as practice, represented by horizon. They illustrate that it is through the broadening of horizon that a practitioner changes the understanding while looking beyond the present standpoint and reconstructing the past. Moreover, the practitioner's own past and that of a specific geographical place spur a move in terms of a broadening of the practitioner's horizon. Practitioners who are involved in implementing a renewed business concept admittedly broaden their horizons. They re-present and reconstruct a past when letting go of old familiar ways of doing strategy; and, when practitioners close in on old ways of doing strategy, a constraining horizon movement is acknowledged.

Since the 'best way to enter a person's lived experience is to participate in it', close observation is a suitable technique for generating lived experience material (Van Manen 1990: 69). As observer *and* participant, the researcher can get close to a particular situation, but he/she must be prepared to step back and reflect on the meaning of the situation at hand.

Protocol-writing, interviewing and observation can help us to transform glimpses of lived experience into an oral or written expression. We need to realize that such expressions are never identical with lived experience, however, because 'lived experience is always more complex than the result of any singular description', and 'there is always an element of the ineffable to life' (Van Manan 1990: 16).

Concluding discussion

As shown in this chapter, history could play a more evident role in strategy-as-practice studies. In this concluding section we summarize and comment on the categories of historical methods presented and on the meaning and implications of a historical approach within an strategy-as-practice perspective.

Reflecting on the method categories

The method category of conventional sources and narratives implies a rereading of accepted accounts but also a different reading of business history sources. As pointed out in reference to the Harvard Honda case (McKenna 2009) and the Minton and Sons case (Popp 2001), this category helps us to pay close attention to a variety of secondary sources, as well as extrapolating them to see how they apply to primary sources. Based on archival sources in the form of a set of auditors' reports, Popp (2001) generated rich material for supplying a narrative of how a family firm survived a period in its history. It is interesting to note, though, that these sources instigated new research questions that led to other sources being found elsewhere in the archive.

Narratives have a powerful naturalizing force but we need to critically reflect on their ability to provide trustworthy interpretations of events in the past. McKenna (2009) has shown that a successive narrative accumulation of interpretations of events can be somewhat misleading. If we tend to overdetermine particular occurrences in the past, the result might be an unjustified glorious image of the present and an exaggerated certainty around specific explanations. When using sources and narratives, the researcher must engage carefully in what can be described as literary detective work.

The method category referring to microhistory has great affinity with the interest of strategy as practice. It directs our attention to the movement between micro and macro levels. Deliberately adopted, this category sets out to find a wider, macro resonance at the smallest, micro level. As researchers, we are then involved in a repeated and ongoing shifting in focus between the particular and the general. As Holt and Popp's study (2013) of the leadership succession strategy at a family firm illustrates, a documentary source, such as a single letter from the founder of the firm to the son, helps not only with the exploration of personal emotions and interpersonal relations associated with the issue of succession; it gives, in addition, insights into strategy formation in a social, political and religious context.

The microhistory category opens up to an understanding of how the micro and macro levels interact and integrate. Applying this method category in practice-based research thus means that we are able to discern an institutional, macro context through a micro context that apparently could be expressed through a letter. When drawing on such a narrow foundation of source, we must combine care and precision with imagination and creativity.

The application of the method category of ego documents also needs to be addressed with caution. Ego documents include letters, diaries, memoirs, wills and other documents expressing personal desires, priorities and values. As these are very problematic sources, they must be read with great care. They cannot be read as direct, unproblematic expressions of desires, priorities and values as they also often reflect codes and languages reminiscent of past times. Further, the authenticity of the access they provide to historical occurrences and an internal self might be elusive. It is worth adding that working with ego documents is a process that is developing slowly, unfolding almost as though in pace with the life being studied.

The method category associated with lived experience implies the use of a qualitative interpretive method involving an ongoing integrative life process with which the practitioner entwines, hermeneutically situated. Akin to the first method category, the lived experience category also provides us with narratives. These narratives originate in an understanding of practitioners' emergent orientation towards that which they see, experience and construct as reality. As Rouleau (2010: 258) makes clear: 'Narratives of practices allow the researcher to dig into the "life-world" of particular actors, such as managers and others, in order to capture the taken-for-granted streams of routines, events and interactions that constitute their social practices.' Narratives also assume a joint performance of and intersection between those talking about their direct involvement in practice and the researcher as listener and interpreter (Barry and Elmes 1997; Boje 1991). Recognizing our own parts as researchers in the conceptualization of reality, we address strategy as practice as a social phenomenon into which valuable insight can be gained as we engage in dialogues with the practitioners through the use of protocol-writing, interviewing or close observation. At the same time, it is necessary to acknowledge the difficulty in directly accessing lived experience and making explicit the practitioners' existential engagement with the world. 'We have only their life expressions as indicators of their own lived experience' (Seebohm 2004: 94).

In addition, it is important to stress the hybridity of these methods, notwithstanding their presentation here in discrete categories. In practice, there is a considerable blurring of lines once we start working. Nonetheless, as we have illustrated, these categories help us to think about how we use sources and narratives, microhistory, ego

documents and lived experience to bring an historical insight into strategy as practice. Our choice of method category will often reflect the starting point from which a research project begins. For example, microhistory could commence with a chance discovery of a document or clue that mystifies us. Rereadings might begin from a sense of dissatisfaction and a subsequent realization that a rereading of a source concerning an issue or event that we thought we understood is indeed possible.

When doing historical work

For those less familiar with the working practices of those doing history, it is important to stress two important points. First, most historical studies work inductively; they begin with the source and not the theory-related question, unlike the practice in most social sciences (Fellman and Popp 2013). Except when working in contemporary history, when it might be possible to collect oral history interviews, we can work only with the sources available. It becomes very difficult to design a study in advance and then simply collect the appropriate data. This is a significant methodological difference, and one to which strategy-as-practice scholars wishing to include a greater historical perspective in their work will need to make some adjustment. The relationship between research question and sources becomes a more open, fluid and multidirectional one. It is not merely a difference in method but to some extent also an epistemological one. It leads to a different (not better or worse) class of truth claims. These qualities ensure that historical studies rarely unfold in a linear fashion; there is, rather, a continuous iteration between source, emergent questions and a deepening knowledge of relevant wider contexts.

Second, doing historical work is a relatively literary endeavour. It is true that, in economic and demographic histories, scholars often work with very large data sets using advanced statistical methods, but the kinds of history relevant to strategy-as-practice scholars are highly textual. In this process it is neither easy nor meaningful to separate out the different phases of data collection, analysis/interpretation and discussion. Historians may not even think in these terms, and interpretation, in particular, may not be a discrete phase at all but, instead, become acts folded into the process of writing. The method categories we have explored in this chapter tend to share this basic characteristic.

Additionally, it is important to stress that methods allowing for a historical perspective open a window for critical reflection on time, providing us with alternatives for evaluating present occurrences. Practice is an inherently temporal experience. A single action at a point of time is not a practice; it is the passage of time that converts action into practice. With temporality and its relationality in focus, there is also a lived, non-linear time (Ericson 2014). It can be argued, then, that any attention to practice also demands an attention to history and, in particular, to time. An area that remains largely unaddressed in the study of strategy as practice is research elaborating on temporality exposed through the variable ways in which practitioners intimately entwine with practice (Sandberg and Dall'Alba 2009). If strategy-as-practice scholars wish to further their interest in time and history, however, then – perhaps counter-intuitively – business historians may not be the first people they should look too. Only very recently has Raff (2013: 436) urged business historians to 'do something with time'. Without sufficient attention to time and our experiencing of it, we (historians and strategy-as-practice scholars) risk stumbling into history's greatest traps: teleology and determinism – a belief that the present explains the past and a conviction that the present we have is the one we were always, in some way, *meant* to have; a present that also, in some way, contains the future. They are traps that strip human actors of agency and make them carriers of destiny. A faith in the generative power of deliberate strategy fits well with these beliefs and convictions.

Strategic decision becomes the vehicle for materializing the underlying explanatory logics driving progress forwards to an ordained end. Agents setting and enacting strategies become prescient, far-seeing prophets able to discern the patterns that foreshadow the coming future. This conception of the power of strategizing to reveal the (preordained) future is obviously embedded within a particular, unidirectional vision of time's flow. Lipartito's (1995: 4) critique that 'we have proceeded on the assumption that business structures [and, de facto, strategies as well] can be thinly described as unproblematic expressions of an underlying, universal process' may be equally applicable to both mainstream strategy scholarship and much business history.

A final comment

In their chapter 'Strategizing and history' in the 2010 edition of this handbook, Ericson and Melin (2010: 326) accepted the challenge to take the strategy-as-practice perspective 'a step further by elevating the historical dimension as a living tradition that shapes present future oriented activities performed by practitioners in their representation and reconstruction of the past'. Our purpose in this chapter is somewhat different, being strongly oriented towards a variety of historical methods, and a presentation and elaboration that deal with the challenges and possibilities of studying strategy as practice from a historical perspective. Nonetheless, it is worthwhile to pick up the points of contact or resonance between the reflections in the chapter on strategizing and history and ours now.

Theoretically, Ericson and Melin (2010: 326) frame their consideration of strategizing in history with an emphasis on *hermeneutical situatedness*, such that the actor becomes a 'social historical being always affected by the testimony of history and under its influence'. Adopting that framing here would suggest a focus on the problem of how such a situatedness can be recovered in historical studies when the living role of history, the discourse of the past and the practitioner's existential being in and 'belongingness' to the world are precisely those elements most likely to be suppressed and muffled by both the hierarchies and silences of the archive and the 'merely ideative representations' of the historian (Gadamer 1989: 168). Remarkably few historians – certainly, very few business historians – are strongly interested in historical tradition and experience as lived. It is indeed the case that they conceive of history as if it were ontologically independent of a subject. Moreover, once we get beyond the period accessible via oral history, it is not obvious how the historians are to listen to what can reach them from the past (Ericson and Melin 2010).

History's strong emphasis on and strengths in contextualization are starting points, however. They provide a kind of situatedness, if not necessarily a temporalized one, as Ericson and Melin (2010) assert. It is hoped that we have pointed the way to some possibilities here. Narratives can be complicated, or even reversed, as McKenna (2006; 2009) has shown; and stories can be told before being disrupted and then retold – a method deliberately employed in the historical-processual studies of entrepreneurship by Popp and Holt (2012; 2013). In either case, the past–present–future nexus becomes more complex, folded in on itself in overlapping pleats and layers. Other routes forward might be found through a different approach to the (business) archive – one that looks again at its content with an eye alert to both the dissonant and the submerged. At the same time we might look to sources traditionally eschewed or dismissed, such as a range of ego texts. Here we can marry microhistory's concern for the exceptional and the normal with the interest in the micro-social within strategy as practice. Finally, by including the notion of lived experience, we may increase our awareness of history as a living cultural tradition with which the practitioner entwines and continuously moves.

References

Adorisio, A. L. M., and Mutch, A. (2013), 'In search of historical methods', *Management and Organizational History*, 8/2: 105–10.

Balogun, J., and Johnson, G. (2004), 'Organizational restructuring and middle manager sensemaking', *Academy of Management Journal*, 47/4: 523–49.

Barry, D., and Elmes, M. (1997), 'Strategy retold: toward a narrative view of strategic discourse', *Academy of Management Review*, 22/2: 429–52.

Bell, E., and Taylor, S. (2013), 'Writing history into management research', *Management and Organizational History*, 8/2: 127–36.

Boje, D. M. (1991), 'The storytelling organization: a study of story performance', *Administrative Science Quarterly*, 36/1: 106–28.

Bourdieu, P. (1990), *The Logic of Practice*. Cambridge: Polity.

Boyce, G. (2010), 'Language and culture in a Liverpool merchant family firm, 1870–1950', *Business History Review*, 84/1: 1–26.

Campbell-Hunt, C. (2007), 'Complexity in practice', *Human Relations*, 60/5: 793–823.

Chandler, A. D. (1962), *Strategy and Structure: Chapters in the History of the American Industrial Enterprise*. Cambridge, MA: MIT Press.

Chia, R. (2004), 'Strategy-as-practice: reflections on the research agenda', *European Management Review*, 1/1: 29–34.

Chia, R., and Holt, R. (2006), 'Strategy as practical coping: a Heideggerian perspective', *Organization Studies*, 27/5: 635–55.

Chia, R., and Rasche, A. (2010), 'Epistemological alternatives for researching strategy as practice: building and dwelling worldviews', in Golsorkhi, D., Rouleau, L., Seidl, D., and Vaara, E. (eds.), *Cambridge Handbook of Strategy as Practice*: 34–46. Cambridge University Press.

Clarke, I., Kwon, W., and Wodak, R. (2012), 'A context-sensitive approach to analysing talk in strategy meetings', *British Journal of Management*, 23/4: 455–73.

Colli, A., Iversen, M. J., and de Jong, A. (2011), 'Mapping strategy, structure, ownership and performance in European corporations: introduction', *Business History*, 53/1: 1–13.

Decker, S. (2013), 'The silence of the archives: business history, post-colonialism and archival ethnography', *Management and Organizational History*, 8/2: 155–73.

Demers, C., Giroux, N., and Chreim, S. (2003), 'Merger and acquisition announcements as corporate wedding narratives', *Journal of Organizational Change Management*, 16/2: 223–42.

Dilthey, W. (1985), *Poetry and Experience*. Princeton University Press.

Dougherty, D. (2004), 'Organizing practices in services: capturing practice-based knowledge for innovation', *Strategic Organization*, 2/1: 35–64.

Ericson, M. (2007), *Business Growth: Activities, Themes and Voices*. Cheltenham: Edward Elgar.
(2014), 'On the dynamics of fluidity and open-endedness of strategy process: toward a strategy-as-practicing conceptualization', *Scandinavian Journal of Management*, 30/1: 1–15.

Ericson, M., and Melin, L. (2010), 'Strategizing and history', in Golsorkhi, D., Rouleau, L., Seidl, D., and Vaara, E. (eds.), *Cambridge Handbook of Strategy as Practice*: 326–43. Cambridge University Press.

Fellman, S., and Popp, A. (2013), 'Lost in the archive: the business historian in distress', in Czarniawska, B., and Löfgren, O. (eds.), *Coping with Excess: How Organizations, Communities and Individuals Manage Overflows*: 216–43. Cheltenham: Edward Elgar.

French, M., and Popp, A. (2010), '"Practically the uniform of the tribe": dress codes among commercial travellers', *Enterprise and Society*, 11/3: 436–67.

Fulbrook, M., and Rublack, U. (2010), 'In relation: the "social self" and ego-documents', *German History*, 28/3: 263–72.

Gadamer, H.-G. (1989), *Truth and Method*. New York: Continuum.

Giraudeau, M. (2008), 'The drafts of strategy: opening up plans and their uses', *Long Range Planning*, 41/3: 291–308.

Gomez, M.-L. (2010), 'A Bourdieusian perspective on strategizing', in Golsorkhi, D., Rouleau, L., Seidl, D., and Vaara, E. (eds.), *Cambridge Handbook of Strategy as Practice*: 141–54. Cambridge University Press.

Gomez, M.-L., and Bouty, I. (2011), 'The emergence of an influential practice: food for thought', *Organization Studies*, 32/7: 921–40.

Hansen, P. (2012), 'Business history: a cultural and narrative approach', *Business History Review*, 86/4: 693–717.

Hendry, K. P., Kiel, G. C., and Nicholson, G. (2010), 'How boards strategise: a strategy as practice view', *Long Range Planning*, 43/1: 33–56.

Holt, R., and Popp, A. (2013), 'Emotion, succession, and the family firm: Josiah Wedgwood & Sons', *Business History*, 55/6: 892–909.

Jarzabkowski, P. (2004), 'Strategy as practice: recursiveness, adaptation, and practices-in-use', *Organization Studies*, 25/4: 529–60.

Jarzabkowski, P., and Spee, P. (2009), 'Strategy-as-practice: a review and future directions for the field', *International Journal of Management Reviews*, 11/1: 69–95.

Johnson, G., Langley, A., Melin, L., and Whittington, R. (2007), *Strategy as Practice: Research Directions and Resources*. Cambridge University Press.

Jones, S. R. H. (2002), 'Routines, capabilities and the growth of the firm: Messrs Ross & Glendining, Dunedin, 1862–1900', *Australian Economic History Review*, 42/1: 34–53.

Jørgensen, B., and Messner, M. (2010), 'Accounting and strategizing: a case study from new product development', *Accounting, Organizations and Society*, 35/2: 184–204.

Kaplan, S., and Orlikowski, W. J. (2013), 'Temporal work in strategy making', *Organization Science*, 24/4: 965–95.

Kipping, M., and Cailluet, L. (2010), 'Mintzberg's emergent and deliberate strategies: tracking Alcan's activities in Europe, 1928–2007', *Business History Review*, 84/1: 79–104.

Kobrak, C., and Schneider, A. (2011), 'Varieties of business history: subject and methods for the twenty-first century', *Business History*, 53/3: 401–24.

Lipartito, K. J. (1995), 'Culture and the practice of business history', *Business and Economic History*, 24/2: 1–42.

(2008), 'The future of Alfred Chandler', *Enterprise and Society*, 9/3: 430–2.

(2013), 'Connecting the cultural and the material in business history', *Enterprise and Society*, 14/4: 686–704.

McGovern, T., and McLean, T. (2013), 'The growth and development of Clarke Chapman from 1864 to 1914', *Business History*, 55/3: 448–78.

McKenna, C. (2006), 'Writing the ghost writer back in: Alfred Sloan, Alfred Chandler, John McDonald and the intellectual origins of corporate strategy', *Management and Organizational History*, ½: 107–26.

(2009), 'Mementos: looking backwards at the Honda motorcycle case, 2003–1973', in Clarke, S., Lamoreaux, N. R., and Usselman, S. (eds.), *The Challenge of Remaining Innovative: Lessons from Twentieth-Century American Business*: 219–42. Redwood City, CA: Stanford University Press.

McKinlay, A. (2013), 'Following Foucault into the archives: clerks, careers and cartoons', *Management and Organizational History*, 8/2: 137–54.

Mintzberg, H. (1989), *Mintzberg on Management: Inside Our Strange World of Organizations*. New York: Free Press.

Peltonen, M. (2001), 'Clues, margins, and monads: the micro–macro link in historical research', *History and Theory*, 40/3: 347–59.

Popp, A. (2001), 'Specialty production, personal capitalism and auditors' reports: Mintons Ltd, *c.* 1870–1900', *Accounting, Business and Financial History*, 10/3: 347–69.

(2012), *Entrepreneurial Families: Business, Marriage and Life in the Early Nineteenth Century*. London: Pickering & Chatto.

(forthcoming), 'The broken cotton speculator', *History Workshop Journal*.

Popp, A., and Holt, R. (2012), 'Entrepreneurship and being: the case of the Shaws', *Entrepreneurship and Regional Development*, 25/1–2: 52–68.

(2013), 'The presence of entrepreneurial opportunity', *Business History*, 55/1: 9–18.

Raff, D. (2013), 'How to do things with time', *Enterprise and Society*, 14/3: 435–66.

Rouleau, L. (2005), 'Micro-practices of strategic sensemaking and sensegiving: how middle managers interpret and sell change every day', *Journal of Management Studies*, 42/7: 1413–41.

(2010), 'Studying strategizing through narratives of practice', in Golsorkhi, D., Rouleau, L., Seidl, D., and Vaara, E. (eds.), *Cambridge Handbook of Strategy as Practice*: 258–70. Cambridge University Press.

Rumelt, R. P. (1974), *Strategy, Structure and Economic Performance*. Cambridge, MA: Harvard University Press.

Sandberg, J., and Dall'Alba, G. (2009), 'Returning to practice anew: a life-world perspective', *Organization Studies*, 30/12: 1349–68.

Schwarzkopf, S. (2012), 'What is an archive – and where is it? Why business historians need a constructive theory of the archive', *Business Archives*, 105/11: 1–9.

Scranton, P. (2008), 'Beyond Chandler?', *Enterprise and Society*, 9/3: 426–9.

Seebohm, T. M. (2004), *Hermeneutics: Method and Methodology*. Dordrecht: Kluwer.

Stensaker, L., and Falkenberg, J. (2007), 'Making sense of different responses to corporate change', *Human Relations*, 60/1: 137–77.

Tosh, J. (2010), *The Pursuit of History*. Upper Saddle River, NJ: Pearson.

Tsoukas, H. (2010), 'Practice, strategy making and intentionality: a Heideggerian onto-epistmelogy for strategy as practice', in Golsorkhi, D., Rouleau, L., Seidl, D., and Vaara, E. (eds.), *Cambridge Handbook of Strategy as Practice*: 47–62. Cambridge University Press.

Vaara, E., and Whittington, R. (2012), 'Strategy-as-practice: taking social practices seriously', *Academy of Management Annals*, 6/1: 285–336.

Van Manen, M. (1990), *Researching Lived Experience: Human Science for an Action Sensitive Pedagogy*. Albany, NY: SUNY Press.

Whittington, R., and Mayer, M. (2000), *The European Corporation: Strategy, Structure, and Social Science*. Oxford University Press.

Whittington, R., Cailluet, L., and Yakis-Douglas, B. (2011), 'Opening strategy: evolution of a precarious profession', *British Journal of Management*, 22/3: 531–44.

Quantitative methods in strategy-as-practice research

TOMI LAAMANEN, EMMANUELLE REUTER, MARKUS SCHIMMER, FLORIAN UEBERBACHER and XENA WELCH GUERRA[1]

Introduction

While most of the prior work in the strategy-as-practice research stream has been conceptual or qualitative in nature, there is also potential in researching strategy practices quantitatively. There are a number of different benefits that can be gained in comparison to a solely qualitative research orientation. Qualitative methods have advanced the strategic management field with groundbreaking theoretical and empirical insights. Their importance in theory-building is uncontestable, as demonstrated by some of the highly influential qualitative articles from our field (for example, Barley 1986; Brown and Eisenhardt 1997; Burgelman 1983b). Despite these advantages, however, the reliance on a single dominant research method can also be constraining. A broader range of methods may be useful in examining the macro-level patterns emerging from the micro-level data, for establishing boundary conditions or in showing that the qualitative insights also have broader generalizability (Edmondson and McManus 2007). Moreover, the innovative use of quantitative methods could also lead to the emergence of novel insights that might not be achievable with purely qualitative research designs.

Strategy-as-practice research has historically had a strong reliance on qualitative data and related research designs in order to go deeper in understanding the micro-level strategy practices that the dominating quantitative research methods could not capture. Bacause of this important mission, an epistemic culture has emerged around the study of strategy practices over time. The term 'epistemic

culture' refers to how a research community generates knowledge. It is an implicit property, and can be inferred from the dominant research practices at work in a research stream (Knorr Cetina 1999). The epistemic culture of strategy-as-practice research has been strongly influenced by sociological practice theory, in which the use of qualitative research methods has been particularly prominent.

While the epistemic culture of a research stream plays a strong role in the choice of a research method, we argue that the maturity of the research focus should also drive decisions on the choice of appropriate research methods. For example, the life cycle perspective distinguishes early, intermediate and mature stages in a research field's life cycle (Edmondson and McManus 2007): At the early stage of a new research field, theory and paradigm development tend to favour inductive theory-building. This stage is typically associated with qualitative methods to develop the foundational concepts and relationships. As the research field then achieves intermediate levels of maturity, concepts and relationships become increasingly refined and precise, enabling the use of both qualitative and quantitative research methods to advance knowledge creation. Further maturity leads to increasing formalization and fine-tuning of the established concepts, and the constructs used to measure them, in order to establish enhanced comparability of the findings across multiple researchers.

From such a life cycle perspective, one could argue that several strategy-as-practice research areas are still in their earlier life cycle stages. While they require intensive qualitative research, early-stage research phenomena can also benefit greatly

---

[1] Authors are listed in alphabetical order.

from the use of quantitative data. Accordingly, mixed-method studies that combine qualitative and quantitative data (see, for example, Jick 1979) would hold major potential in the field of SAP research. In this regard, adding quantitative data to qualitative studies may help in providing more and different types of evidence and in producing further generality for exploratory findings (for example, Creswell 2008).

The chapter proceeds as follows. We start by briefly reviewing and discussing the use of quantitative research methods in closely related strategy research streams, such as upper echelons research, which focuses on top management teams; research on middle management; strategic decision-making research; research on strategic consensus; and research on strategic issues and initiatives. After synthesizing the lessons learned with the established quantitative methods, we also discuss a number of innovative quantitative research methods that could be used to further advance strategy-as-practice research. These methods include computer-aided content analysis, network analysis, sequence analysis, event history analysis and event study methodology. We offer a brief introduction to each method and highlight possible avenues to study strategy practices. In addition, we discuss some of the more novel sources of quantitative data, such as the use of e-mail data and press release data streams extracted from different news sources. The discussion of the different quantitative research methods and novel data sources is by no means meant to be exhaustive. Instead, we focus on a set of quantitative research methods, both established and novel, that strategy-as-practice researchers can potentially use to enrich their research designs.

Quantitative work in related streams

Despite the scarcity of quantitative research on strategy practices, there is extensive research in closely related research streams that one can build on. In particular, the prior research on top management teams, middle management, strategic decision-making, strategic consensus, and strategic issues and initiatives provide important related

research streams in this respect on which to build one's own research on strategy practices. As strategy-as-practice research focuses on the practices, praxis, and practitioners, these research streams are also interested in the role of the practitioners (TMT and middle management), practices (strategic issue management, strategic initiative practices), and praxis (strategic decision-making, consensus formation).

When making the move from a qualitative research design to a quantitative one, the central decisions relate to (1) the choice of the object of analysis, (2) the development or use of established constructs that can be measured and replicated across the different objects of analysis, (3) the development of appropriate control variables to account for alternative theoretical explanations and to control for the contextual differences across the different objects of analysis, and (4) the logic of reasoning as to how the different objects of analysis could cause the outcome variable of interest. We discuss these choices briefly in the context of the related research streams.

Top management teams

The common objects of analysis in the research on top management teams are the team members – such as CEO, CFO, COO or CSO (Menz and Scheef 2014) – or the top management teams across firms. Since Hambrick and Mason (1984) first brought up the idea that the demographic backgrounds of top management team members are likely to matter in terms of their behaviour, the quantitative research into TMTs has expanded rapidly. The ease of measurement has enabled researchers to develop different kinds of quantitative research settings, which have helped deepen the understanding of the effects of TMT member characteristics and heterogeneity on the top management team dynamics across firms. Over time increasingly sophisticated constructs have emerged to go beyond the original demographic variables. On the one hand, research has gone deeper into measuring and examining personality characteristics of top management team members (Chatterjee and Hambrick 2007, 2011; Hayward and Hambrick 1997). On the other hand, the emergence of a construct measuring managerial discretion has enabled researchers to explain why CEOs and TMTs do not always matter equally (Carpenter and Golden 1997; Finkelstein and Hambrick 1990).

It has also been found that, for example, the construct of managerial discretion is highly context-dependent and could play out differently in different cultural contexts (for example, Crossland and Hambrick 2011). Moreover, connecting different constructs to outcomes requires an understanding of the interdependences and the processes with which the TMT interacts, which has led to research on TMT interdependences and team processes (Barrick *et al.* 2007). The relationship of the research on top management teams and strategy as practice is intriguing. When making sense of the relationship, Don Hambrick noted in his keynote speech at the European Academy of Management conference in June 2014 that he sees himself as an epidemiologist, aiming to understand the overall patterns in the data, and strategy-as-practice research as work by microbiologists trying to figure out the specific biological mechanisms at play.

Middle management

The common object of analysis in the research on middle management is an individual middle management representative (see, for example, Wooldridge and Floyd 1990; Wooldridge, Schmid and Floyd 2008). Similarly to the research on top management, middle management and its role represent a fruitful arena for quantitative analysis. It is, in some respects, even easier to do quantitative research on middle managers, because it is often possible to create a sufficiently large sample for quantitative analysis even from within one firm. We see this as a still underutilized research opportunity.

Even though there is already an extensive body of quantitative research on the role of middle management (for a review, see Wooldridge, Schmid and Floyd 2008), there is still significantly less work on it than, for example, on the role of top management teams. Some of the most central constructs of this research stream relate to the roles of the middle managers in relation to strategy and the nature of involvement in strategy development (Collier, Fishwick and Floyd 2004; Floyd and

Wooldridge 1992; Wooldridge and Floyd 1990). While there has also been work on the contextual determinants of the roles of middle managers in different organizational contexts (Currie and Procter 2005; Floyd and Wooldridge 1992), there is still a major further research opportunity on this front as well. Finally, the common logic of reasoning in the research on middle management tends to be that involvement in the strategy process tends to create the highest commitment and that middle management behaviours play a major role in either advancing or slowing down strategy implementation (for example, Guth and Macmillan 1986; Mantere 2008; Ren and Guo 2011).

Strategic decision-making

The common object of analysis in strategic decision-making research is either an individual strategic decision or the process that led to the decision. The central constructs in this research stream relate to the formalization (Papadakis, Lioukas and Chambers 1998), comprehensiveness (Atuahene-Gima and Li 2004; Fredrickson 1984; Fredrickson and Mitchell 1984) and speed (Baum and Wally 2003; Eisenhardt 1990) of the analyses and the process. The moderating influence of different environmental and organizational contexts – dynamic versus mature – on strategic decision processes and strategic decision-making performance has also been extensively studied, with somewhat mixed results (Hough and White 2003; Papadakis, Lioukas and Chambers 1998). The common logic of reasoning in strategic decision-making research is that comprehensiveness and rationality contribute to decision-making performance, in general, and that the speed of decision-making contributes to strategic decision-making performance in fast-moving, turbulent environments. These would be interesting findings to deepen further with the strategy-as-practice lens.

Strategic consensus

Research on strategic consensus can in some respects be seen as an integrative area that cuts across the above research streams. The common object of analysis in strategic consensus research is either a strategic decision around which the consensus is formed or a set of teams or organizations that either reach or do not reach consensus (Bourgeois 1980; Dess 1987; Iaquinto and Fredrickson 1997; Kellermanns *et al.* 2005). The most central constructs of the quantitative research on strategic consensus relate to the locus and content of consensus (for example, Kellermanns *et al.* 2005), and extensive research shows that the performance implications of consensus are context-, organization- and decision-dependent (Henderson and Mitchell 1997; Homburg, Krohmer and Workman 1999; Kellermanns *et al.* 2005).

The common logic of reasoning in this research is that reaching consensus is positively related to team and firm performance and that the relationship is moderated by organizational and environmental context. Recently a group of researchers from Rotterdam University has put forward an innovative quantitative method for mapping organizational consensus in a multi-team setting (Tarakci *et al.* 2014). Using a survey of different teams' rankings of their own priorities regarding firms' strategy, the authors were able to use multidimensional scaling to map the different team-level cognitions in the organization and demonstrate how different teams' priorities differ from each other. The method provides an interesting way to examine organizations simultaneously on three levels – organization, team and individual – and to develop an understanding of the effects of strategic interventions on the changes in the priorities and strategic consensus.

Strategic issues and initiatives

Finally, the common objects of analysis in research on strategic issues and initiatives tend to be the strategic issues that a firm is facing (Chattopadhyay, Glick and Huber 2001; Dutton and Ashford 1993; Dutton *et al.* 1997; Thomas and McDaniel 1990) or the strategic initiatives that it is launching and running (for example, Lechner and Floyd 2012; Lechner, Frankenberger and Floyd 2010). The common constructs in the strategic issue research stream relate to the characteristics of the strategic issues according to management's sensemaking, such as whether they are perceived as opportunities or threats (Jackson and Dutton 1988) or from the perspective of issue feasibility and uncertainty (Julian and Ofori-Dankwa 2008).

In contrast, the research on strategic initiatives tends to be more focused on the effects of the explorative versus exploitative nature of the initiatives (Lechner and Floyd 2007; 2012), how they are coordinated on the corporate level (Lechner and Kreutzer 2010) or how they are positioned in the intergroup networks inside the firm (Lechner, Frankenberger and Floyd 2010). Both research streams are interested in the contextual influences, either in terms of strategic issue interpretation or strategic initiative performance, and the common logic of reasoning being tested is that the nature of the issue or initiative and how it is being managed are related to the performance of the firm. Taking into account the large number of issues and initiatives that even individual large firms are running, there is a major further research opportunity in this research area to go deeper into analysing the strategy practices associated with the management of strategic issues and initiatives.

As a whole, the five related research streams can be seen as the foundation on which one can build one's own quantitative research on strategy practices. While the research on strategy practices adds the more micro-level sociological lens to the study on organizational phenomena, the five related research streams provide a wealth of established constructs, tested relationships and an understanding of some of the most important contextual moderators on which to build one's own quantitative research project.

Lessons learned for strategy practice research

A number of criteria for assessing the quality of quantitative research have emerged over time, and strategy-as-practice scholars can take these on as 'best practices' when examining focal processes and phenomena through a quantitative lens. These include (1) using established constructs, (2) avoiding common method bias, (3) controlling for unobserved outliers, (4) examining reverse causality and (5) avoiding endogeneity. Countering these potential biases when developing the empirical research design of one's paper helps alleviate some of the most common challenges that typically emerge in the journal review process stage. We discuss them briefly below.

The use of established constructs As there are typically extensive, contextually rich data available on a firm's strategy practices and the context surrounding them, it is easy to get distracted by the richness of the data. In order to be able to build on prior work and to provide a basis for future studies in similar and different contexts, it would be useful to be able to complement the richness of the explanation with a quantitative analysis using established pre-tested constructs. In case such constructs do not exist that would be useful for analysing the phenomenon of interest, the creation and testing of new constructs could in itself be an important contribution and develop the research area onwards.

Common method bias When one carries out surveys, either within a single organization or across multiple organizations, there is a danger of the results being confounded by the common method bias. If, for example, one measures both the dependent and the independent construct based on the perception of the same respondent without external data, there is a danger that the characteristics of the respondent affect the results more than the relationships that one is interested in studying.

Unobserved outliers As there are often multiple other events going on in parallel in an organization, it is important to be able to control for the other events occurring at the same time. For example, a firm could be engaging in particular types of strategy activities because of increasing competitive pressure from the market, but in reality it could be the market pressure affecting the dependent variable more than the strategy practices.

Reverse causality When doing cross-sectional data collection it is commonly impossible to show the direction of causality when two variables relate to each other. In order to be able to say something about the cause and the effect, it would be useful to have multiple waves of surveys at different points in time and then examine how a change in the independent variable related to the change in the dependent variable. Another alternative would be to mix the quantitative survey-based evidence with qualitative research in order to help interpret the relationship.

Endogeneity Endogeneity is a common problem in most strategy research, because many organizational behaviours are path-dependent. An example of a possible endogeneity problem would be an analysis of a strategic issue management team's capabilities in which one compared the capabilities of the strategic issue management team on the successful resolution of the strategic issue. One might be surprised to then find that the relationship is statistically significantly negative. This might not be because better-quality strategic issue management teams do not do good work, however. Rather, it could be that the difficulty of the strategic issue affects both the type of issue management team that is assigned to the task – a more capable team for the more difficult strategic issues – and the difficulty of reaching a successful outcome. There are a number of ways to alleviate endogeneity, ranging from two-stage regression analysis to the inclusion of further control variables. Often, however, the influence of endogeneity cannot be fully eliminated from the analyses.

Innovative research methods for quantitative research on strategy practices

Strategy-as-practice research typically involves the mapping of individual- or group-level activities in the process of strategizing, potentially complemented through links to meso- or macro-level outcomes or events. Reflecting the need to do in-depth research, descriptive, process and case studies tend to dominate current research on strategy practices. They offer the richness of explanation necessary to uncover novel phenomena and to understand them holistically. Quantitative methods are useful in complementing the qualitative empirical approaches. They enable one to move from a focus on micro-level patterns and principles to developing causal theories, making predictions, adding contingencies and yielding external validity to the research (Kaplan 2007). In this section we present several quantitative methodologies and their usefulness in (1) quantifying qualitative data surrounding strategy practices, (2) formalizing the sequential nature and temporal aspects of strategizing processes and (3) creating a formal link to meso- or macro-events, outcomes or antecedents. Several quantitative methods seem particularly promising in assisting the realization of these goals:

- computer-aided content and text analysis: to quantify qualitative textual data, such as texts, video data, images, etc., on strategy practices;
- network analysis: to quantify the relational nature of strategy practice data – for example, patterns of interactions between practitioners through the study of communication networks, etc.;
- sequence analysis techniques: to uncover and formalize the sequential patterns with which strategy practices unfold over time;
- event history analysis: to model the durational aspects with which strategy practices unfold over time and the circumstances that increase/decrease the likelihood for this process; and
- event study analysis: to test the effects of certain strategy practices, as discrete events, on firms' stock market evaluations (the external evaluation most important to the majority of large firms).

These five methods are not substitutes for qualitative in-depth studies or for each other. They can be used in multiple complementary ways. Content, text or network analyses can serve to translate qualitative data to the quantitative research domain. Optimal matching algorithms are able to capture sequences and patterns, whereas event history analysis models the transition rate of moving from one state to another and helps explicate how other variables affect this transition rate. Finally, event study analysis can be used to link discrete events from data streams to stock market performances. The different methods can be combined with each other or with qualitative data sources in mixed-method research designs. Alternatively, they could be integrated into set-theoretic approaches to study organizational configurations and explore asymmetric causality (Fiss 2007; Ragin 2014).

In the following sections we briefly introduce this quantitative methodological toolkit, link it to common threads in strategy-as-practice research, discuss how to use the methodologies and provide pointers for further literature and some of the available toolkits. We place the 'application-focused' part of our writing into separate boxes.

Computer-aided content analysis

Computer-aided content analysis (CCA) has found wide application in research across the social sciences. CCA ranges from methods that aim to reconstruct the content of textual data by looking for the prevalence of certain keywords to methods that construct relational maps of language use. While the first makes strong assumptions about how concepts are expressed in texts, the second is based on a theory about how causal relationships are expressed in text. Great potential is seen for future research as algorithms become increasingly capable of 'understanding' the meaning of text. The quantification of narrative, semantic and semiotic analyses helps us go beyond keyword-based content analysis to the analysis of structural and relational features of language use. In this regard, keyword in context analyses, quantitative narrative analysis (Franzosi 2010) and text-based network analyses have proved particularly useful and insightful. To date, however, automated quantification is still primarily dictionary- or keyword-based, which will be outlined next.

The underlying idea of standard computer-aided text analysis (CATA) is that the frequency of word use is a reflection of cognitive saliency (Huff 1990). Categories of language or of images reflect how people perceive the world. Thereby, we can learn something about the issuer of a textual artefact by looking closely at its vocabulary. As such, content analytical techniques are particularly worthwhile for capturing cognitive, cultural, communicative or discursive processes and phenomena (see mechanics in Box 30.1). For instance, several highly cited discourse-analytic studies rely on CATA to substantiate or complement their findings (for example, Fiss and Hirsch 2005). Although CATA offers higher reliability than human coding with lower cost and greater speed, a review of content analysis in organizational studies finds that fewer than 25 per cent of the articles in major management journals in the past twenty-five years used CATA in their content analysis processes (Duriau, Reger and Pfarrer 2007).

When working with CATA tools, there are two main choices: developing custom dictionaries, which is an iterative and time-consuming process, or making use of existing dictionaries (Neuendorf 2002). The predefined dictionaries in the DICTION software programme, for example, have been used to examine the language of charismatic leadership (Bligh, Kohles and Meindl 2004). Alternatively, the LIWC software has been used to capture the (positive or negative) tenor of newspaper data in order to study, for instance, an actor's legitimacy, reputation or celebrity (Pfarrer, Pollock and Rindova 2010). As Pfarrer, Pollock and Rindova (2010: 1146) emphasize,

[C]ontent analysis techniques can help bridge the gap between large-sample archival research, which may suffer from internal validity issues, and small sample research, which allows for the collection of primary data and in-depth analyses but may suffer from external validity problems. Analyzing the content of press releases, media coverage, or stakeholder blogs can enhance archival research (which has been criticized for failure to provide insight into cognitive processes), while maintaining the advantages of using large samples.

Although Short et al. (2010) highlight that construct validity is still often a problematic issue in content analysis, they provide specific guidelines for ensuring construct validity in the application of CATA tools. Human coding procedures remain relevant when working with automatized content analysis tools, however, for the origination of content analysis schemes that eventually become CATA algorithms, for the measurement of highly latent constructs and for the ongoing validation of CATA measures. For instance, to ensure internal and external validity, scholars have combined qualitative, semiotic and quantitative content analyses in the study of cultural registers and related keywords (Weber 2005). Others have used card-sorting techniques to study concept categories

---

Box 30.1   Mechanics explained: computer-aided text analysis

The most comprehensive and current review of techniques and applications of content analysis is maintained by the University of Georgia's Terry College of Business (see www.terry.uga.edu/management/contentanalysis). This project also links to the most common text analysis tools, such as Yoshikoder (see http://conjugateprior.org/software/yoshikoder), Harvard University's General Inquirer, the Linguistic Inquiry and Word Count programme (see www.liwc.net) and various web services.

Text analysis typically serves one of two purposes: the categorization of texts or the scaling of texts according to some scale of interest – for example, the conservative–liberal spectrum. For instance, Figure 30.1 illustrates the relative distributions of

words that may serve as indicators, such as for underlying conceptualizations of a technological change, across companies A, B and C. This, for example, enables researchers to compare differences in attention allocation patterns across companies.

Structure of analyses: for conducting respective analyses, algorithms typically require the body of texts and an analysis scheme that specifies the parameters of the study to be performed – for instance, keyword lists. Here one can either draw from predefined dictionaries or build one's own dictionaries of keywords that require validation to ensure internal validity beforehand. Frequently used examples of software for CATA are the following: LIWC, DICTION, Prosuite, Word Stat, QDA Miner and General Inquirer.

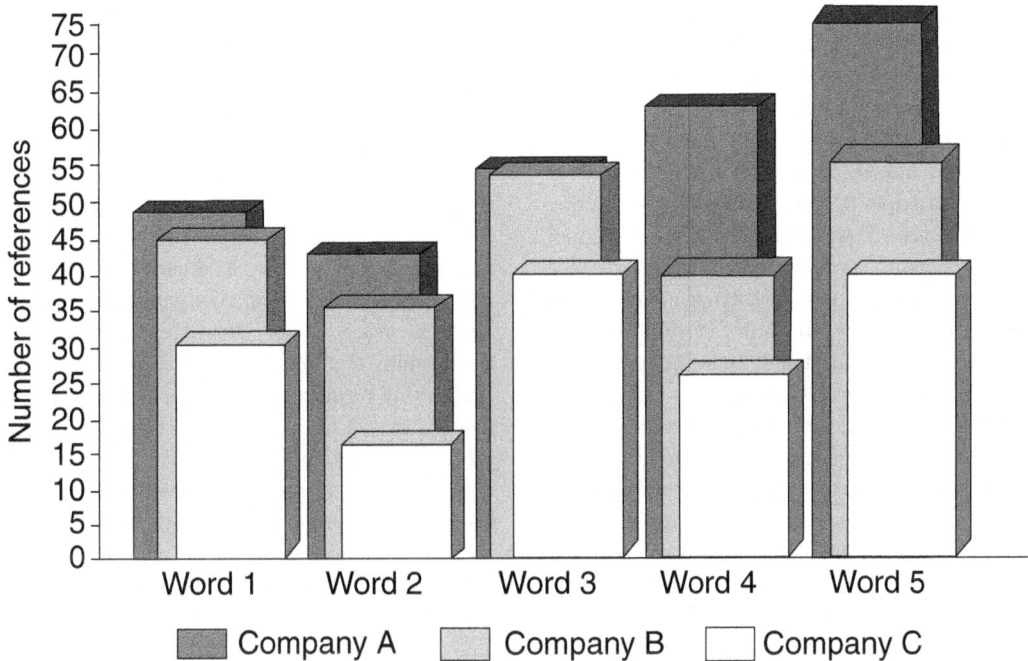

Figure 30.1 Word counts as differing attention allocations, stratified by companies
Source: Huff (1990: 18).

(Nadkarni and Barr 2008). The application of machine-learning methods has also been advanced as an alternative to creating extensive dictionaries beforehand (see Kabanoff and Brown 2008).

Recently traditional CATA has been extended to account for innovative forms of data and for new forms of data analysis. As an extension to traditional CATA, content analyses of image use in language (see Emrich *et al.* 2001; Seyranian and Bligh 2008), of visual images (ICA) and of videos (VCA) provide avenues for future research and novel data sources that might be of particular interest for studying strategizing phenomena from a strategy-as-practice lens. For example, content analysis of images may differentiate between compositional analyses and semiotic analyses.

In SAP research, content analysis could be used in multiple ways.

- Content analysis tools enable one to effectively and reliably analyse vast amounts of text, video and image data about strategizing activities, such

as meetings, plans and presentations, e-mails, company websites, intranets, internal documents, etc. These kinds of data sources may help shed light onto the micro-level dynamics of strategy practices and connect them to strategy process phenomena. For example, content analysis may help uncover the nature, sequence patterns or effects of speech practices (see Seyranian and Bligh 2008) on strategic change implementation or on consensus-building within strategic decision-making teams. It may further help identify the nature, sequence patterns or effects of consulting practices on initiative success.

- Further avenues for the application of CATA in strategy-as-practice research constitute the study of media coverage – for example, text and image – and their relation to strategic responses engaged in by the firm. Content analysis tools help uncover the distinct practices with which firms react to media tenor, discourse, etc.
- Bligh, Kohles and Meindl (2004), for instance, examined the rhetorical content of President

George W. Bush's public speeches before and after the terrorist attacks of 11 September 2001 in combination with changes in the media's portrayal of President Bush. To conduct the study, a sample of 117 text passages from presidential speeches and 442 newspaper articles and television transcripts from before and after the crises were analysed with the DICTION 5.0 tool, which 'due to its microscopic nature…is ideal for uncovering aspects of language that even the trained human eye may not readily perceive' (Bligh, Kohles and Meindl 2004: 214). This tool allowed them to statistically test whether, for example, speeches after the terrorist attacks contained more references to the continuity between past and present, to values and moral justifications, to collectives instead of individual self-interest and to intangible future goals instead of concrete and tangible outcomes. Overall, their study represents a good example for how CATA may help to develop a better understanding of collective sensemaking processes, particular in situations of crises (Huff, Neyer and Möslein 2010).

Network analysis

Over the past thirty years or so network analysis has become an ubiquitous methodology across the social sciences. As such, classes in network analysis are a mandatory component in most PhD programmes in sociology, and increasingly also in management and strategy (see mechanics in Box 30.2). In social network analysis, social structures such as teams, organizations and industries are conceptualized and analysed as networks. Hereby, a network is typically defined as a set of nodes that are connected by dyadic ties of the same type. Nodes typically represent individuals, groups or organizations. Ties, in turn, can represent flows of information, communication or resource exchanges between nodes as well as attitudes between dyads of nodes, such as friendship or trust.

For sociological practice theorists, quantitative network analysis has always been a legitimate tool. Bourdieu, in particular, repeatedly relied on network analytic methods in his surveys and for structuring and quantifying his qualitative field observations. It is thus unsurprising that some of Bourdieu's most central theoretical concepts, such as social capital, social position and social field, can be well captured with network analytic methods. In addition, Giddens' theory of structuration has been empirically explored by means of network analysis in very fruitful ways. For instance, Barley's (1986) landmark study of structuration processes in hospital organizations – arguably a role model for strategy-as-practice scholarship (see Johnson et al. 2007) – receives much of its succinct empirical grounding from the dyadic network analytic methods it employs. Additionally, symbolic interactionism and network analysis can yield fascinating research insights – as shown, for instance, in a study of the micro-level communicative turns in meetings among middle and top managers (Gibson 2005).

In strategy and management research, network analytic methods have gained a strong foothold (Brass et al. 2004). Hereby, Granovetter's studies on how the 'embeddedness' of actors shapes their economic outcomes provide several important foundations (Granovetter 1985). As such, network analysis constitutes one important way for conceptualizing the possibilities of strategic influence and agency, thereby mediating between both over-socialized and under-socialized accounts of actorhood. For instance, with regard to the streams related to strategy-as-practice research that we outlined above, research suggests that such important topics as the quality and innovativeness of strategic decisions, the influence of middle managers in strategy-making and the success of strategic initiatives and strategy implementation efforts all depend on the types of networks that enable and constrain the actors involved (for example, Battilana and Casciaro 2012; Burt 2004; Lechner, Frankenberger and Floyd 2010; McDonald and Westphal 2003; Shi, Markoczy and Dess 2009). Much may thus be gained from SAP research that builds on network analytic methods to distinctively refine and extend these lines of research.

Network analysis is not limited to the analysis of *social* networks, however; it is also increasingly being applied for investigations of some of the

Box 30.2 Mechanics explained: network analysis

There are several authoritative sources on how to design and conduct network analytic studies that strategy-as-practice scholars can draw on when developing and implementing their research designs (for example, Borgatti, Everett and Johnson 2013; Wasserman and Faust 1994).

(1) Data collection One of the biggest differences between network analysis and other widely applied quantitative analysis techniques is the nature of the data that need to be collected: instead of collecting information about individual *cases* (for example, managers, groups, organizations), as would be required for more traditional methods of data analysis, network analysis requires the collection of information about the *relationship* between actors.

Important steps in the data collection procedure include the identification of the population of nodes that the focal study comprises as well as the determination of appropriate data sources. With regard to determining an appropriate population, setting the right boundary for the study is most important. Boundaries can, for instance, be determined by theoretical criteria or by attribute-based criteria, such as top management team members or strategic initiatives. Because of the possibility of collecting data in very detailed and fine-grained ways, fascinating network analytic studies have, for instance, been developed based on data collected about members of a single case organization (for example, Krackhardt 1990). For the latter, network analytic studies can draw on various data sources, including archival data, interviews, observations and surveys. In any case,

network analysis often goes hand in hand with ethnographic immersion in a focal research context. Ethnography at the front end can, for instance, help in selecting the right research questions to investigate, while an ethnographic investigation at the end can help scholars in interpreting the results of the quantitative analysis.

(2) Data analysis For the analysis of collected data, network analysis draws from two distinct areas of mathematics: matrix algebra, to record and analyse relations between notes as variables; and graph theory, to analyse the collection of ties among nodes and to calculate such concepts as paths. Scholars have developed a distinctive set of softwares for the quantitative analysis of networks. Among these, UCINET and NetDraw are perhaps most widely applied. UCINET relies on matrix algebra for calculating various network-related measures – for example, the 'centrality' of a node in a given network, or the 'cohension' of a given network – and can also be used for testing hypotheses. In turn, NetDraw is a network visualization software. Relying on graph theory, NetDraw allows for the graphic representation of networks including relations and attributes. In addition, there are several other software packages that fulfil more specialized roles in the analysis of networks. WordNet, for instance, is a software package that can be applied for various types of semantic network analysis (and thus for the analysis of, for instance, discourses, narratives and cognitive maps). Moreover, SIENA is also of particular interest, as it allows modelling and analysing how networks evolve and change over time.

cultural or *cognitive* structures – such as discourses, narratives and mental models – that have been important research foci for strategy-as-practice scholars. In this case, macro-level discourses, narratives and micro-level mental models have all been conceptualized and analysed as *interrelated* networks of topics or concepts. One can thus rely on semantic network analysis to investigate, for instance, the centrality of a focal topic in a given discourse, or the complexity of a given story or mental model (for example,

Blaschke, Schoeneborn and Seidl 2012; Liu *et al.* 2012; Martens, Jennings and Jennings 2007; Pachucki and Breiger 2010; Pentland and Feldman 2007).

To conclude, network analysis constitutes a fascinating avenue for future strategy-as-practice research. It offers several important advantages that can help scholars push the boundaries of our understanding of strategy formation in organizations, as well as of extant applications of social practice theories more generally.

Sequence analysis using optimal matching

Sequence analysis can be used to study how 'things' 'emerge, develop, grow or terminate over time' and across patterns (Langley *et al.* 2013). Sequence analyses allow the capture of varying units of analysis, such as processes, individuals and organizations (Biemann and Datta 2014). By formalizing sequence patterns (see mechanics in Box 30.3), it can be readily complemented with inferential statistics to link sequence patterns to antecedents and outcomes.

Optimal matching analysis is the 'canonical' technique for sequence analysis in the social sciences (Abbott and Forrest 1986; Abbott and Hrycak 1990). The optimal matching algorithm can be meaningfully applied to sequences with any finite set of different states. It is also possible to code more than one dimension simultaneously, however (Biemann and Datta 2014), meaning that each coded entity within a sequence can be categorized according to different characteristics. The optimal matching algorithm itself calculates distances among sequences by computing the number of insertions, deletions and substitutions that are needed to transform one sequence into the other. It is thus usually applied in combination with cluster analysis to inductively derive groups of resembling sequence patterns. Therefore, it is fundamentally an exploratory tool, which helps to make sense of large amounts of process data.

With this general structure, the method has proved to be very versatile. Although initially developed in biology to identify patterns in DNA sequences, optimal matching soon migrated to sociology and was used to study topics as diverse as transition from school to work (McVicar and Anyadike-Danes 2002; Scherer 2001), links followed in website visits (Wang and Zaïane 2002), time use (Wilson 2006), the interplay of housing, employment, marriage and fertility (Pollock 2007) and lynching incidents in the American South (Stovel 2001). Strategy and organizational researchers have not made comprehensive use of the technique, however, despite various calls for increasing the use of sequence analysis methods (Langley *et al.* 2013). Recent exceptions include studies on patterns in acquisition and alliance behaviour (Shi and Prescott 2011), on pathways in the development of organizational networks (Stark and Vedres 2006) and on the sequences of job experiences (Leung 2014).

For strategy-as-practice researchers, these capabilities may imply promising avenues for formalizing processual aspects and temporal dynamics in the

---

Box 30.3   Mechanics explained: optimal matching analysis

Optimal matching analyses study data describing sequences of states by calculating distance metrics between individual sequences. Typical applications of this capability are:

(1) the clustering of sequences into data-driven typologies; and
(2) the comparison of sequences to theoretically or empirically derived reference sequences

In both these applications the optimal matching algorithm uses dynamic programming techniques to determine the 'cheapest' – for example, least number – of edits to transform one sequence into the other. As different types of edits may imply different 'costs'/weights, the total costs of edits, which represents the resulting distance measure, may vary with scholarly choices.

While the calculation of the distance measure is taken care of by the statistical software package used – for example, the Stata community offers an ado-file for sequence analysis: SEQCOMP – the scholar needs to specify the coding logic of the sequences as well as which sequences should be compared with each other. For this, he/she needs to define the dimension of interest and its respective coding scheme. Further, the scholar needs to theoretically justify the reference object against which he/she seeks to compare individual observations. In the example illustrated by Figure 30.2, the stylized strategic planning process (T) and the rhythmic pattern (G) would need to originate from sound theoretical reasoning. Recommended tools for applying this method are Stata, DTA and TraMineR.

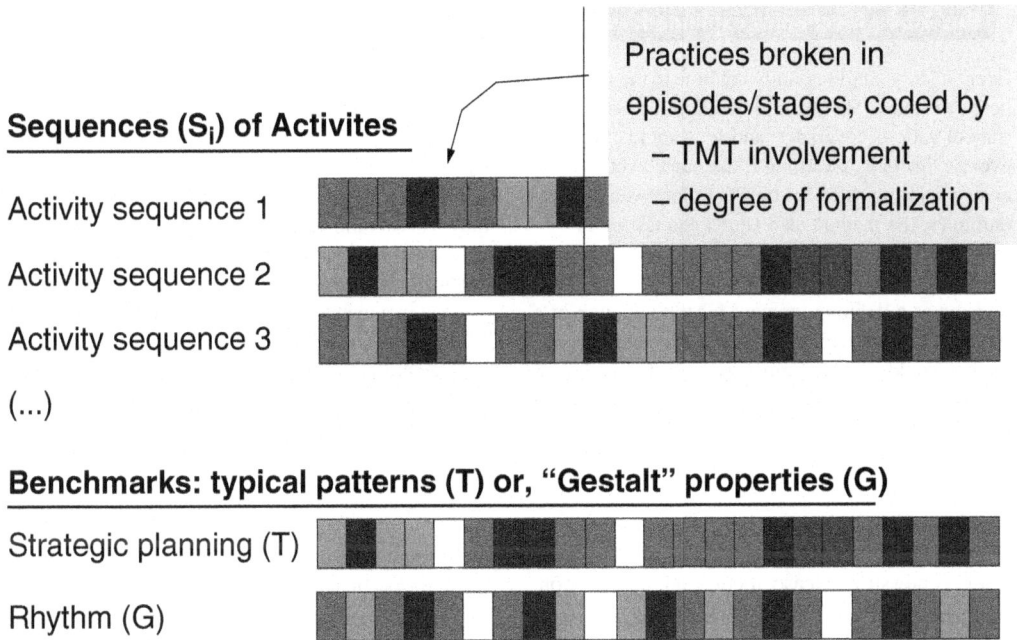

Figure 30.2 Optimal matching analysis for sequence analysis

study of praxis, practices and practitioners (Whittington 2006). Several areas of application come to mind.

- Strategizing unfolds in episodes, such as meetings, strategy events, investor presentations or awaydays (Jarzabkowski, Balogun and Seidl 2007). Furthermore, strategy practices tend to be highly ritualized (Johnson *et al.* 2010). A sequence analysis may enable the identification of a range of prototypical dramaturgies with which strategic episodes and underlying rituals unfold. For example, detailed meeting observations can be coded according to the use of certain tools or ceremonial gestures or the prevalence of certain themes. Eventually, some dramaturgies might be more conducive to successful meeting outcomes than others.
- Consensus among strategists positively shapes team and organizational outcomes (Kellermanns *et al.* 2005). Optimal matching might be used to study how sequences of discursive processes, communicative interactions or behavioural dynamics and associated practices shape the emergence of consensus among strategy practitioners over time.

- A core concern of the SAP lens has been to identify the roles of strategy practitioners and professionals – for example, consultants, strategy directors and the like – that are more than organizational roles (Whittington 2007). Optimal matching techniques lend themselves particularly well to shedding light onto strategy practitioners' career trajectories and developmental paths. In this regard, Abbott and Hrycak (1986), for example, studied the careers of German musicians in the eighteenth century, while Blair-Loy studied women's careers in finance (1999).

Stovel's historical analysis of lynching incidents (2001) is an excellent example for demonstrating the potential usefulness of optimal matching techniques in future strategy-as-practice research. Stovel used rich descriptive narratives of lynching events and categorized them according to a scale of participation and according to the use of rituals. Stovel's study is based on the coding of yearly data for each of the 395 counties in the Deep South between 1882 and 1930. The optimal matching analysis revealed the existence of several distinct temporal profiles in the local lynching histories,

---

Box 30.4   Mechanics explained: event history analysis

Event history analyses study the time to the transition between states. The method therefore considers the state of various covariates, and so is apt to explain an event's 'history', awarding it the name event history analysis. Using different types of clock variables as dummies, the method also allows the testing of dynamic theories on strategy practices. Figure 30.3 illustrates such a case. Using a firm's strategy revision as a defining moment for the initiation of sequences of strategic practices, the event history method could provide formal evidence for managers' increased inclinations to engage in strategic practices following strategy revisions.

The method requires material preparatory work in the form of data transformations. Specifically, it requires the scholar to generate for each firm or actor a series of 'spells' (durations in time units between the transition steps of interest) that stretches across the study's observation period. After this step, the overall set of spells needs to be brought into a cross-sectional sample, for which time-varying covariates need to be assigned in a manner that reflects the covariates' changing values over time. Recommended tools for applying this method are STATA, SPSS and SAS; the transformation of spells can also be done easily using a spreadsheet programme.

---

which she conceptualizes as an attention cycle model, a pressure release model, an acceleration model and a learning model. Overall, this approach allowed her to systematically analyse 'semi-rare and historically transformative events' and 'remaining sensitive to both local level context and the enterprise of generalization' (Stovel 2001).

The example of Stovel's study also emphasizes the iterative nature of the interpretation and algorithmic distance calculation that characterize the optimal matching method. Although it starts with an interpretative process to develop the initial categorization scheme, it also requires interpretation in the end to transform the numerically derived temporal profiles into meaningful conceptualizations of developmental paths.

Event history analysis

Many theories involve arguments on the effect of time to the occurrence of discrete events. Methodologically, this reflects the question of how the transition rate of moving from one state to another state is affected by other variables of interest. To investigate this question, event history methodology[2] derives conditional

likelihoods for moving from one state to another from properties of the underlying data, notably from the time spans between individual transition events (typically referred to as 'spell lengths') and all covariates considered (see mechanics in Box 30.4). Strategy scholars have made use of event history analyses in, for instance, the study of firm competitive behaviours (for example, Hsieh and Chen 2010; Schimmer 2012). In organization theory, event history analysis constitutes the standard methodology in ecological research (see Tuma and Hannan 1984). Organization scholars have also used this method to uncover, for example, the diffusion of practices within a given context (Greve 1996; 1998) and the patterns of attention allocation to emerging industry trends (Eggers and Kaplan 2009; Maula, Keil and Zahra 2013). As event history models consider one transition at a time, the method is less suited for studying processes with recurring events. In these cases, each transition has to be modelled separately and the covariates need to be assigned appropriately each time. This factually renders the longitudinal character of the analysis cross-sectional, such that time dummy variables may be needed to restore the procedural character of longer event sequences. If the research focus lies on such full sequences of multiple transitions – for example, because one wants to investigate if the stages of the sequence fit together – optimal matching analysis is potentially the more appropriate method.

---

[2] The methodology is further referred to as survival analysis, duration analysis (economics), failure time analysis, hazard time analysis, transition analysis and reliability analysis (engineering).

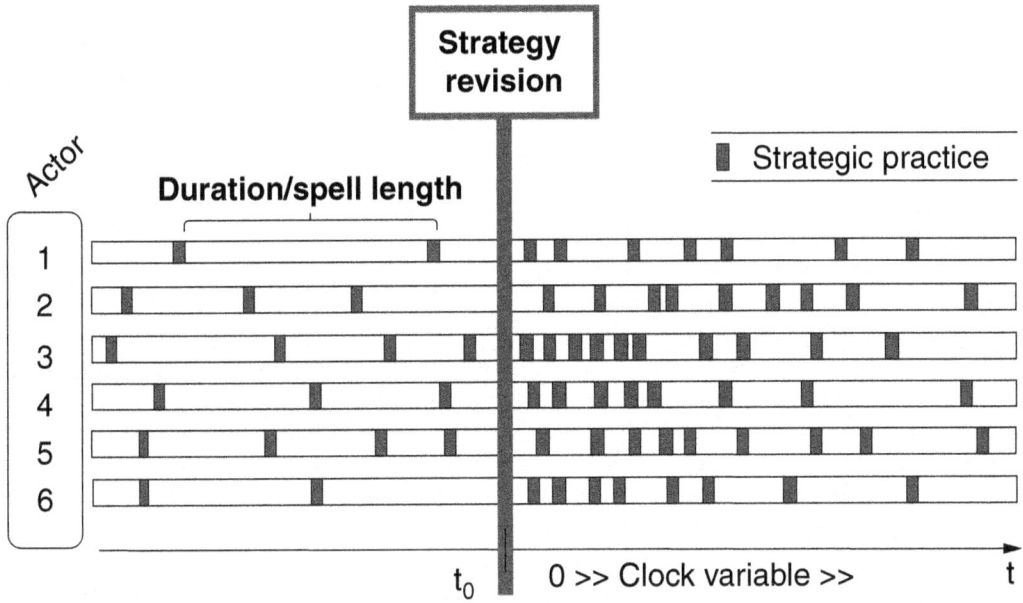

Figure 30.3 Event history analysis for sequence analysis

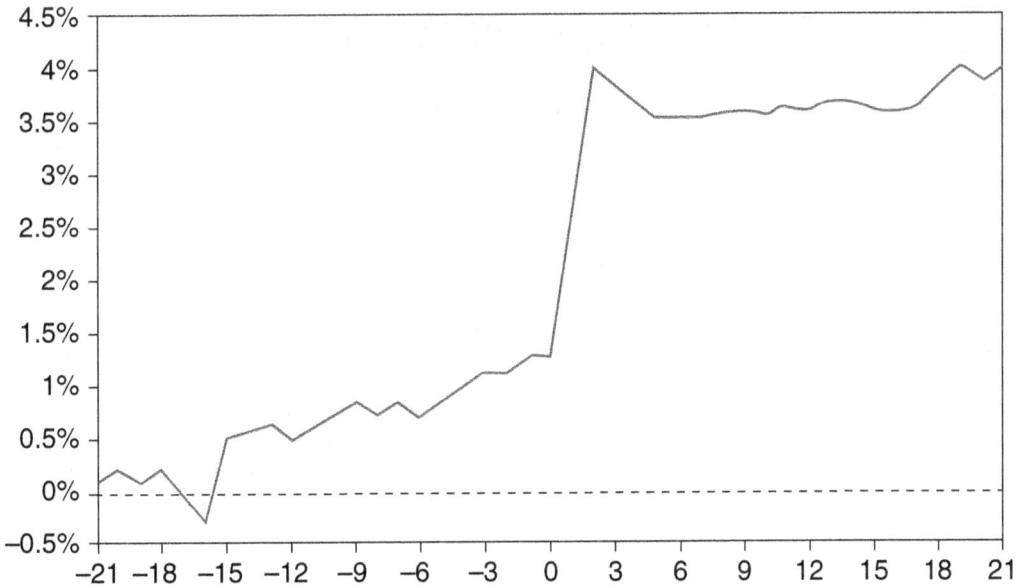

Figure 30.4 Average abnormal returns of strategic plan presentations

For strategy-as-practice researchers, these capabilities may imply promising avenues for uncovering durational aspects of strategizing practices, practitioners and praxis. Exemplary areas of application might be the following.

- An important application of event history analysis in SAP research may, for instance, constitute future research on strategy implementation. In this regard, one could conceptualize and analyse strategy implementation in terms of the diffusion of novel strategy concepts and practices within the organization. Although this topic has been considered at the industry level, there has been less research so far considering the diffusion of practices, their antecedents and outcomes *inside* the organization. For example, consider an organization undergoing a large strategic change. In this regard, event history analysis could be used to model the time to adoption of novel concepts and practices among certain – for example, resistant to a greater or lesser extent – groups, departments or units.

- Event history analysis can also be used to pave the way for new directions in research on strategic issues: A survival analysis may, for instance, uncover how the strategic agenda of organizations evolves and changes over time. As such, one can model the rate at which strategic priorities 'die' within the organization and leave the strategic agenda, as well as antecedents that enhance or mitigate this survival rate.

- Strategy work goes with dominant discursive practices (Mantere and Vaara 2008). Event history analyses may enable the modelling of discursive episodes and shifts in dominant discourses, as well as antecedents that enhance or mitigate the likelihood of such shifts.

Event study methodology

The event study methodology (see mechanics in Box 30.5) quantifies the effect that discrete events have on firms' stock market returns (MacKinlay 1997). To quantify this effect, which is labelled as an abnormal return, the methodology predicts theoretical returns that would have materialized if the event of interest had not taken place and deducts these from the actual stock returns observed. There are several variants of the method, mostly differing with regard to the model used for predicting normal returns.

Box 30.5   Mechanics explained: event study methodology

Event study analyses study how stock markets respond to new information implied or revealed by discrete events. Discrete events can be anything from market shocks to the presentation of firms' strategic plans. Typically, the response is captured in terms of abnormal returns. Alternative forms, however, also capture events' effects on stock trading volumes, currency exchange rates or other economic figures for which sufficient time series data are available. Typical scientific applications are:

(1) the study of investor behaviours and capital market (in)efficiencies; and
(2) the study of stock market response determinants for individual event types.

Conducting event studies implies a fairly structured sequence of analytical steps, which can either be implemented in spreadsheet software or dedicated event study tools. The respective analytical steps implied are as follows. (1) Identify or define the date upon which the capital market has received the news associated with the event of interest. (2) Specify the returns of the individual firms' stocks for the scenario that the event had not

taken place – that is, in the absence of the news about the event. This step implies the choice of a 'normal return model', which predicts the returns for the analysed stocks for the event window. (3) Calculate the difference between the actual observed returns and the 'normal/no-news' returns for each firm and day in the event window. This yields the 'abnormal returns' (ARs) that can be attributed to the occurrence of the event of interest. (4) These single-day 'abnormal returns' can then be further aggregated across time to 'cumulative abnormal returns' (CARs), or cross-sectionally to 'average abnormal returns' (AARs). Aggregating the abnormal returns across both time and firms yields the 'cumulative average abnormal returns' (CAARs). (5) In a final step, significance testing then establishes whether the abnormal returns found at any of the AR, AAR, CAR or CAAR levels are statistically significant. Recommended tools for applying this method are Excel (for small-event studies), Eventus and eventstudytools.com. Stata and SPSS are not well suited to accommodate different parameters for individual events.

For strategy-as-practice scholars, the methodology may offer several useful applications. When strategic practices are publicly observable, the methodology allows the capture of the capital market opinion on these practices. This opinion may, in turn, be conceptualized as the firm's social evaluation in one of its most important stakeholder environments and thus as contributing to (or diminishing) the firm's reputation, status or legitimacy. Whittington and Yakis-Douglas (2012), for example, have used the method to discriminate between the quality of strategic plans and propose to more extensively draw on the qualitative dimension revealed by such analyses in strategic planning research. Further, they suggest making more use of less conventional publicly available documents, such as strategic plan presentations (see the next section, on novel sources of research data).

For SAP researchers, using the event study methodology makes sense only when there is a time series of a variable at hand for which it is fair to assume that it reflects a timely response or effect based on the event, action or practice under study. Typically, this variable holds the closing prices of the studied firm's stock or the trading volumes of the same stock. To our knowledge, Whittington and Yakis-Douglas (2012) were the first to use the methodology to capture public opinion on distinct occurrences of one important strategy practice: the creation and communication of strategic plans. More generally, future research could rely on this method to uncover the effect of very influential new strategy practices (such as strategy presentations, investor meetings and conference calls) on the sentiments and evaluations of one important external resource-holder.

- More specifically, other applications of the method in strategy-as-practice research could focus on alternative discrete incidents when explicit descriptions of strategic practices are communicated to the capital market and it is likely that this communication represents material news. Aside from strategic plans, other types of firm strategic artefacts may reveal information about firms' strategic practices, and thus could be worth being studied from a capital market perspective.

- Furthermore, it may be worth investigating whether capital markets in general appreciate higher degrees of transparency on firm strategic practices.[3]

- Moving away from the direct study of stock market responses to the mentioning of strategic practices, one could also internally study the practices of firms and use event study methodology as a means to merely assess the quality of the eventual outcomes of strategizing, as materialized in different types of firm actions.

- This methodology offers the possibility of studying managerial attempts to induce certain stock market movements, by purposefully crafting a narrative or by diluting the effect of a particular unfavourable announcement by releasing a number of favourable news items at the same time.

- The methodology can also be used to conduct a detailed comparison of rhetorical strategies in the announcement of particularly sensitive events, such as earning warnings, CEO dismissals, corporate scandals or in the context of macroeconomic or environmental crisis. Here, event study methodology offers a novel approach to studying how interactive sensegiving and sensemaking unfold in situations of high uncertainty (as Huff, Neyer and Möslein suggest in Chapter 13).

- The methodology can be used to study the dramaturgy of investor conferences in combination with immediate stock market responses and other sources of immediate feedback, such as Twitter feeds or blog entries.

Novel sources of research data

Novel databases

Besides the trend to tap into unstructured data, novel data sources also offer potential for empirical innovation in strategy-as-practice research

---

[3] Technically, this would imply scanning the firm's communication for strategic practices, creating a 'strategic transparency score' that reflects how clearly each competitive move is linked to strategic practices and conducting an event study to test how stock markets price this practice link (see Box 30.6).

Box 30.6   How to source and study corporate news streams as a data source

Using corporate news streams as research data implies several critical challenges, including the sourcing, structuring and pre-analysis of news data. Most of these challenges go back to the unstructured nature of press releases, which are more and more mitigated by the rapid advancement of web-crawling and semantic text analysis tools, such as Newsanalytics (www.newsanalytics.net) and Semantria (https://semantria.com). Novel web services and tools help in implementing the sequence of tasks that is implied by conducting news-based research (see Figure 30.5).

Based on a sampling strategy that reflects the research purpose, firms' press releases need to be sourced. This can be done either through web-

crawling of the firm's press release archives using respective crawling tools or by means of some pre-processing service, such as Factiva. When sourced from firms' press release archives, the consolidation of news streams and the allocation of individual news items in time represent further challenges. Regular expression-based date identification can resolve the latter (Friedl 2006), whereas computer-aided text analysis of announcement texts (Hilliard, Purpura and Wilkerson 2008) helps to identify practices of interest or characterize individual release texts. If the market reception is relevant for the respective research project, an event study analysis (MacKinlay 1997) could be conducted to capture public acceptance of the individual news items released.

(Box 30.6 outlines the mechanics on how to source and study corporate news streams). Such data sources provide fertile ground for mixed-methods studies employing both qualitative and quantitative research. Data service providers such as Thomson Reuters are scaling their product portfolios by integrating more and more data sources. One new database notable from an SAP perspective is Thomson Reuters StreetEvents. The database holds a wide range of information on corporate events, including transcripts of analyst meetings, conference calls, audio files and Q&A session transcripts. Scholars may draw on this data as complementary elements in broader research projects. Whittington and Yakis-Douglas (2012), for example, sourced and compiled 1425 strategic plans from Thomson Reuter StreetEvents, First Call, SEC files, Factiva and Lexis/Nexis.

E-mail data

One other type of data that typically holds coherent sets of information is e-mail data. Each e-mail comes with a timestamp, a sender, one or multiple recipients (direct recipients and hidden ones) and a body of text, which, ideally, serves one main purpose. With these characteristics, e-mail data lend themselves as a great input for content analysis, sequence analysis and network analyses.

Kleinbaum and Stuart (2014) offer a great example of a recent e-mail-based study with great relevance for strategy-as-practice research. Studying the corporate headquarters of a single large firm, they secured access to data on 3.3 million dyadic internal e-mail communications. Based on this data source, they reconstructed the relationship between corporate staff and line functions as communication networks and tested hypotheses on the likely communication patterns of corporate strategists. More generally, quantitative studies that draw on e-mail data may inform research on strategy practices as well as on strategy practitioners. For instance, when studying strategic issues, researchers could draw on top managers' e-mail data to analyse when and how strategic issues 'enter' organizations, to examine how top managers mobilize political tactics for achieving consensus around a certain issue or for studying how conceptions of issues change once they are 'translated' according to the functional or cultural backgrounds of certain managers or departments.

Press release streams

With the rapid progression in the volume and accessibility of web-based data, the internet is moving more and more into the empirical focus of academics in various disciplines. Finance

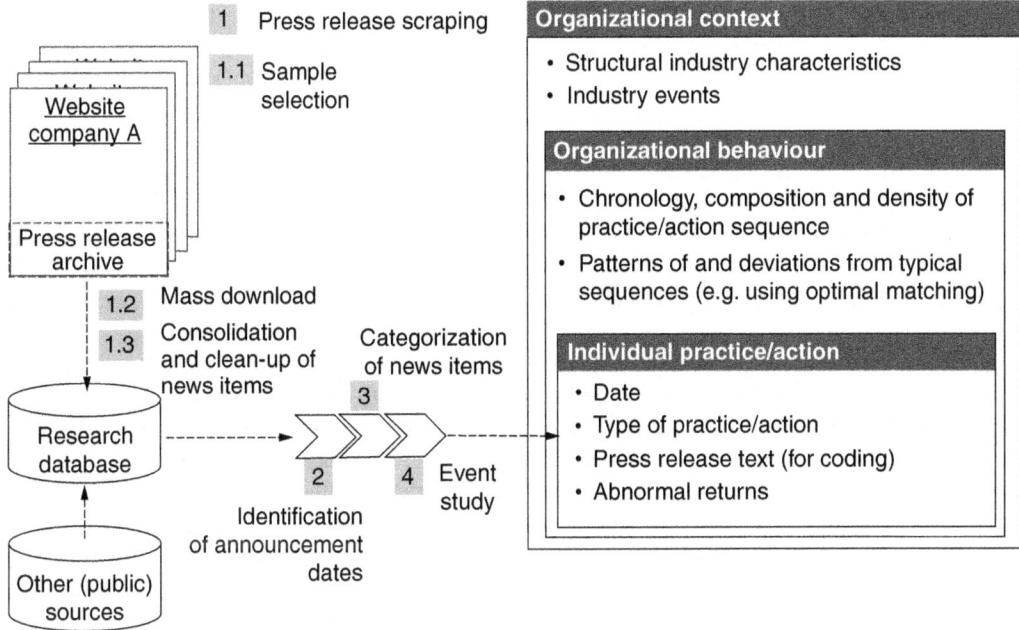

Figure 30.5 News analytics framework for studying organizational behavior and practices under consideration of the industry level
Source: Adapted from www.newsanalytics.net.

scholars study the efficient market hypothesis by scrutinizing corporate news streams (Prast and de Vor 2005; Tetlock 2007; 2010; 2011), management scholars reconstruct firm competitive behaviours from press releases (Bresser 2008; Duriau, Reger and Ndofor 2000; Yu 2003) and sociologists study the digital traces of online social activity (for example, Huy and Shipilov 2012). For strategy-as-practice scholars, the internet may also hold valuable informational fabrics for contextual or focal research elements. While firm strategizing processes are activities internal to firms, the outcomes and contexts of strategizing, as well as potential triggers, may be externally visible in the communication of firms or third parties. Strategy scholars from different domains increasingly tap into web-based information flows – be it press releases or media texts more generally – that describe firms' behaviours or stakeholders' perspectives on the materialized strategies of firms.

The content of firms' news streams is rich – so rich that investment banks trade on quantified

metrics from individual news items in real time (Macquarie; Ravenpack). Further, the firms' news streams are broad, including not only the competitive actions performed by firms but also information geared to guiding the capital market appraisal of firms, including descriptions of firms' strategic practices, such as analyst meetings (Macquarie). Morover, as news streams map the timely occurrence of firms' materialized strategies, they reveal information about the corporate calendar and the firms' decision-making practices. Lastly, when considered at the industry level, collective firm behaviours provide the most comprehensive maps of firms' competitive market contexts, and thus constitute a relevant contingency factor for firms' strategizing (Huff, Neyer and Möslein 2010).

Conclusion

We have argued in this chapter that, even though most of the prior work in strategy-as-practice research has been conceptual or qualitative in nature, there would be major potential in researching strategy practices quantitatively as well. The related research on behavioural strategy (for example, Gavetti 2012; Powell, Lovallo and Fox 2011) and the micro-foundations of strategy (Eisenhardt, Furr and Bingham 2010; Felin and Foss 2009; Felin et al. 2012; Foss and Lindenberg 2013; Greve 2013) has made good progress in combining the conceptual work with both qualitative and quantitative methods.

There are a number of different benefits that could be gained in comparison to a solely qualitative research orientation. Expanding the use of quantitative methods in studying strategy practices would further enable the development and validation of constructs for the study of strategy practices and verification of the applicability of the results across different contexts, and, as a whole, lead to a more effective and integrative accumulation of the empirical evidence in relation to the broader research community it contributes to. Moreover, applying innovative quantitative methods could also lead to the emergence of novel insights that might not be achievable with purely qualitative research designs.

Our chapter offers a number of distinctive contributions to SAP research. First, we outline several related strategic management research areas that co-align well with the strategy-as-practice research agenda and that have used quantitative methods extensively to examine practitioner and practices. Over the years these areas have accumulated a wealth of constructs and measures that SAP scholars can draw from and connect their research to in order to develop quantitative strategy-as-practice research. This would not only enable a more straightforward accumulation and formalization of strategy-as-practice research findings but also a better integration of these findings into the broader strategy research field.

Second, we have also introduced several quantitative research methods that could help SAP scholars go one step further in examining the antecedents, occurrence and implications of strategy practices. Our selection of these research methods is not meant to be exhaustive but, rather, to introduce a set of methods that may be particularly insightful for strategy-as-practice scholarship. Together, these methods help advance the strategy-as practice agenda by providing a toolkit for the holistic quantitative analysis of strategy practices. As such, this toolkit provides robust means for strategy practices' content (with content analysis), context (with network analysis), occurrence (with event history analysis), sequences (with optimal matching analysis) and outcomes (with event study analysis). Moreover, these methods can be mixed and matched in a number of ways.

Finally, we have outlined a number of important contemporary sources of data for quantitative strategy-as-practice analysis, including, for instance, e-mail and blog data, that can be easily quantified and with which the above analysis can be run in many insightful ways. In this regard, future research may unleash the potential that there is in the use of the extensive internal and external data to analyse the antecedents, occurrence and consequences of strategy practices.

Overall, we hope that our chapter helps scholars in also pursuing quantitative SAP research. Developing a more balanced epistemic culture that encourages and accepts not only qualitative but also quantitative research holds a wealth of potential, and will greatly facilitate the further development and effectiveness of strategy-as-practice research.

References

Abbott, A., and Forrest, J. (1986), 'Optimal matching methods for historical sequences', *Journal of Interdisciplinary History*, 16/3: 471–94.

Abbott, A., and Hrycak, A. (1990), 'Measuring resemblance in sequence data: an optimal matching analysis of musicians' careers', *American Journal of Sociology*, 96/1: 144–85.

Atuahene-Gima, K., and Li, H. Y. (2004), 'Strategic decision comprehensiveness and new product development outcomes in new technology ventures', *Academy of Management Journal*, 47/4: 583–97.

Barley, S. R. (1986), 'Technology as an occasion for structuring: evidence from observations of CT scanners and the social order of radiology departments', *Administrative Science Quarterly*, 31/1: 78–108.

Barrick, M. R., Bradley, B. H., Kristof-Brown, A. L., and Colbert, A. E. (2007), 'The moderating role of top management team interdependence: implications for real teams and working groups', *Academy of Management Journal*, 50/3: 544–57.

Battilana, J., and Casciaro, T. (2012), 'Change agents, networks, and institutions: a contingency theory of organizational change', *Academy of Management Journal*, 55/2: 381–98.

Baum, J. R., and Wally, S. (2003), 'Strategic decision speed and firm performance', *Strategic Management Journal*, 24/11: 1107–29.

Biemann, T., and Datta, D. K. (2014), 'Analyzing sequence data: optimal matching in management research', *Organizational Research Methods*, 17/1: 54–76.

Blair-Loy, M. (1999), 'Career patterns of executive women in finance: an optimal matching analysis', *American Journal of Sociology*, 104/5: 1346–97.

Blaschke, S., Schoeneborn, D., and Seidl, D. (2012), 'Organizations as networks of communication episodes: turning the network perspective inside out', *Organization Studies*, 33/7: 879–906.

Bligh, M. C., Kohles, J. C., and Meindl, J. R. (2004), 'Charisma under crisis: presidential leadership, rhetoric, and media responses before and after the September 11th terrorist attacks', *Leadership Quarterly*, 15/2: 211–39.

Borgatti, S. P., Everett, M. G., and Johnson, J. C. (2013), *Analyzing Social Networks*. London: Sage.

Bourgeois, L. J. (1980), 'Performance and consensus', *Strategic Management Journal*, 1/3: 227–48.

Brass, D. J., Galaskiewicz, J., Greve, H. R., and Tsai, W. (2004), 'Taking stock of networks and organizations: a multilevel perspective', *Academy of Management Journal*, 47/6: 795–817.

Bresser, R. (2008), 'Performance implications of delayed competitive responses: evidence from the US retail industry', *Strategic Management Journal*, 29/10: 1077–96.

Brown, S. L., and Eisenhardt, K. M. (1997), 'The art of continuous change: linking complexity theory and time-paced evolution in relentlessly shifting organizations', *Administrative Science Quarterly*, 42/1: 1–34.

Burgelman, R. A. (1983), 'A process model of internal corporate venturing in the diversified major firm', *Administrative Science Quarterly*, 28/2: 223–44.

Burt, R. S. (2004), 'Structural holes and good ideas', *American Journal of Sociology*, 110/2: 349–99.

Carpenter, M. A., and Golden, B. R. (1997), 'Perceived managerial discretion: a study of cause and effect', *Strategic Management Journal*, 18/3: 187–206.

Chatterjee, A., and Hambrick, D. C. (2007), 'It's all about me: narcissistic chief executive officers and their effects on company strategy and performance', *Administrative Science Quarterly*, 52/3: 351–86.

—— (2011), 'Executive personality, capability cues, and risk taking: how narcissistic CEOs react to their successes and stumbles', *Administrative Science Quarterly*, 56/2: 202–37.

Chattopadhyay, P., Glick, W. H., and Huber, G. P. (2001), 'Organizational actions in response to threats and opportunities', *Academy of Management Journal*, 44/5: 937–55.

Collier, N., Fishwick, F., and Floyd, S. W. (2004), 'Managerial involvement and perceptions of strategy process', *Long Range Planning*, 37/1: 67–83.

Creswell, J. W. (2008), *Research Design: Qualitative, Quantitative, and Mixed Methods Approaches*. Thousand Oaks, CA: Sage.

Crossland, C., and Hambrick, D. C. (2011), 'Differences in managerial discretion across countries: how nation-level institutions affect the degree to which CEOs matter', *Strategic Management Journal*, 32/8: 797–819.

Currie, G., and Procter, S. J. (2005), 'The antecedents of middle managers' strategic contribution: the case of a professional bureaucracy', *Journal of Management Studies*, 42/7: 1325–56.

Dess, G. G. (1987), 'Consensus on strategy formulation and organizational performance: competitors in a fragmented industry', *Strategic Management Journal*, 8/3: 259–77.

Duriau, V. J., Reger, R. K., and Ndofor, H. (2000), 'Content analysis of firms' web sites: methodological foundations, software solutions, and implementation issues', paper presented at Academy of Management annual meeting, Toronto, 8 August.

Duriau, V. J., Reger, R. K., and Pfarrer, M. D. (2007), 'A content analysis of the content analysis literature in organization studies: research themes, data sources, and methodological refinements', *Organizational Research Methods*, 10/1: 5–34.

Dutton, J. E., and Ashford, S. J. (1993), 'Selling issues to top management', *Academy of Management Review*, 18/3: 397–428.

Dutton, J. E., Ashford, S. J., Wierba, E. E., Oneill, R. M., and Hayes, E. (1997), 'Reading the wind:

how middle managers assess the context for selling issues to top managers', *Strategic Management Journal*, 18/5: 407–23.

Edmondson, A. C., and McManus, S. E. (2007), 'Methodological fit in management field research', *Academy of Management Review*, 32/4: 1155–79.

Eggers, J., and Kaplan, S. (2009), 'Cognition and renewal: comparing CEO and organizational effects on incumbent adaptation to technical change', *Organization Science*, 20/2: 461–77.

Eisenhardt, K. M. (1990), 'Speed and strategic choice: how managers accelerate decision-making', *California Management Review*, 32/3: 39–54.

Eisenhardt, K. M., Furr, N. R., and Bingham, C. B. (2010), 'Microfoundations of performance: balancing efficiency and flexibility in dynamic environments', *Organization Science*, 21/6: 1263–73.

Emrich, C. G., Brower, H. H., Feldman, J. M., and Garland, H. (2001), 'Images in words: presidential rhetoric, charisma, and greatness', *Administrative Science Quarterly*, 46/3: 527–57.

Felin, T., and Foss, N. J. (2009), 'Organizational routines and capabilities: historical drift and a course-correction toward microfoundations', *Scandinavian Journal of Management*, 25/2: 157–67.

Felin, T., Foss, N. J., Heimeriks, K. H., and Madsen, T. L. (2012), 'Microfoundations of routines and capabilities: individuals, processes, and structure', *Journal of Management Studies*, 49/8: 1351–74.

Finkelstein, S., and Hambrick, D. C. (1990), 'Top-management-team tenure and organizational outcomes: the moderating role of managerial discretion', *Administrative Science Quarterly*, 35/3: 484–503.

Fiss, P. C. (2007), 'A set-theoretic approach to organizational configurations', *Academy of Management Review*, 32/4: 1180–98.

Fiss, P. C., and Hirsch, P. M. (2005), 'The discourse of globalization: framing and sensemaking of an emerging concept', *American Sociological Review*, 70/1: 29–52.

Floyd, S. W., and Wooldridge, B. (1992), 'Middle management involvement in strategy and its association with strategic type: a research note', *Strategic Management Journal*, 13/S1: 153–67.

Foss, N. J., and Lindenberg, S. (2013), 'Microfoundations for strategy: a goal-framing perspective on the drivers of value creation', *Academy of Management Perspectives*, 27/2: 85–102.

Franzosi, R. (2010), *Quantitative Narrative Analysis*. Thousand Oaks, CA: Sage.

Fredrickson, J. (1984), 'The comprehensiveness of strategic decision processes: extension, observation, future directions', *Academy of Management Journal*, 27/3: 445–66.

Fredrickson, J., and Mitchell, T. R. (1984), 'Strategic decision processes: comprehensiveness and performance in an industry with an unstable environment', *Academy of Management Journal*, 27/2: 399–423.

Friedl, J. (2006), *Mastering Regular Expressions*. Cambridge, MA: O'Reilly.

Gavetti, G. (2012), 'Toward a behavioral theory of strategy', *Organization Science*, 23/1: 267–85.

Gibson, D. R. (2005), 'Taking turns and talking ties: networks and conversational interaction', *American Journal of Sociology*, 110/6: 1561–97.

Granovetter, M. (1985), 'Economic action and social structure: the problem of embeddedness', *American Journal of Sociology*, 91/3: 481–510.

Greve, H. R. (1996), 'Patterns of competition: the diffusion of a market position in radio broadcasting', *Administrative Science Quarterly*, 41/1: 29–60.

(1998), 'Managerial cognition and the mimetic adoption of market positions: what you see is what you do', *Strategic Management Journal*, 19/10: 967–88.

(2013), 'Microfoundations of management: behavioral strategies and levels of rationality in organizational action', *Academy of Management Perspectives*, 27/2: 103–19.

Guth, W. D., and Macmillan, I. C. (1986), 'Strategy implementation versus middle management self-interest', *Strategic Management Journal*, 7/4: 313–27.

Hambrick, D. C., and Mason, P. A. (1984), 'Upper echelons: the organization as a reflection of its top managers', *Academy of Management Review*, 9/2: 193–206.

Hayward, M. L. A., and Hambrick, D. C. (1997), 'Explaining the premiums paid for large acquisitions: evidence of CEO hubris', *Administrative Science Quarterly*, 42/1: 103–27.

Henderson, R., and Mitchell, W. (1997), 'The interactions of organizational and competitive influences on strategy and performance', *Strategic Management Journal*, 18/1: 5–14.

Hilliard, D., Purpura, S., and Wilkerson, S. (2008), 'Computer assisted topic classification for mixed methods social science research', *Journal of Information Technology and Politics*, 4/4: 31–46.

Homburg, C., Krohmer, H., and Workman, J. P. (1999), 'Strategic consensus and performance: the role of strategy type and market-related dynamism', *Strategic Management Journal*, 20/4: 339–57.

Hough, J. R., and White, M. A. (2003), 'Environmental dynamism and strategic decision-making rationality: an examination at the decision-level', *Strategic Management Journal*, 24/5: 481–9.

Hsieh, K.-Y., and Chen, M.-J. (2010), 'Responding to rivals' actions: beyond dyadic conceptualization of interfirm rivalry', paper presented at Academy of Management annual meeting, Montreal, 10 August.

Huff, A. S. (1990), *Mapping Strategic Thought*. Chichester, UK: John Wiley.

Huff, A. S., Neyer, A.-K., and Möslein, K. (2010), 'Broader methods to support new insights into strategizing', in Golsorkhi, D., Rouleau, L., Seidl, D., and Vaara, E. (eds.), *Cambridge Handbook of Strategy as Practice*: 201–16. Cambridge University Press.

Huy, Q. N., and Shipilov, A. (2012), 'The key to social media success within organizations', *MIT Sloan Management Review*, 54/1: 73–81.

Iaquinto, A. L., and Fredrickson, J. W. (1997), 'Top management team agreement about the strategic decision process: a test of some of its determinants and consequences', *Strategic Management Journal*, 18/1: 63–75.

Jackson, S. E., and Dutton, J. E. (1988), 'Discerning threats and opportunities', *Administrative Science Quarterly*, 33/3: 370–87.

Jarzabkowski, P., Balogun, J., and Seidl, D. (2007), 'Strategizing: the challenges of a practice perspective', *Human Relations*, 60/1: 5–27.

Jick, T. D. (1979), 'Mixing qualitative and quantitative methods: triangulation in action', *Administrative Science Quarterly*, 24/4: 602–11.

Johnson, G., Langley, A., Melin, L., and Whittington, R. (2007), *Strategy as Practice: Research Directions and Resources*. Cambridge University Press.

Johnson, G., Prashantham, S., Floyd, S. W., and Bourque, N. (2010), 'The ritualization of strategy workshops', *Organization Studies*, 31/12: 1–30.

Julian, S. D., and Ofori-Dankwa, J. C. (2008), 'Toward an integrative cartography of two strategic issue diagnosis frameworks', *Strategic Management Journal*, 29/1: 93–114.

Kabanoff, B., and Brown, S. (2008), 'Knowledge structures of prospectors, analyzers, and defenders: content, structure, stability, and performance', *Strategic Management Journal*, 29/2: 149–71.

Kaplan, S. (2007), 'Review of *Strategy as Practice: An Activity-Based Approach*, by Paula Jarzabkowski', *Academy of Management Review*, 32/3: 986–90.

Kellermanns, F. W., Walter, J., Lechner, C., and Floyd, S. W. (2005), 'The lack of consensus about strategic consensus: advancing theory and research', *Journal of Management*, 31/5: 719–37.

Kleinbaum, A. M., and Stuart, T. E. (2014), 'Inside the black box of the corporate staff: social networks and the implementation of corporate strategy', *Strategic Management Journal*, 35/1: 24–47.

Knorr Cetina, K. (1999), *Epistemic Cultures*. Cambridge. MA: Harvard University Press.

Krackhardt, D. (1990), 'Assessing the political landscape: structure, cognition, and power in organizations', *Administrative Science Quarterly*, 35/4: 342–69.

Langley, A., Smallman, C., Tsoukas, H., and Van de Ven, A. H. (2013), 'Process studies of change in organization and management: unveiling temporality, activity and flow', *Academy of Management Journal*, 56/1: 1–13.

Lechner, C., and Floyd, S. W. (2007), 'Searching, processing, codifying and practicing: key learning activities in exploratory initiatives', *Long Range Planning*, 40/1: 9–29.

(2012), 'Group influence activities and the performance of strategic initiatives', *Strategic Management Journal*, 33/5: 478–95.

Lechner, C., Frankenberger, C., and Floyd, S. W. (2010), 'Task contingencies in the curvilinear relationships between inter-group networks and performance', *Academy of Management Journal*, 53/4: 865–89.

Lechner, C., and Kreutzer, M. (2010), 'Coordinating growth initiatives in multi-unit firms', *Long Range Planning*, 43/1: 6–32.

Leung, M. D. (2014), 'Dilettante or Renaissance person? How the order of job experiences affects hiring in an external labor market', *American Sociological Review*, 79/1: 136–58.

Liu, L. A., Friedman, R., Barry, B., Gelfand, M. J., and Zhang, Z.-X. (2012), 'The dynamics of consensus building in intracultural and intercultural negotiation', *Administrative Science Quarterly*, 57/2: 269–304.

MacKinlay, A. C. (1997), 'Event studies in economics and finance', *Journal of Economic Literature*, 35/3: 13–39.

Macquarie, 'Quantamentals: Macquarie events compendium', Macquarie Equity Research, www.ravenpack.com/research/white-papers/document_Fdetail/macquarie-quantamentals-macquarie-events-compendium.

Mantere, S. (2008), 'Role expectations and middle manager strategic agency', *Journal of Management Studies*, 45/2: 294–316.

Mantere, S., and Vaara, E. (2008), 'On the problem of participation in strategy: a critical discursive perspective', *Organization Science*, 19/2: 341–58.

Martens, M. L., Jennings, J. E., and Jennings, P. D. (2007), 'Do the stories they tell get them the money they need? The role of entrepreneurial narratives in resource acquisition', *Academy of Management Journal*, 50/5: 1107–32.

Maula, M. V. J., Keil, T., and Zahra, S. A. (2013), 'Top management's attention to discontinuous technological change: corporate venture capital as an alert mechanism', *Organization Science*, 24/3: 926–47.

McDonald, M. L., and Westphal, J. D. (2003), 'Getting by with the advice of their friends: CEOs' advice networks and firms' strategic responses to poor performance', *Administrative Science Quarterly*, 48/1: 1–32.

McVicar, D., and Anyadike-Danes, M. (2002), 'Predicting successful and unsuccessful transitions from school to work by using sequence methods', *Journal of the Royal Statistical Society, Series A, Statistics in Society*, 165/2: 317–34.

Menz, M., and Scheef, C. (2014), 'Chief strategy officers: contingency analysis of their presence in top management teams', *Strategic Management Journal*, 35/3: 461–71.

Nadkarni, S., and Barr, P. S. (2008), 'Environmental context, managerial cognition, and strategic action: an integrated view', *Strategic Management Journal*, 29/13: 1395–427.

Neuendorf, K. (2002), *The Content Analysis Guidebook*. Thousand Oaks, CA: Sage.

Pachucki, M. A., and Breiger, R. L. (2010), 'Cultural holes: beyond relationality in social networks and culture', *Annual Review of Sociology*, 36: 205–24.

Papadakis, V. M., Lioukas, S., and Chambers, D. (1998), 'Strategic decision-making processes:

the role of management and context', *Strategic Management Journal*, 19/2: 115–47.

Pentland, B. T., and Feldman, M. S. (2007), 'Narrative networks: patterns of technology and organization', *Organization Science*, 18/5: 781–95.

Pfarrer, M. D., Pollock, T., and Rindova, V. P. (2010), 'A tale of two assets: the effects of firm reputation and celebrity on earnings surprises and investors' reactions', *Academy of Management Journal*, 53/5: 1131–52.

Pollock, G. (2007), 'Holistic trajectories: a study of combined employment, housing and family careers by using multiple-sequence analysis', *Journal of the Royal Statistical Society, Series A, Statistics in Society*, 170/1: 167–83.

Powell, T. C., Lovallo, D., and Fox, C. (2011), 'Behavioral strategy', *Strategic Management Journal*, 32/13: 1369–86.

Prast, H. M., and de Vor, M. P. H. (2005), 'Investor reactions to news: a cognitive dissonance analysis of the euro–dollar exchange rate', *European Journal of Political Economy*, 21/1: 115–41.

Ragin, C. C. (2014), *The Comparative Method: Moving beyond Qualitative and Quantitative Strategies*, rev. edn. University of California Press.

RavenPack, 'RavenPack news analytics', RavenPack, www.ravenpack.com/products/ravenpack-news-analytics.

Ren, C. R., and Guo, C. (2011), 'Middle managers' strategic role in the corporate entrepreneurial process: attention-based effects', *Journal of Management*, 37/6: 1586–610.

Scherer, S. (2001), 'Early career patterns: a comparison of Great Britain and West Germany', *European Sociological Review*, 17/2: 119–44.

Schimmer, M. (2012), 'From crisis to opportunity: how market shocks impact interfirm rivalry', paper presented at Academy of Management annual meeting, Boston, 7 August.

Seyranian, V., and Bligh, M. (2008), 'Presidential charismatic leadership: exploring the rhetoric of social change', *Leadership Quarterly*, 19/1: 54–76.

Shi, W., Markoczy, L., and Dess, G. G. (2009), 'The role of middle management in the strategy process: group affiliation, structural holes, and tertius iungens', *Journal of Management*, 35/6: 1453–80.

Shi, W., and Prescott, J. E. (2011), 'Sequence patterns of firms' acquisition and alliance behaviour and their performance implications', *Journal of Management Studies*, 48/5: 1044–70.

Short, J. C., Broberg, J. C., Cogliser, C. C., and Brigham, K. H. (2010), 'Construct validation using computer-aided text analysis (CATA): an illustration using entrepreneurial orientation', *Organizational Research Methods*, 13/2: 320–47.

Stark, D., and Vedres, B. (2006), 'Social times of network spaces: network sequences and foreign investment in Hungary', *American Journal of Sociology*, 111/5: 1367–411.

Stovel, K. (2001), 'Local sequential patterns: the structure of lynching in the Deep South, 1882–1930', *Social Forces*, 79/3: 843–80.

Tarakci, M., Ates, N. Y., Porck, J. P., van Knippenberg, D., Groenen, P. J. F., and de Haas, M. (2014), 'Strategic consensus mapping: a new method for testing and visualizing strategic consensus within and between teams', *Strategic Management Journal*, 35/7: 1053–69.

Tetlock, P. C. (2007), 'Giving content to investor sentiment: the role of media in the stock market', *Journal of Finance*, 62/3: 1139–68.

(2010), 'Does public financial news resolve asymmetric information?', *Review of Financial Studies*, 23/9: 3520–57.

(2011), 'All the news that's fit to reprint: do investors react to stale information?', *Review of Financial Studies*, 24/5: 1481–512.

Thomas, J. B., and McDaniel, R. R. (1990), 'Interpreting strategic issues: effects of strategy and the information-processing structure of top management teams', *Academy of Management Journal*, 33/2: 286–306.

Tuma, N. B., and Hannan, M. T. (1984), *Social Dynamics: Models and Methods*. Orlando: Academic Press.

Wang, W. N., and Zaïane, O. R. (2002), 'Clustering web sessions by sequence alignment', in *Proceedings of the 13th International Workshop on Database and Expert Systems Applications*: 394–8. Washington, DC: IEEE Computer Society.

Wasserman, S., and Faust, K. (1994), *Social Network Analysis: Methods and Applications*. Cambridge University Press.

Weber, K. (2005), 'A toolkit for analyzing corporate cultural toolkits', *Poetics*, 33/3: 227–52.

Whittington, R. (2006), 'Completing the practice turn in strategy research', *Organization Studies*, 27/5: 613–34.

(2007), 'Strategy practice and strategy process: family differences and the sociological eye', *Organization Studies*, 28/10: 1575–86.

Whittington, R., and Yakis-Douglas, B. (2012), 'Strategic disclosure: strategy as a form of reputation', in Barnett, M., and Pollock, T. (eds.), *The Oxford Handbook of Corporate Reputation*: 402–19: Oxford University Press.

Wilson, C. (2006), 'Reliability of sequence-alignment analysis of social processes: Monte Carlo tests of ClustalG software', *Environment and Planning A*, 38/1: 187–204.

Wooldridge, B., and Floyd, S. W. (1990), 'The strategy process, middle management involvement, and organizational performance', *Strategic Management Journal*, 11/3: 231–41.

Wooldridge, B., Schmid, T., and Floyd, S. W. (2008), 'The middle management perspective on strategy process: contributions, synthesis, and future research', *Journal of Management*, 34/6: 1190–221.

Yu, T. (2003), 'Dynamics of multinational rivalry', doctoral dissertation. College Station: Texas A&M University.

PART V

Substantive Topic Areas

Strategic planning as practice

ANN LANGLEY and MARIA LUSIANI

Strategic planning is an archetypal strategy tool or practice that has been at the core of strategy scholarship since the emergence of strategic management as a structured academic field. While some have questioned its value (Mintzberg 1994), its prevalence has persisted over the years (Ocasio and Joseph 2008; Rigby and Bilodeau 2013). After a brief review of earlier literature, this chapter will examine recent research on strategic planning viewed as a social practice. The chapter aims to consolidate emerging knowledge on the nature of strategic planning, and to examine how, why and with what consequences it is used in organizations.

Before proceeding, it is important to consider what is meant by the notion of strategic planning. Anthony (1965: 16) has defined it as 'the process of deciding on the objectives of the organization, on changes in these objectives, on the resources used to obtain these objectives and on the policies that are to govern the use and disposition of these resources'. Later definitions have tended to insist more clearly on the nature of the process involved, however, describing it as 'explicit' (Armstrong 1982: 198), 'formalized' (Mintzberg 1994: 12) or involving 'deliberative disciplined effort' (Bryson 2011). There is, therefore, an implication that strategic planning is not something that chief executives do informally in their heads, but that it involves a form of systematic and explicit analysis and that 'strategic planning' produces an 'articulated product' (Mintzberg 1994: 12), in the form of texts or 'strategic plans'. Wolf and Floyd (forthcoming) define strategic planning as 'a more or less formalized, periodic process that provides a structured approach to strategy formulation, implementation, and control'. This definition adds two other dimensions not necessarily present in all definitions but potentially significant (Wolf and Floyd forthcoming): strategy planning is here described as 'periodic' and as encompassing not simply strategy formulation but also 'implementation and control'.

The discussion above suggests that there is still some fuzziness around what strategic planning is and means. We take this to be a reflection of the socially constructed, ambiguous and unstable nature of management terms (Giroux 2006). We therefore do not provide our own final 'definition', at least in the sense intended above. It seems to us that 'strategic planning' is essentially a *label* that is applied to a varied and shifting set of practices that have something to do with the articulation of organizational strategic intent in the form of 'strategic plans'. In other words, there is no final 'correct' or stable definition. Nevertheless, the set of practices associated empirically with the label are of central interest to strategy-as-practice scholars. It is their shape, content and dynamics that will be the central focus of this chapter.

Early perspectives on strategic planning

The first treatises on strategy in the 1960s hailed 'strategic planning' as a critical corporate function (Ansoff 1965; Steiner 1979). They viewed formal internal and external analyses and the establishment of objectives, goals and means as intrinsic to strategy formulation and indispensible for a firm's performance and competitive advantage. Strategic planning was seen as the discipline within which an organization's strategy was formed, so that optimal choices of structure, processes and markets for growth and change could be made (Andrews 1971; Ansoff 1965; Anthony 1965; Steiner 1979).

Given the forceful advocacy of strategic planning by its early proponents, the question of its effectiveness naturally came under scrutiny, notably in the 1980s and 1990s. Countering the enthusiasm, certain writers argued that effective strategic action emerges informally and incrementally as actors learn from their experiences (Mintzberg 1978; Mintzberg and Waters 1985;

Quinn 1980) and that such a process might or might not be supported by formalized planning systems (Mintzberg 1994; Zan 1987).

Stimulated by this debate, several scholars attempted to investigate the strategic planning/firm performance relationship through survey research (Armstrong 1982; Boyd 1991; Miller and Cardinal 1994; Pearce, Freeman and Robinson 1987), sometimes contrasting more formal and less formal approaches (Brews and Hunt 1999). In these studies, questionnaire responses were used to determine the degree to which firms planned, or not, with little investigation of what that implied. Overall, these efforts led to weak and conflicting results. While Miller and Cardinal (1994) conclude, based on a meta-analysis of extant studies, that the planning/performance relationship was generally positive, they also note that research methodology was the most important factor determining whether or not researchers found positive results. Among other things, the analysis showed that, when performance was self-assessed, correlations with planning were much higher, raising serious questions about the role of common method bias in these more positive studies.

Other studies shifted attention to the 'roles of strategic planning'. Researchers began to notice that strategic planning concerned several organizational processes that sometimes had little to do with strategy-making as such (Quinn 1980). For example, strategic planning was found to be a useful tool for 'public relations' to legitimize organizations with external stakeholders (Langley 1988; Stone and Brush 1996). It might also serve as a platform for internal communication, potentially performing what Langley (1988) describes as a 'group therapy' role. Strategic planning was also found to involve retrospective sensemaking of decisions already taken, and could be seen as a tool for 'self-knowledge' (Langley 1988; Mintzberg and Waters 1985; Zan 1987). Others noted that strategic planning often seemed to be more about ensuring strategy implementation and control rather than strategy formulation (Allaire and Firsirotu 1990; Langley 1988). Thus, far from being a simple technical tool to achieve rational goals, strategic planning appears to be a fully *social* practice, in that its meaning and role depend

on the way it is inserted into the organization's social system.

This growing evidence led Mintzberg (1994) to announce the death of strategic planning as a tool for strategy formulation in his influential treatise on its 'rise and fall'. Despite his critique, however, and the virtual disappearance of academic interest in relating planning to performance, Mintzberg's verdict appears to have been premature. As Whittington and Cailluet (2008) note, strategic planning discourse and practices have continued to flourish in strategy consulting firms (Ocasio and Joseph 2008), appear to be widespread in many organizations (Rigby and Bilodeau 2013) and have been widely adopted in new industries (Whittington and Cailluet 2008), including the public and not-for-profit sectors (Ferlie 2002; Whittington 2003).

The persistence of practices labelled 'strategic planning' in organizations despite bad press has attracted renewed academic attention to the topic, but this time with a different focus. In particular, strategy-as-practice scholars have begun conducting more fine-grained analyses, opening up the black box of strategic planning to reveal its inner workings, and recognizing it as a complex social practice rather than a narrowly defined technical tool. This recent work is the central focus of the rest of this chapter.

Strategic planning as practice: a framework for analysis

As we noted above, a central aspect of any strategic planning activity concerns the production of text or a set of texts (in particular, 'strategic plans') that in some way articulate organizational strategic intent. Thus, we argue that a full understanding of strategic planning as a social practice requires a consideration of both the nature of strategy texts themselves *and* the processes associated with their production and consumption (Fenton and Langley 2011; Pälli, Vaara and Sorsa 2009), along with an appreciation of how these processes evolve over time. Thus, we propose to organize the extant knowledge on strategic planning as practice around four main foci (see Figure 31.1): *textual practices*

Discourses about strategy process and content

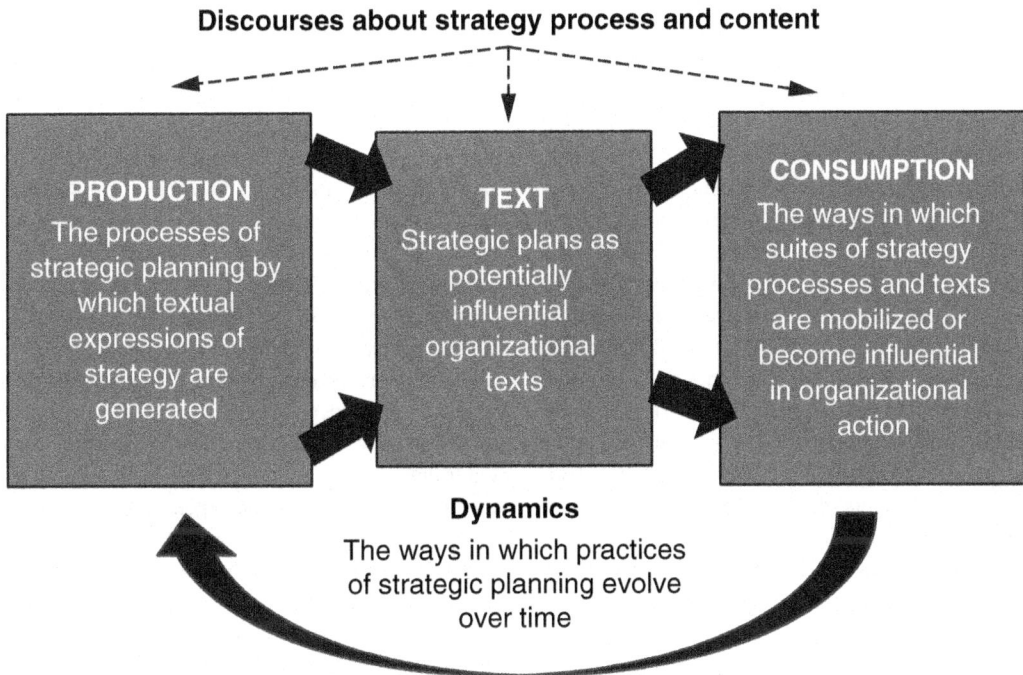

Figure 31.1 A framework for considering strategic planning as a social practice

(grouping research that examines strategic plans as potentially influential textual expressions of strategy); *production practices* (studies that address strategic planning as the process of generating strategy texts); *consumption practices* (studies that focus on whether and how strategy texts are mobilized, potentially influencing organizational action); and *dynamics* (research that addresses the ways in which practices evolve over time and are influenced by ongoing societal discourses). This approach enables a deeper consideration of how and why strategic planning may be related to strategic action by breaking down the process into several complementary parts.

We have focused our framework around 'text' because this is a central element of strategic planning around which the activity generally revolves. Through the analysis of production and consumption practices, however, we reach beyond the text itself to capture the social practices surrounding it. We treat production and consumption practices generically in this chapter, and do not

plunge deeply into specific phenomena that may be involved in them, such as meetings, workshops and tools, which are amply covered in other chapters of this volume. With its emphasis on certain communicative elements, our chapter is also complementary to that by Cooren, Bencherki, Chaput and Vasquez. In contrast to this chapter, however, Cooren *et al.* emphasize not the broad phenomenon of formalized strategic planning processes but the more ephemeral communicative moments in which strategy becomes an object of concern.

Textual practices

To understand strategic planning as practice, an obvious departure point is to look at the textual expression of these practices in the form of strategic plans. Strategic plans can, in fact, be seen as constituting a particular 'genre' of communication (Cornut, Giroux and Langley 2012; Pälli, Vaara and Sorsa 2009) that has certain central, distinctive and institutionalized features. This genre exhibits some variation that may be related to specific contexts and purposes, however, such as variations in the narrative or rhetorical qualities of plans (Chanal and Tannery 2007; Lounsbury and Glynn 2001; Martens, Jennings and Jennings 2007; Shaw, Brown and Bromiley 1998), in their relative degree of openness or ambiguity (Abdallah and Langley 2014; Denis, Langley and Lozeau 1991; Stone and Brush 1996) or in their physical supports, which may include any or all of traditional reports, PowerPoint decks (Kaplan 2011), tabular summaries, web documents and sometimes even physical artefacts – such as the 'strategy cube' described by Molloy and Whittington (2005), when key strategies were inscribed in an object that could be placed on managers' desks. In this review, we first consider what we know about the central generic qualities of strategic plans before exploring some of the important sources of variation.

Central tendencies: the strategic plan as a distinctive 'genre' of communication

Just as mystery novels and romances are two genres of literary writing that have distinctive and recognizable forms, there are distinctive institutionalized genres of business writing: organizational charts, job advertisements, recommendation letters – and strategic plans. Bhatia (2004: 87) defines a 'genre' as a set of 'conventionalized discursive actions in which participating individuals or institutions have shared perceptions of communicative purposes as well of constraints operating on their construction, interpretation and conditions of use'. Drawing on this definition, Cornut, Giroux and Langley (2012) and Pälli, Vaara and Sorsa (2009) attempted to explore the nature of the strategic plan as a genre of communication empirically.

Cornut, Giroux and Langley's (2012) textual analysis of a corpus of public and third-sector organizations' strategic plans finds distinctive linguistic and lexical features, including a prototypical move structure that corresponds to the set of professional norms diffused in business guides to strategic planning (Olsen 2007); for example, it includes sections referring to strategic planning

processes, mission and vision, context, strategies, goals and measures. Cornut, Giroux and Langley (2012) suggest that displaying strategy language in the text has the effect of expressing rigour and professionalism and ensuring legitimization. Similarly, for Pälli, Vaara and Sorsa (2009), the use of linguistic forms recognizable as the strategy genre (textual structures and concepts such as 'vision', 'mission', 'critical success factors', 'strengths and weaknesses') is not arbitrary but motivated by social convention. By conforming to the genre, an organization's proposed actions are easily understandable, thus gaining legitimacy among stakeholders.

At the same time, conformity to the genre also contributes to reproducing a certain managerialist ideology, sometimes at the expense of other voices or rationalities (MacCallum 2008; Vaara, Sorsa and Pälli 2010). Vaara, Sorsa and Pälli argue that distinctive strategy terminology has performative effects. This creates not only legitimacy for the document and its content but also specific power positions: plans (and strategy texts in general) are 'powerful devices through which specific objectives, values and ideologies – and not others – are promoted and legitimated' (Vaara, Sorsa and Pälli 2010: 699). Thus, as strategic planning moves from business firms to public and not-for-profit sectors, it carries along with it some of the managerial assumptions inherent to the genre, with potentially significant effects on how individuals see their roles and their organizations (Oakes, Townley and Cooper 1998).

Nevertheless, a detailed analysis of planning texts in public and non-profit sectors, at least those studied by Cornut, Giroux and Langley (2012), suggests a form of writing that incorporates but also reaches beyond the managerial rationality conveyed by the generic set of strategy moves derived from the textbook. In comparing strategic plans with other forms of documents, Cornut, Giroux and Langley note an emphasis on inspirational and unifying language centred on collaboration, optimism and achievement. The linguistic tone and expression of these documents was inclusive and promotional, suggesting an orientation towards gaining consensus and commitment from organizational members (Stone and Brush 1996).

In their detailed study of a city strategic plan, Ericksson and Lehtimäki (2001) see similar emphasis on consensus and cooperation, as well as on what they call 'developmental optimism'. Using a critical lens, however, they interpret this as a form of 'participation by command' in which planning is presented as participative but in reality is clearly mandated and controlled from the top. They note that, despite the emphasis on collaboration and consensus, orientations are presented according to a 'rhetoric of necessity' (expressions such as 'must', 'require' and 'demand') in which potential alternatives are suppressed. Vaara, Sorsa and Pälli (2010) refer to this phenomenon as 'deonticity' – that is, a form of disguised imperative, in which the final text serves as the formal closure of a (forced) consensus on priorities, despite individual differences of opinion in the process. Clearly, a central feature of the genre is the production of a list of strategies that expresses what the organization will do, and this necessarily appears to eliminate alternatives, turning proposals into 'facts' (Cornut, Giroux and Langley 2012). Nevertheless, as we shall see later, this does not imply that plans eliminate uncertainty or ambiguity.

Overall, Bhatia's (2004) definition of a genre of communication emphasizes that different generic elements may serve different communicative purposes. Earlier studies concerning the roles of strategic planning introduced above (Langley 1988; Mintzberg 1994) suggest that plans may play many roles and have many audiences. While the basic generic set of moves may remain the same, each of the different audiences and communicative purposes may reorient the emphasis of the writing. In addition, the evolution of techniques and discourses for strategy development (for example, scenario planning versus balanced scorecard methods) and of media (such as PowerPoint versus Word documents versus graphics) will also result in different textual forms, suggesting that, although the strategic plan follows certain generic patterns, those patterns may allow variation and evolve over time (see Figure 31.1). Different types of organizations may also generate different types of writing. Indeed, because of availability issues, studies of the textual features of strategic plans in private-

sector organizations are less frequent, and merit further investigation. Below, we elaborate on two other ways in which communicative purposes and textual forms may be interrelated.

Rhetorical variations: narratives, lists and other devices

Within the overall genre, a number of studies have focused on specific rhetorical forms. For example, strategic plans can be written in the form of a narrative or story, or, rather, emphasizing a listing of goals. The bullet point 'list' form may actually be increasing with the pervasive use of PowerPoint for planning documents. Overall, however, studies suggest that the more plans are written extensively and coherently, the more they are able to convey meaning and persuade (Lounsbury and Glynn 2001; Martens, Jennings and Jennings 2007; Shaw, Brown and Bromiley 1998).

For example, by analysing the contents of several strategy texts in which a manager was communicating a group's strategy to the relevant stakeholders, Chanal and Tannery (2007) argue that the reasoning underlying the overall strategic direction is at least as important as the specification of concrete actions and performance measurement. In contrasting strategic plans presented in the form of 'stories' with those written in bullet point form, Shaw, Brown and Bromiley (1998) argue that, in order to convey meaning in a strategic plan, a narrative connecting the firm's situation and challenges with its future actions is needed in which the organization is implicitly conceived as a 'hero' and the proposed strategy is depicted as the solution (see also Barry and Elmes 1997). Besides an overall narrative structure, the features of 'narrative probability' (the internal coherence of the narrative) and 'narrative fidelity' (whether the narrative rings true with what is already known) are raised by Lounsbury and Glynn (2001) and Martens, Jennings and Jennings (2007) as elements that are more likely to persuade readers. Thus, resonance with expectations, alignment with cultural norms or grand narratives and credibility with third parties will contribute to persuasiveness. In particular, in a study of the business plans for new ventures, Martens, Jennings and Jennings (2007) find that plans that construct a 'comprehensible identity for the organization', that provided links between the past and the future in a plausible sequence and that combined new and unfamiliar elements in a coherent way are more likely to be financed by venture capitalists than those that do not have these features.

Researchers have explored a number of other rhetorical features and their effects. For example, a particular feature of plans in public or non-profit contexts may be the use of what Pälli, Vaara and Sorsa (2009) refer to as 'metadiscourses' – for example, segments explaining the logic of strategic planning and justifying why a strategy document is needed. These metadiscourses contribute to legitimizing the plan and its contents in sectors in which such tools are less familiar. In addition to emphasizing specific rhetorics, Chanal and Tannery (2007) stress the ability to alternate different rhetorical forms within the same text – such as means–ends arguments/value or symbolic arguments/evaluation arguments – as a device to persuade heterogeneous stakeholders simultaneously. The challenge of producing plans in multi-stakeholder settings is best captured, however, through the notion of 'strategic ambiguity', discussed next.

Strategic plans as open and ambiguous versus closed and selective

Another form of textual variety is associated with the degree of openness and ambiguity of planning texts. For example, strategic plans may be written to be more inclusive (aiming to satisfy a variety of stakeholders) or more exclusive (prioritizing certain choices and not others) in the array of strategies and goals displayed. They may be ambitious or rather specific and they can be explicitly open to subsequent interpretation and rethinking to a greater or lesser extent. Abdallah and Langley (2014) relate these features to the notion of 'strategic ambiguity', introduced by Eisenberg (1984), to describe situations in which communicators deliberately formulate messages so as to allow multiple interpretations. In contrast to received views, in which ambiguity in communication is perceived as undesirable, Eisenberg argues for its benefits, suggesting that ambiguity

in communication stimulates creativity, facilitates 'unity in diversity' (by permitting a variety of people with different perspectives to value the message) and enables change.

As several authors have suggested, the more inclusive plans are, and the more unfocused and ambitious their goals, the more they allow for conflict absorption (Abdallah and Langley 2014; Denis et al. 2011; Denis, Langley and Lozeau 1991). On paper, such plans seem to offer 'something for everyone', although they may not provide a basis for prioritization. Conflict absorption through inclusiveness and broad ambitious goals may be particularly common for strategic plans in public contexts, professional bureaucracies or other pluralistic settings in which power is diffuse and top management needs to minimize conflict while seeking some kind of consensus around strategic directions (Denis et al. 2011).

Ambiguity in textual representations can take a variety of linguistic and semantic forms (Giroux 2006). Abdallah and Langley (2014) emphasize three that were present in the documents they studied: the presence of dualities (that is, elements that seemed to be in partial contradiction with one another; see also Daigle and Rouleau 2010), the use of equivocal language (that is, undefined words or phrases subject to multiple interpretations) and content expansiveness (that is, large numbers of strategies with no limitations or precise goals). Other devices that may signal ambiguity include equivocal commitments from stakeholders to the document expressed in signatures with escape clauses and loopholes (Denis et al. 2011; Wodak 2000), strategies that propose further study or otherwise postpone critical issues (Denis et al. 2011) and the extensive use of metaphors and labels (Kelemen 2000). Such devices, intentional or not (and there is often little evidence about intention), have been found in many studies of strategic plans (Abdallah and Langley 2014; Chanal and Tannery 2007; Daigle and Rouleau 2010; Denis et al. 2011; Denis, Langley and Lozeau 1991) and have often been considered by the authors as ways to overcome difficulties in achieving agreement, or sometimes as devices to stimulate creativity (Davenport and Leitch 2005; Gioia and Chittipeddi 1991). Ambiguity of meaning seems, in the end, to be a frequent and essential part of strategy work manifested in texts themselves, but, as we shall see later, also partly constructed through the production and consumption of these texts.

Overall, we see that strategic plans have a certain generic form, in which strategies are described and justified on the basis of a set of distinctive rhetorical moves. Strategic plans are generally written in a way that expresses seemingly consensual 'organizational' orientations, suppressing alternatives and disagreements. Moreover, the more they express a coherent narrative, the more they are likely to be appealing to outsiders. The need for consensus may also be associated with ambiguity and content expansion, however, especially in pluralistic settings. We now explore in more detail the social practices of production that generate these texts.

Production practices

Most of the research on strategic planning as a social practice has focused on the practices of *production* of strategic plans – that is, on the processes through which textual expressions of strategy are generated: the 'writing' or formulation of plans. Studies have focused on the formal processes adopted (Grant 2003; Ocasio and Joseph 2008), the involvement of different types of people (Lusiani and Langley 2013; Nordqvist and Melin 2008), and the analytical, communicative, interactive and material elements that contribute to the construction of formalized and articulated expressions of strategy (Jarzabkowski and Balogun 2009; Kaplan, 2011; Spee and Jarzabkowski 2011). In this review, we emphasize two dimensions: the shape of participation and the mechanisms of integration that enable convergence on a unique strategic document.

Indeed, underlying the practices that generate strategic plans is the idea that, whoever actually pens their specific content, the texts that emerge from these processes represent the strategic intent of the collective units that own them – in most cases, the organization, but possibly also an organizational subunit (business unit, division or department). In other words, strategic planning

processes 'construct' a macro-actor with ostensibly shared collective intent, regardless of any fragmentation that may underlie the textual representation of unity. For example, Kornberger and Clegg (2011: 150) claim that, in the creation of a strategy document for the city of Sydney, '[t]he strategy process simultaneously constituted a community and made claim to represent the voice of that community'. Similarly, Pälli, Vaara and Sorsa (2009) show how the 'City of Lahti' was constructed as an identifiable whole in that city's strategic plan. Indeed, beyond representing the collective intent of an already existing organization, strategic plans may sometimes contribute to establishing the existence of new identities. For example, Bryson, Crosby and Bryson (2009) describe a case involving the formulation of mission, goals and strategies for MetroGIS, an organization specifically created to foster the widespread sharing of geospatial information among a large number of public organizations of two main towns. This coordinating entity did not exist prior to the planning process, and the production of a plan served to give this new organization life, identity and legitimacy. In general, however, the construction of credible collective intent implies some kind of legitimate participation of the collective or its representatives in determining it, raising interesting questions about the shape of participation, as well as about the mechanisms by which convergence is achieved among potentially divergent perspectives. We now pursue these questions.

The shape of participation

Traditionally, producing strategic plans has usually been considered to be the business of top management, and senior managers are de facto central to their formulation and to their legitimacy (Mantere and Vaara 2008). The explicitly *'organizational'* character of strategic plans implies that they need to draw together and incorporate information and ideas from multiple sources, however. Thus, depending on the nature of the organizational context (centralization of power; size and complexity in terms of divisions and subunits; the dispersion of expertise and knowledge), participation in planning processes may be more or less widely diffused. Participation may also take various forms and be more or less open and democratic (Whittington, Cailluet and Yakis-Douglas 2011) or technical, channelled and ritualistic (Mantere and Vaara 2008). It remains the case, however, that, in many situations, multiple individuals are likely to be mobilized to participate in the formulation of strategic plans. The literature reveals several patterns of participation varying along vertical and horizontal dimensions of organization.

At one extreme, a first type of production practice is top-down driven strategic planning, which we label 'purely hierarchical', in which it is top management alone that formulates the goals and the directions of a company. This pattern appears most likely for smaller entrepreneurially driven firms. For example, Nordqvist and Melin's (2008) study of middle-sized family businesses shows how strategic planning was led top-down by knowledgeable 'champions': a consultant, in one case, and a board member, in the other – people who clearly had the ear of the chief executive and whose interventions were largely directed to assisting him/her with training, systematic strategic analysis and the application of strategy tools. In a somewhat more diffuse version of hierarchical planning in a utility company, Langley (1988) notes that the central thrust of the strategic plan was mainly inspired by the CEO, who established overarching goals yet involved planning staff in collating insights and information from other managers. Middle managers were required to specify initiatives that would meet key goals. The planning process certainly involved others, enabling the development of commitment and legitimizing the process, but the overall parameters remained negotiable only at the margins.

The larger and the more complex the firm in terms of units and geographical spread, the more likely it is that general managers at unit levels will exert autonomy in the development of strategies, yet these strategies are also likely to be negotiated amongst levels in a form that we label 'composite hierarchy'. In this form, hierarchy remains central, though initiative is partially devolved locally. For example, Jarzabkowski and Balogun (2009) describe various kinds of negotiated interactions between levels in their study of market strategy

development in a multidivisional consumer products firm. Grant (2003) finds that, by the late 1990s, strategy formulation in the oil majors was occurring mostly at the business unit level and outside the central corporate planning system, with strategic decisions being made in response to environmental stimuli that appeared locally, and only subsequently incorporated into corporate strategic plans. He calls this 'planned emergence' and describes it at that time as a feature of the modern practice of strategic planning. A similar trend is reported by Ocasio and Joseph's (2008) reconstruction of the strategic planning process at General Electric over six CEO regimes, between 1940 and the present: strategic planning became increasingly shared between corporate executives and operating unit managers. In essence, the production of strategic plans, at least in large, multidivisional companies, is, rather, a process of top-level coordination and control of the strategies that are formulated vertically by middle managers at the unit level.

As can be seen, this form of vertically interactive planning process inherently embeds an element of control in which written commitments from lower-level managers, negotiated through planning, become explicit or implicit contracts for subsequent action (Allaire and Firsirotu 1990). We return to this later, but for the moment we note that the more planning systems are embedded in hierarchical control arrangements (especially if they are connected to incentives), the more the issues of gaming and conservatism critiqued by Mintzberg (1994) may take hold as people come to realize that their collaboration can have potentially undesirable consequences in terms of the demands that may be placed on them later. There are clearly feedback loops between patterns of consumption of strategic plans and subsequent production.

While initiative to engage in strategic planning is almost always top-down, in some types of organizations production practices may be formally organized to be even more widely and explicitly participative than we have indicated so far (Mantere and Vaara 2008; Whittington, Cailluet and Yakis-Douglas 2011). For example, in pluralistic settings such as hospitals (Denis *et al.*

2011; Denis, Langley and Lozeau 1991; Langley 1988; Lusiani and Langley 2013), arts organizations (Abdallah and Langley 2014; Langley 1988; Oakes, Townley and Cooper 1998), cities (Kornberger and Clegg 2011; MacCallum 2008; Vaara, Sorsa and Pälli 2010), universities (Gioia and Chittipeddi 1991; Gioia *et al.* 1994; Spee and Jarzabkowski 2011) and not-for-profit organizations (Stone and Brush 1996), reports of planning practices reveal not only substantial processes of vertical consultation between levels but also, and perhaps more significantly, collective horizontal negotiations and consultations involving potentially competing interests. Indeed, it is clear that, in such settings, no formal strategic planning document claiming to represent the collective would be likely to achieve some level of minimal legitimacy without some form of organized participation among professionals or other key stakeholders, with the relative importance and involvement of different groups depending on the particular context as well as on the choices made by senior managers.

Clearly, though, the wider the ostensible participation, the more difficult it is to bring divergent perspectives together, enhancing the need for some kind of mechanism of convergence. The next section considers more carefully the research that has looked at modes of integration.

Mechanisms of integration and convergence

Several authors have suggested that the openness of strategic planning processes has often been exaggerated, and that processes that are claimed to be participative are often carefully channelled (Lusiani and Langley 2013), or even manipulated (Kornberger and Clegg 2011), to achieve a predetermined result. For example, from a critical perspective, Kornberger and Clegg (2011) describe how the production of a strategy document in the city of Sydney was constructed through an extensive consultation process based on focus groups, town hall meetings and online discussion forums, but at the same time how the plan organized the voices of both 'experts' and 'the public', so that the former would contribute authority and the latter

legitimacy to the process. Participation here was carefully orchestrated in such a way as to reinforce the power of those at the centre. For example, experts with opposing opinions were not invited to participate in the same meetings, and the public's participation was oriented towards issues of long-term development rather than immediate problems that might have created greater tension.

Similarly, Denis, Langley and Rouleau (2006) show how a planning process aimed at closing hospitals within a large city was orchestrated through extensive public hearings. Their study reveals several mechanisms that can contribute to convergence and integration in planning processes despite their openness. These included, in this case, the mobilization of apparently objective quantitative indicators. The bringing to bear of selected 'evidence' – the analytical dimension of strategic planning – can clearly serve as a valuable mechanism to influence shared understanding, as has also been noted by other observers of planning practices such as Giraudeau (2008) and Kaplan (2011), as well as those adopting a more normative view of strategic planning.

Even so, Denis, Langley and Rouleau (2006) suggest that, on their own, numbers and objective evidence are not enough. They argue that the framing of options in ways that aligned majority interests and values with the desired result, as well as the timing of the presentation of these options, contributed to channelling participants towards a particular outcome. In addition, the public demonstration of competence, consistency and transparency among the plan's proponents as they argued their position and listened to others further enhanced its legitimacy and potential for acceptance. Similarly, Kaplan (2011) uses the term 'cartography' to describe how controllers of PowerPoint decks could orient decisions by deciding which slides to present in which order and how. Clearly, control over the agenda and process of strategic planning, as well as ultimate control over the pen that formulates the final text, remain sources of power whatever transpires in between (Pälli, Vaara and Sorsa 2009; Spee and Jarzabkowski 2011).

Beyond the persuasive efforts of top managers (whether through rational argument supported by numbers, political savvy or agenda manipulation), participative processes will not be fully legitimate unless some actual movement and negotiation occurs, and can be seen to have occurred, as plans are debated. Thus, studies of strategic plan production practices have also looked at the nature, content and consequences of such negotiations. A particularly interesting study in this genre is that by Spee and Jarzabkowski (2011), who recorded the deliberations of a strategic planning committee in a university over a period of twelve months in real time. Interactive discussions around the text, and debates over wording, were eventually restructured into a new text that, in turn, tended to structure subsequent interactions. Spee and Jarzabkowski suggest that, as a result, authority is given to the text, and legitimacy to certain courses of action, while previously conflicting value issues are apparently resolved. An interesting question is what happens to texts when such negotiations occur. There are suggestions in Spee and Jarzabkowski's work, and in other analyses of communicative interactions around strategic planning (see Denis et al. 2011; Tracy and Ashcraft 2001; Wegner 2004), that wording disputes may not always be resolved in ways that clarify meanings but, rather, in ways that may multiply interpretive possibilities in order to accommodate the perspectives of different stakeholders.

This brings us to a related integration mechanism: that of strategic ambiguity – a notion that we introduced in the previous section as inherent to strategic planning texts, especially those emerging in pluralistic settings. There is clear evidence that extensive negotiations among people with divergent goals will tend to favour both the proliferation of planned initiatives and their framing in ways that provide opportunities for reinterpretation. Thus, participative planning may alter the shape of strategic plans in several ways. On the one hand, as Jarzabkowski and Balogun (2009) show, groups that lay the strongest claims to autonomy in strategic planning are likely to exert pressure to be heard, and may acquire significant influence on plans, while nevertheless compromising to a degree with top-down requirements. On the other hand, plans are likely to become more complex

and unwieldy overall, as writers struggle to integrate diverse perspectives.

Finally, another mechanism that may facilitate integration in participative situations is the use of 'boundary spanners' – that is, actors who can contribute by finding ways to harmonize different views, in part because of their location in the organization, and/or because of their personal experience and qualities. Lusiani and Langley (2013) highlight the contribution of planning staff in the case of a hospital they studied. These professionals, led by a person with medical training, acted at the borders between the accounting/management functions and the clinical/professional values of physicians. In the participative planning system of this organization, the planners provided far more than technical support: they were able to translate the logic of resources, goals and targets into a language that was meaningful for physicians, and at the same time they could make physicians' needs and initiatives transparent or understandable to the administration. Although they were acting in the shadows, boundary spanners such as these could clearly be a valuable and influential resource for the construction of a collective within a planning process.

In summary, the present section has explored research on practices of production of strategic plans, focusing in particular on the social contexts of their production (the shape of participation) and the mechanisms that enable passage from the disparate individual understandings, motivations and intentions of organizational stakeholders and a collective expression of organizational intent that has a certain authority and legitimacy. In the next section we consider what happens next. Once plans are produced, how are they consumed?

Consumption practices

In theory, plans are intended to be guides for action. The relationship between plans and subsequent organizational actions is one of the least studied areas of strategic management, however. Surprisingly, even studies that attempt to examine the relationship between strategic planning and performance have paid very little attention to whether or not plans have been implemented, or whether and how they are used or exert their influence.

To discuss the practices associated with the appropriation and use of strategic plans, we draw here on the notion of 'consumption', suggested by de Certeau (1988), to refer to how people are able to creatively take an imposed product of any kind, such as a strategic plan, and 'read' it in their own particular, individualistic ways, mobilizing it in their everyday practices in ways that were perhaps not foreseen by its originators. There is, therefore, a strong relationship between the notion of 'consumption' and that of 'affordance', in the sense that the latter implies the former.

Among studies that have considered the consumption practices associated with strategic plans, several have focused on affordances created by the way they are written, in particular the role of ambiguity in enabling a variety of forms of consumption. For example, Giraudeau (2008) emphasizes the potentially creative nature of strategic plans as approaches to sensemaking that leave room for collective reflection, flexibility and development. Others have noted the multiple ways in which ambiguity in strategic orientations may be received. For example, Jarzabkowski, Sillince and Shaw (2010) examined how members of a business school consumed the strategically ambiguous goal of 'internationalization', and they show that modes of interpretation varied along two dimensions: breadth (narrow or broad interpretations) and accommodativeness (emphasis on personal or broader interests). Drawing on the same data, Sillince, Jarzabkowski and Shaw (2012) show how academics and managers differentially constructed ambiguity around a strategic goal either to protect themselves from having to do anything (for example, by doubting its value, denying its personal relevance or condemning its lack of clarity), to invite others to participate (for example, by arguing for inevitability or assigning responsibilities) or to take an 'adaptive stance' (by presenting the goal as an impression management activity). These studies show how ambiguity can be exploited by individual readers but also reconstructed by them in different ways.

In their study of strategic planning in an arts organization, Abdallah and Langley (2014)
identify four modes of consumption or readings of strategic plans: interpretive, instrumental, value-driven and detached. 'Interpretive' readings are characteristic of those whose staff-related jobs are associated with attempting to ensure the implementation of strategic plans, and they involve efforts to stamp out ambiguity and use planning documents to structure the work of other managers and staff to establish control and direction. 'Instrumental' readings are those in which people draw on planning documents to determine and justify their own personal actions. It is here that plans are perhaps most influential, as people define themselves and their roles with respect to the plan. For these people, the plan essentially creates well-defined 'subject positions' that suggest specific modes of behaviour (see also Fenton and Langley 2011). 'Value-based' readings are those in which the principles and values of the plan are perceived as relevant, offering opportunities and encouragement to pursue preferred objectives, but in which there are few limitations or boundaries on the ways in which initiatives may be pursued; plans are treated as broad reference points rather than specific guides for action. Finally, 'detached' readings are more cynical. Plans are read as irrelevant or as reproducing orientations that are already well established. While resistance may not be overt, detached readers denigrate strategic plans as political management tools of limited value and may undermine attempts to impose particular interpretations.

Thus, Abdallah and Langley (2014) reveal that multiple forms of consumption of the same strategic plan may coexist in any given situation. These forms possess a certain generality that might be found among potential consumers in a variety of settings. By way of comparison, in an interview study across three organizations, Suominen and Mantere (2010) note three forms of consumption of the notion of strategy, which they label instrumental, playful and intimate. These bear some relation to those mentioned above.

While Abdallah and Langley's (2014) findings suggest some generic forms of consumption that might occur in a variety of settings, the authors further show how these interact and how ambiguity in strategy texts may lead to a paradoxical pattern of outcomes. They observe that, although strategic ambiguity initially produces positive consequences because of its enabling qualities, in terms of promoting unity in diversity and stimulating strategic change (see also Gioia and Chittipeddi 1991; Gioia, Nag and Corley 2012), over the longer term it becomes problematic, as multiple interpretations increasingly conflict and as the ambitious and wide-ranging set of activities enabled by ambiguous plans encounter resource constraints. The paradoxical effects of ambiguity are also revealed in Denis et al.'s (2011) study of strategic planning in a large teaching hospital. The tension here lay between the short-term benefits of creating the appearance of consensus during the production process and the long-term problems of attempting to implement complex, interdependent recommendations that embedded profound contradictions. Clearly, there are important interactive effects between practices of production, the textual forms they produce and their future consequences.

In considering modes of consumption of strategic plans, it is also important to be aware that, despite their embeddedness in formal texts, their immutability across space and time as reflections of organizational strategic intent can be fragile. As Aggerholm, Asmuß and Thomsen (2012) illustrate, written plans can be recontextualized in various other kinds of communication, and such recontextualizations may well reopen truces and resurrect ambiguities that had previously been absorbed within collectively generated texts. Strategic plans are likely to maintain their power and influence only to the extent that the discourse reflected within them is continually and consistently reinforced and reproduced through sensegiving practices. When the principal authors and writers of strategic plans renege on their own writing in their own consumption practices, it may be particularly hard to sustain commitment from others.

In summary, while the literature has suggested a variety of different modes of consumption and has hinted at their relationship with textual and production practices, there appears to be a need for further research on consumption practices. The relative lack of research in this area may

perhaps derive from a suspicion that many strategic planning exercises have limited lifetimes beyond their production. It would seem important to better understand the linkages between strategic planning and strategic action, however, even if the answers may lie in unexpected places. For example, it could be that strategic action often precedes or accompanies planning rather than following it, and it could be that strategic plans serve more to legitimize and consolidate strategic directions than to determine them. These issues remain to be investigated further, however.

Dynamics

Another area in which studies of strategic planning as a social practice is limited concerns the dynamics of these practices over time, both within particular organizations and beyond. As illustrated in Figure 31.1, strategic practices, including those of strategic planning, are influenced by a wide variety of societal discourses. Strategic planning is far from a stable practice. Different tools and techniques have come and sometimes gone (for example, portfolio matrices, learning curves, SWOT analysis, five forces, shareholder value calculations, scenarios and the balanced scorecard) but the label 'strategic planning' has stuck, and it remains as an umbrella concept covering all of these. We need to better understand how different toolkits channel the shape and form of strategic planning practices in different ways. As tools have come and gone, so have different societal concerns that might influence the content of strategies. For example, issues of social responsibility and environmental impact have increasingly penetrated understandings of what strategy is about, with further potential consequences for planning practices. Even so, there is still an overall conception of strategic planning as a practice that has a unified and permanent meaning.

Beyond developing a more general understanding of how planning practices have evolved over time, there would also be value in examining how strategic planning practices evolve more specifically within individual organizations, influenced not just by these societal discourses but also by developments within the firm, and through learning and adaptation processes over time. Ocasio and Joseph's (2008) archival study of strategic planning at General Electric achieves this to some extent, showing how turnover in CEOs was regularly associated with shifting patterns of strategic planning (including relabeling, shifting the roles of staffs and redesigning formal procedures) even as certain elements of the practice were continued over sixty years.

Although Ocasio and Joseph's (2008) paper is instructive, its reliance on archival data does not allow a fine-grained understanding of how and why planning practices evolve over time in the same organization. We suggest that dynamic feedback effects may be under-researched. For example, we know that some firms install 'planning cycles' that are repeated annually or at regular intervals. Repetition is likely to create boredom, however, as well as learning about how to game the system. For example, conservatism is likely to set in if people realize from one cycle to the next that inputs they have made to the plan will be turned into demands that they would rather not have. Conversely, people may begin to realize that any projects they may want to invest in will need to be incorporated into the document if they are to receive attention, creating an inflationary rush. Either way, strategic planning systems are likely to lose their freshness over time, demanding constant renewal and rethinking.

Vaara, Sorsa and Langley (2012) have begun to analyse these issues in a city organization, examining the successive adaptation of strategic planning practices over four different iterations. This work is still under way. The findings suggest that changes in strategic planning practices are responsive to learning at all levels over time, however. The perception of the influence of strategic plans at one point in time tends to stimulate interest in them later. Because of their 'organizational' and influential status, it becomes important for individuals to ensure that their perspectives are incorporated into future documents in ways that fit their needs. Thus, the preparing of strategic plans becomes imbued with political struggles to control their shape and destiny. Moreover, while some struggle to reinforce the clarity of strategic plans, others work

to reduce it. The need to ensure participation to achieve legitimacy means that no one in the end fully masters the tool or its effects. The history of strategic planning is imbued with these struggles, as well as with changing fashions and preoccupations at the more macro level.

In summary, there is clearly a need for further research on the evolution of strategic management tools over time within the same organizational context. Feedback loops from one episode of planning to another have been largely neglected. As these examples suggest, however, they may be significant and worthy of greater attention.

Conclusion

This chapter has attempted to open up the black box of strategic planning as a social practice in organizations, by reviewing more recent literature that has examined in some depth the nature and form of planning texts, the practices associated with their production and consumption and their dynamics over time. As can be seen, the different components of the practice have received uneven attention in the literature. We know more about how plans are produced and their textual form than how they are consumed, or how planning practices evolve over time.

In concluding, we draw attention to three final points that have important implications for future research. First, researchers need to stop considering strategic planning as a static and immutable practice the shape and form of which are uniform across all organizations. The benefits of undertaking more studies that relate planning with performance are limited at best, therefore, as they would necessarily be comparing apples and oranges. Moreover, since the practice is far from static over time, there is little hope that such studies could accumulate evidence. Studies from the 1970s, 1980s, 1990s, 2000s and 2010s are probably dealing with entirely different beasts without really knowing exactly how they differ.

Second, as a social practice, strategic planning clearly has political implications that need to be understood and captured in future studies.

Because what is written in plans expresses collective strategic intent, stakeholders in and around organizations will inevitably struggle to ensure that the expressed 'collective intent' fits with their own needs, interests and values. The very term 'planning' seems to imply rationality and systematic analysis; as we have seen throughout this chapter, however, it is imbued with politics, and this is important to understand and recognize in future research.

Third, we still know surprisingly little about the link between strategic planning and strategic action. It seems as if all extensive research relating planning to performance has skipped over this 'detail'. With their interest in 'what people actually do', strategy-as-practice scholars would seem well placed to begin filling this gap. There is a need for more study both of how strategic plans are consumed and of how strategic action emerges through, within or peripherally to the influence of strategic plans. For, as Cooren, Bencherki, Chaput and Vasquez's chapter in this volume suggests, in some situations strategic plans may not be constructed in managerial interactions as objects of strategic concern, while, at the same time, clear objects of strategic concern reveal themselves in other interactions, escaping the discipline of planning.

This leads finally to a comment on methodology. It is perhaps not surprising to find that some types of practices (such as textual and production practices) have been more intensively studied and understood than others (such as consumption practices), because these are the practices that are most easily observed and tracked down. Texts are physically available to be examined. Production practices take place, at least in part, in well-defined locations, such as meetings, to which researchers may gain access. Even here, however, practice scholars need to be aware of the informal locations in which 'meta-planning' may be taking place – that is, where people strategize backstage about how they will intervene in the front-stage planning arena. As Gioia and Chittipeddi (1991) note, access to such locations can greatly enhance understanding and may be most feasible in ethnographic studies in which a member of the research team has some form of 'insider' status.

Consumption practices, on the other hand, are diffuse, imprecise and potentially sporadic and unpredictable. Tracking them down is more difficult through observational methods, as it is hard to arrange to be present in all the dispersed locations where incidents of consumption may actually take place. Studies that focus on consumption have therefore tended to rely more extensively on interviewing (Abdallah and Langley 2014; Sillince, Jarzabkowski and Shaw 2012), with the result that the fine-grained subtleties of these practices may be easier to miss. Nevertheless, there may be ways to enhance the study of these practices by targeting specific issues within strategic plans that are most likely to sustain organizational attention – for example, those that are disruptive or controversial. Following over time the fate of specific strategic issues expressed in terms of different levels or priority or of ambiguity might be valuable to better understand how the framing of collective intent influences the ways in which texts are mobilized in practice.

The way in which strategic planning processes evolve over time through repeated cycles within the same organizational setting is also an understudied issue that deserves greater attention. Examining such issues methodologically ideally requires a commitment to studying the same organization over long periods of time. While retrospective methods can help, real-time analysis is likely to generate much richer and stronger insights into these processes. Although this may appear intimidating, we note that it can be achieved successfully and without shutting down a scholar's career! For example, Robert Burgelman's ongoing engagement with Intel since the 1980s has given rise to multiple successive contributions in the area of strategic management, with each study building on the findings of the previous ones (Burgelman 1991; Burgelman 1994; Burgelman 2002; Burgelman and Grove 2007). SAP scholars are known, among other things, for their many insightful analyses of micro-level interactions and fleeting moments. These analyses are valuable and should be pursued, but there is also potential to contribute at the other end of the temporal spectrum by adopting a longer-term perspective on strategic planning as a social practice.

References

Abdallah, C., and Langley, A. (2014), 'The double edge of ambiguity in strategic planning', *Journal of Management Studies*, 51/2: 235–64.

Aggerholm, H. K., Asmuß, B., and Thomsen, C. (2012), 'The role of recontextualization in the multivocal, ambiguous process of strategizing', *Journal of Management Inquiry*, 21/4: 413–28.

Allaire, Y., and Firsirotu, M. (1990), 'Strategic plans as contracts', *Long Range Planning*, 23/1: 102–15.

Andrews, K. R. (1971), *The Concept of Corporate Strategy*. Homewood, IL: Dow Jones-Irwin.

Ansoff, H. I. (1965), *Corporate Strategy: Business Policy for Growth and Expansion*. New York: McGraw-Hill.

Anthony, R. N. (1965), *Planning and Control Systems: A Framework for Analysis*. Cambridge, MA: Harvard Business School Press.

Armstrong, J. S. (1982), 'The value of formal planning for strategic decisions: review of empirical research', *Strategic Management Journal*, 3/3: 197–211.

Barry, D., and Elmes, M. (1997), 'Strategy retold: toward a narrative view of strategic discourse', *Academy of Management Review*, 22/2: 429–52.

Bhatia, V. (2004), *Worlds of Written Discourse: A Genre-Based View*. London: Continuum.

Boyd, B. K. (1991), 'Strategic planning and financial performance: a meta-analytic review', *Journal of Management Studies*, 28/4: 353–74.

Brews, P. J., and Hunt, M. R. (1999), 'Learning to plan and planning to learn: resolving the planning school/learning school debate', *Strategic Management Journal*, 20/10: 889–913.

Bryson, J. M. (2011), *Strategic Planning for Public and Nonprofit Organizations: A Guide to Strengthening and Sustaining Organizational Achievement*, 4th edn. San Francisco: Jossey-Bass.

Bryson, J. M., Crosby, B. C., and Bryson, J. P. (2009), 'Understanding strategic planning and the formulation and implementation of strategic plans as a way of knowing: the contributions of actor–network theory', *International Public Management Journal*, 12/2: 172–207.

Burgelman, R. A. (1991), 'Intraorganizational ecology of strategy making and organizational adaptation: theory and field research', *Organization Science*, 2/3: 239–62.

(1994), 'Fading memories: a process theory of strategic business exit in dynamic environments', *Administrative Science Quarterly*, 39/1: 24–56.

(2002), 'Strategy as vector and the inertia of co-evolutionary lock-in', *Administrative Science Quarterly*, 47/2: 325–57.

Burgelman, R. A., and Grove, A. S. (2007), 'Let chaos reign, then rein in chaos – repeatedly: managing strategic dynamics for corporate longevity', *Strategic Management Journal*, 28/10: 965–79.

Chanal, V., and Tannery, F. (2007), 'La rhétorique de la stratégie: comment le dirigeant crée-t-il un ordre pour l'action', *Finance Contrôle Stratégie*, 10/2: 97–127.

Cornut, F., Giroux, H., and Langley, A. (2012), 'The strategic plan as a genre', *Discourse and Communication*, 6/1: 21–54.

Daigle, P., and Rouleau, L. (2010), 'Strategic plans in arts organizations: a tool of compromise between artistic and managerial values', *International Journal of Arts Management*, 12/3: 13–30.

Davenport, S., and Leitch, S. (2005), 'Circuits of power in practice: strategic ambiguity as delegation of authority', *Organization Studies*, 26/11: 1603–23.

De Certeau, M. (1988), *The Practice of Everyday Life*. Berkeley: University of California Press.

Denis, J.-L., Dompierre, G., Langley, A., and Rouleau, L. (2011), 'Escalating indecision: between reification and strategic ambiguity', *Organization Science*, 22/1: 225–44.

Denis, J.-L., Langley, A., and Lozeau, D. (1991), 'Formal strategy in public hospitals', *Long Range Planning*, 24/1: 71–82.

Denis, J.-L., Langley, A., and Rouleau, L. (2006), 'The power of numbers in strategizing', *Strategic Organization*, 4/4: 349–77.

Eisenberg, E. M. (1984), 'Ambiguity as strategy in organizational communication', *Communication Monographs*, 51/3: 227–42.

Eriksson, P., and Lehtimäki, H. (2001), 'Strategy rhetoric in city management: how the presumptions of classic strategic management live on?', *Scandinavian Journal of Management*, 17/2: 201–23.

Fenton, C., and Langley, A. (2011), 'Strategy as practice and the narrative turn', *Organization Studies*, 32/9: 1171–96.

Ferlie, E. (2002), 'Quasi strategy: strategic management in the contemporary public sector', in Pettigrew, A. M., Thomas, H., and Whittington,

R. (eds.), *Handbook of Strategy and Management*: 279–98. London: Sage.

Gioia, D. A., and Chittipeddi, K. (1991), 'Sensemaking and sensegiving in strategic change initiation', *Strategic Management Journal*, 12/6: 433–48.

Gioia, D. A., Nag, R., and Corley, K. G. (2012), 'Visionary ambiguity and strategic change: the virtue of vagueness in launching major organizational change', *Journal of Management Inquiry*, 21/4: 364–75.

Gioia, D. A., Thomas, J. B., Clark, S. M., and Chittipeddi, K. (1994), 'Symbolism and strategic change in academia: the dynamics of sensemaking and influence', *Organization Science*, 5/3: 363–83.

Giraudeau, M. (2008), 'The drafts of strategy: opening up plans and their uses', *Long Range Planning*, 41/3: 291–308.

Giroux, H. (2006), '"It was such a handy term": management fashions and pragmatic ambiguity', *Journal of Management Studies*, 43/6: 1227–60.

Grant, R. M. (2003), 'Strategic planning in a turbulent environment: evidence from the oil majors', *Strategic Management Journal*, 24/6: 491–517.

Jarzabkowski, P., and Balogun, J. (2009), 'The practice and process of delivering integration through strategic planning', *Journal of Management Studies*, 46/8: 1255–88.

Jarzabkowski, P., Sillince, J., and Shaw, D. (2010), 'Strategic ambiguity as a rhetorical resource for enabling multiple interests', *Human Relations*, 63/2: 219–48.

Kaplan, S. (2011), 'Strategy and PowerPoint: an inquiry into the epistemic culture and machinery of strategy making', *Organization Science*, 22/2: 320–46.

Kelemen, M. (2000), 'Too much or too little ambiguity: the language of total quality management', *Journal of Management Studies*, 37/4: 483–98.

Kornberger, M., and Clegg, S. (2011), 'Strategy as performative practice: the case of Sydney 2030', *Strategic Organization*, 9/2: 136–62.

Langley, A. (1988), 'The roles of formal strategic planning', *Long Range Planning*, 21/3: 40–50.

Lounsbury, M., and Glynn, M. A. (2001), 'Cultural entrepreneurship: stories, legitimacy, and the acquisition of resources', *Strategic Management Journal*, 22/6–7: 545–64.

Lusiani, M., and Langley, A. (2013), *Professionals as Strategists? Channelling and Organizing Distributed Strategizing*, Working Paper no. 32/2013. Venice: Ca' Foscari University.

MacCallum, D. (2008), 'Participatory planning and means–ends rationality: a translation problem', *Planning Theory and Practice*, 9/3: 325–43.

Mantere, S., and Vaara, E. (2008), 'On the problem of participation in strategy: a critical discursive perspective', *Organization Science*, 19/2: 341–58.

Martens, M. L., Jennings, J. E., and Jennings, P. D. (2007), 'Do the stories they tell get them the money they need? The role of entrepreneurial narratives in resource acquisition', *Academy of Management Journal*, 50/5: 1107–32.

Miller, C. C., and Cardinal, L. B. (1994), 'Strategic planning and firm performance: a synthesis of more than two decades of research', *Academy of Management Journal*, 37/6: 1649–65.

Mintzberg, H. (1978), 'Patterns in strategy formation', *Management Science*, 24/9: 934–48.

(1994), *Rise and Fall of Strategic Planning*. New York: Free Press.

Mintzberg, H., and Waters, J. A. (1985), 'Of strategies, deliberate and emergent', *Strategic Management Journal*, 6/3: 257–72.

Molloy, E., and Whittington, R. (2005), 'Practices of organising: inside and outside the processes of change', *Advances in Strategic Management*, 22/8: 491–515.

Nordqvist, M., and Melin, L. (2008), 'Strategic planning champions: social craftspersons, artful interpreters and known strangers', *Long Range Planning*, 41/3: 326–44.

Oakes, L. S., Townley, B., and Cooper, D. J. (1998), 'Business planning as pedagogy: language and control in a changing institutional field', *Administrative Science Quarterly*, 43/2: 257–92.

Ocasio, W., and Joseph, J. (2008), 'Rise and fall – or transformation? The evolution of strategic planning at the General Electric Company, 1940–2006', *Long Range Planning*, 41/3: 248–72.

Olsen, E. (2007), *Strategic Planning for Dummies*. Hoboken, NJ: John Wiley.

Pälli, P., Vaara, E., and Sorsa, V. (2009), 'Strategy as text and discursive practice: a genre-based approach to strategizing in city administration', *Discourse and Communication*, 3/3: 303–18.

Pearce, J. A., Freeman, E. B., and Robinson, R. B. (1987), 'The tenuous link between formal strategic planning and financial performance', *Academy of Management Review*, 12/4: 658–75.

Quinn, J. B. (1980), *Strategies for Change: Logical Incrementalism*. Homewood, IL: R. D. Irwin.

Rigby, D., and Bilodeau, B. (2013), *Management Tools and Trends 2013*. Boston: Bain.

Shaw, G., Brown, R., and Bromiley, P. (1998), 'Strategic stories: how 3M is rewriting business planning', *Harvard Business Review*, 76/3: 41–54.

Sillince, J., Jarzabkowski, P., and Shaw, D. (2012), 'Shaping strategic action through the rhetorical construction and exploitation of ambiguity', *Organization Science*, 23/3: 630–50.

Spee, P., and Jarzabkowski, P. (2011), 'Strategic planning as communicative process', *Organization Studies*, 32/9: 1217–45.

Steiner, G. A. (1979), *Strategic Planning: What Every Manager Must Know*. New York: Free Press.

Stone, M. M., and Brush, C. G. (1996), 'Planning in ambiguous contexts: the dilemma of meeting needs for commitment and demands for legitimacy', *Strategic Management Journal*, 17/8: 633–52.

Suominen, K., and Mantere, S. (2010), 'Consuming strategy: the art and practice of managers' everyday strategy usage', in Baum, J. A. C., and Lampel, J. (eds.), *Advances in Strategic Management*, vol. XXVII, *The Globalization of Strategy Research*: 211–45. Bingley, UK: Emerald.

Tracy, K., and Ashcraft, C. (2001), 'Crafting policies about controversial values: how wording disputes manage a group dilemma', *Journal of Applied Communication Research*, 29/4: 297–316.

Vaara, E., Sorsa, V., and Langley, A. (2012), 'The constitution and dynamics of organizational agency in a city organization: the interplay of discursive, socio-political, and textual agency in strategy formation', paper presented at the fourth International Symposium on Process Organization Studies, Kos, Greece, 22 June.

Vaara, E., Sorsa, V., and Pälli, P. (2010), 'On the force potential of strategy texts: a critical discourse analysis of a strategic plan and its power effects in a city organization', *Organization*, 17/6: 685–702.

Wegner, D. (2004), 'The collaborative construction of a management report in a municipal community of practice text and context, genre and learning', *Journal of Business and Technical Communication*, 18/4: 411–51.

Whittington, R. (2003), 'The work of strategizing and organizing: for a practice perspective', *Strategic Organization*, 1/1: 117–26.

Whittington, R., and Cailluet, L. (2008), 'The crafts of strategy: special issue introduction by the guest editors', *Long Range Planning*, 41/3: 241–7.

Whittington, R., Cailluet, L., and Yakis-Douglas, B. (2011), 'Opening strategy: evolution of a precarious profession', *British Journal of Management*, 22/3: 531–44.

Wodak, R. (2000), 'From conflict to consensus? The co-construction of a policy paper', in Mungtigl, P., Weiss, G., and Wodak, R. (eds.), *European Union Discourses on Un/Employement*: 73–114. Amsterdam: John Benjamins.

Wolf, C., and Floyd, S. W. (forthcoming), 'Strategic planning research: toward a theory-driven agenda', *Journal of Management*.

Zan, L. (1987), 'What's left for strategic planning?', *Economia Aziendale*, 6/2: 187–204.

Meetings and workshops as strategy practices

DAVID SEIDL and STÉPHANE GUÉRARD

Introduction[1]

From the strategy-as-practice perspective, strategy is what people *do* in organizations (Jarzabkowski, Balogun and Seidl 2007; Johnson *et al.* 2007; Johnson, Melin and Whittington 2003; Vaara and Whittington 2012; Whittington 2006), and one thing people tend to do often in organizations when they strategize is to take part in meetings. This is hardly surprising, considering that meetings represent one of the most pervasive practices in organizations (Schwartzman 1989). Some early studies on meetings found that they occupy between 59 per cent and 69 per cent of managers' time (Dahl and Lewis 1975; Mintzberg 1973). Moreover, many studies stress that meetings undeniably offer space in which different strategic views can be shared and disputed (Gailbraith 1973; Guetzkow and Kriesberg 1950; Kwon, Clarke and Wodak 2014; Mintzberg 1973).

Surprisingly, it was only relatively recently that researchers began to take an interest in how meetings and workshops affect strategizing practices (Hodgkinson *et al.* 2006; Jarzabkowski and Seidl 2008). In fact, meetings were traditionally seen as useless and irrelevant or as nothing more than a 'neutral' frame for decision-making processes (see Schwartzman 1989 for more details). Now, however, it is widely recognized that meetings shape the activities that take place within their span. Recent studies have examined from various angles how meetings influence strategy. The most often researched topics include: how meetings and the discursive practices associated with them affect the development of shared views on strategic

issues (Clarke, Kwon and Wodak 2012; Kwon, Clarke and Wodak 2014; Wodak, Kwon and Clarke 2011), how meetings enable 'strategy talk' and the production of 'strategy text' (Spee and Jarzabkowski 2011), how the display of emotions in meetings influences the way in which strategic issues are discussed and evaluated (Liu and Maitlis 2014), how strategic meetings bring middle and senior managers together to negotiate over and agree on consistent collective action (Hoon 2007), how board meetings influence strategy-making (McNulty and Pettigrew 1999), how 'rituals' in workshops affect strategic outcomes (Johnson *et al.* 2010) and how strategy is changed and stabilized through series of meetings (Jarzabkowski and Seidl 2008). All these studies indicate that meetings and workshops have become an established and important research area within the field of strategy as practice.

Among the several theoretical perspectives on which researchers draw, many place a strong emphasis on communication traditions. Studies in this stream of literature have mobilized particularly discourse analysis (Clarke, Kwon and Wodak 2012; Liu and Maitlis 2014), critical discourse analysis (Kwon, Clarke and Wodak 2014; Wodak, Kwon and Clarke 2011), the communicative constitution of organizations perspective (Spee and Jarzabkowski 2011) and conversation analysis (Boden 1994; 1995). In addition, we find many studies that take a sociological perspective, drawing on social interactionism (Asmuß and Oshima 2012; Hoon 2007), ethnomethodology (Boden 1994; 1995) and systems theory (Jarzabkowski and Seidl 2008). Finally, some works analyse meetings through the lens of ritual theory, which has been borrowed from the anthropological tradition (Bourque and Johnson 2008; Johnson *et al.* 2010), or through that of information-processing

[1] We thank the Swiss National Science Foundation for having funded this research project (SNF number: 100014_130338).

theory (Eisenhardt 1989), which stems from classic management studies (for an overview of the different theoretical perspectives on meetings, see also Dittrich, Guérard and Seidl 2011b).

Some strategy researchers (for example, Kwon, Clarke and Wodak 2014; Wodak, Kwon and Clarke 2011) focus on meetings that are explicitly labelled 'strategic' – such as 'strategy meetings' or 'strategy workshops' – and considered to constitute part of an organization's 'official' strategy-making process. Even when meetings are not explicitly labelled 'strategic', however, they may still be of interest to the strategy researcher as sites of strategy work, if they involve strategic issues or strategists as participants (see, for example, Clarke, Kwon and Wodak 2012; Jarzabkowski and Seidl 2008). Finally, even 'ordinary' meetings – that is, those not labelled 'strategic' – that neither concern explicitly strategic issues nor involve strategists may be of interest to strategy researchers, insofar as they have an impact on the direction of the firm; for example, meetings that concern operational issues might affect the emergent strategy of an organization (see, for instance, Eisenhardt 1989).

The above overview shows that the literature on meetings is rich and diverse. In this chapter we synthesize the extant literature on the role of meetings in the context of strategy, discuss the insights it has generated so far and suggest how this line of investigation can be further developed. We begin with a review of the main generic characteristics of meetings and go on to examine the functions that meetings have in organizations. Following that, we review the literature on internal meetings and awayday workshops and on how these influence strategy. We conclude with a look at the avenues that are open to future research on meetings.

Characteristics and functions of meetings

Characteristics of meetings

In the existing literature, different researchers understand meetings in slightly different ways. For instance, Boden (1994: 84) describes the formal meeting as 'a planned gathering, whether internal or external to an organization, in which the participants have some perceived (if not guaranteed) role, have some forewarning (either long-standing or quite improvisatorial) of the event, which has itself some purpose or "reason", a time, place, and, in some general sense, an organizational function'.

Highlighting somewhat different aspects, Schwartzman (1989: 7) defines the meeting as 'a communicative event involving three or more people who agree to assemble for a purpose ostensibly related to the functioning of an organization or group... A meeting is characterized by multi-party talk that is episodic in nature, and participants either develop or use specific conventions for regulating this talk. Participants assume that this talk in some way relates to the ostensible purpose of the meeting and the meeting form frames the behaviour that occurs within it as concerning the "business" of the group or organization.'

Drawing on these two descriptions, we can list the defining characteristics of meetings. A meeting is:

(1) *planned*; an informal encounter on the corridor, for example, does not constitute a meeting;
(2) *episodic*, which implies that it has a beginning, a conduct and an end;
(3) *focused on talk*, though it may also involve other forms of interaction;
(4) *a gathering*: for Schwarzman (1989) there have to be at least three people, but this seems an unnecessary restriction; for Boden (1994) a meeting may involve only two people;
(5) *an event that presupposes the co-location of people in the same actual or virtual space*; and
(6) *an event that has an official purpose*: formally, the purpose of meetings relates to the functioning of an organization or group.

Combining these different elements, we define the practice of meeting as follows.

A planned and episodic communicative event that involves several participants co-located in the same (physical or virtual) space and whose purpose is ostensibly related to the functioning of the organization or group.

While this definition is specific enough to distinguish the meeting from other social practices, it is also broad enough to capture the many different forms that meetings can take. For example, meetings may be on- or off-site, open or closed, regular or irregular, strategic, operational or administrative, organizational or inter-organizational.

Various studies have highlighted the different ways in which meetings affect the interaction among the participants. An obvious aspect of meetings is selectivity. Given that the participants must be co-located in the same space, it follows that meetings 'bracket in' some people while 'bracketing out' others (Boden 1994; Schwartzman 1989). A second aspect is that each participant brings to the meeting his/her own set of skills, expertise and access to resources, which can influence profoundly the capacity of every participant to affect the outcome (Angouri and Bargiela-Chiappini 2011; Asmuß and Oshima 2012). The differences in skills, expertise and resource access create an asymmetry among the participants, which is reflected in the turn-taking patterns that are peculiar to meetings. In informal conversations turn-taking is managed between participants (Sacks, Schegloff and Jefferson 1974), but in formal meetings the appointment of a chairperson endows this individual with the power to influence the flow of the conversation among the participants by allocating, monitoring and even truncating turns with the aid of various linguistic devices (Barnes 2007; Bilbow 1998; Boden 1994), such as questioning (Boden 1994); in other words, chairpersons have the power to structure conversations (Angouri and Marra 2010).

The chairperson is not the only participant who can control turn-taking in a meeting, however; the other participants also employ questioning, as well as other linguistic devices, to encourage participation, interrupt the turn of someone speaking and manage conflicts (Kwon, Clarke and Wodak 2014; Larrue and Trognon 1993). Meetings rest largely on talk; they are also the site of text production, however. For example, in many meetings one person is assigned the task of taking down the minutes; moreover, people who attend a meeting often take notes (Bothin and Clough 2012), on the basis of (some of) which the minutes of the meeting may be modified (Fear 2012). Considering that writing is necessarily a selective process, the production of text in meetings is not trivial. On the contrary, it is likely to influence the way in which various issues will be addressed in subsequent meetings.

Generally, meetings are held so that participants can talk about and reflect on certain topics, which are usually announced before the meeting and constitute the meeting agenda (Angouri and Marra 2010). Because the meeting agenda includes some topics but excludes others, it too has a 'bracketing' effect, in the sense that it determines what will be discussed in the meeting (Boden 1994). Of course, as the meeting unfolds, the conversation may drift away from the topic under discussion. This may force the chairperson to intervene in order to bring the discussion back to the agenda (Holmes and Stubbe 2003). A formal meeting may often be preceded by informal talk; typically, participants tend to gather in a room before – and after – the meeting and chat informally (Mirivel and Tracy 2005), often about trivial matters not necessarily connected to the meeting agenda (Boden 1994).

As mentioned earlier, a central characteristic of meetings is that they have a clearly defined beginning and end, and are thus temporally delimited: at the beginning of the meeting it is already clear that it will end at some point, which is predefined in terms of a specific time or of an objective that has to be achieved, or of a combination of both (Hendry and Seidl 2003). Thus, the end of the meeting is itself part of the meeting, and many of the activities within the meeting are undertaken in view of its end. Drawing on Luhmann's systems theory (1995), and particularly on his concept of episodes, Hendry and Seidl (2003) have proposed a framework for studying meetings more systematically. The proposed framework focuses on three critical aspects of meetings: initiation, conduct and termination. The authors argue that meetings are structured on the basis of these three aspects. *Initiation* refers to how a meeting is set up – that is, to how it is decided which people and topics are 'bracketed in' and which are 'bracketed out'. It also refers to the process that determines the degree of decoupling between the structures of the meeting and those of the organization as a whole. *Conduct* refers to the specific ways in which the interactions within the meeting are carried out and to the specific ways in which turn-taking is structured. *Termination* refers to the specific ways in which a meeting is terminated and recoupled to the organization. The process of termination also determines the extent to which the various aspects and outcomes of the meeting are transferred to the organization.

Apart from being temporally delimited, meetings are also spatially delimited and embedded in materiality. In organizations, they typically take place in meeting rooms that can seat between five and twenty participants (Asmuß and Svennevig 2009). Materiality – the material aspect of meetings, such as the types of furniture and equipment used – is important, because it pre-structures the meeting physically in a way that can influence how many people can attend, as well as who can speak. For example, the way in which tables and chairs are arranged in the room may inhibit or promote interaction among the participants. In addition, the type of artefacts that are available to participants may restrict or encourage creativity or formalism. For example, whiteboards and flip charts (Whittington *et al.* 2006) may help the participants visualize creative solutions, while projectors and presentation software such as PowerPoint may hinder the ability of participants to think 'outside the box'. Finally, using documentation, such as reports, may force participants to focus on specific issues and can thus also influence the way in which a meeting is conducted.

The functions of meetings

An extensive review of the literature on meetings has revealed that, in organizations, meetings fulfil a wide variety of functions, among which five stand out: meetings may serve coordination, sensemaking, political, symbolic or social purposes (Dittrich, Guérard and Seidl 2011a; 2011b). Often a single meeting fulfils multiple organizational functions simultaneously. Moreover, apart from the explicitly stated or official functions, a meeting can fulfil latent or unofficial functions (Schwartzman 1989), as explicitly stated functions may mask the participants' real agenda.

Perhaps the most obvious role of meetings in organizations is *coordination*. People arrange meetings in order to be able to align or synchronize their activities (Boden 1995; Brinkerhoff 1972), coordinate future action (Huisman 2001; Mintzberg, Raisinghani and Theoret 1976) and pool and distribute information (Schwartzman 1989; Tepper 2004) or tasks (Kaplan 2010; Mirivel and Tracy 2005). A second function is that of *sensemaking*. As Weick (1995) has pointed out, because meetings are the setting in which participants discuss various issues and put forward their arguments, they constitute a central sensemaking device. Meetings have been shown to stimulate critical thinking (Hendry and Seidl 2003; Mezias, Grinyer and Guth 2001) and to help participants generate and develop new ideas (Jarzabkowski and Seidl 2008), as well as become aware of organizational issues (Hodgkinson *et al.* 2006; Schwartzman 1989; Terry 1987) and explore solutions (Mintzberg, Raisinghani and Theoret 1976; Seibold 1979).

Meetings in organizations also have a *political* function, in the sense that they allow participants to promote certain issues and interests at the expense of other interests and to advance a certain agenda (Adams 2004; Tepper 2004). Meetings also enable participants to form alliances (Kangasharju 2002), negotiate (Boden 1995), exert influence (Wodak, Kwon and Clarke 2011), repetitively reschedule some topics on the agenda until an opportunity for decision arises (Tepper 2004) and suppress new ideas (Jarzabkowski and Seidl 2008).

Meetings can also have a symbolic, and typically latent, function. For example, meetings might symbolically confirm the established organizational order: Bailey (1965) and Schwartzman (1989) argue that, when an organizational member agrees to participate in a meeting without questioning its format or without overtly disagreeing about the setting of the meeting, implicitly he/she agrees to the established order that is embedded in that meeting. Other authors have emphasized that meetings with ritualistic elements may signal symbolically a certain status or change in status (Bourque and Johnson 2008; Johnson, Prashantham and Floyd 2006). Starker (1978), for example, shows that in the United States the conferences organized by certain health professional

Table 32.1 The various roles of meetings

Functions	Specific dimensions	Representative studies
Coordination	Synchronization	(Boden 1994; Brinkerhoff 1972)
	Determination of future action	(Clifton 2009; Huisman 2001; Mintzberg, Raisinghani and Theoret 1976)
	Pooling and distribution of information	(Boden 1994; Eisenhardt 1989; Schwartzman 1989)
	Distribution and monitoring of tasks	(Christiansen and Varnes 2007; Mirivel and Tracy 2005)
Sensemaking	Critical reflection	(Abzug and Mezias 1993; Hendry and Seidl 2003; Mezias, Grinyer and Guth 2001)
	Generation and development of new ideas	(Hodgkinson et al. 2006; Jarzabkowski and Seidl 2008)
	Recognition of issues/problems and their importance	(Mezias, Grinyer and Guth 2001; Schwartzman 1989; Terry 1987)
	Search for and screening of solutions	(Mintzberg, Raisinghani and Theioret 1976; Seibold 1979)
Political	Setting and advancing the agenda	(Adams 2004; Tepper 2004)
	Exerting influence	(Clifton 2009; van Praet 2009)
	Bargaining	(Boden 1995; Mintzberg 1973)
	Keeping topics on the agenda	(Jarzabkowski and Seidl 2008; Tepper 2004)
	Suppression of new ideas	(Jarzabkowski and Seidl 2008; Schwarz 2009)
	Formation of alliances; building support	(Adams 2004; Kangasharju 1996; 2002)
Symbolic	Legitimization/validation of the established order	(Boden 1994; Schwartzman 1989)
	Ritual	(Hendry and Seidl 2003; Johnson et al. 2010; Starker 1978)
	Status and status change	(Schwartzman 1989; van Praet 2009)
Social	Establishment of networks and relationships	(Hodgkinson et al. 2006; Mirivel and Tracy 2005; Tepper 2004)
	Development of group identity and organizational identity	(Bürgi, Jacobs and Roos 2005; Mirivel and Tracy 2005; Schwartzman 1989)
	Formation of social values, norms and beliefs	(Bürgi, Jacobs and Roos 2005; Mirivel and Tracy 2005; Schwartzman 1989)
	Display of emotions	(Kangasharju and Nikko 2009; Tracy 2007; van Vree 1999)

Source: Based on Dittrich, Guérard and Seidl (2011a; 2011b).

associations served as a kind of 'rite of passage' for new members of the association.

Finally, meetings may have a social function, in that they serve as a hub that makes it easier for participants to develop networks and relationships (Hodgkinson et al. 2006; Tepper 2004) and form social values, norms and beliefs (Mirivel and Tracy 2005). Meetings also foster group and organizational identity (Bürgi, Jacobs and Roos 2005; Schwartzman 1989) and provide space in which participants can display emotion (Kangasharju and Nikko 2009; Liu and Maitlis 2014; Tracy 2007). Table 32.1 summarizes the five functions of meetings (for more details, refer to Dittrich, Guérard and Seidl 2011a; 2011b).

The role of internal meetings in strategizing

Research on the role of meetings in the context of strategy can be divided into two groups: one group of studies deals with traditional meetings inside the organization, such as strategy review meetings, strategic planning meetings and boardroom meetings. The second group of studies focuses on strategy workshops, such as awaydays, as a particular kind of meeting that takes place outside day-to-day routines and, typically, outside the organizational premises. In this section we concentrate on the former group of studies, while the latter is addressed in the following section.

Practices used in internal meetings

Much of the research on the role of internal meetings in strategy aims primarily to identify the practices that are applied during a meeting and their effects on strategy (Jarzabkowski and Seidl 2008). The large palette of practices applied in a meeting can be divided into two main categories: discursive practices and orientation practices.

Discursive practices, the patterns of saying and the discursive devices that people use, are the focus of most studies in this body of literature. In two consecutive studies, Clarke, Kwon and Wodak have examined how various discursive practices that senior managers use in meetings shape strategic issues. In their first study, Wodak, Kwon and Clarke (2011) focus on the discursive practices that chairpersons employ in order to shape the strategic decision-making process, namely *bonding*, *encouraging*, *directing*, *re/committing* and *modulating*. *Bonding* is reflected in the use of the pronoun 'we' instead of 'I', in order to help build consensus in the course of the meeting. *Encouraging* consists in soliciting opinions, advice and knowledge to support participation in the exploration and development of ideas. *Directing* refers to the practice of challenging or critically interrogating participants by means of closed questions in order to bring the discussion to an end. *Re/committing* is the practice of getting people to make promises or reminding them of their obligations, with the aim of ensuring that, once consensus has been reached, action will follow. Finally, *modulating* describes the practice of influencing the perception of participants by striking the right balance between *encouragement* and *direction* in order to achieve the right 'amount of urgency' that will enable the participants to reach a strong consensus. Their study suggests that chairpersons with an egalitarian style of leadership tend to combine these practices in a balanced way, and thus usually succeed in reaching consensus over a decision.

In their second study, Kwon, Clarke and Wodak (2014) identify five discursive practices that seem to play a particularly important role in the development of a collective view on strategic issues. *Equalizing* reduces hierarchical difference and increases participation. *Re/defining* encourages participants to express new information and perspectives on an issue, and thus refine it. *Simplifying* reduces complexity. Finally, *legitimizing* involves boosting the credibility of a particular view of an issue, and *reconciling* is the practice of dissociating participants from their position to minimize differences between them. These five discursive practices are mobilized dynamically in meetings and fulfil specific goals. Meeting participants tend to employ the practices of *re/defining* and *simplifying* in order to limit the scope of the discussion relative to strategic issues. The practices of *equalizing* and *legitimizing*, in turn, tend to 'balance the opening-up and narrowing-down of understanding of the strategic issue' (Kwon, Clarke and Wodak 2014: 19), while *reconciling* minimizes conflict among the participants. Furthermore, in their case study, the authors find that participants couple each of these practices with 'linguistic devices' such as humour, metaphors, irony, sarcasm, politeness, self-deprecation, expert language and scenarios in order to make the main discursive practices identified above more effective.

A number of studies have also examined the effect of different modes of turn-taking on strategy. In their study of strategy meetings, Jarzabkowski and Seidl (2008) show that different modes of turn-taking have different effects on the emergence and development of new strategic ideas. Distinguishing between four generic modes of discussion, they show that *free discussions* (that is, without interventions from the chairperson) are associated with the emergence and development of new ideas, whereas *administrative discussions* (that is, discussions about existing, previously agreed or non-contentious strategic items), *restricted discussions* (discussions strictly controlled by the chairperson) and *restricted free discussions* (those subtly steered by the chairperson) tend to limit the possibilities for new ideas to emerge and be developed.

In addition to the studies that examine discourse in meetings, there is a separate, emerging stream of research that focuses on practices associated with the display of emotions. The study by Liu and Maitlis (2014) shows that the display of positive emotions in meetings, such as 'energetic exchange' or 'amused encounter', is associated with more collaborative strategizing, in which actors engage in open discussion, generate multiple proposals or bond with the leader. In contrast to that, the display of negative emotions, such as 'discord interaction', 'recurrent confrontation' and 'depleting barrage', leads to antagonized strategizing, which increases the distance between the participants, hinders the exploration of alternatives and results in truncated strategic discussions.

Orientation practices: when meetings are set up and conducted with the aid of certain forms of logistic support, these are referred to as orientation practices. Selecting the location where the meeting will take place is such a practice (Schwartzman 1989). In their study of strategic meetings in three British universities, Jarzabkowski and Seidl (2008) show that, when meetings are held in the building where top managers work, the authority of the latter is perceived as being increased. This has certain implications for an organization's strategy, because it indicates that the choice of location may lend the views of top managers greater weight at the expense of other opinions. Setting the agenda and selecting the chairperson also have a strong influence on how strategic meetings are conducted. In the same study, Jarzabkowski and Seidl argue that, when top managers set the agenda for and chair strategic meetings, it is more likely that the university's strategies will serve the interests of managers, rather than those of teaching staff.

Other practices are (ostensibly) oriented more towards moving things after a meeting. The same authors (Jarzabkowski and Seidl 2008) have demonstrated that, in the context of universities, *rescheduling* – that is, the practice of deferring the discussion about a specific item on the agenda to a future meeting – and *setting up working groups* allow new strategic ideas to be kept alive and further developed until they reach a stage at which they can be seriously considered. In the same study, *voting* (that is, making a decision over an issue, by raising hands, for example) and *stage-managing recoupling* (that is, the practice of adjusting the presentation of new strategic ideas to the legitimate social structures of the organization) are shown to play a particularly important role in the final selection of new ideas.

Interestingly, at least in the university context in which the study was conducted, voting is shown to be associated with the deselection of new ideas, either because a proposed idea gets negative votes or because the margin between positive and negative votes does not suffice for the university to implement the decision. The authors attribute this finding to the fact that, in this setting, the practice of voting tends to be reserved for controversial issues. In contrast to this, the practice of 'stage-managing recoupling', for example, by carefully presenting new strategic directions to increase their acceptability by some stakeholders, tends to be associated with the adoption of the new idea by the university at large.

How internal meetings relate to their context

Apart from the strategic role of different practices in meetings, strategy scholars have also examined the way in which meetings relate to their context, which itself consists of other practices, such as strategic planning (Hoon 2007; Spee and Jarzabkowski 2011). In an interesting study, Clarke, Kwon and Wodak (2012) show that discursive practices in strategic meetings serve as the site at which the larger context is manifested: strategic meetings are 'influenced not only by the logic of argumentation and discursive skills of the participants' (Clarke, Kwon and Wodak 2012: 470) but also by the contextual factors that surround and cross the meeting. These include inter-discursive relationships (for example, previous talks), the extra-linguistic social and institutional context of the meeting (that is, the situation of the meeting, the conditions within the room or the hierarchical position of the participants) and the broader socio-political and historical context (Clarke, Kwon and Wodak 2012).

In their study of preparatory meetings involving the CEO and the human resources manager of a company, Asmuß and Oshima (2012) show that the participants' hierarchical positions in the organization (that is, institutional roles) determine to some degree their right to make spontaneous proposals in order to finalize and modify a strategic document. The authors find that in some instances the proposals, and the right to make proposals, are accepted because the person who makes them is hierarchically superior (the CEO, in this case). By contrast, in order to modify the strategic document, subalterns (the HR manager, in this case) need to negotiate this right first. This indicates that, in meetings, hierarchy and institutional roles more generally are locally recognized.

A few studies have examined how talk within a strategic meeting is influenced by conversations that take place outside the meeting. In particular, in her study of committee meetings, Hoon (2007) shows that the formal discussion in a meeting is shaped by informal conversation that takes place outside the meeting. She also shows that these external 'strategic conversations' positively impact talk in the meeting by increasing understanding among the participants, by creating alignment in the discussion of strategic issues and by giving participants the chance to make prearrangements for the formal meeting.

In a similar study that focuses particularly on boardroom meetings, McNulty and Pettigrew (1999) examine how the informal interactions of part-time board members outside the boardroom influence the dynamics of the meetings. The authors show that the high percentage of proposals accepted and ratified in the boardroom (about 90 per cent) is a result of the informal interactions that take place outside the boardroom, in the course of which board members exercise their influence. For example, the tendency of executives to consult board members before the meeting enables board members to shape and change the content of the strategy proposals, and allows executives to increase the likelihood of their proposals being accepted in the boardroom meeting.

More recently, some authors have begun to examine the interrelations of meetings over time. In the area of strategy as practice, Jarzabkowski and Seidl (2008) studied how different meetings link up to form a series. Following the development of fifteen new initiatives over time in the setting of British universities, they show that topics 'travelled' across different meetings before they were eventually either dismissed or taken up in the organization at large. Because each stage in the life cycle of a topic – namely its emergence,

development and selection – required different practices, the fate of strategic topics depended on how the different meeting practices were combined across the entire series of meetings. The authors identify three general paths (that is, combinations of practices over time), one of which favoured new ideas and thus led to strategic change, while the other two favoured the deselection and questioning of new ideas, and thus stabilized the existing strategic orientation. Overall, these studies look at how meetings and their context influence each other.

Some researchers have examined how meetings relate to practices that have a broader scope, such as strategic planning. For example, Spee and Jarzabkowski (2011) studied how meetings, as the site at which strategic plans are drafted, relate to strategic planning. In particular, the authors examine the interplay between text and talk in the process through which a strategy plan is produced. As they show, the development of a strategic plan in textual form is based on earlier textual versions of that plan. While the practice of talking about such a text involves the recontextualization (Ricœur 1981) or the interpretation of the text within the meeting, and takes into account who participates in the meeting, once the amendments that need to be made to a text have been decided the text becomes decontextualized – that is, the original intention of the speaker can no longer be identified. Thus, the production of the text (the plan) fixes (or decontextualizes) the talk that has taken place in the strategic planning meeting. In sum, Spee and Jarzabkowski's (2011) study shows how the movement from text to talk (recontextualization) and from talk to text (decontextualization) enables participants to exert power by influencing the content of the plan, which, once written, will travel across time, space and actors.

The role of strategy workshops in strategizing

Characteristics of strategy workshops

Over the last few years strategy scholars have been showing an increasing interest in the role and function of strategy workshops in the strategy process

(Langley 2010). This is hardly surprising, considering that strategy workshops are a common organizational practice. Moreover, they are often invested with 'high expectations for influencing strategy formulation and implementation', and, in turn, 'they represent significant resource investments' (Healey *et al.* forthcoming: 1). Strategy workshops are a particular type of meeting that takes place outside the regular organizational routines. Hodgkinson *et al.* (2006) describe them as 'the practice of taking time out from day-to-day routines to deliberate on the longer-term direction of the organization'. To date, two extensive surveys in the United Kingdom (Healey *et al.* forthcoming; Hodgkinson *et al.* 2006) and Germany (van Aaken *et al.* 2013) have shown that strategy workshops 'play a substantial role in the management of strategy in organizations' (Hodgkinson *et al.* 2006: 482). The surveys revealed that more than 70 per cent of the surveyed companies in the United Kingdom and Germany run strategy workshops, and for most of them at least once a year. The new term 'workshopping' (Whittington *et al.* 2006: 619) is indicative of the frequency with which they take place.

Strategic workshops typically last between half a day and several days and tend to be dominated by top managers, which has led Hodgkinson *et al.* (2006: 490) to refer to them as 'elite forums for strategy debate'. Typically (though not necessarily), they take place outside the organizational premises (van Aaken *et al.* 2013). The same surveys (Healey *et al.* forthcoming; Hodgkinson *et al.* 2006) also reveal that strategy workshops can serve a number of different purposes, ranging from the initiation of strategic change to the communication of a particular strategy and to strategy implementation. Most existing research concentrates on workshops that focus on the initiation of strategic change.

Strategy workshops and the suspension of organizational structures

In an attempt to capture the role of strategy workshops in the organization, researchers have mobilized the concept of 'strategic episodes', which was originally developed in a conceptual paper on strategic change by Hendry and Seidl (2003). In this study, episodes are described as sequences of events defined by a beginning and an end, which are points of structural change. In general, the beginning of a strategy workshop is marked by some degree of decoupling between the ordinary structures and routines of the organization and those of the workshop. This means that at the beginning of the workshop the ordinary structures and routines of the organization are temporally suspended, to be reinstated after the workshop has ended. In this sense, 'the basic function of the episode is simply to make [it] possible to suspend and replace structure for a certain time period' (Hendry and Seidl 2003: 183). By providing a space outside the organizational structures and routines, the workshop gives participants the opportunity to interact and communicate about the organization in new ways, and thus provides a platform for reflexive strategic discourse. For example, the traditional authority structures are often suspended during the workshop, which allows participants to dare to express opinions, new ideas or criticism. In line with earlier studies, such as those by Mezias, Grinyer and Guth (2001) and Doz and Prahalad (1987), Hendry and Seidl (2003) argue that the process of decoupling from the established organizational structures is important for strategic change. Strategic change 'usually requires stepping out of the existing management process – since these processes are set to sustain the "old" cognitive perspective' (Doz and Prahalad 1987: 75).

Several other studies have refined the concept of strategic episodes. For example, drawing on two case studies, Schwarz and Balogun (2007) argue that strategic workshops involve partial decoupling, which does not create a 'structural void'. As a result of 'structural decoupling', workshops are characterized by what Brown and Eisenhardt (1997) term 'semi-structures' – that is, very general structures that provide participants with some guidance but still leave space for new forms of interaction to emerge. As Schwarz and Balogun (2007: 8–9) explain, '[A] certain degree of structure may support the coordination of change activities and a balance between order and disorder. Semi-structures [are] rigid enough to allow change to be organized, but not so rigid that change is prevented from happening.' In another study, Seidl, MacLean and MacIntosh (2011) examined the mechanisms through which structural decoupling is achieved. Drawing on an in-depth case study, they show that the suspension of organizational structures is not achieved instantly at the start of a workshop but through an effortful and highly emotional process, in which facilitators and participants must actively inhibit the existing organizational structures. If they do not make this effort, the participants inevitably fall back into existing behavioural patterns.

Other studies examined how decoupling the workshops from the organization affects behaviour. Johnson and colleagues (Bourque and Johnson 2008; Johnson et al. 2010), who examined in more detail what happens within workshops, compare workshops to rituals. The episodic character of strategy workshops, they argue, generates in participants what they call a 'liminal experience' – that is, a state of 'ambiguity and social limbo', which they liken to the state that people experience in religious rituals. According to the authors, it is this kind of 'liminal experience' that leads to new ideas. Drawing on the theory of rituals (Turner 1982) and on empirical observations of strategy workshops, they show that the extent to which workshop participants have liminal experiences depends on how far three criteria are met. First, the workshop must be ritualized. This includes (1) perceived removal, which is reflected in the geographic distance of the workshop from the workplace, in the differentiation of activities and in symbolic removal, such as the turning off of mobile phones; (2) the use of liturgy – that is, prescribed forms of behaviour or interaction, such as the use of scenario techniques and other specific tools; and (3) the presence of specialists, such as workshop facilitators. Second, the specialists and the 'liturgy' must be legitimate – that is, they must be perceived as appropriate by the participants. Third, figures of authority, such as the CEO, must signal the suspension of structural roles – in other words, that the participants do not have to conform to the established roles. As a result of this action, sometimes the hierarchical order may even be reversed. The authors argue that

the more these three criteria are met, the stronger the participants' liminal experience.

This type of liminal experience is also associated with two behavioural patterns. The first results in the emergence of anti-structure – that is, 'the temporary suspension of participants' normal social status' (Johnson et al. 2010: 1592). In other words, people leave their normal roles, and especially their hierarchical positions. The second is that of 'communitas' – that is, the communal commitment of the participants to the purpose of the workshop. Johnson et al. (2010) have demonstrated that the combination of anti-structure and communitas is critical: in the context of an anti-structure, people will interact differently and, as a consequence, may express challenging new ideas. Whereas under normal conditions such challenges would lead to emotional conflict, communitas creates a social bond that keeps the participants together even in the face of criticism; in other words, it allows the conflict of opinions without affective conflict. Thus, liminal experience can render the strategic workshop a particularly fruitful context for the emergence of new ideas.

While workshops can lead to many new ideas through the suspension of organizational structures, these ideas are seldom transferred back to the organization at large. Because of this, it is often the case that a strategy workshop is considered to have failed, even though it is perceived to have been successful as such. This has been termed the 'effectivity paradox' of strategy workshops (MacIntosh, MacLean and Seidl 2010). As Johnson, Prashantham and Floyd (2006: 27, emphasis added) explain: '[T]he very separation and anti-structure that [strategy workshops] foster *may hinder the transfer of ideas and plans back to the everyday work situation.*' Thus, paradoxically, the more a workshop is decoupled from everyday organizational structures and routines, the greater the likelihood that it will lead to new ideas; at the same time, however, the greater the degree of decoupling, the harder it will be to bring these ideas into the organization at large. Conversely, the lower the degree of decoupling, the easier it is to bring into the organization new ideas from the workshop, but, because of the lack of decoupling, there may be no ideas to bring back. Indeed, this argument is supported by empirical evidence (Healey *et al.* forthcoming), and, acknowledging this problem, various researchers have tried to identify workshop designs that allow this paradox to be resolved (MacIntosh, MacLean and Seidl 2010).

The effects of different workshop designs

The effectiveness of different workshop designs in generating tangible outcomes has been examined in a host of recent studies, which, as Healey and colleagues (forthcoming) point out, generally distinguish three different types of outcome. *Organizational outcomes* can be defined as the impact of the workshop on the organization's strategic direction. Thus, a workshop might 'bolster strategic continuity or, alternatively, stimulate strategic change' (Healey *et al.* forthcoming: 3). *Interpersonal outcomes* can be defined as a workshop's 'impact on relations among key actors, [since] workshops can exert a direct impact on relations among those executives, managers and employees involved in the formal proceedings' (Healey *et al.* forthcoming: 4). *Cognitive outcomes* refer to the 'impact on participants' understanding of strategic issues, [which] includes [the] understanding of the organization's strategic position and direction, the strategic issues it faces, and the wider business environment' (Healey *et al.* forthcoming: 4).

Most research on the effectiveness of workshops has focused on organizational outcomes, especially how plans or ideas are transferred from the workshop to the organization at large. In this context, workshop designs that manage to circumvent the effectivity paradox are of particular interest. In one of these studies, MacIntosh, MacLean and Seidl (2010) examined ten organizations that conducted strategy workshops with the particular purpose of effecting strategic change. Some of these organizations arranged a single workshop, while others ran a series of up to thirty-four workshops. We summarize the results of their study in Table 32.2.

MacIntosh, MacLean and Seidl (2010) observe that, even though the workshops produced many new ideas in all ten cases, only in three cases did these ideas have some organizational impact. In four cases they saw initial signs of change, which did not subsequently materialize, however, and in three cases the workshops had no impact at all. Having analysed these ten cases in depth, MacIntosh, MacLean and Seidl identify three aspects of workshop design that seem to explain the difference in their effects: the duration of the interval between the first and last workshops in a series, the frequency of the workshops and the seniority of the participants – that is, workshops with some senior participants are more likely to produce an impact on the organization.

As Table 32.2 shows, all successful workshops were part of a series whose span was fairly long (see 'Duration'). The shortest time lapse between the first and last workshop in a series was twelve months. In addition, in all successful series the

Table 32.2 The effectiveness of workshop designs in ten organizations

Organization	Number	Seniority	Frequency	Duration	Effect
A	34	High	High	18 months	*Change*
B	32	High	High	30 months	*Change*
C	9	High	Medium	12 months	*Change*
D	7	High	High	3 months	*Only initial change*
E	4	Initially high	Low	24 months	*Only initial change*
F	3	High	Low	14 months	*Only initial change*
G	2	High	Medium	3 months	*Only initial change*
H	6	Low	High	3 months	*No impact*
I	1	High	–	1.5 days	*No impact*
J	1	High	–	2 days	*No impact*

Source: Based on Macintosh, MacLean and Seidl (2010).

frequency of the workshops never fell below what the authors describe as 'medium', corresponding to an interval of five to nine weeks between workshops, and the seniority of participants was high. In the other seven cases, which led to no change, at least one of these criteria was not met. For example, organization D organized a series of seven workshops with a high degree of frequency and seniority, but the interval between the first and the last workshop was only three months. By contrast, in organization F the duration was long and the degree of seniority was high, but the frequency of the workshops was low, whereas in organization J, although the degree of seniority was high, only one workshop was organized – that is, the duration was minimal.

On the basis of their analysis, MacIntosh, MacLean and Seidl (2010) draw several conclusions. First, single workshops are unlikely to yield organizational outcomes; on the contrary, workshops are effective only when they are part of a series. The authors argue that 'such series appear to allow separation and reconnection to occur over the course of several workshops' (MacIntosh, MacLean and Seidl 2010: 304), because serialization enables the workshops and ongoing organizational processes to become gradually interwoven. Moreover, the earlier workshops in a series can be clearly separated from ongoing activities, enabling the emergence of new ideas, while later workshops can gradually approach the everyday context, allowing at the same time these ideas to develop. Without adequate time and opportunities for participants to discuss new ideas, these ideas are unlikely to be developed and adjusted to the organizational context, or, indeed, to be transferred to the organization. This finding is confirmed in subsequent quantitative studies (Healey et al. forthcoming; van Aaken et al. 2013), but only for workshops on strategy formulation. Healey et al. (forthcoming: 17) argue 'that "serialization" [of workshops] amplifies the time and energy focused on particular strategic issues, increasing the likelihood of learning, while providing the requisite space to build commitment to new ideas'. Second, the frequency of workshops is also considered important in these studies, because it affects the rhythm and momentum of the discussions: if the interval between workshops is too long, the momentum gets lost, both cognitively, because the participants are likely to forget the details of what has already been discussed, and psychologically, because their 'emotional' energy will be lost (MacIntosh, MacLean and Seidl 2010). Third, in these studies, having senior participants is found to be important, in that it affects the degree to which new ideas are perceived as 'legitimate' when transferred to the organization (MacIntosh, MacLean and Seidl 2010).

Subsequent quantitative studies have identified several additional aspects of workshop design that appear to contribute to the effectiveness of workshops in terms of whether they yield organizational outcomes. One of these aspects concerns the integration of workshops into the formal strategic planning process. Van Aaken and colleagues (2013) find that workshops that are part of the ordinary strategic planning process have significantly higher positive organizational effects than workshops organized outside the context of this process. They argue that integrating workshops into the planning process increases the likelihood that their results will be processed by the wider organization, counterbalancing the effect of the extraneousness of the workshop. At the same time, van Aaken et al.'s (2013) study finds no evidence that holding a workshop outside the organizational premises has any significant effect on its outcomes. According to Healey et al. (forthcoming), the most important predictor of whether the outcome of a workshop will be perceived as successful is the degree to which a workshop's objectives are clearly presented. The authors argue that it is necessary to communicate clear objectives in order to 'restrict the scope of discussions' and to prevent participants from being unclear 'about what to focus upon or how to progress' (Healey et al. forthcoming: 5).

There is also evidence that high numbers of workshop participants are negatively correlated with organizational outcomes (van Aaken et al. 2013), even though, as Healey et al. (forthcoming) find, they are positively correlated with interpersonal outcomes, such as changes in the relations among key actors. Van Aaken et al. find no evidence that the use of analytical tools, the duration of the workshop or the perceived pressure to achieve results has any effect or organizational outcomes. More generally, there is evidence for differences in the effectiveness of workshops relative to their purpose. Healey *et al.* find that workshops focusing on implementation tend to be more positively associated with organizational outcomes than workshops focusing on formulation. Van Aaken *et al.* report that certain aspects of workshop design seem to be more relevant to formulation workshops, while others are more relevant to implementation workshops. For example, the serialization of workshops seems to affect the outcome of formulation workshops more than it affects the outcome of implementation workshops, whereas the correlation between high numbers of participants and negative organizational outcomes is significant in the case of workshops on formulation, but not in those on implementation.

In addition to organizational outcomes, Healey *et al.* (forthcoming) identify certain features of workshop design that affect cognitive and interpersonal outcomes in particular. For example, the serialization and duration of workshops, the degree of cognitive effort they induce and the use of cognitively challenging tools are positively correlated with cognitive workshop outcomes – that is, they all have an impact on how and to what degree participants understand the strategic issues that a workshop involves. Moreover, stakeholder involvement and, surprisingly, particularly high and particularly low numbers of participants are positively correlated with interpersonal outcomes – that is, with the strength of the relationships between participants.

Another aspect that several authors (Schwarz 2009; Whittington *et al.* 2006) have stressed is the importance of the particular skills that the workshop participants bring with them. Whittington *et al.*, for instance, show that the effectiveness of strategy workshops depends on a variety of practical skills; an example is having 'skilled control over detailed activities such as seating, time-tabling and flip-charting' (Whittington *et al.* 2006: 620). Finally, let us note that it is not necessarily always desirable for workshop results to be carried over to the wider organization; in particular, when the discussions that take place within a workshop are

highly controversial and emotive, 'an abrupt ending of the episode without any repercussions outside it may be functional' (Hendry and Seidl 2003: 186).

Conclusion and directions for future research on meetings

By way of conclusion, we summarize the main points of our overview of past research on the role of meetings and workshops in strategizing, and we point out opportunities for future research in this important field of inquiry. First, here is a summary of the seven key points of our overview of the literature on this topic.

(1) Past research has investigated in depth several aspects of the different practices associated with meetings and of the functions that meetings can serve in the organization.

(2) Past research has confirmed that meetings do have an impact on strategy, both in terms of stabilizing an organization's existing strategy in the face of new ideas and in terms of effecting strategic change.

(3) Various researchers have shown that the broader context in which meetings are embedded shapes the processes that take place within a meeting and thus affects its strategic outcomes.

(4) There is evidence that the effect of meetings on the organization's strategy often depends on the way in which individual meetings are integrated into series of meetings.

(5) Previous studies have shown that strategy workshops, as a particular form of meetings, serve as a mechanism for suspending organizational structures and routines and creating a platform for strategic reflection.

(6) Some studies have identified a so-called *effectivity paradox*, namely a clash between the conditions that allow new ideas to emerge and the conditions that ensure their transfer to the wider organization.

(7) Certain studies have identified several variables of the design of strategic workshops that seem to increase the effectiveness of such workshops in terms of organizational, interpersonal and cognitive outcomes.

Notwithstanding the numerous insights of past research into the strategic role of meetings and workshops, there is still much room for investigation. We would even argue that research on the strategic role of meetings and workshops is still in its infancy. In most of the areas identified above, more research is needed to develop these insights further. In addition, we would hope to see future research investigate the five areas we outline below.

(1) *The relation between the different functions of meetings*: in addition to further exploring the different functions that meetings might serve in the organization, we need to know more about the various ways in which these functions can be combined, both at the same time and over time.

(2) *Which functions meetings have and which relevant practices are applied on different organizational levels*: most strategy research to date has focused on meetings at the top management level, paying little attention to the particular characteristics of meetings on other organizational levels. Nevertheless, knowing, for example, that managers on lower levels use meetings differently from top managers (Cohen and March 1986; Doyle and Straus 1976; Mintzberg 1973), we expect that there are significant differences in the role of meetings in the strategizing process, depending on the level on which they are used.

(3) *Meetings on the inter-organizational level*: there is some empirical evidence that organizations engage increasingly in inter-organizational workshop activities when faced with 'meta-problems', such as the problem of water supply affecting several industries (Werle and Seidl 2012). We expect inter-organizational workshops to be characterized by particular practices and to play a specific role in an organization's strategizing processes, not least because such meetings are not integrated into any pre-existing organizational structures and the participants typically do not possess any formal decision-making powers within the organizations involved.

(4) *Comparative studies of meetings and workshops in different contexts*: we expect that there are differences between the specific functions of and practices related to meetings in different organizational contexts, depending on the type of organizations, on the country in which they are located and so on. Although there are some studies on meetings in different types of organizations, such as universities and commercial and public organizations, these studies do not examine systematically these differences. For example, it would be interesting to compare the characteristics of meetings that Jarzabkowski and Seidl (2008) identify in the context of British universities to those of meetings in other kinds of private and public organizations. Moreover, given that most existing studies have been carried out in Western countries and that many of the practices associated with meetings are affected by the organization's broader cultural context (Bilbow 1997), we expect there to be significant differences in the ways in which meetings affect strategy in other cultural contexts.

(5) *The role of materiality and the body in meetings*: while there are several studies on how materiality – such as physical artefacts (Whittington *et al.* 2006), textual artefacts (Vaara, Sorsa and Pälli 2010) or tools such as PowerPoint (Kaplan 2010) – affects the strategizing process, little is known about how materiality and the body (for example, looking at participants, turning the body towards the chairperson or raising hands) affect meetings. Researchers interested in examining the strategic role of materiality in meetings might draw on research from other fields – particularly ethnomethodology – that have a long tradition in studying the role of materiality in human interactions, albeit not explicitly in the domain of strategy.

In order to investigate the areas outlined above, researchers who focus on strategy as practice can choose from a wide range of different methodological options that have already been applied fruitfully in research on meetings. Such options include surveying (Hodgkinson *et al.* 2006; van Aaken *et al.* 2013), interviewing participants (van Praet 2009; 2010), applying ethnographic methods

(Jarzabkowski and Seidl 2008; Schwartzman 1989), shadowing (Mintzberg 1973) and action research (Ackermann and Eden 2011). We also note the need for applying new methods that can capture more effectively how body, materiality and discourse interact in meetings and how they relate to strategy formation. In this respect, video-ethnography seems to be a promising tool that can greatly enhance the scope of research on meetings and how they relate to strategy (Cornelissen and Cienki 2010). Similarly, methods such as asking participants to keep a diary of their reflections on a meeting before, during and after the event (Balogun, Huff and Johnson 2003) have the potential to provide new insights into series of meetings and into the underlying, often hidden, dynamics within meetings. Moreover, such methods hold out the promise of helping researchers gain a fuller and more integrative understanding of meetings, which could help advance the development of this field as a whole.

References

Abzug, R., and Mezias, S. J. (1993), 'The fragmented state and due-process protections in organizations: the case of comparable worth', *Organization Science*, 4/3: 433–53.

Ackermann, F., and Eden, C. (2011), 'Negotiation in strategy making teams: group support systems and the process of cognitive change', *Group Decision and Negotiation*, 20/3: 293–314.

Adams, B. (2004), 'Public meetings and the democratic process', *Public Administration Review*, 64/1: 43–54.

Angouri, J., and Bargiela-Chiappini, F. (2011), '"So what problems bother you and you are not speeding up your work?" Problem solving talk at work', *Discourse and Communication*, 5/3: 209–29.

Angouri, J., and Marra, M. (2010), 'Corporate meetings as genre: a study of the role of the chair in corporate meeting talk', *Text and Talk*, 30/6: 615–36.

Asmuß, B., and Oshima, S. (2012), 'Negotiation of entitlement in proposal sequences', *Discourse Studies*, 14/1: 67–86.

Asmuß, B., and Svennevig, J. (2009), 'Meeting talk: an introduction', *Journal of Business Communication*, 46/1: 3–22.

Bailey, F. G. (1965), 'Decisions by consensus in councils and committees: with special reference to village and local government in India', in Banton, M. (ed.), *Political Systems and the Distribution of Power*: 1–20. London: Tavistock.

Balogun, J., Huff, A. S., and Johnson, P. (2003), 'Three responses to the methodological challenges for studying strategizing', *Journal of Management Studies*, 40/1: 198–224.

Barnes, R. (2007), 'Formulations and the facilitation of common agreement in meetings talk', *Text and Talk*, 27/3: 273–96.

Bilbow, G. T. (1997), 'Cross-cultural impression management in the multicultural workplace: the special case of Hong Kong', *Journal of Pragmatics*, 28/4: 461–87.

(1998), 'Look who's talking: an analysis of "chair-talk" in business meetings', *Journal of Business and Technical Communication*, 12/2: 157–97.

Boden, D. (1994), *The Business of Talk: Organizations in Action*. Cambridge: Polity.

(1995), 'Agendas and arrangements: everyday negotiations in meetings', in Firth, A. (ed.), *The Discourse of Negotiation: Studies of Language in the Workplace*: 83–100. Oxford: Pergamon Press.

Bothin, A., and Clough, P. (2012), 'Participants' personal note-taking in meetings and its value for automatic meeting summarisation', *Information Technology and Management*, 13/1: 39–57.

Bourque, N., and Johnson, G. (2008), 'Strategy workshops and "away days" as ritual', in W., Starbuck, W., and Hodgkinson, G. (eds.), *The Oxford Handbook of Organizational Decision Making*: 552–64. Oxford University Press.

Brinkerhoff, M. B. (1972), 'Hierarchical status, contingencies, and the administrative staff conference', *Administrative Science Quarterly*, 17/3: 395–407.

Brown, S. L., and Eisenhardt, K. M. (1997), 'The art of continuous change: linking complexity theory and time spaced evolution in relentlessly shifting organizations', *Administrative Science Quarterly*, 42/1: 1–35.

Bürgi, P. T., Jacobs, C. D., and Roos, J. (2005), 'From metaphor to practice in the crafting of strategy', *Journal of Management Inquiry*, 14/1: 78–94.

Christiansen, J. K., and Varnes, C. J. (2007), 'Making decisions on innovation: meetings or networks?', *Creativity and Innovation Management*, 16/3: 282–98.

Clarke, I., Kwon, W., and Wodak, R. (2012), 'A context-sensitive approach to analysing talk in strategy meetings', *British Journal of Management*, 23/4: 455–73.

Clifton, J. (2009), 'Beyond taxonomies of influence: "doing" influence and making decisions in management team meetings', *Journal of Business Communication*, 46/1: 57–79.

Cohen, M. D., and March, J. G. (1986), *Leadership and Ambiguity*. Cambridge, MA: Harvard Business School Press.

Cornelissen, J., and Cienki, A. (2010), 'Sensegiving in entrepreneurial contexts: the use of metaphors in speech and gesture to gain and sustain support for novel business ventures', *International Small Business Journal*, 30/3: 213–41.

Dahl, T., and Lewis, D. R. (1975), 'Random sampling device used in time management study', *Evaluation*, 2/1: 20–2.

Dittrich, K., Guérard, S., and Seidl, D. (2011a), 'Meetings in the strategy process: toward an integrative framework', paper presented at the seventy-first annual meeting of the Academy of Management, San Antonio, Texas, 12 August.

(2011b), *The Role of Meetings in the Strategy Process*, Business Working Paper no. 102. University of Zurich.

Doyle, M., and Straus, D. (1976), *How to Make Meetings Work: The New Interaction Method*. New York: Wyden Books.

Doz, Y., and Prahalad, C. K. (1987), 'A process model of strategic redirection in large complex firms: the case of multinational corporations', in Pettigrew, A. M. (ed.), *The Management of Strategic Change*: 63–82. Oxford: Blackwell.

Eisenhardt, K. M. (1989), 'Making fast strategic decisions in high-velocity environments', *Academy of Management Journal*, 32/3: 543–76.

Fear, W. J. (2012), 'Discursive activity in the boardroom: the role of the minutes in the construction of social realities', *Group and Organization Management*, 37/4: 486–520.

Gailbraith, J. R. (1973), *Designing Complex Organizations*. Reading, MA: Addison-Wesley.

Guetzkow, H., and Kriesberg, M. (1950), 'Executive use of the administrative conference', *Personnel*, 26/1: 318–23.

Healey, M. P., Hodgkinson, G. P., Whittington, R., and Johnson, G. (forthcoming), 'Off to plan or out to lunch? Relationships between design

characteristics and outcomes of strategy workshops', *British Journal of Management*.

Hendry, J., and Seidl, D. (2003), 'The structure and significance of strategic episodes: social systems theory and the practice of strategic change', *Journal of Management Studies*, 40/1: 175–95.

Hodgkinson, G. P., Whittington, R., Johnson, G., and Schwarz, M. (2006), 'The role of strategy workshops in strategy development processes: formality, communication, co-ordination and inclusion', *Long Range Planning*, 39/5: 479–96.

Holmes, J., and Stubbe, M. (2003), *Power and Politeness in the Workplace*. London: Longman.

Hoon, C. (2007), 'Committees as strategic practice: the role of strategic conversation in a public administration', *Human Relations*, 60/6: 921–52.

Huisman, M. (2001), 'Decision-making in meetings as talk-in-interaction', *International Studies of Management and Organization*, 31/3: 69–90.

Jarzabkowski, P., Balogun, J., and Seidl, D. (2007), 'Strategizing: the challenges of a practice perspective', *Human Relations*, 60/1: 5–27.

Jarzabkowski, P., and Seidl, D. (2008), 'The role of meetings in the social practice of strategy', *Organization Studies*, 29/11: 1391–426.

Johnson, G., Langley, A., Melin, L., and Whittington, R. (2007), *Strategy as Practice: Research Directions and Resources*. Cambridge University Press.

Johnson, G., Melin, L., and Whittington, R. (2003), 'Guest editors' introduction: micro strategy and strategizing: towards an activity-based view', *Journal of Management Studies*, 40/1: 3–22.

Johnson, G., Prashantham, S., and Floyd, S. W. (2006), *Towards a Mid-Range Theory of Strategy*, Working Paper no. 035. London: Advanced Institute of Management Research.

Johnson, G., Prashantham, S., Floyd, S. W., and Bourque, N. (2010), 'The ritualization of strategy workshops', *Organization Studies*, 31/12: 1589–618.

Kangasharju, H. (1996), 'Aligning as a team in multi-party conversation', *Journal of Pragmatics*, 26/3: 291–319.

(2002), 'Alignment in disagreement: forming oppositional alliances in committee meetings', *Journal of Pragmatics*, 34/10–11: 1447–71.

Kangasharju, H., and Nikko, T. (2009), 'Emotions in organizations: joint laughter in workplace meetings', *Journal of Business Communication*, 46/1: 100–19.

Kaplan, S. (2011), 'Strategy and PowerPoint: an inquiry into the epistemic culture and machinery of strategy making', *Organization Science*, 22/2: 320–46.

Kwon, W., Clarke, I., and Wodak, R. (2014), 'Micro-level discursive strategies for constructing shared views around strategic issues in team meetings', *Journal of Management Studies*, 51/2: 265–90.

Langley, A. (2010), 'The challenge of developing cumulative knowledge about strategy as practice', in Golsorkhi, D., Rouleau, L., Seidl, D., and Vaara, E. (eds.), *Cambridge Handbook of Strategy as Practice*: 91–106. Cambridge Universtiy Press.

Larrue, J., and Trognon, A. (1993), 'Organization of turn-taking and mechanisms for turn-taking repairs in a chaired meeting', *Journal of Pragmatics*, 19/2: 177–96.

Liu, F., and Maitlis, S. (2014), 'Emotional dynamics and strategizing processes: a study of strategic conversations in top team meetings', *Journal of Management Studies*, 51/2: 202–34.

Luhmann, N. (1995), *Social Systems*. Redwood City, CA: Stanford University Press.

MacIntosh, R., MacLean, D., and Seidl, D. (2010), 'Unpacking the effectivity paradox of strategy workshops: do strategy workshops produce strategic change?', in Golsorkhi, D., Rouleau, L., Seidl, D., and Vaara, E. (eds.), *Cambridge Handbook of Strategy as Practice*: 291–309. Cambridge University Press.

McNulty, T., and Pettigrew, A. M. (1999), 'Strategists on the board', *Organization Studies*, 20/1: 47–74.

Mezias, J., Grinyer, P., and Guth, W. D. (2001), 'Changing collective cognition: a process model for strategic change', *Long Range Planning*, 34/1: 71–96.

Mintzberg, H. (1973), *The Nature of Managerial Work*. New York: Harper & Row.

Mintzberg, H., Raisinghani, D., and Theoret, A. (1976), 'The structure of "unstructured" decision processes', *Administrative Science Quarterly*, 21/2: 246–75.

Mirivel, J. C., and Tracy, K. (2005), 'Premeeting talk: an organizationally crucial form of talk', *Research on Language and Social Interaction*, 38/1: 1–34.

Ricœur, P. (1981), *Hermeneutics and the Human Sciences: Essays on Language, Action and Interpretation*. Cambridge University Press.

Sacks, H., Schegloff, E., and Jefferson, G. (1974), 'A simplest systematics of the organization of turn-taking for conversation', *Language*, 50/4: 696–735.

Schwartzman, H. B. (1989), *The Meeting: Gatherings in Organizations and Communities*. NewYork: Plenum.

Schwarz, M. (2009), 'Strategy workshops facilitating and constraining strategy making', *Journal of Strategy and Management*, 2/3: 277–87.

Schwarz, M., and Balogun, J. (2007), *Strategy Workshops for Strategic Reviews: A Case of Semi-Structured Emergent Dialogues*, Working Paper no. 054. London: Advanced Institute of Management Research.

Seibold, D. R. (1979), 'Making meetings more successful: plans, formats, and procedures for group problem-solving', *Journal of Business Communication*, 16/4: 3–20.

Seidl, D., MacLean, D., and MacIntosh, R. (2011), 'Rules of suspension: a rules-based explanation of strategy workshops in strategy process', paper presented at seventy-first annual meeting of the Academy of Management, San Antonio, Texas, 15 August.

Spee, P., and Jarzabkowski, P. (2011), 'Strategic planning as communicative process', *Organization Studies*, 32/9: 1217–45.

Starker, S. (1978), 'Case conference and tribal ritual: some cognitive, social, and anthropologic aspects of the case conference', *Journal of Personality and Social Systems*, 1/1: 3–14.

Tepper, S. (2004), 'Setting agendas and designing alternatives: policymaking and the strategic role of meetings', *Review of Policy Research*, 21/4: 523–42.

Terry, L. D. (1987), 'The conference as an administrative strategy for building organizational commitment: the CWA experience', *Labour Studies Journal*, 26/1: 48–61.

Tracy, K. (2007), 'The discourse of crisis in public meetings: case study of a school district's multimillion dollar error', *Journal of Applied Communication Research*, 35/4: 418–41.

Turner, V. (1982), *From Ritual to Theater: The Human Seriousness of Play*. New York: PAJ.

Vaara, E., Sorsa, V., and Pälli, P. (2010), 'On the force potential of strategy texts: a critical discourse analysis of a strategic plan and its power effects in a city organization', *Organization*, 17/6: 685–702.

Vaara, E., and Whittington, R. (2012), 'Strategy-as-practice: taking social practices seriously', *Academy of Management Annals*, 6/1: 285–336.

Van Aaken, D., Koob, C., Rost, K., and Seidl, D. (2013), 'Ausgestaltung und Erfolg von Strategieworkshops: eine empirische Analyse', *Zeitschrift für betriebswirtschaftliche Forschung*, 65/7: 588–616.

Van Praet, E. (2009), 'Staging a team performance: a linguistic ethnographic analysis of weekly meetings at a British embassy', *Journal of Business Communication*, 46/1: 80–99.

—— (2010), 'The dual voice of domination: ritual and power in a British embassy', *Text and Talk*, 30/2: 213–33.

Van Vree, W. (1999), *Meetings, Manners and Civilization: The Development of Modern Meeting Behaviour*. Leicester University Press.

Weick, K. E. (1995), *Sensemaking in Organizations*. London: Sage.

Werle, F., and Seidl, D. (2012), *Interorganizational Strategizing as Extension of Sensemaking Capacities*, Business Working Paper no. 317. University of Zurich.

Whittington, R. (2006), 'Completing the practice turn in strategy research', *Organization Studies*, 27/5: 613–34.

Whittington, R., Molloy, E., Mayer, M., and Smith, A. (2006), 'Practices of strategising/organising: broadening strategy work and skills', *Long Range Planning*, 39/6: 615–29.

Wodak, R., Kwon, W., and Clarke, I. (2011), '"Getting people on board": discursive leadership for consensus building in team meetings', *Discourse and Society*, 22/5: 592–644.

The role of materiality in the practice of strategy

JANE LÊ and PAUL SPEE[1]

Introduction

While spatial and material aspects are fundamental to accomplishing any organizational activity and process, these have largely been neglected or treated as mere background in theoretical accounts that explain phenomena such as strategic change. This dearth of research exploring the role of materials has inspired 'material turns' in the fields of social studies of finance (for example, MacKenzie 2006; Pinch and Swedberg 2008), organizational routines (for example, D'Adderio 2011; Pentland *et al.* 2012) and technology studies (for example, Orlikowski 2007; Orlikowski and Scott 2008). Although multiple approaches exist that could shed light on the consequentiality of materiality for strategizing, at present these are not explicitly discussed in the literature.

To establish a research agenda for strategy as practice scholars, this chapter provides an overview of different philosophical approaches and empirical traditions to materiality,[2] explaining the assumptions inherent in each approach and how these assumptions alter the way we understand and study strategizing. When possible, we illustrate the approaches with examples from strategy as practice. In so doing, we develop a typology of materiality that researchers might draw upon to guide their own work. Critically, while this typology is conceptually helpful to better understand the different ways in which one may view and work with materiality, we do not see the approaches as abso-

lutely distinct. Rather, we see them as operating on a sliding scale; some approaches may be blended relatively effortlessly, while others would be impossible to combine given their opposing assumptions. In introducing these approaches, we aim to critically engage with the notion of materiality, encouraging the reader to see materiality as something that goes beyond mere physicality.

In line with these aims, our chapter is structured as follows. We briefly review the philosophical foundations of materiality to demonstrate the rich and diverse origins of the construct. We then introduce four empirical traditions to materiality: the communications approach, the technological approach, the sensemaking approach and the positivist approach. Reflecting on these approaches and their utility to SAP research, we draw up an agenda for future research. Herein we suggest the following as particularly fruitful avenues for research: time and space, and emotion and identity; connecting important levels of analysis, such as institutions and practice; drawing on innovative methods; and, most critically, using materiality to prompt new research questions that will significantly alter our understanding of organizations.

Philosophical approaches to materiality

The roots of strategy as practice are the philosophical traditions of social practice theorists, which Postill (2010) separates into a first generation (for example, Bourdieu, de Certeau, Foucault, Garfinkel and Giddens) and a second generation (for example, Pickering, Reckwitz, Rouse and Schatzki). Some social practice theorists equate the material with the symbolic orders of a society's social structure (for example, Giddens). Here, material/social structures are seen as carriers of

---

[1] The author order is purely alphabetical; the contribution is equal.

[2] We distinguish philosophical approaches from empirical traditions, as some work may draw on selected constructs within a philosophical tradition without necessarily adhering to a specific empirical tradition (for example, Kaplan 2011; Jarzabkowski, Spee and Smets 2013).

meaning that become objects of knowledge and require interpretation (Reckwitz 2002: 202). Thus, objects only 'become visible in the context of systems of meaning (categories, discourse, communicative action)' (Reckwitz, 2002: 197). Such assumptions background physical things and artefacts in social inquiry. For other theorists, however, such as Heidegger, things, materials or equipment – 'Zeug', as he calls it – play a substantive role in constituting a 'practice'. In short, materials are part of bodily doings, and individuals' practical understandings shape their use (Schatzki 2002).[3] Thus, materials and bodily doings are entangled and cannot be treated separately. There are a few examples of using this approach to unpack strategic practices. For instance, Kaplan (2011) draws on Heidegger's distinction of 'tools ready-to-hand' and 'tools present-at-hand' (see also Knorr Cetina 1997) to demonstrate the affordances of PowerPoint that create discursive spaces to discuss a telecommunication firm's strategy. Further, Jarzabkowski, Spee and Smets' (2013) Schatzki-inspired study develops a typology of strategy practices that illustrates managers' situated use of mundane artefacts to strategize.

Of course, there are additional approaches to the relation between materiality and practice. For instance, de Certeau has put forward the notion of *bricolage*, which refers to the appropriation of material artefacts (for example, Boxenbaum and Rouleau 2011) or the appropriation of strategy discourse (for example, Abdallah and Langley 2014). Further approaches, such as those put forward by Latour (1987) and Pickering (1995), assume that materials and practice are inextricably entwined. While these approaches to materiality vary in ontological and epistemological assumptions, each provides a fruitful ground for the study of 'practice' as phenomenon. Each philosophical approach provides a fruitful stance to further explore the way materiality accomplishes, or is part of accomplishing, strategizing activities. As recent research points out (for example, Dameron, Lê and LeBaron 2015; Jarzabkowski, Burke and Spee 2015; Jarzabkowski, Spee and Smets 2013; Paroutis, Franco and Papadopoulos 2015; Werle and Seidl 2015), strategists not only draw upon but also struggle to deal with the 'ordinary' stuff used during strategizing episodes. Garnering better understanding of these issues requires drawing on appropriate constructs within a selected philosophical approach while paying heed to its ontological assumptions.

Empirical traditions of materiality

So many different empirical traditions to materiality exist that offering a comprehensive review goes beyond the scope of this chapter.[4] Instead of focusing on a particular empirical approach, we introduce a range of different empirical traditions that have already fruitfully informed strategy as practice research and, we believe, will continue to do so. The four approaches we introduce are: communication, technology, sensemaking and positivism. In presenting these approaches,[5] we maintain the pluralism that characterizes strategy as practice (Golsorkhi *et al.* 2010). We illustrate each approach using examples from SAP research.

In what follows, we thus acknowledge two broad definitions of materiality. First, materiality may refer to mere physicality – that is, material is something that exists separately from the mind; it is an object with physical properties that occupies space (Oxford dictionary). Second, materiality may

---

[3] As noted elsewhere (for example, Nicolini 2013), the philosophical roots of social practice theory are largely built upon Heidegger and Wittgenstein's work. The influence of both philosophers' works are strongly interwoven and reflected in Schatzki's approach to theorizing social practice as constitutive of reality, which is gaining prominence in the realm of practice-based studies (see, for example, Jarzabkowski, Spee and Smets 2013, Jarzabkowski, Lê and Van de Ven 2013; Orlikowski 2007; Zundel and Kokkalis 2010).

[4] The following sources contain overviews of diverse approaches exploring the issue of materiality in sociology (Law and Mol 1994), economic sociology (Pinch and Swedberg 2008) and workplace studies (Dale and Burrell 2008).

[5] We do recognize the incongruence between some of these empirical traditions and the philosophical approaches to strategy as practice, particularly the positivistic approach.

refer to the quality of being relevant or significant – that is, material is something that is inseparable from the mind; it is the object of our attention and may or may not have distinct physical properties but, rather, gains meaning on the basis of the characteristics we ascribe to it (Oxford dictionary). Both definitions are drawn upon in organization studies and can be useful for strategy as practice scholars seeking to work with materiality.

In explaining each of the four approaches, we adopt the following structure. We outline the disciplinary and theoretical origins, summarize the key contributions of each approach, establish its empirical focus and methods and discuss the implications for strategy as practice. We conclude by using exemplar studies to bring each approach to life, thereby demonstrating its potential to make contributions. A summary of the approaches is presented in Table 33.1. This table should be viewed as complementary to the text.

The communication approach

One perspective on materiality originates in the field of organizational communication; it is referred to as the communicative constitution of organization (Cooren, Taylor and Van Every 2006; Putnam and Nicotera 2008; Robichaud, Giroux and Taylor 2004). Instead of assuming that communication occurs within an organization, organization is seen as an ongoing accomplishment, generated in a recursive interaction between 'site' and 'surface' (Taylor and Van Every 2000). The term 'site' refers to the conversational layer that generates 'organization' by continuously negotiating and establishing a common purpose; 'surface' refers to the textual layer that represents the organization. To highlight their mutual constitution, 'it is *in* conversation that organization is literally achieved and *through* texts that they are recognized' (Ashcraft, Kuhn and Cooren 2009: 21; emphasis in original). A material dimension is added through the distinction of verbal, non-verbal and written texts. This has informed studies within strategy as practice (for example, Aggerholm, Asmuß and Thomsen 2012; Spee and Jarzabkowski 2011). For instance, Spee and

Jarzabkowski explore the interplay between talk and text and the ways it enabled and constrained unfolding planning conversations.

Grounded in conversations and narratives (for a detailed overview, see Robichaud and Cooren 2013), materiality focuses on 'objects, sites, and bodies' (Ashcraft, Kuhn and Cooren 2009: 2). *Objects* are differentiated by their material and ideational qualities. Several types of objects, textual or otherwise, have been studied to uncover their influence on coordinating behaviour and control. *Sites* refer to the physical locations of work that are filled with materials (Parker and Clegg 2006). For instance, Kuhn (2006) contrasts spatio-cultural locations and their impact on workers' identity formation. Containerizing the site as mere background should be avoided, however (Taylor and Spicer 2007). A focus on the relation of bodies and materiality requires going beyond crude bodily characteristics such as gender, race, ethnicity, age, etc. Instead, it hones in on the ways *bodies* take shape in communication (see also Dameron, Lê and LeBaron 2015). Examples of such work include studies on the embodiments of femininity or masculinity influenced by organizational discourses, often manifested in documents (Ashcraft 1999; Wolkowitz 2006).

Strategy as practice scholars have recently started to reinstate the constitutive role of communication in strategizing (for example, Aggerholm, Asmuß and Thomsen 2012; Fauré and Rouleau 2011; Fenton and Langley 2011; Spee and Jarzabkowski 2011). Adopting this approach has implications for how SAP research on materiality might be conducted. Theoretically, the study of materiality rests on the analytical separation of talk from text, which provides the basis for examining a plan's appropriation or persistence over time. Such focus reinvigorated the interest in the role of strategic plans in strategy practices. For instance, Cornut, Giroux and Langley (2012) have reconceptualized the plan as a communicative genre by exploring its textual expressions in public- and third-sector organizations. Studies might also explore a plan's textual agency (Cooren 2004). This focus reintroduces the question of how authority is established and constituted, so that one can speak of 'organization' and on its

Table 33.1 Overview of empirical approaches to materiality

Approach	Theoretical background	Degree of materiality	Level of analysis	Implications for strategy as practice/consequentiality	Exemplars
The communication approach (communication as constitutive of organization)	• Speech act theory • Language in use • Assumptions based on actor–network theory	• Textual agency • Materials influence and are influenced by interactions	• Situated speech in action	**Theory**: discourse analysis moving towards communication **Empirical**: emphasizes context and detail; communication-based micro-ethnography	Cooren (2004); Schoeneborn (2013); Seidl (2007); Spee and Jarzabkowski (2011)
The technology approach –science and technology studies –sociomateriality	• Performativity of objects • Assumptions based on actor–network theory	• Interaction of human and non-human • Distributed cognition	• Performativity of artefacts and practitioners • Entanglement beyond communication	**Theory**: relationality; agencement; entanglement **Empirical**: focuses on the performativity and accomplishing of the strategic plan or strategy tools, such as the BCG matrix	D'Adderio (2008); Kaplan (2008); Kornberger and Clegg (2011); Leonardi (2011); Orlikowski and Scott (2013); Whittle and Mueller (2010)
The sensemaking approach	• Knowledge theory of social practice • Cognition-based	• Knowledge embedded in material (boundary object; epistemic object) • Knowledge creates boundaries • Inter-group dynamics (power); who controls the information	• Individuals interact with materials • Cognition-focused • Backgrounding material • Inter-group focus	**Theory**: use of tools; moving to knowledge inscribed in tools; other objects **Empirical**: group dynamics; ethnography	Bechky (2003); Heracleous and Jacobs (2008a); Stigliani and Ravasi (2012)
The positivist approach	• Economic psychology • Behavioural theory	• Physical, material • Objective	• Individual/team/group focus • Response/outcome focus (impact of independent variable on dependent variables)	**Theory**: impact of tools; cause and effect **Empirical**: objects in own right; e.g. quasi-experiment	Jarzabkowski et al. (2012); Wright, Paroutis and Blettner (2013)

behalf (see Taylor 2008; Nicotera 2013). Such insights might inform studies of how strategic plans become authoritative texts (Kuhn 2008). It might also explain how people become strategists (Chia and Holt 2009; Whittington 2006) and the potential conflict over meaning that arises through different genres of communication, such as PowerPoint (for example, Schoeneborn 2013). Empirically, a CCO perspective on materiality has implications for how strategy as practice research is conducted. In an attempt to further our understanding of the human–object interaction in strategizing, CCO defines 'objects' in a way that places distinct emphasis on artefacts, which often fall below the analytic radar. Similarly, a reinvigorated aspect of 'site' encourages us to further explore the growing interest in the characteristics enabling or constraining strategic episodes such as strategy workshops (for example, Jarzabkowski and Seidl 2008; Healey et al. 2015; Hoon 2007). Finally, a focus on 'bodies' provides grounds for future research to investigate the way strategists' emotions shape strategizing (for example, Liu and Maitlis 2014) through a stronger engagement with video-ethnographic methods (for example, Streeck, Goodwin and LeBaron 2011; Jarzabkowski et al. 2014).

The technology approach

The field of science and technology studies emerged in response to growing dissatisfaction with the extant focus solely on technologies and their properties, particularly software, as this did not explain their use. Technology studies are strongly influenced by Giddens' structuration theory (for example, Barley 1986; Orlikowski 2000), aiming to identify reasons for failure in technology adoption and to understand the situated use of technologies such as photocopiers (for example, Suchman 2007). Early studies examining 'technology-in-use' suffered from two difficulties, however. First, they positioned technological effects as exceptional, rather than as continuously present and part of work practices. Second, they artificially separated human activity and technology, resulting in either a technology-centric view that overemphasized the effects of technologies or

a human-centric view that overstated the influence of humans over the technology (Orlikowski 2007). Recent studies have adopted a more radical approach that foregrounds the intertwined relation of technology and humans. Despite this, the field remains fragmented. Thus, we review two distinct strands of the literature: science and technology studies (STS) and sociomateriality. While both approaches reject the dualism of the human and object relationship, sharing a relational ontology (Cooper 1997), the degree of this relation differs subtly across the research agendas.

With regard to materiality, *science and technology studies* build on the notion of distributed cognition across humans and non-humans (for example, Law and Mol 1994). This idea is encapsulated in the construct of sociotechnical agencement, which is comprised of human beings (bodies) as well as material, technical and textual devices (Çalişkan and Callon 2010). For instance, steering a boat or landing an aeroplane is not carried out by humans alone, but includes a number of non-human actors participating in actions and cognitive processes (see, for example, Hutchins 1995). Rejecting the division between macro and micro, the notion of agencement makes changes in size intelligible: '[S]ize and strength are compound realities that can be studied and elucidated by analysing agencements' (Çalişkan and Callon 2010: 10). Moreover, STS emphasizes the performativity of models that render the phenomena of day-to-day activities visible. For instance, a growing body of work (for example, Knorr Cetina and Preda 2012) illustrates how the market is performed by economists and traders through their respective models rather than by assuming that a market of abstracted and aggregated actors exists (see also Çalişkan and Callon 2009; 2010). The locus of such studies is to examine how electronic trading platforms or algorithmic formulae changed the way practices such as trading were perceived and conducted, and how products such as financial futures gained legitimacy (for example, MacKenzie 2006; Preda 2009).

Recently the field has taken a further step away from determinism and individualism (Leonardi and Barley 2010; Orlikowski and Scott 2008). Scholars advocating *sociomateriality* within technology studies centre on the human–technology relation, materializing in the notions of entanglement (Orlikowski and Scott 2008; Scott and Orlikowski 2013) and imbrication (Leonardi 2011). The constructs of entanglement and imbrication highlight the interwoven relationship of humans and technology, which enact a particular work practice. For instance, Leonardi (2011) illustrates how the car safety check routine evolved as the affordances of the simulation shaped the enactment of the routine, which in turn resulted in amendments to the simulation's properties, which in turn shaped subsequent enactments of the routine.

Adopting the approaches put forward by STS and scholars advocating sociomateriality has implications for how strategy as practice research on materiality might be conducted. These areas are still largely underexplored in the SAP field, however. Theoretically, these approaches provide grounds for future research to throw light on additional aspects of performing strategy, for instance by studying the distributed nature of agency across humans and non-humans. Further, studies might explore aspects around the performativity of strategy. A first example is provided by Kornberger and Clegg (2011). Their study of a strategy project to make Sydney sustainable by 2030 illustrates the performativity of strategy, which shaped its subjects and objects. Empirically, it might shed light on the role of technologies, such as scenario planning and its effects on strategizing. Instead of assuming its accuracy in forecasting, scholars might explore the negotiation of meaning around particular scenarios and the mobilizing of the political dimension around its use. Some of the concepts introduced above might further our understanding of the temporal and spatial aspects of strategizing (for example, Kaplan and Orlikowski 2013).

The sensemaking approach

A sensemaking perspective offers an alternative view of materiality. Although it still studies material in its own right – that is, as something with tangible, concrete and physical properties – the focus here is very much on how material is used in sensemaking[6] and sensegiving processes (Cornelissen, Mantere and Vaara 2014; Stigliani and Ravasi 2012). Thus, studies in this area have focused on the link between material and cognition, account or interpretation. This has included connecting material and knowledge in order to better understand organizing and coordinating (Brown and Duguid 2001). Recent studies on epistemic objects even suggest that knowledge may be embedded in material (Ewenstein and Whyte 2009; McGivern and Dopson 2010; Miettinen and Virkkunen 2005). Material may therefore guide and be guided by knowledge processes. Indeed, scholars suggest that material contains memory traces that afford recognition or remembrance, priming actors to certain meanings and actions (Stigliani and Ravasi 2012). Similarly, work on boundary objects shows that material can be used to create and cross boundaries (Bechky 2003; Carlile 2002; 2004). As such, this approach emphasizes studying not just materials in isolation but also the way these materials interact with interpretive processes to drive behaviour.

Contemporary studies suggest that material properties necessarily require sensemaking, partially because organizational actors operate in a context of ambiguity and contradiction (Stigliani and Ravasi 2012). It is therefore important to understand why actors engage with the material and what the outcome of this interaction is. Recent work by Stigliani and Ravasi (2012) suggests that physical engagement with material – which embodies cues and ideas – facilitates engagement with mental content. In short, working with material allows you to augment understanding. Material artefacts may thus be thought of as cognitive extension. Similarly, Kaplan (2011) demonstrates that PowerPoint is not just a technology but also a vehicle for actors to negotiate meaning in the

---

[6] Originating with Weick's (1995) seminal study, sensemaking and sensegiving are two related processes for interpreting the environment. Sensemaking refers to the process of interpreting changes in the environment, whereas sensegiving refers to the process of shaping others' interpretations of changes in the environment (see also Gioia and Chittipeddi 1991; Maitlis 2005; Maitlis and Lawrence 2007).

context of uncertainty. It allows for ideas to be adjusted and recombined, and engages multiple actors. Other materials studied in this way include academic publications (McGivern and Dopson 2010), concepts and models (Miettinen and Virkkunen 2005) and sketches and pictures (Stigliani and Ravasi 2012).

Studies grounded in this approach establish the link between materials and interpretation or sensemaking. As sensemaking occurs at the individual and at the group level (Weick 1995), individuals' interactions with materials are often assessed at both these levels. Although materials are studied in this approach, they are in some ways backgrounded, as a tool used to 'make sense' of the world, while primacy is given to the interpretive social processes that shape meaning more broadly. Methodologically, studies based on this perspective tend to involve ethnographies and interviews, with some focus on cognitive methods such as diaries, maps and grids (Balogun and Johnson 2004) and discursive techniques (Heracleous and Jacobs 2008a; 2008b).

Adopting this approach has implications for how SAP research on materiality might be conducted. Theoretically, it suggests that objects – despite stable characteristics – might produce different sensemaking processes and, indeed, may be appropriated (Kaplan 2011; Stigliani and Ravasi 2012). This indicates that it matters who controls material objects. We thus need to pay greater attention to intergroup dynamics, including politics and power (see Whittle et al. 2014). Empirically, this perspective promotes the study of materials alongside social and interpretive processes. While the focus in strategy as practice has traditionally been on how tools are used in strategizing, attention is shifting towards how knowledge is inscribed in strategy tools (Spee and Jarzabkowski 2009) and the way these shape unfolding processes (for example, Jarzabkowski, Spee and Smets 2013). This calls for more cognitive methods and empirical group dynamics approaches.

One area in which we have seen application of the sensemaking approach to materiality in strategy as practice is strategic representations. For instance, Jacobs and Heracleous (2008), in their work on embodied metaphors, demonstrate how organization members use toy construction material to build physical representations of strategy. The physical character of these constructions – in terms of the elevation, centrality, proximity, directional uniformity, structures, colours and solidity – matters for how strategy is interpreted and understood. It shows the role that material objects can play in interpretive processes and how materials can purposefully be appropriated by organizational members. From this perspective, objects are seen as possessing stable characteristics, which are largely relevant in relation to the interpretations and behaviours they invoke.

The positivist approach

Although the recent turn towards materiality in organization studies has a strong interpretive flavour (Dameron, Lê and LeBaron 2015; for an exception, see Thomas and Ambrosini 2015), the study of material also has a rich tradition of positivism (Dameron, Lê and LeBaron 2015). Indeed, disciplines such as environmental psychology (Mehrabian and Russell 1974), cognitive psychology (Treisman and Gelade 1980; Kahneman, Treisman and Gibbs 1992), psychophysics (Green and Swets 1966), consumer psychology (Bloch 1995) and marketing (Bitner 1992) have studied the power of material for centuries. These studies are united in their efforts to identify relationships between physical stimuli or conditions on human emotion, cognition and behaviour (Bechtel and Churchman 2002; Bitner 1992; Gifford 2007; Stokols and Altman 1987). Thus, work conducted under this approach demonstrates that there are common trends in the way that we perceive and respond to material (Bechtel and Churchman 2002). As a result, material is largely conceived and studied as a physical representation with objective qualities and predictable impact. While the approach acknowledges differences between people in their perception of the environment, of course, it also assumes that there are predicable trends in the way that humans respond to physical material. The approach therefore emphasizes the importance of studying the context in which individuals operate in order to understand the impact of materiality.

For instance, psychophysics examines the relationship between dimensions of the physical world on aspects of sensation and/or perception (Fechner 1860; Stevens 1957). Researchers in this field worked to identify the 'threshold' at which we can perceive light or sound (Green and Swets 1966). Similarly, environmental psychology examines the relationship between individuals and their physical environment, both built and natural (Hellpach 1911; Step, van den Berg and de Groot 2013; Sundstrom *et al.* 1996). The focus on the built environment is particularly interesting to organization scholars; studies have established the impact of basic environmental conditions, such as the colour of walls on physiological responses such as skin arousal (Wilson 1966) and affective responses such as mood (Wexner 1954). Studies have also shown that office design features (Campbell 1979) and desk arrangement (Rosenfield, Lambert and Black 1985; Zweigenhaft 1976) matter because they influence our perception and behaviour. Research also demonstrates that numerical estimates people provide are heavily influenced by arbitrary numbers visible in the periphery (Tversky and Kahneman 1974) and that financial transactions can be influenced by pleasant smells (Li *et al.* 2007).

Perhaps unsurprisingly, studies grounded in this approach tend to try to establish cause-and-effect relationships – or, at least, correlations. The level of analysis is most often individual, but may also be group-based (see Proshansky 1987). Accordingly, laboratory experiments, simulation studies, field studies and questionnaires constitute commonly used methods (Step, van den Berg and de Groot 2013). Increasingly, we also see researchers incorporating neuroscience methods, which study the brain processes underlying thoughts and actions using tools such as computer tomography, electroencephalography, magnetic resonance imaging and eye-tracking technology (for example, Heatherton and Wheatly 2010).

Adopting this approach has implications for how strategy as practice research on materiality might be conducted. Theoretically, it suggests that objects have stable characteristics that, under similar conditions, will provoke similar responses from individuals. It also suggests that we can identify cause-and-effect relationships in the way that material influences people and the way that people influence material. Empirically, this perspective promotes the study of objects in their own right and validates methodological approaches such as survey design and questionnaire studies, as well as calling for quasi-experimental research designs.

One area in which we have seen application of a positivistic approach to materiality in strategy as practice is the study of strategy tools. For instance, Wright, Paroutis and Blettner (2013) adopted a survey approach featuring the repertory grid technique to study how and in what way strategy tools are useful. They find that managers have a tendency to think in opposing dualities and, consequently, prefer multiple tools that offer different perspectives and that support connected thinking, complexity and peripheral vision. The features of strategy tools are thus critical both in terms of how managers use the tools and the effect they have with them. Similarly, Jarzabkowski *et al.* (2013) try to discern broader trends in tool use using a survey method. In a large-scale study of strategy alumni, they find that demographic characteristics – specifically, educational factors such as level of, and time elapsed since, formal education – drive tool adoption. Using these findings, the authors develop a 'predictive model' of strategy tool adoption. A key feature of both studies is the effort to be representative and offer generic observations about tool use. From this perspective, the strategy tool is seen as a material that is used by strategists based on objective features such as the characteristics of strategy tools or strategy tool users. Indeed, Wright, Paroutis and Blettner (2013: 115) suggest that strategy tools act as 'knowledge artefacts' that impose 'cognitive dimensions' on users. In other words, the material nature of the tool influences how people perceive and use a strategy tool.

Future directions

These four approaches and their implications for how we conduct SAP research suggest a number of new avenues for research. First and foremost, these views of materiality suggest that we should ask significantly different research questions, and that answering these questions has the potential to significantly alter the way we view strategy and organizations. Indeed, they suggest that we need to pay greater attention to the physical aspects of the contexts in which we operate, but also remind us of the powerful role of interpretation in ascribing meaning to elements. These approaches also push us to think beyond physicality to consider the power of less visible but perhaps equally 'material' elements of context, such as power relationships, group dynamics, institutions, emotions and identities. We cannot review all fruitful avenues for explorations within the limits of a single chapter, so we focus on four areas that we think hold much promise to further our understanding of strategizing.

First, materiality reintroduces concepts that have been somewhat neglected in organization studies, including concepts such as time and space. Time is interesting because, though acknowledged as critical in organizations, it is itself rarely studied (Butler 1995; Pedersen 2009; Zaheer, Albert and Zaheer 1999). This is because there are two ways to conceptualize time: absolute time and relative time (Butler 1995; Cunliffe, Luhman and Boje 2004; Lee and Liebenau 1999; Levine 1997). While we often incorporate absolute time into our research designs, for instance by using process research methods to study how events and activities unfold over time (for example, Jarzabkowski, Lê and Feldman 2012), less attention has been paid to relative time. There is evidence, however, that the subjective experience of time – the past, the present and the future – will influence perceptions and responses (Barry and Elmes 1997; Cunliffe, Luhman and Boje 2004; Kaplan and Orlikowski 2013; Pedersen 2009; Wright 2005). This emerging stream of research offers a strong complement to existing strategy traditions, such as path dependence research (David 1985; Flaherty and Fine 2001; Mahoney 2000; Sewell 1992; Stinchcombe 1965). It also raises interesting questions about the materiality of time – both absolute and relative – to strategizing. Another area currently re-emerging as a topic of interest is that of space. Physical spaces have a material nature that enables and constrains strategy processes. Indeed, our surroundings are known to impact how we perceive and respond to stimulus. For instance, physical aspects of boardrooms are known to impact strategy processes (Hodgkinson and Wright 2002). Similarly, Stensaker, Balogun and Langley (2012) demonstrate that the nature of working on an offshore oil platform and the space it provides for strategizing affect managers' change agency (see also Clegg et al. 2013). We therefore need to better understand strategizing spaces and how they enact effects.

Second, a focus on materiality as a construct that expands beyond mere physicality to looking at significance and impact will help invigorate emerging research on identity (Oliver and Roos 2007) and emotion (Liu and Maitlis 2014). Human dynamics such as resistance (Courpasson, Dany and Clegg 2012), politics (Whittle et al. 2014) and tension (Jarzabkowski, Lê and Van de Ven 2013) are known to influence strategizing processes. In other words, they have a material impact on what we do when we do strategy. It is thus important to understand these processes in greater depth, particularly how identity and emotional dynamics are elicited, and the effect they create during strategizing episodes. It provides the basis for speaking to a broader area of research that attempts to connect studies on identity with strategy research. So far, strategy has merely provided a setting for the research dynamics on organizational identity formation and change. Approaches that bring materiality to the fore provide fruitful grounds to shed light on the relation of aspects of strategizing and organizational identity formation and change.

Third, materials may enable us to finally connect the micro and macro levels of analysis effectively. For instance, objects may be one way to link institutions and practices. Indeed, we know that institutional pressures affect structures (Scott 1995), meanings (Zilber 2008) and practices (Jarzabkowski, Lê and Van de Ven 2009). Thus, the role of structures and objects has long been acknowledged but rarely studied. This is partially because the types of data sets that institutional theorists draw on tend to lack sufficient detail to connect these three elements (Suddaby, Seidl and Lê 2013). The unique constellation of these structures, meanings and practices is likely to result in significant variance in how organizations respond to institutional pressures, however. Indeed, 'organizational structures and systems are not neutral but are underpinned by interpretive schemes which reflect the values and beliefs of members. As a result, change involves not only changing structural elements of organization but also underlying values and beliefs' (Ransom, Hinings and Greenwood 1980, as cited by Slack and Hinings 1994: 821). Similarly, Zilber (2012: 90) suggests that the 'process of institutionalization...connotes active efforts at sense-making, involving the appropriation of structures, practices, and their meanings into local contexts'. Studying material such as structures and objects is therefore likely to illuminate the relationship between the macro and micro contexts that organizational actors operate in.

Finally, engaging seriously with materiality will require methodological innovation. We need to think carefully about which tools and methods can be used to analyse and account for material, however defined. This may require us to visit other research domains, such as psychology, phenomenology or neuroscience, for inspiration, and will result in the proliferation of existing approaches, such as visual analysis (Meyer *et al.* 2013; Ray and Smith 2012) and video-ethnography (Streeck, Goodwin and LeBaron 2011).

Conclusion

Materiality is important not just because it is increasingly gaining prominence within the strategy as practice community and organization studies more broadly. Materiality is important because of the far-reaching implications it has for how we study organizations. A materiality perspective redefines what is substantial and substantive in organizations, thereby directing our attention to new areas and elements. Critically, it underlines and reinvigorates the importance of adopting a dynamic view of strategy in which recursive relationships – in this case the relationship between the subject and the material – are critical to strategizing processes and outcomes. As our review suggests, what is 'material' is not solely determined by whether something is physical or not. Indeed,

non-physical artefacts can be as 'material' as physical artefacts. We see this as an analytical rather than a philosophical distinction, because the physical and non-physical may well be inseparable in terms of how actors engage in practice. While engagement with 'material' may appear seamless, it may very well be effortful and non-linear. We therefore need more studies into different types of materiality and their impact on strategizing. This means being brave by asking bigger questions and using more innovative methods.

As SAP scholars begin to engage with materiality they need to bear in mind the important distinction between practice as phenomenon, perspective and philosophy (see Orlikowski in this volume). One of the core challenges of completing the material turn in strategy as practice research is going to be which audience it engages when adding materiality to the equation. Understanding the different perspectives on materiality will be critical to formulating ontologically, epistemologically and methodologically sound work. As indicated in the sections above, the perspective taken on materiality influences what is seen as relevant and brings to the fore different aspects of the observed phenomenon. Rather than prescribing 'one best way', narrowing the possibilities for the study of materiality in strategizing, we consider the variety in perspective as fruitful and stimulating. The philosophical traditions of the perspective ought to be respected and well integrated, however, to ensure a coherent argument. If we are able to do this, and conduct strong research on materiality, we may go beyond making significant theoretical contributions and also help narrow the gap between scientific research and the practices in organizational reality, offering real value to practitioners. Indeed, as Heracleous and Jacobs (2008a) aptly demonstrate, artefacts can be a key tool enabling collaboration and the joint development of future strategic endeavours.

In short, we would like to see materiality used not as a label to study objects in organizations but, rather, as a new perspective that allows us to collapse categories, challenge conceptions and shake up fields. This will enhance our ability to make theoretical *and* practical contributions to strategy and beyond.

References

Abdallah, C., and Langley, A. (2014), 'The double edge of ambiguity in strategic planning', *Journal of Management Studies*, 51/2: 235–64.

Aggerholm, H. K., Asmuß, B., and Thomsen, C. (2012), 'The role of recontextualization in the multivocal, ambiguous process of strategizing', *Journal of Management Inquiry*, 21/4: 413–28.

Ashcraft, K. L. (1999), 'Managing maternity leave: a qualitative analysis of temporary executive succession', *Administrative Science Quarterly*, 44/2: 240–80.

Ashcraft, K. L., Kuhn, T. R., and Cooren, F. (2009), 'Constitutional amendments: "materializing" organizational communication', *Academy of Management Annals*, 3/1: 1–64.

Balogun, J., and Johnson, G. (2004), 'Organizational restructuring and middle manager sensemaking', *Academy of Management Journal*, 47/4: 523–49.

Barley, S. R. (1986), 'Technology as an occasion for structuring: evidence from observations of CT scanners and the social order of radiology departments', *Administrative Science Quarterly*, 31/1: 78–108.

Barry, D., and Elmes, M. (1997), 'Strategy retold: toward a narrative view of strategic discourse', *Academy of Management Review*, 22/2: 429–52.

Bechky, B. A. (2003), 'Object lessons: workplace artifacts as representations of occupational jurisdiction', *American Journal of Sociology*, 109/3: 720–52.

Bechtel, R. B., and Churchman, A. (eds.) (2002), *Handbook of Environmental Psychology*. New York: John Wiley.

Bitner, M. J. (1992), 'Servicescapes: the impact of physical surroundings on customers and employees', *Journal of Marketing*, 56/2: 57–71.

Bloch, P. (1995), 'Seeking the ideal form: product design and consumer response', *Journal of Marketing*, 59/1: 16–29.

Boxenbaum, E., and Rouleau, L. (2011), 'New knowledge products as bricolage: metaphors and scripts in organizational theory', *Academy of Management Review*, 36/2: 272–96.

Brown, J. S., and Duguid, P. (2001), 'Knowledge and organization: a social-practice perspective', *Organization Science*, 12/2: 198–213.

Butler, R. (1995), 'Time in organizations: its experience, explanations and effects', *Organization Studies*, 16/6: 925–50.

Çalışkan, K., and Callon, M. (2009), 'Economization, part 1: shifting attention from the economy towards processes of economization', *Economy and Society*, 38/3: 369–98.

——(2010), 'Economization, part 2: a research programme for the study of markets', *Economy and Society*, 39/1: 1–32.

Campbell, D. E. (1979), 'Interior office design and visitor response', *Journal of Applied Psychology*, 64/6: 648–53.

Carlile, P. R. (2002), 'A pragmatic view of knowledge and boundaries: boundary objects in new product development', *Organization Science*, 13/4: 442–55.

——(2004), 'Transferring, translating, and transforming: an integrative framework for managing knowledge across boundaries', *Organization Science*, 15/5: 555–68.

Chia, R., and Holt, R. (2009), *Strategy without Design: The Silent Efficacy of Indirect Action*. Cambridge University Press.

Clegg, S., Cunha, M. P., Rego, A., and Dias, J. (2013), 'Mundane objects and the banality of evil: the sociomateriality of a death camp', *Journal of Management Inquiry*, 22/3: 325–40.

Cooper, R. (1997), 'Relationality', *Organization Studies*, 26/11: 1689–710.

Cooren, F. (2004), 'Textual agency: how texts do things in organizational settings', *Organization*, 11/3: 373–93.

Cooren, F., Taylor, J. R., and Van Every, E. J. (eds.) (2006), *Communication as Organizing: Empirical and Theoretical Explorations in the Dynamic of Text and Conversation*. Mahwah, NJ: Lawrence Erlbaum.

Cornelissen, J., Mantere, S., and Vaara, E. (2014), 'The contraction of meaning: the combined effect of communication, emotions, and materiality on sensemaking in the Stockwell shooting', *Journal of Management Studies*, 51/5: 699–736.

Cornut, F., Giroux, H., and Langley, A. (2012), 'The strategic plan as a genre', *Discourse and Communication*, 6/1: 21–54.

Courpasson, D., Dany, F., and Clegg, S. (2012), 'Resisters at work: generating productive resistance in the workplace', *Organization Science*, 23/3: 801–19.

Cunliffe, A. L., Luhman, J. T., and Boje, D. M. (2004), 'Narrative temporality: implications for organizational research', *Organization Studies*, 25/2: 261–86.

D'Adderio, L. (2008), 'The performativity of routines: theorising the influence of artefacts and distributed agencies on routine dynamics', *Research Policy*, 37/5: 769–89.

(2011), 'Artifacts at the centre of routines: performing the material turn in routines theory', *Journal of Institutional Economics*, 7/S2: 197–230.

Dale, K., and Burrell, G. (2008), *The Spaces of Organisation and the Organisation of Space: Power, Identity and Materiality at Work*. Basingstoke: Palgrave Macmillan.

Dameron, S., Lê, J. K., and LeBaron, C. (2015), 'Materializing strategy and strategizing material: why matter matters', *British Journal of Management*, 26/S1: 1–12.

David, P. (1985), 'Clio and the economics of QWERTY', *American Economic Review*: 75/2: 332–7.

Ewenstein, B., and Whyte, J. (2009), 'Knowledge practices in design: the role of visual representations as "epistemic objects"', *Organization Studies*, 30/1: 7–30.

Fauré, B., and Rouleau, L. (2011), 'The strategic competence of accountants and middle managers in budget making', *Accounting, Organizations and Society*, 36/3: 167–82.

Fechner, G. T. (1860), *Elemente der Psychophysik*, vol. I. Leipzig: Breitkopf und Härtel.

Fenton, C., and Langley, A. (2011), 'Strategy as practice and the narrative turn', *Organization Studies*, 32/9: 1171–96.

Flaherty, M. G., and Fine, G. A. (2001), 'Present, past, and future: conjugating George Herbert Mead's perspective on time', *Time and Society*, 10/1: 147–61.

Gifford, R. (2007), 'Environmental psychology and sustainable development: expansion, maturation, and challenges', *Journal of Social Issues*, 63/1: 199–212.

Gioia, D. A., and Chittipeddi, K. (1991), 'Sensemaking and sensegiving in strategic change initiation', *Strategic Management Journal*, 12/6: 433–48.

Golsorkhi, D., Rouleau, L., Seidl, D., and Vaara, E. (eds.) (2010), *Cambridge Handbook of Strategy as Practice*. Cambridge University Press.

Green, D. M, and Swets, J. A. (1966), *Signal Detection Theory and Psychophysics*. New York: John Wiley.

Healey, M. P., Hodgkinson, G. P., Whittington, R., and Johnson, G. (2015), 'Off to plan or out to lunch? Relations between the design characteristics and outcomes of strategy workshops', *British Journal of Management*, 26(3): 507–528.

Heatherton, T. F., and Wheatley, T. (2010), 'Social neuroscience', in Baumeister, R. F., and Finkel, E. (eds.), *Advanced Social Psychology: The State of the Science*: 575–612. New York: Oxford University Press.

Hellpach, W. (1911), *Geopsyche*. Leipzig: Engelmann.

Heracleous, L., and Jacobs, C. D. (2008a), 'Crafting strategy: the role of embodied metaphors', *Long Range Planning*, 41/3: 309–25.

(2008b), 'Understanding organizations through embodied metaphors', *Organization Studies*, 29/1: 45–78.

Hodgkinson, G. P., and Clarke, I. (2007). 'Conceptual note: exploring the cognitive significance of organizational strategizing: a dual-process framework and research agenda', *Human Relations*, 60/1: 243–55.

Hodgkinson, G. P., and Wright, G. (2002), 'Confronting strategic inertia in a top management team: learning from failure', *Organization Studies*, 23/6: 949–77.

Hoon, C. (2007), 'Committees as strategic practice: the role of strategic conversation in a public administration', *Human Relations*, 60/6: 921–52.

Hutchins, E. (1995), *Cognition in the Wild*. Cambridge, MA: MIT Press.

Jarzabkowski, P., Burke, G., and Spee, P. (2015), 'Constructing spaces for strategizing work: a multimodal perspective', *British Journal of Management*, 26/S1: 26–47.

Jarzabkowski, P., Giulietti, M., Oliveira, B., and Amoo, N. (2013), '"We don't need no education" – or do we? Management education and alumni adoption of strategy tools', *Journal of Management Inquiry*, 22/1: 4–24.

Jarzabkowski, P., Lê, J. K., and Feldman, M. S. (2012), 'Toward a theory of coordinating: creating coordinating mechanisms in practice', *Organization Science*, 23/4: 907–27.

Jarzabkowski, P., Lê, J. K., and Van de Ven, A. H. (2009), 'Doing which work? A practice approach to institutional pluralism', in Lawrence, T., Leca, B., and Suddaby, R. (eds.), *Institutional Work: Actors and Agency in International Studies of Organizations*: 284–316. Cambridge University Press.

(2013), 'Responding to competing strategic demands: how organizing, belonging, and performing paradoxes coevolve', *Strategic Organization*, 11/3: 245–80.

Jarzabkowski, P., LeBaron, C., Phillips, K. and Pratt, M. (2014), 'Call for papers: feature topic: video-based research methods', *Organizational Research Methods*, 17/1: 3–4.

Jarzabkowski, P., and Seidl, D. (2008), 'The role of meetings in the social practice of strategy', *Organization Studies*, 29/11: 1391–426.

Jarzabkowski, P., Spee, P., and Smets, M. (2013), 'Material artifacts: practices for doing strategy with "stuff"', *European Management Journal*, 31/1: 41–54.

Kahneman, D., Treisman, A., and Gibbs, B. J. (1992), 'The reviewing of object files: object-specific integration of information', *Cognitive Psychology*, 24/2: 175–219.

Kaplan, S. (2008), 'Framing contests: strategy making under uncertainty', *Organization Science*, 19/5: 729–52.

—— (2011), 'Strategy and PowerPoint: an inquiry into the epistemic culture and machinery of strategy making', *Organization Science*, 22/2: 320–46.

Kaplan, S., and Orlikowski, W. J. (2013), 'Temporal work in strategy making', *Organization Science*, 24/4: 965–95.

Knorr Cetina, K. (1997), 'Sociality with objects: social relations in postsocial knowledge societies', *Theory, Culture and Society*, 14/4: 1–30.

Knorr Cetina, K., and Preda, A. (eds.) (2012), *The Oxford Handbook of the Sociology of Finance*. Oxford University Press.

Kornberger, M., and Clegg, S. (2011), 'Strategy as performative practice: the case of Sydney 2030', *Strategic Organization*, 9/2: 136–62.

Kuhn, T. (2006), 'A "demented work ethic"and a "lifestyle firm": discourse, identity, and workplace time commitments', *Organization Studies*, 27/9: 1339–58.

—— (2008), 'A communicative theory of the firm: developing an alternative perspective on intra-organizational power and stakeholder relationships', *Organization Studies*, 29/8–9: 1227–54.

Latour, B. (1987), *Science in Action: How to Follow Scientists and Engineers through Society*. Cambridge, MA: Harvard University Press.

Law, J., and Mol, A. (1994), 'Notes on materiality and sociality', *The Sociological Review*, 43/2: 274–94.

Lee, H., and Liebenau, J. (1999), 'Time in organizational studies: towards a new research direction', *Organization Studies*, 20/6: 1035–58.

Leonardi, P. M. (2011), 'When flexible routines meet flexible technologies: affordance, constraint, and the imbrication of human and material agencies', *MIS Quarterly*, 35/1: 147–67.

Leonardi, P., and Barley, S. R. (2010), 'What's under construction here? Social action, materiality, and power in constructivist studies of technology and organizing', *Academy of Management Annals*, 4/1: 1–51.

Levine, A. (1997), *A Geography of Time: The Temporal Misadventures of a Social Psychologist, or How Every Culture Keeps Time Just a Little Bit Differently*. New York: Basic Books.

Li, W., Moallem, I., Paller, K. A., and Gottfried, J. A. (2007), 'Subliminal smells can guide social preferences', *Psychological Science*, 18/12: 1044–9.

Liu, F., and Maitlis, S. (2014), 'Emotional dynamics and strategizing processes: a study of strategic conversations in top team meetings', *Journal of Management Studies*, 52/2: 202–34.

MacKenzie, D. A. (2006), *An Engine, Not a Camera: How Financial Models Shape Markets*. Cambridge, MA: MIT Press.

Mahoney, J. (2000), 'Path dependence in historical sociology', *Time and Society*, 29/4: 507–48.

Maitlis, S. (2005), 'The social processes of organizational sensemaking', *Academy of Management Journal*, 48/1: 21–49.

Maitlis, S., and Lawrence, T. B. (2007), 'Triggers and enablers of sensegiving in organizations', *Academy of Management Journal*, 50/1: 57–84.

McGivern, G., and Dopson, S. (2010), 'Inter-epistemic power and transforming knowledge objects in a biomedical network', *Organization Studies*, 31/12: 1667–86.

Mehrabian, A., and Russell, J. A. (1974), *An Approach to Environmental Psychology*. Cambridge, MA: MIT Press.

Meyer, R. E., Höllerer, M. A., Jancsary, D., and Van Leeuwen, T. (2013), 'The visual dimension in organizing, organization, and organization research: core ideas, current developments, and promising avenues', *Academy of Management Annals*, 7/1: 487–553.

Miettinen, R., and Virkkunen, J. (2005), 'Epistemic objects, artefacts and organizational change', *Organization*, 12/3: 437–56.

Nicolini, D. (2013), *Practice Theory, Work, and Organization: An Introduction*. Oxford University Press.

Nicotera, A. M. (2013), 'Organizations as entitative beings: some ontological implications of communicative constitution', in Robichaud, D., and Cooren, F. (eds.), *Organization and Organizing:*

Materiality, Agency and Discourse: 66–89. New York: Routledge.

Oliver, D., and Roos, D. (2007), 'Beyond text: constructing organizational identity multimodally', *British Journal of Management*, 18/4: 342–58.

Orlikowski, W. J. (2000), 'Using technology and constituting structures', *Organization Science*, 11/4: 404–28.

(2007), 'Sociomaterial practices: exploring technology at work', *Organization Studies*, 28/9: 1435–48.

Orlikowski, W. J., and Scott, S. V. (2008), 'Sociomateriality: challenging the separation of technology, work and organization', *Academy of Management Annals*, 2/1: 433–74.

(2013), 'What happens when evaluation goes online? Exploring apparatuses of valuation in the travel sector', *Organization Science*, 25/3: 868–91.

Parker, B., and Clegg, S. (2006), 'Globalization', in Clegg, S., Hardy, C., Lawrence, T., and Nord, W. (eds.), *The Sage Handbook of Organization Studies*, 2nd edn: 651–74. London: Sage.

Paroutis, S., Franco, L. A., and Papadopoulos, T. (2015), 'Visual interactions with strategy tools: producing strategic knowledge in workshops', *British Journal of Management*, 26/S1: 48–66.

Pedersen, A. R. (2009), 'Moving away from chronological time: introducing the shadows of time and chronotopes as new understandings of "narrative time"', *Organization*, 16/3: 389–406.

Pentland, B. T., Feldman, M. S., Becker, M. C., and Liu, P. (2012), 'Dynamics of organizational routines: a generative model', *Journal of Management Studies*, 49/8: 1484–508.

Pickering, A. (1995), *The Mangle of Practice: Time, Agency, and Science*. University of Chicago Press.

Pinch, T., and Swedberg, R. (2008), *Living in a Material World: Economic Sociology Meets Science and Technology Studies*. Cambridge, MA: MIT Press.

Postill, J. (2010), 'Introduction: theorising media and practice', in Bräuchler, B., and Postill, J. (eds.), *Theorising Media and Practice*: 1–34. Oxford: Berghahn.

Preda, A. (2009), *Framing Finance: The Boundaries of Markets and Modern Capitalism*. University of Chicago Press.

Proshansky, H. M. (1987), 'The field of environmental psychology: securing its future', in Stokols, D., and Altman, I. (eds.), *Handbook of Environmental Psychology*, vol. II: 1467–88. New York: John Wiley.

Putnam, L. L., and Nicotera, A. M. (eds.) (2008), *Building Theories of Organization: The Constitutive Role of Communication*. London: Routledge.

Ransom, S., Hinings, B., and Greenwood, R. (1980), 'The structuring of organizational structure', *Administrative Science Quarterly*, 25/1: 1–17.

Ray, J. L., and Smith, A. D. (2012), 'Using photographs to research organizations: evidence, considerations, and application in a field study', *Organizational Research Methods*, 15/2: 288–315.

Reckwitz, A. (2002), 'Toward a theory of social practices: a development in culturalist theorizing', *European Journal of Social Theory*, 5/2: 243–63.

Robichaud, D., and Cooren, F. (eds.) (2013), *Organization and Organizing: Materiality, Agency and Discourse*. London: Routledge.

Robichaud, D., Giroux, H., and Taylor, J. R. (2004), 'The metaconversation: the recursive property of language as a key to organizing', *Academy of Management Review*, 29/4: 617–34.

Rosenfield, P., Lambert, N. M., and Black, A. (1985), 'Desk arrangement effects on pupil classroom behaviour', *Journal of Educational Psychology*, 77/1: 101–8.

Schatzki, T. R. (2002), *The Site of the Social: A Philosophical Account of the Constitution of Social Life and Change*. University Park: Pennsylvania State University Press.

Schoeneborn, D. (2013), 'The pervasive power of PowerPoint: how a genre of professional communication permeates organizational communication', *Organization Studies*, 34/12: 1777–801.

Scott, W. R. (1995), *Institutions and Organizations*, 2nd edn. Thousand Oaks, CA: Sage.

Scott, S. V., and Orlikowski, W. J. (2012), 'Reconfiguring relations of accountability: materialization of social media in the travel sector', *Accounting, Organizations and Society*, 37/1: 26–40.

(2013), 'Sociomateriality: taking the wrong turning? A response to Mutch', *Information and Organization*, 23/2: 77–80.

Seidl, D. (2007), 'General strategy concepts and the ecology of strategy discourses: a systemic-discursive perspective', *Organization Studies*, 28/2: 197–218.

Sewell, W. H. (1992), 'A theory of structure: duality, agency, and transformation', *American Journal of Sociology*, 98/1: 1–29.

Slack, T., and Hinings, B. (1994), 'Institutional pressures and isomorphic change: an empirical investigation', *Organization Studies*, 15/6: 803–27.

Spee, P., and Jarzabkowski, P. (2009), 'Strategy tools as boundary objects', *Strategic Organization*, 7/2: 223–32.

——— (2011), 'Strategic planning as communicative process', *Organizational Studies*, 32/9: 1217–45.

Stensaker, I., Balogun, J., and Langley, A. (2012), 'Influences on identity work space in the context of major strategic change', paper presented at the twenty-eighth European Group for Organizational Studies colloquium, Helsinki, 7 July.

Step, L., van den Berg, A. E., and de Groot, J. I. M. (2013), *Environmental Psychology*. Oxford: Blackwell.

Stevens, S. S. (1957), 'On the psychophysical law', *Psychological Review*, 64/3: 153–81.

Stigliani, I., and Ravasi, D. (2012), 'Organizing thoughts and connecting brains: material practices and the transition from individual to group-level prospective sensemaking', *Academy of Management Journal*, 55/5: 1232–59.

Stinchcombe, A. L. (1965), 'Social structure and organizations', in March, J. G. (ed.), *Handbook of Organizations*: 142–93. Chicago: Rand McNally.

Stokols, D., and Altman, I. (eds.) (1987), *Handbook of Environmental Psychology*, 2 vols. New York: John Wiley.

Streeck, J., Goodwin, C., and LeBaron, C. (eds.) (2011), *Embodied Interaction: Language and Body in the Material World*. Cambridge University Press.

Suchman, L. A. (2007), *Human–Machine Reconfigurations: Plans and Situated Actions*. Cambridge University Press.

Suddaby, R., Seidl, D., and Lê, J. K. (2013), 'Strategy as practice meets neo-institutional theory', *Strategic Organization*, 11/3: 329–44.

Sundstrom, E., Bell, P. A., Busby, P. L., and Aasmus, C. (1996), 'Environmental psychology 1989–1994', *Annual Review of Psychology*, 47: 482–512.

Taylor, J. R. (2008), 'Communication and discourse: is the bridge language? Response to Jian et al.', *Discourse and Communication*, 2/3: 347–52.

Taylor, J. R., and Van Every, E. J. (2000), *The Emergent Organization: Communication as Site and Surface*. Mahwah, NJ: Lawrence Erlbaum.

Taylor, S., and Spicer, A. (2007), 'Time for space: a narrative review of research on organizational spaces', *International Journal of Management Reviews*, 9/4: 325–46.

Thomas, L., and Ambrosini, V. (2015), 'Materializing strategy: the role of comprehensiveness and management controls in strategy formation in volatile environments', *British Journal of Management*, 26/S1: 105–24.

Treisman, A. M., and Gelade, G. (1980), 'A feature-integration theory of attention', *Cognitive Psychology*, 12/1: 97–136.

Tversky, A., and Kahneman, D. (1974), 'Judgment under uncertainty: heuristics and biases', *Science*, 185: 1124–31.

Weick, K. E. (1995), *Sensemaking in Organizations*. Thousand Oaks, CA: Sage.

Werle, F., and Seidl, D. (2015), 'The layered materiality of strategizing: epistemic objects and the interplay between material artefacts in the exploration of strategic topics', *British Journal of Management*, 26/S1: 67–89.

Wexner, L. B. (1954), 'The degree to which colors (hues) are associated with mood-tones', *Journal of Applied Psychology*, 38/6: 432–5.

Whittington, R. (2006), 'Completing the practice turn in strategy research', *Organization Studies*, 27/5: 613–34.

Whittle, A., and Mueller, F. (2010), 'Strategy, enrolment and accounting: the politics of strategic ideas', *Accounting, Auditing and Accountability Journal*, 23/5: 626–46.

Whittle, A., W. Housley, A. Gilchrist, P. Lenney and F. Mueller (2014). 'Power, politics and organizational communication: an ethnomethodological perspective'. In F. Cooren, E. Vaara, A. Langley and H. Tsoukas (eds), *Language and Communication at Work: Discourse, Narrativity, and Organizing*. Oxford, UK: Oxford University Press.

Wilson, G. D. (1966), 'Arousal properties of red versus green', *Perceptual and Motor Skills*, 23/3: 947–9.

Wolkowitz, C. (2006), *Bodies at Work*. London: Sage.

Wright, A. (2005), 'The role of scenarios as prospective sensemaking devices', *Management Decision*, 43/1: 86–101.

Wright, R. P., Paroutis, S., and Blettner, D. P. (2013), 'How useful are the strategic tools we teach in business schools?', *Journal of Management Studies*, 50/1: 92–125.

Zaheer, S., Albert, S., and Zaheer, A. (1999), 'Time scales and organizational theory', *Academy of Management Review*, 24/4: 725–41.

Zilber, T. B. (2008), 'The work of meanings in institutional processes and thinking', in Greenwood, R., Oliver, C., Sahlin, K., and Suddaby, R. (eds.), *The Sage Handbook of Organizational Institutionalism*: 151–69. London: Sage.

(2012), 'The relevance of institutional theory for the study of organizational culture', *Journal of Management Inquiry*, 21/1: 88–93.

Zundel, M., and Kokkalis, P. (2010), 'Theorizing as engaged practice', *Organization Studies*, 31/9–10: 1209–27.

Zweigenhaft, R. L. (1976), 'Personal space in the faculty office: desk placement and the student–faculty interaction', *Journal of Applied Psychology*, 61/4: 529–32.

Strategy-as-practice research on middle managers' strategy work

LINDA ROULEAU, JULIA BALOGUN and STEVEN W. FLOYD

Advancing research on middle managers, strategy and strategic change is particularly important given the fast-changing strategic contexts in which many organizations operate. Unlike top managers, who are recognised as having formal strategic roles, middle managers' strategizing actions are often informal, occurring across many different organizational subunits throughout the strategy process (Balogun and Johnson 2004). Given that they cannot rely exclusively on formal authority, middle managers need to draw on a diverse set of resources and skills to influence the development of the firm's competitive advantage (Lechner, Frankenberger and Floyd 2010; Huy 2011; Rouleau and Balogun 2011). This raises an interesting question: what do middle managers do in their strategy work and how do they do it? This question speaks directly to the research agenda of the strategy-as-practice perspective (Jarzabkowksi, Balogun and Seidl 2007; Vaara and Whittington 2012). By looking at middle managers' strategy work (Whittington 2006) – or, put differently, at their 'practices' or their 'situated' formal and informal strategic activities – strategy-as-practice researchers studying middle managers are opening the black box of their strategic roles (Mantere 2008). They are consequently providing a better understanding of what kinds of resources and skills it takes to enact these roles.

Since the papers written by Balogun and Johnson (2004; 2005) on middle managers and strategic change, strategy-as-practice research on middle managers has burgeoned (see, for example, Besson and Mahieu 2011; Thomas, Sargent and Hardy 2011; Beck and Plowman 2009; Nielsen 2009; Hoon 2007). This chapter reviews this growing body of research and suggests directions for its future development. The review shows existing research to provide important insights into the

multiple ways middle managers draw on their skills in doing their strategy work. This chapter argues that there remain five main challenges that should be addressed in order to develop the full potential of SAP research on middle managers. First, there is a need for more theoretical depth in drawing on social practice theories for studying middle managers' strategy work. Second, the methodologies used might be more innovative. Third, the lack of coherence and consistency in describing middle manager practices impedes the development of cumulative middle manager strategy-as-practice research. Fourth, research has failed to examine how middle manager practices are embodied and materially mediated. Fifth, middle manager SAP researchers have not put sufficient emphasis on developing critical reflection and discussing the practical relevance of their findings.

The chapter is organized as follows. We start by discussing why it is important to better understand middle managers' strategy work. We then review the existing research on middle managers, strategy and strategic change from a strategy-as-practice perspective. To date, four theoretical lenses have been used by SAP researchers: sensemaking, discursive, political and institutional. Finally, we discuss the five main challenges for middle manager strategy-as-practice research and suggest ways that future research could begin to meet such challenges.

Why study middle managers in strategy as practice?

Middle managers have not always been seen to be as significant strategically as they are now. During the 1980s middle managers became the target of

598

many critics. In a context of delayering and down-sizing, many researchers were even predicting the death of middle managers (Pinsonneault and Kraemer 1997; Dopson and Stuart 1990; 1992). Nevertheless, extensive research (such as Dutton et al. 2001; Floyd and Wooldridge 1992; 1994; 1997) about this period has shown that, even in the traditional hierarchical and bureaucratic organizations common in the 1980s, the importance of the middle manager role was underestimated. Such research was already showing that, in fact, middle managers were a strategic asset, important for their ability to synthesize information and champion strategic ideas, as well as facilitating adaptability and implementing change.

Far from disappearing, middle managers are more present than ever. While the flattening of hierarchies in the 1980s may have reduced the numbers of middle managers, other changes have subsequently increased them. In the more global organizations of today, in which technology and ease of travel have changed spans of control and levels of autonomy, more senior managers are drawn into the middle manager net, becoming middle managers of the corporation rather than autonomous country-based subsidiary managers. Furthermore, there is no longer an archetypal middle manager profile, as there was for the role of middle managers in traditional bureaucratic organizations. As Wooldridge, Schmid and Floyd (2008) suggest, they now form a heterogeneous group that includes, beside the middle manager as a hierarchical position, general line managers (for example, divisional or business unit managers), functional line managers (such as a vice president of marketing) and even project-based managers. Therefore, their roles and functions in strategic change have been largely transformed. The strat-egy-as-practice perspective provides a way of exploring how middle managers are evolving as a professional group along with the evolution of their organizations.

There are many reasons for focusing more atten-tion on the strategic role middle managers play in contemporary organizations. In contemporary organizations middle managers *face a complex set of new issues*, while they are often asked to do more *with less resource* (Balogun 2007; Hassard

and McCann 2004). Since organizations are becoming ever more customer-oriented, *middle managers have to find in their day-to-day activities different ways to accommodate the organizational logic of control with the operational flexibility needed in such contexts* (Sharma and Good 2013; Bryant and Stensaker 2011; Fauré and Rouleau 2011; Ling, Floyd and Baldridge 2005). Not only are they acting as linking pins between top and lower management but, in decentralized and net-worked organizations, they are also frequently interacting with colleagues from other departments and divisions, and even from other organizations (Rouleau and Balogun 2011; Neilsen 2009; Laine and Vaara 2007; Frow, Marginson and Ogden 2005).

While there are many small and medium-sized enterprises, there remain many large organizations that in comparison to their predecessors are flatter, more team-based and more international with greater diversity, changing spans of control and creating a need for management of geographically distant and dispersed teams and team members. Moreover, organizations are becoming pluralistic (Denis, Langley and Rouleau 2007) and their frontiers seem to be more permeable than before (Balogun et al. 2005). Therefore, exploring the work of boundary-spanning middle managers res-onates with the call of Vaara and Whittington (2012) for a better understanding of how practi-tioners are acting through an interlocked web of practices that can be micro- or macro-organizational and even institutional (Frow, Marginson and Ogden 2005; Sharma and Good 2013; Teulier and Rouleau 2013).

The invasion of new communication technolo-gies – such as e-mails, cellphones and the internet – also impacts on how middle managers interact with their superiors, peers and subordinates within and outside the organization. Nowadays middle man-agers interact with virtual teams scattered around the globe, and they also deal with a huge amount of information available on the internet for promoting their projects and retaining the attention of their superiors. Communication technologies transform the ways middle managers play their role in com-plex organizations. Instant messaging, electronic monitoring and filtering tend to complement and/or even sometimes displace the usefulness of informal face-to-face conversation around the coffee machine. All these technical changes are impacting on the way middle managers accomplish their strategic role in organizational settings. The multiple ways through which practitioners are communicating in different contexts are of major importance in SAP research (Bryant and Stensaker 2011; Wooldridge, Schmid and Floyd 2008; Rouleau and Balogun 2011). Since strategy as practice is concerned with the sociomateriality of strategy-making (Jarratt and Stiles 2010; Jarzabkowski, Spee and Smets 2013; Spee and Jarzabkowski 2009), studying middle managers is of great interest, as they are pivotal to the activation of the organizational strategic infrastructure.

Furthermore, middle managers' lack of formal power in comparison to senior managers brings to the surface skills that all strategic players need but are less obvious in those with formal power. Thus, studying them teaches us something about strategic work that is not so obvious (though undoubtedly still needed) in others. As strategy-as-practice research is interested in looking at the skills and activities of practitioners (Jarzabkowski, Balogun and Seidl 2007), research on middle managers is essential for better understanding the social construction of the organizational world. In their daily activities, middle managers have to meet conflicting demands and respond to contradictory logics (Bryant and Stensaker 2011; Lüscher and Lewis 2008). To resolve different organizational and managerial paradoxes, they are developing more or less intentionally discursive and political strategies and tactics that need to be highlighted (Balogun et al. 2005; Hope 2010). Consequently, studying middle managers in SAP research appears to be a way to highlight the essence of managerial work in complex organizations.

As part of the developing strategy-as-practice research agenda, it is also necessary to understand more about the nature of middle manager agency, since current research ignores what enables or constrains middle managers from fulfilling role expectations. Mantere (2008) identifies particular enablers of middle management agency, but also finds that, for middle manager agency to take place, reciprocal actions by top management is needed for the fulfilment of roles. Similarly, Mantere and Vaara (2008) reveal that certain discourses impede or promote participation in strategy work by middle managers. Again, as organizations change, and the nature of middle managers and their relationships with others – particularly senior managers – also changes, then what impedes or promotes their agency and participation may also change. Strategy as practice is a particularly beneficial lens for such research, since it encourages a focus on both agency and structure, by considering not just the strategic work of strategy practitioners but also the practices guiding and fuelling this activity (Mantere 2005).

To sum up, given that middle managers play a central role in the strategy-making process, SAP research is interested in the multiple ways in which middle managers enact their roles, and how they accomplish them on a daily basis. Put differently, those researching middle managers and strategy as practice are interested in opening the black box of middle manager strategic roles in order to look at their 'practices' or their 'situated' formal and informal strategic activities, accomplished through their daily tasks in different contexts and at different levels of the organization. This is why in this chapter we talk in terms of middle managers' strategy work (Whittington 2006) instead of middle managers' strategic role. We next review the research to date on strategy-as-practice middle manager research, to see how this research has until now answered these questions and what contributions it has provided since the beginning of the 2000s.

Researching middle managers through four lenses

Middle managers' strategy work is complex and requires them to draw on numerous relational skills as they seek to maintain their pivotal or boundary role between departments, divisions and even organizations. To study what middle managers do when they are strategizing, strategy-as-practice researchers have until now used four theoretical lens: the sensemaking lens (Table 34.1), the discursive lens (Table 34.2), the political lens

	Theoretical definitions and influences	Methods (type of strategic change)	Types of middle managers (relations with others)	Processes, practices and skills
Balogun (2003)	Sensemaking and change (a range of activities for interpreting the strategic change intent)	Diaries, interviews, focus group – longitudinal case study (organizational restructuring)	Middle managers in a hierarchical position (lateral and downward)	Undertaking personal change Keeping the business going Helping others through change Implementing change through departments
Balogun and Johnson (2004)	Sensemaking and change (process through which people create and maintain an intersubjective world)	Diaries, interviews, focus group – longitudinal case study (organizational restructuring)	Middle managers in a hierarchical position (lateral interactions)	Sensemaking schema development (moving from 'shared' to 'clustered' and finally 'recomposed' sensemaking)
Balogun and Johnson (2005)	Sensemaking and change (process referring to the level of intersubjective face-to-face conversations and interactions)	Diaries, interviews, focus group – longitudinal case study (organizational restructuring)	Middle managers in a hierarchical position (lateral interactions)	Middle managers' sensemaking processes leads to both intended and unintended change outcomes (two levels of sensemaking)
Rouleau (2005)	Sensemaking and knowledge (a set of micro-practices anchored in implicit and contextual knowledge)	Organizational ethnography, interviews – longitudinal case study (strategic reorientation)	Selling directors (organizational boundary, customers)	Translating the orientation Over-coding the strategy Disciplining the client Justifying the change
Ling, Floyd and Baldridge (2005)	Issue-selling and cultural embeddedness (directing top managers' attention to issues and helping them to understand these issues)	Extensive literature review	Local subsidiary managers (upward relations with multinational managers)	Issue-selling practices are embedded in national cultures (16 propositions are elaborated)
Lüscher and Lewis (2008)	Sensemaking, change and paradox (efforts to interpret and create coherence)	Action research (organizational restructuring)	Production managers (downward to employees)	Paradox of performing, belonging and organizing
Beck and Plowman (2009)	Sensemaking and unusual events (assigning meanings to events collectively)	Extensive literature review (referring to the space shuttle Columbia disaster)	Middle managers in a hierarchical position (multi-level and multi-stage)	Encourage divergence in interpretations during early stages of the change and blend and synthesize the divergent interpretations during later stages
Smith, Plowman and Duchon (2010)	Sensegiving and values (everyday effort to influence and shape the meaning constructions of others)	In-depth interviews and on-site visits of 11 manufacturing companies (strategic continuity)	Successful plants managers (downward with employees)	Valuing people Valuing openness Valuing being positive Valuing being part of a larger community
Rouleau and Balogun (2011)	Strategic sensemaking (an ability to craft and share a message in order to influence others)	In-depth interviews (organizational restructuring) and focus groups (organizational change)	A production manager and a coordinator (upward and downwards) A functional line manager and a project manager (lateral and upward interactions)	Performing conversation Setting the scene

Table 34.2 Strategy-as-practice research on middle managers: a discursive lens

	Theoretical definitions and influences	Methods (type of strategic change)	Types of middle managers (relations with others)	Processes, practices and skills
Hoon (2007)	Strategic conversations (discussions on strategic issues and informal interactions around committees)	Management meetings, interviews and documents – longitudinal case study (radical change)	Middle managers in a hierarchical position (upward and downward)	Generating an understanding of the issue; Aligning towards an issue; Making pre-arrangements
Nielsen (2009)	'Talk-in-interaction' (possibility for creating a context for the employees to manoeuvre in)	Department meetings in 5 firms (15 meetings recorded and others); 6 excerpts are analysed (organizational change)	Department heads (downward)	Labelling; Categorizing; Introducing new words; Making conversational repairs
Davis, Allen and Dibrell (2012)	Strategy messages (means for transmitting ideas about the organizational position in the market place)	Questionnaire to top, middle and boundary personnel (change in customer services)	Middle managers in a hierarchical position (multi-level)	The influence middle managers exercise on boundary personnel's strategic awareness depends on the clarity of their messages
Besson and Mahieu (2011)	Strategic dialogue (managers' discussions in situations of exploration) and controversies (discursive processes related to competing views of change)	Action research – longitudinal case study (radical change)	Middle managers responsible for operational units (in interaction in committee with top managers)	Becoming a strategist entails the construction of new systems of roles and identities, along with development of appropriate dialogue modes; Developing a new strategy necessitates transformating the organization's social fabric
Thomas, Sargent and Hardy (2011)	Dialogue (communicative interactions in which meanings are debated, contested and/or agreed upon by participants)	Workshop observation, interviews and documents – longitudinal case study (organizational restructuring)	Middle managers in a hierarchical position (in interaction in committee with top managers)	A set of 13 communicative practices (inviting, affirming, clarifying and so on) from which two coexisting dialogue patterns deduced: a generative and a degenerative pattern
Fauré and Rouleau (2011)	Conversations (strategic competence referring to the knowledge of the strategy drawn in daily activities)	Conversation analysis of 3 budgeting conversations – longitudinal field study (introduction of a partnership strategy)	Middle managers and accountants (lateral interactions)	Invoking the usefulness of numbers to activate local projects; Constructing the acceptability of numbers to report them to external partners; Authorizing the plausibility of numbers to reconcile local contingencies and global coherence

(Table 34.3) and the institutional lens (Table 34.4). We use these lenses to synthesize the SAP middle manager research in this review.

The sensemaking lens

Following the foundational work of Floyd and Wooldrige (1997), as well as that of Dutton and her colleagues (2001), much strategy-as-practice middle manager research has adopted a sensemaking perpsective. This research draws on a Weickian view of sensemaking and explores how middle managers contribute to sensemaking in and of strategic change in two different ways (Table 34.1). The first group of studies explores processes of sensemaking accompanying strategic change, and examines how middle managers contribute to the recreation of order and the stabilization of equivocal views of strategic change over time (Balogun and Johnson 2004; 2005; Beck and Plowman 2009). The second group of studies explores sensemaking as a set of activities (Balogun 2003; Ling, Floyd and Baldridge 2005), micro-practices (Rouleau 2005) and skills and efforts (Rouleau and Balogun 2011; Lüscher and Lewis 2008; Smith, Plowman and Duchon 2010). These studies seek to explain how middle managers contribute to the creation of a collective sense of shared meanings and interpretations through a focus on what they do in terms of activities and practices. While the authors generally do not make any formal distinction between sensemaking and sensegiving, some studies are nevertheless more concerned than others as to the ways middle managers give sense and influence others (Ling, Floyd and Baldridge 2005; Rouleau 2005; Smith et al. 2009; Rouleau and Balogun 2011).

Several of these studies combine sensemaking with literature on organizational change (Balogun 2003; Balogun and Johnson 2004; 2005; Lüscher and Lewis 2008). This is because of the fact that middle managers were studied in a context mainly related to significant restructuring projects. Except for two papers presenting a set of propositions and arguments based on extensive literature reviews (Beck and Plowman 2009; Ling, Floyd and Baldridge 2005), only the study done by Smith et al. (2009) has been conducted in a context of strategic continuity. Most of the empirical papers were drawn from longitudinal studies using narrative methods such as interviews, diaries and focus groups. Surprisingly, only two studies are based on organizational ethnography and action research (Rouleau 2005; Lüscher and Lewis 2008). Even though the middle managers studied under the sensemaking lens seem to be traditional middle managers as defined by their hierarchical position in large organizations, they nevertheless point to the importance of middle manager lateral and multi-level relations when they are making sense of change, rather than exclusively focusing on their upward and downward relationships during the change.

In terms of research outcomes, the strategy-as-practice research on middle managers and sensemaking has highlighted patterns in the process by which middle managers make sense of a change. For example, Balogun and Johnson (2004) identify a sensemaking development process that goes from 'shared' (before the change) to 'fractured and clustered' (during the change) and finally ends up as 'recomposed' (after the change) sensemaking. More recently, Beck and Plowman (2009) have shown how middle managers encourage divergence in interpretations across hierarchical levels during the early stages of a strategic change yet, during the later stages, tend to blend and synthesize divergent interpretations.

Research that explores the activities, micro-practices and skills of middle managers in interpreting and diffusing strategic change provides empirical findings related to what Rouleau (2005) calls the 'third-order explanation of sensemaking' in three ways. First, sensemaking is locally and culturally embedded, drawing on tacit knowledge (Ling, Floyd and Baldrige 2005; Rouleau 2005). Second, middle managers' strategic sensemaking depends on their capacity to deal with paradoxical demands related to their organizational position and that of others as well as the tasks that they need to accomplish during strategic change (Balogun 2003; Lüscher and Lewis 2008). Third, strategic sensemaking is related to the performance

Table 34.3 Strategy-as-practice research on middle managers: a political lens

	Theoretical definitions and influences	Methods (type of strategic change)	Types of middle managers (relations with others)	Processes, practices and skills
Balogun et al. (2005)	Power is relational, and knowledgeable agents are constituted by networks as well as they mobilize resources, processes and meaning for acting upon them	Diaries, focus groups, interviews (organizational change)	Change agents (intra-organizational boundary and multi-level)	Adjusting management systems Aligning agendas selling Engaging in stage management Gathering intelligence Managing up
Laine and Vaara (2007)	Power as discursive struggle over subjectivity	Participant observation, interviews, documents – longitudinal case study (strategic development)	Middle managers in a hierarchical position (upward and lateral influence)	Middle managers resist discursive hegemony by initiating a strategic discourse of their own (an entrepreneurial discourse) to create room for manoeuvring in controversial situations
Smith et al. (2009)	Political skill as interpersonal style combining social astuteness, ability to relate well, network ability and apparent sincerity	In-depth interviews and on-site visits of 11 manufacturing companies (strategic continuity)	Successful plant managers (downward with employees)	Effective plant managers use their political skills and the unobtrusive and systemic power to achieve both affective and substantive outcomes
McCabe (2010)	Power and resistance relations; power exercised is ambiguous and contradictory in that it both supports and disrupts managerial purposes	Interviews and documents – longitudinal case study in financial services (re-engineering and customer service change)	Middle managers in a hierarchical position (upward resistance)	The ambiguities, contradictions and uncertainties involved in strategizing illuminate the possibility of interrogating and challenging claims to power; ambiguity also has the potential to amplify conflict and resistance
Vickers and Fox (2010)	Power as an attribute of networks, not centrally diffused but arising in interactions (enrolment and counter-enrolment through unofficial networks)	Self-ethnography – longitudinal case study (post-acquisition strategy)	Human resource managers (lateral and multi-level interactions)	The unofficial network of middle managers effectively changed the top management strategy for the benefit of the organization
Hope (2010)	Power as resource, process and the management of meaning in creating a perception of legitimacy	Diaries and interviews – longitudinal case study (organizational change)	Heads of sections and department heads (downward relations)	Disobeying management Handpicking loyal and skilled personnel Taking control over staffing project Placing trusted man in strategic position Taking control over the information Developing a memo for justifying reasons and positions Manipulating the flow of information Etc.
Bryant and Stensaker (2011)	Exploration of the negotiation processes through which middle managers manage competing roles	Theoretical paper (literature review on middle managers' competing roles and presentation of theory of negotiated order)	Hierarchical middle managers (multidirectional)	Using negotiated order theory for studying middle managers involves an understanding of the negotiation contexts in which middle managers are engaged and an understanding of their negotiations at three levels : new ways of working, negotiation within the self and negotiation of boundaries

Table 34.4 Strategy-as-practice research on middle managers: an institutional lens

	Theoretical definitions and influences	Methods (type of strategic change)	Types of middle managers (type of relations with others)	Processes, practices and skills
Kellog (2009)	Institutional change and social movement literatures	Observation, interviews, documents – 2 longitudinal case studies (change under a new regulation)	Middle manager surgeons (mutual influence)	In one hospital, 'relational spaces' enabled middle manager reformers and their subordinates to change the daily practice targeted by the new regulation, but not in the other
Bjerregaard (2011)	Institutional theory and Bourdieu	Interviews and participant observation – 2 longitudinal case studies (introduction of a new public management strategy)	Middle managers in a hierarchical position (downward and lateral relations)	Differential institutional orders are maintained by middle managers and front-line staff despite exposure to the same demands
Sharma and Good (2013)	Institutional work, institutional logics and sensemaking	A conceptual paper for explaining how middle managers managed the tensions between social and profit logics	Middle managers in a hierarchical position (relations with external stakeholders)	Reflexivity, sensemaking and sensegiving based on middle managers' capacities for integrative, emotional and behavioural complexity
Teulier and Rouleau (2013)	Scandinavian institutional school of translation and sensemaking	Video-ethnography, interviews and documents – longitudinal case study (the introduction of a 3D software platform)	Technical directors (external sectoral stakeholders and software publishers)	Four 'translation spaces' and a set of editing practices (framing problems, staging the collaboration, adjusting their vision, materializing the change, selling the change, speaking for the technology, stabilizing meanings and taking absent stakeholders into account)

of discursive skills by middle managers in the course of their action (Rouleau and Balogun 2011, Smith, Plowman and Duchon 2010).

By focusing on middle managers' interactions with others, this body of research from a sensemaking perspective has indubitably provided us with a deeper understanding of the strategizing activities, practices and skills of middle managers. Nevertheless, this research presents a rather neutral view of sensemaking (Mills, Thurlow and Mills 2010), underestimating issues of power and knowledge at play as middle managers, in and through their relations with others, try to make sense of change in their organizations. Moreover, research interested in the concrete set of activities and abilities through which middle managers make sense of change provides us with empirical findings that seem to be quite specific and diverse from one study to another.

The discursive lens

The discursive perspective is rooted in Westley's (1990) seminal paper, from a quarter of a century ago, on middle managers' strategic conversations. Strategy-as-practice researchers who have adopted a discursive lens (Table 34.2) are interested in the discrete talk and communicative actions of middle managers in meetings and conversations to do with strategy development and change (Hoon 2007; Nielsen 2009; Davis, Allen and Dibrell 2012; Besson and Mahieu 2011; Thomas, Sargent and Hardy 2011; Fauré and Rouleau 2011). These studies draw on diverse discursive metaphors, such as conversations (Hoon 2007; Nielsen 2009; Fauré and Rouleau 2011), messages (Davis, Allen and Dibrell 2012) and dialogue (Besson and Mahieu 2011; Thomas, Sargent and Hardy 2011), for describing the middle managers' communication-based interactions. Conversations, messages and dialogue are seen as strategic in the sense that middle managers draw on these communicative practices to achieve their goals through discussions with others.

Most of the strategy-as-practice research on middle managers using a discursive lens has been conducted through longitudinal studies of organizational and strategic change. For example, Hoon (2007) and Besson and Mahieu (2011) have targeted the meetings-based interactions between top and middle managers in order to show the importance of formal and informal interactions for reframing the strategy and building new identities. While these studies are mainly presented in the form of case studies, in two other studies one can also find variants of conversation analysis using a small number of excerpts in order to depict specific communicative practices (Nielsen 2009; Fauré and Rouleau 2011). These fine-grained conversation analyses allow the researchers to show how, through conversations, middle managers do strategic leadership and reframe understandings of their roles and those of others. Contrary to SAP studies on middle managers' sensemaking that mainly focus on traditional middle managers engaged in downward and lateral relations, research adopting a discursive lens has a strong interest in exploring the verbal negotiations between middle managers and their superiors during particular strategy episodes, such as meetings related to change.

The strategy-as-practice research on middle managers adopting the discursive lens describes a diverse set of communicative practices that seem to be central to the accomplishment of middle managers' strategy work. Even though the studies show a high level of variation, the communicative practices identified reveal the importance in middle managers' strategy work of choosing words and negotiating them (Nielsen 2009; Besson and Mahieu 2011; Hoon 2007). The choice of words is part of the set of middle managers' relational skills, however, and is not entirely intentional (Fauré and Rouleau 2011). Rather than being simply sold or transmitted, the communicative practices of middle managers are debated and contested as much by top managers and subordinates

in the course of verbal exchanges. According to Thomas, Sargent and Hardy (2011), this process may or may not be generative for accomplishing strategic change.

Overall, these studies adopting a discursive lens seem to be poorly anchored in language or other practice theory. Most of them offer a rather objectivist view of language and communication. The notions of conversation, message and dialogue are often used with managerial categories – for example, time or agenda of dialogue, sources and efficacy of messages, budgeting conversations – rather than being constructed and used as a specific perspective on communication and language. In this regard, the studies by Thomas, Sargent and Hardy (2011) and Fauré and Rouleau (2011) are exceptions. They adopt, respectively, a Foucauldian and a Giddensian view of communication, but they both deal with it as a resisting and competent practice.

The political lens

Middle manager research has identified the importance of their political behaviours (see, for example, Burgelman 1983; Floyd and Wooldridge 1997) to the evolution of strategy. Middle managers do not have the formal authority to impose their views, as is the case for top managers. Therefore, they constantly have to influence others and negotiate with them in their strategy work (Table 34.3). Strategy-as-practice research on middle managers adopts two broad views on power: the relational and the control-resistance perspectives. In the relational view of power, middle managers are considered as autonomous or knowledgeable subjects, able to mobilize resources, processes and meanings on the basis of the room for manoeuvre provided by the context in which they interact (Balogun et al. 2005; Smith et al. 2009; Hope 2010; Bryant and Stensaker 2011). In the control-resistance view of power, middle managers achieve their goals and fulfil their interests less by using the available resources and meanings related to their hierarchical positions and more by formally or informally resisting the official discourse of strategic change (Laine and Vaara 2007; McCabe 2010; Vickers and Fox 2010).

Hope (2010) explores how middle managers in an insurance company seek to influence strategic change outcomes through the political management of meanings. Adopting a negotiated order approach, Bryant and Stensaker (2011) look at how middle managers navigate between competing roles on a day-to-day basis, and propose a framework for better understanding how they negotiate these roles in their work, within the self and when intervening at the multiple organizational boundaries. Balogun *et al.* (2005) show how middle managers exercise their power as boundary-shakers in the networks they belong to. Vickers and Fox (2010) provide a fine-grained analysis of the resistance, enrolment and counter-enrolment practices of an unofficial network of managers, who used a formal human resource management programme to resist the official strategy of the firm. The critical approach taken by Laine and Vaara (2007) highlights how middle managers and organizational members effectively resisted new top-down strategy, subjectively distancing themselves by drawing on competing discourses. McCabe (2010) shows that power is exercised in contradictory ways that support middle managers' initiatives and, at the same time, create possibilities for resistance.

To explore the political side of middle managers' work, strategy-as-practice researchers have until now drawn on a variety of theoretical definitions of power and politics, ranging from negotiated order (Smith *et al.* 2009; Hope 2010; Bryant and Stensaker 2011) to network (Balogun *et al.* 2005; Vickers and Fox 2010) and critical theories (Laine and Vaara 2007; McCabe 2010). Not surprisingly, the SAP research on middle managers from a political perspective draws on similar methodologies used by researchers associated with the sensemaking and the discursive lenses. The collection of interview data in longitudinal studies of change remains the standard. Strategy-as-practice research on middle managers adopting a political lens studies middle managers occupying heterogeneous positions in organizations for whom lateral and multi-levels relations are central.

In terms of outcomes, the SAP research on middle managers under the political lens provides us with an understanding of a set of political

activities (Balogun *et al.* 2005; Hope 2010), skills (Smith *et al.* 2009) and resistance practices (Laine and Vaara 2007; Vickers and Fox 2010; McCabe 2010). These studies show how middle managers are active movers, and even shakers, of networks. We now know that their power depends on their interpersonal skills and their capacity to negotiate their competing roles during the strategic change. The main outcome is related to the rehabilitation of middle managers' resistance, however. Contrary to the general belief that middle managers are resistant to change, the research on middle managers and strategy as practice adopting a political lens shows us that their resistance might also have positive organizational effects.

Overall, the research still largely takes a managerial view of strategy and power, as if these are essentially the prerogative of senior management, thus leaving hidden how inequality and discrimination are perpetuated through the dominant strategic discourse. Even in the two critical papers in our sample (Laine and Vaara 2007; McCabe 2010), power as domination and discipline is not the pillar of the analysis. It is important to note that these critical papers are not explicitly designed as middle management research. In these studies, middle managers represent only an organizational group with divergent interests, instead of being studied under a middle manager perspective.

The institutional lens

Nowadays middle managers increasingly have to be involved in inter-organizational collaboration with various stakeholders in order to position their organization in a fast-changing environment (Teulier and Rouleau 2013). In so doing, they contribute to change in their institutional environment – or, put differently, we can also say that they are doing some kind of institutional work (Lawrence and Suddaby 2006). The classic study in strategic management by Daniels, Johnson and de Chernatony (2002), about institutional influences on senior and middle managers' mental models of competition, was in some ways a precursor to the middle manager research from the institutional lens (Table 34.4). Research on middle managers' institutional practices follows the recent calls to build bridges between institutional theory and strategy-as-practice research (Vaara and Whittington 2012; Suddaby, Seidl and Lê 2013).

To our knowledge, there are to date only four strategy-as-practice studies on middle managers under this lens (Kellog 2009; Bjerregaard 2011; Sharma and Good 2013; Teulier and Rouleau 2013), and so the review of these studies is by necessity briefer than the others. While the first two studies examine the role of middle managers in implementing institutional change in two health care organizations, the other two were conducted in the private sector and look at the relationships between middle managers and their external stakeholders. At the organizational level, the existence of relational spaces in which middle managers construct new identities with others (Kellog 2009) and their previous experiences with the institutional logics embodied in habitus (Bjerregaard 2011) explain why some organizations are more successful in implementing institutional change at the organizational level. At the inter-organizational level, it is either by maintaining the hybridity between the profit and social institutional logics during the implementation of corporate social initiatives (Sharma and Good 2013) or by strategically using sets of editing practices that are specific to the different 'translation spaces' in which they are involved that middle managers make sense of the institutional change (Teulier and Rouleau 2013).

Besides institutional theory influences, these studies draw on social movement theory (Kellog 2009), Bourdieu (Bjerregaard 2011) and sensemaking (Sharma and Good 2013; Teulier and Rouleau 2013). Again, longitudinal cases studies based on observation, interviews and documents are the main methods used, though Teulier and Rouleau (2013) innovate in drawing on video-ethnography data. While the papers by Bjerregaard (2011) and Sharma and Good (2013) look at traditional middle managers in hierarchical positions, the two others propose a larger view of middle managers having higher status and more resource access (Kellog 2009; Teulier and Rouleau 2013). For most of them, however, middle managers interact with others in a multidirectional way.

Research within the institutional lens draws attention to the broader contexts in which middle managers are intervening, rather than focusing analysis on their managerial actions and interactions, as we have seen in papers belonging to the other lenses. Therefore, institutional studies present a richer view of middle manager organizational activities and practices. Not only are middle managers playing their managerial role, they also have to act in different kinds of interactive 'spaces', in which their capacities and competences are strategic for answering the institutional demands of their environment.

Given the small number of strategy-as-practice studies on middle managers that use an institutional lens, it is difficult to criticize their content. Their main challenges remain the theoretical difficulties of linking the macro and the micro levels of analysis when looking at what middle managers do in practice. Supportive theory and clear definitions of institutional work will certainly be needed for advancing research on middle managers under the institutional lens.

Challenges and a future agenda

Without any doubt, strategy-as-practice research on middle managers now constitutes a lively and burgeoning sub-stream on which we can build cumulatively. At first glance, this review reveals the importance of the sensemaking lens, even though other theoretically informed approaches have been added over time. It also confirms the fact that middle managers constitute a heterogeneous group, formed not only by managers in traditionally placed hierarchical roles but also by managers in more diverse, mediating positions. This transformation of middle managers' organizational positions invites us to pay specific attention to their boundary practices, and specifically when interacting with external stakeholders. Moreover, this review indicates that we still know little about how middle managers deal with paradoxes and their competing roles in fast-changing environments. There is at least one study in each of our four lenses above that explores this, but more needs to be done (Lüscher and Lewis 2008;

Mc Cabe 2010; Thomas, Sargent and Hardy 2011; Bryant and Stensaker 2011; Sharma and Good 2013).

Nevertheless, five challenges facing SAP middle manager research fall out of this review. First, our review shows that there is little research on strategy as practice and middle managers that explicitly adopts a practice theory approach, and, as a result, many of the studies take a managerialist approach to the study of the strategic work of middle managers. Second, the review shows that the methodologies used could be more innovative, using alternatives to longitudinal case studies and interviews. Third, there is a lack of coherence and consistency in describing middle manager strategic practices, preventing the drawing together of research to develop a cumulative perspective. Fourth, research to date has under-examined how the practices described are materially mediated and embodied, even though they have to deal with new technological ways of communicating and interacting with others. Fifth, middle manager strategy-as-practice research has not put sufficient emphasis on developing a critical reflection and discussing the practical relevance of the findings.

Taking a social practice approach

In line with the practice turn (Schatzki 2011), strategy as practice involves a recognition that the practice of strategy occurs in a broader context (Balogun et al. 2014). Strategizing comprises those 'actions, interactions and negotiations of multiple actors and the *situated practices* that they draw upon in accomplishing that activity' (Jarzabkowski, Balogun and Seidl 2007: 8, emphasis added). As argued above, however, existing research on middle managers' strategic work and roles still largely takes a managerial view of strategy, thus leaving hidden, for example, issues such as how inequality and discrimination are perpetuated through the dominant strategic discourse, and how strategists are shaped by and shape the social and economic institutions in which they are embedded. Of course, there are exceptions (Bjerregaard 2011); Kellog 2009; McCabe 2010; Lüscher and Lewis 2008; Rouleau 2005; Thomas, Sargent and Hardy 2011). Mantere (2008) explicitly sets

out to explore the influence of role expectations on the work of middle managers, both their own and that of their senior managers, thereby starting to bring together considerations of how the strategic work of middle managers is embedded in a wider structure (here, role expectations).

Accordingly, there is more to be done by adopting social-practice-based and discourse approaches. As the foregoing discussion suggests, part of what is needed involves incorporating other social theories (de Certeau, Latour, Bakhtine and so forth) and a dose of epistemological pluralism. A fuller picture of middle manager strategy practice, for example, should go more deeply into the fine-grained analysis of their practices while connecting them with economic, social and environmental outcomes. This may require the incorporation of ideas from social sciences domains, as well as organizational economics and governance theory that have heretofore been seen as distant from, or even antagonistic towards, the strategy-as-practice agenda. Pursuing this opportunity will require an epistemological dialogue and, ultimately, a translation of such constructs into epistemologically consistent terms.

Increasing the range of methods

The above review reveals the extent to which current work relies on interviews, and, in fact, retrospective interviews in particular. More work is needed that, for example, observes middle managers in action or draws them in as co-researchers. Johnson, Melin and Whittington argued back in 2003, in the first special journal issue on strategy as practice, that most research followed a 'recipe' founded in the process tradition, based on case study and ethnographic research – approaches with data collection centred on interviews, observation and documentation. This is even true of much strategy-as-practice research on middle managers. The calls by Balogun, Huff and Johnson (2003) for innovation in methods to get closer to practice, in order to encourage greater self-reflection from respondents, have largely been ignored when researching middle managers.

Balogun, Huff and Johnson (2003) in particular call for the use of interactive discussion groups such as focus groups, self-report methods such as diaries, and practitioner research in which respondents become collaborators. Some have used such methods for researching middle managers (Balogun and Johnson 2004; 2005; Hope 2010). Others have called for the use of narratives of work life stories (Rouleau 2010). These methods remain rare, however. Other kinds of self-reports, such as personality instruments, would be useful in building an understanding of how constructs such as core self-evaluation and self-confidence, which have been studied among top managers, relate to middle manager willingness to engage in risky practices, such as those associated with resistance towards induced strategic change. Even a method such as repertory grid technique (Huff 1990) and the construction of so-called mental maps would be useful for a better understanding of how middle managers think about the institutional contexts within which strategy practices are embedded. In sum, recognizing that practices are thoughtful phenomena implies a search for links between the inner and outer worlds of middle manager strategy praxis.

Methodological innovation has recently occurred in strategy-as-practice research, through the use of video and video-ethnography in particular. This is allowing researchers to get closer to the practice of strategy by middle managers (Teulier and Rouleau 2013). Such methods position the researcher as interpreter, however, and do not encourage greater reflection by practitioners themselves. Furthermore, methodological innovation needs to extend beyond data collection. Langley and Abdallah (2011) explore templates in qualitative strategy research and reveal how much research either follows the Gioia method (in-depth longitudinal single-site case studies) or the Eisenhardt method (multiple case studies). Both these approaches come with particular epistemological foundations and a specific logic, which influences not just how data are collected but also how they are then analysed and presented. These templates become 'iron cages' and a straightjacket in themselves, as others seek to emulate approaches that have apparently led to successful publication. There are alternatives for analysis, presentation and write-up in middle manager research, however, such as the use of vignettes (Balogun et al. 2005; Rouleau and Balogun 2011).

Improving coherence and consistency

The third challenge is a lack of coherence and consistency in strategy-as-practice research on middle managers, preventing the drawing together of research to develop cumulative SAP research on middle managers. As seen in the literature review, research generally identifies diverse sets of practices and activities that are generally very specific to the middle managers in the context studied. As we have been able to group these studies through four lenses, there are certainly some communalities or consistency between them. Nevertheless, there is a need for future strategy-as-practice research on middle managers not only to take the position of opening the black box of their roles but also to make a specific effort to build on existing knowledge about them. Moreover, there is a need to advance our knowledge of the concepts developed by strategy-as-practice researchers related to middle managers' strategy work, such as, for example, strategic conversations (Hoon 2007), discursive competence (Rouleau and Balogun 2011), the paradoxes of performing, belonging and organizing (Lüscher and Lewis 2008) and generative dialogue (Thomas, Sargent and Hardy 2011). These notions might help strengthening the coherence and consistency challenges that a research stream faces as it grows (Rouleau 2013).

Another way to increase the coherence and consistency of strategy-as-practice research on middle managers is, according to Balogun, Huff and Johnson (2003), to draw together multiple data coming from diverse in-depth case studies. To our knowledge, though, there is only one example in the SAP field in which different research projects are drawn together to throw light on an aspect of strategy work, and, coincidentally, it is a middle manager study (see Rouleau and Balogun 2011). The multiplicity of theoretical approaches does make it hard to draw together existing studies to make a coherent statement about particular aspects of middle manager strategic work. On the other hand, Rouleau and Balogun (2011) show that, even when data are collected through different methods, it is then possible to bring together the two different data sets to throw light on a common phenomenon. This does require collaboration between researchers, however, and not just the reading of each other's work. We would suggest that, given the number of data sets that now exist on middle managers, drawing these data sets together to synthesize conclusions about the nature of middle manager strategic practice could be a valuable endeavour for researchers in the field.

Paying attention to sociomateriality and embodiment

Building on the practice turn, strategy as practice is also concerned with sociomateriality – how tools and locations, for example, configure strategic interactions between bodies and things (Balogun *et al.* 2014; Jarzabkowski, Spee and Smets 2013). This challenge is being taken up in the field more generally, but it is still absent from middle manager research, although as Balogun *et al.* (2014: 29) point out, it is not that sociomateriality is absent from existing studies but, rather, that it has not been the focus. Research on middle managers and sensemaking, for example, reveals the significance of material items and practices. Rouleau's (2005) middle managers were working with clothes from a fashion range when seeking to engage and discipline their customers. Rouleau and Balogun (2011) reveal the role of, for example, room arrangements and gestures in middle manager discursive competence.

We still need to do more to understand how middle manager strategic practices are embodied and materially mediated, however, and how this situation differs – if it does – for middle managers as opposed to more senior managers. In addition, we should explore how middle manager emotions, and their display, influence their strategic practice, though the exploration of emotions and strategy work remains in its infancy (see, for example, Liu and Maitlis 2014). Such research will simultaneously advance what we know about middle managers' sensemaking and their discursive, political and even institutional practices.

Encouraging critical reflection

We point out above that a criticism of much research on middle managers, and strategy-as-practice research in general, is that it does not encourage reflection and engagement by the participants involved. As Ketokivi and Mantere (2010) suggest, the goal of researchers in the organizational sciences is scientifically informed prescription, and this is likely to require links between middle manager strategy practices and outcomes recognized by practitioners as worth pursuing. Therefore, we still need to engage more fully with methods that encourage participants to provide their point of view on what is critical (through, for example, self-report methods: see Balogun, Huff and Johnson 2003), or that encourage participants to explore their understandings of their situation and their work together, encouraging deeper reflection (through, for example, focus groups), or to even become co-researchers, exploring themselves and their practices alongside the academics. Such approaches may have more potential for use among middle managers than among senior executives, purely because the greater number of middle managers makes it more feasible to bring together a group of them in an organization. There are also other means through which we can build greater critical reflection into research on middle managers (though this is not unique to middle manager research). For example, we should consider working in partnership with organizations. Research supported by consortia of organizations can be used to encourage the organizations to reflect on and challenge the interpretations of researchers on data collected in their organizations.

As suggested by Vaara and Whittington (2012), we should also develop a more critical view of strategy-as-practice research in general and on middle managers in particular. For example, we started this chapter by highlighting the changing nature of the discourses on middle managers and the nature of their role. While research is increasingly recognizing the strategic nature of their work, this is not always the case in organizations. How, then, do the traditional discourses, which typically devalue the nature of middle managers and their roles yet pervade organizations, and even extend into the institutional realm, affect the strategic work of middle managers? How is this different in organizations taking a more participative view of middle managers (Canales 2013; Mantere and Vaara 2008)? How do the more general discourses about organizations, and the forms they should take in response to a more global world, lead to restructuring in organizations, including the redefinition of middle manager roles and degrees of autonomy and participation? How do middle managers promote and resist this (Balogun, Jarzabkowski and Vaara 2011)?

Addressing the challenges

Addressing these challenges demands an ambitious research agenda. We would suggest that future research should be designed to respond in an integrative way to all five challenges. The most impactful work is likely to arise out of studies that take practice theory as a starting point, are motivated in the context of prior work, employ innovative methods, incorporate sociomateriality and draw on managers' critical reflections. For example, more work is needed that extends what we know about middle manager practices in their various strategic activities. Imagine that video recordings of middle managers' meetings, either with their superiors, subordinates or colleagues, could be played back to middle manager participants in groups and/or as individuals with an eye towards seeking their self-understandings of what they do to participate in the meeting. Moving beyond discursive practices, self-interpretations could yield insights into practices that would otherwise be difficult to observe, such as those associated with influence attempts, coalition-building and resistance. Such a robust data set is likely also to address so far unanswered questions about differences between senior and middle manager practices, the impact of physical space, the body and material objects, and the role of middle managers' emotions. Coupled with videos of the meetings themselves, interview, archival and observation data of middle manager efforts to design and orchestrate meetings could provide the kind of 360-degree interpretations required to get a holistic

sense of how institutionalized structures interact with middle manager agency to influence meeting outcomes such as shared intentionality regarding deliberate strategic change.

References

Balogun, J. (2003), 'From blaming the middle to harnessing its potential: creating change intermediaries', *British Journal of Management*, 14/1: 69–83.

(2007), 'The practice of organizational restructuring: from design to reality', *European Management Journal*, 25/2: 81–91.

Balogun, J., Gleadle, P., Hope Hailey, V., and Willmott, H. (2005), 'Managing change across boundaries: boundary-shaking practices', *British Journal of Management*, 16/4: 261–78.

Balogun, J., Huff, A. S., and Johnson, P. (2003), 'Three responses to methodological challenges of studying strategizing', *Journal of Management Studies*, 40/1: 197–224.

Balogun, J., Jacobs, C. D., Jarzabkowski, P., Mantere, S., and Vaara, E. (2014), 'Placing strategy discourse in context: sociomateriality, sensemaking, and power', *Journal of Management Studies*, 51/2: 175–201.

Balogun, J., Jarzabkowski, P., and Vaara, E. (2011), 'Selling, resistance and reconciliation: a critical discursive approach to subsidiary role evolution in MNEs', *Journal of International Business Studies*, 42/6: 765–86.

Balogun, J., and Johnson, G. (2004), 'Organizational restructuring and middle manager sensemaking', *Academy of Management Journal*, 47/4: 523–49.

(2005), 'From intended strategy to unintended outcomes: the impact of change recipient sensemaking', *Organization Studies*, 26/11: 1573–601.

Beck, T. E., and Plowman, D. A. (2009), 'Experiencing rare and unusual events richly: the role of middle managers in animating and guiding organizational interpretation', *Organization Science*, 20/5: 909–24.

Besson, P., and Mahieu C. (2011), 'Strategizing from the middle in radical change situations: transforming roles to enable strategic creativity', *International Journal of Organizational Analysis*, 19/3: 176–201.

Bjerregaard, T. (2011), 'Institutional change at the frontline', *Qualitative Research in Organizations and Management*, 6/1: 26–46.

Bryant, M., and Stensaker, I. (2011), 'The competing roles of middle management: negotiated order in the context of change', *Journal of Change Management*, 11/3: 353–73.

Burgelman, R. A. (1983), 'A process model of internal corporate venturing in the diversified major firm', *Administrative Science Quarterly*, 28/2: 223–44.

Canales, J. I. (2013), 'Constructing interlocking rationales in top-driven strategic renewal', *British Journal of Management*, 24/4: 498–514.

Daniels, K., Johnson, G., and de Chernatony, L. (2002), 'Task and institutional influences on managers' mental model of competition', *Organization Studies*, 23/1: 31–62.

Davis, P. S., Allen, J. A., and Dibrell, C. (2012), 'Fostering strategic awareness at an organization's boundary', *Leadership and Organization Development Journal*, 33/4: 322–41.

Denis, J.-L., Langley, A., and Rouleau, L. (2007), 'Strategizing in pluralistic contexts: rethinking theoretical frames', *Human Relations*, 60/1: 179–215.

Dopson, S., and Stewart, R. (1990), 'What is happening to middle management?', *British Journal of Management*, 1/1: 3–16.

— (1992), 'The changing role of the middle manager in the United Kingdom', *International Studies of Management and Organization*, 22/1: 40–7.

Dutton, J. E., Ashford, S. J, O'Neill, R. M., and Lawrence, K. A. (2001), 'Moves that matter: issue selling and organizational change', *Academy of Management Journal*, 44/4: 716–36.

Fauré, B., and Rouleau, L. (2011), 'The strategic competence of accountants and middle managers in budget making', *Accounting, Organizations and Society*, 36/3: 167–82.

Floyd, S. W., and Wooldridge, B. (1992), 'Middle management involvement in strategy and its association with strategic type: a research note', *Strategic Management Journal*, 13/S1: 153–67.

— (1994), 'Dinosaurs or dynamos? Recognizing middle management's strategic role', *Academy of Management Executive*, 8/4: 47–57.

— (1997), 'Middle management's strategic influence and organizational performance', *Journal of Management Studies*, 34/3: 465–85.

Frow, N., Marginson, D., and Ogden, S. (2005), 'Encouraging strategic behaviour while maintaining management control: multi-functional project teams, budgets, and the negotiation of shared accountabilities in contemporary enterprises', *Management Accounting Research*, 16/3: 269–92.

Hassard, J., and McCann, L. (2004), 'Middle managers, the new organizational ideology and corporate restructuring: comparing Japanese and Anglo-American management systems', *Competition and Change*, 8/1: 27–44.

Hoon, C. (2007), 'Committees as strategic practice: the role of strategic conversation in a public administration', *Human Relations*, 60/6: 921–52.

Hope, O. (2010), 'The politics of middle management sensemaking and sensegiving', *Journal of Change Management*, 10/2: 195–215.

Huff, A. S. (1990), *Mapping Strategic Thought*. London: John Wiley.

Huy, Q. N. (2011), 'How middle managers' group-focus emotions and social identities influence strategy implementation', *Strategic Management Journal*, 32/13: 1387–410.

Jarratt, D., and Stiles, D. (2010), 'How are methodologies and tools framing managers' strategizing practice in competitive strategy development?', *British Journal of Management*, 21/1: 28–43.

Jarzabkowski, P., Balogun, J., and Seidl, D. (2007), 'Strategizing: the challenges of a practice perspective', *Human Relations*, 60/1: 5–27.

Jarzabkowski, P., Spee, P., and Smets, M. (2013), 'Material artifacts: practices for doing strategy with "stuff"', *European Management Journal*, 31/1: 41–54.

Johnson, G., Melin, L., and Whittington, R. (2003), 'Guest editors' introduction: micro strategy and strategizing: towards an activity-based-view', *Journal of Management Studies*, 40/1: 3–22.

Kellog, K. C. (2009), 'Operating rooms: relational spaces and microinstitutional change in surgery', *American Journal of Sociology*, 115/3: 657–711.

Ketokivi, M., and Mantere, S. (2010), 'Two strategies for inductive reasoning in organizational research', *Academy of Management Review*, 35/2: 315–33.

Laine, P.-M., and Vaara, E. (2007), 'Struggling over subjectivity: a discursive analysis of strategic development in an engineering group', *Human Relations*, 60/1: 29–58.

Langley, A., and Abdallah, C. (2011), 'Templates and turns in qualitative studies of strategy and management', in Bergh, D. D., and Ketchen, D. J. (eds.), *Research Methodology in Strategy and Management*, vol. VI, *Building Methodological Bridges*: 201–35. Bingley, UK: Emerald.

Lawrence, T. B., and Suddaby, R. (2006), 'Institutions and institutional work', in Clegg, S., Hardy, C., Lawrence, T. B., and Nord, W. R. (eds.), *The Sage Handbook of Organization Studies*, 2nd edn: 215–53. London: Sage.

Lechner, C., Frankenberger, K., and Floyd, S. W. (2010), 'Task contingencies in the curvilinear relationships between intergroup networks and initiative performance', *Academy of Management Journal*, 53/4: 865–89.

Ling, Y., Floyd, S. W., and Baldridge, D. C. (2005), 'Toward a model of issue selling by subsidiary managers in multinational organizations', *Journal of International Business Studies*, 36/6: 637–54.

Liu, F., and Maitlis, S. (2014), 'Emotional dynamics and strategizing processes: a study of strategic conversations in top team meetings', *Journal of Management Studies*, 51/2: 202–34.

Lüscher, L. S., and Lewis, M. W. (2008), 'Organizational change and managerial sensemaking: working through paradox', *Academy of Management Journal*, 51/2: 221–40.

Mantere, S. (2005), 'Strategic practices as enablers and disablers of championing activity', *Strategic Organization*, 3/2: 157–84.

(2008), 'Role expectations and middle manager strategic agency', *Journal of Management Studies*, 45/2: 294–316.

Mantere, S., and Vaara, E. (2008), 'On the problem of participation in strategy: a critical discursive perspective', *Organization Science*, 19/2: 341–58.

McCabe, D. (2010), 'Strategy-as-power: ambiguity, contradiction and the exercice of power in a UK building society', *Organization*, 17/2: 161–75.

Mills, J. H., Thurlow, A., and Mills, A. (2010), 'Making sense of sensemaking: the critical sensemaking approach', *Qualitative Research in Organizations and Management*, 5/2: 182–95.

Nielsen, M. F. (2009), 'Interpretative management in business meetings: understanding managers' interactional strategies through conversation analysis', *Journal of Business Communication*, 46/1: 23–56.

Pinsonneault, A, and Kraemer, K. L. (1997), 'Middle management downsizing: an empirical investigation of the impact of information technology', *Management Science*, 43/5: 659–79.

Rouleau, L. (2005), 'Micro-practices of strategic sensemaking and sensegiving: how middle managers interpret and sell change every day', *Journal of Management Studies*, 42/7: 1413–41.

(2010), 'Studying strategizing through narratives of practice', in Golsorkhi, D., Rouleau, L., Seidl, D., and Vaara, E. (eds.), *Cambridge Handbook of Strategy as Practice*: 258–70. Cambridge University Press.

(2013), 'Strategy-as-practice research at a crossroads', *M@n@gement*, 16/5: 547–65.

Rouleau, L., and Balogun, J. (2011), 'Middle managers, strategic sensemaking, and discursive competence', *Journal of Management Studies*, 48/5: 953–83.

Schatzki, T. R. (2011), 'Landscapes as temporalspatial phenomena', in Malpas, J. (ed.), *The Place of Landscape: Concepts, Contexts, Studies*: 65–90. Cambridge, MA: MIT Press.

Sharma, G., and Good, D. (2013), 'The work of middle managers: sensemaking and sensegiving for creating positive social change', *Journal of Applied Behavioral Science*, 49/1: 95–122.

Smith, A. D., Plowman, D. A., and Duchon, D. (2010), 'Everyday sensegiving: a closer look at successful plant managers', *Journal of Applied Behavioral Science*, 46/2: 220–44.

Smith, A. D., Plowman, D. A., Duchon, D., and Quinn, A. M. (2009), 'A qualitative study of high-reputation plant managers: political skill and successful outcomes', *Journal of Operations Management*, 27/6: 428–43.

Spee, P., and Jarzabkowski, P. (2009), 'Strategy tools as boundary objects', *Strategic Organization*, 7/2: 223–32.

Suddaby, R., Seidl, D., and Lê, J. K. (2013), 'Strategy-as-practice meets neo-institutional theory', *Strategic Organization*, 11/3: 329–44.

Teulier, R., and Rouleau, L. (2013), 'Middle managers' sensemaking and interorganizational change initiation: translation spaces and editing practices', *Journal of Change Management*, 13/3: 308–37.

Thomas, R., Sargent, L. D., and Hardy, C. (2011), 'Managing organizational change: negotiating meaning and power–resistance relations', *Organization Science*, 22/1: 22–41.

Vaara, E., and Whittington, R. (2012), 'Strategy-as-practice: taking social practices seriously', *Academy of Management Annals*, 6/1: 285–336.

Vickers, D., and Fox, S. (2010), 'Towards practice-based studies of HRM: an actor–network and communities of practice informed approach', *International Journal of Human Resource Management*, 21/6: 899–914.

Westley, F. (1990), 'Middle managers and strategy: microdynamics of inclusion', *Strategic Management Journal*, 11/5: 337–51.

Whittington, R. (2006), 'Completing the practice turn in strategy research', *Organization Studies*, 27/5: 613–34.

Woolridge, B., Schmid, T., and Floyd, S. W. (2008), 'The middle management perspective on strategy process: contributions, synthesis, and future research', *Journal of Management*, 34/6: 1190–221.

Participation in strategy work

PIKKA-MAARIA LAINE and EERO VAARA

Introduction

This chapter examines participation in strategy research in general and in strategy-as-practice research in particular. Participation is arguably a key issue in strategy process research because it helps to create commitment to strategies, and its absence may have a negative impact on the quality of decision-making (Floyd and Wooldridge 2000). It may also take other forms, as in emergent strategies (Burgelman 1983; Mintzberg and Waters 1985) or in autonomous strategy work (Mirabeau and Maguire 2014), that are important in process studies. Participation is also a central issue in SAP research that examines the activities of multiple actors and the practices they draw upon in strategy work (Mantere 2008). From a more critical perspective, it can be seen as closely connected to subjectivity (Ezzamel and Willmott 2010; Knights and Morgan 1991) and resistance (McCabe 2010; Ezzamel and Willmott 2008). It may also be regarded as a deeper-level ethical issue in terms of (in)equality linked with organizational decision-making and managerial dominance.

Nevertheless, participation has received relatively little explicit attention in strategy research. Hence, it is the purpose of this chapter to provide an overview of research on participation. As relatively few studies have explicitly focused on this issue (Mantere and Vaara 2008), in this overview we will include a number of studies that have only touched upon participation. Our point of departure is to argue that different streams of research offer fundamentally different conceptions of strategic decision-making, strategy processes and strategic practices, and thus of participation as a social and organizational phenomenon. Accordingly, we spell out four perspectives on participation: participation as a non-issue; participation as a part of strategy process dynamics; participation as produced in and through organizational practices; and participation

as an issue of subjectivity. First, within conventional strategy research, strategy has mostly been understood as decision-making accomplished by top management (Ansoff 1965; Chandler 1962; Hambrick and Mason 1984). Since they are top managers who participate in strategic practices, the participation of others is a non-issue within this stream of research. Second, strategy process studies have examined strategy both as intended and emergent (Burgelman 1983; Mintzberg and Waters 1985), which provides us with an understanding of others – especially middle managers (Floyd and Wooldridge 1992; 2000; Ketokivi and Castañer 2004) – as part of strategy-making. In this view, participation can be seen as an essential part of strategy process dynamics. Third, SAP research further extends the understanding of strategy by conceptualizing it as a praxis of involving various actors. This research has examined micro-level activities and patterns of action related to participation as well as social practices that enable or impede participation (Jarzabkowski 2008; Mantere 2005; 2008). Fourth and finally, we also spell out a critical post-structuralist view, the full potential of which has not yet been fully realized. This perspective builds on the view that strategy discourses and social practices are historically produced and constitutive of strategy and strategic actors. The studies focuses especially on subjectivity – that is, the rights, responsibilities and identities of the actors involved in strategy work (Knights and Morgan 1991). In this view, participation entails various modes of engagement or non-engagement (Ezzamel and Willmott 2008; Kornberger and Clegg 2011; Laine and Vaara 2007; Thomas, Sargent and Hardy 2011).

On this basis, we also offer ideas for future research on participation. These include extending strategic agency to non-managerial actors, focusing on co-orientation in the interaction of actors in multifaceted strategy processes, analysing institutional and cultural differences in participation, studying sociomateriality and its role in enabling or promoting participation, analysing polyphony and dialogicality and developing the critical perspectives needed to deal with issues such as resistance and empowerment in a more comprehensive manner.

After this introduction, we elaborate on the four approaches to participation in existing research. This is followed by a research agenda that spells out ideas for future research on participation. We conclude by arguing for a need to promote participation in research, organizational practice and management education alike.

Approaches to participation

The conventional view: participation as a non-issue

Traditionally, strategy has been examined from the perspective of top management decision-making. In this view, top management is the strategic actor, and so others assume at best the role of implementers in the process. Thus, top managers are the strategists, and they mainly involve others in implementation (Andrews 1987; Ansoff 1965; Chandler 1962). A large part of the strategy literature since then has focused on finding effective ways of formulating strategies. This has especially characterized the planning and positioning literatures in strategic management (Mintzberg, Ahlstrand and Lampel 1998; Whittington 1993). Subsequent upper echelon research has continued the study of top management as a maker of strategic decisions (Carpenter, Geletkanycz and Sanders 2004; Finkelstein and Hambrick 1996; Hambrick and Mason 1984; Hart and Banbury 1994). This research has in particular focused on the interactive dynamics and group processes within top management teams, and thus elucidated how demographic or professional backgrounds and personal characteristics impact participation among top managers (Chatterjee and Hambrick 2007; 2011; Hayward and Hambrick 1997).

This focus on top managers or key decision-makers has also characterized newer streams of research, such as micro-foundations (Felin and Foss 2005; Felin *et al.* 2012) and behavioural strategy research (Gavetti 2005; Powell, Lovallo and Fox 2011). These streams have helped us better understand the micro-level dynamics of strategic decision-making (Felin *et al.* 2012) and the various cognitive and behavioural biases that it may involve (Powell, Lovallo and Fox 2011). These streams of research have been less interested in the social or organizational processes, however, and thus participation has remained a non-issue both in mainstream strategy research and in some more recent approaches.

Participation as part of strategy processes

The conventional view on strategic decision-making was challenged when researchers started to pay attention to the social aspects of strategy processes (Pettigrew 1973; 1992; Mintzberg 1978). In the landmark studies of strategy process, research scholars focused not only on planned or formulated strategies but also on emergent strategies (Bower 1970; Burgelman 1983; Mintzberg and Waters 1985). This meant underlining the role of others – mainly of middle management – as strategic actors. In an early study, Bower (1970) was already arguing that planning in large, diversified companies took place on various levels of the organization: corporate, divisional, business unit and departmental. In this view, middle managers play a crucial role, as only they are able to assess whether an issue was relevant in its context. Mintzberg and his research team (Mintzberg 1978; Mintzberg and Waters 1985) examine strategy as a pattern of actions and decisions in the organization and stress the role of middle management. Burgelman (1983; 1991; 1994) emphasizes the entrepreneurial potential of middle management, who introduce their own initiatives for strategic change, thus acting as agents. He shows that successful projects may begin with the initiatives of experts such as engineers. Lower middle management can then provide the technical and commercial skill needed for the success of the new projects, and the upper middle management conceptualize the strategic impact of the projects for top management. In fact, in this kind of emergent process, the role of top management is mainly to create a context to support innovation.

These early strategy process studies led to a stream of research on middle management, focusing on its role as a strategic actor. Floyd and Wooldridge (1992; 1996; 2000) classify the actions of middle management into roles linked to both top-down and bottom-up strategizing and to either the integration of ideas or their diversification. In an early study, Wooldridge and Floyd (1990) examine the link between middle management participation and corporate performance. Their research shows that decision-making by middle management may lead to superior strategy formulation, which could be seen as the successful integration of diverse ideas. Contrary to expectations, however, their analysis demonstrates that middle management in their study did not necessarily show commitment to strategy, and in fact also considered it important to maintain a critical stance towards strategy proposals. In their subsequent study, Floyd and Wooldridge (1997) conclude that successful performance requires most of the middle managers to play integrative strategic roles and only some of them to perform divergent strategic roles. In a large-scale statistical analysis of participation, Ketokivi and Castañer (2004) examine the process of strategic planning as a means of integrating a variety of goals in an organization. They show that participation in strategic planning and the subsequent communication of its results reduce position bias and, consequently, the likelihood that employees might engage in sub-goal pursuit and cause an integration problem. They contend that this is likely to lead to greater integration and less diversification of goals and also to increase commitment to the organization's objectives. Andersen (2004), for his part, demonstrates that the autonomy of middle managers to take initiatives in the face of environmental changes is linked to positive economic performance. Moreover, distributed decision-making authority seems to be more efficient when the company has a formal strategic planning process that integrates strategic actions. The participation of middle management in strategic decision-making, which may be seen as time-consuming and resource-demanding, did not seem conducive to positive performance however.

Others have then focused on the sensemaking processes involving middle managers. Westley (1990) provides an analysis of strategy conversations, and elaborates on the antecedents and implications of inclusion around strategic issues. She elucidates how middle managers experience inclusion as motivating and energizing if they are allowed to dominate, or at least co-determine, some aspects of the conversation. Dutton et al. (2001) show how middle management use strategic, normative and relational contextual understanding in the process of constructing issues as strategic and, thus, promoting change.

Relatedly, studies have described how a low hierarchy, organizational status or network position supports the autonomy and proactiveness of middle management. Carney (2004) argues that middle managers experience a low organization hierarchy as an enabler of their participation in strategic development. Hornsby et al. (2009) show that top management and middle management experience more opportunity for entrepreneurial activity than lower-level management. Kodama (2005), in turn, describes how middle managers build and lead informal strategic networks in and across firms for open innovation. The study by Pappas and Wooldridge (2007) parallels this; they demonstrate how middle managers in key external and internal network positions have increased opportunities to influence strategy. They also show that managers who lack an external network position but have a central internal network postion contribute to divergent strategic activity.

Still others have linked middle management's engagement with management control systems. Marginson (2002) describes how management systems affect the proactiveness of middle management. He classifies management systems – according to Simons (1991; 1994) – into the following categories: belief and boundary systems; administrative controls and role responsibilities; and performance measures and monitoring. Marginson contends that the values, purpose and direction of the organization communicated by top management enhance the proactiveness of middle management. Administrative control systems in turn affect the location of strategic initiative; some managers are assigned to make strategies concrete, while others are held accountable for assuring the efficiency of current activity. In strategy-making, multiple key performance indicators nevertheless lead middle managers to favour some measures at the expense of others. A study by Currie and Procter (2005) confirms part of the results of Marginson's study. Currie and Procter find that ambiguity of role expectations among stakeholders, including top managers, does in fact prevent middle managers from enacting their strategic roles. The authors also point out, however, that the training of middle managers contributes to the development of active strategic leadership on their part.

The active role of middle managers has also been examined in studies of implementation. Huy (2002), for example, examines how the handling of the emotions of middle management affects how they implement change. He shows how middle managers promote change by committing passionately to goals, assist their subordinates in understanding the change and deal with their negative feelings related to it. Huy later shows (Huy 2011) how the emotional identification of middle managers with various groups in the change (such as newcomers versus veterans or English speakers versus French speakers) persuaded them to either support or covertly dismiss a particular strategic initiative even when their immediate personal interests were not directly under threat.

In all, strategy process research has thus conceptualized middle management participation as an inherent part of strategy processes, both in terms of more formal processes and in the case of emergent strategies. This view has been limited mostly to middle managers, however, whereas the role of other organizational members has mainly been seen as that of implementers.

Participation as part of strategic practices

Although the distinction between process and practice perspectives is to some extent arbitrary (Floyd *et al.* 2011; Vaara and Whittington 2012), the emergence of strategy-as-practice research has brought with it another kind of understanding of strategy work in general and of participation in particular. Linked with process studies, a part of SAP research has elaborated on the micro-level

activities related to participation. Some of the studies have also drawn from a more practice-theoretical understanding of how specific practices enable or impede participation.

Studies have examined how top management involves middle managers in strategizing (Jarzabkowski 2008; Jarzabkowski and Balogun 2009; Paroutis and Pettigrew 2007; Vilà and Canales 2008). Jarzabkowski (2008) examines how top management use interactive actions such as discussions and meetings between management and other actors and procedural actions such as planning, control and monitoring to change strategy. She demonstrates that a change in strongly institutionalized strategy requires a simultaneous pattern of interactive and procedural strategizing, whereas a sequential pattern of interactive and procedural strategizing is enough to change a weakly institutionalized strategy. She concludes that constant discussions among many levels and parts of an organization combined with structural changes supportive of new strategies facilitate strategic change. Jarzabkowski and Balogun (2009) in turn elucidate how a centralized strategy process guides the action of middle management and how the actions of middle management then alter the strategy process so that consensus is constructed and goals are integrated. When managers of larger market areas resisted centralized marketing strategy by appealing to their competence and the profitability of their business, the strategy process was altered so that middle managers were able to take part in the definition of a market-specific application of strategy. The study by Jarzabowski and Baloguin (2009) thus confirms the view that integration arises only from active negotiations and compromises between actors.

Furthermore, Paroutis and Pettigrew and Vilà and Canales describe how the participation of middle managers in the strategy process develops their strategic proactiveness and capability. Paroutis and Pettigrew (2007) show the development of the actions and practices of division-level strategy teams in the course of a corporate strategy process, which then led them to increase their proactiveness and top management to reduce their directiveness. Vilà and Canales (2008) describe how an organization constantly included more middle managers in a strategic planning process with the aim of developing their capacity for strategizing. They show how the process of strategic planning evolved as the competences and expectations of the participants developed. Eventually, middle managers initiated the process themselves. When analysis became more of a routine, they concentrated on discussion of the strategic initiatives in the process.

Other studies have focused on how middle managers take the initiative in strategizing (Balogun and Johnson 2004; 2005; Hoon 2007; Kaplan and Orlikowski 2013; Mirabeau and Maguire 2014; Regnér 2003). Balogun and Johnson examine how middle managers strategize among themselves by making sense of strategic structural change initiated by top management. The first study (Balogun and Johnson 2004) describes how middle managers make sense of each other's actions, rumours and gossip and how they negotiate to develop a shared understanding of strategic change. The study thus emphasizes the construction of strategy within the horizontal interaction of middle management. In their second study, Balogun and Johnson (2005) focus on demonstrating the co-constitutive process of shared understandings and sensemaking actions. Regnér (2003) describes how middle managers develop business at the unit level by reacting flexibly to situations and emerging opportunities whereas strategizing at the centre is more predefined. Hoon (2007) focuses on the proactiveness of middle management as the initiator of strategizing with top management. She explains how middle management create the context for official strategy committees in unofficial discussions between official meetings, thereby enabling eventual implementation of the strategies. Kaplan and Orlikowski (2013) provide a thorough case description of how strategy-making involved various and differing interpretations of the past, present and future of multiple organizational actors in practice and over time. They trace patterns of temporal work – that is, the continuous reframing of the past, present and future – in extensive strategic projects, and conclude that the intensity of temporal work among various participants produced a greater degree of change in strategy. Moreover, Mirabeau and Maguire (2014) demonstrate the construction of emergent strategies from the

autonomous strategic behaviour of middle managers. They elucidate the practices of mobilizing wider support for the projects and altering the structural context for their embeddedness. They especially emphasize the discursive practices of middle managers in and through which the new initiatives were embedded into the strategic context of the company.

To some extent, SAP research has also examined how others in addition to managers participate in strategizing. By examining the participation of strategy consultants in the strategy process, Melin and Nordqvist (2008) offer a rare focus on the actions of these strategy practitioners. Rouleau (2005) in turn elucidates how middle managers involve customers in strategizing by examining how middle managers enact strategy in everyday routines and discussions with customers. She indentifies the micro-practices of sensegiving and sensemaking in and through which middle management demonstrate the cultural and contextual capability needed to shape strategy according to customer preferences. Rouleau and Balogun (2011) examine how middle managers involve subordinates – in addition to management and colleagues – by skilfully communicating strategy. The authors identify two components in the discursive competence of middle management: 'performing the conversation' and 'setting the scene'. They especially emphasize that these two activities are underpinned by the ability of middle managers to draw implicitly on symbolic and verbal representations and the sociocultural systems to which they belong. Hence, the studies of Rouleau and her colleagues underline the contextual understanding of middle managers in strategic communication with other actors. Drawing on an understanding of strategy as practical coping (Chia and Holt 2006), Jarzabkowski and her colleagues (Jarzabkowski, Spee and Smets 2013; Jarzabkowski, Burke and Spee 2015) in turn focus on knowledge workers as strategic actors in an insurance company. They elaborate on how the strategies of the companies are enacted through the everyday practical coping actions of these professionals.

There are also studies that focus on examining the discursive, social and material practices that enable or restrict participation in strategy work (Kaplan 2011; Mantere 2005; 2008; Thomas,

Sargent and Hardy 2011). Mantere (2005) identifies strategy practices that seem to impede or enable progress in strategic matters. He divides them into three categories: practices related to the formation of strategy, to the concretization of goals and responsibilities, and to the measurement and monitoring of results. Mantere concludes that upper management and middle management feel that practices within which strategy is discussed encourage their strategic agency. In contrast, operative actors feel that their strategic agency is fostered by practices that make strategy more concrete. In a later study, Mantere (2008) examines how institutional role expectations (Floyd and Wooldridge 1992; 2000) guide middle managers to expect a certain kind of behaviour on the part of top management so as to enable the strategic agency of middle managers. Their role as strategy implementor is supported if top management explain the strategic goals (narrativization), assist in placing them in context (contextualization), appreciate operative activity and see it as the arena for the implementation of strategy (respect) and provide the resources (resource allocation) that enable implementation of the goals. Middle management are able to make syntheses of local activities and situations for top management when top management take note of feedback from them and react to it (responsiveness). The facilitative role of middle management is possible if top management are confident that initiatives will emerge from the organization (trust). Middle management can introduce strategic initiatives when top management involve them in strategic planning (inclusion) and assess their initiatives (refereeing).

Yet other studies focus on discursive practices that enable or restrict participation. (Jarzabkowski and Sillince (2007) demonstrate how top management use various kinds of linguistic practices to enhance commitment to strategic goals and actions. Thomas, Sargent and Hardy (2011), in turn, identify two patterns of communicative micro-practices in the strategy workshop between top and middle managers. They elucidate how one pattern created generative dialogue in which strategy was co-constructed between top and middle managers, whereas another pattern created degenerative dialogue in which there were two polarized

meanings for implementation. Even though they conclude that generative dialogue requires counter-offers from both groups, their study demonstrates that the impact of a particular communicative practice depends upon who is employing it, when and in response to what. Relatedly, in a rare study of strategy meetings, Wodak, Kwon and Clarke (2011) identify five discursive strategies that the chair of a strategy meeting used to create consensus: bonding, encouraging, directing, modulating and re/committing. Kwon, Clarke and Wodak (2014) in turn highlight the discursive strategies used by teams to develop shared views around strategic issues in meetings; these include re/defining, equalizing, simplifying, legitimizing and reconciling.

Finally, there are studies that have focused on the role of materiality in participation. Whittington *et al.* (2006) show how a cardboard cube, as a material artefact, was created and distributed to an organization so as to communicate strategic messages to the personnel. Heracleous and Jacobs (2011) demonstrate how the formulation of strategy in a metaphorical material structure enables various interpretations and discussion of them. Kaplan (2011), for her part, demonstrates that the use of PowerPoint enables the participation of many in the construction of strategy. In a rare study involving the entire personnel in strategizing, Stieger *et al.* (2012) show how information technology was used in the strategy process of a medium-sized Austrian technology company.

In all, studies focusing on the social and organizational practices have thus elucidated the micro-level activities and practices that enable or impede participation. Whereas this stream of research has also elaborated on the roles of the actors, the subjectivities and identities have been the focal point in more critical post-structuralist analyses that we turn to next.

The critical view: participation as subjectivity

Finally, linked with the previous studies, participation has also been examined from more critical post-structuralist perspectives. In this view, participation is discursively constructed, and it is therefore important to examine the development of the discourses and practices as they define the subjectivities – that is, the rights and responsibilities and identities of focal actors. Some of the studies have pointed out how dominant understandings of strategic decision-making are historically constructed (Ezzamel and Willmott 2010; Knights and Morgan 1991). In their groundbreaking article, Knights and Morgan (1991) suggest how strategy discourse and practices define both objects of strategizing and strategists and create a hierarchical and an unequal power relationship between the actors. The concept of strategy is rooted in warfare, in which it has been used to determine a mode of action that would defeat the enemy or lead to success in the operating environment. In this context, strategy has been the task of generals. In business, too, strategy has been defined as the function of top management. After World War II management and researchers began to describe the operations and goals of companies in strategic terms. Strategy language was used to examine and determine the relationship between the organization and its operating environment, combining models of the military and rational decision-making. The analysis by Knights and Morgan (1991) specifically helps us to understand the creation of subject positions in and through this discourse. In particular, their analysis highlights the following effects:

> (a) It provides managers with a rationalization of their successes and failures; (b) it sustains and enhances the prerogatives of management and negates alternative perspectives on organizations; (c) it generates a sense of security for managers; (d) it reflects and sustains a strong sense of gendered masculinity for male management; (e) it demonstrates managerial rationality to colleagues, customers, competitors, government and significant others in the environment; (f) it facilitates and legitimates the exercise of power; (g) it constitutes the subjectivity of organizational members as particular categories of persons who secure their sense of reality through engaging in this discourse and practice (Knights and Morgan 1991: 262–3).

Others have then followed this kind of critical perspective and studied the creation of subjectivities and identities in strategy processes and practices. In an early study, Eriksson and Lehtimäki (2001) demonstrate how the rhetorical strategies of a strategy document produced by city authorities impeded the participation of city residents in construction of the city's future. Laine and Vaara (2007) examine the discursive construction of subjectivity in strategic change and highlight three different ways in which organizational members engaged with strategy discourse. Top management used strategy discourse to launch change and to gain control of the organization. Some middle managers resisted this development and worked on their own business-unit-level strategies in secrecy. Finally, some experts took distance from the strategy discourse to maintain their identity and power positions as key actors in the organization. Kornberger and Clegg (2011) provide another illuminating analysis of subjectivation in a case study of strategic planning in Sydney. Their analysis shows that, although the process included an unprecedented number of stakeholders (local residents and representatives of organizations and businesses), consultants and strategy experts controlled which issues were defined as strategic, thereby diminishing the strategic agency of other participants. Consultants and strategy experts defined issues such as the growing need for housing as too difficult for public discussion and called on experts to resolve them. They also deemed the individual and acute concerns of local residents to be non-strategic. Furthermore, the diverse and conflicting views of Sydney residents regarding the future of their city were bypassed; the consultants and strategy experts reduced them to integrated goals. The city's future was defined through economic discourse. This meant that issues inexplicable in economic terms were excluded from the process, and the concerns of culture and ecology were harnessed to promote the economy. Hence, the strategy process objectified the citizens into subjects who were supposed to define all spheres of life with economic discourse.

In a rare analysis focusing explicitly on participation, Mantere and Vaara (2008) identify six discourses of impeding or enabling participation. Participation is impeded by mystification (the obfuscation of organizational decisions through various discursive means), disciplining (the use of disciplinary techniques to constrain action) and technologization (imposing a technological system to govern the activities of individuals as resources). In contrast, participation is supported by self-actualization (discourse that focuses attention on the ability of people as individuals to outline and define objectives for themselves in strategy processes), dialologization (discourse integrating top-down and bottom-up approaches to strategizing) and concretization (discourse that seeks to establish clear processes and practices in and through strategizing). Others have then elucidated the role of accounting practices that define power relations and subjectivities. For example, Ezzamel and Willmott (2008) show how accounting practices may gain strategic significance and how they influence what is considered strategic, and how organizational members can participate in strategy processes. Whittle and Mueller (2010) examine the role of management accounting systems in determining what is strategic and on whose terms.

Finally, Dameron and Torset (2014) focus on how the subjectivity of a 'strategist' is constructed. They identify and elaborate on three types of subjectivity that managers frequently reproduced in their interviews: mythicizing subjectivity, concretizing subjectivity and dialogizing subjectivity. Their analysis does not focus specifically on the participative aspects of these subjectivities, however. Laine *et al.* (forthcoming), in turn, draw on Butlerian theorization of subject formation to examine the performative construction of strategists' identity in and through the talk of top managers. They conclude that the persistence of dominant understandings in identity construction tends to impede participation in strategy-making.

Still others have elucidated the role of resistance in strategy processes (Ezzamel and Willmott 2008; McCabe 2010). For instance, Ezzamel and Willmott (2008) show how resistance may involve slow-down tactics, being less cooperative and being resentful. McCabe (2010) focuses on resistance in his empirical study of a UK building society. He shows how power is exercised in ambiguous and contradictory ways, both supporting and hindering management's initiatives. His study thus shows that, without examining power

and resistance in a detailed and nuanced manner, our understanding of strategic processes and practices and the actions of various participants remains superficial. Interestingly, Dick and Collings (2014) have in turn shown that resistance to strategy discourse happens not only among lower-level managers undermining strategy discourse but also by top managers in specific 'breakdown' situations.

In all, by elucidating the ways in which subjectivities are constructed, this critical view has greatly advanced our understanding of the underpinnings of participation and also shed light on the related power dynamics. Nevertheless, these studies also indicate that there is a need to go further in critical analysis – for example, by focusing attention on the role of non-managerial organizational members and the multiple ways in which coping and resistance can be seen as key parts of participation within strategy processes and practices.

An agenda for future research

On the basis of this overview, we now elaborate on the following specific topics for future research on participation: the extension of strategic agency to non-managerial actors; co-orientation in the interaction of actors in multifaceted strategy processes; institutional and cultural differences in participation; sociomateriality enabling or impeding participation; polyphony and dialogicality; and further development of critical perspectives to facilitate dealing with issues such as resistance and empowerment.

Extending strategic agency beyond managerial ranks

It is well established that strategy processes are shaped by participation and that the nature of participation is closely linked and even determined by organizational practices. The focus of research has so far been on top and middle managers as strategic actors, however; only a few studies have examined the involvement of other internal or external stakeholders in strategy work. This is a theoretical and practical deficiency that limits our understanding of strategic agency.

Accordingly, future studies should focus more attention on organizational members beyond managerial ranks. While there are studies that have already begun to do so (Ezzamel and Willmott 2008; Jarzabkowski, Spee and Smets 2013; Laine and Vaara 2007; Mantere 2008; Mantere and Vaara 2008; Nordqvist and Melin 2008; Rouleau 2005; Stieger *et al.* 2012), there is a need to develop a more comprehensive understanding of how exactly various types of organizational actors could influence strategy-making. Ideally, such analyses would also include personnel and other stakeholders of the organization, such as partners, customers, industry professionals and consultants. The aim would be to problematize the prevailing limited notions of what is seen as strategic and to extend our current conceptualizations of strategy processes and strategy work. Such analyses could lead to a more comprehensive and nuanced understanding of the origins of strategic ideas, how they are formed, made sense of and legitimized and how various actors through their interactions contribute to these processes. Importantly, this would involve the analysis of processes that are not conventionally seen as 'strategic'.

Such analyses could also focus on the specific ways in which these actors exercise influence. Existing research has already pointed to the importance of rhetorical (Samra-Fredericks 2003; 2005), discursive (Rouleau and Balogun 2011) and narrative (Kaplan and Orlikowski 2013) skills in strategy work. Although these competences are probably important for other actors, too, they also exercise influence in other ways. For instance, coping and resistance (Ezzamel and Willmott 2008; McCabe 2010) are essential ways for employees to exercise power and influence. Future studies should also focus more attention on non-engagement and deliberate distancing (Laine and Vaara 2007).

Our call resonates with a request for opening strategy, which draws its analogy from open innovation (Chesbrough and Appleyard 2007; Whittington, Cailluet and Yakis-Douglas 2011). Whittington, Cailluet and Yakis-Douglas (2011) demonstrate a trend towards greater openness in strategy processes.

They conclude that there is now more transparency in the strategic communication of top management both inside the company and towards other stakeholders. Inside the company, top management circulate and share strategy documents (Whittington and Yakis-Douglas 2012) and present strategy in blogs (Cox, Martinez and Quinlan 2008). Active share markets also expect proposals on strategy (Davis 2009; Whittington and Yakis-Douglas 2012). Furthermore, in line with our presentation, Whittington, Cailluet and Yakis-Douglas (2011) also note the increased inclusion of internal and external stakeholders in strategy processes. Thus far, we have mainly focused on internal inclusion in strategy-making. As stated by Whittington and his colleagues, however, new technology is especially important for increasing the possibilities of crowdsourcing in strategy-making. This remains one of the interesting research avenues for more intensive participation in strategizing.

Co-orientation in multifaceted strategy processes

Prior research has examined the creation of shared views, consensus and commitment in strategy work (Jarzabkowski and Balogun 2009; Kwon, Clarke and Wodak 2014; Rouleau and Balogun 2011). This stream of research has helped us to better understand how shared views are formed in strategy processes. Strategy process research has focused on consensus and commitment to strategies as a key part of it (Wooldridge, Schmid and Floyd 2008). Recent research has elaborated on the micro-dynamics through which shared views are formed. For example, Thomas, Sargent and Hardy (2011) have explained how shared views may or may not be co-constructed, depending on the dynamics of strategy conversations, and Kaplan and Orlikowski (2013) have explained how the formation of shared views involves an ongoing construction of the past, present and future. Wodak, Kwon and Clarke (2011), Aggerholm, Asmuß and Thomsen (2012) and Kwon, Clarke and Wodak (2014) have in turn elaborated on the discursive practices involved in reaching shared views. This work could be extended, however, to allow a better understanding of participation by a number of actors in space and time.

One alternative to further analysis of this kind is offered by the notion of co-orientation (Cooren 2010; Taylor and Robichaud 2004). This concept comes from work on the communicative constitution of organizations inspired by actor–network theory (see Cooren, Bencherki, Chaput and Vásquez in this volume). The key idea in co-orientation is that it allows one to conceptualize processes of participation without requiring fully shared meanings or creating consensus around any particular issue. Thus, it would allow the analysis of participation involving actors with different orientations – such as positions, interests or frames – in multifaceted and sometimes loosely coupled strategy processes over time. Although recent studies on autonomous strategy work (Mirabeau and Maguire 2014) and the communicative processes of strategy-making (Fenton and Langley 2011) provide interesting examples, more work on co-orientation is needed to develop a more comprehensive understanding of the ways in which multiple actors participate in strategy work and influence outcomes.

Institutional and cultural differences in practices of participation

Previous studies have elaborated on the nature of participation in strategy process as well as the practices that may promote or impede participation (Mantere and Vaara 2008; Thomas, Sargent and Hardy 2011). It is important to complement this stream of research with new studies focusing on new contexts. It may well be that research in this area has thus far assumed that the dynamics of participation would be similar across different industries and institutional and cultural contexts. This is probably not the case, however.

Future research on participation could thus examine and elaborate on differences across various institutional contexts. The prevailing conceptions and practice of strategy work have been developed in the business context, especially in the context of large corporations. In recent decades such practices have been adopted by others, such as government organizations, universities, hospitals, churches, schools, kindergartens and NGOs.

It would therefore be interesting to examine how the various practices of decision-making, strategy work and participation are interlinked, and, for instance, focus on the conflicts or struggles that they may entail.

While prevailing conceptions of strategy work are predominantly of Western origin, it would be important to examine the processes and practices in different cultural contexts. For instance, the Chinese and Japanese patterns of participation appear to differ from Western ones. In addition, different institutional contexts, for example in Europe, probably do imply different types of norms and expectations for participation. Such analyses could also include critical perspectives to examine the ethnocentric and even post- or neocolonial assumptions related to Western ways of conceptualizing participation.

Sociomateriality enabling or impeding participation

Some studies have already pointed to the central role of management systems and technology in enabling or impeding participation (Ezzamel and Willmott 2008; Jarzabkowski and Kaplan 2015; Jarzabkowski, Burke and Spee 2015; Jarzabkowski, Spee and Smets 2013; Kaplan 2011; Laine and Parkkari forthcoming; Stieger et al. 2012; Whittle and Mueller 2010). There is a need to go further, however, with an analysis of the sociomaterial aspects of strategy work and how they affect participation. Sociomateriality means 'the constitutive entanglement of the social and the material in everyday organizational life' (Orlikowski 2007: 1438). The sociomaterial aspects of strategy work involve material artefacts, technologies and embodied practices that enable and constrain participation.

Jarzabkowski and Kaplan (2015) have examined the dynamics of strategy tools-in-use by showing that there is a reciprocal relationship between the agency of actors and the selection, application and outcomes of using the tools – the three strategic phases that Jarzabkowski and Kaplan distinguish between. In the three phases, they identify the interpretive flexibility of strategy tools as one of the key elements enabling actors to select and use tools to cope with uncertainty in the environment. The affordances of the tools together with the agency of the actors affect the selection and implementation of tools and determine which are successful.

In spite of these studies, there is still a lack of systematic analysis of the role of sociomateriality in promoting or impeding participation. In addition to strategy tools and other material artefacts (Heracleous and Jacobs 2011), it would be important to examine the spatial arrangements of participation. Sociomateriality also provides the ability to focus on bodily aspects of inclusion and exclusion, the importance of which have have been elucidated in other contexts than strategy (Kenny and Bell 2011; Meriläinen, Tienari and Valtonen 2015). Given that the role of technology is becoming more and more central in contemporary organizations in general and strategy work in particular, it is paramount to focus on these aspects and the ways in which they influence participation. It is also noteworthy that specific management control systems have been developed to promote participation in strategy processes (Stieger *et al.* 2012), and it would be interesting to study whether and to what extent these systems work as intended. Furthermore, more and more organizations are becoming virtual or resemble online communities. In such contexts, the role of technological systems is of course particularly central and requires closer analysis (Whittington, Cailluet and Yakis-Douglas 2011).

Polyphony and dialogicality in strategy work

Thus far, studies in this area have assumed that strategy work is all about creating consensus, shared views and commitment. The co-orientation perspective outlined above provides another kind of approach, but here we propose looking at participation from yet another angle: that of polyphony. In terms of participation, it is also possible to focus attention on the various interpretations and articulations of organizational strategy. Polyphony means multiple voices, and strategy work may in fact be characterized by a diversity of ideas and initiatives. Ideally, polyphony increases discussion about strategic choices and gives voice to people who may easily be marginalized in organizational decision-making. Such polyphony may also be naturally linked with internal politics and conflict, however, and prevent consensus on future

directions. The point here is that a better understanding of polyphony requires scholarly attention to the ways in which various actors may participate in strategy work.

One way to study polyphony is provided by a narrative perspective (Barry and Elmes 1997; Boje 2008; Vaara and Pedersen 2014). This perspective allows examination of the various ways in which actors produce and consume narratives that provide alternative and competing bases for an organization's strategy. Some of these narratives may be seen as 'antenarratives' – that is, as fragments of discourse that may or may not reproduce or create meanings in a given context (Boje 2001). They are thus 'bets', in the sense that when articulated it is not known whether they will have any impact on the organization. Other narratives may then become more widely spread 'living stories' (Boje 2008) that are disseminated through organizational storytelling. This kind of analysis can also focus on dialogicality – that is, on the ways in which multiple voices and narratives are linked together over time in more formal strategy processes as well as around them. This would provide a better understanding of the ways in which voices are heard or marginalized and how organizational strategies are enacted in and through collective dialogical storytelling.

The development of critical perspectives on participation

Studies of subjectivity (Knights and Morgan 1991; Laine *et al.* forthcoming; Laine and Vaara 2007) and resistance (Ezzamel and Willmott 2008; Dick and Collings 2014; McCabe 2010) have been critical in orientation and elucidated aspects of participation that would otherwise easily pass unnoticed in strategy research. These ideas can be developed further. One interesting avenue for future research would be to connect coping and resistance more directly with the dynamics of strategy processes. Traditionally, organizational resistance has been examined as an activity impeding strategy implementation, and, as such, an obstacle to be overcome. Resistance can also be seen as an essential and even productive part of strategy processes, however. In particular, resistance may be needed to question specific ideas and to offer new alternatives. Furthermore, resistance, at least in some of its forms, may also be an important ingredient of strategy conversations; it can provide the 'traction' needed to engage and involve people and make strategies 'alive'. For instance, Thomas, Sargent and Hardy (2011) have demonstrated the role of facilitative resistance between top and middle management in the co-production of strategies. From an ethical perspective, resistance can also be seen as a right in and of itself that all people should be able to exercise, at least in voicing opposition. Moreover, participation may also be approached as an issue of empowerment, which in its broader meaning should involve opportunities to resist the imposition of ideas. Thus, it would be important to continue to study various forms of resistance and to connect existing studies of managerial roles and identities in strategy processes (Floyd and Wooldridge 2000; Mantere 2008).

Conclusion

Participation is a theoretical and practical issue that needs the attention of strategy research. In this chapter we have provided an overview of four perspectives that each involve specific conceptions of strategy work and the role of managers and other actors in it. The conventional view in strategic management focuses on managerial decision-making and tends to regard participation as a non-issue. Strategy process studies have elucidated the different ways in which middle managers in particular may participate in strategy-making – either in more formal planning or in autonomous strategy work. Strategy-as-practice research has focused on the micro-level activities of strategy processes that have themselves further elucidated the roles of various actors, and a stream of research has specifically elaborated on the social and discursive practices that enable or impede participation. Finally, other studies have concentrated on the social and discursive construction of subjectivity and identity and thus facilitated our understanding of how specific actors may or may not become strategists.

We have also argued that, in addition to all these studies, participation will require explicit attention in

future research, and proposed avenues for this research. These include extending strategic agency beyond managerial ranks, which is important for a better understanding of participation and of how influence and power are exercised in strategy work more generally. We have also suggested that a focus on co-orientation may help to better conceptualize and empirically examine multifaceted strategy processes involving various kinds of actors. In addition, we have maintained that an analysis of patterns of participation and the very practices that enable or impede participation should involve institutional and cross-cultural comparison. We have also argued that the enabling and constraining effects of tools and technologies and other sociomaterial practices should be given special attention in future research. Moreover, we maintain that there is a need to further develop and pursue critical perspectives to better understand the role of resistance in strategy processes and how participation is linked with empowerment.

Finally, it is important to consider the broader implications of participation, or the lack of it, in organizations. The dominant conception of strategic management still treats participation as a non-issue in the sense that it emphasizes the role of top management in strategy work, whereas the role of others is mainly to implement the strategic ideas. This view is also reproduced in the popular management literature and the media, which tend to focus on top leaders and their decisions and actions. We can as researchers, however, offer alternative views that emphasize the role of others in strategy processes in organizational practices, and act as critics of the prevailing approaches. Management education is precisely the arena in which we can make a difference in spreading alternative views on strategy work and participation.

References

Aggerholm, H. K., Asmuß, B., and Thomsen, C. (2012), 'The role of recontextualization in the multivocal, ambiguous process of strategizing', *Journal of Management Inquiry*, 21/4: 413–28.

Andersen, T. J. (2004), 'Integrating decentralized strategy making and strategic planning processes in dynamic environments', *Journal of Management Studies*, 41/8: 1271–99.

Andrews, K. R. (1987), *The Concept of Corporate Strategy*, 3rd edn. Homewood, IL: R. D. Irwin.

Ansoff, I. (1965), *Corporate Strategy*. New York: McGraw-Hill.

Balogun, J., and Johnson, G. (2004), 'Organizational restructuring and middle manager sensemaking', *Academy of Management Journal*, 47/4: 523–49.

— (2005), 'From intended strategies to unintended outcomes: the impact of change recipient sensemaking', *Organization Studies*, 26/11: 1573–601.

Barry, D., and Elmes M. (1997), 'Strategy retold: toward a narrative view of strategic discourse', *Academy of Management Review*, 22/2: 429–52.

Boje, D. M. (2001), *Narrative Methods for Organizational and Communication Research*. London: Sage.

— (2008), *Storytelling Organizations*. London: Sage.

Bower, J. L. (1970), *Managing the Resource Allocation Process*. Cambridge, MA: Harvard University Press.

Burgelman, R. A. (1983), 'A process model of internal corporate venturing in the diversified major firm', *Administrative Science Quarterly*, 28/2: 223–44.

— (1991), 'Intraorganizational ecology of strategy making and organizational adaptation: theory and field research', *Organization Science*, 2/3: 239–62.

— (1994), 'Fading memories: a process theory of strategic business exit in dynamic environments', *Administrative Science Quarterly*, 39/1: 24–56.

Carney, M. (2004), 'Middle management involvement in strategy development in not-for profit organizations: the director of nursing perspective', *Journal of Nursing Management*, 12/1: 13–21.

Carpenter, M. A., Geletkanycz, M. A., and Sanders, G. W. (2004), 'Upper echelons research revisited: antecedents, elements, and consequences of top management team composition', *Journal of Management*, 30/6: 749–78.

Chandler, A. D. (1962), *Strategy and Structure: Chapters in the History of the American Industrial Enterprise*. Cambridge, MA: MIT Press.

Chatterjee, A., and Hambrick, D. C. (2007), 'It's all about me: narcissistic CEOs and their effects on company strategy and performance', *Administrative Science Quarterly*, 52/3: 351–86.

— (2011), 'Executive personality, capability cues, and risk taking: how narcissistic CEOs react to their successes and stumbles', *Administrative Science Quarterly*, 56/2: 202–37.

Chesbrough, H. W., and Appleyard, M. (2007), 'Open innovation and strategy', *California Management Review*, 50/1: 57–65.

Chia, R., and Holt, R. (2006), 'Strategy as practical coping: a Heideggerian perspective', *Organization Studies*, 27/5: 635–55.

Cooren, F. (2010), *Action and Agency in Dialogue: Passion, Incarnation and Ventriloquism*. Amsterdam: John Benjamins.

Cox, J. L., Martinez, E., and Quinlan, K. (2008), 'Blogs and the corporation: managing the risk, reaping the benefits', *Journal of Business Strategy*, 29/1: 4–16.

Currie, G., and Procter, S. J. (2005), 'The antecedents of middle managers' strategic contribution: the case of a professional bureaucracy', *Journal of Management Studies*, 42/7: 1325–56.

Dameron, S., and Torset, C. (2014), 'The discursive construction of strategists' subjectivities: towards a paradox lens on strategy', *Journal of Management Studies*, 51/2: 291–319.

Davis, G. F. (2009), *Managed by the Markets: How Finance Reshaped America*. Oxford University Press.

Dick, P., and Collings, D. G. (2014), 'Discipline and punish? Strategy discourse, senior manager subjectivity and contradictory power effects', *Human Relations*, 67/12: 1513–36.

Dutton, J. E., Ashford, S. J., O'Neill, D. R., and Lawrence, K. A. (2001), 'Moves that matter: issue selling and organizational change', *Academy of Management Journal*, 44/4: 716–36.

Eriksson, P., and Lehtimäki, H. (2001), 'Strategy rhetoric in city management: how the central presumptions of strategic management live on?', *Scandinavian Journal of Management*, 17/2: 201–23.

Ezzamel, M., and Willmott, H. (2008), 'Strategy as discourse in a global retailer: a supplement to rationalist and interpretive accounts', *Organization Studies*, 29/2: 191–217.

— (2010), 'Strategy and strategizing: a poststructuralist perspective', in Baum, J. A. C., and Lampel, J. (eds.), *Advances in Strategic Management*, vol. XXVII, *The Globalization of Strategy Research*: 75–109. Bingley, UK: Emerald.

Felin, T., and Foss, N. J. (2005), 'Strategic organization: a field in search of microfoundations', *Strategic Organization*, 3/4: 441–55.

Felin, T., Foss, N. J., Heimericks, K. H., and Madsen, T. L. (2012), 'Microfoundations of routines and capabilities', *Journal of Management Studies*, 49/8: 1351–74.

Fenton, C., and Langley, A. (2011), 'Strategy as practice and the narrative turn', *Organization Studies*, 32/9: 1171–96.

Finkelstein, S., and Hambrick, D. C. (1996), *Strategic Leadership: Top Executives and Their Effects on Organization*. New York: West.

Floyd, S. W., Cornelissen, M. W., Wright, M., and Delios, A. (2011), 'Processes and practices of strategizing and organizing: review, development, and the role of bridging and umbrella constructs', *Journal of Management Studies*, 48/5: 933–52.

Floyd, S. W., and Wooldridge, B. (1992), 'Middle management involvement in strategy and its association with strategic type: a research note', *Strategic Management Journal*, 13/S1: 153–67.

(1996), *The Strategic Middle Manager: How to Create and Sustain Competitive Advantage*. San Francisco: Jossey-Bass.

(1997), 'Middle management's strategic influence and organizational performance', *Journal of Management Studies*, 34/3: 465–85.

(2000), *Building Strategy from the Middle: Reconceptualizing Strategy Process*. Thousand Oaks, CA: Sage.

Gavetti, G. (2005), 'Cognition and hierarchy: rethinking the microfoundations of capabilities development', *Organization Science*, 16/6: 599–617.

Hambrick, D. C., and Mason, P. A. (1984), 'Upper echelons: the organization as a reflection of its top managers', *Academy of Management Review*, 9/2: 193–206.

Hart, S., and Banbury, C. (1994), 'How strategy-making processes can make a difference', *Strategic Management Journal*, 15/4: 251–69.

Hayward, M. L. A., and Hambrick, D. C. (1997), 'Explaining the premiums paid for large acquisitions: evidence of CEO hubris', *Administrative Science Quarterly*, 42/1: 103–27.

Heracleous, L., and Jacobs, C. D. (2011), *Crafting Strategy: Embodied Metaphors in Practice*. Cambridge University Press.

Hoon, C. (2007), 'Committees as strategic practice: the role of strategic conversation in a public administration', *Human Relations*, 60/6: 921–52.

Hornsby, J. S., Kuratko, D. F., Shepherd, D. A., and Bott, J. P. (2009), 'Managers' corporate entrepreneurial actions: examining perception and position', *Journal of Business Venturing*, 24/3: 236–47.

Huy, Q. N. (2002), 'Emotional balancing of organizational continuity and radical change: the contribution of middle managers', *Administrative Science Quarterly*, 47/1: 31–69.

(2011), 'How middle managers' group-focus emotions and social identities influence top-down implementation of a new strategy', *Strategic Management Journal*, 32/13: 1387–410.

Jarzabkowski, P. (2008), 'Shaping strategy as a structuration process', *Academy of Management Journal*, 51/4: 621–50.

Jarzabkowski, P., and Balogun, J. (2009), 'The practice and process of delivering integration through strategic planning', *Journal of Management Studies*, 46/8: 1255–88.

Jarzabkowski, P., Burke, G., and Spee, P. (2015), 'Constructing spaces for strategizing work: a multimodal perspective', *British Journal of Management*, 26/S1: 26–47.

Jarzabkowski, P., and Kaplan, S. (2015), 'Strategy tools-in-use: a framework for understanding "technologies of rationality" in practice', *Strategic Management Journal*, 36/4: 537–58.

Jarzabkowski, P., and Sillince, J. (2007), 'A rhetoric-in-context approach to building commitment to multiple strategic goals', *Organization Studies*, 28/11: 1639–66.

Jarzabkowski, P., Spee, P., and Smets, M. (2013), 'Material artifacts: practices for doing strategy with "stuff"', *European Management Journal*, 31/1: 41–54.

Kaplan, S. (2011), 'Strategy and PowerPoint: an inquiry into the epistemic culture and machinery of strategy-making', *Organization Science*, 22/2: 320–46.

Kaplan, S., and Orlikowski, W. J. (2013), 'Temporal work in strategy making', *Organization Science*, 24/4: 965–95.

Kenny, K., and Bell, E. (2011), 'Representing the successful managerial body', in Jeanes, E., Knights, D. and Yancey Martin, P. (eds.), *Handbook of Gender, Work and Organization*: 163–76. Chichester, UK: John Wiley.

Ketokivi, M., and Castañer, X. (2004), 'Strategic planning as an integrative device', *Administrative Science Quarterly*, 49/3: 337–65.

Knights, D., and Morgan, G. (1991), 'Corporate strategy, organizations, and subjectivity: a critique', *Organization Studies*, 12/2: 251–73.

Kodama, M. (2005), 'Knowledge creation through network strategic communities: case studies on new product development in Japanese companies', *Long Range Planning*, 38/1: 27–49.

Kornberger, M., and Clegg, S. (2011), 'Strategy as performative practice: the case of Sydney 2030', *Strategic Organization*, 9/2: 136–62.

Kwon, W., Clarke, I., and Wodak, R. (2014), 'Micro-level discursive strategies for constructing shared views around strategic issues in team meetings', *Journal of Management Studies*, 51/2: 265–90.

Laine, P.-M., Meriläinen, S., Tienari, J., and Vaara, E. (forthcoming), 'Mastery, submission, and subversion: on the performative construction of strategist identity', *Organization*.

Laine, P.-M., and Parkkari, P. (forthcoming), 'Dynamics of strategic agency and participation in strategy-making: the entanglement of human actions, IT, and other materialities', *International Journal of Innovation in the Digital Economy*.

Laine, P.-M., and Vaara, E. (2007), 'Struggling over subjectivity: a discursive analysis of strategic development in an engineering group', *Human Relations*, 60/1: 29–58.

Mantere, S. (2005), 'Strategic practices as enablers and disablers of championing activities', *Strategic Organization*, 3/2: 157–84.

(2008), 'Role expectations and middle manager strategic agency', *Journal of Management Studies*, 45/2: 294–316.

Mantere, S., and Vaara, E. (2008), 'On the problem of participation in strategy: a critical discursive perspective', *Organization Science*, 19/2: 341–58.

Marginson, D. E. W. (2002), 'Management control systems and their effects on strategy formation at middle-management levels: evidence from a UK organization', *Strategic Management Journal*, 23/11: 1019–31.

McCabe, D. (2010), 'Strategy-as-power: ambiguity, contradiction and the exercise of power in a UK building society', *Organization*, 17/2: 151–75.

Meriläinen, S., Tienari, J., and Valtonen, A. (2015), 'Headhunters and the "ideal" executive body', *Organization*, 22/1: 3–22.

Mintzberg, H. (1978), 'Patterns in strategy formation', *Management Science*, 24/9: 934–48.

Mintzberg, H., Ahlstrand, B., and Lampel, J. (1998), *Strategy Safari: A Guided Tour through the Wilds of Strategic Management*. London: Prentice Hall.

Mintzberg, H., and Waters, J. A. (1985), 'Of strategies, deliberate and emergent', *Strategic Management Journal*, 6/3: 257–72.

Mirabeau, L., and Maguire, S. (2014), 'From autonomous strategic behavior to emergent strategy', *Strategic Management Journal*, 35/8: 1202–29.

Nordqvist, M., and Melin, L. (2008), 'Strategic planning champions: social craftspersons, artful interpreters and known strangers', *Long Range Planning*, 41/3: 326–44.

Orlikowski, W. J. (2007). 'Sociomaterial practices: exploring technology at work', *Organization Studies*, 28/9: 1435–48.

Pappas, J. M., and Wooldridge, B. (2007), 'Middle managers' divergent strategic activity: an investigation of multiple measures of network centrality', *Journal of Management Studies*, 44/3: 323–41.

Paroutis, S., and Pettigrew, A. M. (2007), 'Strategizing in the multi-business firm: strategy teams at multiple levels and over time', *Human Relations*, 60/1: 99–135.

Pettigrew, A. M. (1973), *The Politics of Organizational Decision-Making*. London: Tavistock.

(1992), 'On studying managerial elites', *Strategic Management Journal*, 13/S2: 163–82.

Powell, T. C., Lovallo, D., and Fox, C. (2011), 'Behavioral strategy', *Strategic Management Journal*, 32/13: 1369–86.

Regnér, P. (2003), 'Strategy creation in the periphery: inductive versus deductive strategy-making', *Journal of Management Studies*, 40/1: 57–82.

Rouleau, L. (2005), 'Micro-practices of strategic sensemaking and sensegiving: how middle managers interpret and sell change every day', *Journal of Management Studies*, 42/7: 1413–41.

Rouleau, L., and Balogun, J. (2011), 'Middle managers, strategic sensemaking, and discursive competence', *Journal of Management Studies*, 48/5: 953–83.

Samra-Fredericks, D. (2003), 'Strategizing as lived experience and strategists' everyday efforts to shape strategic direction', *Journal of Management Studies*, 40/1: 141–74.

(2005), 'Strategic practice, "discourse" and the everyday interactional constitution of "power effects"', *Organization*, 12/6: 803–41.

Simons, R. (1991), 'Strategic orientation and top management attention to control systems', *Strategic Management Journal*, 12/1: 46–62.

(1994), 'How new top managers use control systems as levers of strategic renewal', *Strategic Management Journal*, 15/3: 169–89.

Stieger, D., Matzler, K., Chatterjee, S., and Ladstätter-Fussenegger, F. (2012), 'Democratizing strategy: how crowdsourcing can be used for strategy dialogues', *California Management Review*, 54/4: 1–26.

Taylor, J. R., and Robichaud, D. (2004), 'Finding the organization into communication: discourse as action and sensemaking', *Organization*, 11/3: 395–413.

Thomas, R., Sargent, L. D., and Hardy, C. (2011), 'Managing organizational change: negotiating meaning and power–resistance relations', *Organization Science*, 22/1: 22–41.

Vaara, E., and Pedersen, A. R. (2014), 'Strategy and chronotopes: a Bakhtinian perspective on the construction of strategy narratives', *M@n@gement*, 16/5: 593–604.

Vaara, E., and Whittington, R. (2012), 'Strategy-as-practice: taking social practices seriously', *Academy of Management Annals*, 6/1: 285–336.

Vilà, J., and Canales, I. J. (2008), 'Can strategic planning make strategy more relevant and build commitment over time? The case of RACC', *Long Range Planning*, 41/3: 273–90.

Westley, F. (1990), 'Middle managers and strategy: microdynamics of inclusion', *Strategic Management Journal*, 11/5: 337–51.

Whittington, R. (1993), *What Is Strategy, and Does It Matter?* London: Routledge.

Whittington, R., Cailluet, L., and Yakis-Douglas, B. (2011), 'Opening strategy: evolution of a precarious profession', *British Journal of Management*, 22/3: 531–44.

Whittington, R., Molloy, E., Mayer, M., and Smith, A. (2006), 'Practices of strategising/organising: broadening strategy work and skills', *Long Range Planning*, 39/6: 615–29.

Whittington, R., and Yakis-Douglas, B. (2012), 'Strategic disclosure: strategy as a form of reputation management', in Barnett, M. L., and Pollock, T. G. (eds.), *The Oxford Handbook of Corporate Reputation*: 402–19. Oxford University Press.

Whittle, A., and Mueller, F. (2010), 'Strategy, enrolment and accounting: the politics of strategic ideas', *Accounting, Auditing and Accountability Journal*, 23/5: 626–46.

Wodak, R., Kwon, W., and Clarke, I. (2011), '"Getting people on board": discursive leadership for consensus building in team meetings', *Discourse and Society*, 22/5: 592–644.

Wooldridge, B., and Floyd, S. W. (1990), 'The strategy process, middle management involvement, and organizational performance', *Strategic Management Journal*, 11/3: 231–41.

Wooldridge, B., Schmid, T., and Floyd, S. W. (2008), 'The middle management perspective on strategy process: contributions, synthesis, and future research', *Journal of Management*, 34/6: 1190–221.

The role of emotions in strategizing

ETHEL BRUNDIN and FENG LIU

Introduction

Emotions have not yet found a forceful way into the field of strategy as practice. This is surprising, since emotions over the years have become a recognized aspect of our organizational life (Elfenbein 2007; Fineman 2000; Bartunek, Balogun and Do 2011), and more and more strategic actors have confessed openly to the importance of emotions in their day-to-day activities. Calls have been made for an emotion angle in strategic management literature in general and in strategizing literature in particular (for example, Hodgkinson and Healey 2011; Huy 2012). For instance, Jarzabkowski and Spee (2009), in their extensive review of the strategy-as-practice field, have invited researchers to bring up more intangible practices such as motivation and emotion in strategizing, and Suddaby, Seidl and Lê (2013) identify emotion as an important behavioural process in strategizing. Even so, emotion as a topic in its own right is still in an immature phase of development within strategizing, although it is an acknowledged perspective per se in organizational studies today. The few studies that do exist within the strategy-as-practice field have highlighted the fact that the emotions that strategists feel and display have a significant influence on the social interactions between them, and thus play an important role in strategy-making and strategic change and can either support or jeopardize strategic intents (for example, Liu and Maitlis 2014; Brundin and Nordqvist 2008; Sloan and Oliver 2013).

With the conviction that emotion is a topic that cannot be neglected, the purpose of this chapter is to review the visibility of emotions in strategizing. Our chapter proceeds as follows. After this introduction, we conduct a review of emotion in strategizing. The review maps out the current state of the art, from which we provide some reflections on the role of emotions within the field in the following section. In the last section we identify missing aspects and suggest avenues along which future strategy-as-practice studies may proceed to further our knowledge on emotion and strategizing.

The role of emotion in current strategizing research

Since emotion is an emerging topic in SAP research, there are only a small number of articles that are directly recognized as investigating emotion's role in strategizing. Thus, we were obliged to expand our review to include a set of empirical and conceptual articles that capture the role that emotions play in strategic or organizational change. We drew the conclusion that thirteen articles were 'spot-on' empirical articles that connect strategists' experienced or displayed emotions at the micro level to macro-level organizational strategic outcomes. These articles constitute the core, and represent the 'bull's eye' of the discussion of the role that emotions play in strategizing. The remaining eighteen articles and five book chapters were not included in the core review because they do not explicitly examine how emotions generated at the micro level influence strategic processes or outcomes at the macro level. These articles did help to draw ideas into our arguments about the future directions of research, however (all thirty-one articles are listed in the Appendix).

The studies categorized as the core of the field of strategizing and emotions are presented in Table 36.1. In order to illustrate emotion's role in different kinds of strategizing activities and ultimately connect emotions with strategic outcomes, we categorized them according to the phenomena they are focused on: discursive practices, top management team dynamics, organizational decision-making and strategic change processes. Most of the

Table 36.1 Core articles on strategizing and emotion

Reference	Strategy phenomenon in focus	Definition of emotion	Approach to emotion and unit of analysis	Key findings
Garetty et al. (2003)	Discursive practices	Emotions are socially constructed and mediated. They link to broader patterns of learning and control. Self-conscious emotions (e.g. guilt, shame, embarrassment and pride) are generated through reflexivity in situations in which the self evaluates itself in relation to a set of perceived social values or norms.	Socially constructed Interpersonal	The power of discourse is mediated through an active, reflexive and often emotional engagement by individuals. By being involved, power relationships are reproduced, resisted or reconfigured. Social controls are mediated through emotions.
Samra-Fredericks (2003)	Discursive practices	No explicit definition. Common-sense emotions. The display of emotions is viewed as a tacit resource for the production of persuasion, which in turn gives rise to positive feelings.	Social Interpersonal	One strategist uses emotion in the rhetoric to influence the strategic process. The strategist expresses and displays emotions at the right time and combined with the use of metaphor and knowledge; the focal strategist can persuade other strategists.
Samra-Fredericks (2004)	Discursive practices	From a sociological perspective, 'emotions' are defined as social 'displays of feelings' (Sturdy 2003: 86, cited by Samra-Fredericks 2004). Emotions are embodied and conveyed in discursive acts.	Social Interpersonal	Managers can make use of four discursive constituents to make the audience take action: an empathetic theme, emotional displays, patterning their utterances and rhetorical tools.
Brundin and Nordqvist (2008)	Board team dynamics	Emotions are socially and culturally ingrained. Emotional processes are triggered by interactions whereby societal and organizational norms and values influence and inform how emotions evolve and are interpreted in emotional displays, emotional states and emotional rules regulating what is appropriate in a given cultural context.	Socially constructed Interpersonal	A board member's emotional energy creates power and status dimensions. The former results in the board member either being the order-giver or the order-taker, and the latter dimension ends up as either exclusion or inclusion, depending on the board member's high or low emotional energy. Depending on the interplay of emotional energy, this has an influence on the board's task performance and effectiveness.
Kisfalvi and Pitcher (2003)	Top management team dynamics	Emotions are visible clues to deeper processes. They play the role of signalling, a sort of early warning system, which sets in action a series of memories (both mental and somatic), thoughts and actions originally related to the very survival of the organism.	Biological/ psychological Interpersonal	A CEO's character, formed by his/her biological and psychological background, including emotionally charged life issues, can 'short-circuit the presumed linkages between diversity, decision-making processes and performance'. Underlying life issues make priorities emotionally meaningful. CEO emotions influence TMT interactions.

Table 36.1 (*cont.*)

Reference	Strategy phenomenon in focus	Definition of emotion	Approach to emotion and unit of analysis	Key findings
Liu and Maitlis (2014)	Top management team dynamics	Displays of emotion are situated contributions to discourse that significantly determine its meaning.	Social Interpersonal Collective (emotional dynamic)	Five different kinds of emotional dynamic are identified in the top team's discussions of strategic issues, each associated with a specific strategizing process. The emotional dynamics vary according to the sorts of emotions displayed, their sequencing and their overall form. The strategizing processes vary in how issues are proposed, discussed and evaluated, and whether decisions are taken or postponed. Team relationship dynamics is a key mechanism linking emotional dynamics and strategizing processes, and issue urgency is another important influence.
Maitlis and Ozcelik (2004)	Organizational decision-making	Negative emotions are intense unpleasant feelings, both experienced and expressed, such as fear, shame, apprehension and anger.	Social Interpersonal	The concept of a toxic decision process connects high-intensity negative affect and decision-making in organizations, and generates widespread negative emotion in an organization through the recursive interplay of members' actions and negative emotions. Toxic decision processes unfold in three phases – inertia, detonation and containment – and are informed by emotions such as anxiety, fear, shame, anger and embarrassment.
Fineman (1996)	Strategic change	Emotions are the socialized display of moved, agitated states, culturally moulded presentations or performances using shared communicative signs such as language nuance, body movements and facial expressions. In this study, the focus is on verbal and non-verbal displays of emotions.	Social Interpersonal	Diverse media that carry green demands evoke different emotional meanings, and pro-environmental organizational changes depend crucially on the emotional meanings that key actors attribute to environmental protection. Some may facilitate green actions, some may stall or block them, and others may lead to green tokenism or to 'doing green' to avoid embarrassment.
Brundin and Melin (2006)	Strategic change	Emotions are socially constructed and situational depending on relationships and social interaction. Emotions are enacted – that is, individuals actively take part in the construction of emotions related to their interpretations of the environment. Emotions are performative.	Socially constructed Interpersonal	High or low levels of emotional energy are created in strategizing, depending on the conformity or discrepancies among the displayed emotions and on their interpretation by the followers. A persistent discrepancy between displayed and experienced emotions on the part of the dominant strategist leaves those close to the strategist bewildered and confused (thus lower emotional energy in the strategist), whereas a persistent congruency makes it easy for people to interpret and act on the emotions involved (thus high emotional energy in the strategist).

Table 36.1 (*cont.*)

Reference	Strategy phenomenon in focus	Definition of emotion	Approach to emotion and unit of analysis	Key findings
Huy (2002)	Strategic change	Emotions are organized psychobiological responses that link physiological, cognitive and motivational systems. Emotions are aroused by issues people consider important to them in a given situation. A use of positive and negative emotions in a common-sense way.	Psychological Interpersonal	By displaying an emotional pattern of being committed to the strategic change project and by attending to employees' emotions, middle managers can facilitate change. Low commitment and low attention leads to inertia or chaos, respectively.
Huy (2011)	Strategic change	Group-focus emotions are individual emotions that managers feel on behalf of a group or fellow group members who experience a specific event, even when they themselves are not personally affected by it.	Psychological Interpersonal	Organization-related social identities such as tenure and language elicit middle managers' group-focus emotions and stimulate them to dismiss or support a specific strategic initiative, even if their direct personal interests are not at stake. Top executives can adjust their strategy implementation actions and improve the odds of success of strategic change if they address the causes of middle managers' group-focus emotions in situ.
Kerosuo (2011)	Strategic change	Feelings connect us to our realities, and emotional experiences emerge on the basis of the reactions that we feel in the circumstances of events. Experiencing is an important means of overcoming crises; emotions are an integral part of a change process.	Psychological Intrapersonal Collective	Individually experienced double binds and crises become a driving force for organizational change when emotions are collectively shared. The process is from individually felt emotion to collectively shared emotions. This process can be eased and/or triggered by facilitators.
Sloan and Oliver (2013)	Strategic change	Trust includes both cognitive and affective dynamics. Affective-based trust is anchored in the emotions and feelings that people have for one another. It reflects genuine care and concern, along with goodwill and benevolence towards others. Similarities in a group are associated with positive beliefs and feelings, and dissimilarities are associated with feelings of threat.	Social Interpersonal	Trust-building is a dynamic process in which emotionality plays a central role. 'Critical emotional incidents' can unexpectedly punctuate the partnership process, and serve as essential turning points in the development of trust. 'Emotional engagement practices' enable the partners to connect on an emotional level, and can transform negative emotions into positive emotions. Unexpected emotionally laden events are key turning points critical to success or failure of the partnership as a whole.

articles view emotions as created, experienced and interpreted in a social setting, meaning that they are situational and that the cultural context is important (see Hoschchild 1983; Fineman 1996). Some of the articles are based on the psychological view of emotions, which holds that emotions are a cognitive construction and that an individual can control his or her emotions by cognitive thinking (see Cornelius 1996). The social and cognitive approaches both often relate emotions to part of identity claims. One study takes the biological perspective, in which emotions are seen mainly as a means to adapt and survive (Fox and Calkins 1993).

Discursive practices of emotions

Some of the early studies on emotion and strategizing focus on the discursive practices of key strategists and explain how the emotions involved in strategists' daily conversations have significant implications for an organization's strategic direction. For instance, Samra-Fredericks (2003) explicitly endorses the strategizing perspective and examines strategizing as a 'lived experience'. She shows how one of the strategists in a set of meetings used his knowledge, talked about what is good and bad or right and wrong, made skilful use of questions, put history to work and used metaphors and the emotional realm. The latter implies that the display of emotions such as anger, frustration and despair constitutes a tacit resource for arguing one's case. Over time, the strategist at the focus of this study was able to persuade other strategists that his proposed strategic actions were the relevant ones by combining displays of intense negative emotion and rational argument. Such a combination also enabled a strategist in another study by Samra-Fredericks to move his listener towards his preferred strategic action (Samra-Fredericks 2004). Thus, 'big' organizational strategic actions were determined in the 'small' moments of emotional conversations between strategists.

This kind of emotional conversation occurs not only between the key strategists but also among other employees. Garrety et al.'s (2003) study shows how an organizational change programme can influence employees' emotions, self-perceptions and behaviour. The authors draw on a Foucauldian approach to power and symbolic interactionism (referring to Mead 1934) and argue that the power of discourse may be changed by active engagement by employees through their emotions. During the change programme the researchers studied how talking about emotions such as fears, mistakes and disguised emotions was encouraged as a way of breaking the existing masculine discourse of toughness in the organization, by creating feelings of embarrassment, shame, guilt and anger. In this way, talking about and displaying emotions that were previously unacceptable in the organization helps to challenge, deconstruct and alter powerful discursive organizational practices.

Emotions in top management and board team dynamics

Our review shows that top management teams and board teams are still the major focus of the strategy-as-practice body of research. The emotions that the CEOs display in their interactions with the board and with other members of the top management team are critical to these teams' strategizing. For instance, Brundin and Nordqvist (2008) followed board meetings over twenty months in a manufacturing firm and examined how a board interacted with a CEO whose performance was not as good as expected and who had been struggling for his survival. Drawing on the emotional energy perspective (Collins 1990; 2004), the authors show not only that felt and displayed emotions are important; they also show the energy that emotions create. For instance, joy, confidence, satisfaction and, for example, frustration and anger typically lead to high emotional energy, and they encouraged the CEO to take an active part in what was going on, whereas sadness, hopelessness and distrust reinforced his low emotional energy and alienation from the board discussion and activities. Over time, both short-term and long-term emotions work as power and status energizers, and in this case they eventually left a de-energized and defeated CEO who was excluded from board strategizing.

In contrast, Kisfalvi and Pitcher (2003) find that a CEO's displayed emotions may enable this person to dominate the strategizing activities and outcomes of a top management team. Taking a biological-cognitive approach, these authors find that the CEO in their case was very emotionally charged when it came to his strategic priorities, and these in turn were affected by his background (Jewish concentration camp, a flight from communism in Poland, a dishonest first business partner in the United States). Thus, the psychological and biological aspects of emotionally charged life issues both formed the character of the CEO himself. This emotionally charged CEO often short-circuited the more intellectual discussions with TMT members, which had a bearing on the decision-making process and, eventually, on the strategic choices.

Liu and Maitlis's (2014) study goes beyond a focus on the CEO and investigates sequences of emotions displayed by multiple team members in their discussion of strategic issues, which they term 'emotional dynamics'. All together they identify five different kinds of emotional dynamic, each shaping a distinct strategizing process. This study shows the variety of ways in which collective emotional processes affect the discussion, evaluation and acceptance of strategic proposals. For Brundin and Nordqvist (2008) and Liu and Maitlis (2014), it is not a single strategic actor's displayed and experienced emotions that shape the strategizing activities; rather, emotions experienced and displayed by multiple top management team members in a dynamic and cyclical manner over time influence the process and outcome of strategizing.

Emotions and organizational decision-making

In a longitudinal, ethnographically inspired study of three symphony orchestras encountering unsatisfactory player performance, Maitlis and Ozcelik (2004) examine the role of negative emotions in the organizational decision-making processes, which involved an even wider range of organizational members at different levels of the organization. They describe what they term 'toxic decision-making processes', triggered by issues that were sensitive, ambiguous and non-urgent and that generated widespread negative emotions in an organization through the recursive interplay of members' actions and negative emotions over time. These processes unfolded in three different phases, each involving a distinct set of interactions between decision-makers and other organizational members. In these phases, emotions went from anxiety, apprehension and fear to more intense emotions of shame, embarrassment, humiliation and pity and eventually to emotions of fear, anger, distrust and suspicion, guilt and defensiveness. This study shows that the build-up of toxicity is generated in everyday activities and through the empathetic transmission of emotions, through the emotional contagion of negative emotions and by the suppression of emotions. It thus describes a process in which negative emotions were widespread among a large number of organizational members, and the implications of this for the organizational decision-making process.

Emotions and the strategic change process

The strategic change process is the field in which most research into emotion in the strategic management field is carried out. Although some of these researchers, such as Fineman and Huy, do not identify themselves as doing strategy-as-practice research, their works illustrate how strategists experience and/or display the influence of emotions and are influenced by more macro strategic phenomena. In a very early study, even before the construct of strategizing was in common use, Fineman (1996) describes how managers attributed meaning to a new initiative in environmental protection and the kinds of emotional reactions triggered. The emotions among managers to a large extent determined the organization's strategy towards this new initiative. Different reactions included: socially responsible managers who enacted a green commitment expressing confidence, enthusiasm, trust or pride; managers who contested green boundaries expressing anger and frustration; managers who defended autonomy from being scrutinized with a mix of emotions of defiance, weariness, threats and admiration; and managers who 'did green' because they had to and wanted to avoid embarrassment. In the same vein, Kerosuo (2011) finds in his study that emotion played a critical role in a transition in which individually experienced double binds and crises became a driving force for organizational change. This is shown in a surgical unit in which the individuals felt caught between a contradictory situation and a crisis by having a waiting list of people who needed operations and the pressure to treat them properly. This brought about feelings of constant failure. When these emotions were unveiled and worked out they became shared, and thus the contradiction was collectively addressed, which led to a change in the division of responsibility.

The unintentional effect of emotions on the strategic outcome is further illustrated by Brundin and Melin's (2006) study, in which two CEOs displayed confidence and frustration, respectively, in a patterned way in a strategic change process over time. The main finding is that emotions that are displayed in an inauthentic way do not promote change, whereas authentic emotions drive change in the way intended by the outlined strategy, even if they are negative emotions. In essence, while the strategic goal may be clearly formulated, the achievement of it can be overthrown by the unintentional and unconscious display of inauthentic emotions, even if it is with the best of intentions at first sight. In this study, a performative view of emotions is crucial, meaning that it depends on how the organizational members interpret the emotions and how they are acted upon (for reasoning about power as performative, see Latour 1986).

While the studies by Fineman (1996), Brundin and Melin (2006) and Kerosuo (2011) treat emotions as naturally occurring and sometimes unpredicted in strategic change, Huy's (2002; 2011) studies treat emotions as something to be managed. Huy's series of studies on emotion and strategic change and implementation suggest that organizations' and managers' abilities to perceive and manage organization members' emotions, and their behaviours in doing so, facilitate smooth strategic change and implementation processes (Huy 2002; 2011). These emotion-based abilities and behaviours include managers' emotional intelligence and organizations' emotional capabilities (Huy 1999;

2005), middle managers' emotional balancing behaviours (Huy 2002) and leaders' emotional aperture, as described in the conceptual paper by Sanchez-Burks and Huy (2009). For instance, Huy posits that an organization can develop its emotional capability, which is defined as the 'ability to acknowledge, recognize, monitor, discriminate, and attend to its members' emotions and it is manifested in the organization's norms and routines related to feeling' (Huy 1999: 325). In the context of strategic change, when strong emotions, usually negative ones, are aroused, routines, such as encouragement, expressions of sympathy and empathy, and the eliciting of positive emotions such as having fun and experiencing hope, foster desirable processes such as receptivity to change, mobilization for change and learning for change (Huy 1999). Huy finds that middle managers as change agents engaged in emotion-balancing behaviours (Huy 2002). On the one hand, they managed their own emotions by being highly emotionally committed to the strategic change, and they displayed excitement and optimism about the change project. They also shared their feelings of disappointment and frustration among themselves. On the other hand, they also attended to employees' emotions by encouraging them to express their unpleasant emotions, such as anger and fear, and organized activities to help employees manage their negative emotions and elicit more positive feelings, such as feelings of calm and sympathy. By doing so, the middle managers facilitated a successful change process. In contrast, when top executives fail to attend to middle managers' emotions it results in middle managers' dismissal of a strategic initiative advocated by the top executives. This is the case even if their immediate personal interests are not directly threatened (Huy 2011). Thus, for Huy, emotions are to be managed in order to achieve the organization's desirable strategic change outcomes.

The above-mentioned studies examine emotion's role within the boundary of an organization's, whereas Sloan and Oliver (2013) illustrate how emotion played a role in between-organization strategizing activities in a six-year longitudinal study of trust in a multi-stakeholder partnership. Trust has both a cognitive and emotional aspect; the authors show that trust-building is a dynamic process in which emotional engagement practices help partners to connect at an emotional level and change negative emotions into positive ones, when unexpected critical emotional incidents may destroy the partnership. Emotional engagement practices are defined as 'practices that impact the emotional valence of the partnership by stimulating a personal engagement with other participants and partnership tasks' (Sloan and Oliver 2013: 1853), and they have the purpose of 'stimulating the flow of positive and negative emotions among the people involved in the partnership in ways that increase their involvement and participation' (1853). The authors argue that these practices increase trust and thereby meet the partnership objectives.

Our review shows that emotion is a powerful lens through which to examine strategizing activities. It also indicates that strategic processes trigger intense emotions in members at different levels of the organizational hierarchy, be it the CEO, the middle managers or members of the staff. Emotion thus provides us with an angle that stimulates our conversation about the more traditional approach to strategic management; this leads us, in turn, to reflect further upon the role of emotions in strategizing, with the review as our point of departure.

Reflections about emotion and strategizing in current literature

Although the strategy-as-practice perspective acknowledges the fact that anybody in an organization can be a strategist, the present studies focus to a high degree on the upper echelons of the organization; thus, the emotions displayed and/or experienced by the CEO, the top management team members and other senior executives dominate these studies. It is, of course, both legitimate and necessary to focus on the upper echelon, since we have limited knowledge about strategizing activities even for this group. From these studies, we learn that the displayed emotions of a key strategist play a critical role in the interactions among senior team members, significantly by enabling or suppressing others' contributions to the strategic

change process. It also means that we may miss other strategists, however, such as the middle managers (Rouleau and Balogun 2011), and, above all, the 'ordinary' employees, who may also play an important role in organizational strategizing.

One of the major challenges for researchers into strategizing is to connect the micro-level activities to macro-level strategic processes and outcomes. This is also the case when it comes to studying emotion and strategizing. As our review shows, these studies try to show how individuals' emotions influence their interactions within a group, such as the board (Brundin and Nordqvist 2008), strategic partners (Sloan and Oliver 2013) or the top management team (Kisvalvi and Pitcher 2003). Only a few studies have attempted to identify some general mechanisms through which to link the individual emotions to collective emotional phenomena. For instance, Liu and Maitlis (2014) have shown how emotional dynamics, defined as sequences of emotions expressed by multiple TMT members in their discussions of strategic issues, influence how these issues are discussed and how decisions are made or postponed; on the other hand, Kerosuo's (2011) study takes a psychological approach to experiencing double binds in crisis situations in which collective emotions become a forceful 'change agent'. In addition, Huy's (2011) study uses 'group-focus emotions' to connect individual emotion and the organizational strategic change process. We consider these studies to be initial attempts to identify mechanisms to connect emotions at the micro level to more macro-level organizational strategic phenomena.

Our review shows that it is possible to 'do emotions' in order to achieve the intended strategic outcomes. This is evident in the theme of discursive practices, in which the comparison with Aristotle's rhetorical tools to put the audience in a specific emotional state is not far-fetched. It is also obvious from some of the articles on the theme of strategic change that managers who are aware of the effect of their emotional displays can more effectively achieve their strategic intent. In some studies, emotions are openly recognized as part of the strategizing process, in which they constitute a 'tool' that can be used to obtain an intended strategic outcome. An example of this is the elites' mini-speeches (Samra-Fredericks 2004), whereby strategists who display the right emotions with the right sense of timing can persuade others and make them act. The power of such discourses can also form a repeated pattern that reproduces, resists or reconfigures power relations in strategizing (Garetty *et al.* 2003). Further, emotions are viewed as something that can be elicited and managed to facilitate desirable strategic outcomes within an organization (Huy 2002; 2011), and they can support inter-organizational strategic initiatives (Sloan and Oliver 2013). In other studies, emotions evolve in a more 'naturally occurring' way, forming a pattern that has implications for the strategic outcome. For example, in the studies by Fineman (1996), Brundin and Melin (2006), Brundin and Nordqvist (2008), Kerosuo (2011), Maitlis and Ozcelik (2004) and Liu and Maitlis (2014), emotions evolve into dynamics such that they either facilitate or inhibit the strategic outcome.

Having a closer look at the theories in use, we find a scattered picture in which social theories dominate. There is no single predominant theoretical approach, however, even if there is some focus on the communication of emotions, such as talk-in-interaction theories (Samra-Fredericks 2003), interaction ritual chain theory (Brundin and Nordqvist 2008), rhetoric (for example, Samra-Fredericks 2004) and the display of emotions (for example, Liu and Maitlis 2014). These foci are not surprising, given the subtlety of emotions, making it easier to study the expression of emotions rather than the experiences. This provides space for a wider range of theories, giving more attention to theories such as those about the sensemaking of emotions (see Fineman 1996) or the affective dimensions of emotions (see Sloan and Oliver 2013). Such a development of the topic of emotion in strategizing could potentially provide even more knowledge about how and why strategists act and decide the way they do, tapping into the territories of the unknown but yet so important human aspects of the way strategists lead and form their organizations.

Methodologically, all the articles are qualitative in character, mostly probably on account of the fact that micro-processes are best studied through ethnographically inspired studies (Samra-Fredericks 2003; 2004; Maitlis and Ozcelik 2004), which are complemented or combined with observations and interviews (Huy 2002; 2011), the diary notes of participants (Brundin and Melin 2006; Brundin and Nordqvist 2008), visual mapping (Kisfalvi and Pitcher 2003), video-taping (Kerosuo 2011; Liu and Maitlis 2014; Sloan and Oliver 2013) and interventions (Garetty *et al.* 2003; Kerosuo 2011). Qualitative method techniques offer a more fine-grained way to study the elusiveness of emotions that can be hidden, masked or faked, or may even be unknowable to the self (see Sturdy 2003). These methods allow researchers to understand both the experienced and the displayed emotions of strategists. The longitudinal design of most of these studies not only enables the authors to provide a more contextualized analysis of emotion and strategizing activities but also makes it possible to argue the connection between emotion and more macro-level strategic phenomena, such as strategic change and decision-making.

Avenues for future research

One major conclusion from our review is that an emotion perspective still has much to offer strategizing; therefore, in this section we suggest avenues for future research. We are inspired by what we have found from the complete review of the thirty-one articles and five book chapters.

Missing themes

The first avenue for future research is to build a strong argument about emotion in order to address the 'So what?' question that has been asked of strategizing research. This can be done by connecting the content of strategy to the emotion it triggers. Thus, it may be worthwhile exploring the content of strategy and examining how initiating and implementing certain kinds of strategic initiative may influence different kinds of emotions triggered in organizations. For example, it would be relevant to see how strategic exit, such as Nokia's exit from its 'Connecting people' mobile

phone strategy, triggers emotions related to loss, such as grief and sadness, in the organization. This can be especially interesting when it denotes political initiatives coupled with power or loss of power, which further complicate the emotional dynamics between organization members.

In addition, drawing on the resource-based view of strategy, there have recently been repeated calls for an exploration of the psychological and behavioural foundations of strategic management. For instance, Hodgkinson and Healey (2011), in the *Strategic Management Journal*'s special issue, argue that, by incorporating intuition, which is an emotion-filled concept, organizations will be able to identify and respond to opportunities and threats more effectively than organizations that rely solely on rational analytical approaches. In addition, they argue that developing emotional commitment to new investment opportunities helps firms seize these opportunities quickly. Incorporating the negative emotion associated with extant courses of action lowers the likelihood of falling prey to an escalation of commitment and related dysfunctional decision traps. Further, the greater the capacity of the organization to regulate identity-based affective responses to change, the greater the likelihood of successful strategic transformation becomes. On the individual level, the strategist may be forced to control his/her emotion to the extent that it leads to emotional exhaustion (see Hochschild 1983), which may in turn lead to dysfunctional behaviour. Novel theories that can explain or illustrate how underlying and unconscious relationships between emotions and practices add valuable knowledge to the field. Such an approach can be found within the psychodynamic realm.

Finally, our review shows that emotion is a topic that is added to the field without any closer scrutiny or criticism. A critical review of emotions in strategizing could be a refreshing theme to consider. Overall, emotion is treated as a way to grasp strategizing and its underlying mechanisms better, and it is taken for granted that the combination of emotion and strategizing is a valuable one (regardless of the strategic outcome). This need not be the case, however; emotion and strategizing may be 'an uneasy marriage of emotionality and

rationality' (Murray 2002: 75). Only a critical scrutiny will add to such a debate. This could have unforeseen implications for strategizing, which would be worthy of further studies. In addition, a critical examination of the methods in use, and addressing the issue of whether it is possible to know the unknowable (see Sturdy 2003), could help researchers to better understand the possible pitfalls when they study emotions.

Missing strategists

In order to understand the whole picture of organizational strategizing, future research could focus on examining the emotions experienced and displayed by organizational members other than top managers and 'appointed' strategists. This would open up possibilities for identifying processes in which emotions are part of strategizing in subtler and less obvious ways – for instance, how employees' moods of depression or their real frustration and anger contribute to the change process (see Klarner, By and Diefenbach 2011). Alternative groups of strategists, active in institutions in which 'institutional practices' (Suddaby, Seidl and Lê 2013) are part of daily activities, are missing as well. This means that future research could focus on key persons with informal power or people involved in latent hotbeds of conflict. Since Hochschild's (1983) seminal piece of work on emotion among flight attendants, research has focused on the role of emotions among, for example, debt collectors and service personnel; this has not been conducted from a strategizing perspective, however. For instance, how do categories such as the police force, shop assistants, medical doctors and judges within the court system form emotional practices on a collective level that have an impact on strategizing?

Missing contexts

Present studies primarily take place in large corporations, and only a couple of them have been carried out in the context of medium-sized companies (Brundin and Melin 2006; Brundin and Nordqvist 2008), but no study has been conducted in small-sized businesses. The size of the organization and the impact this may have are not, therefore, brought into focus. Furthermore, the majority of studies have taken place in publicly owned organizations in which the ownership factor is not problematized at all. Different types of ownership operate under different logics, however (Brundin, Florin-Samuelsson and Melin 2014). In family-owned firms, characteristics that go beyond formal ownership, such as the visibility of the owner, the long-term focus, fast decision-making and identification with the firm, supposedly have implications for managerial practices, including the emotion patterns. Future studies could take size and ownership into account, as the role of emotions in strategizing in contexts such as family firms and entrepreneurial companies may evolve and take different forms from those in the large and publicly owned firms.

The major part of present research on the role of emotions and strategizing takes place in the Western hemisphere (western Europe and the United States) and has 'bought into' the Western discourse of emotions. The way of 'doing emotions' elsewhere may differ substantially, depending on the cultural and societal contexts. In the cultural contexts of east Asia the contextual factors are considered to be more important than in the Western sphere (Masuda et al. 2008). This may have considerable implications when it comes to displaying and interpreting emotions where norms and values are deeply ingrained in practices and strategic actors. Moreover, Masuda et al. (2008) claim that there are differences between western Europeans and North Americans, whereby the former are more analytical and sensitive and the latter are more expressive with authentic emotions. In the studies reviewed here, possible cultural implications are seldom mentioned, and we suggest that they ought to be studied as a subject in their own right, and/or, at least, the impact of them should be incorporated into studies.

Missing links from individual emotions to collective strategizing phenomena

In order to connect individuals' displayed and experienced emotions with macro-outcomes, we believe that a longitudinal design is necessary. In this lies the challenge of studying emotions at the interpersonal level, especially if researchers argue for them to be part of social interaction. Emotions are both transient and evolve over time (Bartunek, Balogun and Do 2011; Frijda 1993; Lazarus, 1991). In addition, strategizing activities are complex phenomena, and they may involve multiple events that occur simultaneously and over time. Thus, the mechanisms that link the long-term effect of group emotions with the macro-level strategic processes and outcomes are of special interest. Accordingly, future studies should examine the unfolding emotions at different stages of specific events and across multiple, sometimes simultaneous, events and investigate their cumulative effect on organizational strategic outcomes (for example, Klarner, By and Diefenbach 2011). In addition, Huy (2005) suggests that organizations that can sequence their emotional management actions are in a better position to facilitate a smoother strategic change process and a desirable outcome.

Further, Sanchez-Burks and Huy (2009) have more recently proposed the concept of 'emotional aperture' – that is, the ability to recognize the composition of diverse emotions in a collective, such as a group or business unit. Collective emotions may emerge among change recipients, perhaps because of emotional contagion (Hatfield, Cacioppo and Rapson 1994) or similar organization-related identities (Huy 2012; Bartunek, Balogun and Do 2011). They argue that leaders who score highly on this ability will respond more effectively to patterns of shared emotions triggered by strategic change. Thus, these conceptual studies have proposed mechanisms that are able to connect emotion, also over time (which is a micro-psychological phenomenon), to collective, organization-level strategic processes and outcomes.

In short, we recommend that future research should identify other emotion-related mechanisms that explain the link from micro to macro.

Missing contributions

The theoretical contributions of all core studies are major in the sense that they have opened the field of strategy to new and important insights and moved the field of strategizing forward. It is not surprising that strategic change and strategic implementation are the main foci of the topic of strategy; nor is the aptness of studying micro-processes such as discursive practices and the display of emotions surprising. As mentioned earlier, however, what we mainly see is conformity, not only in the methods used and approaches to emotions but also when it comes to the theoretical contributions of the studies. The field of emotion and strategizing is today characterized by the 'contribution of theory' rather than 'contribution to theory'. By the former we refer to studies in which researchers 'borrow' theories from other fields and disciplines, which is done in most of the studies of emotions, such as from sociology, psychology, organization theory and biology. This implies that the studies make use of and combine emotion constructs with different strategy frameworks, such as strategic and organizational change and strategic decision-making. In this sense, there is an improvement to existing theories. The term 'contribution to theory' refers to when researchers borrowing from one field return to this field with an improved and elaborated version of what was borrowed (see Sharma 2004). We see little evidence in current studies of developed emotion constructs making contributions 'to theory' to further our knowledge about emotion per se. Even if strategizing is the main focus, it is vital for the field of strategy as practice to move beyond the mere application of novel topics. However relevant and important this may be, there is also a need to move the strategizing field forward by showing that not only are the process and its end products relevant but that strategy as practice has more to offer.

Concluding remark

In this chapter we set out to review the visibility of emotions in strategizing. We have done so through examining a set of studies in which we have identified certain commonalities, but we have also identified a need to go more deeply into the emotion-strategizing field and to open doors that have not yet been opened. An emotion perspective on strategizing thus holds much promise for an

area that has not yet been explored. Even if we suggest a set of future avenues for the topic of emotions in strategizing, we want to emphasize that it is equally important to continue exploring emotions and the strategizing activities of top/board teams, middle managers and similar strategic positions, for the simple reason that we still possess only limited knowledge of the role that emotion plays in these contexts.

Appendix – Reviewed articles and book chapters

The review was conducted in five different stages. First we turned to Scopus, where we limited the search to titles, abstracts and key words within social sciences and humanities, specifically within business, management and accounting, and within the timeframe of 1983 to 2014. The search words were *emotion*, *strategizing*, *strategy*, *strategic change* and/or *organizational change*. This rendered 403 hits. The second stage was a purposeful sampling from the Institute for Scientific Information's list of management ranking, sorted by impact factor, of the 100 most cited journals in management research. We chose the twenty most highly ranked journals in order to make sure that we did not miss any article of importance, and this provided an additional eleven articles. The third stage was to go through three journals that are known to be 'strategy-as-practice-friendly', since members of the SAP research community have to a high degree driven the academic debate in these journals. These journals, which are among the top 100 most cited journals, were *Human Relations*, *Strategic Organization* and *Organization Studies*. This search did not give us any new hits. The fourth stage was a review of *Research on Emotion in Organizations* – a book series that had its first volume (of eleven so far) published in connection with the first world conference on emotion, in 2000. From this series, we found five relevant articles. Finally, we went through the *International Journal of Work Organization and Emotion*, which is a niched journal on emotion, and found one article. After a critical review of all the articles and book chapters at hand, we ended up with

Articles: strategizing and emotions (13 articles)	Articles: empirical articles on strategic/ organizational change and emotions (11 articles/book chapters)	Articles: conceptual articles on strategic/ organizational change and emotions (12 articles/book chapters)
Brundin and Melin (2006)	Barner (2008)	Ashton-James and Ashkanasy (2008)
Brundin and Nordqvist (2008)	Bryant and Cox (2006)	Bartunek, Balogun and Do (2011)
Fineman (1996)	Clarke, Hope Hailey and Kelliher (2007)	George and Jones (2001)
Garetty et al. (2003)	Cox (1997)	Hodgkinson and Healey (2011)
Huy (2002)	Harris and Gresch (2010)	Huy (1999)
Huy (2011)	Kiefer (2002)	Huy (2005)
Kerosuo (2011)	Lawlor (2012)	Huy (2012)
Kisfalvi and Pitcher (2003)	Liu and Perrewé (2005)	Kimberley and Härtel (2007)
Liu and Maitlis (2014)	Smollan (2012)	Kirsch, Parry and Peake (2010)
Maitlis and Ozcelik (2004)	Vince (2006)	Klarner, By and Diefenbach (2011)
Samra-Fredericks (2003)	Vince and Broussine (1996)	Metcalf and Benn (2012)
Samra-Fredericks (2004)		Sanchez-Burks and Huy (2009)
Sloan and Oliver (2013)		

thirty-one articles and five book chapters that we deemed useful and falling within the area of study: thirteen of these deal with strategizing and emotions; eleven are empirical articles on strategic/organizational change and emotions; and the remaining twelve are conceptual articles on strategic/organizational change and emotion (see table).

References

Ashton-James, C. E., and Ashkanasy, N. M. (2008), 'Affective events theory: a strategic perspective', in Zerbe, W. J., Härtel, C. E. J., and Ashkanasy, N. M. (eds.), *Research on Emotion in Organizations*, vol. IV, *Emotions, Ethics and Decision-Making*: 1–34. Bingley, UK: Emerald.

Barner, R. (2008), 'The dark tower: using visual metaphors to facilitate emotional expression during organizational change', *Journal of Organizational Change Management*, 21/1: 120–37.

Bartunek, J. M., Balogun, J., and Do, B. (2011), 'Considering planned change anew: stretching large group interventions strategically, emotionally, and meaningfully', *Academy of Management Annals*, 5/1: 1–52.

Brundin, E., Florin-Samuelsson, E., and Melin, L. (2014), 'Family ownership logic: framing the core characteristics of family businesses', *Journal of Organization and Management*, 20/1: 6–37.

Brundin, E., and Melin, L. (2006), 'Unfolding the dynamics of emotions: how emotion drives or counteracts strategizing', *International Journal of Work Organization and Emotion*, 1/3: 277–302.

Brundin, E., and Nordqvist, M. (2008), 'Beyond facts and figures: the role of emotions in boardroom dynamics', *Corporate Governance*, 16/4: 326–41.

Bryant, M., and Cox, J. W. (2006), 'The expression of suppression: loss and emotional labour in narratives of organisational change', *Journal of Management and Organization*, 12/2: 116–30.

Clarke, C., Hope Hailey, V., and Kelliher, C. (2007), 'Being real or really being someone else? Change, managers and emotion work', *European Management Journal*, 25/2: 92–103.

Collins, R. (1990), 'Stratification, emotional energy, and the transient emotions', in Kemper, T. D. (ed.), *Research Agendas in the Sociology of Emotions*: 27–57. Albany, NY: SUNY Press.

(2004), *Interaction Ritual Chains*. Princeton University Press.

Cornelius, R. R. (1996), *The Science of Emotion: Research and Tradition in the Psychology of Emotion*. Englewood Cliffs, NJ: Prentice Hall.

Cox, J. W. (1997), 'Manufacturing the past: loss and absence in organizational change', *Organization Studies*, 18/4: 623–54.

Elfenbein, H. A. (2007), 'Emotion in organizations', *Academy of Management Annals*, 1/1: 315–86.

Fineman, S. (1996), 'Emotional subtexts in corporate greening', *Organization Studies*, 17/3: 479–500.

(ed.) (2000), *Emotion in Organizations*. London: Sage.

Fox, N., and Calkins, S. (1993), 'Multiple-measure approaches to the study of infant emotion', in Lewis, M., and Haviland, J. M. (eds.), *Handbook of Emotions*: 167–84. New York: Guilford Press.

Frijda, N. (1993), 'Moods, emotion episodes, and emotions', in Lewis, M., and Haviland, J. M. (eds.), *Handbook of Emotions*: 381–404. New York: Guilford Press.

Garetty, K., Badham, R., Morrigan, V., Rifkin, W., and Zanko, M. (2003), 'The use of personality typing in organizational change: discourse, emotions and the reflexive subject', *Human Relations*, 56/2: 211–35.

George, J., and Jones, G. (2001), 'Towards a process model of individual change in organizations', *Human Relations*, 54/4: 419–44.

Harris, S. G., and Gresch, E. B. (2010), 'The emotions of change: merger sentiments, pleasure, and emotional expression', in Zerbe, W. J., Härtel, C. E. J., and Ashkanasy, N. M. (eds.), *Research on Emotion in Organizations*, vol. VI, *Emotions and Organizational Dynamism*: 189–220. Bingley, UK: Emerald.

Hatfield, E., Cacioppo, J. T., and Rapson, R. L. (1994), *Emotional Contagion*. Cambridge University Press.

Hochschild, A. R. (1983), *The Managed Heart: Commercialization of Human Feeling*. Berkeley: University of California Press.

Hodgkinson, G. P., and Healey, M. P. (2011), 'Psychological foundations of dynamic capabilities: reflexion and reflection in strategic management', *Strategic Management Journal*, 32/13: 1500–16.

Huy, Q. N. (1999), 'Emotional capability, emotional intelligence, and radical change', *Academy of Management Review*, 24/2: 325–45.

(2002), 'Emotional balancing of organizational continuity and radical change: the contribution of middle managers', *Administrative Science Quarterly*, 47/1: 31–69.

(2005), 'An emotion-based view of strategic renewal', *Advances in Strategic Management*, 22/1: 3–37.

(2011), 'How middle managers' group-focus emotions and social identities influence strategy implementation', *Strategic Management Journal*, 32/13: 1387–410.

(2012), 'Emotions in strategic organization: opportunities for impactful research', *Strategic Organization*, 10/3: 240–7.

Jarzabkowski, P., and Spee, P. (2009), 'Strategy-as-practice: a review and future directions for the field', *International Journal of Management Reviews*, 11/1: 69–95.

Kerosuo, H. (2011), 'Caught between a rock and a hard place', *Journal of Organizational Change Management*, 24/3: 388–99.

Kiefer, T. (2002), 'Analyzing emotions for a better understanding of organizational change: fear, joy, and anger during a merger', in Ashkanasy, N. M., Zerbe, W. J., and Härtel, C. E. J. (eds.), *Managing Emotions in the Workplace*: 45–69. New York: M. E. Sharpe.

Kimberley, N., and Härtel, C. E. J. (2007), 'Building a climate of trust during organizational change: the mediating role of justice perceptions and emotion', in Härtel, C. E. J., Ashkanasy, N. M., and Zerbe, W. J. (eds.), *Research on Emotion in Organizations*, vol. III, *Functionality, Intentionality and Morality*: 237–640. Bingley, UK: Emerald.

Kirsch, C., Parry, W., and Peake, C. (2010), 'The underlying structure of emotions during organizational change', in Zerbe, W. J., Härtel, C. E. J., and Ashkanasy, N. M. (eds.), *Research on Emotion in Organizations*, vol. VI, *Emotions and Organizational Dynamism*: 113–38. Bingley, UK: Emerald.

Kisfalvi, V., and Pitcher, P. (2003), 'Doing what feels right: the influence of CEO character and emotions on top management team dynamics', *Journal of Management Inquiry*, 12/1: 42–66.

Klarner, P., By, R. T., and Diefenbach, T. (2011), 'Employee emotions during organizational change: towards a new research agenda', *Scandinavian Journal of Management*, 27/3: 332–40.

Latour, B. (1986), 'The powers of association', in Law, J. (ed.), *Power, Action and Belief: A New Sociology of Knowledge?*: 264–80. London: Routledge & Kegan Paul.

Lawlor, J. (2012), 'Employee perspectives on the post-integration stage of a micro-merger', *Personnel Review*, 42/6: 704–23.

Lazarus, R. S. (1991), 'Cognition and motivation in emotion', *American Psychologist*, 46/4: 352–67.

Liu, F., and Maitlis, S. (2014), 'Emotional dynamics and strategizing processes: a study of strategic conversations in top team meetings', *Journal of Management Studies*, 51/2: 202–34.

Liu, Y., and Perrewé, P. L. (2005), 'Another look at the role of emotion in the organizational change: a process model', *Human Resource Management Review*, 15/4: 263–80.

Maitlis, S., and Ozcelik, H. (2004), 'Toxic decision processes: a study of emotion and organizational decision making', *Organization Science*, 15/4: 375–93.

Masuda, T., Ellsworth, P. C., Mesquita, B., Leu, J., Tanida, S., and Van de Veerdonk, E. (2008), 'Placing the face in context: cultural differences in the perception of facial emotion', *Journal of Personality and Social Psychology*, 94/3: 365–81.

Mead, G. H. (1934), *Mind, Self and Society: From the Standpoint of a Social Behaviorist*. University of Chicago Press.

Metcalf, L., and Benn, S. (2012), 'Leadership for sustainability: an evolution of leadership ability', *Journal of Business Ethics*, 112/3: 369–84.

Murray, B. (2002), 'Understanding the emotional dynamics of family enterprises', in Fletcher, D. E. (ed.), *Understanding the Small Family Business*: 75–93. London: Routledge.

Rouleau, L., and Balogun, J. (2011), 'Middle managers, strategic sensemaking, and discursive competence', *Journal of Management Studies*, 48/5: 953–83.

Samra-Fredericks, D. (2003), 'Strategizing as lived experience and strategists' everyday efforts to shape strategic direction', *Journal of Management Studies*, 40/1: 141–74.

— (2004), 'Managerial elites making rhetorical and linguistic "moves" for a moving (emotional) display', *Human Relations*, 57/9: 1103–43.

Sanchez-Burks, J., and Huy, Q. N. (2009), 'Emotional aperture and strategic change: the accurate recognition of collective emotions', *Organization Science*, 20/1: 22–34.

Sharma, P. (2004), 'An overview of the field of family business studies: current status and directions for the future', *Family Business Review*, 17/1: 1–36.

Sloan, P., and Oliver, D. (2013), 'Building trust in multi-stakeholder partnerships: critical emotional incidents and practices of engagement', *Organization Studies*, 34/12: 1835–68.

Smollan, R. K. (2012), 'Trust in change managers: the role of affect', *Journal of Organizational Change Management*, 26/4: 725–47.

Sturdy, A. (2003), 'Knowing the unknowable? A discussion of methodological and theoretical issues in emotion research and organizational studies', *Organization*, 10/1: 81–105.

Suddaby, R., Seidl, D., and Lê, J. (2013), 'Strategy-as-practice meets neo-institutional theory', *Strategic Organization*, 11/3: 329–44.

Vince, R. (2006), 'Being taken over: managers' emotions and rationalizations during a company takeover', *Journal of Management Studies*, 43/2: 343–65.

Vince, R., and Broussine, M. (1996), 'Paradox, defense and attachment: accessing and working with emotions and relations underlying organizational change', *Organization Studies*, 17/1: 1–21.

Index

Entries for figures, tables and boxes are denoted in bold typeface.

Lightning Source UK Ltd.
Milton Keynes UK
UKOW05f0509161117
312837UK00014B/328/P